HISTORICAL DICTIONARIES
OF U.S. POLITICS AND POLITICAL ERAS

Jon Woronoff, Series Editor

From the Great War to the Great Depression, by Neil A. Wynn, 2003.
Revolutionary America, by Terry M. Mays, 2005.
Old South, by William L. Richter, 2006.
Early American Republic, by Richard Buel Jr., 2006.
Jacksonian Era and Manifest Destiny, by Terry Corps, 2006.
Reagan–Bush Era, by Richard S. Conley, 2007.
Kennedy–Johnson Era, by Richard Dean Burns and Joseph M. Siracusa, 2008.
Nixon–Ford Era, by Mitchell K. Hall, 2008.
Roosevelt–Truman Era, by Neil A. Wynn, 2008.
Eisenhower Era, by Burton I. Kaufman and Diane Kaufman, 2009.
Progressive Era, by Catherine Cocks, Peter C. Holloran, and Alan Lessoff, 2009.
Gilded Age, by T. Adams Upchurch, 2009.
Political Parties, by Harold F. Bass Jr., 2010.
George W. Bush Era, by Richard S. Conley, 2010.
United States Congress, by Scot Schraufnagel, 2011.
Colonial America, by William Pencak, 2011.
Civil War and Reconstruction, Second Edition, by William L. Richter, 2012.

Historical Dictionary of the Civil War and Reconstruction

Second Edition

William L. Richter

The Scarecrow Press, Inc.
Lanham • Toronto • Plymouth, UK
2012

Published by Scarecrow Press, Inc.
A wholly owned subsidiary of The Rowman & Littlefield Publishing Group, Inc.
4501 Forbes Boulevard, Suite 200, Lanham, Maryland 20706
http://www.scarecrowpress.com

Estover Road, Plymouth PL6 7PY, United Kingdom

British Library Cataloguing in Publication Information Available

Library of Congress Cataloging-in-Publication Data

Richter, William L. (William Lee), 1942-
 Historical dictionary of the Civil War and Reconstruction / William L.
Richter. -- 2nd ed.
     p. cm. -- (Historical dictionaries of U.S. politics and political eras)
  Includes bibliographical references.
  ISBN 978-0-8108-7817-4 (cloth : alk. paper) -- ISBN 978-0-8108-7959-1 (ebook)
  1. United States--History--Civil War, 1861-1865--Dictionaries. 2. Reconstruction (U.S.
history, 1865-1877)--Dictionaries. I. Title.
  E468.R53 2012
  973.703--dc23
                                                2011020751

Printed in the United States of America

to
Lynne

Contents

Editor's Foreword

When the Civil War and Reconstruction are presented in a sufficiently superficial manner, pretty much the sort of presentation most of us received in school or the cinema, the situation appears pretty clear. You know who was good and who was bad, who was noble and who was a scoundrel, and certainly who won and who lost . . . although just who was who will vary with the sources of the presentation. As it happens, and as this very welcome volume shows, the situation was anything but simple, and any conclusions are anything but clear. It is not so easy to say who was good or bad, or at least how good or bad, or who acted out of noble or base motives, or even who won or lost. For this was not only the most decisive period in American history, it was also the most complex, and our views have not ceased evolving. So, the biggest of many advantages of this *Historical Dictionary of the Civil War and Reconstruction* is not to have simplified but rather to have amplified the many complexities and contradictions so we can seek a deeper understanding.

This was done, first, through a very extensive, almost blow-by-blow chronology that passes the whole period in review. Next, an introduction shows how our views have changed about events that have remained the same. Then the dictionary section delves into the details and highlights the nuances of a colorful cast of characters, North and South (or both), civilian and military (or both), good and bad (or both), sometimes on the top only to slip to the bottom, or vice versa. There are also entries on major battles and campaigns, significant legislation, the various political parties and other organizations, as well as many of the issues and some of the jargon. The various appendixes provide useful background. And the bibliography includes most of the better works on the subject, which, although they do not always agree, broaden our range of opinions and help us formulate our own conclusions.

This amazingly thorough analysis of the period was written by William L. Richter, who studied in Arizona and received a doctorate at Louisiana State University. Unlike most of our authors, he was only briefly an academic, teaching history at Cameron University in Oklahoma, before settling down as the owner and operator of Bill's Farrier Service. But he has written as much as, maybe more than, most academics on the Civil War and Reconstruction, starting with his dissertation, passing through numerous articles and book reviews, and culminating in several books, one on the Army in Texas, another on the Freedmen's Bureau in Texas, and a third, *The ABC-Clio Companion to American Reconstruction*. That may explain why the style is refreshingly unacademic and at times nearly literary, leaving us with not only with an understanding of the period but an almost palpable "feel" for it. And this second edition only adds to this.

Jon Woronoff
Series Editor

Acknowledgments

One of the nice things that writers encounter when creating a book is a lot of wonderful people, who go out of their way to help you. Joseph G. Dawson III of Texas A&M University, an old comrade from our days as graduate students under the illustrious T. Harry Williams at Louisiana State University, kindly suggested I do this topic for Scarecrow Press and brought me together with series editor Jon Woronoff. Another longtime friend, Bruce Dinges of the Arizona Historical Society, was ever ready to share his knowledge of the Civil War, in this case, particularly his analyses of Confederate General John Bell Hood and Civil War cavalry operations. Jason Roth, an editor at *Blue & Gray Magazine*, affably took time out of his busy schedule to help a stranger with numerous bibliographic questions. Todd Hallman of ABC-Clio graciously permitted me to excerpt materials from my earlier book, *The ABC-Clio Companion to American Reconstruction, 1862–1877*. Edward C. Fields and Tony J. Lewis of the Wyles Collection of Periodicals at the University of California at Santa Barbara generously came to my aid by looking up citations that were not available in Arizona, saving me many days of research and a long automobile trip. And my old college friend, Harve Mankopf of Chicago, once again enthusiastically filled in the gaps that remained. As always, my wonderful wife, Lynne, shared in my writing, line by line, providing much-needed suggestions, encouragement, love, and friendship to keep me going. To them all I owe a great deal of thanks. What good this volume possesses is due to them. As usual, the errors and shortcomings are mine.

Select Chronology

1846   8 August: Wilmot Proviso introduced in House of Representatives as a rider on the $2 million appropriations bill for the War with Mexico.

1847   29 December: Lewis Cass announced that he was for popular sovereignty on the question of slavery in the territories.

1848   22 May: Democratic Convention at Baltimore nominated Lewis Cass of Michigan for president. **7 June:** Whig Party Convention at Philadelphia nominated war hero Maj. Gen. Zachary Taylor for president. **22 June:** Antislavery Democrats, meeting at Utica, New York, nominated Martin Van Buren for president. **9 August:** Liberty Party supporters, Antislavery Democrats, and Conscience Whigs met at Buffalo, New York, and formed the Free Soil Party and jointly nominated Van Buren for president. **8 November:** Whig candidate Zachary Taylor won election of 1848.

1850   29 January–20 September: Compromise of 1850. **29 January:** Senator Henry Clay of Kentucky introduced a series of resolutions calling for compromising on a multitude of issues concerning slavery. **5–6 February:** Senator Henry Clay of Kentucky spoke in favor of compromise, North and South. **4 March:** Senator John C. Calhoun of South Carolina spoke in favor of the Non-Exclusion Doctrine and equal Southern rights to the territories. **7 March:** Senator Daniel Webster of Massachusetts spoke for no action on slavery in the territories, because climate determined it would not last there. **11 March:** Senator William H. Seward of New York spoke for a Higher Law that justified excluding slavery from the West. **8 May:** Clay's committee in the Senate introduced the Omnibus Bill covering slavery in the territories and a second bill prohibiting the slave trade in the District of Columbia, but they failed to be passed. **10 June:** Nashville Convention. **9 July:** Anti-compromise President Taylor died, allowing pro-compromise Vice President Millard Fillmore to become president. **13 August–7 September:** Led by Senator Stephen A. Douglas of Illinois, the Compromise of 1850 is passed as a series of individual acts, the first of which was the admission of California as a free state. **15 August–6 September:** Under Texas and New Mexico Territory

Act, Texas Republic debt assumed by United States and Texas surrendered all claim to Santa Fé, with no mention of slavery. Utah Territory Act created a new territory with no mention of slavery. **23 August–12 September:** Fugitive Slave Act provided for the return of all fugitives as an exclusive Federal prerogative. **16–17 September:** Abolition of the slave trade in District of Columbia act passed. **13–14 December:** Georgia Platform called for adherence to Union until the North ignored any part of the Compromise of 1850.

1851   1 September: Narciso López executed in Havana, Cuba, for leading numerous filibustering expeditions.

1852   Young American Movement became a national passion. **20 March:** Harriet Beecher Stowe's *Uncle Tom's Cabin* published and became a bestseller. **1 June:** Democratic Convention at Baltimore nominated Franklin Pierce of New Hampshire for president, standing for the Compromise of 1850 and popular sovereignty deciding slavery in the territories. **16 June:** Whig Convention at Baltimore nominated Lt. Gen. Winfield Scott for president, standing for the Compromise of 1850 and an end to further antislavery agitation. **11 September:** Free Soil Party met at Pittsburgh and nominated U.S. Sen. John P. Hale of New Hampshire for president, condemned the Compromise of 1850, and stood for Free Soil and Free Men. **2 November:** Franklin Pierce selected with the abandonment of the Whig Party by the South.

1853   4 March: Pierce inaugurated calling for support of the Compromise of 1850 and acquisition of more territory by peaceful means. **30 December:** Gadsden Purchase annexed all of present-day Arizona and New Mexico below the Gila River.

1854   23 January–30 May: Passage of the Kansas–Nebraska Act under the leadership of Democratic Senator Stephen A. Douglas of Illinois. **28 February:** Spanish seized the *Black Warrior* over an error in its manifest. **28 February–13 July:** Organization of the Republican Party in several states. **31 March:** Treaty of Kanagawa opened up Japan to U.S. trade. **26 April:** Eli Thayer organized the Massachusetts Emigrant Aid Society, which was reorganized as the New England Emigrant Aid Society on 21 February 1855. **16 October:** Abraham Lincoln's first public denunciation of slavery in the territories in a speech at Peoria, Illinois. **18 October:** Ostend Manifesto called for U.S. annexation of Cuba by purchase or force.

1855   30 March: First election for a territorial legislature in Kansas dominated by Missouri "Border Ruffians." **June:** President Pierce appointed Andrew Reeder as first governor of Kansas Territory. **June–October:** William

Walker exploited a local civil war to subjugate Nicaragua. **31 July:** President Pierce appointed Wilson Shannon of Ohio governor of Kansas Territory. Reeder removed as too pro-slavery. **5 September:** Antislavery convention at Big Springs, Kansas Territory, repudiated acts of pro-slavery legislature. **23 October–5 November:** Topeka Convention drew up antislavery constitution for Kansas. **26 November–7 December:** Wakarusa War ends in stalemate.

1856   **24 January:** President Pierce condemned the Topeka government as illegal. **11 February:** President Pierce warned Free Staters and Border Ruffians to disperse. **22 February:** The American (Know Nothing) Party met at Philadelphia and nominated Millard Fillmore for president on a Nativist platform. **14 May:** After repudiating William Walker's takeover of Nicaragua, President Pierce received his emissary, a virtual recognition. **19–20 May:** Sen. Charles Sumner of Massachusetts delivered his "Crime against Kansas" Speech. **21 May:** Sacking of Lawrence, Kansas. **22 May:** Congressman Preston Brooks of South Carolina assaulted Sen. Charles Sumner on the floor of the Senate for insulting a relative. **24 May:** Pottawatomie Massacre of five nonslaveholding Southern settlers led by John Brown. **2 June:** Democratic Party convention met at Cincinnati and nominated James Buchanan for president on a platform of popular sovereignty and support for the Kansas–Nebraska Act. **4 June:** Gov. Shannon ordered all armed bodies to disperse in Kansas. **17 June:** Republican Party met at Philadelphia and nominated John Charles Frémont for president on a platform opposing the twin evils of slavery and polygamy in the territories and a Free State Kansas. **3 July:** House of Representatives passed a bill to admit Kansas as a pro-slave state, which was rejected in the Senate. **18 August:** Unable to stop reoccurring guerrilla warfare, Gov. Shannon resigned, to be replaced by John W. Geary of Pennsylvania. **15 September:** Gov. Geary had U.S. Army intercept 1,500 Border Ruffians, bringing temporary peace to Kansas. **17 September:** Whig Party met at Baltimore and nominated Millard Fillmore of the American Party for president. **4 November:** James Buchanan elected president of the United States.

1857   **4 March:** Geary resigned as Kansas Territory governor, citing disagreements with President Pierce. President Buchanan inaugurated, pledged Federal non-interference and popular sovereignty in the territories. **6 March:** Dred Scott *v.* Sandford decided by U.S. Supreme Court, ruling that African-Americans were not citizens, that slavery had an extraterritorial quality, and that the South was correct in its doctrine of Federal non-interference with slavery in the territories. **26 March:** President Buchanan appointed Robert J. Walker of Mississippi as Kansas Territory governor. Walker pledged a fair vote in Kansas. **1 May:** Filibusterer William Walker surrendered to U.S.

Navy after being run out of Nicaragua by Cornelius Vanderbilt, his original sponsor. **15 June:** Elections in Kansas return a pro-slave majority to the constitutional convention to meet in October. **15 July:** Free Staters meeting at Topeka in their own constitutional convention agreed to wait and let Gov. Walker try for a fair election to territorial legislature. **5 October:** Territorial elections, strictly supervised by Gov. Walker, gave a Free State Majority in legislature in Kansas. **19 October–8 November:** Ignoring Gov. Walker and recent legislative elections, the state convention in Kansas drew up the pro-slave Lecompton Constitution. **25 November:** William Walker landed at Greytown, Nicaragua, only to be expelled by the U.S. Navy. **7 December:** The Free State Kansas territory legislature called for a new election in January 1858 to vote on the Lecompton Constitution. **17 December:** Gov. Walker resigned when President Buchanan supported the Lecompton Constitution. **21 December:** With Free Staters boycotting the election, pro-slave voters in Kansas approved the Lecompton Constitution.

1858   **4 January:** A second election in Kansas, with all parties participating for the first time, rejected the Lecompton Constitution with or without slavery. **2 February:** President Buchanan submitted the Lecompton Constitution to Congress for approval of Kansas's admission as a slave state. **3 February:** Sen. Stephen A. Douglas rejected the Lecompton Constitution as a perversion of democracy and popular sovereignty, causing a Democratic Party split. **23 March:** Senate approved the admission of Kansas as a slave state under the Lecompton Constitution. **1 April:** House of Representatives ordered that the Lecompton Constitution be resubmitted to the voters in Kansas Territory. **30 April:** House of Representatives passed the English Bill, requiring a new popular election over the Lecompton Constitution, accompanied by a large Federal land grant and a warning that to refuse to vote for it would delay Kansas statehood until its population reached 90,000. **4 May:** Senate endorsed the English Bill over the opposition of Sen. Douglas. **16 June:** In Springfield, Illinois, Abraham Lincoln accepted Republican Party nomination to run for U.S. Senate with "House Divided" speech. **2 August:** Voters in Kansas decisively rejected the Lecompton Constitution once again. **21 August–15 September:** Lincoln–Douglas Debates over the election to the U.S. Senate. **27 August:** Lincoln asked Douglas the Freeport Question, and Douglas stated the Freeport Doctrine, that slavery can be stopped in a territory before the vote on a state constitution, winning Illinois (the only Democrat to win in the North, except for some in Indiana) but losing the South in 1860.

1859   **9–19 May:** Southern Commercial Convention met at Vicksburg and called for reopening of the African Slave Trade. **16-18 October:** John

Brown's Raid on Harper's Ferry, Virginia, suppressed by U.S. Marines led by Army Col. Robert E. Lee. **2 December:** After a trial, Virginia hanged John Brown for committing treason against the state.

1860 **27 February:** Lincoln's Cooper Union Address introduced him to the eastern voters in the North for the first time. **23 April–3 May:** Democratic Party met in Charleston and adopted the Cincinnati Platform of 1856, but could not come to an agreement on a presidential candidate, with the Deep South States walking out. **9 May:** The former Whig–American Party met at Baltimore as the Constitutional Union Party and nominated John Bell of Tennessee as its presidential candidate, condemning sectionalism and standing for Constitution and Union. **16 May:** Republican Party met in Chicago and nominated Abraham Lincoln of Illinois as its presidential candidate on a platform of economic improvement and the Wilmot Proviso. **18 June:** Democrats met again in Baltimore and, after another Southern walkout, nominated Stephen A. Douglas of Illinois for president. **28 June:** Meeting at Richmond since 11 June, Southern Democrats nominated Vice President John C. Breckinridge of Kentucky as their presidential candidate for 1860, standing for non-exclusion of slavery from the territories and the acquisition of Cuba. **12 September:** William Walker executed in Honduras after landing in August to subjugate the country. **6 November:** Abraham Lincoln elected president of the United States with a majority of the electoral vote and only 39 percent of the popular vote. **10 November:** South Carolina state legislature called a convention to meet on 17 December to consider secession from the Union. **13 November:** South Carolina state legislature voted to raise 10,000 volunteers to defend the state. **15 November:** Major Robert Anderson appointed to command U.S. garrison at Charleston. **18 November:** Georgia state legislature voted to raise $1 million to arm the state. **1 December:** Florida state legislature met to consider questions of Union. **4 December:** President James Buchanan delivered State of the Union message. House of Representatives named special Committee of Thirty-three to compromise issues of the day. **8 December:** President Buchanan appointed Philip F. Thomas of Maryland as secretary of the treasury. Howell Cobb of Georgia resigned. **12 December:** Secretary of State Lewis Cass of Michigan resigned from Buchanan's cabinet. **13 December:** Seven senators and 23 Representatives from the South urged secession and creation of a Southern Confederacy. **14 December:** Georgia state legislature asked South Carolina, Mississippi, Alabama, and Florida to appoint delegates to a convention to establish a Southern Confederacy. **17 December:** President Buchanan appointed Jeremiah Black of Pennsylvania as attorney general. **18 December:** Crittenden Compromise presented to U.S. Senate. **20 December:** South Carolina seceded. Vice President John C. Breckinridge appointed and referred Crittenden Compromise to a Committee of Thirteen. President Buchanan named Edwin McM. Stanton as attorney general to replace Jeremiah Black, who had become secretary of state. **26 December:** Maj. Anderson transferred the Federal garrison at Charleston from Fort Moultrie on the mainland to Fort Sumter in the bay. **29 December:** Secretary of War John Floyd of Virginia resigned.

1861 **4 January:** Alabama state militia seized Federal arsenal at Mt. Vernon and Forts Gaines and Morgan at Mobile the next day. **6 January:** Florida state militia took Federal arsenal at Appalachicola. **8 January:** Secretary of the Interior Jacob Thompson resigned. **9 January:** Mississippi seceded. Merchant vessel *Star of the West* tried to land men and supplies for Fort Sumter but was driven off by South Carolina troops. **10 January:** Florida seceded. Louisiana state militia seized Federal arsenal at Baton Rouge and Forts St. Philip and Jackson at the mouth of the Mississippi River. **11 January:** Alabama seceded. President Buchanan appointed John A. Dix of New York as secretary of the treasury to replace Philip F. Thomas, who resigned. **14 January:** The Committee of Thirty-three and the Committee of Thirteen were unable to reach a compromise, but the House reported the Corwin Amendment. **18 January:** President Buchanan appointed Joseph Holt of Kentucky as secretary of war. **19 January:** Georgia seceded. **20 January:** Mississippi state troops took Ship Island and Ft. Massachusetts. **24 January:** Georgia state militia took Federal arsenal at Augusta. **26 January:** Louisiana seceded. **29 January:** Kansas admitted to the Union under the Free State Wyandotte Constitution. **1 February:** Texas seceded, with a referendum of the people to be held 23 February. **4 February:** Seceded states met at Montgomery. Washington Peace Conference convened. **7 February:** Choctaw Nation seceded. **8 February:** Constitution of the Confederate States of America adopted at Montgomery. Arkansas state troops seized Federal arsenal at Little Rock. **9 February:** Montgomery Convention elected Jefferson Davis of Mississippi and Alexander H. Stephens of Georgia as provisional president and vice president of the Confederacy. Tennessee voters refused to call secession convention. **18 February:** Jefferson Davis inaugurated president of the provisional government. Bvt. Maj. Gen. David E. Twiggs surrendered all Federal troops and posts in Texas at San Antonio. **22 February:** Lincoln learned of the Baltimore Plot and agreed to be smuggled into Washington overnight, arriving safely the next day. **23 February:** Texas voters approved secession. **27 February:** Washington Peace Conference sent its proposals for six constitutional amendments to Congress. **3 March:** Confederacy took over at Charleston under Brig. Gen. P. G. T. Beauregard. **4 March:** Lincoln inaugurated as president of the United States. **11 March:** Confederate Convention acting as a provisional congress accepted the Constitution of the Confederate States of America and sent it out for ratification. **18 March:** Sam Houston resigned as governor of Texas, refusing to take loyalty oath to the Confederacy. Arkansas state convention refused to secede, but voted to allow voters to decide in August election. **1 April:** Union Secretary of State William H. Seward submitted "Thoughts for the President's Consideration" in a bid to become a prime minister. **2 April:** Morrill Tariff Act passed Congress and was amended higher in 1862 and 1864. **4 April:** Virginia refused to secede. **6 April:** Lincoln informed South Carolina he would succor Ft. Sumter. **11 April:** Confederates demanded the surrender of Ft. Sumter; Maj. Anderson refused. **12 April:** Confederates fired upon Ft. Sumter; Ft. Pickens at Pensacola reinforced without incident. **13 April:** Maj. Anderson surrendered Ft. Sumter to the Confederacy. **14 April:** Formal surrender of Ft. Sumter. **15 April:** Lincoln called up 75,000 state militia, each state receiving a quota. **17 April:** Virginia seceded, with a popular referendum to be held on 23 May. **19 April:** Baltimore rioted against parade of Sixth Massachusetts Infantry. Lincoln declared blockade of South. **20 April:** Federal sailors and marines evacuated from Gosport Navy Yard. **22 April:** Maj. Gen. Robert E. Lee named head of Virginia troops. **27 April:** Lincoln suspended the writ of *habeas corpus* along the railroad running from Washington to Philadelphia. **29 April:** Lincoln issued an executive proclamation creating martial law in Maryland. Maryland refused to secede. **30 April:** Indian Nations abandoned by Federal troops, leaving the Five Civilized (i.e., slaveholding) Tribes to Confederate influence. **3 May:** Lincoln called up 42,000 volunteers for three years' service, also for eight new three-battalion regiments of regular infantry, one regiment of regular artillery, and 18,000 seamen. In Great Britain, Foreign Minister Lord John Russell informally met with the Yancey–Rost–Mann Delegation from the Confederacy. Bvt. Lt. Gen. Winfield Scott issued the "Anaconda Plan" to subdue the South. **6 May:** Arkansas seceded. Britain recognized the Confederacy as a belligerent but not as a nation. **7 May:** Tennessee seceded as Gov. Isham Harris submitted an alliance with the Confederacy, with a popular referendum set for June 8. **10 May:** St. Louis riot against the Federal capture of Camp Jackson. **13 May:** Maj. Gen. Benjamin Butler's Federal troops occupied Federal Hill in Baltimore without orders. **20 May:** North Carolina seceded. Gov. Beriah Magoffin of Kentucky issued proclamation of neutrality. Confederate Congress voted to move its capital to Richmond. **21 May:** Price–Harney Agreement in Missouri restored equilibrium to the state. **22 May:** Gen. Benjamin F. Butler sent to command Fortress Monroe in Virginia. **23 May:** Virginia voters approved of secession. **25 May:** Gen. Butler declared escaped slaves to be contraband of war. **28 May:** *Ex parte* Merryman, Chief Justice Roger B. Taney issued his circuit court opinion challenging President Lincoln's arbitrary arrest policy toward suspected Confederate sympathizers. **31 May:** Bvt. Brig. Gen. Nathaniel Lyon replaced Brig. Gen. William S. Harney in Missouri. **1 June:** Britain refused to receive

Confederate privateer prizes. **3 June:** Stephen A. Douglas died of typhoid fever and exhaustion. Union victory in the Battle of Philippi in western Virginia. **8 June:** Voters in Tennessee approved secession. Gen. Robert E. Lee became military advisor to President Davis. **10 June:** Rebels won the Battle of Big Bethel near Fortress Monroe. **11 June:** Pro-Union elements met at Wheeling. **17 June:** Union victory in Battle of Booneville, Missouri. **19 June:** Francis Pierpont named governor of loyal Virginia at Wheeling Convention. **27 June:** City Marshal of Baltimore George P. Kane arrested as pro-Confederate. **28 June:** Incorporation of the Central Pacific Railroad at Sacramento, California, to build a transcontinental line. **2 July:** Lincoln suspended the writ of *habeas corpus* along the railroad lines from Washington to New York City. **4 July:** Lincoln finally called Union Congress into Special Session. **5 July:** Rebels won Battle of Carthage, Missouri. **8 July:** Brig. Gen. Henry H. Sibley ordered to conquer Union Territory of New Mexico. **11 July:** Yankees win Battle of Rich Mountain in western Virginia. **12 July:** Confederate Commissioner Albert Pike signed treaties with Choctaw and Chickasaw tribes in the Indian Nations. **13 July:** Federals win Battle of Carrick's Ford in western Virginia. **18 July:** Confederates repulsed Yankees at Blackburn's Ford, Virginia. **21 July:** Rebels won First Battle of Manassas. **25 July:** Crittenden Resolution passed Congress, that goal of war was Union not emancipation. **26 July:** Federals surrendered Ft. Fillmore in New Mexico Territory. **27 July:** Maj. Gen. George B. McClellan assumed command of what would become the Army of the Potomac. **31 July:** Convention of Missouri loyalists elected Hamilton R. Gamble governor of the state to replace Claiborne F. Jackson, gone to the Confederacy. **1 August:** Col. John R. Baylor named all of New Mexico south of the 34th parallel the Confederate Territory of Arizona. **2 August:** Union Congress passed first income tax. **5 August:** Tax Law passed by U.S. Congress levied on the seceded South, too. **6 August:** First Confiscation Act passed U.S. Congress. Federal Congress approved all executive measures Lincoln had issued since Battle of Ft. Sumter. **10 August:** In Missouri, Confederates won Battle of Wilson's Creek. **14 August:** Maj. Gen. John Charles Frémont declared martial law in Missouri. **19 August:** Confederate Congress agreed to a military alliance with Rebel Missouri. **20 August:** Convention at Wheeling established a new state, to be called Kanawha. **30 August:** Frémont freed slaves in Missouri by unauthorized military proclamation. **2 September:** Lincoln requested Frémont to modify his emancipation order. **3 September:** Confederate forces entered Kentucky and took Columbus. **6 September:** Federals took Paducah, Kentucky. **10 September:** Federals won Battle of Carnifax Ferry in western Virginia. **11 September:** Federals won Battle of Cheat Mountain in western Virginia. **12 September:** Lincoln ordered the arrest of certain disloyal members of the Maryland legislature to prevent secession. **20 September:** Gen. Price and his

Rebels captured Lexington, Missouri. **20 October:** Union lost the Battle of Ball's Bluff on the Potomac in Virginia. **24 October:** Transcontinental telegraph completed. **31 October:** Missouri formally seceded from the Union. **1 November:** McClellan replaced Scott as general-in-chief. **2 November:** Lincoln removed Frémont from Missouri in quarrel over emancipation, in favor of Maj. Gen. David Hunter. **4 November:** Confederate Maj. Gen. Thomas J. Jackson took command in the Shenandoah Valley. **5 November:** Gen. Robert E. Lee sent to command the South Atlantic Coast. **6 November:** Confederate election of 1861 selected a permanent government and Congress. **7 November:** Reconstruction began in the Confederate South with a Union invasion of the South Carolina Sea Islands. Brig. Gen. U. S. Grant fought first battle at Belmont, Missouri. Confederate commissioners to Britain and France, James M. Mason and John Slidell, taken from the British mail ship *Trent* by Capt. Charles Wilkes of U.S.S. *San Jacinto*. **9 November:** Lincoln appointed Maj. Gen. Henry W. Halleck to command Mississippi Valley and Maj. Gen. Don Carlos Buell to command Army of the Cumberland, replacing Maj. Gen. William T. Sherman, removed for medical reasons. **18 November:** Hatteras Convention of loyalists met in North Carolina and elected Unionist Marble Nash Taylor as congressional representative, but he was refused a seat in Congress. **18 November:** Kentucky Confederate soldiers voted to secede. **21 November:** Judah P. Benjamin of Louisiana appointed secretary of war to replace Leroy P. Walker of Alabama, who resigned. Thomas Bragg of North Carolina became attorney general, replacing Judah P. Benjamin. **26 November:** The convention at Wheeling adopted a new constitution for the proposed state of West Virginia.

1861   4 December: U.S. Senate expelled Sen. John C. Breckinridge of Kentucky from its body as an avowed Rebel. **9 December:** U.S. Congress created the Joint Committee on the Conduct of the War. **10 December:** Kentucky formally seceded from the Union. **26 December:** Lincoln ordered the release of Confederate diplomats James M. Mason and John Slidell.

1862   10 January: Senate expelled Senators Waldo P. Johnson and Trusten Polk of Missouri for pro-Confederate proclivities. **11 January:** Lincoln accepted the resignation of Secretary of War Simon Cameron for wartime corruption and appointed him Minister to Russia, replacing Cassius Marcellus Clay, a Kentucky abolitionist. **15 January:** Edwin McM. Stanton confirmed as U.S. secretary of war. **19 January:** Yankees won Battle of Mill Springs or Logan's Crossroads. **27 January:** President Lincoln ordered Union armies to advance in General Orders No. 1. **30 January:** U.S.S. *Monitor* launched at Greenpoint, New York. **31 January:** Lincoln ordered Gen. McClellan to advance Army of Potomac in Special Orders No. 1 by February 22. **5 Febru-**

ary: U.S. Senate expelled Senator Jesse Bright of Indiana for Confederate sympathies. **6 February:** Ft. Henry surrendered to gunboats of the Union freshwater navy. **8 February:** Union victory at Battle of Roanoke Island, North Carolina. **11 February:** Confederates evacuated Bowling Green, Kentucky. **13 February:** Grant's Federal forces laid siege to Ft. Donelson. **14 February:** Adm. Foote's Federal gunboats beaten back in attack. **15 February:** Grant attacked by Confederates at Ft. Donelson; many Rebels escaped. **16 February:** Ft. Donelson surrendered unconditionally to Grant. **20 February:** Lincoln's son William Wallace "Willie" died of typhoid. **21 February:** Confederate victory at Val Verde, New Mexico Territory. **22 February:** Inaugural of permanent Confederate government at Richmond. **23 February:** Lincoln appointed Andrew Johnson military governor of Tennessee. **25 February:** Federal forces under Maj. Gen. Don Carlos Buell took Nashville. **27 February:** Confederate Congress gave President Davis power to suspend writ of *habeas corpus*. **2 March:** Confederates abandoned Columbus, Kentucky. Confederates under Gen. Sibley entered Albuquerque, New Mexico Territory. **4 March:** Confederates under Gen. Sibley entered Santa Fé, New Mexico Territory. **6 March:** Lincoln offered Federal aid to any state that would abolish slavery gradually. Lincoln issued General Orders No. 2, that McClellan leave sufficient forces to guard Washington in any operation against the Rebels. **6–8 March:** Confederates lost Battle of Pea Ridge in northern Arkansas. **8 March:** Ironclad C.S.S. *Virginia* wrought havoc on Federal blockade fleet of wooden ships at Hampton Roads. **9 March:** Ironclad U.S.S. *Monitor* saved the blockade by fighting C.S.S. *Virginia* to a standstill (often erroneously called the *Monitor* and the *Merrimack).* Confederates withdrew from Centerville Virginia, revealing that many of their cannon were fakes or "Quaker" guns. **11 March:** Lincoln issued General Orders No. 3, removing McClellan as general-in-chief. **14 March:** Federals under Maj. Gen. John Pope took New Madrid, Missouri. Federals under Gen. Burnside took New Berne, North Carolina. **18 March:** Confederate President Davis sent Judah P. Benjamin to the State Department to replace R. M. T. Hunter, who resigned to be senator from Virginia; appointed George W. Randolph secretary of war to replace Benjamin; and made Thomas H. Watts of Alabama attorney general, replacing Thomas Bragg of North Carolina, who resigned. **23 March:** Federals under Brig. Gen. Nathaniel Banks defeated Confederates under Maj. Gen. Stonewall Jackson at Kernstown. **26 March:** Union won the Battle of Apache Canyon, New Mexico Territory, but withdrew. **28 March:** Confederates won the Battle of Glorieta in New Mexico Territory at Pigeon's Ranch, but lost their supply column at Johnson's Ranch. **5 April:** On the Virginia Peninsula, McClellan began the Siege of Yorktown. **6–7 April:** Union Gen. Grant won Battle of Shiloh. **7 April:** Union Gen. Pope took Island No. 10 on the Mississippi River. **9 April:** Confederate Congress passed

First Conscription Act. **11 April:** Union Brig. Gen. Quincy A. Gillmore destroyed Ft. Pulaski at Savannah, demonstrating the power of rifled cannon against brick fortifications. **12 April:** In Great Locomotive Chase, 22 Federals captured a Confederate train in northern Georgia and raced north to destroy a Rebel supply line, but close pursuit rendered the attempt useless. Union Gen. Hunter, in command in South Carolina and Georgia Sea Islands, declared all slaves near Ft. Pulaski to be confiscated and free, one of several such orders Lincoln overturned. **15 April:** Confederate rearguard action at Peralta in New Mexico Territory to protect Rebel retreat, while other Confederates retreated from the Battle of Picacho in Arizona Territory in face of approach of the Union California Column. **16 April:** Confederate President Davis signed First Conscription Act. U.S. Congress abolished slavery in the District of Columbia and all Federal territories. **24 April:** After several day's preparatory bombardment, Union Adm. David Farragut's fleet passed the Confederate forts below New Orleans. **25 April:** Union Adm. Farragut arrived at New Orleans and took over the city. **1 May:** Union Gen. Benjamin F. Butler began the occupation and Reconstruction of the southeast third of Louisiana and other sites along the Gulf. **3 May:** Gen. Joseph Johnston's Confederates evacuate Yorktown, ending the siege. **5 May:** Battle of Williamsburg ended in a tie, but Confederates continued to retreat. **7 May:** Battle of Eltham's Landing ended with Confederate retreat. **8 May:** At Battle of McDowell in western Virginia, Confederate Gen. Jackson slapped Frémont's troops back to protect his left and rear in the First Shenandoah Valley Campaign. **9 May:** Union Gen. Hunter freed all slaves in his command area along the South Atlantic Coast, an order overturned by Lincoln on 19 May. **10 May:** Confederate fleet defeated in Mississippi River Battle at Plum Run near Ft. Pillow. **12 May:** Union Adm. Farragut's fleet occupied Natchez, Mississippi. **15 May:** Confederates beat back Union naval attack at Richmond's Drewry's Bluff. Union Gen. Butler issued General Orders No. 28, the "Woman Order." **18 May:** Union Adm. Farragut attacked Vicksburg, which refused to surrender. **19 May:** President Lincoln appointed Unionist Edward Stanly as provisional governor of North Carolina. **20 May:** Homestead Act passed Congress. **23 May:** Confederate Gen. Stonewall Jackson defeated Yankees at Front Royal, Virginia. **25 May:** Confederate Gen. Jackson defeated Gen. Nathaniel Banks at Winchester. **27 May:** Confederate Gen. Jackson demonstrated in front of Harper's Ferry. **30 May:** Union Gen. Halleck took Corinth, abandoned by the Confederates. **31 May–1 June:** Battle of Seven Pines and First Fair Oaks resulted in stalemate in front of Richmond and wounding of Gen. Joseph E. Johnston. **1 June:** Gen. Lee took command of the Army of Northern Virginia. **5 June:** Union troops captured the abandoned Ft. Pillow. **6 June:** Confederate river fleet defeated at Memphis. **7 June:** Union Gen. Butler hanged William Mumford at New Orleans for pulling Federal flag down.

8 June: Confederate Gen. Stonewall Jackson won Battle of Cross Keys. **9 June:** Confederate Gen. Jackson won Battle of Port Republic, ending the First Shenandoah Valley Campaign. **12–15 June:** Confederate cavalry Gen. J. E. B. Stuart rode a reconnaissance around McClellan's army, chased by his own father-in-law. **17 June:** Gen. Braxton Bragg named head of the Army of Tennessee. **22 June:** Tax Law passed by Congress, creating special tax commissioners to collect sums owed in arrears in the seceded South. **25 June:** Lee struck McClellan at the Battle of Oak Grove and got a stalemate. **25 June–1 July:** Seven Days Campaign. **26 June:** Lee attacked in Battle of Mechanicsville and won with slaughter. **27 June:** Lee attacked in the Battle of Gaines' Mill and won with slaughter. **28 June:** Adm. Farragut bypassed Vicksburg to meet the Federal river fleet north of the city. **29 June:** After losing contact with McClellan for a day, Confederate Gen. Robert E. Lee stuck him again at Savage's Station, taking numerous injured prisoners. **30 June:** McClellan escaped Lee at the drawn Battle of Frayser's Farm at Glendale. **1 July:** Lee defeated at Battle of Malvern Hill with slaughter. Pacific Railroad Act passed Congress and amended in 1864. **2 July:** U.S. Congress passed Morrill Land Grant College Act. **8 July:** President Lincoln met with McClellan at Harrison's Landing. **11 July:** Lincoln named Maj. Gen. Henry W. Halleck general-in-chief. **14 July:** Union Gen. John Pope moved his Army of Virginia south from Washington with bombastic addresses to troops and Confederate civilians. **17 July:** Second Confiscation Act passed Congress. **18 July:** The Dix–Hill Cartel on exchange of prisoners of war drawn up. **19 July:** President Lincoln appointed John S. Phelps provisional governor of Arkansas. **22 July:** President Lincoln presented first draft of the Emancipation Proclamation to his cabinet, agreed to await a military success before going public with it. **24 July:** Union Adm. Farragut withdrew his oceangoing fleet from the Mississippi. **28 July:** Confederate governors of the Trans-Mississippi requested a commanding general and arms, money, and munitions for self-defense. **29 July:** The Confederate cruiser C.S.S. *Alabama* escaped from English port to be outfitted for war at sea. **31 July:** President Lincoln stressed that Louisiana was to be brought back into the Union as soon as possible. **3 August:** McClellan's Union army ordered to join Gen. Pope via Aquia Creek or Washington. **5 August:** Confederates lost the Battle of Baton Rouge. **6 August:** Confederate ironclad C.S.S. *Arkansas* sunk at Baton Rouge. **9 August:** Confederate Gen. Stonewall Jackson barely defeated Union at Battle of Cedar Mountain. **14 August:** In front of a committee of black leaders, President Lincoln called for colonization of freed American blacks in Central America. **17 August–23 September:** Sioux Uprising in Minnesota. **20 August:** Horace Greeley claimed that abolition of slavery was the "Prayer of Twenty Millions." **26 August:** Confederate Gen. J. E. B. Stuart's cavalry outflanked Gen. Pope and struck Manassas Junction. **27 August:** Confederate Gen. Stonewall Jackson's infantry followed his cavalry around Pope to Manassas Junction. **28 August:** Confederate Gen. Jackson attacked Pope's confused men at Groveton. **29 August:** In Kentucky, Confederate Gen. Kirby Smith defeated Yankees at Richmond. **29–30 August:** Confederate Gen. Robert E. Lee won the Second Battle of Manassas. **1 September:** At the Battle of Chantilly, Confederate Gen. Jackson forced Union troops into the defenses around Washington. **2 September:** President Lincoln restored Gen. McClellan to field command, replacing Pope, who was sent to Minnesota to fight the Sioux. **6 September:** Lee's Confederate army at Frederick, Maryland. **9 September:** Lee issued General Orders No. 191, splitting up his army to conquer the Union garrison at Harper's Ferry and hold the Cumberland Valley in Maryland. **13 September:** Lee's "Lost Order" found by Union soldiers at Frederick, Maryland. **14 September:** Union Gen. McClellan attacked and defeated Lee's men at the Battles of South Mountain and Crampton's Gap. **15 September:** Confederate Gen. Stonewall Jackson took Harper's Ferry. **17 September:** Lee and McClellan met at the Battle of Antietam. In Kentucky, Gen. Bragg's invading Confederate army captured Mumfordville. **19 September:** Lee retreated to Virginia after daring McClellan to attack him again. Union Gen. William S. Rosecrans won Battle of Iuka, Mississippi. **22 September:** President Lincoln issued the preliminary Emancipation Proclamation, giving the South until New Year's to surrender or lose its right to slavery. **24 September:** President Lincoln sought to have an asylum for the freed black race outside the United States. President Lincoln issued a new suspension of the writ of *habeas corpus* throughout the North. **25 September:** Union Gen. Buell's army got to Louisville ahead of Bragg's invading Rebels. **27 September:** Confederate Congress passed the Second Conscription Act. Union Gen. Butler enrolled allegedly free Negroes in First Regiment of Louisiana Native Guards. **1–4 October:** President Lincoln visited Gen. McClellan at Antietam battleground. **3–4 October:** Union victory by Gen. Rosecrans at Battle of Corinth, Mississippi. **4 October:** Confederate Gov. Richard Hawes inaugurated at Frankfort, Kentucky. **8 October:** In Kentucky, Union Gen. Buell sort of won the Battle of Perryville. **9–12 October:** Confederate cavalry Gen. Stuart rode around McClellan's Union force for the second time in the war. **14 October:** Union congressional elections resulted in Republican losses in Ohio, Indiana, and Pennsylvania, and a Republican victory in Iowa. **19 October:** In Tennessee, Gen. Bragg's retreating Confederates reached Cumberland Gap. **24 October:** Angered by his lackadaisical pursuit, President Lincoln replaced Gen. Buell as head of the Army of the Cumberland with Gen. Rosecrans. **1 November:** Union Gen. McClellan re-entered Virginia. **3 November:** Along the South Atlantic Coast, Union Col. Thomas W. Higginson employed the First South Carolina (Colored) Regiment from local ex-slaves. **4 November:** In the North, the Republicans lost congressional elections in New York, New Jersey,

Illinois, and Wisconsin, and won in New England, the Border Slave States, California, and Michigan. **7 November:** Lincoln replaced Gen. McClellan with Maj. Gen. Ambrose E. Burnside. **15 November:** Confederate Secretary of War George W. Randolph resigned over President Davis' constant interference with his department. **21 November:** Confederate President Davis appointed James Seddon of Virginia as new secretary of war. **1 December:** President Lincoln asked Congress to consider gradual emancipation of slaves by 1 January 1900, compensation for the owners, and deportation of freed slaves out of the nation. **3 December:** Louisiana elected its first loyal congressmen, B. F. Flanders and Michael Hahn, who were seated in Congress until its adjournment in March 1863. **4 December:** Confederate Gen. Joseph Johnston assumed command in the Western theater. **7 December:** Union victory at the Battle of Prairie Grove, Arkansas. **10 December:** U.S. Congress passed bill to authorize the creation of state of West Virginia. **11 December:** Burnside's Federal army occupied Fredericksburg, Virginia. **13 December:** Confederates won lopsided victory at Battle of Fredericksburg. **15 December:** Union army evacuated Fredericksburg. **16 December:** Bvt. Maj. Gen. Nathaniel P. Banks became commander of the Department of the Gulf, including Louisiana, to forward Reconstruction. **18–20 December:** Collamer Committee called on President Lincoln in attempt to force Secretary of State William H. Seward out of cabinet, which failed. **20 December:** Confederate Gens. Earl Van Dorn and Nathan Bedford Forrest raided Holly Springs, Mississippi, and Jackson, Tennessee, and forced an end to Grant's first attempt to capture Vicksburg. **24 December:** Union forces took Galveston, Texas. **26 December:** President Lincoln ordered 38 Sioux leaders hanged at Mankato, Minnesota, for rebellion. **29 December:** Union forces under the command of Maj. Gen. William T. Sherman attacked and lost the Battle of Chickasaw Bayou at Vicksburg. **31 December:** Confederate Gen. Braxton Bragg attacked Union Gen. Rosecrans at Murfreesboro, Tennessee, on the banks of Stone's River.

1863   1 January: Emancipation Proclamation freed all slaves in Confederate territory. **2 January:** Second day of the Battle of Stone's River ended in Confederate defeat. **3 January:** Union Maj. Gen. John McClernand assumed command of Sherman's men and began an unauthorized campaign up the Arkansas River toward Little Rock. **11 January:** Union Gen. McClernand took Ft. Hindman at Arkansas Post. **14 January:** Confederate Gen. Kirby Smith ordered to take command of the Trans-Mississippi Department. **15 January:** Provisional Governor Edward Stanly of North Carolina resigned because of lack of sympathy with Emancipation. **19–22 January:** Burnside's Federal army attempted to outflank Lee to his north and west in what came to be called the "Mud March." **21 January:** Union Gen. Fitz John Porter, a

McClellan advocate, court-martialed and cashiered for failing to follow Pope's orders at Second Manassas. **25 January:** President Lincoln replaced Burnside in Virginia with Maj. Gen. Joseph Hooker. **29 January:** Confederate Congress authorized the Erlanger Loan for $15 million. **22 February:** Ground broken in California on the Central Pacific Railroad. **25 February:** National banking system created by Congress and amended in 1864. **26 February:** Cherokee Grand Council repealed its secession ordinance and declared for the Union. **3 March:** Lincoln signed Federal Conscription Act into law. Captured and Abandoned Property Act passed Congress. U.S. Congress authorized suspension of the writ of *habeas corpus* for any reason determined by the president during the war. **10 March:** Prize Cases, in which U.S. Supreme Court recognized Lincoln's right to deal with the Confederacy as a belligerent without legitimizing the Rebel government. **17 March:** Battle of Kelly's Ford, Virginia, Federal cavalry fought the Rebel horsemen well for the first time in the Eastern Theater. **26 March:** Voters in West Virginia authorized the gradual emancipation of their slaves. **2 April:** Women of Richmond engaged in the "Bread Riot" over food shortages. **7 April:** U.S. Navy attacked Charleston Harbor but was repulsed. **11 April:** Lt. Gen. James Longstreet's Corps from Lee's Army of Northern Virginia absent for one month at Suffolk siege. **16 April:** Union Gen. Grant sent his troops by land down the west bank of the Mississippi and had his river naval force bypass the batteries at Vicksburg. **17 April:** Union cavalry Brig. Gen. Benjamin Grierson began his raid through central Mississippi. **20 April:** President Lincoln endorsed the admission of the state of West Virginia on June 20. **24 April:** General Orders No. 100, issued by the Adjutant General's Office promulgating the Lieber Code, the American rules of war. **28 April:** Union Gen. Hooker began Chancellorsville Campaign. **29 April:** Battle of Grand Gulf lost by Union Mississippi River fleet. **30 April:** Gen. Grant's army crossed the Mississippi to the east bank at Bruinsburg. **1 May:** Grant's forces defeated Confederates at Port Gibson, Mississippi. **1–4 May:** Gen. Lee won the Battle of Chancellorsville. **2 May:** Grierson's Raid ended with Union cavalry entering Baton Rouge. Gen. Stonewall Jackson severely wounded by his own men after dark at Chancellorsville after crushing Union right flank. **3 May:** Union Col. Abel D. Streight and his raiders surrendered to Forrest's outnumbered Rebel cavalry in Alabama. **4 May:** Battle of Salem Church completed Lee's Confederate victory at Chancellorsville. **5 May:** War protestor and Ohio congressman Clement L. Vallandigham arrested by Maj. Gen. Burnside for speaking against the war in public. **7 May:** Gen. Grant decided to have his army live off the land in Mississippi. **10 May:** Gen. Stonewall Jackson died at Guiney's Station, Virginia. **12 May:** Gen. Grant won the Battle of Raymond, Mississippi. **13 May:** Grant sent McClernand to Fourteen Mile Creek to freeze the Vicksburg Confederate garrison, while the rest of his army headed to Jackson.

14 May: Grant won the Battle of Jackson, routing Gen. Joe Johnston's Rebels. Union Gen. Banks left New Orleans to besiege Port Hudson. **16 May:** Grant's Union army intercepted Gen. John C. Pemberton's Rebel army from Vicksburg at Champion's Hill, winning a major battle. **17 May:** Grant struck Pemberton's Confederates at Big Black River Bridge, driving them back to Vicksburg. **18 May:** Grant laid siege to Vicksburg. **19 May:** Grant impatiently assaulted Vicksburg, to be driven back with loss. President Lincoln changed Clement L. Vallandigham's sentence to banishment to the Confederacy. **21 May:** Gen. Banks laid siege to Port Hudson. **22 May:** Grant assaulted Vicksburg for a second time, to be driven off with loss. **25 May:** Vallandigham turned over to Confederates in Tennessee. **27 May:** Gen. Banks assaulted Port Hudson, to be driven off with loss. **30 May:** Gen. Lee reorganized the Army of Northern Virginia into three corps to cope with the loss of Stonewall Jackson. **3 June:** The first black regiment raised in the North, the 54th Massachusetts (Colored) Infantry arrived at Charleston, for battle. **9 June::** Realizing that Lee's Confederates were on the move, Gen. Joseph Hooker sent the Union cavalry against them at Brandy Station, the largest cavalry battle of the Civil War. **11 June:** Clement L. Vallandigham, now in Canada having run the blockade, nominated *in absentia* for governor on Democratic ticket. **14 June:** Lee's army in Shenandoah Valley won Second Battle of Winchester. In Louisiana, Union Gen. Banks assaulted Port Hudson again, being driven back with loss. **15 June:** Battle of Stephenson's Depot resulted in severe Union loss in prisoners. **16 June:** Lee's Confederates crossed the Potomac and headed north. **20 June:** President Lincoln appointed Unionist Francis S. Pierpont provisional governor of Virginia upon creation of West Virginia as a state. **21–22 June:** Cavalry battles at Aldie, Middleburg, and Upperville as Federals probed Lee's line of march. **23 June:** In the West, Union Gen. Rosecrans began his march upon Chattanooga with the Tullahoma Campaign. **25 June:** Lee's Cavalry under Stuart rode around the Union army a third time, not rejoining Lee until July 2 on the field at Gettysburg. **27 June:** In the East, Gen. George G. Meade replaced Hooker as commander of the Army of the Potomac. **1–3 July:** Union army won Battle of Gettysburg. **3 July:** Surrender negotiations at Vicksburg. **4 July:** Lee retreated from Gettysburg. Grant accepted the surrender of Vicksburg. **7 July:** Confederates retreated to Chattanooga, Tennessee, after Gen. Rosecrans' Tullahoma Campaign. **8 July:** Confederates surrendered Port Hudson, Louisiana, opening the Mississippi River. Confederate cavalry raider John H. Morgan and his men crossed the Ohio into Indiana. **10 July:** Union operations against Battery Wagner in Charleston Harbor began. **11 July:** First Union assault on Battery Wagner at Charleston failed. **13 July:** Morgan's Confederate raiders in Ohio. **13–14 July:** Lee's Confederates crossed the Potomac into Virginia. **13–15 July:** New York anti-draft riots. **18 July:** Second Union assault against Battery Wagner at Charleston failed. **19 July:** President Lincoln revoked appointment of John S. Phelps as provisional governor of Arkansas. **26 July:** Morgan's raiders captured in Ohio. **8 August:** Confederate President Davis rejected Gen. Lee's offer to resign because of the loss at Gettysburg. **16 August:** Union Gen. Rosecrans moved on Chattanooga. **17 August:** Union long-range artillery bombarded Ft. Sumter. **19 August:** Federal authorities resumed the draft in New York City. **21 August:** Confederate guerrillas sacked Lawrence, Kansas. **25 August:** Union Gen. Thomas Ewing issued General Orders No. 11, which forced all civilians in certain pro-Confederate counties in Missouri to leave their homesteads; crops, houses, and barns were burned. **29 August:** Confederate submarine *H. L. Hunley* sank with whole crew at Charleston. **2 September:** Union forces under Gen. Burnside took Knoxville, Tennessee. **6 September:** Britain retained the Laird Rams, preventing their transfer to the Confederate navy. **7 September:** Confederate forces evacuated Battery Wagner and all of Morris Island at Charleston. **8 September:** Confederates defeated Union naval attack at Sabine Pass, Texas. **9 September:** Gen. Rosecrans entered Chattanooga, having outflanked it through the mountains of northern Alabama and Georgia. Confederate President Davis decided to send Gen. Longstreet and his corps to Tennessee to aid Gen. Bragg. **10 September:** Union troops captured Little Rock, Arkansas. **15 September:** President Lincoln suspended the writ of *habeas corpus* nationwide. **18 September:** President Lincoln confirmed that colonization of freed slaves outside the United States was still his primary policy on race. **19–20 September:** Confederates won Battle of Chickamauga, driving Yankees from field in a rout as Longstreet's men debarked from trains right into the fight. **23 September:** President Lincoln agreed to send XI and XII Corps from Army of the Potomac under Gen. Hooker to Tennessee to help Rosecrans, besieged at Chattanooga. **9–22 October:** Gen. Lee launched his Bristoe Station Campaign. **13 October:** Union Party candidates won in North, especially in Ohio, where John Brough bested Clement L. Vallandigham, and in Indiana, Iowa, and Pennsylvania. **15 October:** Confederate submarine *H. L. Hunley* sank in Charleston again, losing all hands, including inventor Hunley himself. **16 October:** President Lincoln appointed Maj. Gen. U. S. Grant commander of all armies in the Western Theater, with right to fire Gen. Rosecrans, if necessary. **17 October:** Grant fired Rosecrans and replaced him with Maj. Gen. George Thomas. **24 October:** Grant arrived at Chattanooga and ordered the opening of a supply line to raise the siege. **27 October:** Federal artillery again bombarded Ft. Sumter in Charleston Harbor for several weeks. **27–28 October:** Grant's forces fought the Battle of Wauhatchie to open up Chattanooga through Brown's Ferry. **5 November:** Free Colored Men of New Orleans petitioned for the right to vote as the Union Radical Association. **9 November:** Confederate Gen. E. W. Gantt switched to Union side in Arkansas and called for an elected convention under Lincoln's Ten Percent Plan. **16 November–3 December:** Confederate Gen. Longstreet unsuccessfully besieged Federals in Knoxville, Tennessee. **19 November:** President Lincoln delivered the Gettysburg Address. **23 November:** Grant's Federals won Battle of Orchard Knob at Chattanooga. **24 November:** Grant's Federals won Battle of Lookout Mountain at Chattanooga. **25 November:** Grant's Federals won Battle of Missionary Ridge at Chattanooga. **26 November–1 December:** Union Gen. Meade launched the Mine Run Campaign in Virginia. **29 November:** Longstreet's Confederates attacked Ft. Sanders at Knoxville, to no avail. **30 November:** Confederate Gen. Bragg resigned his field command in north Georgia. **7 December:** Loyal Virginia legislature called election of constitutional convention for 21 January 1864. **8 December:** Lincoln issued Proclamation of Amnesty and Reconstruction. **16 December:** Confederate President Davis swallowed his hatred of Gen. Joseph Johnston and sent him to command Army of Tennessee, replacing Bragg. **18 December:** Union Gen. Rosecrans named commander in Missouri.

1864   **4 January:** Beginning of Arkansas state constitutional convention under Presidential Reconstruction. **19 January:** Arkansas state convention adopted an antislavery clause. **20 January:** State convention elected Unionist Isaac Murphy provisional governor of Arkansas. **23 January:** President Lincoln recognized the concept of free labor in contract relations between ex-slaves and plantation owners and ordered the army to encourage such and supervise their operations. **31 January:** President Lincoln urged Gen. Banks to adopt any rule that would encourage the vote of all loyal free men, even if they could not take the oath. **1 February:** President Lincoln called up 500,000 men under the Conscription Act to serve three years or the duration of the war. Congress revived the rank of lieutenant general. **3 February:** Gen. Sherman began his Meridian, Mississippi, campaign. **7 February:** Confederate Congress authorized the enrollment of blacks, slave or free, as military laborers. **9 February:** Led by Cols. Thomas Rose and Abel A. Streight, over 100 Federal officers made a massive prison break from Libby Prison in Richmond. **14 February:** Gen. Sherman took Meridian, Mississippi. **15 February:** *Ex parte* Vallandigham, the U.S. Supreme Court upheld the Confederate sympathizer's arrest, military trial, and exile to the Confederacy. **17 February:** C.S.S. *H. L. Hunley* sank the U.S.S. *Housatonic* off Charleston Harbor and was lost itself—first combat use of a submarine in history. **20 February:** Confederates won Battle of Ocean Pond near Olustee, Florida. **22 February:** Confederate Gen. Forrest soundly defeated U.S. forces at West Point and Okolona, Mississippi, forcing Sherman to abandon Meridian area. **24 February:** Confederate Gen. Braxton Bragg became general-in-chief under President Davis.

27 February: Andersonville Prison opened at Americus, Georgia. **28 February:** Union Kilpatrick–Dahlgren Raid, to free prisoners held in Richmond and kidnap or execute members of the Confederate government, began. **1 March:** Kilpatrick–Dahlgren failed, and its controversial orders fell into hands of the Confederates. **2 March:** U.S. Grant confirmed as lieutenant general and general-in-chief. **4 March:** Unionist Michael Hahn inaugurated first Free State governor of Louisiana. **8 March:** Gen. Grant arrived in Washington. **11 March:** Under Special Orders No. 9, Adj. Gen. Lorenzo Thomas codified employment practices regarding contrabands in the Mississippi Valley. **12 March:** Union's Red River Campaign began. **13 March:** President Lincoln suggested that Louisiana consider permitting very intelligent blacks to vote. **14 March:** Union Gen. Banks captured Ft. DeRussy on Red River. President Lincoln called up 200,000 men for naval and army reserve service. **16 March:** Gen. Banks occupied Alexandria, Louisiana. **18 March:** Gen. William T. Sherman to command Western Theater. **23 March:** Union Gen. Fred Steele began the Camden Campaign in Arkansas. **26 March:** Gen. Grant established his headquarters with the Army of the Potomac in the field. **28 March:** Louisiana elected delegates to a constitutional convention under Lincoln's Ten Percent Plan. **4 March:** Grant appointed Maj. Gen. Philip H. Sheridan to command Union cavalry in the Army of the Potomac. **6 April:** Louisiana constitutional convention held at New Orleans to write a free state document. **7 April:** Confederate Gen. Longstreet ordered to rejoin Lee's Army of Northern Virginia for first time since early September 1863. **8 April:** Gen. Banks' army defeated at Sabine Crossroads near Mansfield, Louisiana. **9 April:** Gen. Banks' army managed to hold on at Pleasant Hill, but retreated. **11 April:** Isaac Murphy elected governor of Free State of Arkansas. **12 April:** Confederate Gen. Forrest attacked and captured Ft. Pillow in Tennessee, putting many black and white captives to the sword. **17 April:** Gen. Grant ordered no more prisoner exchanges. **18 April:** Confederate cavalry captured 198 Union supply wagons at Poison Springs, Arkansas, striking a heavy blow at the Camden Campaign. **25 April:** Confederates defeated Gen. Steele at Marks' Mills in Camden Campaign. **27 April:** Confederate President Davis sent Jacob Thompson and Clement C. Clay to Canada as special commissioners to coordinate secret operations behind the Union lines. **28 April:** Confederate Gen. E. Kirby Smith granted supreme civil executive and military powers in Trans-Mississippi area. **29–30 April:** Battle of Jenkins' Ferry ended Union Camden Campaign in defeat. **1 May:** Gen. Banks' army retreated to Alexandria after nearly a month of Confederate skirmishing on its flanks and rear. **4 May:** In Virginia, Gen. Grant crossed the Rapidan into the Wilderness. **5 May:** Gen. Butler landed at City Point, Virginia, to threaten Richmond. **5–6 May:** Grant and Lee fought the Battle of the Wilderness to a stalemate. **7 May:** Gen. Sherman began his campaign to capture Atlanta. **8–19 May:** At Battles for Spotsylvania Court House, Grant and Lee fought to a stalemate after Grant nearly broke through Lee's lines twice. **9 May:** At Alexandria, Louisiana, Union engineers constructed numerous coffer dams to save beached Union river fleet. Gen. Sherman failed to breach Snake Creek Gap in Georgia and trap Johnston's opposing army. **11 May:** Gen. Sheridan's cavalry hit J. E. B. Stuart's Southerners at Yellow Tavern, defeating them and killing him. **12 May:** Confederate Gen. Johnston retreated from Dalton, Georgia, to escape potential encirclement. **13–17 May:** Gen. Sherman failed to corner Rebels again at Resaca, Georgia. **15 May:** In Shenandoah Valley, Union Gen. Franz Sigel defeated at Battle of New Market. **18 May:** Confederate Gen. Beauregard bottled up Union army at Bermuda Hundred. At Cassville, Georgia, Confederate Gen. Hood botched up Gen. Johnston's attack against Sherman's Union forces. **19 May:** Union Red River Campaign ended in failure. **20 May:** President Lincoln ordered that the army and navy not interfere with trade with the Confederacy carried on under treasury department guidelines. **21 May:** Arkansas U.S. senators and representatives presented credentials to Congress and put off in prolonged debate. **23–26 May:** Gen. Lee caught Grant's army astride the North Anna River but failed to coordinate an attack against it. **25 May–4 June:** Gen. Sherman attempted to flank Johnston at Dallas or New Hope Church, Georgia. **26–30 May:** Gen. Lee stopped Grant at Totopotomy Creek. **31 May:** Radical Democracy's Cleveland Convention nominated John Charles Frémont to oppose Abraham Lincoln for president. **1–3 June:** Grant lost heavy casualties attempting to overrun Lee's Confederate lines at Battle of Second Cold Harbor. **5 June:** In the Shenandoah Valley, Union Gen. David Hunter soundly defeated Rebels in the Battle of Piedmont. **7–9 June:** The National Union Party convention met at Baltimore to nominate Lincoln for president and Andrew Johnson of Tennessee for vice president. **10 June:** Confederate Gen. Forrest soundly whipped a Union force at the Battle of Brice's Crossroads, Mississippi. Confederate Congress passed Third Conscription Act. **11–12 June:** Gen. Sheridan's cavalry turned back from reinforcing Hunter in the Valley at the Battle of Trevillian's Station. **14 June:** Gen. Grant's forces began to cross the James River to the south bank. **15–18 June:** Gen. Grant's initial assaults on Petersburg failed and siege began. **17–18 June:** Confederate Gen. Jubal Early defeated Federal force under Gen. Hunter at Lynchburg, Virginia. **19 June:** U.S.S. *Kearsarge* sank C.S.S. *Alabama* at Cherbourg, France. **22–23 June:** Gen. Grant attacked the Jerusalem Plank Road and the Weldon Railroad. **24 June:** Maryland constitutional convention voted to abolish slavery. **27 June:** In Georgia, Gen. Sherman fought and lost Battle of Kennesaw Mountain. **28 June:** President Lincoln signed a congressional bill repealing the Fugitive Slave Acts. **28–**

28 June: Gen. Grant's attack at First Deep Bottom failed. **30 June:** Union Secretary of the Treasury Salmon P. Chase left the Lincoln cabinet, ostensibly over appointments but in reality to run for president. **1 July:** President Lincoln appointed William P. Fessenden as secretary of the treasury. **5 July:** Confederate Gen. Early crossed the Potomac into Maryland at Harper's Ferry. Because of Copperhead activities, President Lincoln suspended the writ of *habeas corpus* for Kentucky. **8 July:** Wade–Davis Bill, the First Congressional Plan of Reconstruction, passed and pocket vetoed by President Lincoln. **9 July:** Gen. Early defeated Union forces at the Battle of the Monocacy River near Frederick, Maryland. Confederate Gen. Johnston fought delaying action at the Chattahoochie River and retreated to Atlanta. **12 July:** President Lincoln came under fire at the Battle of Fort Stevens, after which Confederate Gen. Early withdrew across the Potomac. **14 July:** Union forces in Mississippi suffered another setback when, after defeating Gen. Forrest, they had to withdraw from their overextended positions. **17 July:** In Georgia, Lt. Gen. John Bell Hood replaced Gen. Johnston as commander of the Confederate army in front of Atlanta. **18 July:** President Lincoln issued a call for 500,000 more men. New York newspaper editor Horace Greeley went to Niagara Falls to discuss peace with Confederate emissaries; it came to nothing. **20 July:** In Georgia, Confederate Gen. Hood attacked Sherman at the Battle of Peachtree Creek and lost. **22 July:** In Georgia, Gen. Hood attacked Sherman at the Battle of Atlanta and lost. **24 July:** In the Shenandoah Valley, Confederate Gen. Early defeated Yankees at the Battle of Second Kernstown. **28 July:** In Georgia, Gen. Hood attacked Sherman at the Battle of Ezra Church and lost. **30 July:** Gen. Grant's attack at the Battle of the Crater failed. Confederate cavalry burned Chambersburg, Pennsylvania, after it could not raise the ransom of $500,000 in cash and $100,000 in gold. **3 August:** Gens. Grant and Sheridan arrived in Washington to put Sheridan in charge of a force to defeat Confederate Gen. Early in the Valley. **5 August:** Wade–Davis Manifesto denounced Lincoln's veto of First Congressional Plan of Reconstruction. Union Adm. Farragut fought and won the Battle of Mobile Bay. **9 August:** Two Confederate secret agents blew up Grant's main supply base at City Point, Virginia. **13–20 August:** Gen. Grant's attack at Second Deep Bottom failed. **18–21 August:** Gen. Grant extended his line south at Petersburg in the Battle of Globe Tavern. **21 August:** Confederate Gen. Forrest captured and held briefly Memphis, Tennessee. **23 August:** President Lincoln had cabinet sign a blind document that promised to cooperate with the Democrats to save the Union if they won the 1864 Election. **25 August:** Gen. Grant's II Corps routed at Battle of Reams' Station. **30 August:** Northern Democrats met at Chicago for their convention, adopting a peace platform and nominating George B. McClellan, who promptly repudiated the platform. **31 August–1**

September: Gen. Sherman fought and won the Battle of Jonesboro, forcing the Confederates to abandon Atlanta the next day. **7 September:** Gen. Sherman ordered civilians to evacuate Atlanta. **16 September:** In Mississippi, Confederate Gen. Forrest began his West Tennessee Raid. **17 September:** In the North, Frémont withdrew from the presidential contest. **19 September:** In the Shenandoah Valley, Gen. Sheridan defeated the Confederates at the Battle of Third Winchester or Opequon Creek. **22 September:** In the Shenandoah Valley, Gen. Sheridan defeated the Confederates at Fisher's Hill. **28–30 September:** Gen. Grant halted at the Battle of Chaffin's Farm. **30 September–2 October:** Gen. Grant extended his lines to the south of Petersburg in the Battle of Peebles' Farm. **5 October:** In Georgia, Gen. Hood's army attacked Sherman's line of supply at the battle of Allatoona Station. Union authorities arrested Lamdin P. Milligan for Copperhead activities and tried and convicted him before a military court. **6 October:** Louisiana state constitutional convention met under the Lincoln Ten Percent Plan. **7 October:** Union Gen. Grant's attack at New Market Heights failed. **9 October:** Harassed by Confederate cavalry, Gen. Sheridan ordered his own horsemen to defeat the Confederates at the Battle of Tom's Brook, which was done so effectively, resulting in the Woodstock Races. **11 October:** Northern elections in Pennsylvania, Ohio, and Indiana went heavily Republican. **12 October:** U.S. Supreme Court Chief Justice Roger B. Taney died. **13 October:** Maryland voters narrowly passed a new state constitution abolishing slavery. **19 October:** After almost losing, Gen. Sheridan decisively defeated Confederate Gen. Early's army at the battle of Cedar Creek. Confederate soldiers raided St. Albans Vermont and fled back to Canada. **23 October:** In Missouri, the Battle of Westport (Kansas City) ended Confederate Gen. Price's Missouri raid in defeat. **27 October:** Gen. Grant could not supply his attack south of Petersburg at the Battle of First Hatcher's Run. **27–28 October:** Gen. Grant's attack at Second Fair Oaks Failed. **4 November:** Confederate Gen. Forrest attacked the Union supply base at Johnsonville, Tennessee, from land and water, using captured Federal gunboats, and disrupted the Yankee supply line to Nashville. **8 November:** Abraham Lincoln reelected president, but not as a Republican, the first Northerner in American history to receive a second term. **14 November:** President Lincoln ordered the military commanders in Louisiana to cooperate more fully with his civilian Ten Percent government there. **16 November:** In Georgia, Union Gen. Sherman reorganized his army into two wings and began the March to the Sea. **21 November:** Confederate Gen. Hood, ignoring the March to the Sea, sent his army back into Tennessee to cut the nonexistent Yankee supply line. Gen. Sherman defeated Georgia state militia at Griswoldville. **25 November:** Confederate secret agents attempted to burn New York City but failed. **29 November:** Confederate Gen. Hood stumbled by allowing Union troops under Maj. Gen. John Schofield, cut off to the southeast, to bypass his position at Spring Hill, Tennessee. **30 November:** As if to make up for the mistake at Spring Hill the day before, Confederate Gen. Hood ordered his army to attack Union troops dug in at Franklin on the road to Nashville, at tremendous loss to the Rebels in men and officers. **6 December:** President Lincoln named Salmon P. Chase as chief justice of the U.S. Supreme Court. **8 December:** On the March to the Sea, one of Gen. Sherman's corps commanders took up a pontoon bridge across Ebeneezer Creek, abandoning black refugees to the scant mercies of attacking Confederate cavalry. **10 December:** Gen. Sherman's March to the Sea concluded with the reaching of Savannah. **13 December:** General Sherman captured Ft. McAllister at Savannah, Georgia. **15–16 December:** After much delay from logistics and weather, Union Gen. Thomas attacked Hood's Confederates at Nashville and routed the Rebels in the only decisive major battle of the war. **20 December:** Confederate troops evacuated Savannah. **24 December:** Union Adm. David D. Porter bombarded Ft. Fisher at Wilmington, North Carolina, the last Confederate port open to the outside world. **25 December:** Federal troops under Gen. Ben Butler landed at Ft. Fisher, only to be defeated by Confederate defenders. **27 December:** What was left of Confederate Gen. Hood's army crossed the Tennessee River into Alabama. **30 December:** President Lincoln gave Gen. Grant the go-ahead to fire Gen. Butler for his fiasco at Ft. Fisher and replace him with Maj. Gen. E. O. C. Ord.

1865   **6 January:** Proposed Thirteenth Amendment abolishing slavery reintroduced in the U.S. House of Representatives, having already passed the Senate. **9 January:** Tennessee state convention voted to abolish slavery, which was confirmed by a popular vote on 22 February. **11 January:** Missouri state constitutional convention voted to abolish slavery. **12 January:** Frank Blair, Sr., a Northern Democratic politician with sons in the Republican Party, conferred with Confederate President Davis on a possible Peace Conference. **13–15 January:** Second attack on Ft. Fisher at Wilmington, North Carolina, led by Union Gen. Alfred Terry was successful. **16 January:** Frank Blair, Sr., reported to President Lincoln on his discussions for peace with Confederate President Davis, but Lincoln refused to act as if there were two nations. Maj. Gen. William T. Sherman issued Special Orders No. 15 creating a 30-mile-wide land zone set aside exclusively for the use of freedmen and their families along the South Atlantic Coast. **18 January:** President Lincoln told Blair that he would talk informally with any representative from the South about peace. **19 January:** General Sherman began his Carolinas Campaign, a duplicate of the March to the Sea. **23 January:** Confederate Congress created the position of general-in-chief, and President Davis appointed Robert E. Lee on 31 January. Confederate Gen. Richard Taylor transferred from Louisiana to the Western Theater as overall commander, but lost his only army, which was sent to the Carolinas. **24 January:** Confederate Congress proposed a prisoner exchange, and Union Gen. Grant agreed, ending a nearly year-long boycott. **30 January:** President Lincoln issued a pass to permit three Confederate peace commissioners to come to Union-held Fortress Monroe, Virginia. **31 January:** Congress passed the Thirteenth Amendment, which would take until December 18 to be approved by the requisite number of states. **1 February:** Confederate Secretary of War Seddon resigned. **2 February:** President Lincoln and Secretary of State Seward met with Confederate Senator R. M. T. Hunter, Assistant Secretary of War John Campbell, and Vice President Alexander H. Stephens aboard the *River Queen* in Hampton Roads to discuss peace, to no avail, and told them that his policy toward freed blacks was that they were now on their own: "root hog, or die." **5–7 February:** Union Gen. Grant's attack south of Petersburg at the battle of Second Hatcher's Run extended his lines. **6 February:** President Davis appointed John C. Breckinridge Confederate secretary of war. **13 February:** Virginia state constitutional convention met under Lincoln's Ten Percent Plan. **17 February:** Union Gen. Sherman blamed Confederate Gen. Wade Hampton as Columbia, South Carolina, burned. Confederates abandoned Charleston, South Carolina. **21 February:** Confederate Gen. Braxton Bragg arrived to defend Wilmington and ordered its evacuation to save troops from capture. **22 February:** At a request from Gen. Lee, Confederate President Davis restored Joseph Johnston to command in the Carolinas. **2 March:** Gen. Sheridan crushed the remnants of Confederate Gen. Early's army at Waynesboro, Virginia. **3 March:** Charter of Freedmen's Savings and Trust Company issued. Creation of the Bureau of Refugees, Freedmen and Abandoned Lands. **4 March:** Governor Michael Hahn of Louisiana accepted election to the U.S. Senate, turning the governorship over to James M. Wells. President Lincoln inaugurated to begin his second term. **8–10 March:** Confederate Gens. Johnston and Bragg attacked Union Gen. Sherman's army at Kinston, North Carolina, to no avail. **11 March:** General Orders No. 23 of the Department of the Gulf codified employment practices for the employment of contrabands in Louisiana. **13 March:** Confederate Congress approved the use of black combat troops. **16 March:** Confederate Gen. Johnston attacked Gen. Sherman's army at Avrasboro, North Carolina, to no avail. **19–21 March:** Confederate Gen. Johnston attacked Gen. Sherman's army at Bentonville, North Carolina, to no avail. **25 March:** Gen. Lee attacked the Union siege lines at Petersburg at Ft. Stedman, but failed. **27 March:** President Lincoln and Gens. Grant and Sherman met aboard the *River Queen* at City Point, Virginia, to discuss peace terms for the Southern armies when they surrendered. **1 April:** Union Gen. Sheridan outflanked Gen. Lee's forces at the

Battle of Five Forks, Virginia. **2 April:** Confederate army and civilian government abandoned the Richmond and Petersburg lines. Union Gen. James H. Wilson defeated Confederate Gen. Forrest at Selma, Alabama. **3 April:** Union army occupied Richmond, Virginia. **4 April:** President Lincoln visited Richmond, Virginia. **5 April:** William G. "Parson" Brownlow elected first loyal governor of a seceded state. **6 April:** Gen. Lee lost half of his army at the Battle of Sayler's Creek. **8 April:** Confederate Spanish Fort fell at Mobile, Alabama. **9 April:** Gen. Lee surrendered his army to Gen. Grant at Appomattox Court House, Virginia. **11 April:** President Lincoln's last public speech from the White House balcony treated Louisiana Reconstruction, seating the Free State government of Louisiana in Congress, and the need for blacks of intelligence and those who served as soldiers to vote. **12 April:** Fall of Mobile, Alabama, as Confederates evacuated the city. **14 April:** President Lincoln shot by John Wilkes Booth at Ford's Theater. Federal flag raised over Ft. Sumter. **15 April:** Lincoln died and was succeeded by Andrew Johnson as president. **18 April:** At Durhan Station, North Carolina, Union Gen. Sherman and Confederate Gen. Johnston signed "Memorandum or Basis of Agreement" that surrendered all Confederate armies, provided for recognition of existing Southern state governments, and established a general amnesty. **19 April:** Funeral services for Lincoln in Washington, followed by a rail tour of his body by the same route he had come to the capital in 1861. **24 April:** Union Secretary of War Stanton rejected Gen. Sherman's treaty with Confederate Gen. Johnston, which Sherman characterized as Lincoln's wishes as revealed aboard the *River Queen* on 27 March. **26 April:** Confederate Gen. Johnston surrendered his army to Gen. Sherman on the same terms given Lee in Virginia. Union cavalry shot and killed John Wilkes Booth at Garrett's farm near Port Royal, Virginia. **27 April:** Steamship *Sultana* blew up on the Mississippi near Memphis, killing as many as 1,900 people, many returning Union prisoners of war, in the worst maritime disaster in U.S. history. **4 May:** Confederate Gen. Richard Taylor surrendered the Confederate Western Theater at Citronelle, Alabama. **9 May:** President Johnson recognized the Pierpont Virginia government. **10 May:** Confederate President Davis and party captured by Union cavalry at Irwinsville, Georgia. **12 May:** Confederates won last land battle of war at Palmetto Ranch, Texas. **23 May:** Grand review in Washington of the Army of the Potomac. **24 May:** Grand review in Washington of Sherman's armies. **26 May:** Surrender of Confederate Gen. E. Kirby Smith's Trans-Mississippi forces. **29 May:** President Johnson's proclamation of amnesty and pardon, which exempted all those worth $20,000 or more unless they made special application. President Johnson appointed Unionist William W. Holden provisional governor of North Carolina. **13 June:** President Johnson appointed Unionist Benjamin F. Perry provisional governor of South Carolina. President Johnson appointed Unionist William

H. Sharkey governor of Mississippi. **17 June:** President Johnson appointed Andrew Jackson Hamilton provisional governor of Texas. President Johnson appointed James Johnson provisional governor of Georgia. **19 June:** Pierpont government moved from Alexandria to Richmond, Virginia. **21 June:** President Johnson appointed Conservative Lewis Parsons provisional governor of Alabama. **23 June:** End of the naval blockade of the Southern states. **7 July:** Execution of the Lincoln conspirators at the Washington arsenal. **13 July:** President Johnson appointed Unionist William Marvin as provisional governor of Florida. **14 August:** Beginning of Mississippi state constitutional convention under Presidential Reconstruction. **12 September:** Beginning of Alabama state constitutional convention under Presidential Reconstruction. **13 September:** Beginning of South Carolina state constitutional convention under Presidential Reconstruction. **27 September:** Radicals met in Louisiana and elected Carpetbagger Henry Clay Warmoth as territorial delegate to Congress (Warmoth would be seated in December when the real Louisiana delegation was refused its seats). **2 October:** Beginning of Georgia state constitutional convention under Presidential Reconstruction. Beginning of North Carolina state constitutional convention under Presidential Reconstruction. Conservative Benjamin G. Humphries elected governor of Mississippi. **11 October:** President Johnson pardoned all captured Confederate executive officials except Jefferson Davis. **18 October:** Conservative James L. Orr elected governor of South Carolina. **25 October:** Beginning of Florida state constitutional convention under Presidential Reconstruction. **6 November:** Confederate cruiser C.S.S. *Shenandoah* surrendered at Liverpool, England. Unionist J. Madison Wells elected governor of Louisiana under President Johnson's Reconstruction plan on both Union and Democrat tickets and switched his party affiliation to Democrat. **9 November:** Conservative Jonathan Worth elected governor of North Carolina. **10 November:** Confederate Capt. Henry Wirtz hanged for war crimes committed as commandant of Andersonville Prison. **15 November:** Conservative Charles M. Jenkins elected governor of Georgia. **29 November:** Florida elected Conservative David S. Walker as governor. **December:** Ku Klux Klan founded at Pulaski, Tennessee. **1 December:** President Johnson ended the suspension of the writ of *habeas corpus* everywhere except in the District of Columbia, the former Confederate States, and the territories of New Mexico and Arizona. **2 December:** Mississippi legislature enacted Black Code. **4 December:** Congress rejected the Confederate Brigadiers as the South's Federal representatives and senators. **13 December:** Conservative Robert M. Patton inaugurated governor of Alabama. **15 December:** Alabama legislature enacted Black Code. **18 December:** Thirteenth Amendment ratified. **20 December:** Louisiana legislature enacted Black Code. **21 December:** South Carolina legislature enacted Black Code.

1866   **15 January:** Florida legislature enacted Black Code. **7 February:** Beginning of Texas state constitutional convention under Presidential Reconstruction. **8 February:** Southern Homestead Act passed by Congress. **19 February:** President Johnson vetoed Freedmen's Bill Renewal. **22 February:** President Johnson's Washington's Birthday Speech announced an open breech with Congress over Reconstruction. **28 February:** Virginia legislature enacted Black Code. **10 March:** North Carolina legislature enacted Black Code. **17 March:** Georgia legislature enacted Black Code. **2 April:** President Johnson declared the Civil War over everywhere except Texas. **9 April:** Civil Rights Act of 1866 passed over Johnson's veto. **16 April:** Norfolk race riot. **26 April:** War of the Rebellion officially ended by President Johnson. **1 May:** Memphis race riot. **13 June:** Fourteenth Amendment passed Congress and sent to the states for ratification. **20 June:** Report of the Joint Committee of Fifteen on Reconstruction issued. **8 July:** Judge R. K. Howell (probably illegally) recalled the Louisiana State Convention of 1864 to meet on 30 July to amend the state constitution allowing African-American suffrage and adopt the Fourteenth Amendment. **16 July:** Freedmen's Bureau Renewal Act passed over Johnson's veto. **24 July:** Tennessee ratified Fourteenth Amendment and restored to Union. **30 July:** New Orleans race riot. **13 August:** Conservative James W. Throckmorton sworn in as governor of Texas. **14 August:** "Arm-in-Arm" Convention, at which the National Union political coalition met to support Johnson's Reconstruction policy. **20 August:** President Johnson declared Civil War over in Texas. **28 August:** Beginning of Johnson's "Swing Around the Circle" tour, which alienated Northern voters. **8 November:** Texas legislature enacted Black Code. **17 December:** *Ex parte* Milligan, U.S. Supreme Court ruled that suspension of civil courts unless area under actual enemy attack was unconstitutional.

1867   **7 January:** Congress began investigation designed to impeach Johnson. **8 January:** Blacks received right to vote in District of Columbia. **14 January:** *Ex parte* Garland, U.S. Supreme Court limited the use of the test oath for practitioners in Federal courts. In Cummings *v.* Missouri, U.S. Supreme Court limited the use of the test oath for clergymen. **Spring:** Union Loyal Leagues organized white and black Republican voters in South. **2 March:** Command of the Army Act passed Congress. First Military Reconstruction Act passed Congress. Fortieth Congress Extra Session Act kept Congress in session to negate any chance that President Johnson would interfere with Military Reconstruction. Tenure of Office Act passed Congress. **11 March:** Commanders of the military districts appointed by President Johnson: First Military District (Virginia), Brevet Major General John Schofield, Second Military District (North and South Carolinas), Brevet Major General Daniel Sickles, Third Military District (Georgia, Alabama, and

Florida), Brevet Major General John Pope, Fourth Military District (Arkansas and Mississippi), Brevet Major General E. O. C. Ord, Fifth Military District (Louisiana and Texas), Major General Philip H. Sheridan. **15 April:** In Mississippi *v.* Johnson, U.S. Supreme Court upheld the president's enforcement of the Military Reconstruction Acts. **22 April:** Bvt. Maj. Gen. John Pope tried to replace Governor Jenkins of Georgia, without success. **23 April:** Second Military Reconstruction Act passed Congress. **30 April:** Alaska purchased from Russia. **13 May:** In Georgia *v.* Stanton, Supreme Court upheld the secretary of war's enforcement of the Military Reconstruction Acts. **3 June:** Major General Philip H. Sheridan appointed Scalawag Republican B. F. Flanders to replace Louisiana Democrat Governor J. Madison Wells, who was removed. **19 July:** Third Military Reconstruction Act passed Congress. **30 July:** Maj. Gen. Philip H. Sheridan appointed Scalawag Republican Elisha M. Pease provisional governor of Texas to replace Conservative James W. Throckmorton, who was removed. **19 August:** President Johnson appointed Bvt. Maj. Gen. Charles Griffin commander of Fifth Military District to replace Gen. Sheridan, who was removed. **5 September:** President Johnson appointed Bvt. Maj. Gen. E. R. S. Canby commander of Second Military District. **16 September:** President Johnson appointed Bvt. Maj. Gen. Joseph Mower commander of Fifth Military District to replace Gen. Griffin, who died of yellow fever. **23 November:** Beginning of Louisiana state constitutional convention under the Military Reconstruction Acts. **29 November:** Maj. Gen. Winfield Scott Hancock replaced Gen. Mower as commander of Fifth Military District and issued his General Orders No. 40, which limited the effect of military government in his command area. **5 December:** Beginning of Alabama state constitutional convention under the Military Reconstruction Acts. **9 December:** Beginning of Georgia state constitutional convention under the Military Reconstruction Acts. **28 December:** Bvt. Maj. Gen. George G. Meade replaced Gen. Pope in charge of Third Military District.

1868   **7 January:** Beginning of Arkansas state constitutional convention under the Military Reconstruction Acts. **9 January:** Beginning of Mississippi state constitutional convention under the Military Reconstruction Acts. President Johnson appointed Bvt. Maj. Gen. Alvan C. Gillem commander of the Fourth Military District to replace Gen. Ord, who was removed. **13 January:** Gen. Meade appointed Bvt. Brig. Gen. Thomas H. Ruger provisional governor of Georgia to replace Charles M. Jenkins. **14 January:** Beginning of South Carolina state constitutional convention under the Military Reconstruction Acts. **20 January:** Beginning of Florida state constitutional convention under Military Reconstruction Acts. **4 February:** Scalawag Republican William H. Smith elected governor of Alabama. **10 February:** In Georgia *v.* Grant *et al.*, Supreme Court upheld the Army's enforcement of the Military

Reconstruction Acts. **17 February:** *Ex parte* McCardle, Supreme Court upheld the Congress's right to alter its appellate jurisdiction. **24 February:** Congress impeached President Johnson. **4 March:** Johnson impeachment trial began. **11 March:** Fourth Military Reconstruction Act passed Congress. **25 March:** President Johnson appointed Bvt. Maj. Gen. Robert C. Buchanan commander of Fifth Military District to replace Gen. Hancock, who resigned. **3 April:** Bvt. Maj. Gen. John Schofield appointed Carpetbag Republican Henry H. Wells governor of Virginia to replace Francis S. Pierpont, who was removed. **16 April:** Carpetbag Republican Robert K. Scott elected governor of South Carolina for a first term. **20 April:** Carpetbag Republican Rufus Bullock elected governor of Georgia. **23 April:** Scalawag Republican William W. Holden elected governor of North Carolina. President Johnson appointed Bvt. Maj. Gen. George Stoneman commander of First Military District to replace Gen. Schofield, who became secretary of war, replacing Edwin McM. Stanton. **16 May:** Johnson found not guilty in impeachment trial. **1 June:** Beginning of first session of Texas state constitutional convention under Military Reconstruction Acts. **4 June:** President Johnson appointed Bvt. Maj. Gen. Irvin McDowell commander of the Fourth Military District to replace Gen. Gillem, who was removed. **15 June:** Gen. Irvin McDowell appointed Bvt. Maj. Gen. Adelbert Ames governor of Mississippi to replace Governor Benjamin G. Humphries, who was removed. **22 June:** Arkansas first state to be readmitted to Union under Military Reconstruction Acts. Mississippi rejected its constitution drawn up under the Military Reconstruction Acts. **24 June:** Gen. Meade appointed Scalawag Republican Governor-elect William H. Smith to replace Conservative Governor Robert M. Patton of Alabama, who was removed. **25 June:** Florida readmitted to the Union under the Reconstruction Acts. Omnibus Bill readmitted North Carolina, South Carolina, Florida, Georgia, Alabama, and Louisiana under Military Reconstruction Acts. **30 June:** Bvt. Maj. Gen. E. R. S. Canby appointed Scalawag Republican Governor William W. Holden governor to replace Jonathan Worth, who was removed. **1 July:** Carpetbag Republican Harrison Reed inaugurated governor of Florida. **2 July:** Carpetbag Republican Powell Clayton inaugurated governor of Arkansas. **4 July:** North Carolina readmitted to the Union under the Reconstruction Acts. **6 July:** Congress extended Freedmen's Bureau for one more year. **9 July:** Louisiana readmitted to the Union under the Reconstruction Acts. South Carolina readmitted to the Union under the Reconstruction Acts. **10 July:** President Johnson reappointed Bvt. Maj. Gen. Alvan C. Gillem commander Fourth Military District to replace Gen. McDowell, who was removed. **13 July:** Alabama readmitted to the Union under the Reconstruction Acts. Carpetbag Republican Henry Clay Warmoth inaugurated governor of Louisiana. **25 July:** Congress closed down all Freedmen's Bureau operations as of 1 January 1869, except for education, and Bvt. Maj. Gen. Oliver O. Howard confirmed as head of Bureau for its duration or until he chose to resign. **28 July:** Fourteenth Amendment ratified. President Johnson appointed Bvt. Maj. Gen. Joseph J. Reynolds commander of Fifth Military District, now consisting of Texas alone. **11 August:** Thaddeus Stevens died. **3 September:** Black members purged from Georgia legislature. **19 September:** Camilla race riot in Georgia. **4 November:** Bvt. Maj. Gen. E. R. S. Canby appointed commander Fifth Military District to replace Gen. Reynolds, who was removed. Governor Powell Clayton of Arkansas declared martial law for four months to fight the Ku Klux Klan, the Knights of the White Camellia, and assorted lawbreakers. **6 November:** First attempt to impeach Governor Harrison Reed of Florida failed. **1 December:** Georgia removed from the Union for violating Military Reconstruction Acts. **8 December:** Beginning of second session of Texas state constitutional convention under Military Reconstruction Acts. **9 December:** Virginia state constitutional convention met under Military Reconstruction Acts. **24 December:** Johnson issued a general amnesty of Confederate soldiers and civil officials.

1869   26 January: Second attempt to impeach Governor Harrison Reed of Florida failed. **7 February:** Military Reconstruction constitution assembled by civilian–military committee. **25 February:** Parson Brownlow resigned as governor of Tennessee to become U.S. senator, appointing Scalawag Republican DeWitt C. Senter to succeed him as governor. **4 March:** Ulysses S. Grant inaugurated as president. **5 March:** President Grant appointed Bvt. Maj. Gen. Thomas Ruger commander of Third Military District. President Grant appointed Bvt. Maj. Gen. Joseph J. Reynolds commander of Fifth Military District to replace Gen. Canby, who was removed. **18 March:** Public Credit Act guaranteed the payment of the U.S. debt in gold or its equivalent. **27 March:** Bvt. Maj. Gen. George Stoneman tried to remove Governor Wells of Virginia and was replaced by Bvt. Maj. Gen. E. R. S. Canby; Wells was reinstated. **12 April:** In Texas *v.* White, U.S. Supreme Court upheld the Military Reconstruction Acts. **10 May:** Transcontinental railroad completed at Promontory Summit, Utah. **31 May:** President Grant appointed Bvt. Maj. Gen. Alfred Terry commander of Third Military District. **6 July:** Conservative Fusionist Gilbert C. Walker elected governor of Virginia on platform of "universal suffrage and universal amnesty." **30 August:** Bvt. Maj. Gen. Joseph J. Reynolds assumed governorship of Texas upon resignation of Elisha M. Pease. **21 September:** Bvt. Maj. Gen. E. R. S. Canby appointed Governor-elect Walker to office in Virginia. **24 September:** "Black Friday" crash on New York Stock Exchange as Jay Gould and Jim Fisk's attempt to corner gold market was thwarted. **4 October:** Tennessee redeemed, Scalawag Republican DeWitt C. Senter changed parties to Conservative Democrat and won the election, after Republicans nominated another. **5 October:** Virginia redeemed, only Southern state to be redeemed before its readmission to the Union under the Military Reconstruction Acts. **25 October:** *Ex parte* Yerger, Supreme Court upheld its jurisdiction in *habeas corpus* cases under the Judiciary Act of 1789 regardless of the intent of Congress during more recent Reconstruction measures. **30 November:** Mississippi voted for its constitution and against disfranchisement of whites of Confederate antecedents, electing Scalawag Republican James L. Alcorn as governor. **22 December:** Congress told Georgia to reassemble the legislature under which it had been readmitted in 1868. **24 December:** Bvt. Maj. Gen. Alfred Terry sent to purge Georgia of rebellious elements.

1870 **18 January:** Scalawag Republican Edmund J. Davis sworn in as governor of Texas. **26 January:** Virginia readmitted to Union under Military Reconstruction Acts. **7 February:** In Hepburn *v.* Griswold, U.S. Supreme Court ruled that greenbacks were legal for debts contracted only after 1862. **23 February:** Mississippi readmitted to Union under Military Reconstruction Acts. **25 February:** Hiram R. Revels became first African-American U.S. senator. **30 April:** Fifteenth Amendment ratified. Texas readmitted to Union under Military Reconstruction Acts. **31 May:** First Enforcement Act passed Congress. **20 June:** Beginning of five-month Kirk-Holden War against the Ku Klux Klan in North Carolina. **14 July:** Funding Act allowed bond holders to exchange wartime-issued bonds bought with inflated greenbacks for new ones redeemable in gold. **15 July:** Georgia readmitted to Union for second time under Military Reconstruction Acts. **4 August:** Conservatives won control of North Carolina legislature. **19 October:** Carpetbag Republican Robert K. Scott elected governor of South Carolina for a second term. **23 October:** Eutaw, Alabama, race riot. **3 November:** North Carolina essentially redeemed with seating of Conservative legislature. **4 November:** Conservative Democrat Robert B. Lindsay elected governor of Alabama, but legislative split (Democrat house, Republican senate) stalemated regime. **12 December:** Joseph H. Rainey became first African-American to sit in U.S. House of Representatives. **15 December:** North Carolina state legislature impeached Governor William W. Holden, found him guilty, and removed him from office on 22 March 1871.

1871 **10 January:** Brooks–Baxter War between rival Republicans in Arkansas began as Powell Clayton went to U.S. Senate. **28 February:** Second Enforcement Act passed Congress. **3 March:** Southern Claims Commission created by Congress. **6 March:** Ku Klux Klan riot at Meridian, Mississippi. In Virginia *v.* West Virginia, U.S. Supreme Court upheld the creation of the new state from the old, alleging Virginia's loyal government had agreed to the separation. **3 April:** In Miller *v.* U.S., U.S. Supreme Court ruled that the Confiscation Acts had been passed against traitors as individuals, not belligerents, and thus had to follow due process of the laws. **20 April:** Third Enforcement (Ku Klux Klan) Act passed Congress. **1 May:** In Knox *v.* Lee, U.S. Supreme Court ruled that greenbacks were legal for all debts, reversing Hepburn *v.* Griswold. **24 May:** *Alabama* Claims settled as Treaty of Washington ratified. **8 July:** Tweed Ring exposed in New York City. **9 August:** At Gatling Gun Convention in Louisiana, Radical Republicans read Governor Henry Clay Warmoth out of the party for being too conservative. **4 September:** Crédit Mobilier scandal broke, involving corrupt financing of the transcontinental railroad. **17 October:** President Grant declared suspension of the writ of *habeas corpus* in select counties of South Carolina to suppress the Ku Klux Klan. **1 November:** Georgia redeemed for second time; Conservative Democrat James M. Smith became governor. **22 November:** African-American Republican Lieutenant Governor Oscar Dunn of Louisiana poisoned under mysterious circumstances; succeeded by African-American Republican and Carpetbagger P. B. S. Pinchback.

1872   10 February: Third impeachment of Governor Harrison Reed of Florida succeeded, but he was never brought to trial. **22 May:** Congress passed a general amnesty Act removing office-holding proscriptions from most (all but 500) Confederate soldiers and civil officials. **1 August:** Scalawag Republican Tod R. Caldwell elected governor of North Carolina with a Conservative state legislature. **16 October:** Scalawag Republican Franklin J. Moses, Jr., elected governor of South Carolina. **5 November:** Carpetbag Republican Marcellus L. Stearns elected governor of Florida. Grant defeated Horace Greeley for president. **7 November:** Scalawag Republican David P. Lewis elected governor of Alabama, but both political parties seated their own legislatures. **30 November:** Death of presidential candidate Horace Greeley before the electoral votes were counted. **9 December:** Governor Henry Clay Warmoth impeached by extra session of Louisiana state legislature vice African-American Republican Carpetbagger P. B. S. Pinchback.

1873   7 January: Confederate Gen. Pierre G. T. Beauregard began the Louisiana Unification Movement, a political alliance between black voters and upper-class whites leaders for clean, conservative government. **9 January:** Carpetbag Republican William Pitt Kellogg inaugurated governor of Louisiana and backed by Federal troops. Democrat Conservative John McEnery also inaugurated with his own shadow government. **14 January:** Texas redeemed; Conservative Democrat Richard Coke became governor. **12 February:** Silver Coinage Act passed by Congress took silver out of circulation, called the "Crime of '73." **11 April:** Bvt. Maj. Gen. E. R. S. Canby became the first American general officer to die in an Indian war. **13 April:** Colfax

Massacre in Louisiana (Easter Sunday). **14 April:** In the Slaughterhouse Cases, U.S. Supreme Court began the process of limiting remedies under the Fourteenth Amendment. **18 September:** Failure of Jay Cooke & Company precipitated the Panic of 1873. **8 October:** After prolonged street fighting, court action, and Federal intervention, Scalawag Republican Elisha Baxter became governor of Arkansas over Carpetbag Republican Joseph Brooks.

1874   21 January: Morrison R. Waite became chief justice of the U.S. Supreme Court. **22 January:** Carpetbag Republican Adelbert Ames inaugurated governor of Mississippi. **30 August::** White League initiated Coushatta Massacre in Louisiana. **14 September:** White League initiated Third Battle of New Orleans. **17 September:** President Grant put down the September White League Rebellion in Louisiana with threat of Federal troops restoring Republicans to control. **15 October:** Carpetbag Republican Daniel H. Chamberlain elected governor of South Carolina. **10 November:** Arkansas redeemed; Conservative Democrat Augustus H. Garland elected governor. **14 November:** Alabama redeemed; Conservative Democrat George S. Houston elected governor, with race riots at Eufala and Mobile. **7 December:** Vicksburg race riots in Mississippi mark rise of the First Mississippi Plan, violence for redemption.

1875   6 January: Maj. Gen. Philip H. Sheridan sent a telegram recommending that Louisiana White Leaguers be declared "banditti." **14 January:** Specie Resumption Act expanded the number of greenbacks in circulation as well as the amount of silver to ease the economic depression caused by the Panic of 1873, pledging to return solely to gold in 1879. **1 March:** Civil Rights Act of 1875 passed Congress. **29 March:** In Minor *v*. Happersett, U.S. Supreme Court ruled that Fifteenth Amendment right to vote did not apply to women, as it referred to race alone. **17 April:** Congressman William A. Wheeler of New York established Wheeler Compromise in Louisiana; it left Republican Carpetbag Governor William P. Kellogg in power but split the state legislature between Democrats (lower House) and Republicans (upper House). **1 September:** White Liners rioted at Yazoo City, Mississippi, driving Carpetbag Republican Albert Morgan from power. **4 September:** White Liners rioted at Clinton, Mississippi. **5 September:** North Carolina met to rewrite its state constitution. **13 October:** So-called "Peace Agreement" between Republicans and Conservative Democrats quelled violence in Mississippi state elections. **2 November:** Conservative Democrats won the Mississippi state legislature, redeeming the state.

1876   2 March: Mississippi state legislature impeached Governor Adelbert Ames, replacing him with Scalawag Republican John M. Stone. **27**

March: In U.S. *v.* Cruikshank, U.S. Supreme Court limited the effect of the Enforcement Acts to curb election violence. In U.S. *v.* Reese, U.S. Supreme Court limited the effect of the Enforcement Acts to curb election fraud. **28 March:** Pryor Compromise, by which Governor Adelbert Ames of Mississippi stepped down as governor and impeachment charges were dropped. **4 July:** Hamburg Massacre in South Carolina. **6 September:** Charleston race riot in South Carolina. **15 September:** Three-day Ellenton race riot in South Carolina. **16 October:** Cainhoy race riot in South Carolina. **7 November:** Conservative Democrat Wade Hampton elected governor of South Carolina but prevented from taking power by the presence of Federal troops. Presidential election deadlocked between Rutherford B. Hayes and Samuel J. Tilden over disputed electoral vote; "visiting statesmen" went South to clear up the count with money. **12 November:** South Carolina redeemed by Red Shirts.

1877   1 January: Conservative Democrat Zebulon Vance inaugurated governor of North Carolina. **2 January:** Florida redeemed; Conservative Democrat George F. Drew elected governor of Florida. **8 January:** Conservative Democrat Francis T. Nicholls inaugurated governor of Louisiana at same time as Carpetbag Republican Stephen B. Packard inaugurated governor of Louisiana, but with Federal troop support. **29 January:** Congress created Electoral Commission to decide how to award disputed electoral votes. **8 February:** Electoral commission rewarded all disputed electoral votes to Hayes on an 8–7 party vote. **26 February:** Wormley House Bargain permitted Congress to agree that Hayes was new president. **2 March:** Congress accepted the Electoral Commission's action, awarding the presidency to "Rutherfraud" B. Hayes. **10 April:** Federal troops began final withdrawal from South Carolina; Conservative Democrat Wade Hampton became governor. **24 April:** Federal troops began final withdrawal from Louisiana, and Conservative Democrat Francis T. Nicholls became governor.

1878   14 January: In Hall *v.* DeCuir, U.S. Supreme Court declared that segregated accommodations on steamboats were permissible. **28 February:** Bland–Allison Act passed Congress, leading to the ratio of silver coins to gold at 16 to 1. **31 May:** Fort Act passed by Congress, returning the U.S. to the gold standard but keeping all silver and greenbacks then in circulation. **18 June:** Posse Comitatus Act passed Congress.

1880   1 March: In Strauder *v.* West Virginia, U.S. Supreme Court upheld parts of the Fourteenth Amendment as guaranteeing right of blacks to serve on juries, failing which the case could be transferred to a Federal court. In Virginia *v.* Rives, U.S. Supreme Court upheld parts of the Fourteenth Amendment as guaranteeing right of blacks to serve on juries, failing which the case could be transferred to a Federal court.

1882   22 January: In U.S. *v.* Harris, U.S. Supreme Court limited the effect of the Enforcement Acts to curb violence.

1883   15 October: In Civil Rights Cases, U.S. Supreme Court ruled that public accommodations could be segregated, as could any act or service initiated by an individual rather than a government entity.

1890   20 March: Blair Federal Aid to Education Bill failed to pass Congress. **2 July:** Lodge Enforcement Act passed House but failed in Senate. **1 November:** Mississippi state constitutional convention disfranchised black voters within the terms of the Fifteenth Amendment.

1895   10 September: South Carolina constitutional convention disfranchised black voters within the terms of the Fifteenth Amendment. **18 September:** Booker T. Washington delivered the Atlanta Cotton States Exposition Address, endorsing development of the races in America in a manner as separate as the five fingers but as united as the hand.

1896   18 May: In Plessy *v.* Ferguson, U.S. Supreme Court ruled separate but equal public accommodations acceptable under Fourteenth Amendment.

1898   11 January: Louisiana elected a constitutional convention that disfranchised black voters within the terms of the Fifteenth Amendment. **25 April:** In Williams *v.* Mississippi, the U.S. Supreme Court upheld Mississippi's disfranchisement of black voters so long as done without direct reference to race. **8 June:** Congress removed proscriptions from all Confederate soldiers and civil officials without exception.

1899   18 December: In Cumming *v.* Georgia, U.S. Supreme Court ruled separate but equal education for races was acceptable under the Fourteenth Amendment.

Introduction

When an American hears the term "Civil War," he or she generally envisions legions of heroic men in blue and gray, led by some of the best and worst generals the nation has ever spawned, contesting in the greatest battles ever fought in the Western Hemisphere. What student of American history does not, at least peripherally, know of Ulysses S. Grant, William T. Sherman, Phillip H. Sheridan, "Fighting Joe" Hooker, Robert E. Lee, "Stonewall" Jackson, J. E. B. Stuart, Nathan Bedford Forrest, and P. G. T. Beauregard? Who has not heard of the thousands of men who were killed or maimed at places like Shiloh Church, First and Second Manassas, Wilson's Creek, Perryville, Antietam, Fredericksburg, Gettysburg, Vicksburg, Chickamauga, the Wilderness, Cold Harbor, the burning of Atlanta, and Appomattox? Some are even familiar with famous units in the armies of either side, like the Pennsylvania Reserves, the Iron Brigade, the Michigan Cavalry Brigade, the Stonewall Brigade, the Irish Brigade, the Texas Brigade, and Morgan's Cavalry Brigade; or acquainted with illustrious units like the Louisiana Tigers 1st Special Battalion, the First Texas Infantry, the 20th Maine Infantry, Rush's 6th Pennsylvania Lancers, and the 1st Virginia Black Horse Cavalry.

Books, magazines, Civil War Roundtables, historical re-enactment units, the movie *Gettysburg*, and the felt kepis of blue and gray sold at every roadside stand and state fair all extol the fascination that Americans have with the Civil War—the *military* side of the Civil War. To suggest that the Civil War is important for more than the battlefields being swallowed up by 21st-century urban sprawl, the timeless soldierly prowess of Grant and Lee, and the intrepid efforts of the men of both sides on the field is to risk a loud guffaw from the multitude of traditional Civil War buffs.

But there *is* so much more to the Civil War than mere war. Society is made up of more than just soldiers. The armies are supported by civilians and the government that organizes them. There are institutions that affect the way that one society deals with another. There are fundamental laws (constitutions) and legislative laws that enshrine what a society finds valuable and eternal. The interplay of these factors is politics. There are more than white males that make up traditional Civil War history. There are women and minorities,

1

blacks, Hispanics, Native Americans, the citizen and the immigrant, the rich and poor, the moral and immoral, the jejune and the extraordinary.

The editor of one outstanding, current Civil War magazine opined that his journal was willing to recognize the existence and the importance of the non-military aspects, but that the events on the battlefield would be at least 85 percent of his magazine's total offering. From a business standpoint, a casual observer might wonder if even that is too much of a concession. After all, it is the Civil *War* that sells his publication. This led noted antebellum and Civil War historian William Freehling to counter with his essay, "Why Civil War Military History Must Be Less Than 85 Percent Military" (*North & South*, 5 [February 2002], 14–24). Freehling suggests that the 15 percent to be devoted to other than purely military matters ought to be doubled.

One easy way to accomplish what Freehling suggests would be to place the war in the context of the whole era in which it occurred. In the case of this volume, that would be 1848–1877, but the dates are flexible. Indeed, one could assert with President Abraham Lincoln that it took "four score and seven years" to create the carnage that he memorialized at the hallowed ground at Gettysburg. Many would argue, in the metaphor of the Reverend Martin Luther King, Jr., that particularly in the case of the race question, the war lives on to this day, its end yet an unsettled "dream." No matter how one looks at it, as the most massive event in American history, the Civil War, military and non-military events notwithstanding, continues to affect the politics, constitutionalism, and societal norms of the United States in an irrevocable way. It probably always will.

ANTEBELLUM

Although there have been many books devoted to the political, economic, and social causes of the Civil War, most of the reasons boil down in the end to one, some aspect of slavery. Although slavery as an institution had been present in the original 13 colonies, by the time of the end of the American Revolution, the states north of the Mason–Dixon Line (the northern boundary of Maryland) had begun the process of abandoning it, while racial (what to do with the numerous enslaved black people, whom most whites believed to be innately inferior, if they were freed) and economic (especially the invention of the cotton gin in the 1790s) reasons caused the southern states to retain and then expand the institution.

By the time of the end of the War with Mexico, the grandchildren of the Founding Fathers, those timeless paragons who had been willing to compromise the issue of bondage for the sake of the Constitution of 1787, were no longer willing to let slavery exist unchallenged. Beyond the moral aspects emphasized by the abolitionists, there were important political aspects that tended to make all northerners antislavery. The government of the United States before 1860 had been inordinately controlled by southerners. Of the 15 presidents in the antebellum period, all but six had been from the South, and four of these had been "doughfaces," northern men willing to overlook the slavery issue. Northerners thought that they saw a "slave power conspiracy" in these numbers and strove to check it.

The most obvious place to challenge slavery was in its spread into the Western territories. This had been done before, when the 1820 Missouri Compromise established free and slave territories divided by the line 36° 30′, the southern boundary of the state of Missouri, in the area of the Louisiana Purchase. When the United States received a large session of land from winning the War with Mexico in 1848, northern congressmen introduced the Wilmot Proviso, suggesting that slavery be denied access to the new West. This caused an uproar, much of the fighting in Mexico having been done by southern volunteers, that was finally mollified in the Compromise of 1850. Although it had many provisions, essentially the North got the new free state of California, which upset the even count of free and slave state senators, and the South obtained a strict Fugitive Slave Law, which returned runaway slaves through the agency of the Federal government. The South figured that it could conquer new lands in Latin America around the Caribbean Basin, the so-called Golden Circle, to make up the loss, through private military expeditions, a process known as filibustering.

On the issue of slavery in the new session, much was left unsaid, figuring that the people in the territories would solve the problem by a simple vote, a concept called squatter sovereignty. But by 1854, the equilibrium in the West was upset again. Southerners realized that northerners could move their individual families into the West faster than southerners could transfer plantation technology. The South saw the territorial stage as one of trusteeship, in which the territory had to be open to all, freemen or slaveholders. The vote for or against slavery by a territorial legislature (*i.e.*, squatter sovereignty) was seen as the action of a body lacking sovereignty, something a territory would not possess until it became a state. The vote had to take place in the first constitutional convention as statehood was being sought. This concept was called popular sovereignty.

The issue came to a head when, after the admission of California, it became imperative to link the Pacific Coast to the rest of the nation through a railroad. Immediately, speculators saw riches in the process, which would involve extensive Federal aid through land grants. The eastern terminus of this railroad would bring economic prosperity wherever it was located. There was one problem—the railroad would be so expensive that only one line could afford to be built, Federal aid or no. This made the whole thing sectional, but because of climate and lower mountains, the southern route would be the cheapest. Any issue involving competition between North or South sooner or later boiled down to slavery.

This caused Senator Stephen A. Douglas of Illinois to make a deal with the southerners who controlled the U.S. Senate. That extra senator from California had turned out to be pro-southern in ideology, causing the South still to reign supreme in Washington, D.C. The deal was that Douglas and certain northern allies would admit to popular sovereignty by opening all of the West to slavery. It would be done by creating two new territories, Kansas and Nebraska. In exchange, the transcontinental railroad would be built out of Chicago (actually Omaha, Nebraska, but the effect would be the same), in Douglas' home state.

This act outraged the antislave North. It repealed the old Missouri Compromise line. It threatened to give the whole West to the slave South. Settlers rushed to Kansas to block the South—successfully, after a miniature Civil War ensued. The established political system of Jacksonian Democrats and anti-Jackson Whigs broke up into one of sectional parties, with Democrats predominantly in the South and "Anti-Nebraska" Republicans in the North. The new, upstart Republicans came within three states of winning the 1856 election, realizing that they did not need a single southern state to win the presidency, because the larger northern population had more electoral votes. The Republicans needed only Pennsylvania and Illinois (think Abraham Lincoln) or Indiana to win in 1860. The North was further inflamed when the U.S. Supreme Court ruled that the southern view on slavery in the territories was correct and constitutional, as was the (to the North) obnoxious Fugitive Slave Law of 1850.

The Republicans ably organized their sectional party, hoping to secure the states with the correct electoral vote for 1860. Southerners watched with growing anger as the North took control of the Congress in the by-elections, and of the executive with only 40 percent of the popular vote and Illinois' Lincoln as their candidate. Worse, although four parties contested the 1860 election, if all of Lincoln's opponents had agreed on one ticket, the Republicans still would have won anyway—the numbers in the electoral college favored them so decisively. If the North (read: abolitionist, antislavery, destroyers of Southern civilization) could take the executive, keep the one seat in California, and do it with impunity, the South would ultimately lose the one branch of the government it had left, the Supreme Court, as old pro-southern justices died and new pro-northern ones were appointed.

Cognizant of losing power, encouraged by the inactivity of the outgoing James Buchanan administration, many southerners, secessionists, urged immediate action. Leave the Union and create their own nation, based on the principles of 1787 embodied in the Constitution. Other southerners, cooperationists, wanted to see if Lincoln would commit an overt act against southern interests first. Lincoln, meanwhile, tried to walk a narrow line between the South and his northern constituents. This made him seem unintentionally vaguer than usual. Compromise efforts in and out of Congress failed. Just by coincidence, the state most desirous of leaving the Union, South Carolina, had a new legislature in session and moved to secede on December 20, 1860. The Deep South, stimulated by South Carolina's example, and urged on by "Fire Eaters " or rabid secessionists, seceded from the Union and organized a provisional government of the Confederate States of America at Montgomery, Alabama, before Lincoln could be inaugurated. Some of the preliminary state votes on secession were close, but all were decisive in the end.

THE CIVIL WAR

1861

Facing the new Confederacy, Lincoln had to sneak into Washington to avoid a convincing plot against his life in Baltimore. This made him a laughing-stock and probably caused him to be a little too flippant about future assas-sination threats. Baltimore blocked the only railroads from the North and fi-nally had to be subdued by military force. But bigger problems faced Lincoln. The North still held several Federal installations within the boundaries of the new Confederacy. The South wanted these properties returned to the states in which they stood. Lincoln could not very well turn tail and run; nor could his counterpart, President Jefferson Davis, allow the United States to deny the Confederate state full sovereignty by permitting Union soldiers to remain in the installations. What seems to have happened was that Lincoln forced Davis to fire the first shot, which the South did on April 12, 1861. Probably neither side thought the other had the guts to shoot, and miscalculated. The war was on.

President Lincoln called up the state militias, each state getting a quota, to suppress the rebellion. His action weighed the scales against the cooperation-ists in the rest of the South. Texas had already assisted secessionists in the Far West to secede and form the Confederate Territory of Arizona. Led by Virginia, the Upper South instituted a second secession movement. Only Mis-souri, Kentucky, Maryland, and Delaware of the slave states remained neutral and in the Union. Lincoln immediately occupied Maryland and arrested its pro-secession legislators, lest Washington, D.C., wind up in the Confederacy.

Lincoln's willingness to avoid constitutional provisions for decisive personal action through presidential proclamations was a hallmark of his administration. While it offered him the choice of immediate action, it demoted Congress to spectator status, a result that angered not only those northern Democrats still in the body, but his own Republicans as well. Nonetheless, Lincoln declared the South to be in rebellion, called up the militia and volunteers, increased the size of the regular Army and the Navy, created a blockade of the southern coast, diverted funds appropriated from other departments to the war effort, and suspended the writ of *habeas corpus* to institute arbitrary arrests of suspected Rebel supporters. All of these items were by location in the Constitution reserved for congressional power. After he had acted, Lincoln called Congress into special session and had them ratify what had been done.

For the rest of 1861, the South won the battle of First Manassas near Washington and Wilson's Creek in far off Missouri and elected a permanent Confederate government in November. Meanwhile, the North managed to secure western Virginia, a section of that state that was pro-Union and eventually would become its own state. In the Far West, a Texas-organized invasion swept to the borders of California and Colorado Territory before being driven back. And utilizing its naval power, the North began to land soldiers on the southeastern Atlantic Coast to enforce the blockade. This meant that the problem of how to reconstruct the Union arose almost as soon as its division. But the shooting served to conceal it from the policymakers and the public for some time.

1862

Also concealed for some time was the plodding route to Union victory in the West, on either side of the Mississippi River. In the Trans-Mississippi, the initial Confederate invasion of Missouri after its victory at Wilson's Creek faltered at Lexington and then folded completely with defeats at Pea Ridge and Prairie Grove, which opened Arkansas north of the Arkansas River.

Similarly, Gen. Ulysses S. Grant's push up the Tennessee River led to the fall of Forts Henry and Donelson and the bloody victory at Shiloh, opening the state of Mississippi to future invasion. His army scattered by unfortunate interference from Washington, Grant checkmated a Confederate counterattack at the twin battles of Iuka and Corinth. The Confederates reorganized their forces, slipped around Grant at Memphis, and went up the Cumberland Valley into Kentucky, where they installed a short-lived Rebel state government. Turned back by advancing Union forces at Perryville, the Confederates retreated into central Tennessee, checkmating the following Yankee army at the three-day battle of Stone's River below Nashville at the end of the year.

But the steady Union conquest of Tennessee was eclipsed by events in the area east of the Appalachian Mountains in Virginia and Maryland. Because of botched opportunities over the winter, Congress entered the war in force by creating the Joint Committee on the Conduct of the War. Although the

Republican members' simplistic solution to defeat was more Republican antislavery generals and fewer Democrats in the field, they did serve to impress on the professional soldiers that few excuses for defeat were valid.

But the defeats in the east came fast and furiously. After picking up Confederate ministers James Mason and John Slidell off the British ship *Trent*, an embarrassed Lincoln was forced to release them to continue their missions. Gen. George B. McClellan was in charge of the Union land effort against the permanent Confederate capital of Richmond. A brilliant organizer, McClellan seemed never to be able to close with the Rebels for the final victory. Taking the army from Washington to Fortress Monroe at the tip of the Virginia Peninsula, McClellan dallied in a month-long siege at Yorktown before closing in on Richmond from the east. The war seemed to be coming to a bad end for the Confederates. But a change of Rebel commanders brought Gen. Robert E. Lee to the fore. Lee had already loosed his subordinate, Gen. Thomas J. Jackson, who had won the sobriquet "Stonewall" for holding at First Manassas until the Confederates could win. In a brilliant campaign again three bigger Union armies, Jackson ran the Union commander ragged as he slashed up and down the Shenandoah Valley west of Richmond.

Jackson caused Lincoln to hold what McClellan thought to be vital reinforcements from him at Richmond. As McClellan stewed, Lee brought Jackson quietly to Richmond and counterattacked McClellan in the Seven Days Campaign. McClellan was driven back to the safety of the Union navy's big guns at Harrison's Landing on the James River. Sending a new army through central Virginia at last, Lincoln was dismayed to see Lee march rapidly north and defeat this force at the Second Battle of Manassas. With the Union army retreating right into Washington, Lee and Jackson crossed the Potomac River into Maryland.

Bringing McClellan back from his self-imposed exile on the James, Lincoln sent him out to stop Lee. At Antietam Creek near Hagerstown, Maryland, Lee and McClellan fought to a standstill before Lee retreated back into Virginia. McClellan's refusal to pursue in a timely manner led Lincoln to sack him one last time. Lincoln took this "victory" as an opportunity to issue his preliminary Emancipation Proclamation. It would be made final by January 1, 1863, and would free all slaves in the Confederacy should the South not return to the Union by then. The policy was as unpopular in the North as in the South, but its ostensible purpose was to make the war one for freedom, against which the meddling British dared not intervene.

Meanwhile, Lincoln and the Republicans in Congress moved on domestic policy, passing laws to finance the Pacific Railroad, create land grant colleges, raise the tariff to protect Northern industries, reestablish a national banking system, set up a homestead act to encourage population of the West, and develop a contract labor law to import foreign labor to build the railroad and keep Northern industry running to win the war. The Republican action was made possible by the absence of the South from the halls of Congress. But his Emancipation Proclamation and continued Union defeats in the East caused the Northern voters to defeat many Republican congressmen in November. The following month, the voters received news of Gen. Lee's defeat of the Union army at Fredericksburg, Virginia, under a new commander, Gen. Ambrose E. Burnside, a completely lopsided victory that cost the attacking Yankees twice the losses of the defending Rebels.

1863

At the end of 1862, Gen. Grant's army made its first attempt to take the mighty Confederate fortress of Vicksburg. Going forward under Gen. Sherman, the Union army was shot to pieces. Grant spent the whole winter trying to crack Vicksburg through the back bayous, only to be turned back at each attempt. In the spring, he had the U.S. Navy send its supporting river craft past the guns at night and crossed his army over south of the city. Then in one of the fastest and most effective campaigns of the war, Grant moved east to block Confederate reinforcements at Jackson, Mississippi, then turned back west to Vicksburg from the rear, bottling up the Rebel army in the forts. A siege of two months produced Vicksburg's surrender on July 4. As Grant took care of Vicksburg, another Union army out of New Orleans moved up Bayou Teche west of the city and looped around Port Hudson, Louisiana. Its fall just after Vicksburg opened up the Mississippi to Union ships and split the Confederacy in half.

Once again, however, the nation's eyes were turned to the east. With a mighty army that outnumbered Gen. Lee two to one, Union Gen. "Fighting Joe" Hooker moved upriver from Fredericksburg and stole a march on Lee. Behind Lee and headed for open country, Hooker inexplicably stopped and rested on his laurels. Lee quickly split his army into three parts and using the Wilderness, a secondary growth of scrub timber, to shield his movements, marched Stonewall Jackson just out of sight right across Hooker's front. When the battle ended, Hooker's mighty force was thoroughly defeated. The only good thing for the North was the death of Jackson as he ran Hooker off the field.

Lee immediately slipped west around the Union force and invaded Pennsylvania. Hooker followed halfheartedly, arguing with Lincoln over who commanded the far-flung Union troops in the East. Lincoln fired Hooker and replaced him with Gen. George Meade. Meanwhile, Lee was blinded by the absence of his cavalry, out on a raid around behind the Union army. Retracting his own scattered forces to a road junction in Pennsylvania called Gettysburg, Lee and Meade accidentally bumped into each other and fought a three-day battle that cost both armies 50,000 casualties. Smashed on the third day in Pickett's Charge, Lee withdrew to Virginia on July 4. Meade followed haltingly, his army as thoroughly beaten up as Lee's.

Meanwhile, in the vast middle ground between Vicksburg and Gettysburg, Union Gen. William S. Rosecrans maneuvered his opponent Gen. Braxton Bragg out of the old Stone's River position and skillfully drove him past Chattanooga into northern Georgia. Reinforced by Confederate troops from Lee's army sent by railroad, Bragg attacked Rosecrans' scattered command at Chickamauga Creek, producing a rout and the greatest Southern victory in that theater for the whole war. Rosecrans was bottled up in Chattanooga, his men starving. Lincoln ordered Grant to come over from Vicksburg and, with reinforcements from Meade below Washington, D.C., also sent by rail, Grant fired Rosecrans, relieved the siege, and drove the Rebels off Missionary Ridge, nullifying the earlier Chickamauga victory.

As Union forces occupied more and more of the South, what to do to reconstruct the Union became of prime importance. Lincoln's Reconstruction Plan was to readmit any Southern state in which 10 percent of the male voting population would permit Union occupation, sign an oath of future loyalty to the United States, and draw up a free state constitution. The only problem was that Congress refused to seat representatives elected under Lincoln's plan, its prerogative under the Constitution, negating Lincoln's Reconstruction.

1864

Realizing that he had finally found his best general, Lincoln put Grant in charge of the whole war effort, with orders to destroy the Confederacy posthaste. Grant envisioned a three-pronged attack, but his planned attack on Mobile was lost to political and economic exigencies, and he turned up the Red River Valley toward Shreveport, Louisiana. Here Lincoln hoped to free numerous slaves and capture massive amounts of cotton, by bringing the war into areas that had remained relatively untouched so far. An attack from Baton Rouge was to be supported by a column heading south from Little Rock. Both columns moved so disjointedly that the same Confederate army defeated them both in consecutive attacks. Then part of the Rebel army launched a drive into Missouri that also failed. Lincoln had promised that the campaign would end successfully and early enough to turn back to Mobile, but this was not to be. The capture of Mobile was left to the U.S. Navy.

The other parts of Grant's plan went more smoothly. Gen. Sherman advanced from Chattanooga upon Atlanta, the transportation hub of the Deep South. Although he was checked by the artful Confederate Gen. Joseph Johnston, public pressure at Johnston's delaying tactics led to his replacement by Gen. John B. Hood. Attacking Sherman's forces three times around Atlanta,

Hood wore his army out against Sherman's bigger number of men. Hood's casualties seemed to confirm the wisdom of Johnston's earlier retreats. After taking Atlanta, Sherman reorganized his army into four columns and marched from Atlanta to the sea, laying waste to all he encountered.

Meanwhile, Grant reserved the Confederacy's greatest field commander, Gen. Lee, for himself. Marching overland through the Wilderness west of the old Chancellorsville battlefield, Grant took on Lee at every turn. Rather than giving the Confederates respite by turning back each time Lee checked his move, as had been the Yankees' habit the past two years, Grant kept coming on. He knew that he could afford the casualties, while Lee could not. It took Grant nearly 100,000 killed, wounded, and missing, but by June he was at the gates of Richmond, where McClellan had been in 1862. Grant then crossed south of the James River on a gigantic pontoon bridge to take Richmond from the rear. Only unimaginative Union field leadership permitted the Rebels to hold him at Petersburg until Lee could bring his army up and force a nine-month siege.

Hoping to repeat the 1862 exploits of Stonewall Jackson in the Shenandoah Valley, Lee detached part of his force under Gen. Jubal Early and marched up the valley (scattering his opponents everywhere), across the Potomac River, then southeast to the Monocacy River (where he defeated a weak defending force), and on to Washington. It was the first and only time in the war that the Confederates actually threatened Washington, made more critical because Grant had removed the large garrison and sent it down to participate in the lengthy Petersburg siege. President Lincoln went out to watch the battle, actually coming under fire.

But Early was too weak to force the issue, especially after Grant sent reinforcements from Petersburg. Still, he lingered embarrassingly close to the national capital, and Grant sent back his cavalry general, Gen. Philip Sheridan, to deal with the problem once and for all. Sheridan drove Early back through the Shenandoah in a series of battles. Just when Sheridan thought he had disposed of Early, the Rebels counterattacked at Cedar Creek. In a day-long battle, Sheridan's men were at first routed, but able to rally and drive Early from the field, once and for all. Sheridan then destroyed the agricultural and industrial capabilities of the Shenandoah, Virginia's breadbasket and iron center.

With Grant bogged down at Petersburg, it was fortunate for Lincoln that Sherman and Sheridan had delivered the victories necessary for him to take the election of 1864. Lincoln was under heavy attack, not only from Democrats who accused him of botching the war in the field and arbitrarily arresting his opponents, but from his own Republican Party, which feared that Lincoln would not make a good candidate because he was not decisive enough, particularly on reconstructing the South. The Radical Republicans, the driving ideologues of the party, had rejected Lincoln's Ten Percent Plan of Reconstruction, substituting the Wade–Davis Plan, which proposed that 50 percent of the voters take an oath of future loyalty to the Union and that only those who could take a special Ironclad Oath (never helping the Confederacy willingly) be allowed to create new state governments in the South. Lincoln pocket vetoed the measure, and its sponsors publicly accused him of being too lax.

Running their own ticket to drive Lincoln out of the party, the Radicals found that they could not control the Republican Convention, which re-nominated Lincoln. Then came victories in the Shenandoah, Atlanta, and Mobile. Lincoln's popularity soared with the Northern voters. The Radicals begged to be let back into the party, and Lincoln threw them a bone, as it were, by asking his postmaster general, an especially hated Negrophobe, to resign. The Democrats, meanwhile, nominated Gen. George B. McClellan on a "peace with the South" platform. McClellan accepted the nomination, but rejected the platform. Lincoln's electoral victory was made all the more satisfying when news arrived that Gen. George Thomas had decisively defeated a Confederate army investing Nashville, driving it clear back across the Tennessee River into Alabama.

1865

The end of the Confederacy was but a matter of time. Grant finally broke through Lee's lines at Petersburg and took Richmond at the beginning of April. A week later, he cornered Lee's retreating army at Appomattox Court House and forced Lee's surrender. A week later, John Wilkes Booth assassinated President Lincoln at Ford's Theater in Washington. After some initial problems with political, reconstruction matters being included in the terms, Sherman, who had marched north through the Carolinas, got Gen. Johnston (recently restored to command) to surrender on the same basis as Lee at Durham Station, North Carolina. Confederate President Jefferson Davis and most of his fleeing government were captured in Georgia. Other Confederate military forces surrendered in the ensuing month, until by May 30, the Confederacy was no more.

RECONSTRUCTION

1865

When Lincoln died, Vice President Andrew Johnson became the new president. At first, he seemed to be just what the Radical Republicans wanted—a tough, no-nonsense sort of man who would punish the South. But Congress was out of session until December, and that gave Johnson a lot of time to reconstruct the South without Congress' help. He called for a majority of voters in each seceded state to take an oath of future loyalty. Then they had to draw up a state constitution that abolished slavery and endorsed the new Thirteenth Amendment, which had replaced the Emancipation Proclamation. Johnson excluded from participation all those voters worth over $20,000, the former slaveholders of the big plantations. They had to make individual application for pardon. But Johnson gave those pardons away wholesale.

The South moved rapidly to meet Johnson's demands, and those elected presented themselves before Congress in December to be seated. But Congress refused. They professed horror that the representatives and senators sent by the Southern states were all ex-members of the Confederate army, derisively called the "Confederate Brigadiers." Congress was also angered that the South had passed in each state a series of laws, the "Black Codes," that set aside inferior positions, economically, politically, and socially, for the freed slaves.

1866

Johnson defended his Reconstruction process, and Congress moved to see if some sort of compromise might be reached. Congress sought to renew a Federal agency set up a year before to assist freed blacks and refugees in the South; Johnson vetoed it as unconstitutional. Congress then tried to nullify the Black Codes with a Federal Civil Rights Act. Johnson vetoed that. Then Johnson spoke publicly and derisively of his congressional opponents. Congress re-passed the Freedmen's Bureau Act and the Civil Rights Act over his veto. Then Congress wrote a Fourteenth Amendment to guarantee that the Civil Rights Act would become a constitutional amendment. Johnson told the South to turn it down. All but Tennessee (Johnson's home state, controlled by his worst political enemy) refused to endorse it. Congress readmitted Tennessee into the Union by seating its representatives and senators. Johnson took to the electoral hustings (presidents were not supposed to do such undignified things in those days), seeking to defeat the Radical Republicans in favor of Democrats, in a campaign call the "Swing Around the Circle." Congress sent speakers to stir up the crowds ahead of his appearances. Johnson sparred with hecklers everywhere. The Republicans won a landslide, unusual for an off-year election.

1867

The Congress saw no need to wait for the new body to be seated in December 1867 to act against the president. The People had spoken. Congress passed a series of measures. It restricted the president's powers to fire cabinet members without congressional approval. It forced the president to give no order directly to any Army officer without getting the commanding general's approval first. It called the next Congress into immediate session in March

1867, so Johnson could not act during recesses as both he and Lincoln had done so often. And it put the Army (which Johnson could not command) in charge of the South and Reconstruction. Under Army supervision, each Southern state (less Tennessee) had to start Reconstruction all over with a new state constitution that recognized the right of African-Americans to vote and had to ratify the pending Fourteenth Amendment. The next Congress refined the initial Military Reconstruction act three times, to cover loopholes inadvertently found in the process.

1868–1871

Contrary to what many Southerners have charged, the Federal government was not interested in putting too many obstacles in the way of Southern readmission to the Union. By July 1868, only three states remained (Texas, Mississippi, Virginia) under the Army. It was a presidential election year, and Republicans wanted to see Southern electoral votes, spirited by the first freed black voters, included for their candidate, Gen. Grant. At the same time, Republicans wanted to settle with President Johnson for the last time. Using his removal of Secretary of War Edwin McM. Stanton as an excuse, charges were brought, and the House of Representatives tried him before the Senate, only to see Johnson beat the rap by one vote. In retaliation, the outgoing president pardoned many Confederates excluded from the voting process and the Lincoln conspirators who were still alive in Federal prison.

Winning the election more narrowly than the Republicans would have liked, President Grant moved to end Reconstruction by readmitting the remaining unreconstructed states as quickly as possible. He also had to see to it that Georgia was reconstructed another time for throwing out blacks elected to the state legislature. The price for their recalcitrance was that they had to approve of the Fifteenth Amendment, prohibiting the denial of the vote to African-Americans.

Meanwhile, Georgia proved to be the quickest of the Southern states to limit the role of blacks in society. Most of this discrimination was accomplished extra-legally through organizations like the Ku Klux Klan. To check this activity, Congress passed the Enforcement Acts, putting the Federal power behind the gains of African-Americans in Reconstruction, with varying degrees of success.

1872–1875

In 1872, Grant won a second term. But his next four years would be marred by scandal and the violent end of Reconstruction in the South. Grant did his best, putting more effort into it than most, but he could not stop the race riots that swept the South and "redeemed" each state for white conservatives by 1876. He was not helped any as the Supreme Court began to develop restrictive interpretations of laws and the Constitution that compromised Reconstruction. Nor was Grant assisted by the corrupt nature of the existing Republican governments in the South. Similar corruption affected the Democrats in the big cities of the North. And, of course, Grant's own administration was shot through with its own form of cabinet-level shenanigans that caused the whole country to question "Grantism," as high-placed corruption came to be called.

1876–1877

By the presidential election of 1876, the Republicans stood a good chance of losing the executive office. Congress had already gone Democrat in 1874. When the election was over, it turned out that the Democrats were one electoral vote from victory. But there were enough questionable electoral votes outstanding that if the Republicans could take them all, they would retain their hold on the presidency. The key was that the votes up for grabs all occurred in the three Southern states still under Republican control, South Carolina, Florida, and Louisiana. Both sides sent lobbyists down to buy the needed votes, but the Democrat, Samuel Tilden of New York, was poorly advised and only wished to pay for one vote. The Republican candidate, Rutherford B. Hayes of Ohio, needed everyone. The questionable votes went with the Republican money.

Outraged, the Democrats had an electoral commission set up to validate the votes, all of which were essentially fraudulent. The commission had seven Republicans and seven Democrats, taken from the House and the Senate and the Supreme Court. The one deciding vote ultimately went to the Republicans once again. The Democrat-dominated house threatened not to count the votes, until the Southern Democrats broke ranks and voted for Hayes. Hayes was derided as "Ol' 8 to 7," and "Rutherfraud" B. Hayes, but he took the oath in March 1877. The story grew up that the deal Hayes and his handlers made was to end military support of Reconstruction, the so-called Compromise of 1877, but Hayes was pledged to end Reconstruction, deal or no. In any case, the Federal government withdrew from the electoral process in the South, and every former Confederate state was now back in the Union and under solid white control.

1878–1900

The years that followed Reconstruction were the New Departure Years and were marked by the Federal government keeping its word and staying out of the internal politics of the states. The Supreme Court followed suit, gutting the guarantees of the Thirteenth, Fourteenth, and Fifteenth Amendments, until by 1900, America had been legally divided into two countries, one white and one black, all allegedly "separate but equal." It never worked that way, and by the end of World War II a Second Reconstruction began that reversed the Southern political, economic, and social victory in Reconstruction, and, by 1965, came much closer to achieving the "Great Society" that the North thought it had won in the first place in 1865.

INTERPRETING THE EVENTS

An old adage holds that historical events, especially wars, are written from the viewpoint of the winners. But there is one era of United States history wherein this axiom has not always rung true. That is the period of the Civil War and Reconstruction, running roughly from the end of the War with Mexico (1848) to the beginning of the Spanish–American War (1898). In fact, the loser, the White South, has dominated much of the historical writing, often in a decisive manner.

The very name "Civil War" is itself a compromise between the participants and those who record their actions and thoughts. It is defined in the dictionary as a struggle between at least two factions of a single nation, a general explanation that really does not denote war guilt or the intensity that either side felt at the time. The study of the American Civil War is typified by the emphasis on brave men fighting for what they believed, on military strategy and tactics, and epitomized by the present generation in numerous battlefield re-enactments. It is history, it is fun, but it is relatively neutral. It is the tale that has been brought into everyone's living room as the fascinating movie *Gettysburg.* In its attempt to avoid blame and exalt the glorious, the brave, and the inventive, and explore the tremendous personalities who fought the war, it is typically modern American—very forgiving.

Contemporaries of the Civil War were not so kind. The war's official name in the North was the War of the Rebellion, as the official printed record of the conflict, *The War of the Rebellion: A Compilation of the Official Records of the Union and Confederate Armies*, makes clear. The implication was that the secession of the South and the ensuing hostilities were illegal, immoral, and downright wrong. It was a war forced upon the nation by a group of conspirators, Southern slaveholders, who fired the first shot at Ft. Sumter, brazenly demonstrating their evilness before the whole world. It was the duty of historians to chronicle this "Slave Power Conspiracy" for posterity, exposing it for the misguided attempt it was to divide the hope of all humankind by destroying the United States. That God was on the side of the North was proven by the ultimate Union victory on the battlefield.

Of course, Southerners were not about to admit to what they saw as a cute piece of Yankee fiction—this alleged War of Rebellion. To them, the war was entirely justifiable—a War for Southern Independence, as clearly moral and necessary as the original War of American Independence had been against the British in 1776, and for the same reasons. It was a noble, legal, constitutional attempt to free the South from a continual, unfair, illegal, and unconstitutional Northern attempt to subjugate it, economically, morally, spiritually, and culturally. Having failed to crush the South politically under the U.S. Constitution, the North now sought to do it through the extra-legal means of military force. The South had no choice but to defend itself from the Yankee aggression brought on by President Abraham Lincoln's refusal to surrender peacefully Ft. Sumter, located within the boundaries of the seceded State of South Carolina, and his call-up of the militia of the several states designed to coerce the South back into the Union.

Those south of the Mason–Dixon Line (most of them, anyway) believed that the North's blatant refusal to follow provisions granted to the South under the U.S. Constitution in 1787, which guaranteed that slavery was a domestic institution removed from Federal control, gave the South the right to terminate the compact through secession. Those state rights that the Southern states had temporarily surrendered to the Federal government were now re-claimed and re-delegated in turn to the Confederate government in an attempt to preserve the intentions of the Founding Fathers in their fullest sense. Although the cause might be lost on the battlefield, former Confederates maintained that it was the duty of historians to reveal Yankee duplicity to its fullest and honor the South's purer legal and moral position in this War Between the States. Thus the veterans published the *Southern Historical Society Papers* to prove their point.

As time moved on, the war's meaning changed among the participants and the historians who recorded it. By the turn of the 20th century, in the wake of America's victory in the War with Spain and its entry onto the stage of world colonialism, the United States was experiencing a revived nationalism, of a nature that had not been seen for 60 years. Both sides of the Civil War made an informal compromise. The finger-pointing stopped. They agreed that all had fought in the Civil War honorably for what they believed in. Neither side had a corner on the market for good or evil. The North was right in the war; the South was right about the Reconstruction that followed. This attitude was assisted by the South's support of the united nation in the Spanish–American War and the North's abandonment of equal rights for African-Americans in light of its colonialism among other colored peoples of the world in Latin America and Asia.

It was a love-feast that would last for the next 60 years. Modern researchers usually take the fangs out of all this War of Rebellion (or whatever) argument by using the shortened title *Official Records* or the even more neutral *O.R.* The still best four-volume *Battles & Leaders of the Civil War* (often cited *B&L*) was an attempt to gather remembrances by participants of both sides, 20 years after the fact. It marked the trend, now pretty much general, to focus on brave men fighting for what they believed in, without any censure as to motives.

Thus the War of Rebellion and the War for Southern Independence became the non-judgmental Civil War. Sadly, the modern analysis went, the war had been an Irrepressible Conflict over slavery in all of its implications, economic, political, and moral. It was good that slavery had been abolished. This freed the undivided nation to expand into the American West and then take the blessings of American religion, industry, culture, and government into the world. As the 20th century progressed, some historians, particularly in the North, came to see the war as a Second American Revolution. Now slavery had little to do with it, beyond holding back an inevitable industrializing of America. The Civil War was a sad, but necessary, event in the march of history. In many ways, the progress represented by industrialization turned out to be subtly pro-Southern in its emphasis. The economic revolution and urbanization of the United States wrought new evils like worker exploitation, child labor, sweatshops, and slums.

Others, however, saw the evils of industry as good. These were Marxist historians who viewed the war as a step toward the classless state. Unlike the Second American Revolution school, this view was decidedly anti-Southern. Relegating the Old South to the ash heap of history, the Marxists praised Northern victory as a vital step to heralding the ultimate struggle between the proletarian worker and the bourgeois industrialist.

During this same period of the first half of the 20th century, Southern historians began to assert their own interpretation of what the war was all about. They affirmed that the war was caused by slavery and that the difficult peace that followed was a result, not of industrialization, but of Northerners not understanding what the social and political implications of freeing African-Americans were all about. This was the same period that saw racial segregation heartily practiced, North and South. It also was the era of the Great Depression, which created many challenges to industrial America and the benefits of industrialization. In the more rural South, many writers trumpeted the advantages of agrarianism, something central to the pre–Civil War plantation South. Industrialism had brought with it wage slavery, societal agitators, and a hypersensitive sectional feeling that had removed Yankees from the old agrarian values of the Founding Fathers.

The Southern agrarians were assisted in their quest by the general disappointment in the results of World War I, with its congressional investigations of the so-called Merchants of Death—industrialists who made money on guns and munitions. A whole generation of Northern and Southern historians,

Revisionists they were called, saw the same war profiteering in the Civil War and its corrupt manufacturers of cardboard shoes, bullets loaded with sand, and cheap shoddy uniforms, all abetted by rotten politicians. Wars were seen as exercises in stupidity and exploitation. Politicians were seen as propagandists and agitators, hiding their industrial profits behind talk of noble objectives that did not really exist. The Civil War became no longer inevitable. It was now the Repressible Conflict. Americans, North and South, had been betrayed by venal politicians and industrialists, who cared little but for profits. They were nothing more than Robber Barons, fleecing average citizens for their own profligate greed.

But the war against Fascism changed all that. World War II was the one and only war in American history that garnered the support of a vast majority of all Americans. There was a New Nationalism. War once again was seen as achieving good things and being necessary to meet certain challenges to civilization. Americans who went abroad saw so many evils and stayed away so long that Jack Goodman edited a volume called *While You Were Gone* to bring servicemen and women back to the reality of what happened in the civilian world while they were overseas. It was presented in 26 easy lessons, written by experts in their fields (labor, industry, politics, sports, youth, media, advertising, and so on). But no book could change the changed climate in post–World War II America. There was a new appreciation that politicians could have prevented war but blundered into it anyway. There was a new outlook on race, inspired by evils the Germans and Japanese had committed against perceived lesser races. It was seen that the Civil War, too, had accomplished the end of slavery and the creation of a new America—and it was not at all a bad thing to have done.

This Nationalist line of thought was increased by the civil rights movement, as African-Americans took to the streets and the Federal courts to gain what had been lost in the aftermath of the Civil War. More and more the Southern view of the war was pushed aside as a new breed of neo-abolitionists presented what might best be described as a politically correct version of the War of the Rebellion. Southern heroes quickly became rabid racists fighting for an outdated, immoral society. This was not hard to accomplish in the case of Nathan Bedford Forrest, the leader of the Ft. Pillow massacre and Grand Wizard of the original Ku Klux Klan, but it even rubbed off on Robert E. Lee, the quintessential gentleman and everybody's Southern hero, who once rivaled the Union's sainted Abraham Lincoln in reputation. Lincoln, in turn, has been denigrated into a conniving, constitution-destroying, war-seeking, vengeful, bisexual, monstrous characterization of a president.

Because it is so intimately related to the Civil War, Reconstruction has gone through many of the same interpretive differences as the Civil War, with some important variations, as befits the history of where black Americans belong in American society. Although this is also a recurrent theme in Civil War history, it has often been obscured by the battlefield and military studies that predominate in that area. But the role and place of African-Americans in the United States is a dominant theme in Reconstruction history. Once again, helped by the North–South compromise in 1898 over the War with Spain and American entry onto the world stage of colonialism to civilize "our little brown brothers" with the Krag army rifle (as the old saw went), the advent of Social Darwinism arguing for superior (white) and inferior (colored) races, and a weariness over seemingly unsolvable 19th-century Civil War issues, the Confederate losers have become the victors in the history books and on the silver screen, until fairly recently. So much so, in fact, that Fawn Brodie, an exasperated historian and biographer of Pennsylvania Radical Republican congressman Thaddeus Stevens, once felt compelled to write a column in the *New York Times* wondering "Who Won the Civil War, Anyway?"

So far as Reconstruction was concerned, Brodie had good reason to ask. Like the Civil War, the first histories of Reconstruction were written by the participants themselves. But unlike the Civil War battlefield participants, the Yankees who came South to preserve the peace were not as certain of their victory. They came to put in place a *r*econstruction that came to be characterized as a *R*econstruction. The capitalization is crucial. It differentiates something good and noble from something bad and ignoble. Many disillusioned reconstructors, like Carpetbagger Albion Tourgée, wrote of their experiences in the postwar South as a lost cause, a "fool's errand." Those who did not were in danger of being dismissed as unbridled idealists or impractical racial amalgamationists. Reinforcing the critics' views at the turn of the 20th century was the entrance onto the literary stage of the first college-educated historians. These Ph.D.s included such men as John Burgess, James Ford Rhodes, James Schouler, and future U.S. president Woodrow Wilson, but by far the most influential was William A. Dunning of Columbia University.

It is not so much what Dunning wrote (he only published two volumes), but whom he influenced that made him famous. Dunning attracted many capable history graduate students, especially from the South, to come and study under him at Columbia. Each candidate selected a Southern state to study for a Ph.D. dissertation. Each had that study published. Often each had grown up in the subject Southern state. And each wrote in more or less the same vein: about corrupt, evil, amalgamating ex-slaves; about corrupt, evil Northerners who came to exploit the prostrate South, the infamous Carpetbaggers; about Southern white trash who turned on their own people and supported the blacks and Yankees in their conniving ways, the hated Scalawags; about the Yankee soldiers, many of them black, who gave the teeth to these nefarious evil-doers through their Bayonet Rule; and about the heroic Redeemers, the Civil War veterans and Ku Klux Klansmen who violently turned back these exploiters at the polls by beating them at their own game. The Dunningites saw President Abraham Lincoln as the advocate of a fair Reconstruction through his Ten Percent Plan, which his successor Andrew Johnson failed to get the venal Radical Republicans to accept. In revenge for Johnson's adherence to Lincoln's noble objectives, the Radicals tried to impeach him, failing by one, slim vote. Later writers made Andrew Johnson into some sort of Christ-like figure, selflessly sacrificing himself to save American Democracy from a grasping, radicalized Congress.

At first, few voices of protest appeared against Dunning and his disciples. Those who did speak out were, appropriately, African-American. One of the first was Alrutheus A. Taylor. Another was W. E. Burghardt DuBois. These men pointed out places where Dunning and his students had gone wrong. They showed that the goals of Reconstruction were more in keeping with equality in American society, not about exploitation of race for political advantage. They demonstrated how most black reconstructionists were quite well-educated and worked for the betterment of democracy and the influence of the lower classes, both black and white. And they proved that Reconstruction failed when privileged upper-class whites played the cards of race and sectional hatred to divide the supporters of political and economic reform. Unfortunately, DuBois, a master writer and researcher, ultimately a more powerful and nationally well-known figure, diluted his influence by placing his study in a strict Marxist framework. This was a stretch, for there was no proletariat and few bourgeois in the Reconstruction South, no matter how much one might search for them. Nonetheless, DuBois' thesis was later simplified by white writer James Allen and novelized by Howard Fast in a work that actually appeared on television in the late 1970s, with charismatic boxer Muhammad Ali credibly appearing in the starring role.

As World War II approached, the black historians' challenge to Dunning gained momentum among white academics. First Francis B. Simkins, then Howard K. Beale pointed out that in many respects, Taylor and DuBois had been correct in their questioning of the Dunning School. The real crime of Scalawags and Carpetbaggers was that they had crossed racial lines in political matters. By and large, however, blacks and whites lived in comparative harmony during Reconstruction. Whatever corruption could be attached to Southern state governments was more than matched in the Northern states. They also believed that the struggle between rich and poor was a more potent theme than race. These men received the moniker Revisionists for their challenge to change the Dunning story of Reconstruction.

After the Allied victory in World War II, the questioning of Dunning's version of Reconstruction revived, egged on by the experiences of the war and the publication of the last great Dunning-like work, E. Merton Coulter's *The South During Reconstruction*. John Hope Franklin, a black scholar, questioned Coulter's ignoring the questions raised by Revisionists. Then Franklin and others began a two-decade-long effort to change the traditional Reconstruction history.

These Revisionists challenged Dunning's picture in several select areas. For one, they focused on the political struggle between political parties during and after the war. Most found that the Radical Republicans, the villains according to the Dunningites, were actually interested in preserving the gains of the war and not necessarily opposed to Lincoln or Johnson's different Reconstruction plans. Indeed, many questioned whether Lincoln actually had a Reconstruction plan and saw Johnson as obstinate rather than heroic in opposing a harsh peace with the South. The Supreme Court was praised for its conservative approach to negating questionable Reconstruction measures, rather than, as the Dunningites saw it, as a body under siege by the Radical Republicans.

The main participants in Reconstruction, the Scalawags and Carpetbaggers, reemerged as heroes rather than miscreants. Indeed, depending on which man and which state was examined, enough variants in behavior among Reconstruction participants existed as historians needed to prove any version of the era's history they might want. The same held true of the Compromise of 1877, which removed the Federal support for the last three Reconstruction governments in the South (Florida, South Carolina, and Louisiana) and placed Republican Rutherford (or was it "Rutherfraud"?) B. Hayes in the White House through the means of an extra-constitutional election board—an election as controversial as, maybe more so, the one in 2000.

But by 1959, historian Bernard Weisberger noted that, while the Revisionists had ably showed that Dunning and his advocates had many holes in their studies, they had yet to produce a comprehensive synthesis of their results. This fault was more than made up for by the issuance of Reconstruction surveys by Hodding Carter II, Kenneth Stampp, John Hope Franklin, Rembert W. Patrick, Avery O. Craven, and Allen W. Trelease in the next 10 or so years.

Yet Vernon Wharton once again chided the Revisionists for their lack of thoroughness. The result was a group of historians known as Post-Revisionists. In their increased examination of Dunning's version of Reconstruction, they came up with something that would have astounded even Dunning himself. They asserted that Reconstruction really changed America little. Yankee racism proved fully as potent as that in the South; Republican politicians acted as politicians normally do and did whatever was necessary to stay in power and obtain local patronage, at the expense of racial principles; and Radical Reconstruction had failed because it was simply not radical enough.

Truly there was a need for something that came to be called the New Synthesis. Utilizing numerous independent historical studies of the Reconstruction roles of African-Americans, historian Eric Foner came up with his *Reconstruction: America's Unfinished Business*. He backdated Reconstruction from the traditional date of 1865 to 1863 (although others had already suggested that the real beginning of the period was in 1862, with the first Union military occupations of the South). But Foner credited blacks with forcing Americans to see Reconstruction as an interracial experiment so revolutionary that nothing in the 19th century could compare with it. Black leadership was seen as capable and organized the black community to cope with the new problems of freedom. The result was such an evolution of racial attitudes in America that many whites, North and South, were willing to cast their political futures with black freedom, Northern economic visions of America's future, and universal social and political equality. But the picture was not as rosy as Foner made it out to be. Critics noted that Republicans were more than willing to leave African-Americans for the building of the industrialized state, which left Reconstruction only half completed—"America's Unfinished Business," in the words of Foner's subtitle.

The massive nature of Foner's study left many with the feeling that there was little left to be done in examining the history of Reconstruction. But there were other themes that needed much work. Foner and those who preceded him usually ignored the fact that Reconstruction was a process that depended on the Army's occupation of the South, an un-American duplication of British policy before and during the American Revolution. This in turn led historians to look at the Army's administration of the Southern states and especially at the work of its adjunct social welfare command, the Bureau of Refugees, Freedmen, and Abandoned Lands. This then led back to the problem of violence in political contests—the Ku Klux Klan, White Leagues, and Rifle Clubs—which, in the end, had overwhelmed the more moderate New Departure Southerners.

Such examinations have revealed two disturbing details in depth. One was that the North did not care more than tenuously about the fate of African-Americans in the South. The other was the possibility that Reconstruction was designed to keep blacks in the South and out of the North. Northerners feared massive African-American migration into the North after the war, this theory goes, as the Underground Railroad had helped before the war with dribbles of escaped slaves. Now freed, all blacks could head for the promised land of the North. To keep African-Americans in the South, Congress provided laws and constitutional amendments to force the South to honor black political, economic, and social rights. This would cause them to stay at home. When the feared migration did not materialize because of the vicissitudes of the share-crop and the lien, the North dropped Reconstruction; made its political Compromise of 1877 with the white South; ignored Jim Crow in the South and intensified it in the North (where it had existed from Revolutionary War days as each Northern state freed its slaves); and went on to industrialize, settle the American West, and eventually become a world power.

The Civil War and Reconstruction have traditionally been seen as America's only national tragedy. Its wartime casualties are only slightly less than those in all other American wars combined (the lynchings during Reconstruction were never fully cataloged). Had the United States lost men in World War II at the rate the North did in the Civil War, it would have lost 2 million—at the rate of the South, 5 million—rather than less than half a million. It also produced the one time that history happened *to* a section of the nation. The Southern whites had been defeated and occupied by a victorious power, much as European countries have suffered many times in their histories.

The Civil War and Reconstruction were, and still remain, the pivotal events of American history. This was the only time when the nation could not compromise with itself. The result was the only major European-style war ever fought within the boundaries of the United States, whose battlefields are fairly well-preserved, although the 21st century may change that. And it was a very personal war, not fought by machines, but by men. It was big, but not overwhelming and far away as most of America's modern wars have been. It is modern enough to be relevant to today's military interests, yet gentlemanly enough to be the last of the great romantic wars. Countless Americans have one or more Civil War veterans hidden in their family trees.

Had it not been followed by the stain of Reconstruction, the Civil War would have been perfect. The North erred only in thinking that Appomattox was a peace treaty, rather than a cease-fire. And in many ways, it can be argued that that peace treaty still eludes us as a nation today, although the election of a black national president in 2008 raises questions about that. That uncertainty may be why the battle studies abound in popularity and the politics is ignored. After all, there was a Civil War Centennial, but none for Reconstruction.

A

AB INITIO. A legal concept of great importance among Radical Republicans (q.v.), which held that all laws passed by an illegal jurisdiction, in this case the Confederacy or any state or locality under it, were automatically null and void from their inception. It was an ideological concept that could have led to much mischief, as it would have negated any legal action in the South during the Rebellion, including marriages. The U.S. Supreme Court negated *ab initio* as a valid concept in Texas *v.* White (q.v.), in all matters that did not promote the Rebellion, but the pure concept still caused much controversy in many Southern state constitutional conventions during Reconstruction, especially in Texas.

ABLEMAN *v.* BOOTH (1859). Two years after the U.S. Supreme Court decided in Dred Scott *v.* Sandford (q.v.) the issue of slavery in the territories in favor of the Southern Non-Exclusion Doctrine (q.v.) embodied in popular sovereignty (q.v.), the Court struck again, deciding the fugitive slave issue in favor of the South, too. The Dred Scott case was a bit of a stretch, the Court having to interpret a complicated rendition of the Ninth and Tenth amendments to the U.S. Constitution. The fugitive issue was easy by comparison, the fugitive clause (art. IV, sect. 2) being openly stated.

Since the fugitive clause was there for all to see, the South held it to be a fundamental constitutional right. Even Abraham Lincoln (q.v.) and the mainstream of the Republican Party agreed to enforce it in 1861, before the war changed things. The Court had ruled on fugitive slaves being returned to their owner upon claim in the 1842 case Prigg *v.* Pennsylvania. Here the court had said that the fugitive return was a Federal matter, over which the state has no authority. Prior to this, the states had been claiming concurrent authority over fugitive slave cases and releasing the fugitives through state action.

In the Compromise of 1850, the South demanded and received a strong fugitive law. Jury trials were denied in fugitive cases, which were heard before a special Federal commissioner, who received twice the fee if the African-American were found to be still a slave. The commissioner's decision was an answer to any state application for a writ of *habeas corpus* (q.v.) from any other court, state or Federal. So states under strong abolitionist influence had passed personal liberty laws, preventing any state official from interfering to assist a Federal officer returning a fugitive. This went so far as to deny sheriffs allowing their jails to be used to house a Federal fugitive slave even momentarily. In addition, states required better procedural guarantees, like requiring the presence of all witnesses and denying the use of depositions, which required planters to come North in person and confront a hostile community to reclaim a slave. After Dred Scott, select Northern states declared no African-American could be a citizen, but many Northern states gave blacks citizenship to nullify that. They also provided public defenders to represent indigent fugitives.

The Booth case came up through Wisconsin. A fugitive had been apprehended by his master in Wisconsin. Newspaper editor Sherman M. Booth led a mob to the jail and freed the slave, whom Booth spirited over the border to British Canada, free country. When Federal courts tried to prosecute Booth for violating the Fugitive Slave Act, Wisconsin state courts intervened with a writ of *habeas corpus*, freeing Booth. On appeal, the Wisconsin supreme court declared the Fugitive Acts to be unconstitutional.

In 1859, Chief Justice Roger B. Taney again wrote the decision in this Wisconsin case, now called Ableman *v.* Booth. Unlike the divided bench in Dred Scott, he spoke for a unanimous Court. He said that the fugitive clause in the U.S. Constitution was a guarantee that no state could violate. He maintained that when Wisconsin joined the Union, it lost its absolute sovereignty and could not interpose to prevent the enforcement of Federal laws. The coming of the Civil War left the Booth case an anachronism until 1957, when the Federal government integrated the public schools in Little Rock, Arkansas. When the state interposed its authority to prevent this, the U.S. Supreme Court read the verdict in Ableman *v.* Booth to state officials in Cooper *v.* Aaron (1959). It is still good case law today.

The significance of Booth and Scott as court cases is that they illustrate that the South actually wished to enhance Federal power before 1860, as regards protection of slavery in the territories and the return of fugitive slaves, while the North wished to limit Federal power in these instances. This is the opposite of what many historians and students believe today.

ABOLITIONISTS. A small group of the antislavery movement in the United States in the 19th century, abolitionists comprised as many as 1,300 groups and around 150,000–200,000 members. They came into being in the 1830s, especially after the publication of William Lloyd Garrison's newspaper, *The Liberator*. Abolitionists differed from the antislavery (q.v.) people in that the abolitionists saw an evil, slavery, that they could not easily eradicate because of the difficulty of amending the U.S. Constitution. Rather than working within the system, abolitionists preferred to withdraw and were more in favor of secession before the Civil War than was the South, seeing the Constitution as a "covenant with death and an agreement with hell."

In an attempt to understand the abolitionists, historians have pointed to some things that they all had in common. They were born between 1790 and 1810. This made them young in the 1830s, when they first came on the American scene in great numbers. Eighty-five percent of the total came from the northeast Atlantic coastal states, 60 percent from New England, and 30 percent from Massachusetts. They came from the professional sector of the middle class (teachers, preachers, doctors, farmers). Few were rich; few were poor. They were highly educated, many having attended college. They were by and large Congregational, Presbyterian, and Methodist in religion. They received their strongest support from areas that had been bypassed economically. The sons and daughters who were abolitionists had seen society pass beyond the influence their fathers and mothers had.

Traditionally, Americans thought that the abolitionists had an unreal picture of what slavery was like. Modern scholars are not so sure. They believe that abolitionists were correct in saying that only they really understood slavery, because they had nothing to gain from it politically, socially, or morally. The abolitionists understood that slaveholders were not merely sinners and evil men, but also good, moral Christians. But when the abolitionists tried to send them tracts and pamphlets explaining the evils of slavery or tried to petition Congress to act, the South blocked their use of the mails and tabled their congressional petitions without allowing them to be heard. The real enemies of free men everywhere, the abolitionists maintained, were the good, north and south, who condoned slavery. Treatment of the slave was irrelevant. Blacks were still slaves, and that was the point.

Abolitionists saw that slavery was a complex institution that had to be ended wisely. Hence, they supported the various philanthropic groups that went south during the Civil War, and especially during Reconstruction, to educate blacks, to teach them cleanliness, religion, and the responsibilities of citizenship. They believed that they had a lot of hard work to do, because slavery was such an arbitrary and absolute power that it thoroughly victimized the African-American. To prove this, the abolitionists circulated the atrocity stories that came north with the runaways. It was not to illustrate that cruelty existed in slavery. It was to show that it was an absolute tyranny that crushed independence and resourcefulness, and fostered adaptation, deceit, and vacillation for personal survival.

Slavery did not just affect the South, said the abolitionists. By not allowing the African-American to produce to his or her best capabilities, it deprived all America of its fullest economic potential. The abolitionists also believed that slavery adversely affected the Southern whites. It made them arrogant, violent, and disdainful of the rights of others. They were bowie-knife-wield-ing grandees, who fought duels and bedded black women. Even respectable Southerners who did not have these poor qualities were corrupted when they lent their reputations to support the slave system.

Abolitionism was a double crusade—it sought freedom for African-Americans and the restoration of themselves as America's moral and social leaders. Like the old Puritans, they stood aside from politics before the war as a biblical "city on a hill," a shining example of what good people should believe and act. But after Northern victory on the battlefield, reconstruction of all of Southern society, black and white, from the ground up was necessary, and many abolitionists got involved. But not all of them. The concept of nationalism that emerged from the Civil War was a limited one. It did not include what we today view as more or less normal, the idea of state-planned reform. Indeed, most Americans and most abolitionists believed in self-help. It was not the government's responsibility to assure social or economic equality. One had to achieve that by oneself. Many believed that the winning of the war was the end of the crusade and did not sign on for the road of political, social, and economic equality that branched off from the highway to freedom.

AFRICAN-AMERICAN SOLDIERS IN THE CONFEDERATE ARMIES, USE OF. The role of African-Americans as laborers and soldiers in the Confederate armies is quite controversial in this day and age. But the fact remains that blacks played an important part in defending the South and might have done more if white Southerners had not permitted race to blind them. There were probably a half million African-Americans of military age in the South at the beginning of the war. Their capacity to serve as soldiers and sailors had already been proven in the American Revolution and the War of 1812. It should never have been doubted by North or South, but it was.

African-Americans on both sides of the Mason–Dixon Line were caught up in the war fervor in 1861. In the South, this was especially true of New Orleans and Mobile, which had a large, well-educated, free, Creole class of mixed color. Louisiana had enrolled blacks in the militia from the beginning of its existence. They had served honorably under Gen. Andrew Jackson at the First Battle of New Orleans in 1815. In 1861, there were three regiments of persons of mixed color in the Louisiana militia. They offered their services, only to be rebuffed in Richmond. White Southerners, especially those not from Louisiana, saw black soldiers as a challenge to the whole society they were defending. Eventually, many of these free men of color would go over to the Union occupation forces. But 3,000 blacks still served in Louisiana Confederate units during the war. North or South, they fought to keep their independent, lucrative, middle position between white freedom and black slavery.

But individual blacks are on the records of numerous Confederate regiments. Yankee soldiers reported them during the Peninsula Campaign in 1862. Black gunners manned cannon in Tennessee and Virginia. Slave body servants often followed the sons of their masters into the field, doing everything from tending camp, cooking, and rescuing the sick and wounded, to fighting. The 1st South Carolina Regiment, raised among the best families of the state, had a body servant present for every man from colonel to private. Men of color, free and slave, loyally drove the wagons that supplied Confederate armies in the field with food, forage, and ammunition. One outside observer guessed that Gen. Robert E. Lee's (q.v.) Army of Northern Virginia had 30,000 blacks supporting it in the field. These numbers are probably exaggerated, but not by much. Witnesses told of seeing at least 3,000 blacks accompanying Lee's army as it moved from Frederick to the gigantic battle at Antietam Creek during the Maryland Campaign (q.v.). The following year, 5 percent of the Rebel combat force at Gettysburg was black.

Other African-Americans served the Confederacy by building fortifications and entrenchments at many locations throughout the South. In fact, every slave who did not flee to the invading Yankee armies helped defend the Confederacy with work done on farms and in industry. But in February 1864, the Confederate Congress decided to make a more regularized use of slave labor, when it passed a law drafting up to 20,000 slaves for laborers. No hope of emancipation was included, but large numbers of slaves were impressed as laborers at the defenses surrounding Richmond, Atlanta, and Charleston.

But there were men of greater vision than that. On January 2, 1864, Maj. Gen. Patrick R. Cleburne of Arkansas proposed that the Confederacy offer blacks freedom for their enlistment in the Confederate army as combat troops. His direct commander, Gen. Joseph E. Johnston (q.v.), tried to hush the matter up, but President Jefferson Davis heard of it in Richmond. Davis asked Cleburne to suppress his petition, and the general obeyed. But Cleburne was just the beginning of what became a movement that was not to be denied. Governors from every Southern state that still had a government loyal to the Confederacy asked that black soldiers be given a try. And liberty ought to be included. After all, the North would free them if it won.

The final argument that moved the Confederacy came from Lee. As general-in-chief, he asked for black soldiers. His Second Corps said that white soldiers would fight alongside of blacks without rancor. On March 13, 1865, the Confederate Congress passed a law drafting up to 300,000 African-Americans as soldiers. No more than 25 percent were to come from any one state. But still seeing the contradiction of blacks fighting for the Confederacy as too much to bear, Congress refused to grant those who served their freedom. Davis signed the law and said that he would see to it that those who served would be freed. He might have also included a small plot of land, because already many slaves indicated that freedom and land were what they most desired.

It is commonplace to laugh at Confederate efforts to enlist blacks as soldiers. Abraham Lincoln (q.v.) did on March 17, at the National Hotel, as the Confederates debated the possibility in Congress. But one gets the impression that he laughed only out of the corner of his mouth. As many as five regiments of blacks in gray uniform did drill near Richmond and served as railroad guards in central Virginia, but there is no record that they ever fought as cohesive units in the war. But if a man with as anti-Negro a reputation as Lt. Gen. Nathan Bedford Forrest (q.v.) could employ eight black soldiers on his personal staff, there may be more to black Confederates than meets the modern eye.

AFRICAN-AMERICAN SOLDIERS IN THE UNION ARMIES, USE OF. Roughly 180,000 African-Americans served in the Union forces during the Civil War. This amounts to 12 percent of all Union troops raised. The blacks comprised 120 regiments of infantry, a dozen heavy artillery regiments, 10 light batteries of artillery, and 7 cavalry regiments. The so-called United States Colored Troops (USCT) lost 68,000, one-third of those who served, of which 2,700 were battle casualties. Twenty-one black soldiers received the Medal of Honor.

Initially, there was much opposition to the use of African-American soldiers. It was looked upon as degrading for white soldiers to serve with blacks, many held that blacks would not fight well, and there was fear in the North that their service would incite a bloody servile insurrection in the South. Moreover, many feared that the border slave states that had remained loyal to the North might secede. But on the other hand, there were compelling reasons to enroll African-American troops. They would strengthen the Federal response to the rebellion, give additional meaning to the nature of American democracy, and assist blacks in gaining full admittance into American society.

There were three premature efforts to organize black regiments before the Abraham Lincoln (q.v.) administration was ready to embrace the notion. Maj. Gen. David Hunter, a personal friend of Lincoln and a devout abolitionist (q.v.), issued an unauthorized order for the emancipation of all blacks in his command area in 1862. Hunter, nicknamed "Black Dave," was in charge of the Department of the South, which included the Sea Islands of the Carolina and Georgia coasts. He organized the 1st South Carolina Colored Regiment in April 1862, using commandeering, confiscating, and impressment. Lincoln refused to pay, muster-in, or assist in equipping these men, and the regiment was dropped in four months.

Out in Kansas, James H. Lane, like Hunter another fervent abolitionist, leader of the Free State militia known as the "Red Legs" from the red leggings they wore to battle, ignored Lincoln's refusal to admit his 1st Kansas Colored Regiment into the service. Lane paid for them himself, using them a full year to suppress Rebel guerrillas in Kansas and Indian Territory, before they were accepted into service.

Like Lane, Maj. Gen. Benjamin F. Butler (q.v.) persisted in organizing black soldiers in Louisiana, despite government discouragement. Louisiana had a long antebellum tradition of enrolling black militia units deriving from the free men of color in New Orleans. Butler himself was not enthusiastic about black enlistments at first, but when his agents succeeded beyond everyone's fondest hopes, Butler adopted the program as his own to win the political credit. Over 1,400 men enrolled as the Louisiana Native Guards, later the Corps d'Afrique. All claimed to be free men of color from before the war, to avoid the problems associated with arming slaves, but no one confirmed their claims of freedom.

On August 25, 1862, Lincoln at last timidly authorized the enlistment of up to 5,000 African-American soldiers. His January 1, 1863, Emancipation Proclamation (q.v.) gave further impetus to the raising of black regiments. The enlistees were paid $7 a month plus $3 a month for clothing (whites received $13–21 a month pay plus a monthly clothing allotment of $3.50). By the summer of 1863, the government regularized recruiting (using far less kidnapping, coercion, and catch dogs) and training and created a Bureau of Colored Troops to supervise the whole thing.

Several factors changed the minds of Northern soldiers and civilians about the use of African-American soldiers. Brig. Gen. Lorenzo Thomas, the adjutant general of the army, became a sort of unofficial head recruiter, going up and down the contraband camps and government-run plantations looking for volunteers. He personally raised 50 regiments of 76,000 men, or 41 percent of the total. Yankee officers began to see the African-Americans as powerful allies. They were needed on the field. White enlisted men, failing to gain promotion in the white army, began to transfer to the USCT to gain commissions. And finally, the blacks performed credibly on the battlefields of the war.

Although many of the black regiments were condemned to labor, enough of them served in combat (the USCT fought in 39 major battles and 410 minor engagements) to end any doubt of whether they would fight. The first major action for the USCT was in the Port Hudson Campaign. The most famous single assault was the one the 54th Massachusetts (Colored) Regiment made in vain at Ft. Wagner near Charleston in 1863.

The black soldiers rarely were taken prisoner in battle. If they surrendered, the Rebels generally shot them on the spot as slaves committing insurrection—or sold them back into slavery. At Olustee, Florida, the UCST stood and died facing the Confederate onslaught. Those who ran from the field with all of their white counterparts suffered death at the hands of angry white blue-coats. At Ft. Pillow, Lt. Gen. Nathan Bedford Forrest's (q.v.) Rebel cavalry shot down without mercy black and white Unionists who tried to surrender. The same happened at Poison Spring and Mark's Mill in Arkansas.

One of the biggest uses of the USCT occurred at the end of July 1864, at the Petersburg Siege. A black division from the Army of the Potomac was trained to clear the Rebel line, after white coal miners blew up the forts. At the last minute, nearby white soldiers were substituted for the assault wave. Lt. Gen. Ulysses S. Grant (q.v.) and Maj. Gen. George G. Meade (q.v.) feared that if the attack failed and a bloodbath ensued, they would suffer the political repercussions. Untrained, the whites did not move through the crater made by the explosion, and the blacks jammed in behind them. The whole thing was a fiasco, but Grant and Meade survived the political ramifications that followed.

But the USCT had a fine day at the decisive Nashville Campaign (q.v.), leading the grand attack that drove the Rebels from the field. More than anything else, the fine service of the USCT ensured that Emancipation would remain a national policy and the promises of Lincoln's Emancipation Proclamation (q.v.) would be secured through the passage of the Thirteenth Amendment (q.v.).

ALABAMA **CLAIMS.** The most notable achievement of Hamilton Fish's tenure as President Ulysses S. Grant's (q.v.) secretary of state was the Treaty of Washington, which settled the contentious *Alabama* claims, held over from the days of the Civil War, with Great Britain. Britain had declared itself neutral during the war but, in certain aspects, its neutrality was decidedly pro-Confederate. The building of ships for thinly disguised Confederate agents was a case in point, as was its recognition of the South as a belligerent. An earlier treaty had attempted to settle these problems, but was marred by the desire of Radical Republicans to have Britain pay off claims of Northern citizens who had had cargoes and ships sunk by British-built raiders flying the Rebel flag. The result was an official standoff that lasted until 1873. When Fish let it be known secretly that he did not agree with the exorbitant sums and land claims against British territory in Canada that the Congress put forward, the British opened up discussions again through the government of Canada. This time the negotiations included other matters like boundaries, fishing rights in the Atlantic, and trade, and they were settled in the 1871 Treaty of Washington (q.v.).

ALABAMA, **C.S.S.** *See* CONFEDERATE SEA RAIDERS.

ALASKA, PURCHASE OF. After the expulsion of the French under Maximilian (q.v.) from Mexico in 1867, Secretary of State William H. Seward (q.v.) began to expand his horizons and his view for the future of the United States in the world. In this, he was perhaps the first to accurately foresee the entrance of America onto the world stage as an imperial power co-equal to any European nation. Seward would not realize this in his lifetime, but he began to lay the essential preliminary foundation upon which his successors would build. And the Monroe Doctrine would be a perfect cover for his activities. Americans on the Pacific Coast had long coveted Russian America, as Alaska was then called. But the Civil War had put off a decision on the purchase of this piece of European-controlled real estate on the shores of North America. Russia, however, was interested in selling Alaska, because it was not a viable economic endeavor and was expensive to maintain and impossible to defend. So Tsar Alexander II found himself in the same position that Napoleon I had been in before his sale of Louisiana to Thomas Jefferson—in need of making the best of a lousy deal. Like the French at the beginning of the century, the Russians found the United States the right power to sell to—small, not too powerful, and not European-based. In short, America was not a competitor. The Tsar promised his minister to the United States, Baron Edouard de Stoeckl, a $17,000 bonus to make the deal, but warned him not to get less than $5 million. Could de Stoeckl convince America to buy?

The answer was an unreserved "yes," as far as Seward was concerned. He had noticed the effects of the Confederate raider *Shenandoah* in the last months of the war as it destroyed the Yankee whaling fleet, ship by ship, aided by the lack of U.S. naval bases in the northern Pacific. With the end of the war, Seward was determined to gain American naval bases in the Pacific and also in the West Indies to curtail the easy pickings that the American merchant fleet posed to a potential enemy, as demonstrated by the Confederates. This made him interested in Alaska, Hawaii, Midway, the Danish West Indies, Cuba, and Santo Domingo (and compelled Presidents Abraham Lincoln [q.v.] and Ulysses S. Grant [q.v.] to look longingly at Santo Domingo more than they ought to have, both as a naval base and a place to send America's blacks for a new start, solving racial discrimination against freedmen at the same time). So Seward went to work lining up Congress ahead of time, reminding it and the American people of their prewar desires to advance into the Orient and the Caribbean.

According to the tale, Stoeckl found Seward one night playing whist. He told the secretary of state that he could sell Alaska to the United States and offered to come by the next day to work out the details. "Why wait?" Seward wanted to know. He said that he would get his staff and Senator Charles Sumner (q.v.), chairman of the foreign relations committee (Seward was not stupid; he knew Sumner was the difference between victory or defeat of the treaty) together, and Stoeckl could round up his own people, too. By the next morning, the treaty was ready and President Andrew Johnson (q.v.) sent it to the Senate. There Sumner gave it his unreserved approval (calling it Alaska for the first time), and it passed 37 to 2.

But it took a year to get the $7.2 million from the House, the proceedings going right through the impeachment proceedings against Johnson. It was Alaska's unfamiliarity and the hatred for anything Johnson did that made its purchase a joke. It was $165,000 in bribes (out of a $200,000 slush fund, which was why the price was $7,200,000, Congress voting in effect to pay itself off) to key congressmen that got it accepted. Of course Seward said he knew nothing about that. But as the public ridiculed "Seward's Ice Box," the secretary also appropriated Midway Island unnoticed, by simply landing a force of sailors and marines on it. But the Danish West Indies would have to wait. The Danes tried to drive a hard bargain, and the problem dragged out past Seward's time in office. President U. S. Grant did not choose to pursue it further, being more interested in Santo Domingo.

ALCORN, JAMES LUSK (1816–1894). A Mississippi Scalawag (q.v.) of importance, James L. Alcorn was born in 1816 in Illinois Territory, where his father ran a freighting service on the Mississippi River. The family moved to Kentucky, where Alcorn was educated in local schools and at Cumberland College. He married twice, first to Mary C. Stewart, by whom he fathered three children (she dying in childbirth with the third), and Amelia Walton Greer, with whom he had five more. After teaching schools and acting as deputy sheriff in Arkansas and Kentucky, Alcorn moved to Mississippi in 1843. There he ran a plantation near Yazoo Pass, founded the Mississippi River Levee system, and was a member of the state legislature as a Whig for 15 years. He tried for the U.S. House in 1856, but lost the election. He also was a delegate to the state constitutional conventions of 1851 and 1861, considering secession. Although Alcorn was against secession personally, he was one of those Whigs who backed the proposal in 1861.

During the Civil War, Alcorn served as brigadier general of Mississippi state troops. Disappointed with the war and never much of a Rebel, he resigned his commission. He sold his cotton to smugglers in violation of U.S. regulations to get a cash advance, upon which he lived during the war. Late in the war, Alcorn supported the notion of arming blacks as Confederate soldiers and rendering them free in return. He supported the Thirteenth Amendment (q.v.) at the end of the war. After he applied in person for a pardon, Alcorn was elected U.S. senator, but his application for a seat in that body was rejected, along with others elected under President Andrew Johnson's (q.v.) Reconstruction plan.

After passage of the Military Reconstruction Acts (q.v.), Mississippi Radical Republicans, with the support of African-Americans, elected Alcorn governor. The canvass was helped immeasurably by General Adelbert Ames (q.v.), military commander of the state, who removed from office any who could be identified as opposed to Alcorn as an impediment to Reconstruction.

Alcorn's platform was quite radical to white Mississippians. He stood for legal equality of all races and comprehensive civil rights laws (but he opposed social equality and public accommodations laws). He backed segregated public education (the all-black Alcorn College was named after him), expanding the judiciary (to protect loyal whites and blacks and give the party much patronage to grease the wheels of government), reduction of taxes on land (to save the old planter class), leasing of convicts (to gain a steady source of labor for a massive public works system), and state aid to the construction of railroads (many of which had been wrecked by the passing armies of blue and gray).

The program passed, and afterward Alcorn resigned his governor's position to assume a U.S. Senate seat. There he made quite a splash by arguing and debating with Ames, resigned from the Army and now the other U.S. senator from Mississippi, over the need for the Enforcement Acts (q.v.), which Alcorn opposed.

By now Alcorn was also opposed at home by more than just white Democrats. Radical Republicans in the form of the Carpetbaggers (q.v.) objected to his squeaky clean government style. Blacks began to oppose him because, while he might grant a certain legal equality, Alcorn was white-only at heart. So when Alcorn came home to run for governor again in 1874, the Democrats, African-Americans, and Carpetbaggers all opposed him and elected Ames, the Carpetbagger who as military commander had helped put Alcorn in office in the first place. Alcorn went back to Washington to serve out the remainder of his U.S. Senate term. He voted continuously with the Republicans on Whiggish matters (economic development of the nation particularly through internal improvements) and for the Compromise of 1877.

After his retirement, Alcorn continued to practice law, served on the state levee commission, and ran for governor again in the 1880s, to no avail. He also was a member of the state constitutional convention in 1890, which disfranchised blacks within the terms of the Fifteenth Amendment (q.v.), a measure that Alcorn supported—again demonstrating his limits on behalf of racial equality. Alcorn naïvely hoped that disfranchisement would turn Mississippi back to a time when the better classes ran the state. Instead, what happened was exactly the opposite, as the "red necks" took over and the state stagnated in a way he never envisioned or would have approved of.

To the end, Alcorn remained a Whig among Whigs rather than a real Republican. It was his example that led 20th-century historians to theorize that many more upper class men like him were the Scalawags of Reconstruction, not the poor white trash that the stereotypical legend indicates. But in reality, Alcorn may have been the exception rather than the rule.

ALDIE, BATTLE OF. *See* PENNSYLVANIA CAMPAIGN.

AMBULANCE SERVICES AND TRIAGE. After the capture of the main Union field hospital at Savage's Station during the Peninsula Campaign (q.v.) and the poor condition of the prisoners returned North by the overwhelmed Confederates, Federal Surgeon General William Hammond replaced Dr. Charles C. Tripler as head of medical services in the Army of the Potomac on July 4, 1862, with an old friend, Dr. Jonathan Letterman.

Letterman's job was to clean up the medical system employed in the army to care for the wounded in battle. Letterman quickly did three things: he centralized all ambulances with the medical services; he standardized all equipment and medicines carried by doctors so that they were interchangeable; and he restructured the medical command system, getting rid of regimental hospitals, and consolidated all regimental doctors in brigade or divisional hospitals. Letterman's system was first used in action in the Maryland Campaign (q.v.) at the Battle of Antietam. Within 24 hours, his reorganized ambulance corps had removed 10,000 wounded from the field for treatment.

Letterman was not through. He attacked the whole treatment system next. Behind the battlefield were the first aid treatment centers, staffed by assistant surgeons. They would give first aid and separate wounded into those who could or could not walk. The latter were put on the ambulances and sent to the consolidated divisional hospitals farther to the rear. Ambulatory patients were expected to walk to this next stop. At this field hospital, three surgeons were in charge of three functions, each with an assistant. One would administer anesthetics; another would coordinate all operations, mostly amputations; and the third would compile a complete record on each patient, including name rank, regiment, wound, and treatment. All other surgeons and assistant surgeons would operate at proper medical tables, not merely doors laid on sawhorses for the time being.

First used at the Battle of Fredericksburg (q.v.), Letterman's expanded system was an instant success. On March 30, 1863, it was placed into Maj. Gen. U. S. Grant's (q.v.) Army of the Tennessee. A year later, Congress mandated by law that the Letterman system be used in all Union armies. The Letterman system was greatly assisted by the improved design of army ambulances. In 1859, the army had authorized the employment of two different two-wheeled carts, based on the Larrey "Flying Ambulance" used during the Napoleonic Wars. Both the Coolidge and the Finley carts were too confining and unstable. The patients rocked about from side to side and front to back so that they arrived at the aid station more motion-sick than injured.

Both carts proved to be too flimsy to last under combat conditions and were replaced with four-wheeled wagons. The prewar Rosecrans wagon held four men on stretchers. It was very light and supplemented with the Tripler, a sturdy wagon that could hold four prone or six seated patients. But the Tripler proved to be too heavy to be used without tiring the horses.

So the army re-worked the Rosecrans wagon into a real ambulance, called the Rucker. It also hauled six seated and four prone men, but had better ventilation and more flexibility. It became the most popular military vehicle of the war, every staff officer wanting one for his own use. The ambulance train was supplemented with an Autenreith medicine wagon, sort of a cowboy chuckwagon-style vehicle, stocked with medicines and implements to provide the materials to make every ambulance train or field hospital functional in the best sense of the word. *See also* DISEASE; MEDICAL DIRECTORS OR SURGEONS GENERAL, CONFEDERATE; MEDICAL DIRECTORS OR SURGEONS GENERAL, UNION; NURSES; UNITED STATES SANITARY COMMISSION; WOUNDS.

AMERICAN COLONIZATION SOCIETY. The returning of enslaved black Americans to their native continent was an idea that became very compelling after the war of 1812. As slavery looked pretty much unprofitable at the time, and the soils in the Southeastern Atlantic states were becoming exhausted by intensive agriculture and the accompanying erosion, it was hoped that many slaveowners would avail themselves of this chance to get rid of the "peculiar institution." In 1816, led by notable politicians like President James Monroe, former President James Madison, and Speaker of the House Henry Clay, the American Colonization Society was formed. It was to free the Negroes from slavery and send them back to a spot on the African coast that eventually became the nation of Liberia. Money for the compensated emancipation would be provided from the tariff on imports, also mentioned as a source of funding for various internal improvements, and would serve the dual purpose of protecting the nation's fledgling industries from the import of cheap foreign goods.

AMERICAN FREEDMEN'S UNION COMMISSION (AFUC). As the sectarian societies moved south, various non-sectarian groups also organized with the notion to send relief to the destitute freedmen. The first again began in New England, but soon others cropped up in many Northern cities, such as Cincinnati, Chicago, Cleveland, Detroit, New York, Philadelphia, and Baltimore. The result was a confusion of well-intended voices that was solved somewhat when the non-sectarian groups united under the banner of the American Freedmen's Union Commission. Their leaders included such men as Levi Coffin, Salmon P. Chase (q.v.), William Lloyd Garrison, Phillips Brooks, John Greenleaf Whittier, Henry Ward Beecher, Edward Everett Hale, Edward Atkinson, John A. Andrew, and Edward L. Pierce. By 1866, with the encouragement of the Federal Bureau of Refugees, Freedmen, and

Abandoned Lands (q.v.), most independent groups had affiliated with the American Missionary Association (q.v.) or the AFUC. Perhaps one-half of the $12 million appropriated to the Bureau by 1872 was turned over to the various benevolent societies.

The secretary of the AFUC was Lyman Abbott, a New Englander who believed in the Northern mission to civilize the South through a revolutionary transformation of people's minds. He liked to work through the reconstructed governments and their superintendents of public instruction. But he found his hardest fight to be among the contributing members, each interested in a different religious "truth" for the freedmen. He soon found that the only way to obtain the cooperation of Southern whites was to renounce the notion of integrated education and concentrate on educating by race alone. But in the end, they probably did not educate more than 10 percent of the blacks who were available to learn between 1865 and 1869.

AMERICAN MISSIONARY ASSOCIATION. The first of the freedmen's societies was the American Missionary Association (AMA), begun in 1846 by such abolitionists as Arthur and Lewis Tappan, Edward Beecher, S. S. Jocelyn, Joshua Leavitt, John Greenleaf Whittier, and Gerrit Smith. Reorganized under George Whipple in 1861, the AMA moved down to Virginia and began administrating to the contraband camps at Fortress Monroe. They were soon followed by Methodists and Baptists, no sect wishing to yield the harvest of souls to another, less-enlightened group.

Typical of the philosophical problems that existed was the claim of the American Missionary Association (AMA) to be interdenominational. It was a fraud, of course, to anyone who was not a Congregationalist, the sponsoring body of the association. And the work of the association belied the claim, as its missionaries openly created Congregational churches everywhere its teachers went. But they were not alone. Baptists, Methodists, Presbyterians, and Quakers all competed for the African-Americans' souls as well as their minds. There was also competition from the secular associations, which claimed to be doing their work without denominational prejudices. This was true to some degree, but a poor church member it was indeed who would not stick a bit of the "true salvation" into his or her work, regardless of the parent association's denial of the same.

AMERICAN PARTY. The American Party was a remnant of the old Whig Party (q.v.), which appeared briefly in the election of 1856 (q.v.), only to disappear in the wake of the slavery controversy that led to the secession (q.v.) of the South in 1860–1861. Contrary to popular conception, in the mid-1850s the American Party was the fastest growing political party in the country, not the Republicans (q.v.). It took 25 percent of the popular vote in the election of

1856, after most Northern Whigs had shifted to the Republicans, only to disappear by 1860. Not all of its problems flowed from the quarrel over slavery in the territories. The Whigs had run as pro-slavery in the South and antislavery in the north, and it worked. Something else had to have influenced the American Party's fate. That factor is found in its nickname, the "Know Nothings."

In fact, the American Party was a response to two factors that dominated the 1850s: the slavery issue and the problem of increased immigration, much of it Roman Catholic. Fear of foreigners, an issue that is still with us, and Catholics, an issue much muted with the election of John F. Kennedy as president in 1960, have been persistent themes in American history. The Puritans legislated again "popery" in the 1600s, both here and in Britain. The British crown tried to segregate the religious issue after their victory in the French and Indian Wars with the passage of the Quebec Act, making the British administration of that largely French Catholic province separate from the Thirteen Colonies. From the writing of the Constitution to 1844, foreigners were tolerated only in small numbers. The Alien and Sedition Acts at the end of the 18th century were an attempt by Whig Party forerunners to limit the political impact of foreigners in domestic political life, a theme taken up by the Anti-Masonic Party in the 1830s. Anti-Catholicism was a constant undercurrent, occasionally surfacing with violence, as in the Philadelphia riots of 1844.

But from 1844 to 1850, the War with Mexico overwhelmed the anti-foreign, anti-Catholic issues. The Mexicans annexed to the United States were too far away to be a major concern. But the failure of the revolutions of 1848 in Europe and the Irish potato famine sent droves of new immigrants to the United States, many of them Catholic. This was exacerbated when the Catholic clergy and hierarchy were seen as too controlled by Rome, an attitude fostered by the refusal of John Cardinal Hughes in New York City to mute his allegiance abroad. When Franklin Pierce appointed a Catholic to his cabinet, as postmaster general, no less, in charge of patronage, Protestants and "Old Americans" went wild. The result was the Know Nothing movement.

Begun in New York state in 1849, the "Order of the Star Spangled Banner," the Know Nothing's official name, was a semi-secret organization of patriotic Americans who came together to support whatever party or politicians were willing to stand by long-accepted values and traditions, whatever they were. A secret ritual and degrees of membership in local, state, and national councils flavored the organization. When asked by outsiders about their rituals, members responded, "I know nothing," hence their popular name. As Northern antislavery Whigs went to the Republicans, those who still wanted to oppose the Democrats' economic policies in favor of the American System went over to the Know Nothings, calling themselves Whig–Americans, or, by 1856, the American Party.

The new party swept state and local elections. The Know Nothings took Delaware and Pennsylvania in 1854, and added Rhode Island, New Hampshire, Connecticut, Maryland, and Kentucky in 1855. Just barely losing out to the Democrats in Tennessee, the American Party swept the South in 1855, winning in Virginia, Georgia, Alabama, Mississippi, and Louisiana. Their total Southern vote was just 16,000 less than the regular Whigs and the Democrats. They were aided by a public perception that the regular Whigs, Democrats, and Republicans failed to offer a solution to the social problems brought on by immigration, like Catholicism, Mormonism, Sunday drinking, the selling of corrupted immigrant votes, and a declining economy, especially in the industrial North. The vagueness of the American Party's platform (what is Americanism, anyhow?) attracted many varying political hues to its party colors.

But once in power, the American Party did nothing—even less than it opponents. The Americans were denounced as "Owe Nothings," "Do Nothings," and "Say Nothings." Then the Kansas–Missouri Border Wars heated up, and everything else took a back seat to slavery in the territories and the Kansas Settlement (q.v.), a crisis that lasted until the advent of the Civil War. The Americans and the regular Whigs endured to 1860 as a party of compromise over the slavery issue, making its last stand as the Constitutional Union Party (q.v.) in the election of 1860 (q.v.) and contributing most of the members to the failed Washington Peace Conference of 1861.

AMERICAN SYSTEM. Developed by the erstwhile leader of the Whig Party (q.v.), Henry Clay, the American System was his program of how the Federal government ought to help guide the development of the United States for the betterment of all through economic growth. The notion and its components were not new with Clay. He based his ideas on those of Alexander Hamilton, the first secretary of the treasury under President George Washington, and economists Friedrich List and Matthew Carey. These men were intellectually opposed to the free economy ideas of *laissez faire* supply and demand Adam Smith theorized in the mid-1700s.

Unlike Smith, Clay did not believe in natural economic laws. Instead, Clay maintained that a nation could control its future by the laws it passed legislatively. He held that it was the duty of governments to provide new jobs, protect old jobs, diversify production, and prevent foreign competition.

Clay's economic development was called the American System, and not by accident. This placed the onus on opponents as backing un-American programs. It had four basic components: a high protective tariff to guard infant American industries against foreign competition; a central banking system to regulate the overall economy and national currency (in those days any bank could issue its own paper money, much of it eventually worthless); a vigorous program of governmentally financed internal improvements (bridges, roads, canals, and railroads); and the distribution of the proceeds from the sales of the public lands (it went at $1.25/acre) back to the states, where they could use it for their own internal improvements or for the liberation and colonization of African-American slaves overseas (q.v.) in Africa.

The American System was the platform of the Whig Party for years. It had many proponents and detractors, particularly the Democrats (q.v.), who believed that an unregulated economy was more in tune with the needs of the common man. But the American System outlived Henry Clay and became the internal program of the Republicans as the Republican Platform of 1860 (qq.v.).

AMES, ADELBERT (1835–1933). Union general, Carpetbag U.S. senator, and governor from Mississippi, Adelbert Ames was born in Rockland, Maine. The son of a sea captain, he had accompanied him on several sea voyages. He had a talent for art and mathematics and a New England horror of the institution of slavery. He was a man with a conscience, a stern sense of duty, and a fastidiousness in personal conduct, dressing impeccably, rarely smoking or drinking, seldom swearing, and always a gallant gentleman with the ladies.

Admitted to West Point, Ames graduated near the top of his class. At First Bull Run, he won the Congressional Medal of Honor for valor on the battlefield. He went on to rise to brevet brigadier general, having fought with distinction on the Peninsula, at Antietam, Fredericksburg (q.v.), Gettysburg, the siege of Charleston and Petersburg (q.v.), and the final attack on Fort Fisher. At the end of the war, he received the permanent rank of lieutenant colonel in the regular Army. He thought of resigning his commission to enter private business, but stayed on in the Army with the occupation forces in South Carolina, then took a leave of absence to tour Europe. He returned to Washington and married Blanche Butler, the lovely, articulate, only child of General Benjamin F. Butler (q.v.), Ames' one-time commanding officer during the war.

Ames' station after his leave was with the occupation forces in Mississippi. His first duty was to assume the task of governing the state, the elected governor having refused to relinquish power under the Military Reconstruction Acts. Ames marched him out of the governor's mansion between two files of soldiers. Ames was now provisional governor of the state as well as military commander of Mississippi.

A lifelong Republican (q.v.), Ames removed 2,000 Mississippians from offices to which they had been elected. He gave the positions to blacks, who made up a majority of Mississippi's population, and loyal white Carpetbaggers. He cut the poll tax to allow poorer people to vote. He applied the poll tax to disabled Confederate veterans, exempt from paying it until now. He put African-Americans on juries for the first time and appointed the first black poll watchers. When the Radicals won with a ticket headed by Scalawag James L. Alcorn (qq.v.), Ames appointed the elected officials to office without waiting for the inauguration date. If they could not take the oath, he appointed their rivals who could. Conservative whites accused Ames of being a Caesar, using his military power for selfish political ends, which in Ames' case, was a seat in the U.S. Senate for the term ending in 1875. He resigned from the Army to accept this new opportunity.

When Alcorn removed certain black Republicans from office and appointed Democrats, Ames took advantage of the Senate recess to go down and campaign for Radicals in the 1871 by-elections. Ames managed to turn out the heaviest African-American vote yet, and more blacks were elected than ever before. But the cost was splitting the Republican Party between Moderates, Scalawags like Alcorn (who had the support of Senator Hiram Revels [q.v.] and wanted to cooperate with the Democrats), and rock-ribbed Radicals like Ames, who relied on Negro and Carpetbag votes.

After the election, Alcorn replaced Hiram R. Revels in the U.S. Senate, where he and Ames debated each other over the Third Enforcement Bill. Ames also introduced a bill to desegregate the Army, one that proved 70 years ahead of its time. Ames believed that he would probably win reelection to the Senate from the Radical-controlled Mississippi state legislature, but decided that if he ran for governor, a popular electoral triumph might solidify his political future.

Ames resigned his Senate seat and spoke out for better black education, the importation of manufacturers, the need for land distribution to the former slaves, and a frugal government. After winning the election, he made some progress in tax equalization and forced the railroads under the tax burden for the first time. He wanted Mississippi to reject drinking with a Blue Law, but had to settle for county option. He vetoed measures that would have given debt and tax relief to farmers in the midst of economic depression, but got them $100,000 in flood relief from Congress.

But the flood that worried Ames most was the storm coming in from white Democrats known as White Liners (q.v.). They had begun to "bulldoze" his black voters in acts of violence that spread throughout the state. Ames called the legislature into special session. But all they did was appeal to President Ulysses S. Grant (q.v.) to send a company of troops to quell the violence. The president accommodated them, but it showed that the Ames administration could do little to preserve order itself. Even the so-called Gatling Gun Bill, allowing the governor to reorganize the militia and purchase fast-firing weapons for defense of the state government and blacks in the backcountry, did not help. The White Liners knew that if they killed enough African-Americans to intimidate the rest but kept the number as low as necessary, they could keep the Grant administration from assisting Ames further.

On election day 1875, the Democrats won a majority of 50,000 votes, demonstrating the efficacy of the First Mississippi or Shotgun Plan (q.v.) in regaining white control through controlled violence. The state was redeemed at last. The legislature was theirs. All that remained was to get rid of the Radical Republican executive branch, most of whom had not been up for reelection that year. Impeachment was the cure. Ames was accused of everything (absenting himself from the state, freeing accused criminals, degrading the judiciary, and so on) but corruption. Even the Democrats knew that would not sell. Blanche Ames came up with the solution. The legislature agreed to drop all of the charges, and Ames would resign the governorship and leave the state. The deal consummated, Ames returned North to become a business success in his father's flour mill in Minnesota and then in textiles and real estate in his father-in-law's business in Massachusetts.

AMES, OAKES. *See* CRÉDIT MOBILIER SCANDAL.

AMNESTY ACT, GENERAL (1872, 1898). *See* PARDON, AMNESTY, AND PAROLE.

ANACONDA PLAN. When the Civil War began, Union President Abraham Lincoln (q.v.) lacked any real concept of military planning. So he turned to the general-in-chief of the army, Bvt. Lt. Gen. Winfield Scott (q.v.), for advice on how to defeat the Confederacy. Scott developed a strategic plan that has come to be called the Anaconda Plan, from its method of operation. What Scott suggested was to use the Union navy, the North's one ace in the hole, to blockade every Southern port to starve the South into submission. Then he would sit back and let Southern Unionists (Scott himself was one from Virginia) destroy the South from within. The one campaign that Scott believed would pay off was to take the line of the Mississippi River, opening Old Northwest trade with the Gulf at New Orleans, cutting the South in half.

Gen. Scott's Plan would be used, but modified by a suggestion presented by Anna Ella Carroll (although historians differ as to how much, if anything, she contributed). She was a Maryland Unionist who had a knack for military matters, having discussed them often with Scott at her father's house. She suggested to Assistant Secretary of War Thomas Scott (no relation) that the Tennessee River flows north, so disabled Union craft would be able to be salvaged. Knowing that the distance from Pittsburg Landing to the Tombigbee leading to Mobile was short, Carroll also suggested that the Mississippi be opened through the back door, down the Tennessee. She even theorized that Vicksburg could be taken the same way, by land where it was weak.

The great defect of Gen. Scott's Anaconda was that it essentially emphasized one axis of attack, so popular among military men of the time. This would allow the Confederates to concentrate their smaller forces more easily to stop its progress. But its basic outline would be carried out with modifications by Maj. Gen. U. S. Grant (q.v.) in his Shiloh and Vicksburg Campaigns (qq.v.). He also wanted to put in effect the Mobile operation in the spring of 1864, but it was rejected in favor of the Red River Campaign (q.v.).

ANDERSONVILLE (GEORGIA). The worst of all Confederate installations that housed Union prisoners of war. *See also* PRISONS.

ANTIETAM CREEK, BATTLE OF. *See* MARYLAND CAMPAIGN.

ANTISLAVERY. A doctrine that a majority of Northerners embraced, which held that slavery should be ended gradually throughout the entire United States, and that no expansion of slavery into the Western territories should be allowed as a logical first step in this process. These people saw slavery as immoral, wrong, and out of step with the advances being made in Western civilization in the 18th and 19th centuries. They conceded that slavery was guaranteed in the U.S. Constitution, but believed that it should be ended through an amendment or individual action, such as colonization (q.v.) of freed slaves overseas. But they saw no guarantee of slavery in the territories, because it was not mentioned in the Constitution. As such they were completely opposed to the pro-Southern Non-Exclusion Doctrine.

Antislaveryites were different in nature and philosophy from abolitionists (q.v.). Antislaveryites believed that political action was a way to achieve their goals. They backed the Liberty Party in 1840 and 1844, and the Free Soil Party in 1848 and 1852 (q.v.). Their program of "Free Men, Free Soil, Free Speech" became part of the Republican platform (q.v.) in 1856 and 1860. These people saw the Federal government as essentially good but corrupted by the Slave Power Conspiracy (q.v.), the undue power of the South in government because three-fifths of all slaves were counted for purposes of representation, and the fact that of the first 15 U.S. presidents, all but six were Southerners, and only the Southerners had held two terms. Indeed, four of the six (Martin Van Buren, Millard Fillmore, Franklin Pierce, and James Buchanan) were so pliable in doing Southern bidding in Washington as to earn the nickname, "doughface." Only John Adams and his son, John Quincy, were truly and consistently anti-slavery and pro-Northern during their single-term presidencies.

APACHE CANYON, NEW MEXICO, BATTLE OF. *See* NEW MEXICO–ARIZONA CAMPAIGN.

APACHE PASS, ARIZONA, BATTLE OF. *See* NEW MEXICO–ARIZONA CAMPAIGN.

APPOMATTOX CAMPAIGN. Since late June 1864, the Union army under Lt. Gen. Ulysses S. Grant (q.v.) and Confederate forces commanded by Gen. Robert E. Lee (q.v.) had been deadlocked in the Petersburg Siege (q.v.), which included the Confederate capital of Richmond. Gradually, Grant had been able to extend his lines to the south, attempting to string Lee's army out so far that it would have to break somewhere. But Lee had managed to repel all attacks.

In 1865, as spring approached, Lee hoped to abandon Richmond, join forces with Gen. Joseph Johnston (q.v.) in North Carolina, and attack and defeat Johnston's opponent, Maj. Gen. William T. Sherman (q.v.). Then, operating from a central position, Lee and Johnston would turn back on Grant and defeat him, regaining Richmond once again. Lee, as general-in-chief of the Confederate armies, believed that if he moved before the ground hardened from winter snows and rains, using the railroads, tearing up the tracks as he passed, Grant's big advantage in cavalry would be nullified by the mud. Then as the ground hardened, Lee could hit Sherman and Grant as they were strung out in columns, trying to find Lee.

What Lee needed was to set Grant back on his heels temporarily, allowing the armies to separate. It is also believed that the Confederate secret service was coordinating a bomb attack on the White House, to mine its basement with gunpowder and blow it up during a cabinet meeting. When the powderman failed to get through Union lines, his contact in Washington, John Wilkes Booth, shot President Abraham Lincoln, seeing his action as the culmination of numerous assassination and kidnapping plots against Lincoln (q.v.).

Lee made his move against Grant on March 25 at Fort Stedman, in the center of the Union position at Petersburg, hoping to draw Grant off Lee's threatened southern flank. At first victorious, Grant reacted quickly and drove off the Rebels, who lost about 5,000 men, half of whom surrendered. The Federal casualties were 2,000. But Grant had so many soldiers that he did not have to shorten his lines to respond to Lee's attack.

Receiving the return of Maj. Gen. Philip H. Sheridan's (q.v.) cavalry from the Second Valley Campaign on March 30, Grant sent Sheridan, his cavalry, and two infantry corps to turn Lee out of Petersburg by turning the southern flank. Lee countered by sending out a force of cavalry and infantry under Maj. Gen. George E. Pickett to drive the Federals back in the region of Five Forks. Successful in their mission on March 31, Pickett and his men camped at Five Forks and smugly awaited the next day. But rather than defeat, Sheridan saw Pickett's force was isolated beyond the main Confederate line by three to five miles and vulnerable to destruction.

On April 1, Sheridan attacked. At first things went badly for the Federals. But the fiery Sheridan came up in person, fired the V Corps commander on the spot, and got the attack going. Pickett and his main generals had spent the night at a shad bake and were absent from the field as the attack began. Sheridan's powerful force overran the Confederate position, taking 5,200 prisoners (over half of Pickett's men) and 11 battle flags. Cavalry maneuvers and skirmishing after the battle only served to confirm that Grant had turned Lee out of Petersburg at last.

Lee immediately abandoned Richmond (April 2) and fled to Amelia Court House. There he hoped to pick up supplies previously placed and turn south to join Johnston, as planned. But Sheridan's cavalry got to Jetersville below Amelia and forced Lee's army and the Richmond garrison west, along the line of the Appomattox River. Lee's men were further disappointed to find that no supplies awaited them anywhere. At least a third of his starving troops got caught at Sayler's Creek on April 6, after they halted to let what supply wagons they had proceed ahead. Lee lost 2,000 battle casualties and at least 5,000 taken prisoner.

Jubilant Yankee pursuit across the High Bridge at Sayler's Creek, and a quick counter attack, cost the Federals 800 prisoners of their own. Lee was not defeated yet. The next day (April 7), he received supplies at Farmville and blunted a Union attack from hastily built trenches. This battle allowed Sheridan's cavalry to get around Lee and stop his withdrawal at Appomattox Court House. Sheridan struck the railroad at Appomattox Station on April 8, capturing all of the supplies stored for Lee's use. On April 9, Sheridan erected earthworks across the road and held off Lee's attacking infantry long enough for Federal infantry to appear. Lee knew that it was all over and informed Grant he wanted to hear his terms for surrender.

Acting under President Abraham Lincoln's (q.v.) earlier orders, given aboard ship as he visited Grant and Sherman at Hampton Roads (q.v.), Grant allowed the Rebels to lay down their arms, excepting officers' sidearms, sign a parole, and go home, to remain undisturbed so long as they observed their paroles. At Lee's request, he allowed those who owned horses to keep them. Grant then issued 25,000 rations to feed Lee's hungry men. These terms became fairly standard for other Confederate armies that surrendered later. Any political terms were rejected by the Union generals in the field or nullified by the War Department. Reconstruction of the nation would be left to the politicians.

APPOMATTOX COURT HOUSE, SURRENDER AT. *See* APPOMATTOX CAMPAIGN.

ARIZONA. *See* SECESSION AND THE CREATION OF ARIZONA TERRITORY.

ARKANSAS CAMPAIGN OF 1864. *See* CAMDEN CAMPAIGN.

***ARKANSAS*, C.S.S.** *See* SHILOH CAMPAIGN.

ARKANSAS POST, BATTLE OF. *See* VICKSBURG CAMPAIGN.

ARM-IN-ARM CONVENTION. The month before President Andrew Johnson (q.v.) undertook his "Swing Around the Circle" (q.v.) political tour, designed to elect his supporters to Congress in 1866, a National Union Party (q.v.) coalition met at Philadelphia to hold a convention of Conservative Republicans, Northern Democrats, and restored Southern Democrats, with the intent of supporting the reelection of the president in 1868. Participants were led onto the floor by James L. Orr of the South Carolina and Darius N. Couch of the Massachusetts delegations, giving it its popular nomenclature, "the Arm-in-Arm Convention."

The basis of their organization would be Johnson's program of Reconstruction, recently challenged by Moderate and Radical Republicans in Congress, who backed the Freedmen's Bureau Acts, the Civil Rights Act of 1866, and the proposed Fourteenth Amendment (qq.v.). The Johnson coalition cut across party lines and relied too much on what many saw as unrepentant Southern Democrats like Orr. Therein lay its weakness.

The speakers were artfully chosen by Johnson's managers, called "the Ring" by Radical Republicans, as if to denote some sort of fraud. The next day a 10-plank platform passed. It denied the Federal government could meddle with the franchise in the states, decried slavery, discredited the Confederate debt and made the Union debt sacred, thanked Federal soldiers and sailors for their service, praised President Johnson's Reconstruction program, and thanked God for ending the war and saving the Union and the Constitution.

In Washington, President Johnson hailed the convention's results and stepped on board the train taking him on the first presidential off-year election campaign tour ever conducted. The "Swing Around the Circle" would prove to be such a disaster that it would take generations before a president ventured into the congressional by-elections again.

ARMY, U.S., AND RECONSTRUCTION. It is one of the ironies of Reconstruction history that an entire century passed after the enactment of the Military Reconstruction Acts (q.v.) before a scholar turned his full attention to the Army's critical role in the era. Although minor investigations had been made along with a few legal studies, James E. Sefton's full-length book for the first time focused on both the national and local aspects of military rule in the South between 1865 and 1877. In so doing, he challenged the perspective of earlier scholars, particularly John Hope Franklin and Harold M. Hyman.

Franklin argued that the power and influence of the Army during Reconstruction was minimal, limited by small numbers of soldiers at the government's disposal; Sefton countered that power and influence were functions of more than mere numbers. A few troops placed in key locations in a rural region could be dominant. In addition, Sefton believed that the blue uniform had an adverse psychological effect on Southern whites. Few men dared attack an Army unit because it could trigger a tremendous response from the Army, the president, and Congress, as the Enforcement Acts (q.v.) demonstrated.

On a different level, Hyman argued that the end of the Civil War saw Congress create two peacetime armies: a congressional force that dealt with Reconstruction and the traditional force controlled by the president as commander in chief that handled all other duties (like guarding the coasts and fighting Native Americans). Hyman maintained that President Andrew Johnson (q.v.), through his allegedly shortsighted Reconstruction policies, alienated the Army's high command, forcing it to assist in the establishment of an independent force outside the president's usual influence. Sefton challenged this view, claiming the president was not as anti-military as supposed. He preferred to see congressional indecisiveness in making up its own Reconstruction policies as the prime reason for the Army's problems in the South. Besides, he concluded, Johnson never lost control of either Army. Even under the Military Reconstruction Acts the president had certain powers, like appointing military district commanders, which he exercised to the limit.

According to Sefton, the Army's role in Reconstruction passed through three stages. The first period ran from the end of the war to the passage of the Military Reconstruction Acts, which corresponds to what is generally known as Presidential Reconstruction. At this time, the Army had to administer the South without any real help from Washington, D.C., while Congress and President Johnson maneuvered for a position of dominance. The result was a great deal of confusion and frequent contradictions in policy between military departments (and even within departments) as totally inexperienced and sometimes incompetent officers sought to cope with the problem of civil affairs.

Next Sefton saw a period known as Military Reconstruction, lasting from 1867 to 1870. During this period, Sefton said, Congress emerged as the dominant branch of the Federal government. In a vague set of laws, the Military Reconstruction Acts, Congress established a new Reconstruction program that finally placed the Army in firm control of the Southern state governments. The new program set up five military districts embracing all of the former Confederacy except Tennessee, which had passed the Fourteenth Amendment (q.v.) and been readmitted into the Union. Military Reconstruction lasted until 1870, when all of the remaining Southern states achieved readmission to the Union by creating new constitutions that junked slavery and electing loyal governments that approved the Fourteenth Amendment (the Carolinas, Florida, Alabama, Arkansas, and Louisiana) and, in some cases (Texas, Virginia, Mississippi, and Georgia), the Fifteenth Amendment (q.v.).

The final era of military influence described by Sefton extended from 1870 to 1877, during which the Army was charged with the unenviable task of preserving the new Republican regimes in each Southern state. The main thrust of this policy was the protection of loyal whites and blacks, upon whose votes these governments depended for their existence. This was done by carrying out the provisions of the Enforcement Acts, patrolling polling places, and even installing one side or the other in power. Sefton found it difficult to call the Army's role in any of these periods a success or a failure. He would rather blame the policy and those who created it for whatever shortcomings the era had. In keeping abreast of the twists and turns of events in the national capital, Sefton concluded that the Army proved to be adaptable and flexible to civilian government's demands, and as an institution it rendered overall a credible, honorable performance.

Prior to Sefton's study, historians satisfied themselves with casual references to "bayonet rule" and went on to the seemingly more exciting tales of the interactions of Southern Rebels, Carpetbaggers (q.v.), Scalawags (q.v.), and African-Americans, and the resulting ills of statehouse corruption. Nowadays they do the same, only the heroes and villains have been reversed. Whether they reviled or found merit in the events they described, few historians examined, and even fewer understood, the role of the Army in the process of Reconstruction. Commentators generally realize that one of Reconstruction's great weaknesses is the Army's administration of civilian government, a unique aspect of the period. The idea of military supervision of civil government, regardless of the nobleness of its objectives, has always been reprehensible to Americans.

Hence any period of time in which the traditional constitutional guarantees of civil laws and courts are superseded by Army supervision tends to be distasteful and unnatural to the American palate. Reconstruction was such an era, in which ultimately, above and beyond the merit of its programs designed to purify the former Confederate South, military interference with civil government became an issue in itself. In the end, it was a crucial point, which undermined the North's plans for Southern rehabilitation and caused Reconstruction to be discredited.

Lacking a solid tradition in martial rule, the Army was plagued throughout Reconstruction by a lack of experience and legal precedent in military occupation and government. What little background the Army possessed evolved out of the brief, dated supervision of government in Louisiana and West Florida before the War of 1812, and in East Florida after that conflict ended. A temporary stint of a similar scope occurred during the Mexican War in the occupied territories of New Mexico and California. Unfortunately, the Army's experience with military government in these regions was not catalogued for later reference, and the personnel involved were either dead, retired, or stationed in areas not connected actively with the Reconstruction era after the Civil War.

Thus, wartime experiences in military government proved tentative at best and inadequate at worst. Without an organized, accepted doctrine of military government, the generals had had to improvise from the beginning of the Southern occupation. The problem ultimately became the concern of various provost marshals in each advancing army. Originally conceived to handle troop discipline and prevent disorder in the ranks, the provost marshal system had fallen into ruin by the time of the Civil War.

The scattered deployment of prewar regiments in frontier duty stations and their isolation from the general public had made the provost marshal an unneeded item in the economy-minded Army. All of this changed with the raising of massive civilian forces, which campaigned the settled areas of the Eastern states. As the conquering Federal soldiers advanced south, someone had to deal with the potentially disloyal Confederate civilians. Commanders casually delegated this responsibility to the provosts, a process that became more formal about the time of Bvt. Maj. Gen. John Pope's Second Manassas Campaign (qq.v.) into Virginia in 1862.

By the following year, it had become obvious to Army higher ups that a more standardized conduct of war and occupation was needed. The Union record thus far was irregular. Officers like Henry W. Halleck, Irvin McDowell, and George B. McClellan (qq.v.) had followed a policy of respecting private property (including slaves, to the disgust of Radical Republicans) and Southern civil rights. Other generals, like Pope, Robert Milroy, and the infamous Benjamin F. Butler (q.v.), had been more harsh. The latter's conduct was so controversial as to cause his replacement by Bvt. Maj. Gen. Nathaniel Banks, who asked the War Department for a formal code of behavior to govern occupation of the South. The result was General Orders No. 100 (q.v.), entitled "Instructions for the Government of Armies of the United States in the Field," the first attempt to codify the rules of war by a Western nation.

The first step toward establishing military governments took place in the disputed border states, areas that the North could not bear to lose after secession of the Lower South. President Abraham Lincoln (q.v.) issued an executive proclamation on April 29, 1861, placing all territory between Washington and Philadelphia (a devious way to say the state of Maryland, especially the hostile pro-Confederate city of Baltimore) under martial law.

Missouri received its introduction to military government in July 1861, when local commanders visited nearby towns and organized pro-Union committees of public safety. In August, Bvt, Maj. Gen. John Charles Frémont (q.v.) declared martial law throughout the state, took over the government (it had fled to the Confederacy anyhow), and freed all of the slaves. Lincoln endorsed all of the declaration except the freeing of the slaves—it would have sent every border state into immediate secession, and practicality was more important than morality at this juncture.

Military rule was expanded in 1862 to apply to all Rebels, insurgents, their abettors, those opposing the draft or enlistment and urging others to do the same, anyone who gave aid or comfort to the enemy, and anyone guilty of disloyal practices (a vague term never defined) anywhere in the United States. The War Department ordered all Federal, state, and local law enforcement officials to arrest anyone who encouraged disloyal practices. Chief Justice Roger B. Taney (q.v.) (a Marylander) issued an opinion (*ex parte* Merryman [q.v.]) while on circuit in 1861 that military arrest could not take place and military commissions could not convene while civil courts were in session and operating freely, but the Army ignored him, and Lincoln refused to enforce the decision.

The Merryman opinion would be restated by the whole court in the 1866 decision *ex parte* Milligan, two years after Taney died, but the war was over and the damage done by then. Martial law and military arrest were so effective that military prisons (labeled the "American Bastille" by dissenters) overflowed with political prisoners, and a special board consisting of Bvt. Maj. Gen. John A. Dix and retired New York judge Edwards Pierrepont had to be convened to investigate the cases and free those not openly pro-Confederate.

Generally military commanders had free rein to impose whatever laws they thought proper, so long as they did not create national policy (Frémont's sin). Most of their edicts were still local and municipal. Then in 1862, President Lincoln began a process that would mark the norm for military government in Reconstruction when he appointed Andrew Johnson to be the military governor of Tennessee. There never had been a military governor of a whole state before. Johnson was given the honorary rank of brigadier general and the job of rooting out disloyalty and forming a loyal government. Lincoln appointed military governors for other states as Federal troops advanced into their areas. Other Federal agencies accompanied the military governors and the armies into the South. Principal among them were Treasury Department agents, who collected back taxes due and confiscated contraband property and goods (primarily cotton), and after March 1865, the agents of the Freedmen's Bureau (q.v.), charged with enforcement of the Thirteenth Amendment (q.v.) and helping refugees with transport and rations.

Military government could be quite all-encompassing. Commanders quickly assumed the executive powers of appointment to and removal from public and even quasi-private offices. The usual method was to administer the ironclad oath. It was given to all officeholders, and those who failed to take it lost their authority and position. Such interference extended to public universities, chambers of commerce, private library associations, and sextons of cemeteries. Local military commanders filled all sorts of political offices and held elections under orders from Washington for others. They supervised the convening of bodies to write state constitutions.

Along with the executive power, the commanders carried out judicial functions through courts martial (usually reserved for soldiers) and military commissions (for the trial of civilians in place of criminal and civil courts). The tribunals usually had from three to five members, and their jurisdictions extended from the ordinary crimes like fraud, embezzlement, bribery, breach of the peace, horse theft, rape, arson, receiving stolen goods, riot, assault, and election fraud to more war-related actions like correspondence with the enemy, blockade running, carrying mail to the Confederacy, running arms to the South, burning bridges and other acts of sabotage, hindering the draft or enlistments, and engaging in guerrilla warfare. President Lincoln even set up his own loyal court in Washington and sent it to Louisiana during the war to administer "loyal" justice.

Besides executive and judicial functions, military officers also got involved with economic matters, like trade, labor, and finance. Often they operated in conjunction with the treasury agents or were in direct competition with them. The Army granted special licenses to trade in war zones and even with the enemy, particularly in cotton. To obtain a license, one had to take the proper oaths, get letters of reference, and file the proper money guarantees with the government. The Army also administered the government farms in the Mississippi Valley and elsewhere, provided black labor in the form of contraband slaves to private contractors, administered the wage arrangements, and provided protection for the operation of loyal plantations. If any black behind the Union lines was not employed in some gainful job, he or she was sent to the contraband camps to become part of the general labor pool. This is one reason so many blacks latched onto a union Army regiment as a cook, preferring this form of quasi-freedom to enforced labor on Army-administered plantations. Military governors also saw to it that no Confederate money exchanged hands in their districts and that all banks operated on specie (gold or silver coin) or greenbacks. The Army also levied and collected local taxes.

The absolute nature of military government during the war, afterward during the more informal Presidential Reconstruction (q.v.), and under the more rigorous Military Reconstruction Acts, was evident to all who came in contact with it. Most commanders operated in a just and wise manner. Military courts were fair and above all speedy in their administration of justice. Some Southerners even voiced their desire to continue under military government indefinitely to avoid rule by the Scalawags, Carpetbaggers, and African-Americans who made up the loyal governments installed after readmission and the end of Army supervision. But the fairness and efficiency of military government begs the real question: Was it the right thing to do?

The election of 1876 (q.v.), the "Crime of '76," was the last straw for those opposed to the military intervention in American government that became so common during the Civil War and Reconstruction. The result was a rider to the Army Appropriations bill for 1878 called the Posse Comitatus Act (q.v.). Posse comitatus was an ancient English common law concept in which the adult male populace of a county was to stand armed and ready to aid the sheriff or marshal in enforcing the law. The use of the United States Army to support the civilian governments in the South fell under this doctrine, the Army acting in place of or as a supplement to the posse comitatus. But under the Posse Comitatus Act, no Army officer of any rank could intervene to assist a local, Federal, or state law enforcement official unless specifically ordered to do so by the Congress or under the Constitution (by executive order of the president). The penalty was two years in jail or a $10,000 fine, or both. Its passage can be seen as a part of the Compromise of 1877, despite the year of the law (1878).

It has been common for historians to trace the collapse of Reconstruction to the race problem. And yet had there been no race problem, Reconstruction would have had to overcome the onus of relying upon the Army to enforce "proper" behavior in the South. Americans traditionally have perceived a distinction between the policeman's executive right to enforce the law through arrest and the power to legislate law and determine guilt. Military Reconstruction demonstrated that even though the Army theoretically possessed absolute power in the South, there were limits to its ability to effect through force a permanent change in the region's culture. That is part of why Reconstruction failed, and the heritage of it goes back to the British reliance on the Intolerable Acts to suppress dissent in 1774.

ASHLEY, JAMES M. (1824–1896). Born to Campbellite parents in Allegheny County near Pittsburgh, James Ashley's father removed the family to Ohio, where he took his son on frequent proselytizing missions in the Ohio Valley. Here Ashley received an education by learning to read the Bible. He later worked as a cabin boy on a river steamer on southern rivers. Ashley found slavery abhorrent, especially the re-enslaving of blacks with free papers, the general cruelty of bondage, and the blatant disregard for the feelings of persons.

Ashley returned to Ohio and worked as a printer and newspaper editor and later as a boat-builder, and shortly thereafter set up a wholesale drug company in Toledo. During his spare time he read law and was admitted to the bar in 1849. At this time, with the annexation of the Western territories that were a part of the Mexican Cession, Ashley became interested in politics. A lifelong Democrat (q.v.), he broke with his party, attended the Republican (q.v.) convention of 1856 that nominated John C. Frémont (q.v.) as the party's first presidential candidate, and stood for Congress as a Republican in 1858. He was reelected four more times during the war and Reconstruction.

In Congress, Ashley developed and led much of the Radical Reconstruction program. He led the way in abolishing slavery in the District of Columbia in 1862. He introduced the Thirteenth Amendment (q.v.) in 1863 and, upon its failure, lobbied enough border state Democrats to change their votes, resulting in its passage two years later. Ashley considered this achievement the greatest triumph of his life. His final contribution was the introduction of the impeachment (q.v.) proceedings against President Andrew Johnson (q.v.). Upon the Senate's failure to convict, Ashley suffered the rebuff of so many other Radicals, losing the election of 1868 (q.v.).

After his defeat, Ashley accepted President Ulysses S. Grant's (q.v.) appointment as governor of Montana Territory. But his outspoken criticism of Grant's Reconstruction policy as weak and corrupt cost him the job. Ashley then shifted his support to Horace Greeley's Liberal Republican (q.v.) campaign in 1872, his last political act. After his political career failed, he entered railroading and built and managed the Ann Arbor line until his death.

ASSASSINATION OF LINCOLN. *See* LINCOLN ASSASSINATION, THE CONFEDERACY AND THE; LINCOLN ASSASSINATION, THE NEW YORK CONNECTION OF THE.

ATLANTA CAMPAIGN. Four days after Lt. Gen. Ulysses S. Grant (q.v.) took to the field in the 1864 Richmond campaign, Maj. Gen. William T. Sherman (q.v.) moved out from Chattanooga against Atlanta, a key rail junction in the heart of Georgia. Like Grant in the East, Sherman had 100,000 men organized into three armies of several infantry corps and cavalry divisions each. His opponent, now that Gen. Braxton Bragg (q.v.) had been kicked upstairs to be President Jefferson Davis' (q.v.) military advisor at Richmond, was Gen. Joseph E. Johnston (q.v.). The Rebels had 64,000 men organized into several infantry corps and cavalry divisions.

Because Johnston had fewer men and the mountains of northern Georgia offer so many natural defensive positions, he awaited Sherman's attack. Sherman realized that to assault Johnston head on would be tantamount to mass suicide for his armies. So he relied on turning movements, utilizing the north–south valleys beyond Johnston's control to march behind Confederate positions and force the Rebel army to retreat to save itself. The first of these occurred at Rocky Face Ridge near Dalton, Georgia, on May 5–9, when Sherman swept around Johnston's left and Johnston fought a delaying action to enable his men to slip southward to Resaca, where the same thing happened again, on May 13–16.

After Resaca, the main valley opened more widely, allowing Sherman to advance on a wide front, each army roughly in line, side by side. This was what Johnston had been waiting for. Now he could take the compact Army of Tennessee and strike Sherman on the east flank. Lt. Gen. John B. Hood (q.v.), a transfer from Robert E. Lee's (q.v.) Army of Northern Virginia and a real fighter, was to lead his corps in the attack. But just as Hood was about to move, he was distracted by the advance of Union cavalry on his own flank. Hood hesitated, and the opportunity to attack was lost. Some have theorized that Hood was less than forthright in his excuse, hoping to embarrass Johnston with failure and to replace him in command.

Whatever the military or political reasons for the failure at Cassville, Sherman closed upon Johnston, forcing him to retreat once more to a good defensive position at Allatoona Pass (May 19–20), where the valley narrowed again. Sherman sent his flanking force way into the mountains and came up on Johnston's west flank at New Hope Church near Dallas. Here, after a brisk fight on May 25–27 and two more weeks of indecisive skirmishing, Johnston pulled back to a fortified position based on Kennesaw Mountain, where a counterattack by Hood was anticipated by Sherman, who dug in to block it. By now, Sherman, just like Grant back East, had become thoroughly frustrated by Johnston's slipperiness and made the head-on assault he had so assiduously avoided until now (June 27). Johnston's men mowed down 2,000 Yankees, at a loss of 450 of their own.

After Kennesaw, Johnston withdrew to the Chattahoochie River (July 4–9), just north of Atlanta. Sherman maneuvered once again, and Johnston was forced to withdraw to Peach Tree Creek. This was too much for the politicians back in Richmond. President Davis hated and distrusted Johnston from former quarrels and saw the general as giving Atlanta up without a fight. He was disturbed that Johnston would abandon Kennesaw Mountain, with its near-impregnable defenses. He wanted a fighter and replaced Johnston with Hood.

In Hood, Davis got what he wanted. Hood immediately attacked Sherman at Peach Tree Creek on July 20, in his First Sortie from Atlanta. He employed a plan left over from Johnston, to hit Sherman as he crossed the stream and divided his forces. Once again, as he had at Chickamauga in the Chattanooga Campaign, Sherman's commander on the spot, Maj. Gen. George Thomas, held fast. Hood lost 2,500 (Sherman claimed the Rebels lost twice that) to Sherman's 1,600. Sherman crossed the creek, and Hood returned to Atlanta.

Somehow, the Federals believed that Hood was in full retreat, leaving the city. As Sherman moved north of Atlanta to cut Hood's "retreat" off, he opened the flank of one of his armies to a counterstroke. Hood attacked on July 22, in his Second Sortie from Atlanta or the Battle of Atlanta. But the attack mistakenly failed to hit behind Sherman's flank and failed. Hood lost another 8,000 casualties, Sherman half that many. Hood's expensive attacks were beginning to make Johnston's defensive stance look good.

Because of the death of Maj. Gen. James B. McPherson, Sherman sought to reorganize his armies. Several officers, including Maj. Gen. Joseph Hooker (q.v.), resigned when they felt they had been passed over. But Sherman managed to effect this reorganization and change his tactics, too. He had invested the north and east of Atlanta, but he needed to cut the railroads to the south and west that supplied Hood's forces in the city. He shifted his largest army across his rear to the west, only to be hit in Hood's Third Sortie from Atlanta at Ezra Church (July 28). The Federals immediately dug in and repulsed a Confederate assault at their front and another attack that hit them in the rear, by simply turning around in their trenches. By now Hood's army had been reduced to 37,000 men and 5,000 Georgia militia. Sherman still had 85,000 in his armies.

On August 5, Sherman again tried to move to cut the railroad supplying Hood. But the Rebels beat him to Utoy Creek, and in a two-day battle, marked by confusion in movement and command arguments as to who was in charge, Hood's men fired from their hastily built trenches and decisively halted Sherman's advance. Both sides worn out from all the fighting, Sherman and Hood resorted to exchanging cavalry raids, each trying to cut the rails that supplied the other. About all this demonstrated to Sherman was that cavalry never completed such a job thoroughly. He had to get his infantry across the rail lines into Atlanta.

On August 25, Sherman began his move. He was across the rails in a matter of days. Hood, meanwhile, only knew the location of about a third of Sherman's force and hit the part at Jonesboro (August 31–September 1). The attack failed with great loss, but Sherman's ground commanders failed to follow up and crush Hood's army. With Sherman's infantry blocking the rails, Hood knew that he was finished at Atlanta. He abandoned the city on the evening of September 1. Sherman pursued until he found Hood entrenched at Lovejoy in a position too strong to attack without great loss. Sherman turned back to Atlanta to consolidate his gains and plan his March to the Sea (q.v.). Hood headed west and then north, hoping to cut Sherman's supply line, the single railroad back to Chattanooga, in the Nashville Campaign (q.v.).

AVERASBORO, THE BATTLE OF. *See* CAROLINAS CAMPAIGN.

B

BABCOCK, ORVILLE (1835–1884). Military and political aide to Lieutenant General and President Ulysses S. Grant (q.v.).

BALL'S BLUFF, BATTLE OF. *See* JOINT COMMITTEE ON THE CONDUCT OF THE WAR.

BALTIMORE CONVENTION (1860). On June 11, 1860, the Democrats (q.v.) met for a second convention to nominate a presidential candidate for the election of 1860 (q.v.), their first attempt at the Charleston Convention (q.v.) six weeks earlier having ended in a shambles. It took a week before enough delegates had arrived so they could legally do business. The Southern delegates met separately in Richmond to await developments. Finally, all states but South Carolina sent delegates, and the convention was called to order. The first thing was to inquire into the credentials of all delegates. The North was still angry at the South's walking out at Charleston, to the cheers of the partisan crowd of spectators. The Baltimore Convention decided to seat all delegates except those from Louisiana and Alabama. Georgia and Florida would be allowed to observe the proceedings, but would have no vote. This was to be punishment for walking out, but in reality, the backers of Sen. Stephen A. Douglas of Illinois, the front runner, wanted to exclude enough anti-Douglas delegates to prevent a reoccurrence of Charleston's disruptiveness.

The effect was exactly the opposite. This time Virginia led the walkout. The Deep (Gulf) South followed, along with North Carolina, Tennessee, California, Oregon, and half of Maryland's delegation. This left the convention with fewer than the 202 votes it took to nominate, according to the Tennessee Proposition agreed to at Charleston. Douglas and his men decided to obtain two-thirds of the votes left, which he did on the second ballot. James B. Fitzpatrick of Alabama was chosen to be the vice presidential candidate, but he refused when informed it would mean he could not go home. Herschel V. Johnson of Georgia then accepted the number two spot on the ticket, being appointed by the party's executive committee.

The determination of the Baltimore Convention to obtain a candidate surprised the delegates who had walked out in Charleston. Under the leadership of William L. Yancey of Alabama, they had been awaiting an invitation to come up and compromise, but now decided to act as the Richmond Convention. Douglas offered to unify the party by stepping down for Alexander Stephens (q.v.) of Georgia. But his backers refused to allow this. They wanted to teach the disruptive Southern Democrats a lesson. The Northerners would win without them. But what the Democrats really did was give the Republicans (q.v.) a golden opportunity to win with a minority vote—if they could find the right candidate at their Chicago Convention (q.v.).

BALTIMORE PLOT (1861). One of the more embarrassing moments for Union President-elect Abraham Lincoln (q.v.) occurred on his trip to the inaugural in Washington in February 1861. It seemed minor at the time, but it affected his administration adversely at the beginning and may have been a factor in his later fatalism about being assassinated. Lincoln took an extended trip through the North, a "Swing Around the Circle" (q.v.), on his way to be inaugurated. It was a way for many people to see him, to publicize his upcoming administration, to introduce him to the Northern electorate, and to reassure people by his calm demeanor. Eventually, the Lincoln party wound up in Philadelphia, Pennsylvania. There, Lincoln met a railroad detective, Alan Pinkerton, who had news of a plot on his life that was to be executed as he passed through Baltimore, Maryland.

The railroads did not pass directly through Baltimore in those days. They all terminated, each at its own station, then the railcars were drawn by horses between the lines, or one had to take a horse-drawn carriage. In any case, the trek was slow and potentially dangerous, especially in one spot where the Lincoln entourage had to pass on foot down a narrow hall-like roadway. According to Pinkerton, pro-secession Marylanders led by an anarchist, Cipriano Fernandina, and abetted by the pro-secession chief marshal of Baltimore, George P. Kane, were going to assassinate Lincoln as he passed through Baltimore. Pinkerton had infiltrated their councils with three agents, one of them a woman, Kate Warne. He recommended that Lincoln alter his schedule at once to foil the plot.

At first, Lincoln tended to doubt the plot, until independent confirmation came to him in the person of Fred Seward, son of William H. Seward (q.v.), his secretary of state designate. Lincoln refused to change his plans for Harrisburg the next day. He was to give three speeches, raise the U.S. flag, and attend a high-profile dinner. But he promised to follow Pinkerton's recommendations afterward. Accordingly, Lincoln was called away from the dinner, never to return.

Playing the part of a sick passenger, dressed in a cape and a slouch hat (instead of his trademark stovepipe hat), and assisted by his "sister," Mrs. Warne, Lincoln and his bodyguard, Ward Lamon, were hustled off in a closed carriage to a special train that met the scheduled train for Baltimore at Philadelphia. The last berth in the last car held New York City Police Superintendent John A. Kennedy, who would block the curious. Then Lincoln got on a locked car coupled to the rear of this train, which was hauled through the streets of Baltimore at 3:30 a.m. to connect to the scheduled overnight Baltimore & Ohio train to Washington, where he arrived at 6:00 a.m. There he was met by Illinois congressman Elihu B. Washburne (who would later recommend a local constituent, U. S. Grant, as a general officer, and never let the country forget it), who took Lincoln to Willard's Hotel.

Lincoln was horrified to find that the press nationwide ridiculed him in print and cartoon for sneaking into Washington at night, wearing a Scot's plaid tam and a cloak, looking every bit the coward. He was especially criticized for permitting Mrs. Lincoln and his sons to take the brunt of ire from the hostile Baltimore crowd the next day—which they did with great aplomb. The disappointed plotters, led by John Merryman, would proceed to burn rail bridges and tear up track to cut Washington off from the rest of the North, and were among the first to be arrested when Lincoln as president would suspend the writ of *habeas corpus* (q.v.) by executive proclamation. Merryman would become famous when he appealed unsuccessfully to U.S. Supreme Court Chief Justice Roger B. Taney to annul his incarceration at old Ft. McHenry in *ex parte* Merryman (q.v.). Lincoln vowed never to allow that kind of foolishness to occur again, which helped lead him straight down the road to Ford's Theater four years later.

BATON ROUGE, BATTLE OF. *See* SHILOH CAMPAIGN.

BAYOU TECHE CAMPAIGN. *See* PORT HUDSON, SIEGE OF.

BEALL, JOHN Y. *See* LINCOLN ASSASSINATION, THE CONFEDERACY AND THE; LINCOLN ASSASSINATION, THE NEW YORK CONNECTION OF THE.

BEAN'S STATION. *See* KNOXVILLE CAMPAIGN.

BEAUREGARD, PIERRE GUSTAVE TOUTANT (1818–1893). Born near New Orleans, Beauregard was educated in private schools at New York City, before going on to graduate second in his class from West Point in 1838. He received an appointment to the artillery, but soon transferred to the engineers. During the War with Mexico, Beauregard served on Maj. Gen. Winfield Scott's (q.v.) staff in the campaign on Mexico City, winning two brevets for bravery. He served as an army engineer in the 1850s and was superintendent of cadets at the Military Academy in 1861. Beauregard was removed from this position for secessionist proclivities and soon resigned his commission to join the Confederacy.

Receiving the rank of brigadier general, he went to Charleston, South Carolina, as the Confederate officer in charge. Under orders from his government, Beauregard opened fire on Fort Sumter (q.v.) and accepted the garrison's surrender two days later. In July 1861, Beauregard was in command of the Confederate forces at First Manassas (q.v.). Reinforced by soldiers from the Shenandoah Valley, Beauregard, under Brig. Gen. Joseph E. Johnston (q.v.), who technically outranked him, was allowed to take command of the field while he forwarded troops to reinforce him.

Although Beauregard was now the premier hero of the Confederacy, having won the first two battles of the war, he, Johnston, and President Jefferson Davis (q.v.) quarreled over rank and strategy. Davis transferred Beauregard to the Western Theater to get him out of his hair. There, Beauregard became second in command to Albert Sidney Johnston (q.v.) and received credit for reorganizing Johnston's army and defenses and for planning and, after Johnston's death, fighting the Battle of Shiloh. He withdrew from the field when he realized that the two Union armies under Maj. Gen. Ulysses S. Grant and Don Carlos Buell (qq.v.) had been united against him. Beauregard withdrew to Corinth, Mississippi, and then farther south, as the combined Union juggernaut, now under the command of Maj. Gen. Henry W. Halleck (q.v.), advanced. Dispirited by his losses, Beauregard took sick leave, further angering President Davis, who accused him of malingering.

In 1863, Beauregard commanded the South Atlantic Coast from Charleston. He was always very popular there, socially and militarily, unlike other officers who preceded and followed him. In 1864, Beauregard was called to Richmond to defend the capital from the Union forces of Maj. Gen. Benjamin F. Butler (q.v.), who was attacking the city up the James River as Lt. Gen. Ulysses S. Grant kept Robert E. Lee's (q.v.) Confederates busy in the overland Richmond Campaign (q.v.). Skillfully outmaneuvering Butler, Beauregard daringly left the city open while he assailed the Union army's flanks, harrying it into the Bermuda Hundred peninsula, where it remained bottled up until 1865. He also saved Petersburg (q.v.) from the initial assaults made upon it when Grant stole a march on Lee, crossed the James River, and nearly took Richmond from the south side.

In 1865, after Union General William T. Sherman (q.v.) turned north into South Carolina following his successful March to the Sea, Beauregard served as second in command to Gen. Joseph Johnston in the Carolinas Campaign (qq.v.). He surrendered at Durham Station with Johnston. After the war he returned to Louisiana. He refused commands of the Romanian and Egyptian armies to engage in railroading and fronting for the Louisiana Lottery. Managing New Orleans public works, he published several volumes of military theory and his campaigns.

BELKNAP, WILLIAM W. *See* BUREAU OF INDIAN AFFAIRS SCANDAL.

BELLE ISLE (RICHMOND). Confederate installation at Richmond in the middle of the James River that housed Union prisoners of war. *See also* PRISONS.

BENJAMIN, JUDAH P. (1811–1884). Born in St. Croix in the West Indies to Sephardic Jewish parents, Benjamin's family moved to Charleston, South Carolina, where he was educated. He also attended Yale College until he was expelled for some unspecified immoral behavior, probably gambling, a lifelong addiction. Benjamin removed to New Orleans, read law, and was admitted to the bar. He married into a prominent Creole family, and he and his wife had one daughter. His wife proved to be a libertine, and eventually they separated, but never divorced, she and the daughter moving to France.

An intellect of great force, Benjamin worked hard at law, wrote a prominent law book, entered planting, and became a prosperous man. A member of the Whig Party (q.v.), he served in the state legislature and attended two state conventions. Eventually, he was elected to the U.S. Senate. He served as a Whig (1853–1859) and a Democrat (1859–1861). He was a devout secessionist, but only after Abraham Lincoln's victory in the election of 1860 (qq.v.), when it appeared that more radical politicians would cut him out of the party. Jefferson Davis (q.v.) appointed Benjamin as attorney general in the provisional government of the Confederacy.

Benjamin soon developed a close relationship with Davis and his wife, becoming the most trusted of Davis' civilian advisors. Benjamin was secretary of war in late 1861 and early 1862, a position in which he did poorly. Then Davis made him secretary of state, a position in which he served with distinction to the end of the war. He negotiated several important foreign loans for the Confederacy and became a key man in developing the Confederate secret service. Just how much he had to do with planning Lincoln's attempted kidnapping and successful assassination (q.v.) is unknown, as Benjamin very carefully destroyed all of his and most of the pertinent state department files.

After the war, Benjamin left the fleeing government party and made his way to Great Britain. There he launched a second successful law career, again publishing a key legal treatise. He eventually went to France to rejoin his family briefly before he died, and he was buried in Paris.

BERMUDA HUNDRED CAMPAIGN. *See* DREWRY'S BLUFF, BATTLES OF.

BIG BLACK RIVER BRIDGE, BATTLE OF. *See* VICKSBURG CAMPAIGN.

BIG BLUE RIVER, BATTLE OF. *See* PRICE'S MISSOURI RAID (1864).

BINGHAM, JOHN A. (1815–1900). Born in Mercer, Pennsylvania, John Bingham was educated in local schools and as a printer's apprentice. He went to Franklin College, a center of abolition early in the 19th century, and read law. He was admitted to the bar in Ohio, to which he had removed, and took up a lifelong residence at Cadiz. He became interested in Whig (q.v.) politics and stumped for William Henry Harrison's "Log Cabin" campaign in 1840. He was a Conscience Whig, against slavery, and by 1854 he had become a Republican (q.v.) and was elected to Congress under that banner the same year. He served every term for the next 18 years, except that of 1862–1864, temporarily losing his seat to the Democrat resurgence because of the Emancipation Proclamation (q.v.). He was one of the prosecutors of the Lincoln assassination (q.v.) conspirators in 1865, and after an initial hesitation, he actively sought the impeachment and removal from office of Andrew Johnson (q.v.) in 1867. His main achievement was his part in the drafting of the Fourteenth Amendment (q.v.), particularly the controversial first section having to do with due process of the laws, equal protection of the laws, and the privileges and immunities of citizenship, all of which were old abolitionist doctrines. In 1872, he lost his seat once more and accepted an appointment as U.S. minister to Japan for 12 uneventful years.

BIRCHARD LETTER. Matthew Birchard was the chairman of a committee of Ohio Democrats protesting the arrest and detainment of Clement L. Vallandigham for anti-war protests and political action. President Abraham Lincoln (q.v.) defended arresting men like Vallandigham without charges being filed, because the war had caused emergency conditions in which the normal laws were ineffective. Vallandigham was in jail for urging resistance to the Conscription Act and desertion. Lincoln said that he would be more than happy to release Vallandigham if he were to sign a standard Union loyalty oath. The case *ex parte* Vallandigham (q.v.) went to the U.S. Supreme Court.

BLACK AND TAN. A code phrase used by Reconstruction's opponents to brand the Republican conventions, governments, and state militias in the readmitted South as "Negro dominated" and unworthy of public support.

BLACKBURN, LUKE. *See* LINCOLN ASSASSINATION, THE CONFEDERACY AND THE; LINCOLN ASSASSINATION, THE NEW YORK CONNECTION OF THE.

BLACK CODES. From a modern perspective, one of the greatest follies the South committed during its self-Reconstruction under Andrew Johnson's (q.v.) plan of reunion was the passage of the Black Codes, which defined the African-Americans' place in society. They demonstrated to the victorious North that the white South would not handle the freed African-Americans fairly, even though many of these prohibitions were also included in Northern states' own Black Laws, as part of a form of early segregation that had evolved when slavery was abolished there after the American Revolution. Similar laws had also arisen in Southern cities, where the slave system often broke down under the anonymity of city life and the economic realities of hiring slaves out, or of slaves hiring themselves out.

The Black Codes began by defining who was legally black. Generally, this was accepted to be anyone of one-eighth "Negro blood," one of those imprecise terms that gives modern sociologists chills, but which white Southerners saw as so precise as to give such a person a name—octoroon. Blacks received certain rights in the Black Codes. Their marriages were legalized (blacks had lived together in family units during slavery, but they had no legality under white law); their right to a family name was tacitly recognized (although many slaves had family names, some of them African in origin, they were not legal); and the emancipated were permitted to draw up contracts, sue or be sued, and attend schools for their race (all illegal activities under slave law).

At the same time, certain activities guaranteed to whites were prohibited to blacks. They could not serve on juries, give testimony in court against a white, or carry firearms. Then the Black Codes restricted the African-Americans' status as free laborers. These sanctions varied from state to state and even by region or town within a state, but generally involved a drastic imposition of the laws against vagrancy. This had been reinforced by the former slaves' wanderings after freedom—aimless to whites, meaningful to blacks—as they sought true freedom and lost family members sold down the river years before.

All vagrants were to be arrested and placed to work on public roads or other projects. One was a vagrant if one had no labor contract with a white employer. Any jurisdiction could forcefully sign black vagrants over to private employers. Other parts of the law allowed double deductions on wages for feigned sickness or theft and forbade disobedience and any but "civil and polite" language to the employer or his or her family. Often blacks could not own property, or only a small town lot. What these provisions did, and Northerners and blacks themselves found so objectionable, was place African-Americans in a position somewhere between slavery and freedom. They could not be owned outright, but neither could they do what they pleased like truly free people.

In retrospect, the Black Codes seem really unwise until one takes a look at where they came from. Essentially the Black Codes were based on U.S. Army occupation regulations regulating black laborers during and immediately after the war. Some recent historians point out that the Southern governments had a different, more sinister intent, but since the laws are almost verbatim copies of Army general orders, this seems untrue. Southerners were a bit surprised when the politicians disallowed them their congressional seats in December 1865 for agreeing with the Army's own labor rules in the South. But Congress was also looking for excuses to reexamine Reconstruction from the ground up, and the Black Codes provided this, no matter who instituted them originally.

BLACK EDUCATION AND RECONSTRUCTION. Reconstruction was begun haltingly and with contradictory methods during the Civil War, not in 1865 as is commonly believed. Similarly, it ended just as disjointedly, not with the usual date of 1877. Nothing illustrates this better than the efforts that were made to bring the glories of freedom through education to the ex-slaves by the dozens of Northern religious and benevolent associations. But what the blacks wound up with was not the Northern Free Soil, Free Labor society the missionaries and teachers desired for them, nor the liberated, self-autonomous world hoped for by the African-Americans. It was a capitalist society with remnants of the feudal slave-based society of the antebellum days intermixed.

In the early years of Reconstruction, missionaries and aid workers came South, seeking to relieve the misery of the contrabands (q.v.) who had fled their homes for freedom. The need was so great that education took second place only to mere survival. But it was never forgotten. Education was seen by the Yankees as the only true route to freedom and self-sufficiency. There were 51 different freedmen's aid societies (q.v.)—20 secular, 31 sectarian—in the South during and after the war. When they took up the burden of education among the contrabands, they often found that the blacks had already established schools of their own, run by literate former slaves who could pass on the basics of literacy to their compatriots. Many times, the incoming Yankees approached these early efforts with a condescending scorn, often reluctantly paying the teacher to continue, other times refusing to associate with the contraband teachers. The societies had problems with their own fellows, too, which centered around the proper way to educate the blacks, which in the spirit of the times included religious training as a key part of all education. A person without moral education was deemed at best half-ignorant. But the various church groups were not about to compromise on what they saw as the only true way to godliness and eventual salvation of the human soul.

There was also competition from the secular associations, which claimed to be doing their work without denominational prejudices. It was true to some degree, but a poor church member it was indeed who would not stick a bit of the "true salvation" into his or her work, regardless of the parent association's denial of the same. The secular associations were eventually united under the guise of the American Freedmen's Union Commission (q.v.), or AFUC. And through their demand for government assistance for a work that was too great in size and intent for uncoordinated, private action, the Congress eventually established the Bureau of Refugees, Freedmen, and Abandoned Lands (q.v.), which had its own department of education that was ideally to synchronize the education efforts among the freed people.

Even the strongest abolitionists had their doubts about what would happen to the African-American as a free person. The assumption was that the former slaves would be able to learn. The fear was that slavery had been such a deadening institution to the human senses that they would not be able to overcome the inferiority that it had implanted in the black psyche. But the gross immorality of slavery demanded that blacks be given the chance to be free Americans.

Education, then, was to Americanize the blacks like any other immigrant group. This was important, because the freed slave was not merely a citizen, but a voting citizen. Political rights were a privilege that had to be exercised responsibly. This would transform the entire South into an idealistic picture of a New England with a Southern drawl. Reconstruction was after all an institutional transformation. Every institution in the Old South would have to give way to the ideal represented by the Yankee victors. Included in this were public schools, democratized politics, proper economic activity (without slavery), and a refined morality. Of course, all of this smugly assumed that the South, white or black, did not possess any concept of this already.

Implicit in this was the question of what education was really for? Was it to make the blacks a docile, obedient part of white society, or was it to truly liberate them to find their own unique way in America? The one thing that black education during Reconstruction was not was African-American liberation, in a modern sense. It was rather to make blacks a sober, clean, industrious, thrifty people who would have a fidelity to contracts. In short, the Yankee teachers hoped to replace the care and control exercised over the African-Americans by their former masters. No wonder the white Southerners attacked school rooms, burned school buildings to the ground, and harassed and murdered teachers and students. No wonder blacks often found disappointment in what they were taught.

There was an economic side to education, too. The creation of a hard-working, stable work force was part and parcel of education. This aspect of education was acceptable to the white South, and many planters sought to have schools placed on their property to have a say in the content of education. Implicit in this was the desire of Northern whites to educate blacks to accept their lot in the South and not follow the thousands who took the underground railroad to the opportunity of a new life in the North. One of the key programs of the Freedmen's Bureau was to achieve economic fairness for the ex-slaves in the South so that they would not want to leave their old homes. But this meant that they would for the most part work on someone else's land, not their own.

The schools set up for the African-Americans by the secular and religious aid societies were coordinated and supported by the Federal government through the Freedmen's Bureau. Its commander, Bvt. Maj. Gen. Oliver Otis Howard (q.v.), compromised the Bureau into extinction, until by 1869, only a weakened education division remained. Howard had agents lecture freedmen on how to behave; he curtailed independent economic activity, placing blacks at the mercy of planters; he stopped much of its judicial regulation of white–black relations; and he increased education activities until the promise of black independence and political and economic power shifted to that of the offer of a schoolhouse. The change brought the bureau more and more into conciliation with the Southern white power structure. This was marked by more and more schools being located on the plantations. This permitted planters to control curriculum, tie blacks to the land, and isolate them from each other. The Bureau also saddled the impoverished African-Americans with more of the costs of education. They had to buy the land, erect the building, and pay the teacher's board. Only then would the Bureau step in to help. In the end, education became another force that limited black aspirations during Reconstruction and the period that followed.

Despite the limitations of black education in the South, hundreds of Northerners, mostly white women, flocked into the service. When they arrived in the South they met a host of problems. The school facilities were primitive (floorless, ill-lit, drafty, cold, often without chalk, slates, maps, and books), as were their living quarters (if any were available at all). There was little chance for social life. The Yankee schoolmarms were isolated from the rest of white society; verbal assaults were common, as were the anonymous vulgar, threatening letters. The black community was often too poor to help out.

Teachers quickly found out that corporal punishment was out of the question—it smacked too much of slavery. But the lack of initial discipline was soon replaced by an eagerness to learn. Few teachers went South for monetary reasons; if they did they were soon cured of that idea. Wages were minimal, running around $40 a month. The better jobs, like superintendent, were reserved for males, who rarely numbered more than 17 percent of the force. (Texas military commanders preferred male teachers, as they were easier to house, not needing the niceties that 19th-century Americans thought were essential for ladies.) Some of the teachers were black, but the agencies and the Bureau tended to send them to remote places in the countryside, reserving the prestigious city jobs for whites. Although Southern whites were accepted if they could take the oath, few volunteered, not desiring the ostracism that went with being a "nigger teacher."

The subjects taught in African-American schools did not differ much from those taught in white schools at the time. They included reading, writing, grammar, diction, history, geography, arithmetic, and singing. The normal colleges added orthography, map drawing, physiology, algebra, geometry, Latin, and Greek, as well as tips on how to teach. The greatest emphasis was on piety, domesticity, temperance, thrift, industry, discipline, order, and regularity in habits. The goal was to create the Anglo–Saxon image as the ideal for the ex-slaves.

The school books gave a few ideas on how the American government worked and a mild history of the American Revolution, but had little to say about democracy, rights of the people, or liberty. They emphasized the evangelical's notion of the African-Americans as docile and tractable children. Regardless of the content of the education that they received, black students (and they ranged in age from 6 to beyond 60) were enthusiastic to learn. Because many of the students were adults, schools were often held at night, to get around work schedules. They were held on Sunday, too, before church, although these were particularly religious in nature, embodying the theory that one could not fully comprehend the Bible if one could not read. Advancement tended to be rapid. Students applied themselves with zeal, as if trying to make up for the years when book learning by slaves was illegal. The community at large made many sacrifices to build a church and school (usually they were the same building). Labor, building supplies, and money that they could ill afford, given the grinding poverty of the postwar South, were provided locally.

But the African-Americans did not limit themselves to schools supported by the Freedmen's Bureau or various aid societies. They often went out and found themselves a teacher and set up a school on their own. Often a member of the local black community, probably an ex-Union soldier, would teach basic skills of reading and writing. In most cases, they would have to find room and board for the teacher, this being impossible among the local white community.

The efforts of students and parents to gain control of their education were often muted by the sponsoring agencies or noted with the adverse comment that the freedmen preferred to send their children to their own private schools of inferior quality. But the real lack of quality came with Redemption (q.v.), when the Southern states' school boards sent whites who could not find employment in a white school to teach blacks. Meanwhile, the missionary societies shifted their support to the several black normal colleges, hoping to turn out African-Americans who could go back and teach their own people.

Reconstruction and the Gilded Age were marked by the development of public education as a viable philosophy for the first time in Southern history. Blacks were included, but kept separate from the whole. And black education, in one of the first successful protest movements after emancipation, was to be conducted by teachers of their own race. African-Americans wanted education; but they wanted equality, liberty, and justice most of all. It was the Northern whites who said that education was the panacea, and when it did not pan out, they blamed the crash on the patient, not the diagnosis. This was made evident in the failure of the Federal education subsidy bill of New Hampshire Representative Henry W. Blair. Promising to help fund public schools in the South, with the money going by race, the Blair bill failed for the last time in 1890 at the same time as the Lodge Federal Elections bill, designed to renew the old Force Acts and protect black voters. With the failure of these two measures, Reconstruction's time truly had passed.

BLACK, JEREMIAH S. *See* SECESSION, BUCHANAN'S CABINET AND.

BLACK LEADERSHIP AND RECONSTRUCTION. As professional historians began to write about Reconstruction at the beginning of the 20th century, they had little good to say about African-American leadership during the era. This despite the fact that between 1870 and 1901, 2 blacks were elected to the U.S. Senate; 20 sent to the House of Representatives; and countless others served in state conventions, state legislatures, and local offices on the county and town levels. To give one an idea of the magnitude and importance of black leadership, there were 240 identifiable black political leaders in New Orleans and another 234 in Charleston alone during Reconstruction. Yet the ability of blacks to do a credible job in leading their people and their states during this era is an important part of Reconstruction that until recently was for the most part lost. Instead the books were filled with stories of "Negro Rule," the corruption of blacks in government, and the blunder and insult of putting the Southern whites under the government of persons, black leaders, considered somehow inferior innately to do more than cultivate cotton.

Black leadership was not unknown before Reconstruction. Even under the slave regime, preachers, sorcerers, gang leaders, drivers and foremen, skilled artisans, house servants, and free people of color all provided leadership among the black community, slave and free, North and South. During the Civil War, black leadership displayed itself in many forms. In areas where Union troops were available to protect them, slaves followed their leaders into the Union lines to freedom. But where the Confederates ruled and could effect bloody reprisals, black leaders counseled caution lest a misstep lead to a massive retaliation by Confederate soldiers.

But nothing so eroded the institution of slavery as the appearance of black men in uniform. This was agitated for and against in 1862 and adopted as policy by the Abraham Lincoln (q.v.) administration in 1863 (and even accepted as a last-ditch proposal by the Confederate Congress in 1865). Blacks, from Frederick Douglass (q.v.) to the most lowly of the escaped slaves, sought the right of blacks to enlist and demonstrate their capacity to fight for their own freedom. By 1863, the Union army had adopted a near conscription policy, going into the contraband (q.v.) camps to compel service. Such activity, plus the fleeing of African-Americans *en masse* to free areas, had practically extinguished slavery in the border states by 1864, making the Thirteenth Amendment (q.v.) a legal recognition of already existing fact.

As blacks had experienced slavery as a common bond, so too they approached freedom as a collective community. Under the slave regime, they had learned to cope with the so-called "peculiar institution" and to hope for freedom. The village had been the center of West African society, and the slave quarters had replaced it during bondage. As with the earlier group experience, African-Americans banded together to help each other face the problems of daily life. Slave weddings, no matter how informal, were important and even encouraged by smart masters as a way to give everyone a stake in remaining at home. Kinship was maintained despite slave sales. Indeed, much of what appeared to whites as useless wandering after slavery ended was actually an effort to reestablish contact with lost family members or a home once loved.

Religion was another unifying factor of the slave community, and exhorters were respected leaders of the local slave community. Drivers in the field, slave foremen who set the pace of work and often had to mete out punishment, also were important leaders. They could make or break the work effort and were listened to by worker and master alike. A slowdown in work could upset a whole year's effort, not to mention the master and, if done without his leadership, the driver. Artisans, carpenters, blacksmiths, wheelwrights, masons, coopers, shoemakers, and tailors, to name but a few, who had special talents that built the plantation and kept it functioning, were instrumental in the education of others and provided role models for the young. Even the house servants, often condemned by some as being allies of the white family, used their position to obtain a book education and pass it on to others. They were also excellent spies and kept the slave community informed about what was going on in the big house and the world at large.

There were Rebels who never could put on the act that made slave survival important. Yet they, too, provided a leadership role. They kept the system honest in a sense—one had to be careful lest the single Rebel turn out to be the whole slave community. But there were other, more subtle, ways in which leadership might be exercised as a Rebel. Feigning sickness or disability was one. Indeed, there is a story about a Mississippi slave who convinced his master he was blind and could not work. After emancipation, he led the county in raising cotton, willing to work for himself but not someone else. Stealing prohibited food was another way one might show leadership for the community. As the old slave saw went, nothing tasted as good as stolen pork. Rather than armed rebellion, American slaves specialized in work slowdowns or fleeing to the woods in a general protest against conditions (sometimes the whole plantation would take off) and then renegotiating their return, much like a modern labor strike. The organizers and negotiators, of course, were examples of early black politicians.

After the rush into freedom, the contraband camp became the new community. There they took up activities that had been prominent among the freed community in the North for years. They organized self-help organizations to acquaint newcomers with primitive social services, eschewing commonly available public charity from benevolent agencies. They protested working conditions on the plantations along the Mississippi, where they were sent by Union military commanders and worked by Yankee contractors. But many preferred to work as stevedores or lease their own five-acre farms (the ultimate recognition of freedom was to obtain a wage-paying job or one's own land). They opened up schools and churches to provide places to train their own future leaders—black soldiers were one source of educators, schooling having been one of the main off-duty goals in black regiments. And they asked for the right to vote—but that would come only years later as a part of Military Reconstruction (q.v.). They also asked for land—a request that would never come to pass except in select parts of the South, particularly along the southeast Atlantic Coast.

Often the quests led blacks off the plantations and into towns especially, in the jargon of the day, "freedmen's villages," where they lived in self-imposed segregation, which offered the farthest they could go beyond constant white supervision. Some were substantial efforts built by white and black laborers, but most were constructed by the blacks themselves out of materials at hand. All of these activities were led by men and women who for the most part remain unknown. But of those who are identifiable, many were skilled artisans from the slave era, and a large portion of the rest came from the ministry of the black church.

The first place that black politicians came into public view was at the state constitutional conventions called at the behest of Congress as a part of Military Reconstruction. The black delegates to the state constitutional conventions were from rural districts with predominantly African-American voting majorities and a higher value in crop lands, or from similarly populated urban areas. Those districts with such a large black voting population that did not send African-American delegates to the conventions, generally sent Carpet-baggers (q.v.), showing some hesitation to trust local whites. The urban areas produced another interesting Reconstruction political type, the black Carpet-bagger, African-Americans from Northern states who came South to take part in the biggest event of their time.

Interestingly, 100 of 192 delegates throughout the South were recognized as mulattos or of mixed race (if this could be determined at all), at a time when such listing in the census was only 13 percent (admittedly census takers were horribly inaccurate in such determinations). This color distinction is im-portant for two reasons: mulattos frequently were among the most articulate and best educated of the African-American population nationally; and their color might suggest a different antebellum status—whether they had been slave or free. Most mulatto delegates had been born free or had bought their freedom prior to the war.

But regardless of their actual color, the African-American delegates were highly educated men—a far cry from the average black of their day. Black historian W. E. B. DuBois estimated that about 5 percent of all blacks were literate at this time, but 85 percent of the delegates could read and write, some of them, particularly in Louisiana, at a university level. Admittedly, once again the statistics are based on much faulty information, but the general drift of them still holds. This challenges the notion that black politicians were illiterate, as critics of Reconstruction had long maintained. This trend con-tinues when their occupations are examined. Of 226 black delegates (whose occupation could be determined), 50 were farmers, but only 12 of these were listed as property-less—the traditional picture of the black politician. The next largest group comprised 47 ministers of the gospel, many of whom came south with Northern benevolent or religious freedmen's aid societies (q.v.). Others of this group were antebellum free men of color. As a group they were not wealthy, but they were among the most articulate in presenting black demands. A third occupational group consisted of 54 skilled laborers. Most of them were carpenters, blacksmiths, barbers, shoemakers, and tailors, occupations open to blacks (slave or free) before the war, and many had been free-born. These were prosperous men, indicating that they were successes in the community from which they came. Finally, there were 41 blacks who worked in the professions or business. The largest bloc of this group were teachers. They often had connections with the Bureau of Freedmen, Refu-gees, and Abandoned Lands (q.v.) or other Northern societies. This group included the most prosperous of all black delegates, particularly merchants from the bigger cities.

In the constitutional conventions, the blacks gained their power from bloc voting on issues. Not infrequently, they were the most unified of all the factions and comprised a critical part of the Republican Party (q.v.). Black delegates failed to gain racial equality because Republican whites, especially Scalawags (q.v.), refused to unite with them to achieve this. As a group, the African-American delegates refused to disfranchise permanently any white Southerner. But they did gain the franchise themselves and become a critical voice in Reconstruction governments throughout the former Confederacy.

In almost all cases, except South Carolina and Louisiana, black legislators had little time in which to serve during Radical Republican Reconstruction (q.v.) before Conservative whites regained political power through the process known as Redemption (q.v.). Nonetheless, they acted in league with white Republicans to advance the party's economic program of public education, internal improvements, and civil rights. Blacks worked together as a bloc on public schools and civil rights, but tended to split up by individual, regional, and socioeconomic preferences on other problems. Indeed, blacks tended to divide among themselves in a conservative–radical manner much as did whites. This meant that differences among black leaders and rank and file appeared immediately after emancipation, and that African-Americans were far from being passive objects upon whom white society could work its will. Blacks refused to follow the rich, white planters in 1867, because they mistrusted their motives as Scalawags.

But as the Republican program changed from revolution to conservatism, the white yeomanry abandoned it in favor of the Democrats (q.v.), racial solidarity, and Redemption of home rule. In a pattern that would become common for the rest of the century, the white yeomanry proved too radical in their demands for debt reduction and a shift of taxes upon the rich. The blacks were then left to work out a conservative economic approach with the remaining Scalawags, the old-time Whigs, the former slaveholders. Hence, during the Gilded Age following Reconstruction, the South was ruled by a coalition of white and black conservatives who worked to nullify white farmer radicalism, forcing them into third-party movements. By the end of the 19th century, the Conservative whites, stampeded by black defections to the Populist Party of farmer radicals, joined with their white enemies to disfranchise the African-Americans. But the disfranchising method had to be biracial to get around the restraints of the Fifteenth Amendment (q.v.), so the poorer whites lost out along with the whole black community through the poll tax and literacy tests, understanding exceptions, grandfather clauses, and the white primary notwithstanding.

As with the states, on the national level the influence of black congressmen was mixed. During Reconstruction, 16 African-Americans represented their districts in the nation's capital, six from South Carolina, three each from Alabama and Mississippi, and one each from Florida, Louisiana, Georgia, and North Carolina. All were Republicans. Like black leaders elsewhere, these men received little attention from white historians, usually in passing. On the other hand, modern historians of the black experience in America have written many pieces designed to refute white racist accounts and attempt to recreate a past of which black Americans might be proud, an unfortunate condescending treatment that has led critics to label this kind of history "Moonlight, Magnolias, and Collard Greens," in reference to the same romantic, fictional "Moonlight and Magnolias" treatment of the white South earlier. The result of this effort has been to describe black congressmen as witty, shrewd, eloquent, charismatic, brilliant, and militant. Yet few actually point out legislation or speeches in which this picture is advanced.

Critics say that as a group the black congressmen tended to support the Republican economic program and spoke out on only one issue that affected them most, political and racial equality. Overall they seemed reluctant to cause trouble and by and large just served. The suggestion is not to study these men but to realize that their ineffectiveness might be one important reason why the Redeemers (q.v.) won out in the end. Proponents of the image of blacks in Congress reply that they did a credible job, especially in light of having been kept out of the political process so long and having to buck a nearly immovable prejudice just to take their seats. The telling item in how much they thought of their section may be that so many of them went back to the South at the end of their terms and engaged in business and law, rather than accepting the inevitable "Negro patronage" jobs that abounded in Washington. They were race protective, Southern-loving, articulate, trained, non-vindictive, and as productive as the average congressman can be.

Black leaders were present in every aspect of Reconstruction, helping to formulate issues and responses that would meet the needs of the African community. That they did not always succeed did not lessen their impact on the Reconstruction process. They constantly strove to direct Reconstruction to their advantage on national, state, and especially local levels. Indeed, the more on the grassroots level they operated, the more likely their success. As they operated within the state and national levels, black politicians tended to get lost in the one big reality that would do in all of Reconstruction—it was a white man's country bent on imperialism on the American continent and finally abroad, and in the 19th century that determined for good or ill the direction the nation would take. *See also* BLACKS, URBAN, IN THE SOUTH DURING RECONSTRUCTION.

BLACK "PERSONALITY" IN SLAVERY AND FREEDOM. African-Americans have the dubious honor of being one of the most psychoanalyzed groups in American history, especially when historians have interpreted the slaves' psychic response to the "peculiar institution" and racism. Did the slaves and freedmen internalize their feigned laziness and inabilities until they became reality, as plantation owners wanted to believe, or was every slave a Nat Turner, fighting the system with guile and dignity, as African-Americans forcefully state today?

Numerous black historians, from the eloquent W. E. Burghardt DuBois to Joseph Carroll to the popular Joel A. Rogers, have asserted the African-Americans' nobility as an enslaved people. But one of the better known is the white Marxist historian, Herbert Aptheker. In his *American Negro Slave Revolts*, Aptheker paints a picture of a continually resisting slave population that attacked the "peculiar institution" in a variety of ways, from sly, day-to-day resistance to outright armed rebellion, but in turn, he has been criticized for arguing beyond the evidence and failing to distinguish among rumor, discontent, and actual rebellion.

One of Aptheker's critics is another white Marxist historian (since turned Conservative), Eugene Genovese, author of the monumental study *Roll Jordan Roll: The World the Slaves Made*. Genovese thinks that black and leftist historians of the 20th century were too impressed by the notion that the masses are noble and ripe for revolt and, if not, can be educated to be so. He notes that it is sacrilege to suggest that slavery was a social system in which the vast majority lived in relative harmony, but he believes that the record shows that there was little organized, massive resistance to the slave regime. Genovese points out that there were bloody slave rebellions in the Caribbean and South America that lasted for decades, had thousands of participants, and cost hundreds of lives. Yet the record for the United States in the 19th century includes only the 1811 Louisiana Revolt (which he does not consider American); Nat Turner's 1831 attempt; and two others that were snuffed out before they got off the ground, one of which, Denmark Vesey's in 1822 Charleston, South Carolina, might not have occurred at all. There was no rebellion between 1831 and 1865, despite the occurrence of the Civil War.

Genovese traces this alleged lack of a black revolutionary tradition to three factors. First, the United States had the only homegrown African slave population in the world, which was even more acculturated to the New World. Second, the ratio of white to black population in the United States was decidedly in favor of the white master class (most Southern plantations had fewer than 20 slaves; few had over 50), which more actively patrolled and isolated blacks and put them at the mercy of white law. Third, the treatment of the slaves by their New World masters—which Genovese finds to be better in the United States than elsewhere—involved more food, leisure time, family units, better housing, and less corporal punishment, epitomized by the feeling of duty and responsibility that saw the slaves characterized as "my people" by their owners. Genovese finds that the American slave system was so repressive and yet so benign that revolt was impossible and impracticable.

Far more controversial than Genovese is the theory put forward by Stanley Elkins, based on earlier work by his mentor, Frank Tannenbaum. Rather than seeing the U.S. slave system as the most benign, Elkins posits that it was the most repressive—so much so that it literally brainwashed the normal, varied psyche of the enslaved African into a new, warped personality, one of child-like meekness, humility, optimism, readiness to laugh and joke, happy, easily satisfied, and full of emotion rather than reason, a character he calls (to the disgust of modern American blacks) "Sambo."

Elkins finds that the same regression to childhood and all the rest also occurred among European Jews incarcerated in Adolph Hitler's World War II concentration camps, which he sees as comparable to the American slave system. Like Genovese, he points out that the rebel slave is a general type in Latin America, while in the United States the individual rebel is a noted exception. Hence U.S. slave revolts are known by those who led them—persons who developed personalities outside the norm—aberrations like Gabriel, Denmark Vesey, and Nat Turner.

But what if the "peculiar institution" was not as closed as the concentration camp, but more like a minimum control prison? The constant terror of the camps was not present in slavery. Execution was not the goal. In such a system, multiple personalities (even a false one to fool the white man, and another real one for life in the slave quarters away from white supervision) would develop as in any "normal" society. This is what many historians think actually happened under the slave regime of the American South. Kenneth Stampp joins other critics of Elkins to find at least four distinct slave personality types: the true Sambo, yielding and accommodating—but the wise master knew that at any moment Sambo might become a rebel; another labeled Banzo, a slave common in ruthlessly exploitive and expanding slave systems, like that in Brazil (from whence the name) or the American Old Southwest, who was overworked and fatigued to the point of not caring about life or punishment; a third called Jack, hard working, efficient, trustworthy, who gloried in the life of the slave quarters, so long as he was treated with respect, honor, and trust; and Nat, the true rebel, a conspirator as well as an individual troublemaker, a class comprised of those never reconciled to the system, including runaways, thieves, arsonists, and saboteurs. Naturally the same types could be male or female, despite their gender-prone names of classification.

The argument about slave African-American personality continued into Reconstruction. Whether the former slaves would be independent-minded or "docile" was very important to the white South after the war. In this the Southern whites evidenced little faith in black abilities to act as free people. Whites envisioned two types of African-American personality—the incorrigible rebel and the cooperative black who "knew his place" as a useful laborer. Those few who believed that African-Americans ought to have a modicum of civil rights or be in constant contact with whites saw this more as a way to insure white control than something all free peoples ought to enjoy. But above all, blacks had to be industrious and happy, just like the old plantation Sambo of myth.

The result was the old distinction between the way in which Northern and Southern whites allegedly approach African-Americans. Northerners view the race as worthy of citizenship and the equal rights and privileges and immunities that conveys. But they have little to do with blacks as individuals. Southerners condemn the race as unworthy of full citizenship, but always know individuals who are meritorious. Indeed, in the white South, finding and identifying the exception became a constant pastime. Those blacks who were worthy, servile, cooperative, hard-working, non-complaining, always with a happy face, would be allowed to remain with whites, while any others were to be isolated until they changed their attitude.

But this was a solution that whites still found as disturbing as it was satisfying. How could one know what the African-Americans were really like, what really motivated them, if they were isolated from contact with whites? It was the uncertainty that segregation established that led to extra-legal attempts to guarantee that whites were not being fooled—things like lynchings, beatings, and burnings of people and property. There was an eternal quest for Sambo, the quintessential "nigger," a search that has led more than one black to echo the words of James Baldwin: "I am not a nigger. I am a man. And the question is, why do you need a nigger?" And from the other side comes the usual condescending protest in the words of Bill Arp, the "every man" character creation of 19th-century humorist Charles Henry Smith: "I ain't agin the nigger. I like him. I'm his friend, and I want him kept jest where he belongs." It is a conundrum that continues to plague the nation today and threatens to stifle its potential for the future.

Modern sociologists have found that this imposed segregation had two different effects upon black people. Some came to hate themselves and their blackness. A lighter skin, straightened hair, and products that guarantee them became a rage. But more often the separation led to an increased black pride and a willingness to establish their own institutions for everyday survival. Black businesses grew in the late 19th century: black-owned streetcars, black churches, black libraries, black social and service clubs, black burial societies, and of course black colleges and universities. In these institutions, blacks could live as adults, free people in every sense of the word, holding office, electing their own representatives, contributing to society in their own segregated way. In the metaphor of Booker T. Washington, blacks and whites were as separate as the five fingers and yet as unified as the whole hand.

But others wanted to go further and break what they saw as an unconscious dependency of blacks upon whites. Although blacks were legally free, these advocates believed that they would never achieve psychological independence unless they acquired a self-esteem that could only come by rediscovering the black's African past and a consciousness of social destiny. W. E. Burghardt DuBois, Harvard's first Negro Ph.D., by emphasizing what he called the "talented tenth" of blacks who were well beyond the world of the cotton patch in intellectual abilities and skills, hoped to develop an indigenous black middle class of white collar workers and business owners, which came to be embodied in the 20th-century North as the "New Negro."

BLACK SOLDIERS. *See* AFRICAN-AMERICAN SOLDIERS IN THE CONFEDERATE [OR UNION] ARMIES, USE OF.

BLACKS, URBAN, IN THE SOUTH DURING RECONSTRUCTION. In Southern cities before the Civil War lived a group of free blacks (as distinguished from the freed blacks, or former slaves emancipated by the war) noted for its industriousness and independent social standing—neither black nor white. The largest populations of free men and women of color lived in the South's two largest cities, Charleston, South Carolina, and New Orleans, Louisiana. Their different status was critical to their response to the conditions of Reconstruction. The Civil War changed more than the white South—it also changed the lives of the free blacks forever.

In Charleston, the antebellum free blacks started Reconstruction with certain advantages over the freed men and women from the plantations of the countryside. The free men and women of color had accumulated property—not much, but a lot to the ex-slaves who had nothing. The free people of color also had a good lineage. Many of them came from liaisons between their mothers and the sons and fathers of the finest white families of the Low Country. This often gave them access to good schools and an education that for some included attending colleges in the North and Europe. Those not as fortunate still learned to read and to a lesser degree to write. This gave them the ability to engage in all sorts of businesses, although most of them were in trades like barbers, butchers, tailors, carpenters, blacksmiths, and other skilled trades. Others were churchmen, teachers, and even a rare few, doctors of medicine.

The average black politico in Charleston had a free background rather than having been a slave. Indeed, slavery in one's past tended to exclude one from leadership. Most were of middle age, but there was an active younger group on the way up and a few oldsters to leaven the age mix with experience. At least half were partly literate; that is to say, they could at least read if not write. But a few had as good an education as anyone could receive in 19th-century America, up to and including college. Two-fifths of the black politicians were skilled craftsmen, concentrated in the trades of tailor, carpenters, and butchers. Other trades, like bricklayer and baker, did not contribute very many to leadership councils. But one-fifth of the leaders were common laborers: draymen, stevedores, and chimney sweeps. It was not uncommon for a man to have held several different jobs, however, which was indicative of the economic fluctuation of the Reconstruction years.

Absent from the Charleston black political leadership (q.v.) were the professional men. There were few doctors, teachers, or ministers involved. But the most important local politicos were ministers. The politicians also tended to be joiners of a variety of social and benevolent societies, like the Brown Fellowship Society, the Humane and Friendly Society, the Veteran Republican Brotherhood, the Colored Young Men's Christian Association, various fire companies, and fraternal and literary guilds. Like the whites of South Carolina before them, the blacks tended to develop family political influence, with the son following the father into political action.

Most interesting of all, 39 of Charleston's black politicians were Democrats (q.v.). These men, like their standard Republican (q.v.) counterparts, represented a broad cross section of the whole black community, but several had had the distinction of owning slaves before the war. This produced much political divisiveness as they competed among themselves and their white Republican allies, who resented the Democrat blacks' assertiveness, and gave the more united Conservative whites an edge in the battles for Redemption.

Nothing could be more different from the Charleston scene than those antebellum free blacks in Louisiana, whose presence, particularly in New Orleans, formed such a critical part of Louisiana Reconstruction. An examination into the postbellum life of the antebellum free colored men and women of the Bayou State illustrates the error of viewing the black reaction to the forces of Civil War and Reconstruction as a cohesive unit. When the Yankees captured the southeastern third of Louisiana, the areas around and including New Orleans, in 1862, they found three populations present, the whites, the slaves soon to be emancipated, and the free men and women of color, whose class existed from the time of the French and was molded by Latin attitudes on race. But by and large, Louisiana's free colored population was the seed of the finest white families of the state, encouraged by custom and the lack of white women and black men in the region. The result was alliances between white men and black women (indeed, New Orleans's renowned quadroon balls were the talk of the nation) that lightened the free colored population until Louisiana's supreme court ruled in 1810 that the whiter the Negro, the more the legal presumption of freedom.

But there was more than light color in the New Orleans free blacks or "Creole colored people," as they were popularly called. They adopted the lifestyle and culture of the Gallic society that created Louisiana in the first place. They were Catholic in religion, spoke flawless French, often attended local private academies, and were tradesmen of the highest skills. The first anthology of black verse published in this country, *Les Cenelles*, was penned by the teachers and students of free colored academies in New Orleans. It never mentioned slavery and was exclusively French in outlook, dominated by the philosophies of La Fontaine, Boileau, Fénelon, Racine, Corneille, and Victor Hugo. Indeed, the free colored population was decidedly not in league with their enslaved brothers and sisters, more than willing to turn over a runaway to the white slaveholders, inform on an insurrectionary plot, or help suppress a revolt. They had their own militia that was a part of the state system and had served with honor at the Battle of New Orleans in 1814. By the time of the war, they were among the finest of the city's tailors, carpenters, shoemakers, jewelers, and masons. But they were more. They were also merchants, businessmen, and property owners. And almost half of the property, usually real estate, was owned by free women of color, the inheritances of their white fathers. And they were slaveholders; some were the biggest planters in the state and reputed to be the cruelest when it came to treatment of bondsmen and women.

One of the oddities of the South was Louisiana's *Code Noire*, the state's law on slavery, which not only defined the "peculiar institution" but granted special distinctions normally reserved only for whites elsewhere on the basis of mixed blood. In the 1850s, when the rest of the South was tightening up on free Negroes and trying to deport them from their boundaries or recommit them to slavery, the Louisiana supreme court once again stated that there was "all the difference between a free man of color and a slave, that there is between a white man and a slave." Truly the free persons of Louisiana were a class apart, without equal anywhere else in the nation. Indeed, when the war commenced, they volunteered their service to defend the state against Yankee invasion. The Confederacy turned them down. But as soon as the Union army and navy took New Orleans, the free colored people adapted readily to the new regime, because there was something akin to the French Revolution in their crusade—the possibility of the free colored men voting, a desire that topped everything in their Reconstruction agenda, presented by Louis C. Roudanez (q.v.), editor of the free colored newspaper, the New Orleans *Tribune*.

But in their quest for the vote, an aspiration that was shared by President Abraham Lincoln (q.v.), the New Orleans free blacks found that they would actually loose status. The Union military commanders and even the Republicans in Congress did not understand their desire not to be included with the ex-slaves in any Reconstruction reforms. In reality, the free persons of color believed that the new state constitution drawn up under the Military Reconstruction Acts (q.v.) lessened their rights as individuals. They now had to ride the Jim Crow (q.v.) streetcars and trains; they could not stand apart under law.

Unlike the free blacks in Charleston, Reconstruction was not a liberating experience for the New Orleans mixed bloods. It was an enslavement. It was the humiliation of being treated like any other black in the South. It resulted in their division, decline, and a search for solace and seclusion. It was no wonder that the people who tried to break segregation by race in the 1890s case Plessy *v*. Ferguson were from the old Louisiana free persons of color, who never felt that they were either white or black, but superior to both, *sui generis*, a class alone. *See also* RECONSTRUCTION, SOUTHERN; RECONSTRUCTION, THEORIES OF.

***BLACK WARRIOR* INCIDENT.** *See* "SPREAD EAGLE" FOREIGN POLICY.

BLAIR EDUCATION BILL. *See* BLACK EDUCATION AND RECONSTRUCTION.

BLAIR, MONTGOMERY (1813–1883). *See* CHASE BOOM; WADE–DAVIS MANIFESTO AND THE ELECTION OF 1864.

"BLEEDING KANSAS." *See* KANSAS–MISSOURI BORDER WARS.

BLOCKADE. *See* PRIZE CASES.

BOOTH, JOHN WILKES (1838–1865). He was called the handsomest man in America before he became the quintessential villain of the 19th century and the first successful assassin of an American president. John Wilkes Booth was the matinee star of his time, and a star who was not shy about speaking his mind on the politics of the day, which were pro-Southern, although he lived and worked in the North.

Born on May 10, 1838, in Harford County, Maryland, Booth was a precocious child and the apple of his mother's eye, as her nickname for him, "Pet," showed. But even though he was his parents' favorite child, none of his brothers and sisters (six lived to adulthood) seemed to mind it. They spoiled him, too. He grew up in a family of actors and directors with a father who was the premier American Shakespearean actor of the first half of the 19th century. His father traveled much, often chaperoned by his older brothers (he was a chronic drunk when left alone and died from cholera-like symptoms on a Mississippi River steamboat), which left Johnny to grow up with a minimum of supervision, most provided by his adoring sister, Asia.

Booth's schooling was pretty good for his day, and if his letters are any indication, he grew more sophisticated after he left school for the stage. He considered himself a Southern gentleman with all the good and bad things that involved—noble, courteous, debonair, high-toned, hot tempered, proud, and racially superior to people of color and whites of inferior breeding (immigrants). But he also sought to operate under the Southern concepts of the Constitution and states' rights in great depth.

At the beginning of the Civil War, Booth, like most Marylanders of Southern extraction, was a cooperationist. He believed that the Constitution protected state sovereignty (q.v.) within the Union, including slavery. But as the war lengthened and the Abraham Lincoln (q.v.) administration encroached on the rights of individual citizens and the states and advanced from Union to Freedom as wartime goals, Booth feared that the authoritarian Lincoln and the Radical Republicans (q.v.) would take the next step to Equality. That he could not abide.

This drove Booth to violate the promise he had made to his mother to stay out of the war, and he renounced his cooperationist stand in favor of secession (q.v.). The only problem was that he was two years behind the times. He informed his mother of the shift, but her quiet acceptance of his politics was challenged by his brothers, Junius and Edwin, leading to many family arguments, especially after Edwin voted for Lincoln's second term in 1864. John surreptitiously ran drugs to the Confederacy, specializing in quinine, creating his own "French connection." How much he was in league with the Confederate secret service is open to argument.

By 1865, Booth had advanced his beliefs once more, to tyrannicide. Seeing the South fall beneath the Yankee juggernaut and Lincoln triumphant caused Booth to espouse the ideas of the British justifier of the execution of King Charles I in the English Civil War (1649), Algernon Sydney. Whether Booth acted to kill Lincoln on his own volition or at the behest of agents provocateur of the so-called New York connection of the Lincoln assassination (q.v.) or the Confederacy and the Lincoln assassination (q.v.), he shot the president on April 14, 1865, Good Friday, operating as a part of a gang that failed in their efforts to execute several of Lincoln's cabinet.

Booth was pursued for a dozen days, finally tracked down by Federal detectives and Union cavalry, and shot at Garrett's Farm in Virginia. Although many believed that he escaped to live a long life until the turn of the century, most accept his death as the end of the story. Eight co-conspirators were tried by military tribunal. Four were hanged at the Washington arsenal in July, three given life terms at Ft. Jefferson in the Dry Tortugas, and one jailed at the same place in that living hell at the end of the Florida Keys for six years. President Andrew Johnson (q.v.) freed all of the living defendants after he beat his impeachment (q.v.), to needle the Radicals, who hungered for his scalp but failed to get it. *See also* BOOTH, JOHN WILKES, AND THE ESCAPE FROM GARRETT'S FARM; BOOTH, JOHN WILKES, POLITICAL VIEWS OF; LINCOLN ASSASSINATION, THE CONFEDERACY AND THE; LINCOLN ASSASSINATION, THE NEW YORK CONNECTION OF THE.

BOOTH, JOHN WILKES, AND THE ESCAPE FROM GARRETT'S FARM. One of the great myths about the Lincoln assassination (q.v.) is that John Wilkes Booth was not killed at Garrett's Farm in Virginia, but escaped to live out a long life under another name, either in the United States or as far off as India. The story became so generally known that a group of historians tried to get Booth's body dug up to confirm it was truly he who was buried in the family plot. Thus Booth joined several other Americans of note, like Jesse James (q.v.), Billy the Kid, and President Zachary Taylor (q.v.). The request in Booth's case was denied in court.

But no one needed Booth's body for the story to go public in a big way. The television show *Unsolved Mysteries* and the movie *The Lincoln Conspiracy* both looked into historical and ahistorical theories of Booth's longevity, following in the footsteps of Henry Ford's Dearborn newspaper, the *Independent*, before Ford's reporter gave up on the trail as relying on superficial information. Unfortunately, his promised "new" evidence to prove these tales was never forthcoming.

But Booth's body was the key to the most famous tale, of his disappearance at Garrett's Farm, his body replaced by another's. This was the infamous tale of David E. George of Enid, Oklahoma Territory, or was it John St. Helen of Granbury, Texas? George died in 1903, confessing on his deathbed that he was actually John Wilkes Booth. A local woman read of the passing in the obituary page, went to the morgue, and said she knew him as St. Helen years before in Texas. This made national news and was picked up in Memphis, Tennessee, by a lawyer, Finis L. Bates, who had met St. Helen in Texas years before, appropriately in a Granbury saloon.

Bates said that St. Helen had told a fantastic story about being Booth, shooting Lincoln, escaping from the Federal authorities in Virginia, traveling to Mexico, California (where he saw his mother and brother, Junius), and living out his life in Texas. Bates smelled money and fame. He contacted the U.S. government for the reward money, but it refused to pay up. So Bates had George's unclaimed body embalmed and sent to Memphis as fast as the trains could run. Then he published a book on the topic and contacted the Federal government again. Again the government could not have cared less.

So there was Bates, sitting in Memphis with a worthless dead body on his hands. But the spirit of American free enterprise reared its profitable head, and Bates contacted Henry Ford, a known assassination buff (he owned the chair Lincoln had sat in when he was shot), but Ford refused to bite, his investigative reporter seeing it all as a fake. Bates went on the road and showed the body at every state fair and sideshow in the country. He finally sold it to a carnival, which displayed the embalmed Booth until well into the 1940s, when Booth finally disappeared—literally—for good.

BOOTH, JOHN WILKES, POLITICAL VIEWS OF. One of the major problems facing anyone who reads anything about John Wilkes Booth (q.v.) is that the essay was probably written by a Northerner educated in the usual high school history viewpoint that the actor was somehow an insane fellow who shot Abraham Lincoln in a moment of unthinking grief and killed the one man who was the South's best friend in 1865. This common view has been attacked by those who posit a different view of Lincoln (q.v.) as a political manipulator and far from the greatest of American presidents, on the one hand, and those who see Booth as a rational man moved by political theories common in the South of the antebellum and Civil War periods, on the other.

Part of this unthinking Booth syndrome comes from a sectional feeling of Yankee superiority over the wayward and backward South, epitomized by H. L. Mencken's famous essay, "Sahara of the Bozarts," which presents the South as a "vast vacuity" of any kind of thought, much less political wisdom. As for Booth in particular, he has been presented by a multitude of authors and analysts (historical and otherwise) as an immature man afflicted by a myriad of psychological (absentee father, competitive brother), sexual (suffering from syphilis), alcoholic (a chronic boozer), and submission to authority (he was his own law) issues. In a phrase, Booth was a mere racist cog manipulated by others, like the Confederate government, Knights of the Golden Circle, Northern Radical politicians opposed to Lincoln, Jesuit order of the Roman Catholic Church—did we leave anyone out? In short, Booth was surely insane. His family especially liked that one because it left them out of the mix.

But in reality, Booth told us what he believed and why he would shoot Lincoln in three missives. The first was the undelivered Philadelphia Speech of December 1860, then his "To Whom It May Concern" letter of November 1864, and finally his "Letter to the Editors" of the *National Intelligencer* newspaper on April 14, 1865. In each of these missives, Booth advanced from Cooperationist to Secessionist to tyrannicide.

But the most important was his 1860 never-given speech, in which he analyzed his political rationale as part and parcel of the state sovereignty (q.v.) theory. Then he wrote a standard justification of secession (q.v.), which naturally flowed from the first. Tragically for historians, his final letter to the *National Intelligencer*, a Washington, D.C., newspaper, was given to a friend to deliver the day after Lincoln was shot. But the carrier, an actor friend, panicked when he read the letter, fearing he would be blamed as a co-conspirator, and burned the document, leaving Booth at the mercy of his friend and the historians—never a good fate for a dead man.

BORDER STATES. *See* SECESSION AND LOYALTY IN THE BORDER SOUTH.

BOURBONS. *See* REDEEMERS.

BRAGG, BRAXTON (1817–1876). Born in North Carolina, Braxton Bragg graduated fifth of 50 in the 1837 class at West Point. All his life he was noted for his foul temper and irascibility, often blamed on dyspepsia and migraine headaches. He loved to look for infractions of the rules and gloried in argument. An old story had him arguing with himself as company commander and post quartermaster over the allotment of supplies. Unable to settle the matter, he wrote up both sides and presented it to the disbelieving post commander for solution.

But Bragg was known as an organizer and brave under fire. He served in the War with Mexico; won laurels at Buena Vista for his artillery fire, which saved the day; and won three brevets. He resigned in 1856 to manage a plantation in Louisiana. He also helped design the state levee system and became a general officer in the state militia. When the war broke out, he failed to capture Ft. Pickens at Pensacola. He asked for and received a transfer to Tennessee to be where the action was. He fought in the Shiloh Campaign (q.v.) and took over the Army of Tennessee after the death of Gen. Albert Sidney Johnston and the departure of Gen. P. G. T. Beauregard (qq.v.) on sick leave.

Bragg headed the Confederate effort in the West during 1862 and 1863. As such, he lost the Perryville Campaign (q.v.), the Battle of Stone's River, and the Tullahoma Campaign; abandoned Chattanooga (q.v.); won the Battle of Chickamauga; but lost the Siege of Chattanooga. Throughout it all, Bragg was hated by his men and officers alike. He lacked military daring, lost opportunities, covered up his mistakes and weaknesses by blaming others, and lost track of his objectives in the midst of battles and campaigns in favor of arguments with subordinates. He was a good organizer and provider, but a lousy leader. He feared making mistakes, which made him indecisive and slow to commit to any course of action. He constantly changed his mind. His weaknesses had never become evident before the war, because he had never had to assume final responsibility.

Bragg survived as long as he did because he was protected by his friend, Confederate President Jefferson Davis (q.v.). When his subordinates refused to follow his leadership any longer, Davis removed him to Richmond, where he became Davis' military advisor. He fled with the Davis government in 1865, only to be captured in Georgia. After his parole, he removed to Texas and lived out his life as a civil engineer.

BRANDY STATION, BATTLE OF. *See* PENNSYLVANIA CAMPAIGN.

BRECKINRIDGE, JOHN C. (1821–1875). Born at Lexington, Kentucky, John C. Breckinridge came from a politically powerful background, his grandfather serving as Thomas Jefferson's attorney general. He had an academy education and studied law at Transylvania College and Yale. He practiced law and taught at Transylvania. He married in 1843. Breckinridge served with a Kentucky regiment in the War with Mexico, came home, and was elected to the Kentucky legislature as a Democrat (q.v.). Almost immediately, Breckinridge was elected to Congress, where he served from 1850 to 1856. In the latter year, he became the youngest vice president the United States has ever had. He ran for president on the Southern Democratic ticket in 1860 but lost. Kentucky sent him to the U.S. Senate, where he worked to compromise the coming war and served until he was expelled and declared a traitor in the fall of 1861 for working to get Kentucky to leave the Union.

Joining the Confederate army, Breckinridge became a brigadier general and fought during the Shiloh Campaign (q.v.) at Pittsburg Landing and Baton Rouge. He also led a division during the Perryville Campaign at Stone's River and at Chickamauga and Missionary Ridge in the Chattanooga Campaign (q.v.). In 1864, he fought in Virginia at New Market, the Richmond Campaign (q.v.), and Jubal A. Early's Raid on Washington (q.v.). In 1865, he became the last secretary of war of the Confederacy. Fleeing Richmond with the Jefferson Davis (q.v.) cabinet, Breckinridge managed to get to Cuba. He lived in exile in Canada until he received permission from the Federal government to return to Kentucky in 1868, where he lived out the rest of his life practicing law without incident.

BRICE'S CROSSROADS, BATTLE OF (JUNE 10, 1864). Determined to eliminate the threat to his lines of communication and supply, Maj. Gen. William T. Sherman (q.v.) organized a column of about 5,000 infantry and 3,000 cavalry under Brig. Gen. Samuel D. Sturgis and sent them to destroy the Rebel forces in Mississippi under Maj. Gen. Nathan Bedford Forrest (q.v.). It proved to be a tall order.

Sturgis ran into Forrest at Brice's Crossroads, where the highway ran across a swampy area on an elevated causeway. The rest of the ground was heavily timbered. This allowed Gen. Forrest to deploy his fewer men on the road and maneuver from behind cover, unseen by the less active Yankees. The Federal infantry was particularly inert, suffering from heat exhaustion from the long march. Forrest managed to hit both flanks of the Union line around 5:00 p.m. and drive them onto the causeway. Confusion reigned as vehicles, cannon, and men collided in one massive traffic jam, intensified by Confederate pursuit. With a loss of about 500 from half as many men as the Bluecoats, Forrest inflicted casualties of nearly 2,500 against Sturgis' column, capturing 16 of 18 cannon and his whole supply train intact.

After his return from the Red River Campaign (q.v.), Maj. Gen. A. J. Smith received orders to accomplish what Sturgis had failed to do. With a force of 11,000 infantry, 3,000 cavalry, and 20 guns, Smith ran into Forrest near Tupelo on July 14 and drove off several Confederate attacks, in what the Yankees thought was an outstanding victory. Short of supplies, Smith withdrew to Memphis. Then he advanced southward on the railroad headed toward Jackson. Sending Brig. Gen. James R. Chalmers to contain Smith at the Tallahatchie River crossing, Forrest took a band of 2,000 picked men and moved on Memphis. He entered the city on August 21 and just barely missed capturing the whole Yankee headquarters staff. Smith was recalled immediately.

Forrest was not through. He now raided into West Tennessee and northern Alabama, destroying Sherman's base of supplies. Then he advanced to the old Ft. Henry position and proceeded to ambush several Union riverboats, so terrorizing the area that the Union garrison at Johnsonville burned its own supply depot. When Forrest had finished, he had captured 150 prisoners and destroyed over $6 million in supplies, 4 gunboats, 20 transports, and numerous barges and smaller craft.

BRISTOE STATION, BATTLE OF. *See* PENNSYLVANIA CAMPAIGN.

BROOKS–BAXTER WAR. In Arkansas, by the election of 1872 (q.v.), assisted by the fact that there were fewer blacks than whites in the state, the Republicans (q.v.) broke into armed factions against one another. The regular Republicans backed Powell Clayton's (q.v.) handpicked successor, Elisha Baxter. Liberal Republicans stood behind Joseph Brooks, in an effort to get rid of the political chicanery and corruption that Clayton represented, paralleling the national scene in the presidential election of 1872. But in Arkansas, both sides began shooting. The conflict ended only when President Ulysses S. Grant (q.v.) backed the party regulars (probably as much to counteract what he had done in Texas as anything) and recognized the Brooks faction as the legitimate group to represent Republicans. But the Republicans were so divided that the Democrats (q.v.) easily took the upcoming state elections at the ballot box. Moderate Republicans and Democrats in Congress recognized the Democrat government, despite frequent waving of the bloody shirt (q.v.) by more Radical Republicans, now called Stalwarts for their backing of Grant and the patronage and corruption his first term had represented.

BROWN, JOHN (1800–1859). Born in Connecticut, John Brown moved with his abolitionist parents to Ohio at the age of five, where he grew up. He was against slavery from familial connections, biblical text, and witnessing of the abuse of slaves during his childhood. He sired 20 children with his two wives, and the whole family without exception was dedicated to the end of slavery. Throughout his life, Brown was an organizer of abolition groups, helping runaways and helping resettle escaped slaves on their own land. With the passage of the Fugitive Slave Act of the Compromise of 1850 (q.v.), he created the "League of the Gileadites" to stand by each other in the rescue of fugitive slaves.

By 1854, the Kansas–Nebraska Act (q.v.) sent Brown and five sons off to Kansas to fight for Free Soil. He settled near Osawatomie, hence one of his nicknames, "Osawatomie John Brown." He fought against terror and voter fraud, opposing the Missouri pro-slave Border Ruffians in the Kansas–Missouri Border Wars (q.v.). He bravely fought for the Free Soil cause against all comers, although his hacking to death of five nonslaveholding settlers from the South stained his cause somewhat. This "Pottawatomie Massacre" provided him with another nickname, "Pottawatomie John Brown."

Brown was financed in Kansas by numerous wealthy Eastern businessmen and philanthropists, and they continued to assist him in his newest scheme, the Subterranean Pass Way. The idea was to form a cadre of dedicated black and white men to invade the South and forcibly end slavery by freeing the slaves. Those who wished to fight would be welcomed into his growing army. Those who did not wish to fight would be sent on into Canada and freedom. Guns and weapons would be obtained by raiding Federal arsenals.

On October 16, 1859, Brown and 22 others made the Harper's Ferry Raid (q.v.) on an arsenal in Virginia to begin his plan. He took several prominent citizens hostage, and forted up in a local fire engine house as locals gathered to shoot at him and his men, awaiting the arrival of state militia and Federal soldiers. Brown surrendered only after he had been shot and, many thought, mortally wounded. Surviving his wounds, Brown was tried for treason against Virginia and hanged at Charlestown in December 1859.

BROWN, JOSEPH E. (1821–1894). A Scalawag (q.v.) politician so flexible in his political principles and so adroit at changing sides that he was, according to historian C. Mildred Thompson, "first in secession, first in reconstruction, and very nearly first in redemption." Joseph E. Brown was born in South Carolina. His family moved to the Georgia backcountry, where his father farmed. Brown was educated at Anderson Academy in South Carolina, taught school briefly, and read law, being admitted to the bar in 1845. He also attended Yale Law School with the support of a benefactor. Before the war, Brown served one term in the state legislature and was appointed to the Georgia superior court in 1855. He resigned to become governor in 1857 and was reelected every two years until his resignation in 1865.

Brown was considered a common man's candidate for governor and a radical state rights advocate. He was a red-hot secessionist, so imbued with leaving the Union that he did not even await the secession of his state before seizing Fort Pulaski near Savannah in December 1860. But although he led the way in seceding from the Union and joining the Confederacy, Brown allied with fellow Georgian, Confederate Vice President Alexander Stephens (q.v.), in opposing Jefferson Davis' (q.v.) hearty prosecution of the war and no-surrender policy, by trying to end the war through direct negotiation with the Yankees.

At the end of the war, Brown was arrested for calling a special session of the state legislature, in violation of military orders. He negotiated his own pardon from President Andrew Johnson (q.v.) by repenting of his secession. Brown pledged to work for the restoration of Georgia to the Union and returned to Georgia to practice law at Atlanta. He accepted the terms of the Military Reconstruction Acts (q.v.) in 1867 and switched to the Republican (q.v.) Party. He used his Republican political connections to dabble in railroad stocks and secure valuable real estate. For these properties to have any future value, Brown believed that Reconstruction had to be completed and Georgia returned to normal times.

In 1868, Brown actively campaigned for Republican gubernatorial candidate Rufus Bullock, and in what critics saw as a blatant political pay-off after he won, Bullock appointed Brown chief justice of the state supreme court. Brown served for a year and a half, ostensibly resigning to devote full time to his businesses. But in reality, Brown had been keeping a close eye on Republicanism in Georgia and found it lacking. The party was unable to prevent the expulsion of black legislators on a trumped-up technicality or to counter rising Ku Klux Klan (q.v.) raids in the countryside. The Republicans had had to call on the Army to reconstruct Georgia a second time by purging Democrats (q.v.) who could not take the ironclad oath, in favor of their Republican runners-up

Seeing that the future was not going to be determined by the feeble Republican administration of Military Reconstruction Acts, Brown took this opportunity to denounce Republicanism and switched back to the Democrats. Of course, he led the way in blaming all corruption on the departed governor, who in reality was a clean as could be, but it allowed Brown to complete a full circle in his political loyalties—Democrat before the war, secessionist in 1861, war opponent in 1863, Johnson and Union man in 1865, Radical Republican in 1867, Liberal Republican in 1872, and Democrat again in 1876.

Exactly what brought Brown together with his post-Reconstruction allies was unclear, until U.S. Senator John B. Gordon, a Confederate war hero and spokesman for sectional reconciliation on the basis of economic exploitation of the South and West, unexpectedly resigned his position. He had only a short time left to serve, but the resignation allowed the governor, Alfred H. Colquitt, to appoint a successor. He picked Brown, still hated for being a Reconstruction Scalawag.

Brown, Gordon, and Colquitt became known as the "triumvirate." From here on out, despite cries of collusion, the general pattern in Georgia was for one to be governor and the other two U.S. senators on an alternating basis, a process that ran Georgia through political patronage, peonage, the convict lease, and other graft and corruption until the Spanish–American War. Hated by many, admired by the rest, Joe Brown had shown an uncanny ability over his controversial lifetime to come to the top with every turn of the wheel and make a fortune doing it.

BROWNLOW, WILLIAM G. (1805–1877). Born in Wythe County, Virginia, William G. Brownlow became one of the most noted Scalawag (q.v.) politicians in the South. His extended family kept moving south and west through the Appalachian highlands until most of it reached eastern Tennessee. By the time he was five years old, both his father and mother had died. Brownlow wound up with his uncle and grew hard and strong in the life of a mountain farmer. He had a rudimentary education, made better by an insatiable desire to read everything he could get his hands on. He apprenticed himself to a carpenter, but found his true calling at a Methodist camp meeting and took up the duties of a circuit rider. Henceforth he would be known as "the Parson." He would have the strong convictions of an evangelical, not only in religion but in his politics. He would speak in the words of religious argument, which made him an effective speaker and writer among people who thought the same, which included most of Tennessee.

Although he was a Tennessee Union man as strong as Andrew Jackson, Brownlow preferred the politics of Jackson's archrival, Henry Clay. Like many border state Southerners, Brownlow backed the Constitutional Union Party (q.v.) in 1860 and its candidate, the former Whig (q.v.) John Bell, from his own Tennessee. When Tennessee joined the Rebel states in May 1861 (before its own secession), he called on every man to vote and give the Rebels the setback of their lives at the polls. But the ordinance of secession carried by two to one. Brownlow kept publishing his newspaper, the Knoxville *Whig*, until he was arrested and held for a short period of time as disloyal to the Confederate cause. Eventually Brownlow was freed and run out of the state.

Returning with the conquering Federal armies, Brownlow reopened his sheet, which he renamed the *Whig and Rebel Ventilator*, and once again castigated the Confederacy and the plantation aristocracy, whom he blamed for the war. Although Tennessee voted in the election of 1864, with white voters proscribed who could not take the ironclad oath, the vote was not counted. Shortly afterward, a convention met at Nashville under the Lincoln plan of Reconstruction and a new state constitution was drawn up without slavery and a separate ordinance drafted to negate the Confederate military alliance. Ten percent (and more) of the voters approved of these measures, and on April 5, 1865, William G. Brownlow became the first elected loyal governor of Tennessee since the war had begun.

In his inaugural address, Brownlow declared himself against slavery as an institution and vowed to promote the power of the Federal government at the expense of the states. He praised the Union victory and promised no quarter for the Confederates. The Tennessee legislature was no Carpetbag (q.v.) body, but perhaps the largest Scalawag institution in the whole nation. Much of its representation came from eastern Tennessee and those in other parts of the state that had remained neutral during the war. The legislature did little to advance the cause of blacks as free persons, beyond passing basic civil rights legislation. But Brownlow did get a law much like the later Federal Enforcement Acts (q.v.) passed, which prohibited the use of the state's roads or one's house for illegal activities and the prosecution of any official who refused to enforce the law or any witness who refused to testify in such cases. His campaigns against the Ku Klux Klan (q.v.) were known locally as the "Brownlow Wars."

An idea of how Brownlow's well-led forces worked can be obtained from Tennessee's passage of the Fourteenth Amendment (q.v.), the only former Confederate state to do so before Military Reconstruction (q.v.). When Democrats boycotted the legislature, denying it a quorum, the speaker had four of them arrested. The detained men got a writ of *habeas corpus* (q.v.). The legislature impeached and removed the judge from office for issuing it and hauled two of the detained into the legislature. A quorum was declared, the two refusing to speak or vote. When the speaker got a sudden, belated attack of fairness and refused to sign the vote, the president pro tem did it, and the speaker was impeached and removed from office. Then Brownlow sent the ratification to Congress: "We have fought the battle and won it, . . . two of Andrew Johnson's (q.v.) tools not voting. Give my respects to the dead dog of the White House!" For its astuteness and Brownlow's leadership, the Republican Congress declared Tennessee to be the first Southern state readmitted to the Union.

In 1869, the Scalawag Republican legislature elected Governor Brownlow to the U.S. Senate, displacing Andrew Johnson's son-in-law, at the same time that President-elect Ulysses S. Grant (q.v.) was replacing Johnson. Although Brownlow's mind was as sharp as ever, his body was worn out by his years of vigorous campaigning for the Union. He did little as senator beyond relish the passage of the Enforcement Acts and call for Tennessee's subjugation under them, which never happened.

It seemed that God had willed that Brownlow live long enough to see his handiwork as the premier Unionist of the South undone. Not only did he live to see the Redemption (q.v.) of the entire region, he also suffered the humiliation of being succeeded by his old Democrat enemy, Andrew Johnson, in the Senate. Brownlow was too vindictive to be considered a statesman, and he lacked the training. He remained a product of his times, Scalawag Union man to the day he died.

BROWN'S FERRY, BATTLE OF. *See* CHATTANOOGA CAMPAIGN.

BRUCE, BLANCHE K. (1841–1898). Born a slave at Farmville, Virginia, Blanche K. Bruce was taken by his owner to Missouri. His early life was much the same as that of his master's son, with whom he played and learned, sharing a tutor (contrary to state laws against teaching blacks to read and write). At the outbreak of the Civil War, Bruce escaped to the Union lines in Kansas and returned as a free man to open a school for blacks at Hannibal and learn the printing trade. He then studied for two years at Oberlin College in Ohio after the war and removed to Mississippi, where he had once lived briefly as a boy, and where, by saving and investing his meager salary, he eventually became a wealthy planter. He leased plantations, founded the town of Floreyville (wisely named after a local Carpetbagger [q.v.] of much political influence), and invested in abandoned lands.

After the passage of the Military Reconstruction Acts (q.v.) in Congress, he entered Republican (q.v.) politics, serving as sheriff, tax collector, county superintendent of schools, and member of the state levee board. He was also commissioner of elections and sergeant at arms in the state senate. Bruce had a dignified bearing, handsome look, and magnificent physique. He always kept vindictive statements and actions out of his policies, which appealed to influential whites from the Delta. All sides competed for him, and finally the Radicals under Carpetbagger Adelbert Ames (q.v.) offered him the lieutenant governorship. Bruce declined; he wanted the U.S. Senate seat, a prized plum. By 1874, he was elected senator and became the first African-American to serve a full term in that body (1875–1881), although Hiram R. Revels (q.v.) of Mississippi had been the first black senator for the short two-year term in 1870 (this was done as a matter of course to stagger the election of senators throughout the South as their states rejoined the Union).

In the Senate, Bruce served on the committees on manufactures, education and labor, pensions, and the improvement of the Mississippi River and its tributaries. He opposed the removal of Federal troops from the South and spoke out against the denial of black civil rights in North and South. He also attacked the Chinese Exclusion Bill and stood for a decent Indian policy, believing that the measures employed against them, like those against black Americans, were contrary to American political principles. A temperance advocate who believed in frugal living habits, Bruce did much to clear up the defunct Freedmen's Savings Bank (q.v.) and distribute its resources among the depositors.

Meanwhile, Bruce formed a triumvirate composed of himself, John R. Lynch (q.v.), and James Hill to wrest control of the Mississippi Republican Party from whites. These three men managed to hold their influence until the 1890s, only losing out after the state disfranchised blacks under the limits of the Fifteenth Amendment (q.v.) by using literacy tests. Oddly, the triumvirate gave most of its political favors to whites, leaving few jobs for black supporters. This went along with Bruce's commitment to black acceptance in American society through assimilation. He opposed the late 1870s Kansas exodus of blacks (mostly from Mississippi) to avoid discrimination and refused support for those who wanted to emigrate to Liberia on the African continent. He maintained that the Negro in the United States was an American and no longer African, any more than any other immigrant who had settled here.

Upon completion of his term, Bruce continued his influence in Washington when he accepted an appointment from President James A. Garfield as registrar of the U.S. treasury, and he remained there until his death in 1898 from diabetic complications.

BRUINSBURG, BATTLE OF. *See* VICKSBURG CAMPAIGN.

BUCHANAN, JAMES (1791–1868). Born to a Scots–Irish family in Pennsylvania, James Buchanan was educated locally and read law. At the same time, he served two terms in the state legislature. Admitted to the bar in 1821, he immediately went off to Congress, where he became a loyal Jacksonian Democrat (1821–1831). He served as minister to Russia (1832–1833), U.S. senator from Pennsylvania (1834–1844), secretary of state (1845–1849), minister to Great Britain (1853–1856), and the last Democrat (q.v.) to be president (1857–1861) for the next 24 years. He was a party hack in many respects, always doing what was right, with little imagination. He was an expansionist, as evidenced by his support of the War with Mexico, the Ostend Manifesto, and the annexation of Cuba. He was also a legalist, always supporting the law and the U.S. Supreme Court. He loved details and liked to supervise everything himself.

Buchanan's main problem was that he entered office with too much confidence. He believed that his 42 years in politics had taught him everything. But he did not understand city politics, speculative interests, and the intensity of Southern nationalism, nor the moral aspects of the antislavery issue. In 1856, Buchanan was old. He represented the past. He was a lifelong bachelor, whose true love had died when her parents prevented their marriage. But he liked feminine company and was lithe on the ballroom floor. His First Lady was his niece, Harriet Lane.

Although he looked ruddy, tall, and hearty, Buchanan was weak in body and spirit. He suffered from the "National Hotel disease," a form of dysentery. He was myopic and always held his head cocked to the left. He had horrible scars on his neck from an operation, which he tried to hide with high, stiff collars. At age 65, he was worried because he had never had a saving religious experience, and he tended to get mean and petulant when crossed.

As president, Buchanan had a lot to be cross about. As a party regular, he believed that the biggest issue he faced was party and personal loyalty. He replaced all those appointed before he took office, even though they were Democrats, because President Franklin Pierce (q.v.) had appointed them. He wasted time on minor party politics when he faced insoluble problems in the territories that led to the Mormon War (q.v.), and the final Free Soil settlement in Kansas, which he opposed. He enforced, some say manipulated, the U.S. Supreme Court's pro-slavery decisions in Dred Scott v. Sandford (q.v.) and Ableman v. Booth (q.v.). He watched the nation suffer through the Panic of 1857 (q.v.), a depression that hit the North harder than the South, erroneously confirming the alleged superiority of the slave economy in Southern eyes, and pushing the drive for secession to be rid of the Yankee albatross of free labor. He supported the John C. Breckinridge (q.v.) Southern Democrats in the election of 1860 (q.v.), believing that the South had many just complaints about the nature of the Union. He was against secession, but his belief in governmental non-interference led him to do little during the Secession (q.v.) Movement in 1861. He retired to his home in 1861, announcing his support of the Abraham Lincoln (q.v.) administration's prosecution of the war for Union and quietly living out his life until his death in 1868.

BUELL, DON CARLOS (1818–1898). Born in Ohio and raised in Indiana, Don Carlos Buell was appointed to the Military Academy, graduating in the lower half of the class of 1841. He was an infantry officer, but spent much of his career in the adjutant general's department, although he served in the War with Mexico, where he gained a brilliant but overinflated reputation and three brevets. Buell lacked personality and had a hard time inspiring volunteer soldiers. He was a cautious man in the field and tended to be pedantic and unimaginative. He was a barrel-chested man of great strength, who could easily bend iron bars in half to impress his staff.

At the beginning of the Civil War, Buell spent time organizing troops around Washington before he was sent to the Department of the Ohio to command its Army of the Cumberland. He advanced slowly into Tennessee, taking Nashville, aided by the more active advance of Maj. Gen. U. S. Grant (q.v.) on his right flank in the Shiloh Campaign (q.v.). Buell sent part of his army over to Grant at Pittsburg Landing, where he saved the day by giving Grant the punch to drive the Confederates back to Corinth. Part of Maj. Gen. Henry W. Halleck's set-piece advance on Corinth, Buell was about to attempt his own drive on Chattanooga, when the quick advance of the Confederate army into Kentucky in the Perryville Campaign (q.v.) caused him to fall back to Louisville and Cincinnati. He nearly lost his command over his withdrawal, but managed to get reinstated and advance to Perryville. His lackluster performance against part of the Confederate army there led to his replacement by Maj. Gen. William S. Rosecrans.

Buell's role in the West was investigated by a military commission, but its report was never published. He was unwilling to accept another position, although Lt. Gen. Grant tried to get him reappointed several times. He spent the rest of his days as a pension agent and an ironworks president in Louisville.

BULLOCH, JAMES E. *See* CONFEDERATE SEA RAIDERS.

BULL RUN, FIRST BATTLE OF. *See* MANASSAS, FIRST BATTLE OF.

BULL RUN, SECOND BATTLE OF. *See* MANASSAS CAMPAIGN, SECOND.

BUREAU OF INDIAN AFFAIRS SCANDAL. Not to be outdone by other executive appointees during the Ulysses S. Grant (q.v.) administration, the Department of War's secretary, William W. Belknap, collected his kickbacks from Indian agents out West (the Bureau of Indian Affairs being a function of the Army in those days). The first bribes actually went to Mrs. Belknap, who had obtained the appointment of C. P. Marsh as agent at the Comanche–Kiowa Agency at Ft. Sill, Oklahoma. But Marsh was smarter than to go out on the Southern Plains to live. He merely wrote the incumbent and told him that for $1,000 a month, Marsh would stay home and let him keep the job (it was an especially lucrative post). The agent agreed, and Marsh paid half of the take to Mrs. Belknap to support her lavish lifestyle in Washington society. When Mrs. Belknap died suddenly, the secretary told Marsh to keep the payments coming. He had married his first wife's sister, and she turned out to be even more expensive to maintain. When the fraud was revealed, Belknap offered to resign. Since he was an old war buddy and Grant got the odd notion that it was all the dead Mrs. Belknap's fault, he let him resign to protect the family's reputation. Of course, this made the whole cover-up Grant's responsibility, and Belknap graciously let him assume the blame for the whole deal. After all, Grant's ever-crooked brother, Orvil, seemed to be implicated as well. Belknap's resignation killed a pending impeachment proceeding. The expected criminal suit went by the board when the Department of Justice said there was insufficient evidence to prosecute.

BUREAU OF REFUGEES, FREEDMEN, AND ABANDONED LANDS (FREEDMEN'S BUREAU). Created in the spring of 1865, the Freedmen's Bureau's goal was, in simplest terms, to provide a shortcut from slavery to freedom for the South's 4,000,000 African-Americans. Established as a bureau in the Army under the secretary of war, the Freedmen's Bureau was a quasi-military organization governed by the articles of war. It consisted of a commissioner (Maj. Gen. Oliver Otis Howard) and his staff in Washington and 10 (later 12) assistant commissioners in the field, who would control the relationship between blacks and whites in 16 states and 2 territories below the Mason–Dixon Line.

Just who made up state and local Bureau policies beyond the general guidelines from Washington is debatable. The responsibility lay with the assistant commissioners, but it is possible that they delegated most of the decision making to unnamed staff officers. The core of bureau work, however, would be conducted by the numerous field agents under the assistant commissioners, another group that wound up making more policy. Their agencies would make direct contact between the ex-slaves and the planters.

The new order the Bureau represented was puzzling to 19th-century Americans, because the Bureau entered the lives of Southern blacks and whites at many levels usually reserved for individual (as opposed to governmental) action. Initially, the Bureau's main job was to assist black and white refugees dispossessed by the war to return home. But the Bureau's refugee responsibilities, which included doling out rations, clothing, tents for temporary shelter, and transportation vouchers, were completed by early 1866.

This left the other functions spelled out in its full title: abandoned lands and freedmen. Throughout the war, a large group of reformers was interested in giving the freed slaves an economic base of independence through the family farm, a concept wrapped up in the slogan, "forty acres and a mule" (q.v.). The former slaves were enthusiastic about the idea. But President Andrew Johnson (q.v.), despite his initial statements about punishing Rebels, was patently against confiscation of property. He forced Howard to temper the Bureau's policy, with the result that the only freedmen who managed to gain any kind of land were those in the sea islands along the South Atlantic Coast.

The biggest responsibility that faced the Bureau after the war was protecting the African-Americans in their freedom. This meant that the new institution took the place of the slavery system. This was not to be a kind system; anyone without a contract and visible means of support was treated like a vagrant and put to forced labor. The Bureau, like the Army before it, did not set down hard-and-fast rules of labor. Basically, as long as local agents negotiated labor agreements that were just and provided for real freedom and impartial enforcement, anything went.

The main problem faced by agents was the contracting process. That contracting could not be left to local law enforcement and courts had been proven by the Black Codes (q.v.). Even though they were established on the basis of Federal military regulations with the desire to restore order to chaos, the Yankees saw their application by Southerners as too discriminatory. The labor contracts varied from plantation to plantation, agency to agency, and state to state. Depending on what a freedman and his family received in advances of goods (food and clothing), implements, and seed, he might get a share of the crop, a monthly wage, or compensation by task. Essentially, the freedmen liked crop shares better than cash, as they saw it as a more tangible form of payment. In many places in the South, the old plantation gang system of labor soon gave way to the croppers and landowning farmers who worked small acreages as their own without supervision, could change jobs at will, and played off landowners against each other for better conditions and wages.

The worst thing about the whole system was that blacks were less than really free, bound to the plantation by the contract, which often spelled out behavior, sick days, and absences as thoroughly as any planter or Army officer had done before Emancipation (q.v.). Often there was a clause that any freedman who was absent before the end of the contract lost all shares. This allowed crooked planters to hire gunmen to run their laborers off at the end of harvest so they could claim the full crop.

Besides labor, the Bureau rendered African-Americans with all sorts of legal protections and basic civil rights not available in local law. That the Bureau did much cannot be denied. The problem was that Bureau personnel had a limited ideological framework from which to operate. Too often they saw compulsion as necessary to make the blacks into their vision of what freedpeople ought to be (as opposed to what blacks envisioned their freedom to be), as had the Army and Southerners before them.

The original Bureau courts (when they had the time and money to operate) consisted of the agent, a representative for the white, and one for the freedman involved. But a shortage of agents soon threw the system onto the indigenous state court systems. The result was that the Bureau was pitted against social, legal, political, and institutional forces that made it questionable whether anything could have been done to guarantee justice for the blacks. As one Texas Bureau agent aptly put it, generally the Negroes got a lot of law but very little justice.

One area in which the Bureau did more uneven work than in justice was the creation of health services in the South. Generally, the farther away from Washington, D.C., a state was, the less in health services it received. As for the Southern states, no one was about to waste tax dollars on caring for African-Americans, when even whites received no state aid. Black health during Reconstruction, when compared to that of whites, was much worse than it had been before the war, and it has stayed that way to the present.

But unlike medicine, the Bureau has received fairly universal praise in its development of educational systems for the Southern blacks. It is instructive that this was its longest running program, lasting until 1872. All other programs had been phased out in 1868. From the beginning, blacks sought to move up the ladder in their own schools. Very important to early African-

American education were the Protestant church societies of the North. Hundreds of schools, some founded by blacks, were adopted by groups like the American Missionary Association (q.v.), individual denominations of Northern churches (who often feuded with each other and the Bureau over jurisdiction and the route to proper salvation), and secular freedmen's aid societies. The schools they founded and operated, providing teachers, books, buildings, and administrators, ranged from elementary to secondary to colleges.

Soon black denominations like the African Methodist Episcopal and AME Zion stepped into the picture. Black A & M universities founded under the Morrill 1862 Land Grant College Act (q.v.) sprang up in most Southern states. The problem for black college graduates was where they were going to find work. The answer was in educating other blacks in schools and churches throughout the South. It is no accident that influential black leaders of the late 19th century were educators and ministers, or both. It is also no accident that one of the places blacks demanded more than the traditional input in American society was their schools, especially the many Negro universities.

Yet although the universities and other schools founded by whites and later funded by whites and run by blacks (Howard, Fiske, Spelman, Atlanta, Lincoln, Morehouse, and Wiley) produced the leadership class of the 20th century (W. E. B. DuBois, James Weldon Johnson, James Farmer, Martin Luther King, Thurgood Marshall), many local black schools never got much above the problems of Reconstruction. Whites sought to subvert the independent black school system and bring it under state control. This was done politically and through clandestine violence against schools, teachers, and individual students. The goal was to control the curriculum and operating funds, keeping blacks a "happy peasantry," always in a subordinate place.

As it was, not more than one-sixth of the eligible black population was reached by educators during Reconstruction. But the education movement did accomplish three things: it awakened the African-Americans to the need of education, it led to the establishment of public education in the South, and it created the black colleges and universities that provided the graduates to expand that system in the future.

Along with school separation, not necessarily wanted by blacks, came certain institutions that they desired to be separate. These revolved around the family and churches, areas in which blacks did not want white supervision but preferred their own institutions and customs. It gave them a needed break from white domination and prejudice. Their religion tended toward the evangelical, often Methodist or Baptist, with local traditions thrown in.

The church became the center of African-American family life, the one place they could be themselves and develop their educational, social, and economic needs as well as the spiritual and moral. Black ministers were community leaders, along with artisans, a process that continued well beyond

Reconstruction. It gave them a voice in the development and ordering of their own affairs. Most important were the aid societies that assisted the not so-well-off after the Bureau stopped relief activities in its first year of operation. The church acted as an employment office and a place for Bureau agents and Northern missionaries to make contact with the black community. It also molded those whites into acting as blacks preferred, rather than handing out edicts from on high.

By its very nature, with the exception of ministrations to white refugees in its first year, the Bureau tended to support segregation. Its services were for blacks only. Its labor policies created sharecropping and the lien, a form of peonage that doomed blacks (and then poor whites) for three generations. Its short-term goals (ending destitution; providing clothing, rations, and shelter) were successful. Its intermediate goals (labor contracts, medical care) were less so. Its long-term goals (stabilizing the status of the African-American, public education, employment opportunity, legal rights for blacks, and African-American voting rights, and the altering of state laws to treat blacks fairly) remained unmet for a century.

What the Bureau achieved during Reconstruction was the freeing of the African-Americans from slavery, but the making of them into second-class citizens. Yet in the words of black historian W. E. Burghardt DuBois, the Bureau represented "one of the most singular attempts to grapple with the vast problems of race and social condition." He and recent historians would say that the effort itself was ennobling, well worth it even though the ultimate ideals were never achieved then and are often lacking today.

BURNSIDE, AMBROSE E. (1824–1881). Born in Indiana and graduating in the middle of his 1847 class at West Point, Ambrose E. Burnside was probably as incompetent an officer as the Union army ever had, and yet he was a confidence-inspiring, warm, and likeable man. He was flashy and handsome, over six feet tall. His long whiskers, which curved from his ear to his upper lip, led to the name burnsides being applied to them, which is nowadays twisted around to sideburns. He wore his revolver on his hip like a gunfighter, high cavalry boots, and a uniform that was sloppy by intent. He also had the amazing ability to fall asleep anywhere on demand. He was sincere, actually very modest despite his dress, and shrank from responsibility, always.

Burnside arrived too late in Mexico City to do any fighting. He did fight the Apaches in New Mexico, where he was wounded. From his Indian campaigns he saw the need for a breech-loading cavalry carbine. He resigned from the army in 1853 and invented one, which was used in the Civil War. But before the war, Burnside was a failure at business and relied on the largess of friends, of whom he had many, for jobs. In 1861, he lived in Rhode Island, a gun manufacturing area, where he was perfecting his carbine. He was appointed colonel of the 1st Rhode Island Infantry, fought credibly at First Manassas, and was made brigadier general in charge of taking Roanoke Island off the Carolina coast.

Transferred to the Virginia mainland, Burnside led his men, now styled as the IX Corps of the Army of the Potomac, in the Second Bull Run Campaign and the Maryland Campaign (q.v.). He performed poorly in the latter, but received the top position leading the whole army after the removal of his friend Maj. Gen. George B. McClellan (q.v.). Burnside protested that he had no ability for the job, a denial that made him all the more attractive to a president and Congress sick of braggarts who did not deliver.

Burnside went on to prove that he had no ability to lead an army in the Fredericksburg Campaign (q.v.). He was pulled out of combat roles and sent to administer the District of Ohio, where he arrested outspoken war opponent Clement L. Vallandigham. Returning to the IX Corps in 1864, Burnside fought in the Richmond Campaign (q.v.) and the Siege of Petersburg (q.v.), where he again proved his incompetence at the Battle of the Crater.

After the war, Burnside became a railroad man and a Rhode Island politician, serving three terms as governor and U.S. senator until his death in 1881.

BUTLER, BENJAMIN F. (1818–1893). New Hampshire–born, cockeyed Ben Butler studied hard and was admitted to the bar after a brief stint at Waterville College (present-day Colby University). He became a cracker-jack criminal lawyer and a Democrat politician. Moving to Massachusetts, Butler represented the poor Catholic mill hands at Lowell in the Bay State. He also fancied himself a military man and wrangled a major generalship of the state militia; he commanded several summer encampments, which gave him the distinction of having as large a body of men as Bvt. Lt. Gen. Winfield Scott (q.v.), the general-in-chief of the whole Federal Army. In 1860, he attended the Democrat (q.v.) convention and voted for John C. Breckinridge (q.v.). His support of the extreme Southern candidate cost Butler the governorship of his adopted state.

Declaring himself a Jacksonian in opposition to secession (q.v.), Butler led some of the initial Union troops to Washington during the critical first days of the war. He was the first to classify the slaves who fled to the Northern lines "contraband of war," which in effect freed them, and gave them their wartime nickname, "Contrabands" (q.v.). Eventually sent to the Department of the Gulf, he commanded the Federal occupation forces at the capture of New Orleans.

His occupation of the Gulf ports and southern Louisiana was highly controversial (he hanged one man for insulting the United States flag), even criminal (he allegedly sacked "Confederate" plantations). The theft of silverware was so common under his command that Butler received the pseudonym,

"Spoons." But he never quite outlived his declaration that women of New Orleans who insulted Federal soldiers would be treated as "prostitutes plying their trade," which led to a death sentence being placed on his head in absentia by the Richmond government and worldwide condemnation. Hence the nickname, "Beast."

Needing to have a less controversial man in charge to initiate Reconstruction in Louisiana, President Abraham Lincoln put Butler in command of an army group that was supposed to cooperate with Lt. Gen. U. S. Grant's (q.v.) 1864 campaign on Richmond, but incompetence on Butler's part led to his force being trapped on the Bermuda Hundred peninsula and a new sobriquet, "the Bottle Imp." Grant fired him after Lincoln's winning of the election of 1864 and Butler's botched campaign against Fort Fisher at Wilmington (q.v.), North Carolina, made his feared political influence superfluous.

After the war, Butler served his state in Congress from 1866 to 1875. He acted with the Radical Republicans to develop Military Reconstruction (q.v.) and impeach President Andrew Johnson (q.v.). He led the way in Johnson's impeachment (q.v.) trial as part of the House prosecution team, where he managed to alienate many and actually made the president a sympathetic figure once again. He was the first to "wave the bloody shirt" (q.v.), literally waving the torn, stained garment of a whipped Carpetbagger (q.v.) above his head and calling for a stricter Reconstruction of the South.

He returned home to run for governor, losing in 1877 and 1879, but winning in 1882. Never one to let principle get in the way of practicality, Butler not only won elections as a Democrat and a Republican (q.v.), but also as a Greenbacker, and he unsuccessfully sought the presidency in 1884 under the label of the Anti-Monopoly Party. He died in Washington in 1893, leaving behind a $7 million fortune and a record for audacity matched by few others.

C

CAMDEN CAMPAIGN. In the spring of 1864, Lt. Gen. Ulysses S. Grant (q.v.) had determined that all Union forces would advance to prevent reinforcement of the major Confederate armies in the field led by Generals Robert E. Lee (q.v.) and Joseph E. Johnston (q.v.). One of the targets was Shreveport and through it, East Texas. Two columns would advance upon Shreveport. One, led by Maj. Gen. Nathaniel Banks, would initiate the Red River Campaign (q.v.) and attack Shreveport from the southeast. The other, headed by Maj. Gen. Fred Steele, would undertake the so-called Camden Campaign, advancing from Little Rock, Arkansas, through Camden to attack Shreveport from the north.

At first, Steele's advance went quite well. Although his progress was contested by enthusiastic Confederate cavalry attacks, he was soon in Camden (April 15), even though he had started three weeks late. There he was alarmed to hear that Banks' columns from New Orleans had been defeated at the Battle of Mansfield. Banks' retreat would allow Confederate Gen. E. Kirby Smith (q.v.) to concentrate his forces to oppose Steele.

Turning back at Camden, Steele's 211 wagons of cotton and booty were intercepted by Confederate troopers at Marks' Mill (April 25). Many of the train guards were black soldiers in blue uniform. The Rebels showed little penchant for quarter, killing even those who surrendered. Steele quickened his pace to cross the Saline River before Kirby Smith's men. The two sides collided at Jenkins' Ferry, as Steele's forces were crossing (April 29–30). Using the 43rd Illinois Infantry as a "fire brigade" to plug holes in the line, Steele managed to hold off the Rebel forays and escape back to Little Rock.

CAMILLA MASSACRE, SEPTEMBER 19, 1868. The black population of Camilla, South Carolina, located in a small white farming area surrounded by former slave plantations, had doubled as African-Americans looked for alternate employment to the backbreaking field work to which they had been restricted as slaves. There was to be a planned Republican (q.v.) gathering at Camilla on September 19. Contingents of African-Americans gathered in neighboring communities and on friendly plantations (owned by Carpetbaggers [q.v.]) to march upon Camilla to hear the speeches. Their white organizers told them that they would have no trouble if it were done quietly.

Meanwhile the news of the black "invasion" panicked white townspeople at Camilla. Rumors had the blacks armed to the teeth. The African-Americans refused to leave their weapons outside town as the sheriff asked, because they had heard that an armed band of whites awaited them. When the blacks arrived in town to go to the courthouse, a lone white ran out and demanded that they stop their fife and drum music. The marchers refused, and the man fired at the musicians. From the side of the street more armed whites appeared and joined in the shooting. The blacks panicked and fled. The whites followed, firing their rifles and shotguns as they came. The shooting continued well into the night, lit up by a full moon. A dozen blacks died during the fray, with uncounted others being wounded.

By election day, the violence had accomplished its goal. Only two Republican votes were cast at Camilla. Fraud took care of the rest of the district. The whole area went to the Democrats (q.v.), not bad considering that black and white Republicans outnumbered them in registration. A similar effect was felt throughout the state, as the fallout from the Camilla Massacre was statewide.

CAMPBELL STATION. *See* KNOXVILLE CAMPAIGN.

CANAL STREET, BATTLE OF. *See* NEW ORLEANS, THIRD BATTLE OF.

CANBY, EDWARD R. S. (1817–1873). Born in Kentucky on the Ohio River, "Sprigg" Canby was raised in Madison, Indiana, at that time a bustling, growing river town. He accepted an appointment to the U.S. Military Academy and graduated second to last in his class of 1839. He served in the Second Seminole War and was a staff officer in the War with Mexico under Maj. Gen. Winfield Scott (q.v.). But more than anything else, Canby was a paper-shuffler, an officer in the adjutant general's office, a man who knew regulations and enforced them. He also served in California and for a time was a recruiting officer. He was with the ill-fated Utah Expedition, sent out to subdue the Latter Day Saints in the so-called Mormon War (q.v.) of the late 1850s. In 1860, Canby was sent to New Mexico to put down trouble between the Navajos and local settlers that had been brewing since the War with Mexico. He had just completed a failed campaign against the tribe when the Civil War broke out in the East.

At the beginning of the Civil War, Canby became colonel of the newly raised Nineteenth Infantry. As such, he was the senior officer left in the Southwest, so when the Confederates invaded in their New Mexico–Arizona Campaign (q.v.), he received the duty of checking their advance. Canby wisely fell back past Santa Fé into southern Colorado, seeking to consolidate the few troops he had left after a disastrous defeat at Valverde in southern New Mexico, and covering his supply line to Denver. As Canby retreated, his supply line got shorter and Colorado reinforcements became closer, until his forces managed to wreck the Confederate supply train after another Union loss at Glorieta Pass outside Santa Fé. The Rebels then found themselves overextended and had to do the same as Canby, falling back all the way to Fort Davis in Texas. The result was that Canby became a war hero in a forgotten theater of the conflict.

In the beginning of 1863, he arrived in Washington, D.C., to become a military advisor to Secretary of War Edwin McM. Stanton (q.v.). Some claimed that Canby was more an assistant secretary of war, but in any case, he signed the order that sent Ohio Copperhead Clement L. Vallandigham (q.v.) into Confederate exile and was on the board that revised the Articles of War.

By summer, Canby was in New York City, where he and a brigade of combat infantry from the Army of the Potomac were charged with administering the draft laws. Although Canby had had nothing to do with the earlier New York draft riot, he was the one who saw to it that it never was repeated, and the rioters enrolled in the draft. In 1864, Canby took over the Division of West Mississippi and led the final successful assault on the forts at Mobile (q.v.) Harbor in Alabama. He then took over the Department of Louisiana and the Department of the Gulf, a bigger command area including Louisiana, with headquarters at New Orleans. In this capacity, he received the surrender of Confederate armies operating east and west of the Mississippi River. He also had to administer Reconstruction for the first time.

A Southerner by birth, Canby had a nebulous position on race. He firmly thought that it was a problem of correct concern to the Federal government, but he was very conservative in that he believed that government help ought to be limited and curtailed at the first opportunity. He had a tendency to require all problems involving African-Americans be handled by the Freedmen's Bureau (q.v.) and all crime by local authorities. But he stepped into both jurisdictions if they failed to act judiciously for all concerned. He knew the rules and demanded that others follow them. As a general, Canby was a good adjutant. He remained monotonously consistent all the time.

At first, Canby expected Reconstruction to go along quickly. But Canby was in Louisiana, and politics there had a way of being unfathomable to outsiders. Taking over from Bvt. Maj. Gen. Nathaniel Banks, Canby found that he was the heir to a program that was to reconstruct the state through an old planter–former Confederate but now allegedly loyal group. This seemed to contradict President Abraham Lincoln's (q.v.) desires to open Reconstruction up to a broader black–white coalition. Lincoln wanted Canby to loosen up the Reconstruction process; Canby sought to follow rules already established. Canby was not averse to letting the Rebels run the country, because they knew how to do it. They would simply have to be watched closely.

But Lincoln's death brought a new hand to the helm in Washington. President Andrew Johnson's Reconstruction Plan (qq.v.), although it was not necessarily envisioned that way, returned power to the prewar elites. Again, Canby saw his role as not to interfere with the political process, unless blacks and loyal whites were adversely affected. Then Canby preferred to cajole the elected officials into doing their duties.

Canby did not like the newly elected government any better than Lincoln's, but he abided by the election. About this same time, Maj. Gen. Philip H. Sheridan (q.v.), whose command area in western Louisiana overlapped with Canby's Department of the Gulf, jealously got Canby transferred to Washington and took over the unified Gulf region.

Back in Washington, Canby headed the "Canby Claims Commission," which looked into property seized by the Federal government during the war under the Confiscation Acts. After the passage of the Military Reconstruction Acts (q.v.), Canby was sent to the Second Military District to replace Bvt. Maj. Gen. Daniel Sickles, who had interfered with operation of the circuit courts administered by Chief Justice Salmon P. Chase (q.v.). Canby arrived in Charleston in the summer of 1867 to begin a portion of his career that would result in the admission of four ex-Confederate states (North Carolina, South Carolina, Texas, Virginia) back into the Union —almost half of those 10 that fell under the Military Reconstruction Acts—and earn him the title "the Great Reconstructor."

Canby considered his job to be a ministerial one, of carrying out policy without regard or favor to anyone. He was not a man to make up his own rules. As always, he followed the rules already set down. The first thing Canby did was reorganize his states into military zones, with a troop contingent in each made up of infantry and cavalry. He refused to put soldiers in all county seats, because that would spread his forces too thin. Instead, he concentrated his men in isolated areas that were most likely to have trouble.

Next, Canby made it a habit to investigate all reports and complaints so as to head off trouble before it started. He prohibited armed civilian groups from drilling, but did not take their arms. He expected local authorities to enforce all laws fairly for blacks and whites. He found that many of the state authorities were not of a quality that he would have liked, so he augmented them with military commissions. Canby made jury duty imperative on all registered voters who paid taxes. Color alone was an insufficient basis to include or exclude.

Canby also was chary of removing officials from office. He seemed to have the Kentuckian's famous ability to talk to both North and South in a diplomatic manner. He never tried to force his actions down the throats of Southern whites by direct military confrontation. He did not try to interfere with the conduct of the conventions. Rather, Canby interested himself in the conditions facing voters, safety, preventing economic discrimination against blacks by their employers (he taxed the county where they were fired for their maintenance on a public dole), and closing down all other governmental functions to assure everyone could go vote.

After the constitutions were approved by state voters, Canby appointed all elected officials to office so that the legislatures might get on with approving the Fourteenth Amendment (q.v.) and electing U.S. senators. This required him to force all elected officials to take the ironclad oath (q.v.), which hurt Democrats (q.v.). But Canby pointed out that it was required under the Military Reconstruction Acts. He also immediately recognized the constitutions as valid. By these methods, Canby kept the Reconstruction process going forward to completion.

After Reconstruction had been completed in 1870, Canby went to the Pacific Coast to command the Department of the Columbia out of Portland, Oregon. In 1871, the Modoc Tribe in southern Oregon complained that the government had treated them unfairly, taking lands in violation of an 1864 treaty. The whites who had settled there treated them poorly, and they did not like it. Led by a chief, Captain Jack, a portion of the tribe left the reservation and refused to return. In a meeting on April 11, 1873, Canby and the commissioners were attacked after the general refused to withdraw the soldiers. Canby fell at the first shot from Captain Jack's revolver. He was the first American general officer to fall in an Indian battle. Canby was buried at Indianapolis, Indiana. The Great Reconstructor had finally found a situation that had resisted his skills in rebuilding.

CAPTURED AND ABANDONED PROPERTY ACT OF 1863. As Federal armies advanced into the South, they captured large amounts of private property, much of it abandoned by fleeing owners. The armies really could not do much with this property, as it had little direct military use. But since a lot of it was cotton that had already been sold or seized by the Confederate government and that had value on the open market, something had to be done. So Congress passed the Captured and Abandoned Property Act on March 3, 1863. It declared that under the "belligerent rights of confiscation," all moveable property of disloyal persons could be picked up by treasury agents, who would remove it for sale to the loyal states. The Department of the Treasury immediately sent out customs officials, agency aids, local agents, and supervisory agents to follow the armies into the Rebel states and seize this property. A general agent in Washington coordinated all of this work. About $30 million worth of property was seized during the war, of which 95 percent was cotton. About $25 million in net proceeds was realized by all parties.

Another aspect of the Captured and Abandoned Property Act was the taking of abandoned plantations. If the owner were absent aiding the Confederacy, treasury agents declared the property abandoned and held it with an eye to possible return to its owner in the future. But although land titles remained undisturbed, the intent was really wartime confiscation. Early on, the Federal government decided to manage this property through a bureau of plantations to give employment to the large numbers of fugitive slaves who had fled to Union lines for freedom and security. Usually these properties were leased out to bidders on an annual basis, all rents and proceeds going to the war effort.

By 1865, administration of this captured or abandoned property passed into the hands of the new Bureau of Refugees, Freedmen, and Abandoned Lands (q.v.). There it was held until claimed (one needed to prove title and loyalty, be it original, amnesty, or pardon) or eventually sold at auction. The owners who had the hardest time proving their loyalty, oddly enough, were the people who actually refused to aid the Confederacy. They often had few witnesses or documents to show, unlike pardoned Rebels.

But in 1871, the U.S. Supreme Court ruled in Smith *v.* Kline that all claimants were to be assumed loyal unless evidence to the contrary could be produced. But the uncertainty of U.S. title in any of the seized or abandoned lands defeated those who wished to grant homesteads to African-Americans during Reconstruction and led to the passage of the Southern Homestead Act (q.v.) in 1866.

CARDOZO, FRANCIS L. (1837–1903). A black officeholder who maintained his integrity amid the excesses usually associated with Reconstruction in South Carolina, Francis L. Cardozo (sometimes rendered erroneously as Cardoza) was born in Charleston as a free man of color. His parents were Lydia Williams, a free woman of color, and Isaac N. Cardozo, a customs house clerk from a well-known Jewish family in the city. Francis Cardozo was educated in a school for free Negroes in Charleston, went abroad, and completed his education at the University of Glasgow and seminaries at London and Edinburgh. He returned to the United States during the Civil War and took over a parsonage in New Haven, Connecticut. At the end of the war, Cardozo returned to South Carolina, where he organized schools for blacks. Upon the passage of the Military Reconstruction Acts (q.v.), Cardozo entered politics and was elected to the state constitutional convention.

Throughout the convention, Cardozo exhibited a moderate attitude and insisted that the floor be opened to all newspapermen so that the proceedings could be fairly reported. He was very solicitous of the public purse, opposing all steps that were unnecessary expenses, like appointing pages to the convention, defraying unlimited expenditures, and permitting lucrative travel monies for members. But he supported a petition to Congress asking for a million dollars to assist freedmen in buying abandoned plantations. Cardozo was also for universal manhood suffrage, opposing penalties against ex-Confederates. He served on the committee on public education and worked out the details of the first tax-supported system of universal education in the state. In 1868, Cardozo was elected as secretary of state on the Republican (q.v.) ticket. His most notable act was to clean up the fraud associated with the state land commission and reserve much land for the freedmen as intended in the original act. An active politico, Cardozo became the head of the Union Loyal League in the state in 1872. He campaigned for the party, despite the monetary extravagances that alienated it from most native whites, asking that the regime be assessed on its merits rather than by the avaricious acts of a few. The result was a resounding approval by the voters at the polls.

In 1873, Cardozo became the state treasurer under the corrupt Franklin J. Moses, Jr. (q.v.), administration. Cardozo's policy was to restore the state's credit by the adjustment and settlement in an equable manner of the state's outstanding debts, resuming payment of the state's bonded debt, and reducing property assessment and rate of taxation by emphasizing a fair collection and disbursing of the state's monies. Much of Cardozo's policy was an able reaction to the legitimate complaints of several statewide taxpayers' conventions. Cardozo also pointed out that while the state debt was almost $16 million, over $7 million had been contracted by Democrat (q.v.) governments in power before the passage of the Military Reconstruction Acts. He was attacked viciously by the Charleston *News and Courier* after he removed the state printing contract from it, but the newspaper's tone soon changed as it became evident that Cardozo was the lone honest man in an administration dominated by a greedy, corrupt governor. Numerous investigations by a hostile Democratic state legislature proved that Cardozo's books were in order and that his policies were honest and good for the state. Nonetheless, the 1876 legislature indicted and convicted him for so-called irregularities when Wade Hampton's Red Shirt Democrats took over the state, forcing Governor Hampton to pardon Cardozo of all charges.

Unwilling to trust himself to Hampton's protection forever, Cardozo left South Carolina and moved to the nation's capital. There he was employed by the post office for a while before becoming superintendent of public schools in the District of Columbia, a position he held until his death in 1903.

CARDOZO, THOMAS W. (1838–1881). The brother of Francis L. Cardozo (q.v.), a black politician in South Carolina during Reconstruction known for his integrity and honesty, Thomas W. Cardozo represented the other side of the coin, corruption and avarice. Born in Charleston the son of a free woman of color, Lydia Williams, and customs house clerk, Isaac N. Cardozo, Thomas Cardozo lived in the much-privileged, yet much-oppressed world of Charleston's free black population. This gave him an ambivalent attitude toward other blacks—he felt an obligation to assist them but at the same time wished to stay a step or two above them on the ladder of society, as his almost-white color seemed to demand. He never wanted to dirty his hands too much with the affairs of his own race. He attended private school in Charleston, but the death of his father sent him and his mother to New York City. There he continued his education and opened up a school for local blacks. At the end of the Civil War, Cardozo became associated with the American Missionary Association (AMA) (q.v.) and supervised their schools in Charleston. It was here that a disturbing penchant for quarreling with others became evident. He also turned out to be quite a womanizer, and an affair with one of his students caused the AMA to give his job to his brother, Francis, forcing Thomas into the grocery business to survive.

Thomas Cardozo made many attempts to atone for his past and regain his stature with the AMA, to no avail. He then went to New York state and became associated with the Freedmen's Union Commission, which sent him and his wife to teach in their schools in North Carolina. The failure of the Commission to finance their operations adequately sent Cardozo over to the rival Federal Bureau of Refugees, Freedmen, and Abandoned Lands (q.v.), again as a teacher. After the passage of the Military Reconstruction Acts (q.v.) in 1867, Cardozo entered Republican (q.v.) politics. He went to Mississippi in 1871, where his wife had relatives. In Vicksburg, Cardozo joined the local Republican Party and taught school until he had gained the proper residency requirements (six months) to run for office. Cardozo got himself elected as clerk of the county court in 1872.

By active campaigning, he managed to get the nomination for the post of state superintendent of education on the Adelbert Ames (q.v.) ticket in 1874. He took a real interest in Mississippi's education system, white and black, and made regular field inspections. He backed local control of schools and statewide adoption of uniform texts. But he did nothing to interfere with the segregated nature of the school system. Unfortunately, the vicious campaign that brought him to office led Conservative whites to charge Cardozo with issuing false certificates to the state and pocketing the money. The indicted Cardozo posted a $22,500 bond that was backed by every prominent Republican in the state. The trial resulted in a hung jury (nine blacks and three whites). Prosecutors tried to bring the case again with a change of venue to Jackson.

The redemption of Mississippi by the White Liners (q.v.) meant that the prosecution would go on, and further investigation resulted in his impeachment. The charges echoed the earlier court case (that he had issued false witness certificates and took the cash), but other new charges appeared, too. Cardozo was accused of embezzling funds from Tugaloo University as its treasurer, accepting bribes and kickbacks in choosing Mississippi's school texts, and cheating on the average daily attendance records, splitting the difference in money with local principals. Cardozo did not await the results; he resigned all offices and left the state, reportedly with $2,000 in state funds, and forfeiting the amount bondholders had previously put up for him. In exchange for his departure, the state legislature dropped all charges. Cardozo went to Newton, Massachusetts, where he lived out his life as a local postal service worker.

CAROLINAS CAMPAIGN. On December 21, 1864, the Confederate army abandoned Savannah, Georgia, to the besieging troops of Federal Maj. Gen. William T. Sherman (q.v.). Having completed his March to the Sea (q.v.), Sherman now proposed to tear the heart out of the Carolinas, eventually coming up behind Robert E. Lee's (q.v.) Rebel army defending against the forces of Lt. Gen. Ulysses S. Grant in the Petersburg Siege (qq.v.). As Sherman moved north, he expected to meet somewhere in North Carolina with Federal forces engaging in the Battle of Wilmington (q.v.).

Sherman crossed the Savannah River in January 1865 with the same two armies (60,000 men) that he had used to cross Georgia, the Army of Georgia (two infantry corps under Maj. Gen. Henry Slocum) and the Army of the Tennessee (two infantry corps led by Maj. Gen. O. O. Howard). As he had done in Georgia, Sherman pushed his armies between his actual objectives, forcing the Confederates to commit their forces to one place while he shifted and took another. There was little actual Confederate resistance—the few Rebel forces were scattered under the command first of Gen. P. G. T. Beauregard and then of Joseph E. Johnston (qq.v.). The cavalry was led by Maj. Gen. Wade Hampton, a prominent citizen of South Carolina and former leader of Lee's cavalry in Virginia. Most of Sherman's trouble came from heavy, incessant rains.

On February 16, Sherman took Columbia, South Carolina. The next day great fires burned much of the business sections of the town. The Federals blamed Hampton's withdrawing cavalry, while Hampton pointed the finger at rowdy Union troops. About this time, the Southern troops abandoned Charleston, which had held off besieging Federals for two years. Northern soldiers and politicians would see Maj. Gen. Robert Anderson raise the flag at Ft. Sumter (now a lump of rubble destroyed by constant artillery fire) on April 14, the fourth anniversary of his surrender in 1861.

To supplement the few Confederate garrison and militia troops that faced Sherman, Johnston managed to get what was left of the old Army of Tennessee to the Carolinas from northern Alabama, where they had remained after their defeat during the Nashville Campaign. As reinforcements began to arrive, Johnston took on Sherman's advance at Kinston (Mar. 10) and Averasboro (Mar 16). The battle was indecisive, the bulk of Sherman's approaching army making Confederate success impossible. With all of the Army of

Tennessee up, Johnston tried to assault the Army of Georgia before Sherman could join his forces. Again, Sherman reacted too quickly, and Johnston fell back, losing 2,600 to Sherman's 1,600. Sherman reached Goldsboro on March 22, joining up with troops just in from the victory at Wilmington. Sherman now had 80,000 men, nearly four times Johnston's number.

Johnston reorganized all of his troops into the Army of Tennessee, but with Sherman's force being so large, and Lee retreating from Richmond, Johnston knew that it was all in vain. On April 13, he asked for an armistice to discuss terms. Sherman offered him a very generous settlement, including such political terms as the recalling of state legislatures to repeal secession. Secretary of War Edwin McM. Stanton (q.v.) was horrified by these sections and nullified the surrender pact. Sherman had to go back to Johnston, greatly embarrassed at his treatment by Stanton. But with the passage of the fleeing Confederate government past his lines and the anger generated by the assassination of President Abraham Lincoln (q.v.), Johnston quietly surrendered his forces on April 26 (the day John Wilkes Booth [q.v.] was killed), at Durham Station, without resuming hostilities. He received the same generous terms that Grant gave Lee.

CARPETBAGGERS. More than any other period of American history, the story of Reconstruction has been told as an encounter of good and evil. The prime villain of any Reconstruction melodrama has to be the Carpetbagger, who, in the words of one commentator, created an era of "cruel chicanery and political upheaval" in his "studied degradation of the conquered South."

According to the stereotype, the Carpetbagger was a low-life Yankee, newly arrived from the North with his total world's belongings stowed in a carpetbag, a popular valise of the time made from carpet materials for sturdiness, from which his nickname came. His intelligence was of a keen, corrupt manner, exceeded in its contemptibility only by his lack of decency and honor. A seeker of power and plunder, the Military Reconstruction Acts (q.v.) gave him his partners in opprobrium, the easily exploitable black voters and low-born Southern white traitors to their section, the Scalawags (q.v.). When the Carpetbagger was driven out of the South by the noble ex-Confederate Redeemers (q.v.), concluded the myth, he left behind a trail of corruption, misgovernment, and disturbed race relations.

Although the evil Carpetbagger is a caricature, it still holds in the popular imagination, North and South. Indeed, historians now like to use the term "outside whites" to get around the evils the stereotype imbues. But among historians of Reconstruction, the Carpetbagger portrait had been changing for the last quarter century, until the stereotype is hardly recognizable. Instead of a poor, low-born adventurer out to exploit the South, these men are now seen as Northerners with money who came South to invest in the land and its potentialities for the good of their communities, men who arrived right after the war and had no notion of entering government, men who were interested in everyday business, not Reconstruction politics. Indeed, the Yankees who came South after Appomattox to invest in plantations and planting had little trouble with their Southern white neighbors beyond a little social ostracism, common in 19th-century American for any outsiders or newcomers to an established area.

The Yankees who came South and stayed saw the place as a new frontier. The South was a land of opportunity, and the Northern emigrants expected to achieve much in business because they condescendingly saw the white and black Southerners as indolent. But the main problem with planting in the South was the weather immediately after the war. Much of the South was under drought conditions. Every planter, neophyte Northerner or experienced Southerner, was at its mercy. A lot of planters were going broke by 1867, and the recently arrived Yankees led the pack. Just as everyone seemed to be going broke (and the Northern newcomers had often invested thousands in their businesses), along came the Military Reconstruction Acts. A new field beckoned. Northerners in the South were among those who could vote without question. They could take any oath required, they were indisputably loyal to the Union, they could hold office at a time when Southern whites were still suspect. They also believed that they had a responsibility to serve. It was like enlisting in the war all over again. And that seems to be the key. To be a Carpetbagger in the Reconstruction sense of the word, one had to be a white Northerner who came south after the Civil War and at some time entered Republican (q.v.) politics.

Southerners and historians later accused the Carpetbaggers of disturbing racial relations in the South. On this account, they are indeed guilty. And this became in the end their real "crime." Carpetbag regimes rested their power on a widened democracy (in that all men could vote and hold office); guaranteed political rights as represented by the Thirteenth, Fourteenth, and Fifteenth Amendments (qq.v.) and the Military Reconstruction Acts; reapportioned representation; election rather than appointment to office (with the notable exception of Louisiana); public schools, although they did their best to avoid the question of integration, which might cost them votes among poorer whites who liked the rest of their program; public accommodations, even though it cost them Scalawag support because it was critical for black votes; Northern emigration to purify the South and help Republicanism politically; and internal improvements like highways and railroads. It was the Carpetbaggers who led the war against the Ku Klux Klan (q.v.) and organized the Union Loyal Leagues (q.v.) and the so-called Negro Militias (q.v.).

Although the Carpetbagger stereotype needs to be taken with a healthy grain of salt lest it continue to be reality and misinterpret the way things really were, it cannot be totally ignored, as more recent commentators would have it. Their role in Reconstruction was way too important for that. It was their need to earn a living through political patronage that gave the era much of its flavor of political factionalism based on personalities rather than ideology and their inability to build up unity in the fledgling Southern Republican Party that was central to Reconstruction's failure. Even though they were a distinct minority within the Republican Party in the South, they were its driving element for a South far different from the one that preceded them and the one that followed.

CARROLL, ANNA. *See* ANACONDA PLAN.

CASS, LEWIS (1782–1866). Born in New Hampshire, Lewis Cass was educated in Exeter Academy. When he was 19, he set out on foot for the Northwest Territory and read law in the new state of Ohio, was admitted to the bar, and served in the state legislature and as U.S. marshal. During the War of 1812, he entered the army and emerged as a brigadier general, instrumental in the battles against the British and Native Americans led by the Shawnee chieftain Tecumseh. From 1813 to 1831, he was the governor of Michigan Territory and President Andrew Jackson's secretary of war, where he directed the Black Hawk War and southeastern Indian removal. He was President Martin Van Buren's minister to Britain, resigning over his disagreement with the Webster–Ashburton Treaty.

In 1844, Cass sought the Democratic Party's (q.v.) presidential nomination by coming out for the annexation of Texas. Losing to James K. Polk, Cass served as Michigan's U.S. Senator 1845–1848, where he backed the annexation of Oregon and the War with Mexico and opposed the Wilmot Proviso (q.v.). Cass' solution to the question of slavery was squatter sovereignty (q.v.), the notion that the people in the territories ought to decide by a vote. But he would allow this at any time in the territorial process, which the South would not abide, preferring the Non-Exclusion Doctrine (q.v.) and a decision in the first state convention, a process later called popular sovereignty (q.v.). This cost Cass the presidency in 1848 to Zachary Taylor (q.v.).

Elected to the U.S. Senate again (1849–1857), Cass favored the Compromise of 1850 (q.v.). He was secretary of state under President James Buchanan (q.v.), resigning when Buchanan refused to take a strong stand against secession.

CASSVILLE. *See* ATLANTA CAMPAIGN.

CEDAR CREEK, BATTLE OF. *See* SHENANDOAH VALLEY CAMPAIGN, SECOND (SHERIDAN'S).

CEDAR MOUNTAIN, BATTLE OF. *See* MANASSAS CAMPAIGN, SECOND.

CHAFFIN'S FARM. *See* PETERSBURG, SIEGE OF.

CHAMBERLAIN, DANIEL H. (1835–1907). A South Carolina Carpetbagger (q.v.), Daniel H. Chamberlain was the next to youngest of 10 children born to a Massachusetts farmer. He grew up working on the farm, receiving a common school education. He also taught school for the money to go to a college prep school and eventually wound up at Yale College, where he worked at speech and debate, English composition, and classical languages (Greek and Latin). He graduated at the top of his class and went on to Harvard Law School. He was a confirmed antislavery Republican (q.v.) by now, but he was kept out of the war initially by the need to complete his education and repay some of the debts it cost him. Finally, the moral obligation of the war against slavery could no longer be denied. He enlisted in the Fifth Massachusetts (Colored) Cavalry, as a lieutenant, but saw little action.

Chamberlain came South in response to the accidental drowning of a friend who was serving as a teacher of freedmen, and stayed on to look things over. He saw the South as a place to make the money he needed to pay off his debts, but was lucky to break even. After two years, the Military Reconstruction Acts (q.v.) opened up another possibility—he could serve in the state convention, as a loyal white delegate. It also gave him a job that made good use of his legal education. He voted as a reformer for debt relief (he knew a lot about that firsthand), redistribution of land among the freedmen, elective state offices rather than appointive, reorganization of the court system, and equal rights.

Chamberlain made a good impression on the Republican delegates. Governor Robert K. Scott (q.v.) appointed him attorney general for the new government. He served on the state railroad and the land commissions. He also appealed to the taxpayers' revolt, setting himself up as an alternative to Scott in 1872. He proposed that corruption be controlled and whites be given a better chance of electing representatives by a system of proportional voting. If Charleston County, for example, had 18 representatives in the state legislature, give each voter 18 votes. He could cast them in any way, up to all 18 for one candidate or in any other proportion he wished. Chamberlain also appealed to Democrats (q.v.) like James L. Orr, who wished to create a single party of whites and blacks dedicated to honesty.

Chamberlain ran against Radical Republican Franklin J. Moses, Jr. (q.v.), in 1872 but lost. After two years of Moses and his cronies stealing the state blind, Chamberlain looked good in 1874. He also strengthened his appeal to black voters when he refused to keep black students out of the state university. He received a majority of nearly 12,000 votes, much less than either Scott or Moses had received, but enough to win a convincing victory.

As governor, Chamberlain tried to walk a narrow line between Republicans and Democrats, probably too difficult a job at that day and time for anyone. But he managed to put together a coalition of reform-minded blacks and whites in the legislature to work for an honest, economically run state government. Even hostile editors were impressed. He defeated many appropriation bills and kept tax rates down. But up-land Democrats wanted an independent, white-controlled party with its own Southern white candidate. They wanted Wade Hampton, a Confederate war hero. Hampton promised an end to Reconstruction and Yankee–Negro government. White militia groups, the Red Shirts (q.v.), began to organize and drill for action.

It soon became evident that the Democrats were not about to lose the election of 1876 in South Carolina to an honest vote. Race riots spread all over the area west of Columbia, those at Hamburg (q.v.) and Ellenton (q.v.) merely being the worst. Blacks were shot down at random, in their homes, on the roads, and in marketplaces. It mattered little that they were not engaged in political activities. Rifle Clubs (q.v.) heard speakers who warned that "the tall poppies will fall first."

When Chamberlain appealed for Federal military assistance, he was refused. Chamberlain issued a proclamation for the Rifle Clubs to disband. Knowing that the appearance of non-violence was more important than reality, Hampton complied. The result was a quiet election and a Democrat landslide. Although the electoral vote went to Rutherford B. Hayes (q.v.) for president, everyone in South Carolina knew that made little difference. It was the state elections that counted, nothing else.

At first, Chamberlain naïvely expected the Hayes administration would not allow Hampton to take over. But when troops were withdrawn from Louisiana, he realized that their removal from South Carolina was but a matter of time. Chamberlain left the state and took the New York bar exam. As time passed, Chamberlain did well for himself as a Wall Street lawyer. He continued to speak out for civil rights for African-Americans.

Then during the 1880s, Chamberlain began to change. Soon he was speaking out on the futility of basing government on the vote of the ignorant black voters. He switched to the Democratic Party and then became an Independent. As he spoke out against "Negro Rule," he lost many friends from his New England days, but heard again from old adversaries in South Carolina, impressed with Chamberlain's newly acquired "wisdom" on race. He was invited back to the Palmetto State and settled in Virginia, where he passed his years bedridden except for a few trips to the Johns Hopkins Medical Center for his health. He died in 1907.

CHAMPION'S HILL, BATTLE OF. *See* VICKSBURG CAMPAIGN.

CHANCELLORSVILLE, BATTLE OF. *See* CHANCELLORSVILLE CAMPAIGN.

CHANCELLORSVILLE CAMPAIGN. After the disastrous Mud March of the Fredericksburg Campaign (q.v.), the demoralized Union Army of the Potomac and its Confederate counterpart, the Army of Northern Virginia, settled down to endure winter, marked by plenty of cold, snow, and internecine snowball fights on each side of the Rappahannock River that frequently swelled to brigade-size conflicts. The demoralized Yankees received a new commander, Maj. Gen. Joseph Hooker (q.v.), an officer with a reputation for taking the war to the enemy, hence his sobriquet, "Fightin' Joe." Hooker proved to be as able an administrator as Maj. Gen. George B. McClellan (q.v.) had been. He reorganized the army, getting rid of Maj. Gen. Ambrose E. Burnside's (q.v.) unwieldy Grand Divisions of two corps each. Hooker reorganized the artillery into brigades attached to each infantry division, with a reserve of four brigades that could be sent to battle hot spots. He also reorganized his cavalry, from whom he expected a lot in the upcoming campaign. He gave much-needed furloughs to all ranks. Hooker was pleased with his results, bragging (as usual) that he commanded the "Finest Army on the Planet."

On the south side of the river, Gen. Robert E. Lee's (q.v.) main problem was feeding his army. As soon as it became apparent in early 1863 that the Federals would not launch any more winter marches, he sent Lt. Gen. James Longstreet (q.v.) and two divisions below Richmond to the Suffolk region. This chance at independent leadership pleased Longstreet, who seemed to have an inflated notion of his abilities to command. These pretensions would become more and more ingrained in his persona during the year 1863, leading to many controversies as to whether he measured up to expectations— his own and others. His attack against Union positions at Suffolk proved extraordinarily unimaginative and kept him out of the upcoming battles at Chancellorsville.

While Lee concentrated on foraging and guarding various river crossings, Hooker developed his plan of attack. Essentially, he would do about the same thing that Burnside had done for his January 1863 Mud March, except on a grander scale and in better weather. Hooker would march west up the Rappahannock and its tributary, the Rapidan, cross behind Lee, march through an area of overlogged forest full of secondary growth known as the Wilderness, and meet on open ground to the South. He hoped to entice Lee to abandon his entrenchments at Fredericksburg in late April 1863 and march south by launching Maj. Gen. George Stoneman's Union cavalry in a raid on undefended Richmond, using all of his horse soldiers but one brigade.

Right away Lee refused to do what Hooker expected him to do. Although the Federal cavalry was attempting to do in Stoneman's Raid what Confederate cavalry leader Maj. Gen. J. E. B. Stuart (q.v.) was an expert at, for the first time in the war in the East, Lee essentially ignored him. Richmond would have to defend itself. He calmly waited at Fredericksburg for Hooker to make his main move, which occurred on May 1, when Hooker's troops began crossing behind Lee. So far things had gone well. Hooker was actually ahead of Lee's response, and with a quick march, his men would be out of the Wilderness in open ground before Lee could stop him. Then Hooker lost his nerve. He ordered his army to stop in the middle of the Wilderness at a crossroads with a single, two-story house, called Chancellorsville.

Since Hooker had left a strong force behind to watch Lee at Fredericksburg, the Confederates could not respond to Hooker's march without doing the same. But since Hooker had stopped inside the forest, and the Confederates had better cavalry reconnaissance (Hooker's single brigade did little but sit around), Lee used the undergrowth to conceal his countermoves and hide the number of men he deployed. After all, one merely had to defend the main roads to foul up any of Hooker's future moves.

Lee immediately sent out a blocking force against Hooker's main thrust and called in his chief subordinate, Lt. Gen. Thomas J. "Stonewall" Jackson (q.v.), whose men had been guarding crossings downstream. By the afternoon of May 1, Hooker was still hesitating to move away from Chancellorsville. Instead, he had set up an unentrenched defensive line along the road heading west from Chancellorsville, with its flank wide open. Hooker was going to spend the night. Lee was off to the southeast, so there appeared no danger. Nothing but small bands of roving Confederate horsemen had been seen so far.

That night, these cavalry units reported Hooker's whole position and its vulnerable open flank to Lee. He and Jackson then thought up the most audacious plan Lee had employed so far. Outnumbered by two to one, Lee had already divided his army once. Now he proposed to divide it again, keeping a reinforced division at Fredericksburg, keeping two divisions himself in front of Hooker, and marching Jackson and three divisions across Hooker's front (concealed by the thick secondary growth), and strike the Federal right in full enfilade.

Jackson set off on May 2. The Wilderness proved not as much cover as he and Lee expected. Federals south of Chancellorsville reported his moves. Hooker was pleased. He thought Lee was retreating on Richmond. His plan was working. Hooker ordered his army in pursuit. They struck the tail of Jackson's column, severely battering his rear guard. But in reality, the farther south Hooker went now, the more he was stepping into Lee's trap.

By late in the afternoon, Jackson's men were in position. They overlapped Hooker's line by a full mile on each side. All warnings by the few alert Yankee units had been ignored. A few nervously turned to face west, just in case. The first warning that something was wrong was the flushing of small game through the Yankee position. Then came the Rebel yell, a bloodcurdling scream reminiscent of the one used by attacking Celts since time immemorial. Those Union units that stood to fight were overwhelmed in an instant. It was all over but the running.

Dusk and a cavalry charge by the 8th Pennsylvania brought an end to the fighting. Union officers worked to stabilize the lines. Jackson and his staff rode forward between the lines to reconnoiter the new Union positions for a possible night attack. They turned to come back into the Confederate lines. The edgy soldiers saw horsemen. Another cavalry charge. They opened fire. Stonewall Jackson and his staff were riddled by bullets. Jackson would have to have his left arm amputated and seemed to be recovering. Then the dreaded pneumonia set in, and he died a week after his greatest victory.

But Jackson or no, Hooker was in deep trouble. Lee was threatening to cut the Union army off from its river crossings. Placing Jackson's men under cavalry leader Stuart, Lee attacked again. Hooker, having been knocked senseless by a cannon shot that struck a pillar against which he had been leaning at the Chancellor House, ordered a retreat. Lee had two goals in mind—to cut Hooker off from crossing the river and to reunite his army, still widely separated. Some senior Union officers suspected that Lee was in more trouble than they, but Lee gave them little time to reconsider Hooker's orders. He attacked at Hazel Grove, rejoining his forces in a single line, at a dreadful cost in killed and wounded. The Federals who had attacked Jackson's rear the day before barely made it back to safety.

Meanwhile, the Federal troops under Maj. Gen. John Sedgwick at Fredericksburg had crossed over and assaulted the Confederate lines at Marye's Heights in the Second Battle of Fredericksburg. It took four tries, but soon Rebel defenders were pulling back in numerous directions. The victorious Sedgwick started for Lee's rear, trapping him between himself and Hooker. But Lee was not to be contained. He shifted his army eastward to meet this new threat, letting Hooker recross the Rappahannock untouched. On May 4, Lee boxed in Sedgwick against the Rappahannock at the Battle of Salem Church. Both Sedgwick and Hooker considered themselves lucky to escape across the river that night.

Casualties on both sides were heavy. Hooker lost 17,000, or 13 percent of his 133, 000. Fortunately for Lee, Hooker had failed to commit his whole force to the fray. Lee lost 13,000 or 22 percent of his 61,000 men available. He had put everyone in the fight, and many units had been completely smashed up in the heavy combat. Worst of all, he had lost the irreplaceable

Jackson. Lee would never be able to replace him. But he would reorganize his remaining army into three corps, instead of two, in an effort to do so. Lee's greatest victory at Chancellorsville would inexorably lead to his worst defeat at Gettysburg in the Pennsylvania Campaign (q.v.), two months later.

CHANDLER, ZACHARIAH (1813–1879). Born and educated in New Hampshire, Zach Chandler moved to Detroit in 1833, opened a general store, and graduated into trade, banking, and land speculation, becoming one of the richest men in Michigan. A Whig (q.v.) in politics, he served in the Zachary Taylor (q.v.) campaign and was elected mayor of Detroit in 1851. He tried for governor the following year, but was defeated. Angered by the slavery issue, he was one of the original organizers of the Republican Party (q.v.) in 1854 and a supplier of arms to the Free Soil settlers in Kansas. In 1856, he attended the Republican convention that nominated John Charles Frémont (q.v.) for the presidency and became a member of the national committee. In 1857, he succeeded Lewis Cass (q.v.) as U.S. senator, a position he held until 1875. In the Senate, Chandler was considered a Radical Republican, although he was not on speaking terms with Charles Sumner (q.v.) of Massachusetts, among others, and was chairman of the committee on rivers and harbors, from which he dispensed much party aid in the form of "pork barrel" legislation and appointments.

At the outbreak of the Civil War, Chandler stood against secession and raised and equipped the First Michigan Volunteer Infantry Regiment. The war gave him a golden opportunity to make himself heard, as he was on the critical Joint Committee on the Conduct of the War (q.v.). He also supported the Republican domestic program, especially the national banking system and the printing of greenbacks to finance the war.

Chandler was bitterly anti-British; he proposed a non-intercourse policy with them for their foot-dragging on the *Alabama* claims (q.v.) and suggested that the United States grant the same rights to any British enemy or colony that rebelled as Great Britain had given the defunct Confederacy. He was a die-hard Republican and chaired the party's national congressional campaign committee from 1868 to 1875. He was merciless in using political patronage to strengthen his own and the party's political base and ran Michigan as his own personal fiefdom. But the Democrat (q.v.) landslide of 1874 broke his power in the state, and he lost the upcoming race for the Senate. He accepted the position of secretary of the interior and partially cleaned up the corrupt and incompetent Indian agent system, until the Ulysses S. Grant (q.v.) administration fell from power in 1877. He was returned to the U.S. Senate in 1879 but died before he could make his influence felt again.

CHARLESTON CONVENTION (1860). The Democratic Party (q.v.) met on April 23, 1860, to select a candidate and a party platform for the election of 1860 (q.v.). The choice of the site was an unfortunate accident. It had been made four years earlier as a concession to Southern Democrats for agreeing to meet in Cincinnati in 1856. Now the bill was coming due. Charleston was the center of rabid Southern nationalism. This meant that the galleries would be filled by people who were close to secession in sentiment, and they would cheer on the most anti-Northern speeches and floor actions. If the convention were to be stampeded by the gallery crowd, it would be pro-Southern in its effect.

Charleston was very friendly to any Southern delegate. Gala parties, open doors to the best accommodations, the kisses of cheering women, all were reserved for delegates from the South. But the delegates from the Northwest and the Northeast had a rougher time of it. They received the worst of accommodations and were snubbed socially. Tammany Hall, the New York City machine, had the right idea. They rented a coastal steamboat and brought all of their fun, women, booze, and such with them. It cost a fortune, but it proved worth it.

As the convention met, delegates from all over the South were worried. They feared that a Republican (q.v.) victory would usher in an era of more Harper's Ferry Raids (q.v.). Murder, rape, and pillage of their homes would be the result. If the Republicans won, they would have control of all Federal offices in the South: postmasters, customs collectors, judges. It was a cinch that the Republicans would not be choosing their representatives from among the established gentry. The Republicans would appoint nonslaveholding whites or send their own people down.

The Southerners who were the most in favor of secession or independent action received the name "Fire-Eaters" (q.v.) They were always pushing at the parameters of decent debate. Many of these men saw a great opportunity in the creation of a new Southern nation, a place where they would have the ruling power. At a minimum, they saw the Democratic Party's leading candidate, Senator Stephen A. Douglas (q.v.), as a liar. His program of popular sovereignty (q.v.) had been revealed by astute questioning of his opponent during the 1858 election, Abraham Lincoln (q.v.), in the Lincoln–Douglas Debates, to be a cleverly constructed plan to exclude the pro-slave South from exploiting the territories equally with the nonslaveholding North. Douglas had said as much in his Freeport Doctrine (q.v.). Southern honor required that a trickster like Douglas be defeated and an honest man run in his place.

Before the convention met formally, delegates from Alabama, Florida, Texas, Mississippi, Arkansas, Louisiana, and Georgia had agreed to stand for the whole convention endorsing the Alabama Platform. This called for the open protection of slavery rights in the territories by active Federal action. This was the Non-Exclusion Doctrine that had been the majority opinion in the U.S. Supreme Court case Dred Scott *v.* Sandford (q.v.).

Northern Democrats knew that anything like the Alabama Platform would doom the party's chances in the North. Republicans would call them "Dough Faces," Northern men who yielded to Southern principles. But the Northerners had a weakness. Some of their number were made up of politicos from big city machines, who would sell their votes to the highest bidder. Furthermore, many of the big eastern cities owed their prosperity to carrying cotton to New England and Old Britain cotton mills. The return to the South with finished goods made in Northern factories, protected by the tariff on goods produced by the European competition, was also profitable. So while the Northern Democrats had the convention's biggest bloc of votes, nothing was guaranteed.

To appease all sides, the Douglas managers agreed to draw up the platform first. Usually the candidate was selected, then the platform passed. The platform committee, with heavy Southern representation, reported a modified Alabama Platform. Northern delegates talked it down on the floor. The galleries booed. The Southern delegates stalled the vote for days, knowing that the floor vote, dominated by Yankees, would be against them. Many Northern spectators and even some delegates had to leave for home, their expenses exhausted.

Finally the vote came, and the Alabama Platform went down to defeat. Instead the floor voted to reuse the 1856 Cincinnati Platform. This called for popular sovereignty, protection of all naturalized citizens to counter the anti-immigrant feeling of the American Party (q.v.), Federal subsidies for a transcontinental railroad, the acquisition of Cuba, and the condemnation of personal liberty laws and enforcement of the fugitive clause of the Compromise of 1850 (q.v.) as called for in the U.S. Supreme Court case Ableman v. Booth (q.v.).

Florida, Alabama, Mississippi, Louisiana, and Texas refused to vote on the platform issues. But they stayed on to get a shot at voting against Douglas' presidential nomination. The audience cheered their stance. When Douglas' managers criticized the Deep South States for their non-participation, Leroy Pope Walker (later in the Confederate cabinet) defended the South. In the North, he would have been shouted down by pro-Douglas galleries. Here he was hailed. Then, led by William L. Yancey, the author of the Alabama Platform, Alabama's delegation walked out of the hall. South Carolina, Florida, Mississippi, Louisiana, and Texas followed. Later Georgia and Arkansas left, too. They all met in another hall and adopted the Alabama Platform. They waited patiently for Douglas to call them back and reach some sort of accommodation.

But Douglas refused to give in. He knew that the Alabama Platform would not even carry the Border South, much less the North. Besides, Douglas had two-thirds of the remaining delegates (the number required for nomination in

CHASE BOOM • 121

the Democratic Party then) and expected to receive the party's nomination. But the Border South was not sure of this being fair. They got the convention to adopt the Tennessee Proposition. No man could receive nomination without two-thirds of the original delegates. That meant Douglas needed 203, not the 169 he had. Douglas and his backers decided to adjourn for six weeks and meet again at Baltimore—far enough South to be fair, but far enough North to be effective in getting Douglas the nod. Meanwhile, Douglas would let Yancey and his bolters stew until the Baltimore Convention (q.v.) met.

CHASE BOOM. In 1864, many Radical Republicans, disillusioned by what they perceived to be a halting policy by the Abraham Lincoln (q.v.) administration to win the war and free the slaves, began to look for an alternate candidate to represent the Republican Party (q.v.) better in the fall presidential elections. The first to present himself to the party was Lincoln's own Secretary of the Treasury Salmon P. Chase (q.v.). A perennial candidate for the White House who had lost out to Lincoln in 1860, Chase had placed his face on the one dollar National Bank note to put a campaign picture in every man's pocket. Now he floated a drive for the 1864 nomination that came to be called the Chase Boom.

In early February 1864, Chase began the boom by persuading fellow Ohio Republican, Sen. John Sherman (brother of the general), to issue a pamphlet, "The Next Presidential Election." It presented Lincoln as an incompetent. The pamphlet was so harsh and obviously untrue that it backfired. Sherman immediately revealed what had happened and denied prior knowledge of its contents. Chase did not flinch. He turned to Sen. Samuel Pomeroy of Kansas, a Radical Republican, who presented the "Pomeroy Circular" to the public. This pamphlet rehashed all of the Radical complaints against Lincoln as noncommittal and hesitant, and called for a more vigorous prosecution of the war by a better man. That man was strongly hinted at as being Chase.

Chase ought to have known that the pamphlet route was a dangerous one by now. Lincoln struck back through Postmaster General Montgomery Blair. A thorough hater of Chase, Blair accused the secretary of the treasury of accepting personal loans from powerful New York banker and financier Jay Cooke, who was the sole distributor of war bonds. Blair also accused Chase of favoritism and kickbacks in selecting treasury agents to purchase cotton from loyal Southern whites.

The result was the refusal of the Ohio state Republican Party to back Chase's candidacy as a favorite son at the National Union Party Convention (a combination of Republicans and War Democrats). Embarrassed at last, Chase offered his resignation to Lincoln, another habit of his when things did not go his way. He told Lincoln falsely that Sherman and Pomeroy had used his name without his knowledge. Lincoln refused to accept the resignation.

But the respite was short. Soon Lincoln and Chase had it out over the appointment to the New York Customs House, a traditional treasury bailiwick. Lincoln gave Chase a list of three candidates. Chase did not like any, because they had been picked by Secretary of State William H. Seward (q.v.), a New Yorker. Lincoln told him to pick one. Chase refused and resigned. This time Lincoln accepted it.

Chase was mortified that his usual ploy had backfired. Then the position of chief justice of the Supreme Court opened up with the death of Roger B. Taney of Dred Scott v. Sandford (q.v.) fame. Chase wanted the job badly. He was well-qualified. Lincoln let him stew for some weeks, before appearing to give in. With this appointment, Chase was brought back into the fold, after the election of 1864 had ended with a Lincoln victory.

CHASE, SALMON P. (1808–1873). Born in New Hampshire, where he received an excellent education in public schools and from a private tutor, Salmon P. Chase went to Ohio under the care of his uncle, the first bishop of the Episcopal church there. Completing his boyhood education under his uncle's guidance, Chase returned to New Hampshire to attend Dartmouth College. Graduating in 1826, he taught school in Washington, D.C., until he read for and passed the bar in 1829. He went back to Ohio to practice and became one of Cincinnati's best-known lawyers in short order. He lectured in the Lyceum and wrote a collection of the laws of Ohio, which greatly enhanced his reputation and became a standard course of study. He gained many lucrative fees representing various banks, but his fees grew so pricey that his business fell off. Meanwhile, he married three women in succession, all of whom died early, and fathered six children, only two of whom lived to adulthood.

About 1840, Chase became interested in the antislavery movement. His main interest was free speech of abolitionists rather then the travails of the African-American or the need of the North to secede from the Union (an early abolitionist doctrine) to end the institution. Chase was a poor orator but a sound thinker and good writer. He worked behind the scenes for the Liberty Party and later the Free Soil Party (q.v.) in preparing speeches and platforms. Chase also gave much work to defending fugitive slaves from being returned South, so much so that he was known as the "attorney general of fugitive slaves." He maintained that the Fugitive Slave Act of 1793 allowed recovery of runaways from the original 13 states, and that states west of the mountains were protected from such measures by the Land Ordinance that preceded the Constitution itself. He maintained that evil laws could not properly be passed, as they went against the superior laws of nature.

Although Chase had been a delegate to the 1832 presidential nominating convention for the coalition that eventually became the Whig Party (q.v.), he stayed out of politics until he joined with the Liberty Party and the Free Soil Party (q.v.) to oppose slavery in the 1840s. He was instrumental in dissolving the Liberty Party and reconstituting it as the Free Soil Party in 1848 and nominating former president Martin Van Buren for president at a convention over which Chase presided. Working to manipulate the fragmented parties represented in the Ohio legislature, Chase managed to get himself elected to the U.S. Senate in 1849. He fought against the Compromise of 1850 and tended to act with the Democrats (q.v.) in organizing the Senate for business. But in reality, he was not happy with either party. He became the leader of the opposition to the Kansas–Nebraska Act (q.v.) in 1854, and in 1855 the "Anti-Nebraska" Convention in Ohio nominated him as a candidate for governor under the new Republican label, after the Democrat-dominated state legislature refused to reelect him to the U.S. Senate. Chase was reelected governor in 1857 and his administrative abilities and stance in favor of black rights made him a power to be reckoned with in the Republican Party (q.v.) nationally. In 1860, as the nation threatened to break up over the slavery issue, Chase was returned to the Senate as a Republican.

But Chase had bigger things in mind. He got bit by the presidential bug in a big way. The rest of his life would see him jockey for the presidency, always unsuccessfully, and often embarrassingly. His greatest asset was the able assistance of his beautiful and knowledgeable daughter, Kate, whose tremendous (some would say prurient) personality often made up for her father's shortcomings. He came up short for the nomination in 1860, but the winner, Abraham Lincoln (q.v.), included him in his cabinet (along with everyone else who had sought the Republican nomination that year, like William H. Seward (q.v.), Simon Cameron, and Edward Bates) as secretary of the treasury. As the head of the Department of the Treasury, Chase was brilliant. He reorganized the almost bankrupt treasury, recommended new taxes, supported confiscation of Rebel property, borrowed money and maintained the national credit, created greenback currency (putting his face on the dollar bill so that every voter might have a miniature campaign poster for the upcoming 1864 presidential race in his pocket), established the national banking system that had been the keystone of the Republican platform, and administered the department so well on a day-to-day basis as to be still considered one of the best secretaries the treasury has ever had.

On the other hand, Chase could not stop seeking the presidency, a process he hoped to abet by advancing a Radical Republican program. He backed Maj. Gen. Benjamin F. Butler' s (q.v.) idea of declaring runaway slaves "contraband," opposed colonization of ex-slaves abroad, supported the Emancipation Proclamation (q.v.), advocated arming blacks as soldiers, criticized the Army's employment of freed blacks in government plantations as re-enslavement, and advocated land redistribution among the freed slaves.

He was especially miffed when President Lincoln tended to ignore his freely offered advice, the president preferring to rely on the more moderate tenets of Secretary of State Seward. He gave secret cabinet discussions to the Radical Republicans, who considered Lincoln to be a foot-dragger on the slavery issue, and claimed that the president's advisors were hopelessly under the hand of the allegedly scheming Seward. When Lincoln called Chase's bluff in front of a congressional delegation (he had to deny that the cabinet was bickering or reveal that he was a congressional mole), Chase resigned his office. Seward had already tendered his resignation to give Lincoln a free hand with Congress, but Lincoln returned both documents and asked the two men to stay on for the good of the country. This began a charade of Chase regularly handing in his resignation during the next year only to see Lincoln refuse it.

Finally, in 1864, Chase foolishly backed the "Pomeroy Circular," which claimed that Lincoln needed to be replaced with a better man (like Chase) to win the election later that year. Once again, Chase felt obliged to resign but Lincoln kept the letter to see the secretary squirm. In July, over a minor patronage problem, Chase resigned once more and this time, considering him no longer a possible opponent for the nomination, Lincoln accepted it. Chase was mortified. Lincoln then dangled the possibility of a Supreme Court seat before Chase and, after an appropriate period of cat and mouse during which Chase begged for the job, Lincoln put him up for chief justice. Many in Congress knew of Chase's duplicitous character and were not pleased with the nomination, but Lincoln insisted.

As chief justice, Chase had his good and bad moments. He continued to be active in his support of the Freedmen's Bureau (q.v.), the granting of the franchise to blacks, and numerous freedmen's benevolent societies. He stayed out of Congress's dispute over the nature of Reconstruction (q.v.) with President Andrew Johnson (q.v.), although he drew up a preliminary draft for what would become the Fourteenth Amendment (q.v.). After the passage of the Military Reconstruction Acts (q.v.), Chase refused to ride circuit in Virginia and North Carolina until they had been readmitted to the Union, fearing that to sit in militarily occupied areas would make the court lose prestige and admit to the veracity of the Johnson government. He refused to sit on the case of Jefferson Davis (q.v.) until after Johnson's pardon of him made the point moot. He declared his own greenbacks as not good enough for legal tender and then saw a reconstituted court reverse him. He dissented from the court majority in key cases concerning Reconstruction, but he wrote the majority opinion in Texas v. White (q.v.), which decided that the nation was an indestructible, perpetual Union of the states. He supervised the impeachment of Johnson and kept the hearing fair. And, of course, he had friends put his name up before the Republican convention in 1868, but lost out to Ulysses S. Grant (q.v.). He also toyed with the possibility of running as a Democrat, but the idea was not well received.

Historians consider the Chase Court to be one of great unity, an amazing feat when one looks at the numerous prickly personalities who served, and Chase himself. Of 170 cases, there was dissent for various reasons in only 20. As usual, Chase proved to be an able administrator. He also managed to walk the Court down a fine line between its own independence as a branch of government and possible domination by a Congress interested in its own supremacy in government. In 1870, Chase suffered a stroke that left him partially paralyzed on his right side and without speech. He refused to resign the bench and, although he missed one term, recovered enough to sit on the bench for two more terms and consider another presidential bid in 1872, as a Liberal Republican (q.v.). Once again the vivacious Kate ran the campaign, trying to convince the skeptical delegates that the chief justice was up to the job. But a second stroke felled him on a campaign trip to New York City, where he died on 6 May 1873. *See also* GRANT, ULYSSES S., ADMINISTRATION—DOMESTIC POLICIES.

CHASE–SHELLABARGER THEORY OF FORFEITED RIGHTS. *See* RECONSTRUCTION, THEORIES OF.

CHATTAHOOCHIE RIVER, BATTLE OF. *See* ATLANTA CAMPAIGN.

CHATTANOOGA, BATTLES OF. *See* CHATTANOOGA CAMPAIGN.

CHATTANOOGA CAMPAIGN. On New Year's 1863, the two armies facing each other in central Tennessee after the conclusion of the Perryville Campaign (q.v.) with the Battle at Stone's River were exhausted. The Confederate Army of Tennessee under Gen. Braxton Bragg (q.v.) had withdrawn south of the Duck River around Tullahoma. President Jefferson Davis (q.v.) had sent Gen. Joseph Johnston (q.v.) to coordinate military activities in the West, but Johnston had little idea of what to do. He proposed that the Rebels be ready to give up ground for consolidation of their 80,000 men scattered about between Vicksburg and Tullahoma, but Davis saw that as politically untenable. Johnston was not helped any by the fact that all commanders reported directly to Davis and not through him. Gen. Bragg was embroiled with his officer corps, still arguing over their roles at Perryville and Stone's River. When Davis asked Johnston to intervene, Johnston refused to get involved. He feared that Bragg would see any move he made as coveting command of the army for himself. And Johnston feared he might actually get command if he threw Bragg out.

Fortunately for the Rebels, the Union Army of the Cumberland under Maj. Gen. William S. Rosecrans (q.v.) sat in Murfreesboro for the next 169 days, without a movement. Washington saw the inactivity of all of its forces as outrageous. President Abraham Lincoln's (q.v.) chief of staff, Maj. Gen. Henry W. Halleck (q.v.), offered a major generalship in the regular army (almost all Union Civil War ranks were in the volunteers and temporary) to any general officer who would bring him the first important victory. Rosecrans found that he (much like Bragg on the other side) was in charge of a "stepchild army," receiving everything only after the forces in the East had been provided for.

But Rosecrans had many problems, not to mention that his army was shot to pieces at Stone's River. He was 170 miles from his supply base at Louisville, the railroad was severely damaged and susceptible to attack from Confederate cavalry raiders, and he lacked cavalry to compete with the famed Rebel horse soldiers of Nathan Bedford Forrest (q.v.) and John Hunt Morgan. With Forrest and Morgan present, Union cavalry was outnumbered four to one. Even when Forrest and Morgan were absent, which was often given Confederate command quarrels and glory-seeking raids, the Federal horsemen were outnumbered two to one.

Rosecrans took to mounting infantry to make up the difference. The first brigade he put on horseback was commanded by Col. Abel D. Streight. When he tried to emulate his confederate counterparts in Streight's Raid, he and his command were promptly captured. Rosecrans had better luck with Col. John Wilder's brigade. Called the Lightening Brigade, Wilder had his men throw in three month's salary to purchase Spencer repeating rifles. Then he and his men rode to battle and dismounted to fight. The Spencers allowed him to maintain the firepower of the 25 percent of his men detached to hold the horses while the others fought on foot. But in spite of Rosecrans' inventiveness, a quarter of his army's entire strength was used up just protecting his supply line.

By mid-June 1863, Rosecrans was ready to move. The Tullahoma Campaign was a Civil War classic. Rosecrans faked against Bragg with his right flank and advanced through the Cumberland Mountains with his left, using Wilder's men and their repeaters as shock troops to turn Bragg out of his prepared positions. Each time Bragg tried to stop and fight, he found Wilder's men in his rear, necessitating a retreat all the way to Chattanooga. Rosecrans' moves were masterful—they were exactly what the theorist Baron Antoine Henri Jomini (q.v.) called for in his book, lots of maneuver and little fighting. (Rosecrans lost just under 600 men in the whole campaign, the Confederates about twice that.) Unfortunately for Rosecrans, his brilliant campaign took place during the Gettysburg and Vicksburg (q.v.) fights and was lost to history.

Rosecrans' next target was Chattanooga, the gateway to Atlanta and the Deep South. In reality, Chattanooga was a fortification that was a trap. Whoever held it could easily be outmaneuvered by any clever opponent who used its hills and parallel mountains to conceal his approach. There were over one hundred crossings of the Tennessee River to watch, and Bragg did not have the strength to do it. Rosecrans did the exact opposite of Tullahoma. This time he faked left and moved right, driving deep into Alabama and threatening North Georgia. On September 10, Wilder's brigade entered Chattanooga without having to fire a shot. Jomini would have been pleased. Lincoln sure was.

But now Rosecrans' cleverness was about to catch up with him. His army was split into three main columns, each hidden from the others as well as the Confederates by the parallel mountain ridges that make up this foot of the Appalachians. The Confederates still suffered from internecine command quarrels. They lacked good intelligence, Rebel cavalry in the West being better at raids than information gathering. But after Gettysburg and Vicksburg, the Union forces stagnated, permitting the Confederates to rush detachments to reinforce Bragg, without the information getting to Rosecrans. Most important was the removal of most of Lt. Gen. James Longstreet's (q.v.) corps from Gen. Robert E. Lee's (q.v.) Army of Northern Virginia. Longstreet and his men took the rails through the Carolinas to Atlanta and rode north to reach Bragg in mid-September.

As reinforcements rolled in, Bragg made three attempts to corner a section of Rosecrans' army in little valleys or hollows, called "coves" in northern Alabama. Rosecrans' men managed to avoid these traps, but Rosecrans came to fear the dispersed nature of his advance and called his army together along the banks of Chickamauga Creek. Bragg hoped to crush the left of Rosecrans' north–south line, driving him away from Chattanooga and trapping him against the mountains. On September 19, the Confederates attacked. But Rosecrans managed to send a Corps under Maj. Gen. George H. Thomas to the left to counter Bragg's move and hold open the door to Chattanooga.

The next day proved to be a disaster for Rosecrans. Longstreet's men arrived, literally jumping from the rail cars into the fray. As Rosecrans adjusted his line toward Chattanooga, his staff mistakenly ordered one division to advance north to line up next to another. Rosecrans had assumed that the two units were side by side and merely needed to adjust slightly to close the line. But in reality there was a third unit in between them. The men on the field suspected something was awry, but Rosecrans had angrily criticized the officer of the moving unit some time before for not carrying out orders with sufficient alacrity. He moved quickly now, despite the fact that the shift north opened an enormous gap in the Union line. And as luck would have it, right through that hole came Longstreet's whole corps.

It was all over but the running. Everyone ran, Rosecrans being carried on ignominiously with the others. They did not stop until they had reached Chattanooga. But suddenly the pursuing Confederates struck a unit that did not yield. It was Thomas on the far left. He and his men held Snodgrass Hill in a horseshoe-like formation. Reinforced by a reserve unit, Thomas managed to blunt the Confederate attack until the rest of the army could retreat off the field. Then he followed them after dark.

Although Thomas had saved the day, he was unwittingly helped out when Longstreet concentrated on him instead of sending men to close off the gap through which the Yankees were fleeing. Moreover, Bragg had become so accustomed to losing, he could not believe he had won. But the victory had not come on the northern flank of the armies as he had planned. So he ignored it, also wasting men assaulting Thomas. It took a day for Bragg to realize he had won. The next day he canceled any pursuit because he believed that Rosecrans would have to abandon Chattanooga. Then it took another day before he realized that Rosecrans, regardless of suffering 16,000 casualties, was going to hold the town.

So Bragg settled down to the prolonged Siege of Chattanooga. Besides, he had more important game in mind. He wanted to settle accounts with his generals once again. The Confederate loss of 17,000, just under a third of his force, the worst loss in numbers engaged of any Confederate army in the war, would ultimately be in vain, because Rosecrans still possessed the objective of the whole campaign, Chattanooga.

While Bragg readied himself to purge his officer corps, Rosecrans had to feed his horses and men trapped in the city. The Rebel encirclement was at first very incomplete. But it was effective. The Tennessee River was unnavigable from low water. The railroad had been smashed for months and was under Confederate fire. A wagon road parallel to the tracks was also under fire. But there was a route open north of the fortress that ran over Walden's Ridge and the Cumberland Plateau to Nashville. Rosecrans put his whole force on two-thirds rations, with local commanders able to reduce this to half rations of their own volition. Everything went well until Confederate cavalry hit Walden's Mountain and wiped out an 800-wagon supply train on October 2.

Meanwhile, back in Washington, Rosecrans was undercutting himself through his political views, which he stupidly put in writing. It seemed innocuous enough. Rosecrans came out in favor of forgiveness to reconstruct Tennessee in time for the 1864 election. It sounded a lot like Lincoln. But Secretary of War Edwin McM. Stanton (q.v.) and others disliked this military interference with politics. It sounded to them a lot like what Maj. Gen. George B. McClellan (q.v.) had done during the 1862 Seven Days Campaign (q.v.). Another Democrat (q.v.) spouting off to compromise Republican (q.v.) rule. But Rosecrans was quite popular in Ohio, and the Republicans needed this to defeat Clement L. Vallandigham (q.v.) for governor. So Stanton swallowed his objections until Rosecrans had helped win the election for John Brough, the Union candidate.

To get more information to use against Rosecrans, Stanton sent Assistant Secretary of War Charles Dana to Chattanooga to spy on headquarters there. Then Stanton met Maj. Gen. Ulysses S. Grant (q.v.) in Ohio to talk over combining his army with Rosecrans' to raise the Siege of Chattanooga. Although Lincoln still had faith in Rosecrans, he agreed that Stanton could send in Grant with two orders, one relieving Rosecrans and one keeping him. Given Grant's dislike of Rosecrans, it was not hard to figure out which order he used. Rosecrans left on October 19, replaced by Thomas.

On the other side of the lines, the Confederate command situation was falling apart. Bragg got to be so petulant that President Davis had to come in from Richmond to straighten things out. Davis decided to keep Bragg on regardless. Davis doubted Longstreet's ability in separate command, and he hated Joseph Johnston and Gen. P. G. T. Beauregard (q.v.), the other possibilities. So Davis permitted Bragg to purge the high command by reorganizing his army and shipping those he disliked to other areas. Often the troops went with their officers, so Bragg was weakening the siege at the same time that Grant was strengthening it with the arrival of Maj. Gen. William T. Sherman (q.v.) and his army from Memphis and two corps under Maj. Gen. Joseph Hooker (q.v.) from the East.

As Bragg was doing his best to lose the siege, Grant did his best to relieve it from his side. In doing so, Grant used a plan first thought up by the now-departed and discredited Rosecrans. He attacked to the west of Chattanooga at Brown's Ferry and Wauhatchie (October 26–27) and opened a road up to the rail head at Bridgeport, Alabama. Troops called this outlet to provisions the "Cracker Line." Bragg, absorbed by his command struggles, did not even deign to notice.

Next, Grant needed room in front of Chattanooga to maneuver. He sent in Thomas' Army of the Cumberland, whose fighting abilities it was no secret he suspected since Chickamauga, on November 23. Thomas' men took the hill with little trouble. Bragg now expected an attack to his right at Tunnel Hill, part of the long Missionary Ridge that faced Chattanooga. But Grant surprised him and attacked Lookout Mountain on Bragg's left flank. Towering above the clouds, Lookout Mountain looked formidable, but that was not so. Its sides were so steep that insufficient rifle fire and no artillery fire could be brought to bear on an attacker. The "Battle Above the Clouds" took place on November 24, everyone uncertain as to its outcome until a parting of the mists revealed the Union flag flying at its summit.

Now Grant hit Tunnel Hill (November 25) with Sherman's force, still doubting the combat abilities of Thomas' Army of the Cumberland. Sherman was checked all day. An attempt to hit the Rebels from Lookout Mountain also failed, a deep creek without fords or unwrecked bridges temporarily blocking the way.

Grant was getting desperate. He asked Thomas to make a spoiling attack to draw Rebels off of Sherman. Thomas sent his men in to take the first rifle pits at the foot of Missionary Ridge. By now the Army of the Cumberland had had it with Grant's condescending attitude toward them. They took the first line of Confederate defense and just kept right on going without orders. They went right over the crest, sending Bragg and his men scurrying for Georgia at a run. The Rebel army was saved when Maj. Gen. Patrick Cleburne and his men, the same who had held up Sherman at Tunnel Hill, drove back the Yankee pursuit at Ringgold Gap (November 27). Each side had lost about 5,000–6,000 men. The Confederates had seen about 2,000–4,000 of their men taken prisoner.

Bragg finally realized that he was finished. He resigned as commander of the Confederate Army of Tennessee on November 28. The Campaign for Chattanooga had settled several things. It was the real turning point of the war, the end of Confederate aspirations. Hereafter, the Rebels fought for survival more than for independence. It revealed Thomas and Sherman to be worthy subordinates to Grant. It paved the way for Grant to become lieutenant general. And it finally proved Bragg, the officer who came out of the War with Mexico with the best reputation of anyone, to be one of the worst the Civil War produced. But he still came out ahead—President Davis called him to Richmond as his personal military advisor.

CHATTANOOGA, SIEGE OF. *See* CHATTANOOGA CAMPAIGN.

CHICAGO CONVENTION (1860). In May 1860, the Republican Party (q.v.) met in its second national political convention. The Democrats (q.v.) had just broken up their Charleston Convention (q.v.) without nominating a candidate. Although the Republicans did not yet know what was about to happen to the Democrats, that they would nominate two separate candidates at the Baltimore Convention (q.v.) and the Richmond Convention, they did know that they had a good chance to win the presidency by taking a minority of the popular vote and the majority of the electoral vote. The election of 1856 (q.v.) had already demonstrated that possibility. By keeping the 95 electoral votes they obtained in 1856, they only needed to add 57 more to win.

The Republicans had two courses they could follow in getting those critical 57 votes. They could go for the border states (59 votes), but this was compromised by their antislavery stance. Or the party could go for Ohio (23), Pennsylvania (27), and either Indiana (11) or Illinois (13). This latter strategy determined who would be nominated.

The Republicans held their convention in Chicago, Illinois. The convention hall was a special 180-by-100-foot building constructed for the convention, called the Wigwam. It held 10,600 spaces in its winding galleries on three sides of the hall for spectators. Its floor sloped so that all those on the floor could see the dais. Since the site was in Illinois, the galleries were packed with supporters of a local man, Abraham Lincoln (q.v.). Every time a supporter of another candidate got up to answer the call of nature, a Lincoln man took his place.

The Republican front runners were William H. Seward (q.v.) of New York and Salmon P. Chase (q.v.) of Ohio. Both men were U.S. senators. Seward was part of the old Whig (q.v.) machine in Upper New York, headed by newspaperman Thurlow Weed. Seward ran by talking radically against slavery at home and operating conservatively in the Senate. But he was well-known and had a lot of baggage to carry. Worst of all, his man had just barely won the New York governor's race by 615 votes. It made him look weak. Chase had his problems, too. He had an overinflated idea of his importance to America. It made him overbearing, transparently ambitious, and smug. Although he had a spot in the Ohio delegation, his home district had elected anti-Chase delegates. He, too, looked weak.

What the Republicans needed was someone reliable who was moderate on every issue of the day. There were several men who might fit the bill. Edward Bates of Missouri was an old-line Whig, but he was too old and a latecomer to the party. He might not be reliable enough. Nathaniel Banks of Massachusetts was an ex-Democrat, but he was too anti-immigrant and might alienate too many new citizens. Simon Cameron of Pennsylvania was an ex-Democrat from a necessary state, but corruption was his middle name. He thought that favors could win any election.

Actually, in hindsight, it is easy to see why Lincoln won. Not only was he from a key state, he was exactly the kind of man the party needed. He was homey, homely, and relatively honest. He stood in the correct spot on all of the issues. He also had a team of excellent managers, Norman Judd and David Davis. Judd isolated Seward's and Chase's delegates so they could influence few undecided men. He saw to it that Lincoln men were in the galleries and gave free transport to any who would come and cheer for Illinois. Davis was the deal maker. He promised appointments to everyone who would abandon another candidate for Lincoln. Some of these deals left a bitter taste in one's mouth, but Lincoln would honor them all.

On the third ballot, Davis got New Jersey to switch to Lincoln. Cameron got on the bandwagon for promised appointments for himself and his cronies. Ohio abandoned Chase and gave Lincoln the last four votes he needed. The vice presidential candidate was Hannibal Hamlin of Maine, to balance Lincoln as a westerner. The Republican platform was a masterpiece of economic promises to every special interest in the North. Only one small section referred to slavery not being allowed in the territories. The proof in the deal making and the platform would come in the election of 1860 (q.v.).

CHICKAMAUGA, BATTLE OF. *See* CHATTANOOGA CAMPAIGN.

CHIRIQUÍ. *See* COLONIZATION OF AFRICAN-AMERICANS OVERSEAS.

CITRONELLE, SURRENDER AT. After the surrender of the Confederate armies, led by Gen. Robert E. Lee (q.v.) (April 9, 1865) at the end of the Appomattox Campaign (q.v.), and Gen. Joseph E. Johnston (q.v.) (April 26) at the end of the Carolinas Campaign (q.v.), the only other major Rebel troops west of the Mississippi River were in the Old Southwest, commanded by Lt. Gen. Richard Taylor. In communication with Federal Maj. Gen. E. R. S. Canby (q.v.) since April 19, Taylor hoped to gain some political advantages (recognition of existing state governments and amnesty for civil officials) for the former Confederacy, as had Johnston in his negotiations with Maj. Gen. William T. Sherman (q.v.). By April 21, Canby informed Taylor that such considerations had been unceremoniously rejected by Secretary of War Edwin McM. Stanton (q.v.). Johnston then had surrendered on the same terms as Lee.

On May 4, after some delay contemplating what the full loss of political rights meant for white Southerners, Taylor met Canby at Citronelle, Alabama, some 40 miles north and west of Mobile. Canby offered Taylor the same terms as those given Lee. Public property was to be turned in to local Union provost marshals, parole given at the same time, with officers to keep their horses and sidearms. Further, Canby agreed to allow Taylor's men to utilize public transportation and draw Federal rations for their trips home. At least 40,000 men came in under Taylor's surrender terms.

CIVIL RIGHTS ACT OF 1866. Drawn up by the Joint Committee of Fifteen on Reconstruction, the Civil Rights Bill of 1866 nationalized citizenship for the first time in American history (it had been a prerogative of the individual states before the Civil War) by defining a citizen as anyone born or naturalized in the United States. All citizens received certain rights, among which were right to jury trial, to sue and be sued, to give evidence, to be on juries, and to receive full protection of the laws. No one could be denied these rights without due process of the law (a court proceeding), and the Federal courts were to have sole jurisdiction in these cases. This measure was a part of Moderate Republican Reconstruction (q.v.) and had to be passed over President Andrew Johnson's (q.v.) veto. His refusal to include this measure voluntarily as a part of Reconstruction caused Congress to put part of this measure in the first section of the Fourteenth Amendment (q.v.) to guarantee its availability to future generations protected from ordinary repeal, and to overcome the possibility that the U.S. Supreme Court might find it contrary to the ruling in an 1857 case, Dred Scott *v.* Sandford (q.v.), which declared blacks, free or slave, not to be American citizens. This was the first major piece of legislation enacted by Congress over a presidential veto in American history.

CIVIL RIGHTS ACT OF 1870. *See* ENFORCEMENT ACT, FIRST.

CIVIL RIGHTS ACTS OF 1871. *See* ENFORCEMENT ACT, SECOND.

CIVIL RIGHTS ACT OF 1875. A lifelong project of Massachusetts Senator Charles Sumner (q.v.), the Civil Rights Act of 1875 was the congressional answer to the Supreme Court's curtailing of the wider implications of the Fourteenth Amendment (q.v.). It was essentially America's first public accommodations law and guaranteed citizens of every race the "full and equal" enjoyment and use of inns, public conveyances, and theaters and other places of public amusement. It also had a section that race was not to be a factor in excluding persons from service on grand (indictment) and petit (trial) juries. But to the disappointment of many, it left out any mention of equal schools, cemeteries, and church attendance. These were politically inexpedient measures so far as Congress was concerned, North and South being filled with voters prejudiced against African-Americans in the more personal areas of American life. Indeed, if the Civil Rights Act of 1875 had not been presented as a memorial to Senator Sumner, who had just died, it might not have been enacted at all. North and South people thought the demands of the bill to be an invasion of individual personal prerogatives. But it went a long way in correcting what blacks and their white allies saw as the shortcomings presented in the restrictions on the Fourteenth Amendment in the Slaughterhouse Cases (q.v.). The Supreme Court gutted the public accommodations sections in the 1883 Civil Rights Cases (q.v.), although it upheld the jury section in Strauder *v.* West Virginia.

CIVIL RIGHTS CASES (1883). In the Civil Rights Cases (1883), the Supreme Court ruled that the Fourteenth Amendment did not in any way imbue Congress with the power to interfere in the domain of state legislation. The amendment instead provided a relief to people adversely affected by certain state legislation. This ruling attacked the equal accommodations section of the Civil Rights Act of 1875 (q.v.) as not operating on a specific state action but instead affecting the desires of private individuals. This was not the purpose of the Fourteenth Amendment, said the Court, although it had earlier (1880) upheld the parts of the Civil Rights Act of 1875 pertaining to the right of blacks to serve on juries (Strauder *v.* West Virginia and Virginia *v.* Rives), which the court saw as a valid exercise of the amendment. But the Court stated that it believed that at some point black Americans had to cease being objects of special treatment under the law and be dealt with the same as any other citizen.

CIVIL SERVICE COMMISSION. *See* GRANT, ULYSSES S., ADMIN-ISTRATION—DOMESTIC POLICIES.

CIVIL SERVICE REFORM. *See* GRANT, ULYSSES S., ADMINISTRA-TION—DOMESTIC POLICIES.

CLAYTON, POWELL (1833–1914). Carpetbag (q.v.) governor of Arkansas, Powell Clayton was from a Pennsylvania family that had come over with William Penn. He studied engineering and went to Kansas in 1855. He was not a fighter in the antislavery wars that plagued that territory. He went to Leavenworth because he disliked the Free Soilers at Lawrence. He was elected as city engineer as a Democrat (q.v.) (his family had been noted Whigs [q.v.]). But although Clayton was not an abolitionist, he was an unequivocal Unionist. When the Civil War came, he raised a company and went off to fight as a captain of infantry. After the short three months' enlistment, he raised a cavalry regiment and rode off to free Arkansas from the Rebels. He rose in rank to brevet brigadier general when he made a name for himself defending Pine Bluff from a Confederate attack in 1863.

After the war, Clayton settled down in Pine Bluff to plant cotton. He married an Arkansas girl, apparently with the blessing of her Rebel parents. As President Andrew Johnson (q.v.) squared off against Congress, Clayton found himself growing disillusioned with the Democratic Party and declined an opportunity to run for Congress on the Democrat ticket. But he was worried by the growing raids of nightriders and the threats against all Yankees. After the passage of the Military Reconstruction Acts (q.v.), Clayton decided that he had to stand for the Union once again and joined with local black and white Republicans (q.v.). He quickly rose to the top of the state's party infrastructure and would dominate it until his death.

Elected governor in 1868, Clayton spoke in favor of transportation projects, especially railroads, public schools, creation of a loyal militia, and encouraging emigration from outside the state. Clayton could not fathom the fear of Negro-dominated government in Arkansas, as but a quarter of the population was black. But Ku Klux Klan (q.v.) attacks on Republicans continued, many of them racially inspired. Unlike other Reconstruction governors, Clayton did not hesitate a moment. He proclaimed martial law and called out the "black and tan" (q.v.) militia and pacified the whole state in a series of military campaigns reminiscent of those he fought successfully during the war, using agents and spies who joined the local klaverns and tipped the militia off to the Ku Klux's next moves. Clayton marked his men with red scarves and hat bands, and their arrests paid off in numerous convictions and hangings that gave the governor a national reputation. He revived the state's credit rating, made the atmosphere congenial for railroad and logging investors, and kept public schools active. Meanwhile, a hunting accident caused him to lose his left hand—after he had emerged from four years of war unscratched.

His real opposition came from fellow Republicans, not Democrats. The anti-Clayton Republicans were led by Lieutenant Governor James M. Johnson, and like him most were Scalawags (q.v.). They claimed that Clayton's administration was filled with bad management, and they began talks with the Democrats on a possible fusion policy. When Clayton left the state on a New York trip to fund the state debt, Johnson started a rumor that he had absconded with the state treasury. Johnson also decided to come into Little Rock from his Ozark home and take over the government. Only a warning from friends and a fast steamboat got Clayton back in time to avert disaster.

Then Clayton went on a political offensive of his own. He challenged Johnson in court to prove that he was entitled to the lieutenant governorship, claiming a technicality disqualified him. Clayton also offered an olive branch of his own to the Democrats. The legislature tried to impeach Clayton, but could find no reason to file charges. In a complicated set of negotiations, Clayton agreed to drop his charges against Johnson, who would resign the lieutenant governorship if Clayton would make him secretary of state. The legislature would elect Clayton to the U.S. Senate, and the governorship would go to the state senate president, one of Clayton's Carpetbag friends. In Washington, Clayton found himself at home with Maine Senator James G. Blaine, who had an interest in Arkansas railroads that would eventually cost him the presidency in 1884.

With Clayton in Washington, the state Republican Party divided up. Both sides assembled armed men to back their point of view. President Ulysses S. Grant (q.v.), thoroughly sick of these petty squabbles from the South, decided to accept Clayton's opponents as the legal government. By now, the Republican Party was so divided that it lost the general election to the Democrat candidate, Augustus H. Garland. With the Republican split and the Democrats in power, Garland's supporters decided to cut a deal with Clayton to divide up offices between them to keep blacks from gaining control in the counties they dominated along the Arkansas and Mississippi Rivers. Clayton agreed. This made him the Republican boss to be reckoned with for years to come.

When he finished his term in the Senate, Clayton returned to Arkansas, where he dabbled in railroads and real estate, making a small fortune. In 1897, he went to Mexico as President William McKinley's ambassador. Clayton retired to Washington, D.C., in 1905, and wrote his own account of the turbulent times of Arkansas' Reconstruction. He died a few days after he finished the manuscript in 1914, which was published the following year.

COLD HARBOR, BATTLE OF SECOND. *See* RICHMOND OR OVER-LAND CAMPAIGN.

COLFAX RACE RIOT. In Louisiana in 1874, the Republicans (q.v.) were in deep trouble in the outlying parishes (counties). As in New Orleans on the state level, dual Democrat–Liberal Republican (Fusion) and Stalwart Republican governments existed. But the weight of force lay with the Fusionists. When Republicans took over the Grant Parish courthouse in central Louisiana and called in local blacks to help them defend it, four or five hundred armed men responded. Rumors of black rebellion brought in armed whites from miles around. The Fusion forces gathered outside and surrounded the courthouse. The black occupants and their Scalawag and Carpetbag (qq.v.) allies refused a call to surrender. The whites assaulted the breastworks around the courthouse, breached the line, and brought up a canon to shell the building. Mistakenly thinking that the Republican forces had surrendered, the whites moved forward to meet a new fusillade. Then everyone went berserk. The attackers set fire to the courthouse, and as the occupants fled, a massacre ensued. Victims were chased into the surrounding countryside. Surrendering men were shot down. Forty blacks who had been taken were led out that night and summarily executed. Over a hundred people died, making it the bloodiest of Reconstruction race riots. Federal troops arrived after the fact to restore order. Federal courts indicted 72 men, but on advice of the U.S. attorney general tried but nine, of whom William Cruikshank and two others were convicted. They appealed their convictions to the U.S. Supreme Court as United States *v.* Cruikshank *et al.* (q.v.)

COLFAX, SCHUYLER (1823–1885). Vice president of the United States during the first Ulysses S. Grant (q.v.) administration, Schuyler Colfax was born in New York City. His father died when Schuyler was a boy, and his mother's new husband took the family to Indiana in 1836. His stepfather was a local politician who appointed Colfax to the position of deputy auditor at South Bend, a position he held for eight years. He was also a newspaper correspondent and a publisher and read law on the side. Like his stepfather, Colfax was a Whig (q.v.). He took an early interest in politics, campaigned for Henry Clay in 1844, and attended the national Whig conventions in 1848 and 1852. He also was a delegate to the Indiana constitutional convention in 1850 and unsuccessfully ran for Congress in 1851. He joined the new Republican Party (q.v.) in 1854 and helped organize it in Indiana, winning a seat in the U.S. House in 1855. He served continuously until 1869, being elected speaker in 1863. He was a proponent of Free Soil in Kansas and organized the first transcontinental mail service as chairman of the committee on post offices and roads. He was strongly urged as postmaster general under Abraham Lincoln (q.v.), but the president turned him down for Edward Bates of Missouri. Upon the death of his first wife in 1863, Colfax married a niece of powerful Republican leader Senator Benjamin Wade (q.v.), a wise political move.

As speaker of the House, Colfax was an advocate of "advanced" positions on the Negro, like emancipation, military service, and the vote, which made him the perfect Radical Republican counterbalance to the moderation of Ulysses S. Grant in 1868. Grant then dumped him from the administration in the election of 1872 (q.v.), when Colfax flirted too long with the Liberal Republicans (q.v.). But Colfax would not have lasted anyhow, as he became involved with the Crédit Mobilier (q.v.) scandal. It turned out that as speaker he had accepted 20 shares of stock, uncounted "dividends," and a campaign contribution of $4,000 from a contractor who supplied envelopes to government offices. Colfax maintained his innocence until the end, but his story was not convincing even to friends. After his forced retirement, he spent much of his time as a paid lecturer and a member of the Odd Fellows lodge. He died suddenly while on a trip to Minnesota in 1885. His body was returned to South Bend for burial.

COLLAMER DELEGATION. *See* ELECTION OF 1862, UNION.

COLONIZATION OF AFRICAN-AMERICANS OVERSEAS. Abraham Lincoln (q.v.) was an advocate of Henry Clay's political and economic policies all his life. On colonization he advanced Clay's notion that there was "moral fitness in the idea of returning to Africa her children, whose ancestors have been torn from her by the ruthless hand of fraud and violence." After his inauguration, Lincoln looked into colonization as a way to handle the large numbers of blacks who had fled to Union lines for protection from their masters. Congress endorsed the president's suggestions on April 16, 1862, when it passed a law to end slavery in the District of Columbia. Part of the measure called for $100,000 to be appropriated to remove such manumitted slaves to Liberia or Haiti, or anywhere they wished to go and would be well received. Each immigrant was to receive not more than $100. Later, on July 16, an additional $500,000 was appropriated to extend the project further. Both equal rights advocates, like Senator Charles Sumner (q.v.) of Massachusetts, and most blacks themselves protested the plan as unfair. But the president mentioned the plan to border state white political leaders as a possible solution to the compensated end of slavery he was recommending to them. Lincoln also tried to interest a delegation of freed blacks in the concept, to no avail.

Nonetheless, Lincoln instructed Secretary of State William H. Seward (q.v.) to look into which nations in the Caribbean or Latin America (either independent republics or colonies of European powers) might be used. Most of Central America and South America beyond New Grenada (present-day Colombia) and Ecuador rejected the idea. But several Caribbean islands (Danish, Dutch, and British), Haiti, and Liberia expressed interest. By this time, however, even Lincoln realized that there could be no forced deportation of African-Americans. So he tried to get volunteers to go and show how it would work and interest others. Two colonies were examined, one at Chiriquí on the Isthmus of Panamá and another at L'Ile à Vache off the coast of Haiti. The Panamanian effort fell because of disputes over the land titles between New Granada and Costa Rica. Besides, no one wanted to go when a prior examination proved that alleged coal fields were of doubtful value. But it also masked an American attempt to stake out a claim to the Isthmus for a future canal.

The L'Ile à Vache project went a lot further. An entrepreneur, Bernard Kock, described the island as 100 square miles of tropical paradise. Sugar, cotton, coffee, and indigo were possible crops. Timber was plentiful. At $50 a head, Kock agreed to take 5,000 American Negroes to the place and set them up in their own independent homeland. Kock promised to establish comfortable homes, garden lots, churches, and schools, and guarantee employment for four years. Then Lincoln heard that Kock was in receipt of fugitive blacks from the American South and had contracted with other entrepreneurs to transport them to L'Ile à Vache, at a hoped-for profit of 600 percent for nine months' work. Lincoln canceled all government contracts with Kock immediately. But another group of capitalists secured a governmental contract to transport up to 500 volunteers from contrabands at Fortress Monroe. The project was plagued by disease from the day the ships sailed. The colonists found that the island was a virtual wilderness, and the Haitian government was hostile to their arrival. More disease put an end to the expedition. In 1864, Lincoln sent another vessel to remove all of the colonists who wished to return home. On July 2 of that year, Congress repealed its appropriations for all colonization efforts.

But that did not end the project, at least according to Benjamin Butler (q.v.), although historians generally dismiss Butler's undocumented assertions as suspect. He reported years later that Lincoln still wanted to advance a colony in 1865, shortly before his assassination. This time the place of interest was Santo Domingo. But Butler looked into the project at the president's behest and found that all of the available U.S. shipping that could be safely used could not transport African-Americans fast enough to beat their own birth rate. James H. Lane suggested that blacks be colonized on land west of the Colorado River in Texas, but this received a lot of hostility in the former Confederate state and Congress. It really did not matter. After blacks had fought in the Civil War for their own freedom, it became morally and politically impossible to propose that they leave the country of their birth. And forceful repatriation was out of the question. So the colonization of American slaves to a colony overseas went on the back burner for a while, only to be resurrected later when the Ulysses S. Grant (q.v.) administration tried to buy

Santo Domingo from its own corrupt dictator. Senator Sumner made the destruction of this scheme a priority during his last years in the Senate.

COLUMBIA, BURNING OF. *See* CAROLINAS CAMPAIGN.

COMMAND OF THE ARMY ACT. As section 2 of the Army Appropriations Act of 1867, the Command of the Army Act provided that the headquarters of the general-in-chief be fixed at Washington, D.C., and that the general, Lt. Gen. Ulysses S. Grant (q.v.), could not be suspended, removed, or reassigned to duty elsewhere, unless he requested it, without the express concurrence of the U.S. Senate. All orders to the army in the field from the president or the secretary of war had to go through the general-in-chief to be valid. To obey any order not so routed could lead to imprisonment of from 2 to 20 years. The notion was to fix Grant in the office (he was leaning toward the Radical Republican view at that time and believed Congress to be the supreme branch of the government and voice of the people) and prevent President Andrew Johnson (q.v.) from interfering with Radical or Military Reconstruction (he had tried to send Grant away to Maximilian in Mexico [q.v.] on a diplomatic mission months earlier). The law was never tested because Grant and Johnson never came to open disagreement over any of the president's requests. Another section of the same measure disbanded all existing militia organizations in the Southern states to prevent armed interference with Reconstruction.

COMMAND SYSTEM, CONFEDERATE WARTIME. The Southern government's military command system was relatively simple, because there were few modern developments. As under the U.S. Constitution, the Confederate Constitution rested all ultimate power in the president as commander-in-chief. He was assisted by two civilian officials, the secretary of war and secretary of the navy. Stephen Mallory of Florida was the only head of the navy department the South ever had, serving the provisional and permanent governments. But the South had five secretaries of the army: Leroy P. Walker (appointed to give Alabama a spot in the original cabinet, and not up to the job), Judah P. Benjamin (q.v.) (Davis' troubleshooter, who was not a military man, and was sacrificed to public opinion for military adversities in 1862), George Washington Randolph (an excellent choice who quarreled with Davis every step of the way), James Seddon (also capable, but sacrificed to public opinion for military adversities in 1864), and John C. Breckinridge (q.v.) (the last one, appointed in consultation with Gen. Robert E. Lee [q.v.]). This reflected less on the secretaries than on the interference of President Jefferson Davis (q.v.) in military minutiae of all kinds.

In 1862, Davis decided that he might need personal military advice as he directed the war. He created the position of commanding general under the president and placed Gen. Robert E. Lee in it. Lee furnished technical advice when Davis asked for it. At this time, Lee had lost western Virginia and the South Carolina sea islands to the Yankees and did not look too able. It is really an open argument just how much influence Lee had outside of Virginia during the war. He did not insert himself actively into Davis' realm unless asked. He soon left this position to take command of the Army of Northern Virginia in June 1862.

From the summer of 1862 to February 1863, Davis handled military matters himself. He formulated strategy, interfering only to make defensive strategy more defensive. He did attempt to modify and modernize command in the field in the Western Theater, when he placed Gen. Joseph Johnston (q.v.) in charge of the armies covering Chattanooga (under Gen. Braxton Bragg [q.v.]) and Vicksburg (Gen. John C. Pemberton). The Western Theater was so far from Richmond and so large that to have an army group commander was a good idea. But Johnston was not up to the job. He refused to control unless he was on the field and superseded the army commander. He did not understand how to direct something he could not see. He was a 19th-century man in a 20th-century job. The same exact problem cursed Gen. Edmund Kirby Smith (q.v.) in the Trans-Mississippi Theater at Shreveport.

In 1864, Davis had to save his friend Bragg, so he brought him east as military advisor—the same position Lee had had—probably as much an act of defiance to his critics, as anything. Bragg was actually pretty good at strategy, but he understood Davis and kept quiet unless asked for advice. He was soon shuffled off to the North Carolina coast, leaving Davis alone again.

By the last year of the war, the Confederate Congress, irritated by Davis' military policies, insisted the Confederacy have a real general-in-chief, independent from the president. They also hinted strongly that Lee was the man for the job. But Lee was too busy defending Richmond against Lt. Gen. Ulysses S. Grant's Siege at Petersburg (qq.v) to do much. He did envision a joint campaign against Maj. Gen. William T. Sherman's Carolinas Campaign (qq.v), but by 1865, it proved too late to save the South militarily.

COMMAND SYSTEM, UNION WARTIME. The Northern command system started out much the same as the Confederate one. President Abraham Lincoln (q.v.) was commander-in-chief under the U.S. Constitution, assisted by two civilian deputies, the secretary of war (Simon Cameron, a corrupt political appointee; then Edwin McM. Stanton [q.v.], a capable tyrant) and the secretary of the navy (Gideon Welles). But he also started right off with a general-in-chief, Bvt. Lt. Gen. Winfield Scott (q.v.), who was assisted by a general staff composed of the heads of various military bureaus.

Unlike Davis, who was his own military expert, Lincoln was only too aware of his military shortcomings. So he turned to Scott for advice on strategy. Scott suggested strangling the South through a blockade, called the Anaconda Plan (q.v.). But Lincoln rejected it as a do-nothing plan. He had to have action immediately. Republicans had already lost elections in several Northern states by sitting still.

Because of his age and health, and the demands of the North for action, Scott resigned in November 1861. He was replaced by Maj. Gen. George B. McClellan (q.v.), who had cleared western Virginia of Confederates. McClellan crassly maneuvered Scott out of office, saying he could do it all. Lincoln gave him a try as general-in-chief. As had Scott, McClellan thought only in one direction. He developed a plan whereby he would use the Union navy and float down the coast to take Richmond from the sea. Then he would do the same to every other Southern state until they all surrendered.

McClellan overlooked the fact that everything depended on one army, the South could concentrate to oppose it, McClellan had no staff to implement it, and the North at this stage of the game could not provide the logistical support to carry it out. What Lincoln wanted was what military men nowadays call a cordon offense, in which several armies attack at once and break through at the enemy's weakest point. But that violated the principle of concentration that Civil War generals adored above all. So when McClellan finally took the field, Lincoln removed him as general-in-chief and let him concentrate on his own army.

For the next half year, Lincoln served as his own general-in-chief. He believed that he could do as well as his generals had done so far. During this time he tried to corner Confederate Maj. Gen. Stonewall Jackson (q.v.) in the Shenandoah Valley with three separate armies directed from Washington, concentrated all troops in the Northern Neck of Virginia under Maj. Gen. John Pope (q.v.), and even experimented with observation balloons and signal fires. Lincoln never ran a one-man show like Davis. He relied on the army bureau heads in Washington for advice. He banded them together as the Army Board, under the leadership of Brig. Gen. Ethan A. Hitchcock. But Lincoln had trouble conveying his ideas to military men in a language they could both understand. He also tended to minimize distances to travel and logistical support needed, and exaggerated the strategic possibilities of given situations. Above all, he asked lousy generals to do too much—win.

Lincoln knew that he lacked the skill to run the military side of the war alone. But he wanted to keep as much control over Union policy as possible, especially in 1862 as Congress was entering the picture with its Joint Committee on the Conduct of the War. In July, Lincoln transferred Maj. Gen. Henry W. Halleck (q.v.) from the Western Theater to Washington to act as general-in-chief. Theoretically Halleck was the perfect man for the job. He had written on strategy and tactics, most of it stolen from the French theorist Baron Antoine Henry de Jomini (q.v.), and he had a fine reputation winning in the West, although Lincoln did not yet realize that it was Halleck's subordinates who had done all the winning. At first Halleck did his job. But during the Second Manassas Campaign, he had a complete physical and mental collapse from the strain. He just could not handle responsibility, especially when all glory went to the field commander and all criticism went to the general-in-chief.

But Halleck could give advice and loved to do it. He could suggest courses of action, provided someone else chose what to do. In effect, he was what Lincoln needed, a military man who understood common English and could translate Lincoln to his generals and the generals back to Lincoln. So the president kept him on as an advisor, and Lincoln was general-in-chief, again. And the generals were mostly unimaginative incompetents. But at least he understood them, now.

In 1864, Lincoln seemed to have found his general at last in Ulysses S. Grant (q.v.). Congress agreed and created the permanent rank of lieutenant general (Scott had been a brevet lieutenant general, *i.e.*, honorary) and Lincoln put Grant in the slot as general-in-chief. The work of winning the war was divided among Grant, Halleck, and Lincoln. Grant was general-in-chief, Halleck became chief of staff, and Lincoln was commander-in-chief under the Constitution.

Grant was in charge of coordinating all the Union armies in the field. He planned strategy. He was supposed to stay in Washington, but Grant disliked the politics and backstabbers. So he accompanied the Army of the Potomac in the field against Confederate Gen. Robert E. Lee (q.v.) and communicated by telegraph.

Halleck got a brand new job and title. He ran the army, transmitted Grant's orders and desires to the other armies, and collected and edited communications from the 17 commanders in the field for Grant's perusal. Halleck excelled at this task, and Lincoln and Grant worked well together because Halleck did his job so well.

Lincoln, meanwhile, handled the political tasks of the presidency. He did not give Grant a totally free hand. He interfered twice to force Grant to act against his own desires. First was when he forced Grant to stop Early's Washington Raid. The second was when he ordered Grant to keep Maj. Gen. George Thomas on at Nashville, after Grant wanted to fire him. Both interferences were warranted.

Usually, Grant generally worked out broad military policies and submitted them to Lincoln for approval. When Lincoln gave him the go-ahead, Grant worked out the details and submitted them to Halleck to carry out. Grant also used the cordon offensive that Lincoln had wanted from the beginning, an attack all along the line, everywhere. "Those not skinning can hold a leg," as Lincoln put it.

The new command arrangement was instrumental in gaining a Union victory in the last year of the war. It combined civilian and military in a smooth system that probably rivaled the Prussian General Staff in Europe at that time.

COMMITTEE OF FIFTEEN. *See* JOINT COMMITTEE OF FIFTEEN ON RECONSTRUCTION.

COMMITTEE OF SEVENTY. *See* TWEED RING.

COMMITTEE OF THIRTEEN. *See* CRITTENDEN COMMITTEE OF THIRTEEN.

COMMITTEE OF THIRTY-THREE. *See* CORWIN COMMITTEE OF THIRTY-THREE.

COMMITTEE ON THE CONDUCT OF THE WAR. *See* JOINT COMMITTEE ON THE CONDUCT OF THE WAR.

COMPENSATED EMANCIPATION. Throughout the 18th and 19th centuries, many Americans, North and South, advocated getting rid of the institution of slavery by paying off the slaveowners to allow emancipation. But the movement's chance of success was already lost even before the radical abolitionists (q.v.) appeared on the American political scene, even though new compensation schemes appeared right up to the end of the Civil War. Very often these compensation schemes included colonization (q.v.) of African-Americans back to Africa or in some tropical clime in the Western Hemisphere, but not always.

The first public suggestions for compensated emancipation occurred shortly after the American Revolution. Thomas Pownall, Anthony Benezet, and Elbridge Gerry of Massachusetts advocated emancipating slaves gradually as monies became available from the sales of Western lands. Ten years later, another Massachusetts representative, George Thatcher, in response to a petition of free blacks from Philadelphia to end the fugitive slave law and the Atlantic slave trade, asked that Congress investigate methods to finance the end of all slavery in the United States.

By the end of the War of 1812, the idea of compensated emancipation had become linked with the notion of sending liberated slaves back to Africa. This was the heyday of the American Colonization Society (q.v.), backed by men like Henry Clay and former presidents Thomas Jefferson, James Madison, and James Monroe. All feared the difficulties of absorbing freed blacks into white society and government and saw transportation overseas as a logical (albeit racist) solution. When the Missouri Controversy came to a head in 1820, Henry

Meigs of New York submitted a proposal that argued it was a good time to get rid of slavery altogether using monies from the sale of public lands, by setting aside 500 million acres, especially earmarked for the ending of slavery. When a master decided to free his bondservants, he would receive a government script that entitled him or his heirs to a land grant from the selected territory. Not only would slavery end, but the settlement of the West would be stimulated thereby. Neither of his proposals received any real consideration. Henry Clay introduced compensated emancipation as a part of his American System of financing economic growth. To overcome Southern opposition, he emphasized that his was not an abolition program but a government effort to allow individual slaveowners a choice of emancipation, if they so desired. Clay would finance his program through the proceeds from public land sales, once again.

In December 1862, in his annual message to Congress, President Abraham Lincoln (q.v.) proposed that Congress pay for slaves in U.S. bonds to the slaveholder of any state that would free their slaves by January 1, 1900. He also asked that no slave freed by any wartime action be re-enslaved at any time. He greatly feared that military actions and his Emancipation Proclamation (q.v.) were unconstitutional without a constitutional amendment and that African-Americans freed under its provisions could be re-enslaved after the war. Finally, Lincoln asked that any blacks freed by any plan be colonized out of the United States, preferably to Latin America. Lincoln's true plan of eradicating slavery failed when, in a close vote, Congress failed to pay Missouri $15 million for freeing its slaves through state action.

No matter how reasonable these compensation plans seem today, at the time they were envisioned wholly as revolutionary as uncompensated abolition. It was not until the blood bath of the Civil War and Lincoln's backing of the Emancipation Proclamation and the Thirteenth Amendment (q.v) that they were seen as the conservative approach they truly were. Lincoln, with the backing of many abolitionists, offered to pay for the slaves of the loyal border states during the war several times, only to be rebuffed.

After Lincoln vainly attempted to reunify the nation through negotiation at the Hampton Roads Peace Conference (q.v.), he returned to Washington. Although Lincoln thought some blacks were worthy of citizenship and the vote, the intelligent and those who had served in the Union army, he asked his whole cabinet once more to agree to propose that Congress appropriate $400 million to pay owners for freeing their slaves if the South rejoined the Union by July 1, 1865. The cabinet was horrified and refused. "You are all opposed to me," Lincoln said. He withdrew the proposal.

It was not until 1865 and the passage of the Thirteenth Amendment (q.v.) that Southerners were willing to consider compensation for their slave property. Many slaveowners held their slaves until 1866, hoping in vain that Congress might vote some form of compensation. But by then it was too late.

COMPROMISE OF 1850. Because of the potency of the slavery issue in the Western territories, which emanated from the introduction of the antislavery Wilmot Proviso, which was countered by the pro-slavery Non-Exclusion Doctrine, both of which were compromised by the idea of squatter sovereignty (q.v.) (letting the residents of the territory decide), the United States was near Civil War by 1849.

The new American president was Zachary Taylor (q.v.), a slaveholding member of the Whig Party (q.v.) and hero of the War with Mexico. But Taylor was not much of a party member—he had never voted—and his views on the key issue of slavery in the territories were unknown. But Taylor was going to have to take a stand. In 1849, gold was discovered in California. Overnight, 100,000 people arrived in the state. California not only wanted to be a territory, it had sufficient population to skip the territorial stage of government and asked to be admitted outright as a state.

And that was Taylor's solution to the problem of slavery in the territories. Make all of the territories taken from Mexico states, eliminating the territorial stage of government and the question of slavery in the territories. Everyone agreed that a state constitutional convention could decide the question of slavery in the to-be-admitted state. But to admit California as a state would upset the 50–50 balance between North and South in the U.S. Senate. Besides, who was the president to dictate to Congress? Taylor was begging the question, the most important issue facing the country.

Actually Taylor's solution was way too simplistic. There were many problems facing the nation by 1850: statehood for California; the problem of slavery in the rest of the Mexican Cession; the question of who was going to pay for the Republic of Texas debt after it had been admitted to the Union, causing the War with Mexico and Texas' claim to Santa Fé and the Río Grande; the problem of slavery and the slave trade in the District of Columbia, especially odious to Northern congressmen of all political hues; and Southern desires for a strongly worded and strictly enforced fugitive slave law, returning escaped slaves to their rightful owners, and negating personal liberty laws in Northern states that interfered with slave catchers.

But Taylor was not to be diverted. Egged on by New York's antislave, Whig, U.S. senator, William H. Seward, Taylor said that California must be admitted as a free state first before anything else was done. He would veto all other measures. John C. Calhoun spoke for Southern hard-liners, pledging no compromise—there must be slavery allowed in all territories until statehood. Henry Clay, the Great Compromiser of the 1820s and 1830s, introduced the Omnibus Bill, rolling all five problems into one massive piece of legislation.

Clay's measure would admit California as a free state; set up territorial governments in Utah and New Mexico under the existing laws of Mexico (no slavery); the United States would assume the Texas Republic debt, and

Texas would give up all land claims along the Río Grande north of El Paso; the slave trade (the most despised part of slavery) would be eliminated from the District of Columbia; and a strict fugitive act would be passed, negating personal liberty laws and paying Federal commissioners who ruled on an African-American's status twice their case amount if they ruled for slavery. But it could not get enough votes to pass. There were enough congressmen and senators against each section to destroy any hope of a legislative majority.

Then two men died, President Taylor from gastroenteritis, and Calhoun of old age. Two new men stepped onto the stage to take control of the Omnibus Bill. Senator Stephen A. Douglas (q.v.) of Illinois realized that each section had a congressional majority so long as it was not combined with the others. He broke the Omnibus Bill into its five parts, changing only the section on New Mexico and Utah to make no mention of slavery in their initial organization. And the new president, Millard Fillmore, after indicating he would sign anything Congress could agree to, signed it all into law.

In response, the Southern states called a unified convention at Nashville. They agreed to the Georgia Platform, that is, to support the Union if the North obeyed each and every part of the Compromise of 1850, including the fugitive act. Combined with the failure of the pro-secession Southern Movement, the Compromise of 1850, at best, postponed the Civil War for 10 years.

COMPROMISE OF 1877. *See* ELECTION OF 1876 AND COMPROMISE OF 1877.

CONFEDERATE BRIGADIERS. With the exception of Texas, which was late in implementing Andrew Johnson's Reconstruction (q.v.) plans, the Southern states elected new "reconstructed" governments in the fall of 1865. Part of this process was to elect congressmen and senators. If they were seated in the upcoming session of Congress, it would signify that the Reconstruction process initiated by the executive branch was recognized as valid by the legislative branch of the Federal government. When Northerners saw the names of the men elected to represent the South, they professed shock. They were pretty much the same men who had led it out of the Union four years before and sustained the Confederacy through the war: the vice president of the Confederacy, 10 generals, 5 colonels, 6 cabinet officers, and 58 congressmen, none of whom was able to take the oath without a special pardon. Up North, they received the disparaging nickname, "the Confederate Brigadiers."

But they were not red-hot secessionists, as contemporary newspapers and later historians assumed. Of 80 new senators and congressmen, only seven had been supporters of secession in 1860 and 1861. Seventy had opposed secession until the election of Abraham Lincoln (q.v.) as president, and 44 had remained opposed until their states had voted to leave the Union. But most had supported the Confederacy after its creation, either as military men or civil functionaries. However, five had been peace candidates during their elections, on platforms that came close to treason to the Confederacy. Fifteen others were openly and consistently Union men throughout the war. Another 16 were openly neutral to the war effort. Of the 11 state governors, only 3 had been secessionists, and 4 more would ultimately become Republicans (q.v.) during Radical Military Reconstruction (q.v.).

These men were willing to admit to the loss of the war, the end of slavery, the supremacy of the Federal government, and a temporarily diminished political role for the South nationally, but none of them, even the most devout Unionists, was willing to concede equal civil rights, much less the vote, to African-Americans. This, more than their antecedents, in the eyes of the Republicans in Congress made them poor choices for Reconstructing the South, as their support for the Black Codes (q.v.) demonstrated.

CONFEDERATE CONSTITUTION. *See* CONSTITUTION, CONFEDERATE.

CONFEDERATE ELECTION OF 1863. *See* ELECTION OF 1863, CONFEDERATE.

CONFEDERATE PROVISIONAL GOVERNMENT. *See* CONSTITUTION, CONFEDERATE.

CONFEDERATE SEA RAIDERS. The Confederacy tried to overcome the effectiveness of the Union naval blockade of its sea ports by building warships overseas in Great Britain. It was permissible for Confederate agents to build and purchase existing vessels, providing they were sold for commercial purposes and armed elsewhere. The Rebels played this loophole for all it was worth. The Confederates wanted a specific kind of ship—one that was fast, oceangoing, and able to carry the guns necessary for commerce destroying. The strategic idea was to hit Northern merchantmen so hard that the U.S. Navy would have to weaken the blockade to guard sea lanes. The idea worked after a fashion, but the North just took the losses and high insurance rates as a cost of war and maintained the blockade.

The man in charge of Confederate ship acquisition in Great Britain was Commodore James E. Bulloch, another example of a lower level diplomatic agent who was of superior caliber. He had served in the U.S. Navy until his resignation in 1854 to manage a commercial mail service. Bulloch would place contracts with British shipyards using fictitious names and registry. Then the ship would be taken out for a trial cruise and never be returned. On the high seas, the crew, guns, and provisions would be added from a mother ship. The most famous ships obtained in this manner were the C.S.S. *Shenandoah*, *Florida*, and *Alabama*. In the case of the latter, Bulloch purchased the hulk of ship 290, which he named the *Erica*, until it was outfitted as the warship C.S.S. *Alabama* on a trial run.

Union minister to the Court of St. James Charles Francis Adams was an able competitor for Bulloch. British law said that if anyone could prove the neutrality law was being intentionally circumvented, the ships would be seized before they sailed. Adams set out to do just that. But Bulloch often moved fast and surreptitiously, and Adams could not stop every case. In 1863, Bulloch contracted with the Laird shipyard to have two ironclad rams built. He hoped to use them to break the blockade. U.S. naval officers took a look at the rams being built, found them to be technological wonders for their time, and told Adams that he had to stop them at all costs.

Unfortunately, the evidence Adams collected on the rams and their true owners was circumstantial at best. Bulloch had covered his tracks well. Adams finally told the British government that if the Laird rams escaped for their trial runs, the United States would consider it a declaration of war. But the British by this time had had second thoughts about the precedent they were setting for a future conflict, with the Americans playing the role of shipbuilder and spoiler. The British navy seized the rams and kept a close watch on other suspicious ship projects, severely limiting Bulloch's effectiveness.

Meanwhile, the Confederates managed to buy an ironclad ram from the French, which they renamed the C.S.S. *Stonewall*. But before it could do any damage, the war had ended. The captain sold the vessel to pay his crew's wages. (Most oceangoing sailors were paid foreign mercenaries, rather than Confederate seamen, like their officers.) The C.S.S. *Shenandoah* took the Confederate flag around the world in its rampage against Federal shipping. Lt. James Waddell took 24 vessels in an assault against the New England whaling fleet in the Bering Sea alone. But it was June 1865. Waddell was planning an assault on San Francisco Bay to hold the city to ransom, when he learned from a captured captain that the war was over. He had a newspaper to prove it. The *Shenandoah* sailed all the way to Britain, avoiding every ship at sea, where it surrendered to the British on November 6.

The C.S.S. *Alabama* had a voyage as fantastic and even more profitable than the *Shenandoah*. It took 64 ships worth $6 million. Finally filled with captured enemy crews, Capt. Raphael Semmes put into port. This gave the Yankees some idea where to look. Much in need of repairs, Semmes headed for Cherbourg, France. He was trapped inside the harbor by the steam frigate U.S.S. *Kearsarge*, under Capt. John Winslow. Semmes decided to give battle and sailed out, only to be sunk on June 19, 1864. After the war, the British settled the *Alabama* claims (q.v.), paying massive damages to erase any precedent and ill feelings their wartime conduct still had.

CONFEDERATE SECRET SERVICE. *See* LINCOLN ASSASSINA-
TION; LINCOLN ASSASSINATION, THE CONFEDERACY AND THE;
LINCOLN ASSASSINATION, THE NEW YORK CONNECTION OF THE;
SECRET SERVICE, CONFEDERATE; *SULTANA*, SINKING OF THE.

CONFISCATION ACT OF 1861. In response to Confederate measures that
confiscated all debts due Northerners (May 21, 1861) and alien property (August 30, 1861), the U.S. Congress began its own confiscation program. The
first Confiscation Act, passed on August 6, 1861, condemned all property
used to further the rebellion against the United States. It was limited in scope
and had to take place through a court proceeding. The U.S. attorney could initiate proceedings or a private citizen could file an information which, if found
true, would entitle the informer to half of the condemned property's proceeds.
Maj. Gen. Benjamin Butler (q.v.) said that he used the ideas expressed in this
act even before its promulgation to confiscate fugitive slaves coming into his
lines at Fortress Monroe, Virginia, in 1861, declaring them to be contraband
of war and leading to blacks being called "contrabands" (q.v.) during the rest
of the war, as a matter of course.

CONFISCATION ACT OF 1862. As the war lengthened and Northern
battlefield losses grew, clamor for a harsher policy of confiscation of Rebel
property arose. The 1861 law was cumbersome in its insistence on court proceedings and gave the benefit of the doubt to the alleged Rebels. The Second
Confiscation Act of July 17, 1862 (expanded in 1864), was designed to be
truly punitive in nature and involved the outright seizure of all property of
those who aided the rebellion. The law caused much debate about its harshness and whether it recognized the Southerners as belligerents, especially
from border slave state Democrats. Indeed, President Abraham Lincoln (q.v.)
once considered vetoing the measure, but in the end he signed it. As passed,
the Second Confiscation Act permitted the immediate seizure of all property
of anyone who was an officer of the Confederacy (civil, military, and naval)
for the offender's lifetime. All others in any part of the United States or occupied territory would be given 60 days to change their allegiance by taking
an oath of loyalty to the Union government. After that time, their property
could be taken if they could be declared Rebels in a court proceeding.

CONGRESSIONAL RECONSTRUCTION. During the Civil War and
Reconstruction eras, Congress put forth three proposals to reunite the nation.
The first was the Wade–Davis Bill (q.v.) of 1864, in response to President
Abraham Lincoln's Ten Percent Plan (qq.v.). The Wade–Davis bill proposed
that Congress have a voice in Reconstruction and questioned whether Lin-
coln's plan really represented a democratic proposal, as it relied on only a

small group of the registered voters in 1860 to get it started. Congress preferred a majority and to restrict initial voting to those who had never rendered support to secession or the Confederacy. By refusing to seat the representatives and senators from Lincoln's Southern governments, Congress had parried the president's attempt to reconstruct the South through his war powers. Lincoln's death left Reconstruction in limbo by 1865, necessitating a new look by the executive and legislative branches.

Congress' response was the second legislative Reconstruction program, called Moderate Reconstruction (q.v.), which included the Fourteenth Amendment (q.v.) and the measures that led up to it, the renewal of the Freedmen's Bureau and the Civil Rights Act of 1866 (qq.v.). When President Andrew Johnson (q.v.) had continued the Lincoln wartime policy of ruling during congressional recess through presidential proclamation, Congress refused to seat the representatives from his Reconstruction program in December 1865.

It instead proposed that the Federal government protect the newly freed blacks through continuing an existing agency, the Bureau of Refugees, Freedmen, and Abandoned Lands, or the Freedmen's Bureau. It also proposed that citizenship and certain civil rights be granted by law to the African-Americans, to counter the effect of discriminatory Southern state laws known as Black Codes (q.v.) and a prewar U.S. Supreme Court decision (Dred Scott v. Sandford, 1857 [q.v.]) that said that blacks were not citizens.

When President Johnson vetoed these acts and ridiculed Congress, the legislators repassed both proposals over his veto and sought to enshrine citizenship and equal rights in a constitutional amendment. All of the Confederate South (except Tennessee) and two border slave states that had remained loyal during the war (Delaware and Kentucky) refused to endorse this program, causing it to fail and forcing Congress to reassess its program once again.

The impasse over the Fourteenth Amendment led to the third congressional Reconstruction plan, Radical or Military Reconstruction (q.v.) This was a demanding program that nullified presidential interference and compelled the South to act as Congress desired under the supervision of the Army of Occupation.

CONGRESSIONAL SUPREMACY. The Republicans took control of the Federal government at a time when the power of the presidency was at a low ebb. Ever since the American Revolution, there had been a strong commitment to legislative supremacy vis-à-vis the executive branch of government. The executive–legislative argument became central to early party battles. Usually the party out of power wants more of the voice of government to come from the Congress—a place where they at least have some say on what is going on. This struggle reached a fever point in the 1830s, when the opposition to Andrew Jackson, the first really strong executive under the Constitution, became angry with his leadership. Jackson believed that he was the only member of the Federal government elected by all the people, hence he had a better right to power than the Congress, which represented small districts of special local interests. The opponents also took up the name Whig (q.v.), a reference to those who had supported the American Revolution, here and in the English Parliament. And because their candidates rarely seemed to win the presidency, the Whigs put forward the idea that Congress, elected by the people every two years, was actually the body of government most answerable to the people. Some state legislatures, particularly in the South, even sent instructions to their congressmen and senators telling them how to vote on certain issues.

By the era before the Civil War, America had gone through a series of political administrations that appeared particularly gutless, especially when compared to Jackson and his student, James K. Polk, who preceded them, and Abraham Lincoln (q.v.), who followed. Taking their cue from the defunct Whigs, the new Republican Party (q.v.) once again proclaimed that the branch of government closest to the wishes of the people was the Congress. The president was charged with enforcing Congress' laws, the courts with interpreting them, leaving all duty of correction and initiation of law to the legislative branch. Lincoln, of course, ruled as much as possible by presidential decree, using the adjournment periods of Congress to make his biggest statements in policy. This so angered the Radical Republicans (and they were not alone in the party, merely the most vocal) in 1864 that they passed the Wade–Davis Bill (q.v.), followed by the Wade–Davis Manifesto (q.v.) in answer to Lincoln's veto, which stated that the problem of Reconstruction was a congressional responsibility. Congress would establish policy through law, the president would enforce those laws, and the Supreme Court would find those measures constitutional.

When Andrew Johnson (q.v.) tried to continue with his independent policy of Reconstruction, Congress impeached him and cut him down. They warned the Supreme Court not to interfere by removing cases from its appellate jurisdiction. The appointment process was watched through the Tenure of Office Act (q.v.), which allowed the Senate to confirm any presidential patronage changes. The veto power was also to be used sparingly, not in a "wholesale manner" like Jackson, Lincoln, and especially Johnson. The result was a parade of presidents whom most students of American history cannot name and whose policies remain basically unknown. It would take a man of the character of Theodore Roosevelt to reassert the idea of executive power that became predominant in the 20th century.

CONIODAL BULLET. *See* LOAD-IN-NINE-TIMES.

CONQUERED PROVINCES THEORY. *See* RECONSTRUCTION, THEORIES OF.

CONSCRIPTION AND DRAFT EVASION, CONFEDERATE. As did the North, the South experienced such an initial enthusiasm for the war that it had to turn down 200,000 men between the ages of 13 and 73 for lack of facilities and weapons. Everyone was in a hurry, because they feared it would all be over in one battle. Southern volunteers believed that the Yankees would not fight, anyhow. Besides, every good Rebel knew one Southern man could defeat at least 5 to 10 Yanks. In March 1861, the Provisional Congress passed a law creating the Provisional Army of the Confederate States. President Jefferson Davis (q.v.) was authorized to accept 100,000 volunteers or militia for 12 months.

One year later, the Confederacy was in real trouble. Enlistments had dropped to nothing after the first bloody battle had been fought. The truly devoted had already joined. Those who had been turned down in the first rush to the colors had had second thoughts, now that the first bloody battle had been fought. Many simply stayed at home, not being in favor of the Confederate cause in the first place. But the Union armies were just beginning their first major offensives. The authorities asked the 12-month men to re-enlist, offering furloughs and $50 bonuses. But too many refused, saying they had done their part, and it was someone else's turn.

Davis then asked Congress to do something revolutionary—pass the first conscription act ever applied on a national level. The draft had been used in some states during the Revolution, but never had a national act been passed. Congress responded with the First Conscription Act (April 16, 1862). All white males between the ages of 18 and 35 were liable for three years' service. Those already in the service had two years added to their 12-month enlistments. A Bureau of Conscription was to administer the act under the assistant secretary of war (former U.S. Supreme Court judge John Campbell). Camps of instruction were set up in every state, and men who dodged the draft were to be hunted down and brought in by force. Cursory medical exams and treatment were provided.

The act provided for substitutes, who could replace the original draftee. If the substitute were called up, the original draftee had to enroll or find another substitute. The corruption became so rampant that substitution was abolished in 1863. One could also apply for an exemption. The trades exempted from service were phenomenal in number, as much as 57 percent of all white males. Many small towns suddenly became homes to doctors, pharmacists, teachers, and livestock tenders, when none could be found there before. But the most controversial was the exemption of one white man for every 20 slaves. The excused had to put up $500, and the law was rarely applied, but it did much to discredit the plantation system among the common nonslave-holding whites, who derisively called it the "Twenty Nigger Law."

The problem was not that the Conscription Act was unneeded. The question was its legality. The Confederate Constitution did not provide for Congress to pass a military draft. States' rights men groused about the law, but had the wisdom not to oppose its enforcement. But it could be circumvented legally. Many men were enrolling in home guards or state militia to escape the draft and serve at home. Most prominent in this effort were Georgia and North Carolina. But desertion was up, especially in the Appalachian Peninsula. Often such men organized themselves into self-defense units to fight the Confederate enrolling agents. Entire military units were pulled from the fronts to deal with this resistance. Pillaging and burning were the order of the day. By 1865, estimates ran as high as 100,000 deserters roaming the South.

In September 1862, after a summer of vicious fighting, a second Conscription Act passed Congress. This raised the upper age exemption to 45. By 1863, the South had 465,000 men in the field, the largest number of the war. It was not until February 1864 that the third Conscription Act passed. Ages were dropped to 17 and raised to 50. Few were actually sent into the front lines under this measure. The idea was for the young and old to serve at home, releasing more desirable age groups for service against the Yankees. In addition, all those in service had their enlistments extended for the duration of the war. There were 200,000 on the rolls, but only 100,000 in the field by the end of 1864.

Nonetheless, most Civil War battles had a rough parity in the numbers fighting on both sides until 1865. The draft was full of defects, but it got the men into the army. It is estimated that at least 900,000 men served in the Confederate armed forces between 1861 and 1865. Something like 258,000 Confederate soldiers died, 94,000 from battle wounds (q.v.), the rest of disease.

CONSCRIPTION AND DRAFT EVASION, UNION. The Federal regular army entered the Civil War pretty much unprepared. It has become customary to blame much of this on the inept and even traitorous administration of President James Buchanan's (q.v.) secretary of war, John Floyd of Virginia. But the real problem lay in the fact that no one expected to have to fight a foreign invasion, and few soldiers were needed to deal with Native American tribes and the Mormon War (q.v.) in the West. Congress compounded the problem by doing nothing until Abraham Lincoln (q.v.) became president in March 1861.

The United States Army during the Civil War was made up of three components. First was the regular army, professional officers and enlisted men who joined through voluntary enrollment. In 1861, this force totaled 16,400, before the officer corps was depleted by resigning Southerners hurrying home to defend the Confederacy. Officers could resign their commissions, but the enlisted men had to serve to the end of their term before they could legally change sides. President Lincoln would triple the size of the army to 39,000, by creating nine new regiments in the spring of 1861.

The first line of reserves for the regular army was the militia of the several states, supposedly all men between 18 and 45 years of age according to the law of May 8, 1792. These men were of mixed quality, many militia musters being little more than a good excuse to get drunk. But some units were crack drill regiments and quite capable of making a good fight. Unfortunately, the good ones were mostly in the South, with the exception of New York and Massachusetts. Lincoln called up 75,000 militia in response to the Confederate capture of Ft. Sumter (q.v.) at Charleston, every state being given a quota. These quotas were enough to stimulate the Second Secession (q.v.) of the South.

But the main force that fought for the Union (and the Confederacy in the South) were the volunteers. In the North, these were partly state-administered units and partly Federal. Usually, state governors appointed higher officers, often political cronies, while the men elected their own non-commissioned officers and other company officers (lieutenants and captains). These regiments were numbered according to their date of muster-in and called after their states of origin, often having nicknames besides. Lincoln asked Congress to confirm his 1861 call for 400,000 volunteers to serve three years. Congress gave him 500,000, patriotism being a contagious thing. Just as in the South, state quotas were over-subscribed until the first casualty reports drifted in. The enlistments fell off. States resorted to bounties for enlistments, but even this expedient was not enough, and more had to be done.

Following the example of the Confederacy, Congress passed the Enrollment Act of March 3, 1863. This drafted all single men aged 20–45 and all married men aged 20–35 for three years, if called. There were occupational exemptions, and substitutes were provided for, or one could pay $300 cash to gain exemption. This meant that any substitute was worth $300 right off. If the substitute's name were called up later, the principal had to serve in his place or get another substitute. The law only provided about one-sixth of Union forces during the war. But it worked indirectly to get men to enlist for state and local bounties. Depending on how many enlisted voluntarily, the draft would be lessened, each state receiving a quota at each draft call.

The Civil War demonstrated the cynicism, corruption, shoddiness, and lack of concern for the public weal that preceded and followed the war and was known as the "Great Barbecue." For example, each man received a cursory physical examination. These were exploited by those who wished to avoid service. One of the necessary physical attributes was a good set of front teeth to tear open the paper cartridge to load the Civil War rifled musket. A forefinger on the right hand to pull the trigger was another. Varicose veins could be faked by applying lye to the lower leg. Pepper and castor oil applied to the anus produced temporary hemorrhoids. Often an inductee would send a ringer who was actually sick to answer to his name.

On the other hand, many could not wait to join up. They exaggerated their ages by placing a paper with "17" on it in their shoe, so they could say under oath that they were honestly "over 17." They put lead in shoes to gain weight, iced hernias so they would not be readily detected, and dosed themselves with digitalis to hide heart disease. Some liked the idea of joining up so much that they would join, desert, and rejoin numerous times to collect the bounties. Entire "bounty rings" were organized to bilk the system wholesale. When doctors tried to mark enlistees to limit the process, street demonstrations caused them to let it go.

But protests at fair medical examinations were minor compared with the violent opposition to the whole concept of conscription throughout the North. The worst of these anti-draft riots occurred in New York City on July 13–16, 1863, just after the tremendous Union victory at Gettysburg in the Pennsylvania Campaign. It overwhelmed local authorities in short order, cost over 1,200 dead, thousands injured and wounded, and some $2 million in property damage. Because local garrison troops had to guard Federal installations to keep weapons from the rioters, the riot had to be put down by 13 infantry regiments and supporting artillery pulled off the field after Gettysburg—the veterans did a fast, thorough, professional job, needless to say.

The riot was a social class affair. The average working man could not afford to hire a substitute or leave his family without support. The targeted were the rich and privileged, many of whom were disloyal Copperheads (q.v.), and the African-Americans, who personified the war to the rioters—many of whom were working-class Irish. After a preliminary attempt to enroll 1,200 drafted men on Friday, July 11, grew ugly, Governor Horatio Seymour wanted the draft suspended until the U.S. Supreme Court ruled on it. President Abraham Lincoln (q.v.) said he welcomed a court case, but that the enrollment would continue until the court issued an adverse decision. On Monday, July 13, at 10:00 a.m., a large crowd gathered to hear the first call-up. Suddenly a shot rang out, and the crowd of 5,000–10,000 became an enraged mob. They burned the draft office; cut telegraph wires to prevent communication with the outside; beat men in uniform; attacked city, state, and Federal officials; looked for newspaper editor Horace Greeley (q.v.) to hang him for supporting the war; and mercilessly lynched every black they could find, burning a black orphanage to the ground with the occupants still in it. The Catholic Church got caught up in the middle, Archbishop John Hughes changing his original stand in favor of the draft to support the rioters, while parish priests tried to stop them.

The second and third days of the riot were even worse, but on July 16, the 10,000 troops from the Army of the Potomac swept the streets with fire and restored order. But New York was just the beginning. Other riots, albeit on a lesser scale, occurred in Wisconsin, Indiana, Massachusetts, Vermont, New Hampshire, and Ohio. Threatened disturbances in Pennsylvania did not come off. Draft resistance continued in the North throughout the war, many acts of violence encouraged by the Order of American Knights and other subversive Copperhead groups. The military trials of their leaders in Indiana led to the landmark U.S. Supreme Court case, *ex parte* Milligan *et al.* (q.v.).

CONSERVATIVE REPUBLICANS. See REPUBLICAN PARTY AND THE CIVIL WAR AND RECONSTRUCTION.

CONSTITUTION, CONFEDERATE. Although each Southern state had seceded individually, there had always been a tacit recognition that they would band together in some sort of overall government. Even before South Carolina made the first move, it consulted with other like-minded states and acted only after it received support from Mississippi and Florida. So no one was surprised when the first six seceded states met at Montgomery, Alabama, to form a single government. Texas, having acted later than the others to secede, would send a delegation that would arrive in March and endorse what the others had done.

Montgomery was to become the first capital of the independent South, "the Cradle of the Confederacy." It was centrally located and far enough inland to be protected from Union naval expeditions, which had excluded Charleston, Mobile, Savannah, and New Orleans. Later, after the Second Secession (q.v.) of the Southern States, the capital would be moved to Richmond, Virginia. Richmond was larger, more cosmopolitan, and, by its location, indicated a commitment to the Border South. This also was a gutsy move, typically Southern in nature, challenging the Yankees to come and take it, if they dared.

The delegates at Montgomery were in a hurry. They had less than a month before Abraham Lincoln (q.v.) would be inaugurated. They wanted to have a government in place by then. The convention did some unusual things. It acted as a constitutional convention, elected a provisional president and vice president, and acted as a provisional unicameral Congress in five sessions from February 18, 1861 to February 22, 1862. Usually, in republican theory, the body that draws up the Constitution does not do all those things. But the convention knew that this was a moment unique in American history.

That the Southerners had to have a written constitution showed how American they were. That is America's great contribution to world political history. They called themselves the Confederate States of America. Confederation implied a looser bond than United States. This was stated in the preamble: "We, the People of the Confederate States, each State acting in its sovereign and independent character." The delegates began by assuming that the U.S. Constitution was the best government ever established until it had been perverted by pernicious Yankee influences. So the delegates made only essential changes in their Constitution, necessary to sustain the principle of the original Founding Fathers.

But the Confederate Constitution ought not to be dismissed as inconsequential. The Confederates changed several key things. First, they made the executive and the legislative bodies closer than in the U.S. Constitution. Cabinet members were permitted to take a seat in either house of Congress, debate, but not vote. The Confederate presidency was actually stronger than under the U. S. Constitution. The president had a six-year term, could not succeed himself, could remove cabinet members and diplomats at his pleasure (all other civil officials could be removed only for cause, not political leanings), and had the right to introduce all appropriations bills. Congress could act to introduce appropriations only with a two-thirds vote. In effect, the Confederate Constitution anticipated the future Twenty-second Amendment, a budgetary system of appropriation, obviated the need to impeach executive officials to remove them from office, and created a protected civil service.

Second, the Confederate Constitution changed the relationship between the states and the central government. Congress could pass no tariffs. This was reserved for the states, acting individually or in cooperation with each other. The amendment process was simplified. Any three states could call for a convention to amend, and only two-thirds were necessary to approve it (the figures in the U.S. Constitution are two-thirds to call the convention and three-fourths to approve the amendment). Any Confederate official could be impeached by the state in which he served, to be tried before the Confederate Senate. There was no mention of secession; not because the Confederacy denied this right to its member states, but because it was so essential it needed no mention.

Finally, Negro slavery or slaves were mentioned openly three times in the Confederate Constitution. Slavery was guaranteed by the central government, although any state could theoretically abolish it. A slaveowner was guaranteed the right to transport his or her slaves throughout the Confederacy, and slavery was guaranteed in any Confederate territory (such as the seceded territory of Arizona).

There were other changes. The Confederate Constitution referred to "the favor and guidance of Almighty God." It omitted any mention of "general welfare," the clause that led to much dispute in interpreting the U.S. Constitution. The first 12 amendments to the U.S. Constitution were placed in the main body of the Confederate text. All laws were to concern one topic, which was to be stated clearly in their titles. The Post Office Department was to be self-sustaining by 1863. And new states could be admitted by a two-thirds vote of both houses of Congress. The Confederates fully expected that many of the Middle Atlantic and Old Northwestern states might wish to join this purified form of government in the future. A Southern Reconstruction (q.v.) was anticipated.

The men selected to be the provisional executive of the new Confederacy were Jefferson Davis (q.v.) of Mississippi as president and Alexander Stephens (q.v.) of Georgia as vice president. Both were regular party men (Davis a Democrat, Stephens an old-line Whig and friend of Abraham Lincoln). The Fire-Eaters (q.v.) were generally excluded from the Confederate government right from the start. This was to be a conservative enterprise, based on tried and true principles inherited from the Founding Fathers of 1776 and 1787, not some wild-eyed, experimental nonsense. That was left up to Yankees and abolitionists (q.v.), who had destroyed what the Founders wrought and caused the Confederacy to be necessary.

CONSTITUTIONAL UNION PARTY (1860). Formed on December 29, 1859, from old Whigs (q.v.), Know Nothings, and American Party (q.v.) members primarily in the Border South (Missouri, Kentucky, Maryland, Delaware). The Constitutional Union Party feared that extremists in the other major political parties would opt for war if they did not get their way in the election of 1860 (q.v.). This war, of course, would be fought on the middle ground between North and South. It would ravage the border states.

The Constitutional Unionists met for their convention on May 1, 1860, in Baltimore. Their goal was to throw the election into the House of Representatives, where each state would have but one vote. This then would hopefully lead to some sort of compromise being sought between North and South to save the nation.

The party had no platform. Such written promises limited deal making and also turned off potential voters. They stood for what their name implied—Constitution and Union. They spoke of enforcing all public laws. Opponents laughed and called them the "Soothing Syrup" Party. In fact, the John Brown Harper's Ferry Raid (q.v.) had pretty much killed reasonableness on all sides already.

As their presidential candidate, the Constitutional Unionists put forward John Bell of Tennessee, an old-time Whig who had served as speaker of the house, secretary of war, and U.S. senator. Moderation was his byline. His vice presidential running mate was Edward Everett of Massachusetts, who would better be remembered as the greatest orator of his time. He was the one who would give the three-hour main speech at the dedication of the national cemetery at Gettysburg in November 1863 before President Abraham Lincoln (q.v.) spoke for two minutes. Although they failed to affect the election, the Constitutional Unionists would be heard from again at the Washington Peace Conference (q.v.).

CONTRABANDS. In May 1861, several fugitives slaves fled to Union lines on the Virginia Peninsula at Fortress Monroe. Their owner soon appeared and demanded that the bondsmen be returned under the Fugitive Slave Act of 1850 (q.v.). The post commandant, Maj. Gen. Benjamin Butler (q.v.), refused. He claimed that the Southerner was from a seceded state, which had lost all right to the benefits of United States law. He also asserted that the fugitives in question had been working on constructing Confederate fortifications and could not be returned. Rather they were "contraband of war" and seizable. His report to headquarters became public, and the term "contraband" was used to refer to any fugitive slave that fled to Union lines for freedom and protection during the war. After the war, it was replaced by the generic term "freedman."

CONTRACT LABOR LAW. The Republican Party had a distinct domestic program designed to appease both its agricultural and industrial supporters. This program had as its basis old Whig (q.v.) economic policies based in part on Henry Clay's American System (q.v.). Part of the program appealed to American industry by creating a source of cheap labor. The Contract Labor Law of 1864 was a response to the decline in immigration caused by the war. This law allowed business to import laborers and to deduct the cost of such immigration from the laborers' wages or as a mortgage on their housing. Most of the labor brought in under this act was Chinese, used in building the Central Pacific and later Northern Pacific Railroads. After the Civil War, Southern planters used this law to create so-called Land, Labor and Immigration companies in an attempt to bring in European labor to replace the freed African-Americans, whom they feared would not work without the compulsion of slavery, but the effort failed.

COPPERHEADS. Those Northerners who vehemently opposed the domestic policies of the Abraham Lincoln (q.v.) administration, such as the suspension of the writ of *habeas corpus* (q.v.), suppression of the hostile press, arbitrary arrests, the conscription act, and the centralization of power in Washington, often organized themselves beyond the normal Democratic Party (q.v.) opposition. This was manifested in secret societies like the Order of American Knights, and its inner action circle, the Sons of Liberty. Since the story was that they identified themselves with special copper coins, they were popularly called Copperheads. That this was also the name of a venomous pit viper common to the Old Northwest that struck (like its cousin, the cottonmouth water moccasin) without benefit of rattles, was no accident. The Copperheads were prevalent in the southern areas of Ohio, Indiana, and Illinois. Confederate agents tried unsuccessfully to organize them to free Rebels held at prisoner-of-war camps, to disrupt conscription, and to upset the

Democratic Convention at Chicago in 1864. Union detectives infiltrated these organizations and arrested their leaders, leading to mass trials, especially in Indiana, which resulted in the landmark U.S. Supreme Court case *ex parte* Milligan *et al.* (q.v.).

CORINTH, BATTLE OF. *See* CORINTH CAMPAIGN.

CORINTH CAMPAIGN. As the Confederates invaded Kentucky in the late summer of 1862, forcing the troops commanded by Maj. Gen. Don Carlos Buell (q.v.) to follow, Maj. Gen. Ulysses S. Grant (q.v.) and his men were spread out across northern Mississippi based on Memphis. The Confederates had brought two forces across the Mississippi River from Arkansas (Maj. Gen. Earl Van Dorn) and Missouri (Maj. Gen. Sterling Price [q.v.]) to keep Grant busy. Since Maj. Gen. John Pope (q.v.) was to go east to fight Confederates under Gen. Robert E. Lee (q.v.), his forces were given to the next senior officer under Grant, Brig. Gen. William S. Rosecrans (q.v.). Grant was still burdened with his drinking reputation and troubled with the surprise at Shiloh (q.v.). Rosecrans had never lost a battle, been drunk, or been surprised. It was natural that the perfectionist Rosecrans and the stubborn Grant would conflict somewhere over something. The Corinth Campaign provided the means.

In August 1862, Rosecrans received orders to send about half of his army to assist Buell in Kentucky. With the rest, he was to go to northern Mississippi. Seeing Grant at Memphis and Rosecrans separated from each other, Confederates under Price moved between them and secured Iuka. Rosecrans saw opportunity here. While Price might defeat either him or Grant in turn, if they cooperated they had Price in a trap between them, provided they could keep Van Dorn from joining Price. The plan was for Grant to keep Van Dorn at bay while half of his men attacked Price at Iuka. Upon hearing the fire, Rosecrans would launch the final blow from south of town.

As often happens in pincer attacks, the two Federal columns lost contact. Rosecrans moved up to Iuka on September 19, only to find that he faced Price's whole force in ambush. Grant was nowhere to be seen. Price eventually retreated out of the trap that Grant and Rosecrans had prepared. Rosecrans was angry. What had happened to Grant? One tale is that Grant was so impressed with the news of Antietam that he tried to negotiate Price into surrender without bloodshed, thinking the war over. Price negotiated with Grant and fought Rosecrans. The other story involves drink. Local tradition holds that Grant was drunk once again, he and his staff celebrating the Antietam victory and the end of the war. The third tale says that Grant was jealous of Rosecrans, a winning, talkative, critical of Grant's shortcomings, publicity-wise rival, and decided to let him lose once.

In any case, Grant and Rosecrans were never quite the same with each other again. Price joined Van Dorn, and under the latter's leadership they marched all over northern Mississippi, confusing the Federals. Finally Rosecrans got smart and realized that the only place worth holding was the rail junction at Corinth. Van Dorn arrived after Rosecrans had occupied the old Confederate fortifications built there after the Shiloh defeat. For two days, October 3–4, 1862, Van Dorn and Price assaulted the earthworks, driving Rosecrans to the inner works, but never able to break his lines. Rosecrans tried to get his men to attack out from the forts, but subordinates failed to move in time, and the opportunity was lost. Van Dorn retreated, losing 8,600 men to Rosecrans' 2,200.

Rosecrans launched a pursuit and drove in Van Dorn's army at Big Hill. Meanwhile, Grant also sent out a pursuing column that was halted by the Confederates at the Tallahatchie River. On October 6, Grant halted the chase lest Van Dorn catch one of the two Union columns strung out unsupported and defeat them in detail. Rosecrans protested. He wanted to head for Vicksburg. Grant, contrary to what Maj. Gen. Henry W. Halleck (q.v.) and President Abraham Lincoln (q.v.) wanted, ordered the halt again. Then he and Rosecrans went after each other verbally after a Cincinnati newspaper called Grant's halt unwise. Grant tried to resign, Lincoln refused him, but Rosecrans received a promotion to major general and took over Buell's spot as head of the Army of the Cumberland. Grant and Rosecrans would quarrel again the following year during the Chattanooga Campaign (q.v.), and this time Grant would win, decisively.

CORNING LETTER. Erastus Corning was the leader of a committee of New York Democrats (q.v.) who protested all arbitrary arrests—those in which the detainees had been denied their ordinary right to the writ of *habeas corpus* (q.v.), such as in the case of *ex parte* Vallandigham (q.v.). Lincoln told Corning that the ordinary courts had proved inadequate during the rebellion, and the Constitution had provided for setting them aside in such emergencies. Lincoln denied that the arrest of Vallandigham was vindictive. It was rather preventative. Vallandigham was not arrested for making speeches, but for inciting others to resist the war effort. Lincoln asked Corning the rhetorical question, must he shoot the draft dodger and not touch those who encouraged him to do the act?

CORRUPTION BEFORE, DURING, AND AFTER THE CIVIL WAR. The American fascination with and horror at corruption in government is older than the nation itself. The Founding Fathers talked of how the British system was corrupting the pure republican institutions of the New World, and such a feeling helped point the way to the American

Revolution. It was a reoccurring theme of the "Revolution of 1800" that put the Jeffersonians in power, and it was an integral part of the Jacksonian Era before the War with Mexico. Both Thomas Jefferson and Andrew Jackson, especially the latter, believed that they were taking the nation back to an earlier time of political purity. Neither really accomplished his goal, but they caused a change in the American party system each time that was critical for the future.

The 1850s marked another era in which the jeremiads of the ills of corruption flowed like molten lava over the American political landscape. The depth of the corruption and the fears of those who opposed it ran deep and were an important undercurrent among the causes of the Civil War. Both the Republicans (q.v.) in the North and the Fire-Eaters (q.v.) (Secessionists) of the South sought to cleanse the nation by getting rid of the ills of slavery or the Slave Power, on the one hand, or the damned Yankee moralists who reputedly sold wooden nutmegs and unnecessarily interfered with a booming cotton economy that drove the nation's progress, on the other.

Political corruption, the illegal obtaining of private profit or advantage through the political system and the subversion of the political process for personal ends beyond those of ambition, helped discredit the Democrats and destroy the Whigs (qq.v.) in the decade before the Civil War. That is to say, the war came as much because of the activities of a "plundering generation" as of the "blundering generation" seen by historians in the past. It assumed a sectional aspect, particularly in the creation of potential railroad routes to the West. As there were insufficient private resources to construct so long a line, and the government could afford to assist only one transcontinental route, where it began was essential. And to the disgust of Northerners, the South had the best possible passage.

To counter this advantage, the North flexed its own political power to prove that the Central Overland route would be the best. Most important was a measure that was to create a territory west of Missouri to entice settlement and negate the South's Texas advantage. But the men who wanted the Northern route did not have the votes needed without Southern support. The result was the Kansas–Nebraska Act (q.v.), which repealed the Missouri Compromise and opened the whole West above the 36°30′ line to slavery. Northern settlers rushed to Kansas to stop the extension of slavery, but the railroad men tried to buy Congress' approval of a pro-slave state constitution for Kansas. On top of that, the U.S. Supreme Court endorsed the Southern position on slavery in the territories in the 1857 Dred Scott case (q.v.). It all looked corrupt, and a lot of it was. But it spurred the organization of a sectional party, the Republicans, dedicated to cleaning out the Slave Power in Washington and substituting its own vision for the development of America. It brought the Civil War that much closer.

The Civil War was full of many contradictions. There was the need to treat the Confederate soldiers as prisoners of war rather than as Rebels to be hanged; the need to trade food and medicines to the South for its cotton to bolster Yankee monetary exchange abroad; the commission system of paying off treasury and tax agents who went South to find these sources of traditional income now cut off by war; the commission agents who could expedite anything for a fee; and the shoddy contractors who sold the government dead cavalry horses, sand in place of gunpowder, cardboard shoes instead of leather, and felt uniforms that fell apart in use rather than the cloth and wool promised. It all expedited the continued use of political "influence," this time into good Republican hands and away from the prewar Slave Power Conspiracy (q.v.).

After the war, Reconstruction offered the Republicans another chance to extend their political influence—this time into the conquered South. But their identification with African-American freedom, equal rights, and the franchise made them anathema to the white South. These freed blacks were a continuing visual reminder that the Confederacy had failed. Yet no matter how the Republicans might want to cut it, they could not win the South without the Rebel white vote. Too few states had a black voting majority; and too few had sufficient white Unionists to help flesh out the count (besides, they hated the freed blacks as much as the Rebs did).

So to counter the racial distaste the party had among whites, the Republicans tried to emphasize economic assistance. The method of Northern economic aid would be the construction of railroads. The new Republican governments went to work to institute the "Gospel of Prosperity." It was an appeal to the voters to adopt the Yankee vision of progress through industrial growth. It was not that the Republicans wished to abandon blacks to their white antagonists. That was not the intent of the Republican program—but that was exactly what happened. In effect, the corruption that greased the wheels of progress subtly changed the emphasis of Reconstruction, just enough to compromise its original idealistic objectives.

It worked in the North as well as, perhaps even better than, in the South. Economic expansion, which was marked by the scandals in Washington in nearly every department of government, both houses of Congress, and most major cities, led to a demand for reform. By 1872, Liberal Republican (q.v.) reform had become the new crusade, and Reconstruction had been branded as a part of the sickness of corruption. In reality, the corruption was no worse than in the 1850s. The reformers were not attacking the system so much as the idea of corruption. The corruption issue gave them an edge over the opposition, but the intent was not to change how government worked so much as who worked it.

Nothing revealed the limits of reform more than the election of 1876 and the Compromise of 1877 (q.v.). To obtain a reform-minded Republican instead of a reform-minded Democrat for president, shameless political corruption was resorted to by both sides. The Republicans did a better job and took the prize, installing Rutherford (or was it "Rutherfraud," as his enemies insisted?) B. Hayes (q.v.) in the White House. But Hayes did not change much in how the system worked. He expected political appointments to contribute to the party; there were spoils for everyone, even the relatives of Benjamin F. Butler (q.v.) of Massachusetts, whose name was synonymous with pay-offs; the Louisiana Returning Board that had voted for Hayes all got Federal jobs; and President Ulysses S. Grant's (q.v.) personal secretary, Orville Babcock, who fairly reeked with the stench of corruption, found a political sinecure courtesy of the "scrupulous" President Hayes. The more things changed, the more they remained the same.

CORWIN AMENDMENT. After the House and Senate tried to compromise the First Secession of the Southern States (q.v.) to no avail, they finally got together and passed the Corwin Amendment, named after Thomas Corwin of Ohio. Essentially, it said that no amendment of the U.S. Constitution as regards slavery ought to be allowed in the future. This was to guarantee slavery where it existed in the Southern states. It had a real problem within its text. Was it possible to prohibit amendment of the Constitution? The nation never got a chance to find out, as the Civil War was on before the Corwin amendment could be submitted to the states for ratification.

CORWIN COMMITTEE OF THIRTY-THREE. When the First Secession of the Southern States (q.v.) began, calls went out that Congress ought to do something to compromise the situation. Congress made an effort. There was no shortage of talent among members, but to have been successful would have been to rectify the errors of a generation. Perhaps it was too much to ask.

The matter was not helped any by the factionalism that existed, especially in the House of Representatives. The Democratic Party (q.v.) was separated into five blocs. There were the Breckinridge Democrats, which included the more aggressive secessionists. There were the Douglas Democrats, who had been strengthened by the 1.2 million popular votes Senator Stephen A. Douglas (q.v.) had received from every section of the country. There were Upper South Democrats, who were badly split over secession's advisability. There were the Pacific Coast Democrats, who were beginning to feel for the first time the growing power of the Far West. Finally, there were the Old Northwest Democrats, who were interested in keeping the Mississippi and the Port of New Orleans open.

The Republicans (q.v.) were also split, but not as badly. There were two groups here. The Radicals or Irrepressibles wanted immediate action taken against the seceding states and felt compelled to answer Southern Fire-Eaters (q.v.) with as much fire of their own. Then there were the Moderate Republicans. They tried to keep silent and remain noncommittal so as not to limit President-elect Abraham Lincoln's (q.v.) options before he was inaugurated. The result was that about 60 percent of the House was against some form of compromise. "We have saved the union so often," said Thaddeus Stevens of Pennsylvania, "that I am afraid we shall save it to death."

But the House felt obligated to try. It set up the Committee of Thirty-three, chaired by Thomas Corwin of Ohio, as soon as South Carolina seceded. Several proposals came out of the committee. One was to open the territories to all citizens, with slavery protected until statehood was achieved, essentially the Southern Non-Exclusion Doctrine, rejected by all Republicans and Douglas Democrats. It was proposed that fugitive slaves be paid for by the states that shielded them. No Northern congressman could vote for that. There were to be no African-Americans granted citizenship or allowed to vote. The Republicans could not abide that, because several Northern states allowed both. Indeed, the longer the Committee of Thirty-three worked, the more it justified its nickname, "the coffin." Everything seemed to die there. This left the Committee of Thirteen in the Senate to act.

COUSHATTA MASSACRE. In 1874, Redemption took another turn to violence in Louisiana's Red River Parish, the power base for a family of Vermont Carpetbaggers named Twitchell (qq.v.). The family had the support of the black voters, who outnumbered whites by four to one, so their tenure looked unbeatable by ordinary electoral methods. The excuse for violence was an argument between whites and blacks at a nearby town that turned bloody. The whites killed their opponents, and the shooting spread to Coushatta. The Red River whites asked for reinforcement from neighboring parishes. Armed whites from the White League (q.v.) arrived and arrested the local Republican (q.v.) officeholders, demanding they resign their positions and be escorted to Texas by a posse of their own choosing. After the Republicans left town, young White League members voiced dissatisfaction with the results. They pursued the Republicans and caught up with them near Shreveport. There the six prisoners, one of whom was a Twitchell, their chosen posse standing aside, were murdered in what became known as the Coushatta Massacre. Governor William Pitt Kellogg (q.v.) asked for Federal help, and a battalion of the Seventh Cavalry arrived and restored the Republicans to power. The cavalry also arrested about 20 whites and charged them with murder and civil rights violations. But the charges were later dropped as state Democrats and White League supporters screamed "military despotism."

COVODE RESOLUTION. *See* IMPEACHMENT.

COX PLAN OF RECONSTRUCTION. By 1865, it was evident that the fall of the Confederacy was only a matter of time. Republicans agreed that the Southern slaveholders were responsible for the rebellion, and they believed that the planters' political power had to be broken and that the freedmen could provide a loyal wedge into Southern politics. But they also believed that they had to maintain white supremacy in the nation.

One of the Republican politicians who sought an answer to the problem of the free black in racist white America was Jacob D. Cox. A war hero at Antietam, major general in the Union army, and experienced in the occupation of the South Atlantic Coast, Cox was an acknowledged "expert" in the "Negro problem." Republicans feared that Andrew Johnson's (q.v.) Reconstruction of the South without reference to the rights of African-Americans would hurt them in state and national elections as "Black Republicans."

Cox believed that he could find a middle ground between the equal rights for African-Americans of Radical Republicans and the no rights stand of Southerners and Northern Democrats. Cox proposed that an area along the Southeastern Atlantic Coast from Charleston to and including all of the Florida peninsula should be cleared of all whites and set aside as an all-black territory. Within its boundaries, blacks would be able to rule themselves politically and economically in peace. So long as blacks stayed in their reserve, they would be equal citizens. Outside this area, they would be second-class citizens, at the mercy of local law.

Unbelievably, Cox had managed to stand for reunion, a secure future; the guarantee of basic rights for African-Americans in their part of the South; and the denial of black social, political, and economic equality in the rest of the nation. This insured him a long and fruitful political career in Ohio, but in a nation that had had its fill of Indian removal in the 1830s, the notion of forcibly removing white and black populations was doomed to failure.

CRATER, BATTLE OF THE. *See* PETERSBURG, SIEGE OF.

CRÉDIT MOBILIER SCANDAL. After the passage of the Pacific Railroad Act in 1862 (q.v.) and its amendment in 1864, railroad investment took on an increasing attractiveness to various entrepreneurs in the United States. As lucrative as the rail investments might be, the construction and management of the transcontinental railroad, the Union Pacific, offered more to those wise in the ways of maximizing profit at public expense. Their efforts went into establishing a construction company to build the railroad across the plains and mountains. It was called the Crédit Mobilier of America, to differentiate it from the corrupt French company involved in the construction of the Suez Canal—which should have been an omen of things to come for President Ulysses S. Grant (q.v.).

The Crédit Mobilier was set up at the behest of financier Thomas Durant. It was a construction company, so far as the public knew, with which the railroad contracted to build the line to the west. What the public did not know was that essentially the Crédit Mobilier was run by the same men who directed the railroad. They bought items cheap and sold them to themselves dear, charging the Federal government the higher price and pocketing the difference. If the profits were not in cash, they came in the form of securities that allowed the men to control the railroad and its land grants, particularly the timber and mineral rights that came with them.

Congressman (House Committee on Pacific Railroads) and shovel-maker Oakes Ames was put in charge. He went around among the government-appointed directors and his political peers and distributed shares in the Crédit Mobilier "where it would do the most good," he said sagely later, free to some, at a small cost to others. Among those blessed with Crédit Mobilier shares were the vice president of the United States, Schuyler Colfax (q.v.); the speaker of the house, future president James A. Garfield; perennial presidential hopeful Senator James G. Blaine; and a slew of normally moralistic Radical Republicans. Everyone was in on the take, except Charles Sumner (q.v.) and his kind. To this day, no one knows the names of all of those involved in the American version of the Crédit Mobilier. Suffice it to say, the estimated six dozen did not lose face in financial wizardry. They came from Boston, Chicago, Philadelphia, and New York City. They included William B. Ogden, John Murray Forbes, Charles Butler, Thomas A. Scott, John Edgar Thomson, Erastus Corning, John V. L. Pruyn, John I. Blair, Russell Sage, August Belmont, J. F. D. Lanier, and Samuel J. Tilden, corporate lawyer and future Democrat candidate for the presidency in 1876 (on an honest government platform, of course).

In 1871, well after the Pacific Railroad had been finished and nearly everyone paid off, a combination of directors elected Thomas A. Scott as president of the Union Pacific. Scott was big in the Pennsylvania Railroad, and his election looked like a nationwide railroad power grab to many. So they backed litigation against Ames and banded together to throw Scott out of his presidency. In revenge, the Scott group then leaked old letters in which Ames stupidly named those whom he had bribed. The story went public with a bang—right in the middle of the election of 1872 (q.v.). President Ulysses S. Grant, all of Congress, and one-third of the Senate were up for reconsideration. And although the president was clean, the rest of his administration was not.

There was no way around it. Congress would have to investigate. Of course everyone professed wide-eyed innocence. But the facts were out, and the government had to take the Crédit Mobilier to court. Naturally the suit was civil, not criminal (one did not send upstanding citizens like congressmen to jail in 19th-century America), and eventually the Supreme Court ruled that the government could not collect even on the fraud until 1895, 30 years after the first bonds went out, as stipulated in the Federal charter. The only ones who really suffered were Oakes Ames and Vice President Colfax. Ames lost his congressional seat—but he kept his cash. Grant won a second term by dumping Colfax from the ticket. But Grant might have gone down the road too had the opposition not backed the ending of Reconstruction and abandoning the former slaves to Southern white rule, something Grant nobly refused to do. But with four more years of scandal in the offing, such compunctions would change mightily in 1876.

CREOLE COLORED PEOPLE. *See* BLACKS, URBAN, IN THE SOUTH DURING RECONSTRUCTION.

"CRIME AGAINST KANSAS." *See* SUMNER, CHARLES.

CRIME OF '73. *See* GRANT, ULYSSES S., ADMINISTRATION—DOMESTIC POLICIES.

CRIME OF '76. *See* ELECTION OF 1876 AND COMPROMISE OF 1877.

CRITTENDEN COMMITTEE OF THIRTEEN. Although the U.S. Senate was not as divided into blocs as the House of Representatives' Committee of Thirty-three (q.v.) when it formed its compromise Committee of Thirteen, chaired by Sen. John J. Crittenden of Kentucky, the forlorn result was the same. About 75 percent of the Senate was against compromise in some form or another. Actually, the real problem was that Northerners, especially President-elect Abraham Lincoln (q.v.), assumed that secession was a bluff. The South would soon enough come to its senses and crawl back into the Union. But in the slave states, secession was the most effective answer to a generation of what it saw as unfair and unconstitutional attacks on its guaranteed institution of slavery.

Crittenden's family personified what the possibility of Civil War would mean. It would divide almost equally between Union and Confederacy. Crittenden hoped to avoid that awful fate. The proposals that came out of the Crittenden Committee of Thirteen were to prevent Congress from ending slavery in any territory surrounded by slave states, to order Congress not to interfere with the domestic slave trade, to have slaveholders who could not recover fugitive slaves be paid by the Federal government, to prohibit any constitutional amendment abolishing slavery in any state where it already existed, and to extend the Missouri Compromise line to the eastern border of California, solving the problem of slavery in the territories.

Most Southerners indicated that they would accept the Missouri Compromise extension. But Abraham Lincoln could not, as it violated his most sacred tenet, the Wilmot Proviso (q.v.), as the solution to the extension of slavery into the West. He also feared that if the line were drawn, the South would spare no effort to extend slave territory into the Caribbean, especially Cuba. Lincoln pledged that he would protect slavery in the states where it existed and enforce the Fugitive Slave Law from the Compromise of 1850 (q.v.), but no more. Crittenden asked that his proposals be voted on in a national referendum, but Lincoln said that the country had to face up to the problem, not avoid it through compromise. This meant that with the failure of the Crittenden proposals, and Corwin's Committee of Thirty-three, some other body than Congress would have to act to stop the coming war. That was the Washington Peace Conference (q.v.), then in session.

CUBAN INSURRECTION. A nasty problem that concerned foreign policy during the Ulysses S. Grant (q.v.) administration was the 10-year-long armed insurrection in Cuba beginning in 1868, which threatened American economic interests, which claimed damages against arbitrary actions of Spanish officials there. These problems occupied Secretary of State Hamilton Fish (q.v.) throughout his eight-year term as secretary and often proved embarrassing. He had to try to get the Spanish to negotiate with the rebels to end the conflict and at the same time prevent the Congress from recognizing them as belligerents, which would extend and deepen the war and damage further American businesses. Fish also wanted to end slavery, which was still legal in the island, which provided the basis for some in Congress to call for American intervention. While Fish was engaged on other matters, President Grant moved to recognize Cuban belligerency. Although Fish was not opposed to this in principle, he preferred to keep it back to prompt Spain to negotiate. Grant agreed after a belated consultation with Fish and allowed the secretary to hold up the promulgation of the decree. There was little else he could do, because the president needed Fish's support on the Santo Domingo situation, and he dared not alienate him over Cuba. Meanwhile, Spain promised reforms on the island and a redress of the rebels' grievances.

In the meantime, the Spanish government had a change in its monarchy. Fish threatened to withhold recognition of King Alfonso XII if an immediate settlement on the Cuban revolutionary mess were not achieved favoring the rebels, as promised earlier. Otherwise, he intimated that outside powers might feel obliged to intervene and force a settlement. Spain quickly agreed to Fish's proposals, which included reform of Spanish government on the island with a view to eventual independence and the abolition of slavery. Spain dragged out the negotiations until it could place enough troops to stop the revolution in its tracks. Then it agreed to an arbitration panel's determination of the amount owed the United States for prior claims, and the Cuban problem was solved until it sprang up anew in the 1890s. *See also* FILIBUSTERING.

CUMMING *ET AL. v.* BOARD OF EDUCATION OF RICHMOND COUNTY, GEORGIA (1899). In 1899, the informal system of separate education in the South and elsewhere received the blessing of the highest court in the land. In the case of Cumming *et al. v.* Board of Education of Richmond County, Georgia (not Plessy *v.* Ferguson [q.v.] as commonly supposed, which handled segregation in public accommodations), public education was determined to be a state and local function as determined by the taxes raised, and beyond the scope of the Fourteenth Amendment's (q.v.) "equal protection of the laws" clause, and that segregation of education *per se* was not on its face discriminatory. The Supreme Court was unanimous in its opinion, unlike *Plessy*, in which Justice John Marshall Harlan of Kentucky had dissented. But the decision gave the green light to the South's unequal approach to segregated education.

CUMMINGS *v.* MISSOURI (1866). *See* GARLAND, *EX PARTE* (1866).

CURTIS, GEORGE W. *See* GRANT, ULYSSES S., ADMINISTRATION—DOMESTIC POLICIES.

D

DABNEY'S MILLS, BATTLE OF. *See* PETERSBURG, SIEGE OF.

DALLAS, BATTLE OF. *See* ATLANTA CAMPAIGN.

DARWIN, CHARLES. *See* SOCIAL DARWINISM.

DAVIS BEND EXPERIMENT. As the Union army moved southward, it came across many abandoned lands and slaves, which promised the possibility of actually improvising a truly radical change in Southern society with free black laborers farming their own land. Unlike the Port Royal Experiment (q.v.), which was located in the South Atlantic sea islands and run by abolitionist (q.v.) idealists from New England (q.v.), wartime western experiments in the Mississippi Valley were more geared to the mainstream of the Republican Party, a hard-hearted practical application of the prewar free labor ideology. None achieved its goals more than the free labor experiment at Davis Bend, Mississippi, located on the Father of Waters about 25 miles south of the Confederate fortress at Vicksburg.

The man in charge of the Davis Bend Experiment during the Civil War was John Eaton (q.v.), an antislavery (q.v.) man but not an abolitionist, whom Maj. Gen. Ulysses S. Grant (q.v.) had placed in charge of the thousands of slaves who had fled slavery for security behind the Union army's lines. Eaton used the old plantation system, hiring gangs of blacks throughout Mississippi, Tennessee, and Arkansas, but he reserved an independent black farmer concept for his showpiece at Davis Bend. The experiment at Davis Bend would be managed by Lt. Col. Samuel Thomas, a brash, young Ohioan "of the right Christian spirit," according to Eaton. Thomas set to work, marked off plots ranging in size from 10 to 150 acres, and doled them out to the freedmen. The project was an instant success. Thomas noted that his black charges worked much harder on their own land plots than on those left on a plantation system.

News of Eaton's experiment soon reached Washington, and an impressed President Abraham Lincoln (q.v.) ordered the project to continue in 1865. Eaton changed the formula somewhat and now established 181 cooperatives of 3 to 25 African-American farmers who were given land in proportion to the size of their companies. Taking a leaf from the management book of the Joseph R. Davis family (his brother, Jefferson Davis [q.v.], was president of the Confederacy), the blacks were allowed to police the farms themselves and punish lawbreakers through their own courts, run solely by their elected leaders. Eaton also brought in teachers and established a half dozen schools at the Bend.

After the war, the Freedmen's Bureau (q.v.) took over the administration of Davis Bend under its state assistant commissioner, Samuel Thomas, the same man who had begun the wartime project at Eaton's behest. The land was eventually returned to Joseph R. Davis, its original owner, and he leased it to his former slave foreman, Benjamin Montgomery, who seemed to grate on Thomas' soul. Perhaps Montgomery was too clever to suit the Yankee Bureau man. Thomas was glad to see blacks succeed, so long as they did it in their proper subordinate place. In the end, Davis and Montgomery combined to get rid of Thomas as head of the Bureau in Mississippi, and Davis sold his land to Montgomery, his former slave, for $300,000 in November 1866.

Davis Bend was one of the few labor experiments in the South that showed what blacks could do on their own, and it became the nucleus for the all-black town of Mound Bayou, when Montgomery's high rental fees drove many blacks away. But it was doomed to failure by forces beyond the control of the successful black farmers, including the pardon policy (q.v.) of President Andrew Johnson (q.v.), which returned the land to the Davis family to be bought by Montgomery, and the conservatism of the Constitution and the Republican Party, which put restraint on such a project as land donation outside the confines of temporary wartime exigencies.

DAVIS, EDMUND J. (1827–1883). The Scalawag (q.v.) governor of Texas during Reconstruction, E. J. Davis was born in St. Augustine, Florida. He moved to Texas with his widowed mother when he was 10 years old. Settling at Galveston, he read law, was admitted to the bar, and practiced his profession at Corpus Christi, Laredo, and Brownsville. He was deputy collector of customs at Laredo in the early 1850s and then elected district attorney at Brownsville. His service impressed the right people, and he was made district judge for the Lower Rio Grande Valley, a position he held until he refused to take an oath to the Confederacy. Davis was defeated in the election to the secession convention, to which some attributed his Union support. But it is more likely that he internalized Union feelings prevalent throughout most of the border region, dependent as it was on the Federal government for its economic activity and protection.

During the war, Davis organized a Union cavalry regiment. He was captured soon after and barely escaped being hanged for treason against Texas and the South. He returned to the First Texas (Union) Cavalry, composed of local Hispanics, Union men, and a few Confederate deserters, and led it on a raid to Laredo, but was defeated by Rebel troops led by Santos Benavides (giving the modern reader some idea of the multicultural recruits employed by both sides in this area). He was then transferred to the Louisiana theater, where he and his regiment served the rest of the war, Davis being promoted to brigadier general. After the war, he declined an appointment to the Texas supreme court offered by Maj. Gen. Philip H. Sheridan (q.v.).

But Davis did take a consistent, loyal position in Texas politics, lamenting the lack of a true Republican Party (q.v.) in 1866, when the state went back to proto-Confederate rule. He recommended that a loyal state militia be organized to protect Texas' Union population, which included a fourth of all whites as well as all of the former slaves. He also took the lead in suggesting that Union men organize their own convention of all males, black and white, pledged to universal manhood suffrage and declaring themselves Republicans. Davis was a man ahead of his time, but his idea was taken up by others at Houston a year later after passage of the Military Reconstruction Acts (q.v.). Delegates of both races from 27 counties attended and agreed to promote the Republican Party through the use of Union Loyal Leagues (q.v.).

In 1868, Davis was elected a delegate to the state constitutional convention, where he became the convention chairman. The Texas convention process was held up by a philosophical division between Republicans that was exploited by Conservative Democrat delegates. Essentially, the Republicans divided over whether they should disfranchise former Confederate whites in the new constitution; divide the state into former Rebel, African-American, and Union white-dominated states (Texas had a special provision in the Compromise of 1850 [q.v.] that permitted it to be divided into as many as five states); and adopt a provision of *ab initio* (q.v.) (declaring all legal acts committed since 1861 secession as null and void). Davis led the Radical Republicans, who favored all three positions.

With Davis using the power of the chair to their advantage, they finally moved the convention to authorize the division of the state through several doubtful parliamentary procedures, including voting without a quorum. Davis also proposed that all voters take an oath that was similar to the Union's wartime ironclad oath—that the voter had never directly or indirectly willingly aided or abetted the Confederate cause. This measure was defeated when four African-American Republicans crossed over and voted with the Moderates. The result was a document that recognized universal manhood suffrage (the delegates had considered offering the franchise to women, but eventually dropped the issue), the supremacy of the U.S. Constitution as amended and all Federal treaties and laws, the full freedom of the blacks, easier access to corporate charter, state financing of internal improvements, and a dual (segregated) public education system.

Meanwhile, the Radicals met in a party convention (boycotted by the Moderates) at Houston and nominated Davis. It was then that E. J. Davis pulled off the most brilliant political maneuver of the election. The Houston platform was almost an exact duplicate of the Moderates', an acceptance of the constitution and everything it stood for. The whole state was aghast. What had the past two years' political infighting been about, anyhow? Where were disfranchisement, division of the state, and *ab initio?* Ultra-Radicals were enraged, but they really had no place to go. They would in the end have to swallow Davis' platform. The Moderates cried foul. The Radicals had stolen their platform. Moreover, the state was rife with rumors that the commander of Texas, Bvt. Maj. Gen. J. J. Reynolds (q.v.), would support the Davis ticket in exchange for a U.S. Senate seat under the new government, a proposal the moderate candidate had already refused to make on his own, over the objections of his political managers. Both sides went to Washington to obtain the support of the Ulysses S. Grant (q.v.) administration. Grant chose to support the Radicals.

The result was a Radical electoral win in December 1869, with the erstwhile support of General Reynolds. The Davis administration, the only Republican administration elected in Texas during Reconstruction, remains highly controversial to this day. It would probably be fair to say that Davis ruled from an impossible position, as he lacked a true majority vote, and that he made some unfortunate decisions, often with the best intentions, that backfired. Continuation of white violence led Davis to call for a black and tan state militia to replace the Army, which now moved to the frontier, and a state police to replace the rebellion-tainted Texas Rangers. Recent studies credit the militia and police with more ability than once supposed, although the state adjutant general absconded to Europe with nearly $40,000 in state funds. The major obstacle to white Texans was their high proportion of black officers and rank and file, and Davis' declaration of martial law to protect African-American and loyal white citizens. But they kept the law, especially around polling time.

Another Davis program, later condemned for its expense, was the creation of the segregated public school system. Like most Reconstruction state institutions in most Southern states, this system was highly centralized, with appointments made in Austin. The Democrats (q.v.) would keep the system after Redemption (q.v.) but return it to local control, which effectively gutted it as far as blacks were concerned. Commerce and industry received a boost from the Republican legislature, and the state debt went up as much from needed expenses for increased public services as fraud. Interestingly the Democrats continued to assist transportation projects as much as the Republicans had after Redemption. Perhaps the dumbest thing that Davis did from a public relations point of view was pardon the Kiowa–Comanche chiefs Satanta and Big Tree, after their companion Satank had been "shot while trying to escape" up at Ft. Sill in Indian Territory.

By 1873, it was obvious that the Republicans were done for in Texas. This time whites would turn out *en masse* to vote for Davis' Democrat opponent, Richard Coke. As expected, the totals showed Coke with a large majority, but Davis seized upon a technicality to sue for retention of his office. His contention was that a new election law had repealed only the first part of the old ordinance, but not the second part that required that the election last for four days (it had not). Since the two sections were separated by a semicolon, punctuation being very important in many types of legal documents, the suit became known as the Semicolon Case. Both sides sent armed men to Austin to defend their man. The Radicals appealed to Grant for military assistance to save Texas from "Ku Klux Democracy." Grant said that the dispute involved state law and the Federal government had no interest in it. He lectured Davis on the need to yield to the voice of the people.

Faced with no help from Washington, outnumbered in the military realm, and with the people and politicians ignoring the Semicolon Case, which Davis had won in a Republican-dominated court, the governor stepped down. The Democrats wisely refrained from any overt violence so that Grant would have no reason to change his mind about Federal intervention. Davis stayed on in Austin and practiced law. He headed the Texas Republican Party until his death, standing for governor once again in 1880 (he lost by 100,000 votes). He was considered for a position in the Chester A. Arthur cabinet, but failed to win a previous congressional election, which caused Arthur to recognize him as a potential political liability. He was never accused of personal dishonesty at any time. His personal and social conduct remained above reproach in every way. His belief in the Union cause never slackened, either. He never thought that his fellow Texans were anything but unreconstructed Rebels. As unchanged as they, E. J. Davis died in 1883, a Scalawag to the end, and proud of it.

DAVIS, HENRY WINTER (1817–1865). Born at Annapolis, Maryland, Winter Davis was the son of an Episcopal rector who was the president of St. Johns College. He was raised in an upper class setting and graduated Kenyon College in 1837 with an education in the classics and an interest and skill in forensics. He went on to study law at the University of Virginia and practiced his profession at Alexandria and then Baltimore, where he lived the rest of his life. A polished orator, Winter Davis was a Baltimore politician of the old Whig Party (q.v.). He was elected to Congress in 1855 and served three terms before being retired for two years and then returned for one more term, which ended just before his premature death. Much of his political power was built on a gang of dockworkers known as the "pug uglies," who often rioted in select places on election day, scaring off opposition voters, to Davis' advantage.

In Congress, he was known for his outspokenness and hatred of the Democrats. He spoke out against the crooked, pro-slave Lecompton Constitution in

Kansas and criticized the James Buchanan (q.v.) administration in every respect. In 1859, he cast his vote for the Republicans to organize the U.S. House of Representatives, giving them control of the body for the first time in their existence. Davis' vote earned him the castigation of "Black Republican," the censure of the Maryland state assembly, and cost him his reelection in 1861.

By his 1863 reelection, Davis appealed to white middle class town dwellers, small farmers, and artisans to rid the state of the anachronism of slavery. He shrewdly pointed out that black soldiers allowed the poorer whites to stay home from the war, while the richer slaveholders could buy an exemption. Using the aid of Federal soldiers to shield his crooked election day antics, Davis and his Radical Republicans elected an emancipationist majority to the state legislature. On November 1, 1864, the drive to free the slaves met with success. Davis went on to champion black suffrage, seeing in the black vote a way for his political machine to move into previously Democrat bastions.

Along with his U.S. Senate ally, Benjamin Wade (q.v.) of Ohio, Davis introduced the Wade–Davis Bill (q.v.) into Congress. When President Abraham Lincoln (q.v.) pocket vetoed the bill, the two men issued their Wade–Davis Manifesto (q.v.). A civil libertarian, Davis believed that President Lincoln had overstepped his powers as president when he denied the writ of *habeas corpus* (q.v.) and relied on military courts to try wartime dissenters. He also stood forthrightly against the notions prevalent then of transporting the freed slaves to the Caribbean or back to Africa, maintaining that they had earned the right to be Americans through their labor and service in the Union armies. At the height of his state power, Davis died of pneumonia in December 1865.

DAVIS, JEFFERSON (1808–1889). Jefferson Davis was born in Kentucky, but his family soon removed to Mississippi. There he was educated in private schools before returning to Kentucky to attend Transylvania College. Receiving an appointment to the United States Military Academy, where he was a contemporary of Robert E. Lee, Joseph E. Johnston, and Albert Sidney Johnston (qq.v), Davis graduated in 1828. He served as an officer for seven years along the Western frontier. In 1835, he married the daughter of his regimental colonel, Zachary Taylor (q.v.). He resigned his commission and took his new wife to a plantation in the Felicianas north of Baton Rouge, Louisiana, where she died of a fever. Heartbroken, Davis lived the life of a recluse for several years at his brother Joseph's landholdings back in Mississippi.

Through the influence of his brother, Davis read widely and reentered public life in 1843, as a candidate for Congress. He lost the election, but did serve as a presidential elector in 1844 for James K. Polk. He stood for Congress again in 1845, won the election, but resigned his seat when the War with Mexico broke out. Davis had the necessary influence and education to become the colonel of the First Mississippi Rifle Regiment, the Red

Shirts. Davis took a conspicuous part in several battles, the most important being Buena Vista.

Davis parlayed his military reputation into a national political career in the 1850s. He was elected to the U.S. Senate, served as chairman of the military affairs committee, spoke out for the retention of all of Mexico conquered by the United States during the war and on behalf of Southern rights in the debates over the Compromise of 1850 (q.v.), and even suggested that the South secede rather than submit to what he saw as Yankee perfidy, stealing the fruits of war by preventing the westward movement of slavery. He resigned his seat and went home to run for governor on the Secessionist ticket, but lost the race to a Union man by less than 1,000 votes.

The loss discredited Davis much, but he recovered when his old friend, Franklin Pierce, invited him to come to Washington and serve as secretary of war. He became one of the most innovative secretaries the Department of War ever had. He experimented with camels as beasts of burden, established numerous forts to protect western travelers, and reorganized the numerous types of mounted regiments (dragoons, mounted rifles, and cavalry) in the Army into five units of modern light cavalry. He also supported the building of a transcontinental railroad and was instrumental in getting the Gadsden Purchase to make it possible to have a Southern route out of New Orleans or Memphis.

At the end of Pierce's term, Mississippi returned Davis to the Senate. There he stood for the repeal of the Missouri Compromise and the extension of slavery to all of the Western territories. In 1860, Davis and other Southerners bolted from the Democratic Party (q.v.) and set up Vice President John C. Breckinridge (q.v.) as their candidate. With a split Democrat Party, the rival Republicans (q.v.) easily elected Abraham Lincoln (q.v.) as president. Davis was mortified, but he urged the nation to stay whole. Unfortunately the crisis had passed beyond the control of the politicians, and the First Secession (q.v.) of the Lower South was the result.

Given his foot-dragging in the cause, Davis was really surprised when he was elected president of the provisional government of the Confederate States of America at Montgomery, Alabama. Davis organized a cabinet made up of conservative Southerners like himself and set about to unify the South behind him. The refusal of the Lincoln government to give up Forts Sumter (Charleston, South Carolina) and Pickens (Pensacola, Florida) forced the Confederates to fire the first shot or look less than independent. The result was to unify the South (and the North) and cause a Second Secession of the Upper South and the eventual popular election of Davis to head the Confederate government, now located at Richmond, Virginia.

Much has been written about Davis' inability to work with people of all beliefs, his favoritism to old West Point cronies, his preference for field command over political leadership (he had a neuralgia of the eye that intensified while he was in Richmond and mysteriously disappeared when he went out into the countryside to campaign or inspect the troops), and his willingness to argue an issue to its fine points. But he did manage to take a nation built from scratch and in four years nearly break up the whole United States. There was probably no other who could have done better.

As president, Davis instituted the first national draft of soldiers (*see* CONSCRIPTION AND DRAFT EVASION, CONFEDERATE), preserved the writ of *habeas corpus* and free speech despite the war and many outspoken opponents in the South (groups against him were either more radical in their pursuit of independence or openly pro-Union), moderated those who wished to reopen the slave trade, kept the tariff low, instituted a secret service that probably surpassed the modern Central Intelligence Agency in its audacity, and obtained the enlistment of black Confederate fighting men in exchange for their independence. He put a million men in the field out of a white population of seven million and required the North to raise twice that number to defeat him. Even as the final campaign began in 1865, Davis and Robert E. Lee were planning to unite with the remaining Rebel forces in North Carolina to defeat the Union armies in detail. Davis fled South, hoping to get out to the western part of the Confederacy but was taken by Union cavalry in Georgia, allegedly dressed in a woman's shawl, which soon became a full set of clothes as the story grew in the Northern yellow journalistic sheets of the day. Some historians believe that the reason he tried to escape was Lincoln's assassination (q.v.). But more recent research revealed his departure was part of an involved plan gone awry, because of Lt. Gen. Ulysses S. Grant's (q.v.) unexpectedly quick pursuit of Lee's army.

Davis spent the next two years under arrest in Fortress Monroe, Virginia. President Andrew Johnson (q.v.) refused to set Davis free, but he and his government did not charge him, either. After much thought, they decided to try Davis for treason. Johnson set up a special board made up of the attorney general and several prominent attorneys to prefer the charges. Meanwhile, Davis' attorney, a prominent Democrat, Charles O'Connor of New York, moved for a writ of *habeas corpus* (q.v.). This would force the government to bring charges against Davis or grant him bail. Finally, special prosecutor William M. Evarts appeared and told the court that the government's case was not ready and that Davis could be put out on bail.

Jefferson Davis was released on May 13, 1867, upon a bail bond signed by Yankee publicist Horace Greeley (q.v.) and other longtime Davis opponents, who were weary with the concept of a harsh peace and hoped his release might bind up the wounds of war and promote black civil rights and the vote. The government team then sought to gain an indictment. The statute of limitations for all crimes then was three years, which was fast approaching. But try as they might, the legal team could not agree on a way to proceed, and the investigators in Virginia did little to help out. Meanwhile, the U.S. Senate impeached President Andrew Johnson, and he employed several of the legal team in his own defense. Davis' trial was delayed again.

A great revival of Davis' reputation had taken place because of his stoic demeanor and apparent willingness to accept his fate. On December 25, 1868, President Johnson issued a blanket amnesty for all those who took part in the rebellion, including Davis. The Virginia circuit court moved a *nolle prosequi* (no further prosecution) motion be entered in the Davis case and the appeal to the Supreme Court be dismissed. On February 26, 1869, Davis was a free man, not liable to prosecution in any jurisdiction of the United States.

Davis traveled for a while, finally settling down in Beauvoir, a home near Biloxi, Mississippi, given to him by a friend. There he lived out his days, writing a defense of his actions as Confederate president (*The Rise and Fall of the Confederate Government*, in two long volumes) and relishing the role of elder statesman who had never surrendered, stripped of his rights as a citizen, unreconstructed to the end. He died in New Orleans on a business trip. His body was later disinterred and shipped to Richmond in a procession across a half dozen Southern railroads that rivaled Abraham Lincoln's journey to Springfield 23 years earlier.

DAY OF JUBILEE. *See* JUBILEE, DAY OF.

DEEP BOTTOM, BATTLE OF FIRST. *See* PETERSBURG, SIEGE OF.

DEEP BOTTOM, BATTLE OF SECOND. *See* PETERSBURG, SIEGE OF.

DEEP RUN, BATTLE OF. *See* PENNSYLVANIA CAMPAIGN.

DEMOCRATIC PARTY. Like their Republican (q.v.) opponents, the Civil War Democratic Party was composed of three major groups (or four, if one wishes to consider the seceded South to be mostly Democratic). First there were the Regular Democrats. These men were the largest group of Democrats, but were often ignored for the extremes. They generally supported the fighting of the Civil War, but reserved the right to criticize and vote against Republican policy in general and specific war measures in particular. They were unwilling to hold office in any fusion group that included Republicans, preferring to retain their independent party label. They might best be thought of as the loyal opposition.

The most important group of Democrats, from the Republican Party point of view, were the War Democrats. They were just like the Republicans on the war issue, so much so that they were willing to fuse with the Republicans in name. Their initial leader was U.S. Senator Stephen A. Douglas (q.v.) of Illinois. After he lost the election to Abraham Lincoln (q.v.), Douglas worked mightily to prevent the war. But when it came, he rushed to Lincoln's side to back him up. Douglas' death in June 1861 prevented Republican utilization of his full potential. But Conservative and Moderate Republicans knew that many more Democrats felt like Douglas. The result was the organization of the National Union Party (q.v.), a combination of Republicans and war Democrats putting forth combined tickets to carry doubtful Northern wartime state and national elections. The best example was the candidacy of War Democrat John Brough against Democrat Clement L. Vallandigham (q.v.) in Ohio in 1864.

The third group within the Democratic party during the Civil War was called the Peace Democrats. All sorts of anti-war, anti-Lincoln administration splinter groups were in this party wing. They were mislabeled "Copperheads" (q.v.) to show their latent disloyalty. Some wanted restoration of "the Union as it was, and the Constitution as it is," without Republican meddling under cover of winning the war. Others wanted to call a national convention to work out peace and limit the power of the national government. Still others wanted an independent Northwest separated from New England and allied with the South. In any case, they dominated the Democratic Convention and party platform in the election of 1864, although they could not force their candidate, George B. McClellan (q.v.), to go along with them. After the war, the peace Democrats would be an albatross to the other regular Democrats, too close to the defeated Confederacy for loyal men to vote their way in the elections of 1868 and 1872 (qq.v.). By 1876, they would win the popular vote but lose the electoral vote in the shenanigans that led to the Compromise of 1877.

DENMARK VESEY SLAVE REBELLION. *See* BLACK "PERSONAL-ITY" IN SLAVERY AND FREEDOM.

DIET AND MALNUTRITION. Lloyd Lewis, a newspaperman-turned-historian who had just finished a biography of Union general William T. Sherman (q.v.) and was beginning on a similar, monumental study of Ulysses S. Grant (q.v.), got to thinking about the diet of Southern soldiers and wondering if it and semi-tropical disease (q.v.) might not have had wider implications for the whole Confederate war effort. Although Lewis died before he could finish his study of Grant, he wrote regular letters to his editor that were collected and published for the benefit of other scholars.

In these letters, Lewis mused over how the Rebels would win the first day's battle and then almost inexplicably seem to falter. Examples are startling: Gettysburg, Shiloh, Perryville, Corinth (qq.v.), Stone's River—the names go on and on. He also observed how first-person accounts would describe how

Confederate soldier often went berserk when they captured Yankee camps, wagon trains, and warehouses, looting the myriad foodstuffs that Union quartermasters specialized in providing for their men in the field.

Lewis theorized that Southern troops were undernourished even when supplied by their own commissariat, so much so that it affected their performance on the battlefield. Perhaps their defeats were caused by a lack of stamina caused by the traditional diet of the poor (white and black) in the South—the three Ms of meat (pork fatback), cornmeal, and molasses. The Yankees, on the other hand, fed on bacon and wheat hardtack, real sugar and coffee, not to mention the beans, desiccated vegetables, canned fruit, and canned milk that adorned their diets at regular intervals.

Lewis posited that the longer the campaign, the more likely a Union victory was, especially as the war lengthened. "I wonder how much of it was pure physical weariness," Lewis mulled, "born of the lack of consistent food, imposed upon physiques not nurtured properly from infancy. They weren't lazy in battle, but they were called lazy in succeeding generations as visitors described them in their upland or swamp houses." It was all in the nutrients common to each section of the nation. *See also* DISEASE.

DIPLOMACY, C.S.—CIVIL WAR. One of the great weaknesses of the Confederacy was its emphasis on domestic politics. This was perhaps understandable, as constitutional arguments over the nature of the Union were the basis of secession (q.v.) in 1860. But once the Confederate government set itself up as an independent entity, foreign policy assumed a key role that the Rebels were essentially ill-equipped to handle.

Neither of the first two secretaries of state, Robert Toombs and R. M. T. Hunter, was deeply interested in foreign policy. Indeed, President Jefferson Davis (q.v.) made many early appointments with an eye to having a politician from each Confederate state in his cabinet, rather than the most capable men. It was under these men that the first ineffectual steps in foreign diplomacy were taken, with the appointment of the William L. Yancey–Pierre Rost–A. Dudley Mann delegation (q.v.) to represent the South on a roving basis in Europe. The main goal in sending this group was to get "Fire-Eater" (q.v.) William L. Yancey out of the country and domestic politics.

The next Confederate attempt to influence Europe was to send one man each to England and France. This was the famous James M. Mason–John Slidell mission that led to their capture and removal from HMS *Trent* (q.v.) on the high seas by the U.S. Navy. After much diplomatic argument, the two Rebels were released and sent on their way. Mason proved to be too much a tobacco-spitting plebian for the British upper crust (those who tended to support an independent South), but the French-speaking Louisianan Slidell fit right in with the French at all levels of society. Unfortunately for the South,

European adventures abroad had to have the support of the British Royal Navy to succeed, and this was lacking for the duration of the war.

In 1863, Judah P. Benjamin (q.v.) became secretary of state for the Confederates, and he ably secured several important French loans by reversing the embargo on shipping Southern cotton overseas. But by this time, the Rebel armies had lost the Perryville, Maryland, Vicksburg, and Pennsylvania Campaigns (qq.v.), making support of the Confederacy a generally bad bet. Benjamin then turned his efforts to behind-the-lines efforts by the Confederate secret service through British Canada and ultimately, many historians believe, the Lincoln assassination (q.v.). *See also* DIPLOMACY, U.S.—CIVIL WAR.

DIPLOMACY, U.S.—CIVIL WAR. The two American presidents of the North and South had common goals in the Civil War—to preserve what the Founding Fathers had wrought. The problem was that they had two different interpretations of the form of government necessary, union or separation. But they both had something else in common. Neither Abraham Lincoln (q.v.) nor Jefferson Davis (q.v.) had any experience in foreign policy. But here Lincoln had an advantage. He tended much more to compromise, to be pragmatic, to understand the relationship between foreign and domestic issues, and he had an instinctive feel for interpersonal relations.

Davis, on the other hand, tended to believe that being in the right, he needed not to compromise, he was hard to get along with, and he never really understood that King Cotton diplomacy had been compromised by the great cotton crops exported to Europe before the war. Withholding cotton meant little until late in the war, and by then other sources within the British Empire filled the void just enough to prevent domestic social unrest at home.

Lincoln had one other advantage. His secretary of state was William H. Seward (q.v.), who became a good foreign policy man. Likewise, his man in London was the urbane Charles Francis Adams, whose family lived and breathed United States foreign policy from the days of the Revolution. Davis was saddled for two years with Robert Toombs and R. M. T. Hunter, who were interested in domestic policy furthering the war effort, before he appointed the brilliant Judah P. Benjamin (q.v.) as secretary of state. By then, it was too late. The first 18 months of the Civil War were crucial to European recognition of Confederate national independence. Confederate foreign policy could not be saved, and tobacco-chewing and spitting James M. Mason ruined the Rebels' image where it counted most, in London.

The South achieved its main triumph immediately, when Lincoln's illegal creation of a blockade without recognizing Confederate nationhood first caused Britain to invoke the Foreign Enlistment Act of 1819. This allowed the Rebels to purchase needed items, even ships, providing that none of the vessels were outfitted in Britain for war. This led to the South purchasing many Confederate sea raiders (q.v.), which wreaked havoc on Union shipping throughout the war.

Both the French and the British were ostensibly allied from their joint participation in the Crimean War of years before. But France was much more interested in regaining the foothold it had had in America before Napoleon I sold Louisiana to the United States in 1803. Hence, it used the non-payment of debts owed it by Mexico to induce Britain and Spain to invade Mexico. But when Britain and Spain withdrew upon pledges to pay, France stayed on and enticed Austria to put one of its many archdukes, Ferdinand Maximilian, on the Mexican throne. This was seen as a pro-Southern development, until one realized that French control of Mexico cut off Southern expansion desires to create a Caribbean empire through the Knights of the Golden Circle. But Britain refused to approve of such French adventures.

The North almost lost the whole ball game when it seized the Confederate commissioners to Europe in the *Trent* affair (q.v.). Here, delayed communications (standard at the time), the willingness of Lincoln and Seward to compromise, and the intervention of Prince Consort Albert, husband to Queen Victoria, saved the day. The main time of concern for the North was when Gen. Robert E. Lee's (q.v.) was sweeping Yankee armies out of northern Virginia. After the Union defeat at Second Bull Run during the Second Manassas Campaign (q.v.), England was ready to move to mediate between the North and South on the basis of Confederate independence. But the Maryland Campaign (q.v.) caused Britain to rethink its position and hold back. Had Lee and the South but known, they would have been well advised to have stayed in Virginia and let developments in the British government work in the South's favor.

The failed drive into Maryland caused Lincoln to issue the Emancipation Proclamation (q.v.). He had held off, maintaining the war was solely for the Union to keep the border states from secession. Now this was no longer a worry. The expansion of war aims from union to freedom changed the political dynamic in Britain and brought working-class Britons over to the Northern cause. But initially the Emancipation Proclamation was seen as encouraging racial rebellion in the South. When this failed to materialize, ruling, upper class Britain changed its stance to favor what it called "Christian civilized progress," namely, freeing slaves.

In the end, the real reason that the Confederacy did not pick up diplomatic recognition was that it offered nothing to Britain or France that made intervention worth the risk. Seward was not shy in transmitting to England, whose Royal Navy was critical to any European success in the New World, the North's willingness to go to war over aid to the Confederacy. It was here that Minister Adams was particularly effective, especially in having London seize the Laird

Rams that could have broken the Union blockade of the South. The South faced a true dilemma in the war. To gain recognition and achieve intervention, it had to win a decisive battle. To win such a battle, it needed recognition and intervention. The North's ultimate advantage was that there was only one decisive battle in the Civil War, the Nashville Campaign (q.v.), and the North won that in December 1864. *See also* DIPLOMACY, C.S.— CIVIL WAR.

DIPLOMACY, U.S.—RECONSTRUCTION. Although foreign policy during the Reconstruction era was overshadowed by domestic issues of the South's readmission to the Union and a national commitment to civil and political rights for the newly freed slaves, there were some gains and defeats for American interests in the post–Civil War world.

When Andrew Johnson (q.v.) took over the government because of the death of Abraham Lincoln (q.v.), he kept Lincoln's cabinet officers in power. William H. Seward (q.v.), the secretary of state, soon became the most important of these holdovers, because of his loyalty to Presidential Reconstruction (q.v.). Seward had much influence domestically with the demise of the king-like powers wielded by Secretary of War Edwin McM. Stanton in the wake of the assassination and Seward's physical incapacity because of injuries suffered in a carriage accident and the attempt on his life.

The first problem that Seward faced was the French incursion into Mexico and the installation of the Austrian Archduke Maximilian (q.v.) as emperor. Seward played a game of bluff against the French, sending U.S. troops to the border and supplying arms and ammunition to the Mexican nationalists led by Benito Juarez. The result, inadvertently aided by European troubles between France and the German states, was the French withdrawal by 1867 and Maximilian's execution.

Seward also began America's first steps in becoming a world power by attempting to buy "coaling stations" for the steam-powered U.S. Navy in the Danish West Indies and Samoa. He also tried to advance American interests in the Isthmus of Panama with an eye to a future canal. But the reluctance of the U.S. Senate to go along with these moves halted Seward's plans.

Part of the Senate's reluctance was because it had swallowed Seward's even bigger annexation, the purchase of Alaska (q.v.). Ridiculed as "Seward's Icebox," the securing of Alaska made Seward look pretty foolish at the time, but future events, like the Alaskan gold rush in 1898 and Alaska's strategic location, would figure prominently in World War II, the Cold War, and the oil energy crisis of the late 20th century.

With the election of Ulysses S. Grant (q.v.) as president in 1868, Seward was succeeded by Hamilton Fish (q.v.), who has the distinction of being the longest serving and most honest and capable of Grant's cabinet appointees. Like Seward, Fish had a mixed bag of results in foreign policy. He failed to gain isthmus canal rights from Colombia (which owned Panama at the time) or Nicaragua or a trade treaty with Korea. Fish also got caught up supporting Grant's corrupt bid for San Domingo, a scandal that distanced him from many Republicans (q.v.).

Fish got involved with the ongoing Cuban insurrection (q.v.), a perennial problem for the United States and Spain from before the Civil War. He worked mightily to gain some independence in government from Spain for Cuba, but he had to step carefully, lest Congress grant belligerent rights to Cuba and extend the scope of the revolt. It was a problem that Spain artfully dragged out and that would not be solved until the Spanish–American War in 1898.

While Fish had many disappointments as secretary of state, his one claim to fame was the solution of the *Alabama* claims (q.v.). Fish let Britain know that he was open to a different approach than Congress, which was pushing an inflated territorial solution for wartime damages from the actions of Confederate sea raiders (q.v.) built or purchased in England. The result was the Washington Treaty of 1871, in which Britain accepted blame for the *Alabama* claims and agreed to certain boundary adjustments with Canada that were mediated to America's advantage by the emperor of the newly unified German States, Kaiser Wilhelm I. *See also* DIPLOMACY, C.S.—CIVIL WAR; DIPLOMACY, U.S.—CIVIL WAR.

DISEASE. By the time of the Civil War, medical researchers had seen all of the dots and rods that cause disease, but no one had yet been able to posit a germ theory of medicine. So the soldiers were left with the same home remedies that had served for centuries, to no real avail in curing the maladies that afflicted all humans. The Civil War merely increased the sicknesses contracted, because it put so many men together in filthy circumstances. About two-thirds of the military deaths were from disease, not wounds (q.v.) from combat. Generally, diseases at this time were listed under two big headings— miasmatic and nonmiasmatic—and everything that did not fit was thrown into something called "unclassified disease."

Miasma was the poisonous gases that arose from swamps and other stagnant places. Everybody guarded against being exposed to miasma. The farther South one lived, the more influential miasma was believed to be. Hence, the best remedy for these types of disease was care in a well-ventilated area and a cathartic to flush the poisons out of the body. Then a slew of home remedies might be employed. But by the time of the Civil War, the only remedy that really worked was quinine administered on a daily basis. The taste was so bitter that it was usually disguised with a healthy dose of whiskey. Under such a system, soldiers took their medicine merely for the liquor ration that went with it. When quinine ran low, the Southern soldier drank a substitute concoction of turpentine and whiskey.

The Civil War soldier was plagued with miasmatic fevers. There were intermittent fevers, usually related to malaria (or *mal aire*), correctly attributed to the proximity of swamps, but not to the mosquito they bred; continued fevers, also known as camp fever or crowd poisoning, such as typhoid and typhus, generally caused by a lack of proper sanitation in unclean camps, food, water, and unwashed persons infected with lice (known by the same moniker as the Confederate soldiers, "graybacks"); and eruptive fevers, related to mumps, measles, chicken pox (all real killers in the rural population that made up Civil War soldiery), smallpox (against which soldiers North and South were vaccinated), erysipelas (associated with stuffy winter quarters, lancing the blisters of which could be complicated by pneumonia, gangrene, and septicemia), yellow fever (especially along the coasts), scarlet fever, glanders, dengue, and milk sickness.

Nonmiasmatic diseases were caused by cold and dampness rather than miasma. Chief among these were pneumonia, assorted if lesser bronchial infections, rheumatism, charley horse from strained muscles, septicemia or blood poisoning, arthritis, and scurvy (the desiccated vegetables designed to combat it lost vitamins A and C in preparation and storage). Nutritional maladies such as night blindness and pellagra also existed. But the most common indicator of the poor sanitation of the Civil War camp was the raging bouts of diarrhea and dysentery, most of which were the result of poor food preparation. It was not uncommon for broth not eaten at one meal to sit unattended the rest of the day to be served again lukewarm and full of bacteria, viruses, and developing parasites.

Then there was a host of ailments that were not classified as miasmatic or nonmiasmatic. One of these was called the "Army Itch," which was scabies. It was, like most Civil War ailments, a hygiene problem. Tetanus, or what the troops called lockjaw, was brought about because so much of soldier life was spent in barns and in horse and cattle-grazing fields. And there was the renowned camp disease of nostalgia, brought on by the monotony of being away from home and literally being bored to death, especially in winter camp.

The latter condition often led to troops doing their best to contract one of the numerous venereal diseases from the numerous camp followers, or prostitutes, who overran any town near an army camp. The problem became so bad in occupied Nashville that the army provost marshals tried to ship the women out. When that did not work, they joined the authorities in Washington, D.C., and began to register the houses and their occupants. In Washington, the whorehouses were actually rated and classified according to cleanliness and services provided.

Because venereal disease is caused by microscopic organisms and bacteria, the very things that the Civil War doctor and patient were ignorant about, diagnosis was complicated until the disease raged full. "Spend the night with Venus and a life with Mercury," went the old saw. Often, the treatment involved inserting a hot wire up the diseased member. Other treatments included potassium iodine, corrosive stimulants, lunar caustic, calomel, black draughts, emetics, blistering, iron, quinine, and chloroform. Home remedies included pokeroots, elder, sarsaparilla, sassafras, Jessamine, prickly ash, silk-weed root, resin, blue vitriol, and God knows what else.

It was estimated that one-third of the veterans who died in Old Soldiers and Sailors Homes after the war, North and South, passed away from the prolonged effects of venereal disease. No wonder, as the programs of veterans' reunions were liberally filled with advertisements to visit local establishments and remember the joys of the war. One medical investigator wondered how many wives and children went to their graves rotted by the hidden stuff brought home by their men. As one soldier lamented years later, he wished his pals had pursued the enemy as eagerly as they did the whores. It would have made for a shorter war.

DISFRANCHISEMENT, ECONOMIC. When it came to observers of the South, two statements seemed almost universal. During the antebellum years, it was said that all Southerners, especially the white nonslaveholders and the enslaved blacks, were lazy. After the Civil War, the comments took the line that most Southerners, white or black, lived in wretched misery. That the slaves sought to do as little work as possible, given the compulsory and personally unprofitable nature of their labor, is not surprising. But what of the Southern white who seemed to do little but lie in the shade and commune with his hounds? Recent investigators have theorized that the Southern nonslaveholders had to do little because they lived a lifestyle based on the herding of wild hogs, derived from the Celtic societies of Britain and Ireland, from which most of their ancestors emanated. The only work required was to mark the yearlings in spring and collect the herd for market in the fall. The diet of pork was augmented by home-grown vegetables, all of which grew wild in the Southern heat and humidity and went to seed each year, keeping agricultural tilling common to the rest of the country to a minimum. In truth, the South had the best of all worlds, economic abundance with little effort. As for being lazy, a term that Yankees condescendingly utilized, Southerners would substitute the descriptive adjective "leisurely."

But when the African-Americans achieved emancipation at the close of the Civil War, they did not inherit the independent life of the nonslaveholding whites. Instead, the planters tried to substitute a form of pseudo-slavery through the Black Codes (q.v.). The idea was to create an agricultural system that resembled slavery as much as possible within the demands of freedom. For the first several years after the war, planters tried to get blacks to live on the plantation in select "towns" and work the staple crops with supervised gang labor, just like before the war, with the difference being that blacks would receive a share of the proceeds at harvest. They were assisted in this by the activities and edicts of the Army (q.v.) and the Freedmen's Bureau, which had taken over the management of black labor on abandoned plantations during the war. But African-Americans refused to work in this fashion. It reminded them too much of slavery. They boycotted the extension of slavery under another guise, and whites condemned them as lazy. Finally, blacks and whites came to an agreement—the blacks would work the land in family units as tenants, each being a small "farm" within the planter's whole plantation, and they would rent their house and land out of their share of the crop.

But the black tenant farmer had a problem—there was no pay day until the crop had been harvested and sold. So he needed credit, supplies, draft animals, and implements until this was accomplished. The planter had the wherewithal to provide the credit, so he loaned the necessary items to the tenant at a healthy, usurious interest rate (at least 50 percent was common). To make the whole process easy and convenient for the tenant, the planter went in with a local store owner to provide these services, or ideally ran the store himself. Prices were double or triple what the goods ordinarily sold for elsewhere (on top of the loan interest). Books were kept and the "deducts" taken from the share of the crop that was owed the tenant at the end of the season, after the landowner's share of the crop was secured.

When the whole process was totaled up at the end of the year, the tenant usually found that his family was short of full payment. Hey, no problem, we'll just make you a little loan on next year's potential crop (called the lien), and you can pay off the whole thing a year from now. All credit was for cash crops like cotton. Food was sold at the store—on credit, of course. So the vicious circle went on until the mountainous debt became unmanageable and was permanently passed on from generation to generation. It was a lot more profitable than slavery, and the tenant took all the risk. Some lucky farmers were able to beat the odds and emerge with their own land or a business, but they were few and far between. It took only one bad year of no rain to be in debt for life.

But the blacks were not alone. Remember that white hog farmer who went off to war to fight for Southern Independence? He came home to find that his livestock had been rustled by the passing Union and Confederate armies and brigands of both races that roamed the South during the conflict. The white farmer found himself in a trap after the war. As the blacks gained their political rights, they combined with the planters to fence off the land, something the big landowners had wanted for years but lacked the political power to achieve before the war. The open range had been essential to healthy hog raising. Now the hogs had to be raised in pens, keeping them in their own feces and urine and out of the cool forests where they had run wild (a hog cannot survive temperatures above 98°F without shade and a mud skin covering), causing them to become unhealthy and passing that ill-health on to their consumers in the form of trichinosis. And fewer hogs could be kept, because feeding them in a confined space cost more money than letting them run wild in the acorn forests. At the same time, the time-honored trail drive as a method of taking hogs to market was curtailed in the interest of the developing railroads. But the small white farmer could not afford to send his hogs to market by rail; it was too expensive. Besides, even if he could, the railroads made money only off long hauls and sent the animals out of state for consumption.

The result was to cause the white farmer to turn to the plow for income. But he needed a loan to get started. The local store was happy to help out a Confederate veteran—for the usual price that blacks had already become familiar with. Can't pay it back at the end of the year? Your farm will be the collateral, and we'll rent it back to you. Grow food? Oh, no, all credit is for cash crops like cotton alone. You can buy all the food you need at the store. We'll give you an advance on this year's crop. By 1890, both white and black farmers were in a real credit crunch. The lucky ones, mostly white because wage jobs were reserved for them by tradition to keep them socially above the poor blacks, got jobs at the textile mills, coal mines, or the lumber mills. Need credit? Do you know about the company store? We'll take the payments right out of your wages, and you won't even miss it. Caught short at the end of the year? More debt than income? Prices just keep going up? No problem. We'll carry your last year's debt and advance you more again this year. We'll just take a lien on what you expect to earn.

With this kind of a bloodsucking credit system (in the end, as the song said, you really did owe your soul to the company store), one might wonder what kept people from packing up and leaving the country for somewhere else. At least one could shop around for a better employer. The answer was that the credit system got its teeth from contract labor laws and the convict lease. Each laborer signed himself and his family up for a one-year stint on a piece of land. This was a legal contract, enforceable in court. Should any other planter (or employer) interfere with the original contract, that person could be taken to court for "enticement" of a laborer in violation of contract and be jailed or fined. Emigrant labor laws kept anyone from taking labor from the state. Vagrancy laws were strictly enforced—no contract, no income, off to jail.

And jail was where a person's real troubles began. Southern penal laws were run on a surety basis. Convicts were put to work within the jail system or contracted out to private companies as a cheap labor pool. Common sentences for vagrancy were 6 to 12 months on the chain gang. Any interested citizen could pay a convict's fine and put him or her to labor until the fine was worked off. It was also possible for a planter or employer to charge a hired contract laborer with a pseudo-crime (like charging him or her with obtaining credit under the "false pretense" of agreeing to labor to work it off and failing to do so "adequately" to the creditor's mind) and then buy out the fine and put him or her back to work cheaper than before. Of course, judges and sheriffs received kickbacks to keep the system well-oiled with an automatic presumption of guilt.

The ironic thing was that the Southern penal system had its inception during Radical Reconstruction (q.v.), when the Scalawag–Carpetbag (qq.v.)–Negro state governments had to improvise to create a prison system that was nonexistent after the war with minimum financial outlays. With the exceptions of Alabama and Texas, which tried to maintain minimal supervision of prisoners leased out, and Virginia and the Carolinas, which were trying to keep actual prisons with indigenous industries, all of the Confederate states plus Missouri and Kansas had a convict lease system that best could be described as brutal and corrupt. Living conditions in these convict lease camps were minimal. The prisoners ate and lived in conditions that made slavery truly look benign. At night they were shackled to their bunks in long communal dormitories. Women prisoners were given over to deserving, obedient males and raped. The pretty ones went to the guards. Life was irrelevant to the keepers; there were always new prisoners being made available. Railroads, local public works, mines, pitch and resin factories, and hemp plants used jail inmates to carry out their tasks, often at great profit to the contractors, who skimped on everything, especially food, but not on discipline.

Many historians wonder whether more decisive Federal action on behalf of the freedmen would have produced better economic results during the period after the Civil War. But historian C. Vann Woodward demurs from this viewpoint. Woodward fears that the confiscation of Southern plantations and doling out the land to the ex-slaves would have merely consigned it to the eventual expropriation of Northern speculators and railroad interests, just as it did to the land obtained by blacks under the Southern Homestead Act (q.v.). He also believes that to have placed African-Americans under a lengthy national benevolent guardianship would have been counterproductive, too, if Federal Indian policy is a fair indication. If he is correct, this means that Reconstruction's shortcomings remain speculative and pretty near unsolvable, given America's 19th-century commitment to white supremacy and untamed exploitation of natural resources. The credit crunch that destroyed the better-off white farmers by the 1890s would have done the same to blacks, regardless of their landholdings.

The result was that by the turn of the century, the South wound up with a system of peonage—involuntary servitude based on debt—that was contrary to an 1867 Federal law and had gone unchallenged since its inception during Reconstruction, except for the Populist Revolt of the 1890s, which had merely caused the powers that be to impose disfranchisement to prevent black and white indebted farmers from interfering with its pernicious effect. Econo-mists have labeled this American Gulag the "Prussian Road" to modernity, one based on compulsion rather than the natural economic laws of supply and demand and mobility of labor. It would take the throes of a half dozen court cases, two world wars, and the Great Depression before the system was crushed and a freer society emerged in the last half of the 20th century.

DISFRANCHISEMENT, POLITICAL, WHITE AND BLACK, OR THE SECOND MISSISSIPPI PLAN. American historians and political scientists who investigate and theorize on the impact of voting statutes usu-ally concentrate on the expansion of the franchise while virtually ignoring the contraction in the franchise that might have occurred. This makes American history a success story, inasmuch as more people are qualified to vote today than could, say, in 1789, when all sorts of property and religious restrictions limited the electorate to the very rich of the "proper" beliefs. The biggest expansions of the vote are usually seen as preceding the Age of Jackson in the 1820s and during the First Reconstruction of the 1860s and the Second Reconstruction (the modern civil rights movement) 100 years later.

But there are regressive periods in American history when the vote was reduced rather than expanded. Two of them are germane to Reconstruction (q.v.). The first occurred during the expansion of the vote to blacks, when the Republicans (q.v.) sought through the Fourteenth Amendment (q.v.) and various state laws that imitated it to limit the right of former Confederates to exercise the franchise and their traditional leadership role in the South, per-mitting Reconstruction to advance unimpeded in its early stages. The second occurred after Redemption (q.v.), when the traditional white leadership of the South limited the vote through legal and constitutional means within the scope of the Fifteenth Amendment (q.v.) to deny the franchise to blacks and certain lower class whites.

White Disfranchisement during Reconstruction: The aims of the Radical Republicans in the Military Reconstruction Acts (q.v.) were predicated on two policies, the enfranchisement of the African-Americans and the dis-franchisement of the leaders of the Confederacy, defined as those who had once taken an oath to the United States and then made a subsequent pledge of loyalty to the Confederate States. It was hoped that the loyal voters might thus be given a chance to reconstruct their state constitutions and govern-ments without the obstructionism of Rebels. Many commentators at the time wondered if this was not throwing the government into the hands of alleg-edly ignorant blacks. But there was a long tradition of American political thinking, beginning with Thomas Jefferson and reaching its culmination with Andrew Jackson, that held that any citizen was smart enough to handle the responsibilities of voting and holding office. Nothing that blacks did in Reconstruction matched the riot that took place during Jackson's first inaugural. Besides, it offered a quick way in which to introduce the Republican Party (q.v.) into the South, perhaps the only viable way available, as Union whites were as much Democrat (q.v.) as Republican and too few in number to affect the Deep South states.

The problem was, who did disfranchisement apply to? Particularly important was what was "aid and comfort" to the enemy. The Military Reconstruction Acts (q.v.) were not explicit about this. Obviously, those who had taken an oath before the war to the United States and then taken a subsequent one to the Confederate States were affected. This also exempted anyone who was under 21 when the war began. So it was left up to the military commander to work things out, which meant that there would be five different notions about who ought to be excluded from the process of Reconstruction. The actual disfranchising came about when one registered to vote. The individual military commanders of the five military districts would have numerous interpretations of their instructions to iron out. It came to be quite an involved process that had many political overtones.

First the military commander had to find enough loyal persons, those who could take the ironclad oath of 1862 (never having given aid or comfort to the enemy). Then these men would make the decision of who was loyal enough to vote. Commanders usually ordered the elected governors (declared provisional by the Military Reconstruction Acts) to submit a list of those who could take the oath in any one electoral district. Then appointments were made from the list. If the appointee accepted, the job was done. But of course there were numerous objections to anyone picked, some valid, most superfluous. The commanders would then promulgate an order that would describe probable exclusionary items in a potential voter's past. These included the double oath, most executive and judicial officers of the state during the war, anyone who voluntarily engaged in the rebellion, and all those who lent aid or comfort to the war effort. Bvt. Maj. Gen. John M. Schofield (q.v.), commander of the First Military District (Virginia), defined the latter not to include parents who gave their son in the army food or clothing for his own use, but to comprise parents who gave such a son a weapon, horse, or something that might be used for a "hostile purpose." This rule probably raised as many questions as it settled, but it gives an idea of what registrars faced in doing their job. No wonder one disgruntled historian described their actions as the "arbitrariness of petty officials" and dismissed them as "little despots."

But any registration board's decision could be appealed up the military chain of command, which mitigated the board's effect. Unless the commander was Maj. Gen. Philip H. Sheridan (q.v.) of the Fifth Military District (Louisiana and Texas). When he inquired as to the restrictions of the law, Lt. Gen. Ulysses S. Grant (q.v.) informed him that the matter was under the domain of Andrew Johnson's (q.v.) attorney general, Henry Stanbery, who was mulling it over before rendering an opinion. Meanwhile, Grant told Sheridan, go ahead and give any interpretation that he wanted. Sheridan decided to disfranchise anyone who held any public office, right down to sextons of cemeteries. When Stanbery's decision called for a milder approach, Congress stepped in and put much of Sheridan's policy into law, as the Third Reconstruction Act.

According to the eighth census (1860), on the basis of male population, only one Southern state, South Carolina, was guaranteed a majority of black voters after the Civil War. Louisiana and Mississippi were so close that they could go either way. But when the disfranchising of whites had taken place, Florida and Alabama joined the black majority, while Georgia, Arkansas, Texas, and Virginia had their white majorities severely reduced. This was a far cry from having state conventions dominated by black delegates. But the black voter did return a large number of Carpetbag and Scalawag (qq.v.) delegates, guaranteeing a Republican majority in most conventions. This allowed the achievement of the Radical Republican goals of punishing the traitorous Southern whites for the war and preventing them from disrupting the councils of the victors. But a large part of the triumph came from the fact that many eligible whites refused to register, and even more refused to vote after registering, giving the reconstructing forces a *de facto* victory.

Despite two and a half centuries of slavery and exploitation, African-Americans did not demand further disfranchisement of their former masters by the state constitutional conventions. Indeed, considering the wrongs that they had faced, American blacks tended to be quite forgiving of the past. It was the Carpetbaggers and Scalawags who looked upon disfranchisement with interest. The severest disfranchisement laws, with the possible exception of Louisiana's, existed in West Virginia, Missouri, and Tennessee. These were states in which white loyalists were plentiful, blacks were relatively few, and disfranchisement laws were written and put into effect during the war, long before the Military Reconstruction Acts were even thought of.

Of the Southern states under the jurisdiction of the Military Reconstruction Acts, Florida, Georgia, South Carolina, North Carolina, and Texas disfranchised very lightly if at all, sticking with the Fourteenth Amendment's provisions of excluding those who took the double oath. And South Carolina had the only state convention with a black majority among its delegates, indicating that African-American politicians were quite astute in recognizing that the long-term effects of vindictiveness were counterproductive. Alabama, Virginia, Mississippi, and Louisiana went far beyond the Fourteenth Amendment, with the worst case scenario being Louisiana. Under section 99 of its 1868 state constitution, Louisiana excluded from the polls anyone who had held a civil or military office under the Confederacy for one year or more, anyone who attended the state secession convention, anyone who had voted for the secession ordinance among the general public, plus anyone who had advocated treason by writing or publishing newspaper articles or preaching a sermon against the United States (not an uncommon "crime" in the Civil War Bayou State). The Louisiana requirements could be lifted if one were willing to swear in writing and file with the secretary of state an oath that he believed that the rebellion and his part in it were morally and politically wrong and that he regretted any aid or comfort he had given the enemy.

Despite such devices as Louisiana's disfranchisement law, African-Americans did not control any government. They only could vote for whites or at best for whites and blacks through an agreed upon division of offices made ahead of time. No black was elected governor of a Southern state, and some even doubt the legality of P. B. S. Pinchback's (q.v.) five-week term in Louisiana. As it was, Republicans could no more count on black voters to blindly elect them than Democrats could on blacks to vote against them. The split of Southern Republicans into Radical and Moderate blocs, usually but not always represented by Carpetbaggers and Scalawags respectively, with blacks caught in between, neutralized much of the force of Republican power and led to Redemption everywhere by 1877. But the initial effect of disfranchisement would be remembered 20 years later and brought out again, this time by establishment Democrats under the guise of "cleansing" Southern elections of opposition elements, both white and black.

Black Disfranchisement after Redemption: The period that followed the Redemption of the South, the restoration of whites (usually referred to as Bourbons, because like the French royal family, they neither learned from nor forgot the past) to political control, did not seal the fate of the Reconstruction reforms in politics, economics, or social contacts among whites and blacks. Indeed, the next 20 years from Reconstruction to the Populist Revolt could best be described as a period of transition—a time of uncertainty and fluctuation. The fear among Southern whites was that the Yankees would pass another civil rights or enforcement (qq.v.) measure to continue the spirit of Reconstruction. A measure like this might emanate from humanitarian motives or political realities. Worse yet, not all white politicians in the South were convinced that the Democratic Party was the forum in which all problems should be raised. The constant flow of Fusionists (willing to combine tickets, usually with Republicans), Independents (unwilling to combine with others lest principle be diluted), Republicans (the regular party, often called the "Black and Tans" from its biracial membership), and so-called Readjusters (interested in refunding the horrendous state debts) merely presaged the ultimate third party, the powerful Populists (agrarian radicals who wished to reform the corrupt establishment) in the 1890s. All of this turmoil gave the

Southern blacks greater political leverage throughout this period than historians (or contemporaries) have been willing to admit.

Throughout the 1870s, the two sections had an equal voter turnout in national elections. But in the 1880s, the North began to forge ahead in voter participation by 10 to 12 percent as the South began to turn to disfranchising laws, extensive fraud, and weaker party competition. By 1896, the North was achieving record voter turnouts, while the South was experiencing record non-participation as the Populist movement collapsed there first. The lull in Southern voter interest became permanent as new restrictive laws and state constitutions took over. By the turn of the century, Southern voter participation was half that of the North, and most of it was in the Democrat column. The one-party South had been achieved, the South that would vote for a "yellow dog" if it should appear on what Texans called the "Jay Bird" Democrat ballot, making the party a sort of private club for whites, especially the rich and better-educated, only. This "Solid South" would endure until the civil rights and Conservative Republican movements of the late 20th century.

Throughout this period until the 1890s, African-American votes were important to Southern political strategies. In nearly every state, a majority of black males voted and a majority of them tallied in the Republican column. The Democrats based their appeal to whites on the basis of this active black vote. In counties with less than 30 percent black residents, 54 percent of whites voted Democrat. But in counties with a black population over 30 percent, white support of the Democrat party topped out at just over 92 percent. These black belt counties (actually named from the color of their fertile soils, not the skin color of the majority population) were the parts of the South where the contrast between the races was most pronounced politically, economically, and educationally. It was here that the revolution represented by Radical Reconstruction (q.v.) had been the most successful, where the black politicians and their white Carpetbag and Scalawag allies had ruled the longest.

After Reconstruction, whites took several approaches to power in the South. Some counties chose the First Mississippi Plan (q.v.) and drove blacks from the polls by force. Others had local governments appointed by the government in the state capital, obviating the need for local elections. The rest took the road of counting the blacks out through corrupt officials and fraudulent election returns; or cutting deals whereby whites and blacks arbitrarily divided up the offices by race, permitting the whites to always achieve a partial victory; or continued the Reconstruction party battles. Sometimes the Republicans and blacks won; other times the Democrats and whites. But intimidation and chicanery were the order of the day and became more so as the decades advanced. It was these black belt counties that had the most to lose if a Fusion Party came to power based on the votes of poorer whites and blacks. Then the whites in the black belt would have to pay taxes to African-American tax collectors, argue cases before black judges and juries, and apply to a Negro legislator for favors. They would even have to pay money to black school districts—as the Southern saw went, to educate "the nigger" was to ruin a good field hand.

But despite the fear that Reconstruction might return, opposition parties abounded in the South. Upper class Bourbons constantly cut back on public services, which harmed and irritated poorer whites and blacks alike. They also backed policies that aided big business, much of it Yankee owned and managed, at the expense of the less well-to-do. These things became more and more regressive as the decades wore on, pushed by the deflation of the late 19th century, the share crop, and the lien, which prevented crop diversification in grasses and food crops in favor of cash staples like cotton, and a regressive, malapportioned tax system that was often corruptly collected and spent. As much as the former Confederate fighting men loved the Lost Cause expounded by Bourbon Democrats, this was too much. As they looked for allies to combat this system, they, like all "outs" in the postwar South, began to look to the Negro at home, and the national Republican Party in Washington, D.C., for Federal patronage.

Even though the Republican support of the Southern party and Reconstruction had wavered, many national party leaders were holdovers from Reconstruction days. Some still had the idealism that led to egalitarianism and a hatred of racial oppression. Others might not be so noble philosophically, but they did want to see a free ballot and fair count down South. Both groups waved the bloody shirt (q.v.) for political advantage and because they believed the atrocity stories emanating from the South. This meant that a lot of Republicans, not the major party bigwigs maybe, but the second echelon, believed that the Federal government owed some form of protection to Southern dissenters regardless of race. National Democrats viewed this Republican proclivity to resurrect Reconstruction as a violation of the Compromise of 1877. They condemned it as an unconstitutional interference with the states, a faulty desire to bring back to life a policy that led to unparalleled corruption and the imposition of "Negro rule" on the white South. Republicans complained that post-Reconstruction Southern state governments had instituted "new forms of servitude" upon blacks (violations of political rights, tenantry and the lien, segregation, and the denial of public services), to whom the North owed a great debt for their loyal service during the Civil War.

The Republican policy toward the South had two contradictory aspects. Some wanted to go the route of the Compromise of 1877 and industrialize the South, bringing the "better classes," the Bourbons, the old-time Whigs, to the party's support by wedding them to economic policies of high tariff and government aid to business, especially internal improvements like railroads, and permitting them to paternally "protect" the African-Americans. This line of thought had produced the later (early 1870s), upper class Scalawags during Reconstruction. The other was to appeal to Southern white dissidents and the traditional black Republican voter by stressing honest elections, fair taxes, support for public education, and racial democracy. This reasoning had been prevalent early in Reconstruction (the late 1860s) and had resulted in the common whites as Scalawag in support of the Republicans. It had crumbled when the traditional upper class former slaveholders absorbed the party leadership and neutralized the revolutionary aspects of Reconstruction.

The first course had been supported by the Rutherford B. Hayes (q.v.) administration. But disillusionment set in when the Redeemers (q.v.) failed to deliver the vote, because economic depression had diluted the willingness of the lower classes of either race to follow. And the Redeemers were disappointed when Hayes failed to honor his promise of economic development. Thereafter, Republican administrations fluctuated among who they thought were the proper party representatives in the South, the upper class whites or the lower class dissidents of both races. Sometimes Republicans did both, depending on local circumstances (issues varied greatly among states). The willingness of the national Republicans and lower class whites to work with the black voters in Fusion, Readjuster, Greenback, and Independent parties nearly caused the Bourbons to lose power everywhere in the South; indeed, they did lose power briefly in Virginia and Tennessee. Only South Carolina Democrats managed to weather the storm through the "eight box law," which forced the voter to place his ballot in the correct box or have it nullified. Of course the order of the boxes was switched often, and the labels were difficult to read.

By the 1890s, the Bourbon Democrats had to do something to hold back the dissident tide. The whole nation was under the greatest political turmoil since the Civil War. Depression had led to the People's Party, the Populists, made up of farmer and labor elements tired of conservative Republicanism and Grover Cleveland Democracy, which amounted to the same thing. Southern Democrats wanted to make the final move to contain the dissident vote within the boundaries of the Fifteenth Amendment (q.v.), before the Populists swept them from power. But the Republicans had taken over both houses of Congress and the presidency in 1888. For the first time in decades, the party had the power to block Southern Democrat interference (intimidation of voters, violence, miscounted ballots, unfair procedures at the polling places) with the electoral process and insure a free vote and a fair count through Federal regulation. The Republicans quickly passed a higher tariff (the McKinley Tariff Act), an anti-trust bill (the Sherman Anti-trust Act), increased pensions ("God help the surplus!" cried its triumphant administrator) for Union veterans of 90 days' service or more (the Dependent Pension Act), and a currency expansion measure (the Sherman silver Purchase Act).

Then the party introduced the Lodge Force Bill or Federal Elections Bill, which would extend the Second Enforcement Act of 1871 (q.v.) providing for Federal election supervisors in 34 Southern and 129 Northern cities, to allow Federal officials to supervise elections and voter registrations in any congressional district in which 100 voters asked for it. Introduced by Massachusetts Senator Henry Cabot Lodge, the measure quickly passed the House, but was defeated on a procedural motion by one vote in the Senate. The Lodge bill was really pretty mild, but it would have guaranteed the election of Republicans or Populists in every Southern state by focusing on cleaning up the electoral process. It would be followed by the second Cleveland administration's repeal of all remaining Federal election statutes in 1894. The way was open for the Bourbons to permanently "fix" Southern electoral processes their way and create a multitude of one-party states ruled by the "correct" whites alone. The extra-legal fraud was to be made legal.

Mississippi did not even wait for the Federal process to be played out. In 1890, it convened the first state constitutional convention since Reconstruction and wrote disfranchisement into the state's fundamental law, the so-called Second Mississippi Plan (q.v.). The rest of the South followed suit, although only South Carolina, Louisiana, Alabama, and Virginia followed Mississippi's example and called constitutional conventions to the job. The rest, and even the states with new constitutions, passed normal laws that did the trick. Numerous devices were tried, each state in effect becoming a laboratory for the others to copy: Florida copied South Carolina's eight box scheme; Alabama and Florida instituted Tennessee's secret (Australian) ballot law; Tennessee, Arkansas, Florida, and Mississippi used the poll tax after Georgia proved it effective. But all of this had to be subtle, because the Fifteenth Amendment prohibited it from being overtly based on race, and the Fourteenth Amendment threatened to reduce the representation of any state should it discriminate against any group of voters.

But there were ways to achieve the reduction of select groups of voters, some of which were also actively used in the North. Frequent registration was one of these. By making voters register every so many years or during a specific month, many were discouraged. More important was granting great discretionary powers to the registrars. It was they who determined the literacy of the applicant and his qualifications for exemption from literacy laws, like Louisiana's Grandfather Clause (if one's grandfather voted before 1867, one could not be turned down—of course only white grandfathers voted before that date) or the understanding clause (the registrar read part of the Constitution to the applicant and the applicant explained what it meant—some parts of the Constitution are more easily understood than others). But not knowing extraneous information, like your neighbor's full name, the exact date of your birth (many blacks were not sure), or your street address (black communities often did not have these) could disqualify a potential voter. The law always called to prove these things "as near as may be," which gave the registrar the ability to be tough on one voter and easier on another. Confederate veterans and their heirs were always given the benefit of the doubt, appealing to the Southern whites' vulnerability to the Lost Cause.

Other disqualifying features included minimum property ownership requirements (blacks and lower class whites were renters) and the payment of fees to vote, like a poll tax. The real crux was to require that the voter show his registration certificate and current poll tax receipt. Some states required that several years of receipts be shown, difficult for sloppy record keepers to do. Residency requirements limited the vote to those who had stable jobs and families and stayed in one place, usually a year in the county and several years in the state (sharecroppers moved about a lot to gain a better contract deal).

The biggest help was the secret ballot. Before the "reforms" of the 1890s, parties handed out their own ballots, encouraging voters to select a straight ticket and not requiring any literacy at all. When a ballot box needed to be stuffed, the Democrats would insert enough undersized, fraudulent ballots, "little jokers" in the parlance of the trade, to win the precinct. When the ballots were tallied, too many for the number of voters would be found. Then a reliable party man would be blindfolded (to keep things "honest") and draw out enough excessive ballots to make the count right. Of course he only pulled out the full-sized ballots, guaranteeing a Democrat victory. But the secret ballot, called the Dortch Law in Tennessee (which had originated this bit of electoral chicanery), was better and more honest. Both parties appeared on it, allowing a split vote. Its format could be made unbelievably long and complicated. But more important, one had to read to fill it out, and no help was allowed (unless one or one's predecessors had voted before the Civil War). Also, voters were limited in the time they could take to mark the secret ballot, and any mistake voided one's vote for that election.

Finally, there was the all-white primary rule. The Bourbons claimed that if blacks were excluded as an independent voting block that shifted from side to side, thus controlling elections (a false charge), whites could then disagree on all issues without the fear of "Negro rule." Elections could be honestly run. In the general election, all participants in the white primary would pledge to vote for the candidates picked in the primary. Often the Democrat Party would be made a private club restricted to members only, like the Jay Bird Association of Ft. Bend County, Texas, and the primary became an exclusive club election. The result was that elections became personality contests, going to the candidate who had the funniest stories, the best singing voice, the firmest handshake, and the broadest smile. With no issue but race, political campaigns soon degenerated into demagoguery, "a sort of legalized knife fight and perpetual stomping contest," in the words of one observer, as each white candidate tried to hang the label of "nigger lover" on his opponent.

With the U.S. Supreme Court's endorsement of disfranchisement on some other basis than race alone, Williams *v.* State of Mississippi in 1898 (q.v.) gave the South the go-ahead to make disfranchisement of blacks an established fact. The various disfranchising methods worked like a charm. By the end of the century, the vote for the Democrats had declined by half, the vote for opposition parties by two-thirds, and the number of Southerners of all races who did not vote was 70 percent of male adults. Some blacks still voted, but their number was so small as to be unimportant. Except for Tennessee and North Carolina, where mountain Republicanism still existed, the Republican Party was a mere cipher. Blacks were totally dependent on national Republican patronage, and this ended in 1913, when Woodrow Wilson, the first Southerner in the White House since Lincoln, became president.

The loss of political power hit the black community hard. It no longer had to be recognized by the state governments. The biggest loss was in education. The governments dispensed school funds to the counties for disbursement to local schools. All too often, little or nothing went to the separate, supposedly equal, black system. By matching funds with localities that were willing to tax themselves, the states contributed to an education system that was poverty stricken in rural areas dominated by poor whites and rich in urban areas of upscale whites. The loss of political power directly affected the access to governmental services. What had started out as an extra-legal system of voter fraud had been entrenched as constitutional prerogative on the state level and allowed to pass for electoral reform in the eyes of the nation. It would take 60 years before the nation saw disfranchisement for what it really was, a contraction of democracy, so humiliating in its effect as to be a contradiction of everything the country prided itself on being for.

DOCTORS' LINE, THE. One of the mainstays of Confederate communications during the Civil War ran from Richmond to Montreal, Canada, where Confederate secret agents gathered at the local St. Lawrence Hotel to coordinate various behind-the-lines activities and to avoid the increasingly more effective ocean blockade as they crossed with messages pertinent to the prosecution of the war. This pathway between the South and Canada and thence to the rest of the world was known as the "secret line" or more familiarly as the Doctors' Line. But it was an open secret. The route received its nickname the "Doctor's Line" because so many Southern country doctors covered up their spying and smuggling by pretending to be visiting patients, using their medical bags to conceal drugs and messages.

It was pretty much a well-defined "trail" between the various cities, beginning with the Richmond & Fredericksburg Railroad out of Richmond (run by Yankee counterspy Samuel Ruth), then veering off to the east to cross the Rappahannock (run by Confederate loyalist William Rollins) and the Potomac to Washington, where it went by rail to Baltimore, New York, crossing the Canadian border to Montreal. The key to the line was slaveholding Maryland, occupied by the Union army then and again, but pretty much the domain of Rebel spies and guerrillas (like Gus Howell, John Boyle, and Sarah Slater), who were shielded in the numerous "safe houses" that dotted the region. It was all organized and run by Confederate agent Thomas Harbin, operating across the river out of Virginia from Elizabeth Quesenberry's plantation, the Cottage.

Many Marylanders had sons in the army of Robert E. Lee (q.v.), and others helped conceal Rebel agents and expedite the exchange of information. Often these agents were slaveholding Catholics, inter-related by marriage and family. Indeed, the whole route south that passed through Surrattsville (run by the John Surratt family), Port Tobacco (John Brawner, Richard Smoot, George Atzerodt), Bryantown (E. D. R. Bean), and Newport (the Adams family), past the plantations of St. Catherine's (Dr. Samuel Mudd), Hagan's Folly (William Bertles), and Rich Hill (Samuel Cox), and three or four points east to Banks O'Dee and Chaptico (William L. Sherburn) along the Potomac, was known locally as the "secret mail line."

Here were kept "stations" manned by civilians and military personnel, equipped by boats of various sizes, that crossed people, letters, and packages of interest to the Confederacy. Several houses (like Thomas Jones' "Huckleberry"), strategically placed upon the heights on both sides of the river, could see and chart the Yankee patrol boats, the double enders that could go either up- or downstream without turning around, for miles. A blanket hung in an upstairs window was all that was needed to convey when it was safe to cross. It was along this line that John Wilkes Booth (q.v.) proposed to hustle the kidnapped Abraham Lincoln (q.v.) in 1865, before his plot was changed to execution of President Lincoln. It was also the route he used to flee for his own life after the assassination.

DOUGLAS, STEPHEN A. (1813–1861). Originally from Vermont, Stephen A. Douglas studied at Canandaigua, New York, Academy before setting out for Illinois. He studied law and taught school at Jacksonville, and was admitted to the bar in 1834. Between 1835 and 1843, he served the Democratic (q.v.) Party and his state as state's attorney, state legislator, secretary of state, and judge of the state supreme court. He was usually addressed as "Judge," but his nickname was the "Little Giant."

In 1843, Douglas was elected to the U.S. House for two terms, and in 1847 he went to the U.S. Senate, where he served until his death 14 years later.

Douglas was an expansionist on both Oregon and Texas, a supporter of the War with Mexico, an opponent of the Wilmot Proviso (q.v.), and an advocate of the Compromise of 1850 (q.v.). Indeed, it was Douglas who got the compromise through the Senate by dividing the Omnibus Bill into its component parts. Through his first wife, he was the manager of a Mississippi plantation with over 100 slaves and thus had a personal connection to slavery in the South.

Douglas was leader of the Young America expansionist movement in the 1850s and a practitioner of "Spread Eagle" foreign policy (q.v.). As chairman on the committee on territories, Douglas came to back popular sovereignty (q.v.), a concept forced upon him by senior Southern Democrats. Douglas sponsored the Kansas–Nebraska Act (q.v.), but he opposed the pro-Southern Lecompton Constitution as a violation of popular sovereignty, which caused him to break with President James Buchanan and alienate the Southern wing of his party.

In 1858, Douglas accepted the challenge to debate his opponent for the U.S. Senate seat from Illinois, Abraham Lincoln (q.v.). Even though the election was by the state legislature, the two men toured the state in seven speeches to influence the vote. In the Freeport Debate, Douglas admitted that a territory could prevent slavery from coming in during the territorial stages of government simply by not passing positive laws in its favor. This "Freeport Doctrine" (q.v.) was a violation of his popular sovereignty concept, which gained him the senatorial election in 1858 but cost him the presidential election in 1860, when the South bolted from the party. Douglas made many attempts to compromise the coming of the Civil War, but to no avail. He died of typhoid in 1861, his body already weakened from exhaustion.

DOUGLASS, FREDERICK (ca. 1817–1895). Born a slave in Talbot County, Maryland, of a black mother, Harriet Bailey, and an unknown white father, and originally named Frederick Augustus Washington Bailey, Frederick experienced the usual travails of slavery—neglect, cruelty, hard work, and some indulgence—but he chaffed most under the very tyranny that was slavery, the restraint of the ambition of a very talented person. He struck back at his cruelest master and learned the value of well-placed resistance. He was sent to Baltimore to become a house servant and learned to read and write with the connivance of his mistress. In 1838, he escaped to New York City and assumed the name under which he became famous, Frederick Douglass.

In New York, Douglass married a free woman of color whom he had met in Baltimore, and they went to Massachusetts, where he worked as a common laborer. There for the first time he came into intimate contact with abolitionists (q.v.); upon hearing him speak to a group of blacks at a local meeting, the Massachusetts Anti-slavery Society hired him as an agent on the spot. He then began what would be a lifelong commitment to free blacks from slavery and the pernicious effects of the second-class citizenship that followed. In the process he was mobbed, beaten, mocked, and humiliated by being refused access to public accommodations, but he never faltered in his task.

Douglass had a commanding presence. He was over six feet in height and did not lower his eyes, mumble apologies, smile, or shyly step back as did so many blacks of his time, slave or free. He was simply too much of a commanding presence to be imagined as ever having been in bondage. To prove his story, Douglass wrote his memoirs of slavery in 1845, a volume that white friends urged him to burn, as it was too daring in content and so self-implicating that they feared he might be reclaimed as a fugitive and resold into slavery. But Douglass published his narrative and then took a vacation to Europe to let the heat die down. In Britain, he noticed immediately how differently he was treated; for the first time in his life he was truly a free man. Here he began to change from a man concerned with emancipation of his people to one who would become the premier spokesman for their social equality and African-American economic and spiritual freedom. Besides abolition, Douglas supported advancing the rights of women and counseled John Brown in his raid on Harper's Ferry (q.v.). The latter incident led to a call in Virginia for his arrest, so Douglass went to Canada and Britain and lectured for the next six months, until the chance of apprehension blew over.

The Civil War brought Douglass to the forefront of black liberation activities. He spoke against slavery as the true cause of the war and called for immediate freedom of all slaves. He worked hard for the right of blacks to enlist and help emancipate themselves. He was instrumental in the organization of the 54th and 55th Massachusetts (Colored) Volunteer Infantry Regiments, to whose service he contributed two sons. He hinted that the war could not have been won but for the help of the black volunteers. He conferred with President Abraham Lincoln (q.v.), which raised his stature to the most important African-American in the country. During Reconstruction, Douglass urged Congress to grant the right to vote and secure civil and social rights to the former slaves. For a while he was marshal and recorder of deeds for the District of Columbia. He also served on the Santo Domingo Commission and as U.S. minister to Haiti.

Throughout the Civil War, Reconstruction, and the rest of the 19th century, Douglass sought to keep the unity of blacks and whites on behalf of the cause of freedom and equality intact. He believed that the war was more than a battle for Union. It was a fight for the proper moral ideology, which had to be guarded against what he saw as the historical amnesia implicit in the Lost Cause myth and the resurgent racism that accompanied it. His whole being demanded that future generations see the conflict from an African-American and abolition perspective, rather than as a war in which all were brave soldiers for their own brand of right.

When he died in 1895, five states adopted resolutions of regret, and two U.S. senators and a Supreme Court justice were among the honorary pallbearers. Douglass recognized that the cause of freedom had suffered a setback in the latter part of the 19th century, but he was not without hope. He never ceased seeing the African-American as the mirror of American democracy, against which all other things must be measured.

DRAFT EVASION. *See* CONSCRIPTION AND DRAFT EVASION, CONFEDERATE; CONSCRIPTION AND DRAFT EVASION, UNION.

DRED SCOTT *v.* SANDFORD (1857). In 1857, the Democrats (q.v.) were the only truly national political party. They fought the Republicans in the North and the Whig–Americans (qq.v.) in the South. The other parties could go all out to the extremes on various issues, especially slavery, but the Democrats had to moderate their views to attract voters from all sections of the country. Perhaps the most controversial decision of the antebellum era, Democrats naïvely hoped that the case of Dred Scott would put the issue of slavery in the territories behind America and allow the country to move on to more pressing political issues, such as settlement of the West and the building of the transcontinental railroad and party building, graft, and corruption as usual back East.

One reason the Democrats were naïve in their expectations was that the Supreme Court had a majority of Southern sympathizers. President James Buchanan (q.v.) violated good protocol when he actively intervened with one justice from Pennsylvania to vote with the Southerners to give the decision a non-sectional appearance. Buchanan even went so far as to hint at the case's outcome in his inaugural speech. He asked all good citizens to submit to the Court's decision, as he would.

The facts of the case were these. Dred Scott was a slave, and had been all his life, in Missouri. He was owned by Dr. John Emerson, an army surgeon. Emerson legally bought Scott while the doctor was employed at Jefferson Barracks near St. Louis. As an army doctor, Emerson changed posts a lot. His next duty station was Ft. Armstrong at Rock Island, Illinois, a free state. Scott took his slave Dred Scott there with him, even though Illinois was free territory under the Northwest Ordinance (1787) and by its own state constitution (1818). Then Emerson was ordered to Ft. Snelling in Minnesota territory, Free Soil under the Missouri Compromise (1820). He took Dred Scott with him. While there, Scott married another slave, Harriet, whom Emerson bought at Dred Scott's request. The two African-Americans had a child, Eliza, born on a Mississippi River steamboat between Iowa and Illinois, both free states (1846, 1818).

After returning to St. Louis, the doctor died in 1843, passing the slave property along to his wife and daughter. Mrs. Emerson's brother was

John F. A. Sandford, who was executor to the estate, and he moved to St. Louis from New York. Sandford regularly hired Dred Scott out, a common practice then in Southern states. Scott even went to Mexico during the war as an officer's aid. Slavery had been illegal there since 1821. Scott came back to St. Louis after the war and asked to buy himself and his family out of slavery. Mrs. Emerson, through Sandford, refused. Dred Scott then sued in state court for his freedom, on the grounds that he had been illegally enslaved in a free territory and a free state. The Missouri district court found him to be free. The state supreme court overturned the decision.

By now, Scott was something of a cause célèbre. He attracted big name lawyers, Frank Blair, Jr., and Edward Bates. They appealed the case to the U.S. Federal courts on the legal fiction that Scott was a citizen of Missouri and Sandford was still a resident of New York. Meanwhile, Mrs. Emerson fell in love with and married Dr. Calvin Chaffee, an abolitionist, and moved with him to his Massachusetts home. He convinced her to set Scott free, no matter what the court's decision was. The U.S. District court ruled Scott was still a slave. Just before the election of 1864, the case went to the nine-member U.S. Supreme Court (seven Democrats—five of whom were slaveholders—one Whig, and one Republican), Chief Justice Roger B. Taney, prominent Maryland slaveholder and Jacksonian Democrat, presiding.

The Court ruled seven to two that Dred Scott was still a slave. But no one could agree as to why. Each judge wrote a separate opinion. For all practical purposes, it was the opinion of the Chief Justice that became the reason why. Taney gave three reasons why Scott was still a slave.

First, Scott had no right to even bring suit. He claimed to be a citizen of Missouri, but no black person could be a citizen of that or most free or slave states. Taney should have stopped right there and thrown the case out of court. But he and the South had been waiting too long for him to quit now.

Second, Taney ruled that Scott's mere residence in a free territory or a free state did not liberate him. This was because the U.S. Constitution gave slaveowners an extraterritorial protection to hold their slaves by law anywhere in the United States. Further, as far as territories went, slavery was legal there until the territory became a state, whereupon the new state could vote to become free or remain slaveholding. Just as Congress could not legislate against slavery without a constitutional amendment, neither could a creature of Congress, like a territory. In other words, squatter sovereignty (the Democratic Party [q.v.] platform of 1848) was wrong, as was the Missouri Compromise in 1820 (q.v.), and popular sovereignty (q.v.) (the Democratic Party platform of 1852 and 1856) was correct, as was the Kansas–Nebraska Act in 1854 (q.v.). The Republican Party (q.v.) platform of 1856 calling for no slavery in the territories was unconstitutional.

Finally, no citizen (white male) could be denied his slave property without due process of law, under the Fifth Amendment, which in the case a of slave in transit or temporary residence would involve the need for a constitutional amendment.

Rather than deciding the slavery issue, Taney caused a firestorm that energized all antislavery (q.v.) proponents throughout the North and caused Abraham Lincoln to campaign against the Dred Scott case in the Illinois U.S. Senate race. He would take on incumbent Stephen A. Douglas (q.v.) in the Lincoln–Douglas Debates (q.v.).

DREWRY'S BLUFF, BATTLES OF. Located just southeast of Richmond on the James River, Drewry's Bluff was the single most important geographical feature defending the Confederate capital from a river-borne assault. Massive naval cannon adorned its heights, sighted in a river bend that made Yankee gunboats inviting targets as they slowed to turn. In 1862, at the beginning of the Peninsula Campaign (q.v.), the Union navy had tried to run the guns and take Richmond ahead of the army, but failed in a hail of accurate cannon fire. As the war progressed, Drewry's Bluff was backed up by Rebel gunboats and ironclad ships and the river blocked by contact and electrically fired torpedoes (q.v.).

In 1864, Lt. Gen. Ulysses S. Grant (q.v.) ordered Maj. Gen. Ben Butler's (q.v.) Army of the James to advance from Fortress Monroe up the south side of the James and operate against the Confederate capital, while Grant held Gen. Robert E. Lee's (q.v.) Confederate army in check on the Rappahannock River farther north. Taking river transports up to City Point and a loop in the river known as the Bermuda Hundred, Butler disembarked his men on May 4, the same day Grant began his own Richmond Campaign of 1864. The Confederate commander in the area was Gen. P. G. T. Beauregard (q.v.), but his temporary illness left the defense in the charge of Maj. Gen. George E. Pickett. He managed to hold off Butler from taking Petersburg in a series of small actions until Butler withdrew into the Bermuda Hundred loop on May 11.

By now Beauregard was on the field. Surmising correctly that Butler was going to bypass Petersburg for a drive on Richmond, he concentrated his men at Drewry's Bluff. Butler managed to drive the Confederates back to the inner ring of fortifications, but then he stopped and set up defensive positions of his own. For the first time in the war, Butler's men strung telegraph wire just off the ground in front of their lines to trip attacking Confederates. The navy planned to assist Butler with gunboats, but the James proved too low to permit them to proceed.

Beauregard now took the offensive. He assaulted Butler's right flank, driving back the Union troops there. But Butler managed to hold on until the end of the day. Then he retreated back to the Bermuda Hundred (May

17). Beauregard followed, and Butler found himself trapped by a growing line of Confederate trenches across the neck of Bermuda Hundred. He was jokingly referred to as the "Bottle Imp," who had been "corked" in place by Beauregard's actions. And there he stayed, his position becoming a part of the Petersburg Siege with the approach of Grant and Lee in June. Butler lost 4,000 in these operations, while the Rebels took 2,500 casualties.

DUBUCLET, ANTOINE (1810–1887). The black treasurer of the state of Louisiana from 1868 to 1878, Antoine Dubuclet was born a free man of color in Iberville Parish. His father was a landholder and slaveholder of some wealth, not a rare occurrence in pre–Civil War Louisiana, whose early death sent the remaining Dubuclets to New Orleans, where his mother hoped to educate them better. Antoine, however, remained behind on the plantation. As eldest son, already educated at home, he managed the sugar production until 1834, when the land was divided up among him and his 10 brothers and sisters. By 1864, his property holdings were worth almost $100,000, including more than 100 slaves. This made him the wealthiest free black in Louisiana and the South, and one of the richest men in all Louisiana, regardless of color, to boot. In the fashion of the time, Dubuclet sent his children to France to be educated free from the baneful influences of slavery and racial discrimination.

The coming of the Civil War caused great changes in the plantation system of the South, particularly in Louisiana. Dubuclet would now have to hire his labor. Although there is no record of his Civil War experiences, civilian or military, Dubuclet emerged during Reconstruction as a loyal supporter of the Military Reconstruction Acts (q.v.) and the Republican (q.v.) regime in the state. Not a member of the conventions in 1864 or 1867, Dubuclet was important enough in party circles to be placed on the Republican ticket as nominee for state treasurer and was elected in 1868 along with the rest of the Henry Clay Warmoth (q.v.) regime.

Dubuclet served as state treasurer under three governors, Warmoth, P. B. S. Pinchback (q.v.), and William P. Kellogg (q.v.). Only the latter could really be seen as interested in assisting Dubuclet in reducing the state's indebtedness, which was accomplished by a funding bill that converted the whole amount owed into bonds redeemable in 40 years. Because Dubuclet's term would be up in 1878, he was retained in office by the Redeemers (q.v.) who took over in the election of 1876. The legislature subjected him and his department to an intensive investigation, but Dubuclet, despite some trifling irregularities, ranks as one of the cleanest politicians of his era. Dubuclet decided not to run in 1878, a divided Republican Party having little success in fielding a winning ticket, anyhow. Dubuclet returned to his Iberville Parish estate, which he eventually sold to his son, and lived there with his mistress, his second wife having died. He passed away in 1887, never entering politics again.

DUNN, OSCAR J. (ca. 1820–1871). Born of an unknown father and a free woman of color who ran a rooming house for white actors, Oscar J. Dunn was apprenticed to a painter and plasterer in New Orleans. He had no formal education, but somewhere along the line, probably from his mother's boarders, he picked up a good command of language, written and oral, and he was noted as an excellent fiddle player. He was not enamored of his life as an apprentice, which was expressed by his running away numerous times. He later took up the trade of barber, buying his own shop, and he also taught music. With the occupation of New Orleans, he established an employment office for the newly freed slaves as freedmen and later worked as an inspector for the Federal Bureau of Refugees, Freedmen, and Abandoned Lands (q.v.). He also registered many blacks to vote and helped sponsor a mock election of all races that sent Carpetbagger Henry Clay Warmoth (qq.v.) to Congress to be seated as Louisiana's "territorial representative" with no vote.

Meanwhile, Dunn became secretary to Freedmen's Saving and Trust Company and organized a People's Bakery, owned by its employees. He was in favor of reconvening the state constitutional convention, and Maj. Gen. Philip H. Sheridan (q.v.) appointed him to the commission council of New Orleans in 1867 under powers granted by the Third Military Reconstruction Act (q.v.). Dunn backed public education and spoke out in favor of a more efficient firefighting system, the appointment of only qualified electors to city patronage posts, and a tighter management of city government under the mayor. When the state Republican (q.v.) convention nominated Henry Clay Warmoth as governor in 1868, it tendered the lieutenant governorship to another politician. But the man refused the post, leaving the position open for Oscar J. Dunn, by now the acknowledged leader of the city's powerful contingent of black voters. The election of the Moderate Republican ticket of Warmoth and Dunn placed the black plasterer in power as the first African-American to hold an executive post in Reconstruction.

Aside from his duty as lieutenant governor of presiding over the state senate, Dunn was president of the board of New Orleans metropolitan police, a member of the senate printing committee, and president of the board of military pensions. He insisted that all members of the state senate take the ironclad oath before being seated, a step that sent several prominent Democrats (q.v.) home.

It was soon evident that Louisiana had three aspirants to the open U.S. Senate seat in 1871: Warmoth, senate president pro tem P. B. S. Pinchback (q.v.) (a black from Ohio), and Dunn. The latter had the leap over the other two, both of whom were Carpetbaggers (q.v.) and hence outsiders to many in Louisiana.

Both Warmoth and Pinchback had the reputation of being political hacks who would sell any position for a price. Dunn was in contrast viewed as an honest man, a fact that endeared him to the Ulysses S. Grant (q.v.) administration nationally and many voters of both races locally. He also managed to take over the Louisiana state central committee of the Republican Party, which held the nomination procedure in its hands. With these assets, Dunn could mount a creditable reform campaign for the open U.S. Senate seat in 1871. Of course, this being Louisiana, Warmoth and Pinchback also claimed to have control of their own well-bought versions of the state central committee, each claiming to be the regular, legal candidate. Suddenly the whole picture changed dramatically, as Dunn took sick and died.

Although Dunn had been attended by several physicians during his sickness, none agreed about the reason for the lieutenant governor's death. The coroner suspected arsenic poisoning (as do modern analyzers), a common voodoo concoction popular in the city. But three doctors (all white, implying to some that they were Warmoth hacks) signed the death certificate, making it official and negating an investigation. Dunn's skilled black doctor, L. C. Roudanez, however, was not among the signers, a fact that caused much suspicion, then and now.

DURHAM STATION, SURRENDER AT. *See* CAROLINAS CAMPAIGN.

E

EARLY, JUBAL (1816–1894). From Franklin County, Virginia, Jubal Early was educated at local academies and the U.S. Military Academy, where he graduated in the top half of the class of 1837. He fought in the Seminole War as an artillery officer, but resigned his commission to read law in southwestern Virginia. He was admitted to the bar and served in the state legislature as a Whig. He volunteered for the War with Mexico and served as a major of infantry. Returning home, he was defeated for the legislature and turned to practicing law. In 1861, he was elected as a Union supporter to the Virginia Convention and voted against secession.

When the war began, Early was commissioned as a colonel of the 24th Virginia Infantry. He fought at First Manassas and received a promotion to brigadier general shortly thereafter. He led his brigade until he replaced his division commander during the Maryland Campaign (q.v.). Promoted to major general, Early led his division brilliantly during the Chancellorsville Campaign, the Pennsylvania Campaign, and the 1864 Richmond campaign (qq.v.). He took over the Second Corps at Cold Harbor as lieutenant general. It was during the Petersburg Campaign (q.v.) that he achieved his reputation as the leader of Early's Raid on Washington (q.v.) and as the loser in the Second Shenandoah Valley Campaign (Sheridan's) (q.v.). He was relieved of command at the time of the Appomattox Campaign (q.v.).

Early refused to surrender after the war, fleeing the United States to Maximilian's Mexico (q.v.) and then Canada. He returned to Virginia to practice law and served on the board of the Louisiana Lottery Company. Never reconstructed, Early wrote his memoirs, became the first president of the Southern Historical Society, instrumental in publishing its papers, to which he contributed much in the form of attacks against Lt. Gen. James Longstreet (q.v.), whom he blamed for losing the Battle of Gettysburg. He was a profane, irascible character who was known to his men as "Old Jube" or "Jubilee."

EARLY'S RAID ON WASHINGTON. *See* WASHINGTON, EARLY'S RAID ON.

EATON, JOHN (1829–1906). Originally from New Hampshire, where he attended Dartmouth College to study theology, John Eaton enlisted as the chaplain of the 27th Ohio Volunteer Infantry. In this capacity, he was appointed by Maj. Gen. Ulysses S. Grant (q.v.) as superintendent of freedmen for Mississippi, northern Louisiana, Arkansas, and western Tennessee, a position he held until the end of the war, winding up as a brevet brigadier general. Eaton worked the contrabands (q.v.) in abandoned fields at Corinth, Mississippi, and Grand Junction, Tennessee, where the largest camps of blacks were, and got into several squabbles with the Army's adjutant general, Lorenzo Thomas, over recruitment of blacks as soldiers and how they should be employed by private contractors on abandoned plantations. At the end of the war, Eaton remained in Tennessee, editing a Memphis newspaper and serving as state superintendent of education. He was also a commissioner for the U.S. Bureau of Education, president of two colleges, and placed in charge of restoring the education system of Puerto Rico after the Spanish–American War. He wrote several accounts on Mormonism (he had been in Salt Lake City for a period of time) and about his wartime experience with black labor. He died in Washington, D.C., in 1906.

EBENEZER CREEK, THE DISASTER AT. *See* MARCH TO THE SEA.

ELECTION OF 1848. Although both major political parties, the Democrats and the Whigs (qq.v.), were bi-sectional and affected by the slavery issue as brought forth in the Wilmot Proviso (q.v.), the Democrats were hit the hardest first during the election of 1848. Party regulars were determined to work out some sort of compromise. Developed by Vice President George M. Dallas of Pennsylvania and publicized by their 1848 presidential nominee, Lewis M. Cass (q.v.) of Michigan, the party regulars' solution was squatter sovereignty (q.v.)—let the people in the territories vote on the slavery issue.

But it would not be that easy. For John C. Calhoun, slowly dying after 40 years of public service, saw the trick in squatter sovereignty—only Mexicans and Yankees occupied the territories. The South and its slaves would be excluded before they could think of moving west. So Southern firebrands, led by William L. Yancey of Alabama, stood foursquare behind the Non-Exclusion Doctrine (q.v.)—that slavery ought to be allowed into the territories until a proposed state constitution was drawn up and the territory admitted to the Union as a state.

Yancey's northern counterparts, called Barnburners in New York state, stood for the Wilmot Proviso—no slavery in any territory. Cass refused to come out for either extreme. He wrote a letter to Democrat stalwart A. O. P. Nicholson and declared he was for the middle route, squatter sovereignty, the rule of the majority. The nomination was his, but the extremists on both sides refused to support him, especially after President James K. Polk created Oregon Territory without slavery because it was north of the Missouri Compromise line. If the South could not trust Polk, a slaveholder, how could they trust Cass, a nonslaveholder?

The opposition Whigs were also rent by the slavery issue, but they took the smart way out. They nominated military hero Gen. Zachary Taylor (q.v.), the victor of Buena Vista, which caused chastened rival Henry Clay to mutter, "I wish I could kill a Mexican!" But Taylor had two problems. He was a slaveholder, which pleased the South. But he had never voted, not once in his whole life. So he declared himself to be a Whig, but not an ultra-Whig. He was for some tariffs, some internal improvements—but not as much as Clay. Taylor received the nomination, but certain Northerners, called Conscience Whigs, bolted from the party.

The Conscience Whigs joined with the Northern Democrats to back the remnants of the old antislavery Liberty Party. At the suggestion of Salmon P. Chase, they met at Buffalo, New York, and styled themselves the Free Soil Party. Their nominee was Martin Van Buren, the man who had created the Democratic Party back in 1828 with slaveholding Andrew Jackson as their front man. Now old Van had seen the light. Southern Democrats voted for Taylor, as did most Whigs, and Taylor won, taking 163 electoral votes to Cass' 127. Van Buren received no electoral votes, but garnered 10 percent of the popular votes.

Taylor's first job would be to solve the question of slavery in the territories. It would be called the Compromise of 1850 (q.v.).

ELECTION OF 1852. Even though President Millard Fillmore had signed the Compromise of 1850 (q.v.), the measure was essentially a creation of the Democrats (q.v.), supported by the Southern Whigs. The Northern Whigs were extremely lukewarm on the Compromise of 1850, their attitude being typified by U.S. Senator William H. Seward (q.v.) of New York. Seward spoke of a "higher law" than the U.S. Constitution that justified opposition to slavery.

The Whigs (q.v.) came together with three possible candidates for president. They were Millard Fillmore (q.v.) of New York, who had signed and promoted the Compromise of 1850; Daniel Webster of Massachusetts, whom many in the North thought of as a moral sell-out because he voted for and spoke on behalf of the Compromise of 1850; and Bvt. Lt. Gen. Winfield Scott (q.v.) of Virginia, who said nothing about the Compromise of 1850, but represented the victory in the War with Mexico that had caused the Compromise to have to come into being.

Both Fillmore and Webster were unacceptable to Seward and his allies. Scott, on the other hand, offered the chance of repeating the 1848 triumph with the military hero of the age. And although not a pro-slave advocate, he was a

Virginian. But Southern Whigs wanted some assurance that Scott would not fall under Seward's thumb and forget he was a Southerner, as had Taylor. Scott refused to give any guarantees. He was who he was, and that was that.

The Democrats, meanwhile, moved to secure the Compromise of 1850 coalition of Northern and Southern Democrats and Southern Whigs. Their man was Franklin Pierce (q.v.) of New Hampshire, a man of several advantages. He was a war hero, too, one of the few New Englanders who had supported it and fought in it as a brigade leader. Like many junior volunteer officers, he hated the pompous, overbearing Scott. A Hampshireman, sold to the American public as the "Young Hickory of the Granite Hills" (a sort of Northern version of "Old Hickory," Andrew Jackson), he appealed to New England and the New York supporters of Martin Van Buren, engendering much party unity. Finally, he was outspokenly in favor of the Compromise of 1850.

The election was over almost before it started. Pierce won by over 200,000 popular votes. His vice presidential candidate was William R. King, a happenstance that brought Southern Whigs into the Democratic fold once more, as it had with the passage of the Compromise of 1850. King would soon die. His functions of office, such as they were, presiding over the Senate, were assumed by Senator David Atchison of Missouri, the Senate's president *pro tempore*, and one of the most rabid pro-slavery proponents in the nation. The South had reason to expect much from the Pierce administration, and it would not disappoint, as its "Spread Eagle" (q.v.) foreign policy and its Kansas–Nebraska Act (q.v.) domestic policy were to affirm.

ELECTION OF 1856. Three parties offered candidates in the national election of 1856. The first was the remnants of the old Whig Party (q.v.), now called the American (q.v.) or Know Nothing Party. The Whigs had been virtually destroyed by the quarrel over the slavery issue. The Conscience Whigs found compromise over slavery to be wrong and impolitic. They joined with the new Republican antislavery party. The Cotton Whigs supported slavery and abhorred what they perceived to be meddling with domestic institutions. They still hoped to oppose the Democrats (q.v.) on traditional economic issues left over from the days of Andrew Jackson. These included a national banking system, government assistance to farmers and education, a high protective tariff, the colonization of freed slaves overseas, and the construction of internal improvements with government support.

But above all, the American Party found its adherents in the Atlantic states, which had been overrun by the massive European immigration that came after the failure of the revolutions of 1848 in the German states and the potato famine in Ireland. These immigrants brought Roman Catholicism as their religion and an affection for the consumption of hard liquors and beer, even on Sundays. This, added to the traditional corruption of the Democratic machines of the big cities, which provided jobs and welfare in exchange for the correct vote, caused many Americans to yearn for the old Protestant values of times past.

The American Party's front runner and eventual nominee was Millard Fillmore. Passed over in favor of Gen. Winfield Scott (q.v.) in 1852, Fillmore's essential honesty and willingness to support the Compromise of 1850 (q.v.) looked good on paper. But Fillmore was from Buffalo, New York. This caused many Southern Whigs to suspect him, especially because he was very much against the Kansas–Nebraska Act (q.v.), which had repealed the Missouri Compromise. Southern Whigs feared that if the South split its vote in 1856, the Republicans (q.v.) might win, and slavery would be challenged again.

The Democrats met in convention on June 2, 1856, in Cincinnati, the "Queen City of the West." This was the first time any political party had met west of the Appalachians. It happened as a concession to western Democrats to support New Englander Franklin Pierce (q.v.) in 1852. The Democrats were a tired political organization in 1852. Years of victory had made the party sluggish, out of touch with the moment, faction-ridden. Its potential nominees illustrated that point well. Franklin Pierce was destroyed by the Kansas–Nebraska Act and the Kansas–Missouri Border Wars (q.v.). He had won in 1852 mainly because he was not Lewis Cass. Cass was still in the offing, but he was old, outdated, and had lost in 1848. Stephen A. Douglas (q.v.) represented the new blood in the Democratic Party. He was young, brassy, pushy, and disliked by old-time party regulars. He was also burdened with originating the Kansas–Nebraska Act. This left James Buchanan (q.v.). A 42-year veteran of the party, Old Buck was crafty, plodding, uninspired, but reliable. He had complete Southern support and was safe on the slavery issue.

Buchanan's nomination was engineered by the Southern wing of the party, which hoped that his party loyalty would stop the factionalism that had haunted the party since the days of Jackson. Since Douglas was the strongest opponent, Buchanan's backers made him a deal. He would yield to Buchanan and receive the nod in 1860, when the currently 65-year-old Buchanan would be too old to serve again. To mollify die-hard Southern supporters of Pierce, the 1860 convention was to be held in Charleston.

The final party to offer a slate in 1856 was the new Republican Party. Only two years old, the Republicans needed to select a man who could take votes from Fillmore and the Americans. They needed someone who was moderately antislavery (q.v.) and nativistic. Old Frank Blair, Sr., once an advisor to Andrew Jackson, but now in the opposition, suggested John Charles Frémont (q.v.). He was attractive, a war hero, the conqueror of California, Western explorer of note, in favor of a transcontinental railroad, U.S. senator from California, and possessed all of the qualities of genius except ability. To assist his nomination, Frémont came out against the Kansas–Nebraska Act for the first time.

The platform the Republicans had Frémont run on included a congressional ban on the twin evils of slavery and polygamy in the territories. There was no reference to nativism, the Missouri Compromise, the Kansas–Nebraska Act, or a ban on slavery in the District of Columbia—all traditional Republican positions. The party slogan was "Free Soil, Free Labor, Free Men, and Frémont." Conveniently, the extreme abolitionists (q.v.) ran their own candidate, which made Frémont look moderate.

The result of the election was close, too close for comfort for the Democrats. Even with complete Southern Democrat and Whig–American support, Fillmore took 8 electoral votes (Maryland) and 25 percent of the popular vote; Frémont took 114 electoral votes (all Northern) and only 30 percent of the popular vote; while Buchanan took 174 electoral votes (North and South) and 45 percent of the popular vote. While Buchanan won, seemingly convincingly, the Republicans discovered that if they could hold the states they carried in 1856 four years later and take Pennsylvania (27 electoral votes) and either Indiana (11) or Illinois (13), their man then would sit in the White House with a majority of the electoral vote and a minority (around 40 percent) of the popular vote.

ELECTION OF 1860. In the election of 1860, for the first time and last time in American history, four parties of potentially equal strength contested the presidency. The Democratic (q.v.) Party had three separate conventions, splintering into two factions based on sectional lines. The Charleston Convention (q.v.) was the first, the city having been picked by prior agreement four years earlier. Sadly for party unity, Charleston was the center of Southern nationalism. Backing the so-called Alabama Platform, the Southern delegates insisted that their view on the non-exclusion of slavery in the territories be adopted. When this failed, the Gulf South walked out, forcing party regulars to adjourn and recall the delegates to the Baltimore Convention (q.v.) six weeks later.

Meanwhile, the Constitutional Union Party (q.v.) took over the reins from what was left of the old Whig, Know Nothing, American Parties (qq.v.). Mainly from the border states, the Constitutional Union Party dropped all pretense at a party platform. It stood for Constitution and unity, the vaguer the better. They nominated John Bell of Tennessee for president and Edward Everett of Massachusetts for vice president. The goal of the Constitutional Unionists was to take enough electoral votes to throw the election into the House of Representatives. There, hopefully, a deal could be made to save the slowly crumbling Union.

The Republicans (q.v.) came next, holding their Chicago Convention (q.v.). Only their second try at the presidency, the Republicans had managed to obtain a majority in the House when Representative Henry Winter Davis (q.v.) of Maryland shifted his vote from Whig–American to Republican. In 1856, the Republicans realized that if they kept the states they had won and added Pennsylvania and either Indiana or Illinois to their column in 1860, they would win with a minority of popular votes, but a majority in the electoral college. Their hopes were placed on Abraham Lincoln (q.v.) of Illinois, a moderate on most issues, but as an old Whig in favor of their economic program and safe on the no slavery in the territories issue.

Finally, the Democrats' Baltimore Convention met. Before they had left Charleston, their leading candidate had agreed to accept the nomination only with a two-thirds majority of the original convention's delegates. But now, Stephen A. Douglas (q.v.) agreed to run as their candidate with two-thirds of those attending. Many Southern delegates had met in Richmond, where they awaited developments in Baltimore. This time there was a second walkout, and Douglas and his Northern Democrats had to contend with another Democrat put forth by the Richmond Convention (q.v.). Their candidate was the current vice president, John C. Breckinridge of Kentucky.

Each party had its own marchers and poll watchers. Lincoln used the "Wide Awakes," which name they borrowed from the Know Nothings of 1856. Douglas had the "Little Giants" (a play on his nickname), Breckinridge had the National Democratic Volunteers (which made him sound like the real party nominee), and Bell had the "Bell Ringers." Lincoln's main advantage was that he only had to run in the North. None of the candidates spoke—the myth was that the office sought the man. But every candidate had his front men, who made all the speeches and false promises necessary to carry a state's electoral vote. The key for Lincoln was to show how the South had blocked Henry Clay's old American System (q.v.), upon which the Republican Platform of 1860 (q.v.) was based. Pennsylvania was sure to be carried with this approach.

In the election of 1860, each state voted on its own timetable, the final states voting by November. It was seen quite early that the Democrats were actually going to increase their number of congressmen. But there was something else that only Douglas, and maybe Bell, seemed to grasp. More and more, the seceders in the South were absorbing the regular Democrats. If Lincoln were elected, the South saw itself opened to domestic violence brought on by Lincoln's own party's abolition wing. Douglas broke with precedent and toured New England and the South in person, hoping to head off extremists on both sides. He offered himself as the only compromise candidate of national stature.

The possible loss of its voice in Federal power was a shock to the South. In a sense, Southerners believed the Republicans' attack on the Slave Power Conspiracy (q.v.) that had controlled American Federal government from the days of George Washington and the Virginia dynasty of presidents who followed him in office. Of the 15 presidents who preceded the Civil War, 6 had been from the North. Only the Southerners had served two terms; the Yankees never served more than one term apiece. And of the six Northerners, only two, John and John Quincy Adams, had been true Northern men. The others had kowtowed to the South in domestic policy, particularly when it came to slavery.

But there was a way to maintain the South in power. That was to secede and form its own nation. The regular Democrats were under terrific pressure. They combated the idea of secession by taking over the support of the radical secessionists, the Fire-Eaters (q.v.) or the Chivalry, with their own men in state after state. The regular Democrats would lead the way to Southern independence as they had led the whole United States from the 1830s. James L. Orr took over from Robert Barnwell Rhett in South Carolina, Jefferson Davis (q.v.) from Albert Gallatin Brown (Mississippi), John Slidell from Pierre Soulé (Louisiana), and Howell Cobb from Alfred Iverson (Georgia). This is what Douglas saw, and it scared him.

Douglas and Breckinridge took 47 percent of the popular vote, up 2 percent from 1856. The Constitutional Unionists captured 14 percent of the popular vote, down 9 percent from 1860. The Republicans took the rest, 39 percent, up 7 percent from 1856. Most important was that the Republicans took every state's electoral vote in 1860 that they had won in 1856, plus they added Pennsylvania's and Illinois'. Put more clearly, Lincoln took the electoral vote of every free state except half of New Jersey's. Even if all the others had created a fusion ticket, Lincoln would have won. He might have lost California and Oregon to a fusion slate, but he had enough slack in the electoral vote to still win. Each state was close for the Republicans, but they won everything they had to. Worse yet for the South, Lincoln and Douglas took 70 percent of the popular vote. This indicated that sometime in the future there would be no slavery in the territories. The slave South was a great minority within the nation as never before.

Just by accident, when South Carolina's legislature, elected in October 1860, met in November at the request of the Governor, William H. Gist, no Fire-Eater by any means, the legislature called for a constitutional convention to consider the concept of secession. It also began to buy weapons to arm an increased state militia. The First Secession (q.v.) movement was on its way. *See also* REPUBLICAN PLATFORM OF 1860.

ELECTION OF 1861, CONFEDERATE. Although the Provisional Congress of the Confederacy had elected Jefferson Davis (q.v.) and Alexander H. Stephens (q.v.) as president and vice president, respectively, and functioned as a unicameral national legislature until February 1862, the Confederate

Constitution (q.v.) called for national elections to select permanent executives and a regular bicameral congress. The provisional congress called for these in November 1861. Despite setbacks in Confederate military operations on the South Atlantic Coast, western Virginia, Kentucky, and Missouri, Jefferson Davis ran unopposed and was easily reelected by popular and electoral vote. Vice President Stephens was another matter. Many saw him as not fully dedicated to winning the war or creating a viable Confederate state. He had opposed secession and was deemed very critical of existing policies. Some saw him as a spoilsman, dedicated to the corrupt (q.v.) policies of the antebellum Union. But although the protests against Stephens raised doubts, they did not produce an opposition candidate or prevent his reelection .

In the congressional elections, each state was allotted its normal number of U.S. representatives elected popularly, plus two senators elected by state legislatures. There were no party labels used, although there were still implications of Whig and Democratic areas, and former political machines were utilized whenever possible. But the Democrats and the Whigs (qq.v.) had long ceased to battle over traditional economic issues and banded together for national independence. States in which Whigs and Democrats had been balanced before the war generally selected their two senators, one from each party. More principled candidates pointed to the distaste that party politics had left in the mouths of the generation of the Revolution of 1776 and tried to avoid such.

Because of the war, election campaigns were considered unseemly. Many voters and commentators groused that the ablest men were off with the armies. Instead, candidates offered themselves as individuals, often with an explanation attached to their names to indicate their patriotic support of independence and the boys in the field. Any other issues were purely local. The Rebel governments of Missouri and Kentucky were in exile, but the governors selected their two senators and encouraged soldiers and refugees to vote whenever possible.

If voting were light in these two states, so was it everywhere. But in the end, the First Confederate Congress was selected to meet in Richmond for four sessions: February 18–April 21, 1862; August 18–October 13, 1862; January 12–May 1, 1863; and November 18, 1863–February 21, 1864.

ELECTION OF 1862, UNION. In the midst of the Civil War, the congressional election occurred. Even though President Abraham Lincoln (q.v.) and the Republicans (q.v.) feared its results, it is instructive that, just as in the Confederacy, no one thought of postponing it.

The election of 1862 is often portrayed as a disastrous loss for the Lincoln administration. On the surface, the numbers are staggering. At least, the Radical Republicans and the Regular Democrats (those lukewarm in support of the "Republican war") thought so. Republicans lost the governorship of New York, the governorship and both house in New Jersey, and both houses of the legislatures in Indiana and Illinois (Lincoln's home state). Democrats also won 35 congressional districts throughout the North. Because not all states elected their local and congressional officials in the even-numbered years, as they do today, the Republicans managed to save Ohio and Pennsylvania for their column.

But that is merely a quick look at the obvious. Because Illinois and Indiana had elected Republican governors for four-year terms in 1860, the Republicans still had the gubernatorial use of the veto there. They also retained control of legislatures and governors in 16 other states. They elected several congressmen from Missouri for the first time and, despite the severe losses, maintained their majority in the House of Representatives and actually gained five U.S. Senate seats. What really happened was that the Republicans had suffered the smallest losses in off-year (non-presidential) elections in 20 years. Best of all, the Democratic (q.v.) majority was small in most states and could be traced to the fact that soldiers had not voted, something that the Republicans would see did happen in 1864.

But the election did have important effects, militarily and politically. Radical Republicans demanded scapegoats for the Democrats' improvement. They probably caused as much of the Republican loss by their split with Lincoln and party moderates, but they saw it otherwise. Radicals blamed the inactivity of the armies, especially those led by Maj. Gen. George B. Mc-Clellan (q.v.) in the East and Maj. Gen. Don Carlos Buell (q.v.) in the West. Then there was what Republicans saw as the Democrats' stranglehold on military patronage as a price for support of the war effort. Finally, Radicals lambasted Lincoln's own "rosewater" policies of compensated emancipation and colonization (qq.v.) of the former slaves overseas, rather than enrolling them openly as soldiers.

Lincoln knew that some of the Radicals' objections to the conduct of the war were valid. He moved right after the election to replace McClellan with Maj. Gen. Ambrose E. Burnside (q.v.), and Buell with Maj. Gen. William S. Rosecrans (q.v.). He also permitted the military court-martial of McClellan's prize subordinate, Maj. Gen. FitzJohn Porter, whom Radicals blamed for the loss of the Second Manassas Campaign. Porter was charged with "disobedience of orders and misconduct in face of the enemy." In reality, Porter had been detached off to the left of Maj. Gen. John Pope's army at Second Manassas and had been reluctant to come in and join a series of futile attacks against Confederate Maj. Gen. Thomas J. Jackson's (q.v.) positions, because he knew that he blocked Gen. Robert E. Lee's (q.v.) other wing from the vicious counterattack that finally won the battle. But facts were not important. The trial was designed to show other officers that no more excuses were to be allowed in not prosecuting the war to its fullest and achieving eventual victory, no matter the cost. Porter was sacked outright, although he was reinstated after the war.

As Lincoln's actions changed the military picture, the Radicals still hoped to prove that he was under some malevolent influence within his official family. They decided that the real problem was that Secretary of State William Seward (q.v.) was to blame for backing poor (read: Democrat) generals, slowing emancipation, and demanding colonization of freed blacks (qq.v.) overseas. How did they know? Because Seward's main rival for Lincoln's attention, Secretary of the Treasury Salmon P. Chase (q.v.), secretly told them so. Congress decided to confront Lincoln with their suspicions and force Seward, by now Lincoln's most loyal cabinet member, out of office. They sent a committee to wait upon Lincoln led by Vermont Senator Jacob Collamer. Lincoln greeted the men and asked if they might not return the next day, when he could give fuller time to their important mission. When the committee returned, the whole cabinet was with Lincoln, less Seward, who had handed in his resignation. Lincoln then asked the cabinet if they were not a harmonious body in general agreement on all issues, met frequently, and no one member exercised undue power. He directed the question first to Chase, who agreed with Lincoln, denying all he had told Congress behind the president's back. The delegation left, angry with Chase's lack of candor.

Chase was so embarrassed by this that he felt compelled to resign. Lincoln refused both Seward's and Chase's resignations. But Chase had the habit of threatening to resign over every little thing. So Lincoln kept his letter to remind him who was really in charge, devastating election or no.

ELECTION OF 1863, CONFEDERATE. Since executive officers had been elected for a six-year term in 1861, the Confederate election of 1863 (held at different times in various states between June and November) concerned only congressmen and senators. By now, elections in the South were truer to form than in 1861. There were still no formal parties, as such, but there were issues to discuss—hotly. Most of them concerned President Jefferson Davis' (q.v.) conduct of the war. Included were such things as conscription, impressment of goods, taxation, military policy, and state rights. But it is critical to keep in mind that amid all of the sound and fury, many opposed Davis, not for being too strong, but for being too weak kneed or downright incompetent. This was especially true of military defeats.

In general, areas occupied by the advancing Union armies and soldiers tended to vote pro-administration. But in other areas, many men who had once been Whigs (q.v.) and cooperationists with the Union in 1861 tended to win. But still there were no real political parties on the ballots. The Rebels eschewed them as solidly as had the Founding Fathers in the *Federalist Papers* of 1787. Men ran as individuals for or against a policy or policies backed by the administration. But if prewar party politics had any relevance (and some historians believe they did not), the Second Congress was less aggressive or pro-secession, that is, more conservative or Whig, than the First, which was more secessionist or Democrat.

In the end, the administration's ability to maintain a working majority was made possible only by members who came from districts threatened or occupied by the Yankees. In these areas, the contrast between nationalism and liberty was more starkly drawn for the electorate. This did not stop Gov. Joseph E. Brown (q.v.) of Georgia or Zebulon Vance of North Carolina from opposing the administration's centralization of power or its war policies, even as Federal armies made their protests moot. It is possible that the nonexistence of political parties, caused President Davis to lack the power he needed to overcome his opponents. The voters could not help, because in elections no one ran as part of the loyal opposition, only as an individual—for Davis on some issues and against him on others. There was no regularity on any issue. There was no party discipline.

The Second Congress met for only two sessions, May 2–June 14, 1864, and November 7, 1864–March 18, 1865. Then the realities of military defeat caught up with the Confederate experiment in independent nationhood.

ELECTION OF 1864. *See* WADE–DAVIS MANIFESTO AND THE ELECTION OF 1864.

ELECTION OF 1868. The late 19th-century Republican Party's (q.v.) strength was reliant on the suffrage of small businessmen and farmers. It also appealed to loyal Union men, black and white, with the slogan, "vote as you shot," and through its main lobby of veterans, the Grand Army of the Republic. There was no unity on economic questions. The party was split over questions of tariff, internal improvements, and the national banking system. But it managed to vote in enough varied economic measures to please a wide audience.

In 1868, the Republican Party was going to stand on its Civil War record and past legislation. It had no new program to offer. Doubters were to be won over by appealing to the patriotism of the supporters of the Union. Standing on their record, repudiating Radicalism as typified by the persecution of Andrew Johnson (q.v.) through his impeachment, the Republicans went to Chicago in 1868 for their national nominating convention. Here they played their trump card, the nomination of the popular war hero, Ulysses S. Grant (q.v.). The scene was prepared by a Soldiers and Sailors Convention held just down the street. As he won the war, he could secure the peace, went the reasoning. The vice president's slot went to Smilin' Schuyler Colfax (q.v.), speaker of the House, who had let Thaddeus Stevens (q.v.) run everything.

It was said that Colfax was so amiable that he never lost a friend or made an enemy, which did not hurt him among party stalwarts. Grant accepted the nomination through the traditional letter. Brilliantly, Grant declared that he would have no policy to enforce against the will of the people, which meant that he would do Congress' bidding as opposed to Johnson's independent actions, which pleased Republican theorists who believed that that was the president's constitutional role. Grant closed with a heart-rending plea to a war-weary, Reconstruction-weary nation: "Let us have peace."

Matching Grant was out of the question for the Democrats (q.v.), still ailing from the political throes of Civil War and Reconstruction. As they met in New York City (they had their own Soldiers and Sailors Convention down the street, too), the party did have several possible courses of action. They could openly challenge the Republicans and Reconstruction, or they could accept Reconstruction and the Negro vote as established facts and nominate a man pledged to constitutional government and state rights. Having been denied the Republican nomination, Salmon P. Chase (q.v.), Lincoln's former secretary of the treasury and currently chief justice of the U.S. Supreme Court, declared that he had been a Democrat all along—he had parted with the party only over the slavery issue. There was a lot of Wall Street support for him within the party—Augustus Belmont, for example—and many admired the national banking system he had set up during the war. Chase sent his radiant daughter, Kate Chase Sprague, to promote the millennium, as it were.

Finally, the Democrats could ignore Reconstruction and battle over prewar economic issues that had been enacted by the Republicans under Abraham Lincoln (q.v.) when the South was out of the Congress. The big issue here was to pay off the war debt in greenbacks unless they specified gold on their face. "The dollar that paid the soldier can pay the bondholder," went the call, issued by George Pendleton of Ohio. There was a lot of appeal to this, and Pendleton's "Ohio Idea" became the main plank of the platform. The Democrats also asked the nation to forget the war, pledged to declare the Military Reconstruction Acts (q.v.) null and void and let all of the states settle their desires on suffrage, and promised to withdraw the U.S. Army's occupation force from the South. But the delegates deadlocked on nominating Pendleton. After numerous votes, the convention finally nominated its speaker, Horatio Seymour of New York. His vice presidential nominee was Frank Blair of Missouri, a political general of some ability from an old family that had put Andrew Jackson in the presidency 40 years earlier.

The Democrat ticket was bottom heavy. Blair was a good man, but he was not the candidate. Seymour, on the other hand, had numerous liabilities. He was little known outside New York, and then only as its governor who had been tarred with the brush of disloyalty during the war, which he had vocally opposed. Worse yet, he was a hard money man who wanted to repay the war bonds in gold, just like the Republicans. The Republicans themselves could not have picked a better pair than Seymour and Blair to run against. The result was a smashing electoral victory for Grant and the Republicans (214–80) and a narrower popular victory of 300,000 votes out of nearly six million cast. Outgoing President Johnson never bothered to show up for the inauguration, as he and Grant were still bitter enemies over the Tenure of Office Act (q.v.).

ELECTION OF 1872. By the time of the 1872 election, the Ulysses S. Grant (q.v.) administration had caused quite a bit of disillusionment among the party and the public at large. Some of it was embarrassing, such as Senator Charles Sumner (q.v.) introducing a constitutional amendment limiting a president to one term. True, it would exempt Grant, but on the other hand, everyone knew at whom it was aimed. Other criticism was of the damned if you do, damned if you don't variety. Grant was lambasted as being soft on civil service reform, associated with the most corrupt elements of the party, too harsh on Reconstruction enforcement, not harsh enough on Reconstruction enforcement, and soft on the protective tariff.

Those who opposed Grantism within the party were called Liberal Republicans (q.v.). Most were journalists, professional reformers, and intellectuals. They lacked political skills but made up for it with a lot of enthusiasm. They were liberal not in the 20th-century sense of wanting government services, but in the traditional definition of desiring honest, constitutional government. They decided not to challenge the political professionals of the Republican Party (q.v.) but to step aside and form a new party to challenge all of the status quo.

Led by German immigrant and former Union political general Carl Schurz (q.v.), the Liberals met at Cincinnati, Ohio. Their platform was full of the reforms of the hour. While they agreed with Reconstruction in principle, they found it lacking in practice. Their solution to the corrupt boroughs of the South was to call for universal amnesty and a withdrawal of Federal troops from the civilian political arena. Another platform plank was the call for civil service reform and a general cleaning up of government. They endorsed the paying of the national debt in gold (real hard money, not inflated greenbacks, was the only honest way). But they met their match on the tariff issue. Some wanted it higher; some wanted it lower. So in the end, the party said they would refer it to the people. This made them look weak and willing to drop principle for expediency. The two regular parties did better in that realm.

Up to this point, the Liberals stood a good chance to win. But then they got down to the process of nominating a candidate—where third parties often fail. He was picked by other men behind the scenes, four newspaper editors known as the "Quadrilateral." These men, who trumpeted reform in their papers, were Murat Halstead of the *Cincinnati Commercial*, Samuel

Bowles of the Springfield, (Massachusetts) *Republican*, Henry Watterson of the Louisville *Courier-Journal*, and Horace White of the *Chicago Tribune*. As they pondered what to do, another editor asked for admittance to their group. He was Whitelaw Reid of the powerful New York *Tribune*. His paper was critical to the reform movement; its influence was nationwide. Soon the persuasive Reid was bending the other four to his way of thinking. The man he believed could lead the Liberals to power was none other than his boss, Horace Greeley (q.v.). And on the sixth ballot, Greeley became the standard bearer. His running mate was B. Gratz Brown, a Missouri Radical Republican and a crony of Schurz.

Greeley's nomination has been dismissed as the work of political amateurs, but this is not wholly true. If there were any real politicians or men who understood American politics, it was the members of the Quadrilateral. Greeley was stronger than he seemed on the surface, but he was kind of a fluke in the process. He was a man of insatiable curiosity, and looked like someone who had just stuck a bobby pin in a light socket—a sort of wide-eyed amazement. Greeley was many things to the American people, but presidential candidate was not high on the list. A whole generation of Democrats had been raised to hate him and his loony ideas. If he were to win against Grant, he had to shed this liability. It was a tall order.

When the Democrats (q.v.) met at Baltimore, the outcome of the election rested in large part with their convention delegates. Following the lead of Civil War Copperhead Clement Vallandigham (qq.v.) of Ohio, the Democrats reluctantly admitted that they could not come up with a man who could take on Grant and Greeley at the same time. So they fell into step and took Greeley, too.

But large numbers of Democrats thought as did former Confederate lieutenant general and soon to be Imperial Grand Wizard of the Ku Klux Klan, Nathan Bedford Forrest (qq.v.). He said he would support Grant, because at least he had not advocated emancipation and hatred of the white South for 20 years before the Civil War. Forrest was not alone, North or South. At the same time, Grant represented a strong Reconstruction and support of black rights, which appealed to many old abolitionists (q.v.) in the North. Politics truly makes for strange bedfellows.

As the Democrats fumed about swallowing the Liberal Republicans, Greeley and all, the regular Republicans met at Philadelphia. Party regulars controlled the convention machinery and saw to it that anti-Grant delegates were scattered about on the floor, where they could not communicate and coordinate their opposition. Grant won on the first ballot and, as a sop to honest government, Smilin' Schuyler Colfax (q.v.), implicated in the Crédit Mobilier (q.v.) scandal, was dropped for Henry Wilson of Massachusetts (who had once dallied with Confederate spy Rose O'Neal Greenhow and prematurely revealed the Yankee advance on First Bull Run). They ran on more of the same, vote the way you shot.

The Republican campaign was not harmed any by Greeley's decision to break with precedent and stump for himself. Grant sat back and let his cronies do it for him, preserving the 19th-century myth that the office sought the man, not the other way around. Greeley screeched in a high squeaky voice at every stop, emphasizing sectional reconciliation, "peace not vengeance." His favorite line was to extend "the hand of reconciliation" to the South. Grant's supporters had a field day with that. The bloody shirt waved often. Especially effective was Thomas Nast's series of cartoons in *Harper's Weekly*, a nationally circulated news magazine. The theme was Greeley's "Hand of Reconciliation"—extended to John Wilkes Booth over Abraham Lincoln's (q.v.) grave; extended to a Confederate soldier over the rotting hell hole of Union prisoners of war at Andersonville; extended to a Ku Klux Klansman over the body of a mutilated black voter. Greeley commented that he hardly knew if he were running for the presidency or the penitentiary. But Nast's attack pretty well blew to pieces the farmer–philosopher that Greeley imitated and revealed what allowing the white South to take control of Reconstruction would mean—for those who had already forgotten about Andrew Johnson's (q.v.) failed program that was based on the same people.

When the results came in, Greeley had lost to Grant worse than Horatio Seymour in the election of 1868 (q.v.). The electoral vote was 286 to 62; the popular vote 3.6 million to 2.8 million. Greeley had exhausted himself during the campaign and died heartbroken three weeks later. When the electoral college met to cast their votes, all but 10 electors pledged to Greeley cast their votes for other living Democrats (completely permissible under the Constitution, as political parties are not recognized under it). Grant had won his second term under conditions that meant the anomalies of his first term would be multiplied in his second term and made much worse. The Great Barbecue was on, and the Era of Good Stealings had just begun.

ELECTION OF 1876 AND COMPROMISE OF 1877. The election of 1876, the "Crime of '76," was one of the most controversial in American history. In 1876, the Republican Party (q.v.) met at Cincinnati determined to take the presidency once again. Initially, backers of President Ulysses S. Grant (q.v.) hoped to run the popular general for an unprecedented third term. But the George Washington two-term limit and the corruption of Grant's cronies during his two terms soon put an end to the effort. Obviously the party would face a clean Democrat (q.v.) candidate, and it would have to preempt the honesty issue if it were to win. Benjamin Bristow, one of those who had worked to clean up Grant's cabinet and the Whiskey Ring, was an obvious choice. But he had angered the old pols during his purge, and Grant responded to their feelings by firing Bristow after he had been blocked at the convention.

The main contenders for the nomination after Bristow and Grant were party regulars, U.S. Senators James G. Blaine of Maine and Roscoe Conkling of New York. Blaine was an expert at waving the bloody shirt. His demise came when one James Mulligan surfaced with letters allegedly written by Blaine concerning the senator's involvement in an Arkansas railroad scandal. Blaine claimed to have a telegram that would clear him, but dared not release it lest others' reputations be unintentionally smeared. It was a great ploy, but it did not wash, and he lost his chance for the nomination.

Blaine's colleague, Roscoe Conkling, had a reputation as a spoilsman, taking his cut of all activities in his state and elsewhere. Of course Conkling had never been trapped publicly in his wheeling and dealing, and no one had caught him in bed with the wrong woman, but rumors abounded. Conkling never admitted or denied anything; he just smiled like the Cheshire Cat and made clever jokes as an aside. But in a year like 1876, the mere hint of scandal was enough to give delegates a second thought, so Conkling went the way of Blaine, just more quietly.

Unlike Blaine or Conkling, the Republicans needed a man who was well-enough known to attract the public and clean enough to keep them interested. But he also had to be a party regular who had not bolted with the Liberal Republicans (q.v.) in 1872. It took seven ballots to get rid of the chaff, but then the party nominated the perfect candidate, Governor Rutherford B. Hayes (q.v.) of Ohio. A former Union officer, Hayes was an Ohio native and a strong Republican supporter who had been elected to the House of Representative while serving with the Army; supported Reconstruction (but believed that the African-Americans needed education before receiving the vote); and had become governor on a platform that advocated civil service reform and efficient, honest government. He had stayed with Grant in 1872, even though his support of the national ticket had cost him reelection. But he regained the governorship in 1875, even though the Democrats had taken the rest of the state. He was a proven vote-getter and, upon accepting the presidential nomination, pledged to clean up Washington and withdraw Federal troops from the South (that is, he would not allow them to prop up allegedly unpopular, corrupt, nonwhite state governments).

Just as Hayes had struck the proper stance for the Republicans, the nomination of Samuel B. Tilden (q.v.) did the same for the Democrats. There was no other candidate to consider, Tilden had the nomination going away. The Democrats backed him with a platform pledged to the end of Reconstruction and the end of governmental corruption at all levels. A New York native, Tilden was a state rights Democrat, a critic of the draft, and a supporter of Andrew Johnson (q.v.) during Reconstruction. But he was smart enough to clean up Tammany Hall and the William M. "Boss" Tweed (q.v.) Ring, which gave him a clean enough look to go on to the governorship of the Empire State in 1874. There he became the quintessential reformer, promoting honest, efficient, economical government.

There was very little to differentiate Hayes and Tilden. They had the same outward image, a bit eccentric but clean in a political sense. Both pledged to clean up Washington and end Reconstruction. Both had reformist backgrounds; both were reliable party regulars through thick and thin. As custom demanded, neither candidate spoke, but let party pros do it for him. Their only substantial discrepancy was that Hayes was married and Tilden was a bachelor; which Republicans tried to make hay of by accusing Tilden of not having enough faith in American women or the future of the nation to wed and father a family.

But that was not enough to base a whole campaign on. This left the usual bloody shirt campaign, a natural against any anti-war Democrat. Unfortunately for the scheming politicians, 1876 was not a normal year. When the votes had been counted, Tilden was the popular choice by a quarter million out of eight and a quarter million votes cast. But the electoral vote was Tilden 184 and Hayes 165, with 20 electoral votes undecided. Hayes had to have all; Tilden needed only one. The votes were scattered among four states: Oregon had one; South Carolina had seven; Florida had four; and Louisiana had eight. Oregon turned out to be open and shut for Hayes because of Democrat irregularities in the original count. This left the 19 votes from the occupied South up for grabs.

The problem in the Southern states was that their electoral votes were authenticated by state institutions known as Returning Boards. State governors appointed these boards, which made their membership essentially Republican. But the Democrats claimed fraud and established their own Returning Boards, which sent in duplicate electoral votes for Tilden. In Louisiana, for example (to cite an extreme case), Democrats claimed to have elected their man as governor last time around, who had been prevented from taking office by the interference of Federal troops on behalf of the Republicans. No problem. He just set up his own shadow regime and appointed his own Returning Board and sent in the "real" vote. To make things really interesting, as they always are in Louisiana politics, there were three other Returning Boards also claiming legality. Similar quirks accounted for duplicate returns elsewhere.

So both parties sent "visiting statesmen" to the South to look into the purchase of the votes necessary to elect their brand of reforming president—kind of ironic for good government men. The Returning Boards were very receptive. In fact, a couple of Republican boards indicated that they would be happy to go for Tilden, the Democrat, for a price. But they would go only as a bloc, and Tilden needed only one vote. Louisiana and Florida would sell out to the

Democrats for $200,000 per entire board. At this juncture, the Democrat visiting statesmen got a bad case of false economy and refused to bribe more than the one elector they needed. In the end, the boards held firm and the stalemate continued, one Republican board and one Democrat board in each state.

The electoral college turned the problem over to Congress. The problem there was who should count the votes. The Constitution did not specifically say. It just said that the votes would be opened and counted in front of both houses. If the House did the counting, the winner would be Tilden, because the speaker of the house was a Democrat. The opposite was true of the Senate. Dominated by Republicans, it would count Hayes in. Again stalemate threatened.

As the process stagnated, there was much fear that organized party militia units would storm Washington to force the count to go their way. In desperation, the leaders in Congress decided to appoint an Electoral Commission of 15 members to go behind the returns and determine which were valid. The Commission was to have fives senators (divided three to two in favor of the controlling Republicans, as each body elected its own members), five from the House (three to two in favor of the Democrats), and five from the Supreme Court (divided two to two, with one "independent" or "neutral" judge who would obviously make all the decisions no one else could face up to).

The important thing was who would be the neutral judge (if there were such a man). Judge David Davis, once the campaign director for Lincoln in 1860, was an independent-minded Republican. The creators of the Commission expected him to be the odd vote. Then the Tilden managers did something stupid, again. They asked the Democrat-controlled state legislature of Illinois to elect Davis to the Senate, hoping to commit him ahead of time to their cause. But Davis had more integrity and probably was a mite thankful for the chance to opt out of the whole process. He resigned his judgeship and accepted the Senate seat, leaving the choice of the fifth man to a court dominated by staunch Republicans. Nominating Judge Joseph Bradley to fill Davis' seat, the Electoral Commission voted eight to seven to accept the Republican Returning Boards' contentions at face value and count all of the 19 disputed votes for Hayes, making him the next president of the United States by one vote (185–184). But the Electoral Commission's decision had to be accepted by both houses of Congress. The Republican-controlled Senate voted quickly to accredit the Commission's decision. But the Democrat-dominated House began a lengthy filibuster (allowed under the rules then but not now) that lasted the whole month of February 1877.

As the House talked the problem to death, the March 1877 inauguration date was fast approaching. Suddenly, as things looked bleakest, Southern Democrats broke with their Northern brethren and voted to end debate and accept the Electoral Commission's decision on behalf of Republican Hayes. The nation had a president. But why was this done? The traditional reason given is that Hayes' managers met with the Southern Democrat leaders at the Wormley Hotel and negotiated an agreement to accept Hayes as president if he would end the Reconstruction and the occupation of the South by Federal troops. But both Hayes and Tilden were already committed to that course. Something more had to be involved.

The real reason was that the Civil War and Reconstruction had warped the political process in the South. There were many Southern Democrats who were really Republicans when it came to economic issues—old Whigs, in effect. But the throes of Reconstruction had driven all whites into the Democrat Party to show a solid front against the reconstructing Republicans, who based their strength on the votes of the former slaves. These Whig-like Southern Democrats met with the Republican managers at the Wormley House and cut a deal. Hayes and the Republican Party would confirm their commitment to withdraw the Federal occupation forces; give Southern Democrats control of patronage in the Southern states by supporting former Confederate general David Key as postmaster general (cutting out the Southern Republican loyalists, black and white); and promise the Southern Democrats Federal aid for internal improvements, letting the Southern whites in on the Great Barbecue (the key was to build the Texas & Pacific Railroad to connect with the Southern Pacific coming out of California). In exchange, the Southern Democrats would make Hayes president by ending the House filibuster and voting for the Electoral Commission's decisions, and elect a Republican speaker (James Garfield) to organize the Democrat-dominated house.

More recent historians question whether the Wormley conference really did anything that was not already an accomplished fact. But it did. It allowed everyone involved to reassure each other that the other side would live up to the deal. And it permitted Southern politicians to keep their white electorate happy by creating the myth of the Wormley House agreement for the press and popular consumption—the withdrawal of the troops and end of Reconstruction on behalf of the white South.

Ending Reconstruction had become a reform of government for the public good. It covered up the betrayal of the African-Americans and made it palatable to North and South. In the end, the deal was only partly consummated. Hayes became president but refused to let the internal improvements, the center of prior corruption, continue. The Southern Democrats retaliated by organizing the House for their own party. But the true significance was that the Wormley House agreement, the real Compromise of 1877, returned American politics to the give and take that was normal until the issues of slavery, Civil War, and Reconstruction prevented splitting the difference in national issues.

ELK HORN TAVERN, BATTLE OF. *See* MISSOURI CAMPAIGN (1861–1862).

ELLENTON (SOUTH CAROLINA) RACE RIOT (1876). Unlike Louisiana and Mississippi, where the Republicans (q.v.) dared not leave their capital cities in 1876, in South Carolina, the Republicans engaged in a vigorous campaign. But right behind them came the Red Shirts (q.v.) (there were nearly 300 white Rifle Clubs in the state), who intimidated, hanged, and shot potential Republican voters, mostly black. The Red Shirts were so active that a fear grew that they might even attack U.S. troops on election day. The worst violence of the campaign occurred in Ellenton in September 1876, in an area where whites had vowed to win the election or kill all the Republicans. A minor assault by two blacks, which Republicans claimed to be a trumped up case, started the action. One of the suspects was captured and identified by a victim and shot on the spot. The other had an arrest warrant filed against him. The Rifle Clubs broke up a Republican meeting the next day, chasing the party members into a swamp. The Red Shirts demanded that the assault suspect be turned over. The blacks refused. After much talk, the two sides agreed to depart amicably, but some blacks shot one of the Red Shirts, and the whites went crazy, shooting up houses all over the county. The fighting spread into Ellenton, where a black state legislator was among the murdered. The arrival of Federal troops finally restored the peace, just as the Red Shirts, many arriving by train, had cornered their opponents for the final kill. Over 100 blacks and a half dozen whites died.

EMANCIPATION. During and after the Revolutionary War, many Americans began to feel very uneasy with the contradictions between the principles of the Declaration of Independence and slavery, which had been legal in all of the thirteen colonies. Gradually, states above the Mason–Dixon Line (the southern border of Pennsylvania) began to abandon the "peculiar institution," a process that took until 1832, the last state to enter the process being New Jersey. Usually the slaves were either freed outright or by the time of their attaining adulthood, between the ages of 18 and 21. Concurrently, Congress organized the Western territories, those northwest of the Ohio River (the Northwest Ordinance of 1787) having slavery excluded from their boundaries upon statehood. There were several exemptions to the territorial exclusion, most involving slaves held by British (as of 1795) and French (as of 1763) colonists before United States assumption of control, but these were relatively minor. The only marring of this emancipation record was in Illinois where, upon its separation from Indiana, the territorial legislature legalized slavery through a lifetime indenture and provided for the "hiring" of blacks originally enslaved in other states. At the same time, free African-Americans were practically prevented from entering the area. The culmination of this process was reached in 1823, when by a close vote slavery was prohibited in the state of Illinois according to the provisions of the Northwest Ordinance.

This process of eliminating slavery in the Old Northwest was well-known to people from the South like the Lincolns, poor nonslaveholding families who fled across the river to get away from the slave-dominated economy of the South. At the time of the War with Mexico, Abraham Lincoln (q.v.) was serving in the Federal Congress, and he sided with those who believed that Congress in its ability to govern the territories could regulate slavery there, even eliminate it. He attempted to test this concept by introducing a bill to eliminate slavery in the District of Columbia (a perpetual territory run by Congress), but the measure was amended to death. Lincoln retired at the end of his term.

Lincoln soon returned to the political fray, in 1854, when the Congress voted to destroy the Missouri Compromise of 1820 (q.v.) and extend slavery into all territories, its existence to be decided by a popular vote in the state convention upon application for statehood. This concept of popular sovereignty (q.v.), developed by Illinois senator and Democrat (q.v.) aspirant for the presidency, Stephen A. Douglas (q.v.), would guarantee slavery in any territory until statehood was petitioned for. It was contrary to Lincoln's avowed stance that Congress could regulate or destroy slavery in any territory under the Constitution. But Lincoln's view was challenged by the 1857 U.S. Supreme Court in the case Dred Scott v. Sandford (q.v.), which declared that popular sovereignty was constitutional, and further that no black could be a citizen of the United States. As Douglas was running for reelection to the Senate the following year, Lincoln agreed to take him on for the Republican Party. During the ensuing Lincoln–Douglas debates (q.v.), Lincoln defended Congress' right to regulate or eliminate slavery in the territories and managed to paint Douglas into a corner, where he had to admit that Congress could deal slavery in the territories a death blow by not actively legislating its protection. This admission would cost Douglas the presidency two years later and gain the then unknown Lincoln a national reputation and the presidency in his own right as a Republican in the election of 1860 (q.v.).

Although the Republicans were willing to guarantee slavery where it existed in the states, the election of Lincoln by a majority vote in the North alone touched off the secession of the South. In the attempted compromises that followed, Lincoln promised to defend every state's right to its own institutions, but he refused to denounce the Republican platform's stand against slavery in the territories and pledged to defend the Union of all the states. The war then became inevitable. Although the war's announced purpose was to save the Union, what to do about slavery became an integral part of it immediately. When slaves fled to Yankee lines for freedom and safety, Union commanders were supposed to return them under the Fugitive Slave Act of 1850 (q.v.). At first many of them did so. But as the war went on, more and more commanders adopted the expedient of Maj. Gen. Benjamin Butler (q.v.) at Fortress Monroe on May 30, 1861. He declared that the slaves were contraband of war, having been employed actively in support of the rebellion, through raising foodstuff and building fortifications (*see* CONTRABANDS). Lincoln did not like this approach, because he feared that it might compromise his efforts to hold the border South in the Union. But Butler's policy was relatively mild when compared to that of Bvt. Maj. Gen. John Charles Frémont (q.v.), Federal commander in Missouri. Prompted by Union victories in the West, Frémont, the first Republican candidate for president in 1854, issued a proclamation freeing all slaves in his command area on August 30, 1861. Lincoln let Butler's policy stand, but Frémont's threatened to drive four more states from the Union. Lincoln asked Frémont to substitute a congressional act. Frémont refused, and Lincoln removed him from command.

The congressional act Lincoln had wanted Frémont to recognize was the first Confiscation Act (q.v.). It allowed the confiscation of property, including slaves, of anyone found in sympathy with and support of the rebellion. But the procedure was not arbitrary—it had to be effected through a court process. Meanwhile, the president tried to convince loyal slaveholders as states and individuals to emancipate their chattels voluntarily through a compensation process. He hoped that Congress might accept such manumissions in lieu of direct taxes in support of the war. Lincoln looked for a laboratory in which to try out his idea and came up with the smallest slave state, geographically and in number of slaves (1,798 in 1861), Delaware. But the hostility of local slaveholders, who saw in this scheme an attempt to introduce total emancipation throughout the South as a war aim, caused its failure. Lincoln then turned to Congress directly. In March 1862, he requested the passage of a joint resolution that the Federal government would cooperate with any state that voluntarily emancipated its bondservants through compensation at $400 per adult slave. Lincoln believed that the cost of the war for a half day would pay for Delaware's slaves; the rest of the border states, Maryland, Kentucky, and Missouri, plus the District of Columbia, could be financed at the same rate for what it cost to run the war for just under three months.

None of the border states appeared interested, and Congress moved to eliminate slavery in the District of Columbia at $300 dollars a head and with a further $100,000 expenses for transporting the freed blacks beyond the borders of the United States to Liberia or Haiti. Meanwhile, on May 9, 1862, another field commander, Bvt. Maj. Gen. David Hunter, freed by military order all the slaves along the Atlantic coastal islands in South Carolina and Georgia. Worse yet, from the perspective of quelling the fears of the border South, he also enrolled males in the first black infantry regiments of the war. Hunter claimed that the enrollment was a matter of military necessity, because he had not sufficient numbers of white troops to defend his military district. Lincoln denied knowledge or responsibility for the order as soon as the news reached Washington. But he used the occasion to admonish the border states to rethink the emancipation problem and to act and receive compensation before the war made such a policy unavailable.

Congress had already given new meaning to Lincoln's warning. On March 13, 1862, it had amended the Fugitive Slave Act of 1850, to make it a violation of law for any military or naval officer or enlisted personnel to return any fugitive slave to its owner. On June 5, 1862, it recognized the nations of Haiti (after the United States, the second nation in the Western Hemisphere to declare it independence from European domination) and Liberia (the home in exile of freed American slaves since the 1820s). The Senate then ratified a treaty between the United States and Great Britain for suppression of the African slave trade. Finally, Congress enacted a bill that freed all slaves in the territories, implementing a key point in the 1860 Republican Platform (q.v.) and Lincoln's lifelong ideal of no slavery in the West.

On July 17, 1862, Congress passed its most severe measure yet, the second Confiscation Act (q.v.). It seized all property (including slaves) of anyone found guilty of treason or rebellion. It also freed any slaves who managed to reach the safety of Union military lines or were captured by the Federal armies or abandoned by their owners. The process was roundabout—the fugitive was declared a prisoner of war under Federal control and then freed by act of Congress. And it authorized the president to employ freed African-Americans in any manner he saw fit to prosecute successfully the end of the war. In effect, it permitted the enrollment of blacks as soldiers, for the first time. Once again, Lincoln warned the loyal slave states to reconsider emancipation on their own with Federal compensation. He cautioned them that if the war continued, he would act to destroy all slavery, with no monetary indemnification.

EMANCIPATION PROCLAMATION. As the Republican-dominated Congress had been debating the concepts of confiscation of Rebel property and its corollary, compensated emancipation, President Abraham Lincoln (q.v.) had already been mulling over total uncompensated emancipation. Congress had already taken preliminary steps in this direction by passing the Confiscation Acts of 1861 and 1862 (qq.v.). In the summer of 1862, Lincoln told Secretary of State William H. Seward (q.v.) and Secretary of the Navy Gideon Welles that he believed that emancipation could be instituted as a war measure against the Confederates. On July 21, he approached the whole cabinet on the measure. He maintained that it would bring a moral outlook to the Union cause that it sadly lacked, especially in the eyes of the monarchies of Europe, which were flirting with recognizing the Confederacy. He believed that field commanders should actively subsist their troops off Southern crops; that African-Americans should be paid for their labor to the Union cause; and that in the end, all blacks ought to be colonized overseas. He once again wished to caution all slaveholders, loyal or Rebel, that the Confiscation Acts provided for the summary seizure of slaves, and stated that he would free all slaves in rebellious areas through an executive proclamation on January 1, 1863. Only Seward and Secretary of the Treasury Salmon P. Chase (q.v.) agreed with his proposals. But Seward suggested that Lincoln await a Union field victory, as the war had been going badly, especially in the East, and emancipation might be seen as a last gasp for Union survival rather than a stand on the higher ground of morality. Lincoln agreed.

Lincoln's more radical and conservative political enemies of both parties leaped on him for indecision in the matter of confiscation. Lincoln intentionally kept them in the dark about his resolve to emancipate all slaves in disloyal areas at the beginning of the New Year. But when popular newspaper editor Horace Greeley (q.v.) of the *New York Tribune* asked him to free all the slaves outright, calling it the "Prayer of 20 Millions," Lincoln replied publicly and quickly. The president said that his main purpose in fighting the war was restoration of the Union in the shortest possible way under the Constitution. If he could do it by freeing some of the slaves, all of them, or none of them, he would.

Lincoln received his victory in September when the Army of the Potomac drove Robert E. Lee's (q.v.) Confederate forces out of Maryland at the Battle of Antietam. It was not much of a victory—Lee had withdrawn more or less voluntarily when he should have been destroyed—but it was all Lincoln had. He seized the moment at once. On September 22, 1862, he issued the preliminary Emancipation Proclamation. It contained all of his previous ideas, including renewal of compensated emancipation for loyal states, voluntary colonization (q.v.) of freed blacks overseas, and military emancipation of all slaves in states in rebellion against Federal forces on January 1, 1863. In the election of 1862 (q.v.), the Republican Party took a drubbing, but it still managed to retain a majority in both houses of Congress. In December, Congress rejected a resolution from Congressman George H. Yeaman of Kentucky, condemning the Emancipation Proclamation as an unwarranted, unconstitutional interference with the domestic institutions of the states and a dangerous war message. It also ignored one last attempt to pass measures of compensated emancipation for the loyal slave states and colonization (q.v.) of all freed blacks overseas. Then it passed a resolution of the exact opposite intent. It was the only vote Congress took on the measure. Lincoln gave copies of the Emancipation Proclamation to his cabinet for final discussion on December 31. With minor revisions, it was issued on January 1, 1863.

Lincoln has been traditionally praised as a forward-looking hero in the egalitarian tradition. But with the advent of the modern civil rights movement in the 1960s, he was seen as morally deficient—a traditional white racist. Unlike the more open racists of his time, Lincoln believed that African-Americans had the ability to govern themselves in their own nation. But Lincoln believed that this quality would not evidence itself in America because of the limiting aspects of white racism. So Lincoln openly advocated Henry Clay's solution to race—a gradual compensated emancipation of the slaves and their colonization overseas. This involved sending the blacks back to Africa (hence the American backing of the nation of Liberia, founded by freed American slaves, and its capital, named after a Virginian with ideas similar to Clay's, James Monroe), or their removal to some allegedly idyllic spot in the Caribbean or Latin America. In the words of one historian, Lincoln saw the Negro as "A Man But Not a Brother," a quality recognized by no less than the great black abolitionist and orator of the 19th century, Frederick Douglass (q.v.).

But having admitted this, it would be incorrect not to recognize Lincoln for the revolutionary that he was. Although as many critics have pointed out, because of stated exemptions to the proclamation's effect, Lincoln freed no slaves through the Emancipation Proclamation except those behind the Confederate lines, over whom he had little or no influence. By exempting the slaves in Tennessee, southeastern Louisiana, and coastal Virginia, Lincoln actually re-enslaved 500,000 slaves who had begun to live as free people. Secretary of the Treasury Salmon P. Chase (q.v.), criticized Lincoln for this, which led to the Collamer Delegation of Radical Republicans challenging the role of Secretary of State William Seward (q.v.), a known Conservative Republican, in cabinet consultations. Recent researchers have established that Lincoln's Emancipation Proclamation liberated about 20,000 bondspersons in parts of nine Confederate states occupied by the Union army and not given exemption. As such, historians generally give Lincoln credit for standing four-square behind the Republican ideology of "Free Men, Free Soil, and Free Labor," and he achieved the biggest revolution in American history by patiently adhering to the unconditional surrender of the Confederacy and its principles. Emancipation was the cornerstone of the revolution that was to be guaranteed through the later Thirteenth Amendment (q.v.).

EMMA SILVER MINE. *See* GRANT, ULYSSES S., ADMINISTRATION—SCANDALS.

ENFORCEMENT ACT, FIRST (MAY 31, 1870). Designed to enforce the right to vote (the Fifteenth Amendment [q.v.]), the First Enforcement Act declared that citizens otherwise qualified should be entitled to vote without distinction of race. It also declared that any prerequisite to voting must be equal for all voters regardless of race. Any official who failed to obey this measure was liable to fine (up to $500) or imprisonment (up to one year) or both (most of these terms were served locally in county jail). It also outlawed any combination or conspiracy to deny, intimidate, or threaten voters. It repeated much of the content of the Civil Rights Act of 1866 (q.v.) as regarded the same right to sue or be sued, give evidence, and to hold and convey property as any white citizen. Any official who acted to deny these rights could be removed from office, in addition to other fines and jail sentences. Finally, it prohibited conspiracies by disguised persons or groups using the public highways to deny anyone a right guaranteed under the Constitution. This part was punishable by a healthy fine ($5,000) and jail term (up to 10 years) in a Federal penitentiary (the Albany, New York, facility was the one generally used in these convictions). Any state crimes (murder, rape, assault, and the like) committed by a Klansman were to be tried in Federal court and sentences applicable in the state of occurrence could be applied by the Federal judge.

ENFORCEMENT ACT, SECOND (FEBRUARY 28, 1871). Republicans (q.v.) realized that the election of 1870 had decreased their majority by some 60 votes. They feared that if they did not act immediately to increase the effect of the First Enforcement Act (q.v.), it might not be done later. Sections of the first act were mutually contradictory and vague, and this measure united them in wording and intent. It permitted no one to deny the right to vote through bribery, the threat of intimidation, or actual intimidation. It standardized penalties at $500 or up to three years' imprisonment, and in any town of 20,000 inhabitants or more, it established a system of poll watchers from each political party, appointed by local Federal judges and assisted by special U.S. marshals to establish order at polls and prevent any irregularities. A state Returning Board was to check all votes to ascertain their validity. All ballots were to be printed in any Federal election to prevent ballot box stuffing or other fraud. It was this law that many historians think was designed to regulate voting in Northern cities, where Democrat (q.v.) machines ruled, rather than assist blacks in the South, as it claimed on its surface.

ENFORCEMENT ACT, THIRD (APRIL 20, 1871). Also known as the Ku Klux Act, the Third Enforcement Act was designed to prevent individuals, state officials, or organized conspiracies from depriving persons of their civil rights, particularly in the South where the Ku Klux Klan (q.v.) rode. Where the Civil Rights Act of 1866 (q.v.) had permitted a criminal remedy, this measure allowed the offended party to take action in civil court, too. It also defined conspiracy as two or more persons using the public roads, wearing a disguise, or violating the property of another to deny someone his civil rights. It permitted the president to use the Army and Navy as a *posse comitatus* to assist U.S. marshals or enforce court orders independently and to suspend temporarily the writ of *habeas corpus* (qq.v.). Any official who failed to use his office to prevent a violation of this measure was declared liable, with fines of $1,000 or more and jail terms of one year to life if the complaining citizen lost his life.

ENFORCEMENT ACTS. After the passage of the Fourteenth and Fifteenth Amendments (qq.v), Congress passed several measures designed to enforce them, sometimes referred to as the Civil Rights Acts of 1870 and 1871. The punitive nature of these laws led them to be popularly called the Force Acts. Congress considered a total of four Enforcement Bills, their formal name, of which three became law. Their implementation became one of the controversial issues of Reconstruction that involved the Federal court system from bottom to top.

ENFORCEMENT BILL. A Fourth Enforcement measure, one that would have given the president the right to suspend the writ of *habeas corpus* (q.v.) in Alabama, Arkansas, Mississippi, and Louisiana for two years, passed in the House. It failed in the Senate, which had its own approach, the Civil Rights Act of 1875 (q.v.), a tribute to Senator Charles Sumner (q.v.) of Massachusetts, who had just died.

ENGLISH BILL. *See* KANSAS–MISSOURI BORDER WARS.

ENROLLMENT ACT OF MARCH 3, 1863. *See* CONSCRIPTION AND DRAFT EVASION, UNION.

ETHRIDGE CONSPIRACY OF 1863. In December 1863, at about the same time that President Abraham Lincoln (q.v.) was to announce his Ten Percent Plan of Reconstruction (q.v.), Emerson Ethridge, acting clerk of the U.S. House of Representatives, put into play a plan to turn over control of the legislative body to a moderate coalition of Democrats and Republicans (qq.v.), by refusing to seat certain Radical Republicans. At the time, the clerk had great power in both houses to determine who had been legally elected through the expedient of reading the roll on the first day. If one's name were omitted, that person was not seated until there was a full investigation into the legality of his election. This cannot be done today, as the powers used 100 years ago have been institutionalized and made nonpolitical. The whole concept was made possible by a measure passed the year before, when Congressman James M. Ashley (q.v.) wanted the clerk to exclude any representative from an occupied state, by refusing to seat Lincoln's "reconstructed" governments in the Mississippi Valley.

Ethridge was a Union man from East Tennessee who had not seceded with his state and resented being treated as less than loyal by Ashley's bill. He was dismayed with the course of the war, too. Militarily, the Union seemed to be in a stalemate at best, losing at worst. Politically, Lincoln seemed to be in the clutches of the Radical Republicans, freeing the slaves through executive proclamation (in the manner by which he ran most of the war), sending Carpetbaggers (q.v.) down to run the loyal Southern border states, and passing Northeastern-business-oriented economic measures (high tariffs, internal improvements, a national banking system). What Ethridge thought the nation needed was a moderate constitutional party of War Democrats and middle-of-the-road Republicans to put a brake on things domestically, until the war was won. He promised the Democrats the speaker's chair, under the Union Party label if they cooperated.

Unfortunately for him and his plan, the Democrats failed to deliver enough votes to confirm his action. The fact that the Radicals could gain the backing of moderates from their own party and several border state Union men, like Henry Winter Davis (q.v.), indicated that the conservative resurgence against the Lincoln domestic and war policies, evident in the Democratic victories in the North in the 1862 congressional elections, was over. The Radicals were to surge forward and send up the harsher Wade–Davis Bill (q.v.) to counter Lincoln's plan of Reconstruction and use Ethridge's idea in reverse to unseat the Andrew Johnson Reconstruction governments in 1865. The Ethridge Conspiracy probably marked the beginning of the end for conservative hopes of a Reconstruction based on the prewar Constitution, even though the Union Party would be the device used to reelect Lincoln in 1864 and to pass the Thirteenth Amendment (q.v.) in 1865.

EUFALA (ALABAMA) RACE RIOT (1876). *See* EUTAW (ALABAMA) RACE RIOT (1876).

EUTAW (ALABAMA) RACE RIOT (1876). Alabama became the testing ground for Redemption (q.v.) by force and white racial solidarity. An 1870 race riot at Eutaw, in which the Scalawag (q.v.) county prosecutor was shot in the head several times by a Ku Klux Klan (q.v.) band, was followed a few months later by a street riot that cost blacks two dead and up to 50 wounded, then violence in 1874 at Mobile, where an election-day brawl marred proceedings, and the Eufala race riot, in which over a half dozen blacks died and nearly 80 were wounded. The stage was set for the final push. Key Union whites and black leaders faced assassination if they campaigned for the Republicans (q.v.). Any black voting Republican was threatened with loss of his job. The Army refused to intervene in any disturbance that was not right at the polls, and even then recent orders prevented much interference. By reducing Republican strength in the "Black Belt" (a rich black soil region that cut across the center of the state from east to west) and in Union counties just below the Tennessee River, Democrats (q.v.) took Alabama. In the few areas won by Republicans, Democrats prevented elected officials from obtaining bonds and forced them to relinquish their posts to Democrat contenders. Congress investigated and found the election to have been carried by fraud and intimidation, but, led by a Democrat insurgency that had repudiated Grantism in the North during the congressional elections of 1874, it refused to intervene. The way was now open for the rest of the unredeemed states of the Deep South to end Reconstruction within their borders.

EXECUTIVE PROCLAMATION, LINCOLN AND THE. Union President Abraham Lincoln (q.v.) demonstrated the powers of his office early on by his use of presidential war powers through the executive proclamation. In so doing, he set the precedent for powerful presidents who would follow in the 20th century. Only they would make their marks in non-war issues, as well. Normally, a president is rated as strong if he can get Congress to enact his legislative proposals into law. Lincoln did not do this. In fact, he intentionally kept Congress out of Washington, refusing to call a special session, until July 4, 1861. This gave him a chance to expand his war power and give everything to Congress as *fiats accompli*. No one dared to challenge his orders in the midst of war, for fear of being perceived incorrectly as against the successful prosecution of that war.

As Lincoln found out, the president as commander-in-chief has vast undetermined war powers. The first thing Lincoln did was to declare war. This is a power specifically reserved to Congress in the Constitution. The president is supposed to ask Congress to declare war. But Lincoln maintained that he could not call Congress into special session until their safety in Washington could be assured—in a sense true, but mighty convenient, too. Technically, the Constitution gave to Congress the power to provide for the militia, but Lincoln called for 75,000 volunteers from the state militias and assigned a quota to all states.

Next, Lincoln declared a naval blockade of the coasts and ports of the seceded states on April 17, 1861, which he extended to cover North Carolina and Virginia on May 27. This was illegal, for two reasons. Technically, he had to close the ports of the South, because to declare a blockade recognized the existence of the independence of the Confederacy, which he assiduously denied. He claimed the Southern states to be in rebellion against the true government of the United States. In addition, paper blockades, in which blockading ships do not actually block entry into the port, are illegal. Both of these principles were instrumental to the American position in the War of 1812. But if Lincoln merely closed the ports, the South would have disobeyed his proclamation and let any ship in. A blockade declaration allowed him to call on the U.S. Navy for action. When Congress endorsed Lincoln's proclamation July 13, the owners of ships seized before that day brought suit in Federal court, resulting in the Prize Cases (q.v.)

Third, Lincoln increased the size of the regular army. Under the Constitution, only Congress can raise and maintain armies. Not only did Lincoln increase the size of the army, he created nine special new "Lincoln Regiments," that were two and a half times (2,400) the size of ordinary ones (1,000). Then, Lincoln authorized General Orders No. 100 (q.v.), which established the rules of war, usurping another congressional power.

Next, Lincoln took money appropriated by Congress for one purpose and diverted it to other purposes he found more important, such as prosecuting the war. Only Congress had the right to raise and spend money. The president can suggest, but Congress has the final say.

But one of Lincoln's more dramatic uses of war powers was against Northern opponents and protesters of the war effort. Lincoln acted decisively through executive proclamation to suspend civil liberties usually constitutionally guaranteed to citizens. Opposition to the war came from the Ohio River Valley, especially in the border slave states (Delaware, Maryland, Kentucky, and Missouri) and the Southern parts of Ohio, Indiana, and Illinois. There was a great sectional consciousness here, in common with the South. The agricultural Northwest had a feeling that the Republicans (q.v.) were acting on behalf of the industrial Northeast.

There was also an uneasiness that Lincoln was using the war as an excuse to create a strong central government at the expense of state rights. The one element that they did not have in common with the South was the propensity for secession. These Northwestern Unionists were Nationalistic States Righters. Most of them came from the Democratic Party (q.v.), and were labeled "Peace Democrats," as distinguished from those "War Democrats" who backed the war and were willing to work with Republicans to put down the rebellion.

The Peace Democrats, rather naïvely, believed that the war would end immediately if the Federal government would unilaterally halt its aggression against the South. They believed that the South would willingly come to the peace table for reunion. They wanted to call a national convention to restrict the powers of the national government as evidenced by Lincoln's use of the executive proclamation. The problem was that all action would be taken by the North. It overlooked the fact that the South could refuse to cooperate and sit back, its independence confirmed by default through Northern inaction.

Some of the more enthusiastic Northern war protesters formed secret peace societies, loosely based on the old prewar Knights of the Golden Circle. Calling themselves the Order of American Knights, although war supporters dismissed them by vilifying them as "Copperheads"(q.v.), a stealthy but deadly pit viper common to the Northwest, these peace groups were by and large harmless, as the disgusted Confederate agents sent to coordinate their antigovernment activities found out. But more radical members, called "Sons of Liberty" after the Patriot organizations of the pre-American Revolution, bushwacked Federal patrols, recruited for the Confederacy, and tried to free Southern soldiers held in the numerous prison camps in the Northwest.

To stalemate such organizations, the Lincoln government infiltrated them with agents. But as Lincoln discovered, ordinary laws and rules of evidence proved inadequate to deal with such men. Usually those charged were merely suspected of wrongdoing. To solve this dilemma, Lincoln resorted to the same expediency the Confederates would use—suspension of the writ of *habeas corpus* (q.v.). Confederate President Jefferson Davis (q.v.) acted through the Confederate Congress. Of course, Lincoln did it by executive proclamation, even though the writ is mentioned in the section of the Constitution dealing with congressional prerogatives. He suspended the writ at first for the rail corridor between Philadelphia and Washington. Later he extended this to New York City, then in September 1862, in time for the congressional by-election, to the whole North. Congress would later endorse Lincoln's action—in 1863. (*see HABEAS CORPUS*).

The writ could be denied a defendant if he or she (in a few cases) were charged with discouragement of enlistment, resisting the conscription acts, or being engaged in any illegal act prejudicial to the successful prosecution of the war. Union authorities held somewhere around 13,000 persons without charges during the war. Opponents accused Lincoln of tyranny. He said that it was necessary to prevent traitors from using the mechanics of the law to shield themselves from prosecution, as he detailed ably in the Birchard and Corning letters (qq.v.). The result was three landmark U.S. Supreme Court cases: *Ex parte* Merryman, *ex parte* Vallandigham, and *ex parte* Milligan (qq.v.).

Finally, in another dramatic act, Lincoln used the executive proclamation to influence Union war goals, through issuance of the Emancipation Proclamation (q.v.). The first goal of the North in the Civil War was to preserve the Union. This was made clear in President Lincoln's First Inaugural speech and when Congress passed the Crittenden Resolution four months later, on July 22, 1861. The main reason that Republicans and abolitionist (q.v.) politicians would go along with this was the fear that the border slave states would secede if emancipation (q.v.) were immediately announced as the war's purpose. But as the war dragged on, Congress and more and more of the Northern civilian population and soldiers began to believe that slavery ought to be struck at as a mainstay of the Confederacy. In December 1861, the Crittenden Resolution failed to be repassed. The Confiscation Acts (qq.v), taking all Rebel property including slaves used to further the war, and the freeing of all slaves in the District of Columbia, soon followed. With the pseudo-victory during the Maryland Campaign (q.v.) at Antietam Creek, Lincoln issued a preliminary Emancipation Proclamation, threatening to free the slaves in all states in rebellion by January 1, 1863, providing they did not return to the Union by then. The South refused to consider such action, and the final proclamation went forward as scheduled.

In spite of Lincoln's critics, it was clear that he could have done more to subdue opposition to the war. He did not prevent the Democrats from running against his administration in the election of 1864, even though he feared he would lose. What Lincoln tried to do was enforce the unity needed in a nation if it is to win a war.

EXTRATERRITORIALITY OF SLAVERY. The constitutional theory that the institution of slavery alone in the U.S. Constitution had an extraterritorial component that adhered to the slave and made Southern slavery legal in all places at all times within the boundaries of the United States, slave or free, and its territories, wherever the owner might take his or her slave. It was an instrumental part of popular sovereignty (q.v.) and the U.S. Supreme Court case Dred Scott *v.* Sandford (qq.v.).

EZRA CHURCH, BATTLE OF. *See* ATLANTA CAMPAIGN.

F

5–20 BONDS. *See* GRANT, ULYSSES S., ADMINISTRATION—DO-MESTIC POLICIES.

FAIR OAKS, FIRST BATTLE OF. Part of a battle, which included the Battle of Seven Pines, First Fair Oaks was a Confederate attempt to cut off Union advanced forces south of the Chickahominy River from their main army north of the river. The attack units were to be led by Maj. Gen. G. W. Smith, but when President Jefferson Davis (q.v.) showed up at army headquarters outside of Richmond, army commander, Gen. Joseph Johnston (q.v.), who could not abide Davis' presence, left to lead the attack in person, resulting in his serious wounding. The attack was initially successful, until Federal troops from north of the river braved bridges that were three feet under water and crossed to take the Confederate attack in the left flank. The next day, Gen. Smith proved unable to measure up to the rigors of command, and more Union troops arrived to pushed the Confederates back to their original positions. In the double battle, Union and Confederate forces engaged were about equal at 41,000 each, but the Rebels lost 6,000 casualties to the Yankees' 5,000. Gen. Robert E. Lee (q.v.) replaced the ineffective Gen. Smith.

FAIR OAKS, SECOND BATTLE OF. *See* PETERSBURG, SIEGE OF.

FARRAGUT, DAVID G. (1801–1970). Orphaned early in life, David Farragut was a Tennessee boy who was adopted by the family of Commodore David Porter, an old navy man. Farragut served as a midshipman and prize master during the War of 1812 and against the pirates in the Mediterranean, the West Indies, and the South Atlantic, before serving in the blockade in the War with Mexico. He established the naval shipyard at Mare Island and was awaiting orders at Norfolk during the secession crisis. When neighbors told him he could not live in Virginia without seceding, Farragut went north and became head of the West Gulf Blockade Squadron.

He was told to open up the Mississippi River by taking New Orleans (q.v.), which he did in April 1862, the first major victory for the North in the war. Farragut sailed up the Mississippi all the way to Vicksburg, but could not subdue its budding defenses. He was promoted to rear admiral, being the first to hold that rank. Farragut was given a hero's welcome in New York City and returned to begin operations against Mobile (q.v.). Entering Mobile bay, Farragut was warned of torpedoes (q.v.) in the channel, to which he allegedly gave the reply, "Damn the torpedoes, full speed ahead!"

Again feted in New York, Farragut was given a home in the city and promoted to vice admiral, a rank created for him. He was among the first to enter Richmond in April 1865. At the end of the war, he was made the first full admiral the navy ever had. He conducted a European goodwill tour with a fleet after the war.

FERNANDINI, CIPRIANO. *See* BALTIMORE PLOT (1861).

FESSENDEN, WILLIAM P. (1806–1869). Born out of wedlock in Boscawen, New Hampshire, William P. Fessenden spent his early years in the care of his grandparents in Maine. When his father finally married, he brought his son into his new family. He was a sharp child, and his entrance into Bowdoin College was delayed merely because of his youth. His diploma was withheld for a year, however, because of bad conduct and swearing while he was a student. Years later, he would receive an honorary doctorate from the same institution and serve on its governing board. He studied law after his graduation and moved to Portland, where he practiced his profession and stayed the rest of his life. He entered politics, running as an anti-Jackson candidate for the state legislature and accompanying Daniel Webster during campaigns, until Fessenden refused to support the swarthy Webster for president in 1852, considering "Black Dan" to be too likely to abuse alcohol.

Meanwhile, Fessenden proceeded to build up one of the finest law practices in New England, in partnership with William Willis. He served a second term in the state legislature and one term in Congress as a Whig (q.v.). In Washington he learned to dislike slavery, and his opposition to the institution grew until he became one of the original organizers of the Republican Party (q.v.). Before that, however, he served two more terms in the state legislature and tried several times unsuccessfully for the U.S. House and Senate. As Maine came more and more to embrace Fessenden's attitude on slavery, he gained stature and was elected to the U.S. Senate as a Republican in 1854. He would hold that seat until his death in 1869, with a brief time out when he served as the secretary of the treasury in 1864 and 1865. In the Senate, Fessenden's real power was in the finance committee, which he came to chair. As such, he helped fund the Union war cause through the backing of higher wartime taxes, the national banking system, and the printing of paper money, which he opposed but admitted had to be resorted to because of the unprecedented emergency of the rebellion. Once the war ended, he led the call for fiscal conservatism and a recall of greenbacks.

During Reconstruction, Fessenden was considered a Radical Republican but without the petulance and viciousness attributed to most of them. He was against outright confiscation of Rebels' property and not as enthused about punishment. But his view of Reconstruction was not far from that of Representative Thaddeus Stevens (q.v.) of Pennsylvania. Fessenden saw Reconstruction as a congressional function, with the South reverting to conquered provinces. He lacked respect for President Andrew Johnson (q.v.). Johnson was just too Southern to suit a die-hard Yankee like Fessenden, who thoroughly disapproved of his policies and conduct as too sympathetic to Rebels. As chairman of the Joint Committee on Reconstruction (q.v.), Fessenden conducted the investigation that led to the Fourteenth Amendment (q.v.) and the justification of the Military Reconstruction Acts (q.v.). But he disapproved of the Tenure of Office Act (q.v.) and the impeachment (q.v.) of the president and refused to vote to convict, despite his position as majority leader. Fessenden faced a storm of criticism, and many doubted if he could win another senatorial term, but he died before the question was raised formally in the Maine state legislature. After his death, many former critics came over to his viewpoint on presidential power and hailed him as a principled man who had voted his conscience on a very difficult issue.

FEUDS, GANGS, AND GUNMEN. In his monumental study of the role of the U.S. Army in the South during Reconstruction (q.v.), historian James E. Sefton remarks several times about the "moral and psychological impact which the blue and gold uniform possessed." Using, among other evidence, passages in the reports of Maj. Lewis Merrill, the senior officer in charge of the Seventh Cavalry during the periodic absences of Lt. Col. George Armstrong Custer as the subject of courts of inquiry and courts martial, Sefton found that the beneficial psychological effect of the presence of Federal soldiers stopped many violent situations in many areas.

This is true. Most members of the Ku Klux Klan, the Red Shirts, White Liners, or White Leaguers (qq.v.) refused to shoot at the Federal officers and men, but the Army was not on the spot in most places at most times, because it had too few troops available to police both the Western frontier and the South. This meant much mischief could be done in its absence. Nowhere was this more true on a consistent basis than in Texas. While it is true that soldiers and Freedmen's Bureau (q.v.) agents generally were not attacked personally—there were only four Bureau men and about a dozen soldiers killed during Reconstruction in Texas out of 288 Bureau agents and employees in the field (identified so far) and elements from over a half dozen infantry and cavalry regiments—Texans were not hesitant to shoot back, ambush, and fight it out with Reconstruction authorities. As one discouraged Texas Union-ist grumbled, "*Blue* was as enraging to secesh eyes . . . as *red* is to the eyes of a turkey gobbler."

Some of this resistance came from several family feuds, like the Taylor–Sutton, Lee–Peacock, and Duncan–Davis quarrels, which often had had one side supporting the Union during the war and the other the Confederacy. But most of the trouble came from organized gangs, beyond the Ku Klux Klan, that bracketed the state after the war. And it also depended on who wore the blue uniform. Regular troops were given some leeway, but the so-called black and tan Negro Militia (q.v.) and Texas State Police, who replaced the rebellion-tainted Texas Rangers, were fair game to all comers. It was not unusual for the anti-Reconstruction forces to be able to field as many as 150 armed men on short notice at any time. This made life in Texas and Arkansas, with its Brooks–Baxter War (q.v.), tenuous, to say the least.

And there were plenty of miscreants, especially in the northeastern part of the Lone Star state, like Elisha Guest, John Duty, Bob Lee, "Indian Bill" English, Ben Bickerstaff, Henry Farrar, Ben Griffith, and, the most notorious of all, the Swamp Fox of the Sulphur River bottoms, Cullen Montgomery Baker, America's first fast-draw artist, who reputedly ran a gunman's school in the cane breaks that flanked that river. These men were assisted by, but not a formal part of, such organizations as the Ku Klux Klan, Knights of the Red Hand, Knights of the White Camellia, Pale Faces, White Brotherhood, and the Constitutional Union Guards. The main target of these diverse men and groups was freed slaves who dared to exercise their rights of citizenship under the Thirteenth, Fourteenth, and Fifteenth Amendments and the Civil Rights Act of 1866 (qq.v.). Whenever the Federal authorities got too close, the gangs would slip over the Red River into Arkansas or the Indian Nations. Whenever competing jurisdictions (army commands generally followed state boundaries) cooperated, citizens would spread the warning, allowing the outlaws to escape.

There may have been only a few Federal officers killed in Texas, but the numbers of black victims of these gangs were uncountable, according to Maj. Gen. J. J. Reynolds (q.v.), Army commandant of the state. For a fee, these men would "discipline" any black who violated his work contract or questioned the division of the crop. Often the planter would have the whole black work force driven off at the end of the harvest, and a local judge would declare them absent without leave in violation of the work contract, and con-fiscate all wages. It was not that other Southern states and Western territories were exempt from this kind of violence. It was that in Texas and southwestern Arkansas it was so common, so consistently, for so long.

Finally, the Army did what it had done in Louisiana, Kentucky, and South Carolina. Roving cavalry commands (much like the striker brigades in Iraq and Afghanistan today) rounded up civilians suspected of hiding gang members, who were hung by their thumbs from tree limbs until they talked. Prisoners were shot while "trying to escape." The Sixth Cavalry team in Texas was so brutal that it became known as "Chaffee's Guerillas," after its commander, Capt. Adna R. Chaffee. The power of the Texas–Arkansas gangs disappeared with the demise of their leaders, as did the Jesse James (q.v.) gang with his assassination in Missouri. But they were all part of the political, personal, and property violence that comprised Reconstruction west of the Mississippi River.

FIFTEENTH AMENDMENT. The Republicans (q.v.) saw the African-American vote as central to a true Reconstruction of the nation after the Civil War. Partly it was because the South would re-enter the Union with the freed slaves counting as a whole person for purposes of taxation. That is to say, the South lost the war and as a reward for freeing the slaves, which was forced upon them by the Emancipation Proclamation and the Thirteenth Amendment (qq.v.), they would actually gain seats in the House of Representatives. This threatened Republican control of the nation when joined with Northern Democrat (q.v.) votes already challenging Reconstruction and other domestic policies (transcontinental railroad, national banking system, land grant colleges, higher taxes and tariffs). Another reason for the African-Americans to vote was that their numbers would help Republicans gain a political toehold in the Southern states that could be obtained no other way. There were too few whites willing to go against the Lost Cause consistently. But blacks had no qualms about voting Republican all the time. Finally, there was the notion that through the ballot and their voting strength, blacks would command a respect for their rights that no other method could obtain. The North knew that it could not police the South with soldiers forever. Sooner or later, the African-Americans would have to guarantee their own rights and economic independence, and the ballot offered a manner in which to achieve this.

But there was a bit of a problem with granting African-Americans the vote. As past elections had shown, Northern voters were unalterably opposed to blacks voting in their precincts. State after state had rejected post–Civil War referenda designed to allow blacks to vote in the North. To insist on blacks voting up North would give the whole ball game to President Andrew Johnson and the Democrats. So something hypocritical, yet eminently wise politically, was needed to fasten the Negro vote on the South but preserve the North for whites only. The result was the Fourteenth Amendment (q.v.), which allowed Congress to reduce a state's representation by the same proportion that it systematically denied the vote to any part of its male population, and the Military Reconstruction Acts (q.v.), which required the South to register and count black voters in all elections and approve of the Fourteenth

Amendment. In the presidential election of 1868 (q.v.), the nation voted with a not-too-subtle double standard that had blacks voting in the Reconstructed South by Federal law but not in the North.

But the elections in 1867, in which Radical Republicans (q.v.) were hit hard, and the presidential election of 1868, in which Ulysses S. Grant (q.v.) was rumored to have won only with the black vote from the South, showed the precarious nature of Republican power in Washington, D.C. Radicals argued that the party was losing many white votes in the North anyhow, so now was the time to extend black voting everywhere. There were compelling reasons beyond mere politics to do it. Blacks had fought willingly for the Union, and it appealed to social justice that all should be treated the same. But others were not so sure. Whites feared political equality would lead to social equality. The matter would have to be rehashed many times before a proper formula could be found to appeal to all factions of the party. The end result was an amendment to the Constitution that was worded in such a manner as to not actually grant the franchise to African-Americans, but also not permit them to be refused the vote solely on the matter of race. The Fifteenth Amendment established *impartial* but not *universal* suffrage. The states could still reject voters on any factor but color or former condition of servitude.

Having produced essentially a weak amendment, the Republicans faced the problem of ratification. At first the process looked good. The New England states, except for Rhode Island, which feared the effect of the measure on stimulating the Irish to vote, voted its strong abolitionist (q.v.) leanings. The South joined in voting for the amendment. Most of the legislatures were Republican, there was a large black vote already, and whites figured that if the South had to let blacks vote, why not the North? The border states disliked the idea immensely. The legislatures dominated by Republicans in West Virginia, Maryland (which already had the Negro franchise through prior state action), and Missouri passed the amendment. The rest (Delaware, Kentucky) voted it down or refused to vote at all (Tennessee). The Far West (California, Oregon) rejected the measure, fearing its effect on allowing the Chinese to vote. Only Nevada, removed from the implications of that question, approved of it. The Middle Atlantic states and the Old Northwest (today's Middle West) split almost equally between Republicans and Democrats, and with a strong Southern heritage in the area along the Ohio River, passed the amendment only as a party measure.

In the end, the required three-fourths of the states was lacking. But there was a solution. Three Southern states (Texas, Mississippi, Virginia) had yet to complete Reconstruction. A fourth, Georgia, had been thrown out a second time when it refused to seat elected black legislators. These states were now required to ratify the Fifteenth Amendment (in addition to the Fourteenth Amendment) to regain their places in the new Union. In this way, the South offset the lack of Northern support, and the Fifteenth Amendment passed and became a part of the Constitution on March 30, 1870.

But almost immediately it began to be ignored in the South. The Congress tried to enforce it and the Fourteenth Amendment through the Enforcement Acts (q.v.), only to see both measures restricted by adverse Supreme Court decisions. By 1898, the Fifteenth Amendment had been totally circumvented in the South by limits on voting that were not overtly by race, like literacy tests, grandfather clauses, the poll tax, and the white primary (primaries were conducted solely under state law or as private club elections). Until the Voting Rights Act of 1965, only in the North did blacks have a chance to vote, courtesy of the Fifteenth Amendment.

FILIBUSTERING. In the Western Hemisphere, the United States of the 1850s followed the same "Spread Eagle" (q.v.) foreign policy as it did in Europe and Asia. It must be accorded one of the miracles of the 19th century that the United States never took the Spanish colonies left over from the Latin American revolutions for independence, Cuba and Puerto Rico, before the Civil War. As Puerto Rico was considered the less valuable of the two, American antebellum interest centered on Cuba, the "Pearl of the Antilles," the fertile island "sugar bowl" that guarded the mouth of the Mississippi River. Indeed, every American president from Thomas Jefferson to William McKinley (with the exception of Abraham Lincoln [q.v.]) offered to buy Cuba from Spain. James K. Polk offered $100 million, far more than the measly $40 million he offered Mexico for New Mexico and California before he took them by force and gave Mexico an even more insulting $15 million.

The War with Mexico merely whetted American appetites for expansion to the south. The Mexican Cession was considered to be nothing but barren desert. But Cuba, that was a prize worth contemplating. It had a slave economy in place and a staple crop (sugar) worth millions. But Spain would not sell, preferring to see Cuba "sink into the ocean" before transferring it to another power. It would be impossible to get a declaration of war through Congress. So the supporters of Cuban revolution used another ploy. They created private armies of conquest called Filibustering expeditions. The men who led them were filibusterers, from *filibustereros* in Spanish, an old corruption of the Dutch word *vribueter*, similar to the English freebooter.

The end of the War with Mexico left a lot of unemployed soldiers, who wished to become adventurers, for the right price. Most Americans believed that Cubans would revolt from monarchical Spain if they had a little support from the freedom-loving slaveholders of the United States. There had been aborted revolutions in the past. One of these had involved Narciso López, a native of Venezuela. Now he came to the United States to recruit followers to conquer Cuba for the aggrandizement of the conquerors.

López was nothing if not persistent. Stopped leaving New York harbor with a force of volunteers in 1849, he transferred his operations to New Orleans, where officials were more understanding. His party reached the Cuban beaches only to find that no one rose to meet them. Pursued by a Spanish fleet, López and his followers reached Key West, where he was arrested for violation of the neutrality laws. The jury found him not guilty. He walked out of court a hero. Men clamored to join him. In 1851, he raised an army of Filibusterers numbering 500. The Spanish were ready. His men were massacred on the beaches. The survivors surrendered to the Spanish, who executed López and 50 of his leaders. These became known in the United States as the "Gallant Fifty-one." President Millard Fillmore (q.v.) had a different view. He apologized and paid Spain $25,000 in damages. Spain released the 100 captives still alive.

When Fillmore left office to be replaced by Franklin Pierce (q.v.), everyone knew something would happen. Pierce was an avowed expansionist. He appointed a man of like demeanor, Pierre Soulé (q.v.) of Louisiana, as American minister to Spain. Soulé was so outspoken on America's right to Cuba that his appointment was an insult to Spain. The European diplomatic corps snubbed him. When the French ambassador in Spain made an insulting remark about the décolletage of Mrs. Soulé's dress, Soulé challenged him to a duel and shot him in the hip, maiming the man for life. Europe was outraged, America thrilled that its honor was upheld.

Soulé soon was in the thick of the Cuban mess. Spain had been enforcing its shipping laws very strictly against American seamen, because of the López affair. After a series of minor incidents, Spain seized the American registered ship *Black Warrior* for lacking a proper cargo manifest. Soulé delivered an abusive note to the Spanish, demanding $300,000 damages. Since he acted on his own volition, Spain ignored him and dealt directly with Washington, where the *Black Warrior's* owners agreed to accept $53,000. But Soulé had scored once again among the expansionist crowd of Young America.

During the Crimean War, Pierce offered Spain $130 million for Cuba. Spain refused again. Secretary of State William Marcy ordered Soulé to detach Cuba from Spain, if possible. Soulé moved to comply. He invited the U.S. ministers from France (John Y. Mason) and Great Britain (James Buchanan) to meet him in secret at Ostend, Belgium. There they issued the so-called Ostend Manifesto, a misnomer in that it was issued in Ostend but it was not a manifesto.

The document made a series of assumptions and suggestions to Marcy to guide future U.S. policy toward Cuba. Cuban possession was necessary to suppress the African slave trade, to promote Cuban–American trade, to prevent further insults to the American flag like the *Black Warrior* incident, and as a strategic location necessary to national security. Hence the island should be bought at once for $120 million. If Spain refused, and it was sure to do so, and Spanish rule became dangerous to United States interests in the Gulf, we would be justified in taking Cuba by force.

The Manifesto was leaked in the press even before Marcy saw it. Europe and the antislavery (q.v.) elements of the U.S. North blew it all out of proportion as a Southern attempt to extend American slavery into new territory. Marcy firmly rejected the suggestions of the manifesto and left his letter asking Soulé to detach Cuba from Spain out of the documents sent to Congress. Soulé resigned in a huff, insulted by Marcy's duplicity. Buchanan and Mason denied culpability. The Democrats (q.v.) lost many seats in the 1854 congressional by-elections, and the new Republican Party (q.v.) looked forward with anticipation to the election of 1856 (q.v.), when it would run its first presidential candidate.

But Cuba was not the only place of American filibustering interest in Latin America in the 1850s. William Walker wished to advance American control into Nicaragua and Honduras. A slight man, five feet six and 100 pounds, Walker was called the "Grey-eyed Man of Destiny." He went to California during the Gold Rush, dabbled in newspaper editing, and hit upon the idea of capturing Central America for the United States to exploit as potential slave territory. There was also the potential for an isthmian canal. After an abortive expedition into Baja California in 1853, Walker led three campaigns into Nicaragua, where he also fronted for the William Vanderbilt interest in railroads and shipping. Nicaragua offered a healthier route across the isthmus than Panamá to the south, albeit longer in land distance. Everything seemed to be going well until Walker revoked the charter of the Vanderbilt company. Vanderbilt was not one to mess with. He financed a nationalist revolution against the Walker dictatorship. After Walker was deposed, he foolishly came back to suffer defeat again. A third try in 1860, this time in Honduras, caused the British to step in, capture him, and turn him over to the Honduran government. His execution soon followed.

As common as Walker's efforts in Central America were other expeditions into the northern Mexican states, like Sonora. There was still a lot of sentiment in the United States that all of Mexico should have been annexed after the 1848 treaty. This feeling was tapped when George W. L. Bickley, a Cincinnati doctor, became president-general of an organization called the Knights of the Golden Circle, named after a mythical crusading force in a popular novel of the 1840s, the *Knights of the Golden Horseshoe*. Bickley organized castles all over the United States, especially in the West and South. He plotted a military expedition of "energetic Anglo-Saxons" to conquer Mexico and "Texas-ize" the area. He thought as many as 25 slave states might be formed from Mexico.

His hair-brained scheme seemed real enough to Northern antislavery people to terrorize them throughout the Civil War and Reconstruction. Many thought that the movement of pro-Southern sympathizers, called Copper-heads (q.v.), against the Union war effort was Bickley's plans come to the fore. Bickley was picked up with a Southern army during the war and spent two years in jail without trial. Afterward he emerged as a broken man. Fili-bustering, although still a popular topic of modern Hollywood, died out with the advent of the real war in 1861.

FILLMORE, MILLARD (1800–1874). Born in upstate New York, Millard Fillmore read law, was admitted to the bar, and moved to Buffalo by 1830. Like fellow upstater and Whig (q.v.) lawyer William H. Seward (q.v.), Fill-more was a student of Thurlow Weed in New York politics, serving in the state assembly and two terms in the U.S. Congress, where he was chairman of the Ways and Means Committee and an advocate of Henry Clay's American System (q.v.). Defeated in a bid to become governor of New York, Fillmore accepted the vice presidency to balance the Whig ticket in 1848 under slave-holding Southerner and war hero Zachary Taylor (q.v.). Unlike Taylor, Fill-more supported the Compromise of 1850 (q.v.). When Taylor died, Fillmore's accession to the presidency cooled his passions considerably, and he signed the Compromise and enforced the Fugitive Slave Act (q.v.) rigorously. This caused him much unpopularity with the Northern branch of the Whig Party, the Conscience Whigs led by Seward, and he lost a renomination for the presi-dency in 1852. He ran as the American Party (q.v.) candidate in 1856, but the slavery issue had divided the old Whigs so badly by then that he stood little chance to win. He retired to Buffalo, where he died some years later.

FIRE-EATERS. Those antebellum Southern politicians who championed the breakup of the Democratic Party (q.v.) and the Union were called Fire-Eaters. They were generally led by William Yancey of Alabama, but included James L. Orr in South Carolina, Albert Gallatin Brown in Mississippi, Pierre Soulé (q.v.) in Louisiana, Alfred Iverson in Georgia, and Louis T. Wigfall (q.v.) in Texas.

FISH, HAMILTON (1808–1893). The son of New York patricians, Ham-ilton Fish grew up to become one of the most important secretaries of state in the nation's history and one of the only decent cabinet picks that Ulysses S. Grant (q.v.) made. Fish had a private education and graduated Columbia University with the highest honors. He read law and entered practice, evolv-ing into Whig (q.v.) politics from a Federalist Party tradition. He ran for state assembly in a Democrat district and lost, but managed to win a congressional seat for one term in 1842. Not returned to Congress, Fish turned to the lieuten-ant governorship of New York, only to lose the race. A special election for the same office a year later proved successful, and in 1848 Fish moved on to the governor's chair, where he opened a statewide free school system and modernized the Erie Canal. He was opposed to the extension of slavery into the territories obtained from Mexico and slated to be placed in President Zachary Taylor's (q.v.) reorganized cabinet, but the president's death ended that.

Although Fish was not renominated as governor, the Whigs put him forward as their candidate for the U.S. Senate. In a hotly contested race in the state legislature, Fish emerged triumphant despite his refusal to denounce the Compromise of 1850 (q.v.), which permitted slavery to advance into the Mexican Cession in contradiction of his own earlier announced position. In Washington, he generally followed the lead of the senior New York Senator, William H. Seward (q.v.), and his back home backer, Thurlow Weed, without much imagination. He became a Republican (q.v.) only because the Whigs were going into demise, but he never embraced the slavery issue as the main concern of American politics. After his Senate term expired, Fish took his family to Europe for a two-year vacation. When he returned, he decided to work actively for the election of Abraham Lincoln (q.v.) and advised the outgoing James Buchanan (q.v.) administration to get tough with the South. During the war, he worked on the New York State defense committee and negotiated the exchange of prisoners of war.

After the war, Fish had no special claim to a position in the Ulysses S. Grant administration beyond the fact that he had entertained the president-elect and knew him personally. In truth, Fish really did not want to serve, having retired from politics. But Grant insisted and sent his personal aide, Orville Babcock, to ask Fish to come aboard. Fish agreed only to help the administration get started, but served as secretary of state for Grant's two terms, during which time he became a pillar of honesty and moderation.

As secretary of state, Fish reluctantly supported Grant's desire to annex the ill-governed republic of Santo Domingo, a stand that cost him an old friendship with opposing Senator Charles Sumner (q.v.). Fish also had much difficulty charting a middle course between Cuban insurrectionists and the government of Spain, which he pressured to recognize legitimate claims for damages filed by American citizens (*see* CUBAN INSURRECTION). He attempted to negotiate a Central American canal with Colombia and Nicaragua in succession, but failed in both efforts. He also failed to obtain a convention with Korea for American trading interests.

But in other areas, Fish was more successful. He acted as a protector of German citizens in France during the Franco–Prussian War and kept the conflict from spreading to their Asian colonies, reduced incursions along the Mexican border with much tact, and had the Russian minister to the United States recalled for interfering with negotiations with Great Britain over its turning a blind eye to Confederate ship-building efforts during the Civil War. These *Alabama* claims (q.v.) in the end became Fish's greatest claim to fame, as he skillfully presented the American viewpoint and carried the negotiations through to a successful conclusion. He also got Britain to agree to the notion that extradition of a wanted person need not be accomplished through charges identical to those in the asking nation's courts, but could be for any other viable reason.

After the end of his tenure as secretary of state, Fish retired to New York to live the life of a man of means, culture, and good taste. He enjoyed his family, and had eight children with his wife, Julia Kean, who was considered a most gracious hostess. He was assisted in many of his public jobs by his son, Hamilton, who became an important man in his own right and achieved special notoriety years later by receiving a personal rebuke from President Franklin D. Roosevelt for his opposition to the New Deal. The senior Fish lived out the rest of the 19th century, serving as a trustee of Columbia University, president-general of the Society of Cincinnati, president of the Union League, and president of the New York Historical Society.

FISHER'S HILL, BATTLE OF. *See* SHENANDOAH VALLEY CAMPAIGN, SECOND (SHERIDAN'S).

FITZ JOHN PORTER CASE. *See* ELECTION OF 1862, UNION.

FIVE FORKS, BATTLE OF. *See* APPOMATTOX CAMPAIGN.

FLOYD, JOHN. *See* SECESSION, BUCHANAN'S CABINET AND.

FORCE ACTS. *See* ENFORCEMENT ACTS.

FOREIGN POLICY. *See* DIPLOMACY, C.S.—CIVIL WAR; DIPLOMACY, U.S.—CIVIL WAR; DIPLOMACY, U.S.—RECONSTRUCTION.

FORFEITED RIGHTS OR SHELLABARGER–CHASE THEORY. *See* RECONSTRUCTION, THEORIES OF.

FORREST, NATHAN BEDFORD (1821–1877). Born in Tennessee and raised in Mississippi, Bedford Forrest grew up in a frontier region with very little formal education. But he made up for it with a lot of spunk. He was a blacksmith and a farmer until he moved to Hernando, Mississippi, and became a planter who dealt in horses and slaves. Then he went to Memphis in the 1850s and made it big in real estate, becoming a town alderman. Through his various travels as a businessman, Forrest came to know the highways and byways of northern Mississippi, Alabama, and southwestern Tennessee like few others.

Forrest enrolled as a private in the Confederate army in 1861. He soon went home to raise and equip his own battalion of cavalry, which he commanded as lieutenant colonel. He first drew notice during the Shiloh Campaign (q.v.), when he refused to surrender his command at Fort Donelson, escaping through the swamps, and commanded the rear guard during the Rebel retreat from Shiloh. Appointed brigadier general in July 1862, he began his raiding behind Union lines, using all those roads and paths he knew so well, for which he became famous.

Forrest was an aggressive personality. Shot by a subordinate during a quarrel, he managed to hold his opponent's gun hand while he opened his pocket knife with his teeth and cut his guts out. Then he cried over the carnage he had wrought as the man died in his arms. He clashed often with more cautious and less imaginative superiors, threatening their lives in no uncertain terms, which finally earned him an independent command and the rank of major general.

He was perhaps the best natural-born soldier from either side in the war. He knew when to bluff and when to fight. He constantly surprised opponents from ambush, took on armed river steamboats, and was always at the forefront of all attacks. He decisively drove back Union forces at Brice's Crossroads (q.v.) and Tupelo, earning him the grudging admiration of Union Maj. Gen. William T. Sherman (q.v.) as "that devil Forrest." Although his career was tarnished by the massacre of prisoners and wounded at Fort Pillow (q.v.) in 1864, he was never defeated until the Selma Campaign (q.v.) in 1865. He ended the war as a lieutenant general, turning himself and his men in as a part of the Citronelle surrender (q.v.).

After the war, Forrest returned to Memphis completely broke. He engaged in planting, railroading, and insurance, but was never able to recoup himself economically. Forrest also involved himself in Reconstruction politics. He was willing to accept the results of the war insofar as slavery was concerned, but he brooked no compromise with the idea that the South would always be a white man's country. He was the first imperial grand wizard of the Ku Klux Klan (q.v.) and stonewalled his way through a congressional investigation that led to the Enforcement Acts (q.v.). He died from typhoid in Memphis.

FORREST'S WEST TENNESSEE RAID. *See* BRICE'S CROSSROADS, BATTLE OF.

FORT ACT. *See* GRANT, ULYSSES S., ADMINISTRATION—DOMESTIC POLICIES.

FORT DeRUSSY. *See* RED RIVER CAMPAIGN.

FORT DONELSON, BATTLE OF. After the fall of Ft. Henry (q.v.) on February 6, 1862, Brig. Gen. Ulysses S. Grant (q.v.) and Flag Off. Andrew Foote moved on Ft. Donelson, located on the Cumberland. As usual, the Navy arrived first, not having to contend with the cold weather and muddy roads. Foote decided to try to bombard Ft. Donelson into surrender before Grant arrived on its land side.

But Ft. Donelson was better sited than Ft. Henry. Its bigger guns smashed Foote's little fleet. Foote drifted out of range and waited for Grant's infantry to invest the land side of the fort. But the Confederates attacked Grant on February 15 and forced open the escape route to Clarksville and Nashville.

At this point, the Confederate command malfunctioned. It needed to continue the attack or retreat immediately to save the men. It did neither. Under the inept Brig. Gen. John Floyd, the Rebel army retreated back into its entrenchments, and Grant reclosed the siege lines. Floyd was overly impressed with his value as a prisoner. So he gave the command to his subordinate, Brig. Gen. Gideon Pillow, and boarded a river steamer to escape with some Virginia regiments. Pillow did the same, passing command to Brig. Gen. Simon B. Buckner. Cavalry leader Col. Nathan Bedford Forrest (q.v.) could smell surrender and led his men out through the swamps.

Meanwhile, Buckner asked Grant for terms, assuming that Grant would remember that Buckner had been an old friend who had once loaned him much-needed money. Grant sent him his famous answer: "unconditional surrender." Buckner reluctantly accepted, and Grant had captured the first of the three Confederate armies (this one about 15,000 strong) he would capture during the war. Up North, he was an instant hero, the press noting the initials of his name matched his unconditional surrender demand. And Johnston immediately retreated out of Kentucky into northern Mississippi to plan a new attack.

FORT FISHER. *See* WILMINGTON, BATTLE OF.

FORT HENRY, BATTLE OF. On February 6, 1862, Brig. Gen. Ulysses S. Grant and Flag Off. Andrew Foote moved on Ft. Henry, the western-most and weakest of the forts commanding the Kentucky–Tennessee border. Commanded by Brig. Gen. Lloyd Tilghman, Ft. Henry was partially inundated by the spring flood. It mounted 17 guns, but was unfinished and commanded by a high plateau to its rear, which Grant hoped to take. Delayed by weather and muddy roads, Grant arrived late to find that Tilghman had sent most of his force over to Ft. Donelson (q.v.) and had surrendered Ft. Henry and 80 men to Foote after a short naval bombardment. Fortunately Foote's naval batteries had outranged the land guns in Ft. Henry, making victory possible.

FORT HINDMAN, BATTLE OF. *See* VICKSBURG CAMPAIGN.

FORT LOUDON. *See* KNOXVILLE CAMPAIGN.

FORT McALLISTER. *See* MARCH TO THE SEA.

FORT PEMBERTON. *See* VICKSBURG CAMPAIGN.

FORT PILLOW MASSACRE (APRIL 12, 1864). With the Confederate cavalry division of Brig. Gen. James R. Chalmers, Maj. Gen. Nathan Bedford Forrest (q.v.) moved in the spring of 1864 to neutralize Ft. Pillow, garrisoned to protect Federal river traffic above Memphis on the Mississippi River. Chalmers began the attack against the 600 defenders, who were divided almost equally between blue-coated African-Americans and loyal Tennessee whites. Supporting the fort was the Union gunboat *New Era.*

The Confederates attacked the installation very carefully, working into positions that afforded the gunboat no field of fire. By 3:30 p.m., Forrest offered the defenders a last chance to surrender. It was refused. The Rebel cavalry overran the fort in short order, and that is when the trouble began.

The Confederates said the severe Federal casualties (231 killed, 100 wounded, 210 prisoners) occurred when the garrison retreated across the open beach to the shelter of the gunboats. The Union men, black and white, said that they tried to give up early on in the attack, but that the Confederates refused to accept their surrender and shot them down. "No quarter! No quarter! Kill the damned niggers! Shoot them down!" the Rebel cavalry shouted. To the Rebels, the African-Americans were escaped slaves in rebellion and the whites were traitors to the South. The U.S. congressional investigation said that murder ran amok, some blacks were buried alive, and wounded of both races were burned alive in their tents. The Confederates countered that it was merely an overwhelming victory against troops who refused to give up. Historians have tended to back the congressional investigation as an accurate story of what really happened.

FORT STEDMAN, BATTLE OF. *See* APPOMATTOX CAMPAIGN.

FORT STEVENS, BATTLE OF. *See* WASHINGTON, EARLY'S RAID ON.

FORT SUMTER, BATTLE OF. With the secession of the Southern states, many Federal garrisons wound up in hostile territory. But by March 1861, the United States held only Ft. Jefferson on the Dry Tortugas off of Key West, Ft. Taylor at Key West, Ft. Pickens at Pensacola, and Ft. Sumter at Charleston. Because of the aggressive nature of South Carolina in asserting its sovereignty over Charleston's numerous forts and arsenals, on December 26, 1860, Maj. Robert Anderson moved his approximately 120 officers, soldiers, and workmen from easily accessible Castle Pinckney in the city and Ft. Moultrie on the bay to unfinished Ft. Sumter on an island of rip-rap near the mouth of the harbor, commanding the main ship channel. The fort had 48 guns emplaced, although the walls were designed to accommodate 140. Twenty-one of the cannon were along the top of the walls and hence quite vulnerable to enemy fire.

Meanwhile, because President James Buchanan's (q.v.) cabinet had been reshuffled in favor of a stronger Northern presence, Buchanan decided to send a supply ship to succor the fort. He sent a commercial ship, the *Star of the West*, to remain as non-threatening as possible. South Carolina gunners drove it off in a hail of fire on January 8, 1861. Buchanan did manage to send supplies to Ft. Pickens. When Abraham Lincoln became president, he would reinforce and hold Pickens, Confederate President Jefferson Davis' commander there. Gen. Braxton Bragg, being as irresolute as ever, refused to make the assault.

But by far the most important symbolically were the several installations in Charleston, the seed-bed of secession. After the organization of the Confederacy, the new government sent Brig. Gen. P. G. T. Beauregard to take command of Charleston. Beauregard received instructions on April 10, 1861, to demand Anderson's surrender or reduce the fort by fire. Anderson said he was fast running out of supplies and would have to yield by noon on April 15. Beauregard went ahead with the bombardment, opening fire on the morning of April 12.

Enduring a 34-hour shelling, which set most of the buildings inside the fort on fire, Anderson yielded on April 14. He was allowed to evacuate his men to an awaiting Federal relief fleet at the mouth of the harbor that had not dared challenge the Confederate batteries. Anderson's losses amounted to two wounded (one of whom died later) and one killed; the latter died when an accidental explosion occurred as Anderson saluted the lowered national ensign, according to surrender terms.

Four years later, on April 14, 1865, Anderson raised the same national flag as Union troops reoccupied Ft. Sumter, it having been turned into rubble amid the numerous assaults made during the war. President Lincoln had been invited, but declined, destiny preferring him to attend Ford's Theater in Washington, D.C., instead.

FORTIETH CONGRESS EXTRA SESSION ACT. A measure passed by the outgoing 2nd Session of the Thirty-ninth Congress to call into extra session the 1st Session of the Fortieth Congress immediately upon its adjournment. The idea was to create a Congress with three sessions that would not adjourn until President Andrew Johnson (q.v.) had been thoroughly defeated in his attempts to reconstruct the South through presidential proclamation. As both Johnson and his predecessor, Abraham Lincoln (q.v.), acted frequently in the gaps between congressional sessions, this would curb executive interference.

"FORTY ACRES AND A MULE." The idea of each head of family receiving 40 acres of farmland and a mule to work it with is one of the most enduring myths of Reconstruction. It is true that Congress in the First Freedmen's Bureau law instructed the Bureau of Refugees, Freedmen, and Abandoned Lands (q.v.) to administer all property abandoned by owners during the war and now under Federal control. It is also true that Congress saw the land being divided up and doled out among the freed slaves. But there was not enough abandoned land to accomplish this prodigious task. And President Andrew Johnson (q.v.) soon pardoned the original owners and returned the property to them. The Civil War was a revolution of sorts, but not uncontrolled anarchy. There would be no violation of property rights guaranteed under the Constitution. Few freedmen beyond those involved in the Port Royal Experiment (q.v.) in the Sea Islands along the South Atlantic Coast received any land, unless they bought it. Blacks refused to abandon their hope until well after Christmas 1865, when the land giveaway was rumored to take place. But it never did.

FOURTEENTH AMENDMENT. Once the Congress had repassed the Freedmen's Bureau and Civil Rights Acts of 1866 (qq.v.) over President Andrew Johnson's vetoes, it had indicated that it would not accept his view on Reconstruction. This meant that Congress now had to suggest an alternative, definitive program, a responsibility that fell on the Committee of Fifteen on Reconstruction (q.v.). Historians have traditionally examined the origins of the Fourteenth Amendment as a sort of plot to advance Reconstruction toward more and more vindictive goals designed to make the process unpalatable to the white South. Modern authors have seen it more as Congress searching for some solution that all could live with now that the president had thrown down the gauntlet on the Freedmen's Bureau and the Civil Rights Act of 1866. The reason it was put forward as an amendment was to insure that a succeeding Congress would not be able to alter it by mere majority vote—a real problem, it turns out, given the tenuous hold of the Republicans (q.v.) on the national and particularly Southern state governments. The reason the seceded states had to endorse the Fourteenth Amendment, even though Congress refused to admit they were full-fledged states in the Union yet and there was legitimate doubt if they could ratify any amendment given their status in limbo, was to signify a sort of Civil War peace treaty (non-existent, then and forever, unless the Compromise of 1877 qualifies).

Even though many commentators today believe that the Fourteenth Amendment was typically American, something quite in the realm of continuing constitutional development, it was a really revolutionary document. It was the first amendment that operated directly upon the states rather than the Federal government. The first section was basically a repetition of the

Civil Rights Act of 1866, which nationalized citizenship. Before the Civil War, citizenship was guaranteed by the states. Now it was nationalized, and the power was given to the states only in the absence of action by the Federal government. And for the states to exercise this power, they had to stay within certain boundaries. They could not make or enforce any law that "abridged the privileges or immunities" of citizens, deny a citizen "equal protection of the laws," or deprive anyone of "life, liberty, or property, without due process of the law." This section overturned Dred Scott *v.* Sandford (q.v.), in which the U.S. Supreme Court had declared that blacks were not citizens and actually threatened the constitutionality of the Civil Rights Act of 1866.

The second part of the amendment handled the problem of Southern representation. Because of racist tendencies among Northern voters, Republicans in Congress did not wish to alienate its constituency by granting the African-Americans the vote outright. Every time some movement to free blacks or expand their rights had taken place during the war, the Republican vote had dropped precipitously in the North. But Republicans knew that to hold onto the nation with the increase in Southern representation that came from freeing the slaves, they would either have to grant blacks the right to vote (they would vote for the party that freed them from slavery, the Republicans assumed, smugly) or somehow reduce this representation. So the second section apportioned representation in Congress among the whole numbers of persons in the several states, recognizing Africans as complete citizens (not three-fifths of one person as before the war). But if any male over the age of 21 and a citizen of the United States was denied the vote (except for participation in rebellion or conviction of a crime), a state's representation could be reduced in direct proportion. This was in effect a bribe to the South to permit blacks to vote or accept a loss in representation in Congress. Its weakness of course was that the white Southern establishment just might accept the deal, deny the African-Americans the rights to vote, and take the loss. And it ignored gender, a matter that did not sit well with the Suffragettes, many of whom had been ardent abolitionists (q.v.) before the war.

The third section treated the whites who had taken an oath to the United States before the war in any capacity and then taken a similar oath to support the Confederacy. These men would be denied the vote until Congress decided by a two-thirds vote at some future date to give them a special amnesty (done at various times between 1872 and 1898). Another section of the amendment validated the Union war debt and nullified the Confederate war debt, implying that the Confederacy never existed as a legitimate entity. The final section allowed Congress to make such laws as it thought necessary to enforce the amendment. It was this section that would permit Congress to pass the Enforcement Acts (q.v.) in 1870 and 1871.

The proposals that made up the final draft of the Fourteenth Amendment were not set in cement. At any point, President Andrew Johnson (q.v.) might have altered the process had he been willing to compromise with the Congress on Reconstruction. But Johnson's opposition led Southerners to vote the amendment down in every Southern state except Tennessee, where the Republicans had by chance obtained a majority in the legislature, which they manipulated mercilessly. In most of the South, the vote against the Fourteenth Amendment was unanimous or so lopsided as to be virtually so. The result was that Congress admitted Tennessee back into the Union and turned to the Military Reconstruction Acts (q.v.) to coerce the South into proper readmission. Part of that admission would be Southern ratification of the Fourteenth Amendment, now so necessary because too many Northern states had rejected it, also. It would achieve final approval on July 28, 1868, right after the readmission of North Carolina, South Carolina, Georgia, Florida, Alabama, Mississippi, and Louisiana into the Union.

FRANKLIN, BATTLE OF. *See* NASHVILLE CAMPAIGN.

FRANKLIN'S CROSSING, BATTLE OF. *See* PENNSYLVANIA CAMPAIGN.

FREDERICKSBURG CAMPAIGN. After the Antietam Campaign, Union President Abraham Lincoln (q.v.) awaited the results of the 1862 congressional elections before he replaced Maj. Gen. George B. McClellan (q.v.) as head of the Army of the Potomac with a close army and business friend, Maj. Gen. Ambrose E. Burnside (q.v.). To his credit, Burnside initially turned down the appointment. For the country's sake and his place in history, he should have tried harder, rather than finally reluctantly accepting. It is claimed that he cried like a baby at his fate and worked very hard to be worthy of it—so hard, in fact, he literally made himself sick.

Burnside took over the army in the East when it was about where it had been the previous summer, stretched out along the Orange and Alexandria Railroad. As usual, that supply and communication line was vulnerable to Confederate cavalry raiders. So Burnside took a page out of the McClellan book and moved his whole force to Fredericksburg. There his supplies and communications were dependent upon the U.S. Navy, and quite reliable. His main base became Aquia Creek Landing.

Burnside actually stole a march on Rebel Gen. Robert E. Lee (q.v.). The idea was for the Union army to cross the Rappahannock River on pontoon bridges and march south overland to Richmond. But for one reason or another, the pontoons were two weeks late, and in that time, Lee recovered and had his whole force lined up along the Rappahannock at every probable crossing.

It was getting late in the year, December 1862, in fact. The army ought to have considered winter quarters. But Burnside knew that the Republicans (q.v.) in Washington expected something to be done before the New Year. So he decided to cross the river and knock Lee's men off the heights behind the town. In reality, Burnside's plan was a bit more complicated than that. He did not expect the troops attacking the Rebel positions on the hills behind the city to make the main attack. They were supposed to hold down that part of Lee's army, while the real push was to be made against Lt. Gen. Thomas J. Jackson's (q.v.) corps on less defensible ground to the south around Hamilton's Crossing. But things have a way of getting out of whack during wars.

When the pontoons arrived, Burnside had them set up in three crossings. The pontooniers worked all night and early in the morning on December 11, until the sun burned off the fog. Then Confederate riflemen began to snipe at the workers, stopping progress. The Federals would fire back, and the bridge builders came out to work, only to be driven off again. Finally, several Infantry units got into the pontoon boats and rowed across to flush the Rebels out of the town permanently. In the process, the whole city was wrecked, much of it maliciously without reason. The war was getting tougher all the time.

By December 13, Burnside was ready to advance. His subordinate generals—he had organized the traditional corps of the Army of the Potomac into three Grand Divisions of two corps each—all doubted his plan. But Maj. Gens. Joseph Hooker (q.v.) and William Franklin of the southernmost two Grand Divisions actually became so surly as to sabotage the attack. Franklins' men broke through Jackson's line, but being unsupported, they were soon driven back. In the north, Burnside made half a dozen assaults, each division being slaughtered by concentrated rifle and artillery fire. It was pure butchery. It has been surmised by some historians that Burnside was so stung by the criticism of his indecisiveness at Antietam Creek that he would not quit until the attacks degenerated from tragedy to farce.

In any case, when December 13 was over, the Union had lost over 12,000 men to Lee's 6,000, most of those occurring in Jackson's corps, where the breakthrough had occurred. Burnside soon withdrew across the Rappahannock to Falmouth and went into winter quarters. Officers went up to Washington on furlough and conspired with the Lincoln administration to have Burnside removed. Lincoln was unsure. He told Burnside to make no moves without prior consultation. Burnside went up to defend himself and asked that Chief of Staff Henry W. Halleck (q.v.) and Secretary of War Edwin McM. Stanton be fired (q.v.), as well as the officers who talked behind his back. Lincoln backed off.

The weather stayed surprisingly mild and sunny. In mid-January, Burnside decided to outflank Lee by advancing up the Rappahannock and crossing behind him. The army started out. But as they all got out on the roads, the weather turned cold, and it began to rain, then snow. Soon a full-fledged blizzard struck the columns. Burnside had to give up, and the men returned to Falmouth, forever cursing this so-called Mud March. They fought for old campsites among themselves, and the Rebels taunted them from across the river. In a rage, Burnside recommended that Lincoln dismiss nine high-ranking officers from the service. Lincoln took the easy route and fired Burnside as army commander instead. Burnside wound up in the Department of Ohio behind the lines, far from the battlefields in the South. But he would be back.

FREDERICKSBURG, FIRST BATTLE OF. *See* FREDERICKSBURG CAMPAIGN.

FREDERICKSBURG, SECOND BATTLE OF. *See* CHANCELLORS-VILLE CAMPAIGN.

FREEDMEN'S AID SOCIETIES. Before the Civil War had barely started, various abolition societies already began to look to the Reconstruction of the Union and the liberation of the slaves. It was to them a great opportunity to purge the nation of what they saw as a grievous sin through blood atonement and the sweat of their brows. They would go South and redeem the freedmen, educate them, and make them black moral counterparts in a little piece of New England society located in a rejuvenated South. Typical of such groups were the American Missionary Association, the American Freedmen's Union Commission, and the Peabody Educational Fund (qq.v.).

FREEDMEN'S BUREAU. *See* BUREAU OF REFUGEES, FREEDMEN, AND ABANDONED LANDS.

FREEDMEN'S BUREAU ACT OF MARCH 3, 1965. Congress passed the initial Bureau act in the waning days of the Civil War. Its main purpose was to give assistance to loyal refugees, black or white, who had been dispossessed by the war. As time went on, however, the Bureau became more of a social agency dedicated to helping freedmen make the transition between slavery and freedom. It was this concept that caused controversy in its renewal. In the 19th century, no group of persons except merchant seamen had ever received government largess. Hence the Bureau was a revolutionary concept that would not become accepted until the throes of the Great Depression caused politicians and citizens to rethink the role of government during the New Deal in the 1930s.

Enacted for the duration of the war and one year after, the Bureau of Refugees, Freedmen, and Abandoned Lands (q.v.) was to be a bureau of the War Department and have jurisdiction in the Rebel states or any territory occupied by the United States Army. The Bureau was to administer the three topics suggested by its title. It was to be headed by a commissioner appointed by the president with the advice and consent of the Senate at a salary of $3,000 a year and have a staff of 10 clerks. Both the commissioner and the chief clerk had to be bonded. The secretary of war was authorized to allow the Bureau rations, clothing, fuel, and temporary shelter by proper requisition.

To help the commissioner in his duties, he was permitted to appoint up to 10 assistant commissioners in the insurrectionary states. These men were to be paid $2,000 annually and post bond with the U.S. attorney general. Any military officer could be detailed to any Bureau position without any increase in his normal salary—a cost-saving measure. Each assistant commissioner was to make written reports to the commissioner and the latter to Congress at the beginning of each session. Special reports were to be made on request of any superior officer or Congress. All officers of the Bureau had to subscribe to the ironclad oath.

The commissioner was authorized to set aside, under the president's direction, any lands abandoned or to which the U.S. government had acquired title to male heads of households, black or white, not to exceed 40 acres, for the next three years, with rent not to exceed 6 percent of the value of the land per year as assessed in 1860. These renters would be given the right to buy the land at any time during its rental.

FREEDMEN'S BUREAU ACT OF JULY 16, 1866. This measure, also known as the Freedmen's Bureau Renewal Act, was to continue in force and amend the act of 1865 for the next two years. The jurisdiction of the Bureau was extended to all loyal refugees and freedmen in any part of the nation. The purpose of Bureau aid was to get families back on an independent footing as soon as possible. Two extra assistant commissioners were authorized beyond the 10 in the first act. The commissioner and his assistants were to cooperate with the religious and secular benevolent associations that sent members south for purposes of educational, religious, and moral instruction, particularly in obtaining the use of select buildings for their use.

The second Bureau act confirmed the possession of lands granted African-Americans in the Port Royal Experiment (q.v.) in sea islands below Charleston, South Carolina, which had been condemned for nonpayment of Federal taxes in September 1863. The plots were to be limited to 20 acres for each family. Those lands in the general area that had been granted to blacks under Maj. Gen. William T. Sherman's Special Field Orders No. 15 (q.v.) were also confirmed in title. Vacant lands in theses areas were to be sold exclusively to African-Americans at $1.50 an acre. Such titles could not be alienated within the first six years of ownership. Other lots in and around the area that once belonged to the Confederate States of America were to be sold at public auction. None of these procedures would affect lands reserved for the exclusive use of the military and naval forces of the United States.

Finally, in all Rebel states the Bureau was to guarantee the rights of every citizen regardless of race to sue or be sued, to make or enforce contracts, to sell or hold property, and to have equal protection under the law. No person could be punished for law violations more than any white person. The president or the Bureau had the authorization to ask for and receive military protection and assistance in enforcing these matters until such time as the former Confederate states were readmitted to the Union by their representation in Congress.

President Andrew Johnson (q.v.) vetoed this measure, only to have Congress override his veto, the first time in U.S. history Congress had so acted against a chief executive.

FREEDMEN'S BUREAU ACT OF JULY 6, 1868. This measure extended the first two Bureau acts for the period of one year more, or until such time as notified otherwise by the secretary of war. All officers serving with the Bureau who had been mustered out of the military service could be retained as civilians at the same rate of pay. The bureau would be phased out in any insurrectionary state when that state was readmitted into the Union, unless conditions warranted its continuance beyond that time. The educational operations of the Bureau were exempt from any closure date and were to be continued until black children were guaranteed a free, public education. All unexpended monies held by the commissioner for any particular jurisdiction after the closure of the Bureau field offices there were to be applied to the educational effort. All buildings owned by the Bureau for education were to be sold to local school trustees and the proceeds returned to the treasury.

FREEDMEN'S BUREAU ACT OF JULY 25, 1868. This act guaranteed that Bvt. Maj. Gen. Oliver Otis Howard (q.v.) would continue as head of the Bureau until his death or resignation. Any successor, civilian or military, would be appointed by the president with the advice and consent of the Senate. All assistant commissioners, clerks, and field agents were to be appointed by the secretary of war on the advice of the commissioner. In case of a vacancy in the office of commissioner, the acting assistant adjutant general of the Bureau would fill in temporarily until a successor could be named. Finally, it closed down all Bureau operations on January 1, 1869, the traditional close of the contract season in the South. The educational functions continued until the Panic of 1873 closed them down also.

FREEDMEN'S SAVINGS BANK. In operation from March 1865 to July 1874, the Freedmen's Savings Bank was an attempt by Reconstruction

America to instill middle class mores in the newly freed slaves. It was to be an investment bank, not one that engaged in day-to-day general banking services. Congress reserved for itself the right to inspect the books at any time and created the first and main office in New York City in April 1865, as well as 33 branches throughout the South, something Congress had not foreseen but did not discourage, either. The original backers of the institution were New York and Boston financiers and philanthropists who had connections with the abolitionist movement, the Freedmen's Bureau, and the American Missionary Association (qq.v.), a benevolent association for freedmen firmly connected with the Congregational Church. These men saw the bank as a moral imperative, a way to imbue the African-Americans with middle class values of self-sacrifice and frugality.

Unfortunately for the bank's future, the safeguards and conservative actions of its founders became lost when the institution transferred its headquarters to Washington, D.C. The result was a new board of directors who were an integral part of the Great Barbecue that plagued any money venture of this period. Under the new law, the directors did not wait long to do as they pleased with the deposits. Speculative stocks and mortgages became the norm for the bank's holdings. The new directors entered an agreement with the powerful Jay Cooke and Company, whose bankers began raiding the Freedmen's Savings Bank of its quality investments and dumping their own poorer investments into the Freedmen's portfolios.

Then the nation slumped into the lengthy Panic of 1873 (it would last five years or more), and one of the first victims was none other than Jay Cooke and Company, disastrously overextended in railroads that had gone broke. Bank directors began to liquidate their own accounts while actively soliciting more from blacks throughout the South. With a portfolio that consisted of outstanding loans from companies that had gone broke in the economic depression, drained assets that had gone to its directors rather than the depositors, and poorly kept records and outright errors in bookkeeping ($40,000 could not be found at all), the Freedmen's Savings Bank was in deep trouble.. Over 61,000 depositors lost nearly $3 million in savings. It was a staggering blow to Southern blacks. Many depositors experienced deprivation of a life's work, a loss of self-respect (Southern whites unfairly gloated that it all proved African-Americans were unready for freedom), and a destruction of their trust in banks, regardless of their management. It left a legacy of suspicion and failure that remained a hot issue in the black community well into the 20th century.

FREE MEN, FREE SOIL, FREE LABOR. The Republican Party's (q.v.) slogan in the election of 1856 (q.v.), borrowed from the defunct Free Soil Party of 1848 and 1852 (q.v.), which became the embodiment of Republican ideology (q.v.) before, during, and after the Civil War. Sometimes included the concept of "Free Speech," opposing Southerners' attempt to prevent abolition petitions from being received by Congress.

FREEPORT DOCTRINE. The answer U.S. senator from Illinois Stephen A. Douglas (q.v.), gave to challenger Abraham Lincoln's (q.v.) Freeport Question (q.v.) is known as the Freeport Doctrine. Douglas asserted that slavery could be kept out of the Western territories if no positive law were enacted in the territory in question endorsing slavery as an institution. Without such a law, slavery could not exist in any locality. His answer revealed Douglas' duplicity on the slavery issue to the South and cost him support for the Democrat nomination in the election of 1860 (qq.v.).

FREEPORT QUESTION. In the 1858 Lincoln–Douglas Debates (q.v.) during the race for the U.S. senatorial seat from Illinois, Republican candidate Abraham Lincoln (qq.v.) asked his Democrat opponent, Stephen A. Douglas (qq.v.), whether slavery could be prohibited in a territory despite the recent U.S. Supreme Court decision in the case of Dred Scott *v.* Sandford, which said it could not. This placed Douglas on the horns of a dilemma. If he answered, "yes," he would probably win reelection to the U.S. Senate and alienate the South and lose its critical support for the presidential election of 1860 (q.v.). If he said, "no," he would keep Southern support for the upcoming presidential election, but probably lose the Senate seat to Lincoln. Douglas took his bridges one at a time and answered in the affirmative, his answer being known as the Freeport Doctrine (q.v.).

FREE SOIL PARTY. By the early 1840s, the antislavery (q.v.) movement had slowly diverged into two wings: those who wanted to use the political system to reform the government and the Constitution to eliminate slavery and those who refused to take part in a system they viewed as too corrupted by slavery to be saved. The former organized themselves as the Liberty Party to contest for local, state, and national political offices. Although the Liberty Party did little in the election of 1840, by 1844, it ran a national ticket for president and vice president, under James G. Birney and Thomas Morris, opposing the annexation of Texas as a slave state. Although its national support was small (63,000), it fielded enough votes in New York and Michigan to shift them from the Whigs (q.v.) to the Democrats (q.v.), giving James K. Polk the presidency.

By 1848, it had become evident that a political party tied closely to abolition (q.v.) would not appeal to enough voters. With the introduction of the Wilmot Proviso (q.v.) proposing that slavery be prohibited from any of the new territories acquired in the War with Mexico, the Liberty Party, led by

Salmon P. Chase (q.v.) and John P. Hale, decided to drop its label and join with Conscience Whigs, led by Charles Sumner (q.v.) and Charles Francis Adams, and Free Soil Democrats, led by ex-president Martin Van Buren and David Wilmot, to become the Free Soil Party. Meeting in Buffalo, New York, the party nominated Van Buren and Adams and declared themselves for "Free Soil, Free Labor, and Free Men" (q.v.) and often expanded to include "Free Speech."

Losing to the national tickets of the Whigs (Zachary Taylor and Millard Fillmore [qq.v.]) and Democrats (Lewis Cass [q.v.]), the election of 1848 (q.v.) for the Free Soil Party was notable for destroying Van Buren's political career (as a born political opportunist, he was not ideologically pure) and sending Chase and Hale to the U.S. Senate and 14 men to Congress, including George W. Julian (q.v.) of Indiana, later Republican (q.v.) congressman of note. These men all opposed the Compromise of 1850 (q.v.), but in vain.

In the election of 1852 (q.v.), led by Hale and Julian, the Free Soil Party ran on opposition to the Compromise of 1850, the national sin and crime of slavery, and the Fugitive Slave Act (q.v.). Losing out again to the Democrats (Franklin Pierce [q.v.]) and Whigs (Winfield Scott [q.v.]), the Free Soil Party merged with the new Republican Party in 1854 and supported it in the election of 1856 (q.v.).

FRÉMONT, JOHN CHARLES (1813–1890). Born in Savannah, Georgia, John Charles Frémont was educated in Charleston, South Carolina. He taught mathematics for the navy before he received a commission as second lieutenant in the army topographical corps. He explored the watershed between the Missouri and the Mississippi Rivers under Joseph N. Nicollet in the late 1830s. In 1841, he married Jessie Benton, the daughter of the influential U.S. senator from Missouri, Thomas Hart Benton, who promoted Frémont's career the rest of his life. His wife was an accomplished publicist and writer in her own right, and she edited Frémont's diaries on his three 1840 Western expeditions that made him a household name in the United States as the "Pathfinder."

Frémont started by exploring the Oregon Trail, then the headwaters of the Arkansas and the Río Grande into the Great Basin, and then a third trip to California. In California, he was ordered out by the Mexican administrators just before the start of the War with Mexico. Informed of the war's start, Frémont (assisted, as in all of his expeditions, by Christopher "Kit" Carson, the mountain man, as scout) returned to play a pivotal role in the Bear Flag Revolution in northern California. Frémont's men campaigned southward, meeting Brig. Gen. Stephen W. Kearney's expedition coming in from the conquest of New Mexico.

The two men quarreled immediately over command arrangements. Frémont considered himself to be independent of Kearney and a representative of the California revolution. Kearney saw only a lieutenant. Frémont went back to

Washington for a court-martial. Despite his father-in-law's influence with President James L. Polk and the president's remission of a guilty sentence for mutiny and disobedience of orders, Frémont needed something to regain his reputation. He undertook a fourth expedition in the mountains of southern Colorado, which turned into disaster when a winter storm isolated the men. Cannibalism was the result as Frémont let every man fend for himself.

Frémont returned to California and served as U.S. senator. He then became the first Republican Party (q.v.) nominee for president in the election of 1856 (q.v.), revealing to the North that it could capture the presidency if it kept what Frémont won and picked up Pennsylvania and Illinois or Indiana in 1860. Unfortunately for Frémont, the man picked to achieve that goal was Abraham Lincoln (q.v.).

Knowing the party's debt to Frémont, Lincoln appointed him to command the Department of the West out of St. Louis. There Frémont revealed himself to be a poor general, befuddled much as he had been when his fourth expedition had foundered in the snow in southern Colorado. But as an intriguer, Frémont was without peer, proving that Kearney had been right in 1848. He handed out military contracts to shady war profiteers, surrounded himself with a bunch of incompetent foreign aides in fancy dress, quarreled with the politically prominent Blair family, and proceeded to free all the slaves in his command area without consulting with Lincoln first.

When Lincoln rescinded the emancipation order and tried to replace Frémont, wife Jessie went to Washington and told Lincoln off. Frémont hid behind his military guards to keep Lincoln's order relieving him from command from getting to him. Finally the adjutant disguised himself as a farmer and served the order.

Frémont went to West Virginia next, had a run-in with Confederate Maj. Gen. Stonewall Jackson (q.v.) in the Shenandoah, and refused to serve under Maj. Gen. John Pope (q.v.), whose commission was newer than his, in the Second Manassas Campaign (q.v.). Frémont spent the rest of the war in New York City awaiting orders that never came. In 1864, he represented the Radical Democracy (q.v.) in opposing Lincoln's renomination for president, only to withdraw his candidacy under pressure. After the war, he served as governor of Arizona Territory (he spent most of his time in the East lobbying for his mining interests) and bilked French investors in the transcontinental railroad (for which he was tried and found guilty in a French court *in absentia*). He hoped to retire to his California ranch, but died from food poisoning in New York state in 1890, after being replaced on the army's retired list as major general.

FRONT ROYAL, BATTLE OF. *See* SHENANDOAH VALLEY CAMPAIGN, FIRST (JACKSON'S).

FT. DELAWARE. The most dreaded Federal installation that housed Confederate prisoners of war, because of the brutality of the guards and the Delaware River's tides, which flooded the prison twice a day. *See also* PRISONS.

FUGITIVE SLAVE ACT OF 1850. Part of the Compromise of 1850 (q.v.), the Fugitive Slave Act rested on the Southern interpretation of the extraterritoriality of slavery (q.v.), which maintained that under the U.S. Constitution, the right of slaveholders was to be secure in holding their slaves beyond their home state in both other slave states and free states. Under this law, jury trials were denied in fugitive cases, which were to be heard before a special, Federal commissioner, who received twice the fee if the African-American were found to be still a slave. The commissioner's decision was an answer to any state application for a writ of *habeas corpus* (q.v.) from any other court, state or Federal. Moreover, the commissioner could call upon any citizen to act with him as a *posse comitatus* to help arrest and hold any fugitive slave. Northern states moved immediately to make it a state crime for any state official to assist a Federal commissioner. These laws were called personal liberty laws. The U.S. Supreme Court ruled in 1859 in Ableman *v.* Booth (q.v.) that the Fugitive Slave Act was a valid application of Federal power against state rights, and that the personal liberty laws were unconstitutional, as the states had given up such rights to join the Union.

FUTURE LOYALTY, OATH OF. *See* OATHS OF ALLEGIANCE.

G

GAINES' MILL, BATTLE OF. *See* SEVEN DAYS CAMPAIGN.

GALVANIZED YANKEES. During the Civil War, Union troops were pulled out of the Plains and the Far West to fight in the east. To make up the shortfall after the Sioux Uprising (q.v.) in Minnesota, the Federals recruited six regiments of Confederate prisoners of war to serve on the Plains as infantry. Numbered the 1st–6th U.S. Volunteers, these "Galvanized Yankees" came from various prisons (q.v.) in the Western Theater, like Camps Douglas, Rock Island, Chase, and Morton. Point Lookout, Maryland, was the only camp in the Eastern Theater to contribute men. They served from September 1864 to November 1866, opening up the trails to Oregon and California, and manned forts in western Minnesota and along the Missouri.

The Galvanized Yankees were formed during the election of 1864, partly to lessen the need of conscription in key Northern states that President Abraham Lincoln (q.v.) had to win to get reelected. Initially it was hoped to get Rebel prisoners to take the oath of future loyalty and serve in the U.S. Navy or in U.S. Army units against the Confederate South. But there was much opposition to enlisting former Confederates in the Union forces and much resistance among Confederates to serving in blue uniform against the Confederacy. Both of these qualms were overcome by sending the ex-Rebels onto the Plains. Although the 11th Ohio Volunteer Cavalry was not too pleased at having several of its companies filled by Confederate recruits, the conduct of all the Galvanized Yankees in the field was exemplary.

GALVESTON, SURRENDER AT. With the surrender of Gen. Robert E. Lee at the end of the Appomattox Campaign, Johnston at Durham Station at the end of the Carolinas Campaign, and Richard Taylor at Citronelle (qq.v.), Alabama, the only organized Confederate army left in the field was that of Lt. Gen. Edmund Kirby Smith (q.v.) in the Trans-Mississippi at Shreveport, Louisiana. Although plenty of military and civilian political leaders wanted to fight on, Kirby Smith really had no choice but to negotiate the best terms he could. His men were deserting in droves and stealing public property without much regard to consequences.

Union military authorities made several efforts to contact Kirby Smith and set up surrender talks. Maj. Gen. John Pope (q.v.) at St. Louis sent an aide who offered to allow Kirby Smith the same terms as given Lee. Kirby Smith refused. As head of the Trans-Mississippi, Kirby Smith had a more governmental function, and he wanted to consult with the governors of the states he defended. On May 13, the same day that the Confederates won the last recognized battle of the Civil War at Palmetto Ranch (q.v.), Kirby Smith and Governors Henry W. Allen of Louisiana, Harris Flanigan of Arkansas, Pendleton Murrah of Texas (through his aide, Col. Guy Bryan, as he was home sick), and Thomas C. Reynolds of Missouri drew up a set of terms that asked for all military officers and men to be allowed to return home, immunity granted for offenses committed against the United States during the war, all surrendered personnel to retain their arms and leave the United States if they so desired, the recognition of existing state governments, and the permission of these governments to preserve all law and order through their own militias.

There was no way that Secretary of War Edwin McM. Stanton (q.v.) would allow such political terms to be negotiated by generals in the field. These were prerogatives of the president of the United States and Congress to discuss and present to the surrendered South as demands for peace. With troops going home, Kirby Smith and the governors lacked the power to do much of anything. So Kirby Smith sent Maj. Gen. Simon Bolivar Buckner to New Orleans to negotiate with Maj. Gen. E. R. S. Canby (q.v.), who had already accepted the surrender of Taylor. After a prolonged discussion, Canby convinced Buckner that no political decisions would be allowed. He proposed to grant the whole Trans-Mississippi the same terms he gave Taylor—all public property to be turned over to Federal provost marshals, the officers and men paroled, and public transportation made available whenever practicable. Buckner accepted these terms on May 26.

Before Buckner could contact Kirby Smith, who was on his way to Galveston, Maj. Gen. John Magruder and Governor Murrah tried to get separate terms for Texas. They sent William P. Ballinger and Col. Ashbel Smith to talk to Canby on May 29. Once again, Canby met and talked but declined to allow any political settlement to be made, such as allowing Texas to rejoin the Union through the convening of its legislature and a convention to repeal secession. Meanwhile, Kirby Smith boarded a United States warship at Galveston and signed the Canby–Buckner Convention. It would be three weeks until an army of occupation could be assembled and landed at Galveston. Maj. Gen. Gordon Granger came over from Mobile on June 19 and took over for the Federal government. One of his first orders of the day was to issue a military edict of emancipation for Texas slaves, the fabled Juneteenth (q.v.), so celebrated to this day in the Great Southwest.

GARLAND, *EX PARTE* (1866). At the same time that it limited the use of military tribunals in wartime in *ex parte* Milligan (q.v.), the Supreme Court ruled on the use of test oaths. If loyalty oaths were administered as a part of punishment, they were unconstitutional bills of attainder or *ex post facto* laws. But if they were drawn up as qualification requirements for public office, loyalty oaths were valid exercises of power by Congress or any state legislature. The problem was, of course, that during Reconstruction the test oaths were being administered as punishment for past actions. At least that is what the Supreme Court believed. In Cummings *v.* Missouri (1866) and *ex parte* Garland (1866), the court ruled that loyalty oaths like the ironclad oath were being used to punish white Southerners for past action rather than as qualifications for a future public position or voting.

Once again, Radical Republicans saw the court as a potential snag in their program for improving civilization in the South by introducing Yankee notions and institutions sanctified by the Northern field victory in the Civil War. The new Federal appellate court for the District of Columbia defied the Supreme Court decisions in Cummings and Garland with a bit of legal sleight-of-hand. They ruled that a member of the D.C. bar under the previous Federal circuit court who had served with the Confederate army had to take the test oath, as he was seeking membership anew under a court that had previously not existed under the same name (even though for all practical purposes it was the same body). There were other foot-draggers (West Virginia refused to admit ex-Confederates to the bar even though the Supreme Court decisions implied that they should), but the problem eventually disappeared by the 1870s, when pardons and new constitutions in the South eliminated the test oath as a requirement.

GEARY, JOHN W. (1819–1873). A Pennsylvanian with influence in the Democratic Party (q.v.), John Geary worked as a surveyor and civil engineer before he volunteered for the War with Mexico. After the war, he went to California to set up its postal system and served as first mayor of San Francisco. Working mines in western Virginia with slave labor, he declined appointment as governor of Utah Territory to go to Kansas at the end of the Franklin Pierce (q.v.) administration. There he managed to put an end to the shooting part of the Kansas–Missouri Border Wars (q.v.) by a judicious use of the army, violating the concept of popular sovereignty. During the Civil War, Geary served as a division commander in the III (Army of Virginia), XII (Army of the Potomac), and XX (Army of Georgia) corps. He fought in the Second Manassas Campaign, the Chancellorsville Campaign, the Pennsylvania Campaign, the Chattanooga Campaign, and the March to the Sea (qq.v.). After the war, he was military governor of Savannah, Georgia, and elected governor of Pennsylvania. He died from the prolonged effect of a war wound suffered in the Second Manassas Campaign at Cedar Mountain.

GENERAL AMNESTY ACT (1872, 1898). *See* PARDON, AMNESTY, AND PAROLE.

GENERAL ORDERS NO. 100. Written by a Prussian immigrant and renowned legal expert, Francis Lieber, reviewed by a board of officers supervised by Bvt. Maj. Gen. Ethan Allen Hitchcock, and edited for distribution by Bvt. Maj. Gen. Henry W. Halleck (q.v.), General Orders No. 100 was based on Bvt. Lt. Gen. Winfield Scott's (q.v.) occupation orders in Mexico, a bit of Grotius, and the wartime experience of various Union generals, with a strong dose of Radical Republican abolitionism (q.v.) for good measure. It was designed to prove Yankee war conduct and objectives were well within the realm of Western morality and international law. Often referred to as the "Lieber Code," General Orders No. 100 defined "civil war" as a conflict between two or more portions of a nation, "each contending for the mastery of the whole, each claiming to be the legitimate government." The South's secession was declared a "rebellion," or "insurrection of a long extent," a rising of a portion of the people against their legitimate government with the desire to "throw off their allegiance to it, and set up a government of their own." The treatment of captured Rebels as prisoners of war, the proclamation of martial law in Rebel territory, the honoring of Rebel flags of truce, or a willingness to negotiate with Rebel leaders did not legitimatize their struggle or promise pardon or amnesty to any or all, a statement that echoed the U.S. Supreme Court's prior holding in the Prize Cases (1863) (qq.v.).

Further, General Orders No. 100 stated that "martial law was the direct outcome of enemy occupation or conquest." It did not have to be formally declared, and it would continue until canceled by special mention in a treaty of peace or by presidential proclamation. Martial law permitted local military officers to suspend the normal civil and criminal laws and substitute "military rule and force" and dictate all laws on the basis of "military necessity." The latter term was defined as "those measures which are indispensable for securing the ends of the war, and which are lawful according to the natural law and useages of war." This allowed the annihilation of armed enemies but prohibited cruelty toward unarmed civilians or the undue destruction of their private property. In return, the conquered population was expected to admit to outward loyalty toward the occupation forces. At all times, the Lieber Code recognized the Army's right to treat those truly loyal persons by a different standard than suspect civil inhabitants. Military commissions were to be established to enforce martial law, but the commander could, if he deemed it reasonable, merely order the continuance of local law and custom under his supervision, rather than replace them with his own ordinances. Technically, however, legislative, executive, and judicial functions of the occupied area's government ceased under martial law. These functions, like the right to tax, for example, were to be administered by the occupation forces.

The effects of General Orders No. 100 are still open to much controversy. The Supreme Court took favorable notice of it a year after it was issued in *ex parte* Vallandigham (1864) (q.v.), it was translated into German at the end of the war (Lieber's native tongue), it was copied by numerous European nations during the last half of the 19th century and made the basis of the Hague Agreements on the civilized rules of warfare (a sort of contradiction in terms) at the turn of the century, it became a standard for the occupation of the Spanish empire during the Spanish–American War at the end of the century and a guide for Army officers suppressing the Philippine Insurrection, and it guided the Rhine Occupation after World War I and the German and Japanese Occupations after World War II. Yet, in spite of this favorable worldwide influence of the Lieber Code and Army efforts to publicize it at the end of the Civil War, there is good reason to doubt that Reconstruction Army officers were fully, if at all, cognizant of its implications. Although the conduct of Union soldiers during the war was by and large in agreement with the code, this may have been accidental rather than intentional. Yankee troop conduct might better be traced to length of service of the soldiers, the weeding out of irresponsible officers, and the zealous efforts of General Halleck to ensure a decent standard of conduct, without necessarily referring to the order itself.

Even if the code were known, there is no record of the high command referring its Reconstruction commanders to the General Orders No. 100. Commanders in the field did not refer to it or suggest its contents to subordinates for a guide. It was not included in any of the orders traditionally passed from one command to another. And the code itself was nothing more than a set of guidelines that left much discretion in behavior by each commander and his subordinates. The main reason may be that military government developed independently and ahead of the Lieber Code.

GEORGIA PLATFORM. *See* COMPROMISE OF 1850.

GEORGIA, STATE OF, *v.* GRANT *ET AL.* (1868). Temporarily foiled in its efforts to get out of enforcing the Military Reconstruction Acts (q.v.) in Georgia *v.* Stanton (q.v.), Georgia refused to advance money from its state treasury to meet the expenses of Reconstruction (particularly in not paying for the state convention required by the Military Acts). This was an attempt to raise the issue of property, the funds of the state treasury ordered by the Army to pay for the state constitutional convention that the Military Reconstruction Acts required the Army to convene. Governor Charles J. Jenkins removed the state's money to New York and filed the suit Georgia *v.* Grant *et al.* (1868) to prevent the Army from recovering it. In return, the Army seized a state-owned railroad to get some money for the convention. But a key question arose as to whether Georgia was really a state with rights to sue, so the case was held off until this question was established under other pending suits.

GEORGIA, STATE OF, v. STANTON (1867). Provisional Governor Charles J. Jenkins of Georgia sued Secretary of War Edwin McM. Stanton (q.v.), the man directly responsible for enforcing the Military Reconstruction Acts (q.v.). Mississippi, defeated in its prior attempt to sue President Andrew Johnson in Mississippi v. Johnson (qq.v.), also filed a separate but similarly argued case against the secretary. They argued that the congressional laws interfered with an already constituted government by imposing an unconstitutional form of military rule. The court dismissed both suits, declaring that determining the republican form of government was properly a political question of sovereignty or the existence of a state and reserved to Congress. The court could only rule as to the rights of persons and property. If Congress seated or refused to seat a state government's representatives, then the question was settled.

GETTYSBURG, BATTLE OF. See PENNSYLVANIA CAMPAIGN.

GLENDALE, BATTLE OF. See SEVEN DAYS CAMPAIGN.

GLOBE TAVERN, BATTLE OF. See PETERSBURG, SIEGE OF.

GLORIETA, BATTLE OF. See NEW MEXICO–ARIZONA CAMPAIGN.

GOLD SCANDAL. During his first administration, the scandals that plagued President Ulysses S. Grant (q.v.) were more about his being too close to the malefactors rather than in with them. For instance, there was the Gold Scandal, which involved Grant's regime with the likes of Jim Fisk and Jay Gould, railroad and financial manipulators of note during the Civil War and Reconstruction.

In 1869, Gould decided to go to work on the biggest "rube" of all, President Grant. In league with Fisk, he began to buy gold, to force up its price. The plan was to buy and buy until the market became overheated and then suddenly sell, leaving the speculators with the crash when reality struck. The whole plan depended on the U.S. government keeping its supply of gold off the market. If the government stepped in, the price would crash prematurely, leaving Fisk and Gould in the lurch, too. The rail magnates thought they had Grant's agreement to hold the treasury in check. But Grant never understood what was going on and finally authorized the treasury to inject its gold into the market to stabilize it. Gould found out about the government move; Fisk did not. Gould saw no reason to tell his partner in crime as he shifted all of his options to sell. The next day, Fisk went under with the rest of the speculators, and Gould alone made money. *See* GRANT, ULYSSES S., ADMINISTRATION—SCANDALS.

GOLDEN CIRCLE, KNIGHTS OF THE. *See* FILIBUSTERING.

GOSPEL OF WEALTH. *See* SOCIAL DARWINISM.

GRAND GULF, BATTLE OF. *See* VICKSBURG CAMPAIGN.

GRANT, [HIRAM] ULYSSES S., LIFE AND MILITARY CAREER (1822–1885). Hiram Ulysses Grant was born at Point Pleasant, Ohio, on 27 April 1822. He came from a solid middle class family; his father was a farmer and a tanner, a trade the young Grant never warmed to. Biographers used to talk of Grant's miserable youth, his happiness constantly interrupted by his braggart father, who kept reminding him of his boyhood blunders. But nowadays historians think that Grant's alleged childhood unhappiness never really existed. He was an excellent horseman by nature, and neighbors liked to have him gentle horses for them. He was a superb rider and teamster at an early age. He attended local schools and academies and had a fairly good education for his day. His father was a local politician of sorts, a talent he would never let go of, and he managed to get his son an appointment at West Point—a free education, and one of the best then available.

According to the tale, Grant took a look at his trunk around the time of the appointment and realized his initials spelled out "HUG." He was aware of the penchant of cadets to make up nicknames, and asked Congressman Thomas L. Hamer to put him down on the appointment sheet as "Ulysses Hiram Grant." But Hamer could not remember the "Hiram" part, everybody called him "Ulyss" anyhow, so he registered the boy as "Ulysses Simpson," that being his mother's maiden name. Grant arrived at the Point and signed in as "Ulysses Hiram Grant" and was informed no such name was on the roll. There was a "Ulysses Simpson Grant," however. Grant, ever practical with nonsensical regulations, scratched out his signature and scrawled "U. S. Grant," and so he stayed the rest of his life. His nickname was "Sam" as in "Uncle Sam"—he could live with all that. Besides, "Ulysses" was too close to his father's cutting, and all-too-commonly used moniker, "Useless," to suit him.

Grant did well at West Point. He excelled in horsemanship, was above average in mathematics and engineering, and survived the rest of the course to graduate 21 out of 39 in 1843. In those days, one did not receive a commission as a second lieutenant automatically. A vacancy had to open up somewhere in the small Army first. So he became a brevet second lieutenant, a temporary appointment, in the Fourth Infantry, and was off to Jefferson Barracks near St. Louis. There he met a local planter's daughter, Julia Dent, whom he would marry when he came home from Mexico. He finally received a full second lieutenancy in the Eighth Infantry and was shipped off to Texas to guard against Mexican intrusions over the Rio Grande into the disputed area south of the Nueces. In this capacity, he fought under Maj. Gen. Zachary Taylor (q.v.) in the early battles of the Mexican War. He learned from the ragged-looking Taylor that calmness under fire and solid thinking meant more than spit and polish in a general.

When the main American campaign against Mexico City was launched, Grant's regiment was transferred to Maj. Gen. Winfield Scott's (q.v.) command. Grant served as his regimental supply officer and learned that an army supply line did not have to stretch to an attackable base if the force could live of the country. Scott also showed that a little imagination and not letting the enemy spook you could pay big dividends in a campaign. He learned from both men that one must not allow oneself to get involved with civilian policy decisions—a matter that cost Taylor and Scott much worry in Mexico. Grant also showed himself to be a brave officer, hauling a small cannon into one of the custom house towers outside Mexico City to cover the infantry assault.

Returning home to marry Julia, Grant served with his regiment at Sackett's Harbor, New York, and then was transferred to the Pacific Coast. He could not afford to take Julia with him, and in California, the lonely captain (having been promoted for bravery in Mexico) took to drink. He became an embarrassment to his colonel, Robert C. Buchanan, a stickler for military discipline, and a man who disliked the young officer from St. Louis days. Buchanan offered Grant a choice of court-martial or resignation. The homesick captain turned in his commission and went back to Julia. In Missouri, Grant worked hard as a farmer and businessman but was wiped out in the Panic of 1857. So he went back to his parents' home, now in Galena, Illinois, and worked in his father's store, a humiliating experience.

When the Civil War came, Grant thought enough of his own abilities to ask for a regimental command and through his congressman, Elihu Washburne, became colonel of the 21st Illinois Volunteer Infantry. His abilities at turning this raw company of men into a top-notch regiment impressed the right people (Congressman Washburne saw to that), and President Abraham Lincoln (q.v.) made him a brigadier general. Grant was on his way to fame. He was a very lucky man, one of the qualities of any good officer, because he got to work his way up from smaller to bigger unit command and from skirmishes to battles. Thus he gained his experience in nice little steps that allowed him to digest the lessons he gained from command. He also happened to be in the right place at the right time to make an impact on the course of the war. His opponents happened to be pretty poor early in the war, which helped him a lot, as at Fort Donelson (q.v.), where he became the first Union general to capture a whole enemy army. His terms to the Confederates, "unconditional surrender," not only jibed with his initials, but made for good news copy.

Grant kept moving south into the Tennessee and Cumberland Valleys, where he was surprised by the Rebel army at Shiloh Church (q.v.) near Pittsburgh Landing, Tennessee. Although Grant's men took a shellacking on the first day, he kept his cool and drove the Confederates back a day later, holding the field. Rumors that Grant was drunk (he was not) caused Lincoln to make the statement to find out what brand of whiskey it was so he could send a barrel to his other generals. Lincoln refused to sack Grant. "He fights" was the president's simple analysis. Instead, Grant got a promotion to major general and the task of taking the Confederate fortress at Vicksburg (q.v.). He kept at the project the better part of a year, finally cutting loose from his supply line and (like Scott in Mexico) moving around the Rebels' south flank to bottle them up in the city. It fell after a short siege on Independence Day, the day after the Union victory at Gettysburg. Grant had captured his second Confederate field army. Later that same year, after Yankee defeats south of Chattanooga (q.v.), Grant transferred there, broke the Rebel siege of the town, and routed their army.

By now, it became obvious to the men at Washington that Grant had to be brought east to fight the Confederacy's first team, Robert E. Lee's (q.v.) Army of Northern Virginia. At the same time, he became lieutenant general and commander of all Union armies. He decided to accompany the Army of the Potomac in the field, both to avoid Washington politics and to keep an eye on the fight against Lee. Although the Richmond or Overland Campaign (q.v.) of 1864 was a frustrating experience for Grant, he never lost sight of his objective. Despite losing nearly 100,000 casualties (earning the nickname "butcher," although he actually lost fewer men proportionally than Lee during the war), Grant kept moving southward and managed to bottle Lee up in Petersburg (q.v.). It would take nine months to force Lee into the open and corner his force at Appomattox Courthouse through a brilliant campaign of rapid maneuver. Lee's surrender marked the third time a Confederate field force had given up to the man whose pre–Civil War experiences one historian characterized as "40 years of failure." Now he was the hero of the Northern war effort.

The Civil War had made Grant. Although the nation was plunged into despair by Lincoln's assassination, Grant allowed it to revive itself by honoring him. He reviewed the massed armies in Washington in May 1865 and toured the North, receiving several college degrees and the plaudits of a grateful nation. During Reconstruction, Grant at first favored President Andrew

Johnson's (q.v.) go-easy plan. He toured the Southeast for the president and reported favorably on the willingness of the South's leaders to come back into the Union and recognize the results of the war. But as Johnson and Congress came to blows over the course of Reconstruction, Grant began to change his course. In the 1866 "Swing Around the Circle" (q.v.), when Johnson took Grant and other dignitaries around the country with him to campaign for Democrat (q.v.) congressmen, Grant backed off halfway through the trip and abandoned the president to his fate. He also deeply resented the president's effort to involve him in the squabble over the Tenure of Office Act (q.v.).

When the Republicans lost the impeachment (q.v.) of Johnson, they began to look around for a candidate who could unite the North behind their Reconstruction efforts. Nominated by acclamation, Grant handily beat his Democrat opponent in the electoral vote, although the popular vote was quite close. As president, Grant made a good general. His inexperience in civil administration, lack of political finesse, and reticence and taciturnity made him defer to Congress in most matters. Actually, unrecognized by most historians, Grant's concept of the presidency (q.v.) was an old Whig theory from the 1830s.

But he tended to defer too much to his alleged friends, and the result was that his administration was tainted with corruption from the start. For cabinet positions, he tended to pick businessmen who little understood government. He appointed them much as a general would his staff, rarely asking them if they could serve and often overlooking their lack of qualifications or conflicts of interest. He deferred to Congress in his domestic policy (q.v.), to the state department in his foreign policy, and to his friends, who led the personally honest president down the road to scandal (q.v.).

Grant's Reconstruction program (q.v.) brought the South back into the nation but led to the Army's policing a series of "rotten boroughs," whose votes went to the highest bidder. Accused by many modern writers of being a racist, Grant had one distinction above most of his day—he honestly believed in equal rights under the law. He just was not a good enough politician to bring it all off. And that remains his tragedy. Sometimes decency is not enough. By the end of his eight years, Grant's reputation as president had been stained so badly that he has yet to come out of it, historically speaking.

Although certain of his cronies spoke of a third term, and Grant himself wanted one as he was flat broke after a prolonged world tour, he retired to New York and went into private business. His success was no better now than before the war. Heavily in debt, the heavy-smoking Grant learned that he was stricken with oral and throat cancer. He had received many boxes of cigars as gifts during the war from a grateful North, and the shy Grant took up smoking so as not to offend his public. The habit had finally caught up with him. He wrote his memoirs to clear up his debts and leave his family with something after his passing, even though Congress had restored him to his rank and voted him a pension. He wrote under tremendous pain, valiantly holding on until the task was finished. Edited by Mark Twain, who found Grant to be a natural writer, the memoirs became a best-seller. But Grant had died in July 1885, before their publication, and was interred in the great mausoleum at Riverside Park in New York City overlooking the Hudson. *See also* DIPLO-MACY, U.S.—RECONSTRUCTION; GRANT, ULYSSES S., ADMINIS-TRATION—CONCEPT OF THE PRESIDENCY; GRANT, ULYSSES S., ADMINISTRATION—DOMESTIC POLICIES; GRANT, ULYSSES S., ADMINISTRATION—RECONSTRUCTION; GRANT, ULYSSES S., AD-MINISTRATION—SCANDALS.

GRANT, ULYSSES S., ADMINISTRATION—CONCEPT OF THE PRESIDENCY. Along with Zachary Taylor (q.v.) and Dwight D. Eisen-hower, Ulysses S. Grant was one of America's three professional military men as president. Many others had military experience, but were not career soldiers. They were generally professional politicians or came through the political world. All of the military presidents were similar in one salient fact—they did not understand the role of the presidency in American politics. They thought as top dog all they had to do was issue an order and it would be carried out. In politics, the order becomes a proposal that may never see the light of day.

Of the military presidents, Grant was especially ignorant of what the po-litical world was like. By the time he caught on, a lot of really bad mistakes had already been made. He started off with the mistaken belief that Congress was the sovereign voice of the people and that the president was merely their deputy. So when Congress spoke out on an issue, Grant felt obliged to go along with it and not throw in his opinion. Of course, the American system is predicated on the president combating Congress to reach a consensus. Like other military presidents, Grant did relatively little with the power he had. He acted as if he were still a general in the Army—he carried out the orders of his superiors, the civilian branch of government. He was little more than an administrative officer. This was Grant's greatest tragedy as president, because he served at a time when America needed an imaginative executive to reconstruct the nation. Without Grant actively taking a role, his administra-tion became bogged down in the morals (or lack of them), economics, corrup-tion, and submission to the desires of big business. Grant was too willing to do the bidding of others. Worst of all, he took the advice of the wrong people.

What Grant wanted was noble. He hoped to help the nation make a transi-tion from war to peace, restore the currency, balance the budget, promote economic expansion, and reunite the North and South without sacrificing the position of black Americans as a freed people in the process. What he found out was that the ways of government are tricky. The few decisions he made got twisted around as they progressed down the ladder of control and came out as unrecognizable from the policy he desired. Actually, the very purity of Grant's motives worked against him. He had to make deals with shabby politicians, whom he disliked, to get anywhere, and by the time he understood all of this, it was too late. He had become a victim of the system.

An example of how Grant worked as president came to the fore almost immediately as he picked his cabinet. In making his appointments, Grant consulted with none of the party big-wigs, or even with the men he chose. Many like to point to this as a sign of Grant's independence from the politicians. But the system works with the politicians being able to funnel patronage to the deserving, those who supported the party with money or deeds. Grant angered both Republicans and Democrats (qq.v.) by ignoring them. He also revealed that he was a babe in the woods, ripe for the plucking in the future.

Grant had two considerations when it came to choosing cabinet members. He wanted to act independently of both parties, and he did not want to be overshadowed by big names, as he felt Abraham Lincoln (q.v.) had been with William H. Seward, Salmon P. Chase, Edwin McM. Stanton (qq.v.), and others (not thinking that Lincoln had relished the challenge and believed that these men were better used in a valuable post where he could keep an eye on them than off somewhere making trouble independently).

Grant got off to a bad start by giving two important cabinet posts out as personal compliments, with the understanding that the recipients would resign shortly. This was great for his old congressman friend, Elihu Washburn, who became secretary of state, and Maj. Gen. John Schofield (q.v.), who took the portfolio of secretary of war. But this cheapened the positions in the eyes of many, especially after Schofield left the post in one week! Washburn was not so abrupt, but eventually the posts went to two important men, State to Hamilton Fish (q.v.), arguably the best single appointment Grant ever made, and War to John Rawlins, the most important person from Grant's old wartime staff. It was Rawlins who made Grant's military staff function, and he who kept Grant on the straight and narrow in a multitude of questions from slavery to not drinking. Perhaps the worst event of Grant's early presidency was Rawlins' unexpected death in 1869. It left him without the political skills that Rawlins supplied and that Grant lacked. Rawlins' presence would have undoubtedly made Grant a better president.

And so it went. Grant delighted in springing cabinet positions upon the unsuspecting and unqualified. A. E. Borie, a Pennsylvania businessman, came into Washington to introduce some friends to the president. Grant asked him if he knew who the man from Pennsylvania was. Borie did not and ignored the question, as it made no sense. The man was Borie himself, as he found out when he read his hometown newspaper and realized he had been nominated for secretary of the navy. He was not asked to serve. Grant gave him an order like a subaltern. Borie declined, then accepted after Grant called it a personal favor. His candidate for the Treasury was department store magnate and party contributor A. T. Stewart. Grant thought a successful businessman would save the country money through good management. But Stewart was ineligible to serve under an old law defining conflict of interest. Grant asked that he be exempted, but the Senate, led by Charles Sumner (q.v.) of Massachusetts, refused, hoping to teach Grant how important advice and consent were.

With such a cavalier attitude, it was no wonder that Grant appointed 25 men (excluding Schofield and Stewart) to serve him in seven cabinet positions over his two terms. (This compares with 29 for Theodore Roosevelt in eight years, 25 for Franklin D. Roosevelt in 13 years, and 23 for John Tyler in four years.) The Grant White House was known for its army camp atmosphere; indeed, his official wartime staff all received comparable positions under Grant as president. He was well aware how a commanding general ought to act, but he never really quite caught on to being a politician—although one of his main biographers thinks that he did better than might be expected in the long run.

GRANT, ULYSSES S., ADMINISTRATION—DOMESTIC POLICIES. The Civil War caused a tremendous business expansion in the North, the problems of which came to a head during the Ulysses S. Grant administration and would result in big business becoming a major voice in the party once dominated by farmers and small businessmen. The two problems of concern to business at this time were taxes and the tariff on foreign imports. The war had caused all taxes to rise precipitously and new ones, like the income tax (q.v.), to be imposed. At the same time, the Republicans (q.v.) had elevated the tariff to new heights as part of the fulfillment of their political platform. Now that the war was over, Americans expected relief on both counts. Everyone wanted taxes reduced, but the tariff was another matter. Business and labor groups wanted to exclude goods from lower-wage-paying producers overseas for better profits to owners and higher wages to American workers.

Grant appointed a blue-ribbon Special Tax Commission under David A. Wells, a professional economist once considered as a possible secretary of the treasury. Grant had promised lower taxes in his inaugural message and pledged economy in government to help reduce costs (as usual for an incoming administration). The Wells Committee took a look at the taxes and suggested that nearly all be repealed or reduced dramatically. This was very good publicity for the Republicans and raised their esteem among the voters. But Wells also suggested that the protective tariff be cut to nothing. He said that the tariff did not so much protect American infant industries from unfair foreign competition as it permitted existing industries to raise prices to just under the tariff costs to foreign competitors for extra unearned profits. Wells correctly saw that the difference came out of the pockets of American consumers.

The Republican Congress thanked Wells for his concern and lowered taxes as he suggested. But it kept the high tariff intact. It was too big a pork barrel issue—too many people of influence in the party were making money off the tariff differential. They all banded together and each voted for the tariff to protect themselves and everyone else. The Republicans were not above playing the tariff card in a wholly arbitrary manner. For example, they cut all tariffs 10 percent in 1872 to assist Republican congressmen win their seats, and then raised them back up after the victory. The tariff would be a political football like this until the New Deal of the 1930s, when Congress turned the tariff-making power over to the president, who used it as a treaty device through the Department of State.

Along with the tariff, civil service reform was a hot issue during the Grant years and after. Ever since the days of Andrew Jackson (1830s) the "spoils system" had been in operation as regarded government jobs on all levels. Jackson had theorized that anyone could work for the government—it took no special skills to push a pencil and file papers—and that for the sake of democracy, the principle of "rotation in office" ought to be practiced. This meant that incoming administrations fired all prior appointees for their own people. It was a great device to give the general public a stake in the outcome of elections and guarantee party loyalty. If a congressman did not vote a party line, someone else would get the patronage to his district. If the voter did not vote right, he could kiss off the local postmaster's job (in those days there was no secret ballot; one voted by public declaration at the polling place—often dangerous, as thugs from both sides supervised the process and administered punishment on the spot).

There had been many criticisms of the winner-take-all approach to government jobs. The problem got so bad that each election caused a hiatus in government services as the incoming new appointees took over and learned the job. Different succeeding presidents of the same party cleaned out their predecessor's job-seekers, regardless of party loyalty, putting it all on a very personal basis. Critics suggested that government jobs were more technical than Jackson had reckoned, and that skills needed to be known to function in them efficiently. Besides, jobs went to party contributors or were bought by competitive bidding, which led to much corruption. Civil Service became an imperative for honest government, although cynics would deem "honest government" an oxymoron.

The first improvement was to put forth merit examinations rather than party affiliation. This system had been introduced in various European countries to great effect, and American intellectuals wanted a similar improvement here. After all, the role of government was increasing and becoming more important year by year. The number of government slots had nearly tripled from the beginning of Abraham Lincoln's (q.v.) administration in 1861 to the end of Grant's in 1877. Grant seemed to agree with this assessment. At first he only appointed people to offices that had become vacant through death or resignation. But Grant's appointees were usually old Army buddies or relatives from his wife's family, the Dents, whose number appeared legion to neutral observers.

Congress did not like this approach. How were they to pay off all those dedicated campaign workers and monetary contributors? Congress found especially offensive the fact that Grant's father, Jesse, came to Washington and sought to control patronage on behalf of his many friends. Indeed, if a civil service exam were instituted, wags suggested, its only questions would be: "Were you a contributor to any of President Grant's three homes?" (he had homes in Galena, Philadelphia, and Washington—he had gotten rid of the one in New York City) and "Are you a member of the Dent family or otherwise connected by blood or marriage to General Grant?"

Grant indicated that he would be open to a deal on civil service appointments—a fairly astute move for a man considered to be too apolitical as president. If Congress would modify the Tenure of Office Act (q.v.), he would consult with congressmen in local appointments. So Congress allowed him the right to remove executive officials more freely without resort to the advice and consent provision, unless it found the change to be especially offensive. And Grant wound up approving as many a 150 appointments a day to local machine positions in consultation with the appropriate congressman, much to everyone's glee on Capitol Hill. But certain Republican reformers (who would later bolt from the party as Liberal Republican [q.v.] in 1872) wanted more. They introduced a civil service reform bill into the Senate, where it languished, bottled up in committee by the spoilsmen.

But Grant ignored the old pols in the Senate and went ahead and established an independent Civil Service Commission under an executive order. It was headed by George W. Curtis of *Harper's Weekly*, an influential national illustrated news magazine, and Joseph Medill of the *Chicago Tribune*, the Middle West's most important newspaper. Both men were active reformers who had trumpeted the civil service issue before the American public. Grant figured that if they wanted to see something done, they ought to do it themselves. The report of the Civil Service Commission arrived in the White House in December 1871. It recommended that Federal jobs be classified and each class divided into two grades. All positions should be filled by competitive exam. Promotions would also be made by a competency test. No political assessments would be levied (a common practice) against any appointee by any political group. Grant announced that the Commission's report seemed fair to him. The problem was that most positions of importance still had political input and came under the advice and consent of the Senate. Although Grant offered to continue the Commission's mandate, both Curtis and Medill realized that he would do little actively to encourage change. Neither Congress nor the public was sufficiently aroused, which postponed the matter until the assassination of James A. Garfield in 1881 changed everyone's perceptions.

But the first assault against public confidence in business and government came in 1873, well before the death of Garfield. The obvious corruption in government, the overextension of investors in railroad stocks of dubious quality, the overbuilding of transcontinental railroads, and the withdrawal of silver from circulation caused a major economic contraction and the failure of several New York banking firms, particularly Jay Cooke and Company. Known as the "Financier of the Civil War," the exclusive seller of government war bonds, and a major contributor to Republican campaign funds, Cooke was overextended in Northern Pacific Railroad stock and could not meet his debts. In his wake there was a run on banks throughout the nation, and some 5,000 businesses worth over $2.28 million failed. The Panic of 1873, as the depression came to be known, saw Grant suggesting a revolutionary concept for the first time in American history—that the government employ the poor to save them from ruination. But the idea was 60 years ahead of its time and dismissed in Congress as the ranting of a naïve general who did not understand reality.

The contraction of the economy meant that the Republican pledge to pay off the war bonds in gold was a heavier burden than usual. Following the rejection of Grant's suggestion of full employment, the public demanded that the government do something inflationary to relieve the stress. This naturally led to a reexamination of the money question. Next to Reconstruction, the money question was the hottest issue of the era. It had originated during the Civil War, when the Abraham Lincoln administration (q.v.) had taken the nation off the gold standard and began to pay its debts in paper currency called greenbacks (the color of the back of the bill). Over $450 million in paper currency was issued in 1862 and 1863 alone, and this created a whole series of problems. First, great inflation occurred that reduced the value of the paper dollar by half. Then there was the problem of redemption—would the government make them as good as gold after the war?

Finally, the money question was related to Civil War bonds. The bonds were issued in such a manner as to throw into question how they were to be paid off. They were 5-20 bonds. That meant that one could receive their face value in five years or hold them 20 years and get face value plus 6 percent interest. The law guaranteed that the interest would be paid in gold, but it was silent as to how the principal would be repaid. Many people favored the suggestion of Ohio congressman George Pendleton to pay off the principal in inflated paper dollars. This Ohio Idea had the appealing slogan, "The dollar that paid the soldier can pay the bondholder" (well, it appealed to veterans, anyhow). But the Republican platform under which Grant was elected pledged to pay off both principal and interest in gold. Grant refused to back down from this promise, as it would affect the reputation of the U.S. government as a borrower in the future. In 1869, Congress backed Grant up with the Public Credit Act, which said that the bonds would be paid in gold or its equivalent, nothing less.

But the bond question was an adjunct to the real debate, over the greenbacks themselves. As Grant well knew, there were two schools of thought on greenbacks. The first were the soft money people. These advocates were against resumption, making the greenbacks equal to gold and taking them out of circulation gradually as they were redeemed. This would contract the currency available in the economy. They preferred to keep the greenbacks in circulation to keep the money supply more flexible and slightly inflationary. This would help debtors who could pay back their loans in paper worth less than when they borrowed it. Several groups supported greenbacks. Politicians, mostly Democrats (q.v.), wanted to get away from the perennial Reconstruction (q.v.) issue and back into the economic questions that had been so good to the party before the Civil War. Oddly enough, some Republicans (especially small businessmen backed by the Radicals) stood with the Democrats here because of the middle class origins of their constituents.

Grant was aware that some businessmen also favored a flexible currency, especially those on the make who needed to borrow to succeed. Moderate inflation would make those debts easier to pay back. Labor also favored greenbacks, because it eased up on credit and made loans easier to pay back. They believed that this would give them an edge over the normally usurious bankers. This had an honored history in American economic thought, especially strong during the Jacksonian Era under a group called the Locofocos. Then there were the farmers. Traditionally, they had been against greenbacks, but the Civil War had changed that. To succeed, farmers now had to invest large sums in the new machines of agriculture, steam tractors, threshers, and cutting devices. Because of the lousy weather and poor prices that followed the war, farmers had gone from being creditors to debtors. They believed that the low prices were being set by gold-minded bankers and sought to attack them through easier credit and cheaper money. It was a fight that would see its 19th-century culmination in the Populist movement of the 1890s.

The second group on the money issue during Grant's presidency was the hard money interest. These people favored specie (actual coin minted from precious metals, usually gold alone, as silver was inflationary like paper, only to a lesser extent). There were all sorts of ways to get the United States back on the gold standard, including redeeming paper on a one-to-one basis and retiring it, but the gold bugs (as they were called) preferred that it be done quickly, cheaply, and as painlessly as possible. They too had several groups that supported their view. First came the Protestant churches. Hard money represented virtue and honesty. It was not right to borrow a dollar worth 100 cents and pay it back years later with dollars worth 50 cents (or whatever) of the original. Another group in favor of hard money were academics, especially economists. At that time, economic theory was closely related to religion, in that it had a strong moral strain and was classified as "moral philosophy." These men believed that capital (goods that made goods) was more important than money supply.

As Grant found out, the reformers of the era also stood behind hard money. These men were Liberal Republicans during Grant's terms and later labeled "mugwumps." They saw easy money as the root of all evil when it came to tempting politicians to go bad. They too wished to restore a moral tone to society and purge it of all corruptions, of which easy money was one. They tended to be based in New England and centered at Harvard University. Finally, certain businessmen were for hard money. These included bankers, merchants, and textile manufacturers; generally men who had money owed them. These were established businessmen, not on the make. They had their wealth and intended to keep it. Many were engaged in international trade, where gold was critical as a common unit of value among all currencies. This was the position of the National Board of Trade, for example.

In the middle of the soft money–hard money fight stood President Grant. He saw Republicans on both sides of an issue that threatened to split party and country, especially after the Panic of 1873 sent the debate to a fever pitch. Secretary of the Treasury Hugh McCulloch, a Republican who had served under Lincoln and Johnson, had been retiring greenbacks gradually since 1867. But the soft money people wanted this stopped. Grant's solution was to make greenbacks equal to gold. This would keep an inflationary amount of money in circulation but make it stable in value. It gave a little to both sides, again demonstrating that Grant was not an entirely stupid politician.

But before he could get Congress to go along, the Supreme Court stepped into the question with the Legal Tender Cases (q.v.). The court had as its chief justice at this time Salmon P. Chase (q.v.), former secretary of the treasury under Lincoln and a man constantly with his eye on the presidency. Chase had written the law in 1862 that had created the greenbacks. But he was always suspicious of them, acting in their favor only as an extreme war measure. He now decided to play for hard money support. In the case Hepburn v. Griswold (1871), he led the court in writing the majority decision that declared greenbacks to be legal tender only for debts contracted after 1862. The implication was that greenbacks might be of doubtful value even after that time, although the case stated otherwise.

The indecision of the Hepburn Case could not be allowed to continue. If greenbacks were later declared illegal for all debts, payments after 1862 would have to be renegotiated and repaid. It so happened that the Hepburn case had been decided by a court that was two members short. Grant had appointed William Strong and Joseph P. Bradley to the bench before Hepburn, but they had been unable to take their seats in time to participate. In 1871, another case, Knox *v*. Lee, arrived before the highest bench in the land. This time, with Strong and Bradley participating, the court reversed itself, the ever-flexible Chase again with the majority. In Knox, the court did the commonsense thing and ruled that greenbacks were legal tender for all debts. The court left it up to Congress as to what the greenbacks were worth compared to gold. Because the votes of Strong and Bradley were critical to the new ruling, Grant was accused of packing the court. This was not so. The president had appointed the two men with other considerations in mind before their views on money were known.

The court decisions threw the money issue back into the political area. In response to the Panic of 1873, Congress passed the Inflation Bill in 1874. This would have increased the number of greenbacks in circulation to alleviate the worst aspects of the depression. But Grant vetoed this as coming too late in the greenback odyssey. He essentially used the Protestant moral argument. But by doing so, he froze the money supply. Congress tried but failed to override his veto. Trying a different tack, Congress passed the Banking Act of 1874, which shifted some existing paper from East to West, where the short money supply had hit people hardest. As it did not increase the existing supply, Grant signed the measure into law. But something had to be done to unite the Republican Party over the money question in the election of 1876. The result was what Grant had originally proposed at the beginning of his administration. In the Specie Resumption Act, Congress provided that all greenbacks already in circulation would be kept until January 1, 1879. Then they could be redeemed in gold. But for each $80 of greenbacks turned in, $100 in new Federal bank notes could be issued. This gave the money a gold base and a moderate inflation and took the money issue out of the 1876 contest, much to the Republicans' relief.

After the election of 1876, the money question cropped up again and played a part in the not-too-cozy alliance of Republicans and Southern Democrats that got Hayes elected as part of the Compromise of 1877. In 1873, the Republicans had taken silver out of circulation in the Silver Demonetization Act. This step, one of deflation in the midst of depression, received the onus of being remembered among soft money people as "the Crime of '73." A myth grew up, begun by Maine Republican George Weston, that a Jewish banker, Ernest Seyd, had bought off Congress with a half million dollars so that foreign bondholders would be paid off in gold instead of paper or silver. This led to a conspiracy theory about U.S. gold reserves being sold off to foreign Jews. In reality, Congress demonetized silver in response to a money theory known as Gresham's law, which states that when two metals are in circulation, the cheaper will drive the dearer out. Interested in protecting gold, Congress dropped the cheaper silver coins.

But with the Compromise of 1877 and the return of home rule to the white South, Southern Democrats decided that they could come out in favor of economic inflation. This was contrary to the understanding of the Wormley Agreement, but the Southerners did not think that the Republicans were keeping their end of the bargain, either. The result was a rejuvenated Democrat Party and the passage of the Bland–Allison Act in 1878. This reintroduced silver coins as legal tender for all debts but kept the ratio of silver to gold at 16–1 to undercut the fears of Gresham's law. Hayes vetoed the measure, but the Democrats repassed it over his protest. When the Democrats threatened to repeal the Resumption Act and keep all greenbacks in circulation without a gold backing, Hayes and the Republicans compromised with them in the Fort Act, which kept resumption but permitted an extra $46 million to be kept in circulation after January 1, 1879, and redeemable in gold. By this time, the effects of the Panic of 1873 had eased and the money issue declined in importance, until the Populists brought it up again in the Panic of 1893.

GRANT, ULYSSES S., ADMINISTRATION—FOREIGN POLICY. *See* DIPLOMACY, U.S.—RECONSTRUCTION.

GRANT, ULYSSES S., ADMINISTRATION—RECONSTRUCTION. The one thing that Grant wanted to do as president was complete what he had begun at Appomattox—to end the Civil War and reunite the nation. So he proceeded to hasten the completion of Reconstruction (q.v.) in those four states that had not finished the process in the summer of 1868. He also came out squarely behind the proposed Fifteenth Amendment (q.v.). The election of 1868 (q.v.) had been marked by a duality on the African-American vote. In the South, black males had the right to vote in all elections because of the Military Reconstruction Acts (q.v.). In the North, however, the state option existed. And in many Northern states, blacks could not vote at all. There were all sorts of idealistic and practical political reasons to have blacks vote nationwide. If African-Americans were good enough to serve 180,000 strong in the Union armies, they were good enough to vote. There was also the belief that everyone ought to have an equal chance in life under the law. It would help the Negroes protect their freedom and other civil rights (q.v.). And it would ensure the Republican (q.v.) Party a source of reliable votes for years to come.

Grant was one of many who believed that the right to vote flowed from the willingness of blacks to serve in the war to gain their freedom and that it would help to guarantee Reconstruction's benefits were lasting. He understood the political angle, too. But there was a catch—many close Northern states might go Democrat (q.v.) over the issue. Wisconsin, Michigan, Ohio,

New York, Connecticut, and Kansas had already defeated proposals for universal male suffrage. It never even came to a vote in Indiana, Illinois, Pennsylvania, and New Jersey. Radicals like Thaddeus Stevens (q.v.) of Pennsylvania had granted the African-Americans the right to vote in the District of Columbia in 1866, but the backlash against it in 1867 had caused a general push by constitutional amendment to lag. But now Republicans figured that if it were done quickly, the fervor against it would subside by the next presidential election. Republican politicians decided to take the chance that since there were relatively few blacks in the North, most of the effect would be to neutralize the hostile white vote in the South. The result was the Fifteenth Amendment, a proposal that did not grant the black vote so much as it restricted how it could be limited. The negative wording would cause problems of political disfranchisement (q.v.) later.

The Fifteenth Amendment passed with much hostility in the North, but with enthusiasm in the South, happy to stick the Yankees with their own reform. The only part of the North that accepted the Fifteenth Amendment readily was New England. The only state there that did not like the amendment was Rhode Island, not because it disliked the Negro vote, which it had had since 1840, but because it did not wish to let the Irish into the polls. In the border states, Tennessee refused to consider it, Delaware and Kentucky rejected it, while Missouri and West Virginia passed it. In the Far West, only Nevada passed it; California and Oregon rejected it because of fear the Chinese would get the vote. In the Middle West, it passed mostly as a party measure, particularly in states with a small black population. In the others, a little political chicanery helped—Illinois, for example, passed it by voting without a legal quorum.

The key areas were the Middle Atlantic states, Ohio, Indiana, and Connecticut, where the Republicans and Democrats were nearly equally divided. This was the section of the country that the Republicans wanted the Fifteenth Amendment for, politically speaking. A small number of votes in the Republican column would guarantee them a victory in the future. Their loss in the elections of 1876 (Connecticut, Indians, and New York), 1884 (same states), and 1894 (those three states plus Illinois) created the Compromise of 1877 and the two Grover Cleveland presidencies for the Democrats. Indeed, with the exception of Cleveland, the Republican political strategy involved in the Fifteenth Amendment held until 1912, when Woodrow Wilson took two terms, and the black vote stayed Republican steadily until 1936 and the second election of Franklin D. Roosevelt, after which it has been firmly in the Democrat column to the present time.

But the close vote on the Fifteenth Amendment meant that the Republicans had to produce four more states to ensure ratification. These were the laggards in Southern Reconstruction, Virginia, Georgia, Mississippi, and Texas, not yet readmitted into the Union. Each state was unique in its problems. Virginia had refused to approve of its Reconstruction constitution because it provided for disfranchisement of Confederate military and civilian officials who had taken the oath to the United States and then one later to the Confederacy. The purpose was to trim the white vote, which outnumbered African-Americans and their white Radical allies. Maj. Gen. John Schofield (q.v.) told the convention that their move would destroy the constitution in the eyes of the voters, but to no avail. But he did convince President Grant, who supported submitting the constitution and the disfranchising sections separately. The voters accepted the constitution and rejected the disfranchisement clause. Then the Republican factions split evenly over the ensuing state election, and a stalemate followed. Grant once again intervened in the process, but in an oblique fashion by meeting with his old foe, Robert E. Lee (q.v.). Although Grant made no public statement, the meeting was seen as an indication that all ought to follow Lee's more moderate course. The Conservative Republicans were elected and ratified the Fifteenth Amendment, ending Virginia's government under the Military Reconstruction Acts.

Unlike Virginia or any other Southern state, Georgia had the dubious privilege of being reconstructed twice. It had been readmitted along with six other states (the Carolinas, Florida, Alabama, Arkansas, and Louisiana) in the summer of 1868 after ratifying the Fourteenth Amendment. Then the Conservative legislature (like Virginia, Georgia had a white majority of voters) refused to expel white members holding office in violation of the Fourteenth Amendment (the double oath clause), rejected Republican favorites for U.S. senators (voted on by the state legislatures until 1914), and expelled all of its black members. It also had the unmitigated gall to vote Democrat in the presidential election of 1868 and had an especially active branch of the Ku Klux Klan (q.v.) roaming the countryside. This led Congress to question the admissibility of Georgia's representatives and to expel them and return Georgia to the jurisdiction of the Army. A board of military officers supervised the cleaning out of the legislature of illegally serving whites, the return of the legally elected blacks to the legislature and local offices, and the reelection of new Republican national representatives. In addition, while they were at it, to show true penance, Congress saw to it that the Georgia legislators ratified the pending Fifteenth Amendment.

After the Georgia fiasco, Grant came to doubt the loyalty of Moderate Republicans (q.v.) in the South. Too many of them had joined with Democrats to proscribe black rights. So Grant decided that he would support the more Radical Republicans hereafter, which affected the results in Mississippi and Texas. In Mississippi, an attempt had been made to disfranchise whites who had taken the double oath (first to the United States, then to the Confederacy). But black delegates to the state constitutional convention refused to allow it and helped vote it down as unfair. Moderate leaders, realizing that Grant was not too prone to see things their way after Georgia, decided to call his bluff. They put at the head of their statewide ticket Lewis Dent, the president's brother-in-law. Grant was a great practitioner of nepotism, and the Moderates felt that he could not go against his own family member. But this was too blatant—to the point of insulting Grant's intelligence. Besides, his cabinet, especially Attorney General E. R. Hoar and Secretary of the Treasury George Boutwell (who had the distinction of being honest men to boot, unlike many of Grant's appointees), were ardently behind his desire to back Radicals. Grant wrote his brother-in-law and explained the political facts of life to him and backed the Radical's James L. Alcorn. Mississippi then ratified the Fourteenth and Fifteenth Amendments and rejoined the Union in 1870.

Unlike Mississippi, which had a majority of blacks registered to vote, Texas was like Virginia and Georgia, where white registrants dominated the polls. The state constitutional convention split over several issues. One was the Radical suggestion that Texas be divided into at least three states (up to five states being allowed by the 1845 Treaty of Annexation). Another was to disfranchise anyone who could not take the ironclad oath or who had taken the double oath. A third was that Radicals wanted all acts committed under the Confederate government declared null and void *ab initio* (q.v.), that is, from their inception. This threatened to open a whole bag of worms (including negating all marriages) that few wished to face. But the radicals were adamant, through two convention sessions that did little but prolong the debate and military rule.

Finally, the convention adjourned without a constitution. Maj. Gen. E. R. S. Canby (q.v.) formed a board consisting of his aide and one Moderate and one Radical Republican to put a constitution together. Grant, meanwhile, decided to return his old West Point classmate, Maj. Gen. Joseph J. Reynolds (q.v.), to Texas to replace the politically unreliable Canby—he was too fair. Reynolds switched patronage to the Radical Republicans; became acting provisional governor when the Moderate Republican E. M. Pease (q.v.) resigned, disgusted with these shenanigans; counted in the Radicals during a controversial election that was noted for its irregularities; and then appointed all those elected to office before Reconstruction ended, so that he could force them all to take the ironclad oath. Those who could not Reynolds replaced with loyal Radical appointees. The new legislature ratified the Fourteenth and Fifteenth Amendments, and Texas rejoined the Union with its sister states. In this way, the South offset the lack of Northern support, and the Fifteenth Amendment passed and became a part of the Constitution on March 30, 1870.

With the readmission of Virginia, Georgia, Mississippi, and Texas and the ratification of the Fifteenth Amendment, Grant had completed the technical process of Reconstruction and the South was back in the Union. But the problems of Reconstruction would haunt Grant and Republicans in Washington in the form of increasing violence in the South, particularly around election time. At first this violence was clandestine, through the Ku Klux Klan (q.v.) and various kindred associations like the Knights of the White Camellia, reflecting the fact that whites were not fully united against Reconstruction. Later this violence would become quite open and blatant, through the Red Shirts, the White Liners, the Rifle Clubs, and the White League (qq.v.) indicating that whites at last were united in their desire to destroy as much of Reconstruction as possible and redeem the South. Through it all, Grant stood valiantly against violence and racism, until in the end his whole administration fell to it as the nation registered its disgust and weariness in the election of 1876.

In 1870, at Grant's insistence, Congress passed the first Enforcement Act (q.v.), the "Force Act" in the vernacular of the day. This measure forbade state officials to discriminate against voters because of race, to bribe or intimidate a voter for any reason, or to use the threat of employment or occupational discrimination to affect votes. Since blacks were tenants on the land, the threat of the landowner to force a "correct" vote was very real, especially as there was no secret ballot at that time in the United States (this was an Australian idea incorporated after 1900 here). The Force Act also prohibited disguised groups on the public highways or on anyone's property with the intent to do anyone harm.

The Force Act did not do the job. Congress had to amend it with new measures. The Second Force Act provided Federal supervision of all voter registration. A Third Force Act soon followed. It prohibited any act or conspiracy to overthrow the Federal government by force. It also forbade the intimidation of any public official or members of a jury. Finally, it allowed the president to suspend the writ of *habeas corpus* in disaffected areas and to use the Army and Navy to put down dangerous and illegal combinations.

President Grant immediately utilized the provisions of the Force Acts to stop the Ku Klux activities in Georgia and South Carolina. Grant put over 40 counties under martial law. The Seventh Cavalry was withdrawn from the Great Plains and sent into Kentucky, South Carolina, and Louisiana to give the laws impact. (General Custer was not with his regiment, being before one of the numerous courts martial on unrelated charges that dotted his short, checkered career.) Hundreds of citizens were arrested, tried, and convicted (one Texas suspect was captured in Canada and extradited to face trial). But in reality, even though Grant saw to it that the Ku Klux was destroyed, it had already accomplished much of its objectives, and the Radical portion of Reconstruction had been blunted. A beginning had been made in restoring white supremacy and establishing "law and order" through traditional racial mores.

As the Ku Klux episode demonstrated, everything in secession, Civil War, and Reconstruction began and ended with the problem of race. The movement for Southern independence was dead. Slavery was over. But race remained behind. It was at the bottom of the antebellum quarrels and still very much alive during Reconstruction. The "American Dilemma," as Swedish sociologist Gunnar Myrdal once called it, was an enduring constant. It is possible that fallible human beings could not solve the race problem directly after the Civil War. But the greatest failing was not that the problem went unsolved, but that a deal was reached among whites North and South not to try to resolve it at all.

But to his credit, Ulysses S. Grant did try. He approached Reconstruction with several advantages, including an instinctive sense of fairness and humanity. He did not believe in punishing the South, he wanted the Union restored quickly, he believed that the African-Americans ought to be protected in their freedom. But the problem was staggering. The South had played its hand poorly. It had acted as if it would re-enslave the blacks. This played into the hands of the most unscrupulous and least responsible men in the North. These people did not care about the African-American's place in society. They merely wished to manipulate blacks and the Southern situation to gain political power, graft, and corruption.

Grant could not keep up with the intricacies of the problem, nor could most Americans. The Negroes' civil rights could not be secured without the vote, so he backed the Fifteenth Amendment. Fraud and intimidation unfairly kept blacks from the polls, so he sent Federal troops to curb these evil conditions. Step by step, repression took the place of reconciliation, and the blacks' rights as free people were lost in the struggle to break the will of the white South. Grant lacked the political skill to keep from being maneuvered into a position where the most extreme measures became his policy and the most violent Northern partisans claimed him as their leader.

Grant did not believe that the African-Americans should be thrown to the wolves. Most Republicans agreed. But most whites did not have any taste for keeping Republican politicians in control of Southern states at the point of a bayonet. In reality, Grant belonged with the Liberal Republicans, who sought a reconciliation with the white South. But he could not cross the gulf between them, which was widened by their opposition to his reelection in 1872. He saw them as narrow-minded, idealistic, and unrealistic reformers. They saw him as a crook involved in constant scandal. But if Grant could not work with the Liberals, he could get along with the Radicals and Stalwarts. They knew how to appeal to his hope that the Union victory was not in vain. When the Ku Klux rode, they portrayed them as ghostly Confederate armies, led by Democrats, who would make the Civil War a useless sacrifice. There could be no retreat in face of that image, and Grant felt it. He made Reconstruction harder and harder, until the Northern populace broke under the strain. This made white America do what always lay under the surface—ignore race and go on to conquer the continent represented by the Great West. Later it became the Imperial Dream overseas, in the Caribbean with Cuba and in the Pacific with the Philippines and the Boxer Rebellion in China.

Grant tried his best. He always maintained that the race problem had to be grappled with and defeated. If Reconstruction were subverted in the end by grasping people for unworthy motives, Grant tried to keep it pointed toward the noble end. He knew that the African-Americans had to be protected in their freedom, and this was the one issue that the extremists used to preserve their power, until they tired like everyone else of the perennial problem and the blacks lost that which they fought for the most. By 1874, the situation was becoming impossible for the Republican Party everywhere in the South. In Texas and Arkansas, both sides claimed to have won state elections, and both sides had private armies to contest for control. Grant's policy was to shore up Republicans as long as he could, but in these two cases, the cause was hopeless. The Democrats soon took control.

The reason that Grant could not act in Texas and Arkansas was his greatest embarrassment. It was the situation in Louisiana, a total puzzle to anyone unfamiliar with its political mysteries and idiosyncrasies. Louisiana had become a national scandal that colored all of Reconstruction. It had the most obvious scoundrels, the most unbelievable fraud, and the worst violence. Neither side was right; neither was worth supporting. The White League, a sort of Ku Klux Klan without the sheets, engaged in open massacres of white and black opponents, employing a professional gunman in one case to shoot Carpetbagger Marshall H. Twitchell (qq.v.) to pieces.

Grant sent Maj. Gen. Philip H. Sheridan (q.v.) down to survey the problem. Sheridan labeled the whites "banditti" and called for the Army to intervene. But the House of Representatives in Washington was controlled by the Democrats, and they refused to fund such an intervention. Grant condemned the House and called upon it to force the South to make good on the promises that had got it readmitted in 1868. But the House would have none of that. It dwelled on corruption, horrors of Carpetbag rule, the un-American nature of military intervention, and alleged African-American rascality and inferiority. It was Grantism exported to the states, and it had to be stopped.

But Grant and his advocates managed to get a Fourth Enforcement Bill passed in the House, one that would give the president the right to suspend the writ of *habeas corpus* in Alabama, Arkansas, Mississippi, and Louisiana for two years. It failed in the Senate, which had its own approach. This was the Civil Rights Act of 1875 (q.v.), a tribute to Senator Charles Sumner (q.v.) of Massachusetts, who had just died. He had wanted it passed in conjunction with the Amnesty Act of 1872—the one an act of forgiveness, the other an act of justice, Sumner had reasoned. It included a public accommodations section preventing discrimination because of race in theaters, streetcars, railways, hotels, schools, cemeteries, churches, and courts of law. Grant threatened to veto it in 1872 as interfering with individual choice. But in 1875 it passed, and Grant signed it when the part on schools and cemeteries was left out. The U.S. Supreme Court would rule it unconstitutional in 1883, claiming that social rights were not matters of government.

In the South in 1875, the style was to organize "Rifle Clubs" to drive out unwanted Carpetbaggers and police the polls, seeing to it that only the whites and a few select blacks got the vote. It was done quite openly, so that the Reconstruction supporters would know whom to fear. It also marked the first time that whites were united in their approach to Reconstruction. No one wanted to see if they could live with it any more. They were going to crush it with violence. As this concept was developed first in Mississippi, it was called the "Mississippi Plan" (q.v.) or the "Shotgun Plan," for the weapon of choice in its enforcement. Louisiana had its White Leagues, who took on the Reconstruction forces in a pitched street battle in New Orleans. South Carolina had Wade Hampton's Red Shirts.

But it was all part and parcel of the same thing. The Carpetbag governor of Mississippi, Adelbert Ames (q.v.), faced a dilemma. He could call up the state militia, primarily composed of black units, and institute a race war, or he could appeal for Federal troops to crush the Rifle Clubs. But the national Republican Party was thinking ahead to the presidential election of 1876 and refused to back Grant if he acted. The state legislature impeached Ames on trumped-up charges and dropped them when he agreed to leave Mississippi. The state went to the Democrats. State after state followed Mississippi, and by 1876, all of the South had been redeemed but Louisiana, Florida, and South Carolina. They would have a lot to say about who should be Grant's successor.

GRANT, ULYSSES S., ADMINISTRATION—SCANDALS. The problem with Ulysses S. Grant's presidency was not that he failed to achieve anything. The problem was not what was done, but rather what was not done. Grant's record has been perpetually darkened with the shadow of a few tragic might-have-beens. Nothing illustrates this more than the scandals that compromised his regime. Great wealth came into power with Grant. It was not old wealth, seasoned with public responsibility, but new, brash, vulgar wealth that gloried in its pursuit of more suckers to be plucked. The Civil War had destroyed more than the Confederacy; it crushed the restraints and decorum that had marked the antebellum era. A man wise in the ways of the world might have been able to see that not only should the ambitious human predators be restrained, they should never be given free rein to corrupt the government itself.

But by the time of Reconstruction (q.v.), the North had spent most of a generation adulating the go-getter, the promoter, the entrepreneur who constructed a new railroad, factory, or business of any kind. The American dream has always gone on a cash basis coupled with the right to do almost anything. One had the right to do better in life than one's father. Grant himself had exacting personal standards in his own world. He could size up an officer or soldier in mere seconds. But he was lost in the civilian world, as marked by his business failures. He could operate a Galena tannery or general store or even supply an army, but he had no concept of how to run a whole industry like the titans of business now emerging in American society. Grant outside the military world became a babe in the woods, overawed and gullible, a rube looking to be had. And it did not take long before the jackals moved to cash in on his innocence.

During his first administration, the scandals that plagued Grant were more of being too close to the malefactors rather than in with them. For instance there was the Gold Scandal, which involved Grant's regime with the likes of Daniel Drew, Commodore Cornelius Vanderbilt, Jim Fisk, and Jay Gould. Once described as a "gaunt, wily, and pious," outwardly appearing man who really was "a shambling, mealy-mouthed coward, saved from mediocrity by the almost insane cunning of his weasel mind," Daniel Drew began his business career driving livestock into New York City. He liked to buy the herds cheaply in the countryside and sell them dearly in the city. One day he dumped salt in the pen where the cattle were held, and shortly before the buyer arrived, he turned them loose to water. When his mark arrived, the cattle looked fat and weighed in the same. When the news of this deal got out, Wall Streeters chuckled and coined a new term, "watered stock." It was a term Drew would make famous again and again. Drew was not exceptional in his ethics, or lack of them. His attitude was standard in the 19th century.

Like Drew, Cornelius Vanderbilt (he signed it "Van Derbilt") was the son of a small farmer and grew up with little education. But his lack of formal education did not hold him back; with a loan from his mother of $100, he bought a small sailboat and operated a ferry between Manhattan and Staten Island. He would move into an area dominated by another company and cut rates until the opposition paid him to go elsewhere. This was considered standard practice at the time, it was widely copied, and it made Vanderbilt a rich man. After the discovery of gold in California, Vanderbilt realized another fortune of $10 million in a fast line to California, his passengers being transferred across the Isthmus at Nicaragua's San Juan River. By the time of the Civil War, Vanderbilt had garnered a fortune in various local and international shipping enterprises. But Vanderbilt had bigger game in mind, as he sold his steamship interests and, in league with Drew, bought a small rail line that eventually became a part of the powerful New Haven empire. Vanderbilt also bought up various Hudson Valley lines between New York City and Albany, consolidated them into the New York Central, and proceeded to extend his empire from Albany to Chicago. It was through Drew that he met Fisk and Gould.

A Vermonter who made money as a peddler, filling supply contracts for the Union army, and buying and selling cotton during the Civil War, Jim Fisk became an agent for the noted stock manipulator, Daniel Drew, in 1866. With Drew's help, Fisk, who had a modicum of formal education but a lot of what is now called "street smarts," opened his own brokerage house and made a small fortune. Later Fisk set himself up at New York's Grand Opera House, where he kept an office connected to the stage by a semi-secret passageway. Here he wined and dined numerous ladies (he wasn't known as Jubilee Jim for nothing). But Fisk's attentions to Josephine Mansfield threatened to blow up all of his private business. She and her boyfriend, Ned Stokes, had been blackmailing Fisk over something. But Fisk had cut off the payments, and now Josephine was bringing him to court over a minor matter in retaliation. Probably as many people wanted to see Fisk asked questions under oath as did not. But neither side got its chance. Stokes shot Fisk dead after a compromising liaison with Josephine at a local hotel. The famous cartoonist Thomas Nast (the one who invented the ass for the Democrats and the elephant for the Republicans) drew a caricature of the funeral, showing Gould and New York Democrat (q.v.) political boss William M. Tweed (q.v.) of Tammany Hall standing over Fisk's grave, looking much relieved. The caption: "Dead Men Tell No Tales."

Once described by a historian as a small, quiet, private, outwardly respectable sort with a "reptilian" looking face, Jim Fisk's pal, Jay Gould, worked in a rural store, became a surveyor, invented a mousetrap (there is something very appropriate in this, given his later life), and even wrote a history of Delaware County, New York. He built a tannery at what is now Gouldsboro, Pennsylvania (named after him), stole money from his partner, and invested in a bank. He cheated his banking partner, too, and the man killed himself in despair. By age twenty-four, Gould was in New York City, looking for bigger and better things. He married Ellen Miller, whose father owned a railroad in upstate New York and Vermont. Gould borrowed cash from his father-in-law and took over the line himself. He improved the railroad and sold it at a profit to what became the Delaware & Hudson. For the rest of his life, Gould saw profit in manipulating railroad stock. And he was good at it. His general pattern was to buy a poor railroad with a strategic location, raise the paper value of the stock, and sell out at a profit. Unlike his father-in-law's railroad, Gould never bothered to improve what he bought. Gould became an expert in forcing stocks down, buying, forcing the price up, and selling. He also learned the fine art of bribing politicians and never letting a friendship stand in the way of profit. He ruined several men on his way up in life, but once started, he never looked back.

Gould's career became synonymous with the New York, Lake Erie & Western Railroad, commonly called the Erie. It ran from New York City to Buffalo by way of Binghamton and Elmira, in direct competition with Cornelius Vanderbilt's New York Central, which followed the old Erie Canal route. To counter Vanderbilt's great influence, Gould ingratiated himself with Drew, who had loaned the Erie some $2 million and called in the loan. The directors could not pay, and Drew and his erstwhile compatriot, Gould, now had their own rail line. But Vanderbilt did not want competition in the trade to and from Buffalo. So he started buying Erie stock. When Vanderbilt controlled enough stock, he took over, keeping Drew and Gould on the board and adding Jim Fisk at Drew's suggestion. There Fisk came into his own as he secretly joined Drew and Gould to swindle Vanderbilt out of his control. Most of the transaction came about through watered stock, and a cartoon of the time pictures the malefactors hard at work printing, with Fisk saying, "If this printing press don't break down, I'll be damned if we don't give the old hog [Vanderbilt] all he wants of Erie." It was typically Fisk: brash boisterous, and a bit crude. He was a high liver, and he did it all in the public eye, by choice.

Vanderbilt swore out a complaint, and the trio of Fisk, Gould, and Drew fled to New Jersey, tipped off by informants. The outraged Vanderbilt pursued them with the police to the dock in lower Manhattan, each man gripping a suitcase and carpetbag full of money and stocks. On the Jersey shore, Fisk garbed himself in a naval uniform and labeled himself "the Admiral," with obvious implications that he outranked the old Commodore. "The Commodore owns New York, the stock exchange, the streets, the railroads, and most of the steamship lines," Fisk told an inquisitive newspaper reporter. "As ambitious young men," he continued with a twinkle in his eye, "we saw there was no chance for us there to expand, and so we came over here. . . . Yes," he concluded with a flourish, "tell Mr. [Horace] Greeley [famous editor of the *New York Tribune*] from us that we're sorry now that we didn't take his advice sooner—about going West."

They also incorporated their Erie system in New Jersey, where Vanderbilt had no influence. Meanwhile, realizing that they could never get back to New York City (where the real action was) without being arrested, Gould slipped off to Albany with a half million dollars of ill-gotten gains to "cultivate" the state legislature (one enterprising legislator took $75,000 from Vanderbilt and $100,000 from Gould). The job was well done, and all of the watered stock was declared legal, leaving Vanderbilt holding the bag. Then Gould and his men bought back Vanderbilt's share. That did it for Drew. He withdrew with Vanderbilt, leaving Gould and Fisk in sole control of the Erie.

Still Vanderbilt sought revenge. He started a rate war against the Erie. Cattle went from Buffalo to the Big Apple at $125 a carload. The Commodore cut it to $100. Erie responded with $75; Vanderbilt dropped it to $50; Erie went to $25; Vanderbilt mercilessly cut it to one dollar. But he reckoned without Gould, who had been buying up all the cattle around Buffalo he could get his hands on. Bumping Erie's rate back up to $125 a carload, to insure no one would ship cattle on it, Gould and everyone else sent their steers over the New York Central. Gould and Fisk made a fortune while the price held. Once again, Vanderbilt was the laughingstock of Americas finance.

But Gould was still busy and decided to go to work on the biggest "rube" of all, President Grant. In league with Fisk, he began to buy gold, to force up its price. The plan was to buy and buy until the market became overheated and then suddenly sell, leaving the speculators with the crash when reality struck. The whole plan depended on the U.S. government keeping its supply of gold off the market. If the government stepped in, the price would crash prematurely, leaving Fisk and Gould in the lurch, too. The Erie magnates thought they had Grant's agreement to hold the treasury in check. But Grant never understood what was going on and finally authorized the treasury to inject its gold into the market to stabilize it. Gould found out about the government move; Fisk did not. Gould saw no reason to tell his partner in crime as he shifted all of his options to sell. The next day, Fisk went under with the rest of the speculators, and Gould alone made money. Fisk died a few years later, shot by his ex-lover's new boyfriend, probably agreeing in the end with Daniel Drew's comment on Gould: "His touch is death." But Vanderbilt went him one better: When asked if he learned anything in his operations with and against Fisk and Gould, the old Commodore said yes, he had: "never kick a skunk."

Grant ought to have taken Vanderbilt's advice to heart, because there was more to come. Right on the heels of the gold scandal was San Domingo. Comprising the eastern two-thirds of the Caribbean island of Hispañola, San Domingo (the present-day Dominican Republic) was the site of one of Christopher Columbus's original settlements in the new world. It had as its ruler in the late 1860s one Buenaventura Baez, a corrupt dictator who stopped at nothing where money was concerned. One day he got the bright idea that he could sell his impoverished country to the United States. The Americans had always evidenced a great interest in the Caribbean, especially before the Civil War, when the Greater Antilles were part of the Golden Circle that would extend Southern slavery and American democracy into the Gulf, as represented by the Ostend Manifesto. Although the Americans seemed more interested in Cuba, Baez believed that with the proper prompting, their interest could be shifted to his island. After all, Abraham Lincoln (q.v.) had tried to set up colonies of freed American slaves on the north coast during the recent Civil War.

So Baez sent word to the U.S. government that the Dominicans were ready for annexation, at the proper price. Grant was interested because

San Domingo was strategically located athwart some of the world's busiest shipping lanes and promised a direct link to the Isthmus of Panamá. Grant also wondered if Lincoln had not been right about the need to colonize African-Americans abroad as the only way for them to truly achieve racial justice. San Domingo was big enough for three or four states for them. But then he blew it. Instead of sending a Department of State envoy to work out the details, Grant sent down his wartime aide-de-camp and now presidential assistant, Orville Babcock. Babcock was sort of a North American version of Baez when it came to monetary items—an expert at getting the fast buck. He also had a glib tongue as far as Grant was concerned. The president instinctively trusted him. Babcock drew up a favorable treaty (from the standpoint of his and Baez's greed), brought in the U.S. Navy to advance Baez's interests against his more democratic opponents, and even sent American military supplies to Baez's forces in their domestic civil war.

If the treaty were to be approved in the U.S. Senate (it needed a two-thirds vote), it had to get a favorable review in the Foreign Relations Committee. Its chairman was none other than one of the great moralists and antislavery men of his day, Senator Charles Sumner (q.v.) of Massachusetts. Since much of the population of San Domingo was black, Sumner was going to safeguard their rights as fully as he did those of African-Americans at home. Grant went over in person to plug the treaty, and when Sumner asked questions that Grant could not answer, he volunteered to send Babcock over to sort it all out. Sumner was agreeable. "Mr. President," he intoned as only Charles Sumner could, "I am an administration man and whatever you do will always find in me a most careful and candid consideration." To Grant's simple ears that was a "yes" on the proposed treaty if he ever heard one.

But Sumner's prying was nothing if not thorough. He soon saw through Babcock's machinations and was horrified at the clipping that the U.S. government was about to take. Baez was not even accepted as the ruler of San Domingo by all of its citizens. He was corrupt, brutal, and a notorious wheeler-dealer to boot. Not only would the Federal government have to guarantee the San Domingo national debt (which was quite large), but it would have to go against the wishes of Haiti, which shared the island, and most of Europe as well. It was too expensive in a monetary sense, in a moral sense, and in a political sense. Sumner recommended that the Senate turn it down, which it promptly did.

Grant was furious. What had happened to the "administration man" that Sumner had sworn he was? As Sumner and Grant carped about loyalty and morality (topics that Sumner had few peers in arguing), the public mistakenly got the notion that Grant had endorsed all of Babcock's crookedness and, indeed, had encouraged Baez and Babcock from the start. The president had not, but he evidenced a great gullibility and a willingness to attach his reputation to lesser mortals who did not deserve his support.

He was beginning to see his star tarnished by men he foolishly considered his friends but who were in reality first-class grifters without a shred of integrity. Nothing showed their true colors more than the Crédit Mobilier scandal (q.v.). After the passage of the Pacific Railroad Act (q.v.) in 1862 and its amendment in 1864, railroad investment took on an increasing attractiveness to various entrepreneurs in the United States. As lucrative as the rail investments might be, the construction and management of the transcontinental railroad, the Union Pacific, offered more to those wise in the ways of maximizing profit at public expense. Their efforts went into establishing a construction company to build the railroad across the plains and mountains. It was called the Crédit Mobilier of America to differentiate it from the corrupt French company involved in the construction of the Suez Canal—which should have been an omen of things to come for Grant.

The Crédit Mobilier was set up in Pennsylvania under charter from the state legislature at the behest of Thomas Durant, a manipulator of stocks in what later became the Rock Island Lines. The Crédit Mobilier was a construction company, so far as the public knew, with which the railroad contracted to build the line to the west. What the public did not know was that essentially the Crédit Mobilier was run by the same men who directed the railroad. They bought items cheap and sold them to themselves dear, charging the Federal government the higher price and pocketing the difference. If the profits were not in cash, they came in the form of securities that allowed the men to control the railroad and its land grants, particularly the timber and mineral rights that came with them.

It was nothing new—business was done that way then, quite openly actually, by today's standards. At first the Crédit Mobilier contracted to lay the rails onto the plains for the first 200 miles at a profit to themselves of just over $5 million. That was a poor show. The Boston investors complained, so congressman (House Committee on Pacific Railroads) and shovel-maker Oakes Ames was put in charge. He laid the next 600 miles of track and overcharged the government and first mortgage common stockholders (the manipulators never used their own money) almost $30 million. The system was beginning to hum. But the problem was the five directors appointed by the Federal government. What if one of them blew the whistle? What if the rumors of profit caused some crusading congressman to investigate? Ames had the solution. He went around among the directors and his political peers and distributed shares in the Crédit Mobilier "where it would do the most good," he said sagely later, free to some, at a small cost to others. This also was not unusual during that era, later remembered by Mark Twain as the "Gilded Age."

Among those blessed with Crédit Mobilier shares were the vice president of the United States, Schuyler Colfax (q.v.); the speaker of the house, future president James A. Garfield; perennial presidential hopeful Senator James G. Blaine; and a slew of normally moralistic Radical Republicans. Everyone was in on the take, except Charles Sumner and his kind. To this day, no one knows the names of all those involved in the American version of the Crédit Mobilier. Suffice it to say, the estimated six dozen did not lose face in financial wizardry. They came from Boston, Chicago, Philadelphia, and New York City. They included William B. Ogden, John Murray Forbes, Charles Butler, Thomas A. Scott, John Edgar Thomson, Erastus Corning, John V. L. Pruyn, John I. Blair, Russell Sage, August Belmont, J. F. D. Lanier, and Samuel J. Tilden, corporate lawyer and future Democrat candidate for the presidency in 1876 (on an honest government platform, of course).

The problem lay in the fact that some of those paid off believed that they had been cheated out of their fair share of the greed. One of them took Oakes Ames to court. Now this was not smart. Trials had a way of engaging the public's usually diverted attention (Jim Fisk had found that out). Then in 1871, well after the Pacific Railroad had been finished and nearly everyone paid off, a combination of directors elected Thomas A. Scott as president of the Union Pacific. Scott was big in the Pennsylvania Railroad, and his election looked like a nationwide railroad power grab to many. So they backed the litigation against Ames and banded together to throw Scott out of his presidency. In revenge, the Scott group then leaked old letters in which Ames stupidly named those whom he had bribed. The muckraking *New York Sun* got hold of the letters, and the story went public with a bang—right in the middle of the election of 1872. President U. S. Grant, all of Congress, and one-third of the Senate were up for reconsideration. And although the president was clean, the rest of his administration was not.

There was no way around it. Congress would have to investigate. Of course, everyone professed wide-eyed innocence. But the facts were out, and the government had to take the Crédit Mobilier to court. Naturally, the suit was civil, not criminal (one did not send upstanding citizens like congressmen to jail in 19th-century America), and eventually the Supreme Court ruled that the government could not collect even on the fraud until 1895, 36 years after the first bonds went out, as stipulated in the Federal charter. The only ones who really suffered were Oakes Ames and Vice President Colfax. Ames lost his congressional seat—but he kept his cash. Grant won a second term by dumping Colfax from the ticket. But Grant might have gone down the road too had the opposition not backed the ending of Reconstruction and abandoning the former slaves to Southern white rule, something Grant nobly refused to do. But with four more years of scandal in the offing, such compunctions would change mightily in 1876.

During Grant's second term, the scandals grew worse and more frequent until, they seemed universal, striking nearly every government department. George M. Robeson of New Jersey was the head of the Department of the Navy. Along with Hamilton Fish in State, Robeson had the distinction of serving the longest, nearly eight years after the resignation of A. E. Borie, who did not want the job. After the election of 1872, someone in Congress noticed that Robeson, a relatively poor man most of his life, was living pretty high on the hog. In fact, closer investigation proved the secretary had cleared $320,000 during his tenure. Unfortunately he received this money as kickbacks from friends to whom he awarded government shipbuilding contracts. But by the time Congress got to the bottom of it, the election of 1876 (q.v.) was on, and there were bigger fish to fry in the pan of governmental fraud. So Robeson left office relatively untouched. But it all happened on Grant's watch, as the newspapers were quick to point out.

Not to be outdone by Navy, the Department of War's secretary, William W. Belknap, collected his kickbacks from Indian agents out West (the Bureau of Indian Affairs being a function of the Army in those days). The first bribes actually went to Mrs. Belknap, who had obtained the appointment of C. P. Marsh as agent at the Comanche–Kiowa Agency at Ft. Sill, Indian Territory (Oklahoma). But Marsh was smarter than to go out on the Southern Plains to live. He merely wrote the incumbent and told him that for $1,000 a month Marsh would stay home and let him keep the job (it was an especially lucrative post). The agent agreed, and Marsh paid half of the take to Mrs. Belknap to support her lavish lifestyle in Washington society. When Mrs. Belknap died suddenly, the secretary told Marsh to keep the payments coming. He had married his first wife's sister, and she turned out to be even more expensive to maintain. When the fraud was revealed, Belknap offered to resign. Since he was an old war buddy and Grant got the odd notion that it was all the dead Mrs. Belknap's fault, he let him go to protect the family's reputation. Of course this made the whole cover-up Grant's responsibility, and Belknap let him assume the blame for the whole deal. Belknap's resignation killed a pending impeachment proceeding. The expected criminal suit went by the board when the Department of Justice said there was insufficient evidence to prosecute.

With War and Navy picking up their share, minor functionaries in the Department of State also wished to get in on the act. But Secretary Hamilton Fish (q.v.) was too honest to let that happen. There was one problem, however: Fish could not regulate the overseas appointments, as they were a presidential perk. The American minister to the Court at St. James was Robert Schenck. A mediocre general under the command of men fully as incapable as he, he ran afoul of Confederate genius Stonewall Jackson (q.v.) in the 1862 Valley Campaign. After that debacle, Schenck resigned and went to Congress, where his talents might better be utilized. His one piece of real fame was that he was reputed to have introduced draw poker to the British upper crust. He also wrote a manual of play, which entitled him to the sobriquet, "America's Literary Ambassador." Finally, not wishing to leave his British friends out of North America's real institution of gambling, the "Great Barbecue," he introduced them to the challenge of American corporate finance. Schenck circulated and sold stocks in the Emma Silver Mine. Since he was a secret member of the board of directors in addition to being American minister, he learned of the mine's demise weeks before the news became public in England. Quickly, Schenck unloaded all of his own stock at a profit to his English friends. The whole thing eventually went public, and the British sent him home in disgrace. Under pressure, Schenck had to resign—a rich man.

Since the executive departments were cleaning up, money-wise, Congress wanted in on the public largesse, too. The scheme was a measure that came to be called the Salary Grab Act of 1873. With the approaching centennial of the American Revolution, executive salaries became an issue. The president was still paid the same $25,000 that George Washington had received. The public sentiment was about evenly divided between those who thought that the office was worth twice as much as President Grant was paid, and those who said that Grant ought to live more simply. Congress had refused to pick up Washington's expenses as president, having learned from his Revolutionary War service that his expenses rivaled those of King George. So the annual salary had been slapped on the office as a cost-saving measure. There had been many efforts to raise the executive salary, but all had failed in the more parsimonious times preceding Reconstruction.

The usual attempt to raise executive salaries would have had a similar fate in 1873, but for the imaginative intervention of Congressman Benjamin Butler (q.v.) of Massachusetts, known for his light-fingered occupation of the Gulf Coast, which won him the moniker "Spoons," after his alleged favorite souvenirs from his soldiers' nocturnal visits to the richest plantation houses. There was money to be made from the sentiment that the president needed a salary hike, Butler knew. So he amended the bill to give Grant a salary increase to $50,000 annually, and the vice president, Supreme Court justices, and the speaker of the House of Representatives to $10,000 and members of Congress to $7,500. Then came the kicker—all salaries were to be retroactive back to 1871. Even the by now numb American public was outraged. The 1874 elections returned a large number of Democrats to Congress, and they promptly lowered only the congressional salaries. But the instigators then sent a bill through that also cut Grant's salary. He vetoed the measure, and the whole salary grab looked like something he had been in cahoots with. He was not, but the raise was the only reason that the president did not leave office greatly in debt.

Although the public blamed Grant for much of the salary grab, it paled in comparison with what happened in the Department of the Treasury. In fact, the Treasury scandals were so big that in the end they took the heat off everyone else. Prior to 1872, the government had awarded a percentage of delinquent taxes to those who reported them. This had led to false charges and blackmail by disgruntled employees, neighbors, and such and had been discontinued in 1872. Instead, a series of contract tax collectors was put in. Secretary of the Treasury W. A. Richardson appointed a crony of Ben Butler, John D. Sanborn, to one of the collector's slots. Sanborn was to ferret out unknown delinquent taxes and take half of what was collected. His entrée into district offices was assured by a letter from Richardson, asking that he be given full cooperation.

Sanborn was no idiot. If the government did not know who was not paying their taxes, he was probably not going to find them out, either. So instead of seeking out the unknown, he took Richardson's letter to the Boston internal revenue office and got a list of already known delinquents. Then he collected their payments and took 50 percent off the top. Then on a hunch, Sanborn made a list of 600 railroads and arbitrarily charged them with delinquent taxes. Surprisingly (well, maybe not), a large number confessed to the accusations and paid up to Sanborn, who took half. Complaints led to a congressional investigation, which revealed that Sanborn had made $213,000 off the government, but that he had not found out any delinquent taxes that the Treasury did not already know of. It was suspected that Ben Butler got a healthy cut of Sanborn's income, but no such evidence could be produced. Congress decided to censure Richardson, who resigned, for President Grant's sake, he said. Grant was appreciative and made Richardson a Federal judge after the whole affair cooled off.

And cool off it did, because Richardson's successor, reformer Benjamin Bristow, went on a clean-up-the-Treasury binge that made him a top contender for president on the honest government ticket in 1876. He found that his biggest obstacle in ridding the department of crooks was that they were all Grant's friends and supported him for an unprecedented third term. Bristow decided that if he exposed them to the public, he could not only straighten out the mess at Treasury, but become president as well. His target was the Whiskey Ring. Composed of brewers and distillers of alcoholic beverages, who were supposed to pay Federal excise taxes, the Whiskey Ring had been in existence for years. Basically, the Ring paid off the revenue men to report less production and accept much reduced taxes in exchange for the usual bribes. It was sort of an entrenched tradition that no one had touched before Bristow made his move in 1875. The secretary had tried for months to catch the Whiskey Ring, but tip-offs from inside the department had allowed the culprits to slip through his hands. The secretary then collected a secret police force loyal only to him and made a bunch of surprise raids at Chicago, Milwaukee, and St. Louis.

The most important catch was the collector of internal revenue at St. Louis, John McDonald. An illiterate political manipulator and astute judge of people, McDonald was an old friend of the president. McDonald had been protected by Missouri Republicans, many of them on the take, but there had been a recent shift in Republican personnel to the Carl Schurz (q.v.) group. And Schurz was the rare man of integrity, a liberal Republican who opposed all graft and corruption. But because the Liberals had been against Grant's reelection in 1872, Grant took Schurz's complaints against McDonald as mere political hogwash. Grant should have known better. McDonald had asked the president for a letter of introduction to Jim Fisk and Jay Gould right after the Gold Scandal. Grant refused the letter, but when McDonald came back with a request to be collector at St. Louis, the president had readily assented. He was a staunch Grant man, and the president hoped that his political savvy would neutralize Schurz and his ally, B. Gratz Brown, in Missouri.

All of that was true, but so was the fact that McDonald was the head of the Whiskey Ring's St. Louis operations. He would put local distillers up on minor charges and then not prosecute them for a kickback. McDonald had confided everything in Grant's most trusted aide, Orville Babcock, but Babcock was very understanding for a price. McDonald found this more than reasonable. He gave Babcock $25,000 right off the top and kept him regularly supplied with cigar boxes of $500 bills, large diamonds, vacations with paid expenses, and even a sylph's charms (a polite way at that time to refer to a practitioner of the world's oldest profession). Fortunately, as Babcock was well aware, Grant had heard "thief" so many times that he refused to believe such charges any longer. He saw everything as politically inspired drivel launched against trusted subordinates by Democrats and Liberal Republicans. Grant was personally so squeaky clean that he could not believe that his trusted aides, men who had stood shoulder to shoulder with him against the Rebels, and cabinet members, men of the business community whom Grant unabashedly admired, could be less trustworthy than he. And led by Babcock, they all played on his soft heart for their own benefit.

Yet Grant made other mistakes. He accepted gifts from these men, especially several prized race horses. He never seemed to realize that the givers might expect something later, or how bad this would look if the public ever found out. He was truly ripe for the plucking. In this state of mind, the president was horrified to find that his secretary of the treasury was in league with his critics. At least that is what Grant thought (guided by Babcock) when Bristow revealed all of his findings in the McDonald matter. But Bristow refused to back down. He presented facts that even Grant could not deny, including a bunch of telegrams informing McDonald of Bristow's failed raids, signed "Sylph." McDonald had to go; Grant accepted his resignation and gave Bristow a free hand to clean up the Whiskey Ring. Bristow informed him that "Sylph" was Babcock. "Let no guilty man escape," Grant said. "No personal consideration should stand in the way of performing a public duty. . . . If Babcock is guilty, there is no man who wants him so proven guilty as I do, for it is the greatest piece of traitorism to me that a man could possibly practice."

But in spite of his declaration to Bristow, Grant kept Babcock in his job, convinced deep down that Bristow was wrong about him. Babcock and Grant had several private and intense talks, the aide showing how Bristow was seeking the presidency over Grant's ruined reputation. He even convinced Grant that the "Sylph" telegrams were he and McDonald working to protect the president from a blackmailing woman (as if Grant ever did anything to be blackmailed about). Babcock asked his old general for a military trial, and the president appointed a board consisting of Generals Alfred Terry, Winfield S. Hancock, and Philip H. Sheridan (qq.v.).

But the St. Louis court would not quash Babcock's indictment there or give Grant's military board any evidence. Babcock condemned the court as "Rebel" led, said political plotters wanted to ruin him to get at Grant, and assisted a private investigation authorized by the president to seek out the "facts." The trial in St. Louis convicted all of the accused except Babcock (McDonald got 18 months), who produced an affidavit from Grant that his aide was as pure as the driven snow. The court did not wish to challenge the president's veracity through a mere deposition and felt obliged to let Babcock go. Babcock and Grant then had a heart to heart conference, after which Babcock resigned to be director of public works for the District of Columbia, where he dropped from the public eye. Grant meanwhile turned his fury on Bristow, whom he allowed to continue in place until after the election of 1876, when the reformer was fired. Once again, the president covered up for his friends' lack of reputation by compromising his own. "Grantism" came to mean the worst in crooked government, a castigation that has endured up to the present day and did much to compromise the continuance of Reconstruction, which he supported. *See also* CORRUPTION BEFORE, DURING, AND AFTER THE CIVIL WAR.

GREELEY, HORACE (1811–1872). The most important newspaper editor and reformer of his time, Horace Greeley was born in Amherst, New Hampshire. His father was a hardscrabble farmer who moved the family to various farms in Vermont and Pennsylvania. Greeley received a modicum of education and was apprenticed to a newspaper editor at age 14. The owner soon died, but Greeley kept at newspaper work the rest of his life. With about $25 and all of his belongings wrapped in a large handkerchief, he arrived in New

York City in 1831. The precocious Greeley was soon writing small pieces independently, and then larger ones and editorial comment, too. He came to the notice of James Gordon Bennett, who offered him a partnership in the New York *Herald*, but Greeley had already started a literary magazine, the *New Yorker*. The sheet was a literary masterpiece and gained in reputation and circulation monthly, but Greeley still worried about debt. Nonetheless, he married Mary Cheney, a schoolteacher, and kept writing, earning a wide reputation for his articles.

Ultimately the *New Yorker* failed, probably a good thing, because literary writing was not Greeley's main interest—politics was. He accepted the challenge from William H. Seward (q.v.), later Abraham Lincoln's (q.v.) secretary of state, and his mentor, Thurlow Weed, probably the most powerful political kingpin in upstate New York, to publish a Whig newspaper in the city. In 1840, he opened up the *Log Cabin*, a sheet dedicated to the election of William Henry Harrison, which became an instant success. Greeley also made speeches and stumped the state for Harrison. After the election, Greeley took stock of the newspaper industry in New York City. There were 12 different papers a day published, but not one was dedicated to the Whig party cause. So Greeley took what was left of the *New Yorker* and the *Log Cabin*, borrowed a thousand dollars, and merged them into one publication, which he named the New York *Tribune* in 1841. The other editors attacked him immediately, and the result was rising subscription and a newspaper that made Greeley not only famous, but also rich.

Greeley proceeded to set a new standard in American journalism. He emphasized good taste, high moral standards, and intellectual appeal. He also made good use of the editorial comment page, writing wholly partisan pieces, but with an appeal to reason and accuracy. But most of all, the newspaper was Greeley's personal sounding board, and he had a lot to sound off about. He at one time or another backed every crackpot idea that circulated in 19th-century America. He was an egalitarian who saw aristocratic plots behind everything. He spoke out on behalf of utopian socialism, advocated communal living, and invested in the movement through its banks. He was for the free distribution of land in the West ("Go west, young man," was ever his advice to those on the make), and against economic advantage to the rich. He railed against railroad land grants, assailed corporate heartlessness, was against the exploitation of workers, and wrote against wage slavery as fervently as he campaigned against chattel slavery. He opposed the death penalty, was for freedom of speech. favored women's rights (so long as they did not get the vote), wanted to restrict the sale of liquor, favored a protective tariff, formed one of the first labor unions for printers in America, and was an avid fan of phrenology (he had an especially bumpy head, sort of a phrenologist's dream, as it were).

Greeley's thinking was never consistent—he was always changing his mind on this or that—but he was never idle. He was a moral leader, a popular teacher, the champion of new ideas. He walked about town, curious about everything. By the time of the Civil War, Greeley's paper was circulated all over the North (his antislavery ideas made it unacceptable to Southern readers). He opposed the War with Mexico as the aggression of slavery, opposed the extension of slavery into the Mexican cession, and was livid about the creation of Kansas and Nebraska (q.v.), with slavery allowed above the old Missouri Compromise (q.v.) line of 36°30′ (the northern border of Arkansas). He assisted abolitionists to arm the Yankees who went out to save Kansas from slaveholders and applauded resistance to the Fugitive Slave Act of 1850. He was one of the first editors to join the Republican (q.v.) Party, giving it instant access to homes all over the North. Of the Dred Scott (q.v.) decision, which declared the African-American as not a citizen, he wrote that it was "entitled to as much moral weight as would be the judgment of a majority of those congregated in any Washington bar-room." He fell out with Seward and Weed, declaring them too moderate on the slavery question, and backed Abraham Lincoln (q.v.) in 1860. Although he was a member of Congress briefly in the late 1840s, otherwise Greeley never served in political office. But he was the best-known politician in the nation because of his constant barrage of editorials on every issue.

The war brought him new opportunities to educate America on its moral duty to clean up the slavery problem. He believed that secession was a right if the great majority of the South wanted it, then professed to see a conspiracy of rich slaveowners as its guiding force. After the war began, Greeley became an instant military genius, in his own eyes at least, and covered the masthead of page one with the slogan "Forward to Richmond!" (although in truth the shibboleth was from one of his editors, Richard Henry Dana). He allied himself with the Radical Republicans and pushed emancipation, regardless of its cost. He called it the "Question of the Day" and begged Lincoln to act in an editorial entitled, "The Prayer of Twenty Millions." But the man who wanted war in 1861 had changed his mind as the conflict dragged on and, by 1864, Greeley had become a peace-at-any-price advocate. Lincoln shrewdly let him go and talk to Confederate peace commissioners, where Greeley found to his chagrin that the South's only uncompromisable condition for ending the war was an independent Confederacy. He also supported Lincoln, whom he had berated for so long as ineffectual on most issues, in the 1864 election (q.v.), which angered the Radicals. By the end of the war, Greeley had been on so many contradictory sides of so many questions that most of the North thought him going daft.

Reconstruction was not much different. Greeley endorsed Radical Military Reconstruction and the Fourteenth and Fifteenth Amendments (qq.v.). He permitted the *Tribune* to support the impeachment of Lincoln's successor, Andrew Johnson (q.v.), but the policy was one of a junior editor rather than Greeley himself. Once again, the great editor was changing his mind. He went in on Jefferson Davis'(q.v.) bail bond, even though the action cost him fully one-half of his subscribers. Greeley was slowly coming to be disenchanted with the corruption that Reconstruction came to embody in the South. He saw Ulysses S. Grant (q.v.) as a weak president of poor leadership qualities. Greeley was in favor of a single presidential term anyway, and he believed that Grant ought to step down in 1872. He also believed that the time had come to let wartime animosities pass. By this time, however, the *Tribune* had become more than Greeley—it was now a great institution in itself. If Greeley did not care where his cockeyed ideas carried the paper, his editors did. But Greeley did not understand the change that was taking place. He knew that he was a good, humane man and represented the idealism that had made America great. And Greeley knew that such a man was what the nation needed in 1872, to bring the country back to its senses as a healed, unified entity.

Led by Whitelaw Reid, one of Greeley's editors, the Liberal Republicans (q.v.), the reform element of the party that bolted when Grant ran for a second term, nominated Horace Greeley for president during the summer of 1872. Greeley had not pushed the nomination, but he did not shrink from accepting it. Resigning from the *Tribune*, Greeley took to the stump. His acceptance was a real shock to the political professionals. In the end, he lost out to the better organized Republican (q.v.) machine, fear from the financial markets that he was economically untrustworthy, and the impossibility of reconciling Democrats and Republican reformers under one banner.

The loss hit Greeley personally. It was compounded by the death of his wife at about the same time. He wandered back to his beloved *Tribune*, only to find Reid and others in power and unwilling to let him back in (was this Reid's motive in nominating him all along?). His mind and body both broke. He died insane on November 30, 1872. In death, the nation paid him the tribute that it never did while he was alive, with a massive funeral procession in New York City. *See also* ELECTION OF 1872.

GRESHAM'S LAW. *See* GRANT, ULYSSES S., ADMINISTRATION—DOMESTIC POLICIES.

GRIERSON'S RAID. *See* VICKSBURG CAMPAIGN.

GRIFFIN, CHARLES (1825–1867). Born at Granville, Ohio, Charles Griffin graduated from West Point in 1847. He arrived too late to fight in the War with Mexico, but he served on the Western frontier in New Mexico Territory before teaching artillery tactics at his alma mater. In 1861, he was a captain in the artillery and placed in charge of the West Point battery of light artillery that gained fame at First Bull Run when it was overrun in the final Confederate attack. Griffin returned to Washington, D.C., where he spent the winter reorganizing his unit and courting Sallie Carroll, whom he would marry. An energetic officer, Griffin transferred to the volunteer service where promotions came faster, and by 1862 he was in command of a brigade of infantry. He participated in every campaign of the Army of the Potomac and by the end of the war was a brevet major general in charge of a corps. Griffin's men took the formal surrender of the Confederates at Appomattox (q.v.).

After the war, like all regular officers, Griffin was reduced in actual rank. He became colonel of the Thirty-fifth Infantry, one of the occupation regiments assigned to Texas. Griffin was known as an unyielding officer of fiery temper, arrogant, egotistical, and very close to insubordinate in most of his public utterances. But he was tough and reliable, and those qualities endeared him to Maj. Gen. Philip Sheridan (q.v.) late in the war. And he was a diehard Union man, which reflected itself in support for the Republican Party, especially the Radicals (qq.v.). After a year of frustration in commanding the occupation forces in Louisiana and Texas, Sheridan became well aware that he needed a subordinate who could run Texas while he kept an eye on Louisiana. He called on Griffin.

When he arrived in Galveston to take charge, Griffin found the Reconstruction of Texas in a shambles. The elected governor, James W. Throckmorton (q.v.), a former Whig (q.v.) who had donned the gray only to fight Indians in the Texas frontier had outmaneuvered Sheridan and his Texas commanders time and time again. The Texas legislature had passed the notorious Black Codes, refused to consider the Thirteenth Amendment, rejected the Fourteenth Amendment (qq.v.) outright, proposed to enroll state troops (former Confederates) ostensibly to fight Indians, and elected two uncompromising Rebels as U.S. senators. There was a lot for Griffin to do.

The general knew that he did not possess adequate authority to move against the Texas state government, but he also was aware that Congress was debating the expansion of his powers through the Military Reconstruction Acts (q.v.). So Griffin bided his time; took over the reins of the semi-independent Freedmen's Bureau (q.v.); and unfairly but effectively blamed its outgoing commander for all of the problems between civilians and soldiers, gave in on the surface to Throckmorton's demands by shifting some troops westward, and secretly planned his countermoves. With the passage of the Military Reconstruction Acts, Griffin began his assault on what he saw as the backsliding of the civilian regime in Texas.

Leaving political removals until later (no one was yet sure that commanders had such powers under the initial Military Reconstruction Acts), Griffin turned to the problem of equal justice. One area in which Griffin took an interest was the number of blacks incarcerated in Texas jails, particularly at the state penitentiary at Huntsville. Under the guise of a Freedmen's Bureau inspection, Griffin recommended that many prisoners be released because they were serving time for crimes that would have merely called for a whipping in slavery days. He believed that they were unfairly convicted, as courts excluded blacks from testifying and being impaneled on juries. Governor Throckmorton was outraged at the idea, which impressed him as fuzzy thinking on how to prevent and punish crime.

The general issued an order that any post commander could take any case out of the civil and criminal courts in which an African-American was a party and send it to Griffin for review. He then required that all jurymen take the ironclad oath to serve, effectively limiting jurors to blacks and pro-Union whites. He issued the only public accommodations law promulgated by any regime in Texas Reconstruction (and later ignored by everyone) and sent his soldiers out into the field to protect loyal citizens and assist Freedmen's Bureau officers in their duties (the only general in Texas to do this as consistently and methodically during the whole Reconstruction period).

Griffin also administered the registration of voters for the election of the new state constitutional convention required under the Military Reconstruction Acts. Registrars were Federal employees and thus had to take the ironclad oath to serve. All voters had to take an oath of future loyalty and not be among the classes excluded from participation under the Fourteenth Amendment (people who had taken an oath to the United States and then to the Confederacy). But Griffin, with Sheridan's approval, allowed the registrars to go further and exclude anyone whom they suspected of latent disloyalty. It was a position that Congress would endorse in the Third Military Reconstruction Act, but it caused much dissatisfaction among Texas whites of the former Confederate variety. But although things looked good on the surface, Griffin and Republicans knew that patronage would be the only way to get rid of ex-Rebels in political positions and cleanse the state of treason. And here they ran into a big problem, General Sheridan. He would not allow the wholesale removals so important to the building of the Republican Party. And no matter how hard he tried, Griffin could not change Sheridan's mind.

But Griffin was vindicated once again in the Third Reconstruction Act. Griffin immediately wrote Sheridan about how Governor Throckmorton had impeded Reconstruction. Sheridan removed Throckmorton from office and replaced him with Unionist Elisha M. Pease (q.v.), the very man who had overwhelmingly lost to Throckmorton in the gubernatorial election the year before. In retaliation, President Andrew Johnson (q.v.) promptly removed Sheridan from office for exceeding his powers and replaced him with known Democrat and opponent to Military Reconstruction, Maj. Gen. Winfield Scott Hancock (q.v.). Pending Hancock's arrival (he had to consult with the president in Washington first), Sheridan turned his position over to Griffin, the next ranking officer, and gave him full power to act in any way he wished, as Sheridan left for reassignment on the Great Plains. Griffin did not delay. He promptly began to clean out all Democrats in the state executive department and the state supreme and district court systems.

Suddenly, as the Texas Republicans seemed at the height of success, a virulent yellow fever epidemic swept up the Gulf Coast from Mexico. Everyone turned to combating the dreaded disease, and Griffin was in the forefront. Army authorities recommended that he move himself and his family away until the epidemic ceased with cooler weather. Griffin refused, likening his leaving to abandoning a post in battle. Griffin's family contracted the disease. His little boy died. Then he fell ill. On September 15, 1867, Charles Griffin died from the complications of yellow fever. His parting was a disaster for Texas Republicans. He had left before his program of removing Democrats and replacing them with Republicans had fairly begun. No one knew if they would see his like again—an Army officer who understood the political realities of the Military Reconstruction Acts and carried them out so as to cause a real change in the South to guarantee the results of the war.

GRISWOLDVILLE, BATTLE OF. *See* MARCH TO THE SEA.

GROVETON, BATTLE OF. *See* MANASSAS CAMPAIGN, SECOND.

H

HABEAS CORPUS. Literally, to have the body. It is a legal concept that one cannot be jailed indefinitely without being brought before a judge and having formal charges brought by an accuser.

In the North, President Abraham Lincoln (q.v.) suspended the writ of *habeas corpus* (q.v.) in Maryland in 1861, later in the railroad corridor between Washington and New York, and finally throughout the nation (1862). This allowed his provost marshals to arrest suspects on mere accusation and hold them indefinitely without accusing them or having to produce proof of their complicity in some crime, beyond their disliked intellectual or political leanings.

Political opponents pointed to this action as typical of Lincoln's tendency to emphasize the executive proclamation (q.v.) at the expense of Congress and the clauses of the U.S. Constitution. Congress later authorized Lincoln's action in the Habeas Corpus Act of 1863 (q.v.).

In the South, President Jefferson Davis (q.v.) asked the Confederate Congress to suspend the writ, which it did three times during the war in the Habeas Corpus Act of 1862 (q.v.).

HABEAS CORPUS ACT OF 1862, CONFEDERATE. One of the issues on which the state rights faction of the Confederate Congress opposed the executive operations of President Jefferson Davis (q.v.) was the suspension of the writ of *habeas corpus* (q.v.). The Confederacy had numerous areas of disaffection that did much to break up the operation of the conscription laws and shield dissenters. Just as in the North, to be able to arrest these people without bringing charges against them, often difficult to prove, would enhance the war effort. Local army commanders acted first in the spring of 1862 by suspending the writ in their individual command area, particularly in east Tennessee. But Davis would have none of that. He nullified such orders and had the arrested released as soon as he learned of them.

It was not that Davis disagreed with the need to suspend the writ. It was who should do it. The Confederate Constitution was the same as the U.S. Constitution here. Nowhere was a specific agency of the government charged with the right of suspension. But suspension of the writ was allowed and mentioned in the section referring to Congress. So Davis asked Congress to do it by passing a suspension law. In this matter, Davis acted exactly the opposite of Union President Abraham Lincoln (q.v.), who suspended the writ by executive action.

The suspension bill was called the Barksdale Act, after its sponsor, Ethelbert Barksdale of Mississippi. The quirk was that the measure allowed Davis to suspend the writ only in certain areas for a limited time. Davis had to go back to Congress each time the act expired or he wanted to widen the areas affected. So the Rebels suspended the writ three times in three separate acts for the periods: February 27–October 13, 1862; October 13, 1862–February 15, 1863; and February 15, 1863–August 1, 1864. After August 1, 1864, Congress refused to allow the suspension, calling Davis a despot for desiring a new bill. His own vice president, Alexander Stephens (q.v.), led the critics and voted against any new suspension. Stephens and his allies maintained that the suspension caused internal dissent, and if the suspension were canceled, the protests would stop. In fact, the exact opposite proved true. It was a case where principle proved more important to Confederate lawmakers than victory.

HABEAS CORPUS ACT OF 1863, UNION. The law entitled "An Act Relating to Habeas Corpus, and Regulating Judicial Proceedings in Certain Cases," or the Habeas Corpus Act of 1863, gave the president congressional authorization to suspend the writ of *habeas corpus* (q.v.). Although President Abraham Lincoln (q.v.) had already been suspending the writ in select areas initially, and then the whole Union, since the beginning of the war by executive proclamation (q.v.), the suspension clause was situated in that part of the U.S. Constitution relating to the powers of Congress, not the executive. This measure, in effect, legalized Lincoln's previous executive action. The act required the secretary of war to compile a list of all non-combatant persons who were detained by order of the president, provided that such persons were citizens of Union states where the Federal courts had not been displaced by the war. This list would be given to the Federal courts of the districts that had jurisdiction over the prisoners.

If a Federal grand jury met and adjourned without indicting a prisoner within its jurisdiction whose name was on the list, then that person was entitled to have the court release him upon taking an oath of future loyalty to the United States. The release could be unconditional, or the prisoner could be released on bond and required to meet periodically with the court so that the court could make sure the released person was behaving properly. In spite of the law, the Lincoln and Andrew Johnson (q.v.) administrations do not seem to have issued lists of detainees. Even so, the Habeas Corpus Act of 1863 allowed any non-combatant prisoner arrested by order of the president to petition a Federal court for release. Upon proof that he was a citizen of a non-Confederate state, that he was not a prisoner of war, and that the grand jury had met without indicting him, the prisoner was entitled to be released, conditionally or unconditionally, upon taking the required oaths.

In *ex parte* Milligan (q.v.), the Supreme Court held that the provisions of the Habeas Corpus Act of 1863 were constitutionally valid, as they contemplated no other trial or sentence than that of a civil court. This, of course, ruled out trials of civilians by military commissions in any loyal, pro-Union jurisdiction where the normal courts were functioning, war or no war. Nonetheless, many arrested non-combatant Confederate supporters, including the Lincoln assassins, were erroneously tried by military tribunal.

HABEAS CORPUS ACT OF 1867, UNION. Because Southern white opponents had used suits brought in state courts to harass freedmen and Army and Freedmen's Bureau (q.v.) officers for interfering with state laws in their the application of Federal Reconstruction measures like the Military Reconstruction Acts and the Civil Rights Act of 1866 (qq.v.), the Congress passed the Habeas Corpus Act of 1867. This measure allowed defendants to appeal adverse decisions made against them by hostile state courts to the Federal courts. Ironically, one of its most noted applications was on behalf of an anti-Reconstruction white newspaperman in the case *ex parte* McCardle (q.v.), which caused Congress to reassess and restrict Supreme Court jurisdiction in this and other similar cases.

HAHN, MICHAEL. *See* LOUISIANA EXPERIMENT.

HALLECK, HENRY WAGER (1815–1872). Born in New York, graduated third in the class of 1839 at West Point, Henry W. Halleck was considered a sort of military genius of his time. His nickname was "Old Brains." Halleck spoke in a halting manner, rubbing his elbows across his folded arms. His eyes were bugged out and constantly watering. He had a bald, melon-shaped head, always tilted to one side; a sallow complexion; stooped shoulders; flabby cheeks; double chins covered by an inadequate, thin line of whiskers; and a pot belly. He translated military books from the French, allegedly at nine cents a page, which according to critics was a true measure of his soul. He translated Baron Antoine Henri Jomini's (q.v.) book and published an edited version of it as his own *Elements of Military Art and Science* in 1846, saw little service during the War with Mexico except in military government, and resigned his commission while in California in 1854.

In California, Halleck came into his own. He drew up the first state constitution, made a fortune as a mining engineer and lawyer, and became a recognized expert on international law. Renowned in 1861, President Abraham Lincoln (q.v.) appointed him major general and sent him to the Western Theater to replace Maj. Gen. John Charles Frémont (q.v.). Halleck was an able administrator but a lousy field commander. No matter; he took full credit for all of his subordinates' victories. In the summer of 1862, Lincoln pulled him back to Washington to become general-in-chief of the Union armies.

In Washington, Halleck quickly folded under all the responsibility of running the war. He loved to tell others how to do things, but he could not do them himself. As one commentator put it, "Halleck originates nothing, anticipates nothing to help others, takes no responsibility, plans nothing, suggests nothing, is good for nothing." But Lincoln decided to keep Halleck on as a sort of military advisor. He translated military jargon and principles for the president, who made all of the decisions. But he only gave advice when directly asked for it. When Lt. Gen. Ulysses S. Grant (q.v.) came east in 1864, he kept Halleck on as chief of staff, to administer the armies behind the lines and allow Grant to supervise the battlefields.

Halleck became a nonentity in Reconstruction. This was partially due to his penchant for alienating everyone he came in contact with and, more important, to his philosophy of military government. During and after the war, the general had demonstrated a fairly conservative approach to Reconstruction, much on the line advocated by his close friend and rare defender, Maj. Gen. William T. Sherman (q.v.). Both men tended to adhere to the notion that Reconstruction was solely a military, not a political, problem. This attitude irritated Secretary of War Edwin McM. Stanton (q.v.), who, in the aftermath of President Lincoln's assassination, removed Halleck as chief of staff and ordered him to Richmond to assume command there. In a vain effort to gain the secretary's favor, Halleck engaged in a brief tenure of absolute power. He went so far as to prohibit church services where the minister would not read a proscribed prayer for the president and refused marriage licenses to anyone who had not taken the oath of future loyalty, "to prevent so far as possible the propagation of legitimate Rebels."

But Halleck soon reestablished his conservative credentials by refusing to seize the Tredegar Ironworks, recommending that freedmen stay at their old places of work, and holding quick civil elections for a new Richmond city government. Believing Halleck's position to be too pro-Confederate, Stanton quietly transferred him to San Francisco, where the general remained harmlessly until 1869 in charge of the Department of the Columbia and Pacific. Then Halleck came east once again to head the Military Division of the South at Louisville. By that time, Reconstruction was all but over in his new command area. He died in 1872 without having made a real contribution to the Reconstruction process.

HAMBURG (SOUTH CAROLINA) MASSACRE (1876). As the majority of black voters in South Carolina was the largest in the South, it became evident that mere fraud would not carry the day. The result was the adoption of the Mississippi Plan (q.v.), which meant in South Carolina the organization of the Red Shirts (q.v.), its own version of the White League (q.v.). The movement got its biggest support in Edgefield County, a hotbed of secession in 1860, the Ku Klux Klan (q.v.) after the war, and now the center of straight-out Democracy. The blacks in "Bloody Edgefield" had organized their own Rifle Clubs (q.v.), so the scene was set for open hostility, as soon as a triggering event could take place.

It occurred in nearby Hamburg. A black militia company paraded in Hamburg's streets for the Fourth of July 1876. Two whites in a buggy told the commander to get his men out of the way. The soldier replied that there was plenty of room on either side of the column. A local court swore out an arrest warrant on the militia officer for blocking a public thoroughfare a couple of days later.

An armed group of 200 or 300 whites showed up for the hearing. They demanded that the black militia surrender its weapons. The militia commander refused. Shooting soon erupted, and the blacks took refuge in a building, which the whites began to shell with a cannon. The blacks fled out the rear, 25 of their number being "arrested." One of the armed white companies executed five black men in its custody, an incident called the Hamburg Massacre.

Although the murder was condemned by Conservatives, they blamed the shootings on the evils flowing from Republican rule. At Carpetbag Governor Daniel Chamberlain's (qq.v.) request, President Ulysses S. Grant (q.v.) sent Federal soldiers to restore order. Then the Republicans instituted court proceedings, indicting 60 whites from the best families of the area for the massacre. The trial, with the defendants appearing in their red shirts, was delayed until after the 1876 election (q.v.) so that passions might cool, when all of the accused were released.

HAMILTON, ANDREW JACKSON. (1815–1875). Originally from Huntsville, Alabama, Andrew Jackson Hamilton was educated locally and admitted to the state bar in 1846. Soon afterward he followed his older brother Morgan Calvin Hamilton to Texas. Morgan had been in Texas since before the Texas Revolution, where he clerked in a store and served as a War Department clerk and secretary of war for the Republic. A. J., as the younger Hamilton was known familiarly, became a lawyer in La Grange before moving to Austin to be with his brother.

Both brothers were ardent Union men during the secession (q.v.) crisis. A. J. fled to Mexico and upon the Federal reoccupation of New Orleans went there, where President Abraham Lincoln (q.v.) appointed him brigadier general and provisional governor of Texas. He pushed for the invasion of Galveston (which failed, defeated on the city's docks) and arranged for his friends to get in on a scheme to invest in confiscated cotton. Such machinations led to his nickname of "Colossal Jack." With the failure of the Red River Campaign (q.v.), A. J. remained a governor in exile until the end of the war.

Hamilton arrived back to Texas in late summer 1865 to take over the provisional government. He was charged with appointing loyal men to all offices, calling a constitutional convention, and supervising an election to choose new officials under the revised constitution to replace the provisional government and ratify the Thirteenth Amendment (q.v.). Because of the size of the state, the relatively small size of the Union occupation army, and Jackson's own meticulous approach to selecting reliable, Union men for office, Texas began a long habit of being late in meeting its Reconstruction responsibilities.

Hamilton was disgusted when the constitutional convention and the ensuing election returned political power to the former Confederates. When the army took over Reconstruction (q.v.), he served as associate justice on the state supreme court. During the writing of a new constitution in 1868–1869, supervised by the army, A. J. broke with his brother and the Radical Republicans and joined with a group of Moderate Republicans and Conservatives, breaking off from doctrinaire Democrats (q.v.), over the *ab initio* (q.v.) issue. This led to A. J. standing for governor against E. J. Davis (q.v.), who was supported by his brother. Backed by General Joseph J. Reynolds (q.v.), the Radicals and Davis were counted in and took over the state in 1870, approving the Fourteenth Amendment as required by the Military Reconstruction Acts (q.v.). In 1871, A. J. led the Tax Payers' Revolt against the costs of the new government until Texas was redeemed in 1874. Colossal Jack died in 1875 of tuberculosis.

HAMPTON ROADS PEACE CONFERENCE. To appease the state rights faction (q.v.) opposed to his policies in fighting the war, Confederate President Jefferson Davis (q.v.) suggested, in response to feelers from Union President Abraham Lincoln (q.v.) delivered through ex-Postmaster General Montgomery Blair of Maryland, that the South and North discuss immediate peace to save lives. Davis appointed his most vocal critic, his own vice president, Alexander Stephens (q.v.), to lead the delegation composed of Stephens, John A. Campbell of Alabama (a former U.S. Supreme Court judge and an assistant secretary of war for the Confederacy), and R. M. T. Hunter of Virginia (a Confederate congressman and senator, formerly secretary of state for the Confederacy). The conference was well-publicized, so when the commissioners came across the lines at the siege of Petersburg (q.v.), headed for the truce ship anchored in Hampton Roads, the troops on both sides rose up and cheered.

While Lincoln was not against talking with anyone, he feared to meet with this commission personally, thinking that to do so would be a recognition of the legitimacy of the Confederate government and secession. He sent

Secretary of State William H. Seward (q.v.) in his place. But the poignancy of the moment proved to be too much. Stephens was an old friend from the days when Lincoln had served in Congress from Illinois. They were both ex-Whigs (q.v.). So Lincoln swallowed his fears and came in person.

There was little that the commissioners could do. Davis had handed them a one-word instruction, "Independence." Lincoln had a one-word guide himself, "Union." So the men sat and talked of older and cheerier times. Finally, Stephens asked Lincoln what he was going to do with the African-Americans once they were freed through his Emancipation Proclamation (q.v.). Lincoln was unsure if the proclamation would have any effect after the war—after all, it was a war measure. The courts would have to decide. But in any case, Lincoln said he would not change one word of the proclamation now. Stephens asked for a deal. Seward said that if the South would quit the war and rejoin the Union, they could block the proposed Thirteenth Amendment (q.v.) by voting against its ratification.

Lincoln suggested that the South could ratify the amendment prospectively and keep their slaves five years more. Then Lincoln said Stephens and the others ought to go back to their states, convene their state legislatures, recall their state troops from the war, elect members to the U.S. Congress and Senate, and ratify the amendment to take effect in five years. He thought it would be legal and would avoid what he called "the evils of immediate emancipation." He pledged that he would not undercut them by enforcing the Confiscation Acts (q.v.) to end slavery. He reminded his Rebel listeners that he had promised when elected not to interfere with slavery where it existed. But the war had changed things.

Then Hunter asked again what would happen to the freed slaves. He maintained that they surely would not work. Surely blacks and whites would starve. Then Lincoln told a little story, about a hog raiser back home who planted potatoes for the hogs to root out for feed, only to have the ground freeze. Mulling over what to do, the hog farmer figured, "Well, it may come pretty hard on their snouts, but I don't see but that it will be root hog or die!" That was his stated prescription for the freed blacks at Hampton Roads. Peace through Union was non-negotiable. Slavery was dead, but what was to take its place was negotiable. The Southern delegates went back home empty-handed to await the inevitable Northern victory.

HANCOCK, WINFIELD SCOTT (1824–1886). A Pennsylvanian, Winfield S. Hancock was graduated from West Point in 1840. He served in the Seminole War and in the War with Mexico, receiving a brevet for bravery at Churubusco. After the War with Mexico, he served on the Western frontier, where he was involved in the Kansas–Missouri Border Wars (q.v.) and wound up as chief quartermaster of the California command. With the outbreak of the Civil War, Hancock was brought east as a brevet brigadier general. He fought on the Peninsula (q.v.), where he earned his nickname, "the Superb," in the sharp fight at Williamsburg. He continued with the Army of the Potomac in every campaign it fought, rising from brigade to corps command. His conduct at Gettysburg, where he selected the Union position and turned back several Rebel assaults including Pickett's Charge, won him the thanks of Congress. His bravery had a price, however, and he was severely wounded, suffering a hip injury that would plague him for years. In 1864, Hancock led his corps on the Richmond Campaign (q.v.), watching them disintegrate at Ream's Station, totally worn out from the incessant fighting around Petersburg (q.v.). Hancock, too, was exhausted. His wound reopened, and he had to retire from front line duty, being placed in charge of the Veteran Reserve Corps made up of wounded men like him, too valuable to lose to the service but unable to fight day in and day out.

Because of his war service, Hancock became the junior major general of the Army after the war. He served on several boards and commissions and was posted to the Great Plains, where he fought the Cheyenne in 1866. A well-known Democrat (q.v.), Hancock was one of many Civil War generals who had doubt as to the wisdom of the Army getting involved with the politics of the Military Reconstruction Acts (q.v.). When President Andrew Johnson (q.v.) became particularly miffed at the pro-Republican stance of Maj. Gen. Philip H. Sheridan (q.v.) in the Fifth Military District (Louisiana and Texas), he pulled Sheridan out and sent him to the frontier to replace Hancock, who had not done well against the Cheyenne. Then Johnson used Hancock to blunt the Radical Republicans' plans for the South by putting him in charge of the Fifth Military District (Louisiana and Texas).

Hancock was well aware what awaited him in Louisiana and Texas. He began upon his arrival at his New Orleans headquarters by issuing General Orders No. 40. In it he stated that it was time for the civil authorities to take power in the South. He saw the Army's role as incidental to theirs, one of support, not policy setting. The Army would not interfere with the right to trial by jury, the writ of *habeas corpus* (q.v.), freedom of the press, freedom of speech, and the right to private property. The Army would act only if the civil authorities refused. Conservative whites hailed Hancock's order as a fresh breath of American liberty. Although little had changed as far as announced policy was concerned, the attitude of Hancock and his staff was decidedly against interfering in local matters except as a positively last resort.

Preceding his arrival, both Texas and Louisiana had had a vigorous cleansing of allegedly disloyal Democrats in favor of Republicans (q.v.). Now in both states the ousted officials, all elected in 1866, petitioned to be restored to their rightful places. But Hancock could not do this without creating an insurmountable storm. So he allowed all things to stay as they were when he arrived. Already Radical Republicans in Congress were moving to cut back the Army by removing the junior major general (Hancock) from the list. But in reality, they could do little. Hancock was acting well within his prerogatives as district commander under Congress' own Military Reconstruction Acts (q.v.).

Hancock next reopened all voter registration and liberalized the grounds upon which whites could be excluded for Confederate service. Several thousand voters were registered under Hancock's move, but it probably did not materially affect politics in either of the states under his command. Then Hancock got into an open tiff with Texas Provisional Governor Elisha M. Pease (q.v.) and Bvt. Maj. Gen. Joseph J. Reynolds (q.v.), his subordinate in Texas. Reynolds had placed the Republicans in control of local politics in Texas just before Hancock's arrival in New Orleans. In answer to complaints from those replaced, Hancock ordered the suspension of all removals from and appointments to office. He also commanded that all military trials, whether by military commission or Freedmen's Bureau (q.v.) agents, be submitted to the civil courts. This of course would put loyal black and white defendants at the mercy of the local courts and their Democrat juries.

When Pease protested Hancock's vision of Texas under civil government, Hancock retorted that Texas was at peace and the civil processes were more than adequate to preserve law and order. Pease retorted that the Military Reconstruction Acts imposed other than ordinary conditions upon the state. There was no legal government in Texas, Pease said, and the concept that Texas was at peace was naïve—there was an open race war on, and it was the Army's duty to stop it. He blamed an outrageous increase in crime on Hancock's General Orders No. 40.

Hancock waited some time before replying to Pease's accusations. He told Pease that his letter reeked of bad temper and illogical conclusions and that just because Pease and the Republicans did not like or agree with elected officials and their policies did not mean that they ought to expect the Army to intervene. That was what elections were for. So stop complaining, Hancock concluded, and get on with the process of making a new constitution and electing new officials.

Hancock's biographers lauded the general's refusal to make Reconstruction a process outside the general principles of American government, which ignores the fact that what he did also spelled death to the Republican Party in any state like Texas that had a white majority. Louisiana Republicans might be able to survive Hancock's approach, but Texas Republicans could not. And, of course, that is exactly what President Johnson had in mind when he sent Hancock down South. Hancock next turned to General Reynolds and ordered him to shift the Army from the Texas interior to the frontier. Then Hancock replaced Bvt. Maj. Gen. Joseph Mower in Louisiana with Bvt.

Maj. Gen. Robert C. Buchanan. Mower had paralleled Reynolds' actions in Texas by placing Republicans in power in Louisiana. Hancock also drove Provisional Governor Benjamin F. Flanders from power, Flanders refusing to cooperate with Hancock's "Democrat" policies.

When the Republican New Orleans city council voted to fill a vacant city office, Hancock moved to clean out this Radical stronghold (once appointed by Sheridan). He telegraphed his action to Lt. Gen. Ulysses S. Grant (q.v.). The Army's commanding general now saw his opening and moved against Hancock, whom he despised for not following Congress' bidding or the will of the people (the Northern people), at least as Grant saw it. He refused to allow Hancock to make his removals and replacements. Grant said that Hancock was going against his own public pronouncements that civil government had been restored in the Fifth Military District and that, as a Federal official, he ought not to interfere with a local government he did not like. Hancock sullenly obeyed the order. Shortly thereafter, Hancock tried to replace the New Orleans street commissioner (a position noted for its access to political graft). Grant once again told him to stop interfering with the local government. Hancock resigned his position, compromised as he saw it by a lack of support from on high.

Hancock would continue in the Army for some years, running the Military Division of the Atlantic and the Department of the Dakotas. He contested for president on the Democratic ticket in the election of 1880 against James A. Garfield, losing narrowly, by 10,000 popular votes. His popularity among the voters and veterans never waned, despite his opposition to Reconstruction and the Republican Party. Democrats saw him as a savior from Radical generals like Sheridan, Charles Griffin (q.v.), Mower, and Reynolds. But Southern Republicans envisioned him as the Devil incarnate, a foolish man who would compromise party principle for some ethereal notion of what the Founding Fathers deemed was the spirit of American government. He could never seem to rise above principle to practicality, the way so many of that era did, and that made him special in a time marked by political and monetary greed. But he also did not understand that the period itself was so unique that it might have called for revolutionary approaches to guarantee the freedom of African-Americans and quash a lingering and incipient rebellion.

HANOVER COURT HOUSE, BATTLE OF. *See* PENINSULA CAMPAIGN.

HARPER'S FERRY RAID (1859). In 1859, voters north and south repudiated the National Democratic Party in state election after state election. Only Stephen A. Douglas (q.v.) survived as the Northern states went Republican (q.v.). In the South, only Virginia stayed with the Democrats (q.v.). Whigs (q.v.) or independents took the other Southern states. But in Georgia, Mississippi, and Louisiana, radical Southern Democrats, often called the Chivalry or Fire-Eaters (q.v.), led by William L. Yancey, won handily. Yancey and his adherents stressed several things in their victories. They pointed out that moderate Republicans, not the antislavery radicals, even spoke about not having a nation half slave and half free (Abraham Lincoln's [q.v.] "House Divided Speech") and how war over slavery between North and South was inevitable (William H. Seward's [q.v.] "Irrepressible Conflict Speech"). Douglas admitted that he had flimflammed the South for years with his support of popular sovereignty in his Freeport Doctrine(qq.v.). Worse yet, Oregon and Minnesota had been admitted as free states, upsetting the balance between North and South in the U.S. Senate.

Most Southerners did not buy Yancey's fear-mongering, until an event occurred that seemed to make all of it come true. This was the raid on the Federal arsenal at Harper's Ferry, Virginia, in October 1859. Organized by John Brown (q.v.), who had made a name for himself by executing nonslaveholding Southern settlers in Kansas, the notion was for a cadre of abolitionists (q.v.) to go south, take arms from Federal arsenals, and free slaves by force. Those who did not wish to join the revolt would be hied north to Canada. Those who wished to join up would be armed and spread the revolution in the South.

The problem was that the local African-Americans did not rise up. Maybe it was because the first man Brown's raiders shot was a black free man of color. But the Federal government and the state of Virginia did. United States Marines from Washington, D.C., surrounded Brown and his original conspirators in a firehouse at Harper's Ferry. President James Buchanan (q.v.) sent a well-known Mexican War hero, Col. Robert E. Lee (q.v.), whose home was across from the national capital at Arlington, to take command. His chief aide was another Virginian who would become better known during the coming Civil War, cavalryman Lt. J. E. B. Stuart (q.v.). After a brief siege, the Marines stormed the engine house and arrested Brown and a half dozen of his men. A half dozen more, including several of Brown's sons, were dead, and several others had escaped over the Potomac to Maryland.

Lee found Brown had maps of the South that marked centers of slave population. Virginia tried Brown in state court and found him guilty of treason. Rumors that his abolition friends would try to release Brown led to a call-up of the state militia to guard the execution proceedings, which went off without a hitch. When confronted with assisting Brown, the so-called "Secret Six," a group of wealthy abolition businessmen and philanthropists, denied any complicity.

It made no difference. The South firmly believed that the North irresponsibly had wanted to create a slave rebellion all along, and now they had their proof. They knew that if a Republican like Lincoln were elected, the South's hard-won victories in the U.S. Supreme Court, Dred Scott *v.* Sandford and Ableman *v.* Booth (qq.v.), would go by the wayside. Secession looked more viable than ever. The Harper's Ferry Raid destroyed the Southern Whig–American Party centrist revival of 1859 and left nothing but Republicans in the North and secession-minded Democrats in the South as viable alternatives in the election of 1860 (q.v.). If the Democrats divided in 1860, and they would, war was likely. And when that war of secession came, Yankee troops would march south singing "John Brown's Body Lies A-moldering in the Grave, But His Soul Goes Marching On." Their catchy little tune would be the basis for the "Battle Hymn of the Republic."

HARRIS, ISHAM G. (1818–1897). Instrumental in Tennessee's secession and defense, Isham Harris was born in Tullahoma in 1818. He clerked in stores in Tennessee and Mississippi and then entered the law. He served in the Mississippi legislature and as a congressman from Mississippi in the late 1840s, before moving to Memphis to increase his law practice. In Tennessee, he entered politics and was elected governor in 1857. Harris was a Democrat (q.v.) and a secessionist all his political life. A realist who saw that Tennesseans would have to be led into leaving the Union gradually, Harris declared the state's neutrality and began to recruit what later became the core of the Army of Tennessee, 24 regiments of infantry and cavalry and 10 batteries of artillery. Harris would go on to raise nearly 100,000 troops for the Confederacy during the war.

On May 7, 1861, Governor Harris drew up an alliance with the Confederacy, but one that left Tennessee responsible for its own defense until July 1861 and even after. The result was for Harris and his inadequately equipped military formations to rely on Kentucky's neutrality to preserve Tennessee's borders. When this failed, the state was completely open to invasion, having only the unfinished Fort Henry and Fort Donelson (qq.v.) on the Tennessee and the Cumberland to stave off the inevitable Yankee attack. Forced out of the state by the Union invasion, Harris served as a military aide to Generals P. G. T Beauregard, Braxton Bragg, Joseph E. Johnston, and John B. Hood (qq.v.).

With the fall of the Confederacy, Harris fled the country to Maximilian's Mexico (q.v.), not returning until 1875. He joined the Redeemers (q.v.) and became a U.S. senator, serving until 1895, until his Populist sentiments made him *persona non grata* in the Democratic Party. He died two years later.

HARRISON'S LANDING LETTER. Sent by Maj. Gen. George B. McClellan (q.v.) to President Abraham Lincoln (q.v.) on July 8, 1862, after the retreat of McClellan's army from the siege of Richmond during the Seven Days Campaign (q.v.), the Harrison's Landing letter marked an unwise injection of an army commander 's opinion into domestic policy. Rather than commenting on war strategy, McClellan, a Democrat (q.v.), attacked Republican (q.v.) policy, like the suspension of *habeas corpus* (q.v.), confiscation of property, interference with slavery, and lack of an overall commander-in-chief, a post from which McClellan had been removed some months before. After this gratuitous criticism, McClellan offered to serve wherever he was needed. The letter was unwise, because it placed McClellan out of touch with the rising sentiment for emancipation (q.v.) in the North and challenged Lincoln's role as commander-in-chief under the Constitution.

HATCHER'S RUN, FIRST BATTLE OF. *See* PETERSBURG, SIEGE OF.

HATCHER'S RUN, SECOND BATTLE OF. *See* PETERSBURG, SIEGE OF.

HAYES, RUTHERFORD B. (1822–1893). Born in Ohio after his father died, Rutherford B. Hayes was raised by his mother and sister with assistance from his uncle, Sardis Birchard. He was educated in a local academy and by private tutors and hoped to attend Yale, until financial realities sent him to local Kenyon College. The result was that he never lost his Midwestern point of view and remained a conservative, cautious man all of his life. He also had a strange, overly dependent relationship with his mother and his sister Fanny, who went insane and died after he married. After graduating college, he read law and finally managed to attend Harvard Law School for a year and a half.

He returned to Ohio and opened a law office near his uncle's home at Lower Sandusky, where he practiced for five years at the time of the War with Mexico. He thought of volunteering for the war to clear up a bronchial condition, but doctors advised against it. After the war, he would travel to Texas and visit Guy M. Bryan, a Harvard classmate and plantation owner, with whom he kept up a lifelong correspondence. In Texas, Hayes came to see slavery as essentially a benign institution of racial control, which may have colored his attitude on the South in years to come. He returned to Ohio, this time setting up a law practice in Cincinnati, from which he grew rich. He married Lucy Webb, a temperance supporter who would ban alcohol from the White House and earn the somewhat derisive moniker "Lemonade Lucy" in later years ("You are sister Fanny now," he told her when his sister passed away later), and began to dabble in local politics as a Whig (q.v.). The growth of the slavery issue, especially its spread into the West, made Hayes a Republican (q.v.) by 1856, although he was reserved in his condemnation of any viewpoint.

Although Hayes hoped to see the Civil War prevented, after its outbreak he became active and eventually accepted the post as major of the 23rd Ohio Volunteer Infantry, eventually advancing to regimental and brigade command. He served against Stonewall Jackson (q.v.) in the Shenandoah Valley in 1862 and was wounded in the arm at the Battle of South Mountain during the Maryland Campaign (q.v.). Hayes and his men then fought guerrillas in the mountains of West Virginia and were important in checking flamboyant Confederate cavalryman John H. Morgan during his 1863 raid in southern Ohio. In 1864, Hayes and his troops were part of the Army of the Shenandoah under Maj. Gen. Philip H. Sheridan (q.v.) and active in sweeping Confederate control from the Shenandoah Valley. He spent the rest of the war in garrison duty, achieving the rank of brevet major general.

In the fall of 1864, Hayes was elected to Congress from Cincinnati, even though he had refused to campaign for the seat. He resigned his military rank and took office in June 1865 only after the surrender of the last of the Rebel forces. He generally voted with the Republican Party on Reconstruction questions, even though he was not a Radical (q.v.) and disapproved of their hostile methods toward the South. He was reelected in 1866, but resigned the position in June 1867 to run for the party as governor of Ohio. Hayes narrowly won the governor's chair, and hampered by a Democrat (q.v.) legislature, he got little done. But he did make some prison reforms and set up a better regulation of charities. His popularity with the voters remained high, and in 1869 Hayes won a second term. Now with a Republican majority in the legislature, Hayes came out against high taxes, reformed the care of the insane, supported creation of a state agricultural college, and attacked railroad management for disregarding the public good. He recognized the principle of merit in political appointments, even going so far as to appoint able Democrats to office; combated election fraud; created a geologic survey department; and encouraged the preservation of historical records. By now he was viewed as a capable administrator of national importance, but Hayes instead chose to retire from the governorship and preserve its two-term tradition. He stood for Congress again but was defeated.

The next few years found Hayes devoting himself to the law, real estate, and local public service. But with the Democrat reinsurgence of 1874, state Republicans approached him offering to back him not only for a third term as governor but for president of the country as well. All of a sudden the man without real ambition felt the bite of the presidential bug in a big way. He won the governorship and offered not only an ability to gain votes, but a reform record as one who had stayed loyal to the party despite his disagreements with it. With the backing of Senator John Sherman (q.v.) and Representative James A. Garfield, Hayes went to the Republican convention, which by able maneuvering was held in his hometown of Cincinnati. He won the nomination after opponents to the candidacy of James G. Blaine settled on him as an attractive yet unoffending alternative. The presidential election of 1876 (q.v.) hinged on Hayes' taking all of the disputed votes in the Republican's "rotten boroughs" of the South plus one in Oregon, a process that was accomplished in the usual shady monetary manner, without Hayes' direct participation.

Essentially what Hayes and his administration did was institute what came to be called the "New Departure" (q.v.). Its central tenet was that the better classes in the South, those old Whigs who had been slaveholders, reluctant to secede, and willing to be Scalawags (q.v.) during Reconstruction, would protect blacks as they had done in the days of slavery. But Yankees either failed to realize the implications of their decision for black freedom or, given the struggle for the black vote in the North before and during Reconstruction, did not care. It was a process both he and Democrat opponent Samuel J. Tilden (q.v.) had promised, but one that was made easier on the nation's psyche by Hayes' war record and party label.

Hayes himself seemed to have an inkling of the evils that the New Departure signified for African-Americans. He almost welshed on the deal until a "special" tour of the South and a private talk with South Carolina's Wade Hampton convinced him that any future bloodshed in a race war would be on his hands and that Southern whites would "take care" of their black population, a process that was assisted by letters, some sycophantic, some sinister, from old friend, and now Texas Redeemer (q.v.), Guy M. Bryan. He withdrew the troops, a policy actually begun by President Ulysses S. Grant (q.v.) when he refused to interfere with elections in state after state as their inevitable Redemptions drew nigh. This meant that troops went into traditional barracks areas in the South and did not police elections, not that they necessarily left the South, although contingents certainly did go from there to the Western frontier.

The New Departure relied on getting Southerners to support Republican economic programs that only the conservative, upper class veneer in the South liked. The average Southern white yeoman was more prone to support radical farmers' groups that promised debt relief and soft money, ideas that Hayes (and the old Southern Whigs) found repugnant. He appointed Democrat David Key of Tennessee as postmaster general (in charge of a legion of political appointments nationwide, but especially important for its implications in the South).

But Hayes' whole policy appalled many Northern Republicans, remnants of the Radicals who had lost their idealism in support of the Negro for the greed of office and were now called "Stalwarts." They were angry that Hayes allowed Postmaster General Key to appoint Democrats to lucrative positions in the South. But the catch was that although the New Departure ignored blacks as a group, Hayes was careful to reward them as individuals with appointments to office. This allowed Hayes to maintain the fiction that he really was on the side of black America and muzzle those who accepted his appointments.

Besides abandoning the Republican promises on race, Hayes issued an executive order (he could not get a congressional law for civil service reform [q.v.]) forbidding monetary assessments and political assignments from appointed officeholders and cleaned up the New York customs house corruption (to the dismay of New York Senator Roscoe Conkling and Chester A. Arthur, the commissioner), used Federal troops to suppress the bloody rail strike of 1877 (to the dismay of union leaders nationwide), vetoed a Chinese exclusion bill (threatening party support in the West), and came out on behalf of the resumption of specie payments and the end to greenbacks (alienating the gold lobby and debtors in general but endearing him to Western silver producers).

By the end of his term, it was obvious that Hayes was going to be a one-term president, something that he did not oppose. He retired to his Ohio home and devoted himself to library work, filling his many speaking engagements and supporting various humanitarian causes, like prison and education reform. His wife died in 1889, a severe blow to him, but he remained active until his own death four years later, which had been hastened by exposure to bad weather while attending a meeting of trustees of the state university. His funeral brought forth accolades for his patriotism and common-sense dedication to reform, overlooking the long-range implications of his failed Southern policy.

HAZEL GROVE, BATTLE OF. *See* CHANCELLORSVILLE CAMPAIGN.

HEPBURN *v.* **GRISWOLD (1871).** *See* LEGAL TENDER CASES.

HICKS, THOMAS H. (1798–1865). Born near East New Market in Dorchester County on Maryland's Eastern Shore, Thomas H. Hicks served as town constable and county sheriff as a Democratic–Republican. With the rise of Jackson, like many conservative Southerners, Hicks switched to the Whig Party (q.v.) and served two terms in the House of Delegates. He then was register of wills for Dorchester County until his election in 1858 as state governor, now under the American Party (q.v.), or the Know Nothings, as it was popularly known at the time.

Hicks as governor reflected the stand of the American Party well. He spoke out against immigration as the ruination of the country, decried the growth of abolitionism in the North, and supported slavery and the constitutionality of the Fugitive Slave Act of 1850 (q.v.), under the concept of state sovereignty (q.v.). When the secession (q.v.) crisis came, Hicks had the habit of referring to secessionists and fellow Southerners as "we" while referring to the Federal government, the Abraham Lincoln (q.v.) administration, and Northerners as "they."

After the Pratt Street riot or Baltimore plot (q.v.) in April 1861, in which citizens attacked Union troops headed to defend Washington, Hicks heeded the warnings of the pro-secession mayor of Baltimore, William Brown, the city marshal, George P. Kane, and a former state governor, E. L. Lowe, to ask the Federal government to send its troops some other way than through

Baltimore, the only rail connection between the North and Washington, D.C. To drive his point home, Hicks ordered the state militia to burn the bridges between Baltimore and Harve de Grace to the north.

Governor Hicks' actions in effect cut off Washington, D.C., from the rest of the nation. Hicks at first denied that he had done anything wrong and asked President Abraham Lincoln (q.v.) to send soldiers some other way besides through Baltimore, and to allow Maryland to stand as neutral, but soon changed his mind when Lincoln arrested the bridge-burning militiamen and refused them the writ of *habeas corpus* (q.v.). This led to the case of *ex parte Merryman* (q.v.), decided by Supreme Court Chief Justice Roger B. Taney on circuit, who deemed that such arbitrary arrests were unconstitutional.

Now many prominent citizens wanted Hicks to call a special session of the state legislature, a process that had led the way to session in the Lower South. Hicks complied with the legislative call, but changed its meeting place from the pro-secession state capital of Annapolis to pro-Union Frederick to the west. As the legislators traveled to Frederick, they found the roads patrolled by Union troops, who quickly arrested the more pro-secession members in violation of Judge Taney's opinion in *Merryman*, which Lincoln, having suspended the writ of *habeas corpus*, ordered them to ignore. The result was that Maryland voted to remain in the Union, occupied by Yankee soldiers to the end.

Hicks became more pro-Union during the war. He was appointed to the vacant U.S. Senate seat in 1862, campaigned for Lincoln's reelection in 1864, and died in Washington, D.C., in early 1865.

HIGH BRIDGE, BATTLE OF THE. *See* APPOMATTOX CAMPAIGN.

HINES, THOMAS. *See* LINCOLN ASSASSINATION; LINCOLN ASSASSINATION, THE CONFEDERACY AND THE; LINCOLN ASSASSINATION, THE NEW YORK CONNECTION OF THE.

HOLDEN, WILLIAM W. (1818–1892). North Carolina has a history of villains ranging from Blackbeard the Pirate to Tom Dully [Dula] of folksong fame, but few have exceeded the hatred inspired by William W. Holden, its Reconstruction governor. Born in Orange County, little is known about Holden's early life. He was largely self-made, attended a "field school," and became a printer's apprentice. Originally a Whig (q.v.) newspaper editor, Holden switched to being a Jacksonian Democrat (q.v.) advocate, if for nothing else than to stimulate debate over political issues of the day. As a writer, he was distinctly partisan and frequently abusive, in the style of the times. As a participant in the 1850s demise of the Whig Party, Holden made many lifelong enemies. It also enhanced his reputation as an opportunistic, bitter, unscrupulous, and arrogant demagogue.

In the late 1850s, Holden entered state politics, running for governor and U.S. senator, failing to achieve either position. In 1860, he backed the presidential aspirations of Stephen A. Douglas (q.v.) and cautioned the red-hot seceders to wait until President Abraham Lincoln (q.v.) did something overt before considering leaving the Union. Upon the firing on Fort Sumter (q.v.), Holden came out wholeheartedly for secession, although he tempered it somewhat by voting for the "right of revolution." But he soon saw that secession Democrats were squeezing him out of the party with the connivance of Confederate President Jefferson Davis (q.v.). This caused Holden to organize the Conservative Party, a combination of Douglas Democrats and ex-Whigs. For their front man they chose Zebulon Vance, who became governor in 1864 on a program that criticized the war. Holden also dabbled with the more radical secret peace society, "The Heroes of America." Once revealed, this association led many, Whigs and Democrats of all hues, to charge him with treason to the Confederacy, but the adverse end of the war saved him from any real embarrassment.

As Reconstruction began, President Andrew Johnson (q.v.) appointed Holden as his first loyal governor in the South. It was not unusual, as Johnson and Holden thought much alike, if Holden's editorials were any indication. But it angered many in the state, who thought that Holden had proved much too flexible in the past to be trusted now. Still, Holden surprised many of his detractors when his administration proved to be one of moderation and feeling. Many feared that to reject him in the election of 1866 would cause the North to misinterpret the sincerity of their submission to defeat. But at the last moment, the Conservatives put forward Jonathan Worth, a relative political unknown of principled Union antecedents who had been serving as state treasurer. The result was a repudiation of Holden at the polls, his past reputation as an unprincipled and "malicious prince of demagogism" doing him in.

But the imposition of the Military Reconstruction Acts (q.v.) on North Carolina gave Holden new political life as the head of the state's Republican Party, in league with other Scalawags, blacks, and Carpetbaggers (qq.v.). Guiding the party to a fairly moderate stance on such issues as disfranchising ex-Confederates (there was none on the state level), Holden ran for and won the governor's chair in 1868, the Republicans also taking over the state legislature.

Although many hated Holden for his support of black civil rights, they were a small minority in North Carolina. The real struggle was among Union (Carpetbag and Scalawag) and Rebel whites over state-backed economic growth subsidies, particularly to railroad companies. Holden inevitably became linked up with two con artists extraordinaire, Milton S. Littlefield (q.v.) and George W. Swepson. Holden was probably monetarily honest, but he became tainted when he issued a series of bonds for a railroad in the Piedmont and Appalachian sections of the state that turned out to be fraudulent. In this

Holden was a lot like President Ulysses S. Grant (q.v.)—he never repudiated his friends and thus was guilty by association, if nothing else.

But the problem that did Holden in was the suppression of the Ku Klux Klan (q.v.) in Alamance and Caswell Counties. Authorized to raise a state militia to protect loyal white and black voters, Holden brought in from East Tennessee George W. Kirk, whom he made colonel in charge. The result was the so-called Kirk–Holden War as Kirk's men attempted to put down Ku Klux violence, with mixed effectiveness. It worked well in the two counties affected (both dominated by white Loyalists), but left the rest of the state (especially the African-American and Republican east) wide open to voter intimidation, unlike the comprehensive and successful attack on Ku Klux-ism that Carpetbag Governor Powell Clayton (q.v.) inaugurated in Arkansas, after which it was modeled. But the criticism of Holden reached a new high as the attack on the Klans came just before the state election of 1870. One critic, newspaper editor Josiah Turner, Jr., went to the scene of the military operations and wrote of how "the devil incarnate," Holden, through Kirk's Republican militia "robbed, despoiled, and plundered the people." Turner dared Holden to have him arrested, and Holden foolishly had it done, making Turner the martyr of the hour and guaranteeing a Conservative victory in the legislative contests.

When the new legislators took their seats, many called for the removal of Holden. The legislature put on an impressive impeachment show trial that ignored the Ku Klux attack on white and black Republicans and portrayed Holden as a violator of civil liberties through his militia campaign and arbitrary arrests. The legislature removed Holden and suspended his political rights in the state. Holden vowed to get his rights restored. This opportunity appeared in 1875, as the state assembled delegates to get rid of the state's Reconstruction constitution. But on a straight party vote (53–56), the delegates refused to remove Holden's political disabilities.

During the 1880s, Holden began to engage in several projects that helped restore his reputation in the state. He gave an address on North Carolina journalism and ignored his own considerable contribution. He reconciled with Zeb Vance and began to write a massive history of North Carolina. But the old man's health began to catch up with him. Holden suffered a stroke that limited his ability to write. He had to dictate all correspondence.

At the end of the decade, he tried one more time to regain his political rights. He approached newspaperman Josephus Daniels. But the attempt merely caused the flare-up of old hatreds and failed. Holden then had another stroke that left him bedridden. He died shortly thereafter. His funeral procession was the only vindication he would ever get—a public procession, the lowering of the flag to half-mast, and a public burial attended by blacks and whites from all political persuasions. Josephus Daniels had written his obituary some time earlier. Holden had "made stronger friends and bitterer enemies than any other man in our history," he concluded, "[but w]hatever people in the future may think of him, one thing is certain—they will think of him."

HOMESTEAD ACT. The Republican Party had a distinct domestic program designed to appease both its agricultural and industrial supporters. This program had as its basis the old Whig (q.v.) economic policies, based in part on Henry Clay's American System (q.v.). Part of the agricultural program was the Homestead Act of 1862. This measure opened up free land in the West, up to 160 acres per head of family. If the land were lived on for five years consecutively and improvements made on it, the title would revert to the settler for the cost of the fees to register it ($26–$34). If one wished to hurry up the process, the land could be bought at $1.25 an acre after six months' residence. There was some westward movement during the war. Kansas was admitted as a free state in 1861, after Southern secession (q.v.). Nevada became a free state on the basis of its silver strikes in 1864. In addition, Montana, Colorado, Dakota, and Arizona Territories were created.

HOOD, JOHN BELL (1831–1879). A Kentuckian who graduated from West Point in 1853 in the bottom quarter of his class, John B. Hood was a blond six footer with a bloodhound-looking face. He had some experience in Indian fighting and had been wounded in action on the frontier. He resigned his commission in 1861 and received a lieutenant of cavalry commission. His first duty station was Yorktown. But in March 1862, he was made brigadier general and put in charge of the Texas Brigade, with which his name would be synonymous. He led it at the Seven Days Campaign, Second Manassas Campaign, and the Maryland Campaign (qq.v.), during which time Hood's Texans became the shock troops of Robert E. Lee's (q.v.) army, always in the hottest positions, always taking the most casualties. In October 1862, he acceded to division command and led his men at Fredericksburg and during the Pennsylvania Campaign (qq.v.), being severely wounded in the arm on the second day of Gettysburg.

Barely recovered from his wound, Hood led his division to the West, where it achieved the breakthrough that led to Confederate victory at Chickamauga. Here Hood lost his right leg. He was present at the siege of Chattanooga (q.v.), but moved north to unsuccessfully assault Knoxville. By the spring of 1864, his division was back in Virginia in time for the Richmond Campaign (q.v.). But Hood himself stayed with the Army of Tennessee as a corps commander (lieutenant general) during the Atlanta Campaign (q.v.). He manipulated to succeed the retreating Gen. Joseph Johnston (q.v.) in command at Atlanta, received the temporary rank of general, and led the Confederates in a series of bloody counterattacks that ultimately lost the city.

After Atlanta, Hood removed his army to the west and charged up into Tennessee, supposedly to take Nashville. Hood botched the whole Nashville Campaign (q.v.), permitting the Yankees to pass him at Spring Hill without challenge and charging headlong across open fields at Franklin, decimating his officer corps. The Union counterattack at Nashville is generally considered the only decisive victory of the war. Relieved at his own request and reverting to lieutenant general, Hood surrendered to Federal authorities at Natchez at the end of the war, while trying to reach Texas.

Hood spent the postwar years in New Orleans, working as a cotton factor and a commission merchant. Under attack from Joseph Johnston in his memoirs, Hood felt compelled to write a book of his own defending, at times quite ably, his course of action during the war, no matter how bloody it seemed in retrospect. But the higher up in command Hood went, the more vague his goals seemed to get. The fact remained that while he excelled at brigade and division command, he did not do well in corps or army command. He was as poor an administrator as he was a good fighter. He, his wife (he had married after the war and sired 11 children in 10 years), and eldest daughter died of yellow fever in 1879.

HOOD'S FIRST SORTIE. *See* ATLANTA CAMPAIGN.

HOOD'S SECOND SORTIE. *See* ATLANTA CAMPAIGN.

HOOD'S THIRD SORTIE. *See* ATLANTA CAMPAIGN.

HOOKER, JOSEPH (1814–1879). Massachusetts-born Joseph Hooker graduated from West Point in 1837 at the middle of his class. He fought in the Seminole War and served on the Maine frontier, before becoming an adjutant at the Military Academy. In the War with Mexico, Hooker served as a staff officer and won three brevets for bravery. Hooker stood by the volunteer generals in their quarrels with Bvt. Lt. Gen. Winfield Scott (q.v.), however, which caused him career problems thereafter.

He resigned his commission in 1853 to become a farmer and an engineer in California. He had a disagreement with Maj. Gen. Henry W. Halleck (q.v.) while in California as a militia colonel, which caused his willingness to serve in the Civil War to be snubbed initially. Eventually he received a brigade command at Washington and a division command in the Peninsula Campaign and the Seven Days Campaign (qq.v.). Hooker's corps missed the Second Manassas Campaign, but he was commander of the I Corps during the Maryland Campaign (q.v.) and of the Center Grand Division (V and III Corps) during the Fredericksburg Campaign (q.v.). His record was sterling to this point, and he constantly lived up to his sobriquet, "Fighting Joe." He was also known for keeping his headquarters in the bar at Willard's fashionable Washington hotel. There is some doubt that the ladies of shady reputation popularly known as "hookers" received their names from his liberal patronization of their skills, but it is a good story, nonetheless.

During and after the fiasco at Fredericksburg, Hooker shamelessly had campaigned to become the head of the Army of the Potomac. He also publicly criticized the Abraham Lincoln (q.v.) regime and called for a military dictatorship. When Lincoln appointed him army chief, the president said that only winners could become dictators. If Hooker would win on the battlefield, Lincoln said he would risk the dictatorship.

Unfortunately for his aspirations, Hooker could not deliver. During the Chancellorsville Campaign (q.v.), he became mentally paralyzed after Confederate Gen. Robert E. Lee (q.v.) flanked his position and even more befuddled after a spent shell hit a post against which he had been leaning. He withdrew his army, causing many to say that Lee had beat Hooker, not the Army of the Potomac. He quarreled with his civilian superiors during the initial moves in the Pennsylvania Campaign (q.v.), and Lincoln relieved Hooker as commander for Maj. Gen. George G. Meade (q.v.). Congress, however, gave him its thanks for his revitalization of the army and the defense of Washington. He was one of fifteen to receive that honor during the war.

Going to the Western Theater with a detachment from the Army of the Potomac, Hooker commanded the XI and XII corps, later combined into the XX Corps. He fought well in the Chattanooga Campaign and the Atlanta Campaign (qq.v.). But when he was passed over in the selection of a commander for Maj. Gen. William T. Sherman's (q.v.) Army of Georgia for the March to the Sea (q.v.), Hooker asked for another assignment. He commanded various army departments until he suffered a paralytic stroke in 1868. Hooker retired from active service and died 11 years later.

HOWARD, JACOB M. (1805–1871). Born in Vermont, Jacob M. Howard was educated in public schools and private academies, receiving a degree from Williams College in 1830. He began to read law and was admitted to the bar in Michigan, where he had moved in 1833. Setting up a practice in Detroit, Howard did well as an attorney, but he much preferred politics, which he entered as a Whig (q.v.) candidate to the state assembly in 1838. Changing to the new Republican (q.v.) Party in 1854, Howard served as state attorney general until 1861. He was then sent to the U.S. Senate, where he served until 1871, as a Radical Republican. Howard drafted the Thirteenth Amendment (q.v.), opposed Presidential Reconstruction (q.v.), and favored extreme punishment of the South through the Fourteenth Amendment and the Military Reconstruction Acts (qq.v.). He was a member of the Joint Committee of Fifteen on Reconstruction (q.v.), in charge of investigating conditions in Virginia and the Carolinas. Howard was an excellent speaker, but somewhat ponderous in his presentation of a topic. He read widely in law, history, classics, and literature and even translated and published the memoirs of the Empress Josephine from the original French. Howard also was interested in transportation and chaired the Senate committee on Pacific railroads. He drew up the final report on President Andrew Johnson's (q.v.) removal of Secretary of War Edwin McM. Stanton (q.v.), which led to the chief executive's impeachment (q.v.) (Howard voted to convict). He died of a stroke within a month of ending his term as senator in 1871.

HOWARD, OLIVER OTIS (1830–1909). Born in Leeds, Maine, Oliver Otis Howard graduated Bowdoin College in 1850 and West Point in 1854. He served as an ordnance officer, fought in the Third Seminole War, and taught mathematics at the military academy until the Civil War broke out. He helped organize and train the Third Maine Volunteer Infantry and served as its colonel and brigade commander at First Manassas (q.v.), the first of 20 major engagements he fought in during the war. He was soon promoted to general officer. On the Peninsula (q.v.) in 1862, at the Battle of Fair Oaks, he lost his right arm. Howard returned to the front within three and a half months and fought as brigade and division commander at all major battles in the East through Gettysburg. He advanced to corps command, taking over the XI Corps of the Army of the Potomac, a hard-luck unit largely composed of German immigrants that ran at Chancellorsville (q.v.) and on the first day of Gettysburg, causing Union defeats.

Howard was sent to the West after the Pennsylvania Campaign (q.v.), where he fought well at Chattanooga and in the Atlanta Campaign (qq.v.), advancing to Army command under Maj. Gen. William T. Sherman. Howard commanded one of the wings in the March to the Sea (q.v.) and continued in this role as Sherman moved through the Carolinas (q.v.), changing his record in the East of "diligent mediocrity" to one of occasional brilliance.

In 1865, Secretary of War Edwin McM. Stanton (q.v.) handed Howard a basket of memos and communications, and he became the first and only commissioner of the Bureau of Refugees, Freedmen, and Abandoned Lands (q.v.). Although recent historians have criticized Howard's condescending racism, summed up in the title "Yankee Stepfather," he was probably as good a man as was available at the time to do the job. He was honest, had the interests of the African-Americans at heart, and approached the problems in the spirit of a devout Christian, which led to another of his nicknames, the "Bible General." Howard fully realized that the change from slave to free society would be a long and arduous one, and he worked ever patiently to achieve it. Like many 19th-century intellectuals and reformers, he put his faith in God and education. He founded several black institutions of higher learning, of which Howard University in the District of Columbia is the best known, and worked tirelessly to keep the Bureau as nonpolitical as possible. It is possible that the Bureau might have continued longer had he made it an adjunct of the Republican Party (q.v.), but he refused. For all of his hard work, he was accused of mismanagement of funds and investigated by Congress, but found innocent of any charges.

Howard went on to the Great Southwest, where he negotiated the end of the Apache Wars by bravely confronting the Chiricahua chieftain, Cochise, alone in his stronghold, and impressing the Apaches with his Christian decency. Unfortunately, the rest of the government did not possess it, and Howard's treaty was unilaterally altered and the reservation he promised given over to the cattle and mining barons. Meanwhile, Howard took over the Department of the Columbia (present-day Washington and Oregon) and was there during the Nez Percé War against Chief Joseph, whom he helped hound into submission. In 1886, he returned to the Department of the East, where he served until his retirement in 1894. He remained interested in the field of black education the rest of his life and wrote several historical books including his memoirs, which he finished two years before his death.

HOTZE, HENRY (1833–1887). Throughout the Civil War, the Confederacy hoped to get foreign recognition. Although Confederate diplomacy often suffered on the higher levels, lower echelon employees were quite good. An example of this was the work of Henry Hotze, a newspaperman who published Confederate propaganda in Great Britain that went to all of Europe. Using his publication, the *Index*, Hotze made much of Confederate victories on the battlefield, Union failures to win, and Federal contradictions in policy, such as putting up an illegal blockade against Southern ports it alleged to be its own. Hotze was very careful to play down the fact that the South held slaves and emphasized Yankee oppression of the liberties of Southern whites. He also made much of King Cotton and its value to the livelihood of the English cotton mill workers.

I

IMPEACHMENT. Even though the Republican Congress had tried to subordinate President Andrew Johnson (q.v.) to its will, by March 1867 through measures like the Command of the Army Act, the Tenure of Office Act, the Military Reconstruction Acts (qq.v.), and the calling of its own next session so as not to allow him latitude to create havoc during the traditional congressional recess, Johnson managed to do much within the limits of the laws to frustrate the Radical program. He relied on appointment and pardoning powers that Congress really could not touch. Most of all, he could guide Reconstruction through the assignment of officers to Reconstruction districts in the South.

The only real method to stop Johnson and completely humiliate him was to impeach him. Impeachment is the bringing of charges against an elected or appointed public official. It is an indictment. In the case of the president, the House of Representatives impeaches and acts as prosecutor. The Senate acts as jury, and the trial is overseen by the chief justice of the U.S. Supreme Court (in this case, Salmon P. Chase [q.v.], a former member of Abraham Lincoln's [q.v.] cabinet and Radical Republican). If found guilty, the accused is removed from office. Then separate civil or criminal charges can be filed in ordinary courts. Until he was removed from office, Johnson would be immune to ordinary prosecution. He could be impeached under the Constitution only for treason, bribery, high crimes, or misdemeanors. What comprised the latter two categories was a vague area and zoned in on immediately by the Radical Republicans.

By 1867, Congress had a new weapon to use against the president, the Tenure of Office Act. It was designed to protect Radical sympathizers in the executive department who spied on Johnson and tipped off Congress as to his possible next moves. But it was especially there to shield Secretary of War Edwin McM. Stanton (q.v.). He was the civilian head of the War Department and thus one of the men through whom orders to the Army had to proceed, according to the Command of the Army Act. Thus Stanton, along with Lt. Gen. Ulysses S. Grant (q.v.), kept the field officers from taking orders that might compromise Reconstruction directly from Johnson (although neither had been able to halt Johnson's annoying habit of appointing military district commanders who disliked congressional policy). Johnson's chance came in the summer of 1867, when the Fortieth Congress figured he was in check and declared a recess from July to November. This was the opportunity for Johnson to remove the various Republican military commanders in the South. For good measure, he removed Stanton, too. Then he informed Congress of his deeds, as the Tenure of Office Act provided, when they had reconvened in December. Congress would then advise and consent.

Johnson was rather clever, too clever as it turned out, in his *ad interim* replacement of Stanton. He was none other than Commanding General of the Army Ulysses S. Grant. The general did not understand the give and take of politics—he believed that Congress was right in any political quarrel with the president as the true representatives of the people. He also found out that if he cooperated with Johnson and they lost their case, he could be fined $10,000 and get five years in jail if he refused to give the office back to Stanton. But hanging tough was essential if Johnson were to get a test case in the Federal courts. Finally, unknown to Johnson, Grant was getting the presidential bug—the Republican presidential bug.

So when the second session of the Fortieth Congress met and voted not to concur in Stanton's removal and ordered him back into office, Grant returned the keys before Johnson could stop him. Thus Johnson had to remove him outright while Congress was still in session, to get what he thought was a good test case. In Johnson's eyes, the secretary was not actually protected by the act, because Lincoln had appointed him and Lincoln had been dead for years beyond the one month after a president left office provision in the law that allegedly protected Stanton.

As Stanton held out valiantly, the House of Representatives passed the Co-vode Resolution, impeaching the president for "high crimes and misdemeanors." The Bill of Particulars had 11 accusations. Eight concerned violations of the Tenure of Office Act. Article 9 was the "Emory Article." It accused the president of violating the Command of the Army Act by sending an order directly to Bvt. Maj. Gen. William H. Emory. The general had refused to obey and reported the attempt to Grant, who told Congress. Article 10 was the "Butler Article." Named after Radical congressman Benjamin F. Butler (q.v.) of Massachusetts, it accused Johnson of using foul language disrespectful of Congress—true, but more a matter of bad taste than a high crime or misdemeanor in anybody's book. Article 11 was the "Omnibus Article." It was a catchall that accused Johnson of not faithfully executing the Military Reconstruction Acts. This was false. He was meticulous in his obedience, although he worked the loopholes patiently and effectively. Everyone knew that the House had a poor case. Johnson was right, the Tenure of Office act did not really apply to Stanton. But the Senate was not supposed to vote as a jury. It was to act as a political body and vote the party line.

Knowing its farcical nature and wishing to keep as much of the executive's traditional independence from the legislative as possible, Johnson refused to patronize the impeachment proceedings. He sent his attorneys, Henry Stanbery (who resigned as attorney general to defend the president) and William Evarts (one of the most respected attorneys of the day). They stuck to the legal facts: Stanton was not under the protection of the Tenure of Office Act because Lincoln, who had appointed him, had been dead (out of office) more than one month; Stanton was still in office anyway, so no crime had been committed; and none of the so-called high crimes and misdemeanors were impeachable offenses, but rather political disagreements natural under the American system of government.

Facing Johnson's attorneys was the prosecution, a group of managers appointed by the House of Representatives. The leaders were Thaddeus Stevens (q.v.) and Benjamin Butler. As Stevens was slowly dying, Butler carried on all of the real work. They had a lousy case, but it mattered little. All they wanted was 36 senators to vote "aye" to remove the president. Chief Justice Chase, as political as anyone, possibly seeking a presidential nomination by the Democrats (q.v.), a party from which he had migrated to become a Radical Republican, kept the proceedings as close to law and Constitution as he dared. The House managers sought to belay this influence by voting on Article 11 first. It was vague; most Republicans believed that Johnson had acted to obstruct Reconstruction, so one could vote "aye" with a clean conscience. But it also would amount to passage of a legislative bill of attainder (punishment of the president for no real impeachable offense as defined in the Constitution), which was unconstitutional in itself.

But only 32 others followed Benjamin Wade (q.v.), Butler, and Stevens. The Senate was one vote short of conviction (35–19). Seven Republicans had broken with their party and voted with the dozen Democrats to acquit. The trial was over. Andrew Johnson was still president. Some historians have pointed to Republican Senator E. A. Ross of Kansas as the one vote that saved Johnson. But in reality, there were others who would have voted to acquit had it been necessary. But only seven had to risk their political careers: young men who could start over, old men who could retire. What it did guarantee was that prominent Radicals like Chase and Wade would not receive the nomination of either party. The Republicans now withdrew from ideology and went for practicality, or what politicians call availability. They turned to war hero Ulysses S. Grant, the man who had refused to stand by Johnson in challenging the Tenure of Office Act. He was a war hero, beloved by the voters, and a believer in congressional domination of government.

INCOME TAX. During the Civil War, both the Union and the Confederacy had three ways available to raise money to carry on the fight: taxes, bonds, and printing paper money. Both sides used a combination of these measures, but the Union introduced a new concept, one familiar to modern Americans, a tax on incomes.

The Federal government passed internal revenue laws three times in the war, in 1861, 1862, and 1864. The 1861 Internal Revenue Act created the first income tax in U.S. history. Income was regarded as any wage, in kind or property payment. In 1861, the rate was a flat one of 3 percent on all incomes above $800. This is something like $19,000 in today's dollar values.

In 1862, the obvious lengthening of the war, brought about by Union losses particularly in the Eastern Theater, led to a revision of the tax code. It created a commissioner of internal revenue and a progressive income tax, repealing the idea of a flat tax. All residents were taxed if their income was over $600 at a rate of 3 percent. Those making over $10,000 were taxed at 5 percent. It also provided that all wages paid by the Federal government were to have the tax withheld by the paymaster before payment of the wage. This included civilian and military persons.

In 1864, the rates, still progressive in nature, became 5 percent on all those earning above $600; for all those earning above $5,000 the rate was 7.5 percent, while all those above $10, 000 were hit with a 10 percent rate. The act expired in 1873 with the panic (depression) of that year. The U.S. Supreme Court ruled the income tax constitutional in 1881 in Springer *v.* U.S., but in 1895, the Court overruled itself in Pollock *v.* Farmers' Loan & Trust Co., deciding that income taxes on rents, dividends, and interest were direct taxes, which had to be apportioned among the states. The Sixteenth Amendment in 1913 exempted income taxes from the constitutional requirements regarding direct taxes.

INDEX, **THE.** *See* HOTZE, HENRY.

INFLATION BILL (1874). *See* GRANT, ULYSSES S., ADMINISTRA-TION—DOMESTIC POLICIES.

INTERNAL DISSENT IN THE CONFEDERACY. Almost immediately the Confederacy had major problems with loyalty in every state. But the biggest area of internal dissent within the Confederacy was the Appalachian Peninsula (mountain chain). This dissent took place in two sections of the mountains, western Virginia and eastern Tennessee.

In the western quarter of Virginia, 32 counties were especially vehement in their opposition to secession (q.v.) and the formation of the Confederacy. The center of anti-Confederate sentiment was in the Kanawha Valley. Even before the popular referendum on Virginia's secession, the people in the west were organizing to resist secession and claiming to represent the loyal state of

Virginia. This process would continue until the creation of the separate state of West Virginia (q.v.).

But already troops were in motion. Recruiters raised loyal Virginia regiments in neighboring Ohio. Under the command of Ohio Maj. Gen. George B. McClellan (q.v.), loyal Ohio and Virginia regiments moved to occupy the Kanawha. On June 3, 1861, the first land battle of the war occurred at Philippi, known as the Philippi Races, because the Confederates ran at the first shots. A new Confederate commander, Brig. Gen. Robert S. Garnett, rallied his men at Rich Mountain and Laurel Mountain. McClellan brought his soldiers up and had Brig. Gen. William S. Rosecrans (q.v.) lead a flanking column against Rich Mountain, where the Rebel position was weakest. On July 11, Rosecrans took the hill, and the Confederates withdrew. McClellan's forces overtook them at Carrick's Ford on the Cheat River, where the Confederates were retreating in disorder after Garnett was killed.

McClellan received much credit for saving West Virginia from Rebel invasion and went east to command all Union armies in the coming year, although many believed that Rosecrans and Brig. Gen. Joseph J. Reynolds (q.v.) had done most of the fighting. His opponent, in charge of overall Confederate operations, had been Gen. Robert E. Lee (q.v.), who came onto the field after Carrick's Ford in an effort to salvage western Virginia for the Confederacy. He lost to Reynolds' entrenched forces at Cheat Mountain before he went east to become President Jefferson Davis' (q.v.) military advisor and troubleshooter and shine in later campaigns.

The other major area of dissent against the Confederate government was eastern Tennessee. Opposition here was led by Andrew Johnson (q.v.), one of Tennessee's U.S. senators, who would later become military governor of occupied Tennessee, then vice president and president of the Union. While Johnson worked in Washington to save eastern Tennessee from Rebel occupation and get its loyal congressmen seated, his main competitor on the ground was Parson William G. Brownlow (q.v.). By early 1862, Brownlow had been arrested and exiled to Union lines, and the Confederate army had occupied the area. Meanwhile, representatives from the same districts served in both the U.S. and C.S. congresses simultaneously. Guerrilla war prevailed in much of Tennessee, the pro-Confederate areas being occupied by Federal forces early on, and the pro-Union areas being held by the Confederates.

It was not until 1864 that all of Tennessee fell to Northern occupation troops. In 1865, as the war drew to a close, Brownlow organized a loyal government with himself elected as governor. Johnson had been so hated—by eastern Tennessee because he supported pro-slave John C. Breckinridge (q.v.) in the election of 1860 (q.v.), and by the rest of the state for refusing to secede and give up his U.S. Senate seat in 1861—he did little to advance the cause of reconciliation. The two men would continue to spar over Tennessee during Reconstruction.

There were other areas of dissatisfaction within the Confederacy. Northern Alabama organized several counties into the "Free State of Winston" and sent men to the Federal armies, who became the 1st Alabama (Union) Cavalry and acted as Maj. Gen. William T. Sherman's (q.v.) bodyguard on the March to the Sea (q.v.). The "Free State of Jones" was a similar area in southwestern Mississippi. Here deserters, draft dodgers, and pro-Union men found refuge, and Confederates steered clear. The Ozarks between Arkansas and Missouri was much the same, as were select areas in northwestern Louisiana. In Texas, the "Big Thicket" in East Texas and the frontier areas refused to cooperate with Confederate authorities. Texas dissidents also raised two regiments and a battalion of Union cavalry.

INTERNAL DISSENT IN THE UNION. *See* EXECUTIVE PROCLAMATION, LINCOLN AND THE.

"IRONCLAD OATH." *See* OATHS OF ALLEGIANCE.

ISLAND NO. 10, BATTLE OF. *See* SHILOH CAMPAIGN.

IUKA, BATTLE OF. *See* CORINTH CAMPAIGN.

J

JACKSON, BATTLE OF. *See* VICKSBURG CAMPAIGN.

JACKSON, THOMAS J. "STONEWALL" (1824–1863). Born on January 21, 1824, in what would become West Virginia, Thomas J. Jackson graduated 17th in his class of 59 at West Point in 1846. He won two brevets for bravery during the War with Mexico, but resigned his commission in 1851 to teach tactics at the Virginia Military Academy. He was a devout Presbyterian, tended to be humorless (he laughed by throwing his head back but making no sound), rarely spoke, believed in predestination, was a fatalist, gave out Sunday school tracts to his students and soldiers alike, disliked fighting on Sundays (although he never delayed engaging in battle on the Lord's Day, especially when victory presented itself), and lived a simple life of hard work and few outwardly perceived enjoyments besides constant prayer.

When Jackson joined in the defense of Virginia at Harper's Ferry in 1861, he presented a not-too-inspiring sight. He wore a broken-brimmed kepi, a threadbare jacket from his War with Mexico days, and a pair of floppy boots of a very large size. He was tall at six feet, and powerfully built. He liked to ride about holding one arm up in the air (allegedly to improve his circulation) and often sucked on lemons while in thought. He was deaf in one ear and could not hear distant sounds. His eccentricities caused the soldiers to give him a multitude of nicknames, from the endearing "Old Jack," to the less loveable "Fool Tom," to "Old Blue Light" for the haunting gaze in his pale eyes.

Jackson was a part of the Valley army that Joseph Johnston (q.v.) brought to reinforce Confederate positions at First Manassas (q.v.). As a brigade commander, he and his men held Henry House Hill "like a stonewall," permitting the Rebel counterattack that swept the Yankees from the field. For this both he and his brigade received the nickname "Stonewall." Returned to the Shenandoah Valley, Jackson spent the winter of 1861 quarreling with his subordinates and engaging in botched campaigns in the West Virginia mountains. The following spring, however, Jackson fought the famous First Shenandoah Campaign (q.v.), in which he defeated three Union armies sent against him. Called to Richmond, Jackson took a lackluster part in the Seven Days Campaign (q.v.). That summer, Jackson was his old self as he led half of Robert E. Lee's (q.v.) army; spearheaded the Confederate Second Manassas Campaign; and held off repeated Union attacks at Antietam Creek, after capturing the Union garrison at Harper's Ferry, during the Maryland Campaign (qq.v.).

Playing a minor part at Fredericksburg, Jackson became the key to Lee's 1863 Chancellorsville Campaign (q.v.), when he and his men circled the Union army and made a crushing flank attack on the second day's battle, driving the Yankee lines back on the river. Going forward with several staff officers in the dusk to reconnoiter enemy positions for the next day's attack, Jackson was mistakenly shot down as he returned to Confederate lines. Losing his left arm, Jackson seemed to be mending well when he suddenly took ill from pneumonia and died at Guiney Station on May 10, 1863. It was a loss from which Lee and the Army of Northern Virginia never really recovered.

JAMES, JESSE W. (1847–1882). Known to most Americans from his Hollywood personae, which is loosely the basis of beginning scenes of Clint Eastwood's "The Outlaw Josey Wales," Jesse James was one of the great outlaws of the late 19th century. In the South, he is remembered for robbing the banks and railroads run by the Yankee Robber Barons of the post–Civil War era and taking revenge on the hated Pinkerton detectives, who often but ineffectually hounded his every move. In the North, he is best remembered as a Confederate partisan fighter whose exploits are best described as murder and an embarrassment to the Confederate government's prosecution of the war.

But rather than tell the time-worn story of Jesse as Border Ruffian, it is better to relate his tale as a part of the battle against Yankee Reconstruction (q.v.), in which he emerges as one of the "social bandits" of his time who saw his crimes as a low-key guerrilla war campaign to gain the Confederate victory that could not be achieved on the battlefields of the war. Jesse was a one-man regulator, a Ku Klux Klansman (q.v.) without robes, just like the White Liners, Red Shirts, and White Leaguers (qq.v.) who brought a violent end to Reconstruction. To hear Jesse and his mother (waving her empty dress sleeve—her arm had been accidentally blown off by a Pinkerton agent's errant bomb) tell it, his targets were the policies of Radical Republicans, Carpetbaggers, Scalawags (qq.v.), tax collectors, bankers, railroad tycoons, and express companies, who were raping the Prostrate South under the guise of a misguided reform called Reconstruction. In reality, he struck at the wealth of his pro-Union neighbors.

Only 16 when he joined William T. "Bloody Bill" Anderson's "black flag" (signifying no quarter) guerrillas, Jesse was a product of what modern psychologists call "violentization." A veteran of the Kansas–Missouri Border Wars (q.v.) of the 1850s and the ensuing Civil War in the bloody Trans-Mississippi region, Jesse resolved to continue his belligerency to preserve home and hearth. His biographer describes the defeated Rebel as a "soulless embodiment of evil." But compared to the feuds, gangs, and gunmen (q.v.) that plagued Texas and Arkansas, Jesse was, perhaps unbelievably to the modern reader, a study in moderation.

Shot down as he sought to surrender at war's end (much as he had done to his Yankee enemies at Centralia during the war), Jesse returned to the ways of his mentors, "Bloody Bill" (whose head now decorated a Union pike), Dave Pool, "Little Archie" Clements, and Charles Fletcher Taylor. Jesse never rode with the infamous William C. Quantrill, although brother Frank did. His bank robberies were copies of Confederate guerrilla tactics of "hoo-rahing" a town—outriders took to the streets, shooting anyone too curious or those who tried to fight back, a select team robbed at will, and everyone rode away in a matter of minutes.

Jesse's nobility to the Lost Cause became the theme of *Kansas City Times* newspaper editor and ex-Confederate soldier John N. Edwards. He and Jesse wrote each other, each feeding off the fame of the other. But while Jesse sought to justify his banditry, Edwards was after bigger game. This can be seen in Missouri state politics. The state had been two-thirds pro-Union during the Civil War. But by 1876, Missouri was thoroughly Confederate Democrat (q.v.), thanks in large part to the activities of Jesse James propagandized by editor Edwards. By 1877, Missouri's political conversion had become nationwide, as Republicans (q.v.) retreated from the throes of Reconstruction (q.v.), sanctified in the election of 1876 and the Compromise of 1877 (q.v.).

JENKINS' FERRY, BATTLE OF. *See* CAMDEN CAMPAIGN.

JERUSALEM PLANK ROAD, BATTLE OF. *See* PETERSBURG, SIEGE OF.

JIM CROW (SEGREGATION) BEFORE, DURING, AND AFTER THE CIVIL WAR. Historians differ as to the origins of racial segregation in the South, the so-called Jim Crow system. Many of the traditional white characterizations of African-Americans had a condescending vaudevillian nature about them, stemming from the old minstrel shows so popular a century and a half ago, that was originally an intentionally concocted racial stereotype designed to help relegate blacks to a second-class place in American society.

They are forgotten now, but two classic minstrel roles were fated to be around longer than the rest of the minstrel genre, Zip Coon and Jim Crow. Zip Coon was the urbane, pseudo-sophisticated city Negro who wore the latest fashion and perambulated about flashing a big grin and spinning his cane. His surname endures in a derogatory term for African-Americans. Jim Crow was his country cousin, poor, dressed in rags, lacking the streetwise demeanor and aggressiveness of Zip Coon, portrayed in the Hollywood movies of the 1930s as the character of "Step 'N' Fetch-it." The more widely known Jim Crow came to describe the informal at first, legal later, system of segregation that permeated American society from the days of slavery to the middle of the 20th century, when the Reverend Martin Luther King Jr. successfully attacked its legal and moral precepts.

Originating in the North, Jim Crow was designed as a system to replace slavery, which had gradually been eradicated there during and after the American Revolution. Segregation spread from the cities, because that is where traditional white control first broke down, in a gradual process that continued until the Civil War. By 1865, the end of formal slavery under the new constitutional amendments meant that a new social, political, and economic provision had to be made for the African-Americans. Few whites considered complete equality the answer. The result was social segregation, political and economic disfranchisement (qq.v.), and peonage. The key to this process was the willingness of the North to assist or acquiesce in the result.

Because the Redeemers (q.v.), now called the Bourbons (like the French monarchy of the same name, they never learned and they never forgot), skillfully played the race card and warned white farmers that if they broke the ranks of racial solidarity, the blacks would rule as they had during Reconstruction (q.v.) with national Republican (q.v.) patronage. Those whites who wished to challenge the Redeemers' control of the post-Reconstruction South had to bolt from the Democrat Party (q.v.) and form third parties like Readjusters (who wanted to reassess taxes on the rich and gain debtor relief), Independents (anyone of any political philosophy who was not a Bourbon), and Greenbackers (those who wanted easier credit through inflated paper money). As the decade of the 1890s approached, the proliferation of these third parties made it evident that the usual system was about to fall apart. The new radical farmer's party, the Peoples' Party or the Populists, began to flirt with a new concept of race. Southern farmers, black and white, at last realized that they were being suckered by the Bourbons into a race war when they ought to be more cognizant of class differences. For the first and last time in 19th-century Southern history, a potentially effective biracial party was formed. The Bourbons were in deep trouble. So they redoubled their efforts, ridiculing those whites who would desert their race and forget all the whites who fought for the Confederacy, and practiced racial intimidation and electoral fraud on a scale heretofore unimagined. They blamed the whole thing on the African-Americans not knowing their "proper place" in society.

Then the Bourbons turned to the white farmers and promised them that, if all whites could agree to remove the "evil" influence of black voters from Southern politics and society, whites could afford to disagree on political issues and have honest, competitive elections. Of course, the very things that disfranchised the black farmers also hit the white farmers. To combat this, the disfranchising laws had exceptions for understanding in lieu of literacy and the grandfather clause (if one's grandfather voted, one could not be disfranchised). But the real effect was to disfranchise both black and white poor (no white in his right mind would admit to being unable to read or write or use the grandfather clause, which amounted to the same thing). So the formal laws on segregation became reality for the first time, 30 years after the end of the war and 20 years after the end of Reconstruction. They gave the poor white a feeling that no matter his actual place in the social, economic, and intellectual life of the region, he and his family were different from the black dregs and part of the superior white ruling class. It was not much, but it was something, and in time it became the only important thing that counted.

Other historians believe that one must distinguish between exclusion (wherein blacks were kept out of a public accommodation) and segregation (wherein blacks were allowed into a public area but restricted as to how, when, and where). Thus segregation becomes a forgotten alternative itself when compared to what else existed—namely, total exclusion. And by creating services for themselves upon being excluded from all-white facilities, blacks contributed to segregation's eventual triumph. After the end of the Civil War, Southern whites saw little need to change things racially from the way they were before the conflict. Blacks received no public services under the slave regime, and few if any under the first governments during Presidential Reconstruction (q.v.). Poorhouses, schools, orphanages, asylums, and institutions for the deaf, dumb, and insane were for whites only. It was the Army and the Freedmen's Bureau (qq.v.) who inadvertently introduced segregation to the South when they insisted that blacks must have their own copies of all services traditionally given to whites. But it was not until the Military Reconstruction Acts (q.v.) appeared in 1867 that the South was forced to truly grant new rights, privileges, and services to blacks. The difference between Conservative white Southern policy and the Republican program can best be seen in three areas: militia service, education, and welfare facilities.

The Republicans were the first in the South to arm African-Americans as members of the state militia (at least since the Louisiana example of using free black militia units in the 1814 Battle of New Orleans). But in deference to Scalawag (q.v.) racial mores, the rank and file were segregated by race and permitted black officers only in black units. Similar events took place in forming black fire companies (which often doubled as militia cadres in those days). The Republicans were the first to provide blacks with public education and opened separate schools in all states but Louisiana and South Carolina (states in which black politicians played decisive roles in Reconstruction governments).

When it came to public welfare services, Republicans once again provided these to blacks for the first time, but facilities were segregated by building or by rooms or wings within a single building. In public conveyances, however, particularly railroads, the races were segregated by car. But the Jim Crow car often did double duty as a smoking car for males of both races. Except in New Orleans, streetcars were segregated by race, with blacks having cars of their own, often marked by a star emblem on the vehicle. Hence segregation replaced exclusion to the benefit of newly freed black citizens.

The theme of Reconstruction was that Republicans provided public services for blacks but under a guise that later would be called "separate but equal." Few Republicans were truly egalitarian. The party as a whole, especially the Scalawag elements, had no desire to "Africanize" the South. Even party celebrations were often racially exclusive. Hence the South fairly bristled at the idea of Charles Sumner's Civil Rights Act (qq.v.) of 1875, which would have guaranteed integrated public accommodations in all aspects of everyday life.

The basic response of the Redeemers was to ignore the implications of the act until the U.S. Supreme Court declared it unconstitutional in the 1883 Civil Rights Cases (q.v.). Instead, they continued the separate but equal notion brought South by the Republicans. Indeed, several states opened up institutions (like schools, orphanages, and asylums) that had never been opened before to blacks within their boundaries during the Gilded Age. But everything was segregated by race. Important here was the construction of separate waiting rooms at railroad stations. In restaurants, hotels, saloons, and prostitution, all services and facilities went from total exclusion of African-Americans to segregation, epitomized by the Jim Crow Bible at the courthouse for use by black witnesses. As Frederick Douglass (q.v.) noted, the Negro had more freedom on steamboats as a slave because "he could ride anywhere, side by side with his master. . . . [A]s a freeman, he was not allowed a cabin abaft the wheel."

As whites persisted in exclusion or segregation of blacks, African-Americans began to respond by opening their own places of services and amusement. They also began to drive whites out of teaching in grammar and secondary schools and sought to administer black colleges themselves. Part of this was a response to exclusion, but much of it was a creation of their own group identity. Custom, then, had separated the races during and after Reconstruction. But there still remained some doubt among whites about the permanency of the informal system. By the 1890s, this was resolved by laws that reinforced what had existed informally all along. The only real forgotten alternative was that segregation replaced total exclusion and thus represented an extension of public accommodations to blacks that had been denied before the war.

No instance came to typify the Jim Crow reality by the 1890s better than the Louisiana case of Homer A. Plessy *v.* Judge John H. Ferguson (q.v.). Louisiana had had a segregated system of streetcars before and during the Civil

War, which had been integrated by a concerted effort during Reconstruction. In 1890, prompted by Congress' failure to pass a new civil rights bill designed to enforce renewed Southern compliance in black rights of citizenship, Louisiana state passed a new law segregating rail cars by race. Plessy himself was classified as an octoroon, one-eighth black, and his participation in the case was no accident, but rather an intentional setup, under the theory that an almost white person might advance the cause with fewer racial hang-ups in the higher courts than an easily distinguished black person. Indeed, the New Orleans blacks had tried to get an earlier case instituted by another light-skinned Negro, Daniel F. Desdunes, and won. But as his destination was outside the state, the Louisiana Supreme Court merely ruled that the law could not be applied to interstate travelers under the interstate commerce provisions of the U.S. Constitution, which left the law intact inside Louisiana. So Homer A. Plessy took a train ride from New Orleans to Covington, purchasing a first-class ticket and sitting in a "whites only" car. He was promptly arrested.

In the ensuing trial, Judge John H. Ferguson held that the case was a state matter and Plessy could be proscribed from riding in all but designated cars. Plessy appealed the case, eventually to the U.S. Supreme Court, as Plessy *v. Ferguson*. There, on May 19, 1896, the highest court in the land ruled that states could separate the races legally, provided that "separate but equal" accommodations were provided for all those so proscribed. Technically, the decision only involved transportation, but other decisions expanded the separate but equal rule into all areas of American life. Custom had become enshrined in law; "separate but equal" had become a constitutional and legal reality as never before.

JOHNSON, ANDREW (1808–1875). Born at Raleigh, North Carolina, Andrew Johnson lost his father at an early age and was apprenticed to a tailor. He became interested in his own education through the promptings of a customer and spent the rest of his youth and part of his early adulthood learning to read and write, encouraged by employers and his wife. He violated the terms of his apprenticeship and removed to Greenville, Tennessee, in 1827, traveling with his mother, for whom he always showed the greatest affection. He met and married Eliza McCardle the following year. He became interested in the problems of his fellow workers and nonslaveholding whites in general and ran for alderman, serving three terms, and succeeded to the mayoralty of Greenville in 1830. He served four terms and was also appointed by the county court to the board of supervisors of Rhea Academy.

Johnson was well liked for his political support of the middle class and poor whites in his area and was sent to the state legislature in the late 1830s, where he worked on the new state constitution of 1839. He had opposed internal improvements as wildly speculative endeavors, which cost him a second term, but the Panic of 1837 proved him right, and he went back to the state legislature, eventually going on to the state senate in 1841. In the senate, he introduced a much-scaled-down measure for internal improvements that passed. He stood for Congress in 1843 and served the next 10 years in the House of Representatives as a Jacksonian Democrat (q.v.). He supported refunding a fine imposed on Andrew Jackson earlier for alleged military improprieties, called for the annexation of Texas, favored the war measures against Mexico asked by James K. Polk, advanced all internal improvements that were national in scope, voted for the lower Tariff of 1842, and introduced a homestead bill that failed to pass. He spoke out on behalf of Polk's use of the veto, calling it a conservative measure that allowed the president, as the only true representative elected by all the voters, to delay unwise, hasty, or unconstitutional legislation until it could be more fully considered by the people. It was a position he would adhere to all his life and very Jacksonian in its origins.

In 1852, Johnson was elected governor of Tennessee, where he made many enemies in the slaveholding parts of the state by his advocacy of the rights of nonslaveholding whites. He went on to the U.S. Senate five years later, a tremendous achievement for a man who came to the state penniless and fleeing an apprenticeship. Much of his success as a politician was due to his stump speaking style, provocative yet intelligent, but always very personal in his attacks on his opponents. While in the U.S. Senate, Johnson reintroduced a homestead measure (which failed again) and became an outspoken advocate for Union in the sectional conflict that was coming to a head. A slaveholder himself by now, Johnson was leery of the constant abolition petitions sent to Washington and the pamphlets that antislave societies wished sent through the mails. He supported the Southern Democrats in 1860, but refused to withdraw with his state in 1861 after the election of Abraham Lincoln (q.v.)— making him the only senator from a seceding state to stay on in Washington.

Johnson's uncompromising Unionism made him an instant man of importance. As Tennessee was one of the first Southern states to be occupied by Union soldiers, Lincoln appointed Johnson as the state's military governor in 1862. His wife and family were still behind Confederate lines, and he was threatened with possible assassination, but Johnson went on with the work of running a loyal government without a second thought. His bravery and outspokenness earned him the vice presidential slot on the Union Party ticket (a wartime combination of Republicans [q.v.] and Northern war-supporting Democrats) during the election of 1864 to draw the votes of border states and wavering Democrat districts in the North. Feeling sick to his stomach at his inaugural, Johnson unwisely took some liquor for strength; he had not eaten since the previous day, and the libation caused him to be woozy and unfairly accused of drunkenness. Within six weeks, Johnson would become president as Lincoln fell mortally wounded to John Wilkes Booth's (q.v.) .44 caliber Derringer.

As the accusations of drunkenness showed, Johnson had (then and now) a controversial reputation. Although it was popular a half century ago to portray him as an embattled hero fighting against vindictive opponents for the good of American democracy, even from the first writers on Reconstruction, Johnson has always had his critics. He was tactless, egotistical, overly self-confident, a gut-fighter on the stump, fond of making shocking off-the-cuff statements, a loner, and somewhat radical in the sense that he was always outside the mainstream of thought in his state and the nation. At first, his uncompromising attitude impressed Republicans who wanted a tougher peace with the South than the seemingly moderate Lincoln proposed. But no sooner did Johnson take office than he began to moderate. Historians blame this variously on the influence of Secretary of State William H. Seward (q.v.) or the responsibilities of the office. But also important was the fact that the rich Southerners, the former slaveholders, Johnson's old political enemies in Tennessee whom he had excluded from the political process unless they pled their cases individually, came forward and begged his forgiveness. And like them, Johnson had little sympathy for black Americans.

That—the mere act of asking—more than anything else seemed to be what Johnson craved most. He forgave them right off. Then these men went back home and proceeded to wreck what chance the South had to Reconstruct itself, by passing the notorious Black Codes (q.v.) proscribing African-Americans participation as free people; electing former Confederate congressmen, generals, and even the Rebel vice president to office; and permitting a series of race riots (q.v.) that were highly publicized in the North. But Johnson himself had a great void in his own Reconstruction thoughts. He was essentially a Democrat, and he had little sympathy for Northern Republicans, who needed some guarantee that they would not be swamped by returning Southern Democrats in congressional votes and policymaking. Johnson should have known better. Already Congress had indicated to President Lincoln that they wanted a voice in Reconstruction with the passage of the Wade–Davis Bill (q.v.) in 1864. And upon Lincoln's pocket veto of this measure, the legislators had issued a Wade–Davis Manifesto (q.v.), warning the executive branch that they would be key participants in the future of Reconstruction, or else.

But Johnson went on to issue his own Reconstruction program, a Proclamation for Reconstruction (q.v.), on May 29, 1865, part of which recognized the Lincoln-appointed governments in Louisiana, Arkansas, and Tennessee. Congress was not averse to the president participating in the Reconstruction process—after all, Johnson had to act when they were out of session. The thing that did him in was his refusal to meet Congress halfway on key measures the Republicans saw as critical to Southern readmission, like the Freedmen's Bureau renewal, the Civil Rights Act of 1866, and the Fourteenth Amendment (qq.v.). People could disagree on the necessity of these measures, but Johnson did not merely argue, he shot off his mouth in public, at the Washington's Birthday Speech (q.v.), accusing the Republican leaders by name of trying to destroy traditional American government, isolating himself from any reasonable compromise effort. Then he went on the campaign trail, the "Swing Around the Circle" (q.v.), and spoke out against his opponents in city after city. Aware of his tendency to respond to hecklers, Republican advance men went around and set up confrontations. Johnson made even more intemperate replies, which so alienated the Northern voters that they returned a veto-proof two-thirds Republican majority to a Congress that had already been called into session by its predecessor to limit the president's ability to act in Congress' traditional absence. Reconstruction policymaking had been transferred from the executive to the legislative branch.

As Congress sought to limit the president's power through acts that limited his removal of executive appointees and his control of the Army in the South and established the Military Reconstruction Acts (q.v.), Johnson acted to enforce these measures, but also took care to obstruct them within the law (like appointing military commanders in the South who were against Army control of civilian government). He also sought to test the validity of the Tenure of Office Act (q.v.) by dismissing Secretary of War Edwin McM. Stanton (q.v.), a deed that led directly to his impeachment (q.v.). The trial was a sloppy proceeding, Congress figuring that the Senate would vote on political questions rather than actual accusations. Johnson conducted an admirable defense through his lawyers and managed to diffuse a lot of animus through moderate appointments and the fear that unpopular Republican Senator Benjamin Wade (q.v.) would become president if Johnson were convicted. He was sustained as president by one vote. Johnson then proceeded to offer himself as a presidential candidate for the Democratic Party, but was rejected as too much of a liability. He retired to Greenville, returning to Washington as a U.S. senator when the Democrats took over Tennessee in 1875. Johnson saw his swearing in before a body that had tried to convict him eight years earlier as a personal vindication. On a trip home in July 1875, he collapsed and died of multiple strokes. He was buried at Signal Hill outside of Greenville, his body wrapped in the American flag and his head resting on a copy of the U.S. Constitution—treasured objects he had defended during the Civil War and Reconstruction.

JOHNSON'S ISLAND (LAKE ERIE). Federal installation that housed Confederate prisoners of war. *See also* PRISONS.

JOHNSTON, ALBERT SIDNEY (1803–1862). Perhaps no other officer had the fine reputation enjoyed by Albert Sidney Johnston at the outbreak of the Civil War. Part of it came from the trip he made from California after he had resigned his U.S. commission. He went alone, eluding Union patrols and hostile Native Americans and nearly being captured, only to arrive out of nowhere as a hero. More of it came from his modest career, which was full of pathos and suffering. He was a knight errant, in many ways, straight out of the pages of a Sir Walter Scott novel. Nothing could endear him more to the antebellum Southern heart.

Johnston was a West Point graduate, a friend of Jefferson Davis (q.v.), whose life paralleled the Confederate president's in many ways. He lost his wife to illness. He had resigned his commission to attend to her. He became a recluse after her death, moved to Texas, and was secretary of war to the Texas Republic, general of the Texas Army, and a volunteer in the War with Mexico who saw little action. A plantation owner, Johnston finally remarried and after the admission of Texas to the Union, rejoined the U.S. Army as a paymaster. When his friend, Jefferson Davis, became secretary of war under the Franklin Pierce (q.v.) administration, Johnston received appointment as a colonel of the new Second Cavalry, a crack regiment, whose second officer was Robert E. Lee (q.v.). Johnston unimaginatively led the U.S. forces that fought the Mormon War in 1857–1858. Posted to California, Johnston resigned his commission when Texas seceded from the Union in early 1861. Reaching Richmond, now President Jefferson Davis sent him to the west to organize an army and defensive line.

Although Johnston was a likeable man, he had various flaws that limited his effectiveness in the Western Theater. He was to a fault gentle in nature, unable to reprimand subordinates, whom he never checked up on to see if they were accomplishing assigned tasks, and way too patient with incompetents. He placed too much stock in cavalry raids, at which Confederate plantation and farm boys excelled, to keep the enemy off balance, to the exclusion of developing a more substantial plan, be it offensive or defensive. The result was that Nashville was not fortified, Ft. Henry incompletely fortified, and Ft. Donelson (qq.v.) not fortified enough. Johnston never realized that the reason his inadequate defensive line held up so long was internecine bickering among opposing Federal commanders.

In the spring of 1862, Johnston's defensive line fell apart when the one Federal officer he had so far ignored, Ulysses S. Grant (q.v.), punched a hole between Bowling Green and Columbus. The fall of Ft. Henry and Ft. Donelson sent Johnston into precipitate retreat. He could not hold Nashville with the fortifications he had planned, unbuilt. The result was that Johnston gave up all of middle and west Tennessee and wound up in Corinth, Mississippi. There he received a new second-in-command, the hero of Ft. Sumter and First Manassas, Gen. P. G. T. Beauregard (q.v.). With Johnston's permission, Beauregard reorganized the western forces into a real army, with brigades, divisions, and corps. It was Beauregard who developed the attack at Shiloh (q.v.)

Church, designed to crush Grant's army before he could be joined by Bvt. Maj. Gen. Don Carlos Buell's (q.v.) men and outnumber the army at Corinth. At the battle, Johnston acted with his usual consummate bravery on the field, but not as overall commander. Rather, he engaged in frontline reconnaissance and directed regiments and brigades under fire, just like any ordinary staff officer. It was in this capacity that he closed in on the fighting at the Hornet's Nest, received a wound, the severity of which was concealed by his boot, and bled to death leading his men on. His death, which the Confederacy so mourned, allowed him to die like a hero, a luckless knight errant to the end.

JOHNSTON, JOSEPH E. (1807–1891). Born in Virginia, Joseph E. Johnston received an exceptional education for his day and graduated 13th of 46 in the same West Point class of 1829 that saw Robert E. Lee (q.v.) matriculate second. He fought in the Black Hawk War before resigning his commission to become a civil engineer in Florida. He returned to the army a year later and fought in the Seminole War and became a topographical engineer. Johnston served with Bvt. Lt. Gen. Winfield Scott (q.v.) in the War with Mexico, where he was wounded five times and received three brevets. He served as inspector general for the Mormon War and then was made quartermaster general of the army.

He resigned his commission when Virginia left the Union and was placed in charge of Virginia troops at Harper's Ferry as brigadier general. In this capacity, he transferred his men to the battlefield of First Manassas in time to assist materially in the Confederate victory there. On August 13, 1861, Johnston was promoted to full general, ranking fourth on the seniority list. The appointment caused a rift between Johnston and President Jefferson Davis (q.v.), because Johnston had been the senior brigadier general before.

Withdrawing from the vicinity of Washington before superior Federal numbers could overwhelm him, Johnston moved his men to oppose the Federal attack during the Peninsula Campaign (q.v.). Seeing an opportunity to strike a portion of the Federal army before Richmond, Johnston led the attack, only to fall seriously wounded. He rejoined the army in late 1862 and was placed in charge of the West, the armies of General Braxton Bragg and John C. Pemberton (qq.v.). But with the continued opposition of President Davis and foot-dragging by Davis' old friends Bragg and Pemberton, Johnston could not effect any cooperation between his forces and saw them go down to defeat after defeat in the Battle of Stone's River, the Siege of Vicksburg, and the Battle of Chattanooga (qq.v.). Only the Battle of Chickamauga stood out as an exception.

No longer able to keep his friend Bragg in command, Davis yielded to reality and placed Johnston over the Army of Tennessee for the Atlanta Campaign (q.v.). Johnston skillfully (or incompetently, depending upon one's point of view) fought a delaying retreat against Maj. Gen. William T. Sherman's (q.v.) advancing army, which outnumbered him greatly. But the constant withdrawals and the botching of a possible counterattack opportunity at Cassville led President Davis to order Johnston's removal from command.

After Gen. John B. Hood (q.v.) destroyed the Army of Tennessee in a disastrous series of attacks at Atlanta and Nashville, Davis yielded once again and appointed Johnston to take over the remnants in South Carolina in January 1865. Johnston employed his usual masterful delaying tactics until after the surrender of Robert E. Lee in Virginia. Then he and his opponent, Sherman, negotiated a surrender of Johnston's army. Using the terms given Lee at Appomattox (q.v.), he and Sherman also wrote in certain political expedients permitting Confederate State governments to meet and repudiate secession. The Union government, in the person of Secretary of War Edwin McM. Stanton (q.v.), repudiated this cartel, and Johnston and Sherman had to renegotiate on the basis of Appomattox alone. Johnston surrendered his men at Durham Station on April 26, even though President Davis had ordered him to fight on.

After the war, Johnston worked in private business in Richmond and Savannah. He returned to Richmond and ran for Congress, serving from 1879 to 1881. He was also the Federal railroad commissioner for President Grover Cleveland. Johnston returned to Richmond, went into insurance, and wrote his account of the War, *Narrative of Military Operations*. He died in 1891 of pneumonia contracted as he stood bare-headed during the funeral of his old foe, William T. Sherman.

JOINT COMMITTEE OF FIFTEEN ON RECONSTRUCTION. Formed in December 1865 to investigate conditions in the former Confederate states and recommend a program to assure their loyalty and readmission to the Union, the Joint Committee of Fifteen on Reconstruction was the body that created both Moderate Republican Reconstruction (renewal of the Freedmen's Bureau Act, creation of the Civil Rights Act of 1866, and the Fourteenth Amendment) and Radical Republican Reconstruction (the four Military Reconstruction Acts) (qq.v.).

The first act of the committee was to investigate the conditions in the South. The purpose was to show that the South remained unrepentant in the face of President Andrew Johnson's Reconstruction program (qq.v.), which had already been completed and had sent representatives to Washington. These men, collectively referred to as the "Confederate Brigadiers" (q.v.), had already been refused seats on the floor of Congress, pending the investigation. The report of the committee was presented in four parts (part 1 was an intensive look at Tennessee; part 2 concerned itself with Virginia and the Carolinas; part 3 covered Georgia, Mississippi, Alabama, and Arkansas; and part 4 examined Florida, Louisiana, and Texas), with a general report added.

The committee's conclusions were that the Confederacy was a disorganized community lacking civil governments or constitutions or any proper relations with the United States beyond that of military conquest; that Congress could not recognize any group of representatives from that area; and that Congress would have to revamp conditions in the South to assure the civil rights of all persons, equality of representation, the purging of all conditions of rebellion and the holding of office by the perpetrators of secession, and the right of suffrage to all loyal persons.

The committee then proceeded to recommend several measures to Congress that made up Moderate Republican Reconstruction. Their go-between was moderate Republican Senator Lyman Trumbull (q.v.) of Illinois, who somehow got the impression that President Johnson would be reasonable and work with Congress in developing a new program. Instead, Johnson met Congress head on, asserting that he would act by executive proclamation and the Congress should merely endorse his plan. Besides, Johnson maintained that the measures proposed by Congress at the recommendation of the Joint Committee were blatantly unconstitutional, as they would upset the Federal system and interfere with prerogatives normally left to the states under the Constitution.

At first, Congress wondered if the president might not have a good case. They upheld his veto of the renewal of the Freedmen's Bureau Bill. But when Johnson got personal in his invective at the Washington's Birthday Speech (q.v.), Congress reconsidered its position. It then repassed the Freedmen's Bureau Act, added the Civil Rights Act of 1866, and wrapped its whole program up in the proposed Fourteenth Amendment to the Constitution, all products of the Joint Committee. When only Tennessee approved of the Amendment, Congress readmitted it to the Union and, reinforced by overwhelming Republican victories in the 1866 congressional elections, brought forth Military Reconstruction to coerce the South into the "proper" course of action.

JOINT COMMITTEE ON THE CONDUCT OF THE WAR. On October 21, 1861, Col. Edward Baker, a personal favorite and friend of President Abraham Lincoln (q.v.) and prominent Republican (q.v.), was killed leading his brigade across the Potomac River north of Washington on an assault of Ball's Bluff. The place was of little military value, and the Union column was ambushed by Confederate troops, who decimated the Yankee formations, taking nearly 1,000 prisoners. Because of Baker's political connections, Congress immediately organized the Joint (*i.e.*, both House and Senate members) Committee on the Conduct of the War. The committee was to investigate what was wrong with the Union war effort, which had failed to achieve much by the end of 1861.

In reality, Ball's Bluff was but an excuse for Radical Republicans to look into the political backgrounds of select Union generals. The Republicans noted that most of the top-ranking officers in the army seemed to be Democrats (q.v.). They especially wanted to know why officers did not hold Republican notions of the war as an opportunity to end slavery. Slow moving, incompetent officers were such because they lacked ideological underpinnings of dedication to Republican antislavery (q.v.) principles. At least that is what the committee thought. The only general whom they liked initially was John Charles Frémont (q.v.), the first Republican presidential candidate in 1856, whose pronouncements freeing slaves in Missouri had been overridden by Lincoln.

Comprised of Senators Benjamin Wade of Ohio, Zachariah Chandler of Michigan, and Andrew Johnson of Tennessee (qq.v.), and four House members, George W. Julian, John Covode, Daniel Gough, and Moses Odell (all Republicans but Johnson), the committee got right to work when it attacked Baker's division commander, Maj. Gen. Charles Stone. The committee had him arrested and held without charges for 189 days. Released finally in late 1862, he never received another assignment of value, even though his qualifications were lauded by Lt. Gen. Ulysses S. Grant (q.v.). He was rumored to have committed treason by informing Rebels of Baker's attack in advance.

But Stone was merely the first officer to run afoul of the committee. Most officers unwisely treated the committeemen as meddlers. What the committee really signified was the need of politicians in a democratic nation to have to explain what war policy was and why their soldiers were not winning. It was a natural response of men who had to stand for election and could not patiently wait for results from generals who were not in a hurry.

To gain information (one of their early targets was the flashy Maj. Gen. George B. McClellan [q.v.], a Democrat), they would go to the old-time generals that McClellan's smart-aleck young generals (men like Stone and Fitz John Porter) had replaced and ask for inside information. They got it. McClellan's men refused to talk before the committee, indicating to the politicians that they had incompetence to hide. Civilian appointees were especially eager to spill the beans, or even lie, about anything to save their lucrative government jobs. The committee kept lists of who knew whom and who would cave in to pressure.

McClellan refused to put up with such shenanigans. But Grant knew better and could permit this kind of interference. Of course, Grant was winning, and McClellan was not, so the committee's attitude varied greatly between the two men. In no other American war has a committee of Congress tried to control so much, right down to military personnel changes. The committee came to grasp strategy, but it never understood tactics. Its meddling was the price of getting the people's support through their representatives for an often confusing war.

JOMINI, ANTOINE HENRI, BARON (1779–1869). There are many who claim that the American Civil War had no real military theory, that the movement of the soldiers was little more than the movement of armed mobs. This is more sarcasm than truth. What military theory existed as far as the American soldier was concerned centered around a French writer, the Baron Antoine Henry Jomini. Born in Switzerland, Jomini's early writing attracted the notice of Napoleon I. He gave him rank and told him to write more. When things started going bad for the French Empire in 1813, Jomini went over to the tsar of Russia. Jomini penned some 27 volumes of military history and theory, the most important of which was his 1838 volume, *Summary of the Art of War.*

But Jomini never forgot Napoleon, whom he idolized in actuality and in print. Because French was the foreign language studied at the U.S. Military Academy, everyone lauded Napoleon as the perfect general, and to read Jomini was to study Napoleon, the *Summary* became a much read, much discussed book in the antebellum military community of the United States. Few if any had heard of the Prussian, Karl von Clausewitz, much less read him. Indeed, Jomini's *Summary* was translated into English, and many American theorists based their thoughts on Napoleon by way of Jomini. Among these were Henry W. Halleck (q.v.), *Elements of Military Art and Science* (1846), the most outright plagiarism of Jomini; Dennis Hart Mahan's *Outpost* (1848); and William J. Hardee's *Rifle and Light Infantry Tactics* (1855), perhaps the most popular of these works.

Jomini affected American military thinking in four ways. First, he believed that a commander ought to concentrate his effort against the enemy in successive theaters of war. No multiple offenses for Jomini. Second, the commander ought to maneuver his collected forces against fractions of the enemy. Third, the commander ought to maneuver his forces to strike the enemy at a decisive point. Fourth, the commander ought to maneuver his forces into battle speedily, together, simultaneously.

There was nothing too amazing about this. It was pretty much common sense. Southern cavalry leader Nathan Bedford Forrest (q.v.), who had never heard of Jomini and could barely read anyhow, would summarize Jomini in one terse sentence: get there first with the most. But Jomini went further than that. He provided a dozen set-piece battle diagrams, which if followed by a commander would allegedly lead to victory. He opposed all entrenchments and fortifications. He believed that if a commander could control three sides of a rectangular theater of operations, within which were other rectangles labeled base zone, zone of operations, supply lines, and so on, he would win the day. Above all, Jomini believed that war was for professional soldiers. Civilians ought to mind their own business and butt out. He believed the involvement of civilians in war was what led to the excesses of the Napoleonic and French Revolutionary wars.

The primary objective for a commander was maneuver, not fighting. The ideal battle would have lots of maneuver and very little combat, which made Maj. Gen. William S. Rosecrans' (q.v.) Tullahoma maneuvers during the Chattanooga Campaign (q.v.) a Civil War military masterpiece. Under Jomini, war became in effect a massive quadrille. This is what caused so many of the problems of the Civil War. The generals were fighting a set-piece gentlemen's war, according to Jomini, trying to take each other's capital. But the actual war is the first of the modern conflicts of the 19th century, and the politicians were playing for keeps. They wanted the destruction of the enemy and his civilian and military capabilities. As French Prime Minister Georges Clemenceau was supposed to have said in World War I, "War is too important to be left to the generals."

JONESBORO, BATTLE OF. *See* ATLANTA CAMPAIGN.

JUBILEE, DAY OF. Tradition has the slaves called in by their masters at the end of the war and told about emancipation (q.v.) and what it meant. The happy blacks then roll their eyes, cry hosannas to Heaven, and began to cry and dance for joy. The suggestion was that they were childlike beings who would never make it on their own. Of course, the problem is that the reaction to emancipation was not described by blacks but whites. Most of the slaves were illiterate (a condition enforced by law), and what they felt was not told until years later—then again often to white men of the Works Progress Administration, interviewing them during the New Deal. Far from freedom meaning a release from work, blacks knew that now they had a chance to work for themselves. It had become worthwhile to labor. But soon a new reality hit them, very hard. With the assistance of the Federal Freedmen's Bureau (q.v.), they soon had to sign annual contracts that gave them a portion of the crop but required them to labor in the fields as before. About the only change the average field hand managed to negotiate was the right to work his own piece of rented land like an independent farmer—so long as he raised the cotton necessary to pay the owner off for the loans in food, seeds, equipment, clothing, and shelter at the end of the year. No reason for the freed men and women to cheer, and indeed few said that they did.

JULIAN, GEORGE W. (1817–1899). Born in a log cabin in Wayne County, Indiana, George Julian came from a Huguenot background (his real family name being St. Julien). His father died when the boy was six, and his mother raised the family. Julian had a common school education and read law, practicing his profession in northeastern Indiana. In 1845, he was elected to the state legislature as a Whig (q.v.), but voted with the Democrats (q.v.) against repudiation of state canal bonds. He also began to speak out and write newspaper pieces attacking slavery. Julian ran for Congress as a Free Soiler, was elected in 1848, and voted against the Compromise of 1850 (q.v.). In 1852, he ran as vice president on the Free Soil ticket. By 1854, Julian was in the lead organizing the Republican Party (q.v.) and actively supported the John C. Frémont (q.v.) ticket in 1856. Four years later, he was elected to Congress where, upon the outbreak of war, he urged the abolition of all slavery as a war measure and was instrumental in the passage of the Homestead Act in 1862 (q.v.). Although he was disappointed in the hesitancy of President Abraham Lincoln (q.v.) to emancipate the slaves and impose harsher conditions on the wartime Reconstruction of the South, Julian never broke with the chief executive as so many other Radicals (q.v.) did in 1864.

Upon Lincoln's assassination, Julian called for harsh punishment of Southerners, particularly through land confiscation and the grant of land (the Southern Homestead Act [q.v.]) and suffrage to the freedmen (he also proposed a constitutional amendment granting the vote to women). He was one of the committee of seven that prepared the impeachment (q.v.) charges against President Andrew Johnson (q.v.). But the waning of radicalism upon the president's acquittal caught Julian full force, and he failed to achieve renomination in 1870. He was a Liberal Republican (q.v.) in 1872 and became a lifelong champion of various reforms. He supported the Democrats in 1876 and was made surveyor general for the Territory of New Mexico, during which time he uncovered many frauds. He supported the Gold Democrats in 1896 and published his political philosophy and speeches and a biography of Joshua R. Giddings, an early abolitionist (q.v.). He died at his Indiana home at the end of the century, ever the principled idealist and anathema to regular party politicians.

JUNETEENTH. A traditional day of freedom from slavery, celebrated by blacks in Texas and the Great Southwest to this day, is June 19, or Juneteenth. The day came from the freedom order Bvt. Maj. Gen. Gordon Granger issued when he took command of the District of Texas and his army occupied Galveston in 1865.

KANE, GEORGE P. *See* BALTIMORE PLOT.

"KANSAS, CRIME AGAINST." *See* SUMNER, CHARLES.

KANSAS–MISSOURI BORDER WARS. By the time of the passage of the Kansas–Nebraska Act in 1854 (q.v.), President Franklin Pierce (q.v.) believed that the issue of slavery in the territories had been laid to rest, permanently. He figured that popular sovereignty (q.v.) would transfer slavery out of Congress and into the territories, away from Washington. But in signing the Kansas–Nebraska Act, he failed to reckon with Northern public opinion. Rather than quieting the issue of slavery in the territories, the Kansas–Nebraska Act raised it to new heights. Very little was thought of Nebraska. Everyone was centered on Kansas and what happened there. Only in Kansas could the North defeat what they perceived to be a pro-slave plot to take over the whole West.

Part of the problem was that Kansas was not just a pro-slave versus Free Soil fight. Whoever controlled the new territorial government would have the power to assign land grants to railroads, issue business licenses, and help select people secure high profits. No one would have legal title until all land ownership was registered. This had yet to be done. So force was often used for other than pro-slave or Free Soil reasons. But that is not what people back East heard. Sooner or later, everything came down to a common denominator—slavery or freedom.

The problem was exacerbated for several reasons. There were poor communications between the West and the East. The frontier was by its very nature lawless. Government appointees were generally men of lesser character, men who had lost elections back home, or minor political hacks out for the Almighty Dollar. And finally, the army was distracted from Kansas issues by the incessant Indian wars of the decade, which stretched from Kansas to Oregon.

Trying to diffuse the issue, President Pierce appointed Andrew Reeder of Ohio as the first territorial governor. He was avowedly soft on the slavery issue. Northerners, irritated until now, applauded the move, but Southerners saw it as a double-cross. Reeder immediately began to sell large blocks of

Native American lands at public auction. He built a new capital for Kansas in the middle of these lands, called Pawnee City. It turned out that one of the largest speculators was the governor himself. Reeder also discovered that Yankees paid a higher price for smaller lots than Southerners. So Reeder declared himself a Free Soiler. He spread false and exaggerated stories of Southern violence. Powerful Senator David Atchison of Missouri (and acting vice president of the United States) demanded Reeder's head. Reeder went to Washington to defend himself.

Pierce wanted to walk down the middle again. So he validated Reeder's actions to appease the North and tried to get Reeder to resign to appease the South. But Reeder refused and went back to Kansas, to find that the territorial legislature had abandoned Pawnee City and moved east to Shawnee Mission. Reeder ordered them to go back to his capital. The legislature refused. Reeder promised to veto any and all legislation until they did. At the suggestion of Secretary of War Jefferson Davis (q.v.) of Mississippi, Pierce fired Reeder.

Reeder's replacement was another northerner lukewarm on Free Soilers, Wilson Shannon. Shannon declared the legislature to have been falsely elected by the Border Ruffians, and, with the help of the army, managed to secure a truce among all sides. But the Free Soilers decided to elect their own legislature at Topeka, without Southern involvement. They also elected Charles Robinson as governor, sent Reeder to Congress as territorial delegate, and petitioned for statehood under a Free Soil constitution. Finally the Topeka government enrolled its own militia under James H. Lane. President Pierce called all of this treason and asked the Army to suppress all "irregular combinations" on both sides.

The result was called the Wakarusa War in November 1855. The incident that triggered the war was a pro-slave man shooting a Free Soiler for illegally cutting timber on the Southerner's land. The pro-slave sheriff, Samuel J. Jones, arrested the Northern man, who promptly escaped. As a former Missourian, Jones asked for volunteers from his home state. Eight hundred armed men responded. The Topeka men called up their own militia. Governor Shannon called up the territorial militia he controlled, mainly Southerners. Then Shannon realized that war was imminent and rushed to the banks of the Wakarusa River to quell it before the shooting started.

In a meeting with Lane and Robinson, Shannon declared that he had not asked for Missouri's help. Sheriff Jones agreed to send the men home, aided by winter weather and the drunkenness of the volunteers. What the Wakarusa War showed was that Pierce's desire to rely on civilian posses would not work. Only the army would do to bring peace to Kansas.

By April 1856, the pro-slave men had had enough of organized Yankee emigration. With the backing of Jefferson Buford and 600 Alabama volunteers who had recently arrived, Judge Samuel D. Lecompte had asked the grand jury to indict members of Free Soil governments for high treason. Sheriff Jones had been ambushed outside of Lawrence when he arrested a half dozen Free Soilers. Buford, Jones, and more Missouri volunteers joined the Alabama men and invaded Lawrence, the center of Free Soil sentiment. There they destroyed several businesses, "Gov." Robinson's house, and the Free State Hotel. Free Soil leaders escaped the mob by fleeing into the hills.

In the North, this was called the "Rape of Lawrence." It inspired the U.S. senator from Massachusetts, Charles Sumner (q.v.), to make a speech he called, "The Crime Against Kansas." In it he attacked Southerners in general, and Andrew P. Butler of South Carolina by name, for being lovers of the harlot of slavery. That imagery was a mite rough for those Victorian days. Since Butler was absent and unable to defend himself, his nephew, South Carolina congressman Preston Brooks, accosted Sumner on the floor of the Senate and beat him unmercifully with his walking stick until it broke over Sumner's bleeding head.

The North was outraged by Brooks' action. The South was thrilled. When Southerners heard that Brooks had lost his cane, they sent him new ones from all over the South, some with slogans like "hit him again" embossed on their shafts. Brooks resigned his seat but was returned without opposition. Sumner went into years of seclusion and medical treatment, much of it more painful than the beating he took. The Massachusetts legislature reelected him *in absentia*. "The Vacant Chair of Sumner" became a token of sectional discord.

Meanwhile, as the South lauded Brooks' chastisement of Sumner, the Free Soilers struck in Kansas. Led by an uncompromising abolitionist, John Brown (qq.v.), eight men visited seven alleged Southerners and hacked them to death in the "Pottawattomie Massacre" on May 24, 1856. In response, Judge Lecompte had the U.S. Army arrest the whole Topeka government. Pierce had the ineffectual Gov. Shannon replaced by a new man, John Geary (q.v.) of Pennsylvania, who had been working mines in western Virginia with slave labor. Geary called in the army to keep everyone apart and asked that Judge Lecompte be replaced. But Lecompte refused to step down or release the Topeka government leaders. Eventually, no one showed up to testify against them, so the whole case became moot, and a bitter Judge Lecompte had to release them.

It was painfully obvious that popular sovereignty was not working. Its cardinal principle was no Federal intervention, but the Army and Pierce's appointment of Geary were all that kept the peace. The Free Soilers skillfully had manipulated the myths and rumors of a shooting war to fix the image of "Bleeding Kansas" indelibly in American history. Everything, from the "Rape of Lawrence" to the "Wakarusa War," had been blamed on Pierce and the Missouri Border Ruffians. The Pierce administration was doomed to be limited to one term.

KANSAS–NEBRASKA ACT. Two things brought about the Kansas–Nebraska Act, the idea of a transcontinental railroad and politics. With the 1849 Gold Rush to California, followed by California statehood as part of the Compromise of 1850 (q.v.), and the fact that it took four and a half months to get to California from the East Coast, a clamor arose to connect the Far West with the center of American population east of the Mississippi. The technological star of the age was the railroad, but railroads were expensive to build and needed customers to make them economically viable. But beyond the 95th meridian, where the Missouri River turns north at Kansas City, few people lived. And until one reached the California gold fields, the land was known as the Great American Desert. But the railroad project was so important that something special had to be done to get it going. It needed the support of the American taxpayer through the Federal government in Washington. The project was so expensive that the government could only finance one route.

There were four likely starting points for the rails west: Chicago, St. Louis, Memphis, and New Orleans. The army had surveyed all four routes and reported the obvious—the only all-weather routes were the routes to the south, and the farther south, the better. Since St. Louis was too steamboat-oriented to care and Memphis was too small, the real choice lay between Chicago and New Orleans. Sectional politics (North vs. South) came quickly to the fore.

Politically, the Whigs (q.v.) had the strongest political position in 1853, but their potential had been gutted by the slavery issue, dividing North from South within the party. The Democrats (q.v.) took the election of 1852 (q.v.), installing Franklin Pierce (q.v.) in the presidency, but they had had to rely on Southern Whigs to do it. They, too, had political divisions, especially in the North—New York and New England. As if to show how tenuous any political alliance was, three Free Soil Party men had been elected in 1848: Salmon P. Chase (q.v.), John P. Hale, and Charles Sumner (q.v.). They were up for reelection in 1854 and needed a hot issue to run on.

Politicians of all stripes were confused as to their political roles in the early 1850s, knocked off course by the slavery issue. Any legislation that might bring on the certainty of new alignments would be seized upon, and the railroad west offered just such an opportunity for all sides.

The man who wished to see New Orleans win the railroad race was Jefferson Davis (q.v.), Pierce's secretary of war and chief advisor. The South had one great advantage over the North. Texas had more population farther west than any other state. Davis saw to it that the Southern route was enhanced when James Gadsden of Alabama negotiated the Gadsden Purchase from Mexico in 1854, securing all the excellent potential rail territory south of the Gila River.

The man who wished to see Chicago win the railroad contest was Illinois U.S. Senator Stephen A. Douglas (q.v.). He needed to negate the Texas population advantage by encouraging people to move onto the Great Plains west of Kansas City. In 1854, he proposed a new territorial government be set up to accomplish just that. He called his new territory Nebraska (present-day Kansas and Nebraska). The measure failed to pass over heated Southern opposition in 1853.

In the Senate, there were Southerners not averse to rails going out of Chicago, if Douglas were willing to pay a price for his victory. That price was the Non-Exclusion Doctrine (q.v.) on slavery in the territories, now given the flashy name popular sovereignty (q.v.). It essentially opened all territories to exploitation by slaveholder and nonslaveholder until a territory applied for statehood. At that point, in the constitutional convention for the new proposed state, and only then, the slavery issue would be decided. Congress then would accept the "voice of the people" and admit the new state with or without slavery as its convention had already voted.

In 1854, Douglas and Pierce needed four votes to pass a Nebraska Act and more to get the Gadsden Purchase treaty confirmed in the Senate. These four votes (all Southern) included Senator David Atchison, president *pro tempore* of the Senate and acting vice president of the United States. Atchison wanted a slave territory on Missouri's western border. He also promised that no legislation would pass until this was done. Douglas, chairman of the committee on territories, caved in. He rewrote his Nebraska Bill to provide for two territories, Kansas directly west of Missouri, and Nebraska west of Iowa and Minnesota. After much dickering, Atchison obtained the open repeal of the Missouri Compromise (no 36°30′ line dividing slave territory from free territory) and the installation of popular sovereignty (no vote on slavery until the territories applied for statehood).

The Kansas–Nebraska Act passed both houses of Congress, with Pierce cracking the patronage whip. Atchison got the Democratic Party he wanted, minus New England support of Van Buren. Southern Whigs began the process of becoming Democrats, although it would take the results of the Civil War and Reconstruction to make a real one-party South, and the Gadsden Purchase confirmation soon followed. The Northern Whigs, the New England Democrats, and the Free Soil men formed the Republican Party.

Douglas (who had been overlooked after Atchison took over the bill) was the only one, seemingly, who understood that popular sovereignty still had a lie deep within it. No matter when the popular vote was taken, in territorial stages or as the territory became a state, antislave Northerners and immigrants would always move west faster than Southerners encumbered by slaves. And slavery probably had reached the limits of its expansion, as determined by geography. One could not grow cotton on the plains. So Douglas played on his cleverness to look pro-slave nationally in Washington and antislave locally in Illinois, until another Illinois politician revealed his duplicity in the Lincoln–Douglas Debates (q.v.) in 1858.

KANSAS SETTLEMENT (1856–1861). President James Buchanan (q.v.) had won his office by standing for popular sovereignty (q.v.). Essentially, this meant that the Federal government was to stay clear of the political problems brought on by the issue of slavery in the territories and permit the people in the territories to settle the problem on their own. But this settlement was to come only when the territory in question was ready to draw up a proposed state constitution. At that point, in the state constitutional convention, the decision on slavery would be made. The convention could vote to come into the Union as a free state. But prior to that, while an area was still a territory, slavery was to be allowed under the Non-Exclusion Doctrine (q.v.).

What the Republicans (q.v.) wanted was for Buchanan to violate popular sovereignty. Thus their 1856 party platform railed against the twin evils of slavery and polygamy in the territories. It was a trap. Republicans wanted Buchanan to subdue the rebellious Mormons in Utah Territory and refuse to interfere against his pro-slave Southern allies in Kansas. Buchanan fell into the snare wonderfully. The result was the Mormon War (q.v.) in Utah and the final Kansas Settlement.

Unlike his predecessor, Franklin Pierce (q.v.), Buchanan realized that his Kansas political appointees had to be top-notch men. For territorial governor in Kansas, Buchanan chose Robert Walker, an old-time Democratic politician who had served as secretary of the treasury under President James K. Polk. Walker was New York born, but had spent most of his adult life as a Mississippi planter. He was a strong supporter of popular sovereignty. Walker was at first unwilling to accept the job, but Buchanan pointed out its importance; Walker's friendliness with all Democrats, especially Senator Stephen A. Douglas of Illinois; and his administrative experience.

To support Walker, Buchanan had the Army send out Brig. Gen. William S. Harney. A veteran of wars against the Seminoles in Florida and the Mexicans, where he had hanged American traitors who had joined the Mexican army, Harney was a no-nonsense officer who would do whatever had to be done in Kansas. He had 1,500 soldiers under his command, but the Mormon War soon cut that substantially. Along with Walker and Harney, Buchanan kept the controversial pro-slave Judge Samuel Lecompte on the bench as a sop to Southerners.

But Walker had an ace up his sleeve. He was to combine popular sovereignty with a substantial land deal to, in effect, buy a Kansas Settlement. Traditionally, any territory received a substantial grant of Federal land within its boundaries when it achieved statehood. Kansas was to received double the usual amount. The appeal of this to speculators, especially in railroads, was obvious. Unfortunately, Walker found that the land scheme was not going to work. He and Buchanan had overestimated the powers of greed and self-interest. Kansas Democrats resented Washington Democrats telling them what to do. Free Soilers were not about to fold the principle that brought them to Kansas for land speculation.

Changing his tack, Walker did his best to be as neutral as possible. He went to the Free Soilers and asked them to hold off resubmitting the Free Soil Topeka Constitution. He also got them to pledge to submit any clause on slavery to the people separately from the constitution itself. When the new constitutional convention met at Lecompton, Walker found himself greatly embarrassed. The Free Soilers had refused to vote (they just could not bear to trust a Mississippian, as they saw Walker), and the members were all anti-Walker Democrats. The result was a pro-slave state constitution. Then the convention sent the document to Washington without submitting it to a vote of Kansas residents.

The committee on territories in Congress realized that this could not be. It sent the Lecompton Constitution back to Kansas. The document was to be voted on with or without slavery. Any slaves already in Kansas were to remain slaves for life, unless freed by their owners. On December 21, 1857, the Lecompton Constitution passed overwhelmingly with the slavery provision. Again, the Free Soilers had refused to vote at all. Southerners were cheered by this rejection of Free Soil doctrine. But Walker refused to acquiesce in the vote. He went to Washington and fought against Congress' accepting the slave state of Kansas.

Walker's insistence on a full vote on any constitution convinced Free Soilers all over the North of his innate fairness. This slaveholder became the antislave hero of the hour. Buchanan was outraged at Walker's stance. He wanted any constitution and statehood fast, to get rid of this divisive issue and get on with other business. It was not his fault that the Free Soilers refused to vote. Kansas should become a slave state, and Buchanan told Congress so. Party loyalty demanded a vote for Lecompton, Buchanan said. Walker said that Buchanan was acting undemocratically and not following the intent of popular sovereignty and resigned in a huff. Buchanan replaced Walker with James W. Denver, who had been commissioner of Indian affairs in Kansas and acting governor in Walker's absence.

But Walker was not the only Democrat to break with Buchanan over the legality of the Lecompton Constitution. Stephen A. Douglas (q.v.) realized that Lecompton had to be stopped. He especially railed against its inherent unfairness in passage and the fact that blacks already enslaved would not be freed no matter what passed, pro- or antislave. He knew that if he backed Lecompton, he would lose the 1858 senatorial election. Buchanan struck back, refusing to give him patronage traditionally due a senator. Stand by the party, Buchanan ordered. "Mr. President," Douglas said, "Andrew Jackson is dead." To another commentator, Douglas growled, "By God, sir, I made Mr. James Buchanan, and by God, sir, I will unmake him."

Meanwhile, in Kansas the Republican-dominated state legislature called for another referendum on the Lecompton Constitution. This time the Free Soilers voted, and Lecompton was overwhelmingly defeated, Democrats refusing to vote. But if the two elections were added together, the vote was 11,000 against the Lecompton Constitution and 6,000 for. It was obvious to all that in an honest, fair vote, Kansas should be admitted as a free state. But Buchanan refused to give in. He proposed that Kansas be admitted under Lecompton as a slave state. Then another vote could be taken on slavery. Douglas and the Northern Democrats who stood with him, now called Anti-Lecompton Democrats, refused. They wanted a free Kansas, as did the people of Kansas, and to act otherwise was to invite irreparable losses up north in the 1858 congressional battles.

Buchanan acted once more to save the Lecompton Constitution, his obstinacy becoming fairly unbearable. Acting through Congressman Alexander Stephens (q.v.) of Georgia, a moderate of sorts, well-liked by Northerners, Buchanan had Representative William English of Indiana introduce the English Bill. It proposed that Kansas be admitted immediately under Lecompton, providing it would accept a much-reduced land grant. If Kansas refused to accept these terms, statehood would be delayed until Kansas' population reached 93,000, or the number represented by one congressman in those days. The problem was that either way, Lecompton was informally recognized. Douglas and the anti-Lecompton Democrats almost took this deal, until they realized what a campaign issue it would give their Republican opponents in 1858.

Douglas voted to reject the English Bill, but it passed both houses of Congress. Those Anti-Lecompton Democrats who voted for the English Bill all went down to defeat in 1858. Douglas credited his holding onto his Senate seat to his vote against the English Bill. Kansas was thus rejected for statehood, but a new state convention drew up a new free state constitution that resulted in Kansas becoming a state in 1861, after the South had seceded.

KELLOGG, WILLIAM PITT (1830–1918). The last Reconstruction governor of Louisiana, William Pitt Kellogg was born in Vermont. Educated at a local military academy, Kellogg left for Illinois in the 1840s. There he studied law and was admitted to the bar. He joined the Republican Party (q.v.), was chairman of his county delegation, and was a political ally of Abraham Lincoln (q.v.). In 1859, Kellogg was a convention delegate and an elector, voting for Lincoln both times. In 1861, Lincoln appointed him chief justice for Nebraska Territory, but Kellogg took leave to organize a regiment of Illinois cavalry. He led them in the Trans-Mississippi Theater of war for two years, until ill-health compelled his resignation. Lincoln then appointed him collector for the Port of New Orleans.

In Louisiana, Kellogg was a mainstay of the state's Republican Party. He was U.S. senator (1868–1872) and governor (1872–1876). But it was his tenure as the last Carpetbag (q.v.) governor that has drawn the most attention, then and now. Although much of his political power in the state was based on the black vote, it was rumored that Kellogg never shook hands with an African-American without putting on his gloves first. His election as governor was tainted by the usual shenanigans that flavor Louisiana politics, but Kellogg was reputed to be personally honest. His election was guaranteed by the Returning Board, supposedly composed of the governor, lieutenant governor, secretary of state, and two state senators—or anyone who claimed to be acting for them. Kellogg was selected by a Republican board while his Democratic (q.v.) opponent was picked by another board, organized by outgoing governor Henry Clay Warmoth. No one really knows who won.

Kellogg was placed in power by possessing a Federal court decree authorizing him to call on Federal troops for help. But the Customs House Faction, which backed Kellogg, was in deep trouble in outlying parishes (counties) of Louisiana. Kellogg's term was marked by violent takeovers of local courthouses by local White League (q.v.) militias. Only the intervention of the U.S. Army prevented the same from happening to Governor Kellogg during the Third Battle of New Orleans (q.v.). The state legislature, dominated by Democrats, threatened to impeach Kellogg, until Maj. Gen. Philip Sheridan (q.v.) came in and purged the membership and declared the Democrats "banditti."

This only caused more uproar. Finally, Congress sent a subcommittee to settle things. In the Wheeler Compromise, the statehouse was divided between parties (Democratic House, Republican Senate) and Kellogg guaranteed the final two years of his term. Kellogg stepped down in 1876 and later served as congressman (1883–1885) and in every Republican national convention from 1876 to 1896. Then he essentially retired, to live the life of an ordinary Louisiana citizen until his death 30 years later.

KENNESAW MOUNTAIN, BATTLE OF. *See* ATLANTA CAMPAIGN.

KERNSTOWN, BATTLE OF. Fought on March 23, 1862, the Battle of Kernstown was Confederate Maj. Gen. Thomas J. "Stonewall" Jackson's (q.v.) successful attempt to prevent the transfer of Union troops from the Shenandoah Valley to the Federal advance upon Richmond in the Peninsula Campaign (q.v.). Jackson hit a portion of the moving Federal column near Winchester at Kernstown in the afternoon. Jackson's plan was to feint with his right and attack with his left. But he mistakenly thought that he faced only one Union brigade, when in fact, he faced three. The Rebels began to run low on ammunition just as the Federals advanced. Jackson ordered his own

Stonewall brigade to hold with the bayonet. In danger of being overrun and destroyed, its commander, Brig. Gen. Richard B. Garnett, ordered his men to retreat, causing the whole Confederate line to yield. Furious, Jackson filed charges against Garnett, who was eventually transferred to Maj. Gen. George Pickett's Division to get him away from Jackson's vindictiveness. Although Jackson lost the battle, he was successful in his objective, causing President Abraham Lincoln (q.v.) to halt the transfer of reinforcements to Gen. George B. McClellan's (q.v.) force besieging Richmond in the Peninsula Campaign. But his conduct toward Garnett illustrated how Jackson could become embroiled with junior officers (at least a half dozen others faced Garnett's fate) in bitter, continuous quarrels.

KIDNAP PLOTS AGAINST LINCOLN. *See* LINCOLN, ASSASSINATION; LINCOLN ASSASSINATION, THE CONFEDERACY AND THE; LINCOLN ASSASSINATION, THE NEW YORK CONNECTION OF THE.

KILPATRICK–DAHLGREN RAID. *See* LINCOLN ASSASSINATION, THE CONFEDERACY AND THE.

KING COTTON DIPLOMACY. *See* DIPLOMACY, U.S.—CIVIL WAR.

KINSTON, BATTLE OF. *See* CAROLINAS CAMPAIGN.

KIRBY SMITH, EDMUND (1824–1893). Appointed to West Point from Florida, E. Kirby Smith graduated in the bottom half of the class of 1845. He served in the War with Mexico, won two brevets, then was a mathematics professor at the Military Academy before working on the Mexican Boundary Commission. He was a major of cavalry before he resigned his commission and became a staff officer with Brig. Gen. Joseph E. Johnston (q.v.) in the Shenandoah Valley. Appointed brigadier general just before First Manassas (q.v.), Kirby Smith had the fortune to lead the last brigade onto the battlefield and save the day for the Rebels, for which he received the nickname the "Blücher of Manassas."

Seriously wounded, Kirby Smith, young, dashing, and handsome, met and married a Virginia girl who made him a shirt. She romantically became called the "Bride of the Confederacy." Kirby Smith was outwardly a nice, humble soldier, but inwardly he craved fame. He at first attributed his arrival on the Manassas battlefield to God's will, then he took some and then all of the credit for the Confederate victory. Supposed to cooperate with Gen. Braxton Bragg (q.v.) in the 1862 Perryville Campaign (q.v.), Kirby Smith jumped the gun and invaded Kentucky on his own. His independence during the campaign did much to lose it. But he managed to get the thanks of Congress and a promotion to lieutenant general, which he wheedled into a department command in the Trans-Mississippi.

As Confederate fortunes waned on the Mississippi, Kirby Smith found his department cut off from the rest of the South with the fall of Vicksburg. Promoted to general in early 1864, Kirby Smith went on to defeat the union Red River Campaign and the Camden Campaign (qq.v.), although he was present more as a coordinator behind the lines than on the field of battle. Because of his isolation from the rest of the Confederate government, Kirby Smith eventually ruled his department through fiat, appointing his own officers, civil and military, and consulting with the deposed Confederate governors of Louisiana, Arkansas, and Missouri from Marshall, Texas, and Shreveport, Louisiana. Eventually, Richmond came to recognize most of what Kirby Smith had done, there being no way around it, although President Jefferson Davis (q.v.) did not like the independent nature of government there in what came to be called "Kirby Smithdom."

Kirby Smith surrendered the last organized Confederate army on June 2, 1865, at Galveston. On his way to New Orleans to give his parole, Kirby Smith heard erroneously that Gen. Robert E. Lee (q.v.) had been arrested. Kirby Smith fled to Maximilian's Mexico (q.v.) and then Cuba before returning to the United States in late 1865. He was in insurance and a telegraph company before they went broke. Then he tried college administration and finally taught mathematics at the University of the South at Sewanee.

KIRK–HOLDEN WAR. *See* HOLDEN, WILLIAM W.

KNIGHTS OF THE GOLDEN CIRCLE. *See* FILIBUSTERING.

"KNOW NOTHINGS." *See* AMERICAN PARTY.

KNOX *v.* LEE (1871). *See* LEGAL TENDER CASES.

KNOXVILLE CAMPAIGN. President Abraham Lincoln (q.v.) had an obsession about East Tennessee that lasted most of the war. It was one of the bigger, more loyal Union areas in the seceded South. Its people were small, nonslaveholding farmers, like his parents were. It had once tried to enter the Union before the 1800s as the state of Franklin, before being melded with greater Tennessee. Yet its fate, because of its strategic location along the shortest rail route to the West, was to be occupied by the Confederate army for most of the war. In 1863, in conjunction with Maj. Gen. William S. Rosecrans' (q.v.) Tullahoma Campaign, Lincoln had sent Maj. Gen. Ambrose E. Burnside (q.v.), the loser of the Battle of Fredericksburg, to recover East Tennessee for the Union and protect Rosecrans' left flank.

Burnside moved into East Tennessee from the upper Cumberland in May 1863. Almost immediately his schedule was interrupted by bigger objectives; in this case, the need of protecting Bvt. Maj. Gen. Ulysses S. Grant's (q.v.) so far successful operations at Vicksburg. Burnside's IX Corps, the major part of his infantry were called to Vicksburg to be part of the outer line that was to protect the besieging force from Confederate attack to their rear. Burnside did not receive his men back until August. He advanced once again, the Confederates retreating before him, occupying Knoxville on September 4, 1863.

As he entered Knoxville, Burnside learned that an independent Confederate force had been left behind in the Cumberland Gap. The Gap was much like Chattanooga. It was a key location, but it could be outflanked and surrounded from a half-dozen directions, the approaching enemy hidden behind the hills nearby. When Burnside turned toward Cumberland Gap, he allowed the larger Confederate force near Knoxville to join Gen. Braxton Bragg (q.v.) at Chickamauga Creek for the upcoming battle there as part of the Chattanooga Campaign (q.v.).

It only took three days (September 7–9) for Burnside to take the Gap. The Rebel troops did not want to fight, they were surrounded, and they had no hope of relief. Their surrender was quite a coup for Burnside. He captured 2,000 men, 3,000 small arms, 12 cannon, and 220,000 rounds of ammunition. Burnside moved back to Knoxville to tighten his hold on East Tennessee.

After the Battle of Chickamauga, Bragg began anew his perennial quarrels with his officers. One he came to despise was Lt. Gen. James Longstreet (q.v.), whose Corps from Robert E. Lee's forces in Virginia had been a key to Confederate victory at Chickamauga. Bragg sent Longstreet and his men away to recapture East Tennessee. This suited Longstreet, because he always yearned for independent command, but never seemed to measure up. What followed was one of the most bungled Confederate campaigns of the war, against a second-rate Yankee general of little talent.

Longstreet's men rode the rails up from Chattanooga to Loudon. There they dismounted and repaired some wrecked bridges. Then they advanced to Lenoir Station, this on November 15, in the mountains, without adequate food, blankets, or clothing. Longstreet had hoped to surprise Burnside in his camp there, but the Union troops and their commander had fled to Knoxville, after making a stand at Campbell Station, noteworthy because Confederate artillery ammunition proved totally defective. Longstreet arrived at Knoxville on November 17. He charged an exposed redoubt and drove Burnside completely into the city.

Longstreet had no maps, but a reconnaissance showed a weak point at Ft. Sanders. After some hesitation, the attack took place on November 28, after a night of freezing rain. The ground was so slick that the Rebels could not scale the fort's walls. They lost 1,300 casualties to Burnside's 700. An approaching Federal relief column caused Longstreet to retreat past Knoxville into Virginia, after trying to lure the Yankees into battle at Bean's Station. Recriminations on the Confederate side followed all winter, with Longstreet preferring charges against some of his best officers, who had served beside him the longest, blaming them unfairly for his own stupidity.

KU KLUX ACT. *See* ENFORCEMENT ACT, THIRD (APRIL 20, 1871).

KU KLUX KLAN, KNIGHTS OF THE. In late December 1865, six young ex-Confederate soldiers sat bored in Pulaski, Tennessee. They wanted something fun to do. One suggested that they organize a secret society. They elected a chairman and a secretary and divided themselves into committees to consider at length such things as ritual, rules, and a name for their club. Hereafter the meeting house would be called a "Den," the den leader would be the "Grand Cyclops," his aide the "Grand Magi," the secretary the "Grand Scribe," the greeter of initiates the "Grand Turk," the den's two guards "Lictors," and the Grand Cyclops' two messengers "Night Hawks," while the rank and file members would be "Ghouls." Finally, one of the men being a scholar of the classics, he suggested a name for the new organization, "Kluklos," Greek for "circle." They spoke some more and eventually settled on the alliterative "Ku Klux Klan" as the name of the new club designed to put some zip in dull old Pulaski.

After the more or less accidental organization of the Ku Klux Klan, the organization spread rapidly throughout the rest of the South, with the purpose of expediting white control of the ex-Confederate states and countering the Republican Union Loyal Leagues. Newspaper stories, pro and con, kept the Ku Klux in the public eye. Fear of that old Southern bug-a-boo, "Negro insurrection," fed its expansion. They saw themselves like the Sons of Liberty of the American Revolution. Their activities mimicked the tarring and feathering of British tax collectors and throwing tea into Boston Harbor, but often with a more murderous twist. Perhaps a more appropriate precedent was the "patrol" instituted among whites in slavery days to watch the roads at night to be sure no blacks roamed freely without a pass or conspired against the powers that be.

The Klansmen were the modern Robin Hoods of white supremacy, glorified by Thomas Dixon's fictional Ku Klux trilogy (*The Leopard's Spots* [1902], *The Clansman* [1905], and *The Traitor* [1907]), which became the basis for D. W. Griffith's first smash-hit movie of the 20th century, "The Birth of a Nation" (which incidentally introduced the notion of the fiery cross into Klan ceremonies, something never used in the Reconstruction Era, but it looked good on film). Rhett Butler rode with the hooded vigilantes in *Gone With the Wind* and was saved from arrest by Yankee troopers on the word of an Atlanta madam that he and his cronies spent the evening with her girls. Hodding Carter spoke of the aura of the Reconstruction Klans best: "Your grandfather, God bless his memory, was one of them. And we hadn't been married more than a year when I sewed his robe together for him and out he would ride, night after night, night after night. Terrible times they were, but we won out in the end."

As the Ku Klux grew, haphazard and undisciplined, new levels of control were added, like the Grand Dragon and his staff of Hydras for each state, culminating in 1867 with the election of former Confederate cavalry Gen. Nathan Bedford Forrest (q.v.) as Grand Wizard, the head of all the Klans, and a staff of 10 Genii. Many names came to be used: the Knights of the White Camellia, the Knights of the Rising Sun, Pale Faces, the Invisible Circle, the Families of the South, and of course the Knights of the Ku Klux Klan. Some organizations were more secret than others, but all had the goal of restoring political and social control of the South to the whites who held it before the loss of the war, by violence if necessary—and it usually was.

Not all wished to be as blunt as General Forrest. The whole thing was covered up by a grand-sounding "Prescript," the Klan's constitution, in which the name of the awesome institution was never mentioned. Like the Prescript, every Ku Klux message and warning was written in code. On a raid, the Klansmen and their horses were disguised with flowing robes. No one was to speak. Instead, each raider carried a throaty-sounding whistle. When at rest, one blast meant move, three blasts meant danger, and a series of short toots was a request for aid. Many groups served under military-like discipline. It soon became apparent that something national had to be done to counteract Klan activities, which had expanded into a conspiracy that covered most of the South, lest the violence and intimidation overthrow the influences of local and state government.

But just as a Democrat (q.v.) state government did not necessarily support the Klan, a Republican (q.v.) government rarely acted with enough force to crush it. Most state officials feared that relying on martial law and a loyal militia that was composed of black and pro-Union whites would institute a race war. The only exception to this rule was in Arkansas, where Governor Powell Clayton (q.v.) used his militia units and an active anti-Klan law to destroy the Klan's influence by the end of 1869. Not everybody had the imagination or the resources to follow Clayton's success in Arkansas. Governor W. W. Holden (q.v.) of North Carolina, a state as fully plagued with Ku Klux activity as Arkansas, sent a request to President Ulysses S. Grant (q.v.) for Federal assistance.

The result was Grant's annual message to Congress in December 1870, asking that it look into the Klan and pass necessary legislation. Congress had already passed the First Enforcement Act (q.v.) on May 31 of that year. Now

Congress moved to look into the problems faced in North Carolina from the Ku Klux Klan. The result was a Second Enforcement Act to tighten up election procedures, and a Third Enforcement Act (the Ku Klux Act) on April 20, 1871 (qq.v.).

The Federal government's efforts against the Klan broke its campaign of terrorism, oddly enough, with the conviction of relatively few Klansmen (continued prosecutions would last until 1897 at the rate of 200 cases a year and relatively few convictions). But it was already too late. The Klan's terror program had already revealed how to return Democrat majorities in most Southern states. The new violence would be quite open, practiced under the guise of the Rifle Clubs, White Leagues, and Red Shirts (qq.v.).

L

LAMON, WARD. *See* BALTIMORE PLOT.

LAND GRANT COLLEGE ACT, MORRILL. The Republican Party (q.v.) had a distinct domestic program designed to appease both its agricultural and industrial supporters. This program had as its basis the old Whig (q.v.) economic policies based in part on Henry Clay's American System (q.v.). Part of the agricultural program was Federal aid to education programs called the Morill Land Grant College Act of 1862. This measure granted each loyal state 30,000 acres of Federal land for each U.S. representative or senator for the endowment of at least one college per state. These colleges had to offer agricultural and military sciences as a part of their curriculum.

LECOMPTON CONSTITUTION. *See* KANSAS–MISSOURI BORDER WARS.

LEE, ROBERT E. (1807–1870). Son of a famous Virginian, Richard Henry "Light Horse Harry" Lee, an inveterate gambler who died early in his son's life, Robert E. Lee was raised by his mother, Anne Hill Carter Lee, in what one commentator called "genteel poverty." In 1829, he graduated second in his class at West Point with a perfect conduct record. He went into the Army Corps of Engineers and spent much of his military career working on rivers and fortifications. During the War with Mexico, he was Bvt. Lt. Gen. Winfield Scott's (q.v.) chief scout, winning many of Scott's battles before they started with timely information on enemy positions and roads to the Mexican rear.

After the war, Secretary of War Jefferson Davis (q.v.) recommended Lee as superintendent of West Point and later as lieutenant colonel of the crack Second Cavalry, but he remained in Virginia caring for his wife, who was ill. Thus Lee was available to lead the Federal troops who recaptured Harper's Ferry from John Brown (qq.v.), after which he finally went to Texas briefly. In March 1861, he was appointed colonel of the First Cavalry, but never took command. He resigned his commission after the firing on Ft. Sumter (q.v.), refusing the command of all Federal forces to put down the rebellion. There is some dispute as to whether Lee actually accepted a position with Virginia state troops before he resigned, but he soon was in command of troops sent to subdue Union loyalists in what later became West Virginia, then received appointment to be the chief military advisor to President Jefferson Davis, who sent him to organize defenses along the South Atlantic Coast in the Carolinas. He handled neither assignment with distinction.

On June 1, with the wounding of Gen. Joseph E. Johnson (q.v.), commanding the forces defending Richmond from attack, and the collapse of his successor, Maj. Gen. G. W. Smith, Davis turned to Lee to save the Confederacy. Renaming his troops the Army of Northern Virginia, Lee proceeded to defeat Maj. Gen. George B. McClellan (q.v.) at the gates of Richmond, then to advance upon Washington, defeating the army of Maj. Gen. John Pope at Second Manassas, before advancing into Maryland to fight McClellan once again at Antietam Creek.

Checked in his invasion of Maryland, Lee withdrew to meet the Federals at Fredericksburg (q.v.), resulting in a lopsided Rebel victory. The following spring of 1863, Lee fought the Union army again at Chancellorsville (q.v.). Outnumbered two to one, Lee and his chief subordinate, Lt. Gen. Thomas J. "Stonewall" Jackson (q.v.), crushed the Federals in a four-day battle. But the death of Jackson and so many soldiers during the battle forced Lee to reorganize his army into three corps for the Pennsylvania Campaign (q.v.). Meeting his opponents at Gettysburg, Lee won the first two days' fighting, only to be repulsed with heavy loss on the third. Narrowly regaining the Virginia shore of the Potomac, Lee engaged in an indecisive move on Washington that fall.

The next spring, Lee fought the reorganized Federal armies, led by Lt. Gen. Ulysses S. Grant (q.v.), to a standstill in the Wilderness, only to be defeated at Spotsylvania, hanging on by a thread. Lee recovered to beat Grant to the North Anna River and Totopotomy Creek and decisively crushed Grant's attacks at Second Cold Harbor. But Grant managed to steal a march on Lee and beat him to Petersburg. However, Grant's subordinates muffed the initial attacks, and Lee recovered to force Grant into a costly nine-month siege.

But, as Lee was well aware, the Siege of Petersburg (q.v.) could only have one outcome. Attempting to break away from Grant to join other Confederate forces in the Carolinas, Lee was stymied by Grant's fast-moving cavalry under Maj. Gen. Philip H. Sheridan (q.v.), who brought Lee and his army to bay at Appomattox Court House. Forced to surrender, Lee received a parole to Richmond and then spent the rest of his life as president of Washington University at Lexington, Virginia. Upon his death in 1870 (Lee had suffered from continual heart attacks of varying import during the war), the institution was renamed Washington and Lee University, and Lee was buried there.

If Abraham Lincoln (q.v.) is the key figure of the North during the war, Lee is surely that of the South. Although he did not always make the best tactical choices on the battlefield, Lee's maneuvers before battle could only be called brilliant. He had a drive, an aggressiveness, and an ability to bring out the best in those officers and men under his command that Lincoln could only envy until Grant came east.

Today, Lee is most admired for his dedication to duty and his continual equanimity in all situations, although he was not above angrily ordering President Jefferson Davis off the battlefields around Richmond and disparaging Maj. Gen. George E. Pickett after the latter's loss at Five Forks. Lee was often too tactful and too willing to permit great latitude to his subordinates once the battle was joined. As Southern losses mounted later in the war, Lee found that the newly promoted officers often did not measure up. He also tended to defer to the civilian government at Richmond, when he should have more forcefully expressed his own views. But then his own views often were that he could not help other theaters of war, either by providing men or military advice.

The worst criticism of Lee has been that he was too expensive for the Confederacy. He lost as many casualties during the Chancellorsville Campaign as men were surrendered at the Battle of Ft. Donelson (q.v.). He lost more men at Gettysburg than were available to the Confederacy in 1862 in Tennessee. He lost 50,000 men in the first three months of his command alone. And this against what many historians think might best be labeled as the second string of Northern generals.

We will probably never know the real Robert E. Lee, any more than we understand the real George Washington or the true Abraham Lincoln. But we do know that Lee demonstrated what an active, able officer can do to deliver paralyzing blows through quick maneuvers with highly mobile forces against enemy lines of communication and supply, and attack decisive enemy positions, all done with inadequate supply and numbers when compared to his opponents. In short, Lee was audacious, imaginative, and possessed of the ability to force his own will upon the enemy. He did this without losing a certain nobility and concept of fair play. That is still called character.

LEE'S "LOST ORDER." An order issued on September 9, 1862, by Confederate Gen. Robert E. Lee (q.v.) during the Maryland Campaign (q.v.) that sent six of his divisions south to invest the Federal garrison at Harper's Ferry and three divisions north to Hagerstown to forage. A copy of the order was found wrapped around some cigars by two Union soldiers in an abandoned Confederate camp at Frederick, Maryland, four days later and placed in Maj. Gen. George B. McClellan's (q.v.) hands, giving him a golden opportunity to split Lee's army with his own and defeat the Confederates in detail.

LEGAL TENDER CASES. Before President Ulysses S. Grant (q.v.) could get Congress to work with him on the money issue after the Civil War, the

Supreme Court stepped into the question with the Legal Tender Cases. The court had as its chief justice at this time Salmon P. Chase (q.v.), former secretary of the treasury under Lincoln and a man constantly with his eye on the presidency. Chase had written the law in 1862 that had created the greenbacks. But he was always suspicious of them, acting in their favor only as an extreme war measure. He now decided to play for hard money support. In the case Hepburn *v.* Griswold (1871), he led the court in writing the majority decision that declared greenbacks to be legal tender only for debts contracted after 1862. The implication was that greenbacks might be of doubtful value even after that time, although the case stated otherwise.

The indecision of the Hepburn case could not be allowed to continue. If greenbacks were later declared illegal for all debts, payments after 1862 would have to be renegotiated and repaid, as would those contracted before then and paid off since in greenbacks. It so happened that the Hepburn case had been decided by a court that was two members short. President Ulysses S. Grant (q.v.) had appointed William Strong and Joseph P. Bradley to the bench before Hepburn, but they had been unable to take their seats in time to participate. In 1871, another case, Knox *v.* Lee, arrived before the highest bench in the land. This time, with Strong and Bradley participating, the court reversed itself, the ever-flexible Chase again with the majority. In Knox, the court did the common-sense thing and ruled that greenbacks were legal tender for all debts. The court left it up to Congress as to what the greenbacks were worth compared to gold. Because the votes of Strong and Bradley were critical to the new ruling, Grant was accused of packing the court. This was not so. The president had appointed the two men with other considerations in mind before their views on money were known.

LENOIR STATION. *See* KNOXVILLE CAMPAIGN.

LETTERMAN SYSTEM. *See* AMBULANCE SERVICES AND TRIAGE.

LEXINGTON, BATTLE OF. *See* MISSOURI CAMPAIGN (1861–1862).

LIBBY (RICHMOND). Confederate installation that housed Union prisoners of war. *See also* PRISONS.

LIBERAL REPUBLICANISM. By the time of the 1872 election, the Ulysses S. Grant (q.v.) administration had caused quite a bit of disillusionment among the Republican Party (q.v.) and the public at large. Those who opposed Grantism within the party were called Liberal Republicans. Most were journalists, professional reformers, and intellectuals. They often lacked political skills but made up for it with a lot of enthusiasm. They were liberal not in the 20th-century sense of wanting government services, but in the traditional definition of desiring honest, constitutional government. Led by German immigrant and former Union political general Carl Schurz (q.v.), they decided not to challenge the political professionals of the Republican Party but to step aside and form a new party to challenge all of the *status quo*. Their beliefs reflected the reforms of the time. While they agreed with Reconstruction in principle, they found it lacking in practice. Their solution to the corrupt boroughs of the South was to call for universal amnesty and a withdrawal of Federal troops from the civilian political arena. The Liberals believed that something basic was amiss with governments that could not appeal on the basis of calm, political argument and the vote of the whole public. Another Liberal idea was civil service reform and a general cleaning up of government. They also believed in the paying of the national debt in gold, not inflated greenbacks, as the only honest way. But on the tariff issue, some wanted it higher, some wanted it lower.

During the 1872 election (q.v.), the Liberal-Regular (or Stalwart Republican) split, represented by their candidates for president, newspaper editor Horace Greeley (q.v.) and President Grant, threatened to swamp the Grand Old Party. But Greeley's eccentricities, the Liberals' willingness to leave the African-Americans to the mercy of the Southern whites (a contradiction in terms easily shown by waving the bloody shirt [q.v.]), and their alliance with the Democrats (q.v.) proved too much for voters to swallow. Grant won a resounding victory.

LIEBER CODE. *See* GENERAL ORDERS NO. 100.

L'ILE À VACHE. *See* COLONIZATION OF AFRICAN-AMERICANS OVERSEAS.

LINCOLN, ABRAHAM (1809–1865). Born near Hodgensville, Kentucky, Abraham Lincoln was the second child of carpenter/farmer Thomas Lincoln and his wife, Nancy Hanks Lincoln. Young Abe was named after a grandfather killed by Indians some years earlier. In 1817, the family moved to southern Indiana, near Gentryville, where Lincoln's mother died of undulant fever. Two years later, his father married Sarah Bush Johnston, a widow with three children of her own. She was a strong, cheerful woman who modernized the Lincoln homestead and brought a love of education, which she imparted to Abe over the objections of his father. Largely self-educated, young Lincoln worked hard at physical labor (he grew to six feet four and was quite muscular and strong all of his life) and clerked at Gentry's store. At age 19, he accompanied the Gentrys downriver on a raft to New Orleans, where he encountered slavery for the first time and gained an uncompromising hatred for the institution. The Lincolns then moved to Illinois. Abe accompanied the family, but soon set out on his own. He was about to accompany another flatboat downriver, but a delay in the trip caused a storekeeper at New Salem to hire Lincoln on as a clerk. Lincoln stayed on at New Salem, where he held down a series of jobs. He was well-liked, and during the Black Hawk War he enlisted as a private, only to be elected captain of the local militia.

The war proved uneventful for Lincoln and his men, and they returned home, where he tried to go into storekeeping himself and failed. He paid off the debt incurred only after he became a congressman, 10 years later. Meanwhile, he was elected to the state legislature as a Whig (q.v.) (those opposed to the policies of Andrew Jackson) and was instrumental in getting the state capital moved from Vandalia to Springfield, in his own district, a town to which he promptly moved. He also read law and was admitted to the bar. Lincoln and many other young men of the town courted a visiting Kentucky belle, Mary Todd. The Todds were definitely upper crust, rich, educated, cultured—as Lincoln reputedly said: "God needed only one 'd' to spell His name; the Todds took two."

The story was that by prior agreement, Lincoln's friend Billy Herndon won the first shot at vivacious Mary, only to ruin his chances when he complimented her on her dancing, likening it to the graceful moves of a serpent. She left him standing alone on the dance floor. Then Lincoln moved in on her, and they eventually were married, even after bashful Abe stood her up at the alter a time or two. The marriage turned out to be rather tumultuous, but they stayed together and raised four sons, three of whom died young. Most of the crazy stories about Mary Lincoln's behavior are traceable to Billy Herndon, Mary's rejected suitor and Abe's law partner. He noted that Abe seemed more and more melancholy as the years passed and blamed it on Mary's temper, dismissing her as the "she-wolf of this section" and the "female wild cat of the age," and explained it with the Anne Rutledge story, Abe's supposedly one and only true love who went to a tragic early death, a tale that has been expanded on by romanticists ever since.

Feuding or not, the Lincolns lived out their adult lives in Springfield, where he earned the reputation of being a cracker-jack courtroom lawyer, and she of being a sharp-tongued woman who dominated her husband at home. Lincoln ran for Congress in 1846 and served one term, being remembered for the "Spot Resolution." This was a Whig attempt to reveal President James K. Polk's message for war on Mexico as a sham by requesting he show the "spot" upon which "American blood had been shed on American soil." The spot was, of course, disputed territory at best, and Mexican soil at worst. Lincoln retired after the one term, supposedly by prior agreement, but his anti-war attitude would probably have cost him the seat in pro-war Illinois, anyway.

Lincoln dabbled in politics and law for some years, until the opening of Kansas to slavery above the old Missouri Compromise line brought him back into the fray full-time. Lincoln helped organize the Republican Party (q.v.) in the state, and it decided that he should take on the architect of slavery in the territories, his old friend and political opponent (and an active suitor of Mary Todd in the old days), Stephen A. Douglas (q.v.). A powerful Democrat (q.v.) and U.S. senator from Illinois, Douglas hoped to make his 1858 reelection the springboard for the presidency in 1860. Lincoln accepted the assignment in his famous "House Divided Speech," in which he said that the United States could not remain half free and half slave and survive as a nation. One side or the other had to come out on top. Because of the expense of the campaign, the Lincolns and Douglases traveled together on a special campaign train and engaged in a series of debates (seven, one in each of Illinois' congressional districts) on the issues of the day.

They made a strange pair, Lincoln a foot taller than the "Little Giant," Douglas' sobriquet, and speaking in a high-pitched voice to Douglas' baritone. Both men used racial prejudice to discredit the other, each trying to avoid being seen as too friendly toward blacks; easy for Douglas (whose wife's family owned slaves); harder for Lincoln, a "Black Republican," in the parlance of the day. Lincoln lost the race, but he made it closer than it should have been. He accomplished this with the so-called "Freeport Question" (q.v.). He asked Douglas if slavery could be legally kept out of the territories in violation of the Little Giant's doctrine of "popular sovereignty" (q.v.), which let it in until the territory voted on statehood. Douglas had to answer "yes" to win the Senate seat, but he had to answer "no" to hold the South in the 1860 presidential race. Douglas crossed his bridges as he came to them and answered "yes." He pointed out that if the territorial legislature never passed any laws condoning slavery, it automatically would cease to exist even before the final vote for statehood. No one could be enslaved without a positive law supporting the institution, Douglas admitted. He won the Senate seat with the support of the Illinois legislature, but lost the support of the South forever, his duplicity revealed by Lincoln's question.

Lincoln's skill in compromising Douglas made him a wanted speaker throughout the North. Soon it became obvious that he could carry three key states (Illinois, Indiana, Pennsylvania) that the Republicans had failed to take in the election of 1856 (q.v.). If this were done, Lincoln and the Republicans could win the presidency without a single electoral vote below the Ohio River. Although several other men had more notoriety than he, none could perform the magic task of taking the three states. This, combined with masterly manipulation of the Republican convention and his rivals knocking each other off in a bitter contest, put Lincoln at the head of the Republican ticket in the 1860 election (q.v.). The Democrats split between the Northern branch of the party, which nominated Douglas, and the Southern branch of the party, which nominated John C. Breckinridge (q.v.). They and the Constitutional Union Party (John Bell) took one million more popular votes combined than Lincoln. But even if everyone had united behind Douglas, Lincoln still would have taken the presidency because of the quirks of the electoral vote, which gave a simple majority to the Northern states that voted for Lincoln in close popular races.

Because of Lincoln's ability as president to make appointments to executive offices and the U.S. Supreme Court, the rabid secessionists in the South decided to leave the Union. Although Lincoln tried to allay their fears with a moderate inaugural speech, he refused to give in on the question of the advance of slavery into the territories or to yield Federal properties still held in the seceded states. The result was war and further secessions as Lincoln assigned a quota of militia to every state to help suppress the rebellion. Lincoln demonstrated his political acuity and self-confidence right off in his appointments to his cabinet (he was "Humble Abe Lincoln" only as a public front). At least four members were political rivals within the Republican Party (Simon Cameron, William H. Seward [q.v.], Salmon P. Chase [q.v.], Edward Bates), and two of them (Seward and Chase) considered themselves superior to him in intellect (Seward would soon come around, but Chase never quite caught on).

The Lincoln presidency was a balancing act of wartime and domestic issues. He had to move on the military issue in such a manner as not to offend the still-loyal border slave states of Missouri, Kentucky, Maryland, and Delaware. Maryland determined Delaware's stand by geography, if nothing else. As Maryland was so critical to Northern control of the nation's capital, it was immediately occupied by Federal troops, and dissidents were arrested. Missouri (q.v.) was held by decisive advances of Federal forces under Frank Blair and Bvt. Brig. Gen. Nathaniel Lyon. Kentucky was so critical to the Confederacy that they occupied it first, breaking its neutrality and permitting quick Federal advances to key points. But Lincoln believed that he could not respond to the demands by many Northerners that he free the slaves immediately as a wartime measure. He feared repercussions that might even extend to the Old Northwest, states above the Ohio River like Illinois and Indiana that contained much negrophobia. Meanwhile, Lincoln carried out much of the domestic Republican program, including internal improvements through the Pacific Railroad Act (q.v.), establishing agricultural and mechanical colleges through the Morrill Land Grant College Act, raising the import duties by the Morrill Tariff Act (q.v.), reorganizing the banking system with the National Banking Act (q.v.), and opening up the West by way of a Homestead Act (q.v.).

The president refused to call Congress into session at the war's start, preferring to rule by executive proclamation (q.v.), a practice he continued throughout the duration of his term and which has drawn much criticism then and now from Democrats, Radical Republicans, and of course proto-

Confederate historians. Lincoln's political success came from an excellent ability to appear anti-Southern, without at the same time seeming pro-Negro. His Emancipation Proclamation (q.v.) freed only the slaves outside the jurisdiction of the Union army. Further, he was willing to grant African-Americans technical freedom without attacking any of the traditional racism of the North. Moreover, the litany goes on, the corruptions of the Republican Era that mar the history of Reconstruction and the Gilded Age began with the Lincoln administration and were justified as necessary wartime measures, like the Pacific Railroad. He reinstituted the economic policies that Alexander Hamilton and Henry Clay had failed to sustain against Southern and Western opposition led by the Jacksonians, which were embodied in the Republicans' domestic programs and heavy taxes, including the first U.S. income tax. The result was that for the first time in U.S. history, creditors had the upper hand over debtors, and the developed East could exploit the developing West and defeated South.

Lincoln also expanded the powers of the presidency in such a manner as to alter the basis of the Federal Union. He was our first "Imperial President," as he summoned the militia, expanded the U.S. Army, decreed an illegal blockade, defied the Supreme Court, suspended the writ of *habeas corpus* (q.v.), and created a Yankee gulag (called the "American Bastille" by his critics); transferred millions of dollars from authorized accounts to his pet projects; and pledged the nation's honor and credit to others—all without the necessary participation of Congress under the Constitution. Some have charged that Lincoln led the North in such a manner as to put the domestic priorities of his political machine ahead of the lives and well-being of his soldiers in the field. He fought and fought until he could find a Republican hero in a field general. The result was the firing of Democrats like George B. McClellan, Don Carlos Buell (qq.v.), Fitz John Porter, and the elevation of mere political hacks to army command, men like Nathaniel P. Banks, Benjamin F. Butler, John C. Frémont (qq.v.), and John A. McClernand. The same held true of his cabinet, especially the original one, in which Simon Cameron stole the Union blind, a process Lincoln covered up as necessary to save the Union. Even one of his hack generals, Henry W. Halleck (q.v.), admitted such command decisions were "little better than murder."

Next, he compromised the integrity of his office to further prosecute the war. Each time peace was in the offing, Lincoln upped the ante or stalled so as to make compromise impossible. Peace could come only on his terms, reasonable compromise take the hindmost. Lincoln's search for an expedient peace cost the nation over 100,000 lives. And worse, the war had been his to start, a responsibility Lincoln sought to transfer to Jefferson Davis (q.v.) by arranging to have the South fire the first shot, after several reasonable attempts by politicians of both sections to compromise the crisis failed from

Lincoln's refusal to consider them. They included a willingness to pay for Ft. Sumter (q.v.) and other Federal installations in the South (which he kept secret from the public) and an offer to keep the Mississippi River open to Midwest commerce.

Finally, Lincoln altered the language of American political discourse so that it was next to impossible to reverse the ill effects of trends set in motion by his executive fiat. He put it all in the rhetoric of scripture, which was confirmed by his own assassination (q.v.), making every "good cause" then and since a reason to increase the scope of government. All that counted was the goal; the means to achieve that goal became irrelevant. That Congress thought it was getting short shrift from Lincoln can be seen in its response to Lincoln's Proclamation of Amnesty and Reconstruction (q.v.). Lincoln proposed that whenever 10 percent of the population of any state occupied by the Union army would take an oath of future loyalty and draw up a new state constitution devoid of slavery and ask Congress for readmission to the Union.

Congress responded with its own Wade–Davis Bill (q.v.), suggesting that 50 percent was a more operable number for the future loyalty oath, and that the actual voters electing the constitutional convention be restricted to those who could swear never to have given aid to the enemy. When Lincoln gave this measure a pocket veto (let it lie on the table 14 days after Congress had adjourned), the two principal sponsors issued the Wade–Davis Manifesto (q.v.), accusing the president of interfering with Congress' prerogative to reconstruct the South and guarantee a republican form of government in the various states. Lincoln responded that he had no real objection to the congressional measure, but did not want to be limited in his approach. Any state that preferred to come in under the Wade–Davis Bill could do so. It was typically Lincoln—almost too clever and quite maddening to his critics.

Despite the "with malice toward none; with charity for all" pledge in the Second Inaugural Speech and the decent terms granted the surrendering Confederate armies, no one really knew what his postwar stance on Reconstruction would have been; it is all conjecture, depending upon the sort of person the speculator believed Lincoln to be. The same still pertains today. An assassin's bullet silenced the only man who really knew where he stood—if indeed he had a position; as one writer put it, he was "the most shut-mouthed man" anyone in Washington had met. Regardless of how one feels about Lincoln, the proof of his policy was in winning the greatest war America has ever fought. He always believed that he had a divine purpose in life, although he would have been the first to admit that he did not know exactly what it was. But he saw himself as impelled by incidents outside his control, rather than as a molder of events. It was the very measures he undertook, to the howl of his critics, that made that victory possible and guaranteed his position as the greatest president next to George Washington that the nation ever had. If nothing else, Lincoln had an amazing ability to mold public thinking into accepting policies that most Americans were opposed to at the start of the war. And it was his very hesitancy in executing them, which so aggravated his Radical Republican critics, that made him a true reflection of how the nation at large felt about what the war was all about.

LINCOLN, ABRAHAM, AND BISEXUALISM. It happens occasionally, the book review is better and more profitable to read than the book. This is true with historian Jean Baker's introduction to C. A. Tripp's *The Intimate World of Abraham Lincoln*. But in fairness to the author, Tripp died before the book completed the editorial process, which left a lot of possible revision undone. But Baker's introduction presents the essence of what Tripp was trying to say, often in more understandable prose.

As Tripp through Baker points out, Lincoln's personal life before the presidency was very vague. Lincoln himself said, "there is not much of me." He dismissed his youth as "'the short and simple annals of the poor.' That's my life, and that's all you or anybody else can make of it." But Tripp finds that Lincoln left out one major fact—he was as queer as the proverbial three dollar bill. And so begins the biggest controversy in Lincoln historiography in the last decade.

According to author Tripp, himself gay and an Alfred Kinsey sex researcher who went on to write the *Homosexual Matrix* in 1975, Lincoln's sexual proclivities had been hinted at for nearly all of his life and forever after, from law partner William Herndon to biographer Carl Sandburg. Actually, to a large degree according to Lincoln apologists, this accusation against Lincoln was ostensibly answered decades before it became trendy in William Herndon's *Life of Lincoln* (Lincoln courted three women and married another) and William E. Barton's volume, *The Women Who Loved Lincoln*. But "[h]is attitude toward women to the last day of his life was but a continuation of his boyhood diffidence," rancorous biographer Edgar Lee Masters maintained in his *Lincoln the Man*, describing Lincoln's relations with women, in a word, as "undersexed." Or as his stepmother once put it, "He was not very fond of girls, as he seemed to me."

But Tripp does more than hint. He presents what he sees as facts, although his critics claim he argues well beyond the actual into the realm of the speculative. With the friendlier modern-day outlook on homosexuality, gays have relished Lincoln's sexual proclivities as presented by Tripp. Before, they had no real presidential idol of kindred spirit to point to, unless it was James Buchanan (q.v.). A lifelong bachelor, Old Buck roomed for years with Alabama U.S. senator and Franklin Pierce's vice president, William R. King, also single, a relationship that titillated the prurient interests of Washington society then, and of historians later. Now they had a real hero, not just some schlub, to brag about.

Employing the Kinsey rating system, in which homosexuality is judged on a seven-point continuum, Tripp scores Lincoln as a five, "predominantly homosexual, but incidentally heterosexual." Tripp points to five incidents where Lincoln (now often denigrated as Gay Abe, or "Gabe" Lincoln) had homosexual contacts with men, most in New Salem or Springfield, Illinois. He slept with and learned grammar from Billy Greene, who in an unguarded moment gushed about Lincoln's perfect thighs. He had less-well-developed relationships with A. Y. Ellis (a local merchant and political admirer) and Henry Whitney (a fellow lawyer), the latter of whom maintained that Lincoln told him the sexual contact was "a harp of a thousand strings" and allegedly went on to prove it.

But these incidents pale in comparison to his reputed four-year affair with roommate and bedmate Joshua Speed in Springfield and torrid summer affair with Army Captain David V. Derickson, with whom Lincoln slept at the Old Soldiers' Home outside Washington, D.C., while wife Mary was off visiting relatives. Lincoln was also a fan (whatever that means) of dashing militia colonel and Zouave drillmaster Elmer Ellsworth. But Ellsworth became one of the war's first martyrs when an irate Rebel hotelkeeper shot him dead for removing the Stars and Bars from his rooftop in Alexandria, Virginia. Ellsworth's death deeply depressed Lincoln for some time afterward, which Tripp sees as meaningful, romantically or sexually speaking.

Many commentators have bought the Tripp story more or less in its entirety, leading to the question: "Will scholars, Civil War buffs, and fans of Honest Abe be content to let the Moral Majority and the self-anointed Lincoln establishment set the agenda for research on our greatest president?" Others have used Lincoln's sexual indiscretions to justify Mary Lincoln's anger at Abe and her own alleged marital infidelities. These historians often wonder why "no amount of irrefutable evidence has dislodged it." They blame that on historians and biographers who wish to preserve "Lincoln's status as an American icon, imbued with virtues revered by viewers, a picture of perfection that resists change."

Unlike Tripp's advocates, other historians and newspaper commentators find *The Intimate Lincoln* "a book that was not worth reviewing." These critics believe that "insofar as Dr. Tripp's book helps disabuse the reading public of the 'legend of Lincoln's happy marriage' it serves a valuable function, but insofar as it leads people to think that Lincoln was gay, it does a disservice to history, for the evidence Dr. Tripp adduced fails to support the case." Yet another historian of the stormy Lincoln marriage points out that the stresses of the time were more than enough to exacerbate short tempers.

Lincoln's sleeping arrangements, for example, were common in the 19th century, especially on the frontier where he lived. His fond salutations in his letters to male friends were also the custom of the time. As for his relations with women, even the sometimes hostile Herndon noted that Lincoln "could scarcely keep his hands off of them." Indeed, his hesitancy to wed Mary Todd was not a homosexual mental tussle but a fear on Lincoln's part that he had contracted syphilis. Others blame Lincoln's hesitancy on his supposed love for another woman. Indeed, other women and Lincoln's friendliness toward them are at the center of Mary Lincoln's jealous temper tantrums that became the talk of the town during the Lincoln presidency.

Even Tripp's original co-author, Philip Nobile, dismisses *The Intimate Lincoln* as a "hoax and a fraud." He calls it a hoax because the inaccurate parts are all prejudiced toward a predetermined goal: proving Lincoln was a homosexual. He condemns it as a literary fraud, because the accurate parts are plagiarized from Nobile himself after their co-authorship ended. He concludes that Tripp wrote more as an advocate than an historian, a view shared by Lincoln biographer David H. Donald in a letter to Tripp. "Throughout you seem to be neglecting the fundamental rule, the historian has to rely on facts." Tripp dismissed Donald's criticism when he alleged that the historian had said that he would not believe Tripp's tale of Lincoln's homosexuality even if he could prove Lincoln said so. Others agree with Donald that Lincoln's homosexuality was "highly unlikely."

Finally, what do Lincoln's sexual proclivities mean in the broader picture? He was obviously an early-developing young man according to Tripp's analysis, and Kinsey showed these types to be strong masturbators with a tendency toward homosexuality. Lincoln's strong feeling here led him to challenge revealed religion and other mores of the time, like the "positive good theory" of slavery, and to do something about it. He was also a man of deep unspoken sorrows, and an extra-soft touch for any mother's story of why her son ought not to be punished by the army for sleeping while on sentry duty, much to the dismay of professional military officers.

"Gabe" constantly lived on the edge in his soul and psyche in more matters than one. If Tripp is correct in his analysis, Lincoln was not homosexual but rather bisexual in his bedroom preferences. As president, however, historians by and large believe that he knew the differences between the essential and the not so, making him in the words of one observer, "a most shut-mouthed man" when it came to the non-fundamental. After all, as modern-day newspaperman Paul Greenburg concludes, "he was a man, not a myth."

LINCOLN, ABRAHAM—A DIFFERENT VIEW. What on earth would cause normally level-headed people like Thomas Harbin, John H. Surratt, Jr. and his mother Mary, Dr. Samuel A. Mudd, David E. Herold, George A.

Atzerodt, and Lewis T. Powell, to get involved with John Wilkes Booth's (q.v.) cockamamie plots against President Abraham Lincoln's (q.v.) person and then his very assassination? To understand this, perhaps one ought to become conversant with an unpopular, alternate history of Abraham Lincoln as president of the United States and how this affected Confederate-sympathizing Maryland during the Civil War.

This different history of Lincoln is really nothing new. Americans North and South were deeply aware of it, but it goes against the Republican "Myth of the Assassinated Lincoln" that passes for history today. Alphonso Taft, future U.S. secretary of war (1876), U.S. attorney general (1876–1877), and 19th-century progenitor of the family that produced a slew of noted Ohio Republican politicians, understood what had to come.

Taft wrote about the necessities of future history in a letter to his home-state U.S. solon, Senator *pro tem* Benjamin Wade, on September 8 1864: "It is to be regretted that history should have to tell so many lies as it will tell, when it shall declare Lincoln's intrigues and foolishness models of integrity and wisdom, his weakened and wavering indecision and delay far-sighted statesmanship, and his blundering usurpation of legislative power Jacksonian courage and Roman patriotism, but one cannot help it. History goes with the powers that be."

The success of the historical spin of the Lincolnites (defined by one disgruntled critic as "those empowered to tell the rest of us rubes what everything really means") would amaze Alphonso Taft and puzzle Booth and his co-conspirators were it to be reincarnated in modern America. Present-day historians regularly vote Abraham Lincoln as one of the top three presidents in the nation's history, usually number one.

Booth would find modern Americans inexplicably infected with something best described as "acute Lincolnitis." As one writer explained it, "After the fall of the Roman Republic, the citizens of Rome were encouraged to worship their caesars as gods. The United States is little different. Rather than Caesar Augustus or Gaius Caligula, Americans (particularly up North) are raised in the Cult of Saint Lincoln."

Lincoln, whom James Russell Lowell characterized as the first real American (born in Kentucky, raised in Indiana, matured in Illinois, and possessing the soul and truth of a Massachusetts man), is commonly seen nowadays as so crucial to America's past, present, and future that historian David H. Donald, 30 years before he penned what is arguably the best one-volume history of the Northern Civil War leader, wrote a pivotal essay about it, entitled, "Getting Right with Lincoln."

Donald's characterization of Lincoln as the great practical, political man, whom all Americans (regardless of political antecedents, Union or Confederate, Republican or Democrat, Independent or Communist) wish and need to be in step with, immediately puts those who questioned or opposed him (be they John Wilkes Booth, Northern and Southern Democrats, or the advocates of the Constitution as it was before Lincoln's accession to power—all of which can be summed up in the hackneyed post–Civil War phrase Rum, Romanism, and Rebellion) at a real disadvantage. It has not done much for historians who challenge Lincoln's role in American history, either, as Montgomery S. Lewis' bluntly titled volume, *Legends That Libel Lincoln* (1946) aptly demonstrated. Critics take on the massive Lincoln historical machine, "a formidable and intimidating task," opined historian Robert W. Johannsen, at great risk to their own reputations.

Nonetheless, Booth would be pleased to find that voices of dissent have risen. Although there were hints that the Lincoln story was not all the public might think in early works by William H. Herndon and Albert J. Beveridge, the modern attack on Lincoln's historical celebrity has taken place on several fronts: one led by white historians like Edgar Lee Masters and Melvin Eustace Bradford; another by African American magazine editor and historian Lerone Bennett, Jr.; and the most recent by white economist and historian Thomas J. DiLorenzo. Actually, there are close to 70 articles and several books that challenge Lincoln's reputation, which has become an industry in itself. But these four present the root arguments that others have built upon.

This alternate picture of the historical Lincoln is something Booth and Southerners and Northern Democrats of the 1860s would have recognized as the Lincoln they knew. "Honest Abe" was a political dissembler and equivocator of the highest order. "It may be a vain task to follow the inconstant mind of Lincoln, but at least its vacillations can be recorded," Masters said, supported by Bradford and Bennett. DiLorenzo agreed, quoting economist Murray Rothbard, "Lincoln was a master politician, which means that he was a consummate conniver, manipulator, and liar."

Nothing, however, beat Lincoln's dissembling over the act for which he is best known, asserted Bennett, emancipating the American slaves. Lincoln spoke out against slavery in principle, went the accusation, but did nothing against it before the war and little during the conflict. Bennett used what Lincoln and his defenders, then and now (whom he characterized as the "Abraham Lincoln Salvage Society"), wrote to show Lincoln as "a potentially great man flawed" by his own racist attitudes. Indeed, Bennett concluded, Lincoln's whole family, his political entourage, and his many friends were racist in talk, attitude, and jokes.

Basically, at best, both Bennett and Masters said that Lincoln wanted to free the slaves and allow them to enter the labor force to earn a living, but they were to be kept subordinate to the white race in all matters in perpetuity, because of perceived physical differences. In reality, Bennett pointed out, Lincoln called for gradual, compensated abolition, with a long apprenticeship program and compulsory colonization abroad in Africa (Lincoln believed that all American slaves originally came from Liberia), Haiti (Isle la Vache), or Central America (where the proposed colony would be named Lincolnia by a cynical press), or perhaps locally in Florida or Texas, for all those freed.

But most historians agreed that, if the slaves were to remain in the United States, Lincoln wanted African-Americans to enjoy life, liberty, and the pursuit of happiness, in their "proper" place—which was not in the North or the Great West, competing side by side with white labor. He was against slavery in the abstract only. He was for leaving the institution be in the South, but he was for keeping it out of the territories, especially above the old Missouri Compromise line. Under Lincoln, Bennett argued, and Bradford and Masters agreed, African-Americans would experience "nothing more than a technical freedom" comprised of "empty words," a sort of Jim Crow (q.v.) version of liberty, common after the Civil War and Reconstruction (q.v.).

When Lincoln announced the preliminary Emancipation Proclamation (q.v.) in late 1862, Masters said, he was merely hoping to hold the Republican majority in Congress. In the Preliminary Proclamation of September 22, 1862, Bennett asserted that Lincoln really pledged that he would preserve slavery if the Confederates would come back into the Union within 100 days. His implementation of the Proclamation on January 1, 1863, was not a seizure of property, Masters proposed, but the urging of domestic slave rebellion.

Even more damning than the path to emancipation, in Bradford's eyes, was Lincoln's role as military leader. "Thousands of Northern boys lost their lives in order that the Republican Party might experience rejuvenation, to serve its partisan goals," Bradford accused. "All Lincoln asked of the ordinary Billy Yank was that he be prepared to give himself up to no real purpose—at least until Father Abraham found a general with proper [Republican] moral and political credentials to lead him to Richmond," Bradford charged.

Moreover, Bradford said, the heroes he found to lead his armies were the most vicious practitioners of war to date, laying the South to waste, presaging the horrible contests of the 20th century. As Lincoln sanctimoniously called for "malice toward none and charity for all" in his Second Inaugural Speech, Masters went on, his armies tore a path of pillage and rapine 60 miles wide through Georgia and South Carolina, burning Atlanta and Columbia, and despoiled the Shenandoah Valley of Virginia, without significant opposition. Lincoln rationalized it all by enunciating the "Hebraic-Puritan principle of assuming to act as one's brother's keeper, when the real motive was to become one's brother's jailer," Masters contended, an assertion that Bradford essentially agreed with.

As with emancipation and military policy, Masters saw Lincoln's economic policy as full of contradictions. Far from being the little man's president as reputed, Lincoln supported and was "supported by great wealth." From his first days in 1832 at New Salem, Illinois, to the end of his life, Lincoln supported the party of privilege and monopoly in the antebellum era, the Whigs (q.v.). "It is something requiring explanation," Masters contended, "that Lincoln, who is held up as an apostle of liberty, who himself along the way said so much of the Declaration of Independence and [Thomas] Jefferson, turned in his youth to the rhetorician [and Whig Party leader] Henry Clay and clung to him into maturity, and followed his lead essentially to the end."

Masters saw Lincoln as essentially a lazy attorney who relied on his partner, Billy Herndon, to do all the leg work on a case. Then Lincoln, who always had the ability to move an audience with his golden words and homey drawl, would sway the jury. Lincoln's laziness made him not an original thinker, Masters claimed, and Bradford and DiLorenzo agreed. Because of this he relied economically on Henry Clay's American System. This was a program, originally developed by economist Matthew Carey (Clay was an indolent thinker, too), that promoted a national banking system, internal improvements, and the liberation of American slaves and their return to Africa.

Clay originally hoped to finance this with a high tariff designed to exclude foreign imports and the sale of land in the Western territories at $1.25 an acre. But by the 1850s, the notion of land sales had evaporated in favor of homesteading the land for free, causing the rest of the program to rely on the tariff alone for its financing—a tariff paid predominantly by the South, which imported European goods in exchange for its cotton.

Under Lincoln, Bradford and DiLorenzo argued, the government became the sponsor of a great transfer of wealth using the protective tariff on foreign imports (which rose from 18.84 percent in 1861 to 47.56 percent in 1865), the massive funding of internal improvements (especially the Pacific Railroad, which led to the Crédit Mobilier [q.v.] scandal), a national banking system (that sponsored the creation of $480 million in fiat paper money to enhance credit for big business at the expense of small businesses and farms and later redeemed it one-to-one for gold), and the Homestead Act (in which less than 19 percent of the lands went to actual farmers, the rest to big businesses).

And that economic program explained why slavery in the United States had to be ended by violence rather than peacefully as in the rest of the Americas, posited DiLorenzo. Everywhere else, the Industrial Revolution had destroyed slavery, a most inefficient type of labor ill-suited to the new order. But in the United States, the Whig version of how to achieve industrialism had been voted down by the American people from the time of Jefferson and was seen as corrupt, a replication of the crooked English colonial approach that had led to the American Revolution, and therefore unconstitutional.

Lincoln was always a High Whig, Masters, Bradford, and DiLorenzo contended, not a modern capitalist as Lincolnites maintain. Indeed, DiLorenzo claimed that Lincoln "seethed in frustration" at the lack of constitutional and popular support for the American system. To justify the Republican war, Dilorenzo asserted that Lincoln had to get the South to fire the first shot to distract Northern opponents from the Republican economic program through a war-inspired patriotism for Union. Lincoln had let the genie of centralism out of the bottle never to be returned, as successive administrations, Republican or Democrat (q.v.), have shown. Ending slavery was a by-product designed to cover the real Republican economic program, government aid to business.

But the corruption (q.v.) was not only economic, Bradford complained. Much of it was governmental, resulting in Lincoln's "expansion of the powers of the presidency and his alteration of the basis for the Federal Union." That envisioned what Masters called Lincoln's unconstitutional and illegal centralization of political authority in the Federal government, which Masters embodied in one word—despotism.

From the very first, Lincoln "was a centralist, a privilegist, an adherent of the non-principled Whig Party, which had laid the foundation of the Republican party," Masters argued. The result, according to Masters, was a bevy of unconstitutional Lincolnian acts in response to the secession of the South that "are glossed over with the remark that what he did before Congress met on 4 July 1861, was validated by that Congress and made lawful for his great purpose of saving the Union."

Lincoln's willingness to be associated with a "higher law" doctrine allowed him to ally his trampling of the Constitution and law with the purpose of God, Masters grumped on. Bradford agreed, calling Lincoln "our first Puritan president." That is to say, Lincoln had the "habit of wrapping up his policy in the idiom of Holy Scripture, concealing within the Trojan horse of his gasconade and moral superiority an agenda that would never have been approved if presented in any other form."

Anticipating Bradford's argument by some 50 years, Masters went on to assert that "in Lincoln's case the subjugation of the South had to be smeared over with religion, . . . with the whole rank and file of Calvinism, with the nauseating piety and sadistic righteousness of America as a Christian nation. . . . The War Between the States was for God," Masters said, "and Lincoln made it so. But there was nothing in Lincoln's philosophy which forbade riches and privileges; rather the contrary. Hence he laid the foundation for . . . missions of irreverence and plunder." Masters adjudged that Lincoln was truly America's patron saint of despotism, big business, and hypocrisy, a thought that Bradford and DiLorenzo seconded.

If it is true that Lincoln achieved apotheosis only after his death, it is quite possible that those who conspired against Lincoln attacked a different being than the man who now exists in our history and legend. This means that, unlike now, 150 years after the fact, when serious scholars are calling for rethinking what the Constitution means in light of its allegedly imperfect democratic nature as revealed by the Civil War (so much for the Founding Fathers' republican government), Lincoln's election and governing were quite a shock to the prewar American political mind, especially that in the slave South. This also means that the modern critics of Lincoln as president might have a few of the answers as to what made John Surratt, his family, their many co-conspirators, and their erstwhile leader, John Wilkes Booth, tick.

Nowhere did the "Real Lincoln" make a bigger impression than on the white people of Maryland, particularly on the Confederate-sympathizing people of Baltimore, the Eastern Shore across the Chesapeake, and south-eastern Maryland in the slaveowning and tobacco-growing counties on the peninsulas between the Potomac River and Chesapeake Bay, where Booth's co-conspirators hailed from. Their attitude is best described in the words of a 20th-century Marylander, critic, writer, and iconoclastic curmudgeon, H. L. Mencken, who once observed, "Every normal man must be tempted at times to spit upon his hands, hoist the black flag, and begin slitting throats." The Civil War was one of those times.

Yet others, like newspaperman Paul Greenburg, are not so sure the critics are on the right path. They decry the small but unchanging corps of Lincoln nay-sayers who spend their nights going through the small print looking for inconsistencies as though they have uncovered some basic flaw in Lincoln's values, when all they prove is his statesmanship. They conclude that to study Lincoln is to realize, in the words of Princeton University historian Christine Stansell, that Lincoln was a man, not a myth.

LINCOLN ASSASSINATION, THE CONFEDERACY AND THE. The assassination of President Abraham Lincoln (q.v.) is too often seen as an event in isolation, committed by a man on the brink of insanity, John Wilkes Booth (q.v.), as a sort of last explosion of frustration to avenge the defeated South. This theory reckons without "Come Retribution," a Confederate secret service (q.v.) plan to kidnap Lincoln and hold him ransom for the South's independence. Revealed in its fullest complications in a recent study by re-searchers William A. Tidwell, James O. Hall, and David W. Gaddy (THG), *Come Retribution* challenges all of the ordinary assumptions and portrays Lincoln's death as a logical outcome of a plan gone awry. Former Army and Central Intelligence Agency operatives, THG took a new look at existing Civil War records and found much historians had overlooked or dismissed as gibberish that immediately drew the eye of experienced intelligence officers like themselves. In this study, THG sought to answer, among other things, "Why did Booth kill Lincoln?"

The South in 1865 had everything to gain from the traditional theory that Booth was a half-crazy man who went berserk. It put an end to a lot of searching into motives that might have embarrassed Southern leaders already resting uncomfortably in Yankee jails. All of this is confused more with the notion that Lincoln was the South's best friend in Washington, as illustrated by his wartime Reconstruction policy, the famed Ten Percent Plan (q.v.). Scores of stories, some professionally researched, some not, have appeared since Otto Eisenschiml's 1938 book *Why Was Lincoln Shot?* linking Booth to Radical Republicans, having him disappear only to resurface again 40 years later to confess his crime before dying, and linking him to an ill-conceived plan to kidnap the president and take him South to save the Confederacy. Only the last is indisputably true, and it formed the basis for the president's assassination and THG's current inquiry.

THG were the first to admit that their story is conjecture. But it has escaped much of the criticism raised against others working in the field. THG believe that the origins of the assassination of the president lay in the Kilpatrick–Dahlgren raid against Richmond in the spring of 1864, a few months before Lt. Gen. Ulysses S. Grant's Overland Campaign (q.v.) against the Confederate capital that would end the war a year later. Led by Brig. Gen. Judson Kilpatrick (a reckless boy general of the stripe of George A. Custer, Wesley Merritt, and Elon Farnsworth) and one-legged Col. Ulrich Dahlgren (whose father, Adm. John Dahlgren, invented a powerful, bottle-shaped naval cannon very popular at the time), the cavalry expedition was to penetrate the Rebel lines at the Rapidan River in northern Virginia and move on Richmond in two columns. Dahlgren's command was to drive across the James River upstream and move on Richmond from the south. Kilpatrick, with the larger command, would head directly for the Confederate capital, drawing upon himself the Confederate pursuit. Kilpatrick and Dahlgren would then attack the Richmond defenses. Kilpatrick was to go in first, clearing the way for Dahlgren's men to come up behind the city and free large numbers of Union prisoners of war held in Richmond.

But the plan went off badly from the start. Miserable weather had caused all rivers to rise to above flood stage. Pursuing Confederate cavalry kept the Union columns moving without time to rest and rethink the situation. The Richmond militia (most regular soldiers were in the field with Gen. Robert E. Lee [q.v.]), proved tougher than expected in defending the city. The result was that Dahlgren could not get across the James and had to follow Kilpatrick in from the north. Kilpatrick attacked without hearing from Dahlgren, assumed that his command had been routed or captured, and withdrew from Richmond. Dahlgren, meanwhile, had followed Kilpatrick without being able to contact him. Alerted by Kilpatrick's earlier foray, the Confederates hit the newly arrived Dahlgren with all they had, scattering his command and killing Dahlgren in the process. In the rain, the colonel's body was left for the Rebels. A search revealed numerous papers about the expedition, including the known objectives of freeing Federal soldiers, burning Richmond and, more important, a secret plan to assassinate Jefferson Davis (q.v.) and his cabinet.

In that age of romantic chivalry, the South was outraged by the Dahlgren papers. Lincoln had lived in a Southern city (Washington) for four years without an assassination even being contemplated. Many in the South urged retaliation. Ostensibly, Southern leaders refused to countenance such a move. But THG maintain that secretly they did. The plan was not one of assassination but of kidnapping. It was conceived as Lt. Gen. Ulysses S. Grant (q.v.) tightened his hold upon Richmond and Petersburg in the fall of 1864, and Confederate chances on the battlefield seemed to be waning with the losses of the Shenandoah Valley in Virginia and Atlanta in Georgia. The idea was that Southern agents would take the president into Richmond, using the Confederate secret mail line known as the Doctors' Line (q.v.), which ran from Washington through southern Maryland to the Potomac at Port Tobacco, crossed to Virginia through Port Royal south of the old Fredericksburg battlefield, and wound up at Ashland Station north of Richmond. The Confederate agent who led the kidnap team (one of his own choosing) was actor John Wilkes Booth.

Unfortunately, Lincoln had the habit of traveling through the District of Columbia relatively unprotected. Relying on his lack of protection, Booth and his conspirators picked a time and spot to make their move. But Lincoln on a whim had changed his route and time of travel, causing the plan to fall flat. It was too late to try again, because it would not correspond with the spring 1865 campaign developed by General Lee and Jefferson Davis. This plan called for the abandonment of Richmond after an attack by Lee's army had thrown Grant back on his heels for a few days. With a day or two head start, Lee hoped to get his army to the railroad behind Richmond, where he had stored supplies.

Then Lee would head south and join with another Confederate force led by Gen. Joseph Johnston (q.v.) and crush the Yankee army under Maj. Gen. William T. Sherman (q.v.) in North Carolina. This accomplished, Lee hoped to utilize his central position to swing back on Grant and defeat him as he struggled to move forward on a lengthy supply line. The war was still winnable, Lee reasoned, if the Confederates could move with the rapidity for which they were famous.

To keep Sherman and Grant from communicating among themselves and with the coordinating general staff and Lincoln in Washington, the Rebels came up with a new wrinkle in "Come Retribution." They would blow up the White House, hopefully with Lincoln and some of his cabinet and military men in it. This would so confuse the situation that the North would be in confusion for days, allowing the Confederate campaign to get under way. Lt. Col. John Singleton Mosby, the famous partisan ranger, as they called guerrillas then, would take Confederate explosives expert Thomas F. Harney to Washington to connect with Booth's agents, who would help him do the job.

The Confederates were great improvisers at explosive devices during the war. They specialized in what we would call land and sea mines today, but were named torpedoes (q.v.) then. They had developed a torpedo so small and powerful that it could be concealed as a piece of coal in a ship's bunker. The device was quite successful, the Union losing many river boats to what was believed were boiler explosions, including the *Sultana* (q.v.), whose destruction at Memphis in 1865 was the costliest single water disaster until the sinking of the *Titanic* in 1912.

But bad luck dogged the Confederates in 1865. Outside Washington, Mosby's escort ran into a Yankee cavalry patrol, and in the ensuing gunfight, explosives expert Harney was captured and jailed in the Old Capitol Prison. Meanwhile, Lee began his break away from Grant, only to find that Grant was faster than he in exploiting the fluid situation before Richmond. In a week of hard marching and numerous fire fights, Grant cut Lee off from his stored supplies and ran his army down, forcing Lee to surrender at Appomattox Court House. This left Booth in a quandary. What was he to do without further orders? He decided on his own to improvise on "Come Retribution" with his own people. With no explosives expert, he would rely on assassination to accomplish the same thing. He did not know that Lee's surrender had made the whole plan superfluous. He picked out President Lincoln, Vice President Andrew Johnson, Secretary of State William H. Seward, and Secretary of War Edwin McM. Stanton (qq.v.) as his targets. He would use many men he had known since childhood (most of whom proved untrustworthy) and escape by way of the same route on which the kidnapped Lincoln was to have been hustled to Richmond.

That Booth failed was the fault of poor personnel. Johnson and Stanton were never attacked. But another compatriot almost killed Seward and his son, and Booth killed Lincoln. Along with Confederate courier Davy Herold, Booth fled out to Surratt's Tavern, down to Dr. Samuel Mudd's house (he was a Confederate sympathizer who knew Booth from before the assassination), where his leg was set, and on to Virginia's Northern Neck just south of Port Royal. At Garrett's farm, a pursuing Yankee cavalry squadron killed him and arrested Herold. The young man was brought to Washington, where he joined the other conspirators, four of whom were hanged (Herold; Mrs. Mary Surratt, who probably knew little or nothing of the plot, although her son John did; Lewis Paine, who nearly killed Seward; and George Azerodt, who was to have killed Johnson but panicked). Four more (the hapless Dr. Mudd, a pair of plotters from Baltimore, and an innocent theater worker) were sent off to a military prison off the Florida Keys in the Dry Tortugas.

Many historians of the Civil War question whether THG have not mistakenly included honorable men like Davis, Lee, and Mosby in the plot. They would rather see a "rogue" member of government as initiating the process without the others knowing. The preferred villain is Judah P. Benjamin (q.v.), variously secretary of state, secretary of war, and attorney general of the Confederacy. But he could not have acted without the cooperation of Davis, who had co-signed the money vouchers according to law, the money financing a secret unnamed project. Davis's main military advisor was Lee. And Lee, Mosby (his prime informant on affairs in northern Virginia), and others like Secretary of War John C. Breckinridge (former vice president of the U.S. under Buchanan) had all been at Richmond at the time that the meetings planning such activities took place. Moreover, THG found that nearly 1,000 men from selected Virginia regiments in Lee's army (all from locations along Booth's route to safety with Lincoln as prisoner) got furloughed home just as the kidnapping was to take place—a unit he sees as a blocking force to hold off expected Union pursuit. These men never surrendered at Appomattox with their parent units. They instead surrendered at Ashland Station, now a Federal provost marshal's head-quarters, in the weeks following the fall of the Confederacy.

If THG and others who agree with them are correct, the Civil War seems to have brought out heretofore unthinkable measures on both sides as they fought desperately for their vision of America's future. Perhaps it was just as well that it took 130 years to unravel the whole story, which THG see as part of the clandestine activities of a Confederate secret service that included in its orga-nization the Rose Greenhow spy ring in Washington; Confederate activities in Canada that led to several attempts to free Confederate soldiers held in Illinois, Delaware, Maryland, and Johnson's Island in Lake Erie; the creation of new explosives and weapons like submarines and motor patrol boats with torpedoes hanging out over their bows on long spars; and a reorganized secret service act passed in 1865 that rivaled anything done in North America until the advent of the Central Intelligence Agency in 1947. A lot of hanging might have resulted had the whole truth been known during Reconstruction. *See also* LINCOLN ASSASSINATION, THE NEW YORK CONNECTION OF THE.

LINCOLN ASSASSINATION, THE NEW YORK CONNECTION OF THE. For decades, historians have known of a ghostly New York City connection to the Lincoln assassination. There were several sources that brought Demill & Co. of 178½ Water Street, R. D. Watson, and J. J. Reford to light, from as early as 1865 to most recently in 2009. Now, for the first time, it turns out that the Water Street connection was not a myth (as many historians have charged).

At 178½ Water Street, in the office/warehouse of Demill & Co., a noted rogue and rascal, J. J. Reford had entered a partnership with the Demills just prior to the 1849 California Gold Rush. The operators of Demill & Co. were commission merchant Thomas Arnold Demill and his sons; the soon-to-be Confederate Maj. William Edward Demill and attorney to the rich and famous, Richard Mead Demill. By 1860, the Demills had made J. J. Reford a virtual member of the family, which specialized in foreign trade between the South (through William and a Maryland whiskey salesman and later Confederate secret agent, Roderick D. Watson), the East Coast, the Pacific Coast, and Europe. Whenever he was asked for his job description, supposedly J. J. Reford's stock answer was that he was a professional minder—a sort of "mob-style" enforcer in the Demill family businesses.

In the spring of 1865, the Civil War threatened to end too soon for the Demills. Heavy investors in both sides, the Demill fortune could double or triple if the war went on a few months more—preferably a few years. In contact with the Confederate government through the always affable and pliable Judah P. Benjamin (q.v.), the Confederate secretary of state and a monetary realist, the Demills requested his help. Benjamin sent his secret service (q.v.) agent, John H. Surratt, Jr., to persuade the head of a Confederate plot to abduct Abraham Lincoln, John Wilkes Booth (qq.v.), to coordinate with the Demill's right-hand man, Reford, in the project. Surratt received his orders through a telegram sent him by R. D. Watson, the old Maryland hand.

John Wilkes Booth's association with New York City was much more than met the eye, courtesy of five men: Roderick D. Watson, George A. Atzerodt, Louis J. Weichmann, Samuel K. Chester, and Richard Mead Demill, the Dutch American man-about-town, who had an unbroken bond of business between the Netherlands Dutch of Amsterdam and the Dutch Americans of New York existing from the city's founding.

If Benjamin could convince the rest of the cabinet members to hang on for a few weeks, the Confederate States of America would be back in business again. In rapid order, the Confederate cabinet had abandoned Richmond, Lee had surrendered to Grant, and sightings of Booth were in short supply. Unfortunately, Reford's conspiring with Booth had proved a dangerous notion. If one pushed Booth too lightly, he was full of himself. If one shoved him too hard, he sulked like a child. Booth's various addictions didn't make it any easier either; sex made him distracted, alcohol made him depressed, and Blue Mass (a mercury compound) and opium made him deranged.

Then, what was supposed to be a day of renewed dreams for the land of Dixie had become a nightmare of mayhem and murder. Booth went off on a plan of his own, an improvisation of one hatched in the Confederate Torpedo Bureau independently of Judah P. Benjamin, to blow up the White House and Lincoln's whole cabinet with it. When the Rebel powder-man failed to show up, Booth decided to carry out the plot, by having his gang assassinate all of the higher ups in the Lincoln government individually.

J. J. Reford swore to Demill that the accursed actor, Booth, had changed the whole darn thing, from capturing to killing. Demill did not care about any reward Washington put on Booth's head for his apprehension alive to be held over for trial, he wanted Booth dead and sent Reford to Virginia to do the job. After all, "dead men tell no tales." Regarding the fables about Booth escaping Garrett's farm (q.v.), Demill and Reford all agreed—Booth's ego and mouth were too big for him to keep in hiding for long. He was truly dead before Demill could have his revenge through Reford.

But there were many others who needed to be silenced before the New York connection faced some future gallows, courtesy of an emotive writer of memoirs. Demill's hatchet-man, Reford, became a veritable serial killer, dispatching nearly a dozen persons who knew too much through a series of providential "accidents." The unsolvable problem, however, was with R. D. Watson's letter to John Surratt. Watson had used the Demill name and the Water Street address. But no one figured this out until late in the next century. The Demills and Booth had each made life-changing errors in judgment: the Demills by giving Reford tacit approval to recruit the actor in the first place; Booth by changing the plot from abduction to assassination.

In the end, it was not so much a "lost cause" as it was "lost coin." And while it can be said that there were many heroes and villains of the Civil War, the Confederate defeat found only one rogue Rebel of any note, as in bank note, left standing in one piece. He was Judah P. Benjamin, who lived in luxury in European exile. He was not called "the brains of the Confederacy" for nothing. The Demills and their New York Dutch American friends did not do badly, either. Nor did the Dutch in Amsterdam's investment houses. They had bet on both sides to win.

The American Civil War is known for the brotherly manner in which the soldiers treated each other between the battles, causing some chroniclers to label them "Civil Warriors." But among historians there is little such camaraderie. If an author's story line does not fit the long-established parameters of what is acceptable in Lincolnology by taking a different view of Lincoln, it is unacceptable. The necessity of molding the Lincoln story for historical and political ends was noted by Alonzo Taft, who posited in the 1870s that the "proper" dead Lincoln can be much more appreciated than the living one ever was. But readers might well heed the wise words of the original Dutch settlers of modern New York City: "If you keep asking the wrong questions, you'll never find the correct answers."

LINCOLN–DOUGLAS DEBATES (1858). In 1858, Stephen A. Douglas' (q.v.) term in the U.S. Senate was up, and he had to stand for reelection. The state's Republican Party (q.v.) put up the man who had stolen it from its organizers in 1856, Abraham Lincoln (q.v.). The vote would be made in the Illinois state legislature, the direct election of U.S. senators being a phenomenon of the 20th century. But nonetheless, Lincoln challenged Douglas to debate the issues of the day, before the state legislature met. Douglas did not have to accept, but he did, hoping to place his stand on slavery in the territories before the South as much as Illinois. Because of Douglas' obvious importance in Washington and the fact that he had been all but promised the Democratic presidential nomination in 1860, and because Lincoln did such a creditable job debating him, Lincoln immediately became known nationwide and a viable possibility for Republican presidential aspirations in 1860.

Lincoln accepted his party's nomination in Chicago on June 16, 1858, with an oration since called the "House Divided Speech." He maintained that the United States could not be forever comprised of part slave and part free states. One or the other had to prevail. Douglas cleverly used this speech to expose to the people of Illinois that Lincoln was an ardent abolitionist (q.v.) who would try to destroy the Union to make a point. This forced Lincoln to make several anti-Negro statements at various debates to prove to the people of Illinois and their legislators that he was one of them, against full citizenship and equality for African-Americans. He wanted to leave slavery alone where it was. He did not want it to spread into the West. And he would not force Illinois to admit free blacks as citizens to vote.

And so it went for seven debates, held between August and October 1858 in the county seats of areas that had gone for American Party candidate Millard Fillmore (qq.v.) in 1856 and were now considered toss-ups. The general format was that each debate lasted three hours. The first speaker received one hour, the second speaker talked an hour and a half, and the first speaker got a half hour of rebuttal. Douglas and Lincoln alternated as first speaker.

Lincoln finally cornered Douglas at Freeport. He asked Douglas if a people of a territory could lawfully exclude slavery before a proposed state constitution were drawn up. That is, would Douglas admit to supporting squatter sovereignty rather than popular sovereignty or the pro-Southern Non-Exclusion Doctrine (qq.v.), as he claimed to do. This has since been known as the Freeport Question (q.v.).

Douglas was on the horns of a dilemma. He had always operated as pro-Southern slave expansion in Washington and against Southern slave expansion at home. He did this because he knew that slavery could be stopped at any stage of territorial development, because Northern antislavery (q.v.) people moved into the West faster and in greater numbers than Southerners burdened with slaves. But now he had to admit this publicly for the first time. To do otherwise would be to lose his U.S. Senate seat. But to win his Senate seat would be to lose his party's nomination for the presidency in 1860.

Douglas' answer became known as the Freeport Doctrine (q.v.). He said that slavery could be blocked at any time in a territory by simply not passing a positive law to establish it. Simply by staying silent, slavery would be denied the laws that made it function. Douglas won his U.S. Senate seat by a vote of 54–46 in the state legislature. Douglas was the only Democrat who voted against the Lecompton Constitution in the Kansas Settlement (q.v.) question to survive politically in the North. Although Douglas may have won in the Illinois legislature, Abraham Lincoln became a national figure in the Republican Party overnight. He had given Douglas a run for his money. Most important, Lincoln was popular with the people of Illinois. He had a homey quality that made him an entertaining stump speaker. Illinois was one of the states that the Republicans had to have to win the presidency in 1860, and the people of Illinois would vote in 1860, not the state legislature. *See also* ELECTION OF 1860.

LITTLEFIELD, MILTON S. (1832–1899). Born in New York, Milton Littlefield moved to Illinois as a young man and read law under Abraham Lincoln (q.v.). He was a captain in the 14th Illinois Infantry, stationed at Memphis, where he illegally traded in cotton and guns with the Confederacy. He then obtained a commission as a colonel in the 21st Colored Infantry. He recruited black soldiers in North Carolina, obtaining a fee for each recruit who was added to Illinois' draft quota to permit whites to avoid the war. He also served during the siege of Charleston, eventually becoming a brigade commander and winding up at Hilton Head. He also served as an inspector general of colored troops.

After the war, Littlefield and a Scalawag partner, George Swepson, became involved in selling devalued railroad bonds in Swepson's native North Carolina. The two men bought up the worthless bonds; bribed the state legislature to back them with the full credit of the state, which raised their value; and resold them at a tremendous profit. Although it appears that Governor William W. Holden (q.v.) was innocent of anything but knowing Littlefield, the scheme helped tarnish his administration as Littlefield associated with and was a prominent Republican (q.v.), himself. Interestingly, most of the money stayed in North Carolina with Swepson and other Democrats (q.v.), who let Littlefield take the blame.

Having exhausted the monetary possibilities in North Carolina, Littlefield moved on to Florida. Here he bought up two worthless railroads and paid off the state legislature to finance them as needed internal improvements. Then he and prominent legislators diverted the appropriated money into their own pockets as the railroads continued to languish. It seems quite likely that Republican Governor Harrison Reed (q.v.) sold his approval of their schemes.

After taking the money, Littlefield ran to Europe, where he sold fraudulent railroad bonds to Dutch investors as a hot tip on a good investment. It is estimated that Littlefield received as much as $6.8 million from his various schemes. He left Europe ahead of the law and retired in New Jersey, which had an innate understanding of how such things work and a disinclination to extradite engaging scoundrels like Littlefield. But while Florida wrote the whole Littlefield fraud off as a bad lesson, North Carolina never stopped trying to get him back into the state to face the courts. Finally, Littlefield agreed to stand trial if all who were involved would be tried along with him. The state prosecutor came up to New Jersey to talk it all over. Littlefield laid the whole matter out before him and his aides. Then the prosecutor checked out the facts and figures and found Littlefield's account to be true. The problem was that 22 prominent North Carolinians, now all prominent Redeemers (q.v.), were culpable. The case was closed without further action.

Littlefield, Swepson, and their henchmen represent the worst of the caricatures of those who exploited Reconstruction for their own ends.

LOAD-IN-NINE-TIMES. North or South, the Civil War soldier carried about the same arms and equipment. The standard shoulder arm carried by the infantryman was a percussion-capped, .58 caliber rifled musket, as opposed to the smooth bore musket soldiers carried in earlier wars. Armies preferred the relatively inaccurate musket to the more accurate rifle because of ease and speed of loading. The smooth bore accepted the bullet with a quick push of the rammer. To engage the grooved rifling, one had to pound the bullet home or use a system of leather or cloth patches.

But science had finally struck the battlefield in full force by 1861. It came in the form of the coniodal bullet developed by Capt. Claude Etiennne Minié, a French soldier. The minnie ball, as the bullet was known in the Americas, was a bullet with a hollowed out case and two or three grooved rings cut around its body near and parallel to its base. This made the bullet weak at the base so it would expand and engage the rifling when fired. What this meant was that the soldier could load it fast and easy like a musket and gain the range and accuracy of the rifle. The result was the rifled musket, a combination of the best of all worlds.

Some Civil War soldiers still used the musket. Usually a .69 caliber weapon, it was usually loaded with buck and ball, a round bullet capped by three buckshot that made the musket a single-barrel shotgun. Since distances for accurate fire were rarely over 100–200 yards, the musket made up with lethality for what it lacked in distant accuracy. Most weapons, rifled musket or smooth-bore musket, were fired by placing a percussion cap of fulminate of mercury over a nipple in the firing mechanism. But some flintlocks were used, especially in the Confederacy, although flintlocks tended to misfire more and worked not at all in the rain.

To charge a muzzle-loading weapon under fire was not easy. It required iron discipline and rote memory. Most Civil War soldiers used paper cartridges, hollow tubes of paper tied off at the top, followed by bullet and powder. The back or base was covered by folding the paper tube over on itself to keep it all in place. The soldier tore the paper open at its base with his front teeth, poured the powder down the barrel, and followed it with the bullet and then the rest of the paper as a wad to seal it all tight with a tap from the ramrod.

But it had to be done to a regular rhythm, lest something be forgotten and the weapon not fire properly. Hence the soldier learned to load by the numbers in nine counts, or load-in-nine-times (it beat the 12 counts that flintlocks and loose powder and bullet required). It went something like this: One—LOAD, the soldier grounded his piece with the ramrod channel under the rifled musket barrel facing him; Two—HANDLE CARTRIDGE, he pulled a cartridge from his cartridge box and inserted the tail in his mouth; Three—TEAR CARTRIDGE, he tore the cartridge and placed it at the muzzle; Four—CHARGE CARTRIDGE, he poured the powder down the barrel and placed the bullet in the muzzle; Five—DRAW RAMMER, the soldier drew the ramrod out of its pocket beneath the barrel, placing its wider head against the bullet point; Six—RAM CARTRIDGE, the soldier rammed the cartridge to the bottom of the barrel, seating it against the powder (veterans marked the correct depth on the rammer); Seven—RETURN RAMMER, the ramrod was replaced in the pocket beneath the barrel; Eight—PRIME, the soldier brought the piece up under his right arm, holding it in his left hand, half cocking it and reaching for a percussion cap in his cap box and placing it on the cap nipple of the piece; Nine—READY, the soldier is ready to fire at command or at will.

A similar drill was followed in the artillery, the piece being much bigger and each step carried out by one man.

LOGAN'S CROSSROADS, BATTLE OF. *See* SHILOH CAMPAIGN.

LONGSTREET, JAMES (1821–1904). A Confederate Civil War hero, James Longstreet became one of the most noted and reviled of Southern Scalawags (q.v.) during Reconstruction. Born in South Carolina and raised in Georgia by his uncle, James Longstreet graduated from the U.S. Military Academy in 1842. He served with the infantry in Mexico and was severely wounded at Chapultepec. After the war, he stayed in the Army and rose to the rank of major in the paymaster's department. Resigning his commission in 1861, Longstreet entered Confederate service as a brigadier general. His brigade was lightly engaged on the flanks of the battlefield at First Manassas (q.v.). He served under Joseph Johnston in the Peninsula Campaign (qq.v.) and fought indecisively at Fair Oaks before Richmond. Under Robert E. Lee (q.v.), who had replaced the wounded Johnston, Longstreet commanded one of the assault divisions that drove the Union army from the environs of the Confederate capital.

Lee then divided up his army between Longstreet and Thomas J. "Stonewall" Jackson (q.v.) for the drive on Washington that resulted in the battles of Second Manassas (q.v.) and Antietam Creek. Retreating to Fredericksburg (q.v.), Longstreet still commanded half of Lee's army when his men defeated the Union forces at the stone wall before Marye's Heights. Always maneuvering for an independent command, but never able to shine alone, Longstreet spent the spring of 1863 at Suffolk, Virginia, where he once again was mediocre in operations. Back with Lee as a corps commander, Longstreet made numerous controversial moves at Gettysburg that critics (spurred on by his becoming a Republican [q.v.] after the war) claimed cost Lee the battle. In the fall of 1863, most of Longstreet's corps went to the Western Theater of war to near Chattanooga (q.v.), where they proved to be a decisive force at Chickamauga for the South. But Longstreet joined the other corps commanders in quarreling with his inept superior, Gen. Braxton Bragg (q.v.), and received an independent assignment to recapture Knoxville (q.v.) from the Yankees. Longstreet bungled the job once again. Back in Virginia with Lee in the 1864 Richmond Campaign (q.v.), Longstreet's corps saved Lee's army at the Wilderness. But the general was severely wounded in the neck by his own men in a friendly fire incident (these were quite common in the Civil War) and missed the rest of the 1864 battles. Rejoining Lee in 1865, Longstreet surrendered with him at Appomattox (q.v.).

At the end of the Civil War, Longstreet was a civilian for the first time in his life. He moved to New Orleans, became a cotton broker, and sold insurance. He was doing reasonably well in business at the time of the Military Reconstruction Acts (q.v.). A local newspaper asked several prominent citizens, including Longstreet, to advise the state on how to proceed in the chaotic times that faced them. Longstreet answered immediately and recommended that New Orleans, Louisiana, and the South follow the congressional plan to the letter. After all, Longstreet reminded his readers, the South had lost the war. Had Longstreet stopped there, nothing more would have been said. But somehow, once started, he could not keep his opinions out of print. He began writing the newspaper on his own volition, and each time he got further and further in trouble. He spoke with the "bluntness of a soldier," when the evasiveness of a diplomat might have served him better.

Longstreet was appalled that citizens and the press had misconstrued him to be a Southern traitor. He tried to explain himself in other letters, but no one was listening anymore. He wrote General Lee and asked his endorsement. Lee refused. He was willing to obey the laws, but he would not endorse the course of "the dominant party" as Longstreet had done, which Lee viewed as "a great mistake." Longstreet's business and social connections fell away. Congress did relieve him of his political proscriptions (some protested because he did not asked that it be done) and when a fellow Army friend, Ulysses S. Grant (q.v.), became president in 1869, he offered Longstreet the post of surveyor of customs for the Port of New Orleans. Broke and out of any job prospects, Longstreet accepted and became the Scalawag in fact as well as name. That the customs house was the center of the most radical and corrupt Carpetbaggers (q.v.) in Louisiana did not help the general's reputation any.

In support of the Republican administration of Louisiana, Longstreet was involved in the final battle against the White League (q.v.) as the forces of Redemption swept the state in 1874. In June, the general led the militia and police in the Third Battle of New Orleans (q.v.) (or the Battle of Canal Street) when the Republicans contested with the pro-Democrat White League for control of the city. Valiantly, Longstreet rode forward to order the White Leaguers to disperse. The front rank pulled him from his horse and opened fire on the Republican militia and police. Without their leader, Longstreet's men broke and ran. The general was hit by a spent bullet, probably from his own men.

Longstreet survived his wound, and the White Leaguers let him go. Republicanism in Louisiana was dead, and his reputation ruined. He moved back to Georgia, where he lived out his long life. He still accepted Federal appointments as his income. He was at various moments in the next 25 years U.S. minister to Turkey, U.S. marshal for Georgia, and U.S. railway commissioner. His political jobs became his livelihood. He remarried late in life, and his new wife became one of his principal defenders as die-hard Democrats attacked him for his wartime command actions. Led by Jubal Early (q.v.), they accused him of dragging his feet at Gettysburg and costing the South the whole war. Longstreet answered his critics in his own volume, *From Manassas to Appomattox*, published eight years before he died, which was reinforced by his wife's biography of him after his death.

LOOKOUT MOUNTAIN, BATTLE OF. *See* CHATTANOOGA CAMPAIGN.

LÓPEZ, NARCISO. *See* FILIBUSTERING.

LOUDON. *See* KNOXVILLE CAMPAIGN.

LOUISIANA EXPERIMENT. Nowhere in the South did Reconstruction last longer than in Louisiana. This was due partly to the fact that the Union forces occupied the southeastern third of the state early in 1862; the complexities of the state's population, which included cosmopolitan New Orleans, with its industrial and laboring classes and the largest group of immigrants outside of New York City; a countryside made up of large slaveholding plantations and small nonslaveholding farms; a large black contingent that not only included slaves of varying skills ranging from farm hands to artisans, but numerous free persons of color, some of whom owned slaves and plantations of their own; the largest and best-educated group of African-Americans in the South, mostly located in New Orleans, and many of whom had the blood of the finest white families of the state in their veins; and the fact that politics in Louisiana can best be described as a blood sport, full of intricacies that boggle the mind of ordinary mortals, which caused the Reconstruction process to last until 1877.

The first military ground commander in Louisiana was the infamous Bvt. Maj. Gen. Benjamin F. Butler (q.v.), fresh from Fortress Monroe, Virginia, where he had declared runaway slaves behind his lines to be contraband, initiating one of the first freedom policies of the war. Butler's first goal in Louisiana was to stabilize the civilian population to prevent it from interfering with the movement of his troops and spreading the dreaded yellow fever so prevalent in the region. As blacks comprised more than half of the population of the area he occupied, he turned his attention to his goal right off. No blacks were allowed in army camps and the city of New Orleans. Those who fled to the Union lines were immediately corralled and shipped back to their home plantations or consigned to augment the work force of nearby plantations. Military power was to enforce this policy, making Butler in Louisiana quite the reverse from the abolitionist (q.v.) general he was later portrayed as based on his Virginia record.

Under fire from subordinates and politicians back North for his re-enslaving policies, Butler made a few modifications in his policy that summer. Goaded on by unruly abolitionist subordinates, the threat of Confederate attack on Baton Rouge, and the Union War Department, Butler enrolled the Louisiana Native Guards in three regiments in the summer of 1862. These were free blacks from New Orleans who had stood side by side with Andrew Jackson during the War of 1812, and whose organization had been kept by the state. Contrary to existing custom in the rest of the nation, the Native Guards had their own black officers, once commissioned by the state of Louisiana.

Having duly astonished his critics on the black soldier issue, Butler rounded up all contrabands (q.v.) and sent them to only loyal citizens' plantations south of New Orleans. All an owner had to do to demonstrate loyalty was sign a contract that regulated hours of labor and stipulated a small salary for the black laborers assigned to him. Past or present political affinities were not important.

By January 1863, President Abraham Lincoln (q.v.) had removed Butler from command and replaced him with a less controversial man, Bvt. Maj. Gen. Nathaniel P. Banks (q.v.), like Butler a Massachusetts Democrat turned Republican (q.v.). Indeed, except for regularizing the rules, all Banks did different from Butler was ask for planter input. He got it. In February 1863, the planters' committee reported. It stressed the need for discipline of the black work force, a restoration of civilian government and the recreation of patrols to search for stray freedmen, and the protection of Federal military units.

Banks promised to hold blacks to their contracts and stifle labor complaints through a new military agency (variously called the Commission of Negro Affairs under the corrupt George Hanks or the Bureau of Free Labor led by the capable Thomas Conway) to supervise the labor contract process. The agency was also to provide for black medical care and education, but the small sums allocated for these functions compromised their importance. Federal troops were provided to keep order in the planting areas.

When it came to the enrollment of black soldiers, Banks altered Butler's program significantly. Butler had enlisted the Louisiana Native Guard with its black officer corps intact. This would not do—making African-Americans officers and by implication gentlemen. No other black regiments in the country had such a luxury. The rule was black troops led by white officers. So Banks began to purge the black officers from the service. He then expanded the "Corps d'Afrique," as he now labeled the Native Guard, into 20 regiments. When necessary, black recruits were dragooned off plantations or the streets of New Orleans. Organized into a brigade under Bvt. Brig. Gen. Daniel Ullmann (who had done most of the recruiting and training), the Corps d'Afrique played a key role in the capture of Port Hudson in 1863, a post north of Baton Rouge that along with Vicksburg had blocked the river for the Confederacy.

The arrival of the Department of the Treasury in the summer of 1862 to engage in the cotton and sugar trade discomfited Banks somewhat more than it had Butler, who ignored it so long as he received his portion of the accompanying graft. But Banks was different—he was basically honest. Seeking to compromise him, the treasury agents protested that Banks was in league with the planters and had virtually re-enslaved the contrabands. Banks retorted that the treasury men were trading across enemy lines and aiding the armies opposed to him. Only the fact that the treasury program relied on Army supplies and protection kept them from Banks' throat. The general helped his case by telling Lincoln that a speedy, easy Reconstruction depended upon keeping the planters on his side.

Hence Banks did not report attempts by black leaders to obtain integrated public services, land, and the right to vote, much of which was cheered by white workers in New Orleans, led by Thomas J. Durant, a Utopian Socialist newspaper editor and labor organizer. Banks ignored Durant and the workingmen of New Orleans for a government based on planter support led by Michael Hahn, a pliable man who did Banks' bidding and created a reconstructed government based on the old 1852 state constitution cleansed of slavery rather than a new document that would have liberalized the representation of working-class whites.

Unfortunately, Banks had to produce a military victory to validate his Reconstruction program, and here he faltered. In the 1864 Red River Campaign (q.v.), Banks lived up to his moniker, "Nothing Positive," and allowed an inferior Confederate force to run his men off the field at Mansfield and Pleasant Hill. A disappointed Lincoln divided his command area in half on the Mississippi River and replaced him with Bvt. Maj. Gen. Stephen A. Hurlbut in the east and Bvt. Maj. Gen. E. R. S. Canby (q.v.) in the west. Under the new administration in 1865, the treasury men proposed new regulations that greatly liberalized discipline and increased wages, but the planters appealed to the local provost marshals, who sided with them. Acting on the provosts' reports, General Hurlbut basically continued Banks' old contract labor program until the arrival of the Freedmen's Bureau (q.v.) later that same year, whose first head in Louisiana would be Thomas Conway, the former head of Banks' Bureau of Free Labor. The wartime labor system in Louisiana, as elsewhere, was not one of slavery; but it was not freedom, either. It set a precedent for the Black Codes (q.v.), tenantry, and the lien that followed.

LOUISIANA UNIFICATION MOVEMENT. Made up of business- and plantation-oriented whites, the Louisiana Unifiers were disgusted by the excesses of the Carpetbagger (q.v.) governments in the state, particularly the high property taxes that went into paying for what the rich saw as unnecessary governmental expense. It was obvious that the major bloc of Reconstruction supporters were the African-Americans. Unlike many other Southern whites, the rich had little to fear from contact or social competition with blacks. They had driven them as slaves; they would never be economically, politically, or socially challenged by them. They "knew" how to "manage" blacks. At least so they thought. These Scalawags (q.v.) offered the blacks civil rights while they received lower taxes and internal improvements (levees and railroads). The union faltered when upper class whites refused to permit social equality as well. This demonstrated to white politicians of all levels that the ultimate redemption of the South would rest with white unity reinforced by the terror instituted by the Knights of the White Camellia and the White League (q.v.).

LYNCHBURG, BATTLE OF. *See* WASHINGTON, EARLY'S RAID ON.

LYNCH, JAMES (1838–1872). Born in Baltimore in 1838 of a free mulatto father, a merchant who had just purchased the freedom of his wife, James Lynch was educated in Maryland and New Hampshire. Lynch entered the ministry at age 19 and served pulpits in Indiana and Illinois. In the latter state, he met and married and then moved with his bride to Philadelphia, where he edited *The Recorder*, a popular Methodist magazine. He stayed in Philadelphia until 1864, when he went to Georgia and set up a church and schools for freedmen at Savannah after its capture by Maj. Gen. William T. Sherman's (q.v.) army. Lynch was an accomplished speaker and organizer, and when he heard that local blacks expected to gain land and live separately from whites, he rebuked them and spoke of the need for an integrated society of all races after the war. Lynch soon returned to Philadelphia and stayed for the next two years. When Congress passed the Military Reconstruction Acts in 1867 (q.v.), he went to Mississippi along with Hiram Revels (q.v.) to be the "religious and moral educator of my race," as he put it. Lynch saw it as his duty to assist the less fortunate blacks in making the transition from slavery to freedom.

Early on, Lynch realized that if he were to have a proper impact on Mississippi Reconstruction, he would have to enter politics. Lynch served as a registrar of voters. He impressed upon Mississippi's blacks the necessity of voting the Republican (q.v.) ballot and trusting in the congressional solution for Reconstruction. But Lynch was against the Union Loyal Leagues (q.v.) as too provocative to whites. Nonetheless, his political organization of freedmen under the party banner brought him to the attention of its leaders, and they made him vice president of the Mississippi Republican Party. Lynch went to work traveling the backcountry and speaking on behalf of the constitutional convention, a courageous act as blacks had never done this before. As Lynch spoke on the necessity of blacks and whites cooperating in the new society, he was received well by both races. Lynch himself did not serve in the convention, but he had done much to give it its Republican majority and many of its 17 black members. Lynch was not happy with the disfranchising and officeholding proscriptions against former Confederates. He believed them wrong in principle and also for the practical reason that they gave Conservative whites a free rallying point. But his church work kept him from influencing the proceedings.

Eventually the Ulysses S. Grant (q.v.) administration adopted the view held by Lynch and Republican moderates in the state and separated the proscriptive clauses from the rest of the constitution. The proscriptions failed, and the constitution passed. Lynch sided with James L. Alcorn (q.v.), Mississippi's Scalawag (q.v.) governor, in a moderate course and opened up the *Colored Citizen*, a newspaper at Jackson of which he was editor. Lynch appreciated the work of the Radical Republicans for blacks' civil rights, but maintained that proscriptions against whites would upset the whole program in the long run.

But there was one point that Lynch was not willing to compromise—the equal treatment of blacks under the law. He also believed that offices should be apportioned among the races so that all would get a chance to serve. For these principles, he was willing to accept segregated schools and individual social preferences. He believed that full access to public accommodations would come in due time as soon as blacks demonstrated their capabilities to rule. Unfortunately, his main problem turned out not to be native Mississippians but Yankee Carpetbaggers (q.v.), who talked up a good program in league with blacks, only to not let them participate. In the new order, however, Lynch was elected secretary of state for the new James L. Alcorn administration. He was responsible for election administration, procurement of election data, state printing (a fine patronage opportunity), accounting for and disposing of state lands (he began to clear up the muddle from before the war and get many assigned to educational purposes), and serving on the state board of education. Lynch also began to look into the pernicious effects of the sharecrop and tenantry system that would plague generations of Southern farmers, black and white.

Lynch took to the stump in the state by-elections of 1871 to campaign for Republican candidates. He seemed to sense that his influence was waning, a conviction made solid when he failed to gain the party's congressional nomination from the Jackson–Vicksburg district in 1872. White Carpetbaggers were unwilling to have a black man of such demonstrated abilities as Lynch's in the party, and enough black partisans went along to try to discredit him for their own gain. New heroes, like the more radical Adelbert Ames and John R. Lynch (qq.v.) (they are unrelated to each other), came to the fore. He campaigned nationally for the Ulysses S. Grant (q.v.) ticket in 1872, and upon his return from the North he was stricken with Bright's disease, complicated by a bronchial ailment. He died in December 1872 at age 34 and was buried in the white Greenwood Cemetery at Jackson.

LYNCH, JOHN R. (1847–1939). John R. Lynch was born on a Louisiana plantation to a slave mother and her white master. His father died before he could complete the formalities of emancipation. The executor of the will promptly sold the boy and mother to Mississippi, and the family was split up, with Lynch working on a plantation outside of Natchez. When Federal occupation troops came into the area in 1863, Lynch and other slaves fled to their camps and became free. He tried to pick up the elements of an education while still a slave, but his owners frowned on bondsmen who appeared to want to know too much. In 1866, he went to school at a Northern white missionary's establishment, but overall Lynch's education remained informal at best, prompted by a curiosity for books and newspapers that never ended. As he read, he learned to convey his thoughts to others, developing an ability for public speaking and debate that would later prove invaluable. In 1867, when the Military Reconstruction Acts (q.v.) opened up the world of politics for the South's blacks, Lynch was just 20 years old. But he became active in political organizations like the Union League (q.v.) and wrote and spoke on behalf of the new state constitution. In 1869, the state's military governor, Bvt. Maj. Gen. Adelbert Ames (q.v.), made Lynch a justice of the peace at age 21.

He was soon elected by local blacks to the state legislature, where he served until 1873. He served on committees on elections, education, justice, and election credentials (which judged if members deserved to be seated from their districts), and advanced to speaker of the house. When the house could not agree to a congressional redistricting plan, it placed the project solely in Lynch's hands. He drew up the districts, and the members agreed that it was well done, with five districts safely Republican and one Democrat (qq.v.). In 1872, he was sent to the Republican national convention and returned home to defeat a white Carpetbagger (q.v.) for the honor of representing Mississippi in Congress. At age 26, he was the youngest member in the Forty-third Congress. His major interest was Charles Sumner's (q.v.) Civil Rights Bill, which would guarantee entrance into public accommodations for all Americans regardless of race, which he saw as "an act of simple justice."

Meanwhile, Democrats took the state government and proceeded to redistrict the state's congressional delegation. This forced him to run against Col. James R. Chalmers, a popular Confederate cavalry leader. Lynch was promptly counted out, and the new Democrat-controlled Congress refused to accept his challenge to the vote totals. In 1880, Lynch ran against Chalmers again. Once again Lynch challenged the final vote count, in which thousands of black votes were challenged and thrown out. This time Lynch's principled appeal was favorably received, and he was seated. But Lynch had to rerun almost at once, because of the length of the appeal. In 1882, he lost a fair race to a white Democrat by 800 votes. Lynch also continued to serve as the head of the state Republican machine, which he ran in league with Blanche K. Bruce (q.v.) and James Hill, two other African-American politicians in Mississippi. During this time, he served as preliminary chairman of the 1884 Republican national convention and in his keynote address publicly condemned Democrats for their continued vote fraud in Mississippi. It would take 74 years before a black man would give a keynote address to another national convention of either party.

Lynch's retirement from politics and the stirrings of disfranchisement of blacks all over the South by 1890 caused him to be active in other ways. He declined a political appointment offered by President Grover Cleveland, because he believed that it was contrary to his political loyalties. He did serve as fourth auditor of the Treasury Department under Benjamin Harrison, a Republican. He bought and sold real estate in Mississippi and actually became quite wealthy. He also began to study law formally and passed the bar exam in 1896 on the second try. But before he could do much with his certificate, the Spanish–American War intervened. Lynch received a commission as an Army paymaster from President William McKinley, whom Lynch knew from his service in Congress. Paymasters got to travel a lot, and since Lynch had recently divorced, he found much diverting pleasure in his job. He stayed in the service until 1911, when he retired and married again. This time, Lynch moved to Chicago and lived a life of retirement. But he kept a hand in politics and became an advisor to Congressmen Oscar DePriest, one of the first blacks elected from a Northern district as a result of the African-American migration northward during the First World War.

Lynch also continued to write and speak on topics of interest to black Americans. He was highly critical of white history of Reconstruction and wrote his own book detailing what had "really" happened in Mississippi after the Civil War. He died in 1939.

M

MALVERN HILL, BATTLE OF. *See* SEVEN DAYS CAMPAIGN.

MANASSAS CAMPAIGN, SECOND. With Maj. Gen. George B. McClellan's (q.v.) Union army idle under the U.S. Navy guns at Harrison's Landing at the end of the Seven Days Campaign (q.v.), Gen. Robert E. Lee (q.v.) sent about a third of his army north under Maj. Gen. Stonewall Jackson (q.v.) to Gordonsville on the Virginia Central Railroad to meet a new threat imposed by the advance of Maj. Gen. John Pope's (q.v.) Army of Virginia. Composed of three corps of Federal soldiers once independently under John C. Frémont, Nathaniel P. Banks (qq.v.), and Irvin McDowell, Pope's army was to advance down the Orange and Alexandria Railroad to draw some of Lee's forces away from Richmond, protect the Shenandoah Valley, and guard Washington from Confederate attack. Frémont refused to serve under Pope, whom he outranked, and was replaced by Maj. Gen. Franz Sigel.

Pope's advance in late summer 1862 marked a new Union get-tough policy in the Civil War. He was to vigorously apply all of the provision of the Confiscation Acts (q.v.) against Confederate civilians, root out partisan activity by punishing the neighborhoods in which they operated, summarily execute anyone who fired upon Federal troops, and arrest any avowedly disloyal males caught behind his lines. Above all, as Pope told his angered soldiers, he was from the West, demanded vigorous execution of his orders, and expected his men to advance and fight against the enemy, not to run and show their backs as they were in the habit of doing so far. The Radical Republicans loved Pope and his harsh pronouncements, and he was received joyously by the Joint Committee on the Conduct of the War (q.v.).

Jackson saw immediately that Pope's three corps were widely scattered. He moved on the closest, commanded by Maj. Gen. Banks, an old Valley opponent (and incompetent), hoping to crush it and then operate between the other two, defeating them in detail. Jackson was in for a surprise, as Banks moved forward quickly and hit him head on at Cedar Mountain, scattering two of his own divisions. It was only when Maj. Gen. A. Powell Hill's large division came up late in the day and threw Banks back that Jackson could claim a victory.

Realizing that McClellan's troops were being withdrawn and sent to Pope, Lee decided to leave a token force at Harrison's Landing and join Jackson to defeat Pope, whose men held the line between Clark's Mountain and Cedar Mountain, before he was reinforced. Lee would assemble behind Clark's Mountain and crush Pope's left, cutting him off from Washington. But the plan was compromised when Pope's cavalry took Brig. Gen. J. E. B. Stuart's (q.v.) men by surprise at Verdiersville, capturing Stuart's fancy, feathered hat as he fled and a copy of Lee's intentions. Pope rapidly withdrew across the Rappahannock River to escape Lee's trap.

Both armies sparred along the Rappahannock. Pope received reinforcements from McClellan's army and even from the North Carolina coast. Finally, Stuart conducted a raid of his own behind Pope to Union headquarters at Catlett's Station and captured Pope's uniform and his plans. Stuart found out that Lee had five days to act before the bulk of McClellan's army arrived to assist Pope.

Lee sent Stuart's cavalry and Jackson with half of his whole army on an extended raid deep behind Poe's position to his supply base at Manassas Junction. Pope saw Jackson leave, but took no action. He saw the rest of Lee's army depart in the same direction the next day, but still held firm on the Rappahannock. Then came news that Stuart and Jackson were destroying the Union supply base at Manassas Junction. Pope immediately sent his forces to the rear, hoping to catch Jackson before Lee could get there. He very nearly made it in time, because his cavalry under Brig. Gen. John Buford held Lee up for six critical hours at Thoroughfare Gap in the Bull Run Mountains. Meanwhile, Jackson marched his units off from Manassas in every direction possible to confuse Pope. But they all met on the evening of August 28, 1862, at Stony Ridge or Sudley Mountain behind Manassas. Then Jackson sent a part of his force down the mountain to attack one of Pope's wandering brigades in the battle of Groveton. Pope ordered everyone to meet at Manassas the next day to destroy Jackson once and for all.

On August 29, Pope launched a series of piecemeal attacks on Jackson's position on the Mountain. Jackson's men fired back until they began to run out of ammunition. Then, in truly Jacksonian fashion, they used the bayonet and threw rocks at the advancing Federals. Pope was so involved that he failed to perceive that Lee and Maj. Gen. James Longstreet had come up on his left flank. When one of McClellan's recent arrivals, Maj. Gen. Fitz John Porter, warned Pope about Longstreet's approach, Pope scoffed and ordered him to move in and assist in the attack on Jackson. This opened the way for Longstreet, by taking Porter in off his flank. The Confederates readjusted their lines, which Pope took to mean that Jackson was retreating. He ordered his whole force to take Jackson the next morning.

The next day, Lee permitted Pope to become thoroughly engaged with Jackson before launching Longstreet forward in a massive attack that swept

Pope's forces from the field. Only a tough rearguard action on Henry House Hill permitted his army to escape. Lee then sent Jackson north around Pope's position at Centerville. Jackson struck a portion of Pope's Army at Chantilly or Ox Hill in a rainstorm. Losing two general officers, Pope accepted reality and retreated into the defenses of Washington, a completely beaten man.

MANASSAS, FIRST BATTLE OF. Spurred on by the newspapers and impatient politicians, President Abraham Lincoln (q.v.) ordered his field commander at Washington, Bvt. Brig. Gen. Irvin McDowell, to advance and take on the Confederate force around Manassas Junction under Brig. Gen. P. G. T. Beauregard (q.v.). There were other troop concentrations in Virginia. Both sides had small armies in the Shenandoah Valley, and the Confederates had forces around Fredericksburg. The basic idea was for the Union troops in the Valley, under Maj. Gen. Robert Patterson, to keep the Rebels under Brig. Gen. Joseph Johnson (q.v.) too busy to reinforce Beauregard at Manassas. But Patterson withdrew his feint prematurely, and Johnston marched most of his men to the Manassas Gap Railroad and rode over to Manassas. It was the first use of trains to effect such a movement in military history.

Technically, Johnston was the senior Confederate officer on the field, but he allowed Beauregard, who knew the terrain, to direct the battle while he forwarded troops to threatened positions. The Rebels were lined up along the banks of Bull Run. The Yankees had probed several fords to the right of the Confederate line on July 18, 1861, but McDowell and Beauregard had essentially the same plan—to fake left and attack right—in effect, they would whirl around like a great wheel. But McDowell moved first, and the Confederates were immediately on the defensive, warned by their signal towers located on key hills in the area.

McDowell's attack initially went quite well. Striking a weak spot in Beauregard's line, the Confederates fell back up the slopes of Henry Hill. At the top stood one of Johnston's brigades under the command of Brig. Gen. Thomas J. Jackson (q.v.). Standing firm, "like a Stonewall," according to one observer, Jackson and his men caused the Union attack to bog down. Meanwhile, numerous reinforcements sent forward by Johnson extended the Rebel line to the left until it overlapped the Federals. Then following a cavalry charge under Col. J. E. B. Stuart (q.v.), the Rebels advanced, with Brig. Gen. Edmund Kirby Smith's (q.v.) infantry brigade leading the way. The Yankees lost two regular artillery batteries and a covering force of Fire Zouaves, elite troops from New York City fire companies.

As the Union soldiers withdrew on July 21, a Confederate artillery battery hit the stone bridge across Cub Run in the center of the retreat and panic ensued, complicated by terrified civilians who had come out from Washington to have a picnic lunch and watch the hoped for Federal victory. The Federals did not stop running until they reached Washington, but the Confederates were too exhausted and inexperienced to pursue. The Rebels lost about 2,000, mostly killed and wounded, while the Union lost 2,600 casualties, including 1,200 prisoners. If nothing else, First Manassas demonstrated that it was going to be a longer war than expected.

MANASSAS, SECOND BATTLE OF. *See* MANASSAS CAMPAIGN, SECOND.

MANIFEST DESTINY. *See* SOCIAL DARWINISM; "SPREAD EAGLE" FOREIGN POLICY.

MANSFIELD, BATTLE OF. *See* RED RIVER CAMPAIGN.

MARAIS DES CYGNES, BATTLE OF. *See* RED RIVER CAMPAIGN.

MARCH TO THE SEA. From the middle of November to the middle of December 1864, Maj. Gen. William T. Sherman (q.v.) conducted his infamous March to the Sea. After the fall of Atlanta, Confederate Lt. Gen. John B. Hood (q.v.) had taken what remained of the Army of Tennessee and begun to raid the rail line that supplied Sherman's forces at Atlanta. Sherman proposed an innovative strategy of sending all of his armies except four infantry corps and one cavalry division back to Nashville. Then Sherman would take 20 days' rations and, living off the land, cut a swath of destruction across Georgia from Atlanta to Savannah. He would organize his infantry into two armies, the Army of Tennessee (led by Maj. Gen. O. O. Howard) and the Army of Georgia (Maj. Gen. Henry Slocum), each with two corps. The cavalry would be under Maj. Gen. Judson Kilpatrick, known as a rambunctious and often irresponsible officer, just the kind of man Sherman said he wanted.

Marching in a wide formation between Augusta and Macon, Sherman sent out special raiding parties, called "bummers," to collect supplies. In the 21st century, the destruction Sherman's soldiers wrought on the civilian population of Georgia is pretty much run-of-the-mill—indeed, fairly mild. But to the genteel, 19th-century mind, what Sherman instituted was a policy of barbarism not equaled since the Thirty Years' Wars of religion in Europe during the 1600s. The main ingredient was terrorism, and Sherman made no apologies for it.

The basic tactic was for a unit of Sherman's army to march between two points until the Confederates committed to defend one. Then Sherman's men took the other. It was a standard tactic, later adopted by the German World War II panzer corps, and they were full of admiration for Sherman's march—and other refinements of the Art of War. Most of the skirmishes (there were no real infantry battles except a small fray with the impotent Georgia Militia at Griswoldville near Macon) were between cavalry units, ranging far ahead of the infantry.

As Sherman marched, so did Georgia's slaves, following the armies to freedom. The bands of freedom-seekers got to be so large that they became an army unto themselves. This interfered with army operations and the soldiers' abilities to feed themselves—or at least the general officers thought so. At Ebenezer Creek, as he approached Savannah, Maj. Gen. Jefferson C. Davis (no relation to the Confederate president, improbable as his name is), one of Sherman's best combat officers and an expert duelist, pulled up the pontoon bridge as soon as his XV Corps crossed, leaving the black refugees behind to enjoy the tender mercies, if any, of pursuing Confederate cavalry.

When confronted, both Davis and Sherman ridiculed such tales as Rebel propaganda. But neither was a known advocate of the civil rights of African-Americans. No one was ever punished for the disaster at Ebenezer Creek, but Jefferson C. Davis never made major general in the regular army, much to his disappointment. The fault is usually credited to his killing another Union general in a Cincinnati hotel, but one wonders if the events at Ebenezer Creek did not haunt his career, just a little.

On December 13, Sherman's men assaulted the Confederate position at Ft. McAllister outside Savannah. They took the fort in 15 minutes, opening contact with the Union blockade fleet and the rest of the outside world. Behind them was a 50- to 60-mile-wide band of destruction, mostly military targets, claimed Sherman. But he saw civilian morale as a military target, which included a lot of wrecked and starving plantations and farms, beyond the usual ruined railroads and factories. But Sherman was not finished with the South. His next target was South Carolina, the seedbed of secession. The Carolinas Campaign (q.v.) would make the March to the Sea seem like a Sunday picnic by comparison.

MARKS' MILLS, BATTLE OF. *See* CAMDEN CAMPAIGN.

MARSH, C. P. *See* BUREAU OF INDIAN AFFAIRS SCANDAL.

MARTIAL LAW. *See* ARMY, U.S., AND RECONSTRUCTION.

MARYE'S HEIGHTS, BATTLE OF. *See* CHANCELLORSVILLE CAMPAIGN.

MARYLAND CAMPAIGN. In the wake of the Second Manassas Campaign (q.v.) in late August 1862, Gen. Robert E. Lee (q.v.) decided to invade Maryland even before his men had recovered from his previous victories.

There were reasons to move fast. The quicker the Rebels moved, the less time the defeated Yankees would have to reorganize. To defeat the Federals, it was necessary to draw them out of the Washington fortifications. An invasion of Maryland would do this, unlike anything else. Maryland was still distrusted by Northern authorities. Lee's presence there would allow the state to declare for the South. Moreover, Maryland had lots of food and storage to feed off of. Lee knew that Virginia needed a respite from the armies to harvest its own crops for the coming winter. Finally, never was Europe, especially Great Britain, so close to recognizing the Confederacy. A Rebel victory in Maryland would do the trick.

There were several problems with the invasion. The Union still held the lower Shenandoah at Harper's Ferry. Lee's army was exhausted and ill-equipped for an invasion. By subsisting off of the land, Lee might alienate the Marylanders more than woo them. Then many of Lee's men decided that they had enlisted to defend the South, not to invade the North. He would go North with fewer men than he had at any time so far. But Lee's arrival in Frederick demonstrated the real problem. No one came in to join the cause. By an accident of geography, the pro-Rebel parts of Maryland were off to the southeast of Washington along the Potomac or in areas of the Eastern Shore across the Chesapeake. Lee had arrived in the pro-Union part of the state. When Lee issued his proclamation for a freed state, nothing happened.

While Lee waited for Rebel Maryland in vain, President Abraham Lincoln (q.v.) knew what had to be done to meet the Confederate onslaught. Maj. Gen. George B. McClellan (q.v.) had to be sent out to rally Maj. Gen. John Pope's (q.v.) dispirited Union troops. Lincoln feared that McClellan would never fight with the army, but he would reorganize it as no one else could. Halleck went to work. How much of a miracle he accomplished in a matter of a week is up to speculation, depending on how disorganized the Army of the Potomac really was. But the job was done, and McClellan had his men fanned out west of Washington in short order, looking to pick a fight with Robert E. Lee and his men.

Meanwhile, Lee decided to consolidate his forces in the Great Valley west of the Catoctin Mountains. He withdrew from Frederick to Boonsboro, sending Maj. Gen. Stonewall Jackson (q.v.) to surround Harper's Ferry and round up the men there whom McClellan had begged Bvt. Maj. Gen. Henry W. Halleck (q.v.) to have withdrawn a week earlier. Jackson lay siege to the town, eventually taking 12,500 Yankees prisoner with scores of artillery, wagons, and thousands of small arms and ammunition.

As McClellan moved his army into Lee's abandoned camps at Frederick, luck handed the general a plum. There on the ground, wrapped around three precious cigars, was a paper with a heading, Special Orders No. 191, Army of Northern Virginia. It was the disposition of Lee's whole force, unit by unit. (*See* LEE'S "LOST ORDER.") McClellan had everything he needed to destroy Lee in short order—if "Little Mac" moved fast. And therein lay a problem. The Army of the Potomac never moved fast, especially under McClellan. But they would give it a try. He decided to wait until morning, not realizing that there were no Confederates holding the road crossing the mountains to Boonesboro.

McClellan sent a small force to strike Crampton's Gap to the south. Strangely, he did not make his main effort there, because it was on a direct route to save Harper's Ferry and lightly held. But the force moved slowly and did not push the Confederates hard, allowing Harper's Ferry to fall. The rest of McClellan's army assaulted the gaps on South Mountain on either side of the old National Road headed toward Boonesboro, now fortified by arriving Confederate troops. The result was an all-day battle won by the Yankees. It was the first Union victory in the East since Hanover Court House outside Richmond in May 1862.

All McClellan had to do was march to Sharpsburg, and he would stand between the wings of Lee's army. He outnumbered the Confederates combined by two to one. It would be a piece of cake. But McClellan stopped on the banks of Antietam Creek for two days, allowing Lee to gather his army at Sharpsburg to oppose him. Then Harper's Ferry surrendered, freeing much of Jackson's force to rejoin Lee. Finally, on September 17, 1862, McClellan moved. He crossed Antietam Creek north of Lee and attacked Jackson. He crossed the creek in the center and hit Maj. Gen. James Longstreet (q.v.). He set up his artillery where it could hit the Rebel positions without being hit back. The Rebels called the battle "Artillery Hell." But the carnage was dreadful on both sides.

All McClellan needed to do to win the day was to strike Lee's right flank near the Potomac. But his commander there, a loveable incompetent, Maj. Gen. Ambrose Burnside (q.v.), sat and stared at a stream that was fordable nearly anywhere and wondered how to cross. Finally, Burnside stormed the stone bridge that has ever since born his name. The troops charged for a keg of whiskey, military reasons being nonsensical to such veterans as they. Then Burnside had to assault an undermanned hill. By three in the afternoon, he had his act together, and the Union lines advanced on Sharpsburg. Lee looked on as his chief lieutenant of the field, Gen. Longstreet, helped load and fire the cannon. It was all over. Then at the last possible moment, Jackson's last division, his biggest, led by his most aggressive commander, Maj. Gen. A. Powell Hill, arrived on the Federals' southern flank. The regiments there were newcomers. They broke at the first volley. Burnside withdrew, leaving the field to the Rebels.

There is an old story that McClellan thought to send in his last unit, the V Corps under one of his best and most loyal subordinates, Bvt. Maj. Gen.

Fitz John Porter. But Porter whispered that he commanded the last unit of the last army of the Republic, or something like that. McClellan held off. Lee showed his contempt by defiantly holding the battlefield one more day, as if to dare McClellan to come on. Then he withdrew over the Potomac, slapping back McClellan's pursuit at Shepardstown Ford. Total casualties were around 25,000 on both sides—making September 17, 1862, the bloodiest single day's combat in the whole war.

Lincoln came out to visit McClellan. He wanted him to push on into Virginia, hunt Lee down. Instead, McClellan had had to suffer Brig. Gen. J. E. B. Stuart's (q.v.) Confederate cavalry ride around his whole army again, just as Stuart had done back in June during the Seven Days Campaign. In October, McClellan decided to move over the Potomac. In November, after the congressional by-elections, which had cost the Republicans (q.v.) many seats, Lincoln fired McClellan. The feared army uprising at the demise of the ever-popular "Little Mac" never materialized. Lincoln had finally taken control of McClellan's army, "McClellan's Bodyguard," as the president had once termed it, forever.

MASON AND SLIDELL. *See* DIPLOMACY, C.S.—CIVIL WAR; *TRENT AFFAIR.*

MAXIMILIAN IN MEXICO. Although the foreign policy of the United States was admittedly not the crucial issue facing the nation during Reconstruction, rating far behind the Southern question and the conquest of the American West, it had important implications for the future. It was during Reconstruction that the country took its first steps toward world power. One of the men most responsible was Secretary of State William Seward (q.v.), the Abraham Lincoln (q.v.) cabinet holdover, who had much domestic influence with President Andrew Johnson (q.v.) and almost uncontested mastery in foreign affairs. The rationale of much of Seward's policy was the Monroe Doctrine, that cardinal principle of American foreign policy, that no European encroachment in the New World would be countenanced. But the Civil War had turned American interest inward so much as to permit the invasion of Mexico by France, on the pretense that French claims arising from the constant, violent changes of government would not be paid unless Mexico were stabilized from the outside. This notion was given much creditability because Mexico had experienced 36 changes of government and 73 presidents in a mere 40 years of independence from Spain. In 1863, France (at first helped by Britain and Spain, who soon withdrew) invaded Mexico and installed the Austrian prince, Ferdinand Maximilian, as emperor of Mexico.

Most Mexicans, especially those interested in republican government, were unwilling to submit to this incursion from the outside. But until the end of the American Civil War, the French pretty much had driven President Benito Juárez and his supporters into the vastness of the Mexican north. There, they were cut off from much of the outside world, a process abetted by the Confederacy, which had hoped for French help on the diplomatic scene in exchange. After the war, mercenaries from both Union and Confederacy drifted south to fight on both sides of the Mexican Civil War. Seward had at first proposed a declaration of war against this act contrary to the Monroe Doctrine, but President Lincoln pointed out that one war at a time was enough and they proceeded to concentrate against the Confederates. The Mexican minister to the United States, Matías Romero, ably pushed the Lincoln administration to regard French invasion as a joint American problem. Just as Lincoln hoped to preserve democracy in the United States by crushing the South, Matías Romero pointed out it would be but half a victory should Juárez go under at the same time south of the border. Unfortunately, Union efforts to capture and hold Texas seemed doomed to defeat; indeed, the last land battle of the war was a Yankee defeat near Brownsville at Palmetto Ranch in May 1865.

Meanwhile, increasing losses in men and money and the maneuverings of Otto von Bismarck to unite the various German states into one kingdom under Prussia had caused France's Napoleon III to reconsider his Mexican venture. But he needed to somehow save face as he pulled out. The Lincoln (and later Andrew Johnson) administrations immediately sent 25,000 troops to the Texas border in the spring of 1865, not only to force Texas into surrendering, but with an eye to threatening the French across the Rio Grande. Dissatisfied with the slowness of negotiations for the removal of the 28,000 French soldiers supporting Maximilian, Maj. Gen. Philip Sheridan (q.v.) took a Federal cavalry contingent right through Texas to the border, creating a graphic realization of what could be done should France drag its feet. An actual raid across the Rio Grande below Brownsville by mercenaries with unofficial Union military support compounded the bleak picture awaiting France's Mexican venture.

In Washington, Matías Romero invited Lt. Gen. Ulysses S. Grant or Maj. Gen. William T. Sherman (qq.v.) to lead an expedition to relieve Juárez, and Grant spoke in favor of it. When he got Bvt. Maj. Gen. John Schofield (q.v.) to accept such a commission, Seward appointed Schofield to a diplomatic post, to prevent a military response. Seward told Schofield to make a nuisance of himself in Paris and tell Napoleon to get out of Mexico. But when Schofield got to France, Seward's minister there, John Bigelow, kept him from the government, probably by prior arrangement with Seward. But the point had been made—the French expedition was as good as over. In January 1866, Napoleon III agreed to a staged withdrawal over an 18-month period. Juárez immediately attacked the withdrawing French, using American military equipment somehow "lost" on the border and "recovered" by the Mexicans for just that purpose. Maximilian unfortunately decided that he had a princely obligation to stay behind to "save" Mexico from itself. The result was his capture and execution at Querétaro, north of Mexico City, in the spring of 1867. His wife, Carlotta, had gone to France to plead for French help, and when she heard of her husband's death, she went insane, dying in 1927.

McCARDLE, *EX PARTE* (1868). If the U.S. Supreme Court case Georgia *v.* Stanton (qq.v.) involved investigating whether it was actually a state and could bring suit, no such difficulty adhered to the litigation in *ex parte* McCardle, which concerned the rights of an individual and was fully within the court's jurisdiction. William H. McCardle was a very vocal newspaper editor in Vicksburg, Mississippi. He was unalterably opposed to the Military Reconstruction Acts (q.v.) and editorialized against them to the point of vituperation. His basic contention was, do not obey these laws, boycott them. He published lists of those whites who cooperated with the Federal authorities, that the town might properly ostracize them. Bvt. Maj. Gen. E. O. C. Ord, commanding the Fourth Military District (Mississippi and Arkansas), had him arrested and charged in front of a military tribunal with disturbing the peace and inciting insurrection. McCardle appealed his case to the U.S. Supreme Court, asking for a writ of *habeas corpus* (q.v.). It looked a lot like the Milligan (q.v.) case, except that there was no Civil War anywhere. If it were ruled upon on the same principles, much of the impact of Reconstruction would be nullified, as arguments before the court on the comprehensiveness and unconstitutionality of a military commander's civil powers under the Military Reconstruction Acts aptly showed.

Congress had gone through too much with President Andrew Johnson (q.v.) to allow a bunch of legal theorists sitting isolated from the realities of the world to derail its intent in Reconstruction. After a few false starts that were definitely too radical for most members, it added an amendment on a simple bill that allowed the Court to review certain laws. The amendment would negate the Court's right to hear appeals under the Habeas Corpus Act of 1867, the measure McCardle had used to sue the Army's carrying out of the Military Reconstruction Acts. Ironically, the act had been passed to protect freedmen and Army and Freedmen's Bureau (q.v.) officers from adverse action in hostile state courts. Now it was being used to protect one of their critics. This changed the case from one concerning Reconstruction and individual rights to one about the right of Congress to change the Supreme Court's appellate jurisdiction, a right guaranteed to Congress in the Constitution and something that the American Bar Association tried repeatedly to change in the 20th century through constitutional amendment, without success (the Court's original jurisdiction is unchangeable and also defined in the Constitution). The Court immediately put off a decision in the case until the following year, when it confirmed Congress' action without examining its motive and dropped the McCardle case completely without decision.

McCLELLAN, GEORGE B. (1826–1885) He had everything handed to him on a silver platter. George Brinton McClellan was born in Philadelphia, had a good education, possessed a fine mind, was handsome, read several modern and classical languages, and had an engaging personality and great energy. He graduated second in the class of 1846 after entering two years underage by special permission, was part of Bvt. Lt. Gen. Winfield Scott's (q.v.) staff in the War with Mexico, won three brevets for heroism, received a prestigious appointment to be among the American board of observers during the Crimean War, wrote an excellent and tactical report of operations there, and invented the cavalry saddle that bore his name and was used by American horse soldiers for nearly a century.

But the pre–Civil War army was no place for a young man as on-the-go as George B. McClellan. He resigned his commission to become a civil engineer and vice president of the Illinois Central Railroad at an unheard of salary for the time of $10,000 annually. One of his corporate lawyers was a relatively unknown Illinois politician named Abraham Lincoln (q.v.). When the war began, McClellan accepted the best position offered him, command of all Ohio state troops. He showed an immediate flare for the organization, administration, and training of men. He led his men south of the Ohio River, into what would become West Virginia, and won several key battles. At least McClellan got credit for the victories. He was rarely on the field. But he had good subordinates, like William C. Rosecrans and Joseph Jones Reynolds (qq.v.). They even defeated Virginia's top general, a man named Robert E. Lee (q.v.).

Then Lincoln called him to Washington. George B. McClellan was just thirty-five years old. He was known by all as the "Young Napoleon." After all, he had won in the mountains just like his namesake had done in Italy, decades before. Initially, McClellan was just the man for the job. He was arrogant and haughty, as only the rich can be, leaving a waiting President Lincoln standing unrecognized as McClellan went past his parlor door and up to bed. But he created a wonderful army, the Army of the Potomac. Again, his ability to organize, administer, and train men shone forth. He loved his men. They loved him and his flashy staff, peopled with flashy foreign dignitaries. He was the only general whom the soldiers would drop everything for to cheer as he passed by, always at a gallop. It would be McClellan's force that would win the war in the East—the one that he set up that winter of 1861. It would be his greatest contribution to the war effort. But he never seemed to realize that it was the nation's army, not his personal bodyguard.

McClellan could get away with his arrogance, provided he produced victories. But he did not. His plans were brilliant. His execution was usually good, but at times slow. But his fighting of battles was horrible. McClellan was always creating problems for himself. He overestimated the size of the Confederate armies facing him, relying on the already exaggerated reports of Alan Pinkerton, famous detective and McClellan's head of military intelligence. He delayed advancing upon the Confederates in front of Washington in 1861 until they had withdrawn, and the nation found out all those enemy cannon were painted tree trunks.

McClellan countered with a fabulous plan to attack Richmond in the Peninsula Campaign (q.v.). Then he allowed the Rebels to finesse him into a prolonged siege, when a quick attack would have won the day. He got trapped away from his base in front of Richmond, changed it to another location, outwitting Robert E. Lee, no mean feat. But he got bogged down writing President Lincoln political advice in his Harrison's Landing letter (q.v.) and lost his army as Lincoln withdrew it and gave it to Maj. Gen. John Pope (q.v.).

When Pope lost the Battle of Second Manassas (q.v.), who but McClellan could ride out to the defeated, dejected army coming in from Centerville and restore its morale by his mere appearance? And it was "Little Mac" who led that revitalized army west out of Washington to fight the Battle of Antietam Creek, the bloodiest single day's combat of the war. His victory there permitted Lincoln to issue the preliminary Emancipation Proclamation (q.v.).

But the problem was what McClellan did not do. He failed to retake the initiative from Robert E. Lee during the Seven Days Campaign (q.v.) after administering a defeat to the Confederates at Mechanicsville. He did the same after administering another defeat to Lee at Malvern Hill. Either move might have won the capture of Richmond. But the worst was Antietam Creek. After decimating Lee's army, which numbered less than half of his own force, McClellan refused to send his last corps into the fight to win and let Lee stare him down the following day, before the Confederates defiantly withdrew across the Potomac without being molested. Then he saw the Confederate cavalry ride around his whole army and get away untouched, just as they had done on the Peninsula, three months earlier. He magnified the reasons why he could not advance. Lincoln removed him at once after the election of 1862 (q.v.), even though he feared an army rebellion might result.

Then in the election of 1864 (q.v.), McClellan accepted the nomination of the Democratic Party (q.v.) for president, running on a peace platform, which he rejected. It was truly his public Waterloo. Not even the men who had cheered him as he rode by just two years earlier voted for him. Indeed, it was the soldiers' vote that defeated him. McClellan retired to Europe, but returned to be the administrator of the New York City docks and governor of the state of New Jersey. At the end of his life he wrote *McClellan's Own Story*, an excellent defense of his military career.

McDONALD, JOHN. *See* GRANT, ULYSSES S., ADMINISTRATION—SCANDALS.

McDOWELL, BATTLE OF. *See* SHENANDOAH VALLEY CAMPAIGN, FIRST (JACKSON'S).

MEADE, GEORGE G. (1815–1872). Born of American parents in Cádiz, Spain, George Meade received his appointment to West Point from Pennsylvania. He graduated in the upper half of the class of 1835 and served a year in the Seminole War before resigning to become a civil engineer for a railroad. Meade continued to work as an engineer, charting the mouth of the Mississippi, and as a surveyor on the northeastern boundary between the United States and Canada. In 1842, he rejoined the army as a topographical engineer. He served on the staffs of Maj. Gen. Zachary Taylor and Bvt. Lt. Gen. Winfield Scott (qq.v.) in Texas and Mexico and continued as a military engineer after the War with Mexico, serving mainly on the Great Lakes.

In 1861, Meade was made a brigade commander in the Pennsylvania Reserve Corps, even though he had little experience working with troops. He was a hawk-nosed man with a hot temper. A run-in with Meade was akin to meeting a snapping turtle, some said. He fought in the Seven Days Campaign (q.v.) and was wounded at Gaines' Mill. Recovering, he served in the Second Manassas Campaign and in the Maryland Campaign (qq.v.), advancing to division command. His unit was the only division to break through Confederate lines at Fredericksburg (q.v.) on the Rebel left flank. He advanced to take over the V Corps in the Chancellorsville Campaign (q.v.).

Because he could not have presidential ambitions, as he was born outside the United States, Meade was given command of the Army of the Potomac during the Pennsylvania Campaign (q.v.) on the eve of the battle of Gettysburg. He fought and won the battle using his predecessor's staff. Meade would continue to command the Army of the Potomac from the 1864 Richmond Campaign, to the siege of Petersburg, through the Appomattox Campaign (qq.v.), Lt. Gen. U. S. Grant giving all orders to the troops through him. He commanded the Military Division of the Atlantic from the end of the war until his death from pneumonia prompted by effects from his old war wound, with the exception of a brief stint as commander of the Third Military District (Florida, Georgia, and Alabama) during Reconstruction.

MECHANICSVILLE, BATTLE OF. *See* SEVEN DAYS CAMPAIGN.

MEDICAL DIRECTORS OR SURGEONS GENERAL, CONFEDERATE. Both Confederate and Federal medical departments were organized on the same basis. The only difference, as with so much of the Civil War, was that the Provisional Government of the Confederacy had to start from scratch. It did this by President Jefferson Davis (q.v.) appointing Dr. David C. DeLeon as surgeon general. Underfunded from the beginning, DeLeon used much of his money to purchase several Richmond buildings as military hospitals. With the battle of First Manassas (q.v.) in 1861, these buildings were soon filled to overflowing. At this juncture, Dr. Samuel Preston Moore arrived in Richmond and volunteered to help out.

Noting that Moore had outranked DeLeon in the old army, and probably dissatisfied with DeLeon's tenure, Davis made Moore surgeon general. DeLeon was kept on as an adjunct officer in the medical department. Moore instituted immediate medical examinations for all surgeons and assistant surgeons, getting rid of the worst in the service. He also received more money from the Confederate Congress and began a major hospital building program, the most important of which was the construction of Chimborazo Hospital east of Richmond. As with all Confederate hospitals, the various wards were devoted to the wounded from one state. The five wards at Chimborazo held wounded from Virginia, the Carolinas, Georgia, and Alabama.

The most important Confederate contribution to field medicine came in the First Shenandoah Valley Campaign (q.v.), when Dr. Hunter McGuire persuaded Maj. Gen. Thomas J. Jackson (q.v.) to treat captured Union medical officers as noncombatants and not liable to be sent to prison in Richmond. Instead, they were allowed to return to Union lines. This principle was later extended to chaplains and codified in the Union Lieber Code rules of war in 1863.

By this time, the Confederate medical system was deteriorating. Supplies grew short, medical furlough became a ruse to avoid further service, supervision of the widely scattered hospitals became impossible, and coordination between departments increased in difficulty as Yankee invasions separated communications. Despite this, Moore managed to vaccinate every Confederate soldier against smallpox and rely on captured supplies and blockade running to keep going. He also published a *Confederate Medical and Surgical Journal* to keep doctors informed as to advances in medical care.

There seems to have been little overall difference in medical care, North or South, during the war. But historians point to two campaigns where medical care may have made a difference in who won. One of these was the Vicksburg Campaign in 1863 (q.v.), where Maj. Gen. Ulysses S. Grant (q.v.) had one-fourth of his men out with illness, compared to one-half of the Confederates. This was made possible by a surplus of medical supplies, especially quinine, and the constant exercise that Grant gave his men during the winter as he tried attempt after attempt to take Vicksburg. Lt. Gen. John C. Pemberton's (q.v.) Confederates sat in garrison and grew debilitated from malaria and weakened physically until in the spring, his army could not keep up with Grant's movements.

The other was the Atlanta Campaign of 1864 (q.v.). Here, Maj. Gen. William T. Sherman's (q.v.) army was the healthiest army in the field on either side during the war. Gen. Joseph Johnston's (q.v.) Confederates, however, wasted away from a lack of quinine and an excess of medical furloughs. Up to 30,000 men were absent from the ranks when needed at Atlanta. Of course many did need to be sent home, but not that many. Johnston could have made good use of them in the field to stymie Sherman, much as Gen. Robert E. Lee (q.v.) held up Grant in Virginia. See also AMBULANCE SERVICES AND TRIAGE; DISEASE; NURSES; WOUNDS.

MEDICAL DIRECTORS OR SURGEONS GENERAL, UNION. The Union had a rougher time of medical administration than the Rebels. On May 15, 1860, Surgeon General Dr. Thomas Lawson, a veteran of the War of 1812, died from natural causes. He was replaced by the next man in the command chain, Dr. Clement A. Finley. None of the higher officers in the medical department seemed to realize what the Civil War portended in the scope of casualties. Indeed, Finley proudly told Congress that he had failed to spend all the monies appropriated for the fiscal year ending June 10, 1861.

But the Battle of First Manassas (q.v.) in August 1861 was the undoing of Finley's ordered world. He received fully the blame for the disastrous treatment of the wounded, a process that lasted for weeks. He actively opposed the works of the U.S. Sanitary Commission (q.v.) and women nurse (q.v.) volunteers. They successfully moved to have Finley replaced by Dr. William A. Hammond.

Under the authority granted him by Congress through the Medical Reform Law of 1862, Hammond instituted a medical examination system to cull the incompetent doctors from military service. It began with a two-hour oral exam on everything under the sun and culminated with a three-hour written exam on medicine and medical procedure of the day. He announced that his department would keep extensive medical records of the war and publish them after the victory. He approved and helped to implement the Letterman system (q.v.) of field hospitals, ambulance coordination, and triage. And he enlarged the hospital system of the army, erecting many new buildings on the pavilion system that kept each ward open to as much ventilation as possible.

Hammond's weakness as surgeon general involved his continual quarrel with Union Secretary of War Edwin McM. Stanton (q.v.). Opposed to Hammond's appointment because the Sanitary Commission had gone over his head to President Abraham Lincoln (q.v.), Stanton and Hammond argued over the scandalous treatment of the wounded at the Second Manassas Campaign (q.v.) in August 1862, which Hammond blamed on Stanton personally. Never one to give in gracefully, Stanton bided his time until Hammond made a mistake. Sending Hammond on an extensive inspection tour, Stanton found a replacement in Hammond's own office, the sycophantic Dr. Joseph K. Barnes. When Hammond came back, Stanton suggested that he retire; Hammond refused. Stanton then had him court-martialed for misappropriation of funds. He had cut through the normal red tape to send beef to various hospitals. That was a no-no in Stanton's world.

Barnes took over permanently after Hammond's leaving the service for private practice in New York City. He completely reorganized the medical bureau, bringing in his own people from all over the occupied South. He appointed new men to handle the unbelievably large number of casualties from the 1864 Richmond Campaign and the Atlanta Campaign. And he ultimately autopsied the body of John Wilkes Booth after he died, pursued by Union cavalry after the assassination of President Abraham Lincoln. He also saw to it that the *Surgical and Medical History* planned by Hammond was published in six massive volumes after the war. *See also* AMBULANCE SERVICES AND TRIAGE; DISEASE; NURSES; UNITED STATES SANITARY COMMISSION; WOUNDS.

MEDILL, JOSEPH. *See* GRANT, ULYSSES S., ADMINISTRATION—DOMESTIC POLICIES.

MEMPHIS, BATTLE OF. *See* SHILOH CAMPAIGN.

MEMPHIS RACE RIOT, MAY 1, 1866. After the race riot at Norfolk (q.v.), Virginia, the next major outbreak of violence was at Memphis, Tennessee, two weeks later. As with Norfolk, Memphis was a bustling port whose black population had increased dramatically, upsetting the traditional racial balance. Indeed refugees, black and white, had nearly doubled the city's inhabitants during and right after the war. There was a large city bond debt that necessitated raising taxes; an economic recession; and a vigorous competition between African-Americans and city whites, particularly Irish, for laboring jobs. There was also another item. The city was garrisoned by black United States soldiers from a relatively ill-disciplined regiment, whom the whites blamed for every disturbance. Local police, white only and predominantly Irish in membership, were not understanding nor gentle in their treatment of alleged or real black lawbreakers. It was a situation ripe for trouble.

The riot came on the heels of African-American complaints of police brutality. A crowd of protesters was met by police, who arrested certain ringleaders. Blacks fired weapons into the arresting officers, who returned fire. General volleys followed from both sides. The police retreated until later in the day, when they returned reinforced by a posse and the county sheriff. The demonstrators were gone, but the residents of a black shanty town were readily available. Revenge was exacted without mercy. As local politicians had criticized the Army, the local commandant refused to interfere with the 160 white soldiers in the garrison headquarters. He finally issued an order two days later for the mob to disperse after Freedmen's Bureau (q.v.) schools and personnel became mob targets. The mob dispersed in the face of threatened troop deployment and the riot, dubbed the "Memphis Massacre" up North, subsided. All sides, including the Army, protested their innocence during the ensuing investigation. The city newspapers justified it as necessary to protect white civilization. The tragedy of Memphis, however, disappeared in a real massacre at New Orleans (q.v.) two months later.

MERRIMACK, U.S.S. A Federal frigate burned in the abandonment of Norfolk's Gosport Navy Yard to the state of Virginia. It was raised and became the keel and lower part of the Confederate ironclad, C.S.S. *Virginia. See also MONITOR*, U.S.S.

MERRYMAN, *EX PARTE* (1861). During the Civil War, with the single exception of *ex parte* Merryman, in which Chief Justice Roger B. Taney railed against military arrest outside the civilian court system of non-military personnel suspected of holding disloyal opinions, the U.S. Supreme Court had essentially endorsed the Yankee war effort. John Merryman was part of what would later be called a Copperhead (q.v.) group that was accused of burning railroad trestles between Baltimore and Philadelphia to prevent Union reinforcement of Washington in early 1861. He was arrested, imprisoned in old Ft. McHenry of "Star Spangled Banner" fame, and denied right to the writ of *habeas corpus* (q.v.). Chief Justice Roger B. Taney (a Marylander) issued an opinion (*ex parte* Merryman) while on circuit in 1861, that military arrest could not take place and military commissions could not convene while civil courts were in session and operating freely, but the Army ignored him, and President Abraham Lincoln (q.v.) refused to enforce the decision. The Merryman opinion would be restated by the whole court in the 1866 decision *ex parte* Milligan (q.v.), two years after Taney died, but the war was over and the damage done by then. Martial law and military arrest were so effective that military prisons (labeled the "American Bastille" by dissenters, in reference to Lincoln's reproducing the tyranny of French kings in Cardinal Armand de Richelieu's prison of terror) overflowed with political prisoners and a special board, consisting of Bvt. Maj. Gen. John A. Dix and retired New York judge Edwards Pierrepont, had to be convened to investigate the cases and free those not openly pro-Confederate.

MESILLA CONVENTION. *See* SECESSION AND THE CREATION OF ARIZONA TERRITORY.

MIDDLEBURG, BATTLE OF. *See* PENNSYLVANIA CAMPAIGN.

MIDDLETOWN, BATTLE OF. *See* SHENANDOAH VALLEY CAMPAIGN, FIRST (JACKSON'S).

MILITARY GOVERNMENT. *See* ARMY, U.S., AND RECONSTRUCTION.

MILITARY RECONSTRUCTION ACT, FIRST, MARCH 2, 1867. Passed the same day as the Command of the Army Act and the Tenure of Office Act (q.v.), the First Military Reconstruction Act divided the South into five military districts, each commanded by a major general appointed by the president. The First Military District was the old state of Virginia; the Second Military District was composed of the former states of North and South Carolina; the Third Military District was comprised of the prewar states of Georgia, Florida, and Alabama; the Fourth Military District had in its boundaries the one-time states of Arkansas and Mississippi; while the Fifth Military District included the old states of Louisiana and Texas. Tennessee alone of the former Confederacy was excluded, because it had approved the Fourteenth Amendment (q.v.), which the rest of the South had rejected. The commanders of the military districts were to protect the civil and property rights of all persons; to suppress all insurrection, disorder, and violence; and to punish or cause to be punished all criminal actions. They could use existing civil and criminal courts, Freedmen's Bureau (q.v.) courts, or military tribunals as they felt necessary.

Existing state governments, established under the Andrew Johnson (q.v.) plan of Reconstruction, were declared to be provisional only and were warned not to interfere with the new reconstructing authorities. Each state was to call an election for delegates to a constitutional convention. The convention was to draw up a new state constitution and provide for universal male suffrage, bringing the state's organic laws into agreement with the results of the war in all respects. Once the acts of the convention were voted for by a majority of the registered voters and a new state government elected, the state legislature would approve of the Fourteenth Amendment. Then the reconstructed states could send their duly elected representatives and two senators to Washington. Congress would review the process and, if satisfied, admit the new state back into the Union. Of the four Military Reconstruction Acts, only this one did not receive President Johnson's veto.

MILITARY RECONSTRUCTION ACT, FOURTH, MARCH 11, 1868. This measure corrected a fault in the first Military Reconstruction Act (q.v.), which stated that constitutions had to be approved by a majority of those registered. This act changed that to a majority of those voting. Whites in several Southern states had registered in large numbers and then refused to vote on the state constitutions, causing the one in Alabama to fail after several close calls in other states. This act marked the desire of Congress to get the Southern states back into the Union (unlike before, when keeping them out was the rule) so that those black voters could assist in electing a Republican (q.v.) president in 1868. The vote up North promised to be close, making Southern blacks critical to a Republican White House. By the time of the election only Virginia, Mississippi, and Texas had fallen behind because of local squabbles in the process and could not vote in the national elections.

MILITARY RECONSTRUCTION ACT, SECOND, MARCH 23, 1867. Because the first measure did not detail the procedure of registering state voters, and the Southern governors dragged their feet in calling for the new convention election, the Second Military Reconstruction Act allowed the military commanders to go ahead without the approval of the governors. A general registration of all voters, including blacks males, was ordered. Voters had to take an oath of future loyalty and not be proscribed in any other manner. The state conventions were to have the same number of delegates as represented in the lower house of the state legislature in 1860, and the commanding general would apportion them according to the 1867 registration figures. The commanding general would appoint as many three-man registration boards as he thought necessary to accomplish the task in short order. The delegates were to assemble within 60 days of their election. This measure was passed over President Andrew Johnson's veto.

MILITARY RECONSTRUCTION ACT, THIRD, JULY 13, 1867. This law made district commanders, registrars, or any person appointed to office under military appointment free from obeying the orders or opinions of an executive official of the United States government. Registrars could disfranchise anybody, whether he could take the oath of future loyalty or not, for prior allegations of disloyal activities. Military commanders could remove from office any state officials who obstructed the Reconstruction process and appoint loyal men in their stead. This law was brought about because of conservative interpretations of the first two Military Reconstruction Acts (qq.v.) by Attorney General of the United States Henry Stanbery that military officers had no power to deny registration or remove local officials, and the inability of military commanders to replace obstructionists in office with loyal men. Congress told commanders and their appointees to be liberal in their interpretations under this law. This measure was passed over President Andrew Johnson's veto.

MILITARY RECONSTRUCTION ACTS. As a part of Radical Reconstruction (q.v.), Congress passed four acts that put supervision of the Reconstruction process in the hands of the U.S. Army that was occupying the South. Military commanders saw to it that the individual Southern states, called military districts now, complied with congressional desires.

MILLER v. UNITED STATES (1871). Asked to rule on the validity of the Confiscation Acts (q.v.), the Supreme Court approved of the confiscation of property as a legitimate purpose of war. But many suspected that the Court would rethink many of these issues (excepting confiscation, although the government would find it politic to return much seized property as part of its pardon policy) after the Rebel surrender.

MILLIGAN *ET AL., EX PARTE* (1866). The problem of the suspension of the writ of *habeas corpus* (q.v.) was fully indicated to Congress and the nation in a wartime case that concerned the activities of an Indiana Copperhead (q.v.) and Peace Democrat, Lamdin P. Milligan, who had been a member of the secret pro-Confederate "Order of American Knights." As with most secret American orders, it seemed that there were more government informants than there were actual members. In any case, tipped off as to Milligan's activities, the Union army arrested him and several compatriots for plotting to free Confederate soldiers being held as prisoners of war and spiriting them back into Confederate jurisdiction.

Tried before a military tribunal, Milligan and two others were sentenced to hang. Naturally they appealed the decision, requesting a writ of *habeas corpus* and demanding a civilian trial. Because of the power of the Democratic Party (q.v.) in Indiana, even the Republican (q.v.) governor who had spearheaded the drive for a military trial (the army was not real happy to get involved) asked that the executions be deferred until the appeal was heard. In *ex parte* Milligan *et al.* (1866), the U.S. Supreme Court ruled that Milligan and his pals had been wrongfully convicted because the military court had no jurisdiction since civil courts were operating and available in Indiana despite the war. This also held true in the occupied postwar South and threatened Army and Freedmen's Bureau (q.v.) jurisdictions, which regularly decided cases on behalf of blacks wronged by whites. Milligan later sued the military officer who arrested him and won damages of a trifling amount.

MILL SPRINGS. *See* SHILOH CAMPAIGN.

MINE RUN. *See* PENNSYLVANIA CAMPAIGN.

MINNIE BALL. *See* LOAD-IN-NINE-TIMES.

MINOR *v*. HAPPERSETT (1875). Virginia L. Minor had been refused the right to register to vote on grounds she was a woman. She appealed under the Fourteenth and Fifteenth Amendments and the Enforcement Acts (qq.v.), but was denied registration as she was not a black male under the Fifteenth Amendment, and the provisions of the other measures were deemed too vague to be enforceable.

MISSIONARY RIDGE, BATTLE OF. *See* CHATTANOOGA CAMPAIGN.

MISSISSIPPI PLAN. There were two Mississippi plans. The first was in the mid-1870s and involved redeeming the state from the Republicans (q.v.) by force and intimidation. The second was in 1890, when the state disfranchised black voters in its new constitution by circumventing the Fifteenth Amendment (q.v.) through such devices as literacy tests, understanding clauses, and poll taxes.

MISSISSIPPI, STATE OF, *v*. JOHNSON (1867). Evidence of the Supreme Court's independence was not long in coming after passage of the Military Reconstruction Acts (q.v.). The provisional governors of the Southern states began a concentrated attack against the laws and asked that the executive branch be enjoined from carrying them out. Governor William L. Sharkey of Mississippi filed a suit asking that President Andrew Johnson (q.v.) refrain from carrying out the dictates of the Military Reconstruction Acts. But in Mississippi *v*. Johnson (1867), the Court refused to issue the order, claiming that the question was not a constitutional one that lay in the Court's domain. The president had done his best to evade the enforcement of the laws by using the constitutional remedy available to him, the veto. It was not the purpose of the Court to tell a co-equal branch of government how to carry out the laws of Congress. The next case would involve a lawsuit to enjoin Secretary of War Edwin McM. Stanton, Georgia *v*. Stanton (qq.v.).

MISSISSIPPI VALLEY EXPERIMENT. As Union forces invaded the Mississippi Valley in late 1862, they encountered large numbers of slaves, who automatically became free under the provisions of the Second Confiscation Act (q.v.). Aware of the promise of freedom, blacks flocked to the protection of Union army camps. By November 1862, the refugee situation threatened to get out of hand. Maj. Gen. Ulysses S. Grant (q.v.), under whose jurisdiction the plantation areas of Northern Mississippi and West Tennessee lay, issued Special Orders No. 15, which authorized Chaplain John Eaton (q.v.) of the 27th Ohio Volunteers to organize the African-Americans into companies to be fed, clothed, and cared for. Eaton was to work the contrabands (q.v.) in abandoned fields at Corinth, Mississippi, and Grand Junction, Tennessee, where the largest camps of blacks were. Grant's main concerns were military, but he also was cognizant of other problems like competing interests among speculators, soldiers, and land owners; ideological concerns for the freedmen's futures; and the moral concern for racial justice. Eaton put the blacks to work gathering corn, cotton, and chopping wood, and introduced a wage labor system for all local plantations still occupied by their Southern owners. Whatever proceeds flowed from this labor went to the Department of the Treasury.

After the Emancipation Proclamation (q.v.) in January 1863, President Abraham Lincoln (q.v.) decided to affirm what had been done locally by several commanders and enroll potential black soldiers into units that became the United States Colored Troops. Lincoln sent Brig. Gen. Lorenzo Thomas, the adjutant general of the Army, to the Mississippi Valley to handle the enlistments. (Eventually some 180,000 blacks served the Union war effort, with 134,000 from the slave states alone). As he enlisted soldiers, Thomas looked into the possibility of creating a more general and permanent labor system than Eaton's. Like Eaton, Thomas decided to hire out all blacks for wages. But the farms would be managed by private investors, rather than the government. Thomas' system led to much corruption—dishonest deductions for food and clothing, stolen wages, and physical abuse.

In October 1863, General Thomas had had enough. He promulgated a whole new set of rules. All abandoned property owned by Rebels was to be seized and leased out to allegedly loyal men. Southerners still on their property were required to take on a loyal man as a business partner. Given the risks of planting when levees were broken, the seizure of all standing cotton until the owner was proved loyal, and Rebel retaliation, most landowners gladly leased their land to Yankees.

To protect the leased plantations from Rebel military, local Federal garrisons were to provide military aid, and blacks were to be enrolled as home guards. If a loyal lessee were robbed by Confederate marauders, a like amount of goods or crops would be seized from the nearest disloyal person (one who had not or could not take the oath). If a loyal lessee were killed, an assessment of $10,000 would be levied on all disloyal plantation owners within 30 miles to defray costs to his family. Since the lease and labor area was so big, Thomas' loyal plantations were hard to protect. On the 95 safest loyal operations alone, the Rebels managed to carry off and re-enslave 1,000 blacks and steal 2,300 head of horses and mules.

In the spring of 1864, after an adverse report by its agent, William Yeats, the Department of the Treasury came in to reform Thomas' system, which seemed to attract the corrupt, venal, and fraudulent, interested merely in profit over the well-being of the African-American workers and their families.

Yeats and another treasury man, William P. Mellon, instituted the Yeats–Mellon system, a collection of plantations (one per treasury district) where blacks could concentrate for mutual protection and negotiated wage employment as free laborers. But according to Thomas, employers refused to hire any but the best of hands, actually increasing those on the dole. President Lincoln stepped in and ordered the Army and the Treasury to cooperate under one plan, jointly developed.

The result was Special Orders No. 9 of March 11, 1864, issued through Thomas' headquarters. It created a three-tier system with various levels of responsibility to the Army (supervisory under the provost marshals), employers (who had to pay overtime for Sunday work, not deduct more than $3 per month for clothing, and permit the freedmen to grow truck in their own small gardens), and freedmen (had to stay on the plantation, be obedient laborers, and work "from day clean [*i.e.*, as soon as one could see] to first dark"). Wages were cut in half from the Yeats–Mellon plan, one-half being held back until the crop was harvested and shipped and to cover any offenses against management. This system lasted until the newly established Freedmen's Bureau (q.v.) took over in 1865.

MISSOURI CAMPAIGN (1861–1862). Like many border slave states, Missouri was unsure of either the pro-Southern quasi-secession stance of John C. Breckinridge (q.v.) or the "black Republican" reputation of his opponent, Abraham Lincoln (q.v.). Missourians preferred the candidates who stood for compromise, Stephen A. Douglas (q.v.) or John Bell. Thus when the crisis of Union came after Lincoln's election, Missouri was badly divided, but most stood in the middle, wanting neutrality or compromise.

Unfortunately for peace in Missouri, the extremes were quite influential. On the unconditional Union side were Frank Blair, Jr., scion of the father who had been one of Andrew Jackson's advisors, and Capt. Nathaniel Lyon, commander of the Federal arsenal and garrison at St. Louis. These men had as the base of their support the antislavery Germans, who had immigrated to the city in the past 10 years and comprised the loyal militia.

The other extreme was made up of the secessionists, led by the state's Lieutenant Governor Thomas Reynolds, who lobbied for immediate disunion. In the middle stood Governor Claiborne Fox Jackson, in favor of secession but wisely aware that to push hard would guarantee Missouri stayed in the Union, and Sterling Price (q.v.), former governor, militia commander in the War with Mexico, and planter, who wanted secession only as a last resort to Yankee invasion.

Under Reynolds' incessant pushing, the state legislature called for a state convention to consider secession (q.v.). Led by men like Price, the convention turned down secession (98 to 1) and a second proposal for Missouri to follow any other border slave states out of the Union in the future. But Governor Jackson firmly rejected President Lincoln's call for troops after the Battle of Ft. Sumter (q.v.). Instead, he called up the state militia to assert Missouri's sovereignty, if necessary.

The militia camped outside St. Louis, a definite threat to Blair and Lyon's Unionist hopes. They flew Confederate flags and named their tented streets "Beauregard" and "Jeff Davis." Lyon had the camp thoroughly scouted—rumor later had the red-bearded Lyon driving through the camp in person, in a heavy veil and skirts, disguised as a lady selling eggs—and attacked it by surprise on May 10, 1861, the day the men were supposed to go home. Arresting all of the militia men with his regulars and the German volunteers, Lyon marched them through St. Louis as prisoners. A mob of pro-Southern citizens gather and jeered Lyon and his men. The usual shot was fired, and when the smoke had cleared, 28 were dead, including women and children.

Price was outraged and joined the secession side, Jackson appointing him major general. The state legislature passed a Military Bill to recruit the militia to its fullest under Price's tutelage. Reynolds wanted the legislature to initiate secession, but this was illegal—the convention had to do it, and it had gone out of session. At this moment, Brig. Gen. William S. Harney, a West Pointer and a Tennessean who had married into a pro-slave St. Louis family years before, took command of all of Missouri for the Federal government, superseding Lyon. He invited Price to come to St. Louis and talk compromise. Price responded favorably at once.

On May 21, the Harney–Price Agreement was negotiated, with both sides agreeing not to initiate military action. This angered the extremists on both sides, but pleased most Missourians. Blair quickly got the Lincoln administration to remove Harney from Missouri, putting Lyon back in power. Prominent citizens asked them to hold off and talk to Price once again. Lyon responded with a safe conduct for Price from Jefferson City to St. Louis and back. All parties met at the Planter's Hotel on June 11. After four hours of heated argument, Lyons (with Blair's connivance) told Price that *his* intransigence meant war. An angry Price went back to Jefferson, prepared to defend Missouri from Yankee occupation.

Lyon wasted no time in advancing to secure the rest of the state. He occupied Jefferson City and defeated Missouri guardsmen at Booneville and Carthage. Although the Confederates were reluctant to support a man as mercurial as Price had been in his allegiances, they did order Brig. Gen. Ben McCulloch, in charge of troops in Arkansas, to assist Price, if it would help secure Arkansas from eventual Federal attack. The two men joined forces in southwestern Missouri on July 29.

A new Union general in charge of Missouri, Maj. Gen. John C. Frémont (q.v.), former Republican (q.v.) presidential candidate in 1856, ordered Lyons to retreat in front of a Rebel gathering that outnumbered him two to one. Lyons refused. On August 6, after Price relinquished his independent command to McCulloch (whom he considered much less able than he), the Confederate force encamped at Wilson's Creek near Springfield.

Faced by the same problems that haunted the Battle of First Manassas (q.v.), the expiration of most of his men's enlistments, Lyon attacked the Confederate camp at Wilson's Creek on August 10. At first the Union attack around the Rebel right flank went well. Then the 3rd Louisiana Infantry stalled Lyon's progress, eventually driving the attackers from the field. But the main thrust at Oak Hill turned into a shooting match, with both sides losing heavily. McCulloch took the Louisianans and some Arkansans and extended his line to the left until they outflanked that Yankee line. Lyon fell during this episode, and the Federals soon withdrew. Losses were 1,100 for the Confederates against 1,200 for the outnumbered Bluecoats.

The disorganized retreat of the Union army left western Missouri open for a Confederate counterthrust. Leaving McCulloch behind to defend Arkansas, Price and the Missourians advanced on Lexington. Although the Federal garrison had a chance to retreat, its commander, Col. James A. Mulligan, refused. Instead, he fortified the town around the Masonic College and fought it out. On September 19 and 20, the Confederates first invested the Federal position and then attacked, rolling massive hemp bales in front of themselves as movable cover. Expecting relief that never came, Mulligan surrendered. Price paroled the 3,500 troops and held Mulligan himself, who refused parole.

Meanwhile, Frémont took the field with a rejuvenated Union army, forcing Price to retire lest he be cut off. The Missourians retreated all the way into Arkansas, unable to halt Frémont's larger force. He would soon retreat, replaced because of his attempt to free Missouri's slaves, against Lincoln administration policy at the time. But by winter, Brig. Gen. Samuel Curtis took command and returned, invading Arkansas itself. In response, Richmond decided that the separate commands of Price and McCulloch needed to be put under the control of one man, Maj. Gen. Earl Van Dorn.

A gutsy man liked by officers and men alike, Van Dorn saw the Federal invasion as an opportunity. As the Rebels moved forward, Curtis retreated to Pea Ridge, an outstanding geographical feature in northern Arkansas, to make a stand. In a two-day battle (March 7–8, 1862), the Confederates attacked around both sides of Pea Ridge, McCulloch losing his life on the first day and his men being crushed by superior Federal artillery. Price advanced upon Elkhorn Tavern the same day, only to be driven back in the same manner the following day. Pea Ridge had allowed Curtis to fight both Rebel columns independently and beat them both. The Yankees lost 1,400 and the Rebels suffered 800 total casualties.

Van Dorn had had enough. He retreated back to Van Buren, on the Arkansas River. There, on March 23, he and Price received orders from Gen. Albert Sidney Johnston (q.v.) to come across the Mississippi River to stop Federal attacks in the Shiloh Campaign (q.v.). After a summer of desultory skirmishing and guerrilla warfare, a Trans-Mississippi Confederate specialty, the newly reorganized Confederate troops in Arkansas came under the control of Maj. Gen. Thomas C. Hindman. Disinclined to allow the Federals to go into winter quarters, Hindman moved on their widely scattered garrisons in northern Arkansas and southwestern Missouri. But Curtis sent James G. Blunt's division into the field, and Blunt slapped back Hindman's cavalry advance at Cane Hill on November 28.

Realizing that Blunt, now below Fayetteville, was well forward of the main Federal force in Missouri and liable to be cut off, Hindman quickly recovered and moved north again. If he could hit Blunt before Brig. Gen. Francis Herron could come south from Springfield to succor him, Hindman could win a cheap victory. But Herron had received orders from Curtis to go to Blunt's relief. He came on at a pace of 35 miles a day, his men eating their rations raw as they marched.

Hindman struck Blunt late in the afternoon of December 6. Then Hindman heard of Herron's approach. He decided to leave a small cavalry covering force to occupy Blunt and attack Herron before the latter expected it. The next day, Hindman and Herron met at Prairie Grove Church near Fayetteville. Hindman did well initially, but suddenly he stopped and took up a defensive position. Several of his Arkansas conscript regiments had refused to advance. This allowed Blunt, who had heard the fighting, to march the eight miles and hit Hindman in the flank just after he had repelled several attacks from Herron and was about to launch a counterattack of his own.

The Rebels managed to halt Blunt's drive, but retreated from the field after dark. Both sides lost about 1,300 men, many of the wounded dying from exposure in the freezing night. Thus ended Prairie Grove Church, often called the "Gettysburg of the West," because it marked the highwater mark of the Confederacy in Arkansas. In six weeks, Hindman would lose the fort named after him at Arkansas Post on the other side of the state as part of the Vicksburg Campaign (q.v.). With the fall of Little Rock in September 1863, Rebel influence in Arkansas would be confined to the southern half of the state.

MISSOURI COMPROMISE (1820). *See* WILMOT PROVISO.

MISSOURI COMPROMISE, REPEAL OF. *See* DRED SCOTT *V.* SANFORD; KANSAS–NEBRASKA ACT.

MOBILE (ALABAMA) RACE RIOT (1876). *See* EUTAW (ALABAMA) RACE RIOT (1876).

MOBILE BAY, BATTLE OF. *See* MOBILE CAMPAIGN.

MOBILE CAMPAIGN. For over two years, Federal Lt. Gen. Ulysses S. Grant (q.v.) had been trying to mount a campaign against the port of Mobile, Alabama, with no success. Finally, in the summer of 1864, Maj. Gen. Gordon Granger and the XIII Corps landed and assaulted Forts Gaines, Morgan, and Powell on the outer islands of the bay, while Adm. David G. Farragut (q.v.) led a column of ironclad and traditional wooden ships into Mobile harbor on August 5. The Confederates defended Mobile with a mixture of army garrisons and the ironclad ship C.S.S. *Tennessee,* an inclined casemate with a half dozen guns of various calibers.

Early in the morning, Farragut's fleet opened up on the harbor forts and passed over the bar into the approach to Mobile Bay. The *Tennessee* moved to intercept the Federals, especially after one of their own ironclads struck a torpedo (mine) and sank with great loss of life. The Union squadron hesitated to advance, prompting Farragut to issue the famous command, "damn the torpedoes, full speed ahead." Farragut led three of his ships in to ram the underpowered *Tennessee,* which was hampered by its own defective ammunition. But the Union ramming attack had little effect. Farragut barely escaped death when his flagship was struck by another Union ship by accident. Union ironclads came up and surrounded the *Tennessee,* pounding her into submission.

Having reduced the outer harbor defenses and the Confederate navy, it took the Yankees another six months to collect enough men and supplies to assault the inner harbor installations, centered on Spanish Fort. Maj. Gen. E. R. S. Canby (q.v.) led the attack on Spanish Fort from the east, taking it by storm on April 8, 1865. He then advanced to the fortified area at Blakely, which fell a day later. This allowed Canby to enter the city itself on April 12. The Confederates retreated from the area, surrendering with Lt. Gen. Richard Taylor on May 4 at Citronelle (q.v.).

MODERATE REPUBLICANS AND RECONSTRUCTION. In December 1865, after being out of session since the previous March, Congress returned to Washington for its normal session according to the Constitution. It had been on the sidelines during the assassination of President Abraham Lincoln (q.v.), the surrender of the Confederate armies, and the initiation of the Andrew Johnson Reconstruction (q.v.). The South, by and large, had completed President Johnson's program (with the exception of Texas, which was still forming a government) and had elected its new congressmen and senators, who arrived to be seated in their respective houses.

But there was real reason to suspect that the Southern men would not be seated in either house of Congress. Congress still smarted because it had had little to say about Reconstruction, either under Lincoln or Johnson. Indeed, that was what the Wade–Davis Bill and the Wade–Davis Manifesto (qq.v.) were all about. Many in Congress, not just Radical Republicans, believed that they should have an input into the Reconstruction program. They feared that Reconstruction had so far been too easy, often based on undemocratic numbers, and ignored the needs of the recently freed slaves. Especially worrisome were the Black Codes (q.v.). In addition to the conduct of the Southern state conventions and the laws of the allegedly reconstructed state legislatures was the personnel that made up the Southern representatives coming to Congress, the "Confederate Brigadiers" (q.v.). When the clerk read the roll call, the first order of business in any session of Congress, he passed over the names of the men from the South. This, in effect, refused them their seats.

After denying the Southerners their seats, Congress then established a Joint Committee of Fifteen (q.v.) members from the House and Senate to examine the credentials of those passed over and look into conditions in the Southern states and then make recommendations, that is, create a Congressional Reconstruction (q.v.) program (the Second Congressional Plan) of their own. Moderate Republicans believed that Congress ought to place more restriction on Southern readmission to the Union. These men wanted to work with the president and reach a compromise. So the committee appointed Illinois Senator Lyman Trumbull (q.v.), who reported that Johnson meant he agreed with Congress' ideas on expanding Reconstruction.

Assured by Trumbull that Johnson would cooperate, the Committee of Fifteen reported two bills to the floor, both designed to put further conditions on the South before readmission. The first was the renewal of the Bureau of Refugees, Freedmen, and Abandoned Lands (q.v.). The Bureau could supervise white–black labor relations, giving some Federal support and protection to African-Americans in the first critical months of freedom. Trumbull introduced the 1866 bill, backed by the Committee of Fifteen, under the impression that Johnson would accept it. But it was not the type of measure that a strict constructionist (one who reads the Constitution literally) could accept without much reservation. Johnson was such a legal-minded person. So he vetoed the bill, and Congress upheld his constitutional reservations by one vote.

Foiled in the expansion of the Bureau, the Committee still wished to compromise with the president and yet provide some protection to the ex-slaves. The committee sent Trumbull back to Johnson and explained their views. The Congress wanted to pass a civil rights measure that would void the Dred Scott decision (q.v.) and the Black Codes. Again, Trumbull reported that the president seemed more than receptive. Congress created the Civil Rights Bill of 1866 (q.v.). The whole Republican Party (q.v.) was for this measure. It seemed conservative, yet it got the job done in the protection of black Americans as free people.

But Johnson read the whole process incorrectly. He saw the upholding of his first veto, but forgot that it was sustained by one slim vote. He vetoed the Civil Rights Bill of 1866 as a gross interference in state rights to legislate and adjudicate as preserved in the Constitution. Congress was not to be denied. Johnson's stubbornness and what Congress saw as his perfidy, given Trumbull's prior reports on his support and a public speech on Washington's Birthday (q.v.), in which he ridiculed key congressmen and their aides by name, drove the Moderate Republicans over to the Radicals. Congress repassed the Civil Rights Act over Johnson's veto, and for good measure brought up a modified version of the Freedmen's Bureau. Johnson vetoed the new Bureau measure, and Congress repassed it over his veto.

But the Committee of Fifteen was not pleased with the narrow margins that secured African-American rights. The gains of the Civil War had to be thoroughly protected. The result was the Fourteenth Amendment (q.v.) to the Constitution. The Congress approved the amendment by a two-thirds vote and sent it to the states, where three-fourths of them had to endorse it to make it part of the Constitution. Even though the Southern states had no representation, Congress sent the proposed Fourteenth Amendment to them, too. It reasoned that if the South accepted the measure, it would show some contrition for their past sins of war, slavery, and racial discrimination. There was also a fear that three-fourths of the states meant every one, regardless of the South's not being seated in Congress.

Congress asked Johnson to advocate approval of the proposed amendment. But President Johnson advised the South, indeed all the states, that the proposed amendment be turned down. The South was more than happy to go along with rejection. There were 36 states at that time. The vote of 10 would negate the proposed Fourteenth Amendment, and the former Confederacy had been composed of 11. The way to disaster was open, especially since the four loyal border states had many of the seceded states' racial proclivities. Of the ex-Confederate states, only Tennessee, led by Johnson's arch-political enemy, William G. Brownlow (q.v.), approved the Fourteenth Amendment. For Brownlow's astuteness, Tennessee was declared to be readmitted to the Union, the only Southern state so honored. But it all went for naught. Delaware and Kentucky joined the ex-Confederacy in turning the amendment down.

By the fall of 1866, there were two plans before the American people as they prepared to vote in the off-year elections, Johnson's and Congress'. Whoever won the electoral contest could declare they had a mandate from the people. But there were serious implications for President Johnson and his supporters—almost always the president's party loses seats in off-year elections. Johnson made an intense personal effort to get his supporters elected that fall. He went to the National Union (q.v.) Convention to rally his supporters.

After the convention, Johnson hit the campaign trail, making a "Swing Around the Circle" (q.v.), a tour that replicated Lincoln's trip to Washington in 1861. A Republican delegation followed a day or two later to make their own speeches against Johnson's Reconstruction policies. The result was an election that returned a veto-proof, hostile Republican Congress to Washington. Worst of all, it influenced the outgoing Congress to get tough in the Lame Duck session to save the results of the war and compromise the president's ability to act between congressional sessions, as he was counting on.

MONEY ISSUE. *See* GRANT, ULYSSES S., ADMINISTRATION—DOMESTIC POLICIES.

MONITOR, **U.S.S.** First Federal ironclad ship, and the name of a class of ships built on the same pattern, it was marked by a low freeboard and flat deck topped by a swiveling turret, which held two large caliber, smooth bore cannons. *See also* PENINSULA CAMPAIGN.

MONITOR, **U.S.S., AND THE C.S.S.** *VIRGINIA*. *See* PENINSULA CAMPAIGN.

MONOCACY RIVER, BATTLE OF. *See* WASHINGTON, EARLY'S RAID ON.

MORGAN, ALBERT T. (1842–1922). A Mississippi Carpetbagger (q.v.) sheriff who was born in upstate New York, Albert Morgan was a student preparing to enter Oberlin College in Ohio when the Civil War broke out. He returned to his family home, now in Wisconsin, where his father had done well in the wheat business, and enlisted in the Second Wisconsin Volunteer Infantry. He served in the Eastern Theater of the war, where his regiment made history as part of the famous Iron Brigade of the Army of the Potomac. Morgan rose from private to lieutenant colonel, was captured and exchanged, was severely wounded in the left thigh, and became sick with malaria. But he always returned to his post and finished up the war in his second enlistment. He had managed to keep his damaged leg, but always walked with a limp and tired easily.

His brother Charles, also a Union war veteran, proposed that the two look around for a new start. Landing at Vicksburg, they heard of land for sale at Yazoo City 100 miles northeast. Soon they were in the planting business in a big way. But Mississippi was one of the unfriendliest places in the South for Northern emigrants. His problems were not eased any when he and his brother made known their ideas on race, protested bad treatment of local African-Americans, established a Negro school, and generally stood up for equal treatment. Meanwhile, the planting went poorly.

Broke and needing a reason to go on, the Morgans took heart at the passage of the Military Reconstruction Acts (q.v.) and the emergence of the Republican Party (q.v.) in Mississippi. Local blacks needed some candidates for their seat in the new state constitutional convention. Morgan's ticket won. He worked actively for black civil rights and for the disfranchisement of all who would not swear an oath to political and civil equality of all men. His massive disfranchisement carried the day and ensured a Republican victory in the first election in 1868.

Morgan managed to get himself elected to the county board of supervisors. He instituted Radical Republican policies, taxed property holders, and set up a system of public education and road repairs. His activity pleased black and Carpetbag voters, who sent him to the state legislature. At Jackson, Republican Gov. Adelbert Ames (q.v.) relied heavily on Morgan for advice as to whom to appoint to local patronage positions. Morgan voted for the Fourteenth and Fifteenth Amendments and for Ames and Hiram Revels (qq.v.) as U.S. senators. He also backed the repeal of the Black Code (q.v.), established a new court system and a public school system, and created new counties (named for such prominent Yankees as martyred President Abraham Lincoln, Senator Charles Sumner, and Vice President Schuyler Colfax [qq.v.], as well as correct principles, like Union). But he opposed a public accommodations law because he feared that it would destroy Republicans, as it had in neighboring Louisiana. He also met a New York school teacher, a mulatto named Carrie Highgate. He married her in short order (which did not endear him at all to white Mississippi), and they went on a honeymoon to New York State. They returned to Yazoo City, where they set up housekeeping and Carrie gave birth to three children in as many years. Two more would come along later. Morgan, meanwhile, was elected county sheriff.

With marriage and family and a rousing political career ahead of him, Morgan thought that he had achieved heaven on earth. But he reckoned without white Mississippi. Even though Morgan had clearly won the election, his opponent, the incumbent (a Mississippi Union man during the war), refused to vacate the office; shooting erupted, and his opponent fell dead. Morgan was spirited away to Jackson under arrest. But Governor Ames set Morgan free to resume office.

Meanwhile, the whites of Yazoo City had been organizing, arming, and training as unofficial militia companies. They won the city elections that fall, where they had a slight majority, although Morgan and his black and white allies carried the county. The only way in which Democrats (q.v.) could take the predominantly black county was through violence, and everyone knew it. Blacks warned him that a mounted force estimated at 900 Ku Klux Klan (q.v.) was searching for him. Morgan escaped to Jackson. But Governor Ames' administration was about to fall, too. Morgan gathered up his wife and children, who had been at a summer home in Holly Springs, and fled the state. Eventually Morgan got a Federal job in Washington, D.C., as a second class clerk in the Pension Office, thanks to Mississippi's second black senator, Blanche K. Bruce. He also wrote of his Mississippi experiences.

But the election of Grover Cleveland as president ended that. He took his family to Kansas, then left them there as he toured the Colorado gold and silver fields as a prospector. He found little wealth. He took up the free silver crusade, changed political parties, campaigned for William Jennings Bryan, and wrote several pamphlets and magazines on behalf of the free silver cause. Meanwhile, Carrie took her four girls (their son had become a railroad clerk) and went on a tour of the East as a singing family. With the exception of a few short meetings with his son, Morgan never saw his wife and family again. He died in Denver in 1922.

MORMON WAR (1857). The Republican Party Platform in the election of 1856 (qq.v.) spoke out against the twin relics of polygamy and slavery in the territories. The former was a reference to the people of the Church of Jesus Christ of Latter-day Saints (Mormons), who had fled to the valley of the Great Salt Lake in Utah to escape violent religious persecution in the settled areas of the East. At the time (1847), the area was Mexican territory. But within years the Mormons were back in the United States, on the direct overland trail to California's gold fields, and in need of territorial government.

At that time, the Mormon state of Deseret included Utah Territory and land north to Idaho's Salmon River and south to San Diego, California. After the Compromise of 1850, the new Utah Territory included all of present-day Colorado west of the Continental Divide and the current states of Utah and Nevada. President Millard Fillmore (q.v.) had more pressing problems. He simply appointed the Mormon's own theocracy as the territorial officials. In everlasting gratitude, the Mormons named one of their counties Millard, and its governing seat is Fillmore. When Franklin Pierce (q.v.) came in, he wanted to appoint a secular government to run the territory, but he was too busy with Kansas and let things slide. James Buchanan (q.v.) would not be so lucky or smart.

The governor of Utah was the Prophet and First President of the Council of Twelve, Brigham Young. At best, one could say that his representation of the interests of the United States was secondary to Church desires. The Mormons were smack in the middle of the proposed transcontinental railroad (if it came out of Chicago, and it would), and in the way of the usual contractors, jobbers, speculators, and investment interests that usually ran Western territories. They not only had to deal with the government in Washington, they had to deal with Young and the Church. And Young was smarter than they. He drove a hard bargain, if they could get one at all.

Actually, the Republican Platform of 1856 was a political trap laid for Buchanan. The Republicans wanted Buchanan to intervene in Utah to show the Democrats' inconsistency in supporting popular sovereignty (q.v.), or non-interference, in Kansas. Buchanan stepped into the trap by appointing a secular territorial government of the usual Democratic Party (q.v.) political hacks. Young ignored them, then threw them out. Then a wagon train of rowdy Gentiles from areas that persecuted the Mormons back East passed through Utah, headed for San Diego. When they reached Mountain Meadows near St. George, Mormon militia and local Native Americans attacked and massacred most of the company. How much Young and the Church had to do with this is arguable, but Buchanan had already decided that a show of Federal force was overdue.

Sending the United States Army out onto the Great Plains to Ft. Bridger, Buchanan placed the expedition under one of the army's top officers, Col. Albert Sidney Johnston (q.v.). Supplies had to be freighted out west from Kansas City. The army contracted with the best company for the job, Russell, Majors, and Waddell. When Johnston's column reached Ft. Bridger, they found it burned out by the Mormon militia. The supply train was next, and Russell, Majors, and Waddell lost so much equipment to the Mormon attack that it began their slow decline into eventual bankruptcy. The Army spent a long, cold, and hungry winter at Ft. Bridger.

Meanwhile, an important Gentile friend of the Mormons, Thomas Leiper Kane of Pennsylvania, went by sea, across the Isthmus of Panamá, and up the trail from San Diego to Great Salt Lake City. He convinced Young that he would have to permit punishment of the leaders of the Mountain Meadows Massacre and let the Army march through Great Salt Lake City to an encampment south of town. He would also have to yield to a new non-church government. The real significance, besides the showing of Army inadequacies that Confederate commanders would demonstrate time and time again, was that the Army was too busy to do much in the Kansas Settlement (q.v.).

MORRILL, JUSTIN M. (1810–1898). Born in Vermont the eldest of 10 children, Justin S. Morrill was educated in local schools and academies. He became a clerk in a local store and began a profitable career in merchandising that allowed him to retire to the life of gentleman farmer and scholar by 1848. Morrill married in 1851, and his wife bore him two sons. He served in county and state committees and was elected to Congress as an antislavery Whig (q.v.) in 1854. He would serve 12 years in the House and 32 in the Senate, the longest unbroken tenure until the 20th century. He soon changed over to the Republican Party. Although against slavery, Morrill's real talent lay in tariff and finance. He wrote the initial bills on funding the debt; the Civil War tariff was designed to protect infant industry and raise revenue (it was thus the highest to that time); and the Land Grant College Act (qq.v.), his proudest achievement, one that was expanded in 1890. It would be fair to say that Morrill had much to do with the passage of the Republican's domestic economic program during the Civil War. During Reconstruction, he came out as a hard money man against free silver or greenbacks and spoke in favor of beautifying the Capitol grounds. Morrill was a literary man and wrote several books and articles on self-improvement. He died in Washington at the end of the century, having won overwhelming election each time he ran.

MOSES, FRANKLIN J., JR. (1838–1906). A South Carolina Scalawag (q.v.), Franklin Moses, probably more than any other man, typified the stereotype of the socially prominent, pleasant, promising, young native white who sold his soul to corruption and turned on his race for personal profit. From a Spanish–Jewish family that had once fled the Inquisition, Moses' father was a prominent Charleston attorney, a state legislator for 20 years before the war, and chief justice of the state supreme court afterward, a Scalawag, too. But he was respected by friend and foe alike. Not so the son. Born Franklin Israel Moses, Jr., Frank dropped his middle name (imitating his father) and substituted the initial "J." No one knows why. The Moseses were never discriminated against because of their ethnicity. Indeed, Charleston Jews were quick to point out that the younger Moses was raised as a Gentile and married outside the faith. After his education, Moses became personal secretary to Governor Francis W. Pickens. It was 1860, and South Carolina was in the process of seceding from the Union, the first Southern state to do so. He represented the governor in negotiations for the surrender of Fort Sumter (q.v.), and after the battle he personally raised the Confederate flag over the captured installation. He later served as military enrolling officer with the rank of colonel. It looked respectable, and it avoided combat.

After the war, Moses was admitted to the bar and joined the Episcopal Church. He edited a newspaper and endorsed President Andrew Johnson's Reconstruction (qq.v.) policies. But with the passage of the Military Reconstruction Acts (q.v.), something went haywire in Moses' normally well-ordered, upper class Charlestonian mind. He grasped the obvious to any ambitious politician, that the key to control of the state would be the new black voters. Moses immediately began to organize Union Loyal Leagues (q.v.) among the former slaves. He criticized his social peers for their stupidity in refusing to submit to Radical Reconstruction. Thankful for his leadership, the blacks from his district sent him to the state constitutional convention, where he became an outspoken Radical Republican. He was elected to the state house of representatives, where he became speaker. Under the new administration, Moses was appointed adjutant and inspector general of the state militia, trustee of the state university, and trustee of the state militia. In each office, Moses made it clear that he could be bought. He took bribes in the house of representatives and dealt in bogus state pay vouchers. As head of the militia, he diverted money raised for arms to his personal use.

In 1872, Moses became governor, again relying on the African-American vote, and defeating a reform candidate, Daniel H. Chamberlain (q.v.). As governor, Moses sold pardons and political appointments and his signature on all legislation. Backed up by his militia, he defied court orders. He hobnobbed with his black constituents on a one-to-one level, wined and dined them all, and wenched the best and worst. He spent so much money that he could hardly steal it fast enough to keep up with his bills. Even his corrupt colleagues became embarrassed by his raucous conduct. At the end of his two-year term, even the worst Republicans had deserted him for Chamberlain. The new governor began his reform administration by refusing to issue Moses his commission for circuit judge, a position to which he had been elected. With the triumph of the Red Shirts, Moses managed to save himself from a prison term by ratting on all of his cronies.

In 1878, Moses lost his wife, who divorced him and left the state, never telling his children who their father was. Some of his kin changed their surnames so as not to be identified with his deeds. Moses wandered from one city to another, running small confidence games, operating as a petty thief, serving several prison terms, and winding up a drug addict. He died in Massachusetts of accidental asphyxiation from a poorly ventilated heater.

MUD MARCH. See FREDERICKSBURG CAMPAIGN.

MUSKET. See LOAD-IN-NINE-TIMES.

N

NASHVILLE, BATTLE OF. *See* NASHVILLE CAMPAIGN.

NASHVILLE CAMPAIGN. After Confederate Lt. Gen. John B. Hood's (q.v.) loss of Atlanta, he remained at Lovejoy, waiting for Federal Maj. Gen. William T. Sherman (q.v.) to make his next move. Sherman stayed in Atlanta, however, consolidating his gains. Hood then decided to force Sherman to abandon the city by attacking the single rail line that supplied the Union army in Georgia. Sherman, cognizant of his vulnerability because of activities of Confederate cavalry leader Lt. Gen. Nathan Bedford Forrest's (q.v.) victories during the battle of Brice's Crossroads (q.v.) and the events that followed, sent Maj. Gen. George Thomas' Army of the Cumberland back up the rails to hold Nashville.

Hood moved northward, attacking the railroad at several points, but failing to hold it for any significant period of time. Sherman followed, but what Hood did not count on was that the Federals had enough soldiers to handle him and to continue to hold Atlanta, too. At this moment, Hood decided to attack Nashville, the base from which Sherman was operating. Sherman, however, was about to embark on his March to the Sea (q.v.). He left Atlanta for the coast at Savannah, reinforcing Thomas with all extra troops and letting him worry about Hood.

Meanwhile, instead of taking the initiative, Hood waited three weeks for Forrest to join him in northern Alabama. Thomas took the time to completely reorganize his department and prepare for the onslaught. On November 19, Hood began to move north, headed for Columbia, Tennessee, hoping to cut off all Federals guarding the rails into Georgia. The weather was cold, with rain, sleet, and snow. Then it would thaw and repeat the process. Hood reached Columbia just as the Federals did. Leaving a corps behind to keep the Union commanders' attention, Hood took the rest of his army to Spring Hill. If he reached it first, the Yankees, led by Maj. Gen. John Schofield (q.v.), would be trapped. Schofield and his commanders figured out what Hood was up to, and Schofield started north, arriving at Spring Hill just ahead of Forrest's cavalry, and holding the town (November 29).

Hood's infantry came up about dark. All he had to do was cross the road and Schofield would be cut off from Nashville. All night long, the Confederates sat and waited to move. No orders came, said Confederate corps commanders. Hood said that he gave the orders, but no one acted upon them. All night long, the Confederates could hear Schofield's men, guns, and wagons fleeing up the road toward Nashville. One spoiling attack by one Confederate division acting on its own volition was not enough. By dawn, Schofield was at Franklin, backed against the raging Harpeth River, with Hood coming up slowly.

Schofield prepared to do battle, while his engineers worked on fords and bridges to get the army across. If Hood did not attack, Schofield would cross the river after dark. Around 3:30 p.m., Hood and his commanders attacked. In a charge that dwarfed what Maj. Gen. George E. Pickett did at Gettysburg in the Pennsylvania Campaign (q.v.), Hood's men charged across two miles of open ground without artillery preparation against actual fortifications. The result was slaughter of the Confederate soldiers and the decimation of their generals (six killed, five wounded, one captured). Hood kept up the futile effort until 9:00 p.m. With equal forces engaged (27,000), Hood lost 6,200 men and 10 battle flags. Schofield lost 2,300.

Schofield finished his march to Nashville, coming under the control of Thomas. Hood followed, but lacked the strength to attack. He drew up outside Nashville—each side entrenched and staring at the other. Thomas patiently prepared to attack Hood, but living up to his nickname, "Old Slow Trot," he took his time. Meanwhile, the authorities in Washington were growing impatient. Lt. Gen. Ulysses S. Grant (q.v.) stepped in and ordered Thomas to attack on December 6. He was not yet ready with his cavalry. He delayed until December 8. Then the ground froze, making movement physically too dangerous. Thomas postponed the attack, again. Grant decided to replace Thomas with Schofield, then with one of Sherman's generals, then he decided that he would go in person to straighten things out on December 15.

But Thomas launched his assault that same day, turning Hood's left flank. The Confederates fell back to two hills south of the city. Hood remained in position overnight. On December 16, Thomas hit Hood's right, but it held. Then Thomas attacked Hood's left, as he had done the day before. Hood's whole army pulled out in the dark. Outnumbering the Rebels 2 to 1, Thomas lost 3,000. Hood suffered 1,500 battle casualties, with another 4,500 being captured. Nashville is generally considered to be the only really decisive battle of the war.

Maj. Gen. James H. Wilson's Cavalry corps continued the pursuit the next day, harrying Hood back into Alabama by December 27, stopped only by high rivers and wrecked bridges. On January 10, 1865, the shattered Army of Tennessee was at Tupelo, where Hood submitted his request to be relieved of command, to the relief of the men under him. The remnants of the Army of Tennessee would eventually be called over to join the Carolinas Campaign, where they surrendered under their old commander, Gen. Joseph E. Johnston (q.v.), at Durham Station, on April 26 (q.v.).

NASHVILLE CONVENTION. *See* COMPROMISE OF 1850.

NATIONAL BANKING ACT (1863, 1864). The Republican Party (q.v.) had a distinct domestic program designed to appease both its agricultural and industrial supporters. This program had as its basis the old Whig (q.v.) economic policies based in part on Henry Clay's American System (q.v.). Part of the program appealed to American industry by creating a centralized national banking system. In the National Banking Act of 1862, the Republicans created a banking system that lasted from the Civil War to the founding of the Federal Reserve in 1914.

Designed to replace the Second Bank of the United States, which President Andrew Jackson had destroyed in the 1830s, and which Democrats (q.v.) had prevented from being recreated until the South seceded, the National Banking Act issued Federal charters to banks under the supervision of the Department of the Treasury. Banks had to have a minimum amount of capital to qualify, and one-third of the capital had to be in U.S. bonds deposited in the U.S. Treasury. In exchange, the government would issue the member bank Federal bank notes up to 90 percent of the deposited sums, to be used as a national currency. The National Banks were limited to $300 million in notes in all. Prior to the war, each bank or state issued its own notes, some of which were backed by specie and some of which were not. As with most Federal laws, member banks agreed to allow inspection and audit by Federal bank authorities.

At first, banks did not wish to be limited by Federal controls, but a 10 percent tax on all non-Federal notes quickly drove all but U.S. issuances out of circulation. This caused a rush to join the national banking system, and by 1865, over 11,000 banks with $200,000 in notes were members. The National Banking Act was good in that it created a regulated currency of the same value everywhere in the U.S., but it was bad in that it was limited to $300 million, and most of this amount circulated in the Eastern states, making the West money poor.

NATIONAL UNION PARTY. To work closely with those from the Democratic Party (q.v.) called War Democrats, who wished to prosecute a vigorous war policy against the Confederacy, Abraham Lincoln (q.v.) and the Republicans (q.v.) dropped the Republican label and adopted the National Union Party as their name. It was a coalition that usually presented War Democrats as candidates in close state and local elections. The use of the National Union Party name allowed Democratic voters to choose pro-war men without the onus of voting directly for the often hated Republican Party. Lincoln ran on this label in the election of 1864 (q.v.), and Andrew Johnson (q.v.) tried to use the same label to oppose Congressional Reconstruction (q.v.) in the by-elections of 1866.

NAT TURNER SLAVE REBELLION. *See* BLACK "PERSONALITY" IN SLAVERY AND FREEDOM.

NAVY. *See* CONFEDERATE SEA RAIDERS; PRIZE CASES.

NAVY CONTRACTS SCANDAL. *See* GRANT, ULYSSES S., ADMINISTRATION—SCANDALS.

NEGRO MILITIAS AND RECONSTRUCTION. After the Civil War, various congressional hearings revealed a shocking discovery to the Northern states—the Southern states' white civilians were armed to the teeth, not necessarily to further rebellion, but as a matter of course. But newly freed black slaves were prohibited from carrying arms by the infamous Black Codes (q.v.). Hence Reconstruction and Redemption (qq.v.) of the South would likely be accompanied by a great deal of violence, most of it directed toward African-American leadership, Southern white Scalawags, Northern Carpetbaggers, and occasionally the U.S. Army (qq.v.).

In order to protect loyalists of all ethnicities, two things had to be done posthaste—disarm the white state militias, tainted by secession and rebellion and still wearing their gray uniforms, and create new blue-uniformed militias comprised of solely loyal elements, regardless of color. In the propaganda of the day, the "Negro militias" were born, even though their enlistees were composed of both races. Part of the Military Reconstruction Acts (q.v.) guaranteed this process would go forward by eliminating any prior-existing Southern state militias.

Part of the appeal for the new Negro militias was that their creation would allow for an end to the role of the Army in Reconstruction. By March 1870, Congress had set up new militia laws that applied to all the reconstructed states except Virginia, Mississippi, Georgia, and Texas. The four laggards had laws passed to reconstitute their militias after their admissions later that same year.

Even though all readmitted Southern states could organize loyal Negro militias, not all of them did. Virginia refused, Alabama and Florida organized units but never armed them, while all other states armed and employed them to varying degrees, with Tennessee being one of the most prolific. Tennessee had the largest organized Negro militia, but it was employed mostly for political reasons to guard the polls and intimidate voters. Louisiana, Arkansas, and

North Carolina employed the Negro militias as state armies and fought anti-Reconstruction forces in the bloody Third Battle of New Orleans (q.v.), the lesser sanguine affair of the Brooks–Baxter War (q.v.), and the Kirk Holden War, respectively.

As the time approached for organizing the Negro militias, the loyal governments in the South began to collect statistics on the amount of violence committed against loyal blacks and whites by those of suspected Confederate antecedents. The militias were to be paid by taxes levied by each state for that purpose. Although there was no real effort made to guarantee this, almost half of the enlistees were black, much to the disgust of native Southern whites. Officer procurement was assisted by bonuses or even auctioned to the highest bidder—a process that did not necessarily attract the best recruits. Arming and equipping the militias became a problem, often assisted by arms shipments from Yankee state arsenals.

The notion of black men under arms infuriated the South, still remembering when such occurrences bespoke of slave rebellion before the war. Negro militia parades, drills, barbeques, and dances only exacerbated white fears. Many black militia units were accused of murder, robbery, arson, assault, and rapes. Such things were so infrequent as to make then virtually nonexistent. But the opposition forces' nighttime ambushes, snipings, and assaults on bivouacs made joining the Negro militias quite dangerous. Being led by less than competent officers did not help militia longevity. Finally, the Southern whites came out from behind the sheets of the Ku Klux Klan (q.v.) as the unreconstructed white counter-militias of the White Leagues, Red Shirts, and White Liners (qq.v.) to win the battles of Redemption (q.v.)

The Negro militia movement was pretty much a failure. And much of it came from the Reconstruction governments' unwillingness to employ the Negro militias in their full force. The Reconstruction governments feared a race war so much that they became impotent to do anything to halt the anti-Reconstruction forces' advance to take over the state houses violently. The fact that the Grant administration's Reconstruction policy was watered down by a Northern Congress tired of the annual wars in the South over elections did not help. Then, Negro militia funds appropriated by Reconstruction governments became an easily identifiable source of corruption (q.v.) in an era that reeked of fraud. So the force that was designed to protect the Reconstructors of the South wound up being their main source of weakness when confronting racism and reform.

NEW DEPARTURE. The idea that whites should rule the South and manage racial affairs locally without interference from Congress or Federal soldiers was the New Departure. *See also* HAYES, RUTHERFORD B.

NEW ENGLAND EMIGRANT AID SOCIETY. Because the North saw the passage of the Kansas–Nebraska Act (q.v.) as some sort of diabolical plot to turn the whole West into a preserve for slavery, a movement arose in the North to save Kansas from this earthly perdition. Eli Thayer, a Massachusetts educator and businessman, organized the New England Emigrant Aid Society. Its goal was to help Free Soil settlers get out to Kansas, settle it, and vote to make Kansas free.

They had to move fast. Already Missouri pro-slave settlers were coming in to create pro-slave centers like Atchison, Leavenworth, and Lecompton. Pro-slave forces easily won the first territorial election on March 30, 1854. Although they accounted for the most population, the Southern cause was helped by border crossers from Missouri, who showed up to vote, many wearing guns. They soon received the name "Border Ruffians" up North. In July 1854, the first 30 settlers arrived and built the town of Lawrence, named for the cotton mill magnate, Amos Lawrence, who financed them. The houses were solidly built of brick and stone, and the Free State Hotel in the center of town was a veritable fortress. It proved to be a wise move. *See also* KANSAS–MISSOURI BORDER WARS.

NEW HOPE CHURCH. *See* ATLANTA CAMPAIGN.

NEW HUMANISTS. *See* SOCIAL DARWINISM.

NEW MADRID, BATTLE OF. *See* SHILOH CAMPAIGN.

NEW MARKET, BATTLE OF. *See* RICHMOND OR OVERLAND CAMPAIGN (1864).

NEW MARKET HEIGHTS, BATTLE OF. *See* PETERSBURG, SIEGE OF.

NEW MEXICO–ARIZONA CAMPAIGN. When Texas seceded from the Union in February 1861 and received the surrender of all Federal troops and installations, most of which were in the West guarding against Indian depredations, the government at Austin sent Lt. Col. John R. Baylor and his Second Texas Mounted Rifles out to secure El Paso in a so-called Buffalo Hunt. Baylor declared all of New Mexico south of the 34th parallel (essentially the old Gadsden Purchase) to be the Confederate Territory of Arizona. The advancing Texans managed to bluff the Federals out of Ft. Fillmore above El Paso and capture its fleeing garrison on the roads the next day. Meanwhile, a convention of like-minded citizens had met in Mesilla, New Mexico, and seceded from the Union, beating four later Confederate states. But in reality, Baylor represented the aspirations of Texans to retake all of eastern New

Mexico, which Texas had yielded to the vicissitudes of sectional harmony during the Compromise of 1850 (q.v.).

Soon, Brig. Gen. Henry H. Sibley arrived, fresh from Richmond, looking to secure the alleged mineral wealth of the Great Southwest for the South. He raised three more mounted regiments and, with Baylor's men, invaded New Mexico up the valley of the Rio Grande. Opposing him were a mixture of Federal regular infantry and New Mexico volunteers under Col. E. R. S. Canby (q.v.), stationed at various small posts throughout the territory. The Spanish-speaking locals had little love for the Union, but they hated the arrogant Texans even more.

The advancing Confederates lured the Federals out of Ft. Craig, the next post north, by cutting their supply lines at a ford on the Rio Grande called Valverde. When the fort's garrison sallied forth, the Rebels won a sharp battle, which sent them scurrying back to the shelter of the fort. Sibley, who had been sick during the fighting, now advanced, headed for Santa Fé and Colorado's mines, but he left Canby's Ft. Craig garrison intact across his line of potential retreat.

Capturing Santa Fé, Sibley turned east to secure Apache Canyon, which led to the roads to Colorado. A series of indecisive skirmishes ensued. The Confederates pushed on to meet the main Federal force, reinforced by Colorado volunteers, at Glorieta. In two sharp fights, the Rebels were victorious at Pigeon's Ranch in the canyon, but lost their supply train to a marauding force of Colorado cavalry at Johnson's ranch to their rear. Meanwhile, Sibley received news that Col. Canby had come up the river behind him with a mobile column. Although Canby was pushed aside at Albuquerque, his arrival forced Sibley to order a general retreat and the abandonment of Santa Fé. Pushed on by a skirmish at Peralta below Santa Fé, Sibley's force now was caught between its pursuers and the remaining Ft. Craig garrison. The Confederates decided to avoid the fort, which Sibley dared not stop to attack, and bypass the fort. This impelled him to leave the relatively fertile Rio Grande valley for the dreaded Jornada del Muerto, a waterless trip through rough country to the west.

By the time the demoralized, thirsty Texans got back to the Rio Grande at El Paso, Canby's Colorado force and the Ft. Craig garrison had received reinforcements from California coming across the overland trail from the Pacific Coast. The California Column had lost a skirmish with portions of Sibley's command at Picacho Pass north of Tucson (generally considered the westernmost battle of the Civil War, although another skirmish at Stanwix Station was closer to Ft. Yuma), but by sheer numbers conquered Tucson and drove off an assault by united Apache tribes at Apache Pass in the mountains east of the town, before arriving at Mesilla. Their approach caused the Confederates to retreat all the way to San Antonio, ending their aspirations for extending a Confederate empire through the Rocky Mountains to the Pacific Coast.

NEW ORLEANS RACE RIOT, JULY 30, 1866. The bloodiest so far, unlike the Norfolk and Memphis race riots (qq.v.), the New Orleans riot was not economic but political. This, plus its long list of casualties, made it the story of the day during the ensuing Northern congressional political campaign of 1866 that doomed President Andrew Johnson (q.v.), his plan of easy reunion, and the South to Congressional Reconstruction (q.v.). Although New Orleans looked on the surface much like Norfolk and Memphis—a Federal occupation early in the war, an increase of population comprised of foreigners and blacks, economic competition between them, and a white population fearing the new order in which they had minimal participation—the rest was quite different.

Louisiana had been President Abraham Lincoln's Reconstruction (q.v.) showpiece. Under the Ten Percent Plan (q.v.), Louisiana had called a constitutional convention in 1864 to create the first Free State Government. The representation was based on whites alone, and for the first time, New Orleans mechanics and small white farmers controlled Louisiana government. They refused to put black suffrage in the new Free State constitution, as it would compromise their political clout, although they permitted a future legislature to do it for them. But that was unlikely, as the legislature was under their control, too. As the convention adjourned, it took an unusual step. It passed an ordnance allowing the convention president or the state legislature to recall the delegates to rework the Free State constitution at some future unnamed date.

The first government elected after the war's close under the Free State constitution was a white male, Democrat (q.v.) regime, complete with a governor who had led the early pro-Union government and now had switched sides (a Louisiana art), J. Madison Wells. He and his legislators passed the Black Code (q.v.) and began to work to crush the nascent Republican (q.v.) Party forever. But there was a forum that the Democrats still did not control—the old 1864 constitutional convention. Opponents of the convention asked the Army to stop the new meeting, scheduled for July 30 at the New Orleans' Mechanics Hall. Bvt. Maj. Gen. Absalom Baird refused to get involved.

Meanwhile, the city officials decided to move on their own, despite the general's warnings. They were determined to prevent this "radical" body from interfering with the constitution and instituting black suffrage.

On the day of the convention, it developed that a quorum was not present and the convention sent the sergeant-at-arms to find the missing members. As they waited, a procession of black demonstrators marched up to the hall, waving banners and chanting in favor of a renewed convention. White bystanders, many of them underage and drunk, exchanged words and blows with the demonstrators. As usual some unidentified person, black or white, fired the first shot. The police returned a volley into the crowd of demonstrators, and the riot was on. The blacks fled into the hall for protection from the white mob that continued to grow in numbers and viciousness outside. The police joined the mob, and the whites assaulted the convention hall. Three times the attackers were driven back with losses before taking the hall. By the time United States troops arrived, the riot was over. General Baird explained their tardiness by claiming that he thought the convention would meet at 6:00 p.m., not noon. The casualty list included 34 blacks killed, 4 whites killed (including Dr. Dostie, who was shot by rioters while in police protection), 119 blacks wounded, and 27 whites wounded.

Both sides blamed the other for the riot. But one thing was sure; the carnage in the streets of New Orleans did much to defeat what was left of President Johnson's plans for Reconstruction and elect the Republican Congress that would enforce the Military Reconstruction Acts (q.v.) drawn up by its predecessor and move to impeach the president in short order. It also showed the white South that violence properly channeled could be quite useful.

NEW ORLEANS RACE RIOT, OCTOBER 24–27, 1868. Unlike the earlier 1866 New Orleans race riot (q.v.), black and white Republicans (q.v.) were better prepared to resist, although the results were about the same. Black leaders were getting sick and tired of newspaper smears against their character, intelligence, and abilities. Although they had a slight majority of registered voters, victory was not guaranteed. Whites believed that Republicans imported blacks from surrounding parishes to vote and take the city (an old Louisiana ploy whites had used before the war among themselves, commonly called "Plaquemining" after the parish from which the ringers came). They also disliked the able leadership that blacks provided in the city, a result of the large educated free black population from before the war. Finally, there were numerous political clubs representing every possible faction of both parties. They did much to keep the pot boiling with their nightly parades and antics, designed to embarrass their opponents.

On Saturday, October 24, two political clubs met by accident in Canal Street. They began to try to out shout each other. Then some white boys fired into the Republicans. Seven died as the blacks retreated. Infuriated, the blacks went home and armed themselves and began attacking every white in sight. Federal soldiers finally put an end to the rioting, after two whites died and several were wounded. No bloodshed occurred the next day, but tensions ran high. But the next three days made up for the 24-hour respite, despite the appeal of leaders of both parties and the Army command to cease political marches and fights. The excuse for the white Democrats was that they were helping patrol the city in the absence of the Metropolitan Police, a largely black force. Gangs robbed and looted homes and businesses until Wednesday, when the Army restored order again. Casualties ran from 63 in the state legislature investigation report down to a more realistic half dozen whites and a dozen blacks. Uncounted others were wounded on both sides. Once again, violence had shown the white South how to defeat Republicanism and redeem white rule. It was a portent of things to come.

NEW ORLEANS, SECOND BATTLE OF. As the biggest seaport of the South and located at the mouth of the Mississippi River, which drained the entire area between the Appalachians and the Rockies, New Orleans became an immediate target for Yankee conquest in the spring of 1862, in what would be called the Second Battle of New Orleans (Andrew Jackson's defense in 1815 being the first).

Confederate efforts at its defense seemed more adequate on paper than they proved in action. The river approaches were guarded by two forts nearer the Gulf, the older Ft. St. Philip and the more modern Ft. Jackson, which contained a total of 500 men and 75 guns. The bastions were reinforced by three river "rams," the *Manassas* (operational), the *Louisiana* (unpowered), and the *Mississippi* (unfinished). A thousand infantry were placed at Jackson's old Chalmette line, but very little was done to guard against an overland expedition from the Lake Pontchartrain area to the east, even though the Yankees had already taken Ship Island and placed 15,000 men for the assault against the Crescent City.

On April 18, 1862, Admiral David G. Farragut (q.v.) assembled a fleet of some 24 wood hulls and small numerous mortar boats to pound the forts into submission and run past them to the city itself. All week long the mortars blasted the forts, doing very little damage. Early in the morning of April 25, before dawn, Farragut decided to chance running the fortifications and destroy the Rebel ships. By first light, he had accomplished his purpose with very little loss.

The Confederates were very demoralized by Farragut's *élan* and success. They quickly abandoned the city, which Farragut's fleet took without opposition. The civil authorities formally surrendered New Orleans on April 29, and the Union ground forces occupied it on May 1, laying the framework for the readmission of Louisiana back into the Union in what would be the Louisiana Experiment (q.v.).

NEW ORLEANS, THIRD BATTLE OF. By 1874, the White League (q.v.) had gained control of the countryside outside of New Orleans by using classic guerrilla tactics, isolating Governor William Pitt Kellogg's (q.v.) supporters in the city itself. The local Democratic Club rechristened itself the Crescent City White League (q.v.), ordered rifles from New York, and awaited the yellow fever season, when U.S. troops would be sent to Holly Springs, Mississippi, for their health. The White League planned to arm, capture Kellogg, and exile him out of the state, installing his former electoral opponent, Democrat John McEnery, as governor. When Kellogg refused to surrender, the White Leaguers threw up barricades and prepared to fight his black state militia and the Metropolitan Police. Led by a noted Scalawag, former Confederate Lt. Gen. James Longstreet (q.v.), the Republican forces attacked the White League position only to be driven back. The White Leaguers then charged and, raising the "Rebel yell," eventually cleared the streets. Longstreet's retreating men forted up in the Customs House, which the White League wisely decided not to attack, it being Federal property. But they took all of the state buildings and set up the McEnery people as the government. The Republican casualties were 11 killed and 60 wounded, while the White League lost 21 killed and 19 wounded.

NEW RATIONALISTS. *See* SOCIAL DARWINISM.

NEW YORK CITY DRAFT RIOT (1863). *See* CONSCRIPTION AND DRAFT EVASION, UNION.

NON-EXCLUSION DOCTRINE. A Southern political theory that held that the U.S. Constitution guaranteed slavery as an institution in the Western territories of the United States until such time as the territory might apply for statehood, whereupon slavery could be confirmed or abolished within the boundaries of the proposed new state by the state constitutional convention or a later popular vote. It was a crucial component of the 1857 U.S. Supreme Court case Dred Scott *v.* Sandford (q.v.). *See also* EXTRATERRITORIAL-ITY OF SLAVERY.

NORFOLK RACE RIOT, APRIL 16, 1866. The first major explosion of racial tension during Reconstruction occurred at Norfolk, Virginia. The local African-American population, which had been augmented by numerous ex-slaves looking for economic opportunity away from the plantation system in this busy port city, planned to march in support of the Civil Rights Act of 1866 (q.v.). Whites saw this march as rubbing their faces in a series of congressional humiliations, the loss of political majority to incoming black refugees, and minor racial clashes. They decided that it was time to strike back. As the blacks wended their way through rainy streets to a speaker's platform, local whites attacked them with rocks and bottles. The proverbial first shot rang out, and the riot was on, both sides returning fire. Both sides blamed the other for starting the incident. After the clash, one of the white ringleaders was killed, and white disciplinary squads returned to the streets to exact vengeance. Only belated military intervention prevented another riot. It was a classic example of rioting to maintain traditional white control that was being lost to the population shifts common during the early part of Reconstruction. It was also an indication that while the Civil War might be over on the battlefield, it had barely begun in the back alleys and byways of the former Confederacy. Ensuing race riots (q.v.) would follow in Memphis and New Orleans (qq.v.)

NORTH ANNA RIVER, BATTLE OF. *See* RICHMOND OR OVER-LAND CAMPAIGN.

NURSES. In both North and South, women volunteered to serve as adjuncts to the battlefields, when they were not actually joining the battle line disguised as men. The primary role for women in the 19th century was as caregivers in the hospitals. In both sections, Roman Catholic orders of nuns were accepted right off, but the armies initially objected to the presence of women as providers of medical services. There was great fear that the naked male body would somehow corrupt their morals and that the gore of the battlefield would cause them to faint away or be marred for life. The women volunteers soon disabused the medical authorities of these misunderstandings of the hardiness of the female character.

In the North, as usual, organization was paramount. Helped by the United States Sanitary Commission (q.v.) and opposed by the medical directors and surgeons general (q.v.), Dorothea Dix, already famous for her work with the insane and a friend of Florence Nightingale of Crimean War renown, got the Union to organize a Women's Nursing Bureau as early as April 23, 1861. Her standards were tough and inflexible. A candidate for nursing had to be 30 years of age or older, be plain to ugly in features, dress simply without bustles, and exhibit a proper decorum while making her rounds. Pay was 40 cents a day plus food. Tragically, Miss Dix was a poor organizer and administrator—one soldier called her a "self-sealing can of horror tied up in red tape." The result was that ultimately she became a figurehead as army administrators took over the department.

But there were plenty of women on both sides who were fully capable of making their marks on Civil War medicine in the fields of wounds and disease (qq.v.) treatment without Miss Dix's encumbrances. Phoebe Pember was a noted administrator and nurse at the big Chimborazo Hospital in Confederate Richmond. Kate Cumming served in Rebel hospitals in the Western Theater and kept a meticulous diary that has been published in several editions. Louisa May Alcott visited and publicized hospitals for the Northern home front. Mary Ann Bickerdyke, called "Mother" by all whom she encountered, was a terror, "the Calico Cyclone," to all incompetent doctors and male nurses who crossed her path. She also revealed the qualities that women brought into the army medical ranks. She liked to make unannounced visits and inspect the facilities available. Then she would go over the heads of the local medical staff until she found a man willing to straighten things out. Then she checked to be sure it was done. When an officer complained to his department commander of her interference, he was referred to President Abraham Lincoln (q.v.). "She outranks me," the general told his disgruntled subordinate.

Others of the same mettle were Mary Jane Stafford, "the Angel of Cairo"; Bette Reynolds, who entered medical school to become a doctor in 1864; Clara Barton, "The Angel of the Battlefield," and founder of the American Red Cross; Elizabeth Blackwell, a doctor who turned her skills to educating nurses; and Dr. Mary Walker, the only commissioned doctor in the Union army, who was awarded the Congressional Medal of Honor for her services. In the early 1900s, when a board was reviewing how medals had been issued to noncombatants and asked her to return hers, as they did of many soldiers, she refused.

These and some 3,200 women served in the Union Nursing Bureau alone during the war. On both sides, the women came to be appreciated because they offered quality in a field, nursing, that seemed to attract the worst among men who volunteered or were assigned the job. *See also* AMBULANCE SERVICES AND TRIAGE; DISEASE; MEDICAL DIRECTORS OR SURGEONS GENERAL, CONFEDERATE; MEDICAL DIRECTORS OR SURGEONS GENERAL, UNION; UNITED STATES SANITARY COMMISSION; WOUNDS.

OAK GROVE, BATTLE OF. *See* SEVEN DAYS CAMPAIGN.

OAK HILL, BATTLE OF. *See* MISSOURI CAMPAIGN (1861–1862).

OATHS OF ALLEGIANCE. Unlike the 20th and 21st centuries, in which loyalty oaths have often been challenged as inimical to individual rights, the era of the Civil War and Reconstruction relied on them without question. They were an essential part to any wartime *habeas corpus* (q.v.) proceeding and central to all plans for readmission of the seceded Southern states to full participation in the restored Union.

There were two oaths used during the Civil War and Reconstruction. The standard loyalty oath was one of future loyalty to the United States government. This was given to all released prisoners, civilian or military. It pledged that one would hereafter be loyal to the United States Constitution, its government, and its policies. This oath was administered to all those who wished to participate in government under the Presidential Reconstruction (q.v.) plans of Abraham Lincoln and Andrew Johnson (qq.v.).

But Radical Republicans preferred that the more restrictive ironclad oath be administered. This pledged that the taker had not voluntarily given aid or succor to the Confederacy in any form whatsoever. This was a key element to congressional plans of Reconstruction like the Wade–Davis Bill (q.v.). Some persons were denied the opportunity to take any oath of loyalty, particularly those proscribed under the Fourteenth Amendment (q.v.), until they went through a program of pardon, amnesty, and parole (q.v.) as prescribed by President Lincoln's Proclamation of Amnesty and Reconstruction (q.v.) or President Johnson's Proclamation of Reconstruction (q.v.), or by Congress as in the General Amnesty Acts of 1872 and 1898.

OHIO IDEA. *See* ELECTION OF 1868.

OLD CAPITOL, THE (WASHINGTON). Federal installation that housed Confederate prisoners of war. *See also* PRISONS.

OMNIBUS BILL. *See* COMPROMISE OF 1850.

ORCHARD KNOB, BATTLE OF. *See* CHATTANOOGA CAMPAIGN.

OSAWATOMIE. *See* BROWN, JOHN.

OSTEND MANIFESTO (1854). *See* FILIBUSTERING; "SPREAD EAGLE" FOREIGN POLICY.

OVERLAND CAMPAIGN. *See* RICHMOND OR OVERLAND CAMPAIGN (1864).

P

PACIFIC RAILROAD ACT. The Republican Party (q.v.) had a distinct domestic program designed to appease both its agricultural and industrial supporters. This program had as its basis the old Whig economic policies based in part on Henry Clay's American System (q.v.). Part of the program appealed to both wings of the party by pledging to build a transcontinental railroad. The Pacific Railroad Act (1862, revised and expanded 1864) sought to give Federal aid to the private entrepreneurs through a land grant system of alternate sections along the right-of-way, 20 miles deep. Each rail company received another $16,000 a mile to build on the flats and $48,000 a mile in mountains. Needless to say, many new, never-before-heard-of mountain ranges sprang up along the survey route. The route used was the Central Overland Route, which had been proved to be passable even in winter by the running of the Pony Express just before the war. The Union Pacific Railroad was chartered to build and operate from Omaha, Nebraska Territory, to the west. The Central Pacific (later the Southern Pacific) Railroad was chartered to build and operate from Sacramento, California, to the east. The land grant was doubled in the 1864 amended act, which also canceled the limit on individual stock ownership, allowed companies to issue first-mortgage bonds of their own, and relegated the government's bonds to a second mortgage.

PALE FACES. This group was a local version of the Ku Klux Klan (q.v.) in many Southern states.

PALMETTO RANCH, BATTLE OF. In November 1863, Union troops landed on the Texas coast at Brownsville to secure the Rio Grande boundary between the United States and Mexico, which was then dominated by a French army sent over by Emperor Napoleon III under the Austrian Arch-Duke Maximilian (q.v.). As the French were partial to the Confederacy, President Abraham Lincoln (q.v.) wished to assert some Federal sovereignty in the area, a sparsely settled sort of no-man's land between nations. There was some effort to extend Union control up the Rio Grande to enforce the blockade, but most of these garrisons were withdrawn to help out in the Red River Campaign. But the ones near Brownsville remained behind.

After defeating a force of Texas Union cavalry at Laredo in the spring of 1864, the Confederates moved down the Rio Grande to Brownsville, which was taken on July 30. As a part of the occupation of Texas in 1865, Federal troops tried to reassert national control over Brownsville. But the Confederates stopped this effort at Palmetto Ranch on May 13, 1865, in the last battle of the Civil War. Two weeks later, a reinforced Federal army landed and took Brownsville, abandoned by the Confederates upon learning of the imminent surrender of Texas at Galveston. These Union soldiers would be joined by the black XXV Corps from Virginia in mid-June, who pushed upriver and occupied all points from Brownsville to Laredo.

PANIC OF 1857. The indecisive Crimean War on Russia's Black Sea had upset the world's economy in 1857 by excluding Russia's wheat from the world markets for several years. The shortfall had been made up by increased American production, but in 1857, this was no longer needed, causing a market glut and a corresponding fall in prices. At the same time, British banking interests decided to cash in their American bonds, draining gold from American banks, most located in the North. Many institutions could not meet the call for cash and folded, sending the New York Stock Market into a tailspin and collapse. But while the North suffered, cotton was booming. This led the South to see its slave economy and staple crop system as stronger than that of the industrial North. The solid Southern economy was of great help to the seceders in 1861, who pointed to 1857 and how the South was actually stronger economically than the North and no longer needed it as an albatross pulling the South down.

PANIC OF 1873. *See* GRANT, ULYSSES S., ADMINISTRATION—DOMESTIC POLICIES.

PARDON, AMNESTY, AND PAROLE. As soon as the South had seceded from the Union, the problem arose of how to get it back in. Implicit in this concept was the notion of forgiveness. The Union could not be made whole once again without it. Forgiveness has several contexts: pardon is generally the forgiveness of an individual for certain acts, amnesty is pardon applied to a class of people, while parole (basically a promise) is reserved for soldiers. Until 1864, a captured enemy of either side was generally imprisoned briefly and exchanged. But in cases of mass surrender (there were three of them during the war, Ft. Donelson, Vicksburg, and Appomattox, all to Lt. Gen. Ulysses S. Grant [q.v.]), logistics demanded that the capturing force take the soldiers' paroles to go home and not fight again until properly exchanged.

Abraham Lincoln (q.v.) was a pardoning president. Perhaps it was because of his Southern background (born in Kentucky, raised in Southern Indiana, an adult in Illinois, where he had strong Southern connections, not the least of which were his wife and her family). Maybe it was a part of his soul. His first public policy of pardon was his December 1863 Proclamation of Amnesty (q.v.), which set into operation his wartime plan of Reconstruction. But he was not weak because of this policy. Lincoln's pardon and amnesty powers were always tempered by restrictions, although many Northerners thought him to be too lenient, as the 1864 Wade–Davis Bill (q.v.) demonstrated. Higher officials of the Confederate government or military could not participate in the initial formation of a loyal government in any Southern state.

Through his amnesty policy, Lincoln essentially sought out loyal persons, those who had fought consistently against secession (q.v.), rather than recanting Confederates. He also had a tendency to forgive minor infractions of military law, such as a soldier who was pardoned for having fallen asleep on sentry duty. He refused, however, to interfere in the death sentence of John Y. Beall, a prominent Marylander who got caught in civilian clothes in an attempt to release Confederate prisoners held at Johnson Island in Lake Erie. But he was against wholesale retribution, maintaining that "blood cannot restore blood, and government should not act for revenge." The surrender terms accorded Robert E. Lee's (q.v.) army at Appomattox are the best example of this.

After Lincoln's murder, President Andrew Johnson (q.v.) seemed to give a harsher application to the problem of forgiveness. He spoke of hanging traitors. Radical Republicans were pleased, but events showed the president not to be the man of retribution they wanted. Johnson's Proclamation for Reconstruction (q.v.) exempted 14 classes of citizens from taking the oath of future allegiance and accepting amnesty. Most of these were common to all plans of Reconstruction, higher officials of the Confederate and state governments, and staff officers of the military establishment. But he also included a special class that exempted all persons worth $20,000 or more from amnesty. Instead, they had to apply for individual pardon.

Johnson reserved particular venom for Confederate president Jefferson Davis (q.v.), who was held at Fortress Monroe for two years, then set free on a writ of *habeas corpus* (q.v.), and admitted to bail while still under indictment. But Davis was included in the general Confederate amnesty that was the final act of the Johnson administration (Christmas 1868). With the exception of Davis, who was never tried, the only other Confederate officials jailed were Vice President Alexander Stephens (q.v.) and Postmaster General John H. Reagan. They were released in a matter of months. Most of those who had fled the United States in fear of their lives returned and lived unmolested, if often unreconstructed, lives.

Because Johnson proved to be almost as liberal as Lincoln in individual cases, those exempt from general amnesty applied in droves to regain their rights. This was essential to protect or regain their employment, property, and patents and copyrights, as Johnson's exemptions included those who practiced 50 common occupations. The procedure was to first make application to the provisional governor of the state (appointed by Johnson) for a recommendation. Then the application and letters of recommendation went to the U.S. attorney general's office, where the papers were reexamined for worthiness. Then everything was forwarded to the president who, if he found the petition worthy, would issue a warrant for pardon, the actual documents being filled out and signed by the U.S. secretary of state. Then the president's signature would be obtained and the documents returned to the state governor, who would convey the pardon to the original petitioner.

It was a long, involved process that had many places where bureaucratic snags might develop, so it became common to hire a pardon broker, an expert who would keep track of developments and push an application forward. (The government had thought of creating a pardon bureau but never got around to it.) President Johnson thought the whole business unseemly, especially since several women were involved, a fact considered rather rakish in staid Victorian America. The pardon was free, but the services of a broker were not. And since the president granted 13,500 pardons (half of which were for persons of the $20,000 and above class) in short order, it was a lucrative, if short-lived, business. Johnson's harsh stance against the Confederate leaders soon evaporated. He had Lincoln's wartime example to live up to; Secretary of State William H. Seward (q.v.) was for it; and most of all, the Southerners exempted groveled magnificently. Johnson's hostility soon became so beneficent that many Northerners, especially Republicans in Congress, began to question his motives. Too many old-time Democrats (q.v.) were being let off the hook.

Congress asked the Joint Committee of Fifteen (q.v.) to investigate the real behavior of the South, and it found that the president's pardoning policy was moving too fast (as Republicans had expected), excusing too many who ought to be proscribed from political participation much longer, and not taking into account sufficiently the potential political and economic rights of African-Americans. The result was the Civil Rights Act of 1866 (q.v.) and the officeholding proscription clause of the Fourteenth Amendment (q.v.). It also repealed the clemency clause of the Second Confiscation Act (q.v.), which had granted President Lincoln (and by extension President Johnson) the right to grant amnesty and pardon, as many in Congress believed that the president did not have such powers without a specific grant from the legislative branch. The Military Reconstruction Act of March 2, 1867 (q.v.), then disfranchised anyone coming under the Fourteenth Amendment's proscription (anyone who took an oath to the United States and then subsequently to the Confederacy) until Reconstruction was completed.

Ever ready to take on Congress, Johnson drafted another amnesty, claiming that he had the power directly from the Constitution and needed no congressional sanction. On September 7, 1867, Johnson pardoned all former Confederates except executive officials of the Confederate government, governors of Confederate states, military officers above the army rank of brigadier general and naval rank of captain, anyone implicated in the assassination of President Lincoln, or anyone who had abused captured Union soldiers or officials. This left some 300 Southerners still without full citizenship. During the impeachment (q.v.) trial, Johnson decided to issue a third amnesty, but he wisely waited until he was acquitted before acting. On July 4, 1868, as the Democrat presidential nominating convention met in New York City and the rest of the nation celebrated Independence Day, Johnson extended amnesty to all former Confederates except anyone under indictment or conviction for treason or any other felony. Everyone pardoned received any seized property except slaves.

Finally, Johnson made a fourth amnesty on Christmas Day 1868 pardoning the few Confederate civil and military officials still under proscription, including people like Jefferson Davis, John C. Breckinridge (who had been vice president of the U.S. under James Buchanan, and was well-hated), and Robert E. Lee (qq.v.). Johnson justified his action by saying the Federal authority had been restored to all of the United States, and that there was no need for any voting proscriptions of any kind. But unlike his other proclamations, which had pardoned Southerners for "rebellion," this one used the term "treason." The term was very odious (to use one of Johnson's favorite descriptive adjectives), but it took care of Jefferson Davis, who was under indictment for treason, without having to mention his name specifically.

With President Johnson's leaving office in 1869 and the reluctance of President Ulysses S. Grant (q.v.) to argue over legislative prerogatives, the question of amnesty became pretty much a congressional one. Persons in the South had appealed to Congress for relief from the inception of Military Reconstruction (q.v.), as soon as it became obvious that Johnson was not going to be able to do as he pleased on any question. Individual petitions had been received and some acted upon favorably. President Johnson had signed off on these, allowing Congress to act under its power under the Fourteenth Amendment (q.v.) to remove officeholding disabilities. Congress approved a new oath especially designed for such men who had held Confederate offices and wished to stand for election or had been elected after the war in July 1868.

By 1871, Congress had exempted some 4,600 from the officeholding proscription of the Fourteenth Amendment. President Grant, reflecting public sentiment, spoke favorably for an overall amnesty in 1871. In May 1872, Congress passed the General Amnesty Act that removed officeholding proscriptions from all but those who had served in the two Congresses just before the Civil War, or had been heads of Federal executive departments, Federal judges, foreign ministers for the United States, or officers in the army and navy. Although Congress denied an attempt to pass a general amnesty upon the death of Andrew Johnson in 1876, it continued to give those exempted from the act individual consideration. Finally, in the shadow of the Spanish–American War, Congress restored everyone still exempted under the Fourteenth Amendment on June 8, 1898. Jefferson Davis, the main impediment to such a measure, had been dead for a decade. The Civil War was officially over at last.

PEABODY EDUCATIONAL FUND. A philanthropic group founded by banking and mercantile magnate George Peabody, who had dedicated three and a half million dollars to educating the freed people, the Peabody Educational Fund was administered by Barnas Sears, a New England Yankee who took a more racial view of education in the South than most Northerners. Sears discovered that he had to face up to the separation of race, if he hoped to accomplish the Fund's goal of reestablishing Southern schools after the war. The Peabody Fund had certain requirements that each helped school had to meet: it had to be public, it had to have a term of at least 10 months, it had to have an attendance rate of 85 percent of those enrolled, and local citizens had to contribute at least twice as much to schools as the Fund. From the beginning, through a series of Southern tours, Sears found that the only way to gain local white support was to separate the races in school. This he unabashedly did, granting less money for an African-American school than for a white one in the same straits. The Peabody Fund also tended to stick to school systems in larger urban areas. This meant that the Fund financed white schools, by and large, and refused to help schools in Louisiana and South Carolina that were integrated by state law.

Sears claimed that the Peabody Fund was going to stay out of politics, a naïve concept, if he ever believed it. He quarreled incessantly with the superintendents of education in Louisiana, Thomas Conway and William G. Brown, who believed that their states qualified for funds despite their integrated systems. He also lobbied to get the integrated education clauses pulled out of the Civil Rights Act of 1875 (q.v.), the public accommodations law. Ignoring Senator Charles Sumner (q.v.) and his allies, who favored a strict integration of all public facilities including education, Sears went to other senators and representatives and convinced them that to integrate schools would drive whites out of the public education system into private schools. An interview with President Ulysses S. Grant (q.v.) found the chief executive in complete agreement with Sears. The result was a public accommodations law without the education clauses and a guarantee that Southern schools would be separate but equal 30 years before the U.S. Supreme Court would endorse the same.

PEACHTREE CREEK, BATTLE OF. *See* ATLANTA CAMPAIGN.

PEA RIDGE, BATTLE OF. *See* MISSOURI CAMPAIGN (1861–1862).

PEASE, ELISHA M. (1812–1883). A Connecticut man who immigrated to Texas in 1835, when it was still a part of Mexico. Pease came for the usual reasons—he was bored with being a postal clerk and saw opportunity in a new land. He settled at Mina, read law, and became involved with the Texas Revolution as secretary of the local committee of public safety. At first hoping for conciliation with Mexico, Pease came out for independence and fought at Gonzalez. He was then secretary to the General Council of the Provisional Government, attended the convention, and helped write the constitution of the Republic of Texas.

Pease served the new government as a clerk in various departments and in the House of Representatives, where he helped write the Republic's criminal code. He declined the postmaster generalship and went back to his law studies, being admitted to the bar in 1837. He then was comptroller of public accounts for the Republic and a successful lawyer.

After the annexation of Texas, Pease served in three legislatures, before becoming a two-term governor of some repute. He created a system of public education, deaf and blind schools, an orphan's home, and a state university. He was a strong advocate of railroad construction. Pease also set up Indian reservations and their own system of education. He began the construction of a new state Capitol and completed a governor's mansion.

A Unionist during the Civil War, Pease stayed quietly at home. But with the advent of Reconstruction, he ran for governor once again, this time unsuccessfully, under the Union Party. Pease then helped establish the Republican Party (q.v.) in the state, and when the elected governor was removed from office by the military government, Pease accepted appointment in his place.

As the militarily appointed governor of Texas, Pease and his superior, Bvt. Maj. Gen. Joseph Jones Reynolds (q.v.), came to an agreement that no other governor before Pease, whether elected by the people or appointed by the army (Union or Confederate), had been willing to make. In his Proclamation of October 25, 1867, Pease announced that his administration was in power only at the army's pleasure, and that the state government was subordinate to Gen. Reynolds and the Congress of the United States. Pease also recognized the validity of all laws passed since secession (q.v.) that did not conflict with the results of the war, a denial of the doctrine of *ab initio* (q.v.) that other Texas Republicans held dear. It was Pease's way of saying that Military Reconstruction (q.v.) would be carried out in a non-ideological way.

But the army let Pease down. Gen. Reynolds began to manipulate the Texas state government between the Radical Republicans with their *ab initio* doctrine and the Moderates (q.v.) represented by Pease. Angling for a U.S. Senate seat, Gen. Reynolds managed to get the Radicals to abandon *ab initio* to win the election of 1869. Pease refused to be connected with such crassness and resigned his seat before the election.

Pease refused to back the Radical administration. He presided over a taxpayers' revolt in 1871, joined the Liberal Republicans (q.v.) against the reelection of President U. S. Grant in 1872, and backed Rutherford B. Hayes (q.v.) in his run for the presidency in 1876. This latter act gained him appointment to be collector of customs at Galveston. With the end of the Hayes administration, Pease retired to Austin, where he practiced law until he died of a stroke in 1883.

PEEBLES' FARM, BATTLE OF. *See* PETERSBURG, SIEGE OF.

PEMBERTON, JOHN C. (1814–1881). Philadelphia-born John Pemberton was educated privately as a child. Although he was of Quaker ancestry, he entered West Point and graduated in the middle of the class of 1837. He fought in the Seminole War and served on the Canadian border. In 1846, he married a Virginia woman, falling in love with not only her, but the South as a civilization. He went off as an artillery officer in the War with Mexico, serving as an aide de camp to Brig. Gen. William Worth. Brevetted twice for bravery, Pemberton spent the 1850s on the Western frontier, serving in the Mormon War (q.v.). He was offered a colonelcy in 1861, but resigned his commission to go south and serve with his wife's state as a lieutenant colonel.

He helped organize Virginia troops in 1861 and received rapid promotions to lieutenant general and command of the Department of Mississippi, Alabama, and East Louisiana. This made him responsible for the defense of Vicksburg. At first he did well, but Pemberton was soon befuddled by Federal Maj. Gen. U. S. Grant's (q.v.) seemingly disconnected strategy and conflicting orders from Gen. Joseph E. Johnston and President Jefferson Davis (qq.v.). He surrendered the fortress on July 4, hoping to gain better terms for his men.

Resigning his generalship, Pemberton served as an artillery officer at Richmond for the rest of the war. There is no record he actually surrendered in 1865. He farmed briefly at Warrenton and then moved to Philadelphia, living quietly until his death years later.

PENDLETON, GEORGE. *See* ELECTION OF 1868.

PENINSULA CAMPAIGN. After the Bull Run debacle, Union President Abraham Lincoln (q.v.) began to seek new blood to infuse the Northern command system with aggressiveness. He believed that he had found it in Maj. Gen. George B. McClellan (q.v.). Fresh from the valleys of West Virginia, "Little Mac," as he was called, seemed to be charming, knowledgeable, and above all, a winner. "I can do it all," he asserted calmly, belying all the doubts that lay hidden in his mind. By November 1, 1861, Bvt. Lt. Gen. Winfield Scott (q.v.) had retired, giving the whole Union command to McClellan alone.

Everyone in Washington wanted the Confederate flags that faced them from across the Potomac removed. But McClellan refused to be buffaloed into moving prematurely or against fortifications. He was also made cautious by his chief intelligence officer's inaccurate counting of Rebel troops facing him. The officer was former railroad detective Alan Pinkerton, now known by his alias, E. J. Allen. Pinkerton had supposedly saved Lincoln from assassination during the Baltimore Plot and was now assisting McClellan to be less than bold. Instead, he bided his time until Lincoln issued an order of his own that the army had to at least make a pretense of moving forward in February 1861. Lincoln followed this order with three more, appointing corps commanders for McClellan's force, another ordering him to move to Manassas in March, and a final, which removed McClellan as head of all Union armies and restricted him to the command of his own Army of the Potomac. When McClellan finally moved on Manassas, he found the formidable trenches empty and the forbidding guns adorning them to be fakes. The Rebel army under General Joseph E. Johnston (q.v.) had stolen a march on Little Mac.

But McClellan really had other notions than a frontal attack against Manassas in mind. He had met a New York officer, Col. Rush Hawkins, from the Carolinas, who had landed in the successful campaign for Roanoke Island. He convinced McClellan that the Union's ace-in-the-hole was the navy, something the Confederates could not match. McClellan developed a plan that called for his army to leave the forts around Washington, embark on ships, land at Urbanna near Fredericksburg, and come in behind the Confederates at Manassas. When Johnston realized his vulnerability and retreated, McClellan changed his plan to land on the Virginia Peninsula (the land between the York and James Rivers) at Union-held Fortress Monroe and advance directly on Richmond. His supplies would be provided by the Navy and his flanks guarded by swamps and gunboats. No more Bull Run turning movements would be left to the Rebels. They would have to slug it out on McClellan's own terms.

It was not that McClellan's plan was not of value. It was that he was so slow to carry it out. There were always the little voices urging caution when more *élan* would have better been the order of the day. He arrived at Fortress Monroe in April and advanced to preliminary Rebel positions at Yorktown. Manned by troops led by "Prince John" Magruder, a former actor and bombast of some note, McClellan allowed Magruder to bluff him into performing a formal siege. His delaying tactics held McClellan up for a month (April 5–May 3), until Johnston could get his army down to help out.

But Johnston was not about to fight it out with McClellan's massive siege guns. He began a precipitate retreat up the Peninsula until he reached the entrenchments outside of Richmond. McClellan followed with some alacrity, for a change, forcing Johnston to turn and fight rearguard actions at Williamsburg and Eltham Plantation. The Confederates, commanded by Maj. Gen. James Longstreet (q.v.), hit the Union pursuit head on at Williamsburg (May 5), forcing the Yankees back until Union Gen. Winfield S. Hancock (q.v.) managed to turn Longstreet's flank. Things looked pretty good until Confederate reinforcements caused a halt to the fighting. Two days later, McClellan sent soldiers by boat up the York to Eltham Plantation to outflank the Williamsburg position, where Johnston slapped them back as his men moved on to Richmond's fortifications.

Meanwhile, the Navy had made some progress of its own. On March 7, 1862, during the Yorktown siege, the Confederate ironclad battleship, the C.S.S. *Virginia*, appeared in Hampton Roads threatening McClellan's rear. Built upon the hull of the burned U.S. frigate *Merrimac*, the *Virginia* was essentially a casemate of 10 guns enclosed by sloping sides. The *Virginia*'s presence had been known for some time, allowing the Yankees to develop their own ironclad, the U.S.S. *Monitor*, to oppose it. The *Monitor* was of unusual construction, being basically a flat deck topped by a two-gun revolving turret. But the *Monitor* was a day late, allowing the *Virginia* to wreak havoc among the blockading Union wooden fleet. The next day, the *Monitor* fought the *Virginia* (often erroneously referred to as the *Merrimac*) to a standstill.

But Johnston's retreat to Richmond caused the Confederates to have to withdraw from Norfolk. In the process, the deep draft *Virginia* had to be destroyed, opening the James to the U.S. fleet. The Navy sallied boldly forth until it reached Drewry's Bluff (q.v.), just below Richmond. Here, in a three-hour gun battle (May 15), the Confederates held off the Union ships, causing them to pull back. Richmond would have to be taken by the army.

As McClellan approached Richmond, he faced a geographic problem. Across his path lay the Chickahominy River. He would have to cross it to get at Richmond. But McClellan did not expect to besiege Richmond long. He wanted a part of his army left behind in the vicinity of Fredericksburg to come south and outflank the Rebel positions. To join with these men, McClellan would have to leave some troops north of the Chickahominy. The rest would have to cross the river possibly under fire, always a dangerous proposition in wartime.

But McClellan also had a political problem. He had promised President Lincoln that he would leave enough Union troops behind to safeguard Washington from a surprise Rebel attack. McClellan did so, but he and Lincoln got to arguing how many men would be necessary, and McClellan double-counted the men who were to advance down to Richmond by land as some of those who would defend Washington. Lincoln was not amused.

Worse yet, in the Shenandoah Valley, Maj. Gen. Thomas J. "Stonewall" Jackson (q.v.) had advanced his small force to Kernstown, near Winchester, and attacked the Union position there. Although Jackson got beat, his attack disturbed Lincoln even more. That was far too aggressive a man to leave unguarded. So Lincoln issued another of his interfering orders, removing the force that was to come down by land behind Richmond from McClellan's control and sending it to the Shenandoah. This came at just the moment that McClellan had defeated a Confederate blocking force north of Richmond at Hanover Court House (May 27), clearing the way for action to the rear of the Richmond siege lines.

McClellan had a military problem, in addition to geography and politics. He had to cross the Chickahominy. Johnston waited patiently until McClellan had divided his army and a vicious rainstorm threatened the bridges that kept the two sections in contact. Then Johnston struck the part of McClellan's force south of the river, the smallest part, with most of his whole force. The resulting battles of Seven Pines and First Fair Oaks (May 31–June 1) were essentially a draw, with the most important casualty being Johnston himself. The Confederate army was essentially leaderless, as McClellan hurried to reinforce his isolated Southern force, with many troops running across bridges near collapse to save the day.

Now McClellan faced the exact reverse situation, militarily, from that at Seven Pines. His army stretched across the Chickahominy, but the larger part was on the south side in front of Richmond, with a small covering force on the north side waiting in vain for overland reinforcement. And the Confederates had a new commander, President Jefferson Davis' (q.v.) personal military advisor, General Robert E. Lee (q.v.).

PENNSYLVANIA CAMPAIGN. After the Confederate victory in the Chancellorsville Campaign (q.v.), the question arose of what to do with Robert E. Lee's (q.v.) Army of Northern Virginia next. Sitting on the defensive seemed nonproductive and yielded too much initiative to the North. Many in the Confederate government figured that Lee, with or without a portion of his army, ought to go to the Western Theater and save Vicksburg or operate with the Army of Tennessee, which lacked an overall commander of talent in Gen. Braxton Bragg (q.v.).

But Lee refused to leave the Eastern Theater. He also opposed giving up part of his army under a corps commander, like Lt. Gen. James Longstreet (q.v.), to operate in the West. Lee proposed instead that he invade the North once again. It would give Virginia a rest, permit the plundering of the Cumberland Valley of its foodstuffs, and force the North to respond, not only with Maj. Gen. Joseph Hooker's (q.v.) Army of the Potomac, but hopefully other troops from the Western Theater as well. This would do much to save Vicksburg, and a victory on Northern soil promised more recognition in the diplomatic realm than anything else.

There was much fear in governmental circles on both sides that not keeping a force in front of the capital would permit the enemy to march directly upon Richmond or Washington or both, in effect, swapping queens as chess players might. For this reason, Lee had to leave a couple of brigades behind in Virginia, which would hamper his operations after battle had been joined in Pennsylvania. Hooker, on the other hand, was restricted in his movements to stay between Lee and Washington at all times and denied independent units at Washington and Harper's Ferry that might have given him more operational flexibility.

Lee began moving his troops north on June 3, 1863. Hooker quickly suspected that things were not as they should be and began to probe Lee's lines in Virginia to confirm any move north. He hit the tail of Lee's army at Franklin's Crossing, a position just south of Fredericksburg at Deep Run reached by pontoon bridges. The results seemed to indicate it was still strongly held. Hooker probed deeper on June 15 farther up the Rappahannock in the middle of Lee's extended army. Crossing at Kelly's and Beverly's Fords, Hooker's cavalry corps attacked Confederate Maj. Gen. J. E. B. Stuart's (q.v.) horsemen at Fleetwood hill near Brandy Station. The combat was hand-to-hand, control of the hill changing several times. Finally, Confederate infantry came up at the end of the day. Hooker had what he wanted to know: Lee was on the move toward the Shenandoah Valley and north.

Meanwhile, Lee's Second Corps, the one commanded by Lt. Gen. Thomas J. "Stonewall" Jackson (q.v.) before his death, under Lt. Gen. Richard S. Ewell was already in the Shenandoah routing slow-moving Yankee garrison troops at the Second Battle of Winchester. As the Federals tried to escape Ewell's juggernaut, he moved around them to Stephenson's Depot, capturing a large number. He seemed to be the very personification of his mentor, Jackson. Lee was pleased.

Hooker continued to probe Lee's advance with spirited cavalry actions at Aldie, Middleburg, and Upperville. At the latter place, Union troopers got to the top of the Blue Ridge and saw Confederate infantry marching north. Hooker shifted his position accordingly, keeping between Lee and Washington. It was still uncertain what Lee's ultimate objective might be—Washington, Baltimore, or Philadelphia. Hooker, being tied to Washington, was greatly disadvantaged, even with the call-up of the Pennsylvania and New York militias.

After screening Lee from Federal interference at the Blue Ridge, Stuart started off on the most controversial move he made during the campaign. His orders read to join the Confederate advance up in Pennsylvania; the path was left up to him. Stuart naturally chose to ride around the rear of Hooker's force between him and Washington and meet Ewell's men at Harrisburg. He in effect rode right out of the campaign for the next nine days. Stuart has received much-deserved criticism for what he did, then and now. But his best defender remains Maj. John S. Mosby, the Confederate guerrilla leader, who aptly observed that Lee had adequate cavalry during the Pennsylvania Campaign, which he used poorly. What Lee missed was not Stuart's men but Stuart himself, whom he relied on so much.

By June 28, Lee was in the Cumberland Valley, the tail of his army at Chambersburg with its head at several points on the Susquehanna. Ewell had orders to cross at the first bridge he could. The Rebels were fairly well behaved in Pennsylvania, especially considering what the Yankees had done in Virginia and the rest of the South to date. They made a special side trip, however, to destroy the Caledonian Forge Ironworks, owned and operated by Radical Republican congressman Thaddeus Stevens (q.v.). Maj. Gen. Jubal Early (q.v.) was disappointed that Old Thad was not present, wanting to take his bones back to Richmond as a curiosity, he said.

Hooker was at Frederick, Maryland. He wanted to march straight west and cut Lee's communications somewhere around Boonesboro. President Abraham Lincoln (q.v.) feared that such a move would leave Washington, Baltimore, and Philadelphia open to attack. He had chief of staff Maj. Gen. Henry W. Halleck (q.v.) refuse Hooker's plan. In a huff at being interfered with so much, Hooker resigned. Lincoln had been hoping to get rid of him, still leery of Hooker's loss of nerve at Chancellorsville. He appointed Maj. Gen. George Meade (q.v.) of the Union V Corps as the new commander.

A Pennsylvanian with an acerbic temper, Meade would have to rely on much of Hooker's staff for the coming battle. It was at best a difficult position to be in. But he moved the Union army up to Pipe Creek in northern Maryland, hoping to entice Lee into attacking him in an already prepared position. But Lee was already changing his plans, having been informed by a scout that Meade was the new Federal commander and that his forces were closer than Lee supposed. Lee quickly recalled Ewell's advance units. The two armies were about to meet quite by accident at a small 12-road junction named Gettysburg.

On June 30, a Federal cavalry division, out looking for Lee's infantry, received news from citizens at Gettysburg that the Rebels were out west on the Cashtown Road. Recognizing the terrain and numerous roads made Gettysburg well worth holding. Federal cavalry commander Brig. Gen. John Buford moved as far out the Cashtown Road as he dared, to force the Rebels to have to fight on July 1 for Gettysburg, delaying them until infantry could reinforce him. Two Union infantry corps joined him in the afternoon on Seminary Ridge, setting back the approaching Confederate troops, coincidentally the same units so used up at Chancellorsville and now lackadaisically commanded. The result was that the Federals dealt Lee's men a temporary defeat that was soon rectified as Ewell's brigades came up on their northern flank and routed the Union troops through the town. Night fell with the demoralized Federals hanging onto Cemetery Hill south of Gettysburg by their fingertips.

The time was now. Everyone in Ewell's Second Corps knew it. Jackson would have attacked headlong into the Federal position. But Ewell had orders from Lee not to bring on a general engagement until the whole army was up. Jackson was a man of imagination who took Lee's orders as guides, not straightjackets. Ewell was one of Jackson's subordinates, who remembered that Stonewall never allowed his own captains such leeway. Ewell would wait until the morrow. Ewell would await a direct order, not Lee's usual, "do what you think practicable." And so he waited.

On the other side, Meade had sent Maj. Gen. Winfield S. Hancock (q.v.) forward to scout out the ground, and Hancock reported that it was worth fighting for. Through the night and early the next day, both sides marched in reinforcements. Meade arrived and extended his line southward with his III Corps under Maj. Gen. Daniel Sickles, a New York politician. Sickles' men had almost been cut off trying to stop Jackson's flank march during the Chancellorsville campaign. He looked out from his assigned position on Cemetery Ridge (an extension south of Cemetery Hill) and saw higher ground before him. He was not about to allow Rebels to move behind those ridges to his flank.

On his own volition, Sickles advanced his whole corps forward in battle formation, flags flying to occupy the Peach Orchard, the Wheat Field, and a collection of rocks called Devil's Den. Meade ordered them back. But it was too late. Lee's First Corps, under Lt. Gen. James Longstreet, fresh men who had missed Chancellorsville, slammed into Sickles' left flank headed for Cemetery Ridge and Gettysburg. Meade threw everything he had into the battle. But the Rebels took Devil's Den, the Peach Orchard and the Wheat Field. It finally took every artillery battery Meade's field commanders could find, lined up wheel hub to wheel hub, to stop the Rebel attack at the face of Cemetery Ridge. And even that would not have worked had not the 20th Maine Infantry held Little Round Top, a hill south of Cemetery Ridge, for the Union.

Meanwhile, Ewell had attacked the other end of the Union line, which now resembled an inverted fishhook, with Little Round Top and its neighbor to the south, Big Round Top, as the eye, and Ewell's attack being made at Culp's Hill, the hook. Ewell's men took the base of Culp's Hill and even part of Cemetery Hill, but darkness stopped the fighting. The next morning, the Federals unceremoniously threw Ewell's men out of both positions.

Overnight, both commanders debated with their officers what to do next. Meade got a vote of no retreat from his subordinates, but Lee was having a more extended debate with Longstreet, who had opposed the attacks on July 2 and now on the morning of July 3 renewed his objections. He hoped for Lee to move to a better location and let the Federals wear themselves out on Lee's position, not the other way around. But Lee knew that there was no way out. Any retreat would signal a Union victory.

Since Longstreet had received Maj. Gen. George E. Pickett's division during the night, he would attack the Federals on Cemetery Ridge in the center of Meade's line, the shank of the fishhook position. Longstreet was aghast. Lee was adamant. Longstreet went forward to organize the attack without enthusiasm. Since Pickett's Division was the one that had to leave two brigades behind to guard Richmond, it was undermanned from the start. So Lee assigned parts of two other divisions to assist, the ones that had been beaten up at Chancellorsville and on July 1.

Even though this attack has gone down in history as "Pickett's Charge," Pickett was not in command of all of it. The troops were lined up with Pickett on the right, with two flank brigades (one his, one from another division) to keep his right flank secure. On Pickett's left were four brigades in line under Maj. Gen. J. Johnston Pettigrew (their original commander, wounded on July 1). Behind him as flank guards were two brigades under Maj. Gen. Isaac R. Trimble (their original commander, also wounded on July 1), who had refused to serve any longer under Ewell after he failed to take Cemetery Hill on July 1. Thus Trimble and Pettigrew were not the regular commanders of the men under them. But their units comprised half of the 15,000 attackers (or of however many attacked—the number is increasingly coming under question nowadays).

After a tremendous artillery preparation, during which most of the guns were sighted incorrectly for maximum effect, the assault units moved forward in perfect alignment. Through the usual mistakes in such situations, the four flank brigades, which were to be lined up in echelon, lined up in line behind the attack units. This allowed individual Union regiments to move forward and enfilade the whole assault. The ineffective Confederate artillery preparation had not subdued Federate cannon, which now moved forward and fired rounds called canister—cans of musket balls—making their pieces work like gigantic shotguns. On top of that, the usual riflemen returned fire. Confederate artillery tried to help out, but cover fire was limited the closer to the Yankees the Confederate infantry got.

The assault made it to the Yankee line, several Union units broke and ran, but it was over after a brief hand-to-hand struggle, the so-called "High-water Mark of the Confederacy." Then came the hard part—getting back to the Confederate positions across the valley. By the end of that retreat, probably a third of those who started were down. Lee met the survivors. He took full responsibility for the attack and its result. Lee feared a Federal counterattack, but they were as used up as Lee's men. On July 4, the two armies stood and stared at each other. On July 5, Lee began the trek back to Virginia, in a pouring rain.

When Lee reached the Potomac at Williamsport, the river was at flood stage and unable to be crossed. Union cavalry had harassed the Confederates all the way, their newfound aggressiveness a real surprise to the Rebels. For two weeks, the Confederates dug trenches and awaited an attack. Finally, on July 14, Lee's army was safely back in Virginia, much to the anger of President Lincoln, who believed that Meade should have destroyed them on the flooded Potomac. All casualties for the North totaled 23,000 men. For the Confederates, the number was 28,000.

As the two armies licked their wounds on opposite sides of the Rappahannock, both governments began to withdraw units from them for other operations. Lee lost Longstreet and two divisions to the Army of Tennessee and the Chattanooga Campaign (q.v.). Meade lost equivalent detachments to the Siege of Charleston and to subdue the New York draft riots (q.v.).

Later that fall, Lee learned that two corps from the Army of the Potomac were being sent to the Chattanooga Campaign. He immediately went on the offensive (October 9), using the same strategy that he had used in the Second Manassas Campaign (q.v.). Meade, however, moved quickly back and occupied a strong defensive position on the old Bull Run battlefield, defeating a part of Lee's army at Bristoe Station (October 14). Meade counterattacked and maneuvered across the Rappahannock near the old Chancellorsville (q.v.) battlefield. But he found Lee entrenched and decided to scrub a planned attack in late November 1863. That ended the Pennsylvania Campaign and its aftermath. The armies went into winter quarters to await what 1864 would bring.

PERALTA, BATTLE OF. *See* NEW MEXICO–ARIZONA CAMPAIGN

PERRYVILLE, BATTLE OF. *See* PERRYVILLE CAMPAIGN.

PERRYVILLE CAMPAIGN. After the combined Federal forces in the West under the leadership of Bvt. Maj. Gen. Henry W. Halleck (q.v.) captured the abandoned fortified town of Corinth, Mississippi, President Abraham Lincoln (q.v.) called Halleck to Washington to be his military advisor. Halleck was deemed by all to be one of the smartest men in the service. He had unabashedly taken credit for all that Bvt. Maj. Gen. Ulysses S. Grant and Bvt. Maj. Gen. John Pope (qq.v.) had accomplished with their victories at Shiloh and Island No. 10, and Lincoln wanted him to be general-in-chief. The result was to leave the armies in the West without a single leadership, and they splintered their efforts. Bvt. Maj. Gen. Don Carlos Buell (q.v.) scattered his Army of the Cumberland across Middle Tennessee, actually occupying Chattanooga briefly, and threatening Rebel control of East Tennessee. Grant did the same in West Tennessee, concentrating his attention on capturing the great river fortress of Vicksburg. As Gen. Pope went east with Halleck to take field command against Robert E. Lee (q.v.), his forces were divvied out to Grant.

The Confederates had two forces in the West, one in East Tennessee commanded by Maj. Gen. Edmund Kirby Smith (q.v.), the "Blücher of Manassas," and the force that had fought the Shiloh Campaign (q.v.), deep in Mississippi, under the control of Gen. Braxton Bragg (q.v.), now that Gen. P. G. T. Beauregard (q.v.) was on sick leave, or what President Jefferson Davis (q.v.) believed to be "French leave." Bragg sent one of his cavalry leaders, Brig. Gen. Nathan Bedford Forrest (q.v.), to raid into Tennessee. Smashing up the Union supply lines, Forrest and his mere 1,000 men caused Halleck from Washington to order Buell to draw his men out of Chattanooga and guard the roads to Louisville, his main headquarters area. This shifted the initiative in the West to the Rebels.

Using the convoluted Confederate rail network, Bragg and his Army of Tennessee rode to Mobile and up through Alabama and Georgia, arriving in Chattanooga on July 31, 1862. Kirby Smith came down from Knoxville, and he and Bragg entered into the Chattanooga Agreement, a vague document that pledged them to mutual cooperation while retaining independent commands. At the same time, Confederate commands from Missouri (Maj. Gen. Sterling Price [q.v.]) and Arkansas (Maj. Gen. Earl Van Dorn) would contain Grant in northern Mississippi, another would come up from Louisiana to join Bragg (Brig, Gen. John C. Breckinridge [q.v.]), and a final force from what would become West Virginia (Brig. Gen. Humphrey Marshall) would join Kirby Smith. Then Bragg and Kirby Smith would invade Kentucky at about the same time Lee was entering Maryland. When Bragg and Kirby Smith reached Frankfort, they would reinstall a rump Confederate state government (created at Bowling Green the previous year by George W. Johnson, who died at Shiloh), under Provisional Governor Richard Hawes.

Anxious to get to Kentucky first and grab the glory of liberating Kentucky for Hawes and the Confederacy, Kirby Smith moved out in August. He hit a Union force at Zion Church on August 30 and captured 5,000 of 6,500 defenders, plus their arms, ammunition, and supply wagons and teams. Panic swept Union Kentucky. On September 1, Kirby Smith was at Lexington. Three days later he was at Frankfort, with Bragg and Hawes still around Chattanooga. Then Kirby Smith stalled, wondering what to do next. Bragg ordered Kirby Smith to hold on at Lexington. He was on his way, at last. Bragg entered Nashville and reinstalled Isham Harris (q.v.) as governor of Confederate Tennessee. He followed up and actually passed Buell's Union army, threatening to beat him to Louisville.

Then Bragg got sidetracked. When his cavalry failed to take a stubborn Federal force holding Mumfordville, Bragg came up with his whole army and changed their minds. But the Yankees insisted on several days' negotiation before they would surrender, and Bragg took another day to celebrate and have a religious revival. Before he knew it, Buell's men had passed him by and got to Louisville first. Even worse from Bragg's point of view was the fact that Kentucky failed to rise in support of the Rebel invasion. So Bragg threw out a defensive line toward Louisville and inaugurated Hawes as governor on October 4.

Meanwhile Buell's reorganized force, reinforced by troops from around Louisville, had cautiously begun moving on Frankfort on October 1. Bragg moved out to meet his approach, his force lacking cavalry for reconnaissance. One wing, under Maj. Gen. William Hardee, stopped at the Chaplin River to take on water, the fall being particularly dry. Informed of a large Union force approaching, Hardee called on Bragg for help.

The next day, October 8, in a confused battle, Hardee's outnumbered Rebels attacked and pushed back Buell's whole force. Buell's Corps commanders failed to make the most of opportunities to counterattack and win. Bragg could not hear the battle (sounds have a funny way of not being heard everywhere at once), and when he discovered from prisoners that Buell's whole force was up he retreated, looking to join with the ever-uncooperative Kirby Smith. Both Confederate forces retreated back toward Chattanooga.

Generals on both sides argued that everyone else but themselves were to blame. Bragg was a close friend of Jefferson Davis (q.v.), so Kirby Smith took the fall and was transferred to the Trans-Mississippi graveyard of disgraced officers. Buell could not survive the effects of the Northern congressional election of 1862. He was replaced by Maj. Gen. William Rosecrans (q.v.), who was arguing with Grant over the summer in northern Mississippi at the Battle of Iuka and the Battle of Corinth (qq.v.) against the Rebels Price and Van Dorn. Breckinridge was lucky. Bragg had left him behind in Chattanooga without orders, in his rush to get to Kentucky, and Breckinridge escaped any political retribution.

Anxious to rebuild his tarnished reputation and justify President Davis' faith in him, Bragg quickly moved into Middle Tennessee to hold the town of Murfreesboro and hopefully take Nashville. But Bragg soon realized that his army was too ill-equipped, ill-fed, and disorganized to advance upon Nashville. He was still quarreling with his corps commanders over everything from supplies to the Perryville fiasco. Although Bragg finally received the addition of Breckinridge's men, he lost a division to the defense of Vicksburg.

Fortunately for the confused Confederates, Buell's old Army of the Cumberland, now under Rosecrans, was also in need of revitalization. Rosecrans had several virtues. He was one of the winningest generals the North had. He was a Democrat (q.v.), which appealed to War Democrats supporting President Lincoln, and he was liked by the Radical Republicans on the Joint Committee on the Conduct of the War (q.v.). But the need of reorganization and resupply (constantly interrupted by Rebel cavalry raiders) forced Rosecrans to hold at Nashville until after Christmas 1862.

By December 30, Rosecrans had his whole force strung out along Stone's River, across from Murfreesboro. To fool Bragg, as the Federals' right flank was not anchored on some strong geographical obstacle, Rosecrans had campfires built out beyond his troops' lines. On December 31, Bragg hit Rosecrans on the Union right. Fooled by the campfires, the Confederate attack actually so overlapped the Union line as to threaten Rosecrans' whole army with annihilation. The Union line crumbled and pulled back until Rosecrans' army was bent back over itself in a "V" along Stone's River and the road to Nashville.

That night, Bragg and his commanders expected the defeated Union army to retreat to Nashville. Bragg was so excited that this victory would mitigate the criticism of him after Perryville that he telegraphed Richmond about the great victory he had won. On the Union side, Maj. Gen. George Thomas, one of Rosecrans' corps commanders, refused to permit the other to talk of retreat. Stiffened by Thomas, Rosecrans' order was to "go to your commands and prepare to fight and die here." The two armies were too exhausted for theatrics. All day, January 1, they faced each other, licking their wounds. Bragg could not believe that Rosecrans would not leave the field.

On January 2, Rosecrans shifted his left flank over Stone's River to a hill that threatened Bragg's whole line. He ordered Breckinridge to drive the Yankees off. The Union troops fought well, finally withdrawing across the river. The Confederates followed, right into the muzzles of 58 cannon. Breckinridge's men were slaughtered and driven back in disarray.

The next day, Bragg pondered whether he ought to attack again. On January 4, he decided to withdraw, making his telegram to Richmond look like a kind of cruel hoax. Rosecrans occupied Murfreesboro a day later. He had lost over 13,000 killed and wounded—more than Union Maj. Gen. George B. McClellan (q.v.) had lost during the Seven Days Campaign (q.v.). Bragg had suffered nearly 10,000 casualties. Minus the killed and wounded, everyone was back right where they had started six months earlier.

PETERSBURG, FINAL ASSAULT OF. *See* PETERSBURG, SIEGE OF.

PETERSBURG, SIEGE OF. Having been stymied at each attempt to destroy Confederate Gen. Robert E. Lee's (q.v.) Army of Northern Virginia in May and June 1864, Federal Lt. Gen. Ulysses S. Grant (q.v.) decided to avoid a lengthy siege at Richmond, the Confederate capital, by moving his army south of the James River and taking Petersburg, an important rail junction. This would cut off Richmond's contact with the rest of the South and open up its weaker south side to attack.

If he moved quickly, Grant had a chance of fooling Lee into thinking that he was still north of the river. If Lee did not react soon enough, Grant would have Richmond and be south of and behind the Confederate army. Victory in the war was in the offing. To effect his move, Grant sent his cavalry under Maj. Gen. Philip H. Sheridan (q.v.) deep into Virginia to wreck the Virginia Central Railroad. Sheridan was to join Maj. Gen. David Hunter's troops in the Shenandoah. But Hunter suffered a defeat at Lynchburg (June 17–18) and retreated into West Virginia, opening the way for Confederate Maj. Gen. Jubal Early's Washington Raid (q.v.). Sheridan himself found his command blocked by Confederate cavalry under Maj. Gen. Wade Hampton at Trevilian Station (June 11–12). Hampton was at first driven back, but a countercharge recovered all he had lost and more. The following day Sheridan, having been unsuccessful in attacking Hampton's now-entrenched troopers, withdrew after Hunter's defeat, to rejoin Grant.

While Sheridan was riding about central Virginia, Grant began constructing the James River Bridge, the longest pontoon bridge ever built to that time. It would stretch 2,100 feet across a deep river with a four-foot tide. It had 101 pontoon boats and three schooners to hold it out of the water. It took 450 engineers four days to build it, in three sections that were floated into position at the last minute. It took eight hours to join the sections into a single span.

Grant began crossing his army behind a cavalry and infantry screen, completing the process on June 16. Lee seemed to have been totally surprised by the scope of the move, having expected Grant to attack Richmond from the east, where his screen was employed. In any case, Lee was slow to react. Grant had stolen a march on the Confederates, at last. He had already attempted to grab the Petersburg defenses on June 9, but the attack had been poorly coordinated, and the troops withdrew without achieving their objective. Now, on June 15, he tried again, using part of Bvt. Maj. Gen. Ben Butler's Army of the James (Bvt. Maj. Gen. W. F. Smith's XVIII Corps) and Maj. Gen. Winfield S. Hancock's II Corps of Grant's Army of the Potomac.

The Confederate general in charge at Petersburg was P. G. T. Beauregard (q.v.). He was also responsible for keeping Butler's army bottled up in the Bermuda Hundred in a loop of the James upriver from Petersburg. He really did not have enough men to do both jobs adequately. He was aided by the attacker's slow preparations, slower movements, and inept and unimaginative generalship. Smith's men took the first line of trenches at Petersburg, but Hancock arrived too late to prolong the attack that day. Instead of attacking at night, Smith waited until dawn. Beauregard pulled every man he had from the Bermuda Hundred line, chancing that Butler would remain inactive. Lee sent a couple of divisions to replace Beauregard, but Butler did nothing during the few hours that Richmond stood wide open.

Beauregard's strength surprised the Yankees the next day, but they soon had reinforcements on the ground. Beauregard managed to hold until dark, when he withdrew to a shorter line in his rear. When the Federals attacked the next morning, they struck the empty trenches and wandered in confusion. When they finally attacked Beauregard that afternoon, the Confederate line held, with Lee's whole army coming up late that day. Grant had lost another opportunity. The result was a lengthy siege, something Lee could not hope to win, but which saved the Confederacy for another year.

The basic problem that faced Lee at Petersburg was to figure out where Grant would attack. Grant had two choices. He could make the assault on the north side of the James and take the direct route into Richmond, or he could strike south of the river near Petersburg and take Richmond from the rear. He had to hit Lee where the Confederate strength was weak. Grant had more men, so if he could fool Lee into placing his reserves at one spot and hit another, Grant might break through. Otherwise, Grant sought to extend his lines south and west to cut off the half dozen rail lines into the area and starve Richmond and Lee out.

Grant first struck at the Jerusalem Plank road outside Petersburg (June 22–23), hoping to isolate the Weldon Railroad. He was only partially successful, tearing up the rails temporarily, but holding the plank road. Then Grant shifted gears and began probing alternatively above and below the James River line, as Lee detached all the men he could under Maj. Gen. Jubal Early (q.v.) to the Shenandoah Valley to block a new Federal advance there and threaten Washington, possibly forcing Grant to relax his grip at Richmond.

First Grant struck north of the James at the Battle of First Deep Bottom (July 27–29). But Union infantry and cavalry moved sluggishly, allowing themselves to be bluffed out of aggressive action until Confederate reinforcements blocked the way. At the same time (July 30), Grant initiated the Battle of the Crater, blowing up a section of the Confederate line in front of Petersburg. This assault, one of the war's major uses of African-American soldiers, failed, too, because of incompetent leadership that resulted in the final removal of Maj. Gen. Ambrose E. Burnside (q.v.), commander of the IX Corps, and the blunderer of the 1862 Fredericksburg Campaign.

On August 13, Grant hit north of the James at the battle of Second Deep Bottom, hoping to capitalize on Early's transfer, which left Lee weak in front of Richmond. A week's stalemate resulted. On August 18, Grant struck south of the James at Globe Tavern. Here he successfully cut the Weldon Railroad. But the Rebels were using the rails and off-loading supplies into wagons farther south. So Grant sent the Union II Corps down to Reams' Station to put an end to this. The result was a smashing defeat of the Union troops, which was indicative (like Deep Bottom) of just how much

Grant's army had been weakened as a coherent combat formation. By now he had lost nearly 100,000 casualties, fully as many men as he had started with back on May 3.

Rebuilding and reorganizing, Grant tried a new combination attack on September 28–30, beginning north of the river at Chafin's farm, identified correctly as lightly held by the Rebels. This attack was repulsed when Federal soldiers reached a network of sub-terra shells (mines, in modern parlance), moats, and abatis, a crude form of sharpened sticks braced in the ground, which served like modern barbed wire. At the same time, Grant attacked south of the James at Peeble's farm, extending his line and stretching Lee's defenses thinner. On October 7, Grant returned north of the river to assault New Market Heights, which ended in another stalemate.

At the end of the month (October 27–28), Grant launched another attack, utilizing his black regiments again. This was repulsed after Union command broke down on the field. Simultaneously, Grant launched an attack, the Battle of First Hatcher's Run, that seized the Boydton Road and the South Side Railroad. But his men were too overextended and could not be resupplied or reinforced in time to prevent their being driven off.

Winter brought a temporary respite to Federal and Rebel alike until early February 1865, when Grant took a chance on brief good weather to fight the Battle of Second Hatcher's Run (Dabney's Mills). This time, the Union troops took and held the South Side Railroad, extending Federal lines once again. By this time, Lee's defenses were stretched to the limit. All Grant would have to do was push hard as soon as better weather arrived in the spring, initiating the Appomattox Campaign (q.v.).

PICACHO PASS, BATTLE OF. *See* NEW MEXICO–ARIZONA CAM-PAIGN.

PICKETT'S CHARGE. *See* PENNSYLVANIA CAMPAIGN.

PIEDMONT, BATTLE OF. *See* WASHINGTON, EARLY'S RAID ON.

PIERCE, FRANKLIN (1804–1869). Known as the "Young Hickory from the Granite Hills," Franklin Pierce at age 49 was the youngest president of the antebellum period. Born in Hillsboro, New Hampshire, he grew up in the world of politics, attended all the right schools (Hancock, Francestown, Phillips Exeter), graduated from Bowdoin College third in the class of 1820 (his schoolmates were Henry Wadsworth Longfellow and Nathaniel Haw-thorne), and studied law under a prominent Jacksonian, Levi Woodbury at Portsmouth. Naturally he was a Democrat (q.v.). Pierce served in the New Hampshire state legislature, Congress, and the Senate. He had boyish good looks, a pleasant personality, and no set view on anything. He rarely made a speech, and when he did, he said nothing.

As a loyal Democrat, he volunteered for the army during the War with Mexico, as a private. His political connections led to his promotion to colonel and then brigadier general, when President James K. Polk needed loyal Democratic officers to offset all of the Whig hero-generals of that conflict. But Pierce really got little glory, although he brought reinforcements from Vera Cruz to Puebla and fought off six guerrilla attacks along the way. Pierce had a penchant for hurting himself before battle or not commanding the attacking units. Pierce saw his nomination and defeat of the Whig candidate, his former commander, Bvt. Lt. Gen. Winfield Scott (q.v.), as vindication of him in the public's eye.

Just before assuming office, he and his wife had been on a train that had rolled off an embankment and tragically saw their young son crushed to death before their very eyes. Mrs. Pierce was never the same afterward. Somehow she got the idea that God had taken the boy so as to leave Pierce untrammeled by any family problems during his presidency. She was not happy as First Lady. Her resentment took away a lot of the buoyant optimism and self-assurance that Pierce had evidenced prior to the election.

Pierce pledged the usual in his inaugural: economic government, upholding the Constitution, and support for the Compromise of 1850 (q.v.) as the only solution to the problem of slavery in the territories. He also spoke out against fanatics who unduly excited the public over the slavery issue. Above all, Pierce desired harmony in his administration and appointed a Catholic as postmaster general to prove it. The rest of his cabinet represented various factions or influential men of the party.

But Pierce's administration proved anything but harmonious. In foreign policy, he was tainted by an expansionist wing of the party, which wished to advance American interests in the Caribbean. Northerners saw this as the expansion of slavery into new climes more favorable than the American West. Domestically, he backed the Kansas–Nebraska Act (q.v.), which repealed the Missouri Compromise and led to an antislavery rush to Kansas to stop slavery expansion there, and the organization of antislavery forces into the new Republican Party (q.v.). He angered Southerners by appointing Northern men to govern the territory, many of whom were incompetent political hacks. By 1856, Pierce had been so discredited that he was not considered for renomination. He spent the rest of his years in quiet retirement, discredited as a "doughface," a Northern man with Southern principles.

PILOT KNOB, BATTLE OF. See PRICE'S MISSOURI RAID (1864).

PINCHBACK, PINCKNEY BENTON STEWART (1837–1921). Born near Macon, Georgia, P. B. S. Pinchback was the eighth child of white planter William Pinchback and his slave, Eliza Stewart. His mother had been manumitted sometime around his birth, but she remained with her lover as he traveled from Virginia to Mississippi. P. B. S. Pinchback was born along the way. He was sent away to boarding school in Cincinnati, Ohio, returning to find his father near death. After he died, mother and children were hustled away to the North, to prevent their being enslaved. His older brother becoming mentally incapacitated, P. B. S. Pinchback went to work at age 12 as a cabin boy on canal boats in Ohio. There he learned all there was to know from some of the sharpest con men of the age. "Pinch," as he was appropriately called, later spoke of himself as legally being a quadroon, or one-fourth Negro. He advanced his position to steward (the highest position that a black could have in slavery days) and augmented his income by taking advantage of the black roustabouts and deckhands along the way. In 1862, he slipped off a riverboat headed up the Yazoo and wended his way down to New Orleans to seek his fortune with the conquering Yankees.

Pinchback soon enlisted and became an officer, but faced with the barrier of racial prejudice, he resigned his commission. He went north to get permission to raise a regiment of the U.S. Colored Volunteers, but the end of the war stopped that project before it fairly started. Pinchback returned to the South, this time to Alabama, where he spoke to black assemblages in Mobile and Montgomery.

With the passage of the Military Reconstruction Acts (q.v.), Pinchback returned to New Orleans, a renowned mecca for any ambitious black man in the South. He organized the Fourth Ward Republican Club and entered politics. The ward sent him to the state constitutional convention. One-half of the convention were African-Americans, most of whom had been free men of color before the war, like Pinchback. Immediately he began to look on blacks of lesser ability than himself with scorn. Pinchback called for all offices to be awarded on merit alone, claiming that racial apportionment would cause trouble later. He also spoke out against disfranchising whites for their Confederate activities. But he never forgot his race when it came to writing the constitution. He drafted the equal rights provision of the document, which also declared for open access to public accommodations.

Pinchback's conduct at the convention brought him much notice among blacks and whites. He was immediately put up for state senator from the second district. Pinchback took his seat as a loyal member of the new Republican administration, with Illinois Carpetbagger Henry C. Warmoth (qq.v.) as governor. In 1868, Pinchback was elected delegate to the national Republican convention in Chicago. Back in the Louisiana state senate, Pinchback introduced civil rights measures opposed by white Republicans and refused to operate as a member of the administration. Relations between him and Governor Warmoth grew tense. Warmoth was no fool. He knew that in Pinchback he had a clever potential rival. Pinchback had the same effect on black Lieutenant Governor Oscar J. Dunn (q.v.). Worse yet, all three men were looking ahead to the U.S. senator's election in 1872. But Pinchback's relations with Warmoth were compounded by the governor's unwillingness to enforce civil rights in the state. Warmoth also vetoed a Pinchback bill that would have made it a crime to discriminate on the basis of race. In return, Pinchback and Dunn combined to defeat Warmoth as president of the party convention of 1870, with Dunn getting the job instead. Pinchback went about the state using his oratorical skills to advance the Republican cause and helping elect a new legislature. He had a longer term as state senator, so he did not have to run.

In the new legislature, Pinchback took his share. Meanwhile, Warmoth went to the Mississippi Gulf Coast for rest from an injury, and Lieutenant Governor Dunn tried to take over the party. Warmoth returned to keep control, but the move was indicative of much unrest by white and black factions alike. Already some thought that the governor ought to be impeached. This was very important to Pinchback, because just recently Lieutenant Governor Dunn had died of poisoning. Pinchback, as president *pro tem* of the state senate, was next in line after Warmoth for the governorship, according to the constitution.

Pinchback, however, faced some problems with legislators in getting them to continue to try to remove the governor. Most saw him as a black version of Warmoth, slick and sticky-fingered. Dunn had offered an honest choice. Now Pinchback and Warmoth split over the election of 1872 (q.v.), Pinchback supporting President Ulysses S. Grant and Warmoth going for Democrat/Liberal Republican Horace Greeley (qq.v.). The national Republican Party called upon Pinchback, a popular orator among party faithful, to come up to New England to speak. There Pinchback consulted with party leaders. Then he discovered that Warmoth had come north to explain his side of the impasse. No mean manipulators themselves, national Republican leaders wondered if Pinchback were willing to return to Louisiana ahead of Warmoth. Since the governor was out of the state, Pinchback would automatically become governor. Warmoth caught on, seemingly too late to catch him.

But Pinchback was a victim of his own pride. As he reached Canton, Mississippi, he was awakened in his rail car and told there was a telegram for the governor of Louisiana. Pinchback had to see what it said. He stepped down and entered the room only to be locked in. Warmoth, meanwhile, had taken special trains by prior arrangement and, when he lumbered into Canton the next morning, Pinchback was let loose. They rode back to Louisiana together, affecting forced charm for each other's company. The Pinchback plot had been foiled.

Meanwhile, to elect a Democrat (q.v.) as the next governor, Warmoth (who had switched parties) now signed one of the reform bills and appointed a new Returning Board, which certified a Democratic victory. This act gave Pinchback the opening he needed to secure Warmoth's impeachment. Warmoth had called a special session of the state legislature, allegedly to secure his election as the next U.S. senator. But Pinchback turned it into an impeachment session, which removed Warmoth from office. This allowed Pinchback to take office for just over a month before the new Republican administration under William P. Kellogg (q.v.) took over. Pinchback thus became (depending on whether one credits all of this by-play with legality—the state supreme court bought it) the only black governor of a Southern state during Reconstruction. Not to be outdone, Warmoth installed the Democrats and their own legislature at the same time. Louisiana now had two governments, both claiming legality.

As part of the deal for supporting Kellogg, Pinchback went to Washington as congressman at large to claim his seat. But after a lengthy investigation, his white Democrat opponent was seated. Never mind. Pinchback also had since been elected to be U.S. senator. He went over to the other side of Capitol Hill to complete his quest. But the Senate was unsure of what to do and tabled the motion to consider. Pinchback was reelected by the state legislature once again. This time, after lengthy debate and much delay, Pinchback's request to be seated was rejected. The Democrats had won the national elections in 1874, and Republicans did not wish to sacrifice their possibilities in 1876 by going with Pinchback. As consolation, he was voted $16,000 in compensation and expenses.

When Pinchback got back to Louisiana, the 1876 national contest for president was on. Pinchback supported the national ticket, but he was less than enthusiastic about the state list, which contained too many of his old Republican enemies. Because the state refused to support him adequately before the U.S. Senate, he transferred his allegiance to the Democrats, after receiving a pledge to promote the educational and material interests of black Louisianans. Pinchback received a few Federal appointments, as an internal revenue agent and as surveyor of customs, and went to several Republican national conventions, having switched parties again. In 1879, he went to the state constitutional convention and worked hard to get acceptance of a commitment to a black state college, which became today's Southern University. In 1886, he was admitted to the bar after studying law for one year, giving some idea as to his acumen and the need he had to support his wife and six children with more regularity. In the mid-1890s, as the South fell under the Jim Crow laws, Pinchback went to New York and became a U.S. marshal. By the turn of the century he was in Washington, D.C., practicing law. He died in 1921 and was taken back to Metarie, Louisiana, where he was buried in the family tomb next to his mother.

P. B. S. Pinchback was fully the equal of any of his white compatriots or opponents in Louisiana during his political career. Of course that is a curse as well as a compliment, because it puts him in a pretty shady group. But he got into the fray with the best and never lost sight of the need to provide for others of his race less lucky and able than he. Unfortunately, he seemed to see the state treasury as just another mark to be played by the old riverboat con man that he had been, which put him beneath black politicians like Dunn and state treasurer Antoine Dubuclet (q.v.). But as Governor Warmoth reminded congressional investigators, corruption was the style back then, and they all could have taken more.

PINKERTON, ALAN. *See* BALTIMORE PLOT; PENINSULA CAMPAIGN.

PIPE CREEK LINE. *See* PENNSYLVANIA CAMPAIGN.

PITTSBURG LANDING, BATTLE OF. *See* SHILOH CHURCH, BATTLE OF.

PLEASANT HILL, BATTLE OF. *See* RED RIVER CAMPAIGN.

PLEASANT HILL LANDING, BATTLE OF. *See* RED RIVER CAMPAIGN.

PLESSY, HOMER A., *v.* JUDGE JOHN H. FERGUSON (1896). No instance has come to typify the Jim Crow reality by the 1890s more than the Louisiana case of Homer A. Plessy *v.* Judge John H. Ferguson. Louisiana had had a segregated system of streetcars before and during the Civil War (called "Star Cars," as they had five-pointed stars to indicate Negro occupancy allowed), which had been integrated by a concerted effort during Reconstruction. In 1890, prompted by Congress' failure to pass Massachusetts U.S. Senator Henry Cabot Lodge's new Enforcement Bill, designed to enforce renewed Southern compliance with black rights of citizenship, Louisiana state passed a new law segregating rail cars by race. Unlike most of the rest of the South, New Orleans had a highly articulate, well-educated population of blacks and mixed bloods, the latter descended from liaisons between some of the best planters and their African-American concubines. The state also had a Latin concept of race that allowed such unions to be made more freely than anywhere else in the country. Plessy himself was classified as an octoroon, one-eighth black, and his participation in the case was no accident, but rather an intentional setup, under the theory that an almost-white person might advance the cause with fewer racial hang-ups in the higher courts than an easily distinguished black person. So Homer A. Plessy took a train ride from New Orleans to Covington, purchasing a first-class ticket and sitting in a "whites only" car. He was promptly arrested.

In the ensuing trial, Plessy's attorney was Albion W. Tourgée (q.v.), a former Carpetbagger (q.v.) in North Carolina who, disillusioned with Reconstruction, had gone to New York and written two novels on the subject, *A Fool's Errand* and *Bricks without Straw*, and whom blacks had brought to New Orleans specifically to plead Plessy's case. He maintained that the Louisiana law violated Plessy's rights under the Thirteenth and Fourteenth Amendments (qq.v.). But Judge John H. Ferguson held that the case was a state matter, and Plessy could be proscribed from riding in all but designated cars. Tourgeé appealed the case, eventually to the U.S. Supreme Court, as Plessy *v.* Ferguson. There, on May 19, 1896, the highest court in the land ruled that states could separate the races legally, provided that "separate but equal" accommodations were provided for all those so proscribed. Technically the decision only involved transportation, but other decisions soon expanded the separate but equal rule into all areas of American life.

PLUM RUN, BATTLE OF. *See* SHILOH CAMPAIGN.

POINT LOOKOUT (MARYLAND). The biggest Federal installation that housed Confederate prisoners of war. *See also* PRISONS.

POMERY CIRCULAR. *See* CHASE BOOM.

POPE, JOHN (1822–1892). Born in Kentucky and appointed to the Military Academy from Illinois, John Pope graduated in the top third of the class of 1842. He served with the topographical engineers, fought in the War with Mexico, and explored the Great Southwest, where he experimented in drilling artesian wells. When the Civil War came, Pope received a brigadier generalship and served in eastern Missouri, where he took over the Army of the Mississippi and, in early 1862, took the key Confederate positions at New Madrid and Island No. 10 during the Shiloh Campaign (q.v.). In the summer of 1862, Pope was Lincoln's only choice to come east and put some vigor in Federal war efforts in Virginia, as Maj. Gen. George B. McClellan's Peninsula Campaign (qq.v.) stagnated.

Taking over the detached Union forces in the Shenandoah Valley, northern Virginia, and what would become West Virginia, Pope organized his Army of Virginia. Maj. Gen. John Charles Frémont (q.v.) refused to serve with Pope, as he outranked the new general. But Pope made his first mistake when he condescendingly told these eastern veterans of campaigning against "Stonewall" Jackson (q.v.) that out west he was used to seeing the backs of the enemy, rather than running from them. He also enthusiastically embraced the war aims of the Radical Republicans, especially as represented in the Confiscation Acts (q.v.), and aimed to take the war to the Confederate civilian population, jailing and hanging those opposed to the Union without trial. This made him unpopular with his own men and the enemy, civilian and military. He became the only Federal general whom Gen. Robert E. Lee (q.v.) felt the need to "suppress."

In August 1862, Pope advanced aggressively to the line of the Rappahannock, nearly getting caught in the triangle formed by the Rappahannock, the Rapidan, and the Blue Ridge. Then he demonstrated how vulnerable a line of supply and communication the Orange and Alexandria was, when Jackson and Brig. Gen. J. E. B. Stuart (q.v.) seized his main supply depot in the Second Manassas Campaign (q.v.). Falling back on his base, Pope seemed so overwhelmed with the rapidity and multiplicity of events that he lost contact with reality. Finally thinking that he had cornered Jackson at Stone Mountain, Pope wasted his army in a two-day assault, leaving his left flank open to a massive Confederate counterattack that swept him and his men from the field. Pope tried to hold Centerville, but was outflanked again on his right and forced to flee into the defenses of Washington. Pope immediately brought charges against Maj. Gen. Fitz John Porter, a McClellan partisan, whom he accused of intentionally undermining him through disobedience of orders on the battlefield.

Lincoln had no choice but to replace his friend from Illinois. Sent to Minnesota, Pope put down the Sioux Uprising (q.v.) and served in various departmental commands in the Great Plains and the Far Northwest. He retired in 1882 and died 10 years later.

POPULAR SOVEREIGNTY. The Southern-favored political concept, which incorporated the Non-Exclusion Doctrine (q.v.) that slavery ought to be allowed in the Western territories of the United States until statehood, whereupon the state convention, while drawing up the new state constitution, could approve or abolish it by a simple vote. U.S. Senator Stephen A. Douglas (q.v.) favored this concept and made it law in the Kansas–Nebraska Act of 1854, which led to the Kansas–Nebraska Border Wars (q.v.), a precursor of the Civil War. It was confirmed as proper and constitutional by the U.S. Supreme Court in the case Dred Scott v. Sandford (qq.v.) in 1857. But Abraham Lincoln (q.v.) showed popular sovereignty to be practically inoperative during the Lincoln–Douglas Debates (q.v.) in 1858 when he forced Douglas, in answer to Lincoln's so-called Freeport Question (q.v.), to admit that slavery would fail everywhere without a positive law enforcing it. This revealed Douglas' duplicity and led to breaking up the Democrat Party (q.v.) in 1860 into Northern and Southern wings, Lincoln's nomination for president on the rival Republican (q.v.) ticket, and eventual Republican victory in the election of 1860 (q.v.).

PORT GIBSON, BATTLE OF. *See* VICKSBURG CAMPAIGN.

PORT HUDSON, SIEGE OF. At the same time that Maj. Gen. Ulysses S. Grant (q.v.) was engaging to open up the Mississippi River during the Vicksburg Campaign (q.v.), a similar operation was taking place 110 miles to the south at Port Hudson, Louisiana. Located at an L-shaped bend in the Mississippi 150 miles above New Orleans, Port Hudson made the Confederate control of the Mississippi complete between it and Vicksburg. Just holding one might block Federal passage on the Mississippi, but both had to be held to guarantee Rebel access to the Trans-Mississippi Confederacy. Besides, Port Hudson not only effectively blocked the Mississippi, it also hindered access to the mouth of the Red River, which flowed into the Mississippi some miles above the fortress.

The Confederate officer in charge of Port Hudson was Maj. Gen. Franklin Gardiner, who took over the post and its garrison of 10,000 in December 1862. Technically he was under the overall control of Gen. John C. Pemberton (q.v.) at Vicksburg, but distance kept their military relationship pretty nominal. In fact, the most Gardiner and Pemberton had in common was the fact that they were both Yankee-born officers who married Southern women and followed their wives' states out of the Union.

The attacking Union forces at Port Hudson were officered by Maj. Gen. Nathaniel P. Banks (q.v.). In exile from Virginia, where he had been accustomed to losing battles to Maj. Gen. Thomas J. "Stonewall" Jackson (q.v.), Banks was sent to Louisiana by President Abraham Lincoln (q.v.) because he was a better politician than a general. His primary goal was to reconstruct the state, end slavery, and bring a loyal Louisiana back into the Union under Lincoln's "Ten Percent" Plan (q.v.). But military operations could not be avoided, and Port Hudson was in Banks' command area.

Banks sent a brigade to guard his left flank on the west side of the Mississippi. The Rebel army here, a small one, but still a menace, under Maj. Gen. Richard Taylor, had to be neutralized. Although Banks' command often defeated Taylor, he kept turning up again, refusing to go quietly into oblivion. This caused Banks to inaugurate an extensive invasion of Taylor's base of support, the Bayou Teche Campaign. Besides getting rid of Taylor, the Teche was a grand plantation area full of staple crops and slaves to be freed and enrolled into the Union army. There was a lot of political reason behind Banks' move. After Taylor was defeated and the Teche secured, Banks would cross the Mississippi north of Port Hudson and invest the post.

Banks invaded the Teche with about 17,000 men to Taylor's 5,000 defenders. There was little Taylor could do to stop Banks, but he made the Union forces as uncomfortable as possible, hitting them hard at Ft. Bisland (April 12, 1863) and Irish Bend (April 14). Banks destroyed much of the Teche's economy in lumber, sugar, foodstuffs, livestock, salt, and slaves as he moved north to Alexandria. But in the process, he was late to invest Port Hudson, an operation that Grant was to help him with before the latter took Vicksburg. Not one to stay idle, Grant moved on to take Vicksburg, leaving Port Hudson for Banks alone.

Having driven Taylor up the Red toward Shreveport, Banks turned east across the Atchafalaya and the Mississippi to join more Union troops coming up the Mississippi from New Orleans. Driving in Gardiner's advance guard in the Battle of Bayou Sara Road, Port Hudson was surrounded in a very well-coordinated operation by May 26. The next day, Banks ordered a general assault. The Rebels cut down the attackers in droves. Banks then did something unique. He ordered his African-American contingents into the fray. They received the same defeat as their white brethren in blue. But this was the first time that black troops had been used in a full-scale battle.

On June 11, Banks tried again to take Port Hudson by assault, striking at 3:00 a.m. But the Confederates were ready and threw the Federals back. On June 13, Banks tried to talk Gardiner into surrendering to save lives. Gardiner refused. Banks attacked immediately and lost 1,800 to the Confederates 47, the worst casualty ratio in the whole war. After a loss of 4,000 so far, Banks settled down to a siege. Conditions inside the fortress were far worse than at Vicksburg. Rats, cats, and dogs were all eaten. Banks' men, camped in malaria-ridden swamps, threatened mutiny. Banks threatened to shoot any slackers.

Meanwhile, Taylor's Confederates returned to the Teche and moved down its back, threatening New Orleans, hoping to relax Banks' hold at Port Hudson. Rebel cavalry operated in the Florida parishes to the east of Port Hudson, often murdering blacks caught in uniform. But Banks refused to move. Finally, news came of Vicksburg's surrender. Gardiner at first refused to believe the news, seeing it as a ruse to induce his surrender. But official confirmation came shortly, and on July 6 Gardiner surrendered Port Hudson, giving the Yankees at least nominal control of the Mississippi River, at last. Banks wanted unconditional surrender, but Gardiner refused, holding out for the same terms that Grant gave at Vicksburg—parole for the men, officers to be held until exchanged.

Oddly, Banks received scant notice for his victory. Vicksburg, Gettysburg, and the New York draft riots (qq.v.) drove Port Hudson into immediate obscurity, from which it has never recovered.

PORT REPUBLIC, BATTLE OF. *See* SHENANDOAH VALLEY CAMPAIGN FIRST (JACKSON'S)

PORT ROYAL EXPERIMENT. After a series of Union military disasters marred the opening summer of the Civil War, the North settled down to utilizing its great advantage, a blockade through its naval strength. The initial problem was that the North had too few ships and sailors to enforce a blockade. But the Southern Atlantic area had a geographical feature that allowed the North to overcome its shortage in ships and men. These were the Sea Islands, a group of detached land masses of varying size in the tidal areas off the main coast in South Carolina and Georgia. Capturing these islands would allow the Union forces to create bases for land and sea operations against Charleston (the center of secession) and Savannah.

On November 7, 1861, the Union fleet arrived, opened fire, and landed a small brigade of infantry under Bvt. Brig. Gen. Thomas Sherman (the "other Sherman" in Civil War terminology—*i.e.*, no relation to William T. Sherman [q.v.]—who made his reputation in coastal operations) to seize Port Royal and Hilton Head Islands. At the first volley of naval gunfire, the entire white population fled the main town of Beaufort (pronounced "Bew' fert" in the local style) for the mainland, leaving behind their slaves. Although there was no policy of Northern liberation, these slaves became contraband of war and confiscable by the Federal government. The problem was now what to do with this large black population of 10,000. As such, the Port Royal Island operations became a microcosm of the formal Reconstruction of the whole South that would follow the war.

Four governmental entities competed with each other for control of Port Royal, with its black residents caught in the middle. The first was the United States Army. The soldiers were not abolitionists (q.v.) and cared little about the African-Americans' problems as freed people. The soldiers were imbued with the racial prejudices of their day and saw the blacks as pawns to be manipulated. Officers (those who cared) had a difficult time controlling their men. The troops robbed, raped, cheated, and fought the blacks and among themselves. Sherman's men compounded their problems when they told the blacks that freedom meant they would not have to work, although that is exactly what the Federal government expected freed blacks to do.

Sherman was soon replaced by Bvt. Maj. Gen. David Hunter, a full-fledged abolitionist who considered President Abraham Lincoln (q.v.) much too hesitant in freeing slaves in the South. So Hunter did it for him in the spring of 1862. Lincoln, worried about losing elections to Democrats (q.v.) in the North and the specter of black rebellion that Hunter's actions implied to race-conscious Northerners and border state Southerners, canceled his orders and removed the general from his post. By that summer, however, Congress got tough and passed the Second Confiscation Act (q.v.), permitting the emancipation of slaves whose owners were engaged in rebellion against the United States. Under Brig. Gen. Rufus Saxton, the new commander at Port Royal, and with

Lincoln's approval this time, the Army enrolled the freedmen once again into self-defense units in August 1862. The theory now was that blacks should fight to guarantee their own freedom. The Army was not too nice about this concept, either, using force to dragoon hesitant African-Americans into regiments that became the nucleus of the United States Colored Troops later in the war.

The second Federal agency that dealt with the blacks at Port Royal was the Department of the Treasury. The interest of the treasury agents was the fine sea island cotton, an especially fleecy, fine grade, that had been pledged to the Confederate war effort. The treasury men were to seize this as contraband of war. The treasury men rivaled the Army in their rough treatment of the former slaves. Black work gangs were forcibly set up, and all of the 1861 cotton crop was harvested and taken to Beaufort for shipment. The African-Americans were supposed to be paid for their labor and receive free public education, but it all got lost in the shuffle to get the cotton crop in. Later audits showed that the agents not only collected the cotton crop for shipment north, but that they sold substantial amounts to nearby Confederate agents, who smuggled it through the blockade for sale in Europe to forward the Rebel war effort. Things were not going too well for the first Reconstruction, and the treasury men were recalled to Washington, D.C.

The next group to confront the aspects of Reconstruction at Port Royal were the members of Northern missionary and benevolent associations out of Boston, New York, and Philadelphia who came down to "civilize" the wayward South. Led by Edward Pierce and the Reverend Mansfield French, the goal of these do-gooders was to remake the South into a copy of New England with public schools, Protestant Christianity, and town meeting style self-government. These reformers (both whites and Northern free blacks) became known as the "Gideonites," for like Gideon's Band, they were few in number bent on doing the Lord's work in a strange and savage land.

Once at Beaufort, they quarreled with the Army and Treasury over decent treatment of the ex-slaves, and among themselves over the proper nature of their religion. But they did establish churches and schools and administer to the physical needs of the already twice-picked over freedmen. The do-gooders, however, were quite outraged when their black charges proved to be, on the one hand, good students with minds and preferences of their own, and, on the other, disappointing in how easily they lapsed into the "faults" of slavery like dissembling, lying, theft, and irresponsibility. Either way, the Gideonites saw the blacks unfairly as ingrates.

The fourth group that exploited the capture of the Sea Islands was the private entrepreneurs, men who saw in the South an economic opportunity to get rich off of intensive agriculture, to carry on "free labor experiments under private auspices." The rules of the land investors smacked a lot of slavery, especially to the Gideonites. Moreover, the African-Americans hated to cultivate the sea island cotton, especially to refertilize the fields, which involved putting fresh swamp mud on the crop, a backbreaking job. The land companies bought sea island land at one dollar an acre in 1863 (for lack of payment of Union wartime taxes by its Confederate owners) and sold it to blacks at five dollars an acre two years later.

Wartime Reconstruction in Port Royal had all of the elements of the process after the Civil War in the rest of the South: exploitation of the freedmen, benevolent assistance, and good intentions. But it also had one element that the rest of the South did not. By the end of the war, they owned three-fourths of the land and could support themselves as truck farmers independently of white overseers, Northern or Southern. But reality struck them during Andrew Johnson's (q.v.) pardons policy, which returned land owning to the prewar status, and the freedmen realized that they would have no land for themselves beyond what they could ill-afford to buy.

POSSE COMITATUS ACT (1878). After the Compromise of 1877 withdrawing Federal troops from interfering in state and local elections in the South, Southern congressmen sought to guarantee the informal agreement with a new law. The result was a rider to the Army Appropriations Bill for 1878 called the Posse Comitatus Act. *Posse comitatus* was an ancient English common law concept in which the adult male populace of a county was to stand armed and ready to aid the sheriff or marshal in enforcing the law. The use of the United States Army to support the civilian governments in the South fell under this doctrine, the Army acting in place of or as a supplement to the *posse comitatus*.

Strong Federal executives had used the *posse comitatus* 70 times, from the beginning of the nation's history under the Constitution of 1789 to the end of Reconstruction in 1877. George Washington used the Army as a *posse comitatus* to suppress the Whiskey Rebellion in 1794, Thomas Jefferson used it to enforce the Embargo Acts in 1807, Andrew Jackson employed it during the Nullification Crisis in 1832, Franklin Pierce found it indispensable during the Kansas–Missouri Border Wars (q.v.) in 1854, and Abraham Lincoln used it to call up the militia in 1861 to suppress the War of Rebellion for Southern Independence.

But under the Posse Comitatus Act, no Army officer of any rank could intervene to assist a local, Federal, or state law enforcement official unless specifically ordered to do so by the Congress or under the Constitution (by executive order of the president). The penalty was two years in jail or a $10,000 fine or both. Its passage can be seen as a part of the Compromise of 1877, despite the year of the law (1878).

Presidents have continued to use the *posse comitatus* even after the passage of the 1878 act. President Rutherford B. Hayes (q.v.) used the Army as a *posse comitatus* during the Lincoln County War in New Mexico Territory in 1878, Grover Cleveland called on it for putting down the rail strikes of 1894 (and his Democrat Party [q.v.] lost an election partly because of it), Theodore Roosevelt employed it during the San Francisco earthquake, Woodrow Wilson made the Army available to the states that sent their national guard troops overseas in World War I, Franklin D. Roosevelt used it to guard the banks during the Bank Holiday in 1933, and Dwight D. Eisenhower used it to enforce the integration of public schools in the South in 1958. Some authorities are now questioning whether the act was not violated by the use of military-provided equipment in the 1993 attack on the Branch Davidian compound at Waco, Texas.

The act has been amended twice since its initial passage. In 1900, because of the Klondike gold strike, Alaska was exempted from its protection, as law enforcement there was so haphazard. In 1947, when the Air Force separated from the Army, the act was extended to include it. As yet no one has been arrested and convicted of violating the 1878 act's provisions.

POTTAWATOMIE MASSACRE. *See* BROWN, JOHN; KANSAS–MISSOURI BORDER WARS.

PRAGMATISM. *See* SOCIAL DARWINISM.

PRAIRIE GROVE, BATTLE OF. *See* MISSOURI CAMPAIGN (1861–1862).

"PRAYER OF TWENTY MILLIONS." *See* EMANCIPATION.

PRESIDENTIAL RECONSTRUCTION. The concept that the president should make Reconstruction policy under the powers of executive proclamation led to two presidential plans of Reconstruction, one advanced by President Abraham Lincoln in his Proclamation of Amnesty and Reconstruction, December 8, 1863 (qq.v.), and the other put forward by his successor, Andrew Johnson, in his Proclamation for Reconstruction on May 29, 1865 (qq.v.). The period before the passage of the Military Reconstruction Acts (q.v.) in March 1867 is generally referred to as Presidential Reconstruction, as opposed to Congressional Reconstruction (q.v.), which followed, and under which the South was readmitted to the Union.

PRESIDENTIAL THEORY OF RECONSTRUCTION. *See* RECONSTRUCTION, THEORIES OF.

PRICE, STERLING (1809–1867). Born and raised in Virginia, Sterling Price attended Hampden-Sidney college and studied law before removing to Chariton County, Missouri, in 1831. There he was a farmer, legislator, and lawyer, before he resigned as speaker of the Missouri house to raise the Second Missouri Volunteer Cavalry for the War with Mexico. He followed Brig. Gen. Stephen W. Kearney down the Santa Fé Trail and was put in charge of New Mexico while the rest of the troops left for Chihuahua and California. Price suppressed a rebellion against the United States takeover led by the Taos pueblo, after the murder of the American governor, whom he succeeded.

Returning to Missouri after the war, Price was elected governor and served on the Missouri banking commission. He was a Union man, but was alienated by the aggressive actions of Bvt. Brig. Gen. Nathaniel Lyons and Republican politician Frank Blair, Jr., in holding Missouri in the Union. As major general of the state militia, Price led his men over to the Confederates in the 1861 Missouri Campaign (q.v.). He was tall but portly, had to travel to battle in a carriage, and although beloved by his men, was considered the most pompous, vain, and egotistic man alive by none other than President Jefferson Davis (q.v.), no mean slouch himself when it came to ego.

Besides his campaigns west of the Mississippi, Price also fought east of the Mississippi in the Iuka and Corinth Campaign, before he returned to west of the Mississippi to fight at Helena, Arkansas, in the Red River Campaign (q.v.) and to make Price's Missouri Raid in 1864 (q.v.). After the war, Price fled to Maximilian's Mexico (q.v.), but returned shortly after his plans for a Confederate colony failed, a broken and impoverished man. He died in 1867.

PRICE'S MISSOURI RAID (1864). In the summer of 1864, as the armies of Ulysses S. Grant (q.v.) and William T. Sherman (q.v.) seemed stuck in their marches upon Richmond and Atlanta, respectively, Grant began to remove forces from the Trans-Mississippi Theater to reinforce these main points of invasion of the South. He pulled the XIX Corps to Virginia and XVI Corps to Mississippi to counter hostile actions by Confederate Gen. Nathan Bedford Forrest (q.v.) against Sherman's rear.

Because of the transfer of so many Union troops to east of the Mississippi, Lt. Gen. Kirby Smith, commander of the Confederate Trans-Mississippi, decided to use the remaining infantry and all of the cavalry left behind to send Maj. Gen. Sterling Price (q.v.) on a raid into Missouri. He hoped to recruit new soldiers, scour the land for horses, capture several points of supply, and install a Confederate government at the Missouri state capital, Jefferson City.

Price was not exactly the best man for the job, but he was the only general available. Price also was the commander of Missouri's Knights of the Golden Circle (q.v.), so he had some spies of his own scouting ahead of his columns. Mounting every man he could, Price set out from south central Arkansas in August, with two divisions of cavalry, soon to become three, as Brig. Gen. O. J. Shelby's men joined the column before it crossed into Missouri. With them rode a Union spy, James Butler Hickok, better known later as "Wild Bill."

The 12,000 Confederates advanced and spread out for miles to forage their way northward. At Pilot Knob, Missouri, Price regrouped and attacked a Federal fort, where he lost 1,500 men to the Yankees' mere 200. Licking its wounds, Price's Confederate army allowed the remaining Union troops to escape that night. Price drove on toward St. Louis, but found out that the flexible Federal river transportation had allowed them to recall part of the XVI Corps from Mississippi. These reserves reached St. Louis first, forcing Price to veer to the west along the Missouri River valley, headed for Jefferson City. All along the way, Price captured or stampeded numerous small Federal detachments and pillaged at will. Active Yankee pursuit made installing a Confederate government at Jefferson City impracticable.

Price pushed his army westward toward Kansas City, followed by the XVI Corps. The Rebels reached the Big Blue River on October 22 and forced a passage, driving defending forces before them. But more and more Federals were arriving from the north, east, and west. With the Missouri River blocking any entry into Kansas City, Price's pursuit of the retreating Yankees was actually drawing Price into a box-like trap at Westport, where they outnumbered him two to one. Here, on October 23, was fought the largest, single battle west of the Mississippi during the war, one almost solely fought by cavalry, the second largest cavalry battle of the war after Brandy Station in Virginia during the Pennsylvania Campaign (q.v.).

But Price finally realized his predicament and turned southward in time to retreat into southeast Kansas and the Indian Nations, thereby avoiding the Federal garrison at Ft. Smith, Arkansas. His retreat was hastened by an active pursuit and a disastrous battle at the Marais des Cygnes (pronounced Mer-da-sin, meaning Swan Swamp) crossings, in which the Confederates lost 1,000 men, four colonels, and two generals, and 10 guns captured. It was the last real battle west of the Mississippi for the rest of the war. But Confederate guerrillas fought on in vain, losing the "Terrible Revolver Fighter" George Todd and "Bloody Bill" Anderson, and scattering William C. Quantrill's men as far as Kentucky. Among the guerrilla survivors were Frank and Jesse James (q.v.), who would carry on the fight after the war's end.

PRISONS. During the Civil War, it had been estimated that Federal troops captured 215, 000 Confederate soldiers, and the Rebels took 195,000 Union soldiers. This is exclusive of those paroled by both sides on the battlefield, particularly by the Federals in the last days of the war. Until mid-1863, the ratio favored the Confederates, who held more Union captives than the reverse.

It was fortunate for the South that they did hold the edge in captives for so long. Early in the war, the Yankees seriously thought of treating captured Confederates as what they were—Rebels liable to be hanged. This was especially true with Confederate privateers, who dominated the early Union captured rolls, and whom the North wished to treat as pirates. But President Jefferson Davis warned President Abraham Lincoln (qq.v.) that no such arbitrary treatment would go unavenged. As the war progressed, it became obvious that neither side was ready to handle the large numbers of enemy soldiers in its hands. But Lincoln refused to treat with a Southern governmental official, lest that be seen as recognizing the legitimacy of the Confederacy.

The compromise was to use military officers to set up a cartel to exchange prisoners. After several failed attempts, the North used Bvt. Maj. Gen. John A. Dix, and the Confederates sent Maj. Gen. Daniel H. Hill. Thus the Dix–Hill Cartel was born. What Dix and Hill agreed to was an even exchange of prisoners, rank for rank, man for man. They also created a table of equivalents (*e.g.*, one colonel was equal to 15 privates) so that whenever there was an excess of men of one rank, they could be exchanged without waiting for the other side to capture men of the same rank.

But the cartel began to break down almost as soon as it was created. The agreement called for prisoners to be exchanged or, if declared to be excess, to be paroled to holding camps until exchanged. This caused many problems with the men who expected to go home rather than be guarded by their own men. When Bvt. Maj. Gen. Ben Butler took over the occupation of New Orleans, he hanged a local citizen for defiantly flying the Confederate flag. President Davis issued an order that he be hanged as a common outlaw if taken. He also ordered that commissioned Union officers held prisoner be held until Butler was taken. Union Secretary of War Edwin McM. Stanton (q.v.) suspended the exchange of Confederate officers in return.

Another cause for disagreement over the Dix–Hill Cartel came when Maj. Gen. U.S. Grant (q.v.) found that at least a division of the Rebels paroled at Vicksburg turned up again at Missionary Ridge at Chattanooga (q.v.). He accused the Confederates of bad faith, the men never having been properly exchanged. The Confederates argued that Grant had paroled them illegally and that any parole he issued was invalid on its face.

Then came the Emancipation Proclamation (q.v.) and the extensive use of blacks, free-born or former slaves, as Union soldiers. Confederate authorities announced that captured black soldiers would be treated as slaves in insurrection. Their white officers were liable to being charged with abetting an insurrection. They could be summarily shot or resold into slavery. This was the last straw to the Yankees. They told the South that the Rebel soldiers currently in prison would be held as hostages to guarantee fair treatment of all Union prisoners of war. Ultimately, the South agreed to treat all freemen, but not slaves, the same as whites.

The result was that the numbers of prisoners on both sides increased markedly. Tales of filth, disease, mental depression, camp disorder, vermin infestation, poor or nonexistent food, and lack of sanitation became commonplace,

North and South. Although more than 150 places were used as prisons, some came to have special meaning. In the North, whose prisons were slightly better than those in the South because they were an organized bureaucratic effort under Brig. Gen. William H. Hoffman (average death rate 12 percent), were Camp Douglas (Illinois); Rock Island (Illinois); Camp Chase (Ohio); Johnson's Island (Lake Erie); Ft. Warren (Boston); Ft. Lafayette (New York City); Ft. McHenry (Baltimore); the Old Capitol (Washington); the biggest, Point Lookout (Maryland); Gratiot Street (St. Louis); Elmira (New York), with the worst death rate and often called "Hell-mira"; and Ft. Delaware, the most dreaded, where the river's tides flooded the prison twice a day.

In the South, where the prison system, in the words of Topsy, "just growed," until late in the war when Brig. Gen. John H. Winder took over (average death rate 15.5 percent), were Castle Thunder (one in Petersburg and another in Richmond); Libby (Richmond); Ligon (Richmond); Belle Isle (Richmond); Lynchburg (Virginia); Danville (North Carolina); Columbia (South Carolina); Florence (South Carolina); Cahaba (Alabama); Shreveport (Louisiana); Camp Groce (Texas); Camp Ford (Texas); Camp Lawton (Georgia); Macon (Georgia); Blackshear (Georgia); Salisbury (North Carolina), which had the worse death rate; and the worst of all, everything considered as a package, Andersonville (Georgia).

The problem got even worse when Lt. Gen. Grant, now in command of all Union armies, announced that no prisoners would be exchanged after April 15, 1864. Grant believed that released Rebels merely meant that veteran soldiers were returning to the ranks. He aimed to whip the South through a war of attrition, especially in manpower.

Continued negotiations through Confederate Vice President Alexander H. Stephens (q.v.) and Special Commissioner Robert Ould with Union representative W. H. Ludlow failed to produce the restoration of an exchange system. Indeed, things got worse as Confederates put black captives to work building fortifications under fire, followed by the Federals doing the same with white Rebels. When the Confederacy proved incapable of moving adequate rations to prison camps, the Yankees retaliated by reducing their rations to prisoners, too. In the fall of 1864, however, both sides sent home without regard to numbers all those too sick to be anything but a burden. Then in January 1865, the Rebels agreed to exchange all prisoners regardless of race. Grant agreed—the war was soon to be over, anyhow. The South had been drained of all white manpower and would soon be calling up slaves to be soldiers.

PRIZE CASES (1863). Immediately after the secession (q.v.) of the South, President Abraham Lincoln (q.v.) issued an executive proclamation establishing a blockade of Confederate sea ports. It was a paper blockade at first, technically illegal under international law, but as more Union ships were built, it soon began to have real teeth. The Union navy was managed by Secretary of the Navy Gideon Welles of Connecticut, one of Lincoln's most effective and loyal cabinet members. His assistant was Gustava V. Fox, a professional navy man, who did the day-to-day chores. Their opponent in the Confederate government was Stephen A. Mallory of Florida. He had been a seaman and on the naval committee of the U.S. Senate. He was one of two (the other was postmaster John Reagan of Texas) to stay in the Jefferson Davis (q.v.) administration the whole war, probably because Davis left all naval matters up to Mallory without interference. It was Welles' responsibility to establish and maintain the blockade and Mallory's to break it. It is a tribute to Welles' abilities and Mallory's difficulties that the Rebels had only two deepwater ports open at the end of 1862, Wilmington and Charleston.

Because he came into office without a fleet, Mallory had to create one that could challenge the blockade. In doing this, he had to overcome two disadvantages, the lack of proper shipyards and a psychological feeling that whatever the Confederate navy did, it would not be enough. He achieved his goal through the utilization of technological innovation. The first thing Mallory did was build ironclad ships that gave his small fleet a leg up on the numerous wooden ships the Yankees had for the initial blockade. He built his own ironclad ships at home, the first being the C.S.S. *Virginia*, used in the Peninsula Campaign (q.v.), and tried to purchase others to act as Confederate sea raiders (q.v.) from Europe. Mallory also invested in a submarine program. Named after its designer, who died in an experimental run, the C.S.S. *Hunley* became the first submarine to sink an enemy ship, the U.S.S. *Housatonic*, in combat, only to go down itself in Charleston harbor.

Like Mallory, Welles embraced technology to improve the blockade. He knew that Mallory was investing heavily in ironclads and did so himself, narrowly getting the U.S.S. *Monitor* into operation in time to save the blockade at Hampton Roads in 1862. In this Welles rejected standard designs of covering a regular ship with iron (U.S.S. *Galena* and U.S.S. *New Ironsides*) and went with a radical new design of a low-riding ship with a flat deck and a modern revolving two-gun turret, because its inventor promised it could be faster than his competitors.

The effectiveness and the legality of the blockade were challenged by those who got caught in court. In the 1863 Prize Cases, the U.S. Supreme Court recognized a belligerent status for the Confederacy, while denying it any more than *de facto* control of a specified land mass (as did Great Britain, earlier). It also endorsed in the same breath President Abraham Lincoln's numerous executive proclamations (q.v.) defining the war effort, proclamations that many in the North, including Republicans (q.v.), believed lacked a constitutional mandate. The court would reaffirm its decision 15 years later in Dow *v.* Johnson (1879).

PROCLAMATION FOR RECONSTRUCTION. Picked as the vice presidential candidate to broaden the appeal of the Union Party (a combination of Republicans and War Democrats [qq.v.]) in 1864 and to get rid of then Vice President Hannibal Hamlin (q.v.), whom President Abraham Lincoln (q.v.) saw as a disloyal spy for his radical opponents within the Republican Party, Andrew Johnson (q.v.) became president upon Lincoln's death. It was bad enough that Johnson might not support the Republican hopes for the future of America. Yet initially Johnson fooled his doubters. He spoke of how "treason must be made infamous." He hated the plantation aristocracy. He hinted at hanging Rebel leaders. Radical Republicans began to wonder if the assassination of Lincoln had not been the judgment of the Lord for his hesitancy in advancing the freedom and civil rights of the slaves. Johnson looked to be all right.

Johnson soon put an end to this rank speculation when he issued his Proclamation for Reconstruction on May 29, 1865. Unlike Lincoln's Proclamation of Amnesty and Reconstruction (q.v.), Johnson issued one for each state, beginning with North Carolina. But all said essentially the same thing. And like Lincoln, Johnson assumed that secession (q.v.) was void from the outset and that the president should take the lead in Reconstruction without waiting for the reconvening of Congress in December 1865. The first thing Johnson did was to recognize the "Lincoln governments" in Louisiana, Arkansas, Tennessee, and Virginia. The rest of his plan, however, was more like the Wade–Davis Bill (q.v.) than Lincoln's wartime measure. Johnson expected a majority of the voters registered in 1860 to take an oath of future loyalty to the United States. No actual figure was stated, but it was implied.

Like all other plans of Reconstruction, Johnson's excluded certain classes from initial participation in forming loyal governments. These included the usual higher officials, civilian and military, of the seceded states and the Confederacy, 14 separate classes in all. But Johnson added a new class. He excluded all persons worth $20,000 or more from the initial amnesty. These persons had to appeal directly to the president for individual pardons. Virtually all of these applicants were former planters, the very men whom Johnson had fought during his political career as the defender of the average nonslaveholding Southern white.

Once Johnson had given the initial amnesty, he appointed a provisional governor for each state. In the case of several states, he accepted the Unionists whom Lincoln had put in power. In others he appointed his own man, always a Union supporter. The provisional governors, with the assistance of the occupying Federal forces, were to supervise the amnesty process (taking the oaths) and then call the elections for a constitutional convention. The convention would write a new state constitution that had to repudiate secession and the Confederate war debt, abolish slavery, and recognize the Thirteenth

Amendment (q.v.). No other action outside the amendment was required as to the African-Americans' status in the reconstructed South. Then a new election would be called, and the voters would vote on the constitution and elect a new slate of state and local officials, congressmen, and U.S. senators.

Johnson was being a bit naïve if he expected his governments to receive anything but the short shrift given Lincoln's governments earlier. As quickly as the Confederate leaders got their presidential pardons, they stood for election and won. Derisively, they were grouped under the label, "the Confederate Brigadiers" (q.v.).

This turn of events shocked even Johnson. But he was not about to admit that he had blundered. This would turn the whole process over to Congress. So he made the best of a lousy situation and accepted all that had passed. He was now controlled by the very men he had tried to exclude from the reconstructing process in the first place.

To understand Johnson's seeming political ineptness, one must remember that he was above all still a Jacksonian Democrat. He became president through an unfortunate assassination of the Republican Party leader, President Lincoln. Johnson was a loyal Union man, but he hated Republicans otherwise. He and the Republicans had in common hatred of secession and the planter aristocracy, and a love of the United States undivided and the end of slavery to break the Slave Power Conspiracy (q.v.). But Johnson was not about to help the Republicans expand their party to the South; he would not support a slow or difficult Reconstruction; he was against the Republican's economic measures (high tariff, high taxes, national banking system, massive internal improvements) enacted during the war, except for the Homestead Act (q.v.); and he was against equal political and civil rights for African-Americans. He wanted the South back in the Union fast so he could get all of those Democratic votes to back him in Congress. Unfortunately, the Congress rules on its own members' suitability for being seated, and the Republicans drew back to look into the advisability of seating any of Johnson's representatives by creating a Joint Committee of Fifteen on Reconstruction (q.v.) to investigate the whole executive Reconstruction phenomenon.

PROCLAMATION OF AMNESTY AND RECONSTRUCTION, DECEMBER 8, 1863. On December 8, 1863, President Abraham Lincoln (q.v.) issued his Proclamation of Amnesty and Reconstruction. The demands of the war necessitated that he do something. But rather than view Lincoln's proclamation as an incontrovertible plan (as Congress and future historians would), it would be better to see it as he did—as a proposal that did not exclude future changes. First, Lincoln said, residents of a seceded state had to take an oath of future loyalty to the United States and recognize all Union wartime acts as regarded slavery. This included the Second Confiscation Act, the Emancipation Proclamation (qq.v.), and Congress' ending of slavery in the territories and the District of Columbia. Lincoln did not require the applying state to end slavery. He doubted he had the power to do this. But by making their applications and recognizing wartime acts, the states did it indirectly anyhow. This was typically Lincoln, working around a problem rather than confronting it head-on and alienating people. But it tied Reconstruction to the ending of slavery, once and for all.

Next, Lincoln's proclamation continued, when 10 percent or more of the voters registered in 1860 swore such an oath of future loyalty, that number could establish a loyal state government (hence the plan's popular and somewhat derogatory nickname, the Ten Percent Plan). They would call a state constitutional convention; elect delegates to the convention; draw up a new state constitution that recognized the wartime acts of the Union; then elect local officials, a state legislature, and a governor, and send their duly elected representatives and senators to the U. S. Congress to be seated. Certain highly placed officials of the Confederate and state government and military could not participate in the process. This was a practical matter and good politics. Someone had to pay for secession and the war. But Lincoln would receive their individual supplications for pardon later, after the readmission process had worked itself out. Finally, Lincoln offered his plan only to states that had been occupied by the Union army. This limited his plan to essentially three areas, the northern half of Arkansas, most of Tennessee, and the southeastern third of Louisiana.

All three areas went through Lincoln's program and presented their representatives and senators for seating in Congress. And here Lincoln's plan ran out of steam. Congress had already protested the ease of Lincoln's program in the Wade–Davis Bill (q.v.), which the president had pocket vetoed, provoking a hostile attack on his refusal to work with Congress on the Reconstruction matter. Now both houses refused to seat the men from Lincoln's allegedly reconstructed states under its constitutional right to investigate and determine if the supplicating states had truly republican governments (the theory, not the party, although critics maintained that the Yankee Congress confused the two). And Congress, wondering if 10 percent was an unusually small number for the American way of majoritarian government, asserted its right to have a part in determining the Reconstruction process and noted that the newly emancipated African-Americans did not have a sufficient part in the program or an assured status in post–Civil War America.

That Lincoln was ready to alter his thinking on the South and Reconstruction was seen in his willingness to accept a more complete plan of military occupation and supervision of the defeated South, particularly in Virginia and North Carolina, that Secretary of War Edwin McM. Stanton (q.v.) presented to him at a cabinet meeting on the morning of the day he was assassinated.

Lincoln asked that the plan be altered somewhat but drawn up formally so that it could be discussed with an eye to the fact that he needed to have a plan in operation before Congress reconvened in December 1865. No, Lincoln was not committed to any specific plan, but he did seem determined that he and not Congress would be the guiding light of Reconstruction. And that would brook all sorts of problems for his successor, Andrew Johnson, when he too tried to present Congress with a similar *fait accompli*, the Proclamation for Reconstruction (q.v.), which lacked the maddening flexibility that was Lincoln's greatest strength.

PRO-SLAVE THEORISTS IN THE ANTEBELLUM SOUTH. Although it has never approached the interest of abolition, pro-slave thought is very important in understanding the Civil War and Reconstruction. Historians have generally popularized the attractive myth that at the end of the American Revolution, the South nearly had abolished slavery, as the North had. Indeed, had it not been for the development of the cotton gin, slavery would have ended nationwide, not just in the North, where cotton culture was unprofitable or impossible because of cold climate.

Because of its position as the largest slave state during this period, Virginia is usually viewed as the key to why slavery continued to endure as an institution. Virginians, including Thomas Jefferson, whom most see as a man desiring slavery's demise, held certain truths about slavery. It was an institution forced upon the American colonies as one of the tyrannies of the British crown, making black and white alike innocent victims. Virginians had always opposed the slave trade, but Great Britain refused to allow this course. This was a convenient notion that overlooked that the end of the international slave trade would cause an inflation in slave prices and prevent fresh arrivals from Africa from infecting the system with notions of recent freedom.

Virginians also questioned the innate ability of Africans to be freed, as they would intermix with whites, which would lower the quality of intelligence and industry to preserve democracy. Finally, few Virginians beyond a certain elite class ever expressed any guilt over the institution. Only one Virginian, St. George Tucker, introduced a plan of gradual abolition, based on freeing all black women at age 28 (slavery passed through the mother, probably a result of white male initiated miscegenation). But the fear of the black and white races being contaminated by their own human inability to stay clear of each other sexually was the basis of most freedom plans being based upon some form of colonization (q.v.) of blacks overseas, somewhere.

It was painfully obvious by the time of the Civil War that some powerful force drove Virginians and the whole South to defend slavery through numerous pro-slave treatises. To whom were these tracts written? Certainly not to Northerners infected with the bug of abolition, immediate or gradual.

Certainly not to Southern nonslaveholders, as some historians have asserted. There were no real differences on race between whites, regardless of social class. In recent years, historians have asserted that the pro-slave writers wrote to convince slaveholders, themselves, secretly guilty of holding fellow humans in bondage in violation of Christianity and the ideology of the American Revolution, especially as represented by the Declaration of Independence. This is often referred to as the great Jeffersonian contradiction. It was the paradox of the slaveholders' devotion to liberty, the Old South twisting and turning upon the rack of slavery.

But in all honesty, there was little slaveholder guilt in being the masters over others, especially those already seen as different and inferior. Indeed, they were more than willing to acknowledge the very cruelties of slavery the abolitionists (q.v.) cried about. If the pro-slave writers were not evidently trying to convince slaveholders who were completely aware of the merits of slavery, to whom were they writing? The answer is that they were writing to themselves. Like every other reform movement of the 1830s, the pro-slave writers longed for a return to what they saw as an idealized past. They sought to return to the agrarian society before the rapidly changing industrialism that infected both urban and rural America. They longed to return to a time when people like them ruled. They were responding to the same impulses as the abolitionists of the North. Hence, pro-slave thought was not a freakish aberration, but a normal response to the quest to find social stability in a rapidly changing world that preceded the Civil War.

PROVISIONAL GOVERNMENT, CONFEDERATE. *See* CONSTITUTION, CONFEDERATE.

PUBLIC CREDIT ACT. *See* GRANT, ULYSSES S., ADMINISTRATION—DOMESTIC POLICIES.

Q

QUEEN OF THE WEST. *See* VICKSBURG CAMPAIGN.

RACE RIOTS. *See* CAMILLA MASSACRE; COLFAX RACE RIOT; COUSHATTA MASSACRE; ELLENTON (SOUTH CAROLINA) RACE RIOT; EUTAW (ALABAMA) RACE RIOT; HAMBURG (SOUTH CARO-LINA) MASSACRE; MEMPHIS RACE RIOT; NEW ORLEANS RACE RIOT (JULY 30, 1866 AND OCTOBER 24–27, 1868); NEW ORLEANS, THIRD BATTLE OF; NORFOLK RACE RIOT; ST. LANDRY RACE RIOT.

RADICAL DEMOCRACY. In 1864, the North faced a presidential election. Many Radical Republicans were hoping that one of their own might replace President Abraham Lincoln (q.v.), whom they considered incapable of the job. The first man to put his name in the ring was Secretary of the Treasury Salmon P. Chase (q.v.). But his Chase Boom (q.v.) was short-lived. So the Radicals decided to split off from the Republican Party and form their own party. They called it the Radical Democracy. Their convention was held at Cleveland, in Ohio's Western Reserve, a hotbed of abolitionism (q.v.).

At Cleveland, the Radical Democracy adopted a platform that expressed their ideas. They demanded that slavery be abolished in all states without compensation to the slaveholders; that Congress guide Reconstruction, soon expressed in the Wade–Davis Bill (q.v.); that Congress protect the political, economic, and social rights of the newly freed slaves; that there be a single term for the president, already in place in the hated Confederacy; that the electoral college be eliminated and the president elected on a direct vote of the people; and that Rebel lands be confiscated and redistributed among soldiers and settlers from the loyal states.

As their candidates, the Radical Democracy chose John Charles Frémont (q.v.) for president and John Cochran of New York for vice president. Frémont had been the first Republican Party (q.v.) candidate in 1856 and was a Radical Republican who tried to abolish slavery by military edict in Missouri in 1862, only to be rebuffed by Lincoln. Cochrane was a former political general who had exposed the fiasco of the Fredericksburg Campaign (q.v.) before the Joint Committee on the Conduct of the War. The result had been his censure and resignation. He was currently attorney general of New York state.

Frémont accepted the nomination and pledged to withdraw if a candidate more to the Radicals' liking, other than Lincoln, were offered at the National Union Party (q.v.) convention of Republicans and War Democrats. But Lincoln was the nominee of the party regulars. Then the bleak picture of battlefield stalemate changed to one of victory in the Mobile Campaign, the Second Shenandoah Valley Campaign, and the Atlanta Campaign (qq.v.). Fearful of being shut out of the party altogether, the Radicals sent Ohio's U.S. Senator Benjamin Wade (q.v.) to ask Lincoln to "throw us a crumb." Lincoln got Postmaster General Montgomery Blair to resign for the good of the party, and the Radicals returned to the fold, momentarily chastened.

RADICAL RECONSTRUCTION. Upon the Republican victory in the 1866 congressional elections (q.v.), which returned a two-thirds majority for the upcoming Fortieth Congress, the Republicans in the outgoing Thirty-ninth Congress went to work in the Lame Duck session (December 1866–March 1867) to clear the way for their new colleagues. Led by the Radical Republicans, the party imposed the measures that would become known as Radical Reconstruction. The first thing was to make sure that the Fortieth Congress did not have to wait until December 1867 to meet, its traditional time to assemble. The congressional recesses were the times that presidents Abraham Lincoln and Andrew Johnson (qq.v.) had used to impose executive proclamations of Reconstruction that had done much to modify the influence of prior Congresses on Reconstruction. So the second session of the Thirty-ninth Congress passed the Fortieth Congress Extra Session Act (q.v.) to assemble the day after it adjourned in March 1867. This would give the Fortieth Congress three sessions instead of the customary two. This was not a special session, because the Constitution reserves such calls for the president. So it became a new regular session, to be followed by the constitutionally called December sessions in 1867 and 1868.

The next order of business was to guarantee that the president could not easily get around congressional desires through other independent executive actions. The Command of the Army Act (q.v.) was added to the Army Appropriations Act. It ordered the Commanding General of the United States Army (then Lt. Gen. Ulysses S. Grant) to have his headquarters in Washington, D.C. But there was another official who was a spy inside the executive departments and the president's cabinet, Secretary of War Edwin McM. Stanton. A Radical Republican, the source of many of the anti-Lincoln stories during the war, Stanton was keeping his Radical cronies informed of anything Johnson discussed behind closed doors in the executive offices. To protect him, Congress passed the Tenure of Office Act (q.v.).

Finally, the last session of the Thirty-ninth Congress passed Radical Reconstruction or the first of the Military Reconstruction Acts (q.v.). The Fortieth Congress received the task of enforcing and expanding the scope of the Military Reconstruction Acts. In March 1867, it passed a Second Military Reconstruction Act (q.v.) and in July, it passed a Third Military Reconstruction Act (q.v.) to deal with loopholes in the first measure. Then in March 1868, a year after the process had begun, a Fourth Reconstruction Act (q.v.) passed Congress. The measure was designed to speed up the Reconstruction process so that black Republicans might assist the party in electing a new president in 1868. By the election, all Southern states except Virginia, Mississippi, and Texas had completed the Reconstruction process and could participate fully in politics on the state and national levels. All that was left was to embarrass President Johnson completely through his impeachment (q.v.) and trial. Then legislative government would be a reality.

RADICAL REPUBLICANS. See REPUBLICAN PARTY AND THE CIVIL WAR AND RECONSTRUCTION.

RAID ON WASHINGTON. See WASHINGTON, EARLY'S RAID ON.

RAINES, GABRIEL. See LINCOLN ASSASSINATION; LINCOLN ASSASSINATION, THE CONFEDERACY AND THE; LINCOLN ASSASSINATION, THE NEW YORK CONNECTION OF THE.

RAINEY, JOSEPH H. (1832–1887). Born in Georgetown, South Carolina, to a mulatto slave family, Rainey's father had purchased his whole family's freedom. Rainey received a rudimentary education through private instruction, and at the outbreak of the war he, like his father, was practicing barbering, a traditional position of leadership in America's black community. For a time he was a steward on a blockade runner, but when he was drafted to work on the military fortifications in Charleston Harbor, he fled to the West Indies, where he awaited the outcome of the war. He returned to South Carolina after the Yankee victory, and with the passage of the Military Reconstruction Acts (q.v.), Rainey became a member of the newly constituted state Republican Party. He was a delegate to the constitutional convention, but played a minor role. Nonetheless, he was elected to the state senate in 1868. He resigned his seat in 1870 to run for Congress. His victory made him the first African-American ever to sit in the U.S. House of Representatives.

In Washington, Rainey was known as a quiet man who defended black rights with logic and forcefulness on the House floor. He did not attempt to humiliate the white South, but insisted on the execution of the Enforcement Acts, the suppression of the Ku Klux Klan, and the holding to the promises of the Fourteenth and Fifteenth Amendments (qq.v.). He also was an advocate of black access to public accommodations and had to be forcibly ejected from a Virginia restaurant when he refused to leave. His most notable speech was a eulogy of Massachusetts Senator Charles Sumner (q.v.) in 1876. Rainey served in Congress until 1879, when he was replaced by a white Democrat (q.v.). He was made special treasury agent for South Carolina until his resignation in 1881. He tried banking and the brokerage business in Washington, D.C., after his political career ended, but financial failure sent him back to his Georgetown home. He died there a few years later.

RAYMOND, BATTLE OF. *See* VICKSBURG CAMPAIGN.

REAM'S STATION, BATTLE OF. *See* PETERSBURG, SIEGE OF.

RECONSTRUCTION, SOUTHERN. Many of the delegates at the Montgomery Convention that drew up the Confederate Constitution (q.v.), considered their efforts to be more than just secession (q.v.). They believed in the essential wisdom and goodness of what they were about, and figured that the new Confederacy would attract many of the Northern states into its fold. In effect, the United States would be reconstituted under the banners of the Confederate States of America. There would be a Southern form of Reconstruction. New England and it pernicious ways would be excluded, of course, but the rest of the North, especially the states of the Old Northwest, were welcome. Some of the more radical delegates at Montgomery tried to stop this by putting in a clause that all new states would have to become slave states, but more conservative men, like Jefferson Davis (q.v.), refused to allow such limitations.

Jefferson Davis believed that Stephen A. Douglas (q.v.) might seek a reunion of the country on the basis of the old Democratic Party (q.v.). At least a commercial union might be in the offing, based on the Mississippi River and its tributaries. Douglas did write up such a concept, which was found in his papers after his premature death in 1861, but no one knows to whom it was made. Under Douglas' proposal, all trade regulations, tariffs, patents, and copyright laws would be uniform in both republics. Proceeds from revenues were to be distributed on the basis of population, counting three-fifths of slaves, as in the original United States Constitution. Each member was to guarantee the other's territorial boundaries. Neither was to add territory without the approval of the other.

It is also possible that Douglas envisioned such a commercial trade union extending beyond the Union and the Confederacy to embrace other Western Hemisphere nations, a sort of 19th-century NAFTA. But the firing on Ft. Sumter (q.v.) and Douglas' death in June 1861 put an end to such musings. Reconstruction would come from North to South, not the other way around.

RECONSTRUCTION, THEORIES OF. There were almost a half dozen theories of Reconstruction's (q.v.) constitutional basis, each with variants of its own, and probably no one then or now can say that any one of them was entirely correct. Nowadays the constitutional theories are considered as important as they were early in the century, but for years few historians bothered to investigate them. Indeed, historians preferred to give Andrew Johnson (q.v.) the best of the argument by default. But others had their ideas, too, as the following will show.

The Presidential Theory—Applied by both President Abraham Lincoln (q.v.) and his successor, Andrew Johnson, the Presidential Theory looked to the executive proclamation for its genesis, something that had great impact during the time of war. Lincoln put forth his Ten Percent Plan (q.v.) as a method to undermine the Southern will to fight. It permitted a small part of the population in any seceded state to apply for restoration if they took an oath of future loyalty, allowed themselves to be occupied by the Federal Army (q.v.), and recognized the wartime acts of Congress and the president. The centerpiece of this theory was that the states never really seceded. But Lincoln and Johnson saw the Presidential Plan as two different things. Lincoln envisioned it as a proposal, not excluding Congress from input, but nothing to be inflexibly tied to forever. Johnson thought of Reconstruction as just the opposite. He expected Congress to go along with his plan and fought with them over modifications that Congress thought would make the South pay for the war, like freedmen's rights.

The real problem was that neither president could get his elected supporters seated without the concurrence of the sitting Congress. That body alone is charged in the Constitution with assuring that each state has a republican form of government (the theory of government, not the party). Lincoln knew this would ultimately give Congress a voice in Reconstruction; Johnson seemed to find this reprehensible—odd coming from a constitutionalist as he was. The result, after Lincoln's death, was a bitter fight between legislative and executive branches over policy, with the Supreme Court caught in the middle. This was something that one suspects Lincoln would have avoided or at least handled with more aplomb and skill than Johnson, who forgot that presidents have great power during the emergency of war but much less during the hum-drum of peace.

The Southern Theory—One of the first doctrines of Reconstruction came from the South, and it naturally was one of the easiest to apply. The South was willing after four years of bloody conflict to admit that dissolution could not physically take place. Therefore, it must submit at once to the Union and its Constitution. With the end of the war, all must revert to the way it was in 1860, with the possible exception of the abolition of slavery. Individuals might be guilty of treason, but the states had the same rights and duties as before, as described in the fundamental document. The governors ought to call their state legislatures into session and sue for peace. They certainly had nothing to lose by this magnanimous gesture.

Oddly, the most famous proponent of the Southern Theory of Reconstruction was none other than Maj. Gen. William T. Sherman, Lt. Gen. Ulysses S. Grant's (qq.v.) right-hand man, the general who "made Georgia howl" as he cut a 60-mile-wide swath of terror and destruction across its heart. Sherman's ideas were embodied in his terms for the surrendering of the South's number two army commanded by General Joseph Johnston (q.v.) at Durham Station, North Carolina. Unaware of Lincoln's explicit orders on the subject of surrender, but cognizant that Lincoln believed in a decent peace, Sherman allowed Johnston's army to disband with all of their equipment, which was to be restored to their state capitals. He also made a sweeping commitment on Reconstruction itself, something Grant did not. He promised a general amnesty, the people would be guaranteed their political and property rights (except in slaves), and no citizen would be molested because of the late war so long as he lived in peace and obeyed Federal laws. He also recognized several Southern provisional state governments. The result was an uproar that even Grant and President Andrew Johnson could not bear. Sherman's peace was immediately repudiated (Secretary of War Edwin McM. Stanton [q.v.] did the honors) and had to be renegotiated on the basis of Grant's offering at Appomattox. A simple return to the United States in 1860 would not suffice. Some kind of notice of the four years between Charleston and Appomattox had to be made.

Conquered Provinces Theory—Almost the exact opposite of the Southern Theory, the Conquered Provinces Theory asserted that the Constitution had been so shattered by the force of the rebellion that it no longer had any application to the South. No longer states in the Union, secession removed their traditional rights and left them conquered provinces, susceptible to the will of the victor. A favorite of Radical Republican Representative Thaddeus Stevens (q.v.) of Pennsylvania, the theory maintained that the states had seceded and a new basis of Union had to be drawn up, no holds barred. The entire South had to be remodeled in the proper manner, to assure that rebellion could never happen again. The Southern states had reverted to the territorial stage, where they could have their very boundaries altered and had to do the bidding of the rest of the states through the Federal administrators in the South. Part and parcel of this was the enfranchising of the African-Americans, as the only truly loyal group in the South. Of course the whole process was to be congressional, not executive, in conception.

Oddly, more Southern whites adhered to this theory than Northerners. Yankees found it repugnant to the very idea of republican government, not the American way. Rebels admired its straightforwardness and its admission that they had seceded and created their own government and fought four years to protect it. It also recognized that the South had altered the nation forever, for better or worse. Actually, Southerners, especially former Confederate soldiers, welcomed military government and occupation. It promised law and order and conservative social stratification, which were sadly missing in the confusion that accompanied the fall of the Confederacy. But it was too removed from the Constitution to suit most Americans and, like the Southern Theory, provided a departure for discussion and little more.

State Suicide Theory—A favorite of Massachusetts Senator Charles Sumner (q.v.), this concept of Reconstruction argued that secession was impossible. Rather, by trying to leave the Union, the states had committed a treasonous form of suicide. Although the United States retained control over these areas, they had reverted to territorial status, where they were at the mercy of Congress. The territorial status was important in both Sumner's and Stevens' plans, because it allowed state institutions (but not boundaries to Sumner) to be altered at the pleasure of Congress. There were no constitutional guarantees to get in the way. Congress would decide what these suicidal brethren must do to return to the Union. And for Sumner as for Stevens, this included some recognition of Negro rights, especially the vote.

Shellabarger-Chase Theory of Forfeited Rights—First conceived by Republican Representative Samuel Shellabarger of Ohio and later used by the U.S. Supreme Court under Chief Justice Salmon P. Chase (q.v.), the Forfeited Rights Theory of Reconstruction held secession to be null and void (no state could ever leave the Union), but admitted that the participant states had forfeited some of their rights by committing this form of treason. It worked under the Supreme Court case Luther v. Borden, from the 1840s Dorr War in Rhode Island. Then two warring factions had appealed to the Court to settle their dispute. The Court held that whichever representatives and senators Congress seated were the legal representatives of the state. Congress received this power directly from the Constitution under its responsibility to provide for a republican form of government in each state. In effect, the Supreme Court ruled that this was a political decision outside its authority to adjudicate. It would side with Congress's decision, and did so in Texas *v.* White (1868), which held that all acts committed under the Confederate Constitution that did not conflict with the results of the rebellion were valid (*e.g.*, marriages, yes; canceling of debts owed to U.S. citizens, no). It was conservative, it made sense to all but ideologues, and it worked.

REDEEMERS. Those whites who overthrew the Reconstruction governments in the South in the 1870s were called Redeemers. They went on to rule their states during the New South movement of industrialization by coercing white and black agrarian radicals through voter fraud and racist appeals. But what they exactly stood for and really did has been a field of argument for historians ever since. That they were important cannot be denied. These Democrats (q.v.) controlled every former Confederate state in the last quarter of the 19th century and composed a voting bloc in Congress (about one-third of both houses) that rivaled Northeastern and Western Republicans in power and dominated the Democrat Party's congressional and national party caucuses. Although it was fairly obvious that they would stand for home rule and undermine Federal protection of blacks in their civil rights (90 percent were veterans of the Confederate army or civil government), how they might vote on the paramount economic issues of the day, the economic legislation of the Civil War that made up the Republican Party's (q.v.) domestic policy (as opposed to the war and foreign affairs), such items as soft money, the national banking system, bond redemption, taxes and tariffs, and railroads and other internal improvements, would determine the fate of the nation.

Southern Republicans (Scalawag, Carpetbagger [qq.v.], and African-American representatives in Washington of the Reconstructed state governments) had failed to deliver on these programs. Northern Republican power brokers had viewed these men with suspicion, excluded them from meaningful councils, and denied them the patronage that would have secured their power back home. Nor were they helped by the burgeoning Liberal Republican (q.v.) movement dedicated to eradicating these programs as the epitome of corruption (q.v.). Realizing that the National Democrats would not grant these subsidies, and having missed out on their share of the Great Barbecue because of the Civil War and Reconstruction, the Redeemers made their own deal to elect Rutherford B. Hayes (q.v.), gain removal of the Federal troops (home rule), and get in on the Federal economic largess denied Southern Republicans. This is often seen as the "Right Fork on the Road to Reunion," an agreement between Conservatives of both sections.

But there was another branch in the Road to Reunion, the so-called Left Fork. This one emphasized a more radical agrarian approach and cooperation with Western elements in the Republican Party. Their program was one of reform of government away from industry and business assistance to help out the little man, the small farmers and laborers who dominated the American landscape in those years. Their program emphasized expanded credit through more paper money and the coinage of silver, a decentralized national banking system, and regulation of railroads. Because of the extended Panic of 1873 (which had lasted several years), the agrarian radicals swept into power in 1877.

From there on out, the Southern states were the center of a quarrel between these two points of view, causing the Southern Democrats in Washington to vary in their stand issue by issue, and usually taking the Left Fork, the agrarian–labor or "radical" one, allying with Western Republicans and Western Democrats to support expanded silver coinage, redemption of bonds with greenbacks instead of gold, reduction of the tariff, restoration of the income tax, an expansive banking system to provide easier credit, and tough regulation of railroads.

They voted with all Democrats to revise the revenue tax code to fall more heavily on the East and curtail African-American civil rights. But this did not affect their desire to industrialize the South. Indeed, the Redeemers managed to attract nearly every economic group from business to agriculture (large and small landholders) to their banner. Reconstruction and the Gilded Age that followed caused the Redeemers to reexamine the fundamental premises of what it meant to be an American. In the process the redeemed South, more than any other section of America, came to have a social unity that was challenged only by the bravest or most foolhardy. When it came to race, the mind of the postbellum South was little different from the antebellum—blacks had a definite place in society and were to stay there. The white South was a unique, separate part of the national whole, driven by racism, paternalism, a personal code of honor, and a Southern nationalism reinforced by a rigid concept of constitutionalism. Whatever the political stand of the Redeemers, whether they took the Left Fork or the Right, they illustrated the persistence of Southern distinctiveness within the nation as a whole.

REDEMPTION. The process by which whites, known as Redeemers (q.v.), took back their state and local governments from the reconstructing Republicans (q.v.) elected by white and black loyalists. Redemption went through two phases. The first took place before 1874 and involved Redemption in Alabama, Arkansas, Georgia, North Carolina, Tennessee, Texas, and Virginia. The second involved Florida, Louisiana (the state with the longest Reconstruction [q.v.], lasting from 1862 to 1877), Mississippi, and South Carolina. Except for Mississippi, this group was redeemed during the election of 1876 and the Compromise of 1877 (q.v.)

At first the Southern ruling classes tried to appeal to blacks to vote with their former masters, but African-Americans would have none of this. They knew where their true interests lay. This meant that Southern whites who lived in black majority states like Louisiana, Mississippi, and South Carolina were in deep trouble. So were select congressional districts and local county governments in any state. The Federal election of 1868 (q.v.) demonstrated that blacks could prove decisive in delivering Southern states' electoral votes to a Republican presidential candidate as well as state and local contenders. It also proved that Northern Democrats (q.v.) could not save the South from its fate. The result was the emergence of the Ku Klux Klan (q.v.) and its allied groups, the Knights of the White Camellia, the Knights of the Rising Sun, the Pale Faces (q.v.), and others. They immediately made their influence felt in

Georgia in the Camilla Massacre and in Louisiana in the St. Landry riot and the New Orleans riot of 1868 (qq.v.).

Although Georgia and Louisiana whites were the only white Southerners well enough organized to make inroads on Republican votes in 1868, the impact of violence was felt in all of the states south of what one modern commentator once aptly called "the Smith and Wesson line," roughly that part of the United States below the Ohio River. If only the campaign of terror could be coordinated, at least at the state level, thought whites. Southerners realized that no matter what they did nationally, Republicans would "count in" the needed Republican vote for the presidential elections by dominating the Returning Boards, which certified the electoral votes. Outside the traditional circles of power, with no nonviolent channels through which to express their hostility, Southern whites exaggerated the power of Republican regimes, their corrupt defects, and especially the hypocrisy of forcing the African-American vote on the South while permitting the state option in the North (eventually stopped by the Fifteenth Amendment [q.v.]).

So out came the stereotypes of the Scalawags (q.v.), native Southern whites who sold out race and section; Carpetbaggers (q.v.), Yankee corruptionists who came south to pluck the defenseless Southern pigeon; Negroes, illiterate ex-slaves one step removed from the jungle, led and coordinated by the Union Loyal Leagues (q.v.); and the Army (q.v.), military men who interfered in the democratic process at the points of bayonets. Together they represented unalloyed evil and justified the acts of violence that became an election time ritual in the South. A favorite tactic was to mob "visiting statesmen" like Pennsylvania congressman and ferrous metals magnate William D. "Pig Iron" Kelley. On a trip to Mobile, Kelley had the stupidity to wave the bloody shirt (q.v.) and dare residents to misbehave, because he had the Army at his back. When the smoke cleared, the crowd had wrecked the dais, and a shaken Kelley had to be kept hidden under military guard until he left the city.

Kelley was not the only supporter of Reconstruction to encounter a violent reception. At least he could go home to safety. Southern Reconstructionists were not so lucky. They had to remain behind and face the wrath of the Ku Klux Klan. Although dissatisfaction with the loss of the war, tougher Congressional Reconstruction, and just plain racism contributed to the Klan's growth, some of it was attributable to the poor economic climate in the agricultural South after the war. The two years before the Klan's entrance onto the scene as a covert political force were marked by crop failures and either too little or too much rain. Some modern researchers believe that the cotton crop, its size, and its price on the market, correlated directly with anti-black activities of white regulator groups like the Klan well into the 20th century.

But there was more than crop failure to the Klan's growth. It did not hurt any that important white Southerners, such as John B. Gordon in Georgia or

Nathan Bedford Forrest (q.v.) in Tennessee, respected by the white community for their war records among other qualities, led Klan activities, at least at first. Indeed, one might posit the thesis that the "better classes" (whatever that entails) of the South have always turned a blind eye to racial vigilante activities. The violence of night riders acted as a trump card for the powers that be. One can discipline those who cannot be touched by the law, yet turn in the perpetrators of violence if they get out of hand, and appear to be liberal and forward-looking proponents of a New South. It was a win-win proposition.

In any case, the Klan directed its activities against black leadership (q.v.), teachers promoting black education (q.v.), and Federal and state authorities who backed the Reconstruction policy. Historians disagree on how united the Klans and other similar groups were. But Congress had no doubt, entitling its 13-volume investigation and report, "the Ku Klux Conspiracy," implying a coordinated, centralized program of anti-Reconstruction violence in the South. Blacks fought back, but their inability to stop the raids was exacerbated by the ineffective efforts of the state and local Reconstruction governments to lend a hand. Southern Republicans wasted their party's energy arguing among themselves over mundane theoretical problems like *ab initio* (q.v.), whether all laws and contracts entered into under the rule of the Confederacy were null and void from their inception or whether they ought to accept everyday activities unrelated to the war effort as done deals.

Indeed, segments of the Southern Republican Party seemed more intent on scoring political and mental victories over their black and white brethren than attacking real problems that affected the vote, like Klan violence. In the end, the Republican Party was a veneer of white Carpetbag and Scalawag leaders and the mass of black rank and file, who were divided among themselves by race as surely as were whites and blacks in the South in general. It did not make for an effective force against united white supremacists.

Republican governors in the South were faced with an impossible problem. They could not allow violence to cut the party's vote, but if they fought back they would have to rely on their own state Negro militias (q.v.), and that would lead to a race war. It is indicative of this problem that the more effective battles against vigilante-style violence occurred in states where there was a large element of loyal whites from the days of the war. But this limited the response to some of Texas, parts of Tennessee, and all of Arkansas, whose governor, Powell Clayton (q.v.), was able to defeat the Klan with a state militia composed of blacks from the Southern part of the state and whites from the pro-Union northern half. But Clayton was the exception. This left the anti-Klan response to the Federal government. The result was the three Enforcement Acts (qq.v.) of the early 1870s. But even though these measures halted the Ku Klux, primarily in South Carolina, the force of the regulators was already spent. It had been disbanded by its own leaders, worried by the increasing amount of extracurricular activity that was being done under its disguises that was irrelevant to its original political goal.

The North's moral, psychological, economic, and political commitment against terrorism had been slowly drained in the campaign against the Klan and kindred organizations. The white South criticized the Enforcement Acts as military-enforced tyranny, protested the arrest and prosecution of key citizens on the word of black or white Republican "traitors," physically attacked marshals and district attorneys who carried out the laws, assassinated witnesses, dragged cases through endless litigation, and got the majority of cases dismissed as *nolle prosequi* (not pursued further than the initial indictment). The Congress refused to "waste" necessary amounts of money on the Southern Question, and the Army was unwilling to risk eventual prosecution by assisting civil authorities in their courses of action, which were more politically than criminally oriented.

The end of the Klan did not mark the end of racial violence in the Reconstruction South. In fact, violence now became more open. Slowly, Conservatives began to get all whites on the side of the Democratic Party by appealing to racial solidarity. Until now, some Southern whites were always willing to cut deals with blacks. Now the Klan had destroyed the Union Loyal Leagues (q.v.) and isolated the Carpetbaggers and African-Americans as the only supporters of Reconstruction. (It was at this time that the stereotypes of Carpetbagger and Scalawag became so potent.) Tennessee, Virginia, North Carolina, and Georgia fell easily to the Redeemers, those whites who had joined together regardless of their political antecedents to restore home rule to the South. Texas Republicans appealed to President Ulysses S. Grant (q.v.) for military support as they strove to maintain power by exploiting a technicality in state electoral law, having lost a recent election. Grant refused, and that state went to the Redeemers, too.

Those historians who fault the lack of support for Reconstruction from the Grant administration overlook the tenacity of Southern white resistance to the process through violence. They were aided in their fight by the weariness of the North to enforce Reconstruction and the rise of a new philosophy, Social Darwinism (q.v.), which precluded welfare or special assistance to any group that could not survive the struggle of life and emerge on top. Yet the Redeemers did not deliver on their promise of a better life for Southern whites. They continued to use the black vote to count out white agrarian radicals and keep the New South in the hands that ran the Old. It would not be until the 20th century that a man named Huey P. Long became the first Southern politician to really deliver on his promises to better the life of those left behind as the South industrialized and tried to cope with the economic problems Reconstruction never solved. *See also* REDEMPTION IN ALABAMA; REDEMPTION IN ARKANSAS; REDEMPTION IN FLORIDA; REDEMPTION IN

GEORGIA; REDEMPTION IN LOUISIANA. REDEMPTION IN MISSIS-
SIPPI; REDEMPTION IN SOUTH CAROLINA.

REDEMPTION IN ALABAMA. *See* EUTAW (ALABAMA) RACE RIOT
(1876).

REDEMPTION IN ARKANSAS. *See* BROOKS–BAXTER WAR.

REDEMPTION IN FLORIDA. The easiest Democratic (q.v.) conquest
occurred in Florida. Blacks represented 49 percent of the vote, so the Republicans had to appeal for some white support. The Republicans (q.v.) initially
fielded two candidates, a prospect that boded well for the Democrats. Eventually, the Republicans united behind their incumbent governor, Marcellus L.
Stearns. The opposition put up a bland, conservative businessman, George
F. Drew. Although there were some rifle clubs (q.v.) in the field, and some
intimidation, the Drew forces relied primarily on vote fraud to gain election.
But their efforts did not assure the presidential vote, which later was declared
to be Republican.

REDEMPTION IN GEORGIA. Military Reconstruction ended in 1868,
but the election of a Republican (q.v.) government under the new state constitution, along with a Republican majority in the legislature, was illusory.
Many party members were Moderates whose ideas corresponded with their
Democrat (q.v.) opponents more than they did with their Radical white and
black colleagues. The Moderate Republicans and Democrats managed to
combine and vote to expel 32 black Republicans, challenging their eligibil-
ity. This made Georgia whites more determined than ever to redeem their
state at all levels during the fall 1868 elections (q.v.). If fraud and violence
had to be used, reasoned the non-Republican whites, so be it. The Second
Congressional District, of which Camilla was a part, had white Carpetbaggers (q.v.) as Republican candidates for Congress and as presidential elector.
They campaigned actively for office, an act of great courage in southwestern
Georgia in those days.

The black population of Camilla, located in a small white farming area
surrounded by former slave plantations, had doubled as African-Americans
looked for alternate employment to the backbreaking field work to which
they had been restricted as slaves. The white town was not very happy with
the increased numbers of black residents. The local Freedmen's Bureau (q.v.)
agent was also uneasy. He had heard that cases of Henry repeating rifles had
arrived at nearby Albany, and he feared that the election was going to be a
hot one. And he wondered if the target was not to be a planned Republican
gathering at Camilla on September 19. Contingents of African-Americans

gathered in neighboring communities and on friendly plantations (owned by Carpetbaggers) to march upon Camilla to hear the speeches. Their white organizers told them that they would have no trouble if it were done quietly.

Meanwhile, the news of the black "invasion" panicked white townspeople at Camilla. Rumors had the blacks armed to the teeth. They sent the local sheriff to meet with the marchers and ascertain their real intentions. The leaders of the march assured the sheriff that those with arms were not hostile, merely carrying guns as was their habit when at home. But they refused to leave their weapons outside town as the sheriff asked, because they had heard that an armed band of whites awaited them. Of course, any armed band was prohibited by gubernatorial proclamation, but all claimed that they were individuals, not a real group. A compromise political meeting site at a plantation outside of town was rejected by the landowner.

When the blacks arrived in town to go to the courthouse, a lone white ran out and demanded that they stop their fife and drum music. The marchers refused, and the man fired at the musicians. From the side of the street more armed whites appeared and joined in the shooting. The blacks panicked and fled to the woods and swamps outside town. The whites followed, firing their rifles and shotguns as they came. Several wounded blacks received the *coup de grace* (a bullet in the head) as they lay along the line of march. The shooting continued well into the night, lit up by a full moon. A dozen blacks died during the fray, with uncounted others being wounded.

As the fleeing marchers reached surrounding communities, blacks angrily decided to arm and go out to save the rest of the marchers and wreak what revenge they could on the whites of Camilla. The Freedmen's Bureau agent tried to hold them back, but his work was made more difficult as nightriders hit black labor camps on surrounding plantations. The raiders justified their actions as preempting a black insurrection from taking place that would threaten the lives of white women and children. The governor refused to send state troops, and the Federal authorities denied the use of the Army (q.v.). Republican candidates could not canvass their district. The Freedmen's Bureau was about to go out of operation in Georgia and the rest of the South, so it did little to assist its agent at Albany. By election day, the violence had accomplished its goal. Only two Republican votes were cast at Camilla. Fraud took care of the rest of the district. The whole area went to the Democrats, not bad considering that black and white Republicans outnumbered them in registration. Similar effect was had throughout the state, as the fallout from the Camilla Massacre was statewide.

But the Camilla Massacre had a bad effect, too. Disturbed by the expulsion of the blacks from the state legislature and the riot at Camilla, Congress decided that Georgia needed to be reconstructed again. Back came a reinvigorated Army, the old state legislature with its black members was reassembled, and Georgia had to pass the pending Fifteenth Amendment (q.v.) to return to the Union. But the purge was only temporary. Within a year, the readmission of the state led to the same conditions as before the Camilla Massacre, and terror and fraud reappeared to help whites redeem the state government again by 1872.

REDEMPTION IN LOUISIANA. Georgia was not alone in its early use of violence to redeem its local governments. Even though St. Landry Parish in central Louisiana west of Baton Rouge had a large black population (three to two in favor of African-Americans), the Republicans (q.v.) had not managed to upset the control of the local government, which remained in the hands of the white power structure before, during, and after the war. Military Reconstruction (q.v.) and the new state constitution had done little but unite whites as never before. It was true that blacks and their white Carpetbag (q.v.) leaders (only one white Scalawag [q.v.] was reported in the parish) had managed to elect many of the state legislative officials, but the parish itself was won narrowly by whites. The Republican Party struggled to gain a base in St. Landry that had never before existed. They were assisted by several antebellum free blacks (slaveholders themselves before the war, a not too uncommon Louisiana oddity), who acted as liaisons between the white Republican and the black rank and file voters. White Democrats (q.v.) knew that they had to attract the African-American vote to keep their hold on the parish—registration figures alone demonstrated this. So they organized barbecues and picnics and sent speakers into the black community to attract their support and counter Republican organizers. At the same time, groups of whites rode at night to emphasize the other alternative for those who would not come over.

The Republicans responded with armed guards to protect their political meetings, and by September 1868, the racial tensions in the parish were ready to explode. Whites threatened to shoot everyone who voted Republican. The Republicans, recognizing that they were outgunned, warned that they would burn out anyone who tried to shoot them. As the threat of racial war increased, a committee of five men from each side met to try to work out the terms for a peaceful presidential election in November. They agreed that members of both sides would be at all political meetings, firearms would not be allowed at gatherings, and the sheriff and his deputies were to guarantee order. But the move was too late. Whites were already convinced that the African-Americans were about to engage in an "insurrection" and moved to stop it before it happened.

The result was the September 28 St. Landry riot (q.v.). It all started when a group of white regulators caned a Republican judge who was an organizer of black schools. Blacks organized to protect themselves and marched on Opelousas. They were met by a white mob, and the shooting started. Total casualties on both sides amounted to five dead and six wounded, although Republicans claimed that nearly 300 died, and Democrats asserted the number was around 30. The blacks quickly withdrew, and the whites sent in a mounted contingent that pursued and "arrested" 29 blacks, whom they lodged in the parish jail. The next night all but two were taken by a mob and shot dead, with the connivance of the sheriff and his deputies, who stood aside.

The St. Landry riot was a typical traditional response of white Southerners to the alleged threat of "Negro insurrection" common from slavery days, when Louisianans had crushed a slave rebellion in 1811 and posted the heads of the Rebels along the river banks. But it had great political impact, too. The remaining leaders of the Republican Party fled the parish for their lives. Black agricultural laborers, stuck in their homes, appealed to the Democrats for protection and withdrew from political participation. In November, the parish, which had given the Republicans a 2,500-vote majority in the April statewide elections, reported not one vote for Ulysses S. Grant (q.v.). A Republican effort to reorganize in the parish the following year also came to naught.

As in St. Landry Parish, violence broke out again during the New Orleans race riot in 1868 (q.v.), as it had two years earlier. But this time the black and white Republicans were better prepared to resist, although the results were about the same. Riot had been a possibility throughout the fall of 1868. Black leaders were getting sick and tired of newspaper smears against their character, intelligence, and abilities. The first scuffle broke out when black Republican clubs took to the streets for Ulysses S. Grant on September 22. White Democrats cheered for Horatio Seymour, and a fight broke out, but it soon stopped. Whites were a bit testy in New Orleans. Although they had a slight majority of registered voters, victory was not guaranteed. Whites believed that Republicans imported blacks from surrounding parishes to vote and take the city (an old Louisiana ploy whites had used before the war among themselves, commonly called "Plaquemining" after the parish from which the ringers came). They also disliked the able leadership that blacks provided in the city, a result of the large, educated free black population from before the war. Finally, there were numerous political clubs representing every possible faction of both parties. They did much to keep the pot boiling with their nightly parades and antics, designed to embarrass their opponents.

On Saturday, October 24, two political clubs met by accident in Canal Street. They began to try to out shout each other. Then some white boys fired into the Republicans. Seven died as the blacks retreated. Infuriated, the blacks went home and armed themselves and began attacking every white in sight. Federal soldiers finally put an end to the rioting, after two whites died and several were wounded. No bloodshed occurred the next day, but tensions ran high. But the next three days made up for the 24-hour respite, despite the appeal of leaders of both parties and the Army command to cease political marches and fights. The excuse for the white Democrats was that they were helping patrol the city in the absence of the Metropolitan Police, a largely black force. Gangs robbed and looted homes and businesses until Wednesday, when the Army restored order again. Casualties ran from 63 in the state legislature investigation report down to a more realistic half dozen whites and a dozen blacks. Uncounted others were wounded on both sides. But the results were felt during voting day when the Democrats carried all polls, blacks having been advised to stay home by their own Republican leaders, according to Democrats. Republicans, on the other hand, claimed that their supporters were kept from the polls by force after the riot. But in any case, as in St. Landry, violence had shown the white South how to defeat Republicanism and redeem white rule. It was a portent of things to come.

By 1874, there was nothing in the nation to compare to the political snakebed in the Bayou State. As many as five different political groups (to call them parties would be overly optimistic) were in the field at a time, all with shifting personnel. The state's infant Republican Party was divided among the Customs House Faction, headed by U.S. Marshal Stephen B. Packard, which relied on Federal patronage in New Orleans; the African-Americans of Louisiana, who had the best-educated black population in the South; and a group controlled by Illinois Carpetbagger and power artist, Henry Clay Warmoth (q.v.). Because by 1872, Warmoth had (or had not, depending on one's viewpoint—there were always developing technicalities in Louisiana politics) been impeached, he now favored working with Conservative men of all stripes (Republicans, former Whigs, and Democrats) in what was called the Fusion Party. Bloodshed was always close at hand, and the active intervention of Federal troops was all that kept the peace.

In the 1872 state elections, the Customs House had put up as its gubernatorial candidate a Vermont Carpetbagger, William Pitt Kellogg (q.v.). This did not necessarily please die-hard Republicans, especially blacks, because Kellogg was rumored never to have shaken hands with an African-American without putting on a glove first. Warmoth's people, knowing that Warmoth could not win, nominated Democrat John McEnery. He also had a burden. He was seen by many to be an old prewar corruptionist of the John Slidell wing. No one really knows who won. Warmoth controlled the process as outgoing governor and declared for McEnery. But Louisiana had several other Returning Boards (allegedly they consisted of the governor, the lieutenant governor, the secretary of state, and two senators, or anyone who claimed to be acting for them), one of which certified ballots that counted in Kellogg. One group offered Warmoth a U.S. Senate seat if he and his Returning Board would abandon McEnery for Kellogg. Other bribes too numerous to mention made the rounds on all levels.

Kellogg then played the Customs House's usual trump card. He wrote the Federal government through William E. Chandler, the National Republican Party chairman, and asked for its support. The Grant administration ordered U.S. troops to stand by and told Marshal Packard to enforce Federal court decrees. There was only one—it ordered Kellogg to take over state government. It had been issued by a friend of his. Armed with this writ, Packard took over the statehouse with a military posse. The court also ordered Warmoth to turn over all of the official ballots. He refused. Kellogg's Returning Board declared him elected governor and Republican candidates to be the new legislature. Meanwhile, Warmoth's supporters did exactly the same for McEnery and the Democrats, and Louisiana had two legislatures and two governors, Kellogg relying on Federal troops, and McEnery upon the state's Negro militia (q.v.), organized earlier by Warmoth. Using Federal soldiers and the New Orleans Metropolitan Police, Kellogg arrested McEnery's legislature and took over the government.

But the Republicans were in deep trouble in the outlying parishes (counties). Here dual governments also existed. But the weight of force lay with McEnery's people. When Kellogg men took over the Grant Parish courthouse at Colfax (q.v.) in central Louisiana and called in local blacks to help them defend it, 400–500 armed men responded. Rumors of black rebellion brought in armed whites from miles around. The Fusion forces gathered outside and surrounded the courthouse. The black occupants and their Scalawag and Carpetbag allies refused a call to surrender. The whites assaulted the breastworks around the courthouse, breached the line, and brought up a cannon to shell the building. Mistakenly thinking that the Republican forces had surrendered, the whites moved forward to meet a new fusillade. Then everyone went berserk. The attackers set fire to the courthouse, and as the occupants fled, a massacre ensued. Victims were chased into the surrounding countryside. Surrendering men were shot down. Forty blacks who had been taken were led out that night and summarily executed. Over 100 people died at Colfax, making it the bloodiest of Reconstruction race riots.

Federal troops arrived after the fact to restore order. Federal courts indicted 72 men, but on advice of the U.S. attorney general tried but nine. Conflicting evidence (blacks swore the men had been leaders of the white attackers; the accused produced witnesses who placed them far from the riot) led to hung juries and a second go around. This time William Cruikshank and two others were found guilty of violating the Enforcement Acts. But Cruikshank appealed his case to the U.S. Supreme Court, which ruled that the Fourteenth and Fifteenth Amendments (qq.v.) prohibited states from interfering with a citizen's civil rights but did not operate against individual action. Cruikshank and his pals beat the rap, and the Enforcement Acts were gutted. The significance of this case was not lost on potential Redeemers (q.v.) in Louisiana and the rest of the white South.

Although Kellogg actually turned out to be a conscientious reformer of Louisiana corruption (q.v.), the Fusionists would not stop in their efforts to unseat him for McEnery. They even attempted assassination, but Kellogg led a charmed life. In the parishes, the Fusionists began to organize a group called the White League (q.v.). Just how cooperative the various parishes were is open to question, but unlike the earlier Knights of the White Camellia (q.v.), the White Leagues operated openly and with full newspaper coverage. Usually the White Leaguers could bluff Republicans to flee their area, but in 1874, Redemption took another turn to violence in Red River Parish. Created recently by an earlier Warmoth state legislature, Red River Parish was the power base for a Vermont Carpetbagger named Marshall H. Twitchell (q.v.). Indeed, the whole extended male part of the family had received political appointments and proceeded to make much money, allegedly from the construction cost overruns of the Coushatta Courthouse. The Twitchells had the support of the black voters, who outnumbered whites by four to one, so their tenure looked unbeatable by ordinary electoral methods. The outvoted whites turned to the White League.

The excuse for violence was an argument between whites and blacks at a nearby town that turned bloody. The whites killed their opponents, and the shooting spread to Coushatta. The Red River whites asked for reinforcement from neighboring parishes. Armed whites came in and arrested the local Republican officeholders, demanding they resign their positions and be escorted to Texas by a posse of their own choosing. After the Republicans left town, young White Leaguers voiced dissatisfaction with the results. They pursued the Republicans and caught up with them near Shreveport. There the six prisoners, one of whom was a Twitchell family member, their chosen posse standing aide, were murdered in what became known as the Coushatta Massacre. Governor Kellogg asked for Federal help, and a battalion of the Seventh Cavalry arrived and restored the Republicans to power. The cavalry also arrested about 20 whites and charged them with murder and civil rights violations. But the charges were later dropped as McEnery's people screamed "military despotism."

By 1874, the White League had gained control of the countryside outside of New Orleans by using classic guerrilla tactics, isolating Kellogg supporters to the city itself. The local Democratic Club rechristened itself the Crescent City White League, ordered rifles from New York, and awaited the yellow fever season, when U.S. troops would be sent to Holly Springs, Mississippi, for their health. The White League planned to arm, capture Kellogg, and exile him out of the state, installing McEnery as governor. When Kellogg refused to surrender, the White Leaguers threw up barricades and prepared to fight his black state militia and the Metropolitan Police. Led by a noted Scalawag, former Confederate Lt. Gen. James Longstreet (q.v.), the Republican forces attacked the White League position, only to be driven back. The White Leaguers then charged and raising the "Rebel yell," eventually cleared the streets. Longstreet's retreating men forted up in the Customs House, which the White League wisely decided not to attack, it being Federal property. But they took all of the state buildings and set up the McEnery people as the government. The Republican casualties were 11 killed and 60 wounded (including Longstreet), while the White League lost 21 killed and 19 wounded.

Meanwhile, the Federal soldiers came back from Mississippi. The White League actually cheered their arrival, never dreaming that the soldiers would overturn their victory. But under the demands of President Ulysses S. Grant (q.v.), that is exactly what happened. Refusing to fight Federal troops, although some of the rank and file voted to do so, McEnery turned the government back to Kellogg and surrendered his men. But 1,500 stand of arms and two howitzers remained unaccounted for and presumably in White League hands for future trouble. It came in the state election of 1874, in which the legality of the returns was once again hotly contested. Grant sent Maj. Gen. Philip Sheridan (q.v.) in to take charge, as only he could. After purging the state legislature of Democrats who had forcibly entered the chambers to claim power, Sheridan suggested that all opponents to Kellogg be declared "banditti" and be arrested for trial by military commission. The result was more tumult, as the shakiness of the Republican hold on the state was revealed. Finally, Congressman William Wheeler of New York and his Congressional Subcommittee on Louisiana worked out a deal. Kellogg was not to be impeached, and the lower house was to have a Democrat majority. The Senate would remain Republican.

The Wheeler Compromise left Louisiana in relative peace for two years, but other unredeemed states watched the Louisiana proceedings with trepidation. Grant appeared to be a military tyrant who would stop at nothing to subvert even those states that already had been redeemed. Yet the real significance was that Grant had given no other state as much Federal aid as Republican Louisiana, and the Reconstructionists had managed to hang on only by a precarious string. Grant had decided to back the Customs House Republicans and through a series of well-intentioned decisions had exhausted and confused support for Reconstruction in the North. Louisiana was now a Republican albatross for the upcoming presidential election in 1876 (q.v.). And Louisiana, although as yet unredeemed, had shown the way for Mississippi, Florida, and South Carolina to combat successfully their own Republican administrations.

As in all Southern states, the national election of 1876 in Louisiana was considered "small potatoes," in the words of a North Carolina politician, as Republicans and Democrats were pledged to end Federal interference in the South. In Louisiana, bands of regulators "bulldozed" blacks into voting Democrat. Republican ballots were unavailable outside New Orleans. Black voters were handed Democrat ballots instead and told to vote right. Parishes that had been the center of Republican strength before had not a single vote for the party ticket in 1876. To unite whites, the Democrats ran war hero Francis T. Nicholls, a man who had lost an eye, arm, and one leg in defense of the Lost Cause. The Republicans, reduced to the Customs House Faction, nominated Samuel B. Packard, the U.S. marshal, as its leader. Claiming victory, as did Nicholls, Packard held on until the presidential election was settled, with Louisiana's electoral vote going to Rutherford B. Hayes (q.v.). Then he abandoned the government to the Democrats, as he lost the support of the Army.

REDEMPTION IN MISSISSIPPI. Building on the Louisiana example, Mississippi produced a more refined version of the White League (q.v.) process, known as the Mississippi or Shotgun Plan (q.v.). The state Republican Party (q.v.) was divided over the usual issues: whether the state ought to share the Carpetbag (q.v.) vision of a Radical Republican Party run in a New England fashion based on black support, or the Scalawag (q.v.) future of a Conservative Republican Party that was a broad coalition of Southern whites who would protect the African-Americans in a select but secondary place in society. With a majority of voters being black, it was not hard to see which direction Mississippi would go. The Carpetbag governor of the state was Adelbert Ames (q.v.), a native of Maine and married to the daughter of Benjamin F. Butler (q.v.). Ames was a Yankee war hero, wearer of the Congressional Medal of Honor, and unlike his father-in-law, who was noted for his sticky fingers during the wartime occupation of the Gulf South, a scrupulously honest, upright man. The Scalawag (q.v.) was James L. Alcorn (q.v.), who had preceded Ames as governor and represented the classic story of the Whig-turned-Republican for conservative, upper class societal and economic values.

By the time Ames became governor in 1873, Mississippi was in an economic downturn, part of the nationwide Panic of 1873. The following year, whites at Vicksburg organized the People's Party and began to intimidate the all-black government and African-American voters, who outnumbered them two to one. The black sheriff asked for military support to counter white military companies. Ames forwarded the request to the Ulysses S. Grant (q.v.) administration, which refused to act. The resulting intimidation and vote fraud saw the People's Party win some offices in Vicksburg and Warren County, a political disaster that Ames blamed upon President Grant's refusal to send in the Army (q.v.). But it was evident that the state itself had done little to police a local election. Ames's reluctance to act on his own merely encouraged more white violence, as did his refusal to disperse a black mob or call for Federal military help in Tunica County near Memphis.

As yet, Mississippi whites did not have anything comparable to Louisiana's White Leagues. Once again, the whites at Vicksburg led the way, demanding that their black sheriff resign and leave the area. The sheriff begged Governor Ames for assistance. Ames told him to form a posse to protect his job, but did little more. When the sheriff organized his posse, whites appealed for help, and 160 volunteers crossed the river to show Mississippi how it was done in Louisiana. The result was a riot that extended well into the night as whites ransacked private homes and killed their black residents. At least 36 dead and wounded came from the daytime riot, but the nighttime casualties remain unknown. The sheriff decided to resign and fled to Jackson. Governor Ames declared Warren County in insurrection and this time got Federal troops to reinstate the sheriff. But he resigned again when an assassination attempt was made against him after the U.S. soldiers withdrew.

As Congress investigated the "Vicksburg Insurrection," U.S. Senator Alcorn "guided" them into looking at alleged corruption in Republican government, the sheriff's inability to control law and order, and Governor Ames's so-called complicity by intentionally provoking violence and backing a corrupt regime against the "will of the people." Yet whites in Mississippi remained divided in their need to destroy Ames's administration. The governor did his best to reform the state, but his program fell in the state legislature, once again revealing him as a weak politician. When he raised a black state militia to protect his administration and local Republican officeholders, the whites in the state decided finally to get rid of Reconstruction at once by concerted white action. These White Liners (q.v.) maintained that they had nothing against black participation in politics, but that the unity of African-Americans behind the Radical regime and its corrupt programs forced them to engage in self-defense to save themselves from being taxed out of existence. But more cautious men wondered if racial strife might not lead to more Federal intervention.

By 1875, renewed violence in Vicksburg set the tone for the state election campaign. Opponents to Ames organized a Conservative Democratic Party and listened to the appeal of Senator Alcorn for racial harmony, acceptance of Negro suffrage, and the Fourteenth and Fifteenth Amendments (qq.v.). The delegates responded by calling for civil and political equality and the redemption of the state—two contradictory notions, but it sounded good up North. Under the motto, "peaceably if we can, forcibly if we must," the Conservatives went forth to take control of the legislature and capture the state treasurer's office, the only statewide contest that year. Gun dealers were sold out during the campaign several times over. Ames pointed out that Conservatives made the color line the issue of the election despite their noble-sounding platform. Democrat U.S. Senator L. Q. C. Lamar preached peace in Washington to fool the nation, while back home the nightriders used the whip, rope, and gun to get the job done.

As in Louisiana, the fight was for the county governments. At Yazoo City, Albert Morgan (q.v.), a Wisconsin Carpetbagger, had engaged in planting, established black schools, married an African-American woman, and become a dominant Republican. In 1873 he was elected sheriff, but his opponent, another Republican, refused to leave office until Morgan took it over at gun point. In the scuffle his opponent was killed. Democrats immediately accused him of murder. They wished to arrest him, but a posse of blacks prevented this. Morgan sought to allay white fears by holding a joint Republican–Democratic political meeting. It soon degenerated into a shooting fray, from which Morgan was lucky to emerge alive. Morgan hid out until the heat was off and fled to Jackson, pleading for help. Ames did nothing, and the Republican Party polled a total of seven votes in November. A similar riot occurred in Clinton outside of Jackson, but its proximity to the Federal garrison stopped the fighting after three whites and four blacks died. Indictments were sought, but a grand jury found no true bill. Later, White Liners struck back by murdering black political and community leaders at night.

Governor Ames hoped that President Grant would see the political expediency in sending Federal troops in to police the election. But Grant refused, saying, "The whole public are tired out with these annual autumnal outbreaks in the South, and the great majority are ready to condemn any interference on the part of the Government." He told Ames to handle the problem himself. Ames found out what Grant was referring to when he considered sending the black militia into the field. He was roundly condemned for trying to settle the election by force (which overlooked the fact that his opponents were doing the same) and bringing on a race war. The militia was not used. Instead, the Democrats proposed a compromise. They warned the governor that if he refused the deal, Jackson's streets would run red with blood. Ames agreed to keep the militia out of the election process, and the Democrats said that they would keep the peace for the rest of the contest.

The political agreement was of little consequence, because the Democrats had already coerced most of the results. Mass meetings and torchlight parades, many complete with private white armies armed with cannon, and constant heckling of Republican candidates and voters kept the heat on. Economic coercion (loss of jobs) and forcing of local Republican officials to resign and go into exile filled out the Conservative program. Men from Alabama and Louisiana "assisted" in keeping the peace with gunfire. Armed companies of whites policed the polls and permitted only those blacks with Democratic passes of good conduct to vote. The rest either stayed home or were hounded from the polling places. The "Rebel yell" went up often as voters passed between lines of white men to vote. The statewide Republican majority of 23,000 in 1873 became a Democrat majority of 30,000—this in a state with a large black majority of registered voters.

Although fraud, violence, and intimidation played a role, whites also mobilized their voters and united them in voting as a bloc for the first time since Reconstruction had begun. Democratic control of the legislature allowed them to impeach Governor Ames. In March 1876, the legislature dropped the charges (they had already convicted Ames's lieutenant governor), and Ames left the state, never to return. He retired to Minnesota and, after Jesse James (q.v.) tried to rob his bank in Northfield, left for his wife's family home in Massachusetts. Ames died in Florida in 1933, bitter that his administration had been doomed because "the inferior race" had to "succumb to the superior race" even though the former had the support of the Federal government. In his condescending referral to his supporters was the real truth—he did not have the support of the United States anymore. Florida, South Carolina, and Louisiana sat in the wings and took note. It would be their votes that determined the election of 1876 and the Compromise of 1877 (q.v.).

REDEMPTION IN SOUTH CAROLINA. The Palmetto State had experienced one of the more corrupt Reconstruction (q.v.) regimes in the South. In the end, everyone was in on the take, a problem Republicans managed to overcome by nominating and electing Carpetbagger Daniel H. Chamberlain (qq.v.) as governor in 1874. He had been a part of the previous administration, and many saw his election as a sign of business as usual. Chamberlain fooled them. He called for clean, economical government and fair assessment of taxes and acted to use the state patronage evenly, appointing some white Conservatives to office. Whites, however, had little faith in Chamberlain's promises. They condemned all Republican-run governments as corrupt rule by ignorant blacks. Unfortunately, although Chamberlain lived in a black majority state, he never developed a good relationship with African-American political leaders.

As the majority of black voters in South Carolina was the greatest in the South, it became evident that mere fraud would not carry the day. The result was the adoption of the Mississippi Plan (q.v.), which meant in South Carolina the organization of the Red Shirts (q.v.), its own version of the White League (q.v.). The movement got its biggest support in Edgefield County, a hotbed of secession in 1860, the Ku Klux Klan (q.v.) after the war, and now the center of straight-out Democracy. The blacks in "Bloody Edgefield" had organized their own Rifle Clubs (q.v.), so the scene was set for open hostility, as soon as a triggering event could take place. It occurred in nearby Hamburg. A Negro militia (q.v.) company paraded in Hamburg's streets for the Fourth of July 1876. Two whites in a buggy told the commander to get his men out of the way. The soldier replied that there was plenty of room on either side of the column. The whites were about to remonstrate when a rain came up, dispersing the column to the porches on the side of the street, and the whites drove on. A local court swore out an arrest warrant against the militia officer for blocking a public thoroughfare a couple of days later.

An armed group of 200 or 300 whites showed up for the hearing. They demanded that the black militia surrender its weapons. The militia commander refused. Shooting soon erupted, and the blacks took refuge in a building, which the whites began to shell with a cannon. The blacks fled out the rear, 25 of their number being "arrested." One of the armed white companies, led by Benjamin R. Tillman, later a U.S. senator better known as 'Pitchfork" Ben, refused to allow the black prisoners to be marched to jail and executed five men in its custody, an incident called the Hamburg Massacre (q.v.). Although the murder was condemned by Conservatives, they blamed the shootings on the evils flowing from Republican rule. At Chamberlain's request, President Ulysses S. Grant (q.v.) sent Federal soldiers to restore order. Then the Republicans instituted court proceedings, indicting 60 whites from the best families of the area for the massacre. The trial, with the defendants appearing in their red shirts, was delayed until after the 1876 election (q.v.) so that passions might cool; all of the accused were then released.

The Hamburg Massacre scuttled all of the cooperation between Chamberlain and Conservative Democrats in the upcoming 1876 election. The Democrats, split between low country Conservatives who wanted a peaceful election and Fire-Eaters from upcountry who wanted more blood, cleverly concealed their differences by nominating Confederate war hero Lt. Gen. Wade Hampton. Their platform recognized the Civil War constitutional amendments and summoned all citizens regardless of color to join in reforming the corruption (q.v.) that had plagued the state. Although Hampton was a reasonable man, he lacked the power and possibly the will to stop the bloodletting that went on, especially upcountry (most of the fighting in the low country was initiated by black militia against their white opponents, a rarity in the Reconstruction history of most states). The Republicans stood with Chamberlain, their best chance of looking like honest reformers, too. Democrats condemned Chamberlain as "a carrion coward, a buzzard and a Puritanical seedy adventurer who came down here to steal our substance."

Unlike Louisiana and Mississippi, where the Republicans dared not leave their capital cities, Chamberlain engaged in a vigorous campaign. But right behind him came the Red Shirts (there were nearly 300 white rifle clubs in the state), who intimidated, hanged, and shot potential Republican voters, mostly black. The Red Shirts were so active that a fear grew that they might even attack U.S. troops on election day. The worst violence of the campaign occurred in Ellenton in September 1876, in an area where whites had vowed to win the election or kill all the Republicans. A minor assault by two blacks, which Republicans claimed to be a trumped-up case, started the action. One of the suspects was captured and identified by a victim and shot on the spot.

The other had an arrest warrant filed against him. The rifle clubs broke up a Republican meeting the next day, chasing the party members into a swamp. The Red Shirts demanded that the assault suspect be turned over. The blacks refused. After much talk, the two sides agreed to depart amicably, but some blacks shot one of the Red Shirts, and the whites went crazy, shooting up houses all over the county. The fighting spread into Ellenton, where a black state legislator was among those murdered. The arrival of Federal troops finally restored the peace, just as the Red Shirts, many arriving by train, had cornered their opponents for the final kill. Over 100 blacks and a half dozen whites died.

Governor Chamberlain responded with a proclamation to the rifle clubs to disperse. They promptly changed their names to things like the Allendale Mounted Baseball Club, Mother's Little Helpers, or the First Baptist Sewing Circle, and rode on. Chamberlain complained to Grant, who ordered the Red Shirts to disband or face Federal troops. The whites quickly drew back and election day passed quietly, barring a small riot put down by U.S. forces in Charleston. Hampton claimed victory, and in some respects he was right. It was amazing how little fight Chamberlain had put up—he never called up the Negro militia, for instance. Yet blacks in South Carolina had put up a better fight, especially in the area in and around Charleston, than Republicans in other states, to no avail. Even though the state Returning Board awarded a majority of seats in the legislature to Republicans, it had to be done under the protection of Federal troops. The state presidential electoral vote went to the Republicans and the governorship to Hampton in a sort of compromise that satisfied no one. Hampton warned Chamberlain that the life of the governor and all other Republicans was in Chamberlain's own hands. Although the state's presidential vote went to Republican Rutherford B. Hayes, without Federal support, the government soon fell to the Red Shirts. South Carolina had been redeemed.

RED RIVER CAMPAIGN (MARCH 10–MAY 26, 1864). Because of the French presence in Maximilian's Mexico (q.v.) and fear of possible French-Confederate cooperation, Abraham Lincoln (q.v.) professed the need to invade Texas. As several coastal expeditions had failed in 1862 and 1863, the route he and his military advisor Bvt. Maj. Gen. Henry W. Halleck (q.v.) settled on was to go up the Red River toward Shreveport. As this took Federal forces away from Mexico, many thought that the real reason for the campaign was to secure cotton and sugar to assist the many speculators believed to have the ear of the White House and the War and Treasury Departments.

The operation was to combine a thrust up the Red, utilizing 27,000 troops from the Union's Gulf and Mississippi Departments under Bvt. Maj. Gen. Nathaniel Banks (q.v.), with a flank attack of 15,000 coming in from Little

Rock in the Department of Arkansas under Bvt. Maj. Gen. Fred Steele. The 30, 000 Confederates were divided into three more or less equal contingents stationed in upper Louisiana, southwestern Arkansas, and along the Texas coast, commanded by Lt. Gen. E. Kirby Smith (q.v.) out of Shreveport.

Banks got a late start up the Bayou Teche, not meeting with Bvt. Maj. Gen. A. J. Smith's Federals out of Vicksburg until March 24. Steele started even later and effectively took himself out of the campaign's time schedule. By then, Smith had already subdued Ft. DeRussy on the lower Red and secured Alexandria, hardly firing a shot. The expedition was to be supported by a naval river fleet of 20 ironclads and wooden gunboats, commanded by Adm. David D. Porter, but the Red's unusually low waters kept the fleet busier with keeping afloat than supporting the attack.

Because of the extremely low water at Natchitoches, Banks' infantry left the security of the fleet's guns and moved inland, headed toward Shreveport. At Sabine Crossroads (Mansfield) near Shreveport, Banks command met and blundered into a premature attack against Maj. Gen. Richard Taylor's Confederates. Just having received reinforcements from Texas, Taylor drove the Yankees back, with heavy loss. Rattled, Banks decided to pull back to a better defensive position at Pleasant Hill. Taylor followed and attacked, receiving heavy casualties in return. Gen. Kirby Smith came onto the field and ordered Taylor to retreat.

But Banks had had enough and moved toward Alexandria before Taylor could reorganize his scattered men. Smith sent a large part of Taylor's men to Arkansas to defeat General Steele in the Camden Campaign (q.v.), while Taylor followed Banks, keeping the pressure on. Taylor also sent his cavalry to the Red River to harass the fleet, particularly at Blair's or Pleasant Hill Landing. Admiral Porter was in much worse position than the Union infantry. His ships were barely clearing the river bottom as they headed to Alexandria to meet Banks' army. Above Alexandria, the ships came to a halt. The rapids were now so shallow as to threaten to leave the fleet for Confederate capture.

Fortunately, an imaginative engineering officer, Col. Joseph Bailey, devised a set of coffer dams to narrow the channel and lift the ships over the rocks. After the army left Alexandria, with the fleet being attacked constantly from the shore, Bailey again proved his worth by using the rescued gunboats as pontoons to bridge the 600-yard-wide Atchafalaya at Simmsport. Smith's forces arrived back in Mississippi by May 22, and Banks reached the safety of Donaldsonville, Louisiana, on May 26. Officers on both sides lambasted their comrades. Kirby Smith relieved General Taylor at his request, and Banks lost his job and faced a congressional investigation.

Kirby Smith hoped to transfer Taylor and his Louisianans east of the Mississippi, but the Yankees had too tight a hold on the river. So Taylor went alone to command in Mississippi and Alabama, receiving a promotion to lieutenant general from Richmond for Mansfield. Instead, he urged Maj. Gen. Sterling Price (q.v.) to take his all-Missouri cavalry and invade his home state, which he did in Price's Missouri Raid (q.v.)

RED SHIRTS. A South Carolina white Democratic Party (q.v.) group of armed gunmen who intimidated black and white Republicans (q.v.) at elections in the mid-1870s, shot rival candidates and their supporters, and watched the polls to limit opposition voting.

REEDER, ANDREW H. *See* KANSAS–MISSOURI BORDER WARS.

REED, HARRISON (1813–1899). Boston-born Harrison Reed was a Florida Carpetbag (q.v.) governor. At the outbreak of the Civil War, he had gone to Washington, D.C., where he served as a nameless Treasury Department bureaucrat. He was a widower, and his daughter had also died young. In January 1863, Reed landed at Fernandina Island off the coast of Florida. His job was to follow Federal forces into the mainland and collect the Federal property tax owed the United States. To pay, one had to take a loyalty oath. To refuse the oath meant that the property in question was liable to seizure and sale by auction by the treasury men. Reed bought lots for himself and his two sons. He and the other commissioners also allowed blacks to bid on places where they were living before the lots opened up to public sale. He quarreled with one of his co-agents over this, and in the end, Reed lost his job.

Reed spent the next two years in Washington as a postal employee. President Andrew Johnson (q.v.) sent him back to Florida after the war as a postal supervisor for the whole state. He advised the president to appoint William Marvin as provisional governor and warned him of pro-Chase electioneering taking place among the treasury men who had run Reed off. Marvin sided with Reed and had the treasury men relieved of their jobs, allowing Reed to get even for his 1863 firing. Reed initially had no desire to use the Military Reconstruction Acts (q.v.), being a good Johnson man at heart, but by 1867, it was obvious that Republicanism was the wave of the future in the South. And to ride that wave he needed black votes. But Radical Republicans, known locally as the Mule Team, had a big jump on him. They had won the most seats at the state constitutional convention.

So Reed began by talking to individual delegates as they arrived at Tallahassee for the convention. He also won over Maj. Gen. George Meade (q.v.), military commander of the Third Military District (Georgia, Alabama, and Florida) and the Freedmen's Bureau assistant commissioner, Thomas W. Osborn. The latter had a good reputation among planters and freedmen alike for running a fair operation. But Reed could not defeat the Mule Team in the convention. So he pulled his delegates (almost all white) out and removed to Monticello to write his own constitution, which gave the governor large appointive powers for local offices. The Radicals of the Mule Team meanwhile wrote theirs. They wanted to make all offices elective and apportion all seats by population. This would give blacks a big voice in what went on, because they almost equaled whites when Confederate disfranchisement was tacked on.

Things looked bad until General Meade arrived from Atlanta. He deployed Federal soldiers and forced the two conventions to meet together. Reed managed to persuade enough Mule Team delegates that his constitution was better, and it passed. The convention also nominated Reed for governor on the Republican ticket. When the Mule Team complained to Congress, Reed went to Washington and convinced Congress that only he possessed the necessary majority to carry the day and complete Reconstruction. Back in Florida, Reed found that the Conservative Democrats had broken off their association with him to run their own candidate. But the radicals also entered the fray as a third party. With the support of the Post Office Department, the Freedmen's Bureau, the Army, and the Congress, Reed's ticket took the contest by a large majority.

But Reed had already reached the high point of his power. When he appointed his cabinet and local offices, he angered everyone. Federal patronage, so important because these jobs paid more, went into the hands of his onetime ally, now U.S. senator, Thomas W. Osborn. But Reed had refused to go along with Osborn's scheme to fund state bonds at a profit he offered to split with Reed. The legislature saw him veto bills to raise their pay and open public accommodations to all races equally. And Democrats (q.v.) hated him for raising a "black and tan" (q.v.) militia to put down the Ku Klux Klan (q.v.). Mysteriously, the arms ordered for the militia were stolen en route from New York, making the troops ineffective.

At this point, the legislature moved to impeach the governor after threats against his life failed to get his resignation. With the connivance of the secretary of state, the lieutenant governor stole the state seal and tried to run Reed out of office. Reed drove the usurper off at gunpoint. After this bout, Reed was still governor, but he was a man without a party. When legislators threatened to impeach him once again, Reed grumbled, "Impeach and be damned!"

But there was an issue upon which impeachment could be based. It had to do with railroad matters, one of the governor's pet projects from the very beginning of his stay in Florida. Reed believed in public aid to private enterprise. The financiers of the railroad projects were two men already on the lam from North Carolina for corruption there, Milton S. Littlefield (q.v.) and George W. Swepson. And Littlefield and Swepson, with Reed's backing, persuaded the state legislature to trade $4,000,000 in state bonds for railroad bonds. Rumors had it that Littlefield paid the governor $7,500 for his signature. Reed called it a personal loan, which he expected to repay. The legislature voted his impeachment unanimously and then adjourned *sine die* (as they had no evidence to hang on Reed), leaving the governor in limbo for the 10 months left of his term.

Reed had to turn the office over to the lieutenant governor under the state constitution. When he learned that the lieutenant governor had come to Jacksonville for a meeting, Reed took a quick train to Tallahassee and got the seal from a cooperative secretary of state. The lieutenant governor then made a mistake. He called the senate into special session. Reed's Republican enemies moved to adjourn. But Democrats called for a trial. Reed's attorney then moved that the charges be dropped. The senate voted 10 to 7 on Reed's behalf, and he left office a free man, having outmaneuvered everyone. Having beaten the impeachment, Reed retired to raise oranges. He had made no money while governor. Indeed, he was in much debt. He struggled on, raising oranges, promoting Florida real estate before it boomed, and dying in 1899, poor as ever.

RELIGION OF HUMANITY. *See* SOCIAL DARWINISM.

REPUBLICAN PARTY AND THE CIVIL WAR AND RECONSTRUC-TION. During the Civil War and Reconstruction, the Republican Party (q.v.) was divided into three factions: the Conservatives, the Moderates, and the Radicals. The Conservatives were old-line Whigs (q.v.), the Conscience Whigs, who could not stand with the South on the slavery issue. Their idols were Henry Clay and Daniel Webster, men who wanted to keep slavery out of national politics in favor of economic issues. They disliked their Radical compatriots as too inflammatory, although if pressed, the Conservatives were as much against slavery as an institution as anyone. They believed that the U.S. government had more important things to do, such as construct the transcontinental railroad, open up the West through free land, or raise the tariff to protect American industry. What they wanted from the war was to destroy Southern political power in Washington, the so-called Slave Power Conspiracy (q.v.), which had blocked these programs for a generation. Their desires were the real basis for the Republican Platform of 1860. Their key man in 1860 was Edward Bates of Missouri. During Reconstruction, the Conservatives wanted very little of black civil rights, probably because they seemed to come from districts with a strong Democratic (q.v.) minority, or sometimes even a majority. At the end of Reconstruction, the election of 1876 and the Compromise of 1877 (qq.v.) marked a return of the Republicans to the Conservative fold.

The Moderates were more a branch of the Conservatives before and during the war. They believed in the Conservatives' economic program, but also leavened it with a strong dose of antislavery feeling. These men held the balance of power in the party during the war. The main difference between the Radicals and the Moderates on the slavery issue was that the Radicals wanted government to attack it boldly, while the Moderates wanted the government to restrict its spread and allow slavery to die a natural death. A lot of what attracted Abraham Lincoln (q.v.) to the party was the Conservative Republican economic program and the prohibition of slavery in the territories. He was a Moderate, which helped him be a compromise candidate in the election of 1860 (q.v.). What he would have been in Reconstruction is hard to say. But during Reconstruction, the Moderates wanted very much to compromise with President Andrew Johnson (q.v.), until Johnson's pro-Southern policies drove them into the arms of the Radicals.

Historians differ as to what most motivated the Radicals, as opposed to the Moderates and the Conservatives. Basically, the Radical Republicans wanted comprehensive social, economic, and political change. They tended to come from safe seats, elected by strong Republican majorities. They could take controversial stands on issues with little fear of the voters at the next election. Thus, before the war they were uncompromisingly Free Soil; during the war they were for immediate and total emancipation; and after the war they took the lead in black social, economic, and political equality. As politicians, they were unusual because they rarely compromised. They were ideologues, moral revolutionaries. They welcomed the war for allowing the North to get rid of slavery legally under the guise of fighting for Union.

The Radicals took the lead in the Republican Party, believing that the Whigs and Democrats were dominated by the Slave Power Conspiracy. This was an important concept. All the North believed that the South had too much political power through slavery and its dominance of national policy. All of the North was willing to destroy the slave oligarchs. They wanted no more slavery in the territories, no more slave states, no more slavery or slave trade in the District of Columbia, no fugitive slave laws, no interstate slave trade. But not all Northerners were willing to concede political, economic, or social rights to blacks after the institution of slavery was destroyed. And therein lay the rub for the success of Reconstruction.

Radical Republicans had several qualities in common during Reconstruction. First, they believed that the full benefits of restoration should be withheld from the South for a period of time. Another thought that Radicals subscribed to was the notion that Reconstruction ought to be determined by the legislative branch of government. The Radicals believed that they represented the people directly, contrary to the Jacksonian ideal that the president, as the single Federal official elected by the whole population, did. Most did not deny the executive branch a contributory role, but it would be subordinate. Moderate and Conservative Republicans parted company with them here, reserving more of a role for the president.

But the one factor that defined a Radical Republican was one's interest in black rights. Not that other Republicans were not interested in black rights.

They were. But Radicals made it the centerpiece of their Reconstruction ideology. The former slaves' right to vote was a part of this. This could be done on the basis of principle or from a practical point of view. It was one way to assure the Republican Party of a toehold in the South. It could also help African-Americans retain their freedom. Another aspect of this picture was black civil rights. This included the right to a fair trial, to sue and be sued, to sit on juries, to own property, and to receive equal protection under the laws—much of what the Civil Rights Law of 1866 (q.v.) promised. Once Congress passed this law, the Federal courts and the blacks' right to vote would secure them forever, in theory.

Another right Radicals believed in was that African-Americans ought to enjoy education. One cannot vote without knowledge, went the theory. Finally, Radical Republicans had an affinity for giving the ex-slaves land. Many wanted to seize all plantations and divide them up among the people who had worked them so long in bondage, seen in the legendary Reconstruction slogan of "forty acres and a mule" (q.v.). Conservative Republicans and Democrats managed to block total confiscation amendments to the Freedmen's Bureau (q.v.) bills, and President Andrew Johnson (q.v.) returned most of the seized properties.

If the black vote, civil rights, education, and land grants defined Radical Republicans, what motivated them? Obviously some operated under the desire for revenge. Southerners were traitors and had to be punished for the sins of slavery and secession against America, God, and Constitution. This often was expressed by the slogan "vote as you shot," through a process usually called "waving the bloody shirt." Another motivation for the Radicals was political. By returning to the Union with the slaves freed, the South actually would pick up seats in Congress. Before the war, slaves were counted as three-fifths of a person for purposes of taxation and representation. Now they would be five-fifths and unable to vote, if the Southern whites had their way. This was a cruel reward for rebellion, indeed. Radicals also operated to protect Republican domestic measures enacted during the war in the absence of Southern Democrats. This included land grant colleges, the national banking system, internal improvements (especially the transcontinental railroad), contract labor, and a high protective tariff.

Important to a lot of Radicals (and many other Northerners) was the fear of a lost peace. This was a major cause of a hard Reconstruction policy. Radicals looked at the Presidential Reconstruction plans (q.v.) and saw governments dominated by planters, Confederate military officers, and secessionists; anti-Negro discrimination guaranteed through Black Codes (q.v.); and a general defiant and undefeated attitude among Southern whites. Many feared that four years of bloody war had settled little, and this attitude was widely shared, as evidenced by the smashing Republican victory in the 1866 congressional elections, led by the Radicals.

Finally, Radicals were motivated by idealism, a desire to help out the unfortunates who suffered the vicissitudes of slavery. This involved the vote, land grants, education opportunities, and civil rights. The prewar and wartime idealism of Republicans did not just die out at Appomattox. It continued throughout Reconstruction. Radicals had a compelling view of what America should be like and saw great logic and justice in their programs. They were also special kinds of politicians. They were men of principle who could not bear to compromise their ideals. There was a strong religious component to Radical thought. They were the conscience of the society of their day.

REPUBLICAN PARTY, BEGINNING OF. Third political parties traditionally have had a high mortality rate in American politics. Before the Civil War, there were the Anti-Masonic Party (1827–1832), the Liberty Party (1840–1848), the Free Soil Party (1848–1856), and the American Party (q.v.) (1854–1856). Generally, the programs of third parties have been absorbed by one or both of the major parties. But the one antebellum exception was the Republican Party, which from its organization at Ripon, Wisconsin, in 1854, went on to become the main competitor to the Democrats ever since.

The Republican Party was a reaction to the Kansas–Nebraska Act and the problem of slavery in the territories that the Franklin Pierce (q.v.) administration sought to solve by popular sovereignty and the Non-Exclusion Doctrine (qq.v.). With the opening of the West to slavery, "Anti-Kansas" meetings were held throughout the North. Hoping to avoid the extremist label that the Free Soil Party had inherited, the Ripon Convention adopted the name "Republican." Immediately, the party put forth a full slate of candidates in the 1854 Wisconsin elections and carried the state.

It is quite possible that the Republicans would never have survived their first electoral victory had not the Kansas–Missouri Wars (q.v.) kept slavery in the territories an issue before the American people. In 1855, the party attracted one of its most important adherents, Horace Greeley (q.v.), a newspaper editor in New York City. Greeley's New York *Tribune* was one of the most widely read and circulated sheets of yellow journalism in the nation. It regularly boasted as many as 200,000 readers of its weekly edition. Greeley's exaggerated stories of the travails of brave, honest, outnumbered antislavery farmers before the juggernaut of vicious, pro-slave, Missouri Border Ruffians and other such Southern ilk made "Bleeding Kansas" an American catchword.

In October 1855, some important politicians threw in their lot with the new party. Salmon P. Chase (q.v.), who ran successfully for governor of Ohio on four party labels (Democrat, Know Nothing, Whig, and Republican), declared himself a Republican. Benjamin F. Wade (q.v.), one of Ohio's U.S.

senators, did likewise. Thurlow Weed, a newspaperman and New York's premier political manipulator for over 30 years, and his front-man, a New York U. S. senator, William H. Seward (q.v.), did, too.

The Republicans cleverly called an "Opposition to Kansas" convention at Pittsburgh on Washington's Birthday in 1856, to cultivate the idea that they were moderately antislavery as opposed to radical abolitionists (q.v.). But no new adherents showed up. Kansas had quieted as an issue. Then, in May 1856, Kansas blew up with the sacking of Lawrence, the Brooks–Sumner affair, the Pottawattomie Massacre led by John Brown (q.v.), and the arrest of the Free Soil Topeka government. New adherents came into the party in droves, including a hack Whig politician in Illinois named Abraham Lincoln (q.v.). Fusing all of the opposition to Democratic U.S. Senator Stephen A. Douglas (q.v.), Lincoln stole the Illinois party from its original 1854 organizers, got rid of its antislavery agitators, and turned it into an anti-Kansas, anti-Douglas organization. It would carry him to the presidency in 1860.

What Lincoln did in Illinois was happening with different personae in every Northern state. In an attempt to shut down the Bleeding Kansas propaganda presented in Greeley's newspaper, the lifeblood of Republican organizers, Georgia representative Robert Toombs introduced a bill in Congress that would have ordered a census taken in Kansas and called a constitutional convention, with all those in the territory three months allowed to vote. Everything was to be supervised by five Federal commissioners. But the Republicans did not want Kansas off the front pages. Nor did they want the antislavery Topeka constitution and government abolished, only to have to start all over again. Toombs' bill never passed. The Republicans were off to place in the election of 1856 and win in the election of 1860 (qq.v.).

REPUBLICAN PARTY, IDEOLOGY OF. The Republicans had three basic elements that made up the core of their political thought. The first was the free labor ideal. The Republicans emphasized over and over that they stood for free labor. They believed that this concept expressed the idea of a good, hard-working, morally motivated society. It was the old Protestant ethic writ large. The Republicans held that free labor meant that if one worked diligently, one could advance one's place in society, improve one's life. It was the opportunity to stop being a wage earner and become a wage payer.

The second element of Republican thought was a critique of Southern society based on the institution of slavery. If the North and free labor were good, it followed that the South and slavery were evil—the exact antithesis of each other. The South failed to cherish the free labor ideal. It lacked economic development, fluidity in social position, and political democracy—at least to Republicans. The South lacked all that made the North vibrant—free schools, canals, railroads, charities, commerce, cities, cultivated areas, and, above all, population—when compared to the North. The reason was obvious. It was the presence of slaves.

It was not the slaves' fault that the South was backward—it was the fault of the whites who owned them or condoned their enslavement. The South cried out for reconstruction on the basis of the Northern model of society. Because this was true, the South and its institutions must be kept out of the Western territories, lest they be harmed before they could develop into miniature replicas of the Northern states under the Republican Platform of 1860 (q.v.). Hence, the Wilmot Proviso (q.v.) was the center of Republican political action before the Civil War.

The third element of Republican political ideas was the Slave Power Conspiracy (q.v.). The South dominated the United States government and its domestic and foreign policy before the Civil War. Slavery was morally wrong, but the slave power in the Federal government permitted the South to interfere with Northern political rights, civil liberties, necessary economic measures to promote industry and trade, and free white labor. The slave power rests its strength on the three-fifths clause of the Constitution and the concept of extraterritoriality (q.v.) of Southern pro-slave institutions. The Republicans feared the ulterior designs of the South to make the whole nation re-embrace slavery, even the North, which had once obliterated it within its own boundaries. One could see this of course in the fervor of the South to expand slavery into the territories and to conquer new lands for slavery, like Mexico, Cuba, Nicaragua, Honduras, and Panama.

The only solution to grasping pro-slave Southern political power was for the North to seize control of the Federal government. It also had to free all men and make them beholden to the Republican Party as voters. It was the distinction between slavery and the slave power that allowed the North to end the South's domination of government and permit racial discrimination afterward. Once the South indicated it would embrace Northern economic and political institutions (in effect, the results of the war, in the Compromise of 1877), the black vote and the African-Americans' place in the postwar unified white society became irrelevant.

REPUBLICAN PLATFORM OF 1860. For a political party that was in theory built on its opposition to slavery in the territories, the Republican Party (q.v.) Platform of 1860 said very little about slavery, but included much from Henry Clay's old American System (q.v.) proposals from the 1830s. The platforms planks were no slavery in the West (for the idealists and white, small farmers); a high protective tariff (to win industrial Pennsylvania, one of the key states the party had to have to carry the presidency); a national banking act (to win over old-time Whigs [q.v.] and New England financiers); a homestead act (to develop the West and provide free land to immigrants and white, small farmers); internal improvements on a large scale, especially a transcontinental railroad emanating out of Chicago (to hold the Old Northwest, especially Abraham Lincoln's [q.v.] state of Illinois, critical to his winning the presidency); and land grant colleges to teach agricultural and military sciences (to carry the old Northwest and the immigrant and farm vote). Unlike many political platforms, which are enunciated and forgotten, the Republicans delivered on every issue by 1865. *See also* ELECTION OF 1860.

RESACA, BATTLE OF. *See* ATLANTA CAMPAIGN.

REVELS, HIRAM R. (1822–1901). Born a free man of color in Fayetteville County, North Carolina, Hiram Revels studied at a seminary and Knox College in Galesburg, Illinois, becoming a preacher for the African Methodist Episcopal Church. He served congregations throughout the Old Northwest. When the war broke out, Revels recruited black soldiers for the Union cause and eventually became a chaplain in one regiment. After the war, he settled in Mississippi and entered Republican politics as an alderman in Natchez. In 1870, as the state was readmitted to the Union, Revels was elected U.S. senator by the state legislature for the short-term seat, the one abandoned by Jefferson Davis (q.v.) in 1860. This made Revels the first black man to occupy a place in the U.S. Senate in American history.

The notion of a black man occupying the senatorial position once held by the president of the Confederacy caught the imagination of the nation and became the subject of a famous Thomas Nast cartoon, playing upon a line in William Shakespeare's *Othello* ("For that I do suspect the lusty Moor hath leap'd into my seat: the thought whereof doth like a poisonous mineral gnaw at my inwards") showing Davis as Iago gazing sinisterly upon Revels (Othello) courting the Yankee senators (the modern Desdemonas), with the title, "Time Works Wonders." Yet the extremely conservative Revels did little that Davis might not have done in the Senate beyond supporting an integrated school system in the District of Columbia. He spoke on behalf of the readmission of states like Mississippi into the Union and an increased Federal levee system. After he stepped down (by prior agreement) at the end of his term, Revels became the editor of the *Southwestern Christian Advocate,* the president of Alcorn A & M College, and a district superintendent of the African Methodist Episcopal Church.

REYNOLDS, JOSEPH J. (1822–1899). A Kentuckian who grew up in Indiana, Joseph J. Reynolds graduated West Point in 1843. He served on the Western frontier and in eastern garrison duty, with a stint as a mathematics instructor at the academy. In 1857, he resigned to teach at Washington University at St. Louis, then went home to assist in the family grocery business in

Indiana. During the war, he served with the Tenth Indiana Volunteer Infantry and soon rose to brigade and division command in the Western Theater of the conflict. He was brevetted for bravery in the Chattanooga Campaign (q.v.) at Chickamauga and Missionary Ridge, where he was chief of staff to the Army of the Cumberland (succeeding future president, Bvt. Maj. Gen. James A. Garfield), and wound up the war commanding the VII Corps in Arkansas. He decided to stay in the service after the war and received the colonelcy of the Twenty-sixth Infantry. By 1867 and the passage of the Military Reconstruction Acts (q.v.), he was in charge of the giant subdistrict of the Rio Grande, with headquarters at Brownsville.

As senior officer after the District of Texas commander, Bvt. Maj. Gen. Charles Griffin (q.v.), Reynolds was in line for the Texas command upon Griffin's death from yellow fever in September 1867. He proceeded to make his headquarters at Austin to be closer to the Texas state government (no general preceding him had ever met personally with Texas ex-governor James W. Throckmorton [q.v.], for example) and to be far from the yellow fever that regularly swept towns along the Gulf Coast. There was much trepidation among the Texas Republicans (q.v.) about Reynolds' attitudes about Reconstruction and party necessities. Griffin had put one of their own men, Elisha M. Pease (q.v.), in the governorship and had just begun to clean Democrats (q.v.) out of the state executive and courts before his untimely death.

Republican leaders immediately contacted the general to find out his views. To their pleasant surprise, Reynolds indicated he was willing to work with them on appointments. Of course there was a price. Provisional Governor Pease issued a unique proclamation declaring that the state government he represented was solely provisional; its authority rested on the Military Reconstruction Acts (q.v.) and any orders promulgated by General Reynolds. Reynolds recognized all persons in office as the current civil government. Most important, Pease agreed in writing to accept what would become the Shellabarger–Chase Theory of Forfeited Rights, which became the basis for the U.S. Supreme Court decision Texas v. White (qq.v.)—that all laws and contracts passed since 1861 not in conflict with the results of the war were valid.

Pease had no time to waste in bickering over Reynolds' conditions for supporting the Republican Party. The ideologues would simply have to swallow the truth—Reynolds was king of the dung heap. Reynolds did not let the party down. Using lists drawn up by loyalists since the end of the war and augmented by Griffin before he died, Reynolds removed 400 Democrats from office and appointed 436 Republicans (some positions had been vacant) to county offices. Republicans had their miracle. They were ensconced in Texas local and state government as never before.

Reynolds now turned to the Texas state constitutional convention. The convention was quickly deadlocked over Pease's acceptance of Reynolds' acceptance of Confederate day-to-day government of the state; possible division of the state into loyal white, African-American, and Rebel areas to guarantee Republican control in two of them; and disfranchisement of ex-Confederate voters. Upon President Ulysses S. Grant's (q.v.) election under the Republican banner, President Andrew Johnson (q.v.) struck back. Bvt. Maj. Gen. Edward R. S. Canby (q.v.), an expert at getting constitutions out of recalcitrant state conventions in the Carolinas, replaced General Reynolds. Canby then forced the convention to hammer out a constitution in a second convention session. Reynolds, meanwhile, went to Washington to greet his old friend, Ulysses S. Grant, now the incoming president of the United States. Texas Republicans petitioned him to remove Canby after he became chief executive. Grant happily complied.

Reynolds' return to Texas meant that Moderate Republican party-building could continue as before. The Moderate Republicans had put forth an electoral ticket consisting of Andrew J. Hamilton (President Johnson's provisional governor back in 1865), which was supported by Provisional Governor Pease. It was opposed by a Radical Republican slate led by convention president Edmund J. Davis (q.v.). But Reynolds indicated that there would be a new price for services rendered. He wanted to become one of the U.S. senators elected by the new state legislature. Hamilton would not agree to the condition.

Reynolds was not to be put off. He went to Edmund J. Davis and the Radicals with the same deal. Davis knew that any election would be a close thing, given the preponderant white voter registration in Texas. So he changed his Radical Party platform to accept Reynolds' moderate philosophy. Then Reynolds wrote to Grant that he had been forced to shift his support from Hamilton to Davis because the former was in bed with obstructionist Rebels. Reynolds began to throw Hamilton supporters out of office and replace them with Davis men. Provisional Governor Pease resigned in a huff. Reynolds assumed the governorship himself. When the election showed that the governor's contest hinged on the votes in two counties, Reynolds threw these votes out of the tally as tainted, and Davis became governor. The Republicans also managed to win three of the four congressional seats.

But Reynolds was not through yet. Acting under the Military Reconstruction Acts, he appointed all men elected to office ahead of time. All had to take the ironclad oath. Because of Hamilton's cooperation with the Democrats, many of his supporters locally who ran for office and won could not take the oath. Too many had Confederate antecedents. Reynolds appointed Davis-approved men to take their places, often the very men who had lost the election to the Hamilton ticket in the first place. Then the state legislature met and finished the Reconstruction process by ratifying the Fourteenth and Fifteenth Amendments (qq.v.). Next they considered electing U.S. senators.

Reynolds was among the front runners. But newspapers castigated him statewide for running for office in a body he had largely manipulated into office. Ultimately, he withdrew his name. Texas rejoined the Union in March 1870, nine years after leaving it.

RICHMOND CONVENTION (1860). Having met in Richmond, the Southern delegates to the Democratic Party's Charleston Convention (qq.v.) (plus some scattered delegates from New York, Pennsylvania, and Minnesota) were surprised to see the Northern wing of the party, meeting in the Baltimore Convention (q.v.), drive out more Southern delegates and the delegations from California and Oregon, too. Operating through the telegraph system, the delegates at Richmond contacted the Baltimore rejects and held their own convention. This Southern wing of the party nominated for their presidential candidate current Vice President John C. Breckinridge (q.v.) of Kentucky. His vice presidential running mate was Joseph Lane of Oregon. They offered themselves to the American people in the election of 1860 (q.v.) on the Alabama Platform, which included opening all territories to slavery before statehood; strict enforcement of the Fugitive Slave Act of the Compromise of 1850 (q.v.), as interpreted by the U.S. Supreme Court in the case Ableman *v.* Booth (qq.v.); the acquisition of Cuba; and Federal aid to a transcontinental railroad.

RICHMOND OR OVERLAND CAMPAIGN (1864). In the spring of 1864, Union President Abraham Lincoln (q.v.) finally found the man he wanted to win the war. This was Maj. Gen. Ulysses S. Grant (q.v.), the victor of Ft. Henry, Ft. Donelson (where he captured his first Confederate army), Shiloh, Vicksburg (where he captured his second Confederate army), and Chattanooga (qq.v.). Grant had several qualities that made him important as a candidate to run the whole war. He produced victories; he saw that the enemy armies, not geographical locations, were the main goals of his armies; and he understood that under the U.S. political system, civilians set policy, while military men merely carried it out. Grant's critics point out that he won because he had never had to fight a first-class Confederate military leader like Gen. Robert E. Lee (q.v.), and that he, unlike most soldiers, was perfectly willing to sell his soul to become a Republican and condone policies that he innately disliked, like emancipation (q.v.); procurement corruption; speculation in the field, particularly in cotton seizures, by treasury and war department agents; and bowing to the wants and desires of special interests with whom he had no real sympathy.

But there was a simplicity about Grant that still appeals. He is the ordinary American who makes good in an unpretentious sort of way. He is dogged in going forward, even if he is defeated time after time. And he shows a quiet brilliance in his profession of soldiering, particularly evident in the Vicksburg

Campaign. He may not have fought a man of Lee's abilities before, but he was willing to do the job, learn from his mistakes, and do it until he won. Lincoln knew that. And so did Congress, when they confirmed Lincoln's appointment of Grant as lieutenant general in charge of the Union war effort on March 9, 1864.

Grant immediately did something smart. He left Washington and all of its politics to the devious hands of Chief of Staff Maj. Gen. Henry W. Halleck (q.v.) and took to the field with the Army of the Potomac. Halleck loved the machinations behind the lines and was good at it. Grant did not need that kind of stuff fouling his mind as he plotted military strategy. Besides, Maj. Gen. George G. Meade (q.v.), the victor of Gettysburg, was still in charge of the Army of the Potomac. Part of the troops Grant was going to use in his campaign against Lee were in Maj. Gen. Ambrose E. Burnside's (q.v.) IX Corps, and Burnside outranked Meade. Grant's presence solved any initial command problems, although Burnside eventually revealed himself as willing to serve under Meade.

Grant assigned his crony, Maj. Gen. William T. Sherman (q.v.), the job of crushing the Army of Tennessee and taking Atlanta. He wanted to send Maj. Gen. Nathaniel Banks (q.v.) out of Louisiana to capture Mobile (q.v.), but politics determined that the Red River Campaign (q.v.) was more important. More cotton and more slaves to be liberated. Bvt. Maj. Gen. Benjamin Butler (q.v.), a political powerhouse of a lousy general, took over the Army of the James, to march out on Richmond behind Lee in northern Virginia, while another political general, Franz Sigel, would subdue Virginia's breadbasket, the Shenandoah Valley.

On May 4, Grant crossed the Rappahannock a bit west of where Bvt. Maj. Gen. Joseph Hooker (q.v.) had done the previous year. Like Hooker, he had to wait for his supply train, even though his base was at Fredericksburg, so he camped with his troops strung out in a north–south line (as opposed to the east–west position Hooker had assumed). He ordered a march through the Wilderness the next morning. But Lee was not about to let this opportunity pass. He brought his troops in on two east–west roads and slammed into Grant's columns the next morning.

Once again, Lee used the secondary growth of the Wilderness to conceal his smaller numbers. But Grant was not about to allow the Confederates to drive him back and deny him the road junctions he held. His men began to fortify their lines, a process both sides would employ more and more, until the last year of the Civil War would begin to resemble the trench warfare of the Western Front in World War I.

For the next two days, Lee and Grant slugged it out in the Wilderness, with Lee driving back a Federal counterattack and smashing Grant's right flank in an attack that petered out in the dark of the second day. The woods caught fire, and many of the seriously wounded burned to death. Grant lost 17,500, while Lee suffered an estimated 8,000 casualties. Lee had given Grant as thorough a drubbing as he had every other opponent he had faced. Both sides lost numerous generals to enemy and friendly fire. Lee lost Lt. Gen. James Longstreet (q.v.) for most of the rest of the war.

By the end of May 6, Grant decided to break off contact. To achieve this he would have to pull back to the east. Men on both sides figured that Lee had won another fight; the Yankees would retreat, lick their wounds, fire Grant, and try again. But then something unexpected happened. Instead of retreating to Fredericksburg and crossing the river, Union troops began to turn south again. Grant was not calling it quits. He was still advancing. The Federals began to cheer. They knew that Grant had just won the war. Deep in his heart, Lee knew it, too. Grant could take the constant battering of daily combat. He could replace all losses. Lee could not. He needed the respite that every Union general before Grant had always allowed his army. He would not get it again.

The next road junction of importance was Spotsylvania Court House. Grant marched hard, but Lee beat him to it. Meade groused that the problem was that Union cavalry had held up the infantry. Grant's cavalry commander, Bvt. Maj. Gen. Philip H. Sheridan (q.v.), said if he were given his head, he would go out and beat his Confederate counterpart. Grant told him to do it. Sheridan immediately pulled his men out of line and headed for Richmond. At Yellow Tavern outside of Richmond, Sheridan beat back Maj. Gen. J. E. B. Stuart's (q.v.) Southern horsemen, killing Stuart in the process.

Back at Spotsylvania once again, the trenches went up. For the next two weeks, the war got even nastier. As Grant brought his men up to Spotsylvania, Lee lengthened his entrenchments until they represented a sort of half circle. On May 9, Grant tried unsuccessfully to go around Lee's left flank. On May 10, Grant sent in troops from the II and V Corps in a mass attack that actually penetrated the Confederate line before dusk ended the action.

But the tactic of massed column assault as opposed to the usual line attack offered intriguing possibilities. On May 12, Grant massed his VI Corps opposite a near 90 degree bend in Lee's line, called variously, "the Salient" or "the Muleshoe." The attack went forward suddenly in a driving rain at dawn and penetrated Lee's line once again. Two thousand men and 20 guns were taken. The whole Confederate position seemed threatened. But the Confederates rallied and, for the rest of the day, men stood face to face, killing each other with knives, guns, bayonets, and fists. Forever after, this spot was known as "the Bloody Angle."

The rain continued for a week, seriously hampering operations by either side. Finally, Lee began to move his line southward, feeling Grant was doing the same. Lee attacked the far northern flank of the Union army at Harris' farm to confirm his suspicions. Grant promised Lincoln that he would keep up his "relentless hammering" of Lee "along this line, if it takes all summer." Then he and his men set off to do just that, headed for the North Anna River crossings, around Lee's right, once again. To keep his supply lines short, he shifted his supply base to Port Royal. If he could get to Hanover Junction beyond the North Anna, he would cut Lee's supply and communication line to Richmond.

But Lee realized what Grant was up to. He got to Hanover Junction first. Grant tried to cross the river above and below Lee, splitting his force. Lee attacked the northern crossing, but his illness and the constant losses of officers and men caused the chance to be lost (May 23–27). Meanwhile, Maj. Gen. John C. Breckinridge's (q.v.) Confederate victory over Sigel at New Market in the Shenandoah Valley (May 15), most notable because cadets from the Virginia Military Academy successfully took a Yankee battery, allowed Lee to be reinforced by two divisions.

Grant did not waste any time. Pulling out of the North Anna trap, he shifted to Totopotomy Creek. Lee was waiting for him, both flanks secured in the swamps along the creek. Grant probed the Confederate lines, but wisely decided against an attack. Instead, he marched around Lee's right to Cold Harbor. Grant was near Richmond on the Chickahominy, near the sight of the old Gaine's Mill battle during the Seven Days Campaign of 1862 (q.v.).

Meanwhile, as with the Shenandoah, Grant's other secondary effort by Gen. Butler to attack Richmond from Lee's rear up the James River had failed at Drewry's Bluff (q.v.), after which the uninspired Butler and his men were bottled up in a loop of the James River at the Bermuda Hundred south of the Confederate capital (May 12–16). Grant decided to take some of Butler's wasted men and use them to reinforce his own army to deal Lee a death blow at Cold Harbor. As usual, Lee had beaten the Army of the Potomac into position and was awaiting Grant's attack. On June 3, Grant sent in his men. They outnumbered Lee's two to one.

In less than a half hour, 7,000 Yankees had been shot down. Lee lost 1,500. The actual advance probably did not last eight minutes. It was the largest loss of men in the shortest time during the war. Grant called it the only assault he ever regretted making. As Grant counted up his losses, he found that the past month had cost the Army of the Potomac 50,000 men. Lee had lost 32,000. Cold Harbor would prove to be Robert E. Lee's last great victory. Although he had lost nearly every battle and maneuver, Grant had Lee at last right where he wanted him, cornered in the defenses around Richmond. It was time to cross the James River and strike at their weakest point, in what would be the Petersburg Siege (q.v.).

RIFLE CLUBS. Groups of armed white gunmen who intimidated black and white Republicans (q.v.) at elections in the mid-1870s, shot rival candidates and their supporters, and watched the polls to limit opposition voting. They often disguised their intent through ludicrous titles like Sewing Clubs, Mounted Baseball Clubs, or Mother's Little Helpers to stay within the bounds of Federal and state law.

RIFLED MUSKET. *See* LOAD-IN-NINE-TIMES.

RINGGOLD GAP, BATTLE OF. *See* CHATTANOOGA CAMPAIGN.

RISING SUN, KNIGHTS OF THE. This group was a Texas version of the Ku Klux Klan (q.v.).

ROCKY FACE RIDGE, BATTLE OF. *See* ATLANTA CAMPAIGN.

ROSECRANS, WILLIAM S. (1819–1898). From Ohio, William S. Rosecrans graduated from West Point in 1842, in the top 10 percent of his class. He served as a military engineer for a couple of years before he returned to the academy to teach engineering. He taught and then worked on more fortifications on the East Coast, missing out on the War with Mexico. He resigned his commission in 1854 to become an architect, an engineer, and a refiner of coal and oil. In 1861, he volunteered to help organize Ohio volunteers for the Civil War. He was a part of the occupation of western Virginia and was instrumental in winning several early battles, the credit for which went to his superior, Maj. Gen. George B. McClellan (q.v.).

After serving as part of the occupying force in what was to become West Virginia, Rosecrans was sent to command the Army of Mississippi, where he fought the battles of Iuka and Corinth (qq.v.) and argued with Maj. Gen. U. S. Grant (q.v.) over the results. They became lifelong enemies. Rosecrans was transferred to the Army of the Cumberland and finished off the Perryville Campaign with the indecisive Battle at Stone's River (q.v.), for which, nonetheless, he received the thanks of Congress. The following spring, he initiated the Chattanooga Campaign (q.v.) with a near-bloodless maneuvering of the Confederates out of Tennessee, taking Chattanooga in the process. Then Rosecrans overextended his lines, which led to his disastrous defeat at Chickamauga.

Besieged in Chattanooga, Rosecrans was replaced when Grant arrived to save the day. Exiled to Missouri, Rosecrans drove back belated Rebel attempts to retake the state. He retired to Cincinnati and was made U.S. minister to Mexico in 1868. He served for many years until he retired to California, where he engaged in ranching as well as being a congressman. In the late 1880s, he was register of the treasury, and his signature was on the bills printed in that period. He died near Redondo in 1898.

ROUDANEZ, LOUIS CHARLES (1823–1890). A black Creole from the area north of New Orleans, Louis Roudanez typifies the free-born men and women of color who were more common in Louisiana than any other part of the pre–Civil War South. He was born to a refugee from the Haitian Revolution, as were many in that period. His parents sent him to New Orleans to learn business as a practical intern. He did so well that he earned the money to go to Paris, where he received a university education and a medical degree. He returned to the United States and attended Dartmouth, where he received a second medical degree before returning to Louisiana, where he lived with New Orleans' sophisticated population of urban blacks.

Roudanez set up a profitable medical practice in the Crescent City and married a free woman of color, by whom he had nine children. Like their father, two of his sons practiced medicine and another dentistry. It seems that some of his children passed for white and moved North, before realizing their Creole roots nearly a century later. With the coming of the Civil War, Roudanez and his wife taught newly freed slaves and ran an orphan asylum, working closely with an order of black nuns.

While his wife continued with their charitable activities, Roudanez and several colleagues established *L'Union*, the first black-owned newspaper dedicated to freedom of the slaves and black civil and political rights. By 1864, threats and harassment caused many of his investors to wish to pull out of the business, and Roudanez bought all of them out and changed the newspaper's name to the New Orleans *Tribune*.

Its editorials called for the right to vote for black people, civil rights for all citizens, and free public education for all citizens, attacked the serfdom labor policy of Gen. Nathaniel P. Banks, the Federal officer in charge of the city's occupation, and planned for economic development. On a more practical level, Roudanez sought unity between the freed and free in the black community, questioned Gen. James Longstreet's (q.v.) conversion to Republicanism (q.v.), opposed Henry Clay Warmoth's (q.v.) corrupt Republican state government, became involved in the Louisiana Unification Movement (q.v.), and carried on a war against President Andrew Johnson's (q.v.) policies by sending copies of the *Tribune* to every member of Congress on a regular basis.

In the early 1870s, editorial infighting and the loss of a government printing contract forced the *Tribune* to close its doors forever. Roudanez withdrew from politics after the failure of the Unification Movement and went back to his lucrative medical practice until his death.

RUBY, GEORGE (1841–1882). Born in New York City, George Ruby maintained that his father was a wealthy white man, but reality points to his parents being Ebenezer and Jemima Ruby, his father a black clergyman and farmer who raised George in Portland, Maine. Ruby grew up receiving a fairly good local school education, but although racial discrimination was not a standard practice in Maine, there was enough to demonstrate to Ruby what being black in America could mean. In 1860, Ruby moved to Boston and became involved in a Haitian immigration project that was to show the world that blacks from the United States could manage on their own. Ruby went to Haiti to report on the group's progress, but the scheme turned out to be a failure. Ruby became a teacher in St. Bernard Parish, in occupied Louisiana. He then went over to the Freedmen's Bureau (q.v.).

In September 1866, as Louisiana schools were plagued with financial problems, Ruby followed many other teachers to a new, more promising field in Texas. Ruby worked in Galveston and the surrounding area. He soon had established himself as a good teacher and a man of integrity, even among local whites. In 1867, Bvt. Maj. Gen. Charles Griffin (q.v.) hired Ruby as a Freedmen's Bureau inspector, with his primary responsibility being education. He also organized black temperance societies as he traveled about the state, extending his influence considerably. With the passage of the Military Reconstruction Acts (q.v.), however, Ruby began to look for a better way to help his people—he would become a politician and help write the constitution and laws of the entire state. Ruby returned to Galveston to organize the Union Loyal League (q.v.), a Republican (q.v.) political front.

In the autumn of 1867, Ruby announced his candidacy for a delegate's position at the state convention and won with Union League support. When Ruby arrived in Austin for the convention, he was elected convention vice president, the first recognition of his talents. After his election, Ruby worked to advance his program of black education, economic development, and legal protection through the curbing of violence.

The convention's failure to either divide the state or disfranchise whites meant that the state would have a majority of white voters, most of whom were quite hostile to black aspirations as free persons. Ruby sided with 22 other delegates to defeat the constitution. As such, he became allied with the Radical Republicans led by E. J. Davis (qq.v.). Ruby asked Davis to delay the election to allow him to mobilize the League and announced his desire to run for state senator from Galveston and several cotton counties to the southwest. Davis appealed to the state military commander, Bvt. Maj. Gen. Joseph J. Reynolds (q.v.), for backing with the Ulysses S. Grant (q.v.) administration. Reynolds got Grant to delay the election and allow him to make numerous appointments to office to assist the Davis ticket during the election. Ruby ran on the Davis ticket and won his seat.

Meanwhile, the whites were becoming more organized against the Davis regime and his backers, like Ruby. Local elections proved that most whites had not voted in 1870, and that the Democrats (q.v.) were going to carry Ruby's district and eventually the whole state. He decided to back a white

Republican for his senate seat and, although local blacks wanted him to run for the house seat from Galveston, Ruby recognized the inevitable defeat and refused to enter the race. After the election, Ruby moved to New Orleans, where racial conditions were a bit more to his liking. But Ruby's influence as a black leader of the late 19th century was cut short when he died in New Orleans of a malarial attack at age 41.

S

SABINE CROSSROADS, BATTLE OF. *See* RED RIVER CAMPAIGN.

SALARY GRAB ACT (1873). *See* GRANT, ULYSSES S., ADMINISTRA-TION—SCANDALS.

SALEM CHURCH, BATTLE OF. *See* CHANCELLORSVILLE CAM-PAIGN.

SANBORN, JOHN D. *See* GRANT, ULYSSES S., ADMINISTRATION—SCANDALS.

SANDERS, GEORGE N. (1812–1873). Born in Kentucky in 1812, George Sanders was named after his grandfather, a Virginian who had led the supporters of the Constitution against the opposition of Patrick Henry in 1787 and 10 years later, after moving west, had introduced the Kentucky Resolves (q.v.), the notion that states, rather than the U.S. Supreme Court, had the right to rule Federal laws unconstitutional. The grandson would live a life imbued with states' sovereignty and slavery (q.v.) and secession (q.v.) in America and Europe. The Sanderses lived on the Ohio River a few miles upriver from Madison, Indiana, then a prosperous steamboat town. On their plantation Grass Hills, they specialized in raising livestock.

George's father subscribed to a states' rights–oriented newspaper published in New York and edited by Anna Reid. The young Kentuckian began a correspondence with her; fascinated by her intellect and writing, he wrote her letters, to which she responded, and fell head over heels in love. Impulsive by nature—it was a Sanders family trait—George was off to New York City, where his proposal was accepted. The miracle was that Anna remained with him to the end, ignoring his unkempt nature, including his reluctance to bathe. The newly married couple returned to Kentucky to live.

Under the influence of his older brother, who had been educated at West Point and had resigned his commission to fight for Texas independence, resulting in his capture and prompt execution by the Mexican authorities, George became interested in a cross isthmus canal and joined the expansionist wing of the Democratic (q.v.) Party, called "Young America" (q.v.). He allied himself with John L. O'Sullivan, a widely read newspaper editor and coiner of the term Manifest Destiny, which epitomized American expansionism before the Civil War. Sanders moved a step further and became a backer of other nationalist movements in Europe of the time that initiated the drive for constitutional governments and spurred on the revolutions of 1848.

The 1848 revolts were soon put down, and the Forty-eighters fled to London and exile. With the election of Franklin Pierce (q.v.) as president in 1852, Sanders received an appointment as consul general to London. Sanders was in his element, surrounded by revolutionaries from nearly every country on the continent and with his American political allies stationed all over Europe (August Belmont in the Netherlands, Pierre Soulé [q.v.] in Spain, O'Sullivan in Portugal, John Y. Mason in France, and James Buchanan [q.v.] as minister to England, with Daniel E. Sickles [q.v.] as his secretary). With a big dinner of dissidents and Young Americans in London leading the way, the Americans, led by Sanders, proposed the assassination of Emperor Louis Napoleon III in France and the seizure of Cuba from Spain in the Ostend Manifesto (q.v.)

Forcibly recalled to the United States, Sanders set up operations in New York City and organized the Mississippi Valley Movement, to unite all those along the mighty river, north and south, against Washington, D.C., regardless of their feelings about slavery. He also participated in the pro-expansionist and pro-slavery Knights of the Golden Circle (q.v.). In the election of 1860 (q.v.), Sanders did his best to keep the Democrats united under Stephen A. Douglas (q.v.) against the Republicans (q.v.), but to no avail. With the election of Abraham Lincoln (q.v.) as president, Sanders went over to the Confederacy (his uncle Richard Hawes was the Confederate "governor" of "seceded" Kentucky).

Although numerous schemes to provide munitions and communications for the Confederacy came to naught, Sanders proposed to President Jefferson Davis (q.v.) that the Confederates operate their entire secret service and spy operations out of British Canada, bypassing the Union sea blockade. In 1864, Sanders along with numerous others went north to be a part of the project. As none of the Confederate operatives could get along, he divided his time between St. Catherines near Niagara Falls and headquarters in Montreal.

In Canada, Sanders represented the Confederates (probably informally) at the Peace Conference at Niagara Falls sponsored by Horace Greeley (q.v.) and received the "To Whom It May Concern" letter from President Lincoln's representative, John Hay. He also coordinated the meetings between Confederate secret service personnel and John Wilkes Booth (q.v.) over Lincoln's proposed kidnapping (although had Sanders known about Lincoln's assassination flowing from this, unlike his compatriots, he would not have balked), and he saw to it the Rebel cavalry raiders who robbed the banks at St. Albans (q.v.), Vermont, were treated as soldiers rather than thieves.

In 1865, Sanders fled to Europe with a price on his head. He was soon bankrupt. After a brief sojourn in France in support of the Paris Commune, he returned to England until the political situation allowed him to come back to his home in New York City. He died there of heart failure in the summer of 1873.

SAN DOMINGO SCANDAL. *See* GRANT, ULYSSES S., ADMINISTRATION—SCANDALS.

SANITARY COMMISSIONS. *See* UNITED STATES SANITARY COMMISSION.

SAVAGE'S STATION, BATTLE OF. *See* SEVEN DAYS CAMPAIGN.

SAVAGE'S STATION LETTER. Written by Maj. Gen. George B. McClellan (q.v.) to President Abraham Lincoln and Secretary of War Edwin McM. Stanton (qq.v.) after the battle of Gaines' Mill during the Seven Days Campaign (q.v.), this letter accused the administration of abandoning McClellan and his army to fight it out with the Rebels without any support. McClellan was especially angry that he had not received the 10,000 reinforcements from Fredericksburg, recently placed under the command of Maj. Gen. John Pope (q.v.) at Washington. McClellan said things like "the government has not sustained this army" and "if I save this army now, I tell you [Stanton] plainly that I owe no thanks to you or any other persons in Washington. You have done your best to sacrifice this army." The army telegrapher cut the last sentence off, and Stanton did not see it until months later, but the damage to relations between McClellan and his superiors was terminal.

SAYLER'S CREEK, BATTLE OF. *See* APPOMATTOX CAMPAIGN.

SCALAWAGS. Scalawags were the native white Southerners who supported Reconstruction and the Republican Party (q.v.). They included obstructionist Union and Confederate deserter elements of the Civil War and those former Confederates who for whatever reason believed that Reconstruction meant the dawn of a new day in the South. But it was the brand of a "traitor." According to the legend, these whites turned against those of their own race and background to support the Carpetbaggers (q.v.), soldiers, and African-Americans who brought about the changes incipient in the Military Reconstruction Acts (q.v.)—essentially the social, economic, and political equality of blacks no longer enslaved. Scalawags were labeled low born, white trash, who backed corrupt government, unprecedented self-aggrandizement, and Yankee military rule. While there might be compassion for the position of newly freed African-Americans and some understanding of the Carpetbagger's (q.v.) role as an outsider, the Scalawag received nothing but condemnation and hatred. No wonder. In the end, it would be shocking to see how much of Reconstruction relied on the Scalawags, the native white Southerners. The term is so well-ingrained in the tale of Reconstruction that even modern historians, who find it reprehensible, confess themselves compelled to use it despite its pejorative context, the term "native white" not being powerful enough to replace it.

Although potential Scalawags could be found early on in the pro-Union areas of each Southern state, there was more to it than that. Unionism could not account for the numerous white Republican voters present in all states during Reconstruction, particularly in the Deep South. Beginning with World War II, historians began to look deeper into the makeup of Scalawag ranks, and they came up with some surprising results. Scalawags were not poorer whites but members of the respected prewar upper classes. The common thread among such men was their support of the antebellum Whig Party (q.v.), the nationalists once led by Henry Clay of Kentucky, who were in favor of strong Federal actions on behalf of business and agriculture, including high protective tariffs, internal improvements (building roads, canals, and railroads), and a national banking system. That is to say, they were adherents of a party that had contributed much to the philosophy of the Republican Party's domestic program passed during the Civil War (both Abraham Lincoln and William H. Seward [q.v.], among other Republicans, being former Whigs [q.v.]). All things considered, Whigs were natural Republicans, because they could swallow the liberation of the slaves, had no fear of their social contamination (any more than they feared the common white socially), and liked the Republicans' notions of rebuilding America through Federal aid and coordination.

But by the 1960s, the Whig thesis of Scalawag identification came under fire. It seemed most persuasive for North Carolina and Tennessee, but its application elsewhere was questionable. Indeed, most of the Scalawag voters seemed to come from hilly, remote, and less prosperous areas of the South, but areas that were full of mineral and timber resources and the water power to utilize them if properly developed. Scalawag voters were small farmers, who had little in common with slavery and slaveholders and could swallow the black vote because it did not exist in their home counties. These people had been Jacksonian Democrats before the war. They believed in equality and reform. The Whig counties from before the war went Republican only if they had Appalachian highlanders or lots of African-Americans from slavery days who voted Republican. It was the white, essentially nonslaveholding farmer of the Piedmont region in the foothills of the Appalachian Mountains who were Scalawags. These people had for generations been angry with the way slaveholders dominated state politics. During the war, many had dodged the draft, deserted the Confederate army, and even fought against the Confederacy.

If so many white Southerners were voting Republican by 1872, what caused this vote to disappear and go over to the opposition within four short years? The loss of the Scalawag vote to Republicans throughout the South became a vital reason Reconstruction failed. Carpetbaggers and blacks alike seemed to see that Southern whites were but temporary Republicans at best, ready to drift away from the party at the first sign of trouble, especially when their opponents made an appeal to race. And Southern whites felt this distrust, especially when it resulted in adverse economic policy that favored the North. They considered it unmanly and unfair and eventually joined Redeemers (q.v.), driven away by the complications of too many interests, few of which were their own. Reconstruction is the most difficult period of American history to understand, and nowhere is that better shown than in the ins and outs of being a Scalawag.

SCHENCK SCANDAL. *See* GRANT, ULYSSES S., ADMINISTRA-TION—SCANDALS.

SCHOFIELD, JOHN M. (1831–1906). Born in New York State, John M. Schofield graduated West Point in 1853, seventh in a class of 52. He served in Florida and taught philosophy at the Military Academy until 1860, when he received a leave to teach physics at Washington University in St. Louis. When the war began, he became chief of staff to Bvt. Brig. Gen. Nathaniel Lyon's small loyal army and fought at the Battle of Wilson's Creek (q.v.). Schofield was elevated to brevet brigadier general of volunteers shortly afterward and put in charge successively of the Military District of Missouri, the Military District of Southwest Missouri, and the Army of the Frontier. By 1864, Schofield had served in numerous command areas but had managed to miss every major battle.

In the spring of 1864, however, he received command of the small Army of the Ohio (actually the XXIII Corps) in Bvt. Maj. Gen. William T. Sherman's (q.v.) advance on Atlanta. Schofield's corps was involved in every major fight on the road to Atlanta (q.v.), often being used as the maneuver or reserve element as Sherman tried to fix the Confederate army with the rest of his force. After the taking of Atlanta, Schofield's units went back to Tennessee. There Schofield was nearly cut off from Nashville (q.v.) by a quick advance of the Confederates under Lt. Gen. John B. Hood (q.v.). But Schofield managed to extricate his force by a quick march past the Rebels at Spring Hill into the fortified town of Franklin, where he stung Hood's attacking forces in a fight that cost the South five generals in an ill-advised charge across two miles of open ground that made Pickett's charge at Gettysburg pale by comparison. Schofield then withdrew to Nashville, followed by Hood. At Nashville, Schofield was a part of the final attack that destroyed Hood's army in one of the truly decisive battles of the war. In 1865, Schofield was transferred to North Carolina and was in on the surrender of the Confederacy's second biggest force at Durham Station (q.v.) to Gen. William T. Sherman (q.v.). Schofield received a regular army brigadier generalship for his war service and later was voted the Congressional Medal of Honor for saving the Union army at Wilson's Creek.

After the Rebel surrender, Schofield was put in charge of the Military District of North Carolina. Having had much administrative and battlefield experience in the South, he was convinced that moderation was the only way in which a lasting peace might be constructed out of the throes of the war. Schofield's feelings were expressed in a letter to Lt. Gen. Ulysses S. Grant (q.v.) in May 1865. Schofield never got a chance to put his plan into operation, because he was sent to Europe to convince France to pull its troops out of Mexico and abandon the usurping government of the Emperor Maximilian (q.v.).

When he returned, he was assigned to command the Department of the Potomac, which included the state of Virginia. Schofield fit in well with the Army's approach to early Reconstruction. Although he was privately against the Fourteenth Amendment (q.v.), to refuse it, said Schofield, would merely lead to harsher conditions for readmission. Virginia failed to heed his advice. The result was the Military Reconstruction Acts (q.v.) within a year. Schofield took over the First Military District, composed solely of Virginia, on March 13, 1867.

Schofield's first order as military district commander continued the existing government in operation. He would make such changes as circumstances demanded. Although the state objected to military rule as a philosophical question, it accepted Schofield as better than most commanders. He refused to let any armed group of any color patrol the roads and streets—that was a job for the Army alone. He was willing to deploy forces to guarantee the African-Americans the right to vote. He warned newspaper editors that he would not allow irresponsible baiting of the Reconstruction process. He refused to permit speeches by known crowd manipulators trying to incite riot and dissension. But in all cases, he allowed the act to take place before moving against it. Whenever a civil office turned up vacant, Schofield appointed a new man in consultation with local leaders. He made few removals.

When it came to registration, Schofield had each three-man board made up of one Army or Freedmen's Bureau (q.v.) officer and two local loyal citizens. Each board had a committee of three whites and three blacks to challenge the enrollment of any voter. Any challenge had to be for a real cause that was written down. Schofield divided Virginia into seven subdistricts, each with its own six or eight sitting military commissioners, granting the commissioners complete judicial authority to act when civil officials refused. Recalcitrant officials would be removed from office and replaced by men who would act. But Schofield used the removal power sparingly, preferring to cajole cooperation.

Schofield then drew up new districts from which delegates would be selected to the state constitutional convention. Shocked at the Radical nature of the convention delegates, whites called their own convention to rally those opposed to any constitution. Schofield wrote General Grant that he feared that a Radical victory would brand the Republican Party (q.v.) for decades as the party of the extreme. He hoped that a second convention might produce a more conservative constitution, with full white participation this time. Meanwhile, Schofield suspended all elections. His cautious course got him in a lot of trouble from the state's Radical Republicans, who wanted the patronage that offices would offer. Schofield then acted to make the one removal he had wanted to make for almost a year. This was of the governor, Francis Pierpont, who had been pardoning blacks convicted by state courts, which in turn had been supervised by Schofield's military commissions. Schofield once thought of taking over the office of governor himself, but instead put Henry H. Wells, a Vermont Carpetbagger (q.v.), in Pierpont's place. He rationalized this bit of philosophical inconsistency by stating that Pierpont was limited to one term by state law, whereas other continuing officials were not.

Then Schofield exercised the right Grant gave him to clean out current office holders when he found conservative men to fill the offices. It was an arduous task. Schofield had removed incumbents and filled nearly 500 offices by May 1868, but he feared that he was running out of qualified men of a moderate to conservative turn of mind on Reconstruction. But he never had to solve that problem, as he was made secretary of war upon the failure to impeach President Andrew Johnson (qq.v.).

After the expiration of Johnson's presidency, Schofield served in various departmental command slots and was superintendent at West Point. In 1896, the grade of lieutenant general, which had expired upon the death of Philip H. Sheridan (q.v.) in the late 1880s, was recreated for him as an honor for his faithful service. Virginia's representatives and senators spoke on his behalf during the hearings on his appointment, fondly remembering his moderate course during Reconstruction. He retired within the year and published his memoirs a year after that, and died nearly a decade later at St. Augustine, Florida.

SCHURZ, CARL (1829–1906). Carl Schurz was born near Cologne, Germany. A highly educated man, he was a doctoral student at the University of Bonn. Schurz got involved in the unsuccessful democratic Revolution of 1848. Fleeing to Switzerland, he returned to Germany to rescue one of his college professors from life imprisonment. The two fled to Britain, the country of choice for revolutionaries at that time. He found the United States offered more promise than Great Britain or his homeland and emigrated in 1852, eventually settling in Wisconsin. He became active in the new Republican Party (q.v.), helped organize it in the hinterlands, and became a strong antislavery (q.v.) advocate. He studied law and was admitted to the bar in 1858.

Intrigued by the Lincoln–Douglas Debates (q.v.), Schurz supported Abraham Lincoln's (q.v.) nomination for the presidency as a state delegate to the 1860 Republican Convention. Lincoln appointed him as U.S. minister to Spain, but Schurz returned to the U.S. after a matter of months to fight for the cause of abolition. He was then made brigadier general and commanded German–American troops in the II Corps of the Army of Virginia during the Second Manassas Campaign (q.v.). He was a part of the XI Corps during the Chancellorsville Campaign (q.v.), suffering its embarrassing rout at the hands of Confederate Lt. Gen. Stonewall Jackson (q.v.). Promoted to major general, Schurz tried to get his men cleared of cowardice but failed. He fought in the Pennsylvania Invasion and the Chattanooga Campaign (qq.v.).

When the XI and XII Corps were combined into the XX Corps, Schurz asked to be relieved and went home to work for emancipation (q.v.) and Lincoln's renomination and reelection in 1864. After a brief return to the army in 1865, Schurz toured the defeated South and made a report on Southern attitudes and conditions for President Andrew Johnson (q.v.). He became a newspaperman and worked as a reporter and editor in the German-language press. An opponent of the scandals of President U. S. Grant's (q.v.) administration, he was U.S. senator from Missouri and sided with the Liberal Republican (q.v.) movement in 1872. He supported Rutherford B. Hayes' (q.v.) policy of reconciliation with the South in 1876 and served as his secretary of the interior.

In 1881, Schurz retired to New York City and re-entered the newspaper world, where he spoke out on behalf of civil service reform. He wrote several books, including a history of Henry Clay, an essay on Lincoln, and his own memoirs.

SCOTT, ROBERT K. (1826–1900). A Freedmen's Bureau agent and Carpetbag (qq.v.) governor in South Carolina, Robert K. Scott was a Pennsylvanian by birth. At 16, he set out for Ohio, where he studied and practiced medicine. He followed the lure of gold to California after fighting in the War with Mexico, where he prospected and reestablished his practice. But failing to strike it rich, he returned to Ohio. Here he became quite prosperous as a physician and surgeon. With the advent of the Civil War, he joined the 68th Ohio Volunteers as a major. He fought in most of the campaigns in the Western Theater of the war, being promoted to brigade leader for his actions at Vicksburg (q.v.). Captured outside of Atlanta (q.v.), Scott tried to escape by jumping from a moving railroad prison car. He hurt his back and was recaptured. Later exchanged, he made the campaign from Atlanta to the sea and through the Carolinas (q.v.). He wound up the war with the rank of brevet major general and an opium drug habit (very common among injured Civil War soldiers and usually revealed by the use of laudanum, a morphine and whiskey mixture), courtesy of his everlasting back trouble.

After the Confederate surrender, Scott received the assignment of assistant commissioner of the Freedmen's Bureau (q.v.) in South Carolina. His job was to reconcile the freedmen with their former masters and gain for the African-American an equal place in American society. His worst task was to examine the titles of over 40,000 blacks in families to lands that they had supposedly bought. Scott and his agents could prove actual title for the families of only 1,565 men, women, and children. The rest went back to their original Rebel owners under President Andrew Johnson's (q.v.) pardon policy or were fraudulent from the outset, having been sold by dishonest Federal agents. Scott then proceeded to supervise the labor contract making process for the year of 1866. He was a fairly decent man in his approach, often liberalizing the terms that his agents agreed to, seeking the illusive ideals of black equality and freedom.

As Military Reconstruction (q.v.) approached in 1867, Scott busied himself with his Bureau responsibilities and the ordering of his large landholdings in Ohio and Michigan (he was worth over $300,000 at that time). He also sought loans and investments from Northerners to help alleviate the constant near-starvation among African-Americans in South Carolina. Scott had already declined an attempt to put his name on the Republican (q.v.) ticket for governor, but prominent South Carolinians of all colors and political philosophies urged him to reconsider. The state convention nominated him over his protests. Once he decided to accept the nomination, he immediately changed his mind about Bureau political meddling. He expected all of his agents to turn out a big black vote for him, and he easily won the election. And the heretofore friendly attitude of whites toward Scott began to change for the worse as the prospect of "Negro rule" became evident.

Scott arrived in Columbia with a national reputation as the best among the Carpetbag governors elected in the 1868 Reconstructed South. He was viewed as well-educated, a man of property, and reasonable in race matters. Scott began his administration by asking that all political disabilities against Confederates be removed. He approved of the end of the Freedmen's Bureau, asked that the Federal government remove the occupying troops, and called for segregated public schools.

The Scott administration opened with much hope for success, but it soon degenerated into a farce, and most of it had little to do with white opposition. As governor, Scott was more typically South Carolinian than might be expected. He shared a longtime dream of state politicians from the days of John C. Calhoun—the idea of a railroad from Charleston to Cincinnati and Memphis. Scott was a real estate agent himself, and along with several high-ranking Republicans, over-invested the state in rights of way and other lands, the latter of which were to be sold to freedmen. Some of the exorbitant prices paid were pocketed by politicians on the government boards that supervised these dealings. The Great Barbecue had arrived in South Carolina, and the governor and a lot of his friends cashed in.

The main impediment to the overthrow of Reconstruction was that black voters outnumbered white by some 30,000. In an honest election, the Republicans should always win. But the more radical blacks and more moderate whites threatened to splinter off from the party. This was balanced by the fact that many Democrats (q.v.) were willing to cooperate with Republicans if the party did not become too Radical. These Democrats were led by James L. Orr, a Confederate war hero, who believed that the only way to appease the blacks was to become a Republican. Orr's defection confused the Democrats greatly. The result was a sort of balancing act in which Scott stood with the blacks and managed to get himself reelected and send three of his four congressional candidates to Washington.

After the 1870 congressional election, Scott faced two more problems. In the white upcountry, the Ku Klux Klan (q.v.) began to ride again, disgusted with Orr's compromising and taking revenge on those who had voted Republican or were members of the state militia. In the low country, led by state Attorney General Daniel H. Chamberlain (q.v.), planters and businessmen protested the higher taxes the spendthrift government cost them. Republican Moderates and Fusion Democrats like Orr begged Scott to turn on his black backers, on whom all of the blame for the fraud of Scott's cronies could be laid. Scott refused. He was investigated by a taxpayers' convention, but nothing could be proven against him personally. Meanwhile, Scott worked with the Federal government, which appointed special prosecutors and sent in the Army to arrest and check the Klan excesses. By the end of 1871, an uneasy peace reigned.

Still, the problem of corruption haunted the Republican Party. Everyone knew it existed; the question was who was behind it and how much Governor Scott knew about it. In December 1871, Scott maintained his own innocence. But the legislature refused to buy Scott's assertions. Members of his own party, angry at political patronage snubs, joined with Democrats to introduce a resolution of impeachment. The goal was to filibuster for the rest of the session and then let Scott face the voters with the suspicion unanswered in 1872. But Scott canceled a debt owed him by the speaker of the house, Franklin J. Moses, Jr., a Scalawag (qq.v.), and the filibuster failed when Moses refused to give the floor to the anti-Scott men. But rumors of bribery were everywhere. At the same time, the railroad venture went broke, and disgusted stockholders took Scott and others to trial for the loss. This also made the Scott regime fodder for the Liberal Republican (q.v.) revolt against the corruption of the Ulysses S. Grant (q.v.) administration nationally.

With public criticism running high, the Republican Party in South Carolina needed a new look. Scott retired to live the life of an ordinary citizen. In 1874, he put himself up as a possible gubernatorial candidate, but the nomination went to Daniel H. Chamberlain (q.v.), attorney general under Scott and an honest man. Chamberlain eventually won the contest. But two years later, Chamberlain and the Republicans lost out to a Democratic landslide, led by Wade Hampton (now governor) and his Red Shirt (q.v.) regulators.

Hampton did not waste much time in purging the state of what remained of Republicanism. He brought charges in criminal court against Chamberlain and Scott. Scott decided it was a good time to take a prolonged "business" trip to Ohio. His wife remained behind to wind up his affairs. Eventually, she and their son went back to Ohio, too. The charges against Scott endured in court for some time before being dropped. Scott continued to sell real estate in Ohio and Michigan, still a relatively wealthy man. He remained living in Ohio, visiting South Carolina once again in 1896, and dying from a cerebral hemorrhage in 1900, just after (indeed almost providentially) joining the Methodist church.

SCOTT, WINFIELD (1786–1866). A Virginian from Dinwiddie County near Petersburg, Winfield Scott graduated from the college of William and Mary in 1805. He read law and practiced, riding circuit around Petersburg. In 1807, he received a captain's commission in the army and began his military career. He fought in the War of 1812 on the Niagara frontier, being captured at Queenstown, exchanged, and becoming a hero for his attacks at Chippawa and Lundy's Lane. At war's end, Scott was a major general. He served on various commissions and military boards, coordinated the Army response in the Black Hawk War, and commanded at Charleston during the nullification crisis. Scott went on to the Seminole War and supervised Cherokee Indian removal. In 1841, he became general-in-chief of the army. In 1839, he first became prominent in Whig Party (q.v.) politics, losing the nomination to William Henry Harrison. He also was involved in the so-called Aroostook War in Maine over the boundary with Canada.

As a Whig and potential presidential candidate, Scott was ignored as long as possible by President James K. Polk during the War with Mexico. But when it became obvious that a campaign had to be launched on Mexico City, and that Maj. Gen. Zachary Taylor (q.v.) might also be a Whig presidential possibility, Polk sent Scott into the field, figuring that in a future presidential race, the two men would nullify each other. The resulting attack from Vera

Cruz to Mexico City is still considered a classic. Scott returned a hero. But instead of allowing the two heroes to knock each other off, the Whigs nominated Taylor for president in 1848 and Scott in 1852, when he lost to one of his subordinates, Franklin Pierce (q.v.).

In 1855, Scott was made brevet lieutenant general, the first man to hold such rank since George Washington. By now his quarrels with subordinates were legendary, justifying his nickname, "Old Fuss and Feathers," and Scott removed army headquarters to New York to get away from what he saw as the nefarious influences of Washington. He also came to weigh around 300 pounds, causing him to have to be lifted onto his horse (a stout beast, no doubt) with an a-frame crane for reviews. He also placated a boundary dispute over Puget Sound in 1859.

When the Civil War began, Scott returned to Washington to supervise the inauguration of President Abraham Lincoln (q.v.) and act as chief military advisor. He brought forth the Anaconda Plan (q.v.) to strangle the South with the blockade and attack the line of the Mississippi River. But Scott was fast becoming more an anachronism than a military genius. He was old and sick. In November 1861, one of the new young bloods of the war, Maj. Gen. George B. McClellan (q.v.), maneuvered himself into the job of general-in-chief, putting Scott on the retirement list. He took a European tour in 1864.

Although Scott was less successful as a politician than as a general, he was universally admired for his Mexican Campaign. He was a prolific writer, putting out everything from military manuals to a self-absorbed autobiography. Appropriately, when he died he was buried at West Point in 1866.

SEARS, BARNAS. *See* PEABODY EDUCATIONAL FUND.

SECESSION AND LOYALTY IN THE BORDER SOUTH. It was of great significance that the border slave states (Delaware, Maryland, Kentucky, Missouri) refused to secede. Psychologically, it set the Confederacy back. That the Confederate States of America did not represent all the slave states made secession look not as convincing as it could have, especially abroad. The failure of the Border South to secede cost the Confederacy great wealth and resources. The population of the border states would have doubled the white population of the Confederacy. Had the South been able to utilize the men from the border states in the Confederate army, it would have given the South 50,000 more men just from Kentucky alone. Finally, the border states would have given the South a better geographic boundary to defend along the Ohio River in the Western Theater and placed the Union capital behind the lines in Maryland. The morale loss would have been great in either case.

Both presidents, Abraham Lincoln and Jefferson Davis (qq.v.), were Kentuckians, and that best illustrates the political problem of the border states.

Kentucky had gone for the Constitutional Union Party's John Bell, then the Northern Democrats' Stephen A. Douglas (q.v.), then the Southern Democrats' John C. Breckinridge (q.v.) in the election of 1860 (q.v.). Its John J. Crittenden was the leader of compromise in the U.S. Senate in the spring of 1861. Governor Beriah Magoffin refused to contribute to Lincoln's call for troops after Ft. Sumter (q.v.), but the state legislature had not asked for a state convention. Kentucky's official stance was neutrality.

But insofar as Kentucky did not secede, it was a victory for the North, as was a state and local election in June. The neutral position lasted from May 1861 until September 1861, until Confederate Maj. Gen. Leonidas Polk moved into Columbus to get its better position for blockading the Mississippi River. Both sides had been recruiting in the state, but now Union troops responded by taking important towns along the Ohio River. The rest of the Confederate army moved into Bowling Green, but secession never happened. Nonetheless, Kentucky got a star on the Confederate battle flag and had representatives in the Confederate Congress, as the Rebels made an effort to install the Confederate governor, Richard Hawes, in Frankfort during the Perryville Campaign (q.v.) in 1862.

Across the Mississippi from Kentucky was another important border state, Missouri. To have Missouri secede would outflank Illinois and put Confederate soldiers halfway to Chicago. Governor Claiborne Jackson and Lieutenant Governor Thomas Reynolds were both ardent secessionists. They had the state legislature call a convention, but it was pro-Union and took no action. Prompt action by Federal officers and politicians based in St. Louis during the Missouri Campaign (1861–1862) forced secession-minded men to head south with Maj. Gen. Sterling Price (q.v.) or become guerrilla raiders. Missouri held for the Union, although it also sent representatives to Richmond, had a government in exile in Shreveport, and merited a star on the Confederate Battle Flag.

Although Kentucky and Missouri were important, Maryland was the key to the Border South. Without Maryland in the Union, Lincoln and Congress would have had to adjourn to Philadelphia or New York City. Most of the population was pro-Union, especially in the western reaches of the state. The Eastern Shore was so far from the South as to be nullified as a military factor. But Baltimore and the peninsulas southeast of Washington were ardently pro-Confederate, contributing soldiers and spies to the Rebel cause.

Fortunately for Lincoln, Governor Thomas Hicks was pro-Union. He refused to call the state legislature until April 1861, and then had it meet in Unionist Frederick rather than Secessionist Annapolis. Lincoln could afford no slip-ups, so he had the army arrest 19 members to ensure a Union majority. He also occupied the city of Baltimore. That fall, when the state voted for a new legislature, Lincoln's soldiers occupied polling places, and Maryland enlistees in the Union army were furloughed home to vote. Maryland stayed in the Union, although it was fortunate that Confederate Gen. Robert E. Lee's Maryland Campaign (qq.v.) was fought in the Unionist areas, where he received little popular support.

Delaware was the last border slave state that remained in the Union. It had little choice, given its geographical position, above Maryland and ensconced in Pennsylvania's southern border. Although Delaware had few slaves, it remained pro-South until late in the war. Delaware always believed that the South ought to have been allowed to secede peacefully.

SECESSION AND THE CREATION OF ARIZONA TERRITORY. The South made no apologies for supporting the "Spread Eagle" diplomacy (q.v.) of the 1850s, and it continued to look west for opportunities to expand into the pro-secession area of Los Angeles in California. There were several reasons for this. The most obvious was mineral wealth, particularly gold, which would have helped combat the wild inflation that hit Southern money during the war, as Nevada silver did for the Union. It was also hoped that possession of West Coast ports would fatally weaken the Federal blockade of the Atlantic and Gulf Coasts. And any conquest could not but help in the struggle to gain European recognition.

To get to California, the Confederates would have to initiate a New Mexico–Arizona Campaign (q.v.). There had been indications that whites in New Mexico Territory were favorably disposed to the South and slavery. The territorial legislature had passed restrictions on the movement of free men of color and enacted a slave code before the war. Newspapers regularly proclaimed the right of secession (q.v.), especially in Santa Fé and Tucson. So it was no surprise when a convention met at Mesilla on March 16 and proclaimed the secession of the territory of Arizona (roughly the area of the Gadsden Purchase south of the Gila River) from the Union, and its attachment to the Confederacy. Arizona's secession preceded that of four Southern states. Later action would extend the claim of the Rebels to the 34th parallel, claiming the southern half of the present-day states of Arizona and New Mexico.

By August 1861, the Confederate army was on its way in the person of John Baylor of Texas. Baylor proclaimed himself military governor of the territory and established its capital at Mesilla (across the Río Grande from Las Cruces). Mesilla was made the first judicial district and Tucson the second. Granville Oury from Tucson was elected territorial delegate to the Confederate Congress in Richmond. His first job was to get Confederate troops to replace the fleeing Yankees and protect the area from marauding Apaches. The Confederate invasion force arrived in February 1862 and sent a small detachment to Tucson to cover its exposed left flank as it proceeded up the Río Grande to Santa Fé. But by May 1862, the Rebel army had been driven back into Texas, and Arizona Territory was under occupation by the Union California Column, which seized and sold the mining property of Oury and his brothers and Sylvester Mowry south of Tucson, and arrested them and 20 others, all rabid secessionists. But Arizona Territory continued to be represented in both Confederate Congresses by Marcus H. Macwillie of Mesilla, a local lawyer and once Baylor's appointment as attorney general of the military government.

By then, the mining areas in what is now northern Arizona had decided to send Charles D. Poston to Washington to lobby for a Yankee territory of Arizona, divided from New Mexico on the 109th meridian (the current boundary). Whether Poston deserves his title as the "Father of Arizona" is an open question, because Union Maj. Gen. Samuel Heintzelman had done much of the preliminary work for him. Heintzelman had represented a Cincinnati, Ohio, gold mining concern while he was commander at Ft. Yuma in the 1850s. These entrepreneurs got Congressman James H. Ashley and U.S. Senator Benjamin F. Wade (qq.v.), both Radical Republicans, to sponsor an Organic Act establishing the Union version of Arizona Territory in February 1863. Its first territorial officials were lame duck Republican politicians who had lost their offices in the disastrous 1862 congressional by-election. On December 29, 1863, the first of these men crossed into Arizona and declared the Union territorial government in force, with its capital at Ft. Whipple near present-day Prescott.

SECESSION, ATTEMPTS TO COMPROMISE. As the likelihood of Civil War became more of a reality, concerned men made several attempts to head off the war. In the U.S. House of Representatives the Committee of Thirty-three (q.v.) formed, in the U.S. Senate the Committee of Thirteen (q.v.) organized, and led by the Border South, particularly Virginia, and the Constitutional Union Party (q.v.), a meeting of interested states met in the Washington Peace Conference (q.v.). Essentially, the compromisers came up with many of the same ideas, the core of which was to extend the old Missouri Compromise line to the eastern border of California, reserving half of the West to free state exploitation and the rest to the slave states. President-elect Abraham Lincoln (q.v.) refused to accept this notion, as it differed from the Republican Platform of 1860 (q.v.) and his own notions of limiting the extension of slavery into new areas.

SECESSION, BUCHANAN'S CABINET AND. Even though President James Buchanan (q.v.) and the 1858 Congress had been defeated in the election of 1860 (q.v.), they would serve until March 4, as the "Lame Duck" government. Then President-elect Abraham Lincoln (q.v.) would be inaugurated, but the Republican-dominated Congress would not meet until December

1860. Believing that the South was bluffing, Buchanan did little to ward off secession (q.v.) until South Carolina left the Union. When Buchanan addressed Congress in December 1860, he gave a long, involved interpretation of the legal aspects of secession that was not inspiring. He decided against proclamation against secession, as Andrew Jackson had done in 1833, when South Carolina had tried to nullify the tariff.

Actually, Buchanan tended to blame the crisis on Northern agitation against slavery. Even though he considered the loss of an election no reason for the South to act so precipitously, he did pledge to uphold all Federal laws, collect customs revenue, and maintain Federal property. Then he turned over the whole problem to Congress, which tried to compromise secession with its Corwin Committee of Thirty-three in the House and Crittenden Committee of Thirteen in the Senate (qq.v.).

Although Buchanan looks weak in hindsight, his speech to Congress was considered an affront by many Southerners, especially members of his cabinet. His seven cabinet members had been divided six to three in favor of Southern Democrats in 1857, but in December 1860, this coalition began to come apart and changed its ratio to five to four in favor of the South. In January 1861, Buchanan's cabinet changed to three to six in favor of the North. The result was that Buchanan got a lot of conflicting advice that increased his irresoluteness. While he never intended to surrender Federal installations in the South, he also did not desire to provoke a fight. It was Lincoln's prerogative to start a war.

Buchanan's latent Unionism was immediately recognized by Secretary of the Treasury Howell Cobb of Georgia. Cobb was Buchanan's closest friend in the cabinet, and his resignation over Buchanan's address to Congress was a blow. Cobb was replaced by Philip F. Thomas of Maryland, but his reluctance to cooperate with New York financiers receiving high profits on certain governmental loans led to his being superseded by the more pliable John A. Dix, a devout Union man. The next resignation came for exactly the opposite reason. Secretary of State Lewis Cass (q.v.) told Buchanan he was too soft on the South and ought to reinforce the Federal installations and hold them by force. His replacement was Attorney General Jeremiah Black, a longtime Democrat (q.v.), who now became Buchanan's closet advisor. At Black's suggestion, the attorney generalship was filled by a strong Ohio Unionist, Edwin McM. Stanton (q.v.) (later to be Lincoln's secretary of war).

The next wave of resignations involved Secretary of War John Floyd of Virginia and Secretary of the Interior Jacob Thompson (q.v.) of Mississippi. Floyd had been revealed to be involved in some shady schemes involving War Department monies. He also surrendered to Texas secessionists, with the aid of Brig. Gen. David Twiggs (of Georgia), the three Federal regiments that Twiggs commanded in Texas. Floyd's resignation was a convenient way to beat the rap. Twiggs was cashiered. Floyd's vacancy was filled by Postmaster General Joseph Holt of Kentucky, an uncompromising Unionist. Holt's job went to Horatio King of New York, another solid Union man. This left Thompson, who was also suspected of financial irregularities. Thompson resigned when Buchanan tried to reinforce Ft. Sumter (q.v.) at Charleston. His position was handled by his chief clerk. Buchanan was now ready to weather the secession crisis, irresolutely, but as a Northerner.

SECESSION OF THE SOUTHERN STATES, FIRST. It was one of the unfortunate coincidences in the election of 1860 (q.v.) that the Republican (q.v.) success in winning the presidency with Abraham Lincoln (q.v.) was concurrent with the usual meeting of the state legislature in South Carolina in November 1860. This meant that the emotions and fears engendered by the national election would not have time to lapse before the state's politicians could act. The incumbent governor of the state was William H. Gist, a moderate. He did not wish to act so quickly, but the legislature called for the December meeting of a state convention to consider South Carolina's relation to the Union. He called the convention and signed a measure to purchase $100,000 in arms and ammunition for state defense.

Then the state legislature, again according to state law, elected a new governor. The man chosen was Francis Pickens, a regular Democrat (q.v.) turned fire-eating Seceder. He had pledges from Mississippi and Florida that they would act to secede in concert with South Carolina. On December 20, 1860, South Carolina unanimously dissolved the bonds of Union and declared itself to be a free and independent state—a nation co-equal to all others in the world. There was little opposition, although one critic opined that the state was too small to be an independent Republic and too large to be an insane asylum.

As promised, Mississippi called its own convention and on January 9, 1861, seceded with a vote of 84–15. The few opponents differed more about the timing than the action, preferring to await the action of other states. Florida followed the next day, voting 62–7. This was the last state to secede with little opposition. The rest of the Southern states had to contend with an active group of Cooperationists, people who wished to wait and see what Lincoln and his Republicans did after taking office.

Alabama seceded on January 11, but its quickness to respond concealed much opposition, especially in the northern counties along the Tennessee River. This area was economically tied to Tennessee, and the population was loath to act without backing from Tennessee. The Cooperationists suggested waiting for the meeting of a Southern states' convention for joint action. But the tactic failed to win over the Seceders. The delay proposal lost 54–45. Then secession won 61–39, some Cooperationists admitting to the inevitable and wishing to show solidarity.

Georgia was the next state to follow Alabama. But it took a week before Georgia acted, because the Cooperationists were very strong. Georgia was the keystone to the Deep South. Without its leaving the Union, the Southern nation (and the Seceders always planned on a Confederacy) would be divided geographically. Georgia would also affect the Cooperationist movement in other states, if it were successful. To give the Seceders a boost, Governor Joseph E. Brown (q.v.) had militia seize the Federal installation at Ft. Pulaski. The state legislature had already voted $1 million for defense. The Cooperationists put up a motion to delay and see what transpired after Lincoln took office. As in Alabama, after much debate, this lost 164–133. Then the Convention united to vote secession 208–89. The South was united geographically.

The first state west of the Mississippi River to act on secession was Louisiana. Both the governor and John Slidell reversed their prior Unionists stances and led the move to secede. Once again, as in other states, the regular Democrats took over the secession movement and came out on top, beating the Chivalry at its own game. Naturally, it being Louisiana, the election of the convention members was crooked. The returns were not published until after the state left the Union. Then the closeness of the Seceders' overall victory (20,000 to 17,000) was apparent. Some suspected that the Cooperationist candidates actually had won.

When the secession movement seemed to lag, Governor Thomas Moore had the militia seize the Baton Rouge arsenal and the New Orleans mint. As in Georgia, technically this was treason, as the state had yet to secede. Louisiana had the only large city in the South, and this gave it a more worldly outlook that caused many to question the wisdom of immediate action. But the Seceders also played on Louisiana's critical location at the mouth of the Mississippi. By seceding, they argued, Louisiana could strike a better deal with the North, especially the Northwest. Spurred on by such actions and arguments, the convention voted 113–17 to leave the Union on January 26. But 10 of the 17 refused to sign the final document. Louisiana also passed a special "Resolution to the Northwestern States." It pledged that river trade would not be stopped. But Mississippi took care of that matter by fortifying Vicksburg and stopping all river movement there.

Louisiana's secession was followed by that of Texas, six days later, on February 1. The Texas convention vote to leave the Union was a smashing 166–8. But it belied the true sentiment of a large portion of the state. Governor Sam Houston was an old Jacksonian Democrat. Calling secession treason and unwise, he refused to issue the call for the secession convention. It could but lead to war, Houston said. But the state legislature was not to be denied; they said that the county judges could issue the call. Houston faced reality and reluctantly agreed to call the convention election. Already irregular pro-secession militia units were seizing Federal installations in San Antonio. Unlike the states that preceded it, Texas was the only one of the Gulf South states to have a public referendum on the convention's actions. It showed that those who lived on the frontier of the state, a band stretching along the Red River and south to San Antonio, roughly 25 percent of the population, were opposed to secession.

The first six seceding states sent delegates to Montgomery, Alabama, in February 1861, to form the Confederate States of America (q.v.). They were joined in March by the Texas delegation, awaiting the results of the referendum and having far to travel, which endorsed their actions and became the seventh state in the Confederacy. Back home, Governor Houston refused to take the oath to the new government and was deposed in favor of his lieutenant governor, who had no such compunctions.

SECESSION OF THE SOUTHERN STATES, SECOND. The effect of the Battle of Ft. Sumter (q.v.) was to close ranks, North and South. President Abraham Lincoln (q.v.) called for 75,000 state militia to come forward for three months' service to put down "combinations" of seven states "too powerful to be suppressed by the ordinary course of judicial proceedings." A quota was sent to every state, including those that had not left the Union. U.S. Senator Stephen A. Douglas (q.v.) of Illinois, Lincoln's opponent in politics, rushed to his side in support. Douglas would travel widely to rally Federal support and die from exhaustion on June 3, 1861.

The South rallied to the cause, too—the Confederate cause. They believed that if the Federal government could coerce the seceded South, they would have no rights either. Virginia was the first to leave in the second batch of secession (q.v.). Although the western part of the state was strongly Unionist, and the state voted for Douglas and Constitutional Union Party (q.v.) candidate John Bell in 1860, Virginia had flirted with secession before. Governor John Letcher had called a convention in January 1861 that had voted 85–45 not to leave the Union on April 4. But they asked the Federal government to make concessions and not coerce the seceded states. Virginia was instrumental in calling the Washington Peace Conference of 1861 (q.v.). On April 17, after the firing on Ft. Sumter, Virginia voted 88–55 to secede (more members had come in from the West). Like Texas, Virginia had a popular referendum on May 23 that endorsed the convention's stand.

Following Virginia's lead was Arkansas. There was a strong Union element in the northern part of the state, but Arkansas had refused to attend the Washington Peace Conference. On March 4, the convention had reached a compromise to let the public vote on secession on August 5. But with the Battle at Ft. Sumter, the convention, still in session, voted 65–5 to secede on May 6.

Like the rest of the Upper South, initially Tennessee was a real problem for the secessionists. Its governor, Isham Harris (q.v.), was strongly for leaving the Union. But Eastern Tennessee was very pro-Union. Although the state legislature had called for a convention on January 19, the vote went against having a convention. Delegates had been elected at the same time, and the state voted for predominantly Union men, a double defeat for secessionists. Even after Ft. Sumter, Harris feared calling another convention, so strong was Union sentiment. Since the state legislature was pro-secession, Harris asked it to pass a secession law, which he signed on May 7. The state's voters were to ratify it on June 8. But Harris also signed a military alliance with the Confederacy on May 7, and the state legislature raised 55,000 men, the Army of Tennessee, to occupy polling places. The June 8 vote was a mere formality, 105,000 for secession, 47,000 against.

The last state of the Upper South to secede was North Carolina. Like Tennessee, it had a strong pro-Union element, and when the governor and the state legislature called for a secession convention, the measure narrowly lost by 1,000 votes. But Lincoln's troop call-up shattered North Carolina Unionism. The governor and the state legislature, meeting in special session, called for a convention, which voted unanimously to secede on May 20. North Carolina, like the rest of the Upper South, believed that Lincoln should have been more conciliatory and avoided a shooting war at Ft. Sumter. The call for troops to put down their Southern brethren had been too much.

SECESSION, THEORY OF. Secession was based on a theory of state rights. The abstract concept of the peoples' sovereignty was exalted as the supreme component of government. All authority of government resided with the people. The supremacy clause of the United States Constitution did not make the Federal government supreme over the people, because the people wrote it in the first place. So long as the national government operated within the limits placed on it by the Constitution and the Ninth and Tenth Amendments, which reserved ultimate power to the people and the states, the Federal government was owed obedience. But the Constitution was a compact that could be nullified whenever the Federal government overstepped its written bounds.

Hence secession was not a revolution. It was but the assertion of immutable rights. But this assertion of sovereignty had to be carried out correctly. A state legislature would authorize the state governor to call a special election to select delegates to a convention, this being the body closest to the people, as it was called for a special purpose. The convention would consider the one issue, secession. After debate, the convention would vote. If it did not vote to secede, things remained the same. If it voted to secede, the union between it and the other states was dissolved. The convention did not have to refer its actions back to the people for referendum, because the people had already spoken when they elected the delegates. Secession was merely taking back sovereign rights given to the Federal government conditionally.

The justification for leaving the Union was unassailable in the South of 1860. The real question was the wisdom of acting at a particular time. Thus there were two groups in each convention, the Seceders and the Cooperationists. They did not differ as to the legality of secession, but the timing. The Cooperationists would have preferred to await an overt act by the Republican Abraham Lincoln (qq.v.) administration before acting. The Seceders wanted to act immediately. This is what differentiated 1860 from 1850, when the South also considered leaving the Union over the issue of the Mexican Cession. In 1850, the Cooperators, mostly Whigs (q.v.), did not admit to the right of secession. Their answer to the North was for the South to industrialize and compete openly in the domestic markets.

But their program and their party collapsed by mid-decade, leaving secession as the only alternative. The big advantage of the Seceders in 1860 was that they offered action. The Cooperators offered more indecision, more delay, to solve a problem, Yankee economic and social dominance, that was already at least 30 years old. Besides, the Seceders reasoned, the North disliked the South so much that it would be glad to see Dixie go. The opposite was believed true also.

SECRET MAIL LINE. *See* DOCTORS' LINE, THE.

SECRET SERVICE, CONFEDERATE. The Rebel secret service's activities varied widely during the Civil War. There were, for example, Brig. Gen. Gabriel Rains and his inventive staff, who created the sub-terra shells (land mines) and torpedoes (sea mines) that defended Richmond and port cities from 1862; Capt. Thomas Hines, who plotted in 1864 to free Confederate prisoners of war held at Camp Douglas and other Midwest installations, only to fail when Northern sympathizers (Copperheads [q.v.]) proved all talk and no action; navy officers Capt. John Wilkinson and Lt. John Y. Beall, who tried to seize the U.S.S. *Michigan* as a base to free Confederate officers held at Johnson's Island, also in 1864, only to find that the Confederate expatriates enrolled to help out were much like the Yankee Copperheads (Beall would later hang when caught for another similar escapade in upper New York State); Hines and his men again, who disrupted the Democratic Convention during the election of 1864 and obtained their support for a peace platform, which was only partially successful, because they got the plank but a pro-war candidate in former Maj. Gen. George B. McClellan (q.v.); Capt. Bennett Young and his men, who in 1864 robbed several banks in the prosperous border town of St. Albans, Vermont, escaping to Canada and being shielded against extradition as soldiers on a legitimate military operation; Col. Robert

M. Martin and his crew, who set incendiary bombs (made by Rains and his bureau) designed to burn New York City to the ground in November 1864, only to have them fail after the arsonists closed their hotel room doors, depriving the fires of needed cross drafts; and Dr. Luke Blackburn, who sent shipments of clothes and blankets infected with yellow fever virus to Washington and coastal military institutions in 1864 to infect their inhabitants, not knowing that mosquitoes were the critical infecting agent.

The last year of the war obviously was a banner time for the Confederate secret service. Over a million extra dollars had been set aside in the office of Rebel Secretary of State Judah P. Benjamin (q.v.) for various clandestine projects, including the kidnapping of Union President Abraham Lincoln (q.v.), which ultimately turned into the financing of John Wilkes Booth's (q.v.) assassination plot. But under Benjamin's supervision, Gen. Raines' laboratories also had other projects on hand. For example, Rains and his operatives had developed coal and wood sticks that blew up in steamboat boilers, one of which adorned the desk of Confederate President Jefferson Davis (q.v.) as a paperweight. Such a device has come to be suspected in the destruction of the Union-hired steamboat *Sultana* (q.v.).

SELMA CAMPAIGN. Nothing tickled Union war leaders more than finally crushing the Confederate cavalry forces of Lt. Gen. Nathan Bedford Forrest (q.v.) in the Selma Campaign. Selma, Alabama, was an important Southern industrial center during the Civil War, making cannons and gunpowder and employing numerous foundries and warehouses. The job of reducing Selma was given to the energetic Maj. Gen. James Harrison Wilson and three Federal cavalry divisions.

Starting from northern Alabama, Wilson's cavalry moved in three columns to hopefully deceive the Rebels and maintain his own speed. But there was little else of value to attack, so Confederate cavalry, including Forrest's command, headed for the Selma area to intercept the Wilson raiders. Forrest tried to interfere with Wilson's march, but possessed too few men to deal with the larger Federal columns.

The Confederates were soon driven into the fortifications around Selma. But Forrest had only three small brigades to fight against Wilson's three divisions. When the Yankees attacked on April 2, 1865, the Alabama militia turned and ran, leaving Forrest and his men to fight it out alone. While the Rebels put up their usual strong showing when led by Forrest, the town fell that same day.

Wilson spent a week in Selma, wrecking anything that might aid the Southern war effort. Then he departed for Montgomery, which he took on April 12. His men then spread out as the Confederate government fell, capturing Confederate President Jefferson Davis (q.v.) at Irwinsville, Georgia, on May 10.

Forrest retreated into Mississippi and was surrendered as a part of Lt. Gen. Richard Taylor's forces at Citronelle (q.v.), Alabama, in early May.

SEMINARY RIDGE, BATTLE OF. *See* PENNSYLVANIA CAMPAIGN.

SEVEN DAYS CAMPAIGN. After the battles of First Fair Oaks and Seven Pines, during which Confederate Gen. Joseph E. Johnston (q.v.) had unsuccessfully struck the smaller part of Maj. Gen. George B. McClellan's (q.v.) Union army investing Richmond during the Peninsula Campaign (q.v.), the Federal army settled down to a formal siege. McClellan managed to receive reinforcements from the Fredericksburg area, which arrived by river, disembarking at McClellan's main supply base at White House on the York River. McClellan sent these troops to the north side of the Chickhominy River, which bisected the Peninsula east of Richmond. The Union army had to cross this river to the south side to attack Richmond. But McClellan's supply line ran north of the river to the York River base. To keep communications open, McClellan had his engineers repair and reconstruct the bridges damaged by recent storms. Also, McClellan now hoped more than ever that he might receive more reinforcements overland to turn the Richmond defenses.

These defenses were growing more formidable each day. The new Confederate commander who took over after the wounding of Johnston at Fair Oaks was Robert E. Lee (q.v.). He insisted that the soldiers dig properly engineered breastworks, redans, and other forts on a daily basis. The white soldiers hated what they derisively thought to be "Negro work." They began to call white-bearded Lee "Granny" and the "King of Spades." At this period, both sides thought of trenches as a cowardly way to fight. In the next two years, the men's views would change—those of them who lived. The trenches and forts gave Lee flexibility. He could hold the ground in front of Richmond now with fewer men and create a mobile force for counterattack.

Lee looked to McClellan's massive base at the White House as the key to saving Richmond. If he could capture it, the Union army would be cut off and destroyed. The problem was, where was McClellan's right flank? Was it anchored or hanging in air? Lee sent his cavalry under Brig. Gen. J. E. B. Stuart (q.v.) to find out. Stuart not only found that the flank was wide open to attack, but he rode completely around the Union army, much to McClellan's embarrassment back home, up North. Lee also called Maj. Gen. Thomas J. Jackson's (q.v.) small army into Richmond from the Shenandoah Valley. The basic plan was for Lee to strike McClellan's smaller force north of the Chickahominy under the command of Maj. Gen. Fitz John Porter with most of his force and outflank them with Jackson. North of the river Lee would have a two to one advantage in numbers.

South of the river, he would have a disadvantage in numbers of one to three. But he counted on the trenches and McClellan's usual caution to safeguard Richmond from attack.

McClellan almost beat Lee to the punch. He struck the Richmond lines on June 25, 1862, at Oak Grove. But Lee's line held—narrowly. Lee struck Porter at Mechanicsville on June 26. Porter had withdrawn his men to a strong defensive position behind Beaverdam Creek. Jackson, who was to maneuver Porter out of his position, was six hours behind schedule. The result was a massacre of the attacking Rebels.

Realizing that they were overextended, McClellan had Porter retreat to Gaines' Mill and set up a new defensive line covering the bridges south to the main army based on Boatswain's Swamp. Lee followed, attacking there on June 27. All day long the Rebels beat themselves to death, again waiting for Jackson to arrive and turn the Federals' right flank. Again Jackson was late. As Porter shifted his weight to meet the approach of Jackson, the Texas Brigade, one of Lee's premier fighting formations, broke through the Union line. Mass panic ensued. Two Union regiments surrendered intact. The rest fled to the rear. Dusk and a cavalry charge saved Porter, who crossed south of the Chickahominy during the night.

Lee had achieved his goal. He assumed that Porter had retreated toward the Union base at White House. He sent infantry and cavalry to block the withdrawal. The Confederates found no one. The cavalry rode on to the York River. There they found McClellan's whole base in ruins. The Yankees had destroyed over a million dollars in supplies. In the economy-conscious army of before the war, such a thing was impossible. But McClellan had done it. He was now falling back on the James River and the Union fleet there. Lee moved to intercept him.

While the majority of Lee's army had been fighting it out with Porter, the troops south of the Chickahominy had been attacking to keep McClellan's southern force occupied. The Rebels struck at Goulding's, Garnett's, and Allen farms. But on June 29, as Lee searched north of the Chickahominy for Federal troops, his men south of the river hit Savage's Station. In a prolonged battle, they finally saw the Federals retreat, leaving behind over 2,500 wounded as prisoners of war. Then McClellan did something strange. He sent a telegram, the Savage's Station letter, to President Abraham Lincoln and Secretary of War Edwin McM. Stanton (qq.v.), renouncing all responsibility for the results of the coming battles. He seemed to realize their ultimate outcome before they had taken place.

Aware that all of McClellan's force was south of the Chickahominy headed for the James, Lee sought to hit the retreating Federals on three sides, north, west, and south, cutting them off from the James and driving them into the White Oak Swamp. The attack was another Confederate debacle on June 30. Jackson in the north failed to push the assault across White Oak Swamp. To the south, Federal gunboats held up his men at Turkey Run. In the center, at Glendale and Frayser's farm, the assault divisions attacked all day long, piecemeal, as McClellan's supply train crossed behind the battlefield headed for the James. McClellan managed to hold his line until dark, when the Union army melted away to the south, ahead of the Confederates, too exhausted to pursue rapidly.

But the Rebels were close enough that McClellan had to make another stand before he could retreat to the James under the safety of the naval guns at Harrison's Landing. On July 1, McClellan drew up Porter's men under the muzzles of every artillery piece he could muster on the brow of Malvern Hill. Lee's attack was once again uncoordinated. His premier combat formations had all been cut up in earlier battles. His second-rate units could not win the day against McClellan's best gunners and sharpshooters. And for the first time, McClellan was on the field personally to direct the operation. That night, the Union army walked away from another victory to the safety of Harrison's Landing.

McClellan had gotten away, but Richmond was saved. The cost of the Seven Days Campaign (named for how long it took) was 16,000 Federals and 20,000 Confederates. But all of Lee's losses were in killed and wounded. McClellan had his cut potentially by 6,000 men taken prisoner, who would one day return to combat after they had been exchanged. Robert E. Lee had saved more than Richmond—he had saved the Confederacy for three more years. On July 7, Lincoln came down to see McClellan and asked him to submit a situation paper on the war's strategy. The next day, McClellan wrote the Harrison's Landing letter (q.v.), which criticized everything Lincoln and the Republicans (q.v.) had done so far, injecting himself into the political side of the war. Lincoln started withdrawing McClellan's troops, sending them to a new army near Washington, commanded by Maj. Gen. John Pope (q.v.), the Hero of Island No. 10. But Little Mac he left behind, to stew in his own juices alone.

SEVEN PINES, BATTLE OF. Part of a two-day battle, which included the battle of First Fair Oaks, fought outside of Richmond on May 31–June 1, 1862, between Confederates led by Gen. Joseph E. Johnston (q.v.) and Federals led by Gen. George B. McClellan (q.v.), Seven Pines was held by the Union IV Corps. After much confusion getting their attack force in place on the few overcrowded roads, the Rebels under Gen. James Longstreet (q.v.) launched their attack in the afternoon and drove the Union troops back, until Federal reinforcements stabilized the situation at dark. On the next day, the attack was supposed to continue, but the wounding of Gen. Johnston and reports of an imminent attack kept things at a standstill.

SEWARD, WILLIAM H. (1801–1872). Born in Orange County, New York, William H. Seward studied for the law at Union College. Graduating in 1820, he soon left the legal practice and went into politics. Prompted by the death of Masonic informer William Morgan, Seward ran on the Anti-Masonic ticket for a seat in the state senate and won. From that time on, he occupied influential elective and appointive offices, usually with the backing of influential upstate newspaper publisher and political king-maker Thurlow Weed. In 1838 (having changed parties), he became the first Whig (q.v.) governor of New York, initiating many reforms, including the removal of political disabilities from foreigners, adjusting high rents that had caused much unrest in cities, establishing the museum of natural history and a program of study, and signing a law that provided for the trial of fugitive slaves by jury with counsel furnished by the state. During the 1840s, he returned to the practice of law but kept his interest in politics up. By 1849, he was elected to the U.S. Senate and became an influential advisor to President Zachary Taylor (q.v.). At this time, Seward gave his "higher law" speech, in which he asserted that there was a law above statute and Constitution that demanded the exclusion of slavery from new states.

Seward's "higher law" speech became one of the battle cries of abolition and antislavery (qq.v.) circles in the North. He continued in the Senate throughout the 1850s, speaking out against slavery as an institution. One of his more famous declarations was the "irrepressible conflict" doctrine, a speech in which he stated his belief that the Union would have to solve the slavery issue and make the nation all free or all slave. His outspokenness made him a presidential candidate for the new Republican Party (q.v.) in 1856 and 1860. But Seward, who was probably too well-known for his seemingly radical pronouncements, scared many potential supporters, and he lost out to John Charles Frémont (q.v.) the first time and to Abraham Lincoln (q.v.) the second. Lincoln won the presidency in 1860, with Seward's support, and appointed him secretary of state. At first Seward thought that Lincoln was a country bumpkin and incapable of handling the leadership of party and nation. He tried to help the new president out, even suggesting that the nation declare war on France and Great Britain to unite itself during the secession crisis. But Lincoln firmly yet kindly put Seward in his place, and Seward went on to become one of the best secretaries of state in American history and a valued advisor to Presidents Lincoln and Andrew Johnson (q.v.).

Seward completely reorganized the diplomatic service and sent brilliant instructions to wise men he recommended for foreign posts. Through his ability, Seward turned the fortunes of the Union around, as many European countries leaned strongly toward recognition of the Confederacy and a divided America. When a Federal naval officer stopped the British ship *Trent* (q.v.) without authorization to remove two Confederate ministers going to

Europe, Seward and Lincoln cleverly released the men and praised Britain for her recognition of American shipping neutrality and exemption from search as announced in the War of 1812. Seward also asserted U.S. rights in the *Alabama* claims (q.v.), eventually getting Great Britain to pay millions in reparations for having built Confederate cruisers in violation of international neutrality law. Seward proved a vigorous defender of the Monroe Doctrine, supporting the Benito Juárez republican regime in Mexico against French incursion under Maximilian (q.v.).

In domestic policy, Seward supported Lincoln's freeing the slaves by executive proclamation (q.v.), suggesting the preliminary Emancipation Proclamation (q.v.) be delayed until a Union victory could make it look forceful rather than a gasp for salvation that could not be guaranteed on the battlefield. He also was most influential in getting the Thirteenth Amendment (q.v.) added to the Constitution to protect the wartime liberation and make emancipation universal throughout the country. On January 31, 1865, Seward managed to cobble together a coalition that passed the amendment through the House by one vote. As the Union victory seemed assured in the spring of 1865, Seward was severely injured in a carriage accident. Thrown from his vehicle, the secretary suffered a broken arm and jaw. The splints and bandages on his wounds probably saved his life when he was attacked as part of the John Wilkes Booth conspiracy to assassinate Lincoln (q.v.) and his government. His son and aide, Frederick, was badly cut as he intervened to protect his father from the knife assault of Lewis Paine. After Lincoln's death, Seward supported Andrew Johnson's Reconstruction (q.v.) policies and opposed the impeachment of the president late in his term. His support of the president led to many imputations and bitter censure in Republican circles. But he supported General Ulysses S. Grant (q.v.) for president and the Republican ticket in 1868.

As secretary of state, Seward was one of the first real expansionists in the last half of the 19th century. He negotiated many treaties for purchasing and annexing new territories (the Dutch West Indies, the Isthmus of Panamá, and Samoa) that failed to gain Senate confirmation and one (Alaska [(q.v.)]) that did. As the secretary was ahead of his time by about 30 years in his expansionism, the new territory received the ungracious nicknames "Seward's Icebox" and "Seward's Folly." But the discovery of gold in the 1890s and the vicissitudes of 20th-century world politics showed the wisdom of his move. Seward retired in March 1869 and died a few years later at his Auburn, New York, home.

SEYMOUR, HORATIO. *See* ELECTION OF 1868.

SHANNON, WILSON. *See* KANSAS–MISSOURI BORDER WARS.

SHELLABARGER–CHASE THEORY OF FORFEITED RIGHTS. *See* RECONSTRUCTION, THEORIES OF.

SHENANDOAH VALLEY. Part of the Great Valley that includes the Cumberland in Pennsylvania, the Shenandoah was a critical geographic feature in Virginia, because of the peculiar fact of its tilting toward Washington and away from Richmond. Hence it was of more military interest to the Confederates, as it offered a covered path to the Federal capital. Union troops in it wound up farther away from the Confederate capital as they progressed southward. It was also the breadbasket for Gen. Robert E. Lee's (q.v.) army, which made it liable to much destruction, particularly later in the war, when that became a key Union policy to limit Confederate offensive and defensive capabilities.

SHENANDOAH VALLEY CAMPAIGN, FIRST (JACKSON'S). Cognizant of Maj. Gen. Thomas J. "Stonewall" Jackson's (q.v.) effect on the Union command system in conducting the Battle of Kernstown, Jefferson Davis' (q.v.) military advisor, Gen. Robert E. Lee (q.v.), got together with Jackson up on the Virginia Central Railroad and planned an even bigger action in the valley to cause President Abraham Lincoln (q.v.) to worry more about the security of Washington and deny McClellan the troops necessary for victory.

Jackson went right to work. Reinforced by the division of Richard S. Ewell, Jackson stationed Ewell at Swift Run Gap in the Blue Ridge in his own camp, pulled his own division out, and marched south to Staunton. There he met the brigade of Brig. Gen. Edward Johnson, and the two men moved west into the mountains to McDowell. Taking position on a prominent hill (May 8, 1862), Jackson fended off attacks of the lead Union units commanded by Maj. Gen. John C. Frémont (q.v.), a former Republican politician turned general. Although Jackson was nearly overrun, he managed to hold on, forcing Frémont into retreat. Jackson sent cavalry raiders all over the West Virginia mountains to cut down trees and block any roads Frémont might use to enter Virginia in the future.

Then Jackson and Johnson rejoined Ewell and began marching up the valley toward Winchester, held by Union Maj. Gen. Nathaniel P. Banks (q.v.). As Jackson marched north, he came upon a peculiar geographic feature in the Valley, Massanutten Mountain. The highway ran to the west of the mountain, which paralleled the Blue Ridge for some miles. In the middle of the mountain was the Luray Gap. Jackson kept his cavalry active to hold Banks' attention on the west side and crossed his infantry to the east. This put him behind Banks, who advanced on what he mistakenly thought was Jackson's main force.

On May 23, Jackson (with Ewell and Johnson) piled into Front Royal, held by only one Union regiment. Facing 16 to 1 odds, the Yankees broke in minutes. Jackson pursued vigorously, meeting Banks at Middletown (May 24), who was falling back toward Winchester posthaste, now that Jackson was in his rear. Jackson pummeled Banks' rear guard and the next day, Jackson hit Banks' force at Winchester. For three hours, the Federals shot up Jackson's and Ewell's men, until finally Richard Taylor's Louisiana brigade hit the Federal right flank. The whole Confederate line advanced, and Banks' entire force ran all the way to Harper's Ferry.

As Jackson's little army threatened Harper's, he found himself in real trouble. President Abraham Lincoln saw it, too. Jackson was north of where two Federal forces, one from the west under Frémont (forced north by Jackson's tree-choppers) and another from Fredericksburg under Brig. Gen. James Shields, could enter the valley farther from Winchester than either of them. If Banks counterattacked and pursued Jackson down the valley, it would be possible to ensnare Jackson's 16,000 in a trap laid by 64,000. Jackson sent his men off marching with a speed that earned them the title "foot cavalry." He beat all of the Federals to Winchester and fell back beyond it. Frémont came in behind him ahead of Banks, who was slow as usual, and Shields turned south at Front Royal, hoping to get to the southern end of Massanutten Mountain ahead of Jackson.

Jackson won this race, too. He crossed the Shenandoah River with his division and defeated Shields at Port Republic (June 9). At the same time Ewell, bringing up the rear, threw back Frémont at Cross Keys (June 8) and retreated, burning the bridges behind him (June 9). The Valley Campaign was over. McClellan did not get his reinforcements, and Jackson was on the east side of the Blue Ridge, bridges burned behind him, ready to reinforce Richmond himself for the Seven Days Campaign (q.v.).

SHENANDOAH VALLEY CAMPAIGN, SECOND (SHERIDAN'S). After Confederate Lt. Gen. Jubal Early (q.v.) had pulled back from the forts surrounding Washington in his 1864 summer raid, he encamped in the Berryville region on the east side of the Blue Ridge opposite Winchester and made life miserable for the Federals and their supporters. Federal Lt. Gen. Ulysses S. Grant (q.v.) finally decided not to rely on half measures and sent one of his chief subordinates, Maj. Gen. Philip H. Sheridan (q.v.), to get rid of Early, permanently.

Sheridan had a powerful force to do the job—the VI Corps from Grant's force at the Petersburg Siege (q.v.), the XIX Corps from Louisiana, and the VIII Corps from Baltimore. In addition, he had a very powerful cavalry contingent from Petersburg and Baltimore. Although Early had been reinforced again from Gen. Robert E. Lee's (q.v.) army at Richmond and Petersburg, Early had a difficult position to defend. Sheridan could come at him from two directions, with men to spare, outnumbering Early four to one.

After an extended time of maneuver and countermaneuver, Early set up defending Winchester from north of the town in the Shenandoah Valley and the gaps east of the town behind Berryville. The battle lasted longer that it ought to have, because Sheridan's attack from the east got clogged up on itself in the Blue Ridge gaps. But by the evening of September 19, 1864, the battle of Third Winchester was over, and Early's men were streaming south in an orderly retreat. Sheridan lost 5,000 casualties to Early's 4,000.

Early stopped his withdrawal at Strasbourg, where the Shenandoah River crowds the valley close to the mountains at Fisher's Hill. He set up his line behind Tumbling Run. Early was weakened by his losses at Third Winchester and the removal of Maj. Gen. John Breckinridge's (q.v.) men from his command. He tried to fill in by using his cavalry as dismounted infantry. Sheridan came up and confronted Early on September 22. Rather than make a head-on attack, Sheridan took all day to laboriously place a corps and his cavalry opposite Early's left. Late in the day they advanced, rolling up Early's whole line. Only darkness and poor Union cavalry commanders saved the Confederate army from annihilation. Sheridan lost 500 men, while Early lost twice that plus 1,100 prisoners and a dozen guns.

Grant proposed that Sheridan advance to Charlottesville and destroy the Virginia Central Railroad, advancing on Richmond from the west. Sheridan feared that this would scatter his command and retired in Winchester, proposing to send reinforcements to Grant as the situation allowed. Sheridan began his withdrawal, his men stripping the valley bare, burning all they could not carry off. Confederate cavalry continued to harass the withdrawal; Sheridan told his horsemen to "whip or get whipped." The two mounted contingents met at Tom's Brook on October 9, where the Yankees defeated the Confederates so thoroughly as to result in the "Woodstock Races," as they tried to escape capture.

Although defeated, Early refused to give up. He still believed that he could give Sheridan a whipping under the correct circumstances. Lee agreed and sent him reinforcements. Meanwhile, the bored Union troops encamped at Cedar Creek near Winchester let their guard down. On October 19, Early's men attacked out of the creek bottom, thoroughly surprising and routing Sheridan's soldiers. Sheridan heard the firing in Winchester and immediately rode to the fight in time to stop the rout late in the day. The starving Confederates, meanwhile, went crazy at the wealth of food left behind in the Union camps and let up their pursuit. The result was that Sheridan led a massive counterattack that sent the disorganized Rebels flying.

Sheridan's men completed their devastation of the valley with little interference, carrying out Grant's instructions, which had also been given to Hunter earlier. Sheridan later bragged that the destruction was so thorough that "even crows will have to carry their own provender." What was left of

Early's army was destroyed at Waynesboro, just before Sheridan left with his cavalry to join Grant for the Appomattox Campaign (q.v.).

SHERIDAN, PHILIP H. (1831–1888). Philip Sheridan is usually said to have been born at Albany, New York, but his family moved a lot, and Massachusetts and Ohio also claimed him. Appointed to West Point from Ohio, Sheridan took five years to complete the four-year course, his academic career being marred by a hot temper. After a one-year suspension, he graduated in 1853 and was sent off to the Pacific Northwest, where he fought in several short, nasty Indian wars. At the beginning of the Civil War, Sheridan was a quartermaster lieutenant with few prospects. He soon faced a court martial for improperly giving out vouchers for supplies, but managed to get out of the command area and back to St. Louis in time to avoid trial. He was a roving horse buyer for the Army when the chance for a combat command opened up, and shortly afterward, Sheridan became the colonel of the Second Minnesota Cavalry.

Sheridan was a master of the battlefield. He had a brigade of cavalry within a week and a division of infantry in the Army of the Cumberland in just over a month. He played a prominent part in the Battle of Perryville and held on at Stone's River when the rest of the Union line ran in confusion, probably saving the day. The Army thought so and made him a brevet major general. Sheridan continued to lead his division at Chickamauga and Missionary Ridge, where he stormed the heights and very nearly captured Confederate Gen. Braxton Bragg (q.v.) and his staff. As it was, only Sheridan's division had the cohesion left after the fight to make a credible pursuit. In the spring of 1864, Lt. Gen. Ulysses S. Grant (q.v.), who had viewed Sheridan's masterful performance at Missionary Ridge, brought the young general east to put some spirit and organization into the cavalry of the Army of the Potomac.

In Virginia, Sheridan bristled at the traditional role of the horsemen as guards and messengers and with Grant's approval took the cavalry off on a raid to Richmond, hoping to entice the Confederate cavaliers of Maj. Gen. J. E. B. Stuart (q.v.) into a fight. Sheridan accomplished his goal and met Stuart at Yellow Tavern, where he slammed into the Rebel cavalry corps and killed Stuart in the process. Sheridan went on to lead the Union Army of the Shenandoah in the Second Valley Campaign (q.v.), where he defeated Maj. Gen. Jubal Early's (q.v.) graybacks at Opequon, Fisher's Hill, and Cedar Creek. Returning to Grant and the Army of the Potomac in 1865, Sheridan took the cavalry corps on a 10-day campaign that finally cornered Robert E. Lee's Army of Virginia at Appomattox (qq.v.) and forced his surrender. At the end of the war he, along with Grant and Maj. Gen. William T. Sherman (q.v.), was one of the best-known Northern generals of the conflict.

But Grant had one more assignment for Sheridan. He was to go to New Orleans and organize an expedition to conquer Texas, as yet unaffected by the war, and overawe the French forces in Mexico under Maximilian (q.v.). Sheridan accomplished the task with his usual aplomb, finding that the rumors that Texas would fight were false and actually opening up communications with Mexico's president, Benito Juárez. Sheridan then proceeded to transfer numerous surplus arms to Juárez, which caused somewhat of a diplomatic scandal, but gave the French notice that the United States was not happy about their Mexican incursion.

After settling down to the more mundane occupation duties, Sheridan got a real surprise that disturbed the deep recesses of his orderly military soul. Southern politicians were sneaky, behind-the-scenes manipulators, friends one day and back-stabbing traitors the next. No matter what reasonable request Sheridan might have, there were always complications and negotiations. These Southern politicians never seemed to recognize an order when they received one. Sheridan especially believed that the elected governors of Louisiana (James Madison Wells) and Texas (James W. Throckmorton [q.v.]) were scoundrels. Louisiana particularly baffled him. There was always a second board, another committee that claimed to be more legal than the first. Both state legislatures passed discriminatory Black Codes and rejected the Fourteenth Amendment (qq.v.), and Texas even tried to raise its own militia composed of ex-Confederate soldiers, ostensibly to protect the state's western frontier. It was all highly "anomalous," to use the general's favorite word to describe anything he did not like (he used it a lot, too).

Sheridan had many anomalies to handle in 1866. He was constantly rushing from trouble spot to trouble spot, putting out political fires. First he was off to the Rio Grande, where black Union soldiers had crossed the river to attack a French garrison inside Mexico led by a former Confederate officer. Then it was back to New Orleans, where the city blew up in a race riot designed to prevent loyal men from having a political meeting to reconvene the wartime convention set up under Abraham Lincoln's Ten Percent Plan (qq.v.). Next it was back to Texas to put down the hostile reaction to soldiers burning the business section in the small town of Brenham. Later it was back to Louisiana to supervise the registration of voters for the new state constitutional convention demanded by the Military Reconstruction Acts (q.v.). Then off to Texas to do the same. It was all very frustrating.

Sheridan sat down and reexamined the congressional legislation to see if he might not clean out some of the political deadwood in Louisiana and Texas to lessen his chores. He targeted Louisiana's Governor Wells first, although Bvt. Maj. Gen. Charles Griffin (q.v.), his Texas subordinate, claimed the right to fire Texas Governor Throckmorton as quickly as possible. Gen. Grant told Sheridan to hold off. He was not sure military commanders had the right to move against elected civil officials. But Grant also said that he might try removing some lower officials to see what good it did. He fired one registration officer in New Orleans for intimidating black voters. He reorganized the New Orleans police to require that half be former Union soldiers. Then he moved on the state levee board. Typically Louisiana-style, there were two boards, one appointed by the governor and another established by the state legislature. Sheridan fired both and set up a third of men of his own choosing. He integrated the street cars in New Orleans. Finally, having weathered these storms, Sheridan fired Governor Wells as a "political trickster and dishonest man" and replaced him with Benjamin F. Flanders. When Wells refused to leave his office, Sheridan told him to git or be dragged out by a squad of infantry. Wells left. The country went wild, both pro and con.

While Sheridan kept the public eye on his removal policy, secretly, along with Grant, he permitted voter registrars to contravene a decision of the U.S. attorney general that would have liberalized the process for ex-Confederates. Sheridan and Grant looked at the ruling as an opinion with which reasonable men could disagree. Sheridan believed that registrars, as the government's representatives in the field, ought to have wide discretion in registration. By summer, however, this policy could no longer be kept secret, and President Andrew Johnson (q.v.) ordered Grant to change it. Then, in July 1867, Congress vindicated Sheridan's desire to replace politicians who were "impediments to Reconstruction." Griffin had been pestering him to move against Throckmorton, who became the first official removed under the new act. In retaliation, President Johnson fired Sheridan and replaced him with a general known for his Democrat politics, Maj. Gen. Winfield Scott Hancock (q.v.).

After his removal from the Fifth Military District, Sheridan was put in charge of subduing the Plains Indians. He went about the job with a ruthless efficiency, turning loose his chief weapon, the Seventh Cavalry under Bvt. Maj. Gen. George Armstrong Custer. The result was the Battle of the Washita, after which many of the Southern Cheyenne came in to surrender. In 1870, Sheridan went to Europe as an American observer for the Franco–Prussian War. He traveled with the Prussian forces and admired their ability to mobilize soldiers using their railroad system. They in turn admired his ability to conduct campaigns in the no-quarter style of the Uhlans, the feared cavalry of the new German Army.

In 1874, Sheridan (Sherman had refused to go) was sent back to Louisiana as a special presidential emissary to make recommendations on suppressing the White League (q.v.) movement. Bvt. Maj. Gen. William Emory was quickly aware that he no longer commanded in the state—all decisions would be up to Sheridan. Sheridan immediately saw to it that five critical seats in the state legislature went to the Republican (q.v.) claimants. The Army escorted the Democrats (q.v.) out of the house by threat of bayonet point. Then Sheridan wrote Grant and suggested that the White Leaguers be declared "banditti" and all be arrested and tried by military commission. But Grant was not about to declare martial law, as the Northern public would not stand for it. And Northern public criticism was mild compared to what Southern whites thought. All Grant could do was disown Sheridan's bluster and call him to Washington for consultation. The result was that Gen. Emory lost his job as a concession to Sheridan's ego and inability to act. Sheridan would return during the crisis in 1876, but accomplish even less. Reconstruction was over, and Sheridan's style of command no longer mattered.

After his trip to the South, Sheridan was once more placed in charge of the West. The 1876 Sioux Campaign that resulted in the battles of the Rosebud and the Little Big Horn was accomplished under his tutelage. Although his men lost every battle, they won the war by forcing the Sioux and their Northern Cheyenne allies to come into the reservations and sue for peace just to eat. Sheridan recognized that the slaughter of the buffalo by the hide hunters was probably the real factor that won the war.

After Sherman's retirement, he took over command of the Army. He was not hesitant to use armed force against any people who seemed to threaten the advance of the American demigod of his day, progress. Whether it was Southern whites challenging the Reconstruction of the South, Native Americans trying to protect their homelands, or Northern laborers trying to protect their jobs and wages through unionization and strikes, Sheridan was more than willing to act as their destroyer for the greed of the government and its politicians, contractors, and agents. He was the perfect military man of 19th-century America.

SHERMAN, JOHN (1823–1900). The brother of Maj. Gen. William T. Sherman (q.v.), John Sherman was born in Lancaster, Ohio. His father died early, and his mother had to farm out her 11 children to relatives and friends to get by. John Sherman lived with a distant cousin of his father, who saw to it the boy received an excellent education at schools in Lancaster and Mt. Vernon. He developed a real talent for mathematics and surveying, and by age 14 Sherman was working on various internal improvements that dotted the Ohio landscape. By age 16, he was a foreman of work on a canal. He was soon dismissed from the job, as he was from a Whig (q.v.) family and the Democrats (q.v.) had just taken the state. It was a sobering experience for the rabble-rousing John, who took a long look at his life and decided to mend his ways. He became a sober, cautious man, read law, and passed the bar by 1844. At the same time, he engaged in lumbering and real estate and got married. The Shermans never had any children of their own, but they did adopt a daughter.

After entering the law, Sherman became interested in Whig politics and worked in the party's state organization, attending the national conventions of 1848 and 1852. He held no public office until the wave of anti-Nebraska hysteria hit the North and carried Sherman into Republicanism and election to Congress.

Although by nature Sherman was not a vindictive man, when it came to the war and Reconstruction, he voted the Radical program of rejection of Southern congressmen and senators in 1866, for the imposition of Military Reconstruction (q.v.) in 1867, and for the guilty verdict on President Andrew Johnson's impeachment (qq.v.) trial in 1868. Why? Because it was dangerous not to do so and expect to be reelected. But Sherman was not shy in imposing his more conservative views on Reconstruction. It was he who wrote the initial Military Reconstruction Acts (q.v.), removing much of their harshness while retaining civil rights for blacks. He also spoke out against impeaching the president over the Tenure of Office Act (q.v.) because, as he astutely pointed out, Johnson had never thrown Secretary of War Edwin McM. Stanton (q.v.) out of office—he still physically held it. But Sherman voted to convict, partly because he did not have to vote to acquit to save the president—seven other Republicans by prearrangement had agreed to save Johnson. His career was saved for the future.

Throughout his public career, Sherman was a careful politician, not taking radical positions, and becoming a student of the money issue (q.v.) and government. Sherman was a hard money man, and his ideas on promoting specie resumption (the so-called Crime of '73) were blamed for the Panic of 1873. But he redeemed himself in 1878 as secretary of the treasury by allowing more inflation and the use of gold and silver coin.

He served in the House (1855–1861); was elected to the Senate in place of Salmon P. Chase (q.v.), who became Abraham Lincoln's (q.v.) secretary of the treasury, and served three terms (1861–1877); was secretary of the treasury under Rutherford B. Hayes (q.v.) (1877–1881); returned to the Senate for three more terms (1881–1897); and ended his long career as secretary of state under William McKinley (1897–1898). Sherman also had a desire to be president. He ran in 1880, 1884, and 1888, only to lose out to other men each time.

SHERMAN, WILLIAM T. (1820–1891). Second only to Lt. Gen. Ulysses S. Grant (q.v.) in his popularity at the end of the Civil War, William Tecumseh Sherman was raised by his neighbor, Thomas Ewing, a politician of some influence who got him his appointment to the U.S. Military Academy. Graduating sixth in the class of 1840, Sherman served in Florida and South Carolina. At the start of the War with Mexico, Sherman wanted to get to the action in Texas, but was sent instead to California by way of Cape Horn, missing the war entirely. After a stint as an adjutant general, Sherman returned to the east and married his foster sister. Transferred to the commissary department, Sherman went to St. Louis. There he learned that he had been made a partner in a local bank. He resigned his commission and became a businessman. Sherman represented the bank in California and practiced law in New York and Kansas, before being appointed to head the Louisiana Military Academy at Pineville. He resigned when the state seceded in 1861.

Sherman was made a colonel of the new 13th Infantry and fought as a brigade commander at the battle of First Manassas (q.v.). He was sent to Kentucky and deemed to be insane because of his prescription that it would take 200,000 men to hold that area for the Union. After a leave home, Sherman wound up in Paducah, Kentucky, under Maj. Gen. U.S. Grant (q.v.). Their professional and private friendship grew day by day thereafter. A division commander during the Shiloh Campaign (q.v.), Sherman was seriously wounded. Returning to Grant's command as a major general, Sherman was made a corps commander during the Vicksburg Campaign and the Chattanooga Campaign (qq.v.). He took over as commander of the Western Theater of the war in 1864, when Grant went east. Sherman then conducted the Atlanta Campaign and the March to the Sea (qq.v.). By making war against civilian property, Sherman is considered one of the first truly modern generals. After reaching Savannah, Sherman turned north in the Carolinas Campaign (q.v.), forcing the surrender of the Confederacy's second most important army at Durham Station (q.v.), North Carolina.

It was during the negotiation for the surrender of this army that Sherman overstepped his bounds and included several political provisions for calling the legislature of the various seceded state into session to repeal secession and rejoin the Union. Sherman believed that he was acting under the guidelines that he had discussed with President Abraham Lincoln (q.v.) previously. But Lincoln was dead, and the result was a severe rebuke from Secretary of War Edwin McM. Stanton (q.v.) and a forced renegotiation of the surrender document.

A well-known negrophobe, Sherman refused to get involved in Reconstruction, preferring to subdue the Native Americans of the plains from his headquarters in St. Louis. He became lieutenant general in 1869, upon Grant's accession to the presidency. Sherman retired in 1884. Extremely antipolitical, he is known for his refusal to be put up as a presidential candidate, "If nominated I shall not run; if elected I shall not serve."

SHILOH CAMPAIGN. When Gen. Albert Sidney Johnston (q.v.) arrived in Tennessee in 1862, he found the situation to be very difficult. Like President Abraham Lincoln (q.v.), the Confederates did not want to violate Kentucky neutrality. But unlike the Union commanders, who could sit behind the Ohio River, the Confederates had no natural geographic barriers to station their defensive lines on. All the rivers ran north and south at the border. Even the mountains did the same. When Confederate Gen. Leonidas Polk moved north on his own volition to the bluffs at Columbus, Kentucky, on September

4, 1861, the whole Kentucky situation became more fluid. The Rebels had violated the sacred neutrality. Now anyone could enter Kentucky, the harm having already been done.

Forced by Polk's unfortunate strategic independence to secure as much of Kentucky as possible, Johnston immediately moved his forces out of Tennessee to the Bowling Green, Kentucky, area. Johnston was obsessed by the idea of Maj. Gen. Don Carlos Buell's (q.v.) Union army coming south through Bowling Green, to the exclusion of all else. This was particularly true when he lost his right flank covering force in the Cumberland Mountains in a sharp battle at Logan's Crossroads and the ensuing disastrous retreat through Mill Springs. This was the first Union victory since the Yankee defeat in the Battle of First Manassas (q.v.) and cost the Confederates what little respect they had in the Tory counties of eastern Tennessee. Johnston's attitude offered the Union commander in Paducah, Brig. Gen. Ulysses S. Grant (q.v.), an opportunity to slip between him and Polk, using the Cumberland and Tennessee Rivers as invasion routes, backed by Flag Off. Andrew Foote's gunboats. Each river was blocked by a fortification—Ft. Henry on the Tennessee and Ft. Donelson (qq.v.) on the Cumberland.

On February 6, 1862, Grant and Foote moved on Ft. Henry, the westernmost and weakest of the forts, which surrendered to Foote after a short naval bombardment. Fortunately, Foote's naval batteries had out-ranged the land guns in Ft. Henry. But Ft. Donelson was better sited and armed than Henry. When Foote tried to force the issue on February 14 with a naval bombardment, Donelson's bigger guns smashed his little fleet. Foote drifted out of range and waited for Grant's infantry to invest the land side of the fort. But the Confederates attacked Grant on February 15 and forced open the escape route to Clarksville and Nashville.

After much argument, the Rebels pulled back into their original lines. Two successive commanders deserted their commands, forcing Brig. Gen. Simon Buckner to ask Grant for terms. Grant sent him his famous answer: "unconditional surrender." Buckner reluctantly accepted, and Grant had captured the first of three Confederate armies (this one about 15,000 strong) he would capture during the war. Meanwhile, Johnston retreated out of Kentucky into northern Mississippi at Corinth to plan a new strategy.

Leaving the occupation of Clarksville and Nashville to Buell's Army of the Cumberland, Grant followed the Tennessee River south to Pittsburg Landing. He sent his men inland to camp around Shiloh Church, in anticipation of a move to Corinth to confront Johnston. Stiffened by the arrival of the hero of Ft. Sumter and Manassas, Major General P. G. T. Beauregard (qq.v.), Johnston surprised Grant by attacking his sleeping camp on April 6. Initially quite successful, the Confederate onslaught was held up by Union defense of a hollow that became known as the Hornet's Nest. While organizing troops for an attack here, Johnston received a leg wound, from which he bled to death. Beauregard took over and pushed the attack on. By nightfall, the Federal forces were holding a line with their backs to the river and swamps, covered by the river gunboats at Pittsburg Landing.

Unfortunately for the Rebels, their attack had been organized with units in line rather than column. This meant that by the end of the day, divisions and corps were so intermingled as to make control all but impossible. It took all night for the mess to be straightened out. Grant, meanwhile, received reinforcements from Buell, which allowed the Yankees to commence their own attack the next morning. The fighting raged all day, but superior Union numbers foretold the result. By nightfall, the Confederate army was in full retreat back to Corinth. An aggressive rear guard action led by Gen. Forrest's cavalry soon stopped all idea of pursuit.

As Grant and Buell pushed up the Tennessee and Cumberland, another Union army led by Brig. Gen. John Pope (q.v.) was advancing down the Mississippi from the abandoned Confederate bastion at Columbus. He faced the dual fortifications of New Madrid, Missouri, and Island No. 10 (Mississippi River Islands were numbered from the north for navigation purposes) at a sharp bend on the Tennessee side of the river. Pope instituted siege operations, forcing the Rebels to abandon New Madrid and concentrate their forces on the mainland behind Island No. 10. Pope proceeded to construct a canal on the Missouri side to bypass the bottleneck at Island No. 10. This accomplished he ferried his men and cannon behind the Confederate position, forced the surrender of 3,500 men on April 7, and opened the river to Ft. Pillow above Memphis. A running gun battle between rival river fleets in a Confederate surprise attack at Plum Run Bend scattered the Union river fleet. But the Yankee rivermen recovered quickly and administered a crushing defeat on the Confederate fleet at Memphis, and the fall of Ft. Pillow and the capture of Memphis soon followed.

Meanwhile, Com. David Farragut's (q.v.) ocean fleet had come up the Mississippi from the Battle of New Orleans (q.v.) to Vicksburg and began to bombard the city's riverside defenses on May 16. A brigade of infantry disembarked on the Louisiana side to try to build a canal across the isthmus on that shore but failed. Although Farragut was joined by the river gunboats fresh from their victory at Memphis, and Confederate defenses were at best piecemeal, the dogged refusal of the Rebels to yield and the withdrawal of Pope's army to the line of the Tennessee River in support of the Corinth push sent Farragut down to the Gulf and the riverboats back up to Memphis by July 26.

The infantry, with Farragut, had disembarked at Baton Rouge, and on August 5 they received a two-pronged attack from land and river, led by Maj. Gen. John C. Breckinridge (q.v.), former vice president under James Buchanan (q.v.) and 1860 Democratic (q.v.) presidential candidate. The Confederates drove the Yankees from their camps around the town cemetery, but had to yield in turn as they came under fire from the river gunboats moored nearby. The ironclad C.S.S. *Arkansas* was supposed to nullify the gunboats' cover fire, but her engines failed as she approached the city and she had to be destroyed by her crew to prevent capture.

Back at Pittsburg landing on the Tennessee, Maj. Gen. Henry W. Halleck (q.v.) arrived on the field. As department commander, he combined the armies of Grant, Buell, and Pope under himself and probed toward Corinth. Each night, the army stopped and entrenched to prevent another Shiloh-style surprise attack. After advancing at the measured pace of about 20 miles in a month, Halleck entered Corinth on June 10, which the outnumbered Confederates had abandoned at the end of May. The Shiloh Campaign was over at last. The Yankees were in northern Mississippi, but because Halleck had unwisely pulled Pope away from the river, the Rebels still blocked the Mississippi River at Vicksburg.

SHILOH CHURCH, BATTLE OF (APRIL 6–7, 1862). In early April 1862, Bvt. Maj. Gen. Ulysses S. Grant (q.v.) and his five-division army were at a small river wharf where the Tennessee River crossed the Tennessee–Mississippi border, called Pittsburg Landing. The men were camped around a small county church named Shiloh. There was no attempt made at setting up a defensive camp. The Rebels were at Corinth, miles to the south. No one expected an attack.

Yet, on April 6 at dawn, Gen. Albert Sidney Johnston's (q.v.) Confederate army slammed into Grant's sleeping men, turning the morning into the bloodiest day the nation had seen so far. Most of the soldiers on both sides were green recruits. The rule was that they would run at the first shot or stay and fight stubbornly to the end. Most of the men on both sides stayed to fight.

The surprised Yankees were overwhelmed at first. But gradually, resistance seemed to increase at a hollow about halfway through the Union position near the Tennessee River that became known as the Hornet's Nest. Grant came down to the battlefield from his quarters at Savannah lower on the river and ordered Brig. Gen. Stephen Prentiss to hold it at all costs. Grant needed time to create a defensive line at the river itself. Prentiss' men held until 5:30 p.m., when 62 Confederate fieldpieces literally blew his men away. The Confederates lost heavily, too, including Gen. Johnston, who was replaced by Maj. Gen. P. G. T. Beauregard (q.v.). Many Union defenders tried to escape capture by retreating through a draw renamed Hell's Hollow after the battle. Another 2,200 surrendered with Prentiss.

Meanwhile, Union officers massed their artillery, large bore siege guns, naval cannon from two gunboats off the wharf, and every fieldpiece they could lay their hands on. Erroneously learning that Grant could not receive reinforcements in time, Beauregard suspended operations until the next day and tried to put some order in the inextricably confused Confederate brigades and divisions.

The next morning, Grant assembled three divisions that had arrived during the night and counterattacked. The Confederates were driven back over the previous day's ground until the fighting stagnated at the little church. Informed that the 20,000 reinforcements that he was expecting to cross the Mississippi from Arkansas were late, Beauregard suspended fighting at dusk and withdrew from the field. A pursuit the next day was stopped by Confederate cavalry led by Col. Nathan Bedford Forrest (q.v.), who was wounded in the fighting.

Shiloh Church was the first real battle of the war. Everything else had been prelude. With losses running at just over 13,500 for the combined Union armies and 10,600 for the Confederates, hospital facilities were overwhelmed. It took over a week just to find the wounded and get them to preliminary treatment. Every town in the Mississippi Valley, North or South, suffered the loss of its sons. Shiloh put an end to the romance of war. It also put an end to the notion of compromise between North and South. The grief had been too great and would grow worse still. It would be a war to the bloody end, winner take all. Shiloh determined that—although not all understood it yet.

SHOTGUN PLAN. After the Enforcement Acts (q.v.) dispersed the Ku Klux Klan (q.v.), the First Mississippi (q.v.) or Shotgun plan came into vogue. Organizations, no longer secret and generally referred to as rifle clubs, like the Red Shirts and the White League (qq.v.), actually fielded armies with cannons and fought openly against Loyalist blacks and whites of the pro-Federal black and tan (q.v.) militia. The most spectacular example occurred in 1874, when the Louisiana White League defeated the Republican Metropolitan Police and loyal militia led by none other than Gen. R. E. Lee's (q.v.) former right-hand man, Lt. Gen. James Longstreet (q.v.), now a Scalawag (q.v.) political appointee. This Battle of Canal Street or the Third Battle of New Orleans (q.v.) guaranteed the redemption of Louisiana, as did the activities of similar groups in South Carolina and Mississippi. Recently there has been much political flak in New Orleans, now about 80 percent black in population, over the efficacy of maintaining the monument that was raised on the battle site at the turn of the century.

SICKLES, DANIEL E. (1819–1914). Born in New York City, Daniel Sickles was an outstanding example of the kind of man of little or no military education who became a political general in the Civil War armies: tough, aggressive, a hard drinker, a patron of prostitutes, a flexible politician when it came to principle—generally an all-around man's man or a jerk, depending on one's point of view. Appropriately, he studied law under the tutelage of Benjamin Butler (q.v.), himself no slouch of a character, either.

Sickles became a member of the New York state legislature in 1843 and gained his law license shortly afterward. He was also a reliable member of the Tammany Hall Democratic (q.v.) machine. In the early 1850s, Sickles met a young lady, Theresa Bagioli, whom he had known when he was a student at New York University with her brother some years before. He immediately fell in love with the accomplished Theresa, who spoke five languages and studied music. Of course, Sickles regularly fell in love with any beautiful woman, regardless of her reputation. Both families opposed the marriage, but the head-strong Theresa went ahead and married Sickles in a civil ceremony. Her family, devout Catholics, gave into the accomplished fact and had the couple remarried by Cardinal John Hughes, the top prelate in the United States.

Sickles received a diplomatic post under the Democratic administrations of Franklin Pierce and James Buchanan (qq.v.). Allegedly he took a prostitute to Europe with him, introduced her to Queen Victoria as his wife, and became involved in the Ostend Manifesto (q.v.), which called for the U.S. takeover of Cuba from Spain. Back in New York, Sickles was elected to the U.S. House of Representatives. He took the beautiful Theresa to Washington with him, but never gave up his usual womanizing. So Theresa responded in the Latin manner; she took a lover of her own, Philip Barton Key, son of the writer of the "Star Spangled Banner."

Someone sent an anonymous letter to Sickles outlining Theresa's extra-curricular activities. Sickles, in a perfect application of the double standard, checked up on his wife and found the tales to be true. So he confronted Key in Lafayette Square and shot him dead. Then Sickles went into the office of the U.S. attorney general and surrendered himself and his weapon. The trial was the sensation of the nation. Led by Edwin McM. Stanton (q.v.), Abraham Lincoln's (q.v.) future secretary of war, Sickles was presented as a man who had temporarily lost his mind over the affair of his wife and shot poor Key to save the pure women of Washington from Key's vile advances. Talk about the wrong man being on trial! But it worked, and Sickles beat the rap, the first successful use of the temporary insanity defense in U.S. history. Then the magnanimous congressman forgave his wayward wife and took her back into his own bed. She would die from tuberculosis a few years later, spurned by all good society.

The nation was outraged at the gall of it all. But the approaching Civil War allowed Sickles to join the army. Naturally he did that in style, too, raising five New York regiments into the "Excelsior" (the motto of New York State) Brigade, with himself as brigadier general in charge. Off to war he went. His brigade became part of a division of three brigades commanded by Maj. Gen. "Fightin' Joe" Hooker (q.v.), a man of Sickles' own domestic predilections.

As it turned out, Sickles was a fairly good volunteer general—at least he led his men into fights, not away from them. By 1863, Hooker commanded the army in the east, and Sickles commanded Hooker's old division, and then the III Corps of the Army of the Potomac.

In the ensuing Chancellorsville Campaign (q.v.), Sickles sat at the south end of the Union line as the whole corps of Confederate Gen. Stonewall Jackson (q.v.) crossed in front of him, forbidden to attack by Hooker. The result was a crushing defeat. During the Pennsylvania Campaign (q.v.), Sickles was in what he saw as the same position south of Gettysburg. The new Union general, George G. Meade (q.v.), refused to let Sickles advance again, fearing his new position would be too exposed. Sickles took the bull by the horns and advanced anyway, creating Sickles' Salient (q.v.). The Rebel attack smashed up his corps, with Sickles losing his leg in the process. Meade and Sickles argued until their deaths over whether Sickles had saved the Union army by breaking up Gen. Robert E. Lee's (q.v.) attack prematurely or nearly lost the whole battle by refusing to hold his original position.

After the war, Sickles reentered politics as a Republican (q.v.). He served as military commander of the Carolinas during Reconstruction, until he was fired for doing his job too tyrannically. He next served as minister to Spain, where he had an affair with Queen Isabella II, sort of tyrant to tyrant. Evidently his missing leg was not relevant to either cause. He returned home to be put in charge of the New York monuments commission until he was fired for corruption (q.v.). He was instrumental in beginning Gettysburg National Military Park, partly as a shrine to his military judgment, no doubt. He died shortly thereafter, age finally having got him down.

SICKLES' SALIENT, BATTLE OF. *See* PENNSYLVANIA CAMPAIGN.

SILVER DEMONITIZATION ACT. *See* GRANT, ULYSSES S., ADMINISTRATION—DOMESTIC POLICIES.

SIOUX UPRISING. In Minnesota during the Civil War, a Santee Sioux hunting party coming home without luck picked up some eggs a stray hen had laid by the roadside. When warned this was stealing from a white man, taunts about who was brave and afraid were exchanged, and four of the 20 hunters became warriors out to prove their bravery, killing several whites coming home from church. The murderers bragged of the deed to their chief, Little Crow. A council was assembled and the topic debated. In the end, the tribe voted to go to war, as all would be blamed for the deaths anyway. Little Crow agreed reluctantly to lead them.

Little Crow's leadership was superlative and deadly. The warriors fell on every white unlucky enough to be caught out, killing the men and children, gang-raping women, scalping all for 30 miles around. An estimated 1,500 whites died. Twenty-three counties were stripped of all human life. An attack on nearby Fort Ridgley failed after 40 of the garrison were dispatched, and the hostiles, now some 800 strong, hit New Ulm, fighting house-to-house. The town was fairly well burned, but the whites held on at the center square, finally repulsing the attackers. The militia and several Civil War veteran regiments under Maj. Gen. John Pope of the Second Manassas Campaign (qq.v.) counterattacked and defeated the Indians' main force, which scattered.

Then the retribution began. Two thousand tribesmen were arrested, 75 percent of whom had nothing to do with the war. Trials lasted less than 10 minutes. In the end, 306 were convicted of murder, rape, and pillage. The local Episcopal bishop begged President Abraham Lincoln (q.v.) to intervene, and he pardoned all but 36 convicted of actual statutory crimes. They were all hanged in one spring of the trap at Mankato, Little Crow managing to escape to Canada. He was later shot from ambush, foolishly having returned to the U.S. His surviving tribesmen, innocent and guilty alike, were sent to a Nebraska reservation.

SLAUGHTERHOUSE CASES (1873). The first litigation under the Fourteenth Amendment (q.v.), the Slaughterhouse Cases, involved a Louisiana abattoir law that had been passed to regulate the slaughter of animals in the city of New Orleans. In an attempt to clean up the city's poor sanitation, the state legislature (after the usual bribes and pay-offs) had decreed that all slaughtering had to take place at one location. Butchers had to pay to use the Crescent City Stock Landing and Slaughterhouse Company that had the monopoly. The city's butchers sued, in a series of cases finally combined into one, citing the measure as a form of involuntary servitude prohibited under the Thirteenth Amendment (q.v.) and a denial of their privileges and immunities as citizens guaranteed under the Fourteenth Amendment.

The court dismissed the claims. First, it stated that the Thirteenth Amendment was related exclusively to black slavery. Then the court disposed of the Fourteenth Amendment's provisions in various ways: "privileges and immunities of citizenship" were declared to be state and Federal, with the Federal being limited to things like protection on the high seas and in foreign lands, use of domestic rivers, and ports, and access to *habeas corpus* (q.v.); "equal protection under the laws" was limited to African-Americans and involved such illegal state matters as the Black Codes (q.v.); while "due process" was satisfied so long as the law in question was correctly considered by the legislative body that passed it. Put bluntly, there were not many individual rights under the Fourteenth Amendment. The Civil Rights Act of 1875 (q.v.), a lifelong project of Massachusetts Senator Charles Sumner (q.v.), was the congressional answer to the court's curtailing of the wider implications of the Fourteenth Amendment.

SLAVE POWER CONSPIRACY. The ability of the South to control much of antebellum national politics through the use of the clause in the Constitution that based representation in Congress on a count of the white population plus three-fifths of the South's slaves led to the notion that there was a conspiracy to deny the more populous North its fair share of national power and came to be seen as the Slave Power Conspiracy. It was a separate problem from slavery in the states or the territories before the Civil War and, ironically, with the end of slavery and the counting of the African-Americans as full persons, actually increased the political power of the South during Reconstruction and after, making the black vote necessary as a loyal, anti-white Democrat, pro-Republican (q.v.) force on the national scene.

SLAVERY AS A POSITIVE GOOD, THEORY OF. By the time of the Civil War, the South looked upon the institution as a positive good for the whole nation. It was this concept that caused great fear among Northerners like Abraham Lincoln and William H. Seward (qq.v.), especially when it seemed to be endorsed by the 1857 U.S. Supreme Court case, Dred Scott *v.* Sandford (qq.v.).

The evolution of slavery into a positive good was as old as the United States itself. Before 1830, the South defended slavery apologetically. Slavery was presented as no crime but as a necessary evil. What opposition existed to slavery in the South was confined to a few speculative thinkers like Thomas Jefferson, who rarely acted upon their convictions, or to others like George Washington, James Madison, and James Monroe, who did free their bondspeople upon their deaths.

In the 1830s, after the slave revolts of Denmark Vesey in Charleston, South Carolina, and Nat Turner in Southampton County, Virginia, two courses of action presented themselves for the South and slavery. In Virginia, the institution was debated to it fullest between the Tidewater and the Mountains, in a prelude to the state's division during the Civil War. Historians like to point to this Great Debate as evidence of slavery having many opponents in the South. But abolition had few proponents in either section of the state, unless emancipation (q.v.) were accompanied by compensation for the slaveowner and transportation of the blacks out of Virginia and/or the nation. An attempt to debate the issue at the Tennessee constitutional convention at the same time failed when the committee reported that slavery was the only way whites and blacks could live together without the terror of a holocaust, as experienced in Haiti early in the century.

But the real trend for the future came out of South Carolina, just as secession would 30 years later. This was the notion that slavery was a positive good, for North and South, white and black. The Positive Good Doctrine was not a response to the abolitionist (q.v.) attack from the North as most believed, but preceded it by some years. The Slavery as a Positive Good argument was based on several principles. The South defined slavery much differently than the North. Slaveholders maintained that their power was limited to property rights alone. Ideally, all the slaves lost was their right in self-ownership. They still enjoyed the rights to life, marriage, happiness, indeed, anything so long as it was consistent with their obligation to render service to the master and mistress for the sustenance they received in return.

There was also the historical argument for slavery. Its existence throughout history in nearly every society, especially Jewish, Greek, and Roman, was evidence of its righteousness. The South was especially interested in the fact that people were often enslaved for losing wars. Their own slaves had originally been the losers in African intertribal wars. It was a condition recognized by international law thinkers for centuries to prevent wholesale slaughter of captives.

There was also the object lesson argument. Slavery or barbarism was a natural condition of the African, world over. In Africa they existed as savages, incapable of modern invention. In Haiti, they reverted to the same condition after gaining their freedom. In the British West Indies, the local economies had faltered upon abolition. At home, the free blacks lived in a condition barely above savagery, unable and unwilling to improve themselves. The latter was especially echoed in the North in its own racist feelings. All of this, of course, overlooked the legal and informal discriminations that forced this condition to occur.

The South made use of what then passed for science to prove its points. Important here was the ethnic factor. Blacks were commonly held to be an inferior order of humankind. If this were not true, many Southerners admitted, slavery would be an abomination. Most important was the idea of craniology, a big favorite in the 19th century. Dr. Samuel G. Morton pointed out that white skulls had a forehead slope that was 80°, whereas blacks' forehead slope was about 70°, and the apes' were 68°. One can see the possibilities. In this pre-Darwinian age, scientists also believed in the diverse origins of the races: several creations, not just one.

Dr. Josiah Nott of Mobile had done much work in this area and had a whole laboratory with the skulls of whites, blacks, and apes lined up for correct comparison. Along with George Glidden, Nott wrote the 1850s classic in the field, *Types of Mankind*. He also followed this with a volume of his own, *Indigenous Races of the Earth*. Another "Negro doctor" (a title that covered a multitude of sins), Dr. Samuel A. Cartwright, held forth that an African, not the proverbial serpent, had tempted Eve in the Garden of Eden, basing his theory on the work of Dr. Adam Clark of Britain, who had postulated that the creature that had tempted Eve walked erect, spoke, and reasoned, and hence was an orangutan. "If he had lived in Louisiana, instead of Britain," said Cartwright, "he would have recognized the NEGRO GARDENER." Evidently, D. H. Lawrence wrote 100 years too late. Much of what Cartwright and Nott asserted was roundly condemned by Dr. John L. Cabell of Virginia.

The biblical justification was a powerful force in 19th-century America and was put to use in the case of slavery justification. Everything from the fourth and tenth Commandments to the usual curse of the descendants of Ham from Genesis was employed. Indeed, John Fletcher of Natchez, Mississippi, had an 1852 tome, *Studies in Slavery in Easy Lessons*, which reviewed the biblical defense in depth, using verses from Genesis, Leviticus, and Joshua in the Old Testament, and Luke and over a half dozen of Paul's Letters, to show that black slavery was divinely inspired.

Finally, there were social justifications of slavery. The South maintained that the relationship between the various classes and races demonstrated the superiority of slave society over free society. Slavery's very existence made all whites more equal. The emphasis upon wealth in the North to differentiate between classes arrayed Northern society into competing haves and have-nots. Those without property toyed instead with various "isms" (Fourierism, anarchism, socialism, free rentism, free love-ism, perfectionism, Seventh Day Adventism, Mormonism, and especially abolitionism) that caused government to have to place restrictions upon the lower classes. James Hammond of South Carolina said that slavery was necessary for black slaves to perform the drudgery of society to free the whites for higher purposes of intellect and governance, and this came to be called the "Mudsill Theory." John C. Calhoun of South Carolina was so adamant about this class struggle aspect of Northern society that he came to be called the "Marx of the Master Class" 100 years later.

Naturally, if slavery were so good for society, it followed that certain reforms would mean more of the good thing for everyone. To make slavery more appealing, the slave codes of the South were amended in the 1850s to improve their "humane" features and protect the slaves from unscrupulous owners. Then the South called for the reopening of the international slave trade, which had been closed in 1808 in the Constitution. After all, such a Positive Good institution with all those wonderful benefits of civilization and Christianization must be spread around. In May 1859, a Southern Commercial Convention meeting at Vicksburg, Mississippi, proposed just that.

SMALLS, ROBERT (1839–1915). Born in slavery at Beaufort, South Carolina, Robert Smalls was educated by his white owners and taken to Charleston, where they permitted him to hire his own time as a waiter, hack driver, and ship's rigger. In 1861, Smalls was impressed into Confederate service aboard the supply ship C.S.S. *Planter*, which sailed the waters between the various Charleston harbor fortifications. Aboard the ship, Smalls took special care to learn to navigate and pilot the boat. Then on May 13, 1862, taking advantage of the fact that the white officers slept ashore, Smalls and other crew members smuggled their families on board and steamed out into the harbor. He gave the normal whistle signal to keep the Confederate batteries from firing on the boat, and as soon as he could, cut loose for the Union blockading fleet.

Smalls became an instant hero. His name and fame spread throughout the North, and he was made a pilot in the Union navy and given a share of the *Planter's* prize money. When the *Planter* was placed in Federal service, Smalls was sent along as pilot. On December 1, 1863, the ship came under fire from shore; the white captain panicked, and Smalls took command and brought the ship safely out of danger. For this act of courage, he was made a captain in the Navy and placed in command of the *Planter,* a post he held until September 1866, when the craft was decommissioned.

Returning ashore, Smalls was a natural as a politician. He was a hero to South Carolina blacks for his war record, and the fact that he harbored little animosity toward Southern whites, was good humored, intelligent, fluent in speech, and moderate in his views on Reconstruction made him the least objectionable African-American in the state to whites. His modesty and lack of education alone kept him out of the state's Republican (q.v.) leadership at the beginning. But the black voters knew and respected him, and he served in the state constitutional convention (1868), both houses of the state legislature (1868–1870 in the house, 1871–1874 in the senate), and the U.S. Congress (1875–1879, 1882–1887). He also served in the state militia and rose to the rank of major general (1865–1887).

Smalls was not a flashy congressman, but he attacked South Carolina Democrats (q.v.) for their violent tactics at election time and supported increased access to public accommodations for his race. He was convicted of accepting a bribe while state senator, but he was admired by so many of both races that South Carolina Democrats prevailed upon Governor William D. Simpson to pardon him without serving jail time. He was a loyal Stalwart Republican, opposed civil service reform (q.v.), and favored increased pensions for Union veterans. He also tried to gain an extra $30,000 for his wartime heroism but failed to convince the rest of Congress. In 1889, Smalls was made port collector at Beaufort, a position he held until 1913, with the exception of President Grover Cleveland's second term (1893–1897). In the interim, he was one of six members to the state constitutional convention, which disfranchised blacks within the scope of the Fifteenth Amendment (q.v.), an action that he opposed.

SMITH, EDMUND KIRBY (1824–1893). From St. Augustine, Florida, Edmund Kirby Smith graduated from West Point in 1845, in the lower half of his class. He fought in the War with Mexico and won two brevets for bravery. In 1849–1852, he taught mathematics at the Military Academy, before being sent to the Western frontier. He served on the Mexican Boundary Commission as a botanist and was captain and major in the prestigious 2nd Cavalry before resigning his commission when Florida seceded.

Kirby Smith began the Civil War with spectacular publicity. His was among the last brigades to outflank the Union right at the Battle of First Manassas (q.v.), where he was severely wounded. He married the winsome young lady who sewed his shirts. The wonderful romance made headlines all over the South.

Recovering from his wounds, Kirby Smith was promoted to major general and sent to eastern Kentucky, where he and Gen. Braxton Bragg (q.v.) quarreled with each other and lost the Perryville Campaign (q.v.). Nonetheless, Kirby Smith received the thanks of Congress for his defense of the South and a promotion to lieutenant general. Unabashedly promoting his own career, Kirby Smith asked to be transferred away from Bragg to an independent command. He eventually became a nuisance, so the government sent him off to command the Trans-Mississippi Department out of Shreveport. He remained there for the rest of the war.

In the Trans-Mississippi, Kirby Smith was cut off from the rest of the Confederacy by the Vicksburg and Port Hudson Campaigns (qq.v.). This made him more than a military department commander out of necessity. He also became a pseudo-president of a part of the Confederacy, working with the governors and their legislatures to write and enforce laws and even promote officers, some of it with Richmond's approval, some not. Eventually people came to call the Trans-Mississippi, "Kirby Smithdom." As a military man, recognizing his separateness and importance, Kirby Smith was promoted to full general in February 1864. He worked to defeat the Union Red River Campaign and then drove back the Camden Campaign in Arkansas (qq.v.). He surrendered the last organized Confederate forces in the war in May 1865.

After the war, Kirby Smith fled to Maximilian's Mexico (q.v.) and then Cuba. He returned from exile in November 1865 and went into business as an insurance agent, but failed. Then Kirby Smith was appointed president of the University of Nashville. He thought about the ministry, but decided that he was too old to go into a new profession. Instead, he went to the University of the South at Sewanee, Tennessee, where he taught mathematics for the next 18 years, raising 11 children.

SOCIAL DARWINISM. Society had become more complex with the advent of Union victory, the machine, and big business, all of which had been accelerated by the need to defeat the Confederacy by any means possible. America was changing rapidly, from a rural to an urban society, with all of the complexities that would become common to the 20th century budding out, like want and destitution, unemployment, wandering street people, noise, and pollution. There might have been poverty in the prewar agricultural society, but farmers could grow and consume their own food. Before the Civil War, life had been romantic and comfortable. Events were seen as God's will.

But during Reconstruction, and accelerating in the eras that followed, all of this began to change. Everyone wanted in on the "Great Barbecue"—everyone wanted to preempt, squander, and exploit. It was an age with a lot of brass but very little gilt. It was fed by the alleged ideas of a British scientist, who had lived for a time on the Galapagos Islands off the coast of Ecuador, named Charles Darwin (1809–1882). In 1859, Darwin had published a book on his observations entitled *The Origin of the Species*. Darwin challenged the multiple biblical creation idea by theorizing that all species (he did not ever talk about humans specifically) evolved from a single act of creation. But he never attacked divine creation or biblical revelation. All he did was propose a theory that the animal world evolved from a single cell, as it were.

The problem was not Darwin, but what others made of Darwin, people who carried his implications into the world of human beings and drew pseudo-scientific conclusions about human society, using selected portions of Darwin's thesis for their own ends. The result was something called Social Darwinism, the foremost advocate of which was Englishman Herbert Spencer. In his volume *Synthetic Philosophy*, Spencer claimed that humans passed through evolutionary stages, just like Darwin's animal kingdom. Written in the vernacular rather than in stilted academic prose, Spencer's ideas were an instant success. He gave a feeling of progress and scientific meaning to life beyond the religious. And it was self-congratulatory. It made successful European nations appear as the fittest, following the so-called natural laws put forth in Darwin's work.

All that was needed was for an American scholar to apply Spencer to the United States directly. That man was William Graham Sumner, a Yale University professor. In his book *Folkways*, Sumner united three elements of intellectual interest in the 19th-century United States: the Protestant ethic (work was good for the soul and pacified and cleansed whoever did it); classical economics (the notion that a natural law, *laissez faire*, ruled the wealth of nations); and natural selection (Darwin via Spencer: a person who survived all challenges could manage without the aid or interference of government or other human cooperative groups).

Sumner put in pseudo-scientific terms something that the United States had believed in for a long time, Manifest Destiny. It gave meaning to the success of the nation and the need for other less fortunate peoples to make way for the superior white culture. It told Americans why the Native Americans and the Mexicans were being defeated in the West. And it gave new poignancy to the defeat of the Confederacy, the failure of Reconstruction, and the subordination of the blacks in the East. The race would improve only if the weak were in effect culled out by failure, a human natural selective process. Equality was a false idea that made for mediocrity. Progress was a notion that made for human happiness and was obtained by following natural laws (which Sumner called by a more friendly term, "folkways"), without government interference.

Once Spencer and Sumner had handled the secular justification, it remained necessary to join them with religion. The result was the Gospel of Wealth. Most American millionaires at that time were Protestant, and a majority of those were Calvinist. Many had a lot to do with their religious denominations. They came to believe that God was only superficially against wealth. Were one to dig deeper in the scriptures, ran the argument, one would find that godliness was in league with wealth and property rights; indeed, one had a duty to labor and become wealthy, for it revealed God's blessing. It also promoted democracy by emphasizing individualism, liberty, and *laissez faire*. Through hard work, sobriety, frugality, initiative, and a pietistic use of wealth to promote a Christian society, survival of the fittest became holy and the American way. Indeed, the assistance to others through God's great gift of personal wealth built one's own personal character.

The fortunate person who gained wealth was obligated to live modestly, shun ostentatious display, provide modestly for one's heirs (the less the better, as it would make them struggle to survive like everyone else), but give the rest back to the less fortunate. Wealth was allowed to accumulate so that one person might use its concentration more effectively with a greater impact than a thousand less wealthy could dream of doing. To die rich was disgraceful, and it took more talent to give one's riches away than it did to earn them in the first place. Hence it was best to divest oneself of wealth during one's own lifetime, to see the job was properly done. If one failed to meet this obligation, some suggested that the government confiscate excess wealth upon the owner's death.

Although many adopted Social Darwinism as their own, the concept was not without its critics. The Religion of Humanity was a secular criticism that admitted to the efficacy of Social Darwinism but preferred to water down its excessive individualism by emphasizing group action. But the churches were not about to lose out to changes in late 19th-century thought. Their response was the Social Gospel, an attack on the rampant individualism of Social Darwinism, through the reorganization of traditional religion. It challenged Christians to respond to slums and wretched economic conditions brought on by industrialism and the development of the cities by walking in the steps of Christ and following the Golden Rule in a united effort of all churches, regardless of denomination.

Other critics, like the New Rationalists or New Humanists, issued the first calls for the welfare state that would be so common in the 20th century. They hoped by applying scientific principles of "dynamic sociology" to curb the excesses of wealth and the industrial revolution and create a heaven on Earth, instead of the hell that currently existed. The main way to achieve any reform of society was through education. Called pragmatism, because it rejected the straitjacket of any one system of ideas as a single truth, this philosophy believed that truth was relative to existing experiences and conditions. The result of the interplay of all of these ideas was a breakdown of the rigid society that existed in America before the Civil War.

SOCIAL GOSPEL. *See* SOCIAL DARWINISM.

SOULÉ, PIERRE (1802–1870). Born and raised in France, Pierre Soulé was educated in Jesuit schools in Toulouse and Bordeaux. He was involved in a plot against Louis XVIII and fled to the Pyrenees, where he worked as a shepherd. Returning with a change of regimes, Soulé became a journalist and wrote a scathing criticism of the ministers of Charles X. This time he beat the police to Britain and then traveled to Haiti and the United States. He lived in Maryland, Kentucky, and Tennessee, working as a gardener and learning English, before he arrived in New Orleans. There he read law and was admitted to the bar.

Soulé was a natural in French-speaking Louisiana. He served in the state senate and then for a term in the U.S. Senate, as a Democrat (q.v.). With the accession of Franklin Pierce (q.v.) to the presidency, Soulé was appointed minister to Spain and was one of the authors of the controversial Ostend Manifesto (q.v.), calling for the annexation of Cuba to the U.S. Recalled, he returned to New Orleans and practiced law. He backed Stephen A. Douglas (q.v.) for president in the election of 1860 (q.v.) and, although a Unionist, he followed his state in secession.

During the Civil War, Soulé made several diplomatic trips for the Confederacy to Europe. He was arrested in occupied New Orleans and faced with a firing squad, but a change in Union commanding generals saved his life. He served as a staff officer for Gen. P. G. T. Beauregard (q.v.) at the Siege of Charleston and evidently tried unsuccessfully to recruit a foreign legion to serve the Confederacy. At the end of the war, he fled to Cuba and sponsored a scheme to settle Confederate veterans in Maximilian's Mexico (q.v.). He later returned to New Orleans and practiced law until his death.

SOUTHERN CLAIMS COMMISSION. One of the oddities of the Civil War was that there was no "Solid South" or "Solid North." Over 300,000 Southerners served in Union blue. Large geographical sections of the

South had pro-Union populations, especially in the Appalachian region of Virginia, North Carolina, and Tennessee; the northern parts of Arkansas; the western parts of Texas; and a smattering of counties in other Confederate states.

In the 50 years that followed the Civil War, Congress received a constant stream of appeals by loyal citizens for claims for goods taken, given, and used by the advancing Union armies under the Confiscation Acts and the Captured and Abandoned Property Act (qq.v.). It was one of the reasons that the Freedman's Bureau (q.v.) had departments for refugees and abandoned lands. The problem became so involved and proof was so often lacking in the form of proper vouchers that in 1871 Congress established the Southern Claims Commission to supervise the process. Its jurisdiction involved the legitimate claims held by loyal Southern whites against the government for services rendered during the war, a recognition that some of the white South had done the "right" thing and suffered unfairly for it.

A three-man commission was established to look into the validity of the claims. President Ulysses S. Grant (q.v.) appointed Judge Asa Owen Aldis of Vermont, ex-Representative Orange Ferris of New York, and ex-Senator James B. Howell of Iowa as the commission members. The board was to last two years, but it soon became evident from the number of claims filed in the first two days that it would have to be continued for many years. Eventually 22,298 claims worth over $60 million were filed.

By 1880, the Southern Claims Commission had paid $4.6 million, which compares to the nearly $10 million allowed by the Federal Court of Claims, which handled cotton and contraband confiscations. This would seem to indicate that the commission was very careful with the government's money, although public newspapers saw it as a vast boondoggle that aided people of dubious loyalty, at best.

SOUTHERN HOMESTEAD ACT OF 1866. After the Civil War, the South became a laboratory for experimentation in the sales of public lands. When the South seceded from the Union, there were nearly 48 million acres of public land held by the states of Alabama, Arkansas, Florida, Mississippi, and Louisiana. All other Southern states had no Federal lands within their boundaries. Generally, it was believed that these Southern lands were fairly worthless to individual farmers. They had been on the market since the 1830s at the standard $1.25 an acre, and in 1854 under the Graduated Land Act, prices had been reduced relative to time on the market to as low as 12.5 cents an acre, with no appreciable increase in sales.

One of the staunchest Radical Republicans of his day was U.S. Senator George W. Julian (q.v.) of Indiana. Julian decided to put his love of black liberty and land for the average American together in the Southern Homestead

Act of 1866. It was a measure designed to reserve the unused portions of the South in 80 acre plots to persons who could take the ironclad oath, that is, loyal whites and especially the freedmen. It would be as close to "forty acres and a mule" (q.v.) as most ex-slaves would get.

The Southern Homestead Act lasted until the end of Reconstruction in 1876. By then it had become obvious to the Redeemers (q.v.) that economic development of these marginal farm lands would depend on their use for lumber or railroads. So as Southern states gained more power in Congress, its senators and representatives began to jockey for the repeal of Julian's program. They were assisted by the facts that Julian had retired in 1870 and was no longer present to wield his considerable influence and the end of Reconstruction fervor on behalf of the freedmen, upon which the individual homesteads had been based. Hence the Southern Homestead Act was repealed, and the lands were sold off to corporations that specialized in the timber business, most of which were Northern owned, particularly in Florida, Mississippi, and Louisiana. The best stands of cypress and yellow pine were in the hands of nonresident speculators who took the cream of the profits, looting the South once more. It is a seamy side of Reconstruction policy that one author cleverly described as the "Era of Good Stealings."

SOUTHERN MOVEMENT. *See* COMPROMISE OF 1850.

SOUTHERN RECONSTRUCTION. *See* RECONSTRUCTION, SOUTHERN.

SOUTHERN THEORY OF RECONSTRUCTION. *See* RECONSTRUCTION, THEORIES OF.

SPANISH FORT, BATTLE OF. *See* MOBILE CAMPAIGN.

SPECIAL FIELD ORDERS NO. 15. Issued by Maj. Gen. William T. Sherman (q.v.) on January 16, 1865, this edict set aside all land between the St. Mary's River in northern Florida and Charleston, South Carolina, and 30 miles inland for the exclusive use of blacks, provided that it had not already been sold for nonpayment of taxes. Individual tracts were not to exceed 40 acres each. This order was later canceled under President Andrew Johnson's pardon policies (qq.v.), but African-Americans managed to purchase large amounts of this land, especially in coastal areas like that near Port Royal (q.v.), which gave them a unique, independent economic base uncommon to the rest of the South.

SPECIAL ORDERS NO. 191. *See* LEE'S "LOST ORDER."

SPECIAL TAX COMMISSION. The Civil War caused a tremendous business expansion in the North, the problems of which came to a head during the Ulysses S. Grant (q.v.) administration and would result in big business becoming a major voice in the Republican Party (q.v.), once dominated by farmers and small businessmen. The two problems of concern to business at this time were taxes and the tariff on foreign imports. The war had caused all taxes to rise precipitously and new ones, like the income tax, to be imposed. At the same time, the Republicans had elevated the tariff to new heights as part of the fulfillment of their political platform. Now that the war was over, Americans expected relief on both accounts. Everyone wanted taxes reduced, but the tariff was another matter. Business and labor groups wanted to exclude goods from lower-wage-paying producers overseas for better profits to owners and higher wages for American workers.

Grant appointed a blue-ribbon Special Tax Commission under David A. Wells, a professional economist once considered as a possible secretary of the treasury. Grant had promised lower taxes in his inaugural message and pledged economy in government to help reduce costs (as usual for an incoming administration). The Wells Committee took a look at the taxes and suggested that nearly all be repealed or reduced dramatically. This was very good publicity for the Republicans and raised their esteem among the voters. But Wells also suggested that the protective tariff be cut to nothing. He said that the tariff did not so much protect American infant industries from unfair foreign competition as it permitted existing industries to raise prices to just under the tariff costs to foreign competitors for extra unearned profits. Wells correctly saw that the difference came out of the pockets of American consumers.

The Republican Congress thanked Wells for his concern and lowered taxes as he suggested. But it kept the high tariff intact. It was too big a pork barrel issue—too many people of influence in the party were making money off the tariff differential. They all banded together, and each voted for the tariff to protect himself and everyone else. The Republicans were not above playing the tariff card in a wholly arbitrary manner. For example, they cut all tariffs 10 percent in 1872 to help Republican congressmen win their seats, and then raised it back up after the victory. The tariff would be a political football like this until the New Deal of the 1930s, when Congress turned the tariff-making power over to the president, who used it as a treaty device through the Department of State.

SPENCER, HERBERT. *See* SOCIAL DARWINISM.

SPOTSYLVANIA COURT HOUSE, BATTLES OF. *See* RICHMOND OR OVERLAND CAMPAIGN.

"SPREAD EAGLE" FOREIGN POLICY. During the administrations of Franklin Pierce and James Buchanan (qq.v.), the United States practiced what was called "Spread Eagle" foreign policy. This involved support for the Monroe Doctrine (Europe to stay out of the Americas, America to stay out of European questions) and expansion into the American West and Latin America, generally under the term Manifest Destiny, which implied that expansion was America's God-given right.

Spread Eagle foreign policy had many guises. One was the belief in "Young America," the concept that the United States was a youthful republic on the rise, as opposed to the "effete monarchies" of Europe, which Americans saw on the decline. As such it was the duty of the United States to back the European revolutionaries of 1848, to give them aid when they were fighting in the streets and citizenship and a new home when they were on the run, after the revolutions failed. Of course, this seemed to violate the Monroe Doctrine, but Americans were very contradictory and unscrupulous about all of this.

One of the qualities of Spread Eagle foreign policy was American interest in trade with the Orient. The United States was to follow the setting sun to riches and glory, went the old saw. Franklin Pierce made the first attempts to annex Hawaii, an important stop on the trip from the Isthmus of Panama to San Francisco. Because of tides and winds, ships for the California coast first sailed to Hawaii, then to their continental destinations. The U.S. Senate refused to go along with Pierce's expansionism.

Another hot spot for Americans was China. Impelled by British concessions won in the Opium Wars, the United States demanded and received trading rights in five Chinese ports as early as 1844 in the Treaty of Wanghia. This treaty was an example of "jackal diplomacy." It guaranteed America the same rights as any other power might receive through any other treaty. In 1858, when Great Britain and France forced the Treaty of Tientsin on China, the United States received the same expanded rights of trade through the earlier Treaty of Wanghia.

The trade with China naturally led to interest in Japan, an important stopover for coal and provisions. Japan had closed her ports to all Westerners after excessive Christian missionary zeal had led to dissatisfaction in the island nation. In 1852, Com. Matthew C. Perry had visited Tokyo Bay with a great fleet, which included the first steam warship the Japanese had ever seen. Perry refused to talk to any but the highest authorities, saying he was carrying letters from the American president to the Japanese emperor. He threatened war if rebuffed, but after 10 days of fruitless negotiation, he sailed away.

The following year, he returned with more ships than ever. Japanese merchants managed to prevail upon their government to agree to the Perry Pact. This called for fair treatment of shipwrecked sailors, fuel and water for ships in need, and some trade. The United States pledged not to ask for extraterritorial rights, as Western powers had in China. Townsend Harris arrived as the first American consul, and after patiently working with the suspicious Japanese, he obtained the Harris Treaty of 1858. This opened more ports, secured trade and residence rights for Americans with extraterritorial judicial privileges, and provided for the exchange of ministers (ambassadors). This treaty would last until 1911.

The other area for expanding American influence in the world was Latin America. But here the United States relied less on formal diplomacy and more on irregular military expeditions, a process called filibustering (q.v.).

SPRING HILL. *See* NASHVILLE CAMPAIGN.

SQUATTER SOVEREIGNTY. The concept that the residents of a territory could abolish slavery at any time before statehood by a popular vote. Its most vocal and noted backer was Lewis Cass (q.v.) of Michigan, who advocated it as the Democrat candidate in the election of 1848 (qq.v.). It ran counter to the Southern-favored concept of popular sovereignty (q.v.). But it was a deceptive non-exclusion (q.v.) formula without the hostility engendered by the Wilmot Proviso (q.v.), as recognized by John C. Calhoun. There were more Yankees than southerners in the territories. Joined with antislave Mexicans, they would control territorial governments and vote for Free Soil.

ST. ALBANS, RAID. *See* LINCOLN ASSASSINATION; LINCOLN AS-SASSINATION, THE CONFEDERACY AND THE; LINCOLN ASSAS-SINATION, THE NEW YORK CONNECTION OF THE.

STANTON, EDWIN MCM. (1814–1869). The eldest son of a Steubenville, Ohio, Quaker physician, Edwin Stanton's father died when the boy was but 13 years old, forcing him to leave school and go to work at a bookstore. Continuing his studies when he could, he finally managed to work his way through Kenyon College and read law. He was admitted to the bar in 1836 and began a small private practice before becoming a partner with Ohio's U.S. senator-elect, Benjamin Tappan. Stanton showed great energy, ingenuity, and fidelity, which allowed him to make much money as an attorney. He moved from Steubenville to Pittsburgh and then Washington, D.C., and began to practice before the U.S. Supreme Court. Stanton's forte was the intense research and labor he put into each presentation and the meticulous way in which he pursued the facts.

Because of Stanton's reputation, he was made attorney general during the waning days of the James Buchanan (q.v.) administration. Stanton had had little to do with politics before that, although he was a Jacksonian Democrat (q.v.). He was against the spread of slavery into the Mexican Cession and disliked the domination of Democratic (q.v.) ruling circles by southerners. Stanton was willing, however, to accept the Dred Scott (q.v.) decision in 1857 (which declared the Missouri Compromise unconstitutional and invalidated claims of Negro citizenship) and support John Breckinridge's (q.v.) presidential campaign in 1860 (the pro-slavery candidate), believing that they offered the only hope of preventing secession (q.v.). But when it came to war, Stanton was in favor of force to hold onto Federal property in the South and force the South back into the Union.

Although he hated President Abraham Lincoln (q.v.) and his Republican cohorts, Stanton came into the cabinet in January 1862 as secretary to clean up the poor administration in the Department of War. A stout man of medium height with thick glasses and a long, stringy beard, Stanton's stern visage would become one of the best known in America by the end of the war. He was fierce in his appearance and attitude, leading one critic to label him the "black terrier." Stanton always made quick decisions and, right or wrong, stuck to them.

As secretary of war, Stanton was controversial, to say the least. He apparently was a pathological liar, playing all sides against the middle. But he was a meticulous administrator, honest in a monetary sense, and loyal to the Union cause, which was what Lincoln needed. Stanton reorganized the whole department, established assistant secretaries to whom he delegated specific tasks, cleaned up the corruption (q.v.) rampant in the procurement system, and railed against anyone in a civilian or military position who was disloyal or not pushing the war effort sufficiently. He was gruff and rude. Influential soldiers and civilians alike feared a penetrating interview by Stanton more than they did an attack by the Rebels. Stanton looked into the background and tactics of generals and cooperated with the powerful congressional Joint Committee on the Conduct of the War (q.v.), firing the slackers and fixing blame for all defeats. He ran the vast system of arrests and incarceration of suspected sympathizers in the so-called American Bastille, disregarding their constitutional rights at will. No modern secret police was more diligent in its work than were Stanton's agents.

In short, the states' rights, unionist Democrat became the most ultra of Radical Republicans. He turned on his friend, Bvt. Maj. Gen. George B. McClellan (q.v.); was the originator of many of the most uncomplimentary nicknames of President Lincoln ("the original gorilla"); and would stab anyone in the back in the most slimy fashion to further what he saw as the proper carrying out of the Union cause. After the war, Stanton pursued the Lincoln assassins, saw to it that the conspirators were tried by a tough military commission rather than a possibly weak civilian jury, and hanged and jailed the guilty (and the innocent, some would say). When Maj. Gen. William T. Sherman (q.v.) gave even milder terms to the Confederate army surrendering in North

Carolina than Lt. Gen. Ulysses S. Grant (q.v.) had given Confederate Gen. Robert E. Lee (q.v.), Stanton nullified the act and made him cut any implied political references to the legality of existing Southern state governments.

After Lincoln's death, President Andrew Johnson (q.v.) asked Stanton to stay on. As during the war, Stanton acted as a Radical Republican spy inside the cabinet, keeping important senators and representatives informed as to Johnson's planned course of action, kissing up to everyone in turn. He urged Johnson to accept Congress' version of Reconstruction from the renewal of the Freedmen's Bureau Bill to the Civil Rights Act of 1866 to the Fourteenth Amendment to the Military Reconstruction Acts (qq.v.), then helped him write his vetoes of the same legislation. Aware of Stanton's importance, Congress responded with the Tenure of Office Act (q.v.), designed to protect presidential appointments from easy removal, although there is some doubt as to whether the act really applied to Lincoln selections like Stanton. Johnson's closest advisors warned him to get rid of Stanton, lest he threaten the whole administration. Stanton ignored Johnson's suggestions that he resign, determined to hold on for the good of the country. This forced Johnson to fire him outright, a process that he initiated when Congress went out of session in late 1867, hoping to have it all completed before Congress reassembled so he could present them with a *fait accompli*. But Stanton outmaneuvered the lackluster man Johnson sent to do the job and held on, fortified behind his office door, which was barricaded like the gate of a city under siege.

Stanton's sacrifice was well appreciated by the Radicals, who recognized it for what it was—a golden opportunity to impeach the president for interfering with Congressional Reconstruction (q.v.). But when the impeachment (q.v.) charges failed, Stanton accepted the inevitable and resigned on May 26, 1868. Stanton's vigor in prosecuting the Civil War and Reconstruction had cost him much of his health. He took a long rest and tried to resume his law practice. He also acted as a political advisor to the first Ulysses S. Grant (q.v.) campaign, for which he was rewarded with a seat on the U.S. Supreme Court. But Stanton died shortly after the Senate confirmed his appointment.

STATE RIGHTS FACTION. Although there were no real political parties in the Confederacy, there were political pressure groups, one of which was the State Rights Faction. This was a group of Southern politicians opposed to what they believed was President Jefferson Davis' (q.v.) unconstitutional centralizing of the government in Richmond to win the war at the expense of state rights principles, for which they believed the Confederacy seceded from the Union in the first place. Of course, this concept ignored the real secession (q.v.) issue, which was fear that Abraham Lincoln's Republicans (qq.v.) would not observe the extraterritorial issue of slavery (*see* EXTRA-TERRITORIALITY OF SLAVERY) as guaranteed in the fugitive clause and the Ninth and Tenth Amendments and confirmed by the U.S. Supreme Court in the case of Dred Scott *v.* Sandford (q.v.).

The State Rights Faction was led by, among others, the vice president of the Confederacy, Alexander Stephens (q.v.). These men believed that President Davis was guilty of centralizing the Confederate government in Richmond, instead of yielding power to the states and the people. They overlooked the fact that to win the war, there would have to be unprecedented cooperation and coordination of national effort in the hands of the executive departments and the presidency. But the States' Rights Faction was more interested in sustaining a principle than securing independence. It was shortsighted. If they thought that the Confederate government did not respect state rights, they surely would not get even a modicum of respect for their views from a reconstructed Union run by Republicans.

The State Rights Faction opposed the Davis administration on three major issues. The first was the Conscription Acts (q.v.). The Confederate Constitution did not give the right to raise troops to the central government, unless the states voluntarily contributed a quota upon request. Conscription was a state right. The problem was not the necessity of the national draft—everyone agreed that it was necessary to continue. The question was its legality.

The State Rights Faction dared not openly obstruct the war effort out of pure spite. Supporters got around it legally. For example, Governor Joseph Brown (q.v.) of Georgia created 2,000 extra justices of the peace and 1,000 new constables, all exempt from the draft. Brown also enrolled 10,000 men in the state militia and kept them in the state for defense. Then, at the height of Union Bvt. Maj. Gen. William T. Sherman's March to the Sea (qq.v.), he furloughed them home for 30 days to harvest crops, which Sherman was burning, anyway. Brown was loved in his state and reelected in 1863 by a large majority.

Like Brown, Gov. Zebulon Vance of North Carolina quarreled over state rights. Vance was elected governor in 1862 on a program of vigorous prosecution of the war. He wanted drafted men to be able to choose their own regiments. He wanted North Carolina troops brigaded together and commanded by North Carolina officers, rather than by "strangers." He refused to permit Confederate officials to collect taxes within the state. He refused to permit Confederate officials to distill medical whiskey from 30,000 bushels of grain because it violated state law. He refused to reserve half of the cargo space in the collection of blockade runners in which he had an interest. He refused to contribute state-owned war supplies to troops from any other state but North Carolina. While Robert E. Lee's (q.v.) men lacked clothing, blankets, and shoes at the Siege of Petersburg (q.v.) during the winter of 1864, Vance stored 92,000 uniforms and uncounted blankets and raw leather for future North Carolina use.

Besides the conscription issue, the State Rights Faction opposed the suspension of the writ of *habeas corpus* (q.v.). Whether by local commanders, Davis himself, or Congress, the state righters viewed the suspension as tyranny against the states by the Confederate government. But the biggest issue between the State Rights Faction and Davis was the peace issue. The state rights men claimed that Davis unnecessarily prolonged the war by failing to take allegedly innumerable chances to make peace with the North. Again, the opposition to Davis centered in Georgia and revolved around Vice President Stephens, his brother, Linton, and Governor Brown.

In 1864, Brown called a special session of the Georgia state legislature, and Linton Stephens led them in denouncing conscription and the suspension of *habeas corpus*, and demanded that President Davis convene a peace conference. If Davis did not move fast, the Georgia legislature threatened to combine with two other states and call a constitutional convention to limit Richmond's power. "Liberty before Independence," was their slogan. Gen. Sherman, invading the state, was so impressed that he offered to meet with any state delegation and discuss separate peace terms for Georgia. Of course, he offered neither liberty nor independence—just abject surrender.

To shut up Vice President Stephens and his cohorts, Davis appointed him to lead a three-man commission to discuss peace with President Abraham Lincoln at the Hampton Roads Peace Conference (q.v.). Nothing came of the effort, and Stephens went home to Georgia and stayed there until the Yankees arrested him at war's end. As Stephens and his allies demonstrated, it was much easier for the North to centralize its war effort than the more individualistic South, if for no other reason than Southerners made a fetish of being individualistic for the sake of individualism.

STATE SOVEREIGNTY AND SLAVERY—THE U.S. SUPREME COURT VINDICATES THE SOUTH AND THE NON-EXCLUSION DOCTRINE. Even with Federal domestic and foreign policy (q.v.) support to abet the expansion of slavery (q.v.) and the cotton culture westward into new lands below the Mason–Dixon Line, as the North abandoned slavery after the American Revolution, the Old South became more and more a conscious white minority within the nation. From the very beginning, there was an argument between those southerners who believed that their right to slaves was best protected within the Union under the Constitution of 1787 and those who thought that the Old South ought to opt to become a nation in its own right, with its own pro-slave fundamental law. The first theory was called state sovereignty, and its success was condemned by the North as the Slave Power Conspiracy. The second was called secession (q.v.), and was always a thorn in the side of southern Cooperators and their Yankee political allies, northern men of southern principles, when it came to slavery and race.

Contrary to popularly held notions of modern Americans, a clear majority of the white South was very much against limiting the power of the Federal government before the Civil War—when it came to protecting slavery as an institution. This was the difference between those who advocated cooperation and those who wanted secession. The Cooperators realized that the Constitution offered the South many advantages in preserving their "peculiar institution." This has been concealed, because historians have usually interpreted the Constitutional Convention as a quarrel between big states and small states. In reality, there was a more important division—between those who opposed slavery and those who wished to protect it, under the Constitution of 1787.

The process was simple. The delegates from South Carolina and Georgia, led by such luminaries as Charles Cotesworth Pinckney of South Carolina, refused to endorse the new document without certain pro-slavery concessions. Sufficient northerners from New England wanted the new document for its free trade, common market advantages badly enough to yield to southern blackmail, and worry about the consequences later. It was a deal that the northerners' grandchildren would refuse to live under, and the southerners' progeny would refuse to modify in 1861.

The South had many reasons to laud the new fundamental document that replaced the Articles of Confederation. Unlike the Articles of Confederation, the new Constitution had a stated and an unstated concept of extraterritoriality, when it came to slavery. The overt statement came through the fugitive clause, which guaranteed the return of anyone held to "service or labor" to his or her state of origin (art. IV, sect. 2). What this phrase did was give slavery an extraterritorial nature. That meant the "peculiar institution" could be enforced outside the boundaries of the slave states in the so-called free states of the North. This was a compulsory thing—quite separate from criminal extradition, a voluntary legal process between states, which the U.S. Supreme Court unanimously upheld in Ableman v. Booth (q.v.) in 1859.

But it was the covert concept of extraterritoriality that brought the final break between North and South. This concerned the advance of slavery into the Western territories. Not only was this attempt subtle, it was very involved. Both sides, pro-slave and antislave, realized that the territories were the key to breaking the Old South's hold on the constitutional argument for an extraterritorial application of slave law in the West.

The question in the West revolved around a problem in the Constitution. The document recognized two legitimate governing authorities existing in the United States, Federal and state. But in reality there were three: Federal, state and territorial. The administration of territories was reserved to the Federal government (art. IV, sect. 3, clause 2), but the Constitution defined Federal territories as only the District of Columbia, Federal forts, and Federal dockyards (art. I, sect. 8, clause 17). The territories in the West were not mentioned.

The key was who would administer the police powers (health, safety, morals, well-being) in the unorganized West. The Old South maintained that powers not specifically defined in the Constitution (art. I, sect. 8) were reserved to the states and the people through the Bill of Rights, especially the Ninth and Tenth Amendments to the Constitution. The Old South admitted that the many states and divers peoples could not enforce the wide variety of state and local law in the territories. So that right had to be granted to the Federal government, not as a sovereign, but as a trustee (agent) of all the states and people.

Hence, the Old South argued that the Federal government had no right to make policy (as it lacked sovereignty), but only to enforce any extraterritorial powers of the sovereign states as recognized in the Constitution. The only such power was the extraterritoriality of slavery, recognized through the fugitive clause.

This meant that of all the theories that Congress entertained over the years that referred to slavery in the West, only one obtained, the southerners' Non-Exclusion Doctrine (q.v.). This held that all territories had to be opened to slavery, until the territory achieved popular sovereignty. That happened only when Congress accepted the territory as a state, after the occupants wrote their state constitution. Only states had the sovereignty the territories lacked and could abolish or keep slavery.

The North argued that the nation ought to accept congressional laws on excluding slavery from the West, and that the precedent had been set even before the Constitution was written. In 1787, under the Articles of Confederation's last gasp, Congress had passed the Northwest Ordinance creating the Old Northwest Territory (current Ohio, Indiana, Illinois, Michigan, Wisconsin, and parts of Minnesota) with slavery excluded from the whole area at its inception. Again, in 1820, under the Constitution, Congress had legislated the Missouri Compromise, which admitted Maine (free state) and Missouri (slave state) into the Union, but excluded slavery in the West, synonymous then with the Louisiana Purchase, north of the southern boundary (36° 30′ line of latitude) of Missouri.

Because Congress had passed the Gag Rule, designed to keep the slavery debate off the floor from 1835 to 1845, and there were no new territories annexed after the acquisition of Florida in 1819 and the enactment of the Missouri Compromise of 1820, the question of slavery in the territories became moot. This lasted until Texas joined the Union in 1845, and Mexico was defeated and dismembered in 1848. With the Mexican Cession (the desert Southwest of today), the problem of slavery in the territories became the single most important issue in the Old South's relation with the free states.

Much of this new land lay south of the Missouri Compromise line and was open to slavery.

To preserve the West for free, white, nonslaveholding men only, free-soil congressmen coalesced around the Wilmot Proviso (q.v.), a northern proposal that no slavery be allowed in the territory won from Mexico (already a sovereign state, Texas was excluded from the measure). In the election of 1848, Democrats (q.v.) proposed that slavery be decided by those living in the territories as soon as a territorial legislature was created. This came to be called squatter sovereignty (q.v.).

But the Old South would have none of that. Non-exclusion of slavery (q.v.) in the territories meant non-exclusion. Southern Democrats countered with the Alabama Platform, which urged popular sovereignty (q.v.)—a popular vote on slavery's permanence in a territory, only after the populace ratified a proposed state constitution and achieved sovereignty or self-rule. Squatter sovereignty cost the Democrats the election of 1848, because the Old South went for the Whig candidate, Louisiana planter and military hero Maj. Gen. Zachary Taylor (q.v.), who was allegedly safe on the slavery question. In the ensuing Compromise of 1850 (q.v.), Congress sought to bury the problem of slavery in the territories by avoiding mention of it altogether. The implication was popular sovereignty, but it was only an unmentioned hint.

The issue sprang up again in the election of 1852 (q.v.). This time, the Democrats adopted popular sovereignty openly and carried the South. Then, southern senators moved to hold the organization of the Great Plains west of the Missouri River hostage. They had four critical votes and forced the creation of two territories, Kansas and Nebraska, implying Kansas to the south was for slaveholders and the other for free staters. The Old South got its way in Congress, because men like Democrat Senator Stephen A. Douglas (q.v.) of Illinois were more interested in developing railroads in the West, come what may on slavery. But, as Kansas was above the Missouri Compromise line (36°30′ north latitude), Congress overrode that limitation in the Kansas–Nebraska Act (q.v.).

Douglas and the Old South had underestimated the impact of the slavery issue. Both North and South headed for Kansas and ignored Nebraska. The resulting Kansas–Missouri Border Wars (q.v.) presaged the coming Civil War, as the few southern settlers struggled in vain against overwhelming numbers of free state settlers to write the first state constitution. Meanwhile, back east, the new Republican Party arose, dedicated to stopping the advance of slavery westward.

Then, the thunderclap of the decade struck. The U.S. Supreme Court ruled on the question of slavery in the territories. The 1857 court case was Dred Scott *v.* Sandford (q.v.). In it the court ruled seven to two in favor of the southern position, the Non-Exclusion Doctrine, on slavery in the West. But the justices could not agree on why. Chief Justice Roger B. Taney (q.v.) of Maryland, a slaveholder who had already manumitted his own chattels, wrote the definitive opinion.

What Taney did was to confirm the southern position on slavery and its extraterritorial rights, direct and implied, in the Constitution. When added to the unanimous pro-southern decision in Ableman v. Booth two years later, legitimizing the 1850 Fugitive Slave Act (q.v.), the Old South's concept of slavery, and the United States government's obligation to support its extraterritoriality, was complete.

The Cooperators believed that each state was sovereign within it own borders, immune to outside control on all domestic matters. But beyond state borders, the Old South held that, because of the extraterritoriality guaranteed to slave institutions through the Constitution, it was the duty of the Federal government to enforce state laws on slavery everywhere in the United States—in the free states and in the territories. This is what Abraham Lincoln (q.v.) referred to in his 1858 "House Divided" speech—that the nation could not exist half slave and half free, but would soon become all one or the other, and the Constitution of 1787, as interpreted by the U.S. Supreme Court, beckoned the nation toward slavery. The case that would decide this, Lemmon v. The People of New York, was already on its way to the Supreme Court, only stopped by the outbreak of the Civil War.

There are historians who theorize that most of this was accidental and not intended by the Founding Fathers. But there would seem to be more to the mix than sharp southern politicians twisting the Constitution to their own liking. The pro-southern tilt was endemic in the original document, merely waiting to be utilized.

STATE SUICIDE THEORY. *See* RECONSTRUCTION, THEORIES OF.

STEPHENS, ALEXANDER H. (1812–1883). A native-born Georgian, Alexander Stephens was privately educated as a child for the ministry. He had changed his mind by the time he graduated from Franklin College (now the University of Georgia) and went into the law. This quite naturally led him into politics as a Whig Party (q.v.) legislator opposed to nullification. He attended the Charleston Commercial Convention and was elected to Congress in 1843. He was for the annexation of the Republic of Texas, but opposed President John Tyler's measure, so he wrote one himself that became the basis for admitting Texas into the Union. He was not in favor of the War with Mexico, working in league with his friend, Congressman Abraham Lincoln (q.v.) of Illinois, to oppose it. But he favored its outcome as good for the South and opposed the limitations of the Wilmot Proviso (q.v.) on southern exploitation of the newly won territories.

In 1850, Stephens opposed the Southern Movement and favored compromise. Stephens wrote the Georgia Platform, declaring that the South would reluctantly accept the Compromise of 1850 (q.v.) and continued Union, but zealously guard its rights hereafter. He refused to support Bvt. Lt. Gen. Winfield Scott (q.v.) as the latter refused to support the Compromise of 1850. In 1854, Stephens piloted the Kansas–Nebraska Bill (q.v.) through the House, breaking the southern Whigs off from their northern brethren. Stephens supported the popular sovereignty stand of President James Buchanan (q.v.), until Buchanan violated its principles in the Kansas Settlement (q.v.). Stephens then resigned his House seat.

In the election of 1860 (q.v.), Stephens supported the candidacy of Stephen A. Douglas (q.v.). In 1861, he encouraged cooperation with the Lincoln administration until it committed an overt act against the South. But when Georgia seceded, Stephens went along. He was elected vice president of the Provisional Government of the Confederacy at Montgomery and again a year later in the Confederate election of 1863. His famous "Cornerstone Speech," delivered at Savannah, declared slavery to be the centerpiece of the Confederacy. Stephens was unable to reconcile his theories of state rights with the realities of fighting the war. The State Rights Faction (q.v.) gathered around him, but rather than leading, Stephens went home to Georgia for most of the war. He thought that the Jefferson Davis (q.v.) administration could make peace if it but tried. Tired of Stephens' carping, Davis sent him to the Hampton Roads Peace Conference (q.v.) in 1865. There Stephens met with his old friend Lincoln and failed to come up with anything short of Southern surrender.

Stephens was arrested at his home and lodged in Ft. Warren at Boston Harbor for six months, then released. He was elected to the U.S. Senate in 1866 as a part of the so-called Confederate Brigadiers (q.v.), but was not seated. He spent the rest of Reconstruction writing his *A Constitutional View of the Late War Between the States*. In 1872, he lost a re-try for the U.S. Senate, but was elected to the U.S. House in 1874 and served until 1882. He was against the Civil Rights Bill of 1874, the election of 1876, and the Compromise of 1877, but advised acquiescence. In 1882, he was elected governor of Georgia but died before the end of his term. No matter his party or his office, Stephens remained consistent in his political principles to the end: state sovereignty, local government, and the greatest liberty to the individual.

STEVENS, THADDEUS (1792–1868). The last of four sons whose father either died or abandoned the family when he was but a small boy (the record is uncertain), Thaddeus Stevens had a hard childhood that was made even more difficult by his poor health and a club foot. Early on, he developed a dislike for the rich and aristocratic, although he aspired himself to become wealthy. He was born in Vermont and raised there and in Massachusetts, growing up on the frontier, educated in local schools, and developing a very individualistic and democratic outlook common to America's backcountry. He entered Dartmouth as a sophomore and graduated in 1814. He also attended the University of Vermont briefly. He had the usual classic training from early American colleges but soon turned to reading law to pass the bar and make a living. He became a forceful public speaker with a great wit that was spiced with an often bitter invective. He moved to York, Pennsylvania, to teach at a local academy and complete his law studies.

After passing the bar examination in 1816, he set up practice at nearby Gettysburg. His law business grew slowly, but by the late 1820s, Stevens had earned a reputation as an inventive and thorough attorney and began to pick up some of the biggest and most lucrative cases in the region. He was a hater of slavery, especially after he won a case to return a fugitive to her master in Maryland. Thereafter Stevens atoned for this moral slip by spending money he had saved for his law library to buy and liberate one slave and gladly defending all fugitives brought before local courts for free. Yet he was also suspected in the mysterious murder of a young slave woman in Adams County, Pennsylvania. But the charge was never proven and never adversely affected his later career, especially after Stevens turned the case into an attack on the Masonic Order, which he claimed was out to destroy him for his opposition to its secret councils.

As his legal practice grew, Stevens entered the iron business with partner James D. Paxton and bought a new forge he named Caledonia Furnace. He served from 1833 to 1841 in the Pennsylvania assembly and became noted for his uncompromising stands on issues, particularly against the Masonic Lodge and slavery (especially in the District of Columbia as the seat of American democracy) and for free public schools, the protective tariff, the right of citizens to petition government, and a constitutional limit on the public debt. He excoriated his opponents regularly with his fiery rhetoric, by now a Stevens' specialty.

He also served in the 1837 state constitutional convention and railed against anything that smacked of privilege or class distinction. In 1841, although he was conceded to be "a giant among pigmy opponents," he retired from politics, probably angry that he did not receive what he saw as a well-deserved cabinet position in the William Henry Harrison administration. He returned to the law and made a small fortune in short order. But the rise of the slavery issue in connection with the Mexican Cession soon brought him back into the political fray. In 1848, he was elected to Congress as an antislavery Whig (q.v.). He soon reestablished his uncompromising stand against slavery, the usual invective against his opponents, and a knack for parliamentary maneuver that set him aside from the run-of-the-mill Free Soil candidate. He wished to ring the slave states with Free Soil, believing that slavery would wither away in a quarter of a century under that pressure. And he attacked northern compromisers as more immoral than the worst of the southern slaveholders.

Stevens was looked upon as a reckless, foul-mouthed, and irresponsible fire brand. Disgusted by what he saw as a weak-kneed stand of the Whigs on slavery, he quit Congress and joined the infant Republican Party (q.v.), which he helped organize in Pennsylvania. In 1858, at age 68, he went back to Congress to enter the last debates on slavery before the Civil War. He spoke out for a high protective tariff and against the extension of slavery to the West. Stevens favored fellow Pennsylvanian Simon Cameron for president in 1860, but turned to Abraham Lincoln (q.v.) when the Cameron drive failed. After Lincoln's election, Stevens spoke in favor of coercion of the South before secession (q.v.) in such a manner that friends in the House had to form a protective barrier around him on the floor to protect his life from harm.

Stevens again hoped for a cabinet seat, but Lincoln chose Cameron instead. In the end this turned out to be Stevens' good fortune, for he had too much power in Congress to accept a subordinate position in the executive branch. He took over the ways and means committee, which gave him control of the entire House legislation. And Stevens was a natural leader who assumed command by consent of all House Republicans. As party leader, the only area in which he agreed with the administration was finance. Stevens backed the funding of the war through greenbacks, the income tax, the direct tax on real estate, and the protective tariff. But when it came to the war, he was positively vindictive in his attitudes. He was one of two who voted against the Crittenden (q.v.) Resolution in 1861, which declared that the war was not fought to subjugate the South or interfere with slavery. He urged total confiscation of Rebels' properties and later favored turning them over to the freedmen. He called for the arming and raising of black soldiers from the war's start. He bitterly criticized Lincoln for replacing Generals John Charles Frémont (q.v.) and David Hunter and negating their military emancipations (q.v.) for Lincoln's go-slow emancipation policy, which Stevens dismissed as "diluted milk and water gruel."

Stevens did all he could to stiffen Northern resolve to not only restore the Union but change its very core of meaning. He called on Lincoln to get rid of Republican compromisers in his administration, like Secretary of State William H. Seward (q.v.) and the Frank Blair family and other border state politicos. He helped organize the Joint Committee on the Conduct of the War (q.v.), which had as its purpose the exposure and removal of "Democrat" generals (those who showed compassion to the occupied regions of the South and slavery) and the promotion of "Republican" ones (those who backed confiscation and emancipation). But the war did not go well despite Stevens' attempts to toughen Northern resolve. In 1863, it came home to Stevens personally, as General Robert E. Lee's (q.v.) army invaded Stevens' home state of Pennsylvania. Confederate soldiers were well aware of Stevens' hostility and made a special trip to the outspoken congressman's iron works, which they thoroughly wrecked and looted. Fortunately Stevens was absent in Washington, because Confederate Lt. Gen. Jubal Early (q.v.), in charge of the expedition, had vowed to hang the old man, "divide his bones, and send them to the several states as curiosities."

As the war went on, Stevens theorized that the Constitution no longer applied to the South, that it was but a conquered province because the Constitution had been so shattered by the force of the rebellion that it no longer had any application. No longer states in the Union, the South had reverted to the territorial stage, where they could have their very boundaries altered and had to do the bidding of the rest of the states through the Federal administrators in the South. Part and parcel of this was the enfranchising of the African-Americans, as the only truly loyal group in the South. Of course the whole process was to be congressional, not executive, in conception, and here he ran head-on into Lincoln's Ten Percent Plan (q.v.) for Reconstruction, which Stevens considered pure nonsense. Stevens much preferred the harsher Wade–Davis Bill (q.v.).

It was only reluctantly that Stevens supported Lincoln's second term, and he received the news of the chief executive's assassination (q.v.) with much equanimity. Stevens was quite thrilled with President Andrew Johnson's (q.v.) initial harsh statements on the content of Reconstruction, but greatly horrified when the new president announced his amnesty and pardon program. Stevens supported the renewal of the Freedmen's Bureau Bill and the passage of the Civil Rights Act of 1866 (qq.v.) and got them passed over Johnson's vetoes; he exchanged bitter words with the president that led up to Johnson's ill-thought-of Washington's Birthday Speech (qq.v.). Stevens ran the whole Radical Republican program in the House, including the Fourteenth Amendment, the Military Reconstruction Acts, the Command of the Army Act, the Tenure of Office Act, and the impeachment (qq.v.).

But the drive to reconstruct the South took a toll on the old man, and his health began to fail him as the impeachment trial drew close. He took little part in the actual trial, even though he was one of the House managers. But when Johnson survived the assault by one vote, it was too much for Stevens. His health sank so rapidly that he could not be carried home but died in Washington, with only his nephew and a mulatto housekeeper, Lydia Smith (about whose actual relation with Stevens all sorts of prurient rumors had abounded), at his bedside. His funeral procession was second only to Lincoln's and attracted thousands of mourners. His self-penned epitaph was dedicated to the principle he had fought for all of his life: "EQUALITY OF MAN BEFORE HIS CREATOR." And in tribute to his memory, the voters of his Pennsylvania congressional district elected him posthumously one last time.

ST. LANDRY RACE RIOT, SEPTEMBER 28, 1868. Although St. Landry Parish (county) in central Louisiana west of Baton Rouge had a large black population (three to two in favor of African-Americans), the Republicans (q.v.) had not managed to upset the control of the local government, which remained in the hands of the white power structure before, during, and after the war. Military Reconstruction (q.v.) and the new state constitution had done little but unite whites as never before. The Republican Party struggled to gain a base in St. Landry that had never before existed.

Because of the prevalence of white nightriders, the Republicans armed guards to protect their political meetings, and by September 1868, the racial tensions in the parish were ready to explode. As the threat of racial war increased, a committee of five men from each side met to try to work out the terms for a peaceful presidential election in November. But the move was too late. Whites were already convinced that the African-Americans were about to engage in an "insurrection" and moved to stop it before it happened.

The result was the September 28 St. Landry riot. Total casualties on both sides amounted to five dead and six wounded, although Republicans claimed that nearly 300 died, and Democrats (q.v.) asserted the number was around 30. The blacks quickly withdrew, and the whites sent in a mounted contingent, which pursued and "arrested" 29 blacks, whom they lodged in the parish jail. The next night, all but two were taken by a mob and shot dead, with the connivance of the sheriff and his deputies, who stood aside. The remaining leaders of the Republican Party fled the parish for their lives. In November, the parish, which had given the Republicans a 2,500-vote majority in the April statewide elections, reported not one vote for Ulysses S. Grant (q.v.).

STONEMAN'S RAID. During the Chancellorsville Campaign (q.v.), one of the hallmarks of Bvt. Maj. Gen. Joseph Hooker's (q.v.) plan was a massive Union cavalry raid behind Gen. Robert E. Lee's (q.v.) lines at Fredericksburg to the Confederate capital at Richmond. The cavalry was to precede the army's operations by two weeks, but a severe rain kept the Rappahannock and Rapidan in flood, and the cavalry crossed on April 29, 1863, almost in step with the infantry. Thus it exerted no effect on Lee's communications during the fight, and its absence prevented Hooker from garnering information that might have assisted him at Chancellorsville.

The cavalry divided into three formations, each assigned a particular railroad or canal or other objective to tear up. One, under Brig. Gen. H. Judson Kilpatrick, actually rode within two miles of Richmond before it reached Union lines at Gloucester, across the York from Yorktown. It would be transferred back to the army by boat. Later, it was learned from escaped Yankee prisoners that Richmond had been totally open to attack, a circumstance that would favor the Kilpatrick–Dahlgren raid the following year.

STONE'S RIVER, BATTLE OF. *See* PERRYVILLE CAMPAIGN.

STRAUDER *v*. WEST VIRGINIA (1880). *See* CIVIL RIGHTS CASES (1883).

STREIGHT'S RAID. In the spring of 1863, as he prepared for the Chattanooga Campaign, Bvt. Maj. Gen. William S. Rosecrans (q.v.), commanding Federal forces at Murfreesboro, Tennessee, was plagued by being outnumbered in Confederate cavalry, which raided his supply lines to Louisville mercilessly. To counter this baleful influence, Rosecrans decided to mount infantry. He put one brigade on horseback, that of Col. John T. Wilder, and another on mules, that commanded by Col. Abel D. Streight.

After some training, Streight proposed to lead his men behind enemy lines in May 1863 and destroy the Confederate supply and communication infrastructure in northern Mississippi and Alabama, hopefully striking all the way to the Western & Atlantic Railroad in northern Georgia, supplying the Confederates in Tennessee. He was to start where the Tennessee River crossed the Alabama–Mississippi line and head east, guided by two companies of Alabama white Unionists. Streight's brigade would bust loose into the Rebel rear areas behind an infantry attack, led by a brigade of infantry from Memphis, all of this turning Confederate attention away from Union Maj. Gen. Ulysses S. Grant's (q.v.) final moves in the Vicksburg Campaign (q.v.).

But the feint failed to fool Confederate Brig. Gen. Nathan Bedford Forrest (q.v.), who ignored the infantry and started after Streight. Although mules are known for their stamina, they cannot move as fast as horses, which allowed Forrest to get around in front of Streight and block his path before he got far. As the Yankees made ready to fight, Forrest proposed a truce and surrender discussions to save life and limb. As he talked, Forrest used a few stratagems of his own, riding his fewer men through clearings, having officers call commands to nonexistent units from concealed positions, and creating dust in the distance by dragging tree limbs. His two cannon kept appearing in front of the conference site, as they circled through the woods to appear again and again.

"Name of God!" Streight exclaimed. "How many cannon do you have? I have counted fifteen already." Forrest looked over at the sweating teams coming past once more and replied, "I reckon that's all that's kept up." The baffled Streight decided that he was vastly outnumbered and surrendered 1,400 men to Forrest's 600, only to discover too late that he had been fooled. "As they say, Colonel," Forrest was alleged to have commented, "all's fair in love and war."

Sent eventually to the Union officers' prison at the Libby tobacco warehouse in Richmond, Streight made a daring escape with dozens of others. He reported on the horrible conditions of Southern wartime prisons to President Abraham Lincoln (q.v.), which was instrumental in Lincoln approving the disastrous Kilpatrick–Dahlgren raid on Richmond to free Union prisoners and capture or kill President Jefferson Davis (q.v.) and his cabinet, which modern writers think may have led to Lincoln's assassination (q.v.).

STUART, JAMES EWELL BROWN "JEB" (1833–1864). A Virginian from Patrick County, Jeb Stuart was the seventh son of a prosperous farmer. He attended local academies and graduated from West Point in 1854. He took to temperance and revival religion and epitomized the 19th-century prewar southern romantic movement. Before the Civil War, Stuart served in New Mexico Territory, western Texas, and Kansas, where he was wounded fighting Native Americans. He was a volunteer aide to Col. Robert E. Lee (q.v.) during the Harper's Ferry Raid (q.v.) in 1859. Stuart resigned his commission to enter the Virginia cavalry in 1861.

Stuart was instrumental in raising and fighting the 1st Virginia "Black Horse" regiment at First Manassas (q.v.), where his charge drove the already demoralized Union army from the field. When Gen. Lee took over the Army of Northern Virginia, Stuart led a reconnaissance against the Union army of Bvt. Maj. Gen. George B. McClellan (q.v.), which was investing the Confederate capital at Richmond. Stuart rode completely around McClellan's force, losing only one man in the process. He taunted his father-in-law, who led the Yankee pursuit all the way. He would later repeat this feat after the Battle of Antietam, precipitating McClellan's final removal from command by President Abraham Lincoln (q.v.)

Stuart and Lee developed a close personal and military relationship. Lee claimed that Stuart never brought him a single piece of false information. As the numbers of cavalry rose, Stuart became a major general. He never reached the lieutenant general's rank that such a corps-sized force entitled him to, probably because horse soldiers were traditionally shortchanged in the Old Army.

Stuart creditably led Lt. Gen. Thomas J. "Stonewall" Jackson's Corps at Chancellorsville (qq.v.) after Jackson had been shot. But he returned to the cavalry in time for the Pennsylvania Campaign (q.v.). He joined Lee on the field at Gettysburg on July 2, after riding around the Union army once again. But this time, he left Lee short of information as to the enemy's intentions. Many historians point to Stuart's unwise bravado as a main reason the Confederates lost the battle, but others defend Stuart and claim that Lee missed Stuart himself, not the cavalry, of which he had plenty.

In the 1864 Richmond Campaign (q.v.), Stuart continued to embarrass Lt. Gen. Ulysses S. Grant's (q.v.) movements again Lee's army. Finally, Grant ordered his own cavalry leader, Bvt. Maj. Gen. Philip H. Sheridan (q.v.), to defeat Stuart. In a wide-ranging raid against Richmond, Sheridan's men smashed the flower of Stuart's horsemen, killing Stuart at the Battle of Yellow Tavern, May 11, 1864.

SUFFOLK, SIEGE OF. *See* CHANCELLORSVILLE CAMPAIGN.

SULTANA, **SINKING OF THE.** Just after midnight on the morning of April 27, 1865, just north of Memphis, Tennessee, the side-wheel steamboat *Sultana* exploded in the darkness of the flooded Mississippi River. More than 1,700 people died in the explosion, ensuing fire, and numbing waters of the icy Mississippi—the worst maritime disaster in U.S. history. Most of them were Union prisoners of war returning from months of captivity in Southern prison (q.v.) pens at Cahaba and Andersonville. The *Sultana* was rated to carry 376 persons, but the exigencies of wartime corruption (the dock contractor and boat captain each received a premium for each person boarded, not counting the usual kickbacks) caused as many as 2,500 to be aboard.

Investigators blamed the explosion on the ship's boilers, one of which had just been patched in hasty repair. But more recent research has turned up the names and surreptitious activities of several members of the Confederate secret service. Most of these men had served time in Gratiot Street Prison in St. Louis for alleged spying and pro-Confederate activities. Late in the war, groups of Confederate powdermen, known as destructionists, received $35,000 for each steamboat they destroyed. It only took one stick or lump of coal, a little black powder, and a fuse.

After the war, a former Rebel spy and secret mail carrier for Confederate Maj. Gen. Sterling Price (q.v.), Robert Louden, claimed that he did the job, putting the fake lump of coal bomb in the onshore bunkers one hour before the ship went up in a flash. A one-time steamboat pilot, Louden was familiar with boats, docks, and refueling processes. He also had narrowly escaped hanging for his wartime spying activities in 1863. If he did it, he was single-handedly responsible for the death of as many Union soldiers as had died on the bloody field at Shiloh (q.v.) in 1862. But the Confederacy was well into its death throes, and it is doubtful that he ever received a penny for the job. He considered it an act of unbridled patriotism.

SUMNER, CHARLES (1811–1874). Born in Boston of parents with all of the proper social credentials, Charles Sumner attended the prestigious Boston Latin School and Harvard College. He showed his greatest aptitude in history, literature, and forensics. He then attended Harvard Law School and was a student of Mr. Justice Joseph Story, a professor when he was not sitting on the U.S. Supreme Court. His acquaintanceship with Story gave Sumner an entrée into Washington social and political circles, and he attended the inner sessions of the Supreme Court when Chief Justice John Marshall was still presiding and heard Daniel Webster and Henry Clay speak on the floor of the U.S. Senate. Although Sumner professed at the time that he had nothing more than "any feeling but loathing" for politics, he had been fatally bitten by the political bug. But he was not fully aware of it yet.

Then, in 1845, he got the opportunity that woke him up. Sumner was selected to give the annual Boston Independence Day (when General Thomas Gage left Boston in March 1776, not the 4th of July) Address. It was a prestigious occasion, and Sumner rose to the challenge. The gist of his speech was that all peace was honorable and all war was dishonorable. Although many believed that he had committed political suicide, it was a typical Sumner speech: taking the war to the enemy, so to speak, in his own lair. Sumner continued to plug away at the world's war-mongers, making an appeal for a congress of nations that would arbitrate all disagreements among countries.

But Sumner went even further. He called for the opposition of all good men to the traditional political parties (calling them an "alliance between the lords of the lash and lords of the loom") and issued a call for support for the Free Soil Party. His outspokenness led a coalition of Free Soilers and Democrats to put his name up for the U.S. Senate. The North had shifted from mere objection to the institution to an attack on its very existence.

Sumner would become a household word in the debates over the Kansas–Nebraska Act (q.v.). Sumner had dropped all other party affiliation and helped organize the Republicans (q.v.). Then he launched into his most famous speech, "The Crime Against Kansas." He not only attacked slavery as an institution, but he named certain southern Senators by name—a hitherto understood no-no. He called Senator Andrew Butler of South Carolina slavery's Don Quixote, paying vows to his Desdemona of slavery, a harlot "polluted in the sight of the world, [but] chaste in his sight." The speech horrified the whole Senate.

Several days later, Preston S. Brooks, a relative of Senator Butler, came onto the Senate floor and proceeded "to chastise" Sumner with his cane. He beat the Massachusetts man until the cane broke, and then proceeded to hit him with the remnants until he was winded. Sumner, a big man (six feet four), was wedged in under his desk and could not rise. Then in one burst of strength brought on by the pain of the beating, Sumner wrenched the desk up from the floor to which it had been attached and fainted from loss of blood.

Badly injured, Sumner was reelected to his seat, even though it would be three years before he could mount up the courage and well-being to attend another session. Meanwhile, he went to Europe again to regain his health, submitting to the painful procedure of Moxa, a Japanese treatment in which the skin was burned by chemical treatment to relocate the pain, once described as "the greatest suffering that can be inflicted on mortal man." Publicists pointed to the "Empty Chair of Sumner" as evidence of the brutality brought on by slavery. When returned on the eve of the election of 1860 (q.v.), he delivered another philippic against slavery. Although many described it as rubbing salt in old wounds, Republicans republished it and distributed it all over the North as an Abraham Lincoln (q.v.) campaign document.

As the South moved to secession, Sumner ignored petitions from tens of thousands that he tone down the rhetoric and try to keep the nation whole. When the South left the Union and the Republican Party finally took over Congress, Sumner received the chair of the committee on foreign relations. In this capacity, he recognized the inevitability of having to free the Confederate Commissioners to Europe, James Mason (author of the Fugitive Slave Act [q.v.]) and John Slidell when an over-zealous Union navy captain illegally took them from the British ship *Trent* (q.v.) on the high seas. In October 1861, he was the first to move that slavery be completely ended throughout the nation, North and South. He continued to pressure the Lincoln administration to issue an emancipation proclamation. He was the first to call for equal rights, including the franchise, for all Americans regardless of color, in early 1862.

At the same time, Sumner advanced his theory of Reconstruction, the state suicide theory (*see* RECONSTRUCTION, THEORIES OF). This concept argued that secession (q.v.) was impossible. Rather, by trying to leave the Union, the states had committed a treasonous form of suicide. Although the United States retained control over these areas, they had reverted to territorial status, where they were at the mercy of Congress. This allowed state institutions (but not boundaries) to be altered at the pleasure of Congress with no constitutional guarantees to get in the way. Congress would decide what these suicidal brethren must do to return to the Union. And essentially, what he believed had to be done was to "civilize" and "Americanize" the South by making it over into an idealized version of New England.

Using his theory of Reconstruction, Sumner was instrumental in blocking any consideration of seating Lincoln's Louisiana Reconstruction government in Congress in 1864. Upon Lincoln's death, Sumner and Thaddeus Stevens (q.v.) in the House were brought into alliance by President Andrew Johnson's Reconstruction (qq.v.) policies. Sumner fought for the recognition of African-American political and social rights and the suffrage. He also spoke in favor of free schools and homesteads for the freedmen. He was lukewarm on impeachment (q.v.), seeing it as a political rather than a judicial proceeding. During the trial, however, he was more vindictive than he would have been in a real court proceeding and voted the party line to convict. Critics called it Sumner at his worst.

When the Ulysses S. Grant (q.v.) administration came into power, one might have expected Sumner and the chief executive to be in harmony at last. But Sumner and Grant never understood each other. Sumner rejected Grant's selection for secretary of the treasury on constitutional grounds. He prevented an early settlement of the *Alabama* claims (q.v.), claiming that Great Britain owed the United States billions of dollars in claims from the destructive actions of Confederate cruisers built there in violation of British laws. And Sumner was patently against the annexation of San Domingo, which he correctly saw as a corrupt action of Grant's inner circle. In retaliation, Grant recalled Sumner's recommended appointment to Great Britain and had Sumner himself thrown off the Senate foreign relations committee. Despite this action, Sumner continued to monitor foreign policy and spoke out in favor of the Treaty of Washington (q.v.), which settled the *Alabama* claims in America's favor and recognized Sumner's hallowed principle of international arbitration.

About this time (1872), Sumner sponsored a bill that seemed out of character with his whole past. He asked that all Civil War battle names on Federal regimental colors be obliterated. Opponents were outraged, and the "bloody shirt" flew openly in Congress, as at first he was verbally condemned and then censured (an act removed from the record two years later). But his action makes more sense when it is paired with the public accommodations act Sumner introduced at the same time, which became the Civil Rights Act of 1875 (q.v.), passed in his honor after his death. Sumner was willing to forgive and forget if the South was willing to do the same and truly free the blacks. But he never lived to see either measure become law. On May 10, 1874, he was felled by a heart attack. He died in Washington the next day. Many a Southern congressman took the opportunity to use his death for ending Reconstruction as they rose and spoke on his behalf. His funeral was at Cambridge.

SUMNER, WILLIAM GRAHAM. *See* SOCIAL DARWINISM.

SURGEONS GENERAL. *See* MEDICAL DIRECTORS OR SURGEONS GENERAL.

SURRENDER OF THE CONFEDERATE ARMIES. *See* APPOMATTOX CAMPAIGN; CITRONELLE, SURRENDER AT.

SWING AROUND THE CIRCLE. In the fall of 1866, President Andrew Johnson (q.v.) took to the campaign trail to elect Democrats (q.v.) to Congress to help him oppose Congressional Reconstruction (q.v.), which was becoming more and more radical, due in no small part to ineptitudes of his own like his Washington Birthday Speech (q.v.). Ostensibly the purpose of the journey was to dedicate the tomb of former Illinois Senator Stephen A. Douglas (q.v.), Abraham Lincoln's (q.v.) old debating partner from 1858.

Johnson took along Secretaries William H. Seward (q.v.) and Gideon Welles, Conservative Republican Senator James R. Doolittle, Generals Ulysses S. Grant (q.v.) and George A. Custer, and Admiral David G. Farragut (q.v.). Friends tried to convince the president not to go. Campaigning so openly for mere congressmen was deemed undignified in those days, and many feared a repeat of the Washington Birthday Speech would destroy what little claim Johnson had left to presidential solemnity.

As expected, the trip, from August 28 to September 15, 1866, proved a disaster. Johnson was essentially a stump speaker in the rough and tumble style of the Southern backcountry, which did not go over in the urban cities of the North. Stump speakers like to be challenged by the audience and reply with bitter invective, often with biting humor.

Almost immediately, Republicans (q.v.) saw to it that professional hecklers were at every stop. Johnson compared himself to the crucified Christ and his opponents to Judas Iscariot. He wrapped his plan for the nation in the flag and Constitution. Grant left the convoy, disillusioned with Johnson and ripe for a Republican conversion. Local politicians of both parties began to call in sick at every stop.

Essentially, the "Swing Around the Circle" saw the president repudiate the party that elected him. It also failed to produce votes for the Democrats the president desperately needed to stop Congressional Reconstruction. It permitted the Moderate and Conservative Republicans of the Thirty-ninth Congress (still seated until March 1867), who had desperately worked for a Reconstruction compromise, to desert the president with clean consciences and join the Radicals to get tough on the South. And it produced a veto-proof majority for the Fortieth Congress to come in 1867. The whole revolutionary idea of presidential railroad campaigning to produce a Congress in league with him had blown up in Johnson's face.

T

"TALENTED TENTH." *See* BLACK "PERSONALITY" IN SLAVERY AND FREEDOM.

TALLAHATCHIE EXPEDITION. *See* VICKSBURG CAMPAIGN.

TANEY, ROGER BROOKE (1777–1864). When Supreme Court Justice John Marshal died in 1835, President Andrew Jackson needed a replacement who would overturn Marshal's decisions. For this reason and for his political loyalty, he nominated Democrat Roger B. Taney (pronounced Taw' ney), a former Federalist. Born, raised, and educated in Calvert County, Maryland, Taney bravely supported unpopular issues, such as defending Gen. James Wilkinson against treason charges under the Thomas Jefferson administration and providing sustenance for his freed slaves.

As treasury secretary, he gained national recognition by helping President Jackson withdraw Federal deposits to destroy the Second Bank of the United States, but when Jackson initially nominated him to the Federal bench, the Whig (q.v.)-dominated U.S. Senate rejected him for disassembling the banking system, so essential to their economic policy. Jackson renominated Taney to the Supreme Court after a Democratic victory in the election of 1836, and the newly elected Senate confirmed him.

As chief justice, Taney was a strict constructionist (a literal reader of the U.S. Constitution), rather than a states' righter. He reinforced the Federal government's jurisdiction over slavery. He did not favor states' rights like secession. Important cases decided under Taney's regime included Prigg *v.* Pennsylvania (1842), in support of the Fugitive Slave Law of 1792; Dred Scott *v.* Sandford (1857 [q.v.]), ruling that slavery could not be excluded in the territories; Ableman *v.* Booth (1859 [q.v.]), reaffirming and reinforcing the Prigg case, in reference to the Fugitive Slave Act of 1850; and *ex parte* Merryman (1861 [q.v.]), protesting President Abraham Lincoln's (q.v.) use of executive orders to institute arbitrary arrests in Taney's home state of Maryland by deciding that only Congress has the power to suspend *habeas corpus*.

TARIFF (1861), MORRILL. The Republican Party (q.v.) had a distinct domestic program, designed to appease both its agricultural and industrial supporters. This program had as its basis the old Whig (q.v.) economic policies based in part on Henry Clay's American System (q.v.). Part of the program appealed to American industry by protecting it from cheaper, more efficient foreign competition through the Morrill Tariff. Before the Civil War, the South had objected to the tariff as an unfair northern tax on products it imported from Europe. Successive Democratic (q.v.) administrations during the decade of the 1850s had reduced the tariff to its lowest rate in the whole antebellum period.

Raising the tariff was a critical issue in guaranteeing the Republicans New York and Pennsylvania votes in the election of 1860 (q.v.). It was one of the first measures passed after the South seceded. The Morill Tariff doubled the rates from the 1857 lows and substituted specific rates for *ad valorem* rates. The Republicans never yielded on the tariff as an issue throughout the Civil War and Reconstruction, often lowering it to gain votes in a specific election, only to raise it after victory. By 1869, the tariff rate averaged 47 percent.

TAXATION IN THE CONFEDERACY. As in the North, fighting the Civil War brought on an increased tax burden in the South. Never before had citizens felt the hand of a central government as during the Civil War. This especially rubbed against the grain of the individualistic and localized South. Taxes were still viewed as they had been when King George III tried to impose them on the British American colonies—tyranny writ large. Most Americans had never seen an official, except postmasters, from Washington or Richmond before the war. Confederate citizens hated monetary taxes, but they especially disliked the tax-in-kind, in which 10 percent of all crop or industrial production was collected in lieu of cash payments. This put an increased burden in addition to the usual land taxes. The real problem was that the tax was not always uniformly collected, and those who got stuck did not like the fact that others did not.

Another form of taxation disliked in the South was the Impressment Act of 1863. This measure was passed to establish uniform prices on all goods the government, particularly the passing armies, took to fight the war. The rates were in Confederate paper currency, which grew more and more worthless each year. The vouchers were easily forged; prices were lowered by intent or inflation; and often the army simply stole what it wanted, to the detriment of the citizen. To act as an impressment agent soon became a risky business, especially in pro-Union areas of the South.

TAX LAW OF 1861. Raised by the Union Congress to pay for the prosecution of the War of the Rebellion, this law applied to land within the Confederacy as well as the rest of the nation. If unpaid, the law allowed the land in question to be sold for taxes owed. Usually Northern companies speculated in this land, often making large profits. Much of the effect of this confiscation was ameliorated by President Andrew Johnson's pardon policy (qq.v.).

TAX LAW OF 1862. Passed on June 22, 1862, this measure expanded the Tax Law of 1861 by creating special tax commissioners to collect revenues owed in insurrectionary sections of the United States. All assessments were as of 1861 values; a 50 percent penalty was added to all accounts in arrears; and upon failure of the owner to pay tax and penalty, the land could be seized and sold to the highest bidder, sale to be a fee simple in the land. Of course, the tax could only be collected in areas of the South occupied by the Union armies. The sales differed from ordinary Federal tax sales, wherein the amount raised above the tax owed was given to the owner. Here it went to the Federal treasury.

TAX SCANDAL, THE. All of the executive department scandals of the Ulysses S. Grant (q.v.) administration paled in comparison to what happened in the Department of the Treasury. In fact, the Treasury scandals were so big that in the end they took the heat off everyone else. Prior to 1872, the government had awarded a percentage of delinquent taxes to those who reported them. This had led to false charges and blackmail by disgruntled employees, neighbors, and such and had been discontinued in 1872. Instead, a series of contract tax collectors was put in. Secretary of the Treasury W. A. Richardson appointed a crony of Ben Butler (q.v.), John D. Sanborn, to one of the collector's slots. Sanborn was to ferret out unknown delinquent taxes and take half of what was collected.

Now Sanborn was no idiot. If the government did not know who was not paying their taxes, he was probably not going to find them out either. So instead of seeking out the unknown, he went to the Boston internal revenue office and got a list of already known delinquents. Then he collected their payments and took 50 percent off the top. Then on a hunch, Sanborn made a list of 600 railroads and arbitrarily charged them with delinquent taxes. Surprisingly (well, maybe not), a large number confessed to the accusations and paid up to Sanborn, who took half. Complaints led to a congressional investigation, which revealed that Sanborn had made $213,000 off the government, but that he had only found out delinquent taxes that the Treasury already knew of. It was suspected that Ben Butler got a healthy cut of Sanborn's income, but no such evidence could be produced. Congress decided to censure Secretary of the Treasury W. A. Richardson, who resigned, for President Grant's sake, he said. Grant was appreciative and made Richardson a Federal judge after the whole affair cooled off.

TAYLOR, ZACHARY (1784–1850). Born in Virginia, but raised and educated by private tutors in Kentucky, Zachary Taylor entered the army in 1808 through the Kentucky militia. He fought in the War of 1812 (holding Ft. Harrison, Indiana, against attack), the Black Hawk War, and the Seminole War (victory at Lake Okeechobee), and commanded the District of Florida. He commanded the Army of Occupation that went to Texas to assert American claims to the Río Grande as the international border. Fired on by Mexican troops, Taylor began a set of spectacular victories that led to the Battle of Buena Vista and the presidency as the Whig (q.v.) candidate in 1848. Once in Washington, the slaveholding Taylor turned out to be very much against the southern legal theorizing, like squatter sovereignty and popular sovereignty (qq.v.), on the question of slavery in the territories. He wanted all the territories admitted as states immediately, bypassing the slavery question. The result was his refusal to consider the Compromise of 1850 (q.v.) until his plan was passed through Congress first. With the country perilously close to Civil War, and Taylor determined to take on all comers, he died suddenly of gastroenteritis just after a July 4 picnic at which he ate prodigiously. His death allowed his vice president, Millard Fillmore, and compromise forces in the Congress led by Senator Stephen A. Douglas (q.v.) of Illinois and Representative Alexander H. Stephens (q.v.) of Georgia to pass the Compromise of 1850 (q.v.), which averted the war for 10 years.

TENNESSEE, C.S.S. *See* MOBILE CAMPAIGN.

TEN PERCENT PLAN. A name given popularly to President Abraham Lincoln's Proclamation of Amnesty and Reconstruction (q.v.), which required 10 percent of the registered voters in any occupied Southern state to take an oath of future loyalty to the Union to begin the process of wartime Reconstruction.

TENURE OF OFFICE ACT. One of several measures designed to limit President Andrew Johnson's (q.v.) ability to interfere with congressional desires in Reconstruction, the Tenure of Office Act provided that executive branch officers appointed with the advice and consent of the Senate could be removed only through the same process. A presidential tenure was defined as the president's possession of office plus one month. This measure was used to protect Secretary of War Stanton (q.v.) and became key in the impeachment of President Andrew Johnson (qq.v.)

TEXAS v. WHITE (1869). The Supreme Court declared the nation to be a Union of indestructible states in Texas *v.* White (1869). The case related to some state bonds sold during the war to finance the buying of military goods for the Confederacy. The problem in Texas and other Southern states was that

Radical Republicans wanted all laws passed between secession and surrender declared null and void *ab initio* (q.v.), since their inception. This would include such mundane things as contracts and marriages made during the war. Of course the Confederacy and the seceded states had done the same with debts owed to Yankees contracted from before the war.

But an even more basic question had to be decided first. Was Texas a state, and could it bring suit before the Supreme Court? The court ruled yes on both counts. Once Texas had joined the Union, it could not leave. Hence secession (q.v.) was null and void. But the court had to admit that, because of the attempted secession, Texas and the other Southern states were not in normal relations with the rest of the United States. These states had forfeited some rights because of the rebellion. It was the duty of Congress, under its mandate of securing a republican government for all states, to decide what conditions the South must meet to come back into normal relations with the rest of the country. Hence Military Reconstruction (q.v.), although unusual, was perfectly legal and constitutional.

Then the court moved on to the second issue, the bonds and *ab initio*. Texas did not have to pay off the bondholders, said the court. To decide such issues, the court said that each problem's purpose had to be looked at. The bonds were designed to support the rebellion and were null and void *ab initio*. But normal relationships of everyday life were not connected to the war, and all of these issues handled during the war were entirely valid. Included were such items as criminal and civil trials and their results, and normal business and personal contracts, like marriages, wills, deeds, and the like, "necessary to peace and good order among citizens." What the court finally did in Texas *v.* White was recognize the Shellabarger-Chase Theory of Forfeited Rights as being the basis of Reconstruction. It was a practical notion that made the deeds pertaining to the war invalid but allowed all other relationships to stand. It was in effect a Moderate Republican (q.v.) version of Reconstruction.

THIRTEENTH AMENDMENT. Although historians traditionally blame Military Reconstruction (q.v.) upon the Radical Republicans, it is possible that as much (if not more) of the blame can be laid at the feet of Abraham Lincoln, Andrew Johnson, and William H. Seward (qq.v.) and their efforts to create a new conservative political party, which led the South to resist Reconstruction excessively and resulted in a harsher Reconstruction program in the long run. This realignment was hinted at by the congressional coalition that Seward assembled to pass the Thirteenth Amendment, which freed the slaves. The Thirteenth Amendment was critical, because Lincoln and Seward believed that the Emancipation Proclamation (q.v.) lacked the necessary clout to endure as more than a temporary war measure. A constitutional amendment was forever.

By the end of the Civil War, Conservative Republicans were on a roll. They had backed and reelected Lincoln in 1864 and, through the person of Secretary of State Seward, supported the president consistently since 1861. The Radical Republicans, however, had the image of party disloyalty. They had opposed Seward's candidacy for president in 1860, tried to oust him from the cabinet in 1862, threatened Lincoln's Reconstruction policy with the Wade–Davis Manifesto (q.v.) in 1864, bolted from the party later that year for John Charles Frémont's so-called Radical Democracy (qq.v.), forced Frank Blair out of Lincoln's cabinet despite the president's confidence in him as the price of their reentry into the party, and tried to block Lincoln's renomination.

So, by 1865, it was possible that new party coalitions might be in vogue. Democrats (q.v.) had opposed the war with their peace faction, and many War Democrats wanted to drop the party label as they had in 1864, supporting the Lincoln–Johnson National Union Party (q.v.) ticket. Republicans were a minority party, capable of winning the presidency, but not a majority in Congress with the return of the South. At stake was the political control of the United States for a generation or more, if the correct political moves were made. No one realized this more than Secretary of State Seward, who assumed a commanding position upon the death of Lincoln through the coalition he had assembled in 1864 and 1865 to garner passage of the Thirteenth Amendment through Congress to guarantee the liberty of the slaves nationwide.

Although the Republicans had managed to get the proposed constitutional amendment through the Senate, the House proved to be another matter. A strong Democratic Party led the opposition operating under the party's slogan in the 1864 presidential election: "The Constitution as it is, and the Union as it was" [i.e., with slavery]. Disliking emancipation (especially through presidential decree) and abolitionists (qq.v.), believing the war was started intentionally to put the Republicans in a congressional majority and pass their domestic program (tariffs, taxes, national banking system, massive internal improvements), and full of racial prejudice endemic in the North, the Democrats could deny the amendment the two-thirds vote necessary for passage.

Seward had warned Lincoln of the opposition in the House to the Thirteenth Amendment, but Lincoln was insistent that it had to pass. So Seward went to work to build a coalition that would do it. It would not be easy. Most Northern Democrats were from border areas, slave states that had remained loyal to the United States in 1861. But there were others, too, some from Seward's native New York State. Sixteen Democrats had deserted their party, 14 of whom were lame ducks (not returned to office in the past November 1864 elections, but serving until March 1865), and six of whom were from New York State. Many suspected bribery carried the day, especially in the form of cash and political appointments. But there was more. Seward let it be known that if the Thirteenth Amendment lobby and cooperation between conservatives of all parties continued, Reconstruction would be short and sweet.

The significance of Seward's manipulations that passed the Thirteenth Amendment is that had he failed, it might have drastically altered American history. Lincoln had threatened to call a special session of Congress in the spring of 1865 to reconsider the amendment had it failed in January. Lincoln always doubted that his Emancipation Proclamation had legality, having been done under the president's war powers by stretching them to their limits. He was not about to condemn blacks to a return to slavery under an adverse decision of the Supreme Court or some later, hostile Congress. (The South held their slaves who had not already run off well into 1866, just in case the amendment failed to be approved by the states.) He had to have an amendment one way or another. Lincoln's special session would have met in March and April 1865, or have been in session when he was assassinated and Johnson took over. It would have prevented Johnson's acting alone under presidential proclamation (q.v.) to institute his Reconstruction program.

In any case, Johnson fell heir to Seward's conservative coalition and its form of Reconstruction: free the slaves, generous terms to the defeated Confederates, quick return of Southern states to the Union, and cooperation between conservatives. It is just that Johnson saw the coalition differently from Seward (who saw it differently from Lincoln). To Johnson, the coalition included all Democrat factions (it had to, because they controlled his governments in the South) and excluded both Moderate and Radical Republicans—a critical mistake, as the Moderate Republicans were the biggest group in both houses of Congress. Seward would have excluded the Radical Republicans (whom Lincoln had desired to work with) and the Southern Secessionist and Northern Peace Democrats (whom Johnson hoped to work with). Seward would reorganize on the basis of all the middle-of-the-road politicians left over. All three men wanted to include the old Northern and Southern Whigs (q.v.), the heart of pre–Civil War conservatism.

Although Lincoln and Seward saw the coalition as Northern controlled, Johnson envisioned it as Southern controlled, as Democrats had been before the war. And Johnson had no desire to grant the freed African-Americans any civil or political rights. Both Seward and Lincoln saw some black rights as essential to freedom. But all conservative Reconstruction proposals had something in common: they all wanted a quick readmission of the South (to form a revitalized Whig Party for Seward and Lincoln, or a greater Democratic Party for Johnson). Essentially, all the South had to do for the conservatives was free the slaves and forget the war.

THOMPSON, JACOB (1810–1885). Born in North Carolina, Jacob Thompson was educated in local academies and the University of North Carolina.

He studied law and was admitted to the bar in 1835. The following years he went to Mississippi to seek his fortune. In 1838, he married it, in the person of Catherine Ann Jones. Thompson lived in Natchez, Pontotoc, and Oxford. At the latter place he was elected to the U.S. House of Representatives as a Democrat (q.v.), where he served from 1839 to 1851. He was chairman of the committee on Indian affairs; a supporter of the War with Mexico; and an opponent of the Compromise of 1850 (q.v.), which he considered offered little to the South.

Franklin Pierce (q.v.) offered Thompson the consulship at Havana, but he declined. He lost a try at the governorship of Mississippi to Jefferson Davis (q.v.) in 1855. When James Buchanan (q.v.) became president, Thompson was made secretary of the interior. He centralized all control of the department in his hands, making him responsible for considerable fraud in the Indian trust fund. He resigned when he charged that Buchanan's cabinet interfered with secession (q.v.) unwisely. His resignation to follow his state into the Confederacy was probably all that saved him from indictment. During the war, he was an aide to Gen. P. G. T. Beauregard and Gen. John C. Pemberton (qq.v.). He was captured at Vicksburg and exchanged.

He served in the Mississippi legislature until 1864, when President Davis sent him to Canada to coordinate secret service activity. There Thompson tried to get various Copperhead (q.v.) organizations, like the Order of American Knights and the Sons of Liberty, to break Confederate soldiers out of prisoner of war camps. He was also accused of backing such things as the plot to burn New York City, and even the financing and organization of the plot to kidnap or assassinate President Abraham Lincoln.

With these charges hanging over his head, Thompson fled to Europe after the war, carrying cash from considerable Confederate expense accounts with him, although he denied it. In 1868, he returned to Mississippi, eventually taking up residence in Memphis, Tennessee. He acquired considerable real estate holdings, which financed his later years. He was never charged with his various alleged wrongdoings.

THROCKMORTON, JAMES W. (1825–1894). In July 1867, Congress vindicated Maj. Gen. Philip H. Sheridan's (q.v.) desire to replace Southern politicians whom he deemed as "impediments to Reconstruction." Sheridan's Texas subordinate in the Fifth Military District (Louisiana and Texas), Bvt. Maj. Gen. Charles Griffin (q.v.), had been pestering him to move against Texas Governor James W. Throckmorton, who became the first official removed under the new Third Military Reconstruction Act (q.v.). In retaliation, President Andrew Johnson (q.v.) fired Sheridan and replaced him with a general known for his Democrat (q.v.) politics, Maj. Gen. Winfield Scott Hancock (q.v.).

Throckmorton did not leave office without protest. He published a 13-page address to the people of Texas in which he defended himself and his regime against charges of impeding Reconstruction. Sheridan had refused Throckmorton's request for a face-to-face meeting with him or Griffin, and Sheridan, said Throckmorton, refused to allow any debate or disagreement as to policy. He instead expected everyone to salute and say "yes, sir" like a boot second lieutenant. If anyone was an impediment to Reconstruction, it was Sheridan and his subordinates, claimed Throckmorton. The governor charged Sheridan with covering up three military–civilian incidents in which guilty soldiers got off with no punishment: the Brenham fire, where troops burned the town in drunken response to not being allowed to attend a town dance while inebriated; the Lindley affair, in which a Waco man shot dead two alleged Rebels under military protection who could testify he was a horse thief; and the Walker affair, in which two black soldiers shot dead a deaf man for no apparent reason.

There was more, Throckmorton continued. Sheridan incorrectly ignored the ruling of the U.S. attorney general and forced all voters to take the iron-clad oath to register; he illegally set aside a state law allowing five judicial districts to disappear by reappointing two Union men and recreating their districts; he permitted military commissions and Freedmen's Bureau (q.v.) courts to interfere with state courts, contrary to the *ex parte* Milligan (q.v.) decision of the U.S. Supreme Court; he refused to permit the state to honor the remains of Confederate Gen. Albert Sidney Johnston (q.v.), an original "Texican," as the body moved from Galveston to Austin for burial; and he wrote a false report in November 1866, which many blamed for providing Congress with the excuse to pass Military Reconstruction (q.v.), alleging that "Pride in the Rebellion" was the motive for any attempt by a civil official to discuss a military order.

Actually, the whole argument boiled down to the charge that Griffin had made against Throckmorton. He simply had not violated any law, but he lacked the proper spirit for reconstructing the state. Throckmorton hurled the same charge back in the faces of the two officers when he decried Sheridan's slurring the state's honor when he made a supposedly scurrilous remark in a San Antonio hotel that if he owned Texas and Hell, he would rent out Texas and live in Hell (actually, Sheridan did have a better sense of humor than his critics gave him credit for—if one were not the butt of his jokes). Sheridan's defenders then and now point out that the general really was not a dictator as charged, but more of a man caught up in a new and novel situation never before contemplated in American government. If he had a fault, it was his dedication to the results of the war and his dealing with second-rate politicians. But this was not wholly true. In the end, Sheridan got caught up in his own web of half-truths. He had to get rid of Wells and Throckmorton or admit that he and Griffin were wrong. He could not do that. So the governors went and Sheridan became, in the words of Richard Taylor, son of one-time President Zachary Taylor (q.v.) and wartime Confederate commandant of Louisiana, "the General of the Radicals."

TILDEN, SAMUEL J. (1814–1886). Born in New Lebanon, New York, Samuel Tilden grew up in a political atmosphere. His father was a storekeeper and postmaster and member of the Albany Regency, the political machine that Martin Van Buren used to build up the Jacksonian Democrat (q.v.) political party. Politics were a constant topic of conversation at the Tilden home and business, and bigwigs in New York's Democratic machine often visited. Tilden's father was a natural hypochondriac, his store sold drugs and patent medicines by the score, and the son soon developed similar tendencies. So Tilden grew up an American patriot devoted to the Democrat Party, with a morbid interest in his health, which he always thought to be poor but really was not. No wonder he never married. He was too baneful to attract any woman into a lifetime commitment.

Tilden's formal education was sporadic. He kept leaving school because he thought he was sick. He went to New York City to live with an aunt, both to continue his studies and to find better medical advice. Tilden was not yet out of his teens when he wrote a paper defending President Andrew Jackson's removal of Federal deposits from the Second Bank of the United States, which was so good that the Democrat Party published it and had it distributed statewide. Tilden tried to go to Yale College, but the environment made him ill, as did the food. So he returned home, settling for an honorary degree, which he received in 1875. He returned to New York City, attended a local college, and spent much time writing on political matters. By 1841, he had studied enough to pass the bar and become a practicing lawyer.

Shortly after Tilden entered law practice, his father died. This, combined with a steady and purposeful life, led him to greater health and well-being. He became a corporate lawyer (one of the first really good ones in the country) and entered Democrat politics. Tilden served in the state legislature (1846–1847) and in the state constitutional convention (1847), and unsuccessfully ran for state attorney general in the mid-1850s. Meanwhile, his law business grew as he participated in many important cases, particularly handling the organization and reorganization of railroads, that made him a very rich, well-known man.

Tilden did not take much interest in the Civil War. He opposed the election of Abraham Lincoln (q.v.) and believed the war to be a mistake. But he did go to Washington at the request of Secretary of War Edwin McM. Stanton (q.v.) to advise him on the management of his department. Tilden told Stanton that he should crush the rebellion by massive force, the North's true advantage against the South. He then returned to New York and ignored the conflict, although he encouraged the Democrats to maintain a constitutional opposition to Lincoln's expansion of the executive branch. After the war, Tilden tended to support President Andrew Johnson's Reconstruction policies (qq.v.) and advised the president often.

But his real reputation came from his prosecution of the William M. "Boss" Tweed Ring (q.v.) that was corrupting New York City during this period. This required some political courage, as Tweed and his henchmen delivered the massive New York City vote for the state Democrats regularly. But as chairman of the party, Tilden believed that it was his obligation to clean up the blatant corruption (q.v.) of the era, no matter who was involved. He also led an investigation of the New York bar association into judges who had backed Tweed, running them out of office. Meanwhile, he kept his own involvement in the transcontinental railroad's Crédit Mobilier (q.v.) payoffs an open secret.

Tilden supported the Horatio Seymour campaign for president in 1868 and the Liberal Republican (q.v.) campaign against President Ulysses S. Grant (q.v.) in 1872. In 1874, Tilden ran for and won the governorship. Here, too, he acted as a reformer, breaking up the "Canal Ring," which was composed of men of both parties who bilked the state out of millions. His cleanup of New York politics fired the imagination of the nation, and his nomination for president on the Democrat ticket in 1876 was inevitable. During the campaign, the Republicans (q.v.) tried to make an issue of everything they could find: Tilden's health and general nuttiness in trying to preserve it, his being a bachelor (showing no faith in American womanhood or the future of the country), and alleged fraud in computing his wartime income tax returns. He ran literally no campaign, so much so that many thought him indifferent to the election's outcome. His unwillingness to buy one of the Returning Boards in the South condemned him to lose the disputed electoral count, although Tilden always maintained that he had been robbed unfairly of the post of chief executive (a view most historians agree with). Tilden spent the rest of his years advising the inner circle of the Democrat Party on an intermittent basis as a retired elder statesman. *See* ELECTION OF 1876 AND COMPROMISE OF 1877.

TOM'S BROOK, BATTLE OF. *See* SHENANDOAH VALLEY CAMPAIGN, SECOND (SHERIDAN'S).

TORPEDOES (CIVIL WAR LAND AND NAVAL MINES). As the war progressed, key Confederate locations like Drewry's Bluff on the James River in Virginia were backed up by Rebel gunboats and ironclad ships, and the river itself was blocked by contact and electrically fired torpedoes (what nowadays would be called naval mines). Brig. Gen. Gabriel Rains and his inventive staff created the sub-terra shells (land mines) and torpedoes (sea mines) that defended Richmond, various river crossings on the Potomac and

Rappahannock, and all port cities from 1862 on both land and sea, wherever the enemy might float or step, over Union protests that such hidden devices were barbarous and contrary to the so-called established (but heretofore undefined) rules of war.

Such "infernal machines" eventually were refined and miniaturized to be placed in wood and coal used to fuel ships and river steamboats and are strongly suspected as causing the loss of the Union steamboat *Sultana* (q.v.) on the Mississippi River above Memphis, Tennessee, in 1865. Another clock-timed ("horological" in the term of the day) torpedo was responsible for destroying much of the Union supply depot at City Point, Virginia, in 1864. A piece of coal hollowed out for such an explosive was found on Jefferson Davis' desk as Union troops occupied Richmond, Virginia, in 1865.

TOTOPOTOMY CREEK, BATTLE OF. *See* RICHMOND OR OVERLAND CAMPAIGN.

TOURGÉE, ALBION W. (1838–1905). A North Carolina Carpetbagger (q.v.), Albion W. Tourgée was born in extreme northeastern Ohio of Huguenot parents. His mother died when he was five. He could not abide his stepmother and left for a relative's home in Massachusetts. There he lost the sight in his right eye when he and a friend were playing with percussion caps. He and his classmates enlisted in a volunteer regiment for the war. He was run over by a gun carriage at First Manassas (q.v.) and paralyzed for a year because of the resulting back injury. He finally was able to walk with crutches, finished his college degree, and studied for the law. Rejoining the war as a lieutenant in an Ohio regiment, Tourgée got hit in the hip at Perryville (q.v.) and was captured at Stone's River, spending four months in a Rebel prison before being exchanged. He returned to the Army and served in the Chickamauga Campaign (q.v.), reinjuring his back at the Battle of Chattanooga (qq.v.). The injury cost him a promotion, so he resigned from the Army in protest. Tourgée practiced law until he received a letter from Provisional Governor William W. Holden (q.v.) of North Carolina. Actually, it was an advertisement sent off to numerous soldiers in the North. It invited them to come to the Tar Heel State and try farming.

A seasick Tourgée arrived in New Bern in the summer of 1865. He rode the train to Raleigh, where he met Holden. The people of the state were broke and willing to rent land cheaply, Holden told Tourgée. He decided to go back north, get some friends, and come back to rent land in the Carolina upcountry to run a plant nursery. They would be pretty much alone there, as most Yankees had stayed in the low country. But Tourgée found the climate more to his liking in Guilford County.

Try as he might to concentrate on farming, political events drew him in. He was a part of a local Union convention that adopted his resolution for impartial suffrage. The convention then sent him to a Union Loyal League (q.v.) convention up at Philadelphia, held to counter the "arm in arm" convention of Andrew Johnson's (q.v.) supporters that had met earlier. Here Tourgée met other North Carolina Scalawags (q.v.) and Carpetbaggers (q.v.), who elected him chairman of the delegation. Tourgée made a credible speech on behalf of Negro suffrage. Then the loyalists decided to send out delegates to follow the president on his "Swing Around the Circle" (q.v.) campaign to elect Democrats (q.v.) to Congress. Tourgée was one of those selected, but a hasty letter from North Carolina convinced him to return there. The whole state was up in arms over his convention speech and his electioneering up North. The nursery was failing because Tourgée and anyone associated with him faced social and economic boycott.

Tourgée and his associates had to sell out. But he refused to leave the state. He tried to sell real estate and opened a loyal newspaper. Both enterprises failed. But Congress had just passed the Military Reconstruction Acts (q.v.). Tourgée became one of those elected to the new state constitutional convention. His outspokenness at the convention made him one of the best-known and notorious Carpetbaggers in the state. Tourgée backed the black vote, which he framed as democracy for all. He helped bring government to the people by standing against having local officials appointed from Raleigh. In the election that followed, Tourgée was elected judge.

For the next few years, Tourgée lived well. He bought a nice brick house at Greensboro, which he named "Carpet Bag Lodge." Other parcels of land followed. Most of it was farm land, so he hired men to cultivate it. Tourgée invested in race horses. Most of the time he rode circuit for his job on the bench. He regularly covered eight counties. And he began a lifelong hobby, writing novels set in the South that revealed the evils of slavery and the shortcomings of Reconstruction.

In 1874, Tourgée's tenure as judge was up. He once again turned to practicing law. But he did not do as well as he had hoped. Reluctantly he went to Washington, D.C., to seek a government job. He received a job as pension agent, which necessitated selling the home in Greensboro and moving to Raleigh. He ran for Congress in 1878, but was beaten by a Confederate veteran, losing every county in the district. In 1879, he left North Carolina forever, going to New York City to see about the publication of his novels. His anonymous novel, *A Fool's Errand,* became a runaway best-seller. His next venture, under his own name, *Bricks without Straw,* did even better.

Bad investments soon drained his cash reserves, forcing him to write more. Tourgée continued to promote political, civil, and social rights for African-Americans. In 1896, he penned his last great missive for black rights when he wrote a brief for the case Plessy *v.* Ferguson (q.v.), which concerned the right of African-Americans to use freely all public accommodations, in this case a whites-only railroad car. The U.S. Supreme Court ignored Tourgée's appeal to enforce the Fourteenth Amendment (q.v.) and declared "separate but equal" to be the law of the land. Tourgée then accepted an appointment as U.S. consul at Bordeaux, France. He died there, still on duty, in 1905.

TRENT AFFAIR. After the failure of the Yancey–Rost–Mann (q.v.) delegation to secure European recognition of the Confederacy as a legal *de jure* government, the Rebels decided that a trio of roving ambassadors was insufficient for their diplomatic needs. In November 1861, President Jefferson Davis (q.v.) sent James M. Mason of Virginia and John Slidell of Louisiana to Great Britain and France, respectively. The two men were smuggled through the blockade at Hampton Roads to Havana, Cuba. There the local press made much of their safe arrival, which came to the notice of Capt. Charles Wilkes of the U.S.S. *San Jacinto*, a steam frigate of the U.S. Navy.

Wilkes determined on his own volition to do something about this perceived insult to the effectiveness of the Federal blockade (q.v.) of the South. He lay in wait on the high seas, and when Mason and Slidell passed in the British mail ship *Trent*, he fired a shot across its bow, forcing the *Trent* to heave to and be boarded. Then U.S. sailors arrested and removed the two Rebels and allowed the *Trent* to go on its way. Wilkes then took Mason and Slidell to Boston to be formally interred, becoming the hero of the hour.

There was a slight problem with what Capt. Wilkes had done. It went contrary to all U.S. principles about freedom of the seas and neutral rights, for which the nation had supposedly fought the War of 1812. Wilkes should have at least taken the *Trent* to a prize court and let a judge rule on their removal. The English were furious when the *Trent* got to its destination—not that they had never done the same. But the most important thing about the *Trent* affair was that it took over a month for the news to criss-cross the Atlantic. This allowed the Northern public to forget about the hero, Capt. Wilkes, and the English not to fret so much over the insult to British sovereignty.

The hostile British note to the Abraham Lincoln (q.v.) government had been softened by Queen Victoria's husband, Prince Consort Albert. Instead of an ultimatum, as the British Foreign Office wanted, it asked for an explanation and an apology. Lincoln and his secretary of state, William H. Seward (q.v.), were more than willing to mollify the British. Since the excitement over Wilkes' heroic action had subsided, Seward replied with the apology, coupled with U.S. congratulations that the British had finally admitted to the traditional American view of the rights of neutrals on the high seas. Mason and Slidell were let go and arrived in Europe.

Mason proved to be the wrong man for Great Britain. He chewed tobacco in public; was loud and boisterous at the wrong times, socially and politically; and an outspoken pro-slave advocate, when subtlety was called for. Although Britain seemed poised to give full recognition to the Confederate States in late summer of 1862, the failure of the Antietam Campaign crushed that hope forever. The British upper classes sympathized with the Confederates, but the rest of Britain was too antislavery for the government to act without a major Rebel victory on the battlefield. This was one of the big reasons Lincoln signed the Emancipation Proclamation (q.v.). Mason achieved little and finally went to France to join Slidell in August 1863, after the failure at Gettysburg in the Pennsylvania Campaign (q.v.).

Unlike Mason, Slidell proved to be an able diplomat. He spoke French, was married to a Louisiana French woman, and fit into French society neatly. He also had an easier task—the French being more disposed to the Confederacy from the beginning. But France was embroiled in the attempt to install Maximilian (q.v.) in Mexico and dared not move without the help or the tacit cooperation of the British Navy. So Confederate diplomacy came to naught.

TREVILIAN STATION, BATTLE OF. *See* PETERSBURG, SIEGE OF.

TRUMBULL, LYMAN (1813–1896). The U.S. senator who acted as the congressional liaison to President Andrew Johnson (q.v.) in the early days of Reconstruction, Lyman Trumbull was born in Colchester, Connecticut. He attended a local academy and went to Greenville, Georgia, to teach school for three years in 1833. He also read law in his spare time; was admitted to the bar in 1836; and began to practice law in Belleville, Illinois, near St. Louis, in 1837. Trumbull soon became interested in politics and was elected to the state legislature as a Democrat (q.v.). He resigned his seat to become Illinois secretary of state for two years before returning to his law practice. He ran for several offices, but was not successful until he was elected judge of the state supreme court. He was reelected to the bench in 1852.

As Trumbull sat on the bench, the nation drifted into crisis over the extension of slavery into the West in the Kansas issue. Trumbull stepped down to run for a seat on the House of Representatives as an anti-Nebraska Democrat (against the extension of slavery into territory north of the old Missouri Compromise line). But before he could go to Washington, the Illinois legislature picked him to be the new U.S. senator. Trumbull won this seat with Whig (q.v.) support, Abraham Lincoln (q.v.) throwing party support behind this Democrat in a three-way race to get a Free Soil man to counter Democrat Senator Stephen A. Douglas (q.v.), already in Washington. Trumbull would be reelected two more times and stay as senator until 1871.

In Washington, Trumbull soon deserted the Democrats for the new Republican Party (q.v.) over the slavery issue. As Lincoln had hoped, Trumbull and Douglas opposed each other over the extension of slavery into the West. Trumbull opposed the admission of Kansas as a slave state under the Lecompton Constitution, while Douglas wanted the population of Kansas to vote on the issue through his doctrine of popular sovereignty (q.v.), and Trumbull believed that until a territory actually became a state, Congress ought to have full authority. Trumbull refused to accept compromise over the secession (q.v.) movement, holding that the South had plenty of guarantees for its position under the U.S. Constitution as it stood. Trumbull acted as a Lincoln advisor during the Civil War, especially advising the president on constitutional and legal matters. He proposed that Congress legalize acts of doubtful constitutionality that Lincoln performed while it was out of session (expanding the army and navy, juggling appropriations from other departments into military expenses, suspending *habeas corpus*), while at the same time he opposed granting Lincoln unlimited power to battle the rebellion. Trumbull backed confiscation of Rebel property and the admission of the Ten Percent government in Louisiana to Congress, and introduced the resolution that would become the Thirteenth Amendment (q.v.), freeing the slaves nationwide.

After Lincoln's death, Trumbull was the man who went to President Andrew Johnson and thought he had obtained his agreement to sign the Freedmen's Bureau renewal bill and the Civil Rights Bill of 1866 (qq.v.), both measures he wrote and believed in as a moderate approach to Reconstruction. He warned Johnson that Congress was less inclined to permit presidential usurpation of its powers during peace than it had been during the war. But Trumbull did not think that Radical Reconstruction (Military Reconstruction) (qq.v.) was necessarily legal, constitutional, or wise. He was one of the seven who voted to acquit the president during the impeachment (q.v.) trial. This action was the last straw for the Republican leadership. They drove Trumbull out of their conferences and straight into the hands of the Liberal Republican (q.v.) movement that opposed President Ulysses S. Grant's (q.v.) reelection in 1872 (q.v.). This move cost Trumbull any chance for reelection, and he retired after stumping the North for Horace Greeley (q.v.) and returned to the practice of law, this time in Chicago.

In 1876, he returned to the Democrat Party and acted as a legal counsel for Samuel J. Tilden (q.v.), the party's candidate in the disputed election of 1876 (q.v.). Trumbull ran for governor of Illinois in 1880 as a Democrat but lost. By the time of his death in 1896, he was flirting with the Populist movement. Trumbull was an admirable man of much importance during the Civil War and Reconstruction, but his devotion to conscience made him an unreliable politician who might bolt from the party line at any time for what he saw as the good of the nation.

TULLAHOMA CAMPAIGN. *See* CHATTANOOGA CAMPAIGN.

TUPELO, BATTLE OF. *See* BRICE'S CROSSROADS, BATTLE OF.

TWEED RING. The Tweed Ring, the first modern big city machine in American politics, had its origins in a New York City fire engine company, Americus No. 6. Organized in 1848 by William M. Tweed (q.v.) and others, the Americus company was a stepping-stone into city politics, like all other fire companies of its day. Its symbol was the head of a Bengal tiger, which in time would become the sign of Tammany Hall, New York City's Democrat (q.v.) club. In 1850, William M. Tweed, a big, burly man with an ability to use his fists when reason failed to carry an argument, became the leader of the "Big 6," as city firemen fondly called the company. Tweed also ran for city alderman in his first grab at the strings of political power, but lost by a small margin. The following year he ran again. This time he showed more of the political acumen that he exercised the rest of his life. He had little chance to win in a two-way race, but he persuaded a friend to run as an independent Whig (q.v.) and thus split their natural majority. Democrat Tweed was on his way to fame and infamy.

The common city council to which Tweed was elected was already known as the "Forty Thieves." Tweed quickly fit into the system of graft for which the council was named, and in 1852, he was elected to a seat in the U.S. Congress. Tweed served only one term in Washington. He preferred municipal politics and the unbridled corruption (q.v.) for which it was renowned.

The Tweed Ring made its votes through its management of welfare for the poor, particularly the Irish immigrants. There was no Federal assistance in those days. In exchange for political loyalty, the Ring handed out city jobs, housing, food, education, and citizenship papers. Tammany Hall would hold out its votes until upstate New York had voted and then deliver the majorities required for the Democrats to win. Then Tammany men would vote the gravestones and send in vote repeaters (they preferred men with full beards who would shave a little each time to look different) and pack the ballot boxes. The "adjusted" figures usually would keep the Democrats in power at Albany as well as in the city. Needless to say, Tweed and his henchmen were heroes to those in need, and New York City had a lot of those.

Tweed ran the Ring out of his mid-town law office. True, Tweed was not much of a lawyer, but he knew people and how they worked. He collected huge "legal fees" from every business that had an office inside the city. The Erie Railroad, for example, paid Lawyer Tweed $100,000 personally for its rights to enter the city. In 1864, Tweed bought up a print shop and required that all businesses patronize it if they wished a license to operate. He also bought into a Massachusetts marble firm, which provided building materials for public buildings at a nice mark-up. Tweed had two mansions in which he lived during various political seasons: one in Albany, recognized as the Democrat headquarters for the whole state, and another up on Fifth Avenue in the city, the real mayor's office. Holding multiple offices was a Tweed specialty, and he also was head of the state Democrat Party, New York school commissioner, president of the county board of supervisors, and commissioner of public streets.

In 1869, the Ring decided that all bills paid by the city would be on the basis of 50 percent going to themselves. It soon appeared that the high standard of living for Ring elders would suffer under such an arrangement, and the ante was raised to 85 percent. Tweed became chairman of the board (without investment) of banks, gas companies, and street railways that operated in his home of Manhattan. He also got the ball rolling on the Brooklyn Bridge for a mere $40,000 in stock, public interest seeming to override the usual massive take. But the true gem of the Tweed Ring was the New York City courthouse. Projected to be an $800,000 building of which the city could be proud, it turned into a $12 million boondoggle that was never finished during Tweed's tenure. It was a testament to his power that when Tweed's daughter got married in 1870, she and her groom cleaned up with over $700,000 in gifts from "grateful" city business and social leaders.

But time was growing short for Tweed and his pals. *Harper's Weekly* magazine began its campaign against the Ring, using the courthouse as its centerpiece. The campaign was reinforced not only by editorials and feature stories, but by the skillful drawings of cartoonist Thomas Nast. With a real penchant for hitting the Ring and its members where it hurt, Nast illustrated the intricacies of government fraud for the uneducated and high society as well. It was not an easy job. At first people refused to believe that the kindly old man at city hall was anything but a near saint. But the *Harper's* campaign, illustrated by Nast's brilliant cartoon drawings, finally took its toll. Rumors of how much Tweed took got two dissatisfied politicos to turn the Ring's secret books, the real accounting, over to the *New York Times*.

With the printing of the account books, it was all over. A public Committee of Seventy formed to coordinate the prosecution, which was ably handled by Samuel J. Tilden (q.v.) and would raise him to presidential candidate in the election of 1876 (q.v.). Tweed was indicted on criminal charges. A civil suit sought to reclaim the fraudulently spent public funds. Tweed's cronies did not wait to see if the Boss could beat the charges; men of little faith in the aroused public, they fled quickly to Canada and Europe. Tweed managed to get a hung jury on the first go-around in court. But a second trial brought in a verdict of "guilty," and Tweed received a dozen years in prison and a $12,500 fine. Able attorneys appealed the verdict and got it reduced to a year and $250, and by 1875 Tweed was out of jail, having served his time and paid his fine.

The significance of the Tweed Ring is that it places the corruption in the Reconstruction South into perspective as a national phenomenon, not merely a sectional blight.

TWEED, WILLIAM MARCY [MAGEAR] "BOSS" (1823–1878). Born of parents of Scottish descent, William Marcy (Magear is his mother's name and now believed to be his real middle name) Tweed was born in New York City. His father was a chairmaker, and after a stint in public school, young Tweed was apprenticed to him to learn the trade. Two years later, the boy went off to a saddler to learn that trade, too. He then went to a private academy in New Jersey to learn bookkeeping and became the accountant of a small brush factory that his father had recently bought. At age 19, he became a partner in the firm, and at 21 he married Mary Jane Skaden, who bore him eight children. Tweed was known as a sober young man and a good husband and father. Outside the home among men, he was noted for being big in size and not averse to using his fists to settle an argument. He became a volunteer fireman and helped create the Americus Fire Company No. 6, known as the "Big 6" in fire circles.

Tweed used the fire company as his entrée into politics, a common path to power in the big cities of the 19th-century United States. Like all Americans of the era, he immediately organized a "ring" of adherents to split up the graft and corruption (q.v.), called the Tweed Ring (q.v.). He was alderman (1852–1853), U.S. congressmen (1953–1955), head of the board of supervisors (1856), school commissioner (1856–1857), street commissioner (1861–1870), commissioner of public works (1870–1871), and state senator (1867–1871).

Under attack from various city newspapers, which suspected the worst but could not prove anything, Tweed was brought down when rumors of the lesser amounts given underlings caused them to have a clerk to copy the real accounts and release them through the *New York Times* to the public. With the truth out, the Tweed Ring began to fall apart. Most of the higher ups in the organization fled the country, leaving Tweed to take the rap. He was sentenced to a dozen years in jail and a stiff fine, but appeals got both reduced. Stymied in the criminal proceedings, the good government Committee of 70 filed a civil suit, prosecuted by Samuel J. Tilden (q.v.), a well-known corporate lawyer. Unable to make bail, Tweed languished in jail until he managed to escape while on a furlough home. He fled to Spain but was recognized by local authorities on the basis of one of Thomas Nast's cartoons, which had been instrumental in his original downfall. Returned to New York City, Tweed found himself convicted of the civil charges and unable to repay the money demanded by the court. He died shortly afterward in his jail cell at age 55.

TWITCHELL, MARSHALL H. (1840–1905). Perhaps no single man personifies what historian Claude Bowers once labeled the "Tragic Era" more than Marshall Twitchell of Vermont. War hero, idealist, capitalist, opportunist, legislator, politician, planter, cozen, victim: Twitchell ran the gamut from good to bad to catastrophic during his participation in the Civil War and Reconstruction.

Twitchell's life, from his birth to stout hearted Yankee, Congregational stock in Vermont on the last day of February 1840, through his childhood on a hardscrabble farm, to his enlistment in the 4th Vermont Volunteer Infantry, and his laudable service in one of the fightingest regiments in the Union Army of the Potomac, was a story of success. But by 1864, First Sergeant Twitchell had been passed over for lieutenant. So he did what hundreds of men in similar circumstances did, he asked for transfer to the U.S. Colored Infantry. Passing through a rigorous physical, mental, and moral examination, that proved his superiors in the 4th Vermont mistaken as to his qualities for promotion, Twitchell was assigned to the 109th Colored Infantry and transferred to Texas for occupation duty along the Rio Grande.

But Twitchell was pulled out of the regiment at Indianola and sent back to New Orleans for a toothache. It was but a short distance from there to the offices of the Freedmen's Bureau (q.v.). Twitchell chose an isolated spot in the Red River Valley near Shreveport for his office. He suffered the usual problems of labor negotiations between white landowner and black employee, had the requisite run-in with Yankee schoolmarms, and was mustered out of the service in 1866—almost. The order miscarried, and Twitchell stayed on to meet Adele Coleman, a local planter's daughter.

Their marriage guaranteed that Twitchell would stay in Louisiana. Adele suffered from consumption, and Vermont had the worst death rates from that disease in the nation. She would die in a few years, anyway. Twitchell took his army money (he had saved nearly all of it), bought land, and became a cotton planter. When the Reconstruction Acts (q.v.) passed through Congress, Twitchell was the only white trusted by local blacks, and the only white with a foot in the governing class through his wife's family. Bienville Parish (county) sent him to the state constitutional convention in New Orleans. He ran for parish judge but lost the election, only to see his opponent disqualified under the constitution Twitchell had helped write.

Twitchell again outmaneuvered his political opponents and bought up Red River bottom lands with inside information. He created a Yankee colony in Coushatta in southern Bienville and then got it placed in a new Red River Parish, which he and his pals dominated politically and economically. When the area went into depression during the Panic of 1873, the rich and politically influential Twitchell bought out those less fortunate than he. None of it was illegal; it was more the style of the era, or "honest graft," as it was seen then.

But his actions made powerful enemies in dangerous times. With the assistance of local authorities, Twitchell's brother and several of his allies were arrested along with numerous black supporters. The whites were ordered out of the parish and escorted to Shreveport. On the way, a White League (q.v.) posse overtook the sheriff's escort, and the white prisoners were murdered in what became known as the Coushatta Massacre (q.v.). Twitchell got himself appointed special commissioner, a sort of state-authorized lawman. He returned with Federal soldiers and began arresting local whites under the Enforcement Acts (q.v.).

But Twitchell knew that he was licked. The White League had defeated the Republican (q.v.) forces in New Orleans. They were kept from complete victory only by the intervention of Federal soldiers. But President Ulysses S. Grant (q.v.) was talking of pulling the Army out of the South. Certainly both candidates in the presidential election of 1876 (q.v.) had made that promise. Twitchell sent his family (almost all of them had come to Louisiana) back to Vermont. Why he did not stay there with them is not known. But he returned to Louisiana and worked feverishly in the state legislature to circumvent the impeachment of the Republican governor, William Pitt Kellogg (q.v.).

Then he very unwisely went to Red River Parish to attend a Police Jury (county board of supervisors, elsewhere) meeting. Crossing the river, Twitchell and others were attacked by a lone gunman. He killed another white and wounded the black boatman. He shot Twitchell to pieces, costing him amputation of both arms. Twitchell returned to Vermont, where he married a childhood sweetheart. Then, through some political influence, he was made U.S. consul in Kingston, Canada. He was quite popular, and the Canadians testified on his behalf to keep the spoils system from taking his job as administrations changed in Washington. He remained there the rest of his life. He had to be helped by his family in everyday matters until the day he died in 1905.

U

UNION LOYAL LEAGUES. With the granting of the vote to African-Americans, it became important for the Republican party (q.v.) to organize and deliver that political power in elections locally and nationally. The vehicle for this was the Union Leagues of America (also known as the Loyal Leagues or the Union Loyal Leagues). First founded in the North during the Civil War for white Republicans supporting the Abraham Lincoln (q.v.) administration after the Democrats' (q.v.) resurgence in the congressional elections of 1862, they spread to white Unionist areas of the South like the Appalachians, hills, and sandy pine barrens by the end of the war. The organization was secret and had a Masonic-like ritual (emphasizing chants involving the 3 L's, League, Loyal, and Lincoln). Although its purpose was purely secular and political, the League often operated behind the front of the local black church or secular benevolent societies for protection.

Initially, the white organizers of local Leagues had great power because of the political inexperience of African-Americans. But it did not take long before blacks began to listen to their own natural leaders and become more attuned to advancing their own concerns. It was they who organized the informal militias to protect themselves against white marauders, the plantation boycotts that forced planters to get rid of the old gang labor system, the schools that educated members in political realities along with the 3 Rs, and the demand that political candidates deliver more (like desegregation of public services) than a mere Republican Party label to get elected. Frequently, the point man for the Leagues was the local Freedmen's Bureau (q.v.) agent. He had the contacts in the black community to get things rolling. He also had the power to sign off on labor contracts, and he knew what political rights the African-Americans had coming. He was assisted in supervision of his agency by League members informing on planters operating in violation of fair labor standards.

By 1867, the Leagues had incorporated the new black voters into their ranks and were the vanguard of Republican Reconstruction (q.v.) support everywhere. As black representation among the Leagues grew, the local white Union men, the original core of the Leagues in the South, began to drop out, giving them a more black flavor. The Leagues did more than just get out the vote. They helped focus black resistance to traditional plantation organization, which blacks hated for its reminders of slavery (gang labor, white supervision, clustered cabins, and minimal personal freedom as emphasized in the Black Codes [q.v.]), and paved the way for the reorganization of the individual agricultural worker into a decentralized family farming system by 1868, whether the land was owned, rented, or sharecropped. Thus the Leagues were important in both a political and agricultural context and strengthened the blacks' resistance to complete white domination, which was not totally defeated by the Ku Klux Klan or Redemption (qq.v.).

UNITED STATES COLORED TROOPS. *See* AFRICAN-AMERICAN SOLDIERS IN THE UNION ARMIES, USE OF.

UNITED STATES SANITARY COMMISSION. Patterned on the British Sanitary Commission, established to improve hospital and field conditions for the common soldier during the Crimean War, the United States Sanitary Commission as a civilian agency had its inception after the Battle of First Manassas (q.v.) showed how disorganized the actual military medical services for the wounded in the Eastern Theater of war were. It had its counterparts in the Western Theater in the Western Sanitary Commission and various Christian commissions affiliated with several denominations.

The commissions grew out of local Ladies Aid Societies. In the more individualistic South, there was little organization beyond the local level. But in the North, led by Dr. Henry Bellows of the Unitarian church of New York, Dr. W. H. Van Bureau of the Physicians and Surgeons of New York Hospital, Dr. Elisha Harris of the Women's Central Association, and Dr. Jacob Larsen of the Lint and Bandage Association, the United States Sanitary Commission became a powerful lobbying and practical organization to promote better conditions at the front and behind it. On June 9, 1861, Union President Abraham Lincoln (q.v.) signed an executive order giving the members, mostly women, of the sanitary commissions access to the hospitals and the camps of the armies, with the power to investigate conditions and recommend solutions. The front man for the United States Sanitary Commission was its secretary, Frederick Law Olmstead, a landscape architect in New York City, designer of Central Park, and the author of several books detailing his first-hand observations in traveling through the antebellum slave South.

The army medical directors and surgeons general (q.v.) disliked civilian meddling in their affairs, especially as the commissions brought about needed changes. These ran the gamut from cleaning up the camps and hospitals to prevent disease (q.v.); to improving field rations; to getting cooks appointed to prepare what food was available correctly; to getting their candidate, Col. William Hammond, appointed as surgeon general, over the objections of Secretary of War Edwin McM. Stanton (q.v.), by going over his head directly to the president. They were also invaluable in getting women into the war zones as nurses (q.v.). *See also* AMBULANCE SERVICES AND TRIAGE; DISEASE; MEDICAL DIRECTORS OR SURGEONS GENERAL; WOUNDS.

UNITED STATES *v.* CRUIKSHANK *ET AL*. (1876). The defendants were among the attackers of blacks and white Republicans forted up in a Louisiana courthouse. A blood bath ensued, known as the Colfax race riot (q.v.). William Cruikshank and others were identified by victims, arrested, and convicted under the Enforcement Acts (q.v.). The Supreme Court found that Cruikshank and his co-defendants had not violated the Fifteenth Amendment (q.v.), because no law in Louisiana prevented blacks from voting. Rather, Cruikshank and his companions were able to be tried under state laws concerning fraud, intimidation, murder, and assault. So long as a state did not interfere with the functioning of the Fourteenth (q.v.) or Fifteenth Amendments (q.v.) formally by law, the illegal actions of individuals should be handled by a local authority. It was only when the state violated the amendment that Federal law could apply directly to actions of individuals.

UNITED STATES *v.* HARRIS (1882). In effect, under the ruling in the United States *v.* Cruikshank *et al*. (q.v.), the Supreme Court put black and white Republicans (q.v.) at the mercy of roaming bands of armed gunmen, because no state could gain a conviction through the jury system for crimes considered by whites to be justifiable. And no state had acted to violate the terms of the Fifteenth Amendment (q.v.). This view was reemphasized a few years later in United States *v.* Harris *et al*. (1882), concerning a mob of 20 men who took four African-Americans accused of various violations of Tennessee law from state authority and hanged them. The court ruled that the Fourteenth Amendment (q.v.) did not go into effect merely because the state had been overwhelmed in its enforcement of the law. Any effort, failed or otherwise, counted. Congress' inability to pass a proposed Fourth Enforcement Bill (q.v.) tightening up the whole process left matters standing as the Court left them.

UNITED STATES *v.* REESE *ET AL*. (1876). A state election official had been accused and convicted of not accepting and counting the vote of a black citizen who had not paid a required poll tax. But the Supreme Court saw the provisions of the Enforcement Acts (q.v.) as being so broad as to punish any interference with the franchise, even though the Fifteen Amendment (q.v.) limited this to interference for race alone. Hence the Enforcement Acts lacked specific authority under the Constitution. Hiram Reese and his two co-defendants were sustained in their refusal to count votes.

UPPERVILLE. *See* PENNSYLVANIA CAMPAIGN.

UTOY CREEK, BATTLE OF. *See* ATLANTA CAMPAIGN.

V

VALLANDIGHAM, *EX PARTE* (1864). Clement L. Vallandigham (1820–1871) was a U.S. representative from Ohio and an active Peace Democrat (q.v.). He was flashy and vocal, a real crowd-pleaser. Vallandigham believed that the interests of the Old Northwest were being subverted by the Republican Party (q.v.), which was attempting to centralize the Federal government while acting under the guise of fighting the Civil War. He spoke out on behalf of slavery as a social system that kept blacks in the South and out of the free states. He maintained that the war could easily be ended through French mediation.

As Vallandigham spoke throughout Ohio, he came to the notice of the U.S. Military Department of the Ohio, commanded by Maj. Gen. Ambrose E. Burnside (q.v.), in exile for the fiasco he had made of the Fredericksburg Campaign (q.v.). Burnside sent officers to listen to Vallandigham and take notes of his most inflammatory statements. Then Burnside arrested Vallandigham under General Orders No. 38, which called for the military arrest and trial of anyone expressing sympathy with the Confederates. Tried in front of a military tribunal, Vallandigham was found guilty and jailed in Cincinnati. He issued a statement from his cell, condemning the "American Bastille" in which he was held.

Burnside's action only served to bring attention to Vallandigham's plight. Declaring himself to be a "Democrat—for the Constitution, for law, for Union, for liberty—this is my only crime," Vallandigham embarrassed President Abraham Lincoln (q.v.). The president noted that those convicted of the Conspiracy Law could be banished from the country, rather than jailed and held. So Lincoln, with much fanfare, sent Vallandigham to the Confederacy under a flag of truce through the military lines in Tennessee. This made Vallandigham more of a joke than a threat. When Union Maj. Gen. William S. Rosecrans (q.v.) turned Vallandigham over to the Rebels, he said that he had provided the exile with a guard to prevent him from coming to harm from Yankee troops under his command. Vallandigham asked to speak to the Union soldiers and he would guarantee that Rosecrans would need the guard, not he. Angrily, Rosecrans said that if he ever saw Vallandigham in his command area again, he would hang him on the spot.

Of course, Vallandigham was doing neither himself nor the Confederates any good in the South. President Jefferson Davis (q.v.) had him smuggled through the blockade to Nassau and from there to Canada. Vallandigham entered the United States during the election of 1864 (q.v.), and spoke to the Democratic Party Convention. He also ran for governor of Ohio on the Democrat ticket against John Brough, a War Democrat and Cooperator with Lincoln's combined Republican and Democratic Union Party. Giving strict orders not to interfere with Vallandigham, Lincoln took pleasure in Brough's victory.

Vallandigham brought suit against the Federal government for his earlier arrest and trial, only to have the U.S. Supreme Court refuse to rule, as it had no authority over military commissions, according to the Judiciary Act of 1789. As Lincoln figured, the eventual Union victory shut Vallandigham up more effectively than any trial. After the war, Vallandigham went back to his law practice. While acting as a defense lawyer in a murder case, Vallandigham wanted to prove to the jury that the deceased had committed suicide. Forgetting to check the revolver in question, Vallandigham convincingly blew out his own brains in front of the astonished jury, winning his case and losing his life.

VALVERDE, BATTLE OF. *See* NEW MEXICO–ARIZONA CAMPAIGN.

VICKSBURG BOMBARDMENT. *See* SHILOH CAMPAIGN.

VICKSBURG CAMPAIGN. One of the more strategic locations in the United States is the Mississippi River basin. The Mississippi drains the Missouri and its tributaries, the Ohio, the Allegheny, and the Monongahela, and the Tennessee and Cumberland. From it one can get to about any spot in the Old Southwest, which was the heart of the Confederacy. Its importance to the Old Northwest should not be underestimated, either. The Mississippi provides an easy trip to the Gulf and transport for the agricultural products of the American interior. The secession of Arkansas, Tennessee, Mississippi, and Louisiana threatened the livelihood of half of the remaining United States. Recognizing this, Louisiana pledged to keep the river open to its customers in the Old Northwest. But Mississippi was not so wise. It closed the river to all traffic at its soon-to-be-giant fortress at Vicksburg.

To open the Mississippi was to cut off from the eastern Confederacy four states and their resources in horses, food, and men. This strategic necessity was recognized in Bvt. Lt. Gen. Winfield Scott's Anaconda Plan (q.v.), and in early Federal onslaughts at New Madrid, Island No. 10, and Memphis. And of course, as an Illinoisan, President Abraham Lincoln (q.v.) knew its importance, too. As a young man, Lincoln had discovered all this in person, when he rafted down the Mississippi to New Orleans. Regardless of how the people of the Old Northwest felt about slavery, they all wanted their shipping route down the Great River to the Gulf back. It had to be controlled by one power. Early American history had shown that, when the Mississippi was controlled by Spain or France, American was held hostage to their every whim.

There were two routes from Memphis to Vicksburg. One led down the river. The other went inland, from the high ground at Memphis around the delta with its swamps and bayous, to the next high ground at Vicksburg. The man in charge of the Union war effort in the Memphis area in the summer of 1862 was Maj. Gen. Ulysses S. Grant (q.v.). He proposed to utilize both routes simultaneously. He would take his main force south through Mississippi by way of the Tallahatchie River, hence its name, the Tallahatchie Expedition. The river passage Grant proposed to use as a feint, to freeze the Confederates' gaze upon Vicksburg until he had crossed the easily defended Tallahatchie crossings.

But Grant would have to learn the hard way what every Union commander soon found out. Long overland supply lines were too vulnerable to roving Confederate cavalry. Divided into two combat groups, cavalry under Maj. Gen. Earl Van Dorn and Brig. Gen. Nathan Bedford Forrest (q.v.) struck deep behind Grant's advancing soldiers at Holly Springs, Mississippi (December 18–26, 1862), and Jackson, Tennessee (December 18, 1862–January 3, 1863), respectively. Grant had nothing to do but fall back to Grand Junction, Tennessee, and start anew. But he noted that much of the Mississippi countryside was so rich in food and forage that his men could live off the land. He would remember that next time.

The problem was that Grant could not tell his river expedition, led by Maj. Gen. William T. Sherman (q.v.), what had happened. Sherman had no communications to his rear except by slow boat. But now Sherman faced Gen. John Pemberton's (q.v.) Confederates alone. Pemberton began shuttling troops south to his subordinate, Brig. Gen. Stephen D. Lee (no relation to the Virginia Lees), at Vicksburg. So when Sherman's men began to assault Chickasaw Bluffs (December 29, 1862), he faced so many Rebels that he was hurled back in bloody defeat. Sherman wanted to try again, but fog and finally word from Grant caused him to retreat up to Millican's Bend, halfway to Memphis on the Arkansas side of the Mississippi.

At Millican's Bend, Sherman ran into Maj. Gen. John McClernand, an Illinois Democrat of some note and a Lincoln political appointment. McClernand had raised most of the troops Sherman was commanding (the Army of the Mississippi) and outranked him, too. So McClernand took over and took Sherman and his men up the Arkansas to attack Ft. Hindman at Arkansas Post on the way to Little Rock. At a loss of some 1,000 casualties, McClernand captured the fort (January 10–11, 1863) and 5,000 Rebel prisoners. His next stop was Little Rock, but Grant was not about to allow that. He came down in person and, as he outranked McClernand, joined his army and McClernand's into the Army of the Tennessee. So long as Grant was present, McClernand could be managed. But if Grant ever left, McClernand would be senior officer in charge in his absence.

Abandoning the Little Rock expedition, the taking of Ft. Hindman and its garrison had already covered his right flank, so Grant turned back to the real prize, Vicksburg. Although it was winter and little could be done militarily, Grant kept his men busy trying to outflank the fortress. Pemberton and his men, meanwhile, sat in Vicksburg and grew lazy and out of physical shape. Come Spring, Grant's men would be ready to march and fight, while the Rebels would be soft and slow moving. Grant tried to dig a canal across De Soto Point, the spit of land opposite Vicksburg, but it was placed in a backwater and never filled up properly to float the Union riverboats. He also dug a canal into Louisiana's Lake Providence, but it also proved too narrow and shallow a route.

On the Mississippi side, Grant sent expeditions into the numerous bayous, looking for a way to outflank Vicksburg on the Yazoo River. The attempt down Yazoo Pass was stopped by a Rebel battery at an improvised emplacement called Ft. Pemberton. Hoping to bypass Ft. Pemberton, another attempt up Steele's Bayou was hit by Confederate sharpshooters and long-range cannon that the Federals could not hit. Finally, Grant went back to Louisiana and dug out the Roundaway Bayou. This route was marginal, but it would allow him to move his troops south of Vicksburg on barges out of sight of Confederate observers in the spring.

As Grant was working on his projects, most of them more or less simultaneously, the river navy was not idle, either. Adm. David D. Porter sent the *Queen of the West* to run the Vicksburg batteries and raid the Mississippi and Red Rivers. The *Queen* captured two Confederate gunboats, which it manned, and the three-boat fleet tried to capture Alexandria, Louisiana, at the loss of the *Queen* and one of the Rebel boats. The survivors met the U.S.S. *Indianola*, an ironclad gunboat that had just run past Vicksburg. Hoping to revisit the exploits of the *Queen*, the *Indianola* was surprised to encounter the *Queen of the West*, refloated by the Confederate navy. In a two-hour battle, the *Indianola* had to surrender. The captured Union rivermen managed to blow her up and escape, but nothing substantial came of these raids.

As spring approached, Grant had his plan to attack Vicksburg well in hand. He would transfer all of his men and ships south of the fortress and slip down to Port Hudson (q.v.) near Baton Rouge and take it first. For the plan to succeed, he had to keep Pemberton's attention to the north and away from the Louisiana shore. To do this, he sent Col. Benjamin H. Grierson and a detachment of Union cavalry in a raid deep into Mississippi, cutting all of the rail lines supplying Vicksburg (April 17–May 2). At the same time, he sent an infantry force back into the bayous, to draw Pemberton's attention northward once again.

Grant had the navy run the Vicksburg guns in two waves, the gunboats on April 16 and the supply ships on April 22. He only lost one ship. Meanwhile, his troops marched or took barges through the Roundaway Bayou area. Sherman stayed behind to keep the old campfires burning and keep Pemberton mystified. Grant had thought to cross the river at Grand Gulf (April 29), but the Confederate batteries there proved too straight shooting to be defeated. Hearing from an escaped slave of a better landing downriver at Bruinsburg, Grant crossed his infantry there (April 30).

Then Grant heard that the Union troops in Louisiana he hoped to cooperate with were locked up in the Teche Campaign. It was then that he came up with one of the finest campaigns of the war. Grant would advance along the south bank of the Big Black River to Jackson, defeat Pemberton's reinforcements there under his department commander, Gen. Joseph Johnston (q.v.), then turn around and smash Pemberton as he emerged from Vicksburg to hit Grant in his proffered back. The plan would work, because Grant cut his supply and communication lines and lived off the land, carrying only extra ammunition with him. Pemberton would have nowhere to threaten his rear area, because there was none.

Grant slammed into fragments of the advancing Confederate army at Port Gibson (May 1), and again at Raymond (May 12). On May 13, he sent McClernand north to Fourteen-mile Creek. This froze Pemberton, who saw this as the main advance, and got rid of McClernand as the ever-reliable Sherman passed behind him on the road to Jackson. Grant sent the rest of his force into Jackson (May 14), scattering Johnston's Confederates. After a night in the state capital, Grant turned completely around and headed toward Vicksburg. He met Pemberton's confused and outnumbered army at Champion's Hill on May 16, defeating them in detail. Pemberton retreated toward Vicksburg, hoping to stop Grant at Big Black River Bridge. But the Yankees overwhelmed the Confederate rear guard (May 17), and everyone was at the Vicksburg trenches the next day.

Because he had Pemberton's men on the run, Grant decided not to wait for a lengthy siege, but to hit the Rebels before they could recover. He assaulted the fortress on May 19 and again on May 22, both times being driven back with losses. At this moment, Grant decided to get rid of McClernand, whose men had actually made the last assault alone, being left out to dry by Sherman and other subordinates. Blaming McClernand for moving too slow at Champion's Hill and too fast in the Second Assault on Vicksburg, Grant fired him. McClernand defended himself, with the support of Governor Richard Yates (a Republican), to Lincoln, but Lincoln refused to go against Grant.

The Rebels tried to retake Millican's Bend (June 7) but failed. Lincoln had troops from all over the West sent to Grant so that the general could build two lines around Vicksburg, one against the fortress and one outside that to defend against any Confederate relief. Grant meanwhile tried to blow a hole in the Vicksburg defenses three times. The first exploded on the Jackson Road (June 25), and the troops fought hand-to-hand for 20 hours before the Federals withdrew. The second went off with no real results (July 1), and the third was never fired, because Pemberton surrendered Vicksburg on July 4, picking that day because he hoped it would give his men the best terms.

Because so many Rebels gave up (37,000), there was no way that they could be sent to prison camps. Grant reluctantly paroled them (he had wanted unconditional surrender as at Ft. Donelson during the earlier Shiloh Campaign [q.v.], but Pemberton refused), most going home to await exchange and never to fight again. Union losses amounted to 8,900 for the whole campaign. The Confederates lost another 10,000 killed and wounded, besides the prisoners. Four days later, Port Hudson surrendered and, in the words of President Lincoln, "the Father of Waters roll[ed] unvexed to the sea."

VICKSBURG INSURRECTION (1874). As yet, Mississippi whites did not have anything comparable to Louisiana's White Leagues (q.v.), but whites at Vicksburg led the way, demanding that their black sheriff resign and leave the area. The sheriff begged Governor Adelbert Ames (q.v.) for assistance. Ames told him to form a posse to protect his job, but did little more. When the sheriff organized his posse, whites appealed for help, and 160 volunteers crossed the river to show Mississippi how it was done in Louisiana. The result was a riot that extended well into the night as whites ransacked private homes and killed their black residents. At least 36 dead and wounded resulted from the daytime riot, but the nighttime casualties remain unknown. The sheriff decided to resign and fled to Jackson. Governor Ames declared Warren County in insurrection and this time got Federal troops to reinstate the sheriff. But he resigned again when an assassination attempt was made against him after the U.S. soldiers withdrew. When Congress investigated the "insurrection," U.S. Senator James L. Alcorn (q.v.) "guided" them into looking at alleged corruption (q.v.) in Republican (q.v.) government, the sheriff's inability to control law and order, and Governor Ames' so-called complicity by intentionally provoking violence and backing a corrupt regime against the "will of the people."

VICKSBURG, SIEGE OF. *See* VICKSBURG CAMPAIGN.

VIRGINIA, COMMONWEALTH OF, *v.* RIVES (1880). *See* CIVIL RIGHTS CASES (1883).

VIRGINIA, COMMONWEALTH OF, *v.* STATE OF WEST VIRGINIA (1871). In Commonwealth of Virginia *v.* State of West Virginia (1871), the issue was whether two counties in the panhandle of West Virginia (Berkeley and Jefferson) had been truly admitted to the new state. West Virginia (q.v.) was kind of an anomaly anyhow. When Virginia had seceded, the western quarter of the state had refused to go along and had formed its own loyal government of Virginia, still in the Union. Then in 1862, this loyal Virginia had given the western counties the permission to form a new state under the supervision and approval of Congress. For all practical effect, since the loyal Virginia was actually the state of West Virginia, it had given itself permission to form. But two of the counties in West Virginia had not voted on inclusion in the new state constitution until after the new state had been created. After the war, secessionist Virginia wanted them back—actually, it repealed the separation legislation and wanted all of the western counties back. When Congress reaffirmed what it had done during the war in 1866, Virginia went to the U.S. Supreme Court, which has original jurisdiction in suits between states. On March 6, 1871, the Supreme Court dismissed the case. It noted that the case had no relation to property or individuals but rested on assertions of sovereignty. These were political matters reserved for Congress under the Constitution, and Congress had taken note—albeit a bit late in the 1866 reaffirmation of West Virginia, but nonetheless valid and entirely within the Forfeited Rights Theory (q.v.) of causing some actions of punishment for committing rebellion.

VIRGINIA, C.S.S. *See MONITOR,* U.S.S.

VIRGINIA EXPERIMENT. Whenever Federal troops occupied the Confederacy, slavery as an institution collapsed. The first place this happened was on the Virginia Peninsula at the massive stone fort of Fortress Monroe. Never abandoned like other Federal military installations, and never attacked like Forts Pickens and Sumter, Fortress Monroe was reinforced with Benjamin Butler's (q.v.) Massachusetts volunteers in May 1861. Other troops soon followed, and Butler became the fortress commander with the rank of brevet major general.

On May 23, three slaves followed a Union patrol back under the protection of the fort's massive guns. They sought protection from their masters and offered their services to the Union cause. Butler had initially sided with slaveowners as his men had moved southward through Maryland. His solicitude had caused Massachusetts Governor John A. Andrew to give him a severe rebuke. Butler replied that Maryland had yet to secede, so he could not rightly interfere with slavery there. But Virginia was another matter.

Soon a Virginia militia officer appeared as the representative of the slaveowners involved and asked for the return of the slaves under the Fugitive Slave Act of 1850 (q.v.). Butler refused. He said that he knew that similar slaves were erecting Confederate earthworks nearby, and he needed such labor, too. So he refused to return the slaves to their masters, preferring to declare them "contraband," seizable under the rules of war. Ben Butler had taken the North's first hesitant step toward emancipation (q.v.), and all slaves escaping to Union lines became "contrabands" (q.v.), in the parlance of the times. Although President Abraham Lincoln (q.v.) and his cabinet endorsed Butler's action, it would take Congress almost a year to forbid the return of fugitive slaves. But Congress did pass the First Confiscation Act in August 1861 (q.v.), which allowed Southern slaves used in a military capacity to be seized (not freed) for the duration of the conflict. Soon afterward, Butler was transferred to the Gulf.

News spread quickly throughout the immediate area, and slaves began to come in droves. Now the Yankees were faced with a problem they had not anticipated—how to care for these black refugees. Many suggested that the contrabands, as all fugitive slaves were called, be collected and sent North to labor. Others, Butler and his successor, Major General John Wool, among them, thought that putting them to work on abandoned plantations and fortifications, paying them a small wage on paper, which could be confiscated and used to feed and house those who could not work, was a better idea. Wool also turned to the American Missionary Association (q.v.) and other similar benevolent societies for aid. These missionaries and other secular do-gooders set up schools, regulated contraband camps, and suggested that the Army increase contraband salaries. They also urged Wool to permit contrabands not employed by the Army to care for themselves by farming garden plots. A similar policy was established at Roanoke Island in North Carolina, another Federal base in the Atlantic South.

Wool was soon replaced by a younger man, Maj. Gen. John Dix. This bothered the benevolent and religious societies, because Dix had associated himself with the preservation of slavery at Baltimore, his last posting. Dix wished to exclude all contrabands from his jurisdiction, but the existence of 15,000 fugitive blacks within his lines and a new, more aggressive congressional policy under the Second Confiscation Act (q.v.) that even hinted at arming the contrabands soon changed the general's philosophy. But Dix tried to protect loyal Virginians in their property rights, a policy that was confirmed in Lincoln's 1863 Emancipation Proclamation (q.v.), which freed only slaves behind Confederate lines. On the other hand, Dix allowed the benevolent societies to pursue their own policies based on those announced by General Wool, so long as he was not bothered by details. He did, however, set up a giant contraband camp at Newport News to isolate the African-Americans from the often malevolent influence of his condescending, racist white troops, who made a sport of harassing African-Americans whenever they were encountered. Those blacks who did not move voluntarily to the new camp were chased down by whooping soldiers and deported by force.

At the new camp, the religious and benevolent societies quarreled over the amount of aid to be given and in what form. Many preferred, for example, giving cloth to be sewn into clothing rather than the actual articles, reasoning that the contrabands would be taught self-reliance as well as succored. By the middle of 1863, the Federal government had decided that its "Negro policy" would be to institute managed work forces on abandoned land or plantations owned or managed by loyal men that placed the blacks in a state of pseudo-freedom for the rest of the war. They would be free to work as they were told; no more, no less. In the midst of this policy change, General Butler returned from his controversial administration of Reconstruction in Louisiana. Butler was more interested in the raising of the new U.S. Colored Troops than in agricultural endeavors. He declared all males between 18 and 45 to be eligible for enlistment. He promised each recruit $10 and subsistence rations for his family. Those who refused to go along with the program would be declared unemployed and liable to arrest for idleness and forced labor on fortifications (General Ulysses S. Grant [q.v.] was about to embark on his Richmond Campaign [q.v.], so the need was great), with no rations for their families.

Despite Butler's policies, most blacks worked on leased plantations during the rest of the war. Yet, as hard as the benevolent societies tried, only a small proportion of contrabands were fully employed. And as the war ended, their owners reappeared and demanded their lands back, dispossessing the blacks of their livelihood. Butler proved to be less than brilliant as a military commander and was replaced by Maj. Gen. E. O. C. Ord, a man noted for his lack of sympathy for freedmen. He sought to make the blacks independent of government aid as quickly as possible, arresting and working at hard labor all those who refused to seek an outside job. Others were signed over to landowners for the remainder of the 1865 season. Similar policies prevailed in North Carolina. And here matters stood until the arrival of the Freedman's Bureau (q.v.) administrators later that year.

VIRGINIA, LOYAL. *See* WEST VIRGINIA, CREATION OF.

VIRGINIA PEACE CONFERENCE (1861). *See* WASHINGTON PEACE CONFERENCE.

W

WADE, BENJAMIN F. (1800–1878). Born in Massachusetts as the second to the last of 10 children, Benjamin F. Wade received little formal education during his childhood, save what his mother and a small local school provided. In 1821, his parents took the family to Andover, Ohio, where Ben Wade went to work as a farmer, drover, and common laborer. He also studied medicine and taught school. Five years later, he took up the study of law and by 1828 was in practice, having been admitted to the bar. He had trouble speaking in public at first but kept at it until he had mastered the art. He was in partnerships with Joshua R. Giddings and Rufus P. Ranney and by 1838 was quite established in northeastern Ohio. In 1841, he married Caroline Rosekrans, who bore him two sons. They set up a home in Jefferson.

Already interested in politics, Wade was an antislavery man who had served as local prosecutor and a term in the state senate. He had been defeated on his second try for the senate but returned to that body in 1841 and was made a circuit judge in 1847. He was a forceful man, whose business-like methods and increasingly popular decisions led the Whig Party (q.v.) to nominate him, apparently with no effort on his own part, for the U.S. Senate. He won the seat in 1851 and remained there until 1869, changing his party allegiance to Republican (q.v.) before his second term. Wade was an unusual man for the antislavery forces in the Senate. He was a rough, coarse, and vituperative man in an arena that thrived on the suave and soft-spoken. Along with two other rough fellows, Zachariah Chandler of Michigan and Simon Cameron of Pennsylvania, Wade became the protector of less-rugged antislave senators who feared to physically fight it out with their duel-prone southern pro-slavery foes. Wade proposed that anyone needing a duel with him fight it out at close range with rifles, each duelist having a bull's eye pinned to his shirt over the heart. Threats of violence subsided quickly as southerners complained of the "unmanly" style of Wade's methods.

As the South moved to secession, Wade became more and more intransigent against compromise. He denounced the Fugitive Slave Act of 1850 (q.v.) and opposed the extension of slavery represented by the Kansas–Nebraska Act (q.v.). He favored the Homestead Bill and opposed the suggestion of the acquisition of Cuba. During the war, he was among the most belligerent of Northern senators. He went down to Virginia to watch the Battle of First Manassas (q.v.) and played a prominent role in stemming the panicked retreat. He badgered ever-cautious Maj. Gen. George B. McClellan (q.v.) to get moving and attack the Confederate armies. He acted as chairman of the Joint Committee on the Conduct of the War (q.v.) and became the terror of all called before its prying eye. He labeled all who dissented from his desires as disloyal to the Union. He was temperamentally incapable of understanding the subtleties of President Abraham Lincoln's (q.v.) war policies (which nearly cost him reelection in 1863 from opposition within the Republican-War Democrat war coalition Union Party), all of which seemed too weak and slow to him. He introduced a more stringent plan of Reconstruction along with Winter Davis (q.v.) of the House (the Wade–Davis Bill) to counter Lincoln's Ten Percent Plan (q.v.) and raged at Lincoln's pocket veto and the message that explained it in the Wade–Davis Manifesto (q.v.). He tried to get Lincoln replaced by Secretary of the Treasury Salmon P. Chase in the 1864 election (qq.v.), only to be rebuffed by his own supporters back in Ohio.

Wade welcomed the change at the presidential helm occasioned by Lincoln's assassination (q.v.), but soon realized that President Andrew Johnson (q.v.) was far worse than Lincoln ever had been. Along with Thaddeus Stevens, Charles Sumner (qq.v.), and others, Wade worked to make Reconstruction tougher. He championed the enfranchisement of blacks in the District of Columbia in 1865 and in the election of 1866 (q.v.) called for it to be a national commitment to freedmen everywhere. Although he was willing to readmit the South once it had ratified the Fourteenth Amendment (q.v.), he was in the vanguard in proposing the Military Reconstruction Acts (q.v.) that followed. In March 1867, he succeeded to the office of president *pro tem* of the senate, next in line to Johnson should he die or be removed from office. But Wade's willingness to push everything to its fullest extreme made him as many enemies as friends. Many commentators believe that the picture of Ben Wade as chief executive in place of an impeached President Johnson actually harmed the final impeachment (q.v.) vote. Wade had no reservations at all and, instead of excusing himself as vested with self-interest in the outcome, voted to convict the president. Indeed, he had already begun to choose his cabinet, so confident was he of ultimate victory. He failed in his presidential ambitions by one vote.

Evidently the party and voters back home were not amused by Wade's antics in Washington. They refused to send him back for a fourth term in the Senate. Wade attempted to gain the vice presidency under a Ulysses S. Grant (q.v.) ticket, but the party convention went for the more amiable "Smilin'" Schuyler Colfax (q.v.) instead. Wade returned to Ohio to practice law until his death 10 years later.

WADE–DAVIS BILL. Also known as the First Congressional Plan of Reconstruction (q.v.), the Wade–Davis Bill was a response to President Abraham Lincoln's Ten Percent Plan (q.v.), then in use in the South to establish loyal governments in the reconquered states of Louisiana, Arkansas, and Tennessee. Although it is now believed that Senator Ira Harris of New York wrote the original measure, it was sponsored by Representative Henry Winter Davis of Maryland and Senator Ben Wade (qq.v.) of Ohio (both Radical Republicans). Working on an earlier theory put forth by Representatives James M. Ashley and John A. Bingham (qq.v.) of Ohio, it assumed that if the South was not out of the Union (which the president claimed), it was so far gone that conditions for reentry, like the end of slavery, could be imposed by Congress, much as if it were handling the admission of a territory to statehood for the first time. Then turning to Harris' ideas, the Wade–Davis plan called for 50 percent of the 1860 registered voters of a reoccupied Southern state to take an oath of future loyalty to the Union. It had the appearance of democracy in its reliance on a majority of registrants, but it also would be difficult to achieve (most Southern states had only been partially occupied by Yankee troops) and would tend to delay Reconstruction after the war's end, when a more thought-out, truly radical plan might be introduced. As with the Lincoln plan, certain high civil and military men were excluded from participation.

Once a majority of 1860 voters had pledged their future loyalty, the state could elect delegates to a state convention. But only part of the oath-takers could vote. These were the men who could take a second oath, the ironclad oath, that they had never willingly given aid, directly or indirectly, to the Confederate cause. That is to say, the Wade–Davis plan relied on the Union men of the South to reform their states without interference from the seceders. The state convention elected by these truly pure had to abolish slavery (Davis assumed that Lincoln's Emancipation Proclamation [q.v.] as a wartime military edict was too radical and such an abolition had to be done by the elected politicians of individual Southern states in convention, not soldiers), disfranchise certain Confederate civil and military leaders (to allow the loyal government to start off without Rebel obstructionists), and repudiate the Confederate war debt (making secession and the Confederacy illegal). This meant that they would invalidate all aspects of Confederate thought. Once the state constitution was drawn up and ratified, everyone who took the original oath of future loyalty could elect a state government and their national representatives. These men could then apply for congressional consideration and be seated, if the whole Congress agreed.

The Wade–Davis Bill did little for the ex-slaves except insist on freedom. Seventeen Republicans abstained from voting on it for this or other reasons, but it received enough votes to pass both houses of Congress on July 2, 1864. When Lincoln came down to the presidential office to sign bills, he refused to ink the Wade–Davis measure. Since Congress had already adjourned for the summer, he pocket vetoed it—let it lie on the table for 10 days, whereupon it automatically expired (had Congress been in session, this ignoring of the bill would have led to its automatic passage). Although a president need not say why he pocket vetoed any bill, Lincoln chose to speak out on the Wade–Davis proposal. He claimed that he did not wish to be committed to any single course of action at that time. He also professed not to be against anything in the bill and said that if any Southern state wished to come in under its provisions, he would be happy to acquiesce in that decision. The subtle, yet important, differences in the approaches of Harris and Wade–Davis to the problem of Reconstruction might be seen in the actual titles to their proposals. Harris called his, "A Bill to guarantee in certain States a republican form of government," while Wade–Davis called theirs, "A Bill to guarantee to certain States, whose governments have been usurped or overthrown, a republican form of government." Such subtleties were the difference between Radical and Moderate Republican (q.v.) approaches to the whole era.

WADE–DAVIS MANIFESTO AND THE ELECTION OF 1864. Although President Abraham Lincoln (q.v.) said he was amenable to any seceded Southern state that desired to apply for readmission to the Union under the Wade–Davis Bill (q.v.), his action of pocket veto angered many of the Radical Republicans, who thought his statement a bit flippant. The Wade–Davis Manifesto accused the president of interfering with Congress' prerogative under the constitutional guarantee of assuring republican governments in the several states to reconstruct the South.

Dissatisfied with failed attempts to compromise the Reconstruction issue after the pocket veto; angered by what they thought was the president's hesitant attempts to end slavery, win the war by scourging the South, and punish the traitors who had rebelled; and piqued by the failure of the Red River Campaign, the Richmond Campaign, and the Atlanta Campaign (qq.v.), Radical Republicans were ready for a candidate other than Lincoln in 1864. There was one man within the president's own cabinet who believed he was the man for the job, Secretary of the Treasury Salmon P. Chase (q.v.). Launching the Chase Boom (q.v.), the secretary fell flat on his face, when the Ohio state Republican Party (q.v.) refused to select him as a favorite son candidate over Lincoln.

The Radicals then decided to withdraw from the Republican Party. Calling their new party the Radical Democracy (q.v.), they turned to a more "reliable" candidate for the party's nomination as president in 1864, John Charles Frémont (q.v.). The "Pathfinder," as Freemont was popularly known from his Western trails experiences, had tried to free the slaves in his military command at St. Louis in the early days of the war, only to suffer Lincoln's rebuff and removal. He had also been the party's first nominee in 1854 and had demonstrated that it could win the presidency only with Northern electoral votes. Running on a platform that criticized Lincoln's reluctance to end slavery at once everywhere, North, South, and in the territories, and turn Reconstruction over to Congress as stated in the Wade–Davis Bill, Fremont also said that he would withdraw his name and rejoin the party if it would but put forth a man other than Lincoln, who could win the war.

But by the fall of 1864, Lincoln's field commanders finally had destroyed the Confederate armies enough to make winning the war a matter of time. It was obvious that he would receive the approval of the Republican Convention and a large popular and electoral majority. Dropping the Republican label to encourage the participation of War Democrats, the National Union Party (q.v.) Convention met at Baltimore. Lincoln received the nomination on the first ballot. His vice presidential running mate was a War Democrat, Andrew Johnson (q.v.) of Tennessee, the only Southern senator from a seceded state who did not leave the Union with his state. Lincoln had intentionally shifted away from Hannibal Hamlin because he was a Radical spy. Johnson, on the other hand, made the war seem like a unified national policy.

The National Union Party's platform called for passing and ratifying the proposed Thirteenth Amendment (q.v.), continuing a vigorous war effort, and using black soldiers. The sixth plank was a sop to the Radicals. It said that only those who supported party principles ought to be elected or appointed to office. Some took this as a slap at Secretary of State William H. Seward (q.v.), but more than likely it referred to Postmaster General Montgomery Blair. Blair was from an important Democrat family and considered soft on the place of freed blacks in American society. The Radicals needed to get back in with the Lincoln supporters in order to have a say in future policy. But they did not wish to crawl too much. Lincoln threw them a sop by removing Blair as postmaster general. Upon Blair's removal (he agreed to step down for the good of the party at Lincoln's request), Frémont withdrew as an independent Republican candidate, and the Radicals came back to the fold.

The Democrats (q.v.) then proceeded to destroy their chances to win the election of 1864 when their convention met in Chicago. Their problem was how to unite the Regular Democrats with the Peace Democrats. Unfortunately, the keynote address was delivered by noted Copperhead (q.v.) orator Clement L. Vallandigham (q.v.). He and his types also wrote the platform, which called for an immediate peace conference to end the war on the basis of reunion with the undefeated South. Then the Democrats confused everyone by nominating as their presidential candidate former general George B. McClellan (q.v.), probably figuring that the great war hero would once again be able to secure support from the army, past and present.

McClellan might have been many things, but a traitor he was not. He accepted the nomination and rejected the party platform. The soldiers voted in the field or at home, if furloughed. They resoundingly chose to stand with Lincoln, who became the first Northern man to be elected to a second term since the nation began.

Lincoln's electoral victory in 1864, the Radicals' return to the party ranks, and Congress' refusal to seat the representatives sent to Washington from the Southern states that had followed Lincoln's Reconstruction plan meant that everything was up for grabs in 1865. There was no Reconstruction plan all could agree on. There were indications that Lincoln was considering some compromise with Congress at the time of his death—maybe a proposal that Congress recognize his governments in Virginia, Louisiana, Tennessee, and Arkansas, and he would reorganize the rest of the South on another basis with congressional input—but his death prevented anyone from knowing what exactly he had in mind. But whatever it was, it was not what his successor, Vice President Andrew Johnson (q.v.), did by taking on Congress with no compromise.

WAITE, MORRISON R. (1816–1888). Born in Lyme, Connecticut, Morrison R. Waite came from an old New England lineage. His father was a local judge who advanced to the state supreme court as chief justice. Inspired by his father's example, Waite graduated Yale College in 1837 with top grades. After reading law with his father for a year, Waite moved to Ohio, where he set up practice as a business attorney in Maumee and then Toledo. In 1840, he married his second cousin, Amelia Warner. An active member of the Whig Party (q.v.), Waite was elected to the Ohio state legislature in 1849.

With the advent of the question of the expansion of slavery (q.v.) into the Western territories, Waite helped form the Ohio Republican Party (q.v.). He supported Abraham Lincoln's (q.v.) nomination over that of home state candidate Salmon P. Chase (q.v.). In 1862, he stood for Congress but was defeated in the Republican primary by James Ashley (q.v.), a more Radical Republican. He worked to elect War Democrat John Brough over Peace Democrat Clement L. Vallandigham, recently returned from Confederate exile. His national reputation came during the *Alabama* claims (q.v.), when he represented the United States along with Caleb Cushing and his old classmate, William M. Evarts. Waite's appointment was partly accidental, a prior candidate having refused the nomination. It was Waite's reply to Lord Rondell Palmerston that clinched the American claim to Britain's liability for allowing Confederate cruisers to re-coal in English ports.

Waite returned to Ohio somewhat of a hero and received an honorary doctor of laws from Yale. In 1873, he was chosen by both parties to be a representative in the Ohio state convention to modify its state constitution. He also served as president of the convention. Later that same year, President Ulysses

S. Grant (q.v.) nominated him to be chief justice of the U.S. Supreme Court, for which he received the unanimous approval of the Senate. During his term, the court decided numerous issues of import, including the constitutionality of the Enforcement Acts (q.v.), the rights of states to regulate railroads (the Granger Cases), Federal control of elections through the Enforcement Acts (q.v.), the Tenure of Office Act (q.v.), repudiation of state debts, the rights of labor unions, Chinese exclusion, and the patent of the telephone. He was a man who liked details and paid the strictest attention to the docket of the court and the nature of upcoming cases, and he had a reputation for fairness above party considerations. Waite fell sick while reading an opinion, stepped down from the bench, and went home and collapsed. He died three weeks later from pneumonia.

WAKARUSA WAR. *See* KANSAS–MISSOURI BORDER WARS.

WALKER, ROBERT. *See* KANSAS–MISSOURI BORDER WARS.

WALKER, WILLIAM. *See* FILIBUSTERING.

WARMOTH, HENRY CLAY (1842–1931). Born in Illinois, Henry Clay Warmoth was a Carpetbag (q.v.) governor of Louisiana during Reconstruction. He grew up with a modicum of education, mostly gleaned from books that his father had lying around and from setting type in a local print shop. When he was almost 18 he left home for Missouri, where he put up a sign and practiced law, having learned a bit of it from his father's law books (he was actually a justice of the peace and a harness maker). As soon as the war broke out, Warmoth went off with the 32nd Missouri regiment to fight for the Union. He fought with the regiment at Vicksburg and Chattanooga and as a staff officer in the Red River Campaign (qq.v.). Warmoth went to Washington to view Abraham Lincoln's (q.v.) second inaugural ball and toured Richmond a few days after the Confederates fled on the road to Appomattox. At the end of the war, he traveled to St. Louis to visit his sisters, and he and his father took a steamboat south to New Orleans to see what they could see.

Warmoth was impressed with the big plantation culture he found in Louisiana. He promised himself one day that such luxury would be his and opened up shop as a lawyer representing those who had had property seized by the War or Treasury Departments. Then Warmoth decided that he should organize a loyal party to reconstruct the state, with the help of Thomas J. Durant, a leader of the wartime Free State movement. In a convention they adopted the name of Republican Party (q.v.) for the first time.

The convention, with black delegates participating, voted to send a territorial representative to Congress. Durant declined, but Warmoth accepted the nomination. Congress actually gave him a seat (but no vote). Then he attended the convention of Southern loyalists held in Philadelphia and toured the North following the "Swing Around the Circle" (q.v.) to negate President Andrew Johnson's (q.v.) campaign and elect Republicans. By the time of the passage of the Military Reconstruction Acts (q.v.), Warmoth was back in Louisiana enrolling black and white Union veterans in the Grand Army of the Republic, a Republican veterans organization. He was the most-known Republican in the state.

Although he was not a delegate to the constitutional convention, he played a major role. He got himself and a few others admitted with full privileges on the floor. The 25-year-old Warmoth got the convention to lower the age requirement for governor from 35 to 25 so that he could run for the office, which he won in 1868. Under Warmoth's guiding hand, the legislature passed laws creating a metropolitan police, a parish constabulary, and a state militia. He also saw to it that the governor was a member of the Returning Board that validated all votes. In the beginning, Warmoth worked smoothly with his fellow Republican legislators and got them to elect William Pitt Kellogg (q.v.), a personal friend and Illinois Carpetbagger, to one of the U.S. Senate seats. The Republican vote had already dropped by half from intimidation, and Warmoth could not hold Louisiana in the Republican column for Ulysses S. Grant (q.v.) or elect any Republicans to Congress in November 1868. But since most local parish jobs were appointive through the governor, Warmoth kept the party in power through his own actions. And all appointees received their commissions only after they submitted a signed, undated letter of resignation to the governor as a guarantee of their loyalty.

But in time, many of the legislators grew to resent Warmoth's concentration of all appointment power for local patronage in his own hands. The governor seemed to give more than their fair share of offices to his Carpetbag (q.v.) friends. The resentment spread from Scalawags (q.v.) to blacks. Then Warmoth had an accident aboard a steamboat that lamed him severely. Rather than healing, the wound grew worse, and he took off to the Mississippi Gulf Coast to heal. In his absence, Lieutenant Governor Oscar Dunn (q.v.), a former slave and now a plasterer by trade, took over the governor's post. Warmoth thought this would be a formality, but Dunn was a true Louisianan. He was in for keeps. Not only that; he plotted the removal of Warmoth's appointees and their replacement by his own. On crutches, Warmoth returned to New Orleans and confronted Dunn before any real damage could be done. He also took the opportunity to dress down all of his opponents (a lengthy process by then) at the so-called Gatling Gun Convention, where rival Republicans hoped to reorganize the party without him.

Warmoth made enemies for other reasons, too, many of them monetary. His opponents accused him of every kind of crooked political deal, from pocketing bribes, to overcharging for state printing (20 times too much, according to one story), to collecting fees from his appointees for the right to continue in office. He also bought depreciated state bonds and got the legislature to fund them, making a killing. In 1872, a congressional investigating committee came down to Louisiana to investigate Reconstruction corruption. Warmoth's testimony— full of all sorts of vagaries—lasted three days and filled 135 pages.

After all of this, Warmoth ran into a bit of luck when Lieutenant Governor Dunn died of suspected poisoning. Warmoth convinced the legislature to elect Pinckney Benton Stewart Pinchback (q.v.) as president *pro tem* of the state senate, in effect lieutenant governor. Pinchback, a sort of Warmoth with a darker skin, had been one of the governor's constant supporters until now. By 1872, it was obvious that if Warmoth expected to gain anything by the end of his term, like a U.S. Senate seat, say, he would have to appeal to the Democrats (q.v.). Oddly enough, there was a fairly easy way to do this. He declared himself to be a Liberal Republican (q.v.) in favor of Horace Greeley's (q.v.) election as president.

By the end of August 1872, Warmoth had worked out a deal to combine the Liberal Republicans with both Democrat factions behind the candidacy of John McEnery for governor. For his political acumen, Warmoth was promised election to the U.S. Senate by the hopefully Democrat legislature. Their real opponent was Kellogg, backed by the Customs House faction led by Stephen B. Packard, the U.S. marshal, and state Senator Pinchback.

Warmoth's Fusion Party won the state by 10,000 votes; at least, that is what his Returning Board said. But the Regular Republicans got a Federal judge to declare their Returning Board was the correct one and to enjoin Warmoth from having anything to do with validating the returns. The U.S. Army took over the statehouse in New Orleans (the Mechanics Institute) and refused to admit anyone to the legislature who was not on the judge's approved list. Pinchback got up before the senate and announced that Warmoth had approached him with a $50,000 bribe the preceding midnight to let his people be seated. Of course, Pinchback said, he had refused the money. The house was informed and quickly impeached Warmoth, suspending him as governor until tried. Pinchback broke into the governor's office and took over. As president *pro tem* of the senate, he was next in line to be governor.

A shoot-out between factions seemed imminent. Then a contingent of Federal soldiers came forward with a telegraphed order from Washington. Pinchback was to be governor for the rest of Warmoth's term, said President Grant. On January 13, 1873, both Kellogg and McEnery took the oath of office as governor of Louisiana, each guarded by their adherents. But Kellogg had an ace up his sleeve. He also had the support of President Grant. The Fusionists would have to wait for 1876 and the removal of the Federal troops by President Rutherford B. Hayes (q.v.).

Warmoth retired to a sugar plantation in the bayou country west of New Orleans, which he had bought with some of his political proceeds. He got married and lived out a long and fruitful life in a style that he had always dreamed of. He remained a power in Louisiana Republican circles, once running for governor in 1888. He wrote his memoirs. He seemed forgotten when he died in 1931, but he was not. He had an unknown admirer who used all of his political tricks to attain power in the state, instructed the legislature on how to vote, sequestered all patronage in the governor's office, and required undated resignations from all appointees. His name was Huey P. Long.

WARNE, KATE. *See* BALTIMORE PLOT.

WASHINGTON, EARLY'S RAID ON. After the defeat of Union Bvt. Maj. Gen. Franz Sigel at New Market, Lt. Gen. Ulysses S. Grant (q.v.) knew that he had to keep pressure on the Confederates by denying them sole occupation of Virginia's Shenandoah Valley. Because of its particular geographical qualities (it ran roughly from the northeast to the southwest), the Valley was not only the breadbasket for Gen. Robert E. Lee's (q.v.) Army of Northern Virginia, it was a direct route for a covered Confederate march on Washington. So Grant placed Federal troops there under Bvt. Maj. Gen. David Hunter, a personal political friend of President Abraham Lincoln (q.v.), as had been Sigel.

Initially, Hunter was all that was expected. He drove back the Confederate force that faced him, which had been depleted to aid Lee in opposing Grant's 1864 Richmond Campaign (q.v.). The Confederates turned to fight at Piedmont on June 5. Hunter used his artillery first to silence the Confederate guns and then to cover an infantry assault. The Confederates counterattacked. As the two sides struggled, Hunter managed to get around the Rebels' flank and roll up the whole Confederate position, killing their commander, Brig. Gen. W. E. Jones. Both sides lost about 700 casualties, but the Southerners also had 1,000 men surrender.

Hunter followed up his victory with a move on the Confederate rail center at Lynchburg. Gen. Lee responded to this threat by returning Maj. Gen. John C. Breckinridge (q.v.) and his command to the Valley. Breckinridge met Hunter near Lynchburg on June 18. Hunter's attack was rebuffed. He retreated, having information that more reinforcements from Lee's army, under Lt. Gen. Jubal Early (q.v.), were arriving. Hunter panicked and withdrew through the mountains into West Virginia, effectively removing all Federal presence from the Shenandoah Valley.

Early quickly gathered all Confederate units together and advanced north to Washington, hoping to reduce Grant's pressure against Lee. He dodged the Federal garrison at Harper's Ferry and moved through Hagerstown, reaching Frederick on July 9. He levied ransoms of $20,000 against Hagerstown and

$200,000 against Frederick. Opposing him across the Monocacy was a small ersatz army commanded by Bvt. Maj. Gen. Lew Wallace, later author of *Ben Hur*. Early's men crossed and in the battle of the Monocacy drove Wallace back toward Baltimore.

Early let Wallace go, turning toward Washington itself. He raided Silver Spring, burning the home of Montgomery Blair, Lincoln's postmaster general. Then Early shook out a skirmish line and attacked Ft. Stevens on Washington's Seventh Street. The fort was held by reinforcements Grant had sent up from Richmond. For a moment or two, President Lincoln himself stood on the parapet under fire. It was the only Rebel attack made on Washington during the war.

But Early was not strong enough to capture Washington. He retreated to the vicinity of Berryville, across the Blue Ridge from Winchester. His presence was as embarrassing to Grant as Lee had hoped, but Grant had sufficient men to handle Early without materially weakening the Petersburg Siege (q.v.). He sent his VI Corps to Washington, where it was joined by the XIX Corps, which had just arrived at Fortress Monroe from Louisiana. The Federals operating against Early came from four different departmental commands. Grant hoped that Chief of Staff Maj. Gen. Henry W. Halleck (q.v.) might coordinate them, but Halleck refused to act. After Lincoln refused several choices, Grant sent Maj. Gen. Philip H. Sheridan (q.v.), his aggressive cavalry commander, to take over. Sheridan was ordered to defeat Early and clear the Valley of Confederates, which he did in the Second Shenandoah Valley Campaign (Sheridan's) (q.v.).

WASHINGTON PEACE CONFERENCE (1861). Foremost among President Abraham Lincoln's (q.v.) announced political policy goals was the restoration of the Union. So for all practical purposes, the minute the South seceded there was the notion of Reconstruction—even during the secession (q.v.) crisis itself.

Lincoln was not alone in his notion of reconstructing the Union before secession led to war. Before his home state of Virginia seceded, U.S. Senator Robert M. T. Hunter suggested an outward alliance between the North and South with separate economic and domestic institutions and a dual presidency, one executive from each section. Congress would be denied power to deal with slavery in the territories (the actual cause of the breakup). Indeed, slavery was to be guaranteed access to all territories, and each territory would decide on its status as slave or free by a popular vote upon its admission to the new Union. To clean up another aggravating problem, Hunter proposed that the Federal government pay for all fugitive slaves who escaped into free states.

Not to be outdone, Illinois' U.S. Senator Stephen A. Douglas (q.v.), Lincoln's old debating opponent in 1858, came forward with a plan of his own. Douglas was solidly behind Lincoln's effort to prevent secession by force. But instinctively he tried to compromise the whole secession crisis, as he had done years earlier in the Compromise of 1850 (q.v.), which had solved the question of slavery in the Mexican Cession. Unfortunately, events moved too fast toward war, and the plan lay dormant in Douglas' personal papers, found after his death in June 1861 (he had exhausted himself to death trying to heal the secession crisis and then rallying the North around Lincoln through personal intervention). Like Hunter, he would have recognized the disunion as fact and substituted an economic union for the old United States. All of the old tariffs, trade regulations, patents, and copyright laws would still obtain uniformly between the two republics. Each country would guarantee the other's territorial integrity, and neither would add territory or change its boundaries without the other's consent. As the tariff was a thorny problem to begin with, its proceeds were to be divided between the two republics on the basis of population, including three-fifths of the slaves, the old Federal formula.

Many of Hunter's and Douglas' ideas in varied forms were presented in the House of Representatives' Corwin Committee of Thirty-three and the Senate's Crittenden Committee of Thirteen (qq.v.) and had already failed there. They came up again in the Washington Peace Conference of 1861, a belated effort sponsored by the border South to head off secession and war (after all, these states knew very well that any North–South war would be fought on their lands). After much talk, the "Old Gentleman's Convention" (many of the sponsors and delegates were elderly ex-Whigs [q.v.]) proposed a Thirteenth Amendment to the Constitution and a reunification of the nation under the old Constitution. This amendment would draw the 1820 Missouri Compromise line of 36° 30′ across the Western territories to the eastern border of California. Above the line, slavery was not to be had. Below the line, slavery was to be guaranteed. Territories would become states in the traditional manner. No new territories could be added to the United States without a majority of senators from both sections concurring.

The proposed amendment also guaranteed slavery in the states where it existed and in the District of Columbia so long as it existed in Maryland. Slavery could not be abolished in any state without concurrence of the slaveholders. All fugitive slaves were to be rendered back to their states of origin. If this could not be done because of mob action or the inaction of state or Federal officials, the Federal government would compensate the slaveholder, which action would end all claims on the fugitive. The slave trade was to be prohibited in the District of Columbia (already done in the Compromise of 1850 by law) and between the United States and foreign countries (done by law in 1808). The amendment could not itself be amended without the agreement of all the states. But many in the North and South were fed up with compromise by this time, and Lincoln's tough inaugural speech put an end to the effort.

In an effort to clarify early wartime policy, Congress passed the Crittenden Resolution in the summer of 1861, which declared that the war was not being fought to subjugate the South or interfere with slavery. But by the following year, an attempt to repass this resolution failed, indicating how far down the road to eventual emancipation Congress had come.

WASHINGTON, TREATY OF (1871). In an effort to resolve the *Alabama* claims (q.v.), held over from the Civil War, President Ulysses S. Grant's Secretary of State Hamilton Fish (qq.v.), during talks initially aimed at resolving the U.S.–Canadian boundary through Puget Sound, emphasized the need of a neutral to use diligence to prevent the arming of belligerent vessels in its ports. When the British refused to admit their fault in advance of a monetary settlement, Fish began to pile on a series of minor claims at the Geneva arbitration hearings that threatened to raise the jackpot considerably. The British decided to admit their failure during the war, and settlement was established at the sum of $15,500,000. Fishing rights and trade proved more enduring and dragged on for years. But the territorial settlement of the boundary through the San Juan Islands in Puget Sound was arbitrated by Kaiser Wilhelm I of Germany in 1872, mostly to America's advantage.

WASHINGTON'S BIRTHDAY SPEECH. Right after President Andrew Johnson (q.v.) had his veto of the renewal of the Freedmen's Bureau (q.v.) sustained by Congress, he spoke to an impromptu audience of serenaders at the White House. It was the first time the public had really seen the president since he was sworn in (staggering from drunkenness or illness or a little of both) as vice president at Abraham Lincoln's (q.v.) second inaugural, almost a year earlier. It was very important, because Johnson crossed the invisible line between good politics and decency by insulting his opponents personally. This meant that any future compromise between the executive and legislative branches over Reconstruction would be next to impossible.

Johnson was preoccupied with himself as a martyr. He used the word "I" 152 times and accused unnamed congressmen of conspiring against him and his plan of Reconstruction, which he pronounced as only just, as the war had ended. Johnson pointed to his pardons and maintained that the Rebels had repented their sins of secession (q.v.) and rebellion. He even compared his plan to what Jesus Christ would have done had He been there—kind, just, forgiving. Then he went on to say that there were men in the North whose disunionist designs were fully as evil as anything put forward by Jefferson Davis (q.v.), Robert Toombs, John Slidell, and "a long list of others."

"Give us their names," came an anonymous voice from the crowd.

Johnson rose to the occasion. "A gentleman calls for their names," he began. "Well, I suppose I should give them. . . . I say Thaddeus Stevens (q.v.)

of Pennsylvania [tremendous applause according to a witness]. I say Charles Sumner (q.v.) [great applause]. I say Wendell Phillips and others of the same stripe are among them," the president continued, naming the great abolitionist (q.v.).

"Give it to Forney," came the voice, referring to John W. Forney, editor of the *Philadelphia Press* and now clerk of the U.S. Senate and the one who would not seat the senators from the South elected under Johnson's "Christlike" plan of Reconstruction.

Johnson bellowed, "Some gentleman in the crowd says 'Give it to Forney.' I have only just to say that I do not waste my ammunition on dead ducks" [laughter and applause].

All Republicans were mortified by Johnson's hasty speaking. "Was he drunk?" inquired a friend of Senator John Sherman (q.v.), the general's brother. Tragically, no. What the president had done was publicize a breach between him and the Congress. This made it official in the eyes of the public and hard to heal. His vetoes would no longer hold up in disagreements over future congressional measures, and it was the first step in the long road to impeachment (q.v.).

WAUHATCHIE, BATTLE OF. *See* CHATTANOOGA CAMPAIGN.

"WAVING THE BLOODY SHIRT." "Waving the bloody shirt" is a colorful phrase of post–Civil War politics that essentially meant accusing white Southern Democrats (q.v.) of wholesale slaughter of white Unionists and black Republicans (q.v.) in the South and Northern Democrats of wholehearted complicity in these deeds by opposing Republican congressional programs in Washington. The term came from Benjamin Franklin Butler (q.v.), a Massachusetts politician better known as the "Beast of New Orleans," for his tough occupation policies and heavy-handed larceny. After the war, Butler supported a harsh Reconstruction and helped manage the impeachment of President Andrew Johnson (qq.v.). During one debate on violence in the South, Butler waved a bloody shirt over his head, asserting that the scourged victim was an Ohio Carpetbagger (q.v.), who had merely tried to obtain justice for African-Americans in Mississippi. The antic was so successful in demonstrating Southern white retaliations on loyal people that the term came to be applied to any attack on the Democrats that emphasized their support of Southern violence and subordination of legitimate black social and political aspirations as free persons.

WAYNESBORO, BATTLE OF. *See* SHENANDOAH VALLEY CAMPAIGN, SECOND (SHERIDAN'S).

WELDON RAILROAD, BATTLES OF. *See* PETERSBURG, SIEGE OF.

WESTERN STATES SANITARY COMMISSION. *See* UNITED STATES SANITARY COMMISSION.

WESTPORT, BATTLE OF. *See* PRICE'S MISSOURI RAID (1864); RED RIVER CAMPAIGN.

WEST VIRGINIA, CREATION OF. Virginia had been two states in many ways from its inception. The west was always cut off from the east by the Blue Ridge and the Alleghenies. The land admitted to small, subsistence farms rather than large, staple-crop plantations, so the numbers of slaves were few, around 18,000 in 1860, depending on what counties were included in the idea of "west." The western part of Virginia had long maintained that the government at Richmond cared little about them, even though they comprised a third of the white population, a quarter of the land area, and all of the mineral wealth of the state. Transportation improved with the building of the Baltimore & Ohio Railroad in the 1850s, but an extension of that line down the heavily populated Kanawha Valley, as promised by the state legislature, had never been built. Taxes on slave property were less than on land, but three-fifths of slaves were counted for the basis of country representation in the state legislature, as in the Federal Constitution.

After the election of 1860 (q.v.), Virginia called a convention, which met on February 13 and rejected secession (q.v.). The firing on Ft. Sumter (q.v.) caused the convention to reconvene, and President Abraham Lincoln's (q.v.) call for troops to suppress the South led to Virginia's convention voting to secede on April 17, becoming the first state to lead in the Second Secession (q.v.) Movement. The ordinance to secede was sent to the people for a referendum on May 23. The eastern part of the state voted overwhelmingly to leave the Union. Western Virginia did not, but its vote was not counted before Virginia joined the Confederacy.

Even before the public vote on secession, which everyone pretty much would be in favor of, delegates from select western counties met at Wheeling to consider a loyal course of action. This First Wheeling Convention decided to adjourn and hold an election after the secession referendum to elect new delegates to a Second Wheeling Convention to meet on June 11. The Second Wheeling Convention decided to act as if it were the loyal state government. It elected Francis Pierpont governor, and John S. Carlile and Waitland T. Riley as U.S. senators. Congressmen already representing the disaffected counties would continue to serve. Then the senators and congressmen presented themselves to Congress, which promptly seated them.

The seating of state officials in Congress is the way state governments gain legality. Lincoln capped off the charade by addressing all official correspondence to Pierpont as governor. Now the new government of Loyal

Virginia would engage in another ploy. According to the U.S. Constitution, no state may be divided without its own consent. After much argument, the Loyal State of Virginia gave its consent to allow the creation of the new state of West Virginia. A public referendum on April 3, again in select counties, omitting many pro-slave areas to be included in the new state, passed. U.S. Senator Riley sanctimoniously introduced the measure to divide Virginia to the Senate on May 29.

After much deliberation over boundaries and its proposed pro-slave state constitution, Congress passed the final bill to create West Virginia on December 10. In all cases, the rationale seemed to be that of Pennsylvania Congressman Thaddeus Stevens, a Radical Republican: unconstitutional but necessary. Lincoln signed the bill with some reluctance on December 31. In the end, he opined that secession to divide the Union may be unconstitutional, but secession to restore part of the Union was certainly constitutional.

But Congress' admission of West Virginia had a condition. The state would not be admitted until it amended its proposed state constitution to get rid of slavery. West Virginia provided for gradual emancipation of slaves without compensation to the owners (made immediate with the passage of the Thirteenth Amendment [q.v.] in 1865), which the voters approved on March 28, 1863. President Lincoln issued a proclamation recognizing West Virginia statehood on April 20, to take effect on June 20, and Congress sat all of its senators and representatives at its next session. Meanwhile, the Pierpont government had moved from Wheeling to Alexandria to keep up the appearance of two Virginias. When it was forcibly returned to the Union, real Virginia sued to regain its western counties in Commonwealth of Virginia v. State of West Virginia (q.v.), but lost the case. Virginia got its revenge in the settlement of state debt; it took West Virginia until World War II to pay off its share.

WHIG PARTY. Originally formed by those who opposed Andrew Jackson's election to the presidency, the Whig Party has often been forgotten in the popular historical record. Named for the American patriots and British politicians who opposed the power of King George III and his ministers during the period of the American Revolution, the 19th-century Whigs called themselves such because they were against "King Andrew I of veto memory," Jackson being the first president to use the veto power to negate other than unconstitutional measures.

The Whigs introduced many things into American politics. They were the first party to have a substantial economic development program, the American System (q.v.), which remained consistent for the years of its existence. They were the first party to use uncannily modern campaign methods based on sloganeering and high profile advertising. They had problems, however, in securing enough votes to win the presidency on the basis of their program alone. So they tended to run military heroes like William Henry Harrison, Zachary Taylor, and Winfield Scott (qq.v.). Otherwise, they were stuck with their perennial candidate, party leader Henry Clay, a man who would rather be right than president, and was neither.

By the end of the War with Mexico, the Whigs got steamrollered by their own diverse membership and factionalized over the issue of slavery. They were composed of two major groups, the northern or antislavery Conscience Whigs, and the southern planter and their northern cotton mill allies, the Cotton Whigs. As the Democrats tended to support southern ideas on the place of slavery in the Constitution and the day-to-day settlement of the West, the Cotton Whigs, at least the southern elements, began to switch to the Democratic Party (q.v.). Some remnants of the Whig Party appeared in the election of 1856 (q.v.) as the American Party, but the process of destroying the Whigs was completed by the election of 1860 (q.v.).

After the Civil War, many native Southern whites, derisively called Scalawags (q.v.), supported the Republican Party (q.v.). Historians have found that one of the bases of support of postwar Republicanism in the Reconstruction South and later was the old prewar Whigs. Since the slavery issue had been eliminated by the results of the war, these persons turned once again to the party that promised economic development through the Republican Platform of 1860, Henry Clay's old American System, enacted into law when the Democrats lost their Southern wing through secession.

WHISKEY RING SCANDAL. *See* GRANT, ULYSSES S., ADMINISTRATION—SCANDALS.

WHITE CAMELLIA, KNIGHTS OF THE. This group was a Louisiana version of the Ku Klux Klan (q.v.).

WHITE LEAGUE. A Louisiana Democratic Party group of armed white gunmen who intimidated black and white Republicans at elections in the mid-1870s, shot rival candidates and their supporters, and watched the polls to limit opposition voting. *See also* NEW ORLEANS, THIRD BATTLE OF.

WHITE LINERS. A Mississippi Democratic Party group of armed white gunmen who intimidated black and white Republicans at elections in the mid 1870s, shot rival candidates and their supporters, and watched the polls to limit opposition voting.

WIGFALL, LOUIS T. (1816–1873). Born to Levi Durand and Eliza Thompson Wigfall in Edgefield, South Carolina, on April 21, 1816, Louis T. Wigfall grew up filled with the notion that the perfect society was led by the planter class based on slavery (q.v.) and the chivalric code. He was highly educated, attending the University of Virginia in the mid-1830s, his schooling interrupted by his service in the Second Seminole War in 1835, in which he earned a lieutenancy. He graduated from South Carolina College in 1837, went back to study law at the University of Virginia, and became a lawyer before the Edgefield bar in 1839. He married Charlotte Maria Cross, who bore him five children.

Wigfall was a good attorney, when he wanted to be. But he had a hot temper, was naturally contentious, and fought several duels, including one in which he was severely wounded. In a wise move, he decided to go to Texas, where he set up a law establishment in Marshall after a brief partnership in Nacogdoches. Wigfall was soon known as an ardent expansionist; a proponent of the War with Mexico; and an opponent of the Wilmot Proviso (q.v.), which would have made the acquired territories from Mexico Free Soil. In this he echoed his earlier stand in South Carolina, where he was one of the "Bluffton Boys," desiring the nullification of the Tariff of 1842 and secession from the Union should Texas not be annexed as a state. The Democrat (q.v.) victories in the election of 1844 solved both problems without such drastic measures.

But Wigfall never forgot that Sam Houston was an opponent to his aggressive policies and made him his eternal enemy, calling Houston a coward and a traitor to the South. Wigfall served in the Texas house of representatives, was instrumental in the defeat of Houston as governor in 1857, and moved up to the state senate in 1858. He promoted a strong pro-slavery stance that helped break up the Know Nothing Party (q.v.) in the same year. Capitalizing on the fear of John Brown's Harper's Ferry Raid in 1859 (qq.v.), Wigfall became Texas' new U.S. senator. His stand on state rights compromised his desire for Federal aid to fight Indians and expand railroads into Texas.

With the election of Abraham Lincoln (q.v.) in 1860, Wigfall used his talent for eloquent, acerbic debate to foil any attempts to mitigate the sectional crisis, leading the so-called "Fire-Eaters" (q.v.) in defense of Southern secession. He wrote the "Southern Manifesto," which said the Union was finished, and the South had to secede for its own honor and salvation and organize the Confederacy. When Texas seceded, Wigfall refused to resign and stayed North to spy, criticize Northern senators, provide arms and ammunition for Texas troops, and persuade Maryland to secede from the Union, as one of the key Apostles of Disunion.

Wigfall set up shop in Baltimore because this was the key point for Union reinforcements to get through to defend and secure the Union government in Washington, D.C. It was also at this time that Wigfall participated in plots to kidnap President James Buchanan (q.v.) and assassinate the incoming chief executive, Abraham Lincoln. It is possible that Wigfall met John Wilkes Booth (q.v.), a kindred spirit in plots and skullduggery, prominent among the

Maryland civilian and militia volunteers for the defense of Baltimore. He was also in direct communication with the provisional president of the Confederacy, Jefferson Davis (q.v.).

The plots against Lincoln and Buchanan fell through, and Wigfall was present for Lincoln's First Inaugural Speech, which the Texan saw as a declaration of war against the Confederacy. Finally resigning from the U.S. Senate in late March 1861, Wigfall went to Charleston, South Carolina, for the impending conflict. Ever the supreme egotist, in the midst of the firing on Ft. Sumter (q.v.), Wigfall rowed out to the fort's sally port and negotiated without authority a cease-fire with the post commander, Maj. Robert Anderson.

With the war on, Wigfall became in quick succession colonel of the First Texas Infantry, brigadier general in charge of the Texas Brigade in Virginia, and member of Congress from Texas. At first an ally of President Jefferson Davis, the two men, both considering themselves military experts without peer, soon became enemies over the conduct of military policy. Wigfall supported Gen. Joseph E. Johnston and Gen. P. G. T. Beauregard (qq.v.), whom Davis disliked, through their informal military-political organization, the Abingdon–Columbia Bloc. Wigfall, contrary to his state rights philosophy, supported a strong central control of military matters. He refused to go along with arming slaves late in the war, as he considered black soldiers unworthy representatives of the Confederacy.

After the fall of the Confederacy, Wigfall returned to Texas, and in 1866 he fled to England. He remained in exile until 1872, when he returned to Baltimore and then Galveston, Texas, where he died of apoplexy in 1873.

WILDERNESS, BATTLE OF THE. See RICHMOND OR OVERLAND CAMPAIGN.

WILKINSON, JOHN. See LINCOLN ASSASSINATION; LINCOLN ASSASSINATION, THE CONFEDERACY AND THE; LINCOLN ASSASSINATION, THE NEW YORK CONNECTION OF THE. .

WILLIAMS v. STATE OF MISSISSIPPI (1898). Shortly after it decided Plessy v. Ferguson (q.v.), the U.S. Supreme Court validated the formal skirting of the Fifteenth Amendment (q.v.) in Williams v. Mississippi (1898). After Congress had dropped the proposed Lodge Force Bill from consideration just before the Spanish–American War, Mississippi decided to take the final step and disfranchise African-Americans within the limits set by the Fifteenth Amendment. Because of the negative wording, the amendment did not actually grant anyone the right to vote. It merely said that race could not be the sole determining factor. This left the states wide latitude to use any other method but race to achieve the same goal. Eventually two devices achieved the endorsement of the court, the literacy test and the poll tax. Two others, the grandfather clause and the white primary, would be declared unconstitutional as they excluded blacks on their face alone.

The Magnolia State led the way with the Second Mississippi Plan—the first was the Shotgun Plan (q.v.) of 1876. The idea was simple. No one could vote without being able to read and write or understand the Federal and state constitutions. Since these requirements on their face did not involve race, the court accepted them in 1898 as acceptable means to regulate elections. With the endorsement of disfranchisement on some other basis than race alone, Williams v. Mississippi gave the South the go-ahead to make disfranchisement of blacks an established fact. South Carolina and Louisiana quickly followed suit with new state constitutions imitating the Second Mississippi Plan. But the South could not keep away from overt racism. The real problem, of course, was that the tests were never given equally, and it was upon this fault that the exclusions would ultimately fail a half century later.

WILLIAMSBURG, BATTLE OF. *See* PENINSULA CAMPAIGN.

WILMINGTON, BATTLE OF. The last major port open on the Atlantic, halfway between Robert E. Lee's (q.v.) Army of Northern Virginia and Confederate forces in South Carolina, Wilmington, North Carolina, was strategically located to succor the last Confederate war effort. With his army bogged down at the Petersburg Siege (q.v.), Federal Lt. Gen. Ulysses S. Grant ordered Bvt. Maj. Gen. Benjamin Butler (qq.v.) to subdue Wilmington and its bastion, Ft. Fisher, in December 1864.

Lee quickly learned of the expedition and sent a division of infantry to help defend the fort. Even though the Federals had touched off 215 pounds of black power in a ship floated close to shore, the blast had little effect on the fort's defenders. But bad weather had delayed the Federal fleet and Butler's infantry until Lee's men approached in time to cause Butler to withdraw his attacking infantry, which had already succeeded in capturing several minor supporting installations near Ft. Fisher. This botched attack permitted Grant, with the concurrence of President Abraham Lincoln (q.v.), to fire Butler, who had been kept on beyond his military usefulness to help Lincoln win the election of 1864.

With the failure of the Butler attempt, Grant sent down a new expedition in January 1865. Again, storms made the trip from the Petersburg Siege to Wilmington slow and hazardous. Led by Bvt. Maj. Gen. Alfred Terry, the Federals landed against a garrison reinforced once again by new Confederate arrivals. On January 13, Terry landed and entrenched to hold his gains. Then, under the cover of a naval bombardment, soldiers, sailors, and marines took the fort by assault on January 15.

The fort commander, Confederate Maj. Gen. W. H. C. Whiting, believed that troops from Lee's army and the District of North Carolina commanded by Gen. Braxton Bragg (q.v.) could have prevented the Union victory had they but jumped into the fray. He angrily asked for a formal investigation into Bragg's role by the Confederate hierarchy from his Yankee prison cell. The attack cost the Federals 1,200 and the Confederates 2,000, most of whom were made prisoners of war.

WILMOT PROVISO (1846, 1848). The Wilmot Proviso was the extreme antislavery view in the northern United States. It simply held that slavery ought not to be permitted in the Western territories won from Mexico as a result of the war. It was introduced in 1846 by David Wilmot, a Pennsylvania congressman in the Democratic Party, as a rider on the Army Appropriations Bill of 1846. Like many northeastern Democrats (q.v.), Wilmot believed that President James K. Polk had stolen the presidential nomination from their man, Martin Van Buren. The idea was to introduce an antislavery measure to isolate Polk and southern Democrats, and reveal the War with Mexico to be one of blatant conquest designed to spread slavery into the West and bring more future slave states into the Union. It created no problem nationally when Wilmot introduced it in 1846, because everyone recognized it as blatant party politics solely within the Democratic Party.

Then in 1848, it was reintroduced for what it could really be—a measure to keep slavery out of all Western territories. This time, it caused all sorts of controversy. Northerners saw it as a reasonable way to limit the spread of slavery. It had been done before under the Articles of Confederation through the Northwest Land Ordinance of 1787, which prohibited slavery north of the Ohio River; and under the Constitution by way of the Missouri Compromise, which prohibited slavery in the West above Missouri's southern border (the 36°30′ line). Southerners saw it as an unfair way to prevent them from enjoying the fruits of the war, one which they had fought much more enthusiastically than the antislave northeast, and they feared the earlier compromises as an unconstitutional denial of their rights in the West.

The issue of slavery's expansion into the West became the key issue of the election of 1848 (q.v.).

WILSON'S CREEK. *See* MISSOURI CAMPAIGN (1861–1862).

WINCHESTER, FIRST BATTLE OF. *See* SHENANDOAH VALLEY CAMPAIGN, FIRST (JACKSON'S).

WINCHESTER, SECOND BATTLE OF. *See* PENNSYLVANIA CAMPAIGN.

WINCHESTER, THIRD BATTLE OF. *See* SHENANDOAH VALLEY CAMPAIGN, SECOND (SHERIDAN'S).

WOMEN'S RIGHTS BEFORE AND DURING THE CIVIL WAR AND RECONSTRUCTION. Along with increased rights for black males, Reconstruction witnessed a rise in women's rights, especially when it came to property. In every Southern state except Virginia that had to rewrite its state constitution under the Military Reconstruction Acts (q.v.), the guarantee of women's property rights, independent of their husbands, was recognized. South Carolina also gave them the right to file for divorce, and Texas even seriously considered granting the right to vote (as did Arkansas and South Carolina in a less solemn way), but that proposal was shelved in a raucous convention that had trouble turning out a normal fundamental law, much less one reformed beyond congressional demands.

Contrary to the picture many Americans hold of antebellum Dixie, the South had actually led the nation in reforms in women's rights before the Civil War. In Alabama, Arkansas, Florida, Louisiana, Mississippi, and Texas, the Reconstruction constitutions merely reconfirmed what those states had had as law before the war. Reconstruction then was but one stage in an ongoing reform that had its inception in Mississippi in 1839. It was so successful because men had a real stake in the outcome, and it had little to do with feminism *per se.* The equality that flowed from these laws was a byproduct of them, not their actual intent. Under common law, a single woman had the same right as a man in property as a matter of tradition. Marriage, however, changed this. Now a woman's possessions and she herself became part of the property of her husband. She could make no independent contracts, could not sue or be sued, and could not execute a valid will.

The gallant Southern men who dominated Reconstruction constitutional conventions feared that a woman could be taken advantage of by unscrupulous men. So they wrote laws to allow women these property rights, and the result was an equality not dreamed of. Another consideration during the Reconstruction period was the vast indebtedness of the South. Indeed, this probably was the reason the states first enacted these laws beginning in 1839. It was a response to another bad economic period, marked by the intense Panic of 1837. These laws protected a woman from losing her property to the collection of debts owed by her husband. So too was it in Reconstruction, except that the earlier laws were now elevated to constitutional status. Three states, Alabama, Florida, and Texas, went even further. They did not allow a husband to sell the family homestead without his wife's permission.

The real problem was that these grants of power to women were done in a fairly vague manner, which left it to the courts to round them out with specific decisions. The first state to do this was Georgia, and it did it with a vengeance. In Huff *v.* Wright (1869), the state ruled that a woman who claimed not to have to pay a debt incurred in 1866 because the promissory note was null and void as she was married at the time, could not claim exemption. The court held that the state constitution confirmed that the law before the war was valid and that the new constitution went so far as to make of husband and wife two separate entities. The wife was no longer subordinate to her husband but free to purchase, hold, and convey property; contract and be contracted with; and sue or be sued, just as if she were a single woman. It would take several decades for case law in all states to catch up with Georgia's, but the right of women in property had been changed forever throughout the South (and the rest of the nation by then) by the actions of the Reconstruction conventions. Admittedly, there were inconsistencies among the various states and sometimes within the states themselves, but the trend toward equality in property rights between the sexes was certain.

WOODSTOCK RACES. *See* SHENANDOAH VALLEY CAMPAIGN, SECOND (SHERIDAN'S).

WORMLEY HOUSE AGREEMENT. *See* ELECTION OF 1876 AND COMPROMISE OF 1877.

WOUNDS. Prior to the 19th century, there were few medical services for the rank and file. It was not until large armies conscripted from the general populations became common that organized military services came into use. Some of the greatest strides came from the medical director of Napoleon I, Dominique J. Larrey. Since Napoleon conquered most of Europe, Larrey's influence was widespread. His memoirs only served to make his methods more well known.

But American military medical science even predated Larrey. During the American Revolution, John Jones, a New York City surgeon, wrote a guide for surgery and public hygiene (1775). All of the advances in military medicine available to the Civil War soldier, however, came a decade before the revolutionary techniques of antisepsis and asepsis were known. Despite the horrendous losses suffered on both sides during the Civil War, two-thirds of the dead expired from disease (q.v.).

Of those who were battle casualties, 94 percent of all reported wounds were from bullets. Artillery fire, torpedoes, and grenades comprise 5.5 percent of the total. The rest were from edged weapons like bayonets and sabers. Of all wounds, 71 percent were in the extremities: legs, feet, arms, or hands. Only 18 percent were in the torso. But Civil War wounds were much more damaging than those incurred in prior wars because of the use of the conoidal bullet, or minnie ball. In the War with Mexico, for example, the old round musket ball would nick a bone. Because of its soft lead content and the speed with which it hit its target, the minnie ball tended to tumble and disintegrate when it hit the body and rip a bigger wound, shattering any bony surface it encountered. The result was a higher chance of infection.

But the pain and disorientation of the battlefield wounding were only a prelude to the horrors of medical treatment. The speed with which the soldier received treatment ranged from slow to better as the war progressed and improved ambulance services and triage (q.v.) came into use. The fortunate thing for the wounded Civil War soldier was that doctors were able to render him unconscious before operating through the use of nitrous oxide, ether, or chloroform (in the order of their effectiveness)—if they were available. Otherwise it was a shot of whiskey, and good luck. Generally, a gauze cone would be placed over the patient's nose and the anesthetic dripped onto it. Then the doctor would probe for the bullet with his finger. If the ball was in too deep, he would use a bullet probe. Once the bullet was encountered, it would be withdrawn with a bullet extractor and the wound cleared of any foreign debris, like the cloth from a shirt or coat. Then the wound would be dressed. Any shock would be treated with a liberal dose of whiskey.

Generally the dressing would consist of some lint followed by a linen bandage. It would not be changed for days and would become quite filthy. Nothing was known about that. Often a bandage would be reused, especially in Confederate hospitals. The Rebels took to boiling the blood and pus out of old wrappings, accidentally sterilizing the old bandages. Such a bandage might prove better than a new, clean one without any sterilization procedure. Bandages were usually applied dampened with cold water. Then if infection set in, the surgeon would change over to hot water. By that time, the soldier might be so weakened by his ordeal that amputation would do little more than kill him.

There were three types of amputation, classified by time period. Primary amputations were completed within 48 hours of the injury. The patients' survival rate was 76 percent. An intermediate amputation occurred from 48 hours to two weeks after the injury. That survival rate was 65 percent. A secondary amputation usually took place in a general hospital later than two weeks after the injury and in addition to the primary amputation, as a correction or supplemental treatment. That survival rate was 71 percent. It was of critical importance to get the wounded off the battlefield, which placed a premium on good, prompt ambulance services and triage. For this reason, many military surgeons advocated immediate amputation before the patient could be debilitated by infection. Amputation was necessary if the blood supply to the lower extremity were adversely affected, if there was excessive bullet laceration, or if there were a bone shattered. The closer to the torso, the less chance one had to survive an amputation, especially in the leg.

There were three types of amputation: circular, oval, or flap. The circular amputation involved cutting through the skin and drawing the inner muscles back so that the bone would be revealed above the wound closer to the torso. Then the bone would be sawed (it sounded a lot like sawing a wood plank), and the skin and muscles allowed to drop below the bone cut. The arteries and major veins would be tied off (a disintegrating catgut was preferred), and the various tissues would be drawn over the bone and stitched together.

If thread were used to tie off the blood vessels, the surgeons would wait several days and pull the thread loose. If the blood vessels had not clotted sufficiently, the wound might have to be reopened and the arteries and veins cauterized or tied off again. In the oval or single flap operation, the leg was cut on one side higher than the other so that there would be a padding of tissues to cushion the wound after it was sewed up. A double flap was an amputation that left a tissue flap on either side of the bone cut that could be drawn over the stump and sewed up. Because of the speed and the ease of closure, the oval flap was the preferred surgical method used in the Civil War.

After the amputation, the patient might remain in the field hospital until he was ambulatory. More serious cases were transferred by train or steamboat to general hospitals in major cities behind the lines. Because of the lack of even basic cleanliness, wounded soldiers quickly developed so-called surgical fevers. Among these were pyemia (death rate of 97 percent), tetanus (90 percent), erysipelas (41 percent), and gangrene (62 percent).

Generally the doctors came to isolate such fevers from the general hospital population, which improved their recovery rate and, in the case of erysipelas, prevented contagion. As hospital cleanliness improved during the war, probably brought on by the involvement of women in the medical care of the wounded, infections lessened. In the case of gangrene, death rates could be brought down to 2.6 percent merely by treating the infected area with bromide injections, rather than using old, outmoded, caustic treatments.

Civil War surgery reached a pre-Listerian zenith. Even with its faults, the death rates for all forms of amputation were 30 percent less than they had been for the Crimean War, a decade before.

Y

YANCEY–ROST–MANN DELEGATION. In March 1861, the Confederacy sent its first diplomatic mission to Europe. Three men were to represent the independent South as roving ambassadors to all nations. These were William L. Yancey, the leading Fire-Eater who broke up the Democratic Convention at Charleston and whom conservative Confederate leaders wanted to get out of their way; Pierre Rost, a Louisiana planter who spoke French but had little else to recommend him; and A. Dudley Mann, a career diplomat who tended toward the bombastic, writing communications twice as long as those of the rest of the diplomatic corps combined.

Although these three men inspired little confidence, they achieved the biggest diplomatic coup of the war when Great Britain declared the Confederate States of America (q.v.) to be a belligerent, a *de facto* political entity making war, not engaged in an illegal rebellion as President Abraham Lincoln (q.v.) asserted. But a *de facto* government is exactly that—one that exercises political control and maintains law and order. This was not actual recognition, which is *de jure* recognition, a fine distinction that the British are very good at making.

By recognizing the Confederacy as *de facto*, the Foreign Enlistment Act of 1819 applied to the American Civil War. A British citizen could not legally enlist in another nation's armies because Britain was neutral. British citizens also could not fit out ships for either side. Such vessels were liable to seizure by the British Navy. Finally, no British ship could sail through a legal blockade. Of course, the Confederates held that the Union blockade of their ports was illegal because it existed on paper only, not in fact. But the increase in the numbers of ships employed made it real enough far too soon to suit Southern consumers, civilian or military.

The Federal government protested the British declaration as more than the Rebels were entitled to, and as an unwarranted interference in U.S. internal affairs. But Britain pointed out that the Federals had declared a blockade against the South of their own volition. One cannot blockade one's own ports under international law; hence, the Lincoln administration had recognized the Confederacy as a *de facto* entity itself. Besides, the Union held Confederate soldiers as prisoners of war, instead of dealing with them as traitors.

The Confederates argued that Britain ought to take the next logical step and recognize it as a *de jure* government, fully independent of the United States. But the British never changed their stance, which led the Confederates to send a separate delegation to both Britain and France, led by James M. Mason and John Slidell, respectively. This led to the next crisis in Union–British foreign relations, the *Trent* affair (q.v.).

YERGER, *EX PARTE* (1868). After the Supreme Court's decision in *ex parte* McCardle in 1868, the problem of the constitutionality of the Military Reconstruction Acts arose once again in *ex parte* Yerger, another Mississippi newspaper editor's case, this one from Jackson. Edward M. Yerger had stabbed to death an Army officer serving as the militarily appointed mayor of the Mississippi capital for seizing a piano for nonpayment of taxes (Yerger was bankrupt). He was tried for murder before a military commission. As the trial proceeded, he applied for a writ of *habeas corpus* (q.v.) from the Federal circuit judge for Mississippi, Associate Justice Joseph Bradley. As the Supreme Court justice sitting on circuit, Bradley denied the plea. Yerger's attorneys applied directly to Chief Justice Salmon P. Chase (q.v.), who at first refused to override Bradley, then acquiesced. The appeal, however, was brought under the Judiciary Act of 1789, not the Habeas Corpus Act of 1867. Thus Yerger would follow a different route to the Supreme Court, regardless of what would happen with a similar case, *ex parte* McCardle (q.v.).

When the Yerger case came up before the whole Court, the judges ruled that they had jurisdiction through a writ of *habeas corpus* aided by a writ of *certiorari*. By now, it was 1870, and Reconstruction was over in all states but Texas and Mississippi, and elections there would be in a matter of months. So the Court cut a deal whereby the Federal government dropped the case and the Supreme Court remanded it to the Mississippi state courts as soon as the state was readmitted to the Union. There Yerger managed to escape authorities and flee to Maryland, where he dabbled in the Liberal Republican (q.v.) movement, published a Baltimore newspaper, and finally died in 1875 of natural causes. He was never brought to trial, many considering that a civil proceeding would constitute double jeopardy after the military commission case.

YORKTOWN, SIEGE OF. *See* PENINSULA CAMPAIGN.

YOUNG AMERICA. Part of the American idea called Manifest Destiny was the concept of "Young America." The revolutions in Europe in 1848 for constitutional government, with or without monarchy, were wildly supported in the United States, almost like the coming of the millennium. The European revolutionaries formed societies, all named after their nations, or hoped-for nations, such as Young Italy, Young Hungary, Young Germany, Young Ireland, and so on.

Naturally, republicans in the United States clamored to support these revolutions, so reminiscent of the American Revolution of 1776. So, in 1850, at the suggestion of Edwin De Leon of South Carolina, they formed Young America and sent munitions and men to join the European revolutionaries. The Federal government appointed A. Dudley Mann, a professional diplomat who later served the Confederacy, as its minister to the Hungarian Revolution (which the Russians brutally suppressed before his arrival). The Austrian government vehemently protested official American interference. Secretary of State Daniel Webster dismissed the Austrian protest, daring Austria to do something about it. In another incident, Martin Koszta, a Hungarian revolutionary who had visited the United States and declared he wished to be a citizen, returned to Europe only to be arrested by an Austrian officer in the Ottoman Empire. A U.S. warship intervened to secure his release.

After the monarchies violently suppressed the revolutions in Europe, Americans opened their arms to the exiled heroes of the hour. Hungarian revolutionary leader Lajos Kossuth visited the United States in 1851, to be greeted with enthusiasm. Over 100,000 persons lined the railroad tracks as he passed, cheering and waving their support. He made an able speech before the Ohio state legislature, declaring 1803 was a great year because both he and the State of Ohio were born then. In Washington, Webster called for Hungarian independence, Hungarian self-government, and Hungarian control of Hungarian destinies. Back in Europe, U.S. Minister to the Court at St. James, dour old James Buchanan (q.v.), entertained Kossuth and all of the European states, although his underling, George Sanders (q.v.), later implicated in helping to plan the Lincoln kidnap and assassination (q.v.) plots during the Civil War, did most of the work.

It was natural for the United States to support all revolutionaries in the world in the 19th century. After all, their ideology was American. And the spread of American ideas was a key part of America's "Spread Eagle" (q.v.) foreign policy of the 1850s.

APPENDIXES: DOCUMENTS RELATED TO THE CIVIL WAR AND RECONSTRUCTION

Presidential Administrations of the United States and the Confederacy, 1849–1877
Constitution of the Confederate States, 1861
Constitution of the United States as of 1860
Amendments to the Constitution of the United States before 1860
Post–Civil War Amendments

Presidential Administrations of the United States and the Confederacy, 1849–1877

UNITED STATES GOVERNMENTS DURING THE ANTEBELLUM ERA, 1849–1861

Table A.1. U.S. Governments during the Antebellum Era, 1849–1861

Party	President	V. Pres.	State	War	Treasury	Post. Gen.	Atty. Gen.	Navy	Interior
Whig, 1849–1851	Zachary Taylor	Millard Fillmore	John M. Clayton	George W. Crawford	William M. Meredith	Jacob Collamer	Reverdy Johnson	William B. Preston	Thomas Ewing
Whig, 1851–1853	Millard Fillmore		Daniel Webster; Edward Everett	Charles M. Conrad	Thomas Corwin	Nathan K. Hall; Samuel D. Hubbard	John J. Crittenden	William A. Graham; John P. Kennedy	Thomas M. T. McKennan; Alexander H. H. Stuart
Democrat, 1853–1857	Franklin Pierce	William R. King	William Hunter; William L. Marcy	Charles M. Conrad; Jefferson Davis	James Guthrie	James Campbell	Caleb Cushing	James C. Dobbin	Robert McClelland
Democrat, 1857–1861	James Buchanan	John C. Breckinridge	Lewis Cass; Jeremiah S. Black	John B. Floyd; Joseph Holt; John A. Dix	Howell Cobb; Philip F. Thomas; Horatio King	Aaron V. Brown; Joseph Holt	Jeremiah S. Black; Edwin McM. Stanton	Isaac Toucey	Jacob Thompson

UNITED STATES AND CONFEDERATE GOVERNMENTS DURING THE CIVIL WAR AND EARLY RECONSTRUCTION ERA, 1861–1869

Table A.2. U.S. and Confederate Governments during the Civil War and Early Reconstruction Era, 1861–1869

Party	President	V. Pres.	State	War	Treasury	Post. Gen.	Atty. Gen.	Navy	Interior
U.S.A., Republican, 1861–1865	Abraham Lincoln	Hannibal Hamlin	William F. Seward	Simon Cameron; Edwin McM. Stanton	Salmon P. Chase; William P. Fessenden	Montgomery Blair; William Dennison	Edward Bates; James Speed	Gideon Welles	Caleb B. Smith; John P. Usher
C.S.A., No Party, 1861–1865	Jefferson Davis	Alexander H. Stevens	Robert Toombs; R. M. T. Hunter; Judah P. Benjamin	Leroy P. Walker; Judah P. Benjamin; George W. Randolph; James Seddon; John C. Breckinridge	Christopher G. Memminger; George A. Trenholm	John H. Reagan	Judah P. Benjamin; Thomas Bragg; Thomas H. Watts; George Davis	Stephen A. Mallory	NONE
U.S.A., Nat'l Union, 1865–1869	Andrew Johnson		William F. Seward	Edwin McM. Stanton; John M. Schofield	Hugh McCullouch	William Dennison; Alexander W. Randall	James Speed; Henry Stanbery; William Evarts	Gideon Welles	James Harlan; Orville H. Browning

UNITED STATES GOVERNMENTS DURING THE ERAS OF RECONSTRUCTION AND REDEMPTION, 1869–1881

Table A.3. U.S. Governments during the Eras of Reconstruction and Redemption, 1869–1881

Party	President	V. Pres.	State	War	Treasury	Post. Gen.	Atty. Gen.	Navy	Interior
Republican, 1869–1877	Ulysses S. Grant	Schuyler Colfax; Henry Wilson	Elihu B. Washburne; Hamilton Fish	John A. Rawlins; William T. Sherman; William W. Belknap; Alphonso Taft; James D. Cameron	George S. Boutwell; William A. Richardson; Benjamin H. Bristow; Lott M. Morrill	John A. J. Cresswell; James W. Marshall; Marshall Jewell; James N. Tyner	Ebenezer R. Hoar; Amos T. Ackerman; George H. Williams; Edwards Pierrepont; Alfonso Taft	Adolph E. Borie; George Robeson	Jacob D. Cox; Columbus Delano; Zachariah Chandler
Republican, 1877–1881	Rutherford B. Hayes	William A. Wheeler	William M. Evarts	George W. McCrary; Alexander Ramsey	John Sherman	David M. Key; Horace Maynard	Charles Devens	Richard W. Thompson; Nathan Goff Jr.	Carl Schurz

Constitution of the Confederate
States of America, 1861

PREAMBLE

We, the people of the Confederate States, each State acting in its sovereign and independent character, in order to form a permanent, Federal Government, establish justice, insure domestic tranquillity, and secure the blessings of Liberty to ourselves and our posterity—invoking the favor and guidance of Almighty God—do ordain and establish this Constitution for the Confederate States of America:

ARTICLE I.

Section I.

All legislative powers herein delegated shall be vested in a Congress of the Confederate States which shall consist of a Senate and House of Representatives.

Section II.

1. The House of Representatives shall be composed of members chosen every second year by the people of the several States; and the electors in each State shall be citizens of the Confederate States, and have the qualifications requisite for electors of the most numerous branch of the State Legislature; but no person of foreign birth, not a citizen of the Confederate States, shall be allowed to vote for any officer, civil or political, State or Federal.
2. No person shall be a Representative, who shall not have attained the age of twenty-five years and be a citizen of the Confederate States, and who shall not, when elected, be an inhabitant of that State in which he shall be chosen.
3. Representatives and direct taxes shall be apportioned among the several States which may be included within this Confederacy according to their respective numbers, which shall be determined by adding to the

whole number of free persons, including those bound to service for a term of years, and excluding Indians not taxed, three-fifths of all slaves. The actual enumeration shall be made within three years after the first meeting the Congress of the Confederate States, and within every subsequent term of ten years, in such manner as they shall, by law, direct. The number of Representatives shall not exceed one for every fifty thousand, but each State shall have, at least, one Representative; and until such enumeration shall be made, the State of South Carolina shall be entitled to choose six—the State of Georgia ten—the State of Alabama nine—the State of Florida two—the State of Mississippi seven—the State of Louisiana six, and the State of Texas six.

4. When vacancies happen in the representation from any State, the Executive authority thereof shall issue writs of election to fill such vacancies.

5. The House of Representatives shall choose their Speaker and other officers; and shall have the sole power of impeachment; except that any judicial or other federal officer resident and acting solely within the limits of any State, may be impeached by a vote of two-thirds of both branches of the Legislature thereof.

Section III.

1. The Senate of the Confederate States shall be composed of two Senators from each State, chosen for six years, by the Legislature thereof, at the regular session next immediately preceding the commencement of the term of service; and each Senator shall have one vote.

2. Immediately after they shall be assembled in consequence of the first election, they shall be divided, as equally as may be, into three classes. The seats of the Senators of the first class shall be vacated at the expiration of the second year, of the second class at the expiration of the fourth, and of the third class at the expiration of the sixth year, so that one-third may be chosen every second year; and if vacancies happen, by resignation or otherwise, during the recess of the Legislature of any State, the Executive thereof may make temporary appointments until the next meeting of the Legislature, which shall then fill such vacancies.

3. No person shall be a Senator who shall not have attained the age of thirty years, and be a citizen of the Confederate States, and who shall not, when elected, be an inhabitant of the State for which be shall be chosen.

4. The Vice President of the Confederate States shall be President of the Senate, but shall have no vote, unless they be equally divided.

5. The Senate shall choose their other officers, and also a President pro tempore, in the absence of the Vice President, or when he shall exercise the office of President of the Confederate States.

6. The Senate shall have the sole power to try all impeachments. When sitting for that purpose, they shall be on oath or affirmation. When the President of the Confederate States is tried, the Chief Justice shall preside; and no person shall be convicted without the concurrence of two-thirds of the members present.

7. Judgment, in cases of impeachment, shall not extend further than to removal from office, and disqualification to hold and enjoy any office of honor, trust or profit under the Confederate States; but the party convicted shall nevertheless be liable and subject to indictment, trial, judgment and punishment, according to law.

Section IV.

1. The times, places and manner of holding elections for Senators and Representatives shall be prescribed in each State by the Legislature thereof, subject to the provisions of this Constitution; but the Congress may, at any time by law, make or alter such regulations, except as to the times and places of choosing Senators.

2. The Congress shall assemble at least once in every year, and such meeting shall be on the first Monday in December, unless they shall by law appoint a different day.

Section V.

1. Each House shall be the judge of the elections, returns and qualifications of its own members, and a majority of each shall constitute a quorum to do business; but a smaller number may adjourn from day to day, and may be authorized to compel the attendance of absent members, in such manner and under such penalties as each House may provide.

2. Each House may determine the rules of its proceedings, punish its members for disorderly behavior, and, with the concurrence of two-thirds of the whole number, expel a member.

3. Each House shall keep a journal of its proceedings, and from time to time publish the same, excepting such parts as may, in their judgment, require secrecy; and the yeas and nays of the members of either House on any question shall, at the desire of one-fifth of those present, be entered on the journal.

4. Neither House, during the Session of Congress, shall, without the consent of the other, adjourn for more than three days, nor to any other place than that in which the two Houses shall be sitting.

Section VI.

1. The Senators and Representatives shall receive a compensation for their services, to be ascertained by law, and paid out of the Treasury of the Confederate States. They shall in all cases, except treason, felony, and breach of the peace, be privileged from arrest during their attendance at the session of their respective Houses, and in going to and returning from the same; and for any speech or debate in either House, they shall not be questioned in any other place.

2. No Senator or Representative shall, during the time for which he was elected, be appointed to any civil office under the authority of the Confederate States, which shall have been created, or the emoluments whereof shall have been increased, during such time; and no person holding any office under the Confederate States shall be a member of either House during his continuance in office; but Congress may by law grant to the principal officer in each of the Executive Departments a seat upon the floor of either House, with the privilege of discussing any measures appertaining to his department.

Section VII.

1. All bills for raising revenue shall originate in the House of Representatives; but the Senate may propose or concur with amendments, as on other bills.

2. Every bill which shall have passed both Houses, shall, before it becomes a law, be presented to the President of the Confederate States; if he approve, he shall sign it; but if not, he shall return it, with his objections, to that House in which it shall have originated, who shall enter the objections at large on their journal, and proceed to reconsider it. If, after such reconsideration, two-thirds of that House shall agree to pass the bill, it shall be sent, together with the objections, to the other House, by which it shall likewise be reconsidered, and if approved by two-thirds of that House, it shall become a law. But in all such cases the votes of both Houses shall be determined by yeas and nays, and the names of the persons voting for and against the bill shall be entered on the journal of each House respectively. If any bill shall not be returned by the President within ten days (Sundays excepted) after it shall have been presented to him, the same shall be a law in like manner as if he had signed it, unless the Congress by their adjournment prevent its return, in which case it shall not be a law. The President may approve any appropriation and disapprove any other appropriation in the same bill. In such case he shall, in signing the bill, designate the appropria-

tions disapproved; and shall return a copy of such appropriations, with his objections, to the House in which the bill shall have originated; and the same proceedings shall then be had as in case of other bills disapproved by the President.

3. Every order, resolution, or vote, to which the concurrence of both Houses may be necessary, (except on a question of adjournment) shall be presented to the President of the Confederate States; and before the same shall take effect, shall be approved by him, or, being disapproved by him, shall be re-passed by two-thirds of both House, according to the rules and limitations prescribed in the case of a bill.

Section VIII.

The Congress shall have power—

1. To lay and collect taxes, duties imposts, and excises, for revenue necessary to pay the debts, provide for the common defense and carry on the Government of the Confederate States; but no bounties shall be granted from the Treasury, nor shall any duties or taxes on importations from foreign nations be laid to promote or foster any branch of industry; and all duties, imposts and excises shall be uniform throughout the Confederate States.

2. To borrow money on the credit of the Confederate States.

3. To regulate commerce with foreign nations, and among the several States, and with the Indian tribes; but neither this nor any other clause contained in the Constitution shall ever be construed to delegate the power to Congress to appropriate money for any internal improvement, intended to facilitate commerce, except for the purpose of furnishing lights, beacons and buoys, and other aids to navigation upon the coasts, and the improvement of harbors and the removing of obstructions in river navigation; in all which cases such duties shall be laid on the navigation facilitated thereby, as may be necessary to pay the costs and expenses thereof.

4. To establish uniform laws of naturalization, and uniform laws on the subject of bankruptcies, throughout the Confederate States; but no law of Congress shall discharge any debt contracted before the passage of the same.

5. To coin money, regulate the value thereof, and of foreign coin, and fix the standard of weights and measures.

6. To provide for the punishment of counterfeiting the securities and current coin of the Confederate States.

7. To establish post-offices and post-roads: but the expenses of the Post-office Department, after the first day of March, in the year

of our Lord eighteen hundred and sixty-three, shall be paid out of its own revenues.

8. To promote the progress of science and useful arts by securing for limited times to authors and inventors the exclusive right to their respective writings and discoveries.
9. To constitute tribunals inferior to the Supreme Court.
10. To define and punish piracies and felonies committed on the high seas and offences against the law of nations.
11. To declare war, grant letters of marque and reprisal, and make rules concerning captures on land and water.
12. To raise and support armies; but no appropriation of money to that use shall be for a longer term than two years.
13. To provide and maintain a navy.
14. To make rules for the government and regulation of the land and naval forces.
15. To provide for calling forth the militia to execute the laws of the Confederate States, suppress insurrections, and repel invasions.
16. To provide for organizing, arming, and disciplining the militia, and for governing such part of them as may be employed in the service of the Confederate States, reserving to the States respectively the appointment of the officers and the authority of training the militia according to the discipline prescribed by Congress.
17. To exercise exclusive legislation, in all cases whatsoever, over such district (not exceeding ten miles square) as may, by cession of one or more States and the acceptance of Congress, become the seat of Government of the Confederate States; and to exercise like authority over all places purchased, by the consent of the Legislature of the State in which the same shall be, for the erection of forts, magazines, arsenals, dockyards, and other needful buildings: and,
18. To make all laws which shall be necessary and proper for carrying into execution the foregoing powers, and all other powers vested by this Constitution in the Government of the Confederate States, or in any department or officer thereof.

Section IX.

1. The importation of negroes of the African race from any foreign country other than the slaveholding States or Territories of the United States of America, is hereby forbidden, and Congress is required to pass such laws as shall effectually prevent the same.
2. Congress shall also have power to prohibit the introduction of slaves from any State not a member of, or Territory not belonging to, this Confederacy.

3. The privilege of the writ of habeas corpus shall not be suspended, unless, when in cases of rebellion or invasion, the public safety may require it.
4. No bill of attainder, ex post facto law, or law denying or impairing the right of property in negro slaves, shall be passed.
5. No capitation or other direct tax shall be laid, unless in proportion to the census or enumeration herein before directed to be taken.
6. No tax or duty shall be laid on articles exported from any State except by a vote of two-thirds of both Houses.
7. No preference shall be given by any regulation of commerce, or revenue to the ports of one State over those of another.
8. No money shall be drawn from the treasury, but in consequence of appropriations made by law; and a regular statement and account of the receipts and expenditures of all public money, shall be published from time to time.
9. Congress shall appropriate no money from the Treasury except by a vote of two-thirds of both Houses, taken by yeas and nays, unless it be asked and estimated for by some one of the Heads of Department and submitted to Congress by the President; or for the purpose of paying its own expenses and contingencies; or for the payment of claims against the Confederate States, the justice of which shall have been judicially declared by a tribunal for the investigation of claims against the Government, which it is hereby made the duty of Congress to establish.
10. All bills appropriating money, shall specify, in Federal currency, the exact amount of each appropriation, and the purposes for which it is made, and Congress shall grant no extra compensation to any public contractor, officer agent or servant, after such contract shall have been made, or such service rendered.
11. No title of nobility shall be granted by the Confederate States and no person holding any office of profit or trust under them, shall, without the consent of the Congress, accept of any present, emolument, office, or title of any kind whatever, from any king, prince or foreign State.
12. Congress shall make no law respecting an establishment of religion, or prohibiting the free exercise thereof; or abridging the freedom of speech, or of the press; or the right of the people peaceably to assemble and petition the Government for a redress of grievances.
13. A well regulated militia being necessary to the security of a free State, the right of the People to keep and bear arms, shall not be infringed.
14. No soldier shall, in time of peace, be quartered in any house, without the consent of the owner; nor in time of war, but in a manner to be prescribed by law.

15. The right of the people to be secure in their persons, houses, papers and effects, against unreasonable searches and seizures, shall not be violated; and no warrant shall issue, but upon probable cause, supported by oath or affirmation, and particularly describing the place to be searched, and the persons or things to be seized.

16. No person shall be held to answer for a capital or otherwise infamous crime, unless on a presentment or indictment of a grand jury, except in cases arising in the land or naval forces, or in the militia, when in actual service in time of war or public danger; nor shall any person be subject for the same offence to be twice put in jeopardy of life or limb; nor be compelled in any criminal case to be a witness against himself, nor be deprived of life, liberty or property, without due process of law; nor shall private property be taken for public use, without just compensation.

17. In all criminal prosecutions, the accused shall enjoy the right to a speedy and public trial, by an impartial jury of the State and district wherein the crime shall have been committed, which district shall have been previously ascertained by law, and to be informed of the nature and cause of the accusation; to be confronted with the witnesses against him; to have compulsory process for obtaining witnesses in his favor, and to have the assistance of counsel for his defense.

18. In suits at common law, where the value in controversy shall exceed twenty dollars, the right of trial by jury shall be preserved, and no fact so tried by a jury shall be otherwise re-examined in any court of the Confederacy than according to the rules of the common law.

19. Excessive bail shall not be required, nor excessive fines imposed, nor cruel and unusual punishments inflicted.

20. Every law, or resolution having the force of law, shall relate to but one subject, and that shall be expressed in the title.

Section X.

1. No State shall enter into any treaty, alliance or confederation; grant letters of marque and reprisal; coin money; make anything but gold and silver coin a tender in payment of debts; pass any bill of attainder, ex post facto law, or law impairing the obligation of contracts; or grant any title of nobility.

2. No State shall, without the consent of the Congress, lay any imposts or duties on imports or exports, except what may be absolutely necessary for executing its inspection laws; and the net produce of all duties and imposts, laid by any State on imports or exports, shall be for the use of the Treasury of the Confederate States; and all such laws shall be subject to the revision and control of Congress.

3. No State shall, without the consent of Congress, lay any duty on tonnage, except on sea-going vessels, for the improvement of its rivers and harbors, navigated by the said vessels; but such duties shall not conflict with any treaties of the Confederate States with foreign nations; and any surplus revenue thus derived shall, after making such improvement, be paid into the common treasury; nor shall any State keep troops or ships of war in time of peace, enter into any agreement or compact with another State or with a foreign power, or engage in war unless actually invaded, or in such imminent danger as will not admit of delay; but when any river divides or flows through two or more States, they may enter into compacts with each other to improve the navigation thereof.

ARTICLE II.

Section I.

1. The Executive power shall be vested in a President of the Confederate States of America. He and the Vice-President shall hold their offices for the term of six years; but the President shall not be re-eligible. The President and Vice-President shall be elected as follows:
2. Each State shall appoint, in such manner as the Legislature thereof may direct, a number of electors, equal to the whole number of Senators and Representatives to which the State may be entitled in the Congress; but no Senator or Representative, or person holding an office of trust or profit under the Confederate States, shall be appointed an Elector.
3. The electors shall meet in their respective States and vote by ballot for President and Vice-President, one of whom at least shall not be an inhabitant of the same State with themselves.—They shall name in their ballots the person voted for as President, and in distinct ballots the person voted for as Vice-President, and they shall make distinct lists of all persons voted for as President and of all persons voted for as Vice-President, and of the number of votes for each, which lists they shall sign and certify and transmit, sealed, to the seat of Government of the Confederate States, directed to the President of the Senate. The President of the Senate shall, in the presence of the Senate and House of Representatives, open all the certificates, and the votes shall then be counted; the person having the greatest number of votes for President shall be the President, if such number be a majority of the whole number of electors appointed, and if no person have such majority, then

from the persons having the highest numbers not exceeding three on the list of those voted for as President, the House of Representatives shall choose immediately by ballot the President. But in choosing the President the votes shall be taken by States, the Representation from each State having one vote. A quorum for this purpose shall consist of a member or members from two-thirds of the States and a majority of all the States shall be necessary to a choice; and if the House of Representatives shall not choose a President, whenever the right of choice shall devolve upon them, before the fourth day of March next following, then the Vice President shall act as President as in case of the death or other constitutional disability of the President.

4. The person having the greatest number of votes as Vice-President shall be the Vice-President, if such number be a majority of the whole number of electors appointed; and if no person have a majority, then from the two highest numbers on the list the Senate shall choose the Vice-President. A quorum for the purpose shall consist of two-thirds of the whole number of Senators, and a majority of the whole number shall be necessary to a choice.

5. But no person constitutionally ineligible to the office of President shall be eligible to that of Vice-President of the Confederate States.

6. The Congress may determine the time of choosing the electors, and the day on which they shall give their votes, which day shall be the same throughout the Confederate States.

7. No person, except a natural born citizen of the Confederate States, or a citizen, thereof at the time of the adoption of this Constitution, or citizen thereof born in the United States prior to the twentieth of December, 1860, shall be eligible to the office of President; neither shall any person be eligible to that office who shall not have attained the age of thirty-five years, and been fourteen years a resident within the limits of the Confederate States as they may exist at the time of his election.

8. In case of the removal of the President from office, or of his death, resignation, or inability to discharge the powers and duties of said office, the same shall devolve on the Vice-President and the Congress may by law provide for the case of removal, death, resignation, or inability, both of the President and Vice-President, declaring what officer shall then act as President; and such officer shall act accordingly until the disability be removed or a President shall be elected.

9. The President shall, at stated times, receive for his services a compensation, which shall neither be increased nor diminished during the period for which he shall have been elected, and he shall not receive within that period any other emolument from the Confederate States, or any of them.

10. Before he enters on the execution of his office, he shall take the following oath or affirmation: "I do solemnly swear (or affirm) that I will faithfully execute the office of President of the Confederate States, and will, to the best of my ability, preserve, protect and defend the Constitution thereof."

Section II.

1. The President shall be Commander-in-Chief of the army and navy of the Confederate States, and of the militia of the several States, when called into the actual service of the Confederate States; he may require the opinion, in writing, of the principal officer in each of the Executive Departments, upon any subject relating to the duties of their respective offices; and he, shall have power to grant reprieves and pardons for offences against the Confederate States, except in cases of impeachment.
2. He shall have power, by and with the advice and consent of the Senate, to make treaties, provided two-thirds of the Senators present concur; and he shall nominate, and by and with the advice and consent of the Senate, shall appoint Ambassadors, other public Ministers and Consuls, Judges of the Supreme Court and all other officers of the Confederate States, whose appointments are not herein otherwise provided for, and which shall be established by law; but the Congress may by law vest the appointment of such inferior officers, as they think proper, in the President alone, in the courts of law, or in the Heads of Departments.
3. The principal officer in each of the Executive Departments, and all persons connected with the diplomatic service may be removed from office at the pleasure of the President.— All other civil officers, of the Executive Department, may be removed at any time by the President, or other appointing power, when their services are unnecessary, or for dishonesty, incapacity, inefficiency, misconduct or neglect of duty; and when so removed the removal shall be reported to the Senate, together with the reasons therefor.
4. The President shall have power to fill all vacancies that may happen during the recess of the Senate, by granting commissions which shall expire at the end of their next session; but no person rejected by the Senate shall be reappointed to the same office during their ensuing recess.

Section III.

The President shall from time to time, give to the Congress information, of the state of the Confederacy, and recommend to their consideration such measures as he shall judge necessary and expedient; he may, on extraordinary occasions, convene both Houses, or either of them; and in case of disagreement between them, with respect to the time of adjournment, he may adjourn them to such time as he shall think proper; he shall receive Ambassadors and other Public Ministers; he shall take care that the laws be faithfully executed, and shall commission all the officers of the Confederate States.

Section IV.

The President, Vice-President, and all civil officers of the Confederate States, shall be removed from office on impeachment for, and conviction of treason, bribery or other high crimes and misdemeanors.

ARTICLE III.

Section I.

1. The judicial power of the Confederate States shall be vested in one Supreme Court, and in such inferior courts as the Congress may from time to time ordain and establish. The Judges, both of the supreme and inferior courts, shall hold their offices during good behavior; and shall, at stated times, receive for their services a compensation, which shall not be diminished during their continuance in office.

Section II.

1. The Judicial power shall extend to all cases arising under this Constitution, the laws of the Confederate States, and treaties made, or which shall be made, under their authority; to all cases affecting Ambassadors, other public ministers and consuls; to all cases of admiralty and maritime jurisdiction; to controversies to which the Confederate States shall be a party; to controversies between two or more States; between a State and citizen of another State, where the State is plaintiff; between citizens claiming lands under grants of different States; and between a State, or the citizens thereof, and foreign States, citizens, or subjects; but no State shall be sued by a citizen or subject of any foreign State.
2. In all cases affecting Ambassadors, other public Ministers and Consuls, and those in which a State shall be a party, the Supreme Court shall have original jurisdiction. In all the other cases b fore mentioned, the Supreme Court shall have appellate jurisdiction, both as to law and fact, with such exceptions and under such regulations as the Congress shall make.

3. The trial of all crimes, except in cases of impeachment, shall be by jury; and such trial shall be held in the State where the said crimes shall have been committed; but when not committed within any State, the trial shall be at such place or places as the Congress may by law have directed.

Section III.

1. Treason against the Confederate States shall consist only in levying war against them, or in adhering to their enemies, giving them aid and comfort. No person shall be convicted of treason unless on the testimony of two witnesses to the same overt act, or on confession in open court.
2. The Congress shall have power to declare the punishment of treason, but no attainder of treason shall work corruption of blood, or forfeiture, except during the life of the person attainted.

ARTICLE IV.

Section I.

1. Full faith and credit shall be given in each State to the public acts, records and judicial proceedings of every other State. And the Congress may by general laws prescribe the manner in which such acts, records and proceedings shall be proved, and the effect thereof.

Section II.

1. The citizens, of each State shall be entitled to all the privileges and immunities of citizens in the several States, and shall have the right of transit and sojourn in any State of this Confederacy, with their slaves and other property; and the right of property in said slaves shall not be thereby impaired.
2. A person charged in any State with treason, felony or other crime, against the laws of such State, who shall flee from justice, and be found in another State, shall, on demand of the Executive authority of the State from which he fled, be delivered up, to be removed to the State having jurisdiction of the crime.
3. No slave or other person held to service or labor in any State or Territory of the Confederate States, under the laws thereof, escaping, or lawfully carried into another, shall, in consequence of any law or regulation therein, be discharged from such service or labor; but shall be delivered up on claim of the party to whom such slave belongs, or to whom such service or labor may be due.

Section III.

1. Other States may be admitted into this Confederacy by a vote of two-thirds of the whole House of Representatives, and two-thirds of the Senate—the Senate voting, by States; but no new State shall be formed or erected within the jurisdiction of any other State; nor any State be formed by the junction of two or more States or parts of States, without the consent of the Legislatures of the States concerned, as well as of the Congress.

2. The Congress shall have power to dispose of and make all needful rules and regulations concerning the property of the Confederate States, including the lands thereof.

3. The Confederate States may acquire new territory, and Congress shall have power to legislate and provide governments for the inhabitants of all territory belonging to the Confederate States lying without the limits of the several States, and may permit them, at such times and in such manner as it may by law provide, to form States to be admitted into the Confederacy. In all such territory, the institution of negro slavery, as it now exists in the Confederate States, shall be recognized and protected by Congress, and by the Territorial Government; and the inhabitants of the several Confederate States and Territories shall have the right to take to such territory any slaves lawfully held by them, in any of the States or Territories of the Confederate States.

4. The Confederate States shall guarantee to every State that now is, or hereafter may become, a member of this Confederacy, a republican form of government, and shall protect each of them against invasion; and on application of the Legislature, or of the Executive when the Legislature is not in session, against domestic violence.

ARTICLE V.

Section 1.

1. Upon the demand of any three States, legally assembled in their several Conventions, the Congress shall summon a Convention of all the States to take into consideration such amendments to the Constitution as the said States shall concur in suggesting at the time when the said demand is made; and should any of the proposed amendments to the Constitution be agreed on by the said Convention, voting by States, and the same be ratified by the Legislatures of two-thirds of the several States, or by Conventions in two-thirds thereof, as the one or the other mode of ratification may be proposed by the General Convention, they shall thenceforward form a part of this Constitution. But no

State shall, without its consent, be deprived of its equal representation in the Senate.

ARTICLE VI.

Section I.

The Government established by this Constitution is the successor of the Provisional Government of the Confederate States of America, and all the laws passed by the latter shall continue in force until the same shall be repealed or modified; and all the officers appointed by the same shall remain in office until their successors are appointed and qualified, or the offices abolished.

Section II.

All debts contracted and engagements entered into before the adoption of this Constitution, shall be as valid against the Confederate States, under this Constitution, as under the Provisional Government.

Section III.

This Constitution and the laws of the Confederate States, made in pursuance thereof, and all treaties made, or which shall be made under the authority of the Confederate States, shall be the supreme law of the land; and the Judges in every State shall be bound thereby, anything in the Constitution or laws of any State to the contrary notwithstanding.

Section IV.

The Senators and Representatives before mentioned, and the members of the several State Legislatures, and all executive and judicial officers, both of the Confederate States and of the several States, shall be bound by oath or affirmation to support this Constitution; but no religious test shall ever be required as a qualification to any office or public trust under the Confederate States.

Section V.

The enumeration in the Constitution of certain rights shall not be construed to deny or disparage others retained by the people of the several States.

Section VI.

The powers not delegated to the Confederate States by the Constitution, nor prohibited by it to the States, are reserved to the States respectively, or to the people thereof.

ARTICLE VII.

1. The ratification of the Conventions of five States shall be sufficient for the establishment of this Constitution between the States so ratifying the same.
2. When five States shall have ratified this Constitution, in the manner before specified, the Congress, under the Provisional Constitution, shall prescribe the time for holding the election of President and Vice-President, and for the meeting of the electoral college, and for counting the votes, and inaugurating the President. They shall also prescribe the time for holding the first election of members of Congress under this Constitution, and the time for assembling the same. Until the assembling of such Congress, the Congress under the Provisional Constitution shall continue to exercise the legislative powers granted them, not extending beyond the time limited by the Constitution of the Provisional Government.

EXTRACT FROM THE JOURNAL OF THE CONGRESS

CONGRESS, March 11, 1861

On the question of the adoption of the Constitution of the Confederate States of America, the vote was taken by yeas and nays; and the Constitution was unanimously adopted, as follows:

Those who voted in the affirmative being Messrs. Walker, Smith, Curry, Hale, McRae, Shorter and Fern, of Alabama, (Messrs. Chilton and Lewis being absent); Messrs. Morton, Anderson and Owens, of Florida; Messrs. Toombs, Howell Cobb, Bartow, Nisbet, Hill, Wright, Thomas R. R. Cobb and Stephens, of Georgia, (Messrs. Crawford and Kenan being absent); Messrs. Perkins, De-Clonet, Conrad, Kenner, Sparrow and Marshall, of Louisiana; Messrs. Harris, Brooke, Wilson, Clayton, Barry and Harrison, of Mississippi; (Mr. Campbell being absent), Messrs. Rhett, Barnwell, Keitt, Chesnut, Memminger, Miles, Withers and Boyce, of South Carolina; Messrs. Reagan, Hemphill, Waul, Gregg, Oldham and Ochiltree, of Texas (Mr. Wigfall being absent.)

A true copy:

J. J. HOOPER,
Secretary of the Congress.

CONGRESS, March 11, 1861.

I do hereby certify that the foregoing are, respectively, true and correct copies of "The Constitution of the Confederate States of America," unanimously adopted this day, and of the yeas and nays, on the question of the adoption thereof.

HOWELL COBB,
President of the Congress.

Constitution of the United States of America as of 1860

PREAMBLE

We the people of the United States, in order to form a more perfect union, establish justice, insure domestic tranquility, provide for the common defense, promote the general welfare, and secure the blessings of liberty to ourselves and our posterity, do ordain and establish this Constitution for the United States of America.

ARTICLE I

Section 1.

All legislative powers herein granted shall be vested in a Congress of the United States, which shall consist of a Senate and House of Representatives.

Section 2.

The House of Representatives shall be composed of members chosen every second year by the people of the several states, and the electors in each state shall have the qualifications requisite for electors of the most numerous branch of the state legislature.

No person shall be a Representative who shall not have attained to the age of twenty five years, and been seven years a citizen of the United States, and who shall not, when elected, be an inhabitant of that state in which he shall be chosen.

Representatives and direct taxes shall be apportioned among the several states which may be included within this union, according to their respective numbers, which shall be determined by adding to the whole number of free persons, including those bound to service for a term of years, and excluding Indians not taxed, three fifths of all other Persons. The actual Enumeration shall be made within three years after the first meeting of the Congress of the United States, and within every subsequent term of ten years, in such manner as they shall by law direct. The number of Representatives shall not exceed one for every thirty thousand, but each state shall have at least one Representative; and until such enumeration shall be made, the state of New Hampshire shall be entitled to chuse [*sic*] three, Massachusetts eight, Rhode Island and Providence Plantations one, Connecticut five, New York six, New Jersey four, Pennsylvania eight, Delaware one, Maryland six, Virginia ten, North Carolina five, South Carolina five, and Georgia three.

When vacancies happen in the Representation from any state, the executive authority thereof shall issue writs of election to fill such vacancies.

The House of Representatives shall choose their speaker and other officers; and shall have the sole power of impeachment.

Section 3.

The Senate of the United States shall be composed of two Senators from each state, chosen by the legislature thereof, for six years; and each Senator shall have one vote.

Immediately after they shall be assembled in consequence of the first election, they shall be divided as equally as may be into three classes. The seats of the Senators of the first class shall be vacated at the expiration of the second year, of the second class at the expiration of the fourth year, and the third class at the expiration of the sixth year, so that one third may be chosen every second year; and if vacancies happen by resignation, or otherwise, during the recess of the legislature of any state, the executive thereof may make temporary appointments until the next meeting of the legislature, which shall then fill such vacancies.

No person shall be a Senator who shall not have attained to the age of thirty years, and been nine years a citizen of the United States and who shall not, when elected, be an inhabitant of that state for which he shall be chosen.

The Vice President of the United States shall be President of the Senate, but shall have no vote, unless they be equally divided.

The Senate shall choose their other officers, and also a President pro tempore, in the absence of the Vice President, or when he shall exercise the office of President of the United States.

The Senate shall have the sole power to try all impeachments. When sitting for that purpose, they shall be on oath or affirmation. When the President of the United States is tried, the Chief Justice shall preside: And no person shall be convicted without the concurrence of two thirds of the members present.

Judgment in cases of impeachment shall not extend further than to removal from office, and disqualification to hold and enjoy any office of honor, trust or profit under the United States: but the party convicted shall nevertheless be liable and subject to indictment, trial, judgment and punishment, according to law.

Section 4.

The times, places and manner of holding elections for Senators and Representatives, shall be prescribed in each state by the legislature thereof; but the Congress may at any time by law make or alter such regulations, except as to the places of choosing Senators.

The Congress shall assemble at least once in every year, and such meeting shall be on the first Monday in December, unless they shall by law appoint a different day.

Section 5.

Each House shall be the judge of the elections, returns and qualifications of its own members, and a majority of each shall constitute a quorum to do business; but a smaller number may adjourn from day to day, and may be authorized to compel the attendance of absent members, in such manner, and under such penalties as each House may provide.

Each House may determine the rules of its proceedings, punish its members for disorderly behavior, and, with the concurrence of two thirds, expel a member.

Each House shall keep a journal of its proceedings, and from time to time publish the same, excepting such parts as may in their judgment require secrecy; and the yeas and nays of the members of either House on any question shall, at the desire of one fifth of those present, be entered on the journal.

Neither House, during the session of Congress, shall, without the consent of the other, adjourn for more than three days, nor to any other place than that in which the two Houses shall be sitting.

Section 6.

The Senators and Representatives shall receive a compensation for their services, to be ascertained by law, and paid out of the treasury of the United States. They shall in all cases, except treason, felony and breach of the peace, be privileged from arrest during their attendance at the session of their respective Houses, and in going to and returning from the same; and for any speech or debate in either House, they shall not be questioned in any other place.

No Senator or Representative shall, during the time for which he was elected, be appointed to any civil office under the authority of the United States, which shall have been created, or the emoluments whereof shall have been increased during such time: and no person holding any office under the United States, shall be a member of either House during his continuance in office.

Section 7.

All bills for raising revenue shall originate in the House of Representatives; but the Senate may propose or concur with amendments as on other Bills.

Every bill which shall have passed the House of Representatives and the Senate, shall, before it become a law, be presented to the President of the United States; if he approve he shall sign it, but if not he shall return it, with his objections to that House in which it shall have originated, who shall enter the objections at large on their journal, and proceed to reconsider it. If after such reconsideration two thirds of that House shall agree to pass the bill, it shall be sent, together with the objections, to the other House, by which it shall likewise be reconsidered, and if approved by two thirds of that House, it shall become a law. But in all such cases the votes of both Houses shall be determined by yeas and nays, and the names of the persons voting for and against the bill shall be entered on the journal of each House respectively. If any bill shall not be returned by the President within ten days (Sundays excepted) after it shall have been presented to him, the same shall be a law, in like manner as if he had signed it, unless the Congress by their adjournment prevent its return, in which case it shall not be a law.

Every order, resolution, or vote to which the concurrence of the Senate and House of Representatives may be necessary (except on a question of adjournment) shall be presented to the President of the United States; and before the same shall take effect, shall be approved by him, or being disapproved by him, shall be repassed by two-thirds of the Senate and House of Representatives, according to the rules and limitations prescribed in the case of a bill.

Section 8.

The Congress shall have power to lay and collect taxes, duties, imposts and excises, to pay the debts and provide for the common defense and general welfare of the United States; but all duties, imposts and excises shall be uniform throughout the United States:

To borrow money on the credit of the United States;

To regulate commerce with foreign nations, and among the several states, and with the Indian tribes;

To establish a uniform rule of naturalization, and uniform laws on the subject of bankruptcies throughout the United States;

To coin money, regulate the value thereof, and of foreign coin, and fix the standard of weights and measures;

To provide for the punishment of counterfeiting the securities and current coin of the United States;

To establish post offices and post roads;

To promote the progress of science and useful arts, by securing for limited times to authors and inventors the exclusive right to their respective writings and discoveries;

To constitute tribunals inferior to the Supreme Court;

To define and punish piracies and felonies committed on the high seas, and offenses against the law of nations;

To declare war, grant letters of marque and reprisal, and make rules concerning captures on land and water;

To raise and support armies, but no appropriation of money to that use shall be for a longer term than two years;

To provide and maintain a navy;

To make rules for the government and regulation of the land and naval forces;

To provide for calling forth the militia to execute the laws of the union, suppress insurrections and repel invasions;

To provide for organizing, arming, and disciplining, the militia, and for governing such part of them as may be employed in the service of the United States, reserving to the states respectively, the appointment of the officers, and the authority of training the militia according to the discipline prescribed by Congress;

To exercise exclusive legislation in all cases whatsoever, over such District (not exceeding ten miles square) as may, by cession of particular states, and the acceptance of Congress, become the seat of the government of the United States, and to exercise like authority over all places purchased by the consent of the legislature of the state in which the same shall be, for the erection of forts, magazines, arsenals, dockyards, and other needful buildings;—And

To make all laws which shall be necessary and proper for carrying into execution the foregoing powers, and all other powers vested by this Constitution in the government of the United States, or in any department or officer thereof.

Section 9.

The migration or importation of such persons as any of the states now existing shall think proper to admit, shall not be prohibited by the Congress prior to the year one thousand eight hundred and eight, but a tax or duty may be imposed on such importation, not exceeding ten dollars for each person.

The privilege of the writ of habeas corpus shall not be suspended, unless when in cases of rebellion or invasion the public safety may require it.

No bill of attainder or ex post facto Law shall be passed.

No capitation, or other direct, tax shall be laid, unless in proportion to the census or enumeration herein before directed to be taken.

No tax or duty shall be laid on articles exported from any state.

No preference shall be given by any regulation of commerce or revenue to the ports of one state over those of another: nor shall vessels bound to, or from, one state, be obliged to enter, clear or pay duties in another.

No money shall be drawn from the treasury, but in consequence of appropriations made by law; and a regular statement and account of receipts and expenditures of all public money shall be published from time to time.

No title of nobility shall be granted by the United States: and no person holding any office of profit or trust under them, shall, without the consent of the Congress, accept of any present, emolument, office, or title, of any kind whatever, from any king, prince, or foreign state.

Section 10.

No state shall enter into any treaty, alliance, or confederation; grant letters of marque and reprisal; coin money; emit bills of credit; make anything but gold and silver coin a tender in payment of debts; pass any bill of attainder, ex post facto law, or law impairing the obligation of contracts, or grant any title of nobility.

No state shall, without the consent of the Congress, lay any imposts or duties on imports or exports, except what may be absolutely necessary for executing it's inspection laws: and the net produce of all duties and imposts, laid by any state on imports or exports, shall be for the use of the treasury of the United States; and all such laws shall be subject to the revision and control of the Congress.

No state shall, without the consent of Congress, lay any duty of tonnage, keep troops, or ships of war in time of peace, enter into any agreement or compact with another state, or with a foreign power, or engage in war, unless actually invaded, or in such imminent danger as will not admit of delay.

ARTICLE II

Section 1.

The executive power shall be vested in a President of the United States of America. He shall hold his office during the term of four years, and, together with the Vice President, chosen for the same term, be elected, as follows:

Each state shall appoint, in such manner as the Legislature thereof may direct, a number of electors, equal to the whole number of Senators and Representatives to which the State may be entitled in the Congress: but no Senator or Representative, or person holding an office of trust or profit under the United States, shall be appointed an elector.

The electors shall meet in their respective states, and vote by ballot for two persons, of whom one at least shall not be an inhabitant of the same state with themselves. And they shall make a list of all the persons voted for, and of the number of votes for each; which list they shall sign and certify, and transmit sealed to the seat of the government of the United States, directed to the President of the Senate. The President of the Senate shall, in the presence of the Senate and House of Representatives, open all the certificates, and the votes shall then be counted. The person having the greatest number of votes shall be the President, if such number be a majority of the whole number of electors appointed; and if there be more than one who have such majority, and have an equal number of votes, then the House of Representatives shall immediately choose by ballot one of them for President; and if no person have a majority, then from the five highest on the list the said House shall in like manner choose the President. But in choosing the President, the votes shall be taken by States, the representation from each state having one vote; A quorum for this purpose shall consist of a member or members from two thirds of the states, and a majority of all the states shall be necessary to a choice. In every case, after the choice of the President, the person having the greatest number of votes of the electors shall be the Vice President. But if there should remain two or more who have equal votes, the Senate shall choose from them by ballot the Vice President.

The Congress may determine the time of choosing the electors, and the day on which they shall give their votes; which day shall be the same throughout the United States.

No person except a natural born citizen, or a citizen of the United States, at the time of the adoption of this Constitution, shall be eligible to the office of President; neither shall any person be eligible to that office who shall not have attained to the age of thirty five years, and been fourteen Years a resident within the United States.

In case of the removal of the President from office, or of his death, resignation, or inability to discharge the powers and duties of the said office, the same shall devolve on the Vice President, and the Congress may by law provide for the case of removal, death, resignation or inability, both of the President and Vice President, declaring what officer shall then act as President, and such officer shall act accordingly, until the disability be removed, or a President shall be elected.

The President shall, at stated times, receive for his services, a compensation, which shall neither be increased nor diminished during the period for which he shall have been elected, and he shall not receive within that period any other emolument from the United States, or any of them.

Before he enter on the execution of his office, he shall take the following oath or affirmation:—"I do solemnly swear (or affirm) that I will faithfully execute the office of President of the United States, and will to the best of my ability, preserve, protect and defend the Constitution of the United States."

Section 2.

The President shall be commander in chief of the Army and Navy of the United States, and of the militia of the several states, when called into the actual service of the United States; he may require the opinion, in writing, of the principal officer in each of the executive departments, upon any subject relating to the duties of their respective offices, and he shall have power to grant reprieves and pardons for offenses against the United States, except in cases of impeachment.

He shall have power, by and with the advice and consent of the Senate, to make treaties, provided two thirds of the Senators present concur; and he shall nominate, and by and with the advice and consent of the Senate, shall appoint ambassadors, other public ministers and consuls, judges of the Supreme Court, and all other officers of the United States, whose appointments are not herein otherwise provided for, and which shall be established by law: but the Congress may by law vest the appointment of such inferior officers, as they think proper, in the President alone, in the courts of law, or in the heads of departments.

The President shall have power to fill up all vacancies that may happen during the recess of the Senate, by granting commissions which shall expire at the end of their next session.

Section 3.

He shall from time to time give to the Congress information of the state of the union, and recommend to their consideration such measures as he shall judge necessary and expedient; he may, on extraordinary occasions, convene both Houses, or either of them, and in case of disagreement between them, with respect to the time of adjournment, he may adjourn them to such time as he shall think proper; he shall receive ambassadors and other public ministers; he shall take care that the laws be faithfully executed, and shall commission all the officers of the United States.

Section 4.

The President, Vice President and all civil officers of the United States, shall be removed from office on impeachment for, and conviction of, treason, bribery, or other high crimes and misdemeanors.

ARTICLE III

Section 1.

The judicial power of the United States, shall be vested in one Supreme Court, and in such inferior courts as the Congress may from time to time ordain and establish. The judges, both of the supreme and inferior courts, shall hold their offices during good behaviour, and shall, at stated times, receive for their services, a compensation, which shall not be diminished during their continuance in office.

Section 2.

The judicial power shall extend to all cases, in law and equity, arising under this Constitution, the laws of the United States, and treaties made, or which shall be made, under their authority;—to all cases affecting ambassadors, other public ministers and consuls;—to all cases of admiralty and maritime jurisdiction;—to controversies to which the United States shall be a party;—to controversies between two or more states;—between a state and citizens of another state;—between citizens of different states;—between citizens of the same state claiming lands under grants of different states, and between a state, or the citizens thereof, and foreign states, citizens or subjects.

In all cases affecting ambassadors, other public ministers and consuls, and those in which a state shall be party, the Supreme Court shall have original jurisdiction. In all the other cases before mentioned, the Supreme Court shall have appellate jurisdiction, both as to law and fact, with such exceptions, and under such regulations as the Congress shall make.

The trial of all crimes, except in cases of impeachment, shall be by jury; and such trial shall be held in the state where the said crimes shall have been committed; but when not committed within any state, the trial shall be at such place or places as the Congress may by law have directed.

Section 3.

Treason against the United States, shall consist only in levying war against them, or in adhering to their enemies, giving them aid and comfort. No person shall be convicted of treason unless on the testimony of two witnesses to the same overt act, or on confession in open court.

The Congress shall have power to declare the punishment of treason, but no attainder of treason shall work corruption of blood, or forfeiture except during the life of the person attainted.

ARTICLE IV

Section 1.

Full faith and credit shall be given in each state to the public acts, records, and judicial proceedings of every other state. And the Congress may by general laws prescribe the manner in which such acts, records, and proceedings shall be proved, and the effect thereof.

Section 2.

The citizens of each state shall be entitled to all privileges and immunities of citizens in the several states.

A person charged in any state with treason, felony, or other crime, who shall flee from justice, and be found in another state, shall on demand of the executive authority of the state from which he fled, be delivered up, to be removed to the state having jurisdiction of the crime.

No person held to service or labor in one state, under the laws thereof, escaping into another, shall, in consequence of any law or regulation therein, be discharged from such service or labor, but shall be delivered up on claim of the party to whom such service or labor may be due.

Section 3.

New states may be admitted by the Congress into this union; but no new states shall be formed or erected within the jurisdiction of any other state; nor any state be formed by the junction of two or more states, or parts of states, without the consent of the legislatures of the states concerned as well as of the Congress.

The Congress shall have power to dispose of and make all needful rules and regulations respecting the territory or other property belonging to the United States; and nothing in this Constitution shall be so construed as to prejudice any claims of the United States, or of any particular state.

Section 4.

The United States shall guarantee to every state in this union a republican form of government, and shall protect each of them against invasion; and on application of the legislature, or of the executive (when the legislature cannot be convened) against domestic violence.

ARTICLE V

The Congress, whenever two thirds of both houses shall deem it necessary, shall propose amendments to this Constitution, or, on the application of the legislatures of two thirds of the several states, shall call a convention for proposing amendments, which, in either case, shall be valid to all intents and purposes, as part of this Constitution, when ratified by the legislatures of three fourths of the several states, or by conventions in three fourths thereof, as the one or the other mode of ratification may be proposed by the Congress; provided that no amendment which may be made prior to the year one thousand eight hundred and eight shall in any manner affect the first and fourth clauses in the ninth section of the first article; and that no state, without its consent, shall be deprived of its equal suffrage in the Senate.

ARTICLE VI

All debts contracted and engagements entered into, before the adoption of this Constitution, shall be as valid against the United States under this Constitution, as under the Confederation.

This Constitution, and the laws of the United States which shall be made in pursuance thereof; and all treaties made, or which shall be made, under the authority of the United States, shall be the supreme law of the land; and the judges in every state shall be bound thereby, anything in the Constitution or laws of any State to the contrary notwithstanding.

The Senators and Representatives before mentioned, and the members of the several state legislatures, and all executive and judicial officers, both of the United States and of the several states, shall be bound by oath or affirmation, to support this Constitution; but no religious test shall ever be required as a qualification to any office or public trust under the United States.

ARTICLE VII

The ratification of the conventions of nine states, shall be sufficient for the establishment of this Constitution between the states so ratifying the same.

Done in convention by the unanimous consent of the states present the seventeenth day of September in the year of our Lord one thousand seven hundred and eighty seven and of the independence of the United States of America the twelfth. In witness whereof We have hereunto subscribed our Names,

G. Washington
Presidt. and deputy from Virginia
New Hampshire:
John Langdon, Nicholas Gilman
Massachusetts:
Nathaniel Gorham, Rufus King
Connecticut:
Wm. Saml. Johnson, Roger Sherman
New York:
Alexander Hamilton
New Jersey:
Wil. Livingston, David Brearly, Wm. Paterson, Jona. Dayton
Pennsylvania:
B. Franklin, Thomas Mifflin, Robt. Morris, Geo. Clymer, Thos. Fitz
    Simons, Jared Ingersoll, James Wilson, Gouv Morris
Delaware:
Geo. Read, Gunning Bedford Jr., John Dickinson, Richard Bassett, Jaco.
    Broom
Maryland:
James McHenry, Dan of St Thos. Jenifer, Danl Carroll
Virginia:
John Blair, James Madison Jr.
North Carolina:
Wm. Blount, Richd. Dobbs Spaight, Hu Williamson
South Carolina:
J. Rutledge, Charles Cotesworth Pinckney, Charles Pinckney, Pierce Butler
Georgia:
William Few, Abr Baldwin

Amendments to the Constitution of the United States before 1860

THE BILL OF RIGHTS

Amendment I (1791)

Congress shall make no law respecting an establishment of religion, or prohibiting the free exercise thereof; or abridging the freedom of speech, or of the press; or the right of the people peaceably to assemble, and to petition the government for a redress of grievances.

Amendment II (1791)

A well regulated militia, being necessary to the security of a free state, the right of the people to keep and bear arms, shall not be infringed.

Amendment III (1791)

No soldier shall, in time of peace be quartered in any house, without the consent of the owner, nor in time of war, but in a manner to be prescribed by law.

Amendment IV (1791)

The right of the people to be secure in their persons, houses, papers, and effects, against unreasonable searches and seizures, shall not be violated, and no warrants shall issue, but upon probable cause, supported by oath or affirmation, and particularly describing the place to be searched, and the persons or things to be seized.

Amendment V (1791)

No person shall be held to answer for a capital, or otherwise infamous crime, unless on a presentment or indictment of a grand jury, except in cases arising in the land or naval forces, or in the militia, when in actual service in time of war or public danger; nor shall any person be subject for the same offense to be twice put in jeopardy of life or limb; nor shall be compelled in any criminal case to be a witness against himself, nor be deprived of life, liberty, or property, without due process of law; nor shall private property be taken for public use, without just compensation.

Amendment VI (1791)

In all criminal prosecutions, the accused shall enjoy the right to a speedy and public trial, by an impartial jury of the state and district wherein the crime shall have been committed, which district shall have been previously ascertained by law, and to be informed of the nature and cause of the accusation; to be confronted with the witnesses against him; to have compulsory process for obtaining witnesses in his favor, and to have the assistance of counsel for his defense.

Amendment VII (1791)

In suits at common law, where the value in controversy shall exceed twenty dollars, the right of trial by jury shall be preserved, and no fact tried by a jury, shall be otherwise reexamined in any court of the United States, than according to the rules of the common law.

Amendment VIII (1791)

Excessive bail shall not be required, nor excessive fines imposed, nor cruel and unusual punishments inflicted.

Amendment IX (1791)

The enumeration in the Constitution, of certain rights, shall not be construed to deny or disparage others retained by the people.

Amendment X (1791)

The powers not delegated to the United States by the Constitution, nor prohibited by it to the states, are reserved to the states respectively, or to the people.

OTHER PRE–CIVIL WAR AMENDMENTS

Amendment XI (1798)

The judicial power of the United States shall not be construed to extend to any suit in law or equity, commenced or prosecuted against one of the United States by citizens of another state, or by citizens or subjects of any foreign state.

Amendment XII (1804)

The electors shall meet in their respective states and vote by ballot for President and Vice-President, one of whom, at least, shall not be an inhabitant of the same state with themselves; they shall name in their ballots the person voted for as President, and in distinct ballots the person voted for as Vice-President, and they shall make distinct lists of all persons voted for as President, and of all persons voted for as Vice-President, and of the number of votes for each, which lists they shall sign and certify, and transmit sealed to the seat of the government of the United States, directed to the President of the Senate;—The President of the Senate shall, in the presence of the Senate and House of Representatives, open all the certificates and the votes shall then be counted;—the person having the greatest number of votes for President, shall be the President, if such number be a majority of the whole number of electors appointed; and if no person have such majority, then from the persons having the highest numbers not exceeding three on the list of those voted for as President, the House of Representatives shall choose immediately, by ballot, the President. But in choosing the President, the votes shall be taken by states, the representation from each state having one vote; a quorum for this purpose shall consist of a member or members from two-thirds of the states, and a majority of all the states shall be necessary to a choice. And if the House of Representatives shall not choose a President whenever the right of choice shall devolve upon them, before the fourth day of March next following, then the Vice-President shall act as President, as in the case of the death or other constitutional disability of the President. The person having the greatest number of votes as Vice-President, shall be the Vice-President, if such number be a majority of the whole number of electors appointed, and if no person have a majority, then from the two highest numbers on the list, the Senate shall choose the Vice-President; a quorum for the purpose shall consist of two-thirds of the whole number of Senators, and a majority of the whole number shall be necessary to a choice. But no person constitutionally ineligible to the office of President shall be eligible to that of Vice-President of the United States.

Post–Civil War Amendments

AMENDMENT XIII (1865)

Section 1.

Neither slavery nor involuntary servitude, except as a punishment for crime whereof the party shall have been duly convicted, shall exist within the United States, or any place subject to their jurisdiction.

Section 2.

Congress shall have power to enforce this article by appropriate legislation.

AMENDMENT XIV (1868)

Section 1.

All persons born or naturalized in the United States, and subject to the jurisdiction thereof, are citizens of the United States and of the state wherein they reside. No state shall make or enforce any law which shall abridge the privileges or immunities of citizens of the United States; nor shall any state deprive any person of life, liberty, or property, without due process of law; nor deny to any person within its jurisdiction the equal protection of the laws.

Section 2.

Representatives shall be apportioned among the several states according to their respective numbers, counting the whole number of persons in each state, excluding Indians not taxed. But when the right to vote at any election for the choice of electors for President and Vice President of the United States, Representatives in Congress, the executive and judicial officers of a state, or the members of the legislature thereof, is denied to any of the male inhabitants of such state, being twenty-one years of age, and citizens of the United States, or in any way abridged, except for participation in rebellion, or other crime, the basis of representation therein shall be reduced in the proportion which the number of such male citizens shall bear to the whole number of male citizens twenty-one years of age in such state.

Section 3.

No person shall be a Senator or Representative in Congress, or elector of President and Vice President, or hold any office, civil or military, under the United States, or under any state, who, having previously taken an oath, as a member of Congress, or as an officer of the United States, or as a member of any state legislature, or as an executive or judicial officer of any state, to support the Constitution of the United States, shall have engaged in insurrection or rebellion against the same, or given aid or comfort to the enemies thereof. But Congress may by a vote of two-thirds of each House, remove such disability.

Section 4.

The validity of the public debt of the United States, authorized by law, including debts incurred for payment of pensions and bounties for services in suppressing insurrection or rebellion, shall not be questioned. But neither the United States nor any state shall assume or pay any debt or obligation incurred in aid of insurrection or rebellion against the United States, or any claim for the loss or emancipation of any slave; but all such debts, obligations and claims shall be held illegal and void.

Section 5.

The Congress shall have power to enforce, by appropriate legislation, the provisions of this article.

AMENDMENT XV (1870)

Section 1.

The right of citizens of the United States to vote shall not be denied or abridged by the United States or by any state on account of race, color, or previous condition of servitude.

Section 2.

The Congress shall have power to enforce this article by appropriate legislation.

Select Bibliography

ABOLITIONISTS AND ANTISLAVERY THEORY

Curry, Richard O. "The Abolitionists and Reconstruction: A Critical Appraisal," *Journal of Southern History*, 34 (1968), 527–45.

Davis, David Brion. "Abolitionists and the Freedmen: An Essay Review," *Journal of Southern History*, 31 (1965), 164–70.

Dillon, Merton L. "The Failure of American Abolitionists," *Journal of Southern History*, 25 (1959), 159–77.

Donald, David H. "Towards a Reconsideration of the Abolitionists," in Donald (ed.), *Lincoln Reconsidered: Essays on the Civil War Era.* New York: Vintage, 1956, 19–36.

Duberman, Martin (ed.). *The Antislavery Vanguard: New Essays on the Abolitionists.* Princeton: Princeton University Press, 1965.

Frederickson, George M. *The Inner Civil War: Northern Intellectuals and the Crisis of the Union.* New York: Harper & Row, 1965.

Magdol, Edward. *The Antislavery Rank and File: A Social Profile of the Abolitionists' Constituency.* Westport, Conn.: Greenwood Press, 1986.

McPherson, James M. "Abolitionists and the Civil Rights Act of 1875," *Journal of American History,* 52 (1965), 493–510.

———. *The Struggle for Equality: Abolitionists and the Negro in the Civil War and Reconstruction.* Princeton, N.J.: Princeton University Press, 1964.

Nye, Russell B. *Fettered Freedom: Civil Liberties and the Slavery Controversy, 1930–1860.* East Lansing: Michigan State College Press, 1949.

Poole, W. Scott. "Memory and the Abolitionist Heritage: Thomas Wentworth Higginson and the Uncertain Meaning of the Civil War," *Civil War History*, 51 (2005), 202–17.

Riddleberger, Patrick W. "The Radicals' Abandonment of the Negro during Reconstruction," *Journal of Negro History*, 45 (1960), 88–102.

Sewell, Richard. *Ballots for Freedom: Antislavery Politics in the United States, 1837–1860.* New York: Oxford University Press, 1976.

Sproat, John G. "Blueprint for Radical Reconstruction," *Journal of Southern History*, 23 (1957), 25–44.

Venet, Wendy Hamand. *Neither Ballots nor Bullets: Women Abolitionists and the Civil War.* Charlottesville: University of Virginia Press, 1991.

Woodward, C. Vann. "Equality: The Deferred Commitment," *The American Scholar*, 27 (1958), 459–72.

————. "Seeds of Failure in Radical Race Policy," in Harold M. Hyman (ed.), *New Frontiers of the American Reconstruction*. Urbana: University of Illinois Press, 1966, 125–47.

ALCORN, JAMES L.

Alexander, Thomas B. "Persistent Whiggery in Mississippi: The Hinds County Gazette," *Journal of Mississippi History*, 23 (1961), 71–93.

Donald, David H. "The Scalawag in Mississippi Reconstruction," *Journal of Southern History*, 10 (1944), 447–60.

Harris, William C. "Mississippi: Republican Factionalism and Mismanagement," in Otto H. Olsen (ed.), *Reconstruction and Redemption in the South*. Baton Rouge: Louisiana State University Press, 1980, 78–112.

————. "A Reconsideration of the Mississippi Scalawag," *Journal of Mississippi History*, 32 (1970), 3–42.

Pereyra, Lillian. *James Lusk Alcorn: Persistent Whig*. Baton Rouge: Louisiana State University Press, 1966.

Wakelyn, Jon L. *Biographical Dictionary of the Confederacy*. Westport, Conn.: Greenwood Press, 1977.

AMES, ADELBERT (1835–1933)

Ames, Blanch Ames. *Adelbert Ames, 1835–1933: General, Senator, Governor*. New York: Argosy-Antiquarian, 1964.

Boatner, Mark M., III. *The Civil War Dictionary*. New York: D. McKay and Company, 1959.

Current, Richard N. *Those Terrible Carpetbaggers: A Reinterpretation*. New York: Oxford University Press, 1988.

————. *Three Carpetbag Governors*. Baton Rouge: Louisiana State University Press, 1967.

Currie-McDaniel, Ruth. "The Wives of the Carpetbaggers," in Jeffrey J. Crow *et al.* (eds.), *Race, Class, and Politics in Southern History*. Baton Rouge: Louisiana State University Press, 1989, 35–78.

Garner, James W. *Reconstruction in Mississippi*. New York: Macmillan, 1901.

Harris, William C. "Mississippi: Republican Factionalism and Mismanagement," in Otto H. Olsen (ed.), *Reconstruction and Redemption in the South*. Baton Rouge: Louisiana State University Press, 1980, 78–112.

Kennedy, John F. *Profiles in Courage*. New York: Harper & Row, 1956.

Sefton, James E. *The United States Army and Reconstruction, 1865–1877*. Baton Rouge: Louisiana State University Press, 1967.

ANACONDA PLAN

Blackwell, Sarah Ellen. *A Military Genius: Life of Anna Carroll of Maryland.* Washington, D.C.: Judd & Detweiler, 1891.

Coryell, Janet L. *Neither Heroine nor Fool: Anna Carroll of Maryland.* Kent, Ohio: Kent State University Press, 1990.

Elliott, Charles Winslow. *Winfield Scott: The Soldier and the Man.* New York: Macmillan, 1937.

Greenbie, Sydney, and Marjorie Latta Greenbie. *Anna Ella Carroll and Abraham Lincoln.* Manchester, Maine: Falmouth Publishing Co., 1952.

Hagerman, Edward. *The American Civil War and the Origins of Modern Warfare.* Bloomington: Indiana University Press, 1988.

Hattaway, Herman, and Archer Jones. *How the North Won.* Urbana: University of Illinois Press, 1983.

Johnson, Timothy D. *Winfield Scott: The Quest for Military Glory.* Lawrence: University Press of Kansas, 1998.

Long, E. B. "Anna Ella Carroll: Exaggerated Heroine?" *Civil War Times Illustrated*, 14 (July 1975), 28–35.

Patchan, Scott C. "Piedmont: The Forgotten Battle," *North & South*, 6 (April 2003), 62–75.

Perret, Geoffrey. "What Anaconda Plan?" *North & South*, 6 (May 2003), 36–43.

Reed, Rowena. *Combined Operations in the Civil War.* Annapolis, MD: Naval Institute Press, 1978.

Safire, William. *Freedom: A Novel of Abraham Lincoln and the Civil War.* Garden City, NY: Doubleday & Co., 1987.

Sydner, Charles McCool. "Anna Carroll, Political Strategist and Gadfly of President Fillmore, *Maryland Historical Magazine*, 68 (No. 1, 1973), 36–63.

Weddle, Kevin J. "The Blockade Board of 1861 and Union Naval Strategy," *Civil War History*, 48 (2002).

Williams, Kenneth P. "The Tennessee River Campaign and Anna Carroll," *Indiana Magazine of History*, 46 (1950), 221–48.

ARM-IN-ARM CONVENTION

Wagstaff, Thomas. "The Arm-in-Arm Convention," *Civil War History*, 14 (1968), 101–19.

ARMY, U.S., AND RECONSTRUCTION

Alderson, William T. "The Influence of Military Rule and the Freedmen's Bureau on Reconstruction in Virginia, 1865–1870." Ph.D. dissertation, Vanderbilt University, 1952.

Ambrose, Stephen E. *Halleck: Lincoln's Chief of Staff.* Baton Rouge: Louisiana State University Press, 1962.

Ashcraft, Alan C. "Role of the Confederate Provost Marshals in Texas," *Texana,* 6 (1968), 390–92.

Bailyn, Bernard. *Ideological Origins of the American Revolution.* Cambridge: Harvard University Press, 1967.

Baker, George T. "Mexico City and the War with the United States: A Study of the Politics of Military Occupation." Ph.D. dissertation, Duke University, 1970.

Ballantine, Henry W. "Martial Law," *Columbia Law Review,* 12 (1912), 529–38.

———. "Unconstitutional Claims of Military Authority," *Yale Law Journal,* 24 (1914–1915), 201–202.

Barr, Alwyn (ed.). "Records of the Confederate Military Commission in San Antonio, July 2–October 10, 1862," *Southwestern Historical Quarterly,* 70 (1966–1967), 93–109, 289–313, 623–44; 71 (1967–68), 247–78.

Benet, Stephen Vincent. *Treatise on Military Law and the Practice of Courts Martial.* 2nd ed. New York: D. Van Nostrand, 1868.

Birkhimer, William E. *Military Government and Martial Law.* 2nd ed. Kansas City: F. Hudson Publishing Company, 1904.

Blair, William Alan. "The Use of Military Force to Protect the Gains of Reconstruction," *Civil War History,* 51 (2005), 388–402.

Bluntschli, Johann Kaspar. *Das Moderne Kriegsrecht der Civilisierten Staaten als Rechtsbuch Dargestellt.* Noerdlingen: C. H. Beck, 1866.

Byrne, Frank L. "'A Terrible Machine': General Neal Dow's Military Government on the Gulf Coast," *Civil War History,* 12 (1966), 5–22.

Carpenter, A. H. "Military Government of Southern Territory, 1861–1865," *American Historical Association Annual Report* (1900), I, 465–98.

Davis, Ronald L. F. *Good and Faithful Labor: From Slavery to Sharecropping in the Natchez District, 1860–1890.* Westport Conn.: Greenwood Press, 1982.

Dawson, Joseph Green, III. *Army Generals and Reconstruction: Louisiana, 1862–1977.* Baton Rouge: Louisiana State University Press, 1982.

Dennison, George W. "Martial Law: The Development of a Theory of Emergency Power, 1776–1861," *American Journal of Legal History,* 18 (1974), 52–95.

Dunning, William A. *Essays on the Civil War and Reconstruction.* New York: Macmillan Company, 1897.

Foner, Eric. *Reconstruction: America's Unfinished Revolution, 1863–1877.* New York: Harper & Row, 1988.

Franklin, John Hope. *Reconstruction: After the Civil War.* Chicago: University of Chicago Press, 1961.

Freidel, Frank. "General Orders No. 100 and Military Government," *Mississippi Valley Historical Review,* 32 (1945–1946), 541–56.

Furman, H. W. C. "Restrictions upon the Use of the Army Imposed by the Posse Comitatus Act," *Military Law Review,* 7 (1959), 85–129.

Futrell, Robert F. "Federal Military Government in the South, 1861–1865," *Military Affairs,* 15 (1951), 181–91.

Garner, James W. "General Orders 100 Revisited," *Military Law Review*, 27 (1965), 1–48.

Gerteis, Louis S. *From Contraband to Freedman: Federal Policy Toward Southern Blacks, 1861–1865*. Westport, Conn.: Greenwood Press, 1973.

Holdsworth, W. S. "Martial Law Historically Considered," *Law Quarterly Review*, 18 (1902), 117–32.

Holladay, Florence Elizabeth. "The Extraordinary Powers and Functions of the General Commanding the Trans-Mississippi Department of the Southern Confederacy." M.A. thesis, University of Texas, 1914.

Hyman, Harold M. "Johnson, Stanton, and Grant: A Reinterpretation of the Army's Role in the Events Leading to Impeachment," *American Historical Review*, 66 (1960), 85–100.

———. *A More Perfect Union: The Impact of the Civil War and Reconstruction on the Constitution.* New York: Alfred A. Knopf, 1973.

Main, Jackson Turner. *The Anti-Federalists: Critics of the Constitution, 1781–1788.* Chicago: Quadrangle Books, 1964.

Majeske, Penelope K. "Virginia after Appomattox: The Unites States Army and the Formation of Presidential Reconstruction Policy," *West Virginia History*, 43 (1982), 95–117.

Maslowski, Peter. "*'Treason Must Be Made Odious'*: Military Occupation and Reconstruction in Nashville, Tennessee, 1862–1865." Ph.D. dissertation, Ohio State University, 1972.

Matthews, Clifford. "Special Military Tribunals, 1775–1865." M.A. thesis, Emory University, 1951.

McDonough, James L. "John Schofield as Military Director of Reconstruction in Virginia," *Civil War History*, 15 (1969), 237–56.

Meek, Clarence I., III. "Illegal Law Enforcement: Aiding Civil Authorities in Violation of the Posse Comitatus Act," *Military Law Review*, 70 (1975), 83–126.

Moore, Wilton P. "The Provost Marshal Goes to War," *Civil War History*, 5 (1959), 62–71.

———. "Union Provost Marshals in the Eastern Theater," *Military Affairs*, 26 (1962), 120–21.

Morrill, James Ray III. "North Carolina and the Administration of Brevet Major General Sickles," *North Carolina Historical Review*, 42 (1965), 291–305.

Rice, Paul Jackson. "New Laws and Insights Encircle the Posse Commitatus Act," *Military Law Review*, 104 (1984), 109–38.

Richter, William L. *The Army in Texas During Reconstruction, 1865–1870.* College Station: Texas A&M University Press, 1987.

———. "'Devil Take Them All': Military Rule in Texas, 1862–1865," *Southern Studies*, 25 (1986), 5–30.

Sefton, James E. *The United States Army and Reconstruction, 1865–1877.* Baton Rouge: Louisiana State University Press, 1967.

Shy, John. *Toward Lexington: The Role of the British Army in the Coming of the Revolution.* Princeton, N.J.: Princeton University Press, 1965.

St. Clair, Kenneth E. "Judicial Machinery in North Carolina in 1865," *North Carolina Historical Review*, 30 (1953), 415–39.

———. "Military Justice in North Carolina, 1865: A Microcosm of Reconstruction," *Civil War History*, 11 (1965), 341–50.

Thomas, Benjamin P., and Harold M. Hyman. *Stanton: The Life and Times of Lincoln's Secretary of War*. New York: Alfred A. Knopf, 1962.

Thomas, David Y. *A History of Military Government in Newly Acquired Territories of the United States*. New York: Columbia University Press, 1904.

Ulrich, John William. "The Northern Military Mind in Regard to Reconstruction, 1865–1872: The Attitudes of Ten Leading Union Generals." Ph.D. dissertation, Ohio State University, 1959.

Weigley, Russell F. *History of the United States Army*. New York: Macmillan, 1967.

ASHLEY, JAMES M. (1824–1896)

Carter, Clarence E. "James Mitchell Ashley," in Allen Johnson *et al.* (eds.), *Dictionary of American Biography* (10 double vols. + 9 supplements, 1964–1981), I, 389–90.

Horowitz, Robert F. "James M. Ashley and the Presidential Election of 1856," *Ohio Historical Quarterly*, 83 (1974), 4–16.

———. "Land to the Freedmen: A Vision of Reconstruction," *Ohio Historical Quarterly*, 85 (1977), 187–99.

Kahn, Maxine Baker. "Congressman Ashley in the Post-Civil War Years," *Northwest Ohio Quarterly*, 36 (1964), 116–33.

ATLANTA CAMPAIGN (1864)

Bonin, John Aubrey. "Lost Victories: Johnston and Sherman at Cassville," *Blue and Gray*, 13 (1996).

Carter, Samuel, III. *The Siege of Atlanta, 1864*. New York: St. Martin's Press, 1973.

Castel, Albert. *Decision in the West: The Atlanta Campaign of 1864*. Lawrence: University Press of Kansas, 1992.

Clauss, Errol MacGregor. "The Battle of Jonesborough," *Civil War Times Illustrated*, 7 (November 1968), 12–23.

Connelly, Thomas M. *Autumn of Glory: The Army of Tennessee, 1862–1865*. Baton Rouge: Louisiana State University Press, 1971.

Daniel, Larry J. *Soldiering in the Army of Tennessee: A Portrait of Life in a Confederate Army*. Chapel Hill: University of North Carolina Press, 1991.

Davis, Stephen. "Atlanta Campaign, Part 3," *Blue & Gray*, 6 (1988–1989), [Special Issue].

Duncan, Kennedy, and Roger S. Fitch. *Supply of Sherman's Army during the Atlanta Campaign*. Ft. Leavenworth, Kans: Army Service Schools Press, 1911.

Fowler, Robert H. (ed.). "The Campaign for Atlanta," *Civil War Times Illustrated*, 3 (July 1964), [Special Issue].

Hicken, Victor. "The Battle of Allatoona," *Civil War Times Illustrated*, 7 (June 1968), 18–27.

Hoehling, A. A. *Last Train from Atlanta*. New York: Thomas Yoseloff, 1958.

Keller, Allan. "On the Road to Atlanta: Johnston vs. Sherman," *Civil War Times Illustrated*, 1 (December 1962), 18–22, 32–35.

Kelly, Dennis. "Atlanta Campaign, Part 2," *Blue & Gray*, 6 (1988–1989), [Special Issue].

McMurry, Richard M. "The Atlanta Campaign in 1864: A New Look," *Civil War History*, 22 (1976), 5–15.

McMurry, Richard M. "Atlanta Campaign, Part 1," *Blue & Gray*, 6 (1988–1989), [Special Issue].

———. "The Battle of Kolb's Farm," *Civil War Times Illustrated*, 7 (December 1968), 20–27.

———. "Cassville," *Civil War Times Illustrated*, 10 (December 1971), 4–9, 45–48.

———. "Confederate Morale in the Atlanta Campaign of 1864," *Georgia Historical Quarterly*, 54 (1970), 226–43.

———. "Kennesaw Mountain," *Civil War Times Illustrated*, 8 (January 1970), 19–34.

———. "Resaca: 'A Heap of Hard Fiten,'" *Civil War Times Illustrated*, 9 (November 1970), 4–12, 44–48.

Newton, Steven H. "Formidable Only in Flight? Casualties, Attrition, and Morale in Georgia," *North & South*, 4 (April 2000), 43–56.

———. "Myths and Realities: Joseph Johnston and Snake Creek Gap," *North & South*, 4 (March 2001), 56–67.

Rowell, John W. "McCook's Raid," *Civil War Times Illustrated*, 13 (July 1974), 4–9, 42–48.

Savas, Theodore, and David A. Woodbury (eds.). *Campaign for Atlanta and Sherman's March to the Sea*. 2 vols. Campbell, CA: Savas Publishers, 1994–1997.

Stanchak, John (ed.). "The Atlanta Campaign," *Civil War Times Illustrated*, 28 (Summer 1989), [Special Issue].

Symonds, Craig L. *Joseph E. Johnston: A Civil War Biography*. New York: Norton, 1992.

BLACK EDUCATION AND RECONSTRUCTION

Abbott, Martin. "The Freedmen's Bureau and Negro Schooling in South Carolina," *South Carolina Historical Magazine*, 57 (1956), 65–81.

Alderson, William T. "The Freedmen's Bureau and Negro Education in Virginia," *North Carolina Historical Review*, 29 (1952), 64–90.

Alexander, Roberta Sue. "Hostility and Hope: Black Education in North Carolina during Presidential Reconstruction, 1865–1867," *North Carolina Historical Review*, 53 (1976), 113–32.

Armstrong, Warren B. "Union Chaplains and the Education of Freedmen," *Journal of Negro History*, 52 (1967), 104–15.

Beatty, Bess. *A Revolution Gone Backward: The Black Response to National Politics, 1876–1896*. New York: Greenwood Press, 1987.

Blassingame, John W. "The Union Army as an Educational Institution for Negroes, 1961–1865," *Journal of Negro Education*, 34 (1965), 152–59.

Butchart, Ronald E. *Northern Schools, Southern Blacks, and Reconstruction: Freedmen's Education, 1862–1875*. Westport, Conn.: Greenwood Press, 1980.

Chang, Perry. "'Angels of Peace in a Smitten Land': The Northern Teachers' Role in the Reconstruction South Reconsidered," *Southern Historian*, 16 (1995), 26–45.

Cornish, Dudley T. "The Union Army as a School for Negroes," *Journal of Negro History*, 37 (1952), 368–82.

Franklin, John Hope. "Jim Crow Goes to School: The Genesis of Legal Segregation in Southern Schools," *South Atlantic Quarterly*, 58 (1959), 225–35.

Halstead, Jacqueline J. "The Delaware Association for the Moral Improvement and Education of the Colored People: 'Practical Christianity'," *Delaware History*, 15 (1972), 19–40.

Hornsby, Alton, Jr. "The Freedmen's Bureau Schools in Texas, 1865–1870," *Southwestern Historical Quarterly*, 76 (1972–73), 397–417.

Jackson, Luther P. "The Educational Efforts of the Freedmen's Bureau and Freedmen's Aid Societies in South Carolina, 1862–1872," *Journal of Negro History*, 8 (1923), 1–40.

Jones, Jacqueline. *Soldiers of Light and Love: Northern Teachers and Georgia Blacks, 1865–1873*. Chapel Hill: University of North Carolina Press, 1980.

———. "Women Who Were More Than Men: Sex and Status in Freedmen's Teaching," *History of Education Quarterly*, 19 (1979), 47–59.

Kimball, Philip Clyde. "Freedom's Harvest: Freedmen's Schools in Kentucky after the Civil War," *Filson Club Historical Quarterly*, 54 (1980), 272–88.

Kousser, J. Morgan. *Dead End: The Development of Nineteenth Century Litigation on Discrimination in Schools*. New York: Oxford University Press, 1985.

———. "Separate But Not Equal: The Supreme Court's First Decision on Racial Discrimination in Schools," *Journal of Southern History*, 46 (1980), 17–44.

Low, W. Augustus. "The Freedmen's Bureau and Civil Rights in Maryland," *Journal of Negro History*, 37 (1952), 221–47.

Morris, Robert C. *Reading, 'Riting, and Reconstruction*. Chicago: University of Chicago Press, 1981.

Newby, Robert G., and David B. Tyack. "Victims without Crimes: Some Historical Perspectives on Black Education," *Journal of Negro Education*, 40 (1971), 192–206.

Pearce, Larry W. "The American Missionary Association and the Freedmen's Bureau in Arkansas, 1868–1878," *Arkansas Historical Quarterly*, 30 (1971), 123–44, 246–61; 31 (1972), 246–61.

Proctor, Samuel. "Yankee 'Schoolmarms' in Post-war Florida," *Journal of Negro History*, 44 (1959), 275–77.

Rabinowitz, Howard N. "Half a Loaf: The Shift from White to Black Teachers in the Negro Schools of the Urban South, 1865–1890," *Journal of Southern History,* 40 (1974), 565–94.

Richardson, Joe M. "The American Missionary Association and Black Education in Civil War Missouri," *Missouri Historical Review,* 69 (1975), 433–48.

———. "The Freedmen's Bureau and Negro Education in Florida," *Journal of Negro Education,* 31 (1962), 460–67.

Schweninger, Loren. "The American Missionary Association and Northern Philanthropy in Reconstruction Alabama," *Alabama Historical Quarterly,* 32 (1970), 129–56.

Sherer, Robert G. *Subordination or Liberation? The Developing Theories of Black Education in Nineteenth Century Alabama.* Tuscaloosa: University of Alabama Press, 1977.

Small, Sandra E. "The Yankee *Schoolmarm* in Freedmen's Schools: An Analysis of Attitudes," *Journal of Southern History,* 45 (1979), 381–402.

Smith, Thomas H. "Ohio Quakers and the Mississippi Freedmen: 'A Field to Labor'," *Ohio History,* 78 (1969), 159–71.

Sparks, Randy J. "'The White People's Arms Are Longer than Ours': Blacks, Education, and the American Missionary Association in Reconstruction Mississippi," *Journal of Mississippi History,* 54 (February 1992), 1–27.

Spivey, Donald. *Schooling for the New Slavery: Black Industrial Education, 1868–1915.* Westport, Conn.: Greenwood Press, 1978.

Swint, Henry Lee. *The Northern Teacher in the South, 1862–1870.* Nashville, Tenn.: Vanderbilt University Press, 1941.

Wesley, Edgar B. "Forty Acres and a Mule and a Speller," *History of Education Journal,* 8 (1957), 113–27.

White, Kenneth B. "The Alabama Freedmen's Bureau and Black Education: The Myth of Opportunity," *Alabama Review,* 34 (1981), 107–24.

BACK LEADERSHIP AND RECONSTRUCTION

Abbott, Martin. "Freedom's Cry: Negroes and their Meetings in South Carolina, 1865–1869," *Phylon,* 20 (1959), 263–72.

Barr, Alwyn. "Black Legislators of Reconstruction Texas," *Civil War History,* 32 (1986), 340–52.

Berry, Mary Frances, and John W. Blassingame. *Long Memory: The Black Experience in America.* New York: Oxford University Press, 1982.

Blassingame, John W. *Black New Orleans, 1860–1880.* Chicago: University of Chicago Press, 1973.

Brown, Canter, Jr. *Florida's Black Public Officials, 1867–1924.* Tuscaloosa: University of Alabama Press, 1998.

Carter, Dan T. "Moonlight, Magnolias, and Collard Greens: Black History and the New Romanticism," *Reviews in American History,* 5 (1977), 167–73.

Cimprich, John. "The Beginning of the Black Suffrage Movement in Tennessee, 1864–1865," *Journal of Negro History*, 65 (1980), 185–95.

———. *Slavery's End in Tennessee, 1861–1865*. Tuscaloosa: University of Alabama Press, 1985.

Cook, Samuel Dubois. "A Tragic Conception of Negro History," *Journal of Negro History*, 45 (1960), 219–40.

Cruden, Robert. *The Negro in Reconstruction*. Englewood Cliffs, N.J.: Prentice-Hall, 1969.

Drago, Edmund. *Black Politicians and Reconstruction Georgia: A Splendid Failure*. Baton Rouge: Louisiana State University Press, 1982.

Foner, Eric. "African-Americans in Public Office during the Era of Reconstruction," *Reconstruction*, 2 (No. 2, 1994), 20–32.

———. *Freedom's Lawmakers: A Directory of Black Officeholders During Reconstruction*. rev. ed. Baton Rouge: Louisiana State University Press, 1996.

Genovese, Eugene D. *Roll Jordan Roll: The World the Slaves Made*. New York: Pantheon Books, 1974.

Hermann, Janet S. "Reconstruction in Microcosm: Three Men and a Gin," *Journal of Negro History*, 65 (1980), 312–35.

Holt, Thomas. *Black over White: Negro Political Leadership in South Carolina during Reconstruction*. Urbana: University of Illinois Press, 1977.

Hosmer, John, and Joseph Fineman. "Black Congressmen in Reconstruction Historiography," *Phylon*, 39 (1978), 97–107.

Jones, Howard James. "Images of State Legislative Reconstruction Participants in Fiction," *Journal of Negro History*, 67 (1982), 318–27.

Klingman, Peter D., and David T. Geithman. "Negro Dissidence and the Republican Party, 1864–1872," *Phylon*, 40 (1979), 172–82.

Kolchin, Peter. *First Freedom: The Responses of Alabama's Blacks to Emancipation and Reconstruction*. Westport, Conn.: Greenwood Press, 1972.

Logsdon, Joseph. "Black Reconstruction Revisited," *Reviews in American History*, 1 (1973), 553–58.

Lowe, Richard. "The Freedmen's Bureau and Local Black Leadership," *Journal of American History*, 80 (1993), 989–98.

Magdol, Edward. "Local Black Leaders in the South, 1867–1875: An Essay toward the Reconstruction of Reconstruction History," *Societas*, 4 (1974), 81–110.

———. *A Right to the Land: Essays on the Freedmen's Community*. Westport, Conn.: Greenwood Press, 1977.

McFarlin, Annjeannette Sophia. *Black Congressional Reconstruction Orators and Their Orations*. Metuchen, N.J.: Scarecrow Press, 1976.

Mohr, Clarence L. "Southern Blacks in the Civil War: A Century of Historiography," *Journal of Negro History*, 59 (1974), 177–85.

O'Brien, John T. "Reconstruction in Richmond: White Restoration and Black Protest, April–June 1865," *Virginia Magazine of History and Biography*, 89 (1981), 259–81.

Pitre, Merline. *Through Many Dangers, Toils, and Snares: The Black Leadership of Texas, 1868–1900*. Austin, Tex.: Eakin Press, 1985.

Rabinowitz, Howard N. (ed.). *Southern Black Leaders of the Reconstruction Era*. Urbana: University of Illinois Press, 1982.

Reid, George W. "Four in Black: North Carolina's Black Congressmen, 1874–1901," *Journal of Negro History*, 64 (1979), 229–43.

Richardson, Joe M. *The Negro in the Reconstruction of Florida, 1865–1877*. Tallahassee: Florida State University, 1965.

Robinson, Armistead L. "Beyond the Realm of Consensus: New Meanings of Reconstruction for American History," *Journal of American History*, 68 (1981), 276–97.

————. "Explaining the Failure of Democratic Reform in Reconstruction South Carolina," *Reviews in American History*, 8 (1980), 521–30.

Smith, Samuel Denny. *Negroes in Congress, 1870–1901*. Chapel Hill: University of North Carolina Press, 1940.

Thornbrough, Emma Lou (ed.). *Black Reconstructionists*. Englewood Cliffs, N.J.: Prentice-Hall, Inc., 1972.

Thorpe, Earl E. *Black Historians: A Critique*. New York: 1971.

Vincent, Charles. "Louisiana's Black Legislators and Their Efforts to Pass a Blue Law during Reconstruction," *Journal of Black Studies*, 7 (1976–1977), 47–56.

Wagandt, Charles L. "The Army versus Maryland Slavery, 1862–1864," *Civil War History*, 10 (1964), 141–48.

————. *The Mighty Revolution: Negro Emancipation in Maryland, 1862–1864*. Baltimore: The Johns Hopkins Press, 1964.

Williamson, Joel. *After Slavery: The Negro in South Carolina during Reconstruction*. Chapel Hill: University of North Carolina Press, 1965.

Woodward, C. Vann. "Clio with Soul," *Journal of American History*, 56 (1969), 5–20.

————. "Flight from History—The Heritage of the Negro," *The Nation*, 201 (1965), 142–46.

BLACKS AND RECONSTRUCTION

Bennett, Lerone, Jr. *Black Power, U.S.A.: The Human Side of Reconstruction*. Chicago: Johnson Publishing Company, Inc., 1967.

Berry, Mary Frances, and John W. Blassingame. *Long Memory: The Black Experience in America*. New York: Oxford University Press, 1982.

Carter, Dan T. "Moonlight, Magnolias, and Collard Greens: Black History and the New Romanticism," *Reviews in American History*, 5 (1977), 167–73.

Donald, Henderson H. *The Negro Freedman: Life Conditions of the American Negro in the Early Years After Emancipation*. New York: Abelard-Schumann Ltd., 1971.

Cruden, Robert. *The Negro in Reconstruction*. Englewood Cliffs, N.J.: Prentice-Hall, 1969.

Franklin, John Hope, and Alfred A. Moss, Jr. *From Slavery to Freedom: A History of the African-American*. New York: Alfred A. Knopf, 1994.

Gutman, Herbert G. *The Black Family in Slavery and Freedom, 1750–1925*. New York: Pantheon Books, 1976.

Hancock, Harold B. "The Status of the Negro in Delaware during the Civil War, 1865–1875," *Delaware History*, 8 (1968), 57–66.

Harris, Robert L., Jr. "Coming of Age: The Transformation of Afro-American Historiography," *Journal of Negro History*, 67 (1982), 107–21.

Litwack, Leon F. *Been in the Storm So Long: The Aftermath of Slavery*. New York: Alfred A. Knopf, 1979.

McPherson, James M. "The Hidden Freedmen: Five Myths in the Reconstruction Era," in James C. Curtis and Lewis L. Gould (eds.), *The Black Experience in America: Selected Essays*. Austin: University of Texas Press, 1970, 68–86.

Saville, Julie. *The Work of Reconstruction: From Slave to Wage Laborer in South Carolina, 1860–1870*. New York: Cambridge University Press, 1994.

Woodward, C. Vann. "Seeds of Failure in Radical Race Policy," in Harold M. Hyman (ed.), *New Frontiers of the American Reconstruction*. Urbana: University of Illinois Press, 1966, 125–47.

BALL'S BLUFF AND THE JOINT COMMITTEE ON THE CONDUCT OF THE WAR

Farwell, Byron. *Ball's Bluff: A Small Battle and Its Long Shadow*. McLean, Va.: EPM Publications, 1990.

Holien, Kim B. *Battle at Ball's Bluff*. Orange, Va.: Moss Publications, 1985.

———. "Battle of Ball's Bluff," *Blue & Gray*, 7 (1989–1990), [Special Issue].

Long, E. B. "The Committee on the Conduct of the War," *Civil War Times Illustrated*, 20 (August 1981), 20–27.

Longacre, Edward G. "Charles P. Stone and the 'Crime of Unlucky Generals,'" *Civil War Times Illustrated*, 13 (November 1974), 4–9, 38–41.

Morgan, James A., III. "A Table Full of Civilians: [The Joint Committee on the Conduct of the War]," *Civil War Times Illustrated*, 45 (June 2006), 50–56.

Williams, T. Harry. *Lincoln and the Radicals*. Madison: University of Wisconsin Press, 1941.

BANKS, NATHANIEL P. (1816–1894)

Harrington, Fred Harvey. *Fighting Politician: Major General N. P. Banks*. Philadelphia: University of Pennsylvania Press, 1948.

Hollandsworth, James G. *Pretense of Glory: The Life of General Nathaniel P. Banks*. Baton Rouge: Louisiana State University Press, 1998.

McDowell, John E. "Nathaniel P. Banks: Fighting Politico," *Civil War Times Illustrated*, 11 (January 1973), 4–9, 44–47.
Williams, T. Harry. "General Banks and Radical Republicans in the Civil War," *New England Quarterly*, 12 (1939), 268–80.

BAYOU TECHE AND PORT HUDSON CAMPAIGN

Cunningham, Edward. *The Port Hudson Campaign, 1862–1863*. Lafayette: Acadiana Press, 1963.
Hewitt, Lawrence Lee. *Port Hudson: Confederate Bastion on the Mississippi*. Baton Rouge: Louisiana State University Press, 1987.
———, and R. Christopher Goodwin. "The Battle of Bisland, Louisiana," *North & South*, 1 (September 1998), 29–45.
Kushlan, Jim (ed.). "July 1863: America Explodes," *Civil War Times Illustrated*, 42 (August 2003), 30–40.
Longacre, Edward G. "Port Hudson Campaign," *Civil War Times Illustrated*, 10 (February 1972), 20–34.
Rudolph, Jack. "Battle in the Bayou [Teche, 1863]," *Civil War Times Illustrated*, 23 (January 1985), 12–21.

BEAUREGARD, P. G. T. (1818–1893)

Current, Richard N. (ed.). *Encyclopedia of the Confederacy*. 4 vols. New York: Simon & Schuster, 1993.
Davis, William C. (ed.). *The Confederate General*. 6 vols. N.p.: National Historical Society, 1991.
Freeman, Douglas Southall. *Lee's Lieutenants: A Study of Command*. 3 vols. New York: Charles Scribner's Sons, 1942–1944.
Warner, Ezra J. *Generals in Gray: Lives of Confederate Commanders*. Baton Rouge: Louisiana State University Press, 1959.
Williams, T. Harry. *P. G. T. Beauregard: Napoleon in Gray*. Baton Rouge: Louisiana State University Press, 1955.

BENJAMIN, JUDAH PHILIP (1811–1884)

Adams, Ephraim Douglas. *Great Britain and the American Civil War*. 2 vols. New York: Russell & Russell, 1925.
Beckles, Willson. *John Slidell and the Confederates in Paris, 1862–1865*. New York: Minton, Balck, 1932.
Bulloch, James D. *The Secret Service of the Confederate States in Europe; or, How the Confederate Cruisers Were Equipped*. 2 vols. New York: Thomas Yoseloff, 1959, repr.

Case, Lynne M., and Warren F. Spencer. *The United States and France: Civil War Diplomacy*. Philadelphia: University of Pennsylvania Press, 1970.

Crook, David Paul. *The North, the South, and the Powers, 1861–1865*. New York: Wiley, 1974.

Daddysman, James W. *The Matamoros Trade: Confederate Commerce, Diplomacy, and Intrigue*. Newark: University of Delaware Press, 1984.

Delaney, Norman. "The Strange Occupation of James Bulloch: 'When Can You Start?'," *Civil War Times Illustrated*, 21 (March 1982), 18–27.

Durkin, J. T. *Stephen R. Mallory: Confederate Navy Chief*. Chapel Hill: University of North Carolina Press, 1954.

Jones, Wilbur D. *The Confederate Rams at Birkenhead: A Chapter in Anglo-American Relations*. Tuscaloosa, Ala.: Confederate Publishing Co., 1961.

Lebergott, Stanley. "Through the Blockade: The Profitability and Extent of Cotton Smuggling," *Journal of Economic History*, 51 (1981), 867–88.

May, Robert E. (ed.). *The Union, the Confederacy, and the Atlantic Rim*. West Lafayette: Purdue University Press, 1995.

Merli, Frank J. *Great Britain and the Confederate Navy, 1861–1865*. Bloomington: Indiana University Press, 1970.

Owsley, Frank L. *King Cotton Diplomacy*. Chicago: University of Chicago Press, 1959.

Spencer, Warren F. *The Confederate Navy in Europe*. Tuscaloosa: University of Alabama Press, 1983.

Surdam, David G. "Cotton's Potential as Economic Weapon: The Antebellum and Wartime Markets for Cotton Textiles," *Agricultural History*, 68 (1994), 122–45.

Thompson, Samuel Bernard. *The Confederate Navy in Europe*. Tuscaloosa: University of Alabama Press, 1983.

BINGHAM, JOHN A. (1815–1900)

Beauregard, Erving E. "The Chief Prosecutor of President Andrew Johnson," *Midwest Quarterly*, 31 (1990), 408–22.

Kendrick, Benjamin B. *The Journal of the Joint Committee of Fifteen on Reconstruction, 39th Congress, 1865–1867*. New York: Columbia University Press, 1914.

McCormick, Thomas D. "John Armor Bingham," in Allen Johnson *et al.* (eds.), *Dictionary of American Biography* (10 double vols. + 9 supplements, 1964–1981), II, 277–78.

Donald, David H. *The Politics of Reconstruction, 1863–1867*. Baton Rouge: Louisiana State University Press, 1965.

Swift, Donald. "John Bingham and Reconstruction: The Dilemma of a Moderate," *Ohio Historical Quarterly*, 77 (1968), 76–94.

Ten Broek, Jacobus. *Equal under Law: The Antislavery Origins of the Fourteenth Amendment*. New York: Collier Books, 1951, 1965.

BLACK "PERSONALITY" IN SLAVERY AND FREEDOM

Aptheker, Herbert. *American Negro Slave Revolts*. New York: Columbia University Press, 1943.

Barr, Alwyn. "The Texas 'Black Uprising' Scare of 1883," *Phylon*, 41 (1980), 179–87.

Dew, Charles B. "Disciplining Salve Ironworkers in the Antebellum South: Coercion, Conciliation, and Accommodation," *American Historical Review*, 79 (1974), 393–418.

———. *Ironmaker to the Confederacy*. New Haven, Conn.: Yale University Press, 1966.

Elkins, Stanley M. *Slavery: A Problem in American Institutional and Intellectual Life*. Chicago: University of Chicago Press, 1959.

Friedman, Lawrence J. "The Search for Docility: Racial Thought in the White South, 1861–1917," *Phylon*, 31 (1970), 313–23.

Genovese, Eugene D. *Roll Jordan Roll: The World the Slaves Made*. New York: Pantheon, 1974.

Lane, Ann J. *The Debate over "Slavery": Stanley Elkins and His Critics*. Urbana: University of Illinois Press, 1971.

Lynd, Staughton. "Rethinking Slavery and Reconstruction," *Journal of Negro History*, 50 (1965), 198–209.

McKenzie, Robert H. "The Shelby Iron Company: A Note on Slave Personality after the Civil War," *Journal of Negro History*, 58 (1973), 341–48.

Meier, August. *Negro Thought in American, 1880–1915*. Ann Arbor: University of Michigan Press, 1966.

Stampp, Kenneth M. *The Era of Reconstruction*. New York: Knopf, 1965.

Tannenbaum, Frank. *Slave and Citizen*. New York: Knopf, 1947.

Toll, William. "Free Men, Freedmen, and Race: Black Social Theory in the Gilded Age," *Journal of Southern History*, 44 (1978), 571–96.

Wagstaff, Thomas. "Call Your Old Master—'Master': Southern Political Leaders and Negro Labor during Presidential Reconstruction," *Labor History*, 10 (1969), 323–45.

Wood, Forrest G. *Black Scare: The Racist Response to Emancipation and Reconstruction*. Berkeley: University of California Press, 1968.

BLACK CODES

Carter, Dan T. *When the War Was Over: The Failure of Self-Reconstruction in the South, 1865–1867*. Baton Rouge: Louisiana State University Press, 1985.

Crouch, Barry A. "'All the Vile Passions': The Texas Black Code of 1866," *Southwestern Historical Quarterly*, 97 (1993), 13–34.

Davis, Ronald L. F. "The U.S. Army and the Origins of Sharecropping in the Natchez District: A Case Study," *Journal of Negro History*, 62 (1977), 60–80.

Dawson, Joseph Green, III. *Army Generals and Reconstruction: Louisiana, 1862–1977.* Baton Rouge: Louisiana State University Press, 1982.

Humphrey, George D. "Failure of the Mississippi Freedman's Bureau in Black Labor Relations, 1865–1867," *Journal of Mississippi History,* 45 (1983), 23–37.

Litwack, Leon F. *North of Slavery: The Negro in the Free States, 1790–1860.* Chicago: University of Chicago Press, 1961.

May, J. Thomas. "Continuity and Change in the Labor Program of the Union Army and the Freedmen's Bureau," *Civil War History,* 17 (1971), 245–54.

Mecklin, John W. "The Black Codes," *South Atlantic Quarterly,* 16 (1917), 248–59.

Nieman, Donald G. "The Freedmen's Bureau and the Mississippi Black Code," *Journal of Mississippi History,* 40 (1978), 91–118.

Perman, Michael. *Reunion without Compromise: The South and Reconstruction, 1865–1868.* New York: Cambridge University Press, 1973.

Richardson, Joe M. "Florida's Black Codes," *Florida Historical Quarterly,* 47 (1969), 365–79.

———. "The Freedmen's Bureau and Negro Labor in Florida," *Florida Historical Quarterly,* 39 (1960), 176–84.

Richter, William L. *Overreached on All Sides: The Freedmen's Bureau Administrators in Texas, 1865–1868.* College Station: Texas A&M University Press, 1991.

Shofner, Jerrell H. "Custom, Law, and History: The Enduring Effect of Florida's 'Black Code'," *Florida Historical Quarterly,* 55 (1977), 277–98.

Wade, Richard C. *Slavery in the Cities: The South, 1820–1860.* New York: Oxford University Press, 1964.

Wilson, Theodore B. *The Black Codes of the South.* Tuscaloosa: University of Alabama Press, 1965.

Wood, George A. "The Black Codes of Alabama," *South Atlantic Quarterly,* 13 (1914), 350–60.

Woodward, C. Vann. *The Strange Career of Jim Crow.* 2nd rev. ed., New York: Oxford University Press, 1966.

BLACK EDUCATION AND RECONSTRUCTION

Abbott, Martin. "The Freedmen's Bureau and Negro Schooling in South Carolina," *South Carolina Historical Magazine,* 57 (1956), 65–81.

Alexander, Roberta Sue. "Hostility and Hope: Black Education in North Carolina during Presidential Reconstruction, 1865–1867," *North Carolina Historical Review,* 53 (1976), 113–32.

Armstrong, Warren B. "Union Chaplains and the Education of Freedmen," *Journal of Negro History,* 52 (1967), 104–15.

Beatty, Bess. *A Revolution Gone Backwards.* New York: Greenwood, 1987.

Blassingame, John W. "The Union Army as an Educational Institution for Negroes, 1961–1865," *Journal of Negro Education,* 34 (1965), 152–59.

Butchart, Ronald E. *Northern Schools, Southern Blacks, and Reconstruction.* Westport, Conn.: Greenwood, 1980.

Cornish, Dudley Taylor. "The Union Army as a School for Negroes," *Journal of Negro History*, 37 (1952), 368–82.

Faulkner, Carol. *Women's Radical Reconstruction: The Freedmen's Aid Movement.* Philadelphia: University of Pennsylvania Press, 2004.

Franklin, John Hope. "Jim Crow Goes to School: The Genesis of Legal Segregation in Southern Schools," *South Atlantic Quarterly*, 58 (1959), 225–35.

Halstead, Jacqueline J. "The Delaware Association for the Moral Improvement and Education of the Colored People: 'Practical Christianity'," *Delaware History*, 15 (1972), 19–40.

Hornsby, Alton, Jr. "The Freedmen's Bureau Schools in Texas, 1865–1870," *Southwestern Historical Quarterly*, 76 (1972–1973), 397–417.

Jackson, Luther P. "The Educational Efforts of the Freedmen's Bureau and Freedmen's Aid Societies in South Carolina, 1862–1872," *Journal of Negro History*, 8 (1923), 1–40.

Jones, Jacqueline. *Soldiers of Light and Love: Northern Teachers and Georgia Blacks, 1865–1873.* Chapel Hill: University of North Carolina Press, 1980.

Kimball, Philip Clyde. "Freedom's Harvest: Freedmen's Schools in Kentucky after the Civil War," *Filson Club Historical Quarterly*, 54 (1980), 272–88.

Kousser, J. Morgan. *Dead End: The Development of Nineteenth Century Litigation on Discrimination in Schools.* New York: Oxford University Press, 1985.

———. "Separate But Not Equal: The Supreme Court's First Decision on Racial Discrimination in Schools," *Journal of Southern History*, 46 (1980), 17–44.

Low, W. Augustus. "The Freedmen's Bureau and Civil Rights in Maryland," *Maryland Historical Magazine*, 47 (1952), 29–39.

Morris, Robert C. *Reading, 'Riting, and Reconstruction.* Chicago: University of Chicago Press, 1981.

Newby, Robert G., and David B. Tyack. "Victims without Crimes: Some Historical Perspectives on Black Education," *Journal of Negro Education*, 40 (1971), 192–206.

Pearce, Larry W. "The American Missionary Association and the Freedmen's Bureau in Arkansas, 1868–1878," *Arkansas Historical Quarterly*, 30 (1971), 123–44, 246–61; 31 (1972), 246–61.

Proctor, Samuel. "'Yankee School Marms' in Post-War Florida," *Journal of Negro History*, 44 (1959), 275–77.

Rabinowitz, Howard N. "Half a Loaf: The Shift from White to Black Teachers in the Negro Schools of the Urban South, 1865–1890," *Journal of Southern History*, 40 (1974), 565–94.

Richardson, Joe M. "The Freedmen's Bureau and Negro Education in Florida," *Journal of Negro Education*, 31 (1962), 460–67.

Schweninger, Loren. "The American Missionary Association and Northern Philanthropy in Reconstruction Alabama," *Alabama Historical Quarterly*, 32 (1970), 129–56.

Sherer, Robert G. *Subordination or Liberation? The Developing Theories of Black Education in Nineteenth Century Alabama.* Tuscaloosa: University of Alabama Press, 1977.

Small, Sandra E. "The Yankee Schoolmarm in Freedmen's Schools: An Analysis of Attitudes," *Journal of Southern History*, 45 (1979), 381–402.

Smith, Thomas H. "Ohio Quakers and Mississippi Freedmen—'A Field to Labor'," *Ohio History*, 78 (1969), 159–71.

Spivey, Donald. *Schooling for the New Slavery: Black Industrial Education, 1868–1915.* Westport, Conn.: Greenwood, 1978.

Swint, Henry Lee. *The Northern Teacher in the South.* Nashville, Tenn.: Vanderbilt University Press, 1941.

Wesley, Edgar B. "Forty Acres and a Mule and a Speller," *History of Education Journal*, 8 (1957), 113–27.

White, Kenneth B. "The Alabama Freedmen's Bureau and Black Education: The Myth of Opportunity," *Alabama Review*, 34 (1981), 107–24.

Williams, Heather Andrea. "'Clothing Themselves in Intelligence': The Freedpeople, Schooling, and Northern Teachers, 1861–1871," *The Journal of African American History*, 87 (2002), 372 ff.

———. *Self-Taught: African American Education in Slavery and Freedom.* Chapel Hill: University of North Carolina Press, 2006.

BLACK LEADERSHIP AND RECONSTRUCTION

Abbott, Martin. "Freedom's Cry: Negroes and Their Meetings in South Carolina, 1865–1869," *Phylon*, 20 (1959), 263–72.

Barr, Alwyn. "Black Legislators of Reconstruction Texas," *Civil War History*, 32 (1986), 340–52.

Berry, Mary Frances, and John W. Blassingame. *Long Memory: The Black Experience in America.* New York: Oxford University Press, 1982.

Blassingame, John W. *Black New Orleans, 1860–1880.* Chicago: University of Chicago Press, 1973.

Carter, Dan T. "Moonlight, Magnolias, and Collard Greens: Black History and the New Romanticism," *Reviews in American History*, 5 (1977), 167–73.

Cimprich, John. "The Beginning of the Black Suffrage Movement in Tennessee, 1864–1865," *Journal of Negro History*, 65 (1980), 185–95.

———. *Slavery's End in Tennessee.* Tuscaloosa: University of Alabama Press, 1985.

Cook, Samuel Dubois. "A Tragic Conception of Negro History," *Journal of Negro History*, 45 (1960), 219–40.

Cruden, Robert. *The Negro in Reconstruction.* Englewood Cliffs, N.J.: Prentice-Hall, 1969.

Drago, Edmund. *Black Politicians and Reconstruction Georgia: A Splendid Failure.* Baton Rouge: Louisiana State University Press, 1982.

Foner, Eric. *Freedom's Lawmakers: A Directory of Black Officeholders During Reconstruction*. 2nd ed. New York: Oxford University Press, 1996.

Genovese, Eugene D. *Roll Jordan Roll: The World the Slaves Made*. New York: Pantheon, 1974.

Hermann, Janet S. "Reconstruction in Microcosm: Three Men and a Gin," *Journal of Negro History*, 65 (1980), 312–35.

Holt, Thomas. *Black over White: Negro Political Leadership in South Carolina during Reconstruction*. Urbana: University of Illinois Press, 1977.

Hosmer, John, and Joseph Fineman. "Black Congressmen in Reconstruction Historiography," *Phylon*, 39 (1978), 97–107.

Jones, Howard James. "Images of State Legislative Reconstruction Participants in Fiction," *Journal of Negro History*, 67 (1982), 318–27.

Kolchin, Peter. *First Freedom: The Responses of Alabama's Blacks to Emancipation and Reconstruction*. Westport, Conn.: Greenwood, 1972.

Logsdon, Joseph. "Black Reconstruction Revisited," *Reviews in American History*, 1 (1973), 553–58.

Magdol, Edward. "Local Black Leaders in the South, 1867–1875: An Essay toward the Reconstruction of Reconstruction History," *Societas*, 4 (1974), 81–110.

———. *A Right to the Land: Essays on the Freedmen's Community*. Westport, Conn.: Greenwood, 1977.

McFarlin, Annjeannette Sophia. *Black Congressional Reconstruction Orators and Their Orations*. Metuchen, N.J.: Scarecrow Press, 1976.

Mohr, Clarence L. "Southern Blacks in the Civil War: A Century of Historiography," *Journal of Negro History*, 59 (1974), 177–85.

O'Brien, John T. "Reconstruction in Richmond: White Restoration and Black Protest, April–June 1865," *Virginia Magazine of History and Biography*, 89 (1981), 259–81 .

Pitre, Merline. *Through Many Dangers, Toils, and Snares: The Black Leadership of Texas*. Austin, Tex.: Eakin, 1985.

Rabinowitz, Howard N. (ed.). *Southern Black Leaders of the Reconstruction Era*. Urbana: University of Illinois Press, 1982.

Richardson, Joe M. *The Negro in the Reconstruction of Florida*. Tallahassee: Florida State University Press, 1965.

Reid, George W. "Four in Black: North Carolina's Black Congressmen, 1874–1901," *Journal of Negro History*, 64 (1979), 229–43.

Robinson, Armistead L. "Beyond the Realm of Consensus: New Meanings of Reconstruction for American History," *Journal of American History*, 68 (1981), 276–97.

———. "Explaining the Failure of Democratic Reform in Reconstruction South Carolina," *Reviews in American History*, 8 (1980), 521–30.

Smith, Samuel Denny. *Negroes in Congress, 1870–1901*. Chapel Hill: University of North Carolina Press, 1940.

Thornbrough, Emma Lou (ed.). *Black Reconstructionists*. Englewood Cliffs, N.J.: Prentice-Hall, 1972.

Thorpe, Earl E. *Black Historians: A Critique*. New York: Morrow, 1971.

Vincent, Charles. *Black Legislators in Louisiana during Reconstruction*. Baton Rouge: Louisiana State University Press, 1976.

———. "Louisiana's Black Legislators and Their Efforts to Pass a Blue Law during Reconstruction," *Journal of Black Studies*, 7 (1976–1977), 47–56.

Wagandt, Charles L. "The Army versus Maryland Slavery, 1862–1864," *Civil War History*, 10 (1964), 141–48.

———. *The Mighty Revolution: Negro Emancipation in Maryland, 1862–1864*. Baltimore, Md.: The Johns Hopkins University Press, 1964.

Williamson, Joel. *After Slavery: The Negro in South Carolina during Reconstruction*. Chapel Hill: University of North Carolina Press, 1965.

Woodward, C. Vann. "Clio with Soul," *Journal of American History*, 56 (1969), 5–20.

———. "Flight from History—The Heritage of the Negro," *The Nation*, 201 (1965), 142–46.

BLACK SOLDIERS, USE OF—CONFEDERATE

Ambrose, Stephen E. "Cleburne's Proposal to Enlist Slaves in the Southern Army," *Civil War Times Illustrated*, 3 (January 1965), 16–21.

Austermann, Wayne P. "Virginia's Black Confederates," *Civil War Quarterly*, 8 (March 1987), 46–54.

Barnickel, Linda. "'No Federal Prisoners Were Included': The Execution of Black Union Soldiers at Jackson, Louisiana," *North & South*, 12 (February 2010), 59–62.

Bergeron, Arthur W. "Free Men of Color in Gray," *Civil War History*, 32 (1986), 247–55.

Berry, Mary F. "Negro Troops in Blue and Gray: The Louisiana Native Guards, 1861–1863," *Louisiana History*, 8 (1967), 165–90.

Blackerby, H. C. *Blacks in Blue and Gray: Afro-American Service in the Civil War*. Tuscaloosa, Ala.: Portals Press, 1973.

Brewer, James H. *The Confederate Negro: Virginia's Craftsmen and Military Laborers, 1861–1865*. Durham, N.C.: Duke University Press, 1969.

Cahill, Carl. "Note on Two Va. Negro Civil War Soldiers, One Union, One Confederate," *Negro History Bulletin*, 24 (1960), 39–40.

Connor, Sam. "Cleburne and the Unthinkable (Enrolling Black Confederate Troops)," *Civil War Times Illustrated*, 36 (February 1998), 45–47.

Durden Robert F. *The Gray and the Black: The Confederate Debate on Emancipation*. Baton Rouge: Louisiana State University Press, 1972.

Escott, Paul D. "'We Must Make Free Men of Them'," *Civil War Times Illustrated*, 49 (June 2010), 44–51.

Hall, Martin H. "Negroes with Confederate Troops in West Texas and New Mexico," *Password*, 3 (Spring 1968), 11–12.

Heisley, Alexia J. "Black Confederates," *South Carolina Historical Magazine*, 74 (July 1973), 184–87.

Jordan, Ervin L., Jr. *Black Confederates and Afro-Yankees in Civil War Virginia.* Charlottesville: University of Virginia Press, 1995.

Levine, Bruce. "Black Confederates: Myth and Reality," *North & South*, 10 (July 2007), 40–45.

———. "Thinking the Unthinkable: 'Confederate Emancipation' and Its Meaning," *North & South*, 8 (November 2005), 14–23.

Mallock, Daniel. "Cleburne's Proposal," *North & South*, 11 (December 2008), 64–72.

Mills, Gary B. "Patriotism Frustrated: The Native Guards of Confederate Natchitoches," *Louisiana History*, 18 (1977), 437–51.

Mohr, Clarence L. "Southern Blacks in the Civil War: A Century of Historiography," *Journal of Negro History*, 59 (1974), 177–85.

Newton, Stephen H. "African Americans Resist the Confederacy: Two Variations on a Theme," *North & South*, 8 (November 2005), 52–60.

Obatala, J. K. "The Unlikely Story of Blacks Who Were Loyal to Dixie," *Smithsonian Magazine*, 9 (1979), 94–101.

Preisser, Thomas M. "The Virginia Decision to Use Negro Soldiers in the Civil War," *Virginia Magazine of History and Biography*, 83 (1975), 98–113.

Quarles, Benjamin. *The Negro in the Civil War*. Boston: Little, Brown, 1955.

Rollins, Richard (ed.). *Black Southerners in Gray: Essays on Afro-Americans in Confederate Armies*. Redondo Beach, Calif.: Rank and File Publications, 1994.

Sallee, Scott E. "Black Soldier of the Confederacy," *Blue and Gray*, 8 (1990), 24–25.

Silverman, Jason. "Blacks in Gray," *North & South*, 5 (April 2002), 35–43.

Spraggins, Tinsley Lee. "Mobilization of Negro Labor for the Department of Virginia and North Carolina, 1861–1865," *North Carolina Historical Review*, 24 (1947), 160–97.

Tyler, Gress. "Rebel Drummer Boy, Henry Brown," *Civil War Times Illustrated*, 28 (February 1989), 22–23.

Wesley, Charles H. "The Employment of Negroes as Soldiers in the Confederate Army," *Journal of Negro History*, 4 (1919), 239–53.

Wiley, Bell I. *Southern Negroes, 1861–1865*. New Haven, Conn.: Yale University Press, 1938.

BLACK SOLDIERS, USE OF—UNION

Aliyetti, John E. "Gallantry under Fire [USCT at New Market]," *Civil War Times Illustrated*, 35 (October 1996), 50–55.

Aptheker, Herbert. *The Negro in the Civil War*. New York: International Publishers, 1938.

Belz, Herman. "Law, Politics, and Race in the Struggle for Equal Pay during the Civil War," *Civil War History*, 22 (1976), 197–213.

Berry, Mary F. "Negro Troops in Blue and Gray: The Louisiana Native Guards, 1861–1863," *Louisiana History*, 8 (1967), 165–90.

Blackerby, H. C. *Blacks in Blue and Gray: Afro-American Service in the Civil War.* Tuscaloosa, Ala.: Portals Press, 1973.

Blassingame, John W. "Negro Chaplains in the Civil War," *Negro History Bulletin*, 27 (October 1963), 23–24.

———. "The Recruitment of Colored Troops in Kentucky, Maryland, and Missouri, 1863–1865," *Historian*, 24 (1967), 533–45.

———. "The Recruitment of Colored Troops in Maryland," *Maryland Historical Magazine*, 58 (1963), 20–29.

———. "The Recruitment of Colored Troops in Missouri during the Civil War," *Missouri Historical Review*, 58 (1964), 326–38.

Cahill, Carl. "Note on Two Va. Negro Civil War Soldiers, One Union, One Confederate," *Negro History Bulletin*, 24 (1960), 39–40.

Coopersmith, Andrew S. "Battlelines and Headlines: The Debate over [Union] 'Negro Soldiers'," *North & South*, 9 (August 2006), 72–82.

Cornish, Dudley Taylor. *The Sable Arm: Negro Troops in the Union Army.* New York: Norton, 1966.

Dye, Brainerd. "The Treatment of Colored Union Troops by the Confederates, 1861–1865," *Journal of Negro History*, 20 (1935), 273–86.

Fletcher, Jack. "The Hard Fight Was Getting into the Fight at All," *Smithsonian Magazine*, 21 (October 1990), 46–61.

Fletcher, Marvin. "The Negro Volunteer in Reconstruction, 1865–1866," *Military History*, 32 (December 1968), 124–131.

Glathaar, Joseph T. *Forged in Battle: The Civil War Alliance of Black Soldiers and White Officers.* New York: Free Press, 1990.

Hargrove, Hondon B. *Black Union Soldiers in the Civil War.* Jefferson, N.C.: McFarland Co., 1988.

McPherson, James M. *The Negro's Civil War: How American Negroes Felt and Acted during the War for the Union.* New York: Pantheon, 1965.

Richardson, Marilyn. "*Glory* and the Distortion of Black History," *Reconstruction*, 1 (No. 2, 1990), 38–42.

Robertson, James I., Jr. "Negro Soldiers in the Civil War," *Civil War Times Illustrated*, 7 (October 1968), 21–32.

Samito, Christian G. "The Intersection between Military Justice and Equal Rights: Mutinies, Courts-martial, and Black Civil War Soldiers," *Civil War History*, 53 (2007), 170–202.

Seraile, William. "The Struggle to Raise Black Regiments in New York State," New York Historical Society, *Quarterly*, 58 (1974), 215–33.

Shannon, Fred A. "The Federal Government and the Negro Soldier, 1861–1865, *Journal of Negro History*, 11 (1926), 563–83.

Stone, Alan A. "*Glory* as a White Man's Movie," *Reconstruction*, 1 (No. 2, 1990), 42–48.

Whyte, James H. "Maryland's Negro Regiments," *Civil War Times Illustrated*, 1 (July 1962), 41–43.

Woodward, Howard C. "Benjamin Butler's Enlistment of Black Troops in New Orleans in 1862," *Louisiana History*, 26 (1985), 5–22.

BLACKS, URBAN, IN THE SOUTH DURING RECONSTRUCTION

Berlin, Ira. *Slaves without Masters: The Free Negro in the Antebellum South.* New York: Panheon, 1974.

Blassingame, John W. *Black New Orleans, 1860–1880.* Chicago: University of Chicago Press, 1973.

Everett, Donald E. "Demands of the New Orleans Free Colored Population for Political Equality, 1862–1865," *Louisiana Historical Quarterly*, 38 (1955), 43–64.

Fitchett, E. Horace. "The Traditions of the Free Negro in Charleston, South Carolina," *Journal of Negro History*, 25 (1940), 139–52.

Fitzgerald, Michael W. *Urban Emancipation: Popular Politics in Reconstruction Mobile, 1860–1890.* Baton Rouge: Louisiana State University Press, 2002.

Harris, Robert L., Jr. "Charleston's Free Afro-American Elite: The Brown Fellowship Society and the Humane Brotherhood," *South Carolina Historical Magazine*, 82 (1981), 289–310.

Hine, William C. "Black Politicians in Reconstruction Charleston, South Carolina: A Collective Study," *Journal of Southern History*, 49 (1983), 555–84.

———. "The 1867 Charleston Streetcar Sit-ins: A Case of Successful Black Protest," *South Carolina Historical Magazine*, 78 (1976), 110–14.

Holt, Thomas. *Black Over White: Negro Political Leadership in South Carolina during Reconstruction.* Urbana: University of Illinois Press, 1977.

McCrary, Peyton. *Abraham Lincoln and Reconstruction: The Louisiana Experiment.* Princeton, N.J.: Princeton University Press, 1978.

Rankin, David C. "The Impact of the Civil War on the Free Colored Community of New Orleans," *Perspectives in History*, 11 (1977–1978), 377–416.

———. The Origins of Black Leadership in New Orleans during Reconstruction," *Journal of Southern History*, 40 (1974), 417–40.

———. "The Tannenbaum Thesis Reconsidered: Slavery and Race Relations in Antebellum Louisiana," *Southern Studies*, 18 (1979), 5–31.

Ripley, C. Peter. *Slaves and Freedmen in Civil War Louisiana.* Baton Rouge: Louisiana State University Press, 1976.

Vincent, Charles. *Black Legislators in Louisiana during Reconstruction.* Baton Rouge: Louisiana State University Press, 1976.

Somers, Dale A. "Black and White in New Orleans: A Study in Urban Race Relations," *Journal of Southern History*, 40 (1974), 19–42.

Wade, Richard C. *Slavery in the Cities.* 1973.

Wikramanayake, Marina. *A World in Shadow: The Free Negro in Antebellum South Carolina.* Columbia: University of South Carolina Press, 1973.

BOOTH, JOHN WILKES (1838–1865)

Alford, Terry L. *Fortune's Fool: The Life of John Wilkes Booth.* New York: Oxford University Press, forthcoming.

Bryan, George S. *The Great American Myth: The True Story of Lincoln's Murder.* Introduction by William Hanchett. Chicago: Americana House, 1990; orig. 1940.

DeWitt, David Miller. *The Assassination of Abraham Lincoln.* New York: Macmillan, 1909.

Hall, James O. "John Wilkes Booth at School," *Surratt Courier*, 16 (July 1991), 3–4.

Head, Constance. "John Wilkes Booth as a Hero Figure," *Journal of American Culture*, 5 (Fall 1982), 22–28.

———. "John Wilkes Booth in American Fiction," *Lincoln Herald*, 82 (Winter 1980), 455–62.

———. "John Wilkes Booth: Prologue to Assassination," *Lincoln Herald*, 85 (Winter 1983), 254–79.

Houmes, Blaine V. *Abraham Lincoln Assassination Bibliography: A Compendium of Reference Materials.* Clinton, Md.: Surratt Society, 1997.

Kauffman, Michael W. *American Brutus: John Wilkes Booth and the Lincoln Conspiracies.* New York: Random House, 2004.

———. "John Wilkes Booth and the Murder of Abraham Lincoln," *Blue and Gray Magazine*, 7 (April 1990 [Special Issue]).

Kimmel, Stanley. *The Mad Booths of Maryland.* 2nd ed., rev. and enlarged. New York: Dover Publications, 1969.

Lewis, Lloyd. *The Assassination of Lincoln: History and Myth.* Lincoln, Neb.: Bison Books, 1994; original 1929.

Niderost, Eric. "Mad as a Hatter: [Boston Corbett Kills John Wilkes Booth]," *Civil War Times Illustrated*, 49 (October 2010), 38–43.

Rhodehamel, John, and Louise Taper (eds.). *"Right or Wrong, God Judge Me": The Writings of John Wilkes Booth.* Urbana: University of Illinois Press, 1997.

Richter, William L. *The Last Confederate Heroes: The Final Struggle for Southern Independence & the Assassination of Abraham Lincoln.* 2 vols. 2nd rev. ed. Edited with introduction by J. E. "Rick" Smith III. Laurel, Md.: Burgundy Press, 2008.

———. *Sic Semper Tyrannis: Why John Wilkes Booth Shot Abraham Lincoln.* Bloomington, Ind.: iUniverse, 2009.

Smith, Gene. *American Gothic: The Story of America's Legendary Theatrical Family—Junius, Edwin, and John Wilkes Booth.* New York: Simon & Schuster, 1992.

———. "The Booth Obsession," *American Heritage*, 52 (September 1992), 105–19.

Steers, Edward, Jr. *Blood on the Moon: The Assassination of Abraham Lincoln.* Lexington: University of Kentucky Press, 2001.

Townsend, George Alfred. *The Life, Crime, and Capture of John Wilkes Booth.* New York: Dick & Fitzgerald, 1865.

Tucker, Glenn. "John Wilkes Booth at the John Brown Hanging," *Lincoln Herald,* 78 (Spring 1976), 3–11.

Wilson, Francis. *John Wilkes Booth: Fact and Fiction of Lincoln's Assassination.* Boston: Houghton Mifflin, 1929.

BOOTH, JOHN WILKES, AND THE ESCAPE FROM GARRETT'S FARM

Balsiger, David and Charles E. Sellier. *The Lincoln Conspiracy.* Los Angeles: Schick Sunn Classic Productions, 1977.

George S. Bryan. *The Great American Myth: The True Story of Lincoln's Murder.* rev. ed. Chicago: Americana House, 1990.

Verge, Laurie (ed.). *The Body in the Barn: The Controversy Over the Death of John Wilkes Booth.* Clinton, Md.: The Surratt Society, 1993.

BOOTH, JOHN WILKES, AND OLIVER WENDELL HOLMES JR., ROBERT LINCOLN, JOHN HAY, AND LUCY HALE

"Booth and Bob Lincoln," *Chicago Inter-Ocean* (June 18, 1878), 4–5.

Morcum, Richmond. "They All Loved Lucy," *American Heritage,* 21 (October 1970), 12–15.

Morris, Clara. "Some Recollections of John Wilkes Booth," *McClure's Magazine,* 11 (February 1901), 299–304.

Richter, William L. *The Last Confederate Heroes: The Final Struggle for Southern Independence & the Assassination of Abraham Lincoln.* 2 vols. 2nd rev. ed. Edited with introduction by J. E. "Rick" Smith III. Laurel, Md.: Burgundy Press, 2008.

BOOTH, JOHN WILKES, POLITICAL VIEWS OF

Bestor, Arthur. "State Sovereignty and Slavery: A Reinterpretation of Proslavery Constitutional Doctrine, 1846–1860," Illinois State Historical Society, *Journal,* 53 (1960), 117–80.

Richter, William L. *The Last Confederate Heroes: The Final Struggle for Southern Independence & the Assassination of Abraham Lincoln.* 2 vols. 2nd rev. ed. Edited with introduction by J. E. "Rick" Smith III. Laurel, Md.: Burgundy Press, 2008.

———. *Sic Semper Tyrannis: Why John Wilkes Booth Shot Abraham Lincoln.* Indianapolis: iUniverse, 2009.

BRAGG, BRAXTON (1817–1876)

Current, Richard N. (ed.). *Encyclopedia of the Confederacy*. 4 vols. New York: Simon & Schuster, 1993.

Davis, William C. (ed.). *The Confederate General*. 6 vols. N.p.: National Historical Society, 1991.

Engel, Stephen D. *Struggle for the Heartland: The Campaigns from Fort Henry to Corinth*. Lincoln: University of Nebraska Press, 2001.

Franks, Edward C. "In Defense of Braxton Bragg," *North & South*, 5 (July 2002), 28–38.

McWhiney, Grady. "Braxton Bragg," *Civil War Times Illustrated*, 11 (April 1972), 4–7, 42–48.

———, and Judith Hallock. *Braxton Bragg and Confederate Defeat*. 2 vols. Tuscaloosa: University of Alabama Press, 1969, 1991.

Warner, Ezra J. *Generals in Gray: Lives of Confederate Commanders*. Baton Rouge: Louisiana State University Press, 1959.

BROWN, JOHN, AND HARPER'S FERRY (1859)

Brown, Salmon. "John Brown and His Sons in Kansas Territory," *Indiana Magazine of History*, 31 (1935), 142–50.

Karsner, David. *John Brown, Terrible Saint*. New York: Dodd Mead, 1934.

Malin, James C. *John Brown and the Legend of Fifty-six*. Philadelphia: American Philosophical Society, 1942.

Oates, Stephen B. *"To Purge This Land with Blood": A Biography of John Brown*. New York: Harper & Row, 1970.

Reynolds, David S. "John Brown, the Election of Lincoln, and the Civil War," *North & South*, 9 (March 2006), 78–88.

Sinha, Manisha. "'His Truth Is Marching On': John Brown and the Fight for Racial Justice," *Civil War History*, 52 (2006), 161–169.

Tucker, Glenn. "John Wilkes Booth at the John Brown Hanging," *Lincoln Herald*, 78 (Spring 1976), 3–11.

Villard, Oswald Garrison. *John Brown, 1800–1859: A Biography Fifty Years After*. New ed. New York: Knopf, 1943.

Von Frank, Albert J. "John Brown, James Redpath, and the Idea of Revolution Civil," *Civil War History*, 52 (2006), 142–160.

Warren, Robert Penn. *John Brown: The Making of a Martyr*. New York: Payson & Clarke, 1929.

Wilson, Hill Peebles. *John Brown, Soldier of Fortune: A Critique*. Lawrence, Kans.: H. P. Wilson, 1913.

Woodward, C. Vann. "John Brown's Private War," in Woodward (ed.), *The Burden of Southern History*. New York: Mentor Books, 1968, rev. ed.

BROWN, JOSEPH E. (1821–1894)

Conway, Alan. *The Reconstruction of Georgia*. Minneapolis: University of Minnesota Press, 1966.

Duncan, Russell. *Entrepreneur for Equality: Governor Rufus Bullock, Commerce, and Race in Post-Civil War Georgia*. Athens: University of Georgia Press, 1994.

Eckert, Ralph Lowell. *John Brown Gordon: Soldier, Southerner, Statesman*. Baton Rouge: Louisiana State University Press, 1989.

Hesseltine, William B., and Larry Gara. "Georgia's Confederate Leaders After Appomattox," *Georgia Historical Quarterly*, 35 (1951), 1–15.

McMurry, Richard M. "Joseph E. Brown of Georgia," *Civil War Times Illustrated*, 10 (November 1971), 30–39.

Nathans, Elizabeth Studley. *Losing the Peace: Georgia Republicans and Reconstruction*. Baton Rouge: Louisiana State University Press, 1968.

Parks, Joseph H. *Joseph E. Brown of Georgia*. Baton Rouge: Louisiana State University Press, 1977.

Roberts, Derrell C. *Joseph E. Brown and the Politics of Reconstruction*. Tuscaloosa: University of Alabama Press, 1973.

Thompson, C. Mildred. *Reconstruction in Georgia, Economic, Social, Political, 1865–1872*. New York: Columbia University Press, 1915.

Wakelyn, Jon L. *Biographical Dictionary of the Confederacy*. Westport, Conn.: Greenwood Press, 1977.

BROWNLOW, WILLIAM G. (1805–1877)

Alexander, Thomas B. "Strange Bedfellows: The Interlocking Careers of T. A. R. Nelson, Andrew Johnson, and William G. (Parson) Brownlow," *East Tennessee Historical Society Papers*, 24 (1952), 68–91.

Bergeron, Paul H. *Antebellum Politics in Tennessee*. Lexington: University of Kentucky Press, 1982.

Bining, F. Wayne. "The Tennessee Republicans in Decline, 1869–1876," *Tennessee Historical Quarterly*, 39 (1980), 471–84; 40 (1981), 68–84.

Coulter, E. Merton. *William G. Brownlow: Fighting Parson of the Southern Highlands*. Knoxville: University of Tennessee Press, 1937.

Haskins, Ralph W. "Internecine Strife in Tennessee: Andrew Johnson vs. Parson Brownlow," *Tennessee Historical Quarterly*, 24 (1965), 321–40.

McKenzie, Robert Tracy. "Secession: Parson Brownlow and the Rhetoric of Proslavery Unionism, 1860–1861," *Civil War History*, 48 (2002), 294–312.

Patton, James Welch. *Unionism and Reconstruction in Tennessee, 1860–1869*. Chapel Hill: University of North Carolina Press, 1934.

Trefousse, Hans L. *Andrew Johnson: A Biography*. New York: W. W. Norton & Company, 1989.

BRUCE, BLANCHE K. (1841–1898)

Harris, William C. "Blanche K. Bruce of Mississippi: Conservative Assimilationist," in Howard N. Rabinowitz (ed.), *Southern Black Leaders of the Reconstruction Era*. Urbana: University of Illinois Press, 1982, 3–38.

Low, W. Augustus, and Virgil A. Clift. *Encyclopedia of Black America*. New York: McGraw-Hill Book Company, 1981.

Mann, Kenneth Eugene. "Blanche Kelso Bruce: United States Senator Without a Constituency," *Journal of Mississippi History*, 38 (1976), 183–98.

McFarlin, Annjeannette Sophia. *Black Congressional Reconstruction Orators and Their Orations*. Metuchen, N.J.: Scarecrow Press, 1976.

Shapiro, Samuel. "A Black Senator from Mississippi: Blanche K. Bruce," *Review of Politics,* 44 (1982), 83–109.

St. Clair, Sadie D. "The National Career of Blanche Kelso Bruce." Ph.D. dissertation, New York University, 1947.

Urofsky, Melvin I. "Blanche K. Bruce: United States Senator," *Journal of Mississippi History*, 29 (1967), 118–41.

BURNSIDE, AMBROSE, AND THE SOUTH
ATLANTIC COAST (1861–1862)

Cullen, Joseph P. "The Very *Beau Ideal* of a Soldier: A Personality Profile of Ambrose E. Burnside," *Civil War Times Illustrated*, 16 (August 1977), 4–10, 38–44.

Luvaas, Jay. "Burnside's Roanoke Island Campaign," *Civil War Times Illustrated*, 7 (December 1968), 4–11, 43–48.

Marvel, William. *Burnside*. Chapel Hill: University of North Carolina Press, 1991.

Poore, Ben Perley. *The Life and Public Service of Ambrose E. Burnside, Soldier, Citizen, Statesman*. Providence, R.I.: J. A. and R. A. Reid, 1882.

Sauers, Richard Allen. "Laurels for Burnside: The Invasion of North Carolina, January–July 1862," *Blue and Gray*, 6 (May 1988), [Special Issue].

BUREAU OF REFUGEES, FREEDMEN, AND
ABANDONED LANDS (FREEDMEN'S BUREAU)

Abbott, Martin. "Free Land Free Labor, and the Freedmen's Bureau," *Agricultural History*, 30 (1956), 150–56.

———. *The Freedmen's Bureau in South Carolina, 1865–1872*. Chapel Hill: University of North Carolina Press, 1967.

Belz, Herman. *Emancipation and Equal Rights: Politics and Constitutionalism in the Civil War Era*. New York: W. W. Norton, 1978.

————. "The Freedmen's Bureau Act of 1865 and the Principle of No Discrimination According to Color," *Civil War History*, 21 (1975), 197–217.

————. *A New Birth of Freedom: The Republican Party and Freedmen's Rights, 1861–1866.* Westport, Conn.: Greenwood Press, 1976.

Bentley, George R. *A History of the Freedmen's Bureau.* Philadelphia: University of Pennsylvania Press, 1955.

Bethel, Elizabeth. "The Freedmen's Bureau in Alabama," *Journal of Southern History*, 14 (1948), 49–92.

Bronson, Louis Henry. "The Freedmen's Bureau: A Public Policy Analysis." Ph.D. dissertation, University of Southern California, 1970.

Carper, N. Gordon. "Slavery Revisited: Peonage in the South," *Phylon*, 37 (1976), 85–99.

Cimbala, Paul A. "The 'Talisman Power': Davis Tillson, the Freedmen's Bureau, and Free Labor in Reconstruction Georgia," *Civil War History*, 28 (1982), 153–71.

————. *Under the Guardianship of the Nation: The Freedmen's Bureau and the Reconstruction of Georgia, 1865–1870.* Athens: University of Georgia Press, 1997.

Cohen, William. "Negro Involuntary Servitude in the South, 1865–1940: A Preliminary Analysis," *Journal of Southern History*, 42 (1976), 31–60.

Cohen-Lack, Nancy. "A Struggle for Sovereignty: National Consolidation, Emancipation, and Free Labor in Texas, 1865," *Journal of Southern History*, 58 (1992), 57–98.

Colby, Ira C. "The Freedmen's Bureau: From Social Welfare to Segregation," *Phylon*, 46 (1985), 219–30.

Cox, LaWanda. *Lincoln and Black Freedom: A Study in Presidential Leadership.* Columbia: University of South Carolina Press, 1981.

————. "The Promise of Land for the Freedmen," *Mississippi Valley Historical Review*, 49 (1958), 413–40.

Crouch, Barry A. *The Freedmen's Bureau and Black Texans.* Austin: University of Texas, 1992.

Currie, James T. "From Slavery to Freedom in Mississippi's Legal System," *Journal of Negro History,* 65 (1980), 112–25.

Davis, Ronald L. F. "The U.S. Army and the Origins of Sharecropping in the Natchez District: A Case Study," *Journal of Negro History*, 62 (1977), 60–80.

DuBois, W. E. Burghardt. "The Freedmen's Bureau," *Atlantic Monthly*, 87 (1901), 254–65.

Farmer-Kaiser, Mary. "'Are They Not in Some Sorts Vagrants?' Gender and the Efforts of the Freedmen's Bureau to Combat Vagrancy in the Reconstruction South," *Georgia Historical Quarterly*, 88 (2004): 25–49.

Finley, Randy. *From Slavery to Uncertain Freedom: The Freedmen's Bureau in Arkansas, 1865–1869.* Fayetteville: University of Arkansas Press, 1996.

Fitzgerald, Michael W. "Wager Swayne, the Freedmen's Bureau, and the Politics of Reconstruction Alabama," *Alabama Review*, 48 (1995), 188–232.

Foster, Gaines M. "The Limitations of Federal Health Care for Freedmen, 1862–1868," *Journal of Southern History*, 48 (1982), 349–72.

Friedman, Lawrence J. "The Search for Docility: Racial Thought in the White South, 1861–1917," *Phylon*, 31 (1970), 313–23.

Gutman, Herbert G. *The Black Family in Slavery and Freedom, 1750–1925*. New York: Pantheon Books, 1976.

Harlan, Louis R. "Desegregation in New Orleans Public Schools during Reconstruction," *American Historical Review*, 67 (1961), 663–75.

Hasson, Gail S. "Health and Welfare of Freedmen in Reconstruction Alabama," *Alabama Review*, 35 (1982), 94–110.

Howard, Victor B. "The Kentucky Press and the Negro Testimony Controversy, 1866–1872," *Register of the Kentucky Historical Society*, 71 (1973), 29–50.

Humphrey, George D. "Failure of the Mississippi Freedman's Bureau in Black Labor Relations, 1865–1867," *Journal of Mississippi History*, 45 (1983), 23–37.

Jackson, Luther P. "The Educational Efforts of the Freedmen's Bureau and Freedmen's Aid Societies in South Carolina, 1862–1872," *Journal of Negro History*, 8 (1923), 1–40.

Kitrell, Irvin, III. "40 Acres and a Mule: [Sherman's Special Field Orders, No. 15, 16 January 1865]," *Civil War Times Illustrated*, 41 (May 2002), 54–61.

Kolchin, Peter. *First Freedom: The Response s of Alabama's Blacks to Emancipation and Reconstruction.* Westport, Conn.: Greenwood Press, 1972.

Lee, Anne S., and Everett S. Lee. "The Health of Slaves and Freedmen: A Savannah Study," *Phylon*, 38 (1977), 170–80.

Low, W. Augustus. "The Freedmen's Bureau and Civil Rights in Maryland," *Journal of Negro History*, 37 (1952), 221–47.

———. "The Freedmen's Bureau in the Border States," in Richard O. Curry (ed.), *Radicalism, Racism, and Party Alignment: The Border States during Reconstruction*. Baltimore: The Johns Hopkins Press, 1969, 245–64.

Lowe, Richard. "The Freedmen's Bureau and Local White Leaders in Virginia," *Journal of Southern History*, 64 (1998), 455–72.

May, J. Thomas. "Continuity and Change in the Labor Program of the Union Army and the Freedmen's Bureau," *Civil War History*, 17 (1971), 245–54.

———. "A 19th Century Medical Care Program for Blacks: The Case of the Freedmen's Bureau," *Anthropological Quarterly*, 46 (1973), 160–71.

McPherson, James M. "White Liberals and Black Power in Negro Education, 1865–1915," *American Historical Review*, 75 (1970), 1357–86.

Messner, William F. "Black Education in Louisiana, 1863–1865," *Civil War History*, 22 (1976), 41–59.

Morris, Thomas D. "Equality, 'Extraordinary Law,' and Criminal Justice: The South Carolina Experience, 1865–1866," *South Carolina Historical Magazine*, 83 (1982), 15–33.

Nieman, Donald G. "Black Political Power and Criminal Justice: Washington County, Texas. 1868–1884," *Journal of Southern History*, 55 (1983), 391–420.

————. *To Set the Law in Motion: The Freedmen's Bureau and the Legal Rights of Blacks, 1865–1868*. Millwood, N.Y.: Kraus International, 1979.

Oakes, James. "A Failure of Vision: The Collapse of Freedmen's Bureau Courts," *Civil War History*, 25 (1979), 66–76.

Olds, Victoria Marcus. "The Freedmen's Bureau as a Social Agency." Ph.D. dissertation, Columbia University, 1966.

Oubre, Claude F. *Forty Acres and a Mule: The Freedmen's Bureau and Black Land Ownership*. Baton Rouge: Louisiana State University Press, 1978.

Pearson, Reggie L. "'There Are Many Sick, Feeble, and Suffering Freedmen': The Freedmen's Bureau's Health-care Activities During Reconstruction in North Carolina, 1865–1868," *North Carolina Historical Review*, 79 (2002): 141–81.

Pierce, Paul Skeels. *The Freedmen's Bureau: A Chapter in the History of Reconstruction*. Iowa City: State University of Iowa Press, 1904.

Raphael, Alan. "Health and Social Welfare of Kentucky Black People, 1865–1870," *Societas*, 2 (1972), 143–57.

Richter, William L. *Overreached on All Sides: The Freedmen's Bureau Administrators in Texas, 1865–1868*. College Station: Texas A&M University Press, 1991.

————. "Who Was the Real Head of the Texas Freedmen's Bureau? The Role of Brevet Colonel William H. Sinclair as Acting Assistant Inspector General," *Military History of the Southwest*, 20 (1990), 121–56.

Ripley, C. Peter. "The Black Family in Transition: Louisiana, 1860–1865," *Journal of Southern History*, 41 (1975), 369–80.

Rodrigue, John C. *Reconstruction in the Cane Fields: From Slavery to Free Labor in Louisiana's Sugar Parishes, 1862–1880*. Baton Rouge: Louisiana State University Press, 2001.

Savitt, Todd L. "Politics and Medicine: The Georgia Freedmen's Bureau and the Organization of Health Care, 1865–1866," *Civil War History*, 28 (1982), 45–64.

Schmidt, James D. *Free to Work: Labor Law, Emancipation, and the Reconstruction, 1815–1880*. Athens: University of Georgia Press, 1998.

Scott, Rebecca J. *Degrees of Freedom: Louisiana and Cuba after Slavery*. Cambridge: Harvard University Press, 2005.

Shlomowitz, Ralph. "'Bound' or 'Free'? Black Labor in Cotton and Sugarcane Farming, 1865–1880," *Journal of Southern History*, 50 (1984), 569–96.

Shofner, Jerrell H. "Militant Negro Laborers in Reconstruction Florida," *Journal of Southern History*, 39 (1973), 397–408

Small, Sandra E. "The Yankee *Schoolmarm* in Freedmen's Schools: An Analysis of Attitudes," *Journal of Southern History*, 45 (1979), 381–402.

Smallwood, James. *Time of Hope, Time of Despair: Black Texans During Reconstruction*. Port Washington, N.Y.: National University Publications, 1981.

Smith, John David. "'The Work It Did Not Do Because It Could Not': Georgia and the 'New' Freedmen's Bureau Historiography," *Georgia Historical Quarterly*, 82 (1998), 331–49.

Smith, Solomon K. "The Freedmen's Bureau in Shreveport: the Struggle for Control of the Red River District," *Louisiana History*, 41 (2000): 435–65.

Stealey, John Edmond, III. "The Freedmen's Bureau in West Virginia," *West Virginia History*, 39 (1978), 99–142.

White, Howard A. *The Freedmen's Bureau in Louisiana*. Baton Rouge: Louisiana State University Press, 1970.

White, Kenneth B. "The Alabama Freedmen's Bureau and Black Education: The Myth of Opportunity," *Alabama Review* 34 (April 1981): 107–24.

———. "Black Lives, Red Tape: The Alabama Freedmen's Bureau," *Alabama Historical Quarterly*, 43 (1981), 241–58.

Woody, Robert H. "The Labor and Immigration Problem of South Carolina during Reconstruction," *Mississippi Valley Historical Review*, 18 (1931), 195–212.

Wynne, Lewis N. "The Role of Freedmen in the Post Bellum Cotton Economy of Georgia," *Phylon*, 42 (1981), 309–21.

BUTLER, BENJAMIN F. (1818–1893)

Boatner, Mark M., III. *The Civil War Dictionary*. New York: D. McKay and Company, 1959.

Butler, Benjamin F. *Autobiography and Personal Reminiscences of Major-General Benjamin F. Butler: Butler's Book*. Boston: A. M. Thayer, 1892.

Hall, James O. "Butler Takes Baltimore," *Civil War Times Illustrated*, 17 (August 1978), 4–10, 44–46.

Holzman, Robert S. *Stormy Ben Butler*. New York: Macmillan, 1954.

Morgan, Michael. "The Beast at His Best: [General Butler Saves Maryland, 1861]," *Civil War Times Illustrated*, 42 (February 2004), 2431.

Longacre, Edward G. "[Butler's] Petersburg Follies, *Civil War Times Illustrated*, 18 (January 1980), 4–9, 34–41.

Nellis, David M. "Benjamin Butler in New Orleans," *Civil War Times Illustrated*, 12 (October 1973), 4–10, 41–47.

Patterson, Gerald. "The Beast of New Orleans," *Civil War Times Illustrated*, 32 (May/June 1993), 28–33, 62–66.

Smith, David R. "The Beast of New Orleans," *Civil War Times Illustrated*, 8 (October 1969), 10–21.

Trefousse, Hans L. *Ben Butler: The South Called Him BEAST!* New York: Twayne Publishers, 1957.

CANBY, EDWARD R. S. (1817–1873)

Alderson, William T. "The Influence of Military Rule and the Freedmen's Bureau on Reconstruction in Virginia, 1865–1870." Ph.D. dissertation, Vanderbilt University, 1952.

Boatner, Mark M., III. *The Civil War Dictionary.* New York: D. McKay and Company, 1959.

Hamilton, Joseph G. de Roulhac. *Reconstruction in North Carolina.* New York: Columbia University Press, 1914.

Heyman, Max L., Jr. "'The Great Reconstructor': General E. R. S. Canby and the Second Military District," *North Carolina Historical Review*, 32 (1955), 52–80.

———. *Prudent Soldier: A Biography of Major General E. R. S. Canby, 1817–1873.* Glendale, Calif.: A. H. Clark, 1959.

Lowe, Richard G. *Republicans and Reconstruction in Virginia.* Charlottesville: University of Virginia Press, 1991.

Maddex, Jack P., Jr. *The Virginia Conservatives.* Chapel Hill: University of North Carolina Press, 1970.

Moneyhon, Carl H. *Texas after the Civil War: The Struggle of Reconstruction.* College Station: Texas A&M Unversity Press, 2004.

Ramsdell, Charles W. *Reconstruction in Texas.* New York: Columbia University Press, 1910.

Richter, William L. *The Army in Texas During Reconstruction, 1865–1870.* College Station: Texas A&M University Press, 1987.

———. "'We Must Rubb Out and Begin Anew': The Army and the Republican Party in Texas Reconstruction, 1867–1870," *Civil War History*, 19 (December 1973), 334–52.

Sefton, James E. *The United States Army and Reconstruction, 1865–1877.* Baton Rouge: Louisiana State University Press, 1967.

Shook, Robert W. "Federal Occupation and Administration of Texas, 1865–1870." Ph.D. dissertation, North Texas State University, 1970.

Simkins, Francis B., and Robert W. Woody. *South Carolina during Reconstruction.* Chapel Hill: University of North Carolina Press, 1932.

CARDOZO, FRANCIS L. (1837–1903)

Richardson, Joe M. "Francis L. Cardozo: Black Educator During Reconstruction," *Journal of Negro Education*, 48 (Winter 1979), 73–83.

Simkins, Francis B., and Robert W. Woody. *South Carolina during Reconstruction.* Chapel Hill: University of North Carolina Press, 1932.

Sweat, Edward F. "Francis L. Cardozo—Profile of Integrity in Reconstruction Politics," *Journal of Negro History*, 46 (1961), 217–32.

———. "Some Notes on the Role of Negroes in the Establishment of Public Schools in South Carolina," *Phylon*, 22 (1961), 160–66.

CARDOZO, THOMAS W. (1838–1881)

Brock, Eugene W. "Thomas W. Cardozo: Fallible Black Reconstruction Leader," *Journal of Southern History*, 47 (1981), 183–206.

CAROLINAS CAMPAIGN, FLORIDA, AND THE BATTLES FOR CHARLESTON, WILMINGTON, AND FORT FISHER

Barrett, John G. *Sherman's March through the Carolinas*. Chapel Hill: University of North Carolina Press, 1956.

"Battle of Bentonville," *Blue & Gray*, 13 (1995–96), [Special Issue].

Beronius, George. "Joe Johnston's Last Charge [Bentonville]," *Civil War Times Illustrated*, 35 (May/June 1996), 44–53.

Bradley, Mark L. "Battle of Averasboro," *Blue & Gray*, 16 (1998–99), [Special Issue].

———. *Last Stand in the Carolinas: The Battle of Bentonville*. Campbell, Calif.: N. Pub., 1996.

Brennan, Patrick. "Assault on Charleston," *North & South*, 6 (May 2003), 62–76.

Burchard, Peter. *One Gallant Rush: Robert Gould Shaw and His Brave Black Regiment*. New York: St. Martin's Press, 1965.

Burton, E. Milby. *The Siege of Charleston, 1861–1865*. Columbia: University of South Carolina Press, 1970.

Fonvielle, Chris. "Wilmington and Fort Fisher," *Blue & Gray*, 12 (1994–1995), [Special Issue].

Gragg, Rod. *Confederate Goliath: The Battle for Fort Fisher*. New York: HarperCollins, 1991.

Lucas, Marion B. *Sherman and the Burning of Columbia*. College Station: Texas A&M University Press, 1976.

Luvaas, Jay. "Bentonville—Last Chance to Stop Sherman," *Civil War Times Illustrated*, 2 (October 1963), 7–9, 38–42.

———. "The Fall of Fort Fisher," *Civil War Times Illustrated*, 3 (August 1964), 5–9, 31–35.

MacDonald, Sharon S., and W. Robert Beckham. "Heroism at Honey Hill [Charleston]," *North & South*, 12 (February 2010), 20–43.

Mallard, M. Stanton. "Assault on Charleston [Secessionville]," *North & South*, 6 (May 2003), 62–76.

Nulty, William H. *Confederate Florida: The Road to Olustee*. Tuscaloosa: University of Alabama Press, 1990.

Reed, Rowena. *Combined Operations in the Civil War*. Annapolis, Md.: Naval Institute Press, 1991.

Wise, Stephen R. *Gate of Hell: Campaign for Charleston Harbor, 1863*. Columbia: University of South Carolina Press, 1994.

CARPETBAGGERS

Abbott, Richard. *The Republican Party in the South, 1865–1877: The First Southern Strategy*. Chapel Hill: University of North Carolina Press, 1986.

Campbell, Randolph B. "Carpetbagger Rule in Reconstruction Texas: An Enduring Myth," *Southwestern Historical Quarterly*, 97 (1993–1994), 586–96.

Current, Richard N. "Carpetbaggers Reconsidered," in David H. Pinckney and Theodore Ropp (eds.), *A Festschrift for Frederick B. Artz*. Durham, N.C.: Duke University Press, 1964, 139–57.

———. *Those Terrible Carpetbaggers: A Reinterpretation*. New York: Oxford University Press, 1988.

———. *Three Carpetbag Governors*. Baton Rouge: Louisiana State University Press, 1967.

Currie-McDaniel, Ruth. "The Wives of the Carpetbaggers," in Jeffrey J. Crow *et al.* (eds.), *Race, Class, and Politics in Southern History*. Baton Rouge: Louisiana State University Press, 1989, 35–78.

Foner, Eric. *Reconstruction: America's Unfinished Revolution, 1863–1877*. New York: Harper & Row, 1988.

Harris, William C. "The Creed of the Carpetbaggers: The Case of Mississippi," *Journal of Southern History*, 40 (1974), 199–224.

Hume, Richard L. "Carpetbaggers in the Reconstruction South: A Group Portrait of Outside Whites in the 'Black and Tan' Constitutional Conventions," *Journal of American History*, 64 (1977–78), 313–30.

Kolchin, Peter. "Scalawags, Carpetbaggers, and Reconstruction: A Quantitative Look at Southern Congressional Politics, 1868–1872," *Journal of Southern History*, 45 (1979), 63–76.

Maizlish, Stephen E. "A Look Inside the Carpetbag," *Reviews in American History*, 17 (1989), 79–84.

Mechelke, Eugene R. "Some Observations on Mississippi's Reconstruction Historiography," *Journal of Mississippi History*, 33 (1971), 21–38.

Powell, Lawrence N. "The Politics of Livelihood: Carpetbaggers in the Deep South," in J. Morgan Lousser and James M. McPherson (eds.), *Region, Race, and Reconstruction: Essays in Honor of C. Vann Woodward*. New York: Oxford University Press, 1982, 315–47.

Scroggs, Jack B. "Carpetbagger Constitutional Reform in the South Atlantic States, 1867–1868," *Journal of Southern History*, 27 (1961), 475–93.

———. "Southern Reconstruction: A Radical View," *Journal of Southern History*, 24 (1958), 407–29.

Stampp, Kenneth M. *The Era of Reconstruction, 1865–1877*. New York: Alfred A. Knopf, 1965.

Thornton, J. Mills, III. "Fiscal Policy and the Failure of Radical Reconstruction in the Lower South," in J. Morgan Kousser and James M. McPherson (eds.), *Region, Race, and Reconstruction: Essays in Honor of C. Vann Woodward*. New York: Oxford University Press, 1982, 349–94.

CAVALRY OPERATIONS IN THE EASTERN THEATER

Alexander, Ted. "Gettysburg Cavalry Operations," *Blue & Gray*, 6 (1988–89), [Special Issue].

Ashdown, Paul, and Edward Caudill. *The Mosby Myth: A Confederate Hero in Life and Legend.* Wilmington, Del.: Scholarly Resources, Inc., 2002.

Brennan, Patrick. "Thunder on the Plains of Brandy (I)," *North & South*, 5 (April 2002), 14–34.

———. "Thunder on the Plains of Brandy (II)," *North & South*, 5 (May 2002), 32–51.

Brooksher, William R., and David K. Snider. *Glory at a Gallop: Tales of the Confederate Cavalry.* McLean, Va.: Brassy's, 1993.

———. "Wade Hampton Turns Cattle-Rustler: A Piece of Rebel Rascality," *Civil War Times Illustrated*, 23 (June 1984), 10–19.

Davis, Burke. *Jeb Stuart: The Last Cavalier.* New York: Rinehart & Co., 1957.

Davis, William C. (ed.). *The Confederate General.* 6 vols. N. p.: National Historical Society, 1991.

Downey, Fairfax. *Clash of Cavalry: The Battle of Brandy Station, June 9, 1863.* New York, David McKay Co., 1959.

Gallagher, Gary W. "Brandy Station: The Civil War's Bloodiest Arena of Mounted Combat," *Blue and Gray*, 8 (1990).

Garavaglia, Louis A., and Charles G Worman. "'Many Were Broken by Very Slight Shocks, as in Mounting and Dismounting': [Civil War Cavalry Shoulder Weapons]," *North & South*, 2 (June 1999), 40–55.

Hall, Clark B. "The Battle of Brandy Station," *Civil War Times Illustrated*, 29 (May/June 1990), 32–42, 45.

Hutton, Paul A. *Phil Sheridan and His Army.* Lincoln: University of Nebraska Press, 1985.

Jones, Virgil Carrington. *Eight Hours before Richmond.* New York: Henry Holt and Co., 1957.

———. *Gray Ghosts and Rebel Raiders.* New York: Henry Holt and Co., 1956.

———. "The Story of the Kilpatrick-Dahlgren Raid," *Civil War Times Illustrated*, 4 (June 1965), 12–21.

———. *Ranger Mosby.* Chapel Hill: University of North Carolina Press, 1944.

Keen, High C., and Horace Mewborn. *43rd Battalion Virginia Cavalry: Mosby's Command.* Lynchburg, Va.: H. E. Howard, 1993.

Klein, Frederic S. "Westminster: Little Skirmish, Big Affair?" *Civil War Times Illustrated*, 7 (August 1968), 32–38.

Long, David E. "Lincoln, Davis, and the Dahlgren Raid," *North & South*, 9 (October 2006), 70–83.

Longacre, Edward G. "Alfred Pleasonton: 'The Knight of Romance,'" *Civil War Times Illustrated*, 13 (December 1974), 10–23.

———. *The Cavalry at Gettysburg: A Tactical Study of Mounted Operations during the Civil War's Pivotal Campaign, 9 June–14 July, 1863.* Rutherford, N.J.: Fairleigh Dickinson University Press, 1986.

———. "Judson Kilpatrick," *Civil War Times Illustrated*, 10 (April 1971), 24–32.

———. *Mounted Raids of the Civil War.* New York: A. S. Barnes and Co., 1975.

———. "The Raid That Failed [Stoneman at Chancellorsville]," *Civil War Times Illustrated*, 26 (January 1988), 14–21, 44–45, 49.

Luvass, Jay. "Cavalry Lessons of the Civil War," *Civil War Times Illustrated*, 6 (January 1968), 20–31.

Lykes, Richard. "Hampton's Cattle Raid, September 14–17, 1864," *Military Affairs*, 21 (Spring 1957), 1–20.

———. "Hampton's Great Beef Raid," *Civil War Times Illustrated*, 5 (February 1967), 4–14. 47–49.

Martin, Samuel. "Kill-Cavalry," *Civil War Times Illustrated*, 38 (February 2000), 23–30, 56–59.

Mewborn, Horace. "Mosby's Confederacy," *Blue & Gray*, 17 (1999–2000), [Special Issue].

———. "Mosby in Maryland and West Virginia," *Blue & Gray*, 18 (2000–2001), [Special Issue].

———. "Stuart's Ride Around McClellan," *Blue & Gray*, 15 (1997–98), [Special Issue].

Morris, Roy. *Sheridan: The Life and Wars of General Phil Sheridan*. New York: Crown, 1992.

Naisawald, L. VanLoan. "Stuart as a Cavalryman's Cavalryman," *Civil War Times Illustrated*, 1 (February 1963), 6–10, 42–45.

Noe, Kenneth W. "Who Were the Bushwackers? Age, Class, Kin, and Western Virginia's Confederate Guerrillas, 1861–1862," *Civil War History*, 49 (2003), 5–31.

Nye, Wilbur S. "The Affair at Hunterstown," *Civil War Times Illustrated*, 9 (February 1971), 22–34.

———. *Here Come the Rebels*! Baton Rouge: Louisiana State University, 1965.

O'Connor, Richard. *Sheridan, the Inevitable*. Indianapolis: Bobbs-Merrill, 1953.

O'Neill, Robert. *The Cavalry Battles of Aldie, Middleburg, and Upperville: Small but Important Riots, June 10–27, 1863*. Lynchburg, Va.: H. E. Howard, 1994.

Poulter, Keith (ed.). "Cavalry Special," *North & South*, 2 (January 1999).

Prowell, George R., *et al. Encounter at Hanover: Prelude to Gettysburg*. Shippensburg, Pa.: White Mane Publishing Co., 1985, repr.

Rafuse, Ethan S. "Culture and Cavalry: Discourse and Reality: Some Observations on the War in the East," *North & South*, 10 (March 2008), 72–86.

Ramage, James A. *Gray Ghost: The Life of John Singleton Mosby*. Lexington: University of Kentucky Press, 1999.

Rhea, Gordon C. "'The Hottest Place I Was Ever In': The Battle of Haw's Shop, May 28, 1864," *North & South*, 4 (April 2001), 42–57.

Ryckman, W. G. "Clash of Cavalry at Trevilian's," *Virginia Magazine of History and Biography*, 75 (1967), 443–58.

Schultz, Duane. *The Dahlgren Affair: Terror and Conspiracy in the Civil War*. New York: Norton, 1998.

Sears, Stephen W. "Raid on Richmond," *MHQ: The Quarterly Journal of Military History*, 11 (1998), 88–96.

Seipel, Kevin H. *Rebel: The Life and Times of John Singleton Mosby*. New York: St. Martin's Press, 1983.

Smith, Everard D. "Chambersburg: Anatomy of a Confederate reprisal," *American Historical Review*, 96 (1991), 432–55.

Starr, Stephen Z. *The Union Cavalry in the Civil War*. 3 vols. Baton Rouge: Louisiana State University Press, 1985.

Swank, Walbrook Davis. *Battle of Trevilian Station: The Civil War's Greatest and Bloodiest of All Cavalry Battle*. Shippensburg, Pa.: Burd Street Press, 1994.

Sword, Wiley. "Cavalry on Trial at Kelly's Ford," *Civil War Times Illustrated*, 13 (April 1974), 32–40.

Thomas, Emory. "The Kilpatrick-Dahlgren Raid," *Civil War Times Illustrated*, 16 (February 1978), 4–9, 46–48; (April 1978), 26–33.

Trout, Robert J. "Galloping Thunder: Horse Artillery of the Army of Northern Virginia," *North & South*, 3 (September 2000), 74–84.

Urwin, Gregory J. *Custer Victorious: The Civil War Battles of General George Armstrong Custer*. Rutherford, N.J.: Fairleigh Dickinson University Press, 1990.

Venter, Bruce. "The Kilpatrick-Dahlgren Raid on Richmond, February 28–March 4, 1864," *Blue & Gray*, 20 (2002–2003).

Wert, Jeffry D. *Mosby's Rangers*. New York: Simon & Schuster, 1990.

Wittenberg, Eric J. "The Cavalry Fight at Samaria Church," *North & South*, 5 (February 2002), 64–75.

CAVALRY OPERATIONS IN THE WESTERN THEATER AND THE TRANS-MISSISSIPPI

Bailey, Anne J. *Between the Enemy and Texas: Parson's Texas Cavalry in the Civil War*. Fort Worth: Texas Christian University Press, 1989.

———. *Texans in the Confederate Cavalry*. Fort Worth: Ryan Place Publishers, 1995.

Brooksher, William R., and David K. Snider. "Morgan Raids Again: Kentucky, 1862," *Civil War Times Illustrated*, 17 (June 1978), 4–10, 43–46.

Brown, D. Alexander. "Grierson's Raid: 'Most Brilliant' of the War," *Civil War Times Illustrated*, 3 (January 1965), 4–11, 30–32.

Brownlee, Richard S. *Gray Ghosts of the Confederacy: Guerrilla Warfare in the West, 1861–1865*. Baton Rouge: Louisiana State University Press, 1958.

Castel, Albert E. *William Clarke Quantrell: His Life and Times*. Baton Rouge: Louisiana State University Press, 1968.

Dinges, Bruce J. "Grierson's Raid," *Civil War Times Illustrated*, 34 (January 1996), 50–64.

———. "Running Down Rebels [Van Dorn's Raid on Holly Springs]," *Civil War Times Illustrated*, 19 (April 1980), 10–18.

Dyer, John P. *"Fightin' Joe" Wheeler*. Baton Rouge: Louisiana State University Press, 1941.

Fellman, Michael. *Inside War: The Guerrilla Conflict in Missouri during the American Civil War*. New York: Oxford University Press, 1989.

Gaines, W. Craig. *The Confederate Cherokees: John Drew's Regiment of Mounted Rifles*. Baton Rouge: Louisiana State University Press. 1989.

Gallaway, B. P. *The Ragged Rebel: A Common Soldier in W. H. Parson's Texas Cavalry, 1861–1865*. Austin: University of Texas Press, 1988.

Hale, Douglas. *The Third Texas Cavalry in the Civil War*. Norman: University of Oklahoma Press, 1993.

Hattaway, Herman. *General Stephen D. Lee*. Jackson: University Press of Mississippi, 1976.

Henry, Robert S. *"First with the Most" Forrest*. Indianapolis: Bobbs-Merrill, 1944.

Holland, Cecil F. *Morgan and His Raiders: A Biography of the Confederate General*. New York: Macmillan, 1942.

Jones, James Pickett. *Yankee Blitzkreig: Wilson's Raid through Alabama and Georgia*. Athens: University of Georgia Press, 1976.

Keller, Allan. *Morgan's Raid*. Indianapolis: Bobbs-Merrill, 1961.

Kushlan, Jim (ed.). "July 1863: America Explodes," *Civil War Times Illustrated*, 42 (August 2003), 30–40.

Lawson, Lewis A. *Wheeler's Last Raid*. Greenwood, Fla.: Penkeville, 1986.

Longacre, Edward G. "Judson Kilpatrick," *Civil War Times Illustrated*, 10 (April 1971), 24–32.

———. "Streight's Raid: 'All's Fair . . . '," *Civil War Times Illustrated*, 8 (June 1969), 32–40.

Luvass, Jay. "Cavalry Lessons of the Civil War," *Civil War Times Illustrated*, 6 (January 1968), 20–31.

Martin, Samuel. "Kill-Cavalry," *Civil War Times Illustrated*, 38 (February 2000), 23–30, 56–59.

Matthews, Duncan K. *The McCook-Stoneman Raid*. Philadelphia: Dorrance, 1976.

Oates, Stephen B. *Confederate Cavalry West of the River*. Austin: University of Texas Press, 1992, repr.

Ramage, James A. *Rebel Raider: The Life of General John Hunt Morgan*. Lexington: University of Kentucky Press, 1986.

Roth, Dave. "Grierson's Raid," *Blue & Gray*, 10 (1992–1993), [Special Issue].

Rowell, John W. "McCook's Raid," 13 (July 1974), 4–9, 42–48.

Starr, Stephen Z. The *Union Cavalry in the Civil War*. 3 vols. Baton Rouge: Louisiana State University Press, 1985.

Sutherland, Daniel E. "Guerrilla Warfare, Democracy, and the Fate of the Confederacy," *Journal of Southern History*, 68 (2002), 259–92.

Van Noppen, Ina Woestemeyer. *Stoneman's Last Raid*. Raleigh: North Carolina State College Print Shop, 1961.

CHAMBERLAIN, DANIEL H. (1835–1907)

Current, Richard N. *Those Terrible Carpetbaggers: A Reinterpretation*. New York: Oxford University Press, 1988.

Fowler, Wilton B. "A Carpetbagger's Conversion to White Supremacy," *North Carolina Historical Review*, 43 (1966), 286–304.

Holt, Thomas. *Black over White: Negro Political Leadership in South Carolina during Reconstruction*. Urbana: University of Illinois Press, 1977.

Melton, Maurice. "The Gentle Carpetbagger: Daniel H. Chamberlain," *American History Illustrated*, 7 (January 1973), 28–37.

Sheppard, William A. *Red Shirts Remembered: Southern Brigadiers of the Reconstruction Period*. Atlanta, Ga.: Ruralist Press, 1940.

Thompson, Henry T. *Ousting the Carpetbagger from South Carolina*. Columbia: University of South Carolina Press, 1926.

Wellman, Manley Wade. *Giant in Gray: A Biography of Wade Hampton of South Carolina*. New York: Charles Scribner's Sons, 1949.

Williams, Alfred B. *Hampton and His Red Shirts: South Carolina's Deliverance in 1876*. Charleston,: Evans & Cogswell Co., 1935.

Woody, Robert H. "The South Carolina Election of 1870," *North Carolina Historical Review*, 8 (1931), 168–86.

Zuczek, Richard. *State of Rebellion: Reconstruction in South Carolina*. Columbia: University of South Carolina Press, 1996.

CHANCELLORSVILLE AND SUFFOLK

Bigelow, John. *The Campaign of Chancellorsville. A Strategic and Tactical Study*. New Haven, Conn.: Yale University Press, 1910.

Cannan, John. *The War in the East: Chancellorsville to Gettysburg, 1863*. New York: New York: Gallery Books, 1990.

Catton, Bruce. *Glory Road: The Bloody Route from Fredericksburg to Gettysburg*. New York: Doubleday and Co., 1952.

Cormier, Steven A. *The Siege of Suffolk: The Forgotten Campaign, April 11–May 4, 1863*. Lynchburg, Va.: H. E. Howard, 1989.

Cullen, Joseph P. "The Battle of Chancellorsville," *Civil War Times Illustrated*, 7 (May 1968), [Special Issue].

Foote, Shelby. *The Civil War: A Narrative*. 3 vols. New York: Random House, 1974.

Freeman, Douglas Southall. *Lee's Lieutenants: A Study of Command*. 3 vols. New York: Charles Scribner's Sons, 1942–1944.

Ferguson, Ernest B. *Chancellorsville, 1863: The Souls of the Brave*. New York: Knopf, 1992.

Goolrick, William K. *Rebels Resurgent: Fredericksburg to Chancellorsville*. Alexandria, Va.: Time-Life Books, 1985.

Lange, James E. T., and Katherine DeWitt, Jr. "Was Stonewall Jackson 'Fragged?'," *North & South*, 2 (April 1999), 10–15.

Longacre, Edward G. "The Raid That Failed [Stoneman at Chancellorsville]," *Civil War Times Illustrated*, 26 (January 1988), 14–21, 44–45, 49.

Luvaas, Jay. The Role of Intelligence in the Chancellorsville Campaign, April-May 1863," *Intelligence and National Security*, 5 (1990), 99–115.

Martin, David G. *The Chancellorsville Campaign, March–May 1863*. Co-shohocken, Pa.: Combined Books, 1991.

McPherson, James M. (ed.). *Battle Chronicles of the Civil War*. 6 vols. New York: Macmillan, 1989.

Stackpole, Edward. *Chancellorsville: Lee's Greatest Battle*. Harrisburg, Pa.: Stackpole Co., 1958.

Wert, Jeffry D. "Lee and His Staff," *Civil War Times Illustrated*, 11 (July 1972), 10–19.

CHASE, SALMON P. (1808–1873)

Blue, Frederick J. "Friends of Freedom: Lincoln, Chase, and the Wartime Racial Policy," *Ohio History*, 102 (1993), 85–97.

———. *Salmon Chase: A Life in Politics*. Kent, Ohio: Kent State University Press, 1986.

Donald, David H. (ed.). *Inside Lincoln's Cabinet: The Civil War Diaries of Salmon P. Chase*. New York: Longmans, Greene & Co., 1954.

Fairman, Charles. *Reconstruction and Reunion, 1864–1888*. 2 pts. New York: The Macmillan Company, 1971–1987.

Gerteis, Louis S. "Salmon P. Chase, Radicalism, and the Politics of Emancipation, 1861–1864," *Journal of American History*, 60 (1973–1974), 42–62.

Kutler, Stanley I. *Judicial Power and Reconstruction Politics*. Chicago: University of Chicago Press, 1968.

Nevin, John. *Salmon P. Chase: A Biography*. New York: Oxford University Press, 1995.

Sefton, James E. "Chief Justice Chase as an Advisor on Presidential Reconstruction," *Civil War History*, 13 (1967), 242–64.

Silver, David M. *Lincoln's Supreme Court*. Urbana: University of Illinois Press, 1956.

CHATTANOOGA CAMPAIGN

Bowers, John. *Chickamauga and Chattanooga: The Battles That Doomed the Confederacy*. New York: HarperCollins, 1994.

Bradley, Michael R. *Tullahoma: The 1863 Campaign for Control of Middle Tennessee*. Shippensburg, Pa.: White Mane Publishing Co., 1999.

Brennan, Patrick. "Hell on Horseshoe Ridge [Chickamagua]," *North & South*, 7 (February 2004), 22–44.

Catton, Bruce. *This Hallowed Ground: The Story of the Union Side of the Civil War*. Garden City, N.Y.: Doubleday, 1956.

Connelly, Thomas M. *Autumn of Glory: The Army of Tennessee, 1862–1865*. Baton Rouge: Louisiana State University Press, 1971.

Cozzens, Peter. *The Shipwreck of Their Hopes: The Battles for Chattanooga*. Urbana: University of Illinois Press, 1994.

————. *This Terrible Sound: The Battle of Chickamauga*. Urbana: University of Illinois Press, 1992.

Daniel, Larry J. *Soldiering in the Army of Tennessee: A Portrait of Life in a Confederate Army*. Chapel Hill: University of North Carolina Press, 1991.

Downey, Fairfax. *Storming the Gateway: Chattanooga, 1863*. New York: David McKay, 1960.

Feis, William B. "The Deception of Braxton Bragg: The Tullahoma Campaign," *Blue and Gray*, X (October 1992), 10–21, 46–53.

————. "Tullahoma Campaign," *Blue & Gray*, 10 (1992–1993), [Special Issue].

Fowler, Robert F (ed.). "The Battle of Chattanooga," *Civil War Times Illustrated*, 10 (August 1971), [Special Issue].

Furqueron, James R. "'Point Blank Business'," *North & South*, 5 (September 2002), 22–42.

Lamers, William M. *The Edge of Glory: A Biography of William S. Rosecrans*. New York: Harcourt, Brace, 1961.

McDonough, James Lee. *Chattanooga: A Death Grip on the Confederacy*. Knoxville: University of Tennessee Press, 1984.

McPherson, James M. (ed.). *Battle Chronicles of the Civil War*. 6 vols. New York: Macmillan, 1989.

Pratt, Fletcher. *Eleven Generals: Studies in American Command*. New York: W. Sloane Associates, 1949.

Robertson, William Glenn. "The Chickamauga Campaign: The Armies Collide," *Blue & Gray*, 24 (2006–2007), [Special Issue].

————. "The Chickamauga Campaign: The Battle of Chickamauga, Day 1," *Blue & Gray*, 24 (2006–2007), [Special Issue].

————. "The Chickamauga Campaign: The Battle of Chickamauga, Day 2," *Blue & Gray*, 25 (2008–2009), [Special Issue].

————. "The Chickamauga Campaign: Bragg's Lost Opportunity," *Blue & Gray*, 23 (2005–2006), [Special Issue].

————. "The Chickamauga Campaign: The Fall of Chattanooga," *Blue & Gray*, 23 (2005–2006), [Special Issue].

Rutherford, Phillip. "Battle Above the Clouds," *Civil War Times Illustrated*, 28 (September/October 1989), 30–39.

Sword, Wiley. "Battle Above the Clouds: The Battle of Lookout Mountain," *Blue & Gray*, 17 (1999–2000), [Special Issue].

————. *Mountains Touched with Fire: Chattanooga Besieged*. New York: St. Martin's Press, 1995.

Tucker, Glenn. "The Battle of Chickamauga," *Civil War Times Illustrated*, 8 (1969), [Special Issue].

———. *Chickamauga: Bloody Battle in the West*. Indianapolis: Bobbs-Merrill, 1961.

Wilson, John. "Miracle at Missionary Ridge," *America's Civil War*, 13 (March 2000), 42–49.

CIVIL RIGHTS ACTS

Beale, Howard K. *The Critical Year [1866]: A Study of Andrew Johnson and Reconstruction*. New York: Harcourt, Brace & Co., 1930.

Clark, John G. "Radicals and Moderates in the Joint Committee on Reconstruction," *Mid America*, 45 (1963), 79–98.

Donald David H. *Charles Sumner and the Rights of Man*. New York: Alfred A. Knopf, 1970.

Ezell, John S. "The Civil Rights Act of 1875," *Mid-America*, 50 (1968), 251–71.

Franklin, John Hope. *Race and History: Selected Essays, 1938–1988*. Baton Rouge: Louisiana State University, 1989.

Hyman, Harold M. "Reconstruction and Political-Constitutional Institutions: The Popular Expression," in Hyman (ed.), *New Frontiers of the American Reconstruction*, 1–39. and critical comment by Alfred H. Kelley, 40–58.

Kelly, Alfred H. "The Congressional Controversy over School Segregation, 1867–1875," *American Historical Review*, 64 (1958–1959), 537–63.

Kendrick, Benjamin B. *The Journal of the Joint Committee of Fifteen on Reconstruction, 39th Congress, 1865–1867*. New York: Columbia University Press, 1914.

McKitrick, Eric. *Andrew Johnson and Reconstruction*. Chicago: University of Chicago Press, 1960.

McPherson, James M. "Abolitionists and the Civil Rights Act of 1875," *Journal of American History*, 52 (1965), 493–510.

Murphy, L. E., "The Civil Rights Law of 1875," *Journal of Negro History*, 12 (1927), 110–27.

Riddleberger, Patrick W. *1866: The Critical Year Revisited*. Carbondale: Southern Illinois University Press, 1979.

U.S., 39th Cong., 1st Sess., H. Rep. 30. "Report of the Joint Committee on Reconstruction." Reprinted, New York: Negro Universities Press, 1969.

Vaughn, William P. "Separate and Unequal: The Civil Rights Act of 1875 and Defeat of the School Integration Clause," *Southwestern Social Science Quarterly*, 48 (1967), 146–54.

Weaver, Valerie W. "The Failure of Civil Rights 1875–1883 and Its Repercussions," *Journal of Negro History,* 54 (1969), 368–82.

Wilson, Kirt H. *The Reconstruction Desegregation Debate: The Politics of Equality and the Rhetoric of Place*. East Lansing: Michigan State University Press, 2002.

Wyatt-Brown, Bertram. "The Civil Rights Act of 1875," *Western Political Quarterly*, 18 (1965), 763–75.

CIVIL WAR, RADICAL REPUBLICANS AND

Benedict, Michael Les. *A Compromise of Principle: Congressional Republicans and Reconstruction, 1863–1869*. New York: W. W. Norton & Co., 1974.

Blackburn, George M. "Radical Republican Motivation: A Case Study," *Journal of Negro History*, 54 (1969), 109–28.

Bogue, Allan G. *The Earnest Men: Republicans of the Civil War Senate*. Ithaca: Cornell University Press, 1981.

Donald, David H. "Devils Facing Zionwards," in Grady McWhiney (ed.), *Grant, Lee, Lincoln and the Radicals*. Evanston, Ill.: Northwestern University Press, 1964, 72–91.

———. *The Politics of Reconstruction, 1863–1867*. Baton Rouge: Louisiana State University Press, 1965.

———. "The Radicals and Lincoln," in Donald (ed.), *Lincoln Reconsidered*. 2nd ed. New York: Vintage Books, 1956, 103–27.

Gambill, Edward L. "Who Were the Senate Radicals?" *Civil War History*, 11 (1965), 237–44.

Hyman, Harold M. (ed.). *The Radical Republicans and Reconstruction*. Indianapolis: Bobbs-Merrill Company, Inc., 1967.

Keys, Thomas Bland. "Profanation of the Constitution: Radical Rule, 1861–1877," *Lincoln Herald*, 90 (Spring 1988), 10–16.

Kincaid, Larry G. "Victims of Circumstance: An Interpretation of Changing Attitudes toward Republican Policy Makers and Reconstruction," *Journal of American History*, 57 (1970), 48–66.

Linden, Glenn M. "'Radicals' and Economic Policies: The Senate, 1862–1873," *Journal of Southern History*, 32 (1966), 189–99.

Trefousse, Hans L. *The Radical Republicans: Lincoln's Vanguard for Racial Justice*. New York: Alfred A. Knopf, 1969.

Williams, T. Harry. "Lincoln and the Radicals," in Grady McWhiney (ed.), *Grant, Lee, Lincoln, and the Radicals*. Evanston, Ill.: Northwestern University Press, 1964, 92–117.

———. *Lincoln and the Radicals*. Madison: University of Wisconsin Press, 1941.

CLAYTON, POWELL (1833–1914)

Boatner, Mark M., III. *The Civil War Dictionary*. New York: D. McKay and Company, 1959.

Burnside, William H. *The Honorable Powell Clayton*. Conway: University of Central Arkansas Press, 1991.

Clayton, Powell. *The Aftermath of the Civil War in Arkansas.* New York: Neal Publishing Co., 1915.

Current, Richard N. *Those Terrible Carpetbaggers: A Reinterpretation.* New York: Oxford University Press, 1988.

Driggs, Orval T. "The Issues of the Powell Clayton Regime, 1868–1871," *Arkansas Historical Quarterly,* 8 (1949), 1–76.

Ellenburg, Martha A. "Reconstruction in Arkansas." Ph.D. dissertation, University of Missouri, 1967.

Harrell, John M. *The Brooks and Baxter War: A History of the Reconstruction Period in Arkansas.* St. Louis: Slawson Printing Co., 1893.

Swinney, Everette. "United States *v.* Powell Clayton: Use of the Enforcement Acts in Arkansas," *Arkansas Historical Quarterly,* 26 (1967), 143–54.

Thompson, George H. *Arkansas and Reconstruction: The Influence of Geography, Economics, and Personality.* Port Washington, N.Y.: National University Publications, 1976.

COLFAX, SCHUYLER (1823–1885)

MacDonald, William. "Schuyler Colfax," in Allen Johnson *et al.* (eds.), *Dictionary of American Biography* (10 double vols. + 9 supplements, 1964–1981), IV, 297–98.

Smith, Willard H. *Schuyler Colfax: The Changing Fortune of a Political Idol.* Indianapolis: Indiana Historical Bureau, 1952.

COMPROMISE OF 1850, THE NASHVILLE CONVENTION, THE GEORGIA PLATFORM, AND THE SOUTHERN MOVEMENT

Brown, Thomas. *Politics and Statesmanship: Essays on the American Whig Party.* New York: Columbia University Press, 1985.

Campbell, Stanley. *The Slave Catchers: Enforcement of the Fugitive Slave Law, 1850–1860.* Chapel Hill: University of North Carolina Press, 1970.

Foster, Herbert D. "Webster's Seventh of March Speech and the Secession Movement, 1850," *American Historical Review,* 27 (1922), 245–70.

Gara, Larry. "Results of the Fugitive Slave Law," *Civil War Times Illustrated,* 2 (October 1963), 30–37.

Grayson, Benson Lee. *The Unknown President: The Administration of President Millard Fillmore.* Washington, D.C.: University Press of America, 1981.

Hamilton, Holman. *Prelude to Conflict: The Crisis and Compromise of 1850.* Lexington: University of Kentucky Press, 1964.

Harmon, George D. "Douglas and the Compromise of 1850," Illinois State Historical Society, *Journal,* 21 (1929), 477–79.

Hodder, Frank H. "The Authorship of the Compromise of 1850," *Mississippi Valley Historical Review,* 22 (1936), 525–36.

Holt, Michael. *The Political Crisis of the 1850s.* New York: John Wiley & Sons, 1978.
———. *Political Parties and American Political Development from the Age of Jackson to the Age of Lincoln.* Baton Rouge: Louisiana State University Press, 1992.
Howe, Daniel W. *The Political Culture of American Whigs.* Chicago: University of Chicago Press, 1979.
Johannsen, Robert W. *Stephen A. Douglas.* New York: Oxford University Press, 1973.
Johnson, Vicki Vaughn. *The Men and Vision of the Southern Commercial Conventions. 1845–1871.* Columbia: University of Missouri Press, 1992.
Leddy, Chuck. "Boston Combusts: The Fugitive Slave Case of Anthony Burns," *Civil War Times Illustrated,* 46 (May 2007), 50–55.
Morris, Thomas D. *Free Men All: The Personal Liberty Laws of the North, 1780–1861.* Baltimore, Md.: The Johns Hopkins University Press, 1974.
Nichols, Roy F. *The Democratic Machine, 1850–1854.* New York: Columbia University Press, 1923.
Petersen, Merrill D. *The Great Triumvirate: Webster, Clay, and Calhoun.* New York: Oxford University Press, 1987.
Potter, David. *The Impending Crisis, 1848–1861.* New York: Harper & Row, 1976.
Sewell, Richard. *Ballots for Freedom: Antislavery Politics in the United States, 1837–1860.* New York: Oxford University Press, 1976.
Sibley, Joel. *The Shrine of Party: Congressional Voting Behavior, 1841–1852.* Pittsburgh: University of Pittsburgh Press, 1967.
Smith, Elbert B. *The Presidencies of Zachary Taylor and Millard Fillmore.* Lawrence: University Press of Kansas, 1988.
Sydner, Charles McCool. "Anna Carroll, Political Strategist and Gadfly of President Fillmore," *Maryland Historical Magazine,* 68 (No. 1, 1973), 36–63.
Waugh, John C. "On the Brink of Civil War [Compromise of 1850]," *North & South,* 6 (November 2003), 36–46.

CONFEDERATE BRIGADIERS

Carter, Dan T. *When the War Was Over: The Failure of Self-Reconstruction in the South, 1865–1867.* Baton Rouge: Louisiana State University Press, 1985.
DuBois, W. E. Burghardt. *Black Reconstruction: An Essay toward a History of the Part Which Black Folk Played in the Attempt to Reconstruct Democracy, 1860–1888.* New York: Harcourt, Brace and Company, 1935.

CONGRESSIONAL RECONSTRUCTION—COMMAND OF THE ARMY ACT

Sefton, James E. *The United States Army and Reconstruction, 1865–1877.* Baton Rouge: Louisiana State University Press, 1967.

CONGRESSIONAL RECONSTRUCTION—GENERAL

Coulter, E. Merton. *The South During Reconstruction, 1865–1877*. Baton Rouge: Louisiana State University Press, 1947.

Craven, Avery O. *Reconstruction: The Ending of the Civil War*. New York: Holt, Rinehart, and Winston, Inc., 1969.

Foner, Eric. *Reconstruction: America's Unfinished Revolution, 1863–1877*. New York: Harper & Row, 1988.

Franklin, John Hope. *Reconstruction: After the Civil War*. Chicago: University of Chicago Press, 1961.

Patrick, Rembert W. *The Reconstruction of the Nation*. New York: Oxford University Press, 1967.

Sefton, James E. *The United States Army and Reconstruction, 1865–1877*. Baton Rouge: Louisiana State University Press, 1967.

Trelease, Allen W. *Reconstruction: The Great Experiment*. New York: Harper & Row, 1971.

CONGRESSIONAL RECONSTRUCTION—FORTIETH CONGRESS EXTRA SESSION ACT

Trefousse, Hans L. *Andrew Johnson: A Biography*. New York: W. W. Norton & Company, 1989.

CONGRESSIONAL RECONSTRUCTION—MILITARY RECONSTRUCTION ACTS

Kincaid, Larry G. "The Legislative Origins of the Military Reconstruction Act, 1865–1867." Ph.D. dissertation, The Johns Hopkins University, 1968.

Main, Jackson Turner. *The Sovereign States, 1775–1783*. New York: New Viewpoints, 1973.

McCormick, Richard P. *The Second American Party System: Party Formation in the Jacksonian Era*. Chapel Hill: University of North Carolina Press, 1966.

White, Leonard D. *The Jacksonians: A Study in Administrative History, 1829–1861*. New York: Macmillan, 1954.

———. *The Republican Era: A Study in Administrative History, 1869–1901*. New York: Macmillan, 1958.

CONGRESSIONAL RECONSTRUCTION—TENURE OF OFFICE ACT

Sefton, James E. *The United States Army and Reconstruction, 1865–1877*. Baton Rouge: Louisiana State University Press, 1967.

Thomas, Benjamin P., and Harold M. Hyman. *Stanton: The Life and Times of Lincoln's Secretary of War*. New York: Alfred A. Knopf, 1962.

CORRUPTION IN ANTEBELLUM, CIVIL WAR, AND RECONSTRUCTION ERAS

Eaton, Clement. *The Waning of the Old South Civilization, 1860s–1880s*. Athens: University of Georgia Press, 1968.

Foster, Gaines M. *Ghosts of the Confederacy: Defeat, the Lost Cause, and the Emergence of the New South, 1865 to 1913*. New York: Oxford University Press, 1987.

Govan, Gilbert E., and James W. Livingood. "Chattanooga under Military Occupation," *Journal of Southern History*, 17 (1951), 23–47.

Johnson, Ludwell H., III. "Contraband Trade during the Last Year of the Civil War," *Mississippi Valley Historical Review*, 49 (1963), 635–41.

———. "Northern Profit and Profiteers: The Cotton Rings of 1864–1865," *Civil War History*, 12 (1966), 101–15.

———. *Red River Campaign: Politics and Cotton in the Civil War*. Baltimore, Md.: The Johns Hopkins University Press, 1958.

Osterweis, Rollin G. *The Myth of the Lost Cause, 1865–1900*. Hamden, Conn.: Archon Books, 1973.

Parks, Joseph H. "A Confederate Trade Center under Federal Occupation: Memphis, 1862 to 1865," *Journal of Southern History*, 7 (1941), 289–314.

Robinson, Armistead L. "Beyond the Realm of Consensus: New Meanings of Reconstruction for American History," *Journal of American History*, 68 (1981), 276–97.

Summers, Mark W. "'A Band of Brigands': Albany Lawmakers and Republican National Politics, 1860," *Civil War History*, 30 (1984), 101–19.

———. *The Era of Good Stealings*. New York: Oxford University Press, 1993.

———. *The Plundering Generation: Corruption and the Crisis of the Union*. New York: Oxford University Press, 1987.

———. *Railroads, Reconstruction, and the Gospel of Prosperity: Aid Under the Radical Republicans*. Princeton, N.J.: Princeton University Press, 1984.

Williams, T. Harry. "An Analysis of Some Reconstruction Attitudes," *Journal of Southern History*, 12 (1946), 469–86.

———. "The Louisiana Unification Movement of 1873," *Journal of Southern History*, 11 (1945), 349–69.

DAVIS, EDMUND J. (1827–1883)

Baenziger, Ann Patton. "The Texas State Police during Reconstruction: A Reexamination," *Southwestern Historical Quarterly*, 72 (1968–1969), 470–91.

Baggett, James Alex. "Birth of the Texas Republican Party," *Southwestern Historical Quarterly*, 78 (1974–1975), 1–20.

———. "Origins of Early Texas Republican Party Leadership," *Journal of Southern History*, 40 (1974), 441–50.

———. "The Rise and Fall of the Texas Radicals, 1867–1883." Ph.D. dissertation, North Texas State University, 1972.

Baum, Dale. *The Shattering of Texas Unionism: Politics in the Lone Star State During the Civil War Era*. Baton Rouge: Louisiana State University Press, 1998.

Campbell, Randolph B. "Carpetbagger Rule in Reconstruction Texas: An Enduring Myth," *Southwestern Historical Quarterly*, 97 (1993–1994), 586–96.

Carrier, John P. "A Political History of Texas during the Reconstruction, 1865–1874." Ph.D. dissertation, Vanderbilt University, 1971.

Crouch, Barry A. "'Unmanacling' Texas Reconstruction: A Twenty Year Perspective," *Southwestern Historical Quarterly*, 93 (1989–1990), 275–302.

Field, William T., Jr. "The Texas State Police, 1870–1873," *Texas Military History*, 5 (1965), 131–41.

Gillette, William. *Retreat from Reconstruction, 1869–1879*. Baton Rouge: Louisiana State University Press, 1979.

Gray, Ronald N. "Edmund J. Davis: Radical Republican and Reconstruction Governor of Texas." Ph.D. dissertation, Texas Tech University, 1976.

Moneyhon, Carl. *Republicanism in Reconstruction Texas*. Austin: University of Texas Press, 1980.

Moneyhon, Carl H. *Texas after the Civil War: The Struggle of Reconstruction*. College Station: Texas A&M University Press, 2004.

Perman, Michael. *The Road to Redemption: Southern Politics, 1869–1879*. Chapel Hill: University of North Carolina Press, 1984.

Rable, George C. *But There Was No Peace: The Role of Violence in the Politics of Reconstruction*. Athens: University of Georgia Press, 1984.

Ramsdell, Charles W. *Reconstruction in Texas*. New York: Columbia University Press, 1910.

Richter, William L. *The Army in Texas During Reconstruction, 1865–1870*. College Station: Texas A&M University Press, 1987.

Russ, William A., Jr. "Radical Disfranchisement in Texas, 1867–1870," *Southwestern Historical Quarterly*, 38 (1934–1935), 40–52.

Sandlin, Betty Jeffus. "The Texas Reconstruction Constitutional Convention of 1868–1869." Ph.D. dissertation, 1970.

Singletary, Otis A. *Negro Militia and Reconstruction*. Austin: University of Texas Press, 1957.

Sneed, Edgar P. "A Historiography of Reconstruction in Texas: Some Myths and Problems," *Southwestern Historical Quarterly*, 72 (1968–1969), 435–48.

Thompson, Jerry Don. *Vaqueros in Blue and Gray*. Austin, Tex.: Presidial Press, 1976.

Wallace, Ernest. *The Howling of the Coyotes: Reconstruction Efforts to Divide Texas*. College Station: Texas A&M University Press, 1979.

Waller, John L. *Colossal Hamilton of Texas: A Biography of Andrew Jackson Hamilton*. El Paso: Texas Western Press, 1968.

Webb, Walter Prescott. *The Texas Rangers: A Century of Frontier Defense*. Austin: University of Texas Press, 1965.

DAVIS, HENRY WINTER (1817–1865)

Belz, Herman. "Henry Winter Davis and the Origins of Congressional Reconstruction," *Maryland Historical Magazine*, 67 (1972), 129–43.

Curry, Richard O. *Radicalism, Racism, and Party Realignment: The Border States during Reconstruction*. Baltimore, Md.: The Johns Hopkins University Press, 1969.

Hentig, Gerald S. "Henry Winter Davis and the Speakership Contest of 1859–1860," *Maryland Historical Magazine*, 68 (1973), 1–19.

———. *Henry Winter Davis: Antebellum and Civil War Congressman from Maryland*. New York: Twayne Publishers, 1973.

Steiner, Bernard C. *Life of Henry Winter Davis*. Baltimore, Md.: The Johns Hopkins University Press, 1916.

Tyson, Raymond W. "Henry Winter Davis: Orator for the Union," *Maryland Historical Magazine*, 58 (1963), 1–19.

DAVIS, JEFFERSON (1808–1889)

Ballard, Michael B. *A Long Shadow: Jefferson Davis and the Final Days of the Confederacy*. Jackson: University of Mississippi Press, 1896.

Bradley, Chester D. "Was Jefferson Davis Disguised as a Woman When Captured?" *Journal of Mississippi History*, 36 (1954), 243–68.

Canfield, Cass. *The Iron Will of Jefferson*. New York: Harcourt Brace Jovanovich, 1978.

Cooper, William J. *Jefferson Davis, American*. New York; Knopf, 2000.

———. "Jefferson Davis and the Politics of Command," *Civil War Times Illustrated*, 47 (August 2008), 34–39.

———. "A Reassessment of Jefferson Davis as War Leader: The Case from Atlanta to Nashville," *Journal of Southern History*, 36 (1970), 189–204.

Crist, Lynda Lasswell. "A 'Duty Man': Jefferson Davis as Senator," *Journal of Mississippi History*, 51 (1989), 281–96.

Cutting, Elisabeth. *Jefferson Davis: Political Soldier*. New York: Dodd, Mead, 1930.

Davis, Jefferson. *The Rise and Fall of the Confederacy*. 2 vols. New York: D. Appleton & Co., 1881.

Davis, William C. *Jefferson Davis; The Man and His Hour*. New York: HarperCollins, 1991.

Eaton, Clement. *Jefferson Davis*. New York: Free Press, 1977.

Eckenrode, Hamilton J. *Jefferson Davis: President of the South*. New York: Macmillan, 1923.

Escott, Paul D. *After Secession: Jefferson Davis and the Failure of Confederate Nationalism*. Baton Rouge: Louisiana State University Press, 1878.

Fleming, Walter L. *Jefferson Davis at West Point*. Baton Rouge: Louisiana State University Press, 1910.

Grimsley, Mark. "'We Will Vindicate the Right': An Account of the Life of Jefferson Davis," *Civil War Times Illustrated*, 30 (July/August 1996), [Special Issue].

Hattaway, Herman, and Richard Beringer. *Jefferson Davis, Confederate President*. Lawrence: University Press of Kansas, 2002.

Hendrick, Burton J. *Statesmen of the Lost Cause: Jefferson Davis and His Cabinet*. New York: Literary Guild of America, 1939.

Langheim, Eric. *Jefferson Davis, Patriot: A Biography*. New York: Vantage Press, 1962.

Mallonee, Frank Buckner, Jr. "The Political Thought of Jefferson Davis." Ph.D. dissertation, Emory University, 1966.

McElroy, Robert. *Jefferson Davis: The Unreal and Real*. 2 vols. New York: Harper and Bros., 1937.

Meade, Robert D. "The Relations between Judah P. Benjamin and Jefferson Davis," *Journal of Southern History*, 5 (1939), 468–78.

Monroe, Haskell M., Jr. (ed.). *The Papers of Jefferson Davis*. 8 vols. Baton Rouge: Louisiana State University Press, 1971.

Neely, Mark E., Jr. *Jefferson Davis and Civil Liberties*. Milwaukee, Wisc.: Marquette University Press, 1993.

Patrick, Rembert. *Jefferson Davis and His Cabinet*. Baton Rouge: Louisiana State University Press, 1944.

Rabun, James Z. "Alexander H. Stephens and Jefferson Davis," *American Historical Review*, 58 (1953), 290–321.

Richardson, James D. *The Messages and Papers of Jefferson Davis and the Confederacy, Including Diplomatic Correspondence, 1861–1865*. 2 vols. New York: Chelsea House, 1966.

Riley, Harris D., Jr. "Jefferson Davis and His Health . . . ," *Journal of Mississippi History*, 49 (1987), 179–202, 261–87.

Roland, Dunbar (ed.). *Jefferson Davis, Constitutionalist: His Letters, Papers, and Speeches*. 10 vols. Jackson: Mississippi Department of Archives and History, 1923.

Sansing, David. "A Happy Interlude: Jefferson Davis and the war Department," *Journal of Mississippi History*, 51 (1989), 297–312.

Schaff, Morris. *Jefferson Davis: His Life and Personality*. Boston: J. E. Luce and Co., 1922.

Tate, Allen. *Jefferson Davis: His Rise and Fall*. New York: Monton, Balch and Co., 1929.

Vandiver, Frank E. *Jefferson Davis and the Confederate State*. Oxford, England: Clarendon Press, 1964.

Wiley, Bell I. "Jefferson Davis: An Appraisal," *Civil War Times Illustrated*, 6 (April 1967), 4–11, 44–49.

DIPLOMACY, C.S.—CIVIL WAR

Adams, Ephraim Douglas. *Great Britain and the American Civil War*. 2 vols. New York: Russell & Russell, 1925.

Beckles, Willson. *John Slidell and the Confederates in Paris, 1862–1865*. New York: Minton, Balck, 1932.

Blumenthal, Henry. "Confederate Diplomacy: Popular Notions and International Realities," *Journal of Southern History*, 32 (No. 2, May 1966), 151–71.

Bonner, Robert E. "Slavery, Confederate Diplomacy, and the Racialist Mission of Henry Hotze," *Civil War History*, 51 (2005), 288–316.

Bulloch, James D. *The Secret Service of the Confederate States in Europe; or, How the Confederate Cruisers Were Equipped*. 2 vols. New York: Thomas Yoseloff, 1959, repr.

Case Lynne M., and Warren F. Spencer. *The United States and France: Civil War Diplomacy*. Philadelphia: University of Pennsylvania Press, 1970.

Crook, David Paul. *The North, the South, and the Powers, 1861–1865*. New York: Wiley, 1974.

Daddysman, James W. *The Matamoros Trade: Confederate Commerce, Diplomacy, and Intrigue*. Newark: University of Delaware Press, 1984.

Delaney, Norman. "The Strange Occupation of James Bulloch: 'When Can You Start?'," *Civil War Times Illustrated*, 21 (March 1982), 18–27.

Durkin, J. T. *Stephen R. Mallory: Confederate Navy Chief*. Chapel Hill: University of North Carolina Press, 1954.

Gentry, Judith Fenner. "A Confederate Success in Europe: The Erlanger Loan," *Journal of Southern History*, 36 (1970), 157–88.

Hubbard, Charles M. *The Burden of Confederate Diplomacy*. Knoxville: University of Tennessee Press, 1998.

Jones, Howard. *Blue and Gray Diplomacy: A History of Union and Confederate Foreign Relations*. Chapel Hill: University of North Carolina Press, 2009.

Jones, Wilbur D. *The Confederate Rams at Birkenhead: A Chapter in Anglo-American Relations*. Tuscaloosa, Ala.: Confederate Publishing Co., 1961.

Lebergott, Stanley. "Through the Blockade: The Profitability and Extent of Cotton Smuggling," *Journal of Economic History*, 51 (1981), 867–88.

May, Robert E. (ed.). *The Union, the Confederacy, and the Atlantic Rim*. West Lafayette, Ind.: Purdue University Press, 1995.

Merli, Frank J. *The Alabama, British Neutrality, and the American Civil War*. Bloomington: Indiana University Press, 2004.

———. *Great Britain and the Confederate Navy, 1861–1865*. Bloomington: Indiana University Press, 1970.

Owsley, Frank. *King Cotton Diplomacy: Foreign Relations of the Confederate States of America.* 2nd ed. Chicago: University of Chicago Press, 1959.

Spencer, Warren F. *The Confederate Navy in Europe.* Tuscaloosa: University of Alabama Press, 1983.

Surdam, David G. "Cotton's Potential as Economic Weapon: The Antebellum and Wartime Markets for Cotton Textiles," *Agricultural History*, 68 (1994), 122–45.

Thompson, Samuel Bernard. *The Confederate Navy in Europe.* Tuscaloosa: University of Alabama Press, 1983.

DIPLOMACY, U.S.—CIVIL WAR

Adams, Charles Francis, Jr. *Charles Francis Adams.* Boston: Houghton Mifflin, 1909.

Adams, Ephraim Douglas. *Great Britain and the American Civil War.* 2 vols. New York: Russell & Russell, 1925.

Bernath, Stuart L. *Squall Across the Atlantic: American Civil War Prize Cases and Diplomacy.* Los Angeles: University of California Press, 1970.

Brauer, Kinley J. "Seward's 'Foreign War Panacea': An Interpretation," *New York History*, 55 (1974), 133–57.

Case Lynne M., and Warren F. Spencer. *The United States and France: Civil War Diplomacy.* Philadelphia: University of Pennsylvania Press, 1970.

Cook, Adrian. *The Alabama Claims: American Politics and Anglo-American Relations, 1861–1872.* Ithaca, N.Y.: Cornell University Press, 1975.

Cortada, James W. "Spain and the American Civil War: Relations at Mid-Century, 1855–1868," American Philosophical Society, *Transactions*, 70 (1980), Pt. 4.

Crook, Carland E. "Benjamin Théron and the French Designs in Texas during the Civil War," *Southwestern Historical Quarterly*, 68 (1964–1965), 432–54.

Crook, David Paul. *The North, the South, and the Powers, 1861–1865.* New York: Wiley, 1974.

Ferris, Norman B. *Desperate Diplomacy: William H. Seward's Foreign Policy, 1861.* Knoxville: University of Tennessee Press, 1977.

Ferris, Norman B., and David M. Pelcher. *The Trent Affair: A Diplomatic Crisis.* Knoxville: University of Tennessee Press, 1977.

Hanna, Kathryn A. "The Roles of the South in the French Intervention in Mexico," *Journal of Southern History*, 20 (1954), 3–21.

Jones, Howard. *Abraham Lincoln and a New Birth of Freedom: The Union and Slavery in the Diplomacy of the Civil War.* Lincoln: University of Nebraska Press, 1999.

———. *Blue and Gray Diplomacy: A History of Union and Confederate Foreign Relations.* Chapel Hill: University of North Carolina Press, 2010.

———. "Republic in Peril: The Threat of Foreign Intervention in the Civil War," *North & South*, 12 (No. 4, 2010), 36–49.

————. *Union in Peril: The Crises over British Intervention in the Civil War.* Chapel Hill: University of North Carolina Press, 1993.

May, Robert E. (ed.). *The Union, the Confederacy, and the Atlantic Rim.* West Lafayette, Ind.: Purdue University Press, 1995.

O'Rourke, Mary M. "The Diplomacy of William H. Seward during the Civil War: His Politics as Related to International Law." Ph.D. dissertation, University of California, 1963.

Pattock, Florence B. "Cassius M. Clay's Mission to Russia, 1861–1862, 1863–1869," *Filson Club Historical Quarterly*, 43 (1969), 325–44.

Taylor, John M. *William Henry Seward.* New York: HarperCollins, 1991.

Warren, Gordon H. *Fountain of Discontent: The Trent Affair and Freedom of the Seas.* Boston: Northeast University Press, 1981.

Woldman, Albert A. *Lincoln and the Russians.* Cleveland: World Publishing. 1952.

DIPLOMACY, U.S.—RECONSTRUCTION

Beisner, Robert L. *From the Old Diplomacy to the New, 1865–1900.* New York: Thomas Y. Crowell Co., 1975.

Campbell, Charles S. *The Transformation of American Foreign Relations: 1865–1900.* New York: Harper & Row, 1976.

Cook, Adrian. *The Alabama Claims: American Politics and Anglo-American Relations, 1861–1872.* Ithaca, N.Y.: Cornell University Press, 1975.

Donald David H. *Charles Sumner and the Rights of Man.* New York: Alfred A. Knopf, 1970.

Dulles, Foster Rhea. *Prelude to World Power: American Diplomatic History, 1860–1900.* New York: Macmillan, 1965.

Ferrell, Robert H. *American Diplomacy: A History.* New York: W. W. Norton, 1969.

Fuller, Joseph V. "Hamilton Fish," in Allen Johnson *et al.* (eds.), *Dictionary of American Biography* (10 double vols. + 9 supplements, 1964–1981), VII, 145–50.

LaFeber, Walter. *The New Empire: An Interpretation of American Expansion, 1860–1898.* Ithaca, N.Y.: Cornell University Press, 1963.

Nevins, Allan. *Hamilton Fish: The Inner History of the Grant Administration.* 2 vols. New York: Dodd, Mead & Co., 1936.

Plesur, Milton. *America's Outward Thrust: Approaches to Foreign Affairs, 1865–1890.* DeKalb: Northern Illinois University Press, 1971.

Spence, Clark C. "*Robert Schenck* and the Emma Mine Affair," *Ohio Historical Quarterly*, 68 (1959), 141–60.

Taylor, John M. *William Henry Seward: Lincoln's Right Hand.* New York: HarperCollins, 1991.

Van Deusen, Glyndon G. *William Henry Seward.* New York: Oxford University Press, 1967.

DISEASE

Bollet, Alfred Jay, M.D. *Civil War Medicine: Challenges and Triumphs*. Tucson, Ariz.: Galen Press, 2000.

Jones, Gordon W. "Sanitation—100,000 Needless Deaths," *Civil War Times Illustrated*, 5 (November 1966), 12–18.

Lloyd, Lewis. *Letters from Lloyd Lewis . . . .* Boston: Little, Brown, 1950.

Lowery, Thomas P. *The Civil War Bawdy Houses of Washington, D.C., Including a Map of Their Former Locations and a Reprint of the Souvemir Sporting Guide for the Chicago, Ill., G.A.R. 1895, Reunion.* Fredericksburg, Va.: Sergeant Kirkland's, 1997.

———. *The Story the Soldiers Wouldn't Tell: Sex in the Civil War.* Mchanicsburg, Pa.: Stackpole Books, 1994.

Steiner, Paul E. *Diseases in the Civil War: Natural Biological Warfare in 1861–1865.* Springfield, Ill.: Charles C. Thomas, 1996.

Wilbur, C. Keith. *Civil War Medicine.* Old Saybrook, Conn.: The Globe Pequot Press, 1998.

DISFRANCHISEMENT, ECONOMIC

Bacote, Clarence A. "Negro Proscriptions, Protests, and Proposed Solutions in Georgia, 1880–1908," *Journal of Southern History*, 25 (1959), 471–98.

Cable, George W. "The Convict Lease System in the Southern States," *Century*, n.s., 5 (1884), 582–99.

Carleton, Mark T. *Politics and Punishment: The Story of the Louisiana Penal System.* Baton Rouge: Louisiana State University Press, 1971.

Carper, N. Gordon. "Slavery Revisited: Peonage in the South," *Phylon*, 37 (1976), 85–99.

Cohen, William. "Negro Involuntary Servitude in the South, 1865–1940: A Preliminary Analysis," *Journal of Southern History*, 42 (1976), 31–60.

Daniel, Pete. "The Metamorphosis of Slavery, 1865–1900," *Journal of American History*, 66 (1979), 88–99.

———. *The Shadow of Slavery: Peonage in the South.* New York: Oxford University Press, 1973.

Eckert, Ralph Lowell. *John Brown Gordon: Soldier, Southerner, Statesman.* Baton Rouge: Louisiana State University Press, 1989.

Goldin, Claudia D., and Frank D. Lewis. "The Economic Cost of the Civil War: Estimates and Implications," *Journal of Economic History*, 25 (1975), 299–326.

Holt, Sharon Ann. *Making Freedom Pay: North Carolina Freedpeople Working for themselves, 1865–1900.* Athens: University of Georgia Press, 2000.

Kolchin, Peter. "Race, Class, and Poverty in the Post-Civil War South," *Reviews in American History,* 6 (1979), 515–26.

Krebs, Sylvia. "Will the Freedmen Work? White Alabamians Adjust to Free Black Labor," *Alabama Historical Quarterly*, 36 (1974), 151–63.

Logan, Rayford W. *The Betrayal of the Negro: From Rutherford B. Hayes to Woodrow Wilson*. New York: Collier Books, 1965.

Magdol, Edward. *A Right to the Land: Essays on the Freedmen's Community*. Westport, Conn.: Greenwood Press, 1977.

Mandle, Jay R. *The Roots of Black Poverty: The Southern Plantation Economy after the Civil War*. Durham, N.C.: Duke University Press, 1978.

McDonald, Forrest, and Grady McWhiney. "The South from Self-Sufficiency to Peonage: An Interpretation," *American Historical Review*, 85 (1980), 1095–1118.

McKelvey, Blake. "Penal Slavery and Southern Reconstruction," *Journal of Negro History*, 20 (1963), 153–79.

Novak, Daniel A. *The Wheel of Servitude: Black Forced Labor after Slavery*. Lexington: University of Kentucky Press, 1978.

Ransom, Roger L., and Richard Sutch. *One Kind of Freedom: The Economic Consequences of Emancipation*. Cambridge, England: Cambridge University Press, 1977.

Reid, Joseph D., Jr. "Sharecropping as an Understandable Market Response—the Postbellum South," *Journal of Economic History*, 33 (1973), 106–30.

———. "White Land, Black Labor, and Agricultural Stagnation: The Causes and Effects of Sharecropping in the Postbellum South," *Explorations in Economic History*, 16 (1979), 31–55.

Roark, James L. *Masters without Slaves: Southern Planters in the Civil War and Reconstruction*. New York: W. W. Norton, 1977.

Schweninger, Loren. "Prosperous Blacks in the South, 1790–1880," *American Historical Review*, 95 (1990), 31–56.

Schmidt, James D. *Free to Work: Labor Law, Emancipation, and the Reconstruction, 1815–1880*. Athens: University of Georgia Press, 1998.

Shlomowitz, Ralph. "The Origins of Southern Sharecropping," *Agricultural History*, 53 (1979), 557–75.

Shofner, Jerrell H. "Custom, Law, and History: The Enduring Effect of Florida's 'Black Code'," *Florida Historical Quarterly*, 55 (1977), 277–98. (1973), 397–408.

Temin, Peter. "The Post-Bellum Recovery of the South and the Cost of the Civil War, Journal of Economic History, *Journal of Economic History*, 36 (1976), 898–907.

Weaver, Herbert. *Mississippi Farmers, 1850–1860*. Nashville, Tenn.: Vanderbilt University Press, 1945.

Wiener, Jonathan M. "Class Structure and Economic Development in the American South, 1865–1955," *American Historical Review*, 84 (1979), 970–92.

Wilson, Theodore B. *The Black Codes of the South*. Tuscaloosa: University of Alabama Press, 1965.

Woodman, Harold D. *King Cotton and His Retainers: Financing and Marketing the Cotton Crop of the South, 1800–1925.* Lexington: University of Kentucky Press, 1968.

———. "Post Civil War Agriculture and the Law," *Agricultural History,* 53 (1979), 319–37.

Woodward, C. Vann. "Reconstruction: A Counterfactual Playback," in Woodward, *The Future of the Past.* New York: Oxford University Press, 1989, 183–200.

Wynne, Lewis N. "The Role of Freedmen in the Post Bellum Cotton Economy of Georgia," *Phylon,* 42 (1981), 309–21.

DISFRANCHISEMENT, POLITICAL, WHITE AND BLACK, OR THE SECOND MISSISSIPPI PLAN

Argersinger, Peter H. "The Southern Search for Order," *Reviews in American History,* 3 (1975), 236–41.

Calhoun, Charles W. *Conceiving a New Republic: The Republican Party and the Southern Question, 1869–1900.* Lawrence: University of Kansas Press, 2006.

Eaton, Clement. *The Waning of the Old South Civilization.* Athens: University of Georgia, 1968.

Edwards, Laura F. "Status without Rights: African Americans and the Tangled Law of Governance in the Nineteenth Century U.S. South," *American Historical Review,* 112 (2007), 265–393.

Foster, Gaines M. *Ghosts of the Confederacy: Defeat, the Lost Cause, and the Emergence of the New South, 1865 to 1913.* New York: Oxford University Press, 1987.

Fredman, L. E. *The Australian Ballot: The Story of an American Reform.* Lansing: Michigan State University Press, 1969.

Hair, William Ivy. *Bourbonism and Agrarian Protest: Louisiana Politics, 1877–1900.* Baton Rouge: Louisiana State University, 1969.

Holmes, William F. "The Leflore County Massacre and the Demise of the Colored Farmer's Alliance," *Phylon,* 4 (1973), 267–74.

Jones, Robert R. "James L. Kemper and the Virginia Redeemers Face the Race Question: A Reconsideration," *Journal of Southern History,* 38 (1972), 393–414.

Key, V. O., Jr. *Southern Politics in State and Nation.* New York: Knopf, 1949.

Kirby, Jack Temple. *Darkness at the Dawning: Race and Reform in the Progressive Era.* Philadelphia: J. B. Lippincott, 1972.

Kousser, J. Morgan. "Ecological Regression and the Analysis of Past Politics," *Journal of Interdisciplinary History,* 4 (1973), 237–62.

———. *The Shaping of Southern Politics: Suffrage Restrictions and the Establishment of the One-Party South, 1880–1910.* New Haven, Conn.: Yale University Press, 1974.

Lewinson, Paul. *Race, Class, and Party: A History of Negro Suffrage and White Politics in the South.* New York: Grosset & Dunlap, 1965.

Mabry, William Alexander. "Disfranchisement of the Negro in Mississippi," *Journal of Southern History*, 4 (1938), 318–33.

Moore, James T. "Black Militancy in Readjuster Virginia, 1879–1883," *Journal of Southern History*, 41 (1975), 167–86.

Osterweis, Rollin G. *The Myth of the Lost Cause, 1865–1900*. Hamden, Conn.: Archon Books, 1973.

Potter, David M. *The South and the Concurrent Majority*. Baton Rouge: Louisiana State University Press, 1972.

Russ, William A., Jr. "Disfranchisement in Louisiana (1862–1870)," *Louisiana Historical Quarterly*, 18 (1935), 557–80.

———. "The Negro and White Disfranchisement During Radical Reconstruction," *Journal of Negro History*, 19 (1934), 171–92.

———. "Radical Disfranchisement in Texas, 1867–1870," *Southwestern Historical Quarterly*, 38 (1934–1935), 40–52.

———. "Registration and Disfranchisement under Radical Reconstruction," *Mississippi Valley Historical Review*, 21 (1935), 163–80.

Simkins, Francis B. *Pitchfork Ben Tillman: South Carolinian*. Baton Rouge: Louisiana State University Press, 1944.

Tindall, George Brown. *The Disruption of the Solid South*. Athens: University of Georgia Press, 1972.

Welch, Richard E., Jr. "The Federal Elections Bill of 1890: Postscripts and Prelude," *Journal of American History*, 52 (1965), 511–26.

Williams, Frank B. "The Poll Tax as a Suffrage Requirement in the South, 1870–1901," *Journal of Southern History*, 18 (1952), 469–96.

Wood, Forrest G. "On Revising Reconstruction History: Negro Suffrage, White Disfranchisement, and Common Sense," *Journal of Negro History*, 51 (1966), 98–113.

Woodward, C. Vann. *Origins of the New South*. Baton Rouge: Louisiana State University Press, 1951.

———. *The Strange Career of Jim Crow*. 2nd ed. New York: Oxford University Press, 1966.

———. *Tom Watson: Agrarian Rebel*. New York: Oxford University Press, 1938.

DISSENT IN THE NORTH—CONSCRIPTION AND RIOTS

Bernstein, Iver. *The New York City Draft Riots: Their Significance for American Society and Politics in the Age of the Civil War*. New York: Oxford University Press, 1990.

Coleman, Charles H., and Paul H. Spence. "The Charleston Riot, March 28, 1864," Illinois State Historical Society, *Journal*, 33 (1940), 7–56.

Cook, Adrian. *The Armies of the Streets: The New York City Draft Riots of 1863*. Lexington: University of Kentucky Press, 1974.

Earnhart, Hugh. "Commutation: Democratic or Undemocratic?" *Civil War History*, 12 (1966), 132–42.

Fried, Joseph P. "The Story of the New York Draft Riots," 4 (May 1965), 4–10, 28–31.

Geary, James W. "Civil War Conscription in the North: A Historiographical View," *Civil War History*, 32 (1986), 208–28.

———. *We Need Men: The Union Draft in the Civil War*. DeKalb: Northern Illinois University Press, 1991.

Haines, J. D. (ed.). "Eyewitness to History: New York City Draft Riots," *America's Civil War*, 13 (May 2000), 66–72.

Hallock, Judith. "The Role of Community in Civil War Desertion," *Civil War History*, 29 (1983), 123–34.

Hanna, William F. "The Boston Draft Riot," *Civil War History*, 36 (1990), 262–73.

Harstad, Peter T. "Draft Dodgers and Bounty Jumpers," *Civil War Times Illustrated*, 6 (May 1967), 28–36.

Kawa, Adam J. "No Draft!" *Civil War Times Illustrated*, 37 (June 1998), 54–60.

Levine, Peter. "Draft Evasion in the North during the Civil War, 1863–1865," *Journal of American History*, 67 (1981), 816–34.

McKay, Ernest A. *The Civil War and New York City*. Syracuse: Syracuse University Press, 1990.

McPherson, James M. (ed.). *Anti-Negro Riots in the North, 1863*. New York: Arno Press, 1969.

Murdock, Eugene C. "Horatio Seymour and the 1863 Draft," *Civil War History*, 11 (1965), 117–41.

———. *One Million Men: The Civil War Draft in the North*. Westport, Conn.: Greenwood, 1980, repr.

———. "Was It a Poor Man's Fight?" *Civil War History*, 10 (1964), 241–45.

Palladine, Grace. *Another Civil War: Labor, Capital, and the State in the Anthracite Regions of Pennsylvania, 1840–1868*. Urbana: University of Illinois Press, 1990.

Pleasants, Samuel A. *Fernando Wood of New York*. New York: Columbia University Press, 1948.

Schneider, John C. "Detroit and the Problem of Disorder: The Riot of 1863," *Michigan History*, 38 (1974), 4–24.

Shelden, Rachel A. "Measures for a 'Speedy Conclusion': A Reexamination of Conscription and Civil War Federalism," *Civil War History*, 55 (2009), 469–498.

DISSENT IN THE NORTH—COPPERHEADS

Abzug, Robert H. "The Copperheads and Civil War Dissent," *Indiana Magazine of History*, 66 (1970), 40–55.

Curry, Richard O. "Copperheadism and Ideological Continuity: Anatomy of a Stereotype," *Journal of Negro History*, 57 (1972), 29–36.

———. *A House Divided: A Study of Statehood Politics and the Copperhead Movement in West Virginia*. Pittsburgh: University of Pittsburgh Press, 1964.

————. "The Union as It Was: A Critique of Recent Interpretations of the Copperheads," *Civil War History*, 13 (1967), 25–39.

Fesler, Mayo. "Secret Societies in the North during the Civil War," *Indiana Magazine of History*, 14 (1918), 183–286.

George, Joseph, Jr. "'Abraham Africanus I': President Lincoln through the Eyes of a Copperhead Editor," *Civil War History*, 14 (September 1968), 226–41.

Headly, John W. *Confederate Operations in Canada and New York*. New York: Time-Life Books, 1984.

Klien, Frederic S. "The Great Copperhead Conspiracy of 1864," *Civil War Times Illustrated*, 4 (June 1965), 21–26.

Klement Frank L. *The Copperheads in the Middle West*. Chicago: University of Chicago Press, 1960.

————. *Dark Lanterns: Secret Political Societies, Conspiracies, and Treason Trials in the Civil War*. Baton Rouge: Louisiana State University Press, 1984.

Lendt, David L. *Demise of Democracy: The Copperhead Press in Iowa, 1856–1870*. Ames: Iowa State University Press, 1973.

Milton, George Fort. *Abraham Lincoln and the Fifth Column*. New York: Vanguard, 1942.

Neely, Mark E., Jr. "Treason in Indiana: A Review Essay." *Lincoln Lore* (February and March 1974), 1–4, 1–3.

Tidwell, William A. *April '65: Confederate Covert Action in the American Civil War*. Kent, Ohio: Kent State University Press, 1995.

————, with James O. Hall and David Winfred Gaddy. *Come Retribution: The Confederate Secret Service and the Assassination of Lincoln*. Jackson: University of Mississippi Press, 1988.

Werthiem, Lewis J. "The Indianapolis Treason Trials, the Elections of 1864, and the Power of the Partisan Press," *Indiana Magazine of History*, 85 (1989), 236–60.

Wubben, Hubert H. *Civil War Iowa and the Copperhead Movement*. Ames: Iowa State University Press, 1980.

DISSENT IN THE NORTH—SUSPENSION OF CIVIL LIBERTIES

Belz, Herman. *Lincoln and the Constitution: The Dictatorship Question Reconsidered*. Ft. Wayne, Ind.: Louis A. Warren Lincoln Library and Museum, 1984.

Klement, Frank L. *Dark Lanterns: Secret Political Societies, Conspiracies, and Treason Trials in the Civil War*. Baton Rouge: Louisiana State University Press, 1984.

Neely, Mark E., Jr. *The Fate of Liberty: Abraham Lincoln and Civil Liberties*. New York: Oxford University Press, 1991.

Towne, Stephen E. "Killing the Serpent Speedily: Governor Morton, General Hascall, and the Suppression of the Democratic Press in Indiana, 1863," *Civil War History*, 52 (2006), 41–65.

Williams, Frank J. "Civil Liberties v. National Security: The Long Shadow of the Civil War," *Civil War Times Illustrated*, 46 (June 2007), 24–29.

DISSENT IN THE NORTH—VALLANDIGHAM AND MILLIGAN CASES

Klement, Frank. *The Limits of Dissent: Clement Vallandigham and the Civil War.* Lexington: University of Kentucky Press, 1970.
Neely, Mark E., Jr. "Treason in Indiana: A Review Essay." *Lincoln Lore* (February and March 1974), 1–4, 1–3.
Shankman, Arnold. "Soldier Votes and Clement L. Vallandigham in the 1863 Gubernatorial Election," *Ohio History*, 82 (1973), 88–104.

DISSENT IN THE NORTH—WAR RESISTANCE

Belz, Herman. *Lincoln and the Constitution: The Dictatorship Question Reconsidered.* Ft. Wayne, Ind.: Louis A. Warren Lincoln Library and Museum, 1984.
Fesler, Mayo. "Secret Societies in the North during the Civil War," *Indiana Magazine of History*, 14 (1918), 183–286.
Frederickson, George. *The Inner Civil War: Northern Intellectuals and the Crisis of the Union.* New York: Harper & Row, 1965.
Freidel, Frank (ed.). *Union Pamphlets of the Civil War, 1861–1865.* 2 vols. Cambridge, Mass.: Harvard University Press, 1967.
Gallman, J. Matthew. *The North Fights the War: The Home Front.* Chicago: Ivan Dee, 1994.
———. "Preserving the Peace: Order and Disorder in Civil War Philadelphia," *Pennsylvania History*, 55 (1988), 201–28.
Klement, Frank L. *Dark Lanterns: Secret Political Societies, Conspiracies, and Treason Trials in the Civil War.* Baton Rouge: Louisiana State University Press, 1984.
McKitrick, Eric L. "Party Politics and the Union and Confederate War Efforts," in William N. Chambers and Walter D. Burnham (eds.), *The American Party Systems: Stages of Development.* New York: Oxford University Press, 1967, 117–51.
Neely, Mark E., Jr., *The Fate of Liberty: Abraham Lincoln and Civil Liberties.* New York: Oxford University Press, 1991.
Shankman, Arnold. *The Anti-War Movement in Pennsylvania, 1861–1865.* Rutherford, N.J.: Fairleigh Dickinson University Press, 1980.
Stanchak, John (ed.). "Dissent: Fire in the Rear," *Civil War Times Illustrated*, 20 (December 1981), [Special Issue].

DOCTORS' LINE, THE

Richter, William L. *The Last Confederate Heroes: The Final Struggle for Southern Independence & the Assassination of Abraham Lincoln.* 2 vols. 2nd rev. ed. Edited with introduction by J. E. "Rick" Smith III. Laurel, Md.: Burgundy Press, 2008.

Smith, Joseph E. "Rick," with William L. Richter. *In the Shadows of the Lincoln Assassination: The Life of Confederate Spy Thomas H. Harbin.* Laurel, Md.: Burgundy, 2007.

Tidwell, William A., James O. Hall, and David W. Gaddy. *Come Retribution: The Confederate Secret Service and the Assassination of Lincoln.* Jackson: University Press of Mississippi, 1988.

DOUGLAS, STEPHEN A. (1813–1861)

Archampeau, Philip G. "The Douglas-Buchanan Feud," Illinois State Historical Society, *Journal*, 25 (1932), 5–48.

Baker, Jean H. *Affairs of Party: The Political Culture of Northern Democrats in the Mid-Nineteenth Century.* Ithaca, N.Y.: Cornell University Press, 1983.

Bestor, Arthur. "State Sovereignty and Slavery: A Reinterpretation of Proslavery Constitutional Doctrine, 1846–1860," Illinois State Historical Society, *Journal*, 53 (1960), 117–80.

Harmon, George D. "Douglas and the Compromise of 1850," Illinois State Historical Society, *Journal*, 21 (1929), 477–79.

Holt, Michael F. *Political Parties and American Political Development from the Age of Jackson to the Age of Lincoln.* Baton Rouge: Louisiana State University Press, 1992.

Johannsen, Robert W. *Stephen A. Douglas.* New York: Oxford University Press, 1973.

———. "Stephen A. Douglas, 'Harper's Magazine,' and Popular Sovereignty," *Mississippi Valley Historical Review*, 45 (1959), 606–31.

Johnson, Allen. *Stephen A. Douglas: A Study in American Politics.* New York: Macmillan, 1908.

Milton, George Fort. *Eve of Conflict: Stephen A. Douglas and the Needless War.* Boston: Houghton Mifflin, 1934.

Nichols, Roy F. *The Democratic Machine, 1850–1854.* New York: Columbia University Press, 1923.

———. *The Disruption of the American Democracy.* New York: Macmillan, 1948.

DUBUCLET, ANTOINE (1810–1887)

Vincent, Charles. "Aspects of the Family and Public Life of Antoine Dubuclet: Louisiana's Black State Treasurer, 1868–1878," *Journal of Negro History*, 66 (1981), 26–36.

DUNN, OSCAR J. (CA. 1820–1871)

Christian, Marcus B. "The Theory of the Poisoning of Oscar J. Dunn," *Phylon*, 6 (1945), 254–66.

Perkins, Archie E. "Oscar James Dunn," *Phylon*, 4 (1943), 105–21.

Vincent, Charles. *Black Legislators in Louisiana during Reconstruction*. Baton Rouge: Louisiana State University Press, 1976.

EARLY, JUBAL ANDERSON (1816–1894)

Current, Richard N. (ed.). *Encyclopedia of the Confederacy*. 4 vols. New York: Simon & Schuster, 1993.

Davis, William C. (ed.). *The Confederate General*. 6 vols. N.p.: National Historical Society, 1991.

———. "'Jubilee': General Jubal A. Early," *Civil War Times Illustrated*, (December 1970), 4–11, 43–48.

Freeman, Douglas Southall. *Lee's Lieutenants: A Study of Command*. 3 vols. New York: Charles Scribner's Sons, 1942–1944.

Warner, Ezra J. *Generals in Gray: Lives of Confederate Commanders*. Baton Rouge: Louisiana State University Press, 1959.

EATON, JOHN (1829–1906)

Bigelow, Martha Mitchell. "Freedmen of the Mississippi Valley, 1862–1865," *Civil War History*, 8 (1962), 38–47.

Eaton, John. *Grant, Lincoln, and the Freedmen*. New York: Negro Universities Press, 1969, repr.

Gerteis, Louis S. *From Contraband to Freedman: Federal Policy Toward Southern Blacks, 1861–1865*. Westport, Conn.: Greenwood Press, 1973.

Ross, Stephen Joseph. "Freed Soil, Freed Labor, Freed Men: John Eaton and the Davis Bend Experiment," *Journal of Southern History*, 44 (1978), 213–32.

Wiley, Bell I. "Vicissitudes of Early Reconstruction Farming in the Lower Mississippi Valley," *Journal of Southern History*, 3 (1937), 441–52.

Williams, Frank B. "John Eaton, Jr., Editor, Politician, and School Administrator, 1865–1870," *Tennessee Historical Quarterly*, 10 (1951), 291–319.

ELECTION OF 1848 AND SQUATTER SOVEREIGNTY

Berwanger Eugene H. *The Frontier against Slavery: Western Anti-Negro Prejudice and the Slavery Extension Controversy.* Urbana: University of Illinois Press, 1967.

Brauer, Kinley. *Cotton versus Conscience: Massachusetts Whig Politics and Southwestern Expansion, 1843–1848.* Lexington: University of Kentucky Press, 1967.

Brown, Thomas. *Politics and Statesmanship: Essays on the American Whig Party.* New York: Columbia University Press, 1985.

Hamilton, Holman. *Zachary Taylor.* Indianapolis: Bobbs-Merrill, 1951.

Holt, Michael F. *Political Parties and American Political Development from the Age of Jackson to the Age of Lincoln.* Baton Rouge: Louisiana State University Press, 1992.

Howe, Daniel W. *The Political Culture of American Whigs.* Chicago: University of Chicago Press, 1979.

Johannsen, Robert W. *Stephen A. Douglas.* New York: Oxford University Press, 1973.

Johnson, Allen. *Stephen A. Douglas: A Study in American Politics.* New York: Macmillan, 1908.

Klunder, Willard Carl. *Lewis Cass and the Politics of Moderation.* Kent, Ohio: Kent State University Press, 1996.

McKinley, Silas Bent. *Old Rough and Ready: The Life and Times of Zachary Taylor.* New York: Vanguard Press, 1946.

McLaughlin, Andrew Cunningham. *Lewis Cass.* New York: AMS Press, 1972.

Morrison, Chaplain. *Democratic Politics and Sectionalism: The Wilmot Proviso Controversy.* Chapel Hill: University of North Carolina Press, 1967.

Potter, David. *The Impending Crisis, 1848–1861.* New York: Harper & Row, 1976.

Rayback, Joseph G. *Free Soil: The Election of 1848.* Lexington: University of Kentucky Press, 1970.

Sewell, Richard. *Ballots for Freedom: Antislavery Politics in the United States, 1837–1860.* New York: Oxford University Press, 1976.

Volpe, Vernon. *Forlorn Hope of Freedom: The Liberty Party in the Old Northwest.* Kent: Kent State University Press, 1990.

Wofford, Frank B. *Lewis Cass: The Last Jeffersonian.* rev. ed. New York: Octagon Books, 1973.

ELECTION OF 1852 AND FRANKLIN PIERCE

Elliott, Charles Winslow. *Winfield Scott: The Soldier and the Man.* New York: Macmillan, 1937.

Gara, Larry. *The Presidency of Franklin Pierce.* Lawrence: University Press of Kansas, 1991.

Howe, Daniel W. *The Political Culture of American Whigs*. Chicago: University of Chicago Press, 1979.

Johannsen, Robert W. *Stephen A. Douglas*. New York: Oxford University Press, 1973.

Johnson, Allen. *Stephen A. Douglas: A Study in American Politics*. New York: Macmillan, 1908.

Johnson, Timothy D. *Winfield Scott: The Quest for Military Glory*. Lawrence: University Press of Kansas, 1998.

Nichols, Roy F. *The Democratic Machine, 1850–1854*. New York: Columbia University Press, 1923.

———. *Franklin Pierce: Young Hickory of the Granite Hills*. Philadelphia: University of Pennsylvania, 1931.

Porter, Kirk Harold, and Donald Bruce Johnson. *National Party Platforms, 1840–1964*. Urbana: University of Illinois Press, 1966.

ELECTION OF 1856 AND THE ORGANIZATION OF THE REPUBLICAN PARTY

Anbinde, Tyler. *Nativism and Slavery: The Northern Know Nothings and the Politics of the 1850s*. New York: Oxford University Press, 1992.

Baker, Jean H. *Affairs of Party: The Political Culture of Northern Democrats in the Mid-Nineteenth Century*. Ithaca, N.Y.: Cornell University Press, 1983.

Blue, Frederick J. *The Free Soilers: Third Party Politics, 1848–1854*. Urbana: University of Illinois Press, 1973.

Brown, Thomas. *Politics and Statesmanship: Essays on the American Whig Party*. New York: Columbia University Press, 1985.

Foner, Eric. *Free Soil, Free Labor, Free Men: The Ideology of the Republican Party before the Civil War*. New York: Oxford University Press, 1970.

Gienapp, William E. *The Origins of the Republican Party, 1852–1860*. New York: Oxford University Press, 1987.

Hesseltine, William B., and Rex G. Fisher (eds.). *Trimmers, Trucklers, & Temporizers: Notes of Murat Halstead from the Political Convention of 1856*. Madison: University of Wisconsin Press, 1961.

Holt, Michael F. *Forging a Majority: The Formation of the Republican Party in Pittsburgh, 1848–1860*. Pittsburgh: University of Pittsburgh Press, 1990, repr.

———. *Political Parties and American Political Development from the Age of Jackson to the Age of Lincoln*. Baton Rouge: Louisiana State University Press, 1992.

———. "The Politics of Impatience: The Origins of Know Nothingism," *Journal of American History*, 60 (1973), 309–31.

Howe, Daniel W. *The Political Culture of American Whigs*. Chicago: University of Chicago Press, 1979.

Johannsen, Robert W. *Stephen A. Douglas*. New York: Oxford University Press, 1973.

Johnson, Allen. *Stephen A. Douglas: A Study in American Politics*. New York: Macmillan, 1908).

Meerse, David E. "James Buchanan, the Patronage, and the Northern Democratic Party, 1857–1858." Ph.D. dissertation, University of Illinois, 1969.

Milton, George Fort. "Indiana in the Douglas-Buchanan Contest of 1856," *Indiana Magazine of History*, 30 (1934), 119–32.

Mulkern, John R. *The Know Nothing Party in Massachusetts: The Rise and Fall of a Peoples' Movement*. Boston: Northeastern University Press, 1990.

Nicholls, Roy F. *The Disruption of the American Democracy*. New York: Macmillan, 1848.

Porter, Kirk Harold, and Donald Bruce Johnson. *National Party Platforms, 1840–1964*. Urbana: University of Illinois Press, 1966.

Sewell, Richard. *Ballots for Freedom: Antislavery Politics in the United States, 1837–1860*. New York: Oxford University Press, 1976.

ELECTION OF 1860

Auer, J. Jeffry (ed.). *Antislavery and Disunion, 1857–1861: Studies in Rhetoric of Compromise and Conflict*. New York: Harper & Row, 1963.

Baker, Jean H. *Affairs of Party: The Political Culture of Northern Democrats in the Mid-Nineteenth Century*. Ithaca, N.Y.: Cornell University Press, 1983.

Crenshaw, Ollinger. "The Speakership Contest of 1859–1860," *Mississippi Valley Historical Review*, 29 (1942), 323–38.

Gienapp, William E. "Nativism and the Creation of the Republican Majority before the Civil War," *Journal of American History*, 72 (1985), 529–59.

Graebner, Norman A. (ed.). *Politics and the Crisis of 1860*. Urbana: University of Illinois Press, 1961.

Hentig, Gerald S. "Henry Winter Davis and the Speakership Contest of 1859–1860," *Maryland Historical Magazine*, 68 (1973), 1–19.

Hesseltine, William B. (ed.). *Three Against Lincoln: Murat Halstead and the Caucuses of 1860*. Baton Rouge: Louisiana State University Press, 1960.

Hicken, Victor. "John A. McClernand and the House Speakership Struggle of 1859," Illinois State Historical Society, *Journal*, 53 (1960), 163–78.

Holt, Michael F. *Political Parties and American Political Development from the Age of Jackson to the Age of Lincoln*. Baton Rouge: Louisiana State University Press, 1992.

Johannsen, Robert W. *Stephen A. Douglas*. New York: Oxford University Press, 1973.

Johnson, Allen. *Stephen A. Douglas: A Study in American Politics*. New York: Macmillan, 1908.

Milton, George Fort. *Eve of Conflict: Stephen A. Douglas and the Needless War*. Boston: Houghton Mifflin, 1934.

Nagel, Paul C. *One Nation Indivisible: The Union in American Thought, 1776–1861*. New York: Oxford University Press, 1964.

Nicholls, Roy F. *The Disruption of the American Democracy*. New York: Macmillan, 1848.

Porter, Kirk Harold, and Donald Bruce Johnson. *National Party Platforms, 1840–1964*. Urbana: University of Illinois Press, 1966.

Potter, David. *The Impending Crisis, 1848–1861*. New York: Harper & Row, 1976.

Sewell, Richard. *Ballots for Freedom: Antislavery Politics in the United States, 1837–1860*. New York: Oxford University Press, 1976.

Stampp, Kenneth M. *The Imperiled Union: Essays on the Background of the Civil War*. New York: Oxford University Press, 1980.

ELECTION OF 1868

Carpenter, John A. *Ulysses S. Grant*. New York: Twayne Publishers, 1970.

Coleman, Charles H. *The Election of 1868: The Democratic Effort to Regain Control*. New York: Columbia University Press, 1933.

Hesseltine, William B. *U. S. Grant: Politician*. New York: Dodd, Mead & Co., 1935.

Logan, Rayford W. *The Betrayal of the Negro: From Rutherford B. Hayes to Woodrow Wilson*. New York: Collier Books, 1965.

McFeely, William S. *Grant: A Biography*. New York: W. W. Norton, 1981.

Richter, William L. "The Papers of U. S. Grant: A Review Essay," *Civil War History*, 36 (1990), 149–66; 38 (1992), 342–48; and 42 (1996), 80–84.

Simpson, Brooks D. *Let Us Have Peace: Ulysses S. Grant and the Politics of War and Reconstruction*. Chapel Hill: University of North Caroline Press, 1991.

ELECTION OF 1872

Carpenter, John A. *Ulysses S. Grant*. New York: Twayne Publishers, 1970.

Downey, Matthew T. "Horace Greeley and the Politicians: The Liberal Republican Convention in 1872," *Journal of American History*, 53 (1966–1967), 727–50.

Hesseltine, William B. *U. S. Grant: Politician*. New York: Dodd, Mead & Co., 1935.

Josephson, Matthew. *The Politicos, 1865–1896*. New York: Harcourt Brace & World, 1938.

———. *The Robber Barons: The Great American Capitalists*. New York: Harcourt, Brace, 1934.

McFeely, William S. *Grant: A Biography*. New York: W. W. Norton, 1981.

McPherson, James M. "Grant or Greeley? The Abolitionist Dilemma in the Election of 1872," *American Historical Review*, 71 (1965–1966), 43–61.

Riddleberger, Patrick W. "The Break in the Radical Ranks: Liberals vs. Stalwarts in the Election of 1872," *Journal of Negro History*, 44 (1959), 136–57.

Simpson, Brooks D. *Let Us Have Peace: Ulysses S. Grant and the Politics of War and Reconstruction.* Chapel Hill: University of North Carolina Press, 1991.

Summers, Mark W. *The Era of Good Stealings.* New York: Oxford University Press, 1993.

ELECTION OF 1876 AND COMPROMISE OF 1877

Benedict, Michael Les. "Southern Democrats and the Crisis of 1876–1877: A Reconsideration of *Reunion and Reaction*," *Journal of Southern History*, 46 (1980), 489–524.

DeSantis, Vincent P. "Rutherford B. Hayes and the Removal of the Troops and the End of Reconstruction," in J. Morgan Kousser and James M. McPherson (eds.), *Region, Race, and Reconstruction: Essays in Honor of C. Vann Woodward.* New York: Oxford University Press, 1982, 417–50.

Fairman, Charles. *Five Justices and the Electoral Commission of 1877.* New York: Macmillan Company, 1988.

Harris, Carl V. "Right Fork or Left Fork? The Section-Party Alignments of Southern Democrats in Congress, 1873–1897," *Journal of Southern History*, 42 (1976), 471–506.

Haworth, Paul L. *The Hayes-Tilden Disputed Presidential Election of 1876.* Cleveland, Ohio: Arthur H. Clark Co., 1906.

House, Albert V. "The Speakership Contest of 1875: Democratic Response to Power," *Journal of American History*, 52 (1965), 252–74.

Peskin, Allan. "Was There a Compromise in 1877?" *Journal of American History*, 60 (1973), 63–75.

Polakoff, Keith Ian. *The Politics of Inertia: The Election of 1876 and the End of Reconstruction.* Baton Rouge: Louisiana State University Press, 1973.

Pomerantz, Sidney I. "Election of 1876," in Arthur M. Schleinger, Jr., and Fred L. Israel (eds.), *History of American Presidential Elections, 1789–1968.* 4 vols. New York: Chelsea House, 1971, II, 1379–1435.

Rable, George C. "Southern Interests and the Election of 1876: A Reappraisal," *Civil War History*, 26 (1980), 347–61.

Shofner, Jerrell H. "Fraud and Intimidation in the Florida Election of 1876," *Florida Historical Quarterly*, 42 (1964), 321–30.

Simkins, Francis Butler. "The Election of 1876 in South Carolina," *South Atlantic Quarterly*, 21 (1922), 225–40, 335–51.

Tunnell, Ted. "The Negro, the Republican Party, and the Election of 1876 in Louisiana," *Louisiana History*, 7 (1966), 101–16.

Williams, T. Harry. *Hayes of the Twenty-Third: The Life of a Volunteer Officer.* New York: Alfred A. Knopf, 1965.

Woodward, C. Vann. *Origins of the New South, 1877–1913.* Baton Rouge: Louisiana State University Press, 1951.

————. *Reunion and Reaction: The Compromise of 1877 and the End of Reconstruction*. Boston: Little, Brown and Company, 1951.

————. "Yes, There Was a Compromise of 1877," *Journal of American History*, 60 (1973), 215–19.

Zuczek, Richard. "The Last Campaign of the Civil War: South Carolina and the Revolution of 1876," *Civil War History*, 42 (1996), 18–31.

EMANCIPATION IN GENERAL

Belz, Herman. *Emancipation and Equal Rights: Politics and Constitutionalism in the Civil War Era*. New York: W. W. Norton, 1978.

————. *A New Birth of Freedom: The Republican Party and Freedmen's Rights, 1861–1866*. Westport, Conn.: Greenwood Press, 1976.

————. *Reconstructing the Union: Theory and Practice during the Civil War*. Ithaca, N.Y.: Cornell University Press, 1969.

Bennett, Lerone, Jr. *Forced into Glory: Abraham Lincoln's White Dream*. Chicago: Johnson Publishing, 2000.

————. "Was Abe Lincoln a White Supremacist?" *Ebony*, 23 (1968), 35–38, 40, 42.

Berlin, Ira. "Emancipation and Its Meaning in American Life," *Reconstruction*, 2 (No. 3, 1994), 41–44.

Blackiston, Harry S. "Lincoln's Emancipation Plan," *Journal of Negro History*, 7 (1922), 257–77.

Bridges, Robert. "Equality Deferred: Civil Rights for Illinois Blacks, 1865–1885," Illinois State Historical Society, *Journal*, 74 (1981), 82–108.

Brink, Dean C. "What Did Freedom Mean? The Aftermath of Slavery as Seen by Former Slaves and Former Masters in Three Societies," *OAH Magazine of History*, 4 (Winter 1989), 31–46.

Current, Richard N. *The Lincoln Nobody Knows*. New York: McGraw Hill Book Co., 1958.

Eberstadt, Charles. "Lincoln's Emancipation Proclamation," *The New Colophon*, 3 (1950), 312–55.

Fehrenbacher, Don E. "Only His Stepchildren: Lincoln and the Negro," *Civil War History*, 20 (1974), 293–310.

Foner, Eric. *Nothing But Freedom: Emancipation and Its Legacy*. Baton Rouge: Louisiana State University Press, 1983.

————. *Reconstruction: America's Unfinished Revolution, 1863–1877*. New York: Harper & Row, 1988.

Franklin, John Hope. *The Emancipation Proclamation*. Garden City, N.Y.: Doubleday & Co., 1963.

Frederickson, George M. "A Man But Not a Brother: Abraham Lincoln and Racial Equality," *Journal of Southern History*, 41 (1975), 39–58.

Guelzo, Allen C. "'Not One Word Will I Recall' [Emancipation Proclamation]," *North & South*, 7 (March 2004), 74–82.

Harris, William C. "After the Emancipation Proclamation," *North & South*, 5 (December 2001), 42–53.

Hesseltine, William B. "Lincoln and the Politicians, *Civil War History*, 6 (1960), 43–55.

———. *Lincoln's Plan of Reconstruction*. Tuscaloosa, Ala.: Confederate Publishing Company, 1960.

Heckman, Richard A. "British Press Reaction to the Emancipation Proclamation," *Lincoln Herald*, 71 (Winter 1969), 150–53.

Johannsen, Robert W. *Lincoln, the South, and Slavery: The Political Dimension*. Baton Rouge: Louisiana State University Press, 1991.

Klement, Frank L. "Midwestern Opposition to Lincoln's Emancipation Policy," *Journal of Negro History*, 49 (1964), 169–83.

Kitrell, Irvin, III. "40 Acres and a Mule: [Sherman's Special Field Orders, No. 15, 16 January 1865]," *Civil War Times Illustrated*, 41 (May 2002), 54–61.

Lucie, Patricia M. L. "Confiscation: Constitutional Crossroads," *Civil War History*, 23 (1977), 307–21.

Lee, Bill R. "Missouri's Fight over Emancipation in 1863," *Missouri Historical Review*, 45 (1951), 256–74.

McPherson, James M. *Abraham Lincoln and the Second American Revolution*. New York: Oxford University Press, 1990.

———. "Who Freed the Slaves?" *Reconstruction*, 2 (No. 3, 1994), 35–40.

Mitgang, Herbert. "Was Lincoln Just a Honkie?" *New York Times Magazine*, February 11, 1968, 34–35, 100–107.

Noyes, Edward. "White Opposition to Black Migration into Civil-War Wisconsin," *Lincoln Herald*, 73 (1971), 181–91.

Oates, Stephen B. *Abraham Lincoln: The Man Behind the Myths*. New York: Harper & Row, 1984.

———. "'The Man of Our Redemption': Abraham Lincoln and the Emancipation of the Slaves," *Presidential Studies Quarterly*, 9 (Winter 1979), 15–25.

Olsen, Otto H. "Abraham Lincoln as Revolutionary," *Civil War History*, 24 (1978), 213–24.

Quarles, Benjamin. *Lincoln and the Negro*. New York: Oxford University Press, 1962.

Randall, James G. *Lincoln the President*. 4 vols. New York: Dodd, Mead & Co., 1945–1955.

Roy, Caesar A. "Was Lincoln the Great Emancipator?" *Civil War Times Illustrated*, 33 (May 1994), 46–49.

Schwalm, Leslie A. "'Overrun with Free Negroes': Emancipation and Wartime Migration in the Upper Midwest," *Civil War History*, 50 (2004), 145–74.

Soodalter, Ron. "Hanging Captain Gordon [the Only American Sent to the Gallows for Slave Trading]," *Civil War Times Illustrated*, 48 (August. 2009), 46–53.

Strickland, Avrah E. "The Illinois Background of Lincoln's Attitude Toward Slavery and the Negro," Illinois States Historical Society, *Journal*, 56 (1963), 474–94.

Striner, Richard. *Father Abraham: Lincoln's Relentless Struggle to End Slavery.* New York: Oxford University Press, 2006.

Stutler, Boyd B. "Abraham Lincoln and John Brown—A Parallel," *Civil War History*, 8 (1962), 290–99.

Trefousse, Hans L. *Lincoln's Decision for Emancipation.* Philadelphia: J. B. Lippincott Co., 1975.

Wagant, Charles. "Election by Sword and Ballot: The Emancipation Victory of 1963," *Maryland Historical Magazine*, 59 (1964), 143–64.

Wiley, Bell I. "Slavery in the Civil War," *Civil War Times Illustrated*, 9 (April 1970), 36–42.

Wubben, Hubert H. "The Uncertain Trumpet: Iowa Republicans and Black Suffrage, 1860–1868," *Annals of Iowa*, 47 (1984), 409–29.

Zilversmit, Arthur (ed.). *Lincoln on Black and White: A Documentary History.* Belmont, Calif.: Wadsworth Publishing Company, 1971.

EMANCIPATION, COLONIZATION
OF AFRICAN-AMERICANS OVERSEAS

Boritt, Gabor S. "The Voyage to the Colony of Lincolniana: The Sixteenth President, Black Colonization, and the Defense Mechanism of Avoidance," *Historian*, 37 (1975), 619–32.

Gallagher, Gary. "The A'Vache Tragedy," *Civil War Times Illustrated*, 18 (February 1980), 4–10.

Gold, Robert L. "Negro Colonization Schemes in Ecuador, 1861–1864," *Phylon*, 30 (1969), 306–16.

Lockett, James D. "Abraham Lincoln and Colonization: An Episode that Ends in Tragedy at L'Ile à Vache, Haiti, 1863–1864," *Journal of Black Studies*, 21 (1991), 428–44.

Neely, Mark E., Jr. "Abraham Lincoln and Black Colonization: Benjamin Butler's Spurious Testimony," *Civil War History*, 25 (1979), 77–83.

Stadenraus, P. J. *The African Colonization Movement, 1816–1865.* New York: Columbia University Press, 1961.

Wesley, Charles H. "Lincoln's Plan for Colonizing the Emancipated Negroes," *Journal of Negro History*, 4 (1919), 7–21.

EMANCIPATION, COMPENSATED

Fishel, Leslie H., Jr. "Repercussions of Reconstruction: The Northern Negro, 1870–1883," *Civil War History*, 14 (1968), 325–45.

Fladeland, Betty L. "Compensated Emancipation: A Rejected Alternative," *Journal of Southern History*, 42 (1976), 169–86.

Litwack, Leon F. *Been in the Storm So Long: The Aftermath of Slavery.* New York: Alfred A. Knopf, 1979.

Myrdal, Gunnar. *An American Dilemma.* new ed. 2 vols. New York: McGraw-Hill, 1964.

Schultz, John H. "Thomas Pownall and His Negro Commonwealth," *Journal of Negro History*, 30 (1945), 400–404.

Stadenraus, P. J. *The African Colonization Movement, 1816–1865.* New York: Columbia University Press, 1961.

Zilversmit, Arthur. *The First Emancipation: The Abolition of Slavery in the North.* Chicago: University of Chicago Press, 1967.

EMANCIPATION, THIRTEENTH AMENDMENT, SEWARD AND

Cox, John H., and LaWanda Cox. *Politics, Principles and Prejudice, 1865–1866: Dilemma of Reconstruction America.* New York: Atheneum, 1963.

Donald, David H. *Lincoln Reconsidered.* 2nd ed. New York: Vintage Books, 1956.

———. *The Politics of Reconstruction, 1863–1867.* Baton Rouge: Louisiana State University Press, 1965.

Horowitz, Robert F. "Seward and Reconstruction: A Reconsideration," *Historian*, 47 (1985), 382–401.

Stampp, Kenneth M. *The Era of Reconstruction, 1865–1877.* New York: Alfred A. Knopf, 1965.

Vorenburg, Michael. *Final Freedom: The Civil War, the Abolition of Slavery, and the Thirteenth Amendment.* Cambridge: Cambridge University Press, 2001.

ENFORCEMENT ACTS

Avins, Alfred. "The Ku Klux Klan Act of 1871: Some Reflected Light on State Action and the Fourteenth Amendment," *St. Louis University Law Journal*, 11 (1967), 331–81.

Cresswell, Stephen. "Enforcing the Enforcement Acts: The Department of Justice in Northern Mississippi, 1870–1890," *Journal of Southern History*, 53 (1987), 421–40.

Fairman, Charles. *Reconstruction and Reunion, 1864–1888.* 2 pts. New York: The Macmillan Company, 1971–1987.

Faulkner, Harold U. *Politics, Reform, and Expansion, 1890–1900.* New York: Harper & Row, 1959.

Frantz, Laurent B. "Fourteenth Amendment against Private Acts," *Yale Law Journal*, 73 (1964), 1353–84.

Gara, Larry. "Slavery and the Slave Power: A Crucial Distinction," *Civil War History*, 15 (1969), 5–18.

Gillette, William. *Retreat from Reconstruction, 1869–1879*. Baton Rouge: Louisiana State University Press, 1979.

Hall, Kermit L. "Political Power and Constitutional Legitimacy: The South Carolina Ku Klux Klan Trials, 1871–1872," *Emory Law Journal*, 33 (1984), 921–51.

———, and Lou Falkner Williams. "Constitutional Tradition Amid Social Change: Hugh Lennox Bond and the Ku Klux Klan in South Carolina," *Maryland Historian*, 16 (1985), 43–58.

Hesseltine, William B. *U. S. Grant: Politician*. New York: Dodd, Mead & Co., 1935.

Kaczorowski, Robert J. "To Begin the Nation Anew: Congress, Citizenship and Civil Rights after the Civil War," *American Historical Review*, 90 (1987), 45–68.

———. *The Nationalization of Civil Rights: Constitutional Theory and Practice in a Racist Society, 1866–1883*. New York: Garland Publishing, Inc., 1987.

Martinez, J. Michael. "An Officer of Great Intelligence: Lewis Merrill, the Man who Exposed the Ku Klux Klan," *North & South*, 10 (July 2007), 70–79.

Richardson, Joe M. "Curbing Voter Intimidation in Florida, 1871," *Florida Historical Quarterly*, 43 (1967), 352–68.

Swinney, Everette. "Enforcing the Fifteenth Amendment, 1870–1877," *Journal of Southern History*, 28 (1962), 202–18.

Williams, Lou Falkner. *The Great South Carolina Ku Klux Klan Trials, 1872–1872*. Athens: University of Georgia Press, 1996.

———. "The South Carolina Ku Klux Klan Trials and Enforcement of Federal Rights, 1871–1872," *Civil War History*, 39 (1993), 47–66.

Woodward, C. Vann. "Seeds of Failure in Radical Race Policy," in Harold M. Hyman (ed.), *New Frontiers of the American Reconstruction*. Urbana: University of Illinois Press, 1966, 125–47.

FARRAGUT, DAVID G. (1801–1870)

Bradford, James C. (ed.). *Captains of the Old Steam Navy: Makers of the American Naval Tradition, 1840–1880*. Annapolis, Md.: Naval Institute Press, 1986.

Lewis, Charles L. *David Glasgow Farragut*. 2 vols. Annapolis: Naval Institute Press, 1941–1943.

Mahan, Alfred T. *Admiral Farragut*. New York: Appleton, 1892.

Martin, Christopher. *Damn the Torpedoes: The Story of America's First Admiral, David Glasgow Farragut*. New York: Abalard-Schuman, 1970.

Mordell, Albert. "Farragut at the Crossroads," *U.S. Naval Institute Proceedings*, 57 (1931), 151–61.

Stevens, William O. *David Glasgow Farragut: Our First Admiral*. New York: Dodd, Mead, 1942.

West, Richard S., Jr. "Admiral Farragut and General Butler," *U.S. Naval Institute Proceedings*, 82 (1956), 635–43.

―――. "Relations between Farragut and Porter," *U.S. Naval Institute Proceedings*, 61 (1835), 985–96.

FESSENDEN, WILLIAM P. (1806–1869)

Robinson, William A. "William Pitt Fessenden," in Allen Johnson *et al.* (eds.), *Dictionary of American Biography* (10 double vols. + 9 supplements, 1964–1981), VI, 348–49.
Jellison, Charles A., *Fessenden of Maine, Civil War Senator.* Syracuse, N.Y.: Syracuse University Press, 1962.

FEUDS, GANGS, AND GUNMEN

Crouch, Barry A. *The Freedmen's Bureau and Black Texans.* Austin: University of Texas Press, 1992.
―――. "A Spirit of Lawnessness: White Violence, Texas Blacks, 1865–1868," *Journal of Social History*, 19 (1984), 217–32.
―――, and Donaly E. Brice. *Cullen Montgomery Baker: Reconstruction Desperado.* Baton Rouge: Louisiana State University Press, 1997.
Jackson, Jack. *Lost Cause: The True Story of the Famed Texas Gunslinger John Wesley Hardin.* Northampton, Mass.: Kitchen Sink Press, 1998.
Kenner, Charles V. "Racial Turmoil in Texas." M.A. thesis, North Texas State University, 1971.
Richter, William L. *The Army in Texas during Reconstruction, 1865–1870.* College Station: Texas A&M Press, 1987.
―――. "'A Dear Little Job': Second Lieutenant Hiram F. Willis, Freedmen's Bureau Agent in Southwestern Arkansas, 1866–1868," *Arkansas Historical Quarterly*, 50 (1991), 158–200.
―――. "'Oh, God, Let Us Have Revenge': Ben Griffith and His Family during the Civil War and Reconstruction," *Arkansas Historical Quarterly*, 57 (1998), 255–86.
―――. *Overreached on All Sides: The Freedmen's Bureau in Texas, 1865–1868.* College Station: Texas A&M Press, 1991.
―――. "'The Revolver Rules the Day!': Colonel DeWitt C. Brown and the Freedmen's Bureau in Paris, Texas, 1867–1868," *Southwestern Historical Quarterly*, 93 (1989–1990), 303–32.
―――. "'This Blood-thirsty Hole': The Freedmen's Bureau Agency at Clarksville, Texas, 1867–1868," *Civil War History*, 38 (1992), 51–77.
Sefton, James E. *The United States Army and Reconstruction, 1865–1877.* Baton Rouge: Louisiana State University Press, 1967.
Smallwood, James M. "When the Klan Rode: White Terror in Reconstruction Texas," *Journal of the West*, 25 (October 1986), 4–13.

————, Barry Crouch, and Larry Peacock. *Murder and Mayhem: The War of Reconstruction in Texas*. College Station: Texas A&M Press, 2003.

FISH, HAMILTON (1808–1893)

Fuller, Joseph V. "Hamilton Fish," in Allen Johnson *et al.* (eds.), *Dictionary of American Biography* (10 double vols. + 9 supplements, 1964–1981), VII, 145–50.
Nevins, Allan. *Hamilton Fish: The Inner History of the Grant Administration*. 2 vols. New York: Dodd, Mead & Co., 1936.

FORREST, NATHAN BEDFORD (1821–1877)

Ashdown, Paul, and Edward Caudill. *The Myth of Nathan Bedford Forrest*. Lanham, Md.: Rowman & Littlefield, 2005.
Bearss, Edwin C. "Battle of Brice's Crossroads," *Blue & Gray*, 16 (1998–99), [Special Issue].
————. *Forrest at Brice's Crossroads and North Mississippi in 1864*. Dayton, Ohio: Morningside, 1991.
Bearss, Margie Riddle. *Sherman's Forgotten Campaign: The Meridian Expedition*. Baltimore, Md.: Gateway Press, 1987.
Brown, Campbell H. "Forrest's Johnsonville Raid," *Civil War Times Illustrated*, 4 (July 1965), 48–57.
Brown, D. Alexander. "The Battle of Brice's Crossroads," *Civil War Times Illustrated*, 7 (April 1968), 4–9, 44–48.
Carney, Court. "The Contested Image of Nathan Bedford Forrest," *Journal of Southern History*, 67 (1998), 601–30.
Current, Richard N. (ed.). *Encyclopedia of the Confederacy*. 4 vols. New York: Simon & Schuster, 1993.
Davis, William C. (ed.). *The Confederate General*. 6 vols. N.p.: National Historical Society, 1991.
Domer, Ronald G. "Rebel Rout of Streight's Raiders," *America's Civil War*, 9 (September 1996), 30–36.
Fuchs, Richard L. *An Unerring Fire: The Massacre at Fort Pillow*. Mechanicsburg, Pa.: Stackpole Books, 2001.
Grimsley, Mark. "The Life of Nathan Bedford Forrest," *Civil War Times Illustrated*, 32 (September/October, November/December 1993; January/February 1994), 58–73; 32–39, 94–95; 34–41, 63–72.
Hattaway, Herman. "Dress Rehearsal for Hell [February 1864 Meridian Campaign]," *Civil War Times Illustrated*, 37 (October 1998), 32–39, 74–75.
Henry, Robert S. *"First with the Most" Forrest*. Indianapolis: Bobbs-Merrill, 1944.

Holmes, Jack D. L. "The Day That Forrest Visited Memphis," *Civil War Times*, 2 (January 1961), 16–18.

Longacre, Edward G. "Streight's Raid: 'All's Fair . . . '," *Civil War Times Illustrated*, 8 (June 1969), 32–40.

McMurry, Richard M. "Sherman's Meridian Campaign," *Civil War Times Illustrated*, 14 (May 1975), 24–32.

Morris, Roy, Jr. "Fort Pillow: Massacre or Madness," *America's Civil War*, 13 (November 2000), 26–32.

Palo, Rani-Villem. "Forrest's Okolona Victory: The Invasion of Mississippi's Black Prairie," *Civil War Times Illustrated*, 24 (April 1985), 32–39.

Stinson, Byron. "The Battle of Tupelo," *Civil War Times Illustrated*, 11 (July 1972), 4–9, 46–48.

Ticker, Glenn. "Forrest—Untutored Genius of the War," *Civil War Times Illustrated*, 3 (June 1964), 7–9, 35–39, 49.

Warner, Ezra J. *Generals in Gray: Lives of Confederate Commanders*. Baton Rouge: Louisiana State University Press, 1959.

Wills, Brian Steel. *A Battle from the Start: The Life of Nathan Bedford Forrest*. New York: HarperCollins, 1992.

FORT SUMTER, THE FIRING ON

Castel, Albert. "Fort Sumter—1861," *Civil War Times Illustrated*, 15 (October 1976), [Special Issue].

Current, Richard N. *Lincoln and the First Shot*. Philadelphia: J. B. Lippincott and Co., 1963.

Gaff, Alan D. "Two Dead at Sumter," *Civil War Times Illustrated*, 40 (March 2001), 46–52.

Hendrickson, Robert. *Sumter: The First Day of the Civil War*. Chelsea, Mich.: Scarborough House, 1990.

Hummel, Jeffrey R. "Why Did Lincoln Choose War?" *North & South*, 4 (September 2001), 38–44.

Meredith, Roy. *Storm over Sumter*. New York: Simon & Schuster, 1957.

Swanberg, W. A. *First Blood: The Story of Fort Sumter*. New York: Charles Scribner's Sons, 1957.

FREDERICKSBURG AND THE MUD MARCH

"Battle of Fredericksburg," *Blue & Gray*, 1 (1983–1984), [Special Issue].

Catton, Bruce. *Glory Road: The Bloody Route from Fredericksburg to Gettysburg*. New York: Doubleday and Co. 1952.

Freeman, Douglas Southall. *Lee's Lieutenants: A Study of Command*. 3 vols. New York: Charles Scribner's Sons, 1942–1944.

Goolrick, William K. *Rebels Resurgent: Fredericksburg to Chancellorsville*. Alexandria, Va.: Time-Life Books, 1985.

McPherson, James M. (ed.). *Battle Chronicles of the Civil War*. 6 vols. New York: Macmillan, 1989.

O'Reilly, Francis Augustine. "Fredericksburg: Attack at the Stone Wall," *Blue & Gray*, 25 (2008–2009), [Special Issue].

———. "Fredericksburg: The Real Battle of Fredericksburg: Stonewall Jackson, Prospect Hill, and the Slaughter Pen," *Blue & Gray*, 23 (2008–2009), [Special Issue].

———. *The Fredericksburg Campaign: Winter War on the Rappahannock*. Baton Rouge: Louisiana State University Press, 2003.

Rable, George C. "Fire in the Streets: The Assault on Fredericksburg," *North & South*, 3 (August 200), 74–86.

———. *Fredericksburg! Fredericksburg!* Chapel Hill: University of North Carolina Press, 2002.

Roth, David E. "The Battle of Fredericksburg, December 13, 1862," *Blue and Gray*, 2/3 (December 1983/January 1984).

Stackpole, Edward J. "The Battle of Fredericksburg," *Civil War Times Illustrated*, 4 December 1965), [Special Issue].

———. *Drama on the Rappahannock: The Fredericksburg Campaign*. Harrisburg, Pa.: The Stackpole Co., 1957.

Whan, Vorin E., Jr. *Fiasco at Fredericksburg*. State College: Pennsylvania State University Press, 1961.

Wert, Jeffry D. "Lee and His Staff," *Civil War Times Illustrated*, 11 (July 1972), 10–19.

Williams, Kenneth P. *Lincoln Finds a General: A Military Study of the Civil War*. 5 vols. New York: Macmillan, 1949–1959.

FREEDMEN'S AID SOCIETIES

Brady, Patricia. "Trials and Tribulations: American Missionary Association Teachers and Black Education in Occupied New Orleans, 1863–1864," *Louisiana History*, 31 (1990), 5–20.

Brown, Ira V. "Lyman Abbott and Freedmen's Aid, 1865–1869," *Journal of Southern History*, 15 (1948), 49–92.

Butchart, Ronald E. *Northern Schools, Southern Blacks, and Reconstruction: Freedmen's Education, 1862–1875*. Westport, Conn.: Greenwood Press, 1980.

Drake, Richard B. "The American Missionary Association and the Southern Negro, 1861–1888." Ph.D. dissertation, Emory University, 1957.

———. "Freedmen's Aid and Sectional Compromise," *Journal of Southern History*, 29 (1963), 175–86.

Harlan, Louis R. "Desegregation in New Orleans Public Schools during Reconstruction," *American Historical Review*, 67 (1961), 663–75.

Kelly, Alfred H. "The Congressional Controversy over School Segregation, 1867–1875," *American Historical Review*, 64 (1958–1959), 537–63.

Richardson, Joe M. "The American Missionary Association and Black Education in Civil War Missouri," *Missouri Historical Review*, 69 (1975), 433–48.

Sparks, Randy J. "'The White People's Arms Are Longer Than Ours': Blacks, Education, and the American Missionary Association in Reconstruction Mississippi," *Journal of Mississippi History*, 54 (February 1992), 1–27.

Vaughn, William P. "Partners in Segregation: Barnas Sears and the Peabody Fund," *Civil War History*, 10 (1964), 260–74.

———. "Separate and Unequal: The Civil Rights Act of 1875 and Defeat of the School Integration Clause," *Southwestern Social Science Quarterly*, 48 (1967), 146–54.

West, Earle H. "The Peabody Fund and Negro Education, 1867–1880," *History of Education Quarterly*, 6 (1966), 3–21.

FREEDMEN'S SAVINGS BANK

Fleming, Walter Lynwood. *The Freedmen's Savings Bank: A Chapter in the History of the Negro Race*. Chapel Hill: University of North Carolina Press, 1927.

Gilbert, Abby L. "The Comptroller of the Currency and the Freedmen's Savings Bank," *Journal of Negro History*, 57 (1972), 125–43.

Lindsay, Arnett G. "The Negro in Banking," *Journal of Negro History*, 14 (1929), 156–201.

Osthaus, Carl L. *Freedmen, Philanthropy, and Fraud: A History of the Freedmen's Savings Bank*. Urbana: University of Illinois Press, 1976.

Story, Ronald D. "'That Damned Pack of Sharpers': Savings Banks and American History in the Nineteenth Century," *Reviews in American History*, 5 (1977), 335–41.

GRANT, [HIRAM] ULYSSES SIMPSON (1822–1885)

Carpenter, John A. *Ulysses S. Grant*. New York: Twayne Publishers, 1970.

Catton, Bruce. "The Generalship of U. S. Grant," in Grady McWhiney (ed.), *Grant, Lee, Lincoln and the Radicals*. Evanston, Ill.: Northwestern University Press, 1964, 3–30.

———. *Grant Moves South*. Boston: Little, Brown & Co., 1960.

———. *Grant Takes Command*. Boston: Little, Brown & Co., 1969.

———. *U. S. Grant and the American Military Tradition*. Boston: Little, Brown & Co., 1954.

Cozzens, Peter. "General Grant's 'Living and Speaking Conscience,' [Brigadier General John Rawlins]," *Civil War Times Illustrated*, 48 (October 2009), 28–33.

Current, Richard N. "Grant without Greatness," *Reviews in American History*, 9 (1981), 507–9.

———. "President Grant and the Continuing Civil War," in David L. Wilson and John Y. Simon (eds.), *Ulysses S. Grant: Essays and Documents*. Carbondale: Southern Illinois University Press, 1981, 1–8.

Fuller, J. F. C. *The Generalship of U. S. Grant*. 2nd ed. Bloomington: Indiana University Press, 1958.

Goldhurst, Richard, *Many Are the Hearts*. New York: Reader's Digest, 1975.

Grant, Ulysses S. *Personal Memoirs of U. S. Grant*. 2 vols. New York: Charles L. Webster, 1886.

Grant, Ulysses S., III. *Ulysses S. Grant: Warrior and Statesman*. New York: William Morrow & Co., 1969.

Grimsley, Mark. "Ulysses S. Grant," *Civil War Times Illustrated*, 28 (January/February 1990), [Special Issue].

Hagerman, Edward. *The American Civil War and the Origins of Modern Warfare: Ideas, Organization, and Field Command*. Bloomington: Indiana University Press, 1988.

Hesseltine, William B. *U. S. Grant: Politician*. New York: Dodd, Mead & Co., 1935.

Lewis, Lloyd. *Captain Sam Grant*. Boston: Little, Brown & Co., 1950.

Mantell, Martin E. *Johnson, Grant, and the Politics of Reconstruction*. New York: Columbia University Press, 1973.

McFeely, William S. *Grant: A Biography*. New York: W. W. Norton, 1981.

Nye, Wilbur S. "U.S. Grant—Genius or Fortune's Child?" *Civil War Times Illustrated*, 4 (June 1965), 5–15, 43–44.

Richter, William L. "The Papers of U. S. Grant: A Review Essay," *Civil War History*, 36 (1990), 149–66; 38 (1992), 342–48; and 42 (1996), 80–84.

Selcer, Richard F. "Battlefield Bulldog, Compassionate Conqueror [Grant's Mastery of the 'Art of Surrender']," *Civil War Times Illustrated*, 46 (February 2007), 46–53.

Simon, John Y. (ed.). *The Papers of Ulysses S. Grant*. 20 vols. Carbondale: Southern Illinois University Press, 1967.

Simpson, Brooks D. "Butcher? Racist? An Examination of William S. McFeely's *Grant: A Biography*," *Civil War History*, 33 (1987), 62–83.

———. *Let Us Have Peace: Ulysses S. Grant and the Politics of War and Reconstruction*. Chapel Hill: University of North Caroline Press, 1991.

Steere, Edward. "Grant's Ideas on Strategy Expressed in Victories," *Civil War Times*, 2 (January 1961), 5, 19.

Zilversmit, Arthur. "Grant and the Freedmen," in Robert H. Abzug and Stephen E. Maizlish (eds.), *New Perspectives on Race and Slavery in America: Essays in Honor of Kenneth M. Stampp*. Lexington: University of Kentucky Press, 1986, 128–45.

GRANT, ULYSSES S., ADMINISTRATION—CONCEPT OF THE PRESIDENCY

Carpenter, John A. *Ulysses S. Grant.* New York: Twayne Publishers, 1970.

Catton, Bruce. *U. S. Grant and the American Military Tradition.* Boston: Little, Brown & Co., 1954.

Cozzens, Peter. "General Grant's 'Living and Speaking Conscience,' [Brigadier General John Rawlins]," *Civil War Times Illustrated,* 48 (October 2009), 28–33.

Current, Richard N. "Grant without Greatness," *Reviews in American History,* 9 (1981), 507–509.

Grant, Ulysses S., III. *Ulysses S. Grant: Warrior and Statesman.* New York: William Morrow & Co., 1969.

Hesseltine, William B. *U. S. Grant: Politician.* New York: Dodd, Mead & Co., 1935.

McFeely, William S. *Grant: A Biography.* New York: W. W. Norton, 1981.

Richter, William L. "The Papers of U. S. Grant: A Review Essay," *Civil War History,* 36 (1990), 149–66; 38 (1992), 342–48; and 42 (1996), 80–84.

Simpson, Brooks D. "Butcher? Racist? An Examination of William S. McFeely's *Grant: A Biography*," *Civil War History,* 33 (1987), 62–83.

———. *Let Us Have Peace: Ulysses S. Grant and the Politics of War and Reconstruction.* Chapel Hill: University of North Caroline Press, 1991.

Zilversmit, Arthur. "Grant and the Freedmen," in Robert H. Abzug and Stephen E. Maizlish (eds.), *New Perspectives on Race and Slavery in America: Essays in Honor of Kenneth M. Stampp.* Lexington: University of Kentucky Press, 1986, 128–45.

GRANT, ULYSSES S., ADMINISTRATION—DOMESTIC POLICIES

Beale, Howard K. "The Tariff and Reconstruction," *American Historical Review,* 35 (1929–1930), 276–94.

Barrett, Don C. *The Greenbacks and the Resumption of Specie Payments, 1862–1879.* Cambridge, Mass.: Harvard University Press, 1931.

Coben, Stanley. "Northeastern Business and Radical Reconstruction," *Mississippi Valley Historical Review,* 46 (1959–1960), 69–90.

Fairman, Charles. *Reconstruction and Reunion, 1864–1888.* 2 pts. New York: The Macmillan Company, 1971–1987.

Friedman, Milton, and Anna Jacobson Schwartz. *A Monetary History of the United States, 1867–1960.* Princeton, N.J.: Princeton University Press, 1963.

Graham, Frank D. "International Trade under Depreciated Paper: The United States, 1862–1879," *Quarterly Journal of Economics,* 36 (1922), 220–73.

Hammond, Bray. *Sovereignty and an Empty Purse: Banks and Politics in the Civil War.* Princeton, N.J.: Princeton University Press, 1970.

Hesseltine, William B. *U. S. Grant: Politician*. New York: Dodd, Mead & Co., 1935.

Hoogenboom, Ari A. *Outlawing the Spoils: A History of the Civil Reform Movement*. Urbana: University of Illinois Press, 1961.

Hurst, James Willard. *A Legal History of Money in the United States, 1774–1970*. Lincoln: University of Nebraska Press, 1973.

McFeely, William S. *Grant: A Biography*. New York: W. W. Norton, 1981.

Nugent, Walter T. K. *The Money Question during Reconstruction*. New York: W. W. Norton, 1967.

Schell, Herbert S. "Hugh McCulloch and the Treasury Department, 1865–1869," *Mississippi Valley Historical Review*, 17 (1931), 404–23.

Sharkey, Robert P. *Money, Class, and Party: An Economic Study of the Civil War and Reconstruction*. Baltimore, Md.: The Johns Hopkins University Press, 1959.

Unger, Irwin. "Businessmen and Specie Resumption," *Political Science Quarterly*, 74 (1959), 46–70.

———. *The Greenback Era: A Social and Political History of American Finance*. Princeton, N.J.: Princeton University Press, 1964.

GRANT, ULYSSES S., ADMINISTRATION—RECONSTRUCTION

Blair, William Alan. "The Use of Military Force to Protect the Gains of Reconstruction," *Civil War History*, 51 (2005), 388–402.

Carrier, John P. "A Political History of Texas during the Reconstruction, 1865–1874." Ph.D. dissertation, Vanderbilt University, 1971.

Carter, Hodding. *The Angry Scar: The Story of Reconstruction*. Garden City, N.Y.: Doubleday & Company, Inc., 1959.

Cox, LaWanda. *Lincoln and Black Freedom: A Study in Presidential Leadership*. Columbia: University of South Carolina Press, 1981.

Dawson, Joseph Green, III. *Army Generals and Reconstruction: Louisiana, 1862–1977*. Baton Rouge: Louisiana State University Press, 1982.

Gillette, William. *Retreat from Reconstruction, 1869–1879*. Baton Rouge: Louisiana State University Press, 1979.

———. *The Right to Vote: Politics and the Passage of the Fifteenth Amendment*. Baltimore, Md.: The Johns Hopkins University Press, 1966, 1969.

Hesseltine, William B. *U. S. Grant: Politician*. New York: Dodd, Mead & Co., 1935.

Olsen, Otto H. "The Ku Klux Klan: A Study in Reconstruction Politics and Propaganda," *North Carolina Historical Quarterly*, 39 (1962), 340–62.

———. "Southern Reconstruction and the Question of Self-Determination," in George M. Frederickson (ed.), *A Nation Divided: Problems and Issues of the Civil War and Reconstruction*. Minneapolis: Burgess Publishing Company, 1975, 113–41.

Rable, George C. *But There Was No Peace: The Role of Violence in the Politics of Reconstruction*. Athens: University of Georgia Press, 1984.

Ramsdell, Charles W. *Reconstruction in Texas*. New York: Columbia University Press, 1910.

Richter, William L. *The Army in Texas During Reconstruction, 1865–1870*. College Station: Texas A&M University Press, 1987.

Sefton, James E. "Aristotle in Blue and Braid: General John Schofield's Essays on Reconstruction," *Civil War History*, 17 (1971), 45–57.

———. *The United States Army and Reconstruction, 1865–1877*. Baton Rouge: Louisiana State University Press, 1967.

Simpson, Brooks D. *Let Us Have Peace: Ulysses S. Grant and the Politics of War and Reconstruction*. Chapel Hill: University of North Caroline Press, 1991.

———. *The Reconstruction Presidents*. Lawrence: University Press of Kansas, 1998.

Taylor, Joe Gray. *Louisiana Reconstructed, 1863–1877*. Baton Rouge: Louisiana State University, 1974.

Trelease, Allan W. *White Terror: The Ku Klux Klan Conspiracy and Southern Reconstruction*. New York: Harper & Row, 1971.

Wallace, Ernest. *The Howling of the Coyotes: Reconstruction Efforts to Divide Texas*. College Station: Texas A&M University Press, 1979.

Williamson, Joel. *After Slavery: The Negro in South Carolina during Reconstruction*. Chapel Hill: University of North Carolina Press, 1965.

Woodward, C. Vann. "Seeds of Failure in Radical Race Policy," in Harold M. Hyman (ed.), *New Frontiers of the American Reconstruction*. Urbana: University of Illinois Press, 1966, 125–47.

Zilversmit, Arthur. "Grant and the Freedmen," in Robert H. Abzug and Stephen E. Maizlish (eds.), *New Perspectives on Race and Slavery in America: Essays in Honor of Kenneth M. Stampp*. Lexington: University of Kentucky Press, 1986, 128–45.

GRANT, ULYSSES S., ADMINISTRATION—SCANDALS

Boynton, H. V. "The Whiskey Ring," *North American Review*, 123 (1876), 280–327.

Donald David H. *Charles Sumner and the Rights of Man*. New York: Alfred A. Knopf, 1970.

Hesseltine, William B. *U. S. Grant: Politician*. New York: Dodd, Mead & Co., 1935.

Mayer, George H. *The Republican Party, 1854–1866*. 2nd ed. New York: Oxford University Press, 1967.

McDonald, John. *Secrets of the Great Whiskey Ring* . . . . St. Louis, Mo.: W. S. Bryan, 1880.

McFeely, William S. *Grant: A Biography.* New York: W. W. Norton, 1981.

Prickett, Robert C. "The Malfeasance of William Worth Belknap, Secretary of War, October 13, 1869 to March 2, 1876," *North Dakota History*, 17 (1950), 5–51.

Spence, Clark C. *"Robert Schenck* and the Emma Mine Affair," *Ohio Historical Quarterly*, 68 (1959), 141–60.

Sproat, John G. *The Best Men: Liberal Reformers in the Gilded Age.* New York: Oxford University Press, 1968.

Tansill, Charles C. *The United States and Santo Domingo, 1798–1873: A Chapter in Caribbean Diplomacy.* Baltimore, Md.: The Johns Hopkins Press, 1938.

Webb, Ross A. *Benjamin Helm Bristow: Border State Politician.* Lexington: University of Kentucky Press, 1969.

Wilson, David L. Ulysses S. Grant and Reconstruction," *OAH Magazine of History*, 4 (Winter 1989), 47–50.

GREELEY, HORACE (1811–1872)

Hale, William Harlan. *Horace Greeley: Voice of the People.* New York: Collier Books, 1950.

Linn, William Alexander. *Horace Greeley: Founder of the New York Tribune.* Indianapolis: Bobbs-Merrill, 1926.

Lunde, Erik S. *Horace Greeley.* Boston: Twayne, 1981.

Nevins, Allan. "Horace Greeley," in Allen Johnson *et al.* (eds.), *Dictionary of American Biography* (10 double vols. + 9 supplements, 1964–1981), VII, 528–34.

Ross, Earle D. "Horace Greeley and the South, 1865–1872," *South Atlantic Quarterly*, 16 (1917), 324–28.

Van Deusen, Glyndon G. *Horace Greeley: Nineteenth Century Crusader.* Philadelphia: University of Pennsylvania Press, 1957.

GRIFFIN, CHARLES (1825–1867)

Baggett, James Alex. "Birth of the Texas Republican Party," *Southwestern Historical Quarterly*, 78 (1974–1975), 1–20.

———. "Origins of Early Texas Republican Party Leadership," *Journal of Southern History*, 40 (1974), 441–50.

Boatner, Mark M., III. *The Civil War Dictionary.* New York: D. McKay and Company, 1959.

Carrier, John P. "A Political History of Texas during the Reconstruction, 1865–1874." Ph.D. dissertation, Vanderbilt University, 1971.

Ramsdell, Charles W. *Reconstruction in Texas.* New York: Columbia University Press, 1910.

Richter, William L. *The Army in Texas During Reconstruction, 1865–1870*. College Station: Texas A&M University Press, 1987.

———. *Overreached on All Sides: The Freedmen's Bureau Administrators in Texas, 1865–1868*. College Station: Texas A&M University Press, 1991.

———. "Tyrant and Reformer: General Charles Griffin Reconstructs Texas, 1866–1867," *Prologue: The Journal of the National Archives*, 10 (1978), 255–41.

Sefton, James E. *The United States Army and Reconstruction, 1865–1877*. Baton Rouge: Louisiana State University Press, 1967.

Shook, Robert W. "Federal Occupation and Administration of Texas, 1865–1870." Ph.D. dissertation, North Texas State University, 1970.

HALLECK, HENRY WAGER (1815–1872)

Ambrose, Stephen E. "Halleck—the Despised 'Old Brains'," *Civil War Times Illustrated*, 2 (1962), 15–16, 33–34.

Ambrose, Stephen E. *Halleck: Lincoln's Chief of Staff*. Baton Rouge: Louisiana State University Press, 1962.

Hattaway, Herman, and Archer Jones. *How the North Won: A Military History of the Civil War*. Urbana: University of Illinois Press, 1983.

Marszalek, John "Henry W. Halleck: The Early Seeds of Failure," *North & South*, 8 (January 2005), 86.

Simon, John Y. "Lincoln and 'Old Brains'," *North & South*, 2 (November 1998), 38–45.

HAMILTON, ANDREW JACKSON

Adkins, Robert. "The Public Career of A. J. Hamilton." M.A. thesis, University of Texas, 1947.

Ashcraft, Allan C. "Texas in Defeat: The Early Phase of A. J. Hamilton's Provisional Governorship, June 17, 1865 to February 7, 1866," *Texas Military History*, 8 (1970), 199–219.

Waller, John L. *Colossal Hamilton of Texas: A Biography of Andrew Jackson Hamilton*. El Paso: Texas Western Press, 1968.

HAMLIN, HANNIBAL (1809–1891)

Rudolph, Jack. "Hannibal Hamlin, Possible President: The Old Carthaginian," *Civil War Times Illustrated*, 20 (February 1982), 22–27.

HAMPTON ROADS PEACE CONFERENCE

Bennett, Lerone, Jr. *Forced into Glory: Abraham Lincoln's White Dream*. Chicago: Johnson Publishing, 2000.

Harris, William C. "The Hampton Roads Peace Conference: A Final Test of Lincoln's Presidential Leadership," *Journal of the Abraham Lincoln Association*, 21 (Winter 2000), 43–44.

Pfanz, Donald C. *The Petersburg Campaign: Abraham Lincoln at City Point, March 20–April 9, 1865*. Lynchburg, Va.: H. E. Howard, 1989.

Sims, Henry Harrison. *Life of R. M. T. Hunter: A Study in Sectionalism and Secession*. Richmond,: William Byrd Press, 1935.

Turner, Justin C. "Peace Conference at Hampton Roads," *Civil War Times*, 3 (January 1962), 12–16.

HANCOCK, WINFIELD SCOTT (1824–1886)

Boatner, Mark M., III. *The Civil War Dictionary*. New York: D. McKay and Company, 1959.

Carrier, John P. "A Political History of Texas during the Reconstruction, 1865–1874." Ph.D. dissertation, Vanderbilt University, 1971.

Dawson, Joseph Green, III. *Army Generals and Reconstruction: Louisiana, 1862–1977*. Baton Rouge: Louisiana State University Press, 1982.

————. "Army Generals and Reconstruction: Mower and Hancock as Case Studies," *Southern Studies*, 17 (1978), 255–72.

Hancock, Almira R. *Reminiscences of Winfield Scott Hancock*. New York: Charles L. Webster, 1887.

Richter, William L. *The Army in Texas During Reconstruction, 1865–1870*. College Station: Texas A&M University Press, 1987.

Sefton, James E. *The United States Army and Reconstruction, 1865–1877*. Baton Rouge: Louisiana State University Press, 1967.

Shook, Robert W. "Federal Occupation and Administration of Texas, 1865–1870." Ph.D. dissertation, North Texas State University, 1970.

Taylor, Joe Gray. *Louisiana Reconstructed, 1863–1877*. Baton Rouge: Louisiana State University, 1974.

Tucker, Glenn. *Hancock, the Superb*. Indianapolis: Bobbs-Merrill, 1960.

HARTFORD CONVENTION (1814)

Banner, James M. *To the Hartford Convention: The Federalists and the Origins of Party Politics in Massachusetts, 1789–1815*. New York: Alfred A. Knopf, 1970.

HAYES, RUTHERFORD B. (1822–1893)

Barnard, Harry. *Rutherford B. Hayes and His America.* Indianapolis: Bobbs-Merrill, 1954.

Eckenrode, Hamilton J. *Rutherford B. Hayes: Statesman of Reunion.* New York: Dodd, Mead & Co., 1930.

Haworth, Paul L. *The Hayes-Tilden Disputed Presidential Election of 1876.* Cleveland, Ohio: Arthur H. Clark Co., 1906.

Hoogenboom, Ari A. *The Presidency of Rutherford B. Hayes.* Lawrence: University Press of Kansas, 1988.

———. *Rutherford B. Hayes: Warrior and President.* Lawrence: University Press of Kansas, 1995.

Nevins, Allan. "Rutherford Birchard Hayes," in Allen Johnson *et al.* (eds.), *Dictionary of American Biography* (10 double vols. + 9 supplements, 1964–1981), VIII, 446–51.

Simpson, Brooks D. *The Reconstruction Presidents.* Lawrence: University Press of Kansas, 1998.

Williams, T. Harry. *Hayes of the Twenty-Third: The Life of a Volunteer Officer.* New York: Alfred A. Knopf, 1965.

——— (ed.). *Hayes: The Diary of a President, 1875–1881, Covering the Disputed Election, the End of Reconstruction, and the Beginning of Civil Service.* New York: D. McKay Co., 1964.

HICKS, THOMAS H. (1798–1865)

Baker, Jean H. *Ambivalent Americans: The Know-Nothing Party in Maryland.* Baltimore, Md.: The Johns Hopkins University Press, 1977.

Radcliffe, G. L. P. *Governor Thomas H. Hicks of Maryland and the Civil War.* Baltimore, Md.: The Johns Hopkins University Press, 1901.

Towers, Frank. "'A Vociferous Army of Howling Wolves': Baltimore's Civil War Riot of April 19, 1861," *Maryland Historian*, 23 (1992), 1–27.

HISTORIOGRAPHY OF THE CIVIL WAR—GENERAL HISTORIES, DICTIONARIES, AND ENCYCLOPEDIAS

Aimone, Alan, and Barbara Aimone. *A User's Guide to the Official Records of the American Civil War.* Shippensburg, Pa.: White Mane Publishing Co., 1993.

Allardice, Bruce S. *More Generals in Gray.* Baton Rouge: Louisiana State University Press, 1995.

Amann, William F. *Personnel of the Civil War.* 2 vols. New York: Thomas Yoseloff, 1961.

Batty, Peter, and Peter Parish. *The Divided Union: The Story of the Great American War, 1861–1865.* Topsfield, Mass.: Salem House, 1987.

Beers, Henry Putney. *The Confederacy: A Guide to the Archives of the Confederate States of America.* Washington, D.C.: National Archives, 1968.

Berringer, Richard E., *et al. Why the South Lost the Civil War.* Athens: University of Georgia Press, 1987.

Boatner, Mark M., III. *The Civil War Dictionary.* rev. ed. New York: McKay, 1988.

Buck, Paul H. *The Road to Reunion, 1865–1890.* Boston: J. B. Lippincott, 1937.

Buel, Clarence Clough, and Robert Underwood Johnson (eds.). *Battles and Leaders of the Civil War.* 4 vols. New York: Century, 1887.

Bush, Richard, *et al.* (eds.). *The Official Records of the Union and Confederate Navies in the War of the Rebellion.* 31 vols. Washington, D.C.: Government Printing Office, 1894–1927.

Catton, Bruce. *The Centennial History of the Civil War.* 3 vols. Garden City, N.Y.: Doubleday 1961–1963.

Civil War Society (ed.). *The American Civil War: A Multicultural Encyclopaedia.* 7 vols. Danbury, Conn.: Grolier, 1994.

Confederate Veteran: Published Monthly in the Interest of Confederate Veterans and Kindred Topics. 43 vols. with index, 1893–1932. Wilmington, N.C.: Broadfoot Publishing, 1990, repr.

Cullum, George W. *Biographical Register of the Officers and Graduates of the U.S. Military Academy.* 2 vols. New York: D. Van Nostrand, 1868.

Current, Richard N., *et al. Encyclopedia of the Confederacy.* 4 vols. New York: Simon & Schuster, 1993.

Curry, Richard O. "The Civil War and Reconstruction: A Critical Overlook of Recent Trends and Interpretations," *Civil War History,* 20 (1974), 446–61.

Davis, George B., *et al.* (eds.). *Atlas to Accompany the Official Records of the Union and Confederate Armies.* Washington, D.C.: Government Printing Office, 1891–1895.

Davis William C. (ed.). *The Confederate General.* 6 vols. New York: National Historical Society, 1991.

Denney, Robert E. *The Civil War Years: A Day by Day Chronicler of the Life of a Nation.* New York: Sterling, 1992.

Dornbusch, Charles E. *Military Bibliography of the Civil War.* 4 vols. Dayton, Ohio: Morningside Press, 1961–1987, repr.

Dyer, Frederick H. *A Compendium of the War of the Rebellion.* 2 vols. New York: Thomas Yoseloff, 1959, repr.

Evans, Clement A. (ed.). *Confederate Military History.* 13 vols. Dayton, Ohio: Morningside Press, 1987, repr.

Foote, Shelby. *The Civil War: A Narrative.* 3 vols. New York: Random House, 1958–1974.

Fox, William F. *Regimental Losses in the American Civil War, 1861–1865.* Albany, N.Y.: Albany Publishing, 1889.

Freehling, William W. "Why Civil War History Must Be Less Than 85 Percent Military," *North & South*, 5 (February 2002), 14–24.

Freeman, Douglas Southall. *The South to Posterity: An Introduction to the Writing of Confederate History*. Wilmington, N.C.: Broadfoot Publishing, 1993, repr.

Griffith, Paddy. *Battle Tactics of the Civil War*. New Haven, Conn.: Yale University Press, 1989.

Guelzo, Allen C. *The Crisis of the American Republic: A History of the Civil War and Reconstruction*. New York: St. Martin's Press, 1995.

Hattaway, Herman, and Archer Jones. *How the North Won: A Military History of the Civil War*. Urbana: University of Illinois Press, 1983.

Heitman, Francis B. *Historical Register and Dictionary of the United States Army*. 2 vols. Washington, D.C.: Government Printing Office, 1903.

Hubbell, John T., and James W. Geary (eds.). *Biographical Dictionary of the Union Leaders of the Civil War*. Westport, Conn.: Greenwood Press, 1995.

Krick, Robert K. *Lee's Colonels: A Biographical Register of the Field Officers of the Army of Northern Virginia*. 4th rev. ed. Dayton, Ohio: Morningside Press, 1992.

Leckie, Robert. *None Died in Vain: The Saga of the American Civil War*. New York: HarperCollins, 1990.

Livermore, Thomas L. *Numbers and Losses in the Civil War in America, 1861–1865*. Boston: Houghton Mifflin, 1900.

Long, E. B., and Barbara Long. *The Civil War Day by Day: An Almanac, 1861–1865*. Garden City, N.Y.: Doubleday , 1971.

Mahan, Harold E. "The Arsenal of History: The Officia! Records of the War of the Rebellion," *Civil War History*, 29 (1983), 5–27.

McPherson, James M. *Battle Chronicles of the Civil War*. 6 vols. New York: Macmillan, 1989.

———. *Battle Cry of Freedom: The Civil War Era*. New York: Oxford University Press, 1988.

———. *Ordeal by Fire: The Civil War and Reconstruction*. New York: Knopf, 1982.

Merideth, Lee W. (ed.). *Guide to Civil War Periodicals*. Twenty-nine Palms, Calif.: Historical Indexes, 1991.

Military Order of the Loyal Legion of the United States. 69 vols., 1887–1915. Wilmington, N.C.: Broadfoot Publishing, 1992–1995, repr.

Moebs, Thomas Truxton (comp.). *Black Soldiers, Black Sailors, Black Ink: Research Guide on African-Americans in U.S. Military History, 1526–1900*. Williamsburg, Va.: Moebs Publishing Co., 1994.

Munden, Kenneth W., and Henry Putney Beers. *The Union: A Guide to Federal Archives Relating to the Civil War*. Washington, D.C.: National Archives, 1962.

Nevins, Alan. *The Crisis of the Union*. 8 vols. New York: Charles Scribner's Sons, 1947–1971.

Parrish, Peter. *The American Civil War*. New York: Holmes & Meier, 1975.

Phillips, Kevin. *The Cousins' Wars: Religion, Politics, and the Triumph of Anglo-America*. New York: Basic Books, 1999.

Pressley, Thomas J. *Americans Interpret Their Civil War*. New York: Free Press, 1965.

Rable, George C. *The Confederate Republic: A Revolution Against Politics*. Chapel Hill: University of North Carolina Press, 1994.

Randall, James G., and David Donald. *The Civil War and Reconstruction*. 2nd rev. ed. Lexington, Mass.: D. C. Heath, 1969.

Rhodes, James Ford. *History of the United States from the Compromise of 1850 to the Final Restoration of Home Rule at the South in 1877*. 7 vols. New York: Macmillan, 1909–1919.

Roland, Charles P. *An American Iliad: The Story of the Civil War*. Lexington: University of Kentucky Press, 1991.

Scott, Robert N., *et al*. (eds.). *The War of the Rebellion: The Official Records of the Union and Confederate Armies*. 128 vols. Washington, D.C.: Government Printing Office, 1881–1901.

Shannon, Fred A. *Organization and Administration of the Union Army, 1861–1865*. Cleveland, Ohio: Arthur H. Clark, 1928.

Sifakis, Stewart. *Compendium of the Confederate Armies*. 5 vols. New York: Facts on File, 1992.

———. *Who Was Who in the Civil War*. New York: Facts on File, 1988.

———. *Who Was Who in the Confederacy*. New York: Facts on File, 1989.

Simpson, Brooks D. *America's Civil War*. New York: Harlan Davidson, 1996.

Smith, Page. *Trial by Fire: A People's History of the Civil War and Reconstruction*. New York: McGraw-Hill, 1982.

Snow, Richard F. (ed.). "The Civil War," *American Heritage*, 41 (March 1990), [Special Issue].

Southern Historical Society Papers. 55 vols., with index, 1876–1910. Wilmington, N.C.: Broadfoot Publishing, 1979, repr.

Stampp, Kenneth M. *The Imperiled Union: Essays on the Background of the Civil War*. New York: Oxford University Press, 1980.

Thomas, Emory M. *The Confederacy as a Revolutionary Experience*. Englewood Cliffs, N.J.: Prentice-Hall, 1970.

———. *The Confederate Nation, 1861–1865*. New York: Harper & Row, 1979.

Tulloch, Hugh. *The Debate on the Civil War Era*. Manchester, England: Manchester University Press, 1999.

U.S. Adjutant General's Office. *Official Army Register of the Volunteer Force of the United States Army for the Years of 1861, '62, '63, '64, '65*. 8 vols. Washington, D.C.: Government Printing Office, 1865–1867.

———, National Archives and Records Administration. *Military Operations of the Civil War: A Guide-Index to the Official Records of the Union and Confederate Armies, 1861–1865*. 5 vols., 9 pts., Washington, D.C.: Government Printing Office, 1966–1980.

Vandiver, Frank E. *Blood Brothers: A Short History of the Civil War*. College Station: Texas A&M University Press, 1992.

————. *Their Tattered Flags: The Epic of the Confederacy*. New York: Harper's Magazine Press, 1970.

Wakelyn, Jon L. *Biographical Dictionary of the Confederacy*. Westport, Conn.: Greenwood Press, 1977.

Warner, Ezra J. *Generals in Blue: Lives of the Union Commanders*. Baton Rouge: Louisiana State University Press, 1964.

————. *Generals in Gray: Lives of the Confederate Commanders*. Baton Rouge: Louisiana State University Press, 1959.

————, and W. Buck Yearns. *Biographical Register of the Confederate Congress*. Baton Rouge: Louisiana State University Press, 1975.

Weigley, Russell F. *A Great Civil War: A Military and Political History, 1861–1865*. Bloomington: Indiana University Press, 2000.

Welcher, Frank J. *The Union Army, 1861–1865: Organization and Operations*. 2 vols. Bloomington: Indiana University Press, 1993.

Wright, John. *List of Field Officers, Regiments, and battalions in the Confederate Army, 1861–1865*. Bryan, N.C.: J. M. Carroll, 1983.

HISTORIOGRAPHY OF THE RECONSTRUCTION—BLACK CRITICS OF WILLIAM A. DUNNING ET AL. AND SOME WHITE SYMPATHIZERS

Allen, James. *Reconstruction: The Battle for Democracy*. New York: International Publishers, 1937.

Bond, Horace Mann. *Negro Education in Alabama: A Study in Cotton and Steel*. Washington, D.C.: Associated Publishers, 1939.

————. "Social and Economic Forces in Alabama Reconstruction," *Journal of Negro History*, 23 (1938), 290–348.

DuBois, W. E. Burghardt. *Black Reconstruction: An Essay toward a History of the Part Which Black Folk Played in the Attempt to Reconstruct Democracy, 1860–1888*. New York: Harcourt, Brace, 1935.

————. "Reconstruction and Its Benefits," *American Historical Review*, 15 (1910), 781–99.

————. "Reconstruction, Seventy-Five Years After," *Phylon*, 4 (1943), 205–21.

Fast, Howard. *Freedom Road*. New York: Duell, Sloan, & Pearce, 1944.

Gray, Daniel Savage. "Bibliographic Essay: Black Views on Reconstruction," *Journal of Negro History*, 58 (1973), 75–85.

Logsdon, Joseph. "Black Reconstruction Revisited," *Reviews in American History*, 1 (1973), 553–54.

Lynch, John R. "Some Historical Errors of James Ford Rhodes," *Journal of Negro History*, 2 (1917), 345–67.

Taylor, Alrutheus A. "Historians of Reconstruction," *Journal of Negro History*, 23 (1938), 16–341.

————. "Negro Congressmen a Generation After," *Journal of Negro History*, 7 (1922), 121–71.

―――. *The Negro in Reconstruction Virginia*. Washington, D.C.: The Association for the Study of Negro Life and History, 1926.

―――. *The Negro in South Carolina during Reconstruction*. Washington, D.C.: The Association for the Study of Negro Life and History, 1924.

―――. *The Negro in Tennessee, 1865–1880*. Washington, D.C.: The Association for the Study of Negro Life and History, 1934.

Williams, George Washington. *History of the Negro Race in America from 1619 to 1880*. New York: G. P. Putnam's Sons, 1883.

HISTORIOGRAPHY OF THE RECONSTRUCTION—THE NEW SYNTHESIS

Anderson, Eric. "Afterward: Whither Reconstruction Historiography," in Eric Anderson and Alfred A. Moss, Jr. (eds.), *The Facts of Reconstruction: Essays in Honor of John Hope Franklin*. Baton Rouge: Louisiana State University Press, 1981, 219–28.

Browne, Thomas J. (ed.). *Reconstruction: New Perspectives on the Postbellum United States*. New York: Oxford University Press, 2006.

Carter, Dan T. "Moonlight, Magnolias, and Collard Greens: Black History and the New Romanticism," *Reviews in American History*, 5 (1977), 167–73.

Cox, LaWanda. "From Emancipation to Segregation: National Policy and Southern Blacks," in John Boles and Evelyn Thomas Nolan (eds.), *Interpreting Southern History: Essays in Honor of Sanford W. Higgenbotham*. Baton Rouge: Louisiana State University Press, 1987, 199–253.

Eric Foner. "The Continuing Evolution of Reconstruction Historiography," *OAH Magazine of History*, 4 (Winter 1989), 1–13.

―――. *Reconstruction: America's Unfinished Revolution, 1863–1877*. New York: Harper & Row, 1988.

Harris, Robert L., Jr. "Coming of Age: The Transformation of Afro-American Historiography," *Journal of Negro History*, 67 (1982), 107–21.

Hosmer, John, and Joseph Fineman. "Black Congressmen in Reconstruction Historiography," *Phylon*, 39 (1978), 97–107.

Kennedy, Stetson. *After Appomattox: How the South Won the War*. Gainesville: University of Florida Press, 1995.

Kolchin, Peter. "The Myth of Radical Reconstruction," *Reviews in American History*, 3 (1975), 228–36.

Magdol, Edward. "Local Black Leaders in the South, 1867–1875: An Essay toward the Reconstruction of Reconstruction History," *Societas*, 4 (1974), 81–110.

McCrary, Peyton. "The Political Dynamics of Black Reconstruction," *Reviews in American History*, 12 (1984), 51–57.

Mohr, Clarence L. "Southern Blacks in the Civil War: A Century of Historiography," *Journal of Negro History*, 59 (1974), 177–85.

Newby, I. A. "Historians and Negroes," *Journal of Negro History*, 54 (1969), 34–47.

Perman, Michael. "Eric Foner's Reconstruction: A Finished Revolution," *Reviews in American History*, 17 (1989), 73–78.

Pressly, Thomas J. "Reconstruction in the Southern United States: A Comparative Perspective," *OAH Magazine of History*, 4 (Winter 1989), 14–31.

Veysey, Lawrence. "The Autonomy of American History Reconsidered," *American Quarterly*, 31 (1979), 455–77.

Woodward, C. Vann. "Clio with Soul," *Journal of American History*, 56 (1969), 5–20.

HISTORIOGRAPHY OF THE RECONSTRUCTION—
THE POST-REVISIONISTS

Belz, Herman. "The New Orthodoxy in Reconstruction Historiography," *Reviews in American History*, 1 (1973), 106–13.

Benedict, Michael Les. *A Compromise of Principle: Congressional Republicans and Reconstruction, 1863–1869*. New York: W. W. Norton & Co., 1974.

———. "Equality and Expediency in the Reconstruction Era: A Review Essay," *Civil War History*, 23 (1977), 322–35.

———. *Fruits of Victory: Alternatives in Restoring the Union, 1865–1877*. Lanham, Md.: University Press of America, 1986.

———. "Preserving the Constitution: The Conservative Basis of Radical Reconstruction," *Journal of American History*, 61 (1974), 65–90.

———. "Southern Democrats and the Crisis of 1876–1877: A Reconsideration of *Reunion and Reaction*," *Journal of Southern History*, 46 (1980), 489–524.

Foner, Eric. "Reconstruction Revisited," *Reviews in American History*, 10 (1982), 82–100.

Genovese, Eugene D. "On Southern History and Its Historians: A Review Article," *Civil War History*, 13 (1967), 170–82.

Meier, August. "Negroes in the First and Second Reconstructions of the South," *Civil War History*, 13 (1967), 114–30.

Perman, Michael. *Reunion without Compromise: The South and Reconstruction, 1865–1868*. New York: Cambridge University Press, 1973.

———. *The Road to Redemption: Southern Politics, 1869–1879*. Chapel Hill: University of North Carolina Press, 1984.

Wharton, Vernon L. "Reconstruction," in Arthur S. Link and Rembert W. Patrick (eds.), *Writing Southern History: Essays in Historiography in Honor of Fletcher M. Green*. Baton Rouge: Louisiana State University Press, 1965, 295–315.

Woodward, C. Vann. "Seeds of Failure in Radical Race Policy," in Harold M. Hyman (ed.), *New Frontiers of the American Reconstruction*. Urbana: University of Illinois Press, 1966, 125–47.

HISTORIOGRAPHY OF THE RECONSTRUCTION—WILLIAM L. DUNNING AND HIS FELLOW TRAVELERS

Bowers, Claude G. *The Tragic Era: The Revolution after Lincoln.* Cambridge, Mass.: Riverside Press, 1929.

Burgess, John W. *Reconstruction and the Constitution, 1866–1876.* New York: Charles Scribner's Sons, 1902.

Caskey, William M. *Secession and Restoration of Louisiana.* Baton Rouge: Louisiana State University Press, 1938.

Coulter, E. Merton. *The Civil War and Readjustment in Kentucky.* Chapel Hill: University of North Carolina Press, 1926.

———. *The South During Reconstruction, 1865–1877.* Baton Rouge: Louisiana State University Press, 1947.

Davis, William W. *Civil War and Reconstruction in Florida.* New York: Columbia University, 1913.

Eckenrode, Hamilton J. *Political History of Virginia during the Reconstruction.* Baltimore, Md.: The Johns Hopkins University Press, 1904.

Ficklen, John. *History of Reconstruction in Louisiana (through 1868).* Baltimore, Md.: The Johns Hopkins University Press, 1910.

Fleming, Walter Lynwood. *Civil War and Reconstruction in Alabama.* New York: Columbia University Press, 1905.

Garner, James W. *Reconstruction in Mississippi.* New York: Macmillan, 1901.

Hamilton, Joseph G. de Roulhac. *Reconstruction in North Carolina.* New York: Columbia University Press, 1914.

Harper, Alan D. "William A. Dunning: The Historian as Nemesis," *Civil War History*, 10 (1964), 54–66.

Lomask, Milton. *Andrew Johnson: President on Trial.* New York: Farrar, Straus & Cudahy, 1960.

Lonn, Ella. *Reconstruction in Louisiana after 1868.* New York: George Putnam's Sons, 1918.

McGinty, Garnie W. *Louisiana Redeemed: The Overthrow of Carpet-bag Rule, 1876–1880.* New Orleans: Tulane University Press, 1941.

Milton, George F. *The Age of Hate: Andrew Johnson and the Radicals.* New York: Howard-McCann, 1930.

Muller, Philip D. "Look Back without Anger: A Reappraisal of William A. Dunning," *Journal of American History*, 61 (1974), 325–38.

Nunn, W. C. *Texas under the Carpetbaggers.* Austin: University of Texas Press, 1962.

Phillips, Ulrich B. "The Central Theme of Southern History," *American Historical Review*, 34 (1928), 30–43.

Ramsdell, Charles W. *Reconstruction in Texas.* New York: Columbia University Press, 1910.

Reynolds, John S. *Reconstruction in South Carolina.* Columbia: University of South Carolina Press, 1905.

Rhodes, James Ford. *History of the United States from the Compromise of 1850 to the Final Restoration of Home Rule at the South in 1877.* 7 vols. New York: Macmillan, 1896–1906.

Schouler, James. *History of the United States of America under the Constitution.* 7 vols. New York: Dodd, Mead & Co, 1880–1913.

Staples, Thomas S. *Reconstruction in Arkansas, 1862–1874.* New York: Columbia University Press, 1923.

Stryker, Lloyd P. *Andrew Johnson: A Study in Courage.* New York: Macmillan, 1929.

Thomas, David Y. *Arkansas in Civil War and Reconstruction, 1861–1874.* Little Rock: United Daughters of the Confederacy, Arkansas Chapter, 1923.

Thompson, C. Mildred. *Reconstruction in Georgia, Economic, Social, Political, 1865–1872.* New York: Columbia University Press, 1915.

Wallace, John. *Carpetbag Rule in Florida: The Inside Workings of the Reconstruction of Civil Government in Florida after the Close of the Civil War.* Gainesville: University of Florida Press, 1964.

Wilson, Woodrow. *A History of the American People.* 10 vols. Harper & Bros., 1902.

Winston, Robert W. *Andrew Johnson: Plebian and Patriot.* New York: Henry Holt, 1928.

HISTORIOGRAPHY OF RECONSTRUCTION—THE REVISIONISTS

Beale, Howard K. "On Rewriting Reconstruction History," *American Historical Review*, 45 (1939–1940), 807–27.

Craven, Avery O. "The Civil War and Reconstruction: A Critical Overlook of Recent Trends and Interpretations," *Civil War History*, 20 (1974), 446–61.

———. *Reconstruction: The Ending of the Civil War.* New York: Holt, Rinehart & Winston, Inc., 1969.

Franklin, John Hope. *Reconstruction: After the Civil War.* Chicago: University of Chicago Press, 1961.

———. "Whither Reconstruction Historiography," *Journal of Negro Education*, 17 (1947), 446–61.

Guelzo, Allen C. *The Crisis of the American Republic: A History of the Civil War and Reconstruction.* New York: St. Martin's Press, 1995.

Hyman, Harold M. (ed.). *The Radical Republicans and Reconstruction.* Indianapolis: Bobbs-Merrill Company, Inc., 1967.

Lindsey, David. *Americans in Conflict: The Civil War and Reconstruction.* Boston: Houghton Mifflin Co., 1974.

Patrick, Rembert W. *The Reconstruction of the Nation.* New York: Oxford University Press, 1967.

Pressley, Thomas J. "Racial Attitudes, Scholarship, and Reconstruction: A Review History," *Journal of Southern History*, 32 (1966), 88–93.

Randall, James G., and David Donald. *The Civil War and Reconstruction*. 2nd rev. ed. Lexington, Mass.: D. C. Heath, 1969.

Simkins, Francis B. "New Viewpoints of Southern Reconstruction," *Journal of Southern History*, 5 (1939), 46–61.

Smith, Page. *Trial by Fire: A People's History of the Civil War and Reconstruction*. New York: McGraw-Hill, 1982.

Stampp, Kenneth M. *The Era of Reconstruction, 1865–1877*. New York: Alfred A. Knopf, 1965.

———— (ed.). *Reconstruction: An Anthology of Revisionist Writings*. Baton Rouge: Louisiana State University Press, 1969.

Trelease, Allen W. *Reconstruction: The Great Experiment*. New York: Harper & Row, 1971.

Weisberger, Bernard A. "The Dark and Bloody Ground of Reconstruction Historiography," *Journal of Southern History*, 25 (1959), 427–44.

Wood, Forrest G. *The Era of Reconstruction, 1863–1877*. New York: Thomas Y. Crowell Co., 1975.

————. "On Revising Reconstruction History: Negro Suffrage, White Disfranchisement, and Common Sense," *Journal of Negro History*, 51 (1966), 98–113.

HOLDEN, WILLIAM W. (1818–1892)

Bogue, Jessie Parker. "Violence and Oppression in North Carolina During Reconstruction." Ph.D. dissertation, University of Maryland, 1973.

Boyd, William K. "William W. Holden," Trinity College Historical Society *Papers*, Series III (1899), 38–78, 90–133.

Ewing, Cortez A. M. "Two Reconstruction Impeachments," *North Carolina Historical Review*, 15 (1938), 197–230.

Folk, Edgar Estes. "W. W. Holden and the Election of 1858," *North Carolina Historical Review*, 21 (1944), 294–318.

————. "W. W. Holden and the North Carolina Standard, 1843–1848," *North Carolina Historical Review*, 19 (1942), 22–47.

————, and Bynum Shaw. *W. W. Holden: A Political Biography*. Winston-Salem, N.C.: John F. Blair, Publisher, 1982.

Hamilton, Joseph G. de Roulhac. *Reconstruction in North Carolina*. New York: Columbia University Press, 1914.

Harris, William C. *William Woods Holden: Firebrand of North Carolina Politics*. Baton Rouge: Louisiana State University Press, 1987.

————. "William Woods Holden: In Search of Vindication," *North Carolina Historical Review*, 59 (1982), 354–72.

Lancaster, James L. "The Scalawags of North Carolina, 1850–1868." Ph.D. dissertation, Princeton University, 1974.

Olsen, Otto H. "The Ku Klux Klan: A Study in Reconstruction Politics and Propaganda," *North Carolina Historical Quarterly*, 39 (1962), 340–62.

Raper, Horace W. *William W. Holden: North Carolina's Political Enigma*. Chapel Hill: University of North Carolina Press, 1985.

Russ, William A. "Radical Disfranchisement in North Carolina," *North Carolina Historical Review*, 11 (1934), 271–83.

Trelease, Allan W. *White Terror: The Ku Klux Klan Conspiracy and Southern Reconstruction*. New York: Harper & Row, 1971.

Tucker, Glenn. *Zeb Vance: Champion of Personal Freedom*. Indianapolis: Bobbs-Merrill, 1965.

Wakelyn, Jon L. *Biographical Dictionary of the Confederacy*. Westport, Conn.: Greenwood Press, 1977.

Walker, Jacqueline Baldwin. "Blacks in North Carolina during Reconstruction." Ph.D. dissertation, Duke University, 1979.

Yates, Richard E. *The Confederacy and Zeb Vance*. Tuscaloosa, Ala.: Confederate Publishing Co., 1958.

Zuber, Richard L. *Jonathan Worth: A Biography of a Southern Unionist*. Chapel Hill: University of North Carolina Press, 1965.

————. *North Carolina During Reconstruction*. Raleigh: North Carolina Division of Archives and History, 1996.

HOOD, JOHN BELL (1831–1879)

Current, Richard N. (ed.). *Encyclopedia of the Confederacy*. 4 vols. New York: Simon & Schuster, 1993.

Davis, William C. (ed.). *The Confederate General*. 6 vols. N.p.: National Historical Society, 1991.

Dyer, John P. *The Gallant Hood*. Indianapolis: Bobbs-Merrill, 1950.

Hood, John Bell. *Advance and Retreat: Personal Experiences in the United States and Confederate States Armies*. Intro. by Bruce J. Dinges. Lincoln: University of Nebraska Press, 1996, repr.

McMurry, Richard M. *John Bell Hood and the War for Southern Independence*. Lexington: University of Kentucky, 1982.

Patterson, Gerard A. "John Bell Hood," *Civil War Times Illustrated*, 9 (February 1971), 12–21.

Warner, Ezra J. *Generals in Gray: Lives of Confederate Commanders*. Baton Rouge: Louisiana State University Press, 1959.

HOOKER, JOSEPH (1814–1879)

Hassler, Warren W. "'Fightin' Joe' Hooker," *Civil War Times Illustrated*, 14 (August 1975), 4–9, 36–37, 41–46.

Hebert, Walter H. *Fighting Joe Hooker*. Indianapolis: Bobbs-Merrill, 1944.

HOWARD, JACOB M. (1805–1871)

Knauss, James O. "Jacob Meritt Howard" in Allen Johnson *et al.* (eds.), *Dictionary of American Biography* (10 double vols. + 9 supplements, 1964–1981), IX, 278–79.

Howard, Hamilton Gay. *Civil War Echoes: Character Sketches and Secrets.* Washington, D.C.: Howard Publishing Co., 1907.

HOWARD, OLIVER OTIS (1830–1909)

Carpenter, John A. *Sword and Olive Branch: Oliver Otis Howard.* Pittsburgh: University of Pittsburgh Press, 1964.

Catton, Bruce. *The Army of the Potomac.* 3 vols. New York: Doubleday & Co., 1951–1953.

Cox, John, and LaWanda Cox. "General Howard and the 'Misrepresented Bureau,'" *Journal of Southern History*, 19 (1953), 427–56.

Howard, Oliver Otis. *Autobiography of Oliver Otis Howard.* 2 vols. New York: Baker and Taylor Company, 1908.

McFeely, William S. *Yankee Stepfather: General O. O. Howard and the Freedmen.* New Haven, Conn.: Yale University Press, 1968.

IMPEACHMENT

Benedict, Michael Les. *The Impeachment Trial of Andrew Johnson.* New York: W. W. Norton, 1973.

———. "The Rout of Radicalism: Republicans and the Elections of 1867," *Civil War History*, 18 (1972), 334–44.

Berger, Raul. *Impeachment: The Constitutional Problems.* Cambridge, Mass.: Harvard University Press, 1973.

Brandt, Irving. *Impeachment: Trials and Errors.* New York: Alfred A. Knopf, 1973.

Brodie, Fawn. *Thaddeus Stevens: Scourge of the South.* New York: W. W. Norton, 1966.

Current, Richard N. *Old Thad Stevens: A Story of Ambition.* Madison: University of Wisconsin Press, 1942.

Korngold, Ralph. *Thaddeus Stevens: A Being Darkly Wise and Rudely Great.* New York: Harcourt, Brace & Co., 1955.

Kutler, Stanley I. "Impeachment Reconsidered," *Reviews in American History*, 1 (1973), 480–87.

Lomask, Milton. *Andrew Johnson: President on Trial.* New York: Farrar, Straus & Cudahy, 1960.

Mantell, Martin E. *Johnson, Grant, and the Politics of Reconstruction.* New York: Columbia University Press, 1973.

Sefton, James E. *Andrew Johnson and the Uses of Constitutional Power.* Boston: Little, Brown & Co., 1980.

Sefton, James E. "The Impeachment of Andrew Johnson: A Century of Writing," *Civil War History*, 14 (1968), 120–47.

Thomas, Benjamin P., and Harold M. Hyman. *Stanton: The Life and Times of Lincoln's Secretary of War.* New York: Alfred A. Knopf, 1962.

Trefousse, Hans L. "The Acquittal of Andrew Johnson and the Decline of the Radicals," *Civil War History*, 14 (1969), 148–61.

———. *Ben Butler: The South Called Him BEAST!* New York: Twayne Publishers, 1957.

———. *Benjamin Franklin Wade: Radical Republican from Ohio.* New York: Twayne Publishers, 1963.

———. *Impeachment of a President: Andrew Johnson, the Blacks, and Reconstruction.* Knoxville: University of Tennessee Press, 1975.

INTELLIGENCE AND SECRET SERVICE OPERATIONS

Ashley, Robert P. "The St. Albans Raid," *Civil War Times Illustrated*, 6 (November 1967), 18–25.

Axelrod, Alan. *The War between the Spies: A History of Espionage during the Civil War.* New York: Atlantic Monthly Press, 1992.

Bakeless, John. "The Enigma: James Harrison," *Civil War Times Illustrated*, 9 (April 1970), 12–20.

———. *Spies of the Confederacy.* Philadelphia: Lippincott, 1970.

Blakey, Arch. *General John H. Winder, C.S.A.* Gainesville: University of Florida Press, 1990.

Bryant William O. *Cahaba Prison and the Sultana Disaster.* Tuscaloosa: University of Alabama Press, 1990.

Canan, H. V. "Confederate Military Intelligence," *Maryland Historical Magazine*, 59 (1964), 34–51.

Davis, William C. "The Conduct of 'Mr. Thompson'," *Civil War Times Illustrated*, 9 (May 1970), 4–7, 43–47.

Feis, William B. *Grant's Secret Service: The Intelligence War from Belmont to Appomattox.* Lincoln: University of Nebraska Press, 2002.

Fishel, Edwin C. "The Mythology of Civil War Intelligence," *Civil War History*, 10 (1964), 344–67.

———. *The Secret War for Union: The Untold Story of Military Intelligence in the Civil War.* Boston: Houghton Mifflin, 1996.

Gaddy, David Winfred. "Gray Cloaks and Daggers," *Civil War Times Illustrated*, 14 (July 1975), 20–27.

Hall, James O. "The Spy Harrison: A Modern Hunt for a Fabled Agent," *Civil War Times Illustrated*, 24 (February 1986), 18–25.

Headly, John W. *Confederate Operations in Canada and New York.* New York: Neal Publishing, 1906.

Horan, James D. *Confederate Agent: A Discovery in History.* New York: Crown Publishers, 1954.

Johnston, Angus J., II. "Disloyalty on Confederate Railroads in Virginia," *Virginia Magazine of History and Biography*, 68 (1955), 410–26.

Kinchen, Oscar A. *Confederate Operations in Canada and the North.* North Quincy, Mass.: Christopher, 1970.

Klein, Frederic S. "The Great Copperhead Conspiracy of 1864," *Civil War Times Illustrated*, 21–26.

Klement, Frank L. *Dark Lanterns: Secret Political Societies, Conspiracies and Treason Trials in the Civil War.* Baton Rouge: Louisiana State University Press, 1984.

Kushlan, Jim (ed.). "Rebel Secret Agents and Saboteurs in Canada," *Civil War Times Illustrated*, 40 (June 2001), [Special Issue].

Levin, Alexandra Lee. "The Canada Contact: Edwin Gray Lee," *Civil War Times Illustrated*, 18 (June 1979), 4–8, 42–47.

Markel, Donald E. *Spies and Spymasters of the Civil War.* New York: Hippocrene Books, 1994.

Mogelever, Jacob. *Death to Traitors: The Story of General Lafayette C. Baker, Lincoln's Forgotten Secret Service Chief.* Garden City, N.Y.: Doubleday, 1960.

Moore, Winton P. "Union Army Provost Marshals in the Eastern Theater," *Military Affairs*, 26 (1962), 120–26.

Pardell, James G. "The Newspaper Problem in Its Bearing upon Military Secrecy during the Civil War," *American Historical Review*, 23 (1918), 303–23.

Radley, Kenneth. *Rebel Watch Dog: The Confederate States Army Provost Guard.* Baton Rouge: Louisiana State University Press, 1989.

Robbins, Peggy. "The Greatest Scoundrel [Jacob Thompson]," *Civil War Times Illustrated*, 31 (November/December 1992), 54–59, 89–90.

Rule, D. H. "*Sultana*: A Case for Sabotage," *North & South*, 5 (December 2001), 76–87.

Scheips, Paul J. "Union Signal Communications: Innovation and Conflict," *Civil War History*, 9 (1963), 399–406.

Singer, Jane. *The Confederate Dirty War: Arson, Bombings, Assassination and Plots for Chemical and Germ Attacks on the Union.* Jefferson, N.C.: McFarland & Company, 2005.

Soodalter, Ron. "Last Raid of a Rebel Pirate," *Civil War Times Illustrated*, 48 (April 2009), 42–47.

Sparks, David. "General Patrick's Progress: Intelligence and Security in the Army of the Potomac," *Civil War History*, 10 (1964), 371–84.

Squires, J. Duane. "Aeronautics in the Civil War," *American Historical Review*, 42 (1937), 635–54.

Steers, Edward, Jr. "Terror—1860s Style," *North & South*, 5 (May 2002), 12–18.

Stuart, Meriwether. "Samuel Ruth and General Robert E. Lee: Disloyalty and the Line of Supply to Fredericksburg, 1862–1863," *Virginia Magazine of History and Biography*, 71 (1963), 35–109.

Taylor, Charles E. *The Signal and Secret Service of the Confederacy*. Harman, MD: Toomey Press, 1986.

Tidwell, William A., with James O. Hall and David Winfred Gaddy. *Come Retribution: The Confederate Secret Service and the Assassination of Lincoln*. Jackson: University of Mississippi Press, 1988.

———. "Confederate Expenditures for Secret Service," *Civil War History*, 37 (1991), 219–31.

INTERNAL DISSENT IN THE CONFEDERACY—APPLACHIAN PENINSULA

Auman, William T. "Neighbor against Neighbor: The Inner Civil War in the Randolph County Area of Confederate North Carolina," *North Carolina Historical Review*, 52 (1984), 327–63.

Bailey, Hugh C. "Disaffection in the Alabama Hill Country, 1861," *Civil War History*, 4 (1958), 183–94.

———. "Disloyalty in Early Confederate Alabama," *Journal of Southern History*, 23 (1957), 522–28.

Noe, Kenneth W. "Red String Scare; Civil War Southwest Virginia and the Heroes of America," *North Carolina Historical Review*, 69 (1992), 301–22.

Shanks, Henry T. "Disloyalty to the Confederacy in Southwestern Virginia," *North Carolina Historical Review*, 21 (1944), 118–35.

Storey, Margaret M. "Civil War Unionists in the Political Culture of Loyalty in Alabama," *Journal of Southern History*, 69 (2000), 71–106.

INTERNAL DISSENT IN THE CONFEDERACY—CIVIL WAR STATE AND LOCAL POLITICS

Baker, Jean H. *The Politics of Continuity: Maryland and Political Parties from 1858 to 1870*. Baltimore, Md.: The Johns Hopkins University Press, 1973.

Barnett, James. *The Civil War in North Carolina*. Chapel Hill: University of North Carolina Press, 1963.

Bergeron, Arthur W. *Confederate Mobile*. Jackson: University of Mississippi Press, 1991.

Bettersworth, John K. *Confederate Mississippi: The People and Politics of a Confederate State*. Baton Rouge: Louisiana State University Press, 1943.

Bill, Alfred H. *Beleaguered City: Richmond, 1861–1865*. New York: Knopf, 1846.

Bowen, Nancy Head. "A Political Labyrinth: Texas in the Civil War—Questions of Continuity." Ph.D. dissertation, Rice University, 1974.

Bragg, Jefferson Davis. *Louisiana in the Confederacy*. Baton Rouge: Louisiana State University Press, 1941.

Bryan, T. Conn. *Confederate Georgia*. Athens: University of Georgia Press, 1953.

Cauthen, Charles E. *South Carolina Goes to War, 1861–1865*. Chapel Hill: University of North Carolina Press, 1950.

Coleman, Kenneth. *Confederate Athens, 1861–1865*. Athens: University of Georgia Press, 1968.

Coulter, Nate. "The Impact of the Civil War upon Pulaski County, Arkansas," *Arkansas Historical Quarterly*, 41 (1982), 67–82.

Dougan, Michael B. *Confederate Arkansas: The People and Politics of a Frontier State in Wartime*. University: University of Alabama Press, 1976.

Frank, Fedora Small. "Nashville during the Civil War," *Tennessee Historical Quarterly*, 39 (1980), 310–22.

Harrison, Lowell. *The Civil War in Kentucky*. Lexington: University of Kentucky Press, 1975.

Johns, John E. *Florida during the Civil War*. Gainesville: University of Florida Press, 1963.

Parrish, William. *Turbulent Partners: Missouri and the Union, 1861–1865*. Columbia: University of Missouri Press, 1963.

Somers, Dale A. "War and Play: The Civil War in New Orleans," *Mississippi Quarterly*, 26 (1973), 3–28.

Thomas, Emory. "Wartime Richmond," *Civil War Times Illustrated*, 16 (June 1977), [Special Issue].

Wiley, Bell I. *Plain People of the Confederacy*. Baton Rouge: Louisiana State University Press, 1944.

Winters, John D. *The Civil War in Louisiana*. Baton Rouge: Louisiana State University Press, 1963.

Wooster, Ralph A., and Robert Wooster, "A People at War: East Texas during the Civil War," *East Texas Historical Journal*, 28 (1990), 3–16.

INTERNAL DISSENT IN THE CONFEDERACY—CONSCRIPTION AND DRAFT EVASION

Harrison, Lowell H. "Conscription in the Confederacy," *Civil War Times Illustrated*, 9 (July 1970), 10–19.

Lonn, Ella. *Desertion during the Civil War*. New York: Century, 1928.

Martis, Kenneth C. *The Historical Atlas of the Congresses of the Confederate States of America, 1861–1865*. New York: Simon & Schuster, 1994.

Moore, Albert Burton. *Conscription and Conflict in the Confederacy*. New York: Macmillan, 1924.

INTERNAL DISSENT IN THE CONFEDERACY—DISAGREEMENT ON CONDUCT OF THE WAR

Bass, James Horace. "The Attack upon the Confederate Administration in Georgia in the Spring of 1864," *Georgia Historical Quarterly*, 18 (1934), 228–47.

Bragg, William Harris. *Joe Brown's Army: The Georgia State Line, 1862–1865.* Macon: Mercer University Press, 1987.

Eicher, David J. "How the Confederacy Fought Itself," *Civil War Times Illustrated*, 46 (January 2008), 52–59.

Escott, Paul D. *After Secession: Jefferson Davis and the Failure of Confederate Nationalism.* Baton Rouge: Louisiana State University Press, 1878.

Faust, Drew Gilpin. *The Creation of Southern Nationalism: Ideology and Identity during the American Civil War South.* Baton Rouge: Louisiana State University Press, 1988.

Fleming, Walter Lynwood. "The Peace Movement in Alabama during the Civil War," *South Atlantic Quarterly*, 2 (1903), 114–124, 246–260.

Harris, William C. *William Woods Holden: Firebrand of North Carolina Politics.* Baton Rouge: Louisiana State University Press, 1987.

Hill, Louise Biles. *Joseph E. Brown and The Confederacy.* Chapel Hill: University of North Carolina Press, 1939.

McKitrick, Eric L. "Party Politics and the Union and Confederate War Efforts," in William N. Chambers and Walter D. Burnham (eds.), *The American Party Systems: Stages of Development.* New York: Oxford University Press, 1967, 117–51.

Parks, Joseph H. *Joseph E. Brown of Georgia.* Baton Rouge: Louisiana State University Press, 1977.

———. "State Rights in a Crisis: Governor Joseph E. Brown versus President Jefferson Davis," *Journal of Southern History*, 32 (1966), 3–24.

Raper, Horace W. "William Woods Holden and the Peace Movement in North Carolina," *North Carolina Historical Review*, 31 (1954), 493–516.

———. *William Woods Holden: North Carolina's Political Enigma.* Chapel Jill: University of North Carolina Press, 1985.

Smith, Mary Shannon. *Union Sentiment in North Carolina during the Civil War.* Raleigh, N.C.: Meredith College, 1815.

Talmadge, John E. "Peace Movement Activities in Civil War Georgia," *Georgia Review*, 7 (1953), 190–203.

Thomas, Emory M. *The Confederacy as a Revolutionary Experience.* Englewood Cliffs, N.J.: Prentice-Hall, 1971.

Thompson, William Y. *Robert Toombs of Georgia.* Baton Rouge: Louisiana State University Press, 1966.

Wiley, Bell I. "The Confederate Congress," *Civil War Times Illustrated*, 7 (April 1968), 22–24.

Yearns, W. Buck. *The Confederate Congress.* Athens: University of Georgia Press, 1960.

INTERNAL DISSENT IN THE CONFEDERACY—EAST TENNESSEE

Bryan, Charles F., Jr. "'Tories' amidst Rebels: Confederate Occupation of East Tennessee," *East Tennessee Historical Society Publications*, 60 (1988), 3–22.

Coulter, E. Merton. *William G. Brownlow: Fighting Parson of the Southern Highlands*. Chapel Hill: University of North Carolina Press, 1937.

Patton, James W. *Unionism and Reconstruction in Tennessee, 1860–1867*. Chapel Hill: University of North Carolina Press, 1934.

Sheeler, J. Rueben. "The Development of Unionism in East Tennessee," *Journal of Negro History*, 29 (1944), 166–203.

White, Edward L., III. "A Question of Security: The Confederacy's Policy in East Tennessee. 1861–1863," *Southern Historian*, 11 (1988), 1–23.

INTERNAL DISSENT IN THE CONFEDERACY—ECONOMIC QUESTIONS, MONETARY TAXATION, GOODS IN KIND, AND IMPRESSMENT

Ball, Douglas B. *Financial Failure and Confederate Defeat*. Urbana: University of Illinois Press, 1991.

Bateman, Fred, and Thomas Weiss. *A Deplorable Scarcity: The Failure of Industrialization in the Slave Economy*. Chapel Hill: University of North Carolina Press, 1981.

Burdekin, Richard C. K., and Farrokh K. Langdana. "War Finance in the Southern Confederacy, 1861–1865," *Explorations in Economic History*, 10 (1993), 352–76.

Engermann, Stanley, "The Economic Impact of the Civil War," *Explorations in Economic History*, 3 (1966), 176–99.

Fogel, Robert W. *Without Consensus or Contract: The Rise and Fall of American Slavery*. New York: Norton, 1989.

Hamilton, Daniel W. "The Confederate Sequestration Act," *Civil War History*, 52 (2006), 373–408.

Johnson, Ludwell H., III. "Blockade or Trade Monopoly: John A. Dix and the Union Occupation of Norfolk," *Virginia Magazine of History and Biography*, 93 (1985), 54–78.

———. "Contraband Trade during the Last Year of the Civil War," *Mississippi Valley Historical Review*, 49 (1963), 635–53.

Lerner, Eugene M. "The Monetary and Fiscal Programs of the Confederate Government, 1861–1865," *Journal of Political Economy*, 62 (1954), 506–22.

Massey, Mary Elizabeth. *Ersatz in the Confederacy*. Columbia: University of South Carolina Press, 1952.

Pecquet, Gary M. "Money in the Trans-Mississippi Confederacy and the Currency Reform Act of 1864," *Explorations in Economic History*, 24 (1987), 218–43.

Todd, R. C. *Confederate Finance*. Athens: University of Georgia Press, 1954.
Weddle, Kevin J. "The Blockade Board of 1861 and Union Naval Strategy," *Civil War History*, 48 (2002), 123–142.

INTERNAL DISSENT IN THE CONFEDERACY— GOVERNMENT AND PRESS

Neely, Mark E., Jr. *Jefferson Davis and Civil Liberties*. Milwaukee, Wisc.: Marquette University Press, 1993.

INTERNAL DISSENT IN THE CONFEDERACY—*HABEAS CORPUS*

Neely, Mark E., Jr. *Jefferson Davis and Civil Liberties*. Milwaukee, Wisc.: Marquette University Press, 1993.

INTERNAL DISSENT IN THE CONFEDERACY—IN GENERAL

Adams, Ephraim Douglas. *Great Britain and the American Civil War*. 2 vols. New York: Russell & Russell, 1925.
Beckles, Willson. *John Slidell and the Confederates in Paris, 1862–1865*. New York: Minton, Balck, 1932.
Bulloch, James D. *The Secret Service of the Confederate States in Europe; or, How the Confederate Cruisers Were Equipped*. 2 vols. New York: Thomas Yoseloff, 1959, repr.
Case Lynne M., and Warren F. Spencer. *The United States and France: Civil War Diplomacy*. Philadelphia: University of Pennsylvania Press, 1970.
Crook, David Paul. *The North, the South, and the Powers, 1861–1865*. New York: Wiley, 1974.
Daddysman, James W. *The Matamoros Trade: Confederate Commerce, Diplomacy, and Intrigue*. Newark: University of Delaware Press, 1984.
Delaney, Norman. "The Strange Occupation of James Bulloch: 'When Can You Start?'," *Civil War Times Illustrated*, 21 (March 1982), 18–27.
Durkin, J. T. *Stephen R. Mallory: Confederate Navy Chief*. Chapel Hill: University of North Carolina Press, 1954.
Jones, Wilbur D. *The Confederate Rams at Birkenhead: A Chapter in Anglo-American Relations*. Tuscaloosa, Ala.: Confederate Publishing Co., 1961.
Lebergott, Stanley. "Through the Blockade: The Profitability and Extent of Cotton Smuggling," *Journal of Economic History*, 51 (1981), 867–88.
May, Robert E. (ed.). *The Union, the Confederacy, and the Atlantic Rim*. West Lafayette, Ind.: Purdue University Press, 1995.

Merli, Frank J. *Great Britain and the Confederate Navy, 1861–1865*. Blooming-ton: Indiana University Press, 1970.

Owsley, Frank L. *King Cotton Diplomacy*. Chicago: University of Chicago Press, 1959.

Spencer, Warren F. *The Confederate Navy in Europe*. Tuscaloosa: University of Alabama Press, 1983.

Surdam, David G. "Cotton's Potential as Economic Weapon: The Antebellum and Wartime Markets for Cotton Textiles," *Agricultural History*, 68 (1994), 122–45.

Thompson, Samuel Bernard. *The Confederate Navy in Europe*. Tuscaloosa: Uni-versity of Alabama Press, 1983.

INTERNAL DISSENT IN THE CONFEDERACY—OTHER AREAS OF DISAFFECTION

Baker, Robin E. "Class Conflict and Political Upheaval: The Transformation of North Carolina Politics during the Civil War," *North Carolina Historical Re-view*, 69 (1992), 148–78.

Brown, Norman D. "A Union Election in Civil War North Carolina," *North Caro-lina Historical Review*, 43 (1966), 381–400.

Bynum, Victoria E. *The Free State of Jones: Mississippi's Longest Civil War*. Chapel Hill: University of North Carolina Press, 2001.

Current, Richard N. *Lincoln's Loyalists: Union Soldiers from the Confederacy*. Boston: Northeastern University Press, 1992.

Dodd, Don. *Winston: An Antebellum Civil War History of a Hill County of North Alabama*. Jasper, Ala.: C. Elliott, 1972.

Durrill, Wayne K. *War of Another Kind: A Southern Community [Washington, County, North Carolina] in the Great Rebellion*. New York: Oxford University Press, 1990.

Elliott, Claude. "Union Sentiment in Texas, 1861–1865," *Southwestern Histori-cal Quarterly*, 50 (1947), 449–77.

Inscoe, John C., and Robert C. Kenzer (eds.). *Enemies of the Country: New Per-spectives on Unionists in the Civil War South*. Athens: University of Georgia Press, 2001.

Kruman, Marc. "Dissent in the Confederacy: The North Carolina Experience," *Civil War History*, 27 (1981), 293–313.

Leverett, Rudy H. *The Free State of Jones*. Jackson: University of Mississippi Press, 1984.

McCaslin, Richard B. *Tainted Breeze: The Great Hanging at Gainesville, Texas, 1862*. Baton Rouge: Louisiana State University Press, 1994.

McMillan, Malcolm C. *The Disintegration of a Confederate State: Three Gov-ernors and Alabama's Wartime Home Front*. Macon, Ga.: Mercer University Press, 1986.

Marten, James. *Texas Divided: Loyalty and Dissent in the Lone Star State*. Lexington: University of Kentucky Press, 1990.

Mills, Gary. "Alexandria, Louisiana: A 'Confederate' City at War with Itself," *Red River Historical Review*, 5 (1980), 23–36.

Moneyhon, Carl H. "Disloyalty and Class Consciousness in Southwest Arkansas, 1852–1865," *Arkansas Historical Quarterly*, 52 (1993), 223–43.

Neely, Mark E., Jr. *Jefferson Davis and Civil Liberties*. Milwaukee, Wisc.: Marquette University Press, 1993.

Robbins, Peggy. "Hanging Days in Texas [Gainesville]," *America's Civil War*, 12 (May 1999), 50–55.

Smith, David P. "Conscription and Conflict on the Texas Frontier," *Civil War History*, 36 (1990), 250–61.

Storey, Margaret. "'I'd Rather Go to Hell': White Unionists, Slaves, and Federal Counter-Insurgency in Civil War Alabama," *North & South*, 7 (February 2004), 70–82.

Taylor, Ethel. "Discontent in Confederate Louisiana," *Louisiana History*, 2 (1961), 410–28.

Walker, Peter F. *Vicksburg: A People at War, 1860–1865*. Chapel Hill: University of North Carolina Press, 1960.

Worley, Ted R. "The Arkansas Peace Society of 1861: A Study in Mountain Unionism," *Journal of Southern History*, 24 (1958), 445–56.

INTERNAL DISSENT IN THE CONFEDERACY—STATE RIGHTS AND THE POLITICIANS, PRO AND CON

Bass, James Horace. "The Georgia Gubernatorial Elections of 1861 and 1863," *Georgia Historical Quarterly*, 17 (1935), 167–88.

Boney, F. N. *John Letcher of Virginia: The Story of Virginia's Civil War Governor*. Tuscaloosa: University of Alabama Press, 1966.

Brown, Norman D. *Edward Stanly: Whiggery's Tar Heel "Conqueror."* Tuscaloosa: University of Alabama Press, 1974.

Cassidy, Vincent H., and Amos E. Simpson. *Henry Watkins Allen of Louisiana*. Baton Rouge: Louisiana State University Press, 1964.

Donald, David H. (ed.). *Why the North Won the Civil War*. Baton Rouge: Louisiana State University Press, 1960.

Dubay, Robert W. *John Jones Pettus, Mississippi Fire-Eater: His Life and Times, 1813–1867*. Oxford: University of Mississippi Press, 1975.

Edmunds, John B., Jr. *Francis W. Pickens and the Politics of Destruction*. Chapel Hill: University of North Carolina, 1986.

Flippin, Percy S. *Herschel V. Johnson of Georgia: States Rights Unionist*. Richmond, Va.: Dietz Printing Co., 1931.

Hill, Louise Biles. *Joseph E. Brown and The Confederacy*. Chapel Hill: University of North Carolina Press, 1939.

Kibler, Lillian A. *Benjamin F. Perry, South Carolina Unionist.*

McCash, William B. *Thomas R. R. Cobb, 1823–1862.* Macon, Ga.: Mercer University Press, 1983.

McKitrick, Eric L. "Party Politics and the Union and Confederate War Efforts," in William N. Chambers and Walter D. (eds.), *The American Party Systems: Stages of Development.* New York: Oxford University Press, 1967, 117–51.

Meiners, Frederika Ann. "The Texas Governorship, 1861–1865: A Biography of an Office." Ph.D. dissertation, Rice University, 1974.

Montgomery, Horace. *Howell Cobb's Confederate Career.* Tuscaloosa, Ala.: Confederate Publishing Co., 1959

Owsley, Frank L. *State Rights in the Confederacy.* Chicago: University of Chicago Press, 1925.

Pearce, Haywood J., Jr. *Benjamin H. Hill: Secession and Reconstruction.* Chicago: University of Chicago Press, 1928.

Pereya, Lillian A. *James Lusk Alcorn: Persistent Whig.* Baton Rouge: Louisiana State University Press, 1966.

Proctor, Ben. *Not without Honor: The Life of John H. Reagan.* Austin: University of Texas Press, 1962.

Rable, George C. *The Confederate Republic: A Revolution against Politics.* Chapel Hill: University of North Carolina Press, 1994.

Rabun, James Z. "Alexander H. Stephens and Jefferson Davis," *American Historical Review,* 58 (1953), 290–321.

Ringold, May Spencer. *The Role of the State Legislature in the Confederacy.* Athens: University of Georgia Press, 1966.

Robinson, William M., Jr. *Justice in Gray: A History of the Judicial System of the Confederate States of America.* Cambridge, Mass.: Harvard University Press, 1941.

Scarboro, David D. "North Carolina and the Confederacy: The Weakness of States' Rights during the War," *North Carolina Historical Review,* 56 (1979), 133–49.

Schott, Thomas E. *Alexander H. Stephens of Georgia: A Biography.* Baton Rouge: Louisiana State University Press, 1988.

Simpson, John Eddins. *Howell Cobb: The Politics of Ambition.* Chicago: Adams Press, 1973.

Sims, Henry Harrison. *Life of R. M. T. Hunter: A Study in Sectionalism and Secession.* Richmond, Va.: William Byrd Press, 1935.

Smith, John I. *The Courage of a Southern Unionist: A Biography of Isaac Murphy, Governor of Arkansas, 1864–1868.* Little Rock: Rose Publishing Co., 1979.

Tucker, Glenn. "A Personality Profile: Zeb Vance," *Civil War Times Illustrated,* 7 (April 1968), 10–19.

———. *Zeb Vance: Champion of Personal Freedom.* Indianapolis: Bobbs-Merrill, 1965.

White, Laura Amanda. *Robert Barnwell Rhett: Father of Secession.* Glouster, Mass.: P. Smith, 1965.

Yates, Richard E. "Governor Vance and the Peace Movement," *North Carolina Historical Review*, 17 (1940), 1–25, 89–113.

———. *The Confederacy and Zeb Vance*. Tuscaloosa, Ala.: Confederate Publishing Co., 1958.

Yearns, W. Buck (ed.). *The Confederate Governors*. Athens: University of Georgia Press, 1985.

INTERNAL DISSENT IN THE CONFEDERACY—WEST VIRGINIA

Curry, Richard Orr. *A House Divided: A Study of Statehood Politics and the Copperhead Movement in West Virginia*. Pittsburgh: University of Pittsburgh, 1964.

———. "The Virginia Background for the History of the Civil War and Reconstruction Era in West Virginia: An Analytical Commentary," *West Virginia History*, 20 (1959), 215–46.

Gooden, Randall Scott. "The Completion of a Revolution: West Virginia from Statehood through Reconstruction." Ph.D. dissertation, West Virginia University, 1995.

Lewis, Virgil A. "How West Virginia Became a Member of the Federal Union," *West Virginia History*, 30 (1969), 598–606.

Lowe, Richard. "Another Look at Reconstruction in Virginia," *Civil War History*, 32 (1986), 56–76.

Moore, George Ellis. *A Banner in the Hills: West Virginia's Statehood*. New York: Appleton Century Crofts, 1963.

Newell, Clayton R. *Lee vs. McClellan: The First Campaign*. Washington, D.C.: Regnery Publishing, 1996.

Shaffer, Dallas S. "Lincoln and the 'Vast Question of West Virginia'," *West Virginia History*, 32 (1970), 86–100.

Steers, Ed, Jr. "Montani Semper Liberi: The Making of West Virginia," *North & South*, 3 (January 2000), 18–33.

Tatum, Georgia Lee. *Disloyalty in the Confederacy*. Chapel Hill: University of North Carolina Press, 1934.

Taylor, Alrutheus A. "Making West Virginia a Free State," *Journal of Negro History*, 6 (1921), 131–73.

Winston, Sheldon. "Statehood for West Virginia: An Illegal Act?" *West Virginia History*, 30 (1969), 530–534.

Woodward, Isaiah A. "Opinions of President Lincoln and His Cabinet on Statehood for West Virginia." *West Virginia History*, 21 (1960), 157–85.

IUKA AND CORINTH, THE BATTLES OF

Allen, Stacy D. "Corinth (Siege and Battle) & Iuka," *Blue & Gray*, 19 (2001–2002).

Castel, Albert. *General Sterling Price and the Civil War in the West*. Baton Rouge: Louisiana State University Press, 1968.

Castel, Albert. "Victory at Corinth," *Civil War Times Illustrated*, 17 (October 1978), 12–22.

Engel, Stephen D. *Struggle for the Heartland: The Campaigns from Fort Henry to Corinth*. Lincoln: University of Nebraska Press, 2001.

Lamers, William M. *The Edge of Glory: A Biography of William S. Rosecrans*. New York: Harcourt, Brace, 1961.

Marszalek, John. "Halleck Captures Corinth," *Civil War Times Illustrated*, 45 (February 2006), 46–52.

Suhr, Robert Collins. "Small But Savage Battle of Iuka," *America's Civil War*, 12 (May 1999), 42–49.

Sunderland, Glenn W. "The Bloody Battle of Corinth," *Civil War Times Illustrated*, 6 (April), 28–37.

Williams, Kenneth P. *Lincoln Finds a General: A Military Study of the Civil War*. 5 vols. New York: Macmillan, 1949–1959.

JACKSON, THOMAS JONATHAN (1824–1863)

Alexander, Bevin. *Lost Victories: The Military Genius of Stonewall Jackson*. New York: Henry Holt and Co., 1992.

Casdorph, Paul D. *Lee and Jackson: Confederate Chieftains*. New York: Paragon House, 1992.

Chambers, Lenoir. *Stonewall Jackson*. 2 vols. New York: William Morrow, 1959.

Current, Richard N. (ed.). *Encyclopedia of the Confederacy*. 4 vols. New York: Simon & Schuster, 1993.

Davis, William C. (ed.). *The Confederate General*. 6 vols. N.p.: National Historical Society, 1991.

Freeman, Douglas Southall. *Lee's Lieutenants: A Study of Command*. 3 vols. New York: Charles Scribner's Sons, 1942–1944.

Henderson, G. F. R. *Stonewall Jackson and the American Civil War*. 2 vols. London: Longmans, Green, 1989.

Krick, Robert K. "Stonewall Jackson's Deadly Calm," *American Heritage*, 47 (January 1997), 56–69, *passim*.

Kushlan, Jim (ed.). "Life After Stonewall," *Civil War Times Illustrated*, 42 (June 2003), [Special Issue].

Robertson, James I., Jr. "Life of Stonewall Jackson," *Blue & Gray*, 9 (1991–92), [Special Issue].

Robertson, James I. *Stonewall Jackson: The Man, the Soldier, the Legend*. New York: Macmillan, 1997.

Royster, Charles. *The Destructive War: William Tecumseh Sherman, Stonewall Jackson, and the Americans*. New York: Knopf, 1991.

Selby, John. *Stonewall Jackson as Military Commander*. Princeton, N.J.: D. Van Nostrand, 1968.

Stanchak, John (ed.). "Stonewall Jackson: The Biography," *Civil War Times Illustrated*, 27 (April 1988), [Special Issue].

Vandiver, Frank E. *Mighty Stonewall*. New York: McGraw-Hill, 1957.

Warner, Ezra J. *Generals in Gray: Lives of Confederate Commanders*. Baton Rouge: Louisiana State University Press, 1959.

JAMES, JESSE W.

Abbott, Edith. "The Civil War and the Crime Wave of 1865–1870, *Social Service Review*, 1 (1927), 212–34.

Bowen, Don R. "Counterrevolutionary Guerrilla War: Missouri, 1861–1865," *Conflict*, (1988), 69–78.

DeArmond, Fred. "Reconstruction in Missouri," *Missouri Historical Review*, 61 (1967), 364–77.

Goodrich, Thomas. *Black Flag: Guerrilla Warfare on the Western Border, 1861–1865*. Bloomington: Indiana University Press, 1995.

Monaghan, Jay. *The Civil War on the Western Border*. Boston: Little, Brown & Co., 1958.

Stiles, T. J. *Jesse James: The Last Rebel of the Civil War*. New York: Alfred A. Knopf, 2003.

Sutherland, Daniel E. "Sideshow No Longer: A Historiographical Review of the Guerrilla War," *Civil War History*, 46 (2000), 5–23.

White, Richard. "Outlaw Gangs of the Middle Border: American Social Bandits," *Western Historical Quarterly*, 12 (1981), 387–408.

JIM CROW (SEGREGATION)

Bacote, Clarence A. "Negro Proscriptions, Protests, and Proposed Solutions in Georgia, 1880–1908," *Journal of Southern History*, 25 (1959), 471–98.

Berlin, Ira. *Slaves Without Masters: The Free Negro in the Antebellum South*. New York: Pantheon, 1974.

Bernstein, Barton J. "Case Law in Plessy v. Ferguson," *Journal of Negro History*, 47 (1962), 192–98.

Blassingame, John W. *Black New Orleans, 1860–1880*. Chicago: University of Chicago Press, 1973.

Calcott, Margaret Law. *The Negro in Maryland Politics, 1870–1912*. Baltimore, Md.: The Johns Hopkins University Press, 1969.

Cartwright, Joseph H. *The Triumph of Jim Crow: Tennessee Race Relations in the 1880s*. Knoxville: University of Tennessee Press, 1976.

Chesteen, Richard D. "Bibliographical Essay: The Legal Validity of Jim Crow," *Journal of Negro History*, 56 (1971), 284–93.

Collins, Charles Wallace. "The Fourteenth Amendment and the Negro Race Question," *American Law Review*, 45 (1911), 830–56.

Dailey, Jane E. *Before Jim Crow: The Politics of Race in Post-Emancipation Virginia*. Chapel Hill: University of North Carolina Press, 2000.

Dethloff, Henry C., and Robert P. Jones. "Race Relations in Louisiana, 1877–1898," *Louisiana History*, 9 (1968), 301–23.

Eaton, Clement. *The Waning of the Old South Civilization, 1860s–1880s*. Athens: University of Georgia Press, 1968.

Fischer, Roger A. "A Pioneer Protest: The New Orleans Street-Car Controversy of 1867," *Journal of Negro History*, 53 (1968), 219–33.

———. "The Post Civil War Segregation Struggle," in Hodding Carter *et al.* (eds.), *The Past as Prelude: New Orleans, 1718–1968*. New Orleans: Tulane University Press, 1968, 288–304.

———. "Racial Segregation in Antebellum New Orleans," *American Historical Review*, 74 (1969), 926–37.

———. *The Segregation Struggle in Louisiana, 1862–1877*. Urbana: University of Illinois Press, 1974.

Foster, Gaines M. *Ghosts of the Confederacy: Defeat, the Lost Cause, and the Emergence of the New South, 1865 to 1913*. New York: Oxford University Press, 1987.

Groves, Harry E. "Separate But Equal—The Doctrine of Plessy *v.* Ferguson," *Phylon*, 12 (1951), 66–72.

Lemmons, Sarah M. "Transportation Segregation in the Federal Courts since 1865," *Journal of Negro History*, 38 (1953), 174–93.

Lewinson, Paul. *Race, Class, and Party: A History of Negro Suffrage and White Politics in the South*. New York: Grosset & Dunlap, 1965.

Litwack, Leon F. *North of Slavery: The Negro in the Free States, 1790–1860*. Chicago: University of Chicago Press, 1961.

Logan, Frenise A. *The Negro in North Carolina, 1876–1894*. Chapel Hill: University of North Carolina Press, 1964.

Logan, Rayford W. *The Betrayal of the Negro: From Rutherford B. Hayes to Woodrow Wilson*. New York: Collier Books, 1965.

McMillan, Neil R. *Dark Journey: Black Mississippians in the Age of Jim Crow*. Urbana: University of Illinois Press, 1989.

Nathan, Hans. *Dan Emmett and the Rise of Early Negro Minstrelsy*. Norman: University of Oklahoma Press, 1962.

Osterweis, Rollin G. *The Myth of the Lost Cause, 1865–1900*. Hamden, Conn.: Archon Books, 1973.

Rabinowitz, Howard N. "From Exclusion to Segregation: Health and Welfare Services for Southern Blacks, 1865–1890," *Social Service Review*, 48 (1974), 327–54.

———. "From Exclusion to Segregation: Southern Race Relations, 1865–1890," *Journal of American History*, 325–50.

Rice, Lawrence D. *The Negro in Texas, 1874–1900*. Baton Rouge: Louisiana State University Press, 1971.

Roche, John P. "Plessy *v*. Ferguson: *Requiescat in Pace?*" *University of Pennsylvania Law Review*, 103 (1954), 44–58.

Somers, Dale A. "Black and White in New Orleans: A Study in Urban Race Relations," *Journal of Southern History*, 40 (1974), 19–42.

Tindall, George B. *South Carolina Negroes, 1977–1900*. Columbia: University of South Carolina Press, 1952.

Wade, Richard C. *Slavery in the Cities: The South, 1820–1860*. New York: Oxford University Press, 1964.

Wharton, Vernon L. *The Negro in Mississippi, 1865–1890*. Chapel Hill: University of North Carolina Press, 1947.

Williamson, Joel. *After Slavery: The Negro in South Carolina during Reconstruction*. Chapel Hill: University of North Carolina Press, 1965.

———. *The Crucible of Race: Black-White Relations in the American South Since Emancipation*. New York: Oxford University Press, 1984.

Woodman, Harold D. "Sequel to Slavery: The New History Views the Postbellum South," *Journal of Southern History*, 43 (1977), 523–54.

Woodward, C. Vann. "The Birth of Jim Crow," *American Heritage*, 15 (1964), 52–55, 100–103.

———. *The Strange Career of Jim Crow*. 2nd rev. ed. New York: Oxford University Press, 1966.

———. "The Strange Case of a Historical Controversy," in Woodward, *American Counterpoint: Slavery and Racism in the North-South Dialogue*. Boston: Little, Brown, 1971, 234–60.

Wynes, Charles E. *Race Relations in Virginia, 1870–1902*. Charlottesville: University of Virginia Press, 1961.

JOHNSON AND PRESIDENTIAL RECONSTRUCTION

Beale, Howard K. *The Critical Year [1866]: A Study of Andrew Johnson and Reconstruction*. New York: Harcourt, Brace & Co., 1930.

Brock, William R. "Reconstruction and the American Party System," in George M. Frederickson (ed.), *A Nation Divided: Problems and Issues of the Civil War and Reconstruction*. Minneapolis: Burgess Publishing Company, 1975, 81–112.

Burgess, John W. *Reconstruction and the Constitution, 1866–1876*. New York: Charles Scribner's Sons, 1902.

Carter, Dan T. *When the War Was Over: The Failure of Self-Reconstruction in the South, 1865–1867*. Baton Rouge: Louisiana State University Press, 1985.

Castel, Albert. *The Presidency of Andrew Johnson*. Lawrence: University Press of Kansas, 1979.

Cox, John, and LaWanda Cox. "Andrew Johnson and His Ghost Writers: An Analysis of the Freedmen's Bureau and Civil Rights Veto Messages," *Mississippi Valley Historical Review*, 48 (1961–1962), 460–79.

———. *Politics, Principles and Prejudice, 1865–1866: Dilemma of Reconstruction America.* New York: Atheneum, 1963.

Dunning, William A. "More Light on Andrew Johnson," *American Historical Review*, 2 (1905–1906), 574–94.

Gipson, Lawrence H. "The Statesmanship of President Johnson: A Study of the Presidential Reconstruction Policy," *Mississippi Valley Historical Review*, 2 (1914–1915), 363–83.

Lomask, Milton. *Andrew Johnson: President on Trial.* New York: Farrar, Straus & Cudahy, 1960.

McKitrick, Eric. *Andrew Johnson and Reconstruction.* Chicago: University of Chicago Press, 1960.

Milton, George F. *The Age of Hate: Andrew Johnson and the Radicals.* New York: Howard-McCann, 1930.

Perman, Michael. *Reunion without Compromise: The South and Reconstruction, 1865–1868.* New York: Cambridge University Press, 1973.

Riddleberger, Patrick W. *1866: The Critical Year Revisited.* Carbondale: Southern Illinois University Press, 1979.

Sefton, James E. *Andrew Johnson and the Uses of Constitutional Power.* Boston: Little, Brown & Co., 1980.

Simpson, Brooks D. *The Reconstruction Presidents.* Lawrence: University Press of Kansas, 1998.

Stryker, Lloyd P. *Andrew Johnson: A Study in Courage.* New York: Macmillan, 1929.

Thomas, Lately. *The First President Johnson: The Three Lives of the Seventeenth President of the United States of America.* New York: William Morrow, 1968.

Trefousse, Hans L. *Andrew Johnson: A Biography.* New York: W. W. Norton & Company, 1989.

Williams, Chad. "Symbols of Freedom and Defeat: African-American Soldiers, White Southerners, and the Christmas Insurrection Scare of 1865," *Southern Historian*, 21 (Spring 2000), 40–55.

Winston, Robert W. *Andrew Johnson: Plebeian and Patriot.* New York: Henry Holt, 1928.

JOHNSON, ANDREW (1808–1875)

Beale, Howard K. *The Critical Year [1866]: A Study of Andrew Johnson and Reconstruction.* New York: Harcourt, Brace & Co., 1930.

Graf, LeRoy P., *et al.* (eds.). *The Papers of Andrew Johnson.* 11 vols. Knoxville: University of Tennessee Press, 1967.

McKitrick, Eric. *Andrew Johnson and Reconstruction.* Chicago: University of Chicago Press, 1960.

Milton, George F. *The Age of Hate: Andrew Johnson and the Radicals*. New York: Howard-McCann, 1930.

Riddleberger, Patrick W. *1866: The Critical Year Revisited*. Carbondale: Southern Illinois University Press, 1979.

Sefton, James E. *Andrew Johnson and the Uses of Constitutional Power.* Boston: Little, Brown & Co., 1980.

Stryker, Lloyd P. *Andrew Johnson: A Study in Courage*. New York: Macmillan, 1929.

Thomas, Lately. *The First President Johnson: The Three Lives of the Seventeenth President of the United States of America*. New York: William Morrow, 1968.

Trefousse, Hans L. *Andrew Johnson: A Biography*. New York: W. W. Norton & Company, 1989.

Winston, Robert W. *Andrew Johnson: Plebeian and Patriot*. New York: Henry Holt, 1928.

JOHNSTON, JOSEPH EGGLESTON (1807–1891)

Current, Richard N. (ed.). *Encyclopedia of the Confederacy*. 4 vols. New York: Simon & Schuster, 1993.

Davis, William C. (ed.). *The Confederate General*. 6 vols. N.p.: National Historical Society, 1991.

Freeman, Douglas Southall. *Lee's Lieutenants: A Study of Command*. 3 vols. New York: Charles Scribner's Sons, 1942–1944.

Govan, Gilbert E., and James W. Livingood. *A Different Valor: The Story of General Joseph E. Johnston*. New York: Bobbs-Merrill, 1956.

Johnston, Joseph E. *Narrative of Military Operations Directed during the Late War Between the States*. Bloomington: Indiana University Press, 1959.

Luvaas, Jay. "An Appraisal of Joseph E. Johnston," *Civil War Times Illustrated*, 4 (January 1966), 5–8, 28–32.

Newton, Steven H. "Why Wouldn't Joe Johnston Fight?" *North & South*, 5 (September 2002), 44–55.

Warner, Ezra J. *Generals in Gray: Lives of Confederate Commanders*. Baton Rouge: Louisiana State University Press, 1959.

JULIAN, GEORGE W. (1817–1899)

Clarke, Grace Giddings Julian. *George W. Julian*. Indianapolis: Indiana Historical Commission, 1923.

Haworth, Paul L. "George Washington Julian," in Allen Johnson *et al.* (eds.), *Dictionary of American Biography* (10 double vols. + 9 supplements, 1964–1981), 245–46.

Julian, George W. *Political Recollections, 1840–1872*. Miami, Fla.: Mneosyne Publishing Co., 1969, repr. of 1884 ed.

Riddleberger, Patrick Williams. "George W. Julian: A Nineteenth Century Reformer as Politician." Ph.D. dissertation, University of California at Berkeley, 1953.

Roark, James L. "George W. Julian: Radical Land Reformer," *Indiana Magazine of History*, 64 (1968), 25–38.

Turnier, William J. "George W. Julian." M.A. thesis, Penn State University, 1967.

KANSAS–NEBRASKA ACT AND KANSAS–MISSOURI BORDER WARS

Archampeau, Philip G. "The Douglas-Buchanan Feud," Illinois State Historical Society, *Journal*, 25 (1932), 5–48.

Andrews, Horace, Jr. "Kansas Crusade: The New England Emigrant Aid Company," *New England Quarterly*, 35 (1962), 497–514.

Beers, Paul. "John W. Geary: A Profile," *Civil War Times Illustrated*, 9 (June 1970), 10–16.

Brown, Salmon. "John Brown and His Sons in Kansas Territory," *Indiana Magazine of History*, 31 (1935), 142–50.

Cooper, William J. *Liberty and Slavery: Southern Politics to 1860*. New York: Knopf, 1983.

Dew, Charles B. *Ironmaker to the Confederacy: Joseph R. Anderson and the Tredegar Iron Works*. New Haven, Conn.: Yale University Press, 1966.

DuBois, James T., and Gertrude S. Mathews. *Glausha Grow: Father of the Homestead Law*. Boston: Houghton Mifflin, 1917.

Fleming, Walter Lynwood. "The Buford Expedition to Kansas," *American Historical Review*, 6 (1900), 39–43.

Fogel, Robert W., and Stanley L. *Time on the Cross: The Economics of American Negro Slavery*. 2 vols. Boston: Little, Brown, 1974.

Gates, Paul W. *Fifty Million Acres: Conflicts over the Kansas Land Policy, 1854–1890*. Ithaca, N.Y.: Cornell University Press, 1954.

Goldin, Claudia Dale. *Urban Slavery in the American South*. Chicago: University of Chicago Press, 1976.

Harlow, Ralph V. "Gerrit Smith and the John Brown Raid," *American Historical Review*, 38 (1933) 32–37.

———. "The Rise and Fall of the Kansas Aid Movements," *American Historical Review*, 41 (1925), 1–25.

Herklotz, Hildegarde R. "Jayhawkers in Missouri, 1858–1863," *Missouri Historical Review*, 17 (1923), 266–84.

Hodder Frank H. "The Railroad Background of the Kansas-Nebraska Act," *Mississippi Valley Historical Review*, 12 (1925), 3–22.

———. "Some Aspects of the English Bill for the Admission of Kansas." American Historical Association, *Annual Report*, I (1906), 202–10.

Hoffert, Sylvia. "The Brooks-Sumner Affair." *Civil War Times Illustrated*, 11 (October 1972), 35–40.

Holt, Michael F. *The Political Crisis of the 1850s*. New York: John Wiley & Sons, 1978.

———. *Political Parties and American Political Development from the Age of Jackson to the Age of Lincoln*. Baton Rouge: Louisiana State University Press, 1992.

Hughey, Jeff. "Black Jack: 1856 [First Battle of the Civil War?]," *Civil War Times Illustrated*, 14 (January 1976), 38–42.

Isley, W. H. "The Sharps Rifle Episode in Kansas History," *American Historical Review*, 12 (1907), 546–66.

Johannsen, Robert W. "Lecompton Constitutional Convention," *Kansas Historical Quarterly*, 23 (1957), 226–234.

———. *Stephen A. Douglas*. New York: Oxford University Press, 1973.

———. "Stephen A. Douglas, 'Harper's Magazine,' and Popular Sovereignty," *Mississippi Valley Historical Review*, 45 (1959), 606–31.

Johnson, Samuel A. *Battle Cry of Freedom: The New England Emigrant Aid Company in the Kansas Crusade*. Lawrence: University Press of Kansas, 1954.

Lampton, Joan E. "The Kansas-Nebraska Act Reconsidered: An Analysis of Men, Methods and Motives." Ph.D. dissertation, Illinois State University, 1979.

Lewis, Lloyd D. "Propaganda and the Missouri Kansas War," *Missouri Historical Review*, 34 (1939), 3–17.

Malin, James C. *John Brown and the Legend of Fifty-six*. Philadelphia: American Philosophical Society, 1942.

———. *The Nebraska Question, 1852–1854*. Lawrence: University Press of Kansas, 1953.

——— "The Pro-Slavery Background of the Kansas Struggle," *Mississippi Valley Historical Review*, 10 (1923), 287–97.

Meerse, David E. "James Buchanan, the Patronage, and the Northern Democratic Party, 1857–1858." Ph.D. dissertation, University of Illinois, 1969.

Milton, George Fort. *Eve of Conflict: Stephen A. Douglas and the Needless War*. Boston: Houghton Mifflin, 1934.

Monaghan, Jay. *Civil War on the Western Border, 1854–1965*. Boston: Bonanza Books, 1955.

Moore, Glover. *The Missouri Controversy, 1819–1821*. Lexington: University of Kentucky Press, 1966.

Nichols, Roy F. *The Democratic Machine, 1850–1854*. New York: Columbia University Press, 1923.

———. *Franklin Pierce: Young Hickory of the Granite Hills*. Philadelphia: University of Pennsylvania Press, 1931.

Parrish, William E. *David Rice Atchison of Missouri: Border Politician*. Columbia: University of Missouri Press, 1961.

Phillips, Christopher. "'The Crime against Missouri': Slavery, Kansas, and the Cant of Southerners in the Border West," *Civil War History*, 48 (2002), 60–81.

Quaife, Milo M. (ed.). "Bleeding Kansas and the Pottawatomie Murders," *Mississippi Valley Historical Review*, 6 (1920), 556–59.

Ramsdell, Charles W. "The Natural Limits of Slavery Expansion," *Mississippi Valley Historical Review*, 16 (1929), 151–71.

Rawley, James A. *Race and Politics: "Bleeding Kansas" and the Coming of the Civil War*. Philadelphia: Lippincott, 1969.

Ray, P. Orman. *The Repeal of the Missouri Compromise, Its Origin and Authorship*. Cleveland, Ohio: Arthur H. Clark, 1909.

Rosenberg, M. "The Kansas-Nebraska Act: A Case Study," *Annals of Iowa*, 26 (1964), 436–57.

Russel, Robert R. *Economic Aspects of Southern Nationalism, 1840–1861*. Urbana: University of Illinois Press, 1923.

———. "The Issues in the Congressional Struggle over the Kansas-Nebraska Bill, 1854," *Journal of Southern History*, 29 (1963), 187–210.

Shenton, James P. *Robert John Walker: A Politician from Jackson to Lincoln*. New York: Columbia University Press, 1961.

[Shoemaker, Floyd C.] "John Brown's Missouri Raid: A Tale of the Kansas Missouri Border Wars Retold with Some New Facts," *Missouri Historical Review*, 26 (1931), 78–83.

Smith, William E. "The Blairs and Frémont," *Missouri Historical Review*, 23 (1929), 36–47.

Starobin, Robert S. *Industrial Slavery in the Old South*. New York: Oxford University Press, 1970.

Stephenson, Wendell Holmes. *The Political Career of James H. Lane*. Topeka: Kansas State Printing Plant, 1930.

Wade, Richard C. *Slavery in the Cities: The South, 1820–1860*. New York: Oxford University Press, 1964.

Weisberger, Bernard A. "The Newspaper Reporter and the Kansas Imbroligo," *Mississippi Valley Historical Review*, 36 (1950), 633–56.

Wolff, Gerald. "The Slaveocracy and the Homestead Problem of 1854," *Agricultural History*, 40 (1966), 101–11.

KELLOGG, WILLIAM PITT (1830–1918)

Gonzales, John Edmund. "William Pitt Kellogg, Reconstruction Governor of Louisiana, 1873–1877," *Louisiana Historical Quarterly*, 29 (1946), 394–495.

Taylor, Joe Gray. "Louisiana: An Impossible Task," in Otto H. Olsen (ed.), *Reconstruction and Redemption in the South*. Baton Rouge: Louisiana State University Press, 1980, 202–36.

———. *Louisiana Reconstructed, 1863–1877*. Baton Rouge: Louisiana State University, 1974.

Tunnell, Ted. *Crucible of Reconstruction: War, Radicalism, and Race in Louisiana 1862–1877*. Baton Rouge: Louisiana State University Press, 1984.

KENTUCKY AND VIRGINIA RESOLVES

Koch, Adrienne, and Harry Ammon. "The Virginia and Kentucky Resolutions: An Episode in Jefferson's and Madison's Defense of Civil Liberties," *William and Mary Quarterly*, 5 (1948), 145–176.

KNOXVILLE CAMPAIGN AND EASTERN TENNESSEE

Franks, Edward C. "In Defense of Braxton Bragg," *North & South*, 5 (July 2002), 28–38.
Kelly, Dorothy E. "Sanders' Raid," *North & South*, 6 (December 2002), 76–86.
Seymour, Digby Gordon. *Divided Loyalties: Fort Sanders and the Civil War in East Tennessee*. Knoxville: University of Tennessee Press, 1963.
Johnston, Terry A., Jr. "Failure Before Knoxville: Longstreet's Attack on Ft. Sanders, November 29, 1863," *North & South*, 2 (September 1999), 56–75.
Klein, Maury. "The Knoxville Campaign," *Civil War Times Illustrated*, 10 (October 1971), 4–10. 40–45.

KU KLUX KLAN

Ayers, Edward L. *Vengeance and Justice: Crime and Punishment in the 19th Century American South*. New York: Oxford University Press, 1984.
Beck, E. M., and Stewart E. Tolnay. "The Killing Fields of the Deep South: The Market for Cotton and the Lynching of Blacks, 1882–1930," *American Sociological Review*, 55 (1990), 526–39.
Budiansky, Stephen. "America's First War on Terror [KKK]," *North & South*, 10 (June 2008), 30–38.
———. "The South Did Rise Again: [Major Lewis Merrill and the Ku Klux Klan]," *Civil War Times Illustrated*, 48 (June 2009), 50–55.
Carpenter, John A. "Atrocities during the Reconstruction Period," *Journal of Negro History*, 47 (1962), 234–47.
Carter, Hodding. *The Angry Scar: The Story of Reconstruction*. Garden City, N.Y.: Doubleday & Company, Inc., 1959.
Chalmers, David M. *Hooded Americanism: The History of the Ku Klux Klan*. Chicago: Quadrangle Books, 1968.
Cresswell, Stephen. "Enforcing the Enforcement Acts: The Department of Justice in Northern Mississippi, 1870–1890," *Journal of Southern History*, 53 (1987), 421–40.
Escott, Paul D. "White Republicanism and Ku Klux Klan Terror: The North Carolina Piedmont during Reconstruction," in Jeffrey J. Crow *et al.*, (eds.), *Race, Class, and Politics in Southern History*. Baton Rouge: Louisiana State University Press, 1989, 3–34.

Grimshaw, Alan. "Lawlessness and Violence in America and Their Special Manifestations in Changing Negro-White Relationships," *Journal of Negro History*, 44 (1959), 52–72.

Hackney, Sheldon. "Southern Violence," *American Historical Review*, 74 (1969), 906–25.

Harcourt, Edward John. "Who Were the Pale Faces? New Perspectives on the Tennessee Ku Klux," *Civil War History*, 51 (2005), 23–66.

Horn, Stanley. *Invisible Empire: The Story of the Ku Klux Klan, 1866–1871*. Boston: Houghton Mifflin Company, 1939.

Jones, Virgil Carrington. "Rise and Fall of the Ku Klux Klan," *Civil War Times Illustrated*, 2 (February 1964), 12–18.

Lewis, Patrick A. "The Democratic Partisan Militia and the Black Peril: The Kentucky Militia, Racial Violence, and the Fifteenth Amendment, 1870–1873," *Civil War History*, 56 (2010), 145–74.

Martinez, J. Michael. "An Officer of Great Intelligence: Lewis Merrill, the Man who Exposed the Ku Klux Klan," *North & South*, 10 (July 2007), 70–79.

Nieman, Donald G. (ed.). *Black Freedom/White Violence, 1865–1900*. New York: Garland Publishing, Inc., 1994.

Olsen, Otto H. "The Ku Klux Klan: A Study in Reconstruction Politics and Propaganda," *North Carolina Historical Quarterly*, 39 (1962), 340–62.

———. "Southern Reconstruction and the Question of Self-Determination," in George M. Frederickson (ed.), *A Nation Divided: Problems and Issues of the Civil War and Reconstruction*. Minneapolis: Burgess Pub. Co., 1975, 113–14.

Peek, Ralph L. "Lawlessness in Florida, 1868–1871," *Florida Historical Quarterly*, 40 (1961–62), 164–85.

———. "Military Reconstruction and the Growth of Anti-Negro Sentiment in Florida, 1867," *Florida Historical Quarterly*, 47 (1968–69), 380–400.

Phillips, Paul D. "White Reaction to the Freedmen's Bureau in Tennessee," *Tennessee Historical Quarterly*, 25 (1966), 50–62.

Sefton, James E. *The United States Army and Reconstruction, 1865–1877*. Baton Rouge: Louisiana State University Press, 1967.

Shapiro, Herbert. "Afro-American Responses to Race Violence During Reconstruction," *Science and Society*, 36 (1972), 158–70.

———. "The Ku Klux Klan during Reconstruction: The South Carolina Episode," *Journal of Negro History*, 19 (1964), 34–55.

———. *White Violence and Black Response: From Reconstruction to Montgomery.* Amherst: University of Massachusetts Press, 1988.

Simkins, Francis B. "The Ku Klux Klan in South Carolina, 1868–1871," *Journal of Negro History*, 12 (1927), 606–47.

Singletary, Otis A. *Negro Militia and Reconstruction*. Austin: University of Texas Press, 1957.

Stagg, J. C. A. "The Problem of Klan Violence: The South Carolina Up-Country, 1868–1871," *Journal of American Studies*, 8 (1974), 303–18.

Swinney, Everette. "Enforcing the Fifteenth Amendment, 1870–1877," *Journal of Southern History*, 28 (1962), 202–18.

Trelease, Allan W. *White Terror: The Ku Klux Klan Conspiracy and Southern Reconstruction*. New York: Harper & Row, 1971.

U.S., 42d Cong., 2d Sess., H. Rep. 22. "Condition of Affairs in the Late Insurrectionary States." Washington, D.C.: Government Printing Office, 1873.

West, Jerry Lee. *The Reconstruction Ku Klux Klan in York County, South Carolina, 1865–1877*. Jefferson, N.C.: McFarland & Co., 2002.

Williams, Lou Falkner. "The South Carolina Ku Klux Klan Trials and Enforcement of Federal Rights, 1871–1872," *Civil War History*, 39 (1993), 47–66.

Woodward, C. Vann. "Seeds of Failure in Radical Race Policy," in Harold M. Hyman (ed.), *New Frontiers of the American Reconstruction*. Urbana: University of Illinois Press, 1966, 125–47.

LEE, ROBERT EDWARD (1807–1870)

Carse, Robert. *Hilton Head Island in the Civil War: Department of the South*. Columbia, S.C.: The State Printing Co., 1961.

Casdorph, Paul D. *Lee and Jackson: Confederate Chieftains*. New York: Paragon House, 1992.

Castel, Albert. "West Virginia in 1861: A Tale of a Goose, a Dog, and a Fox," *North & South*, 7 (November 2004), 44–55.

Connelly, Thomas L. *The Marble Man: Robert E. Lee and His Image in American Society*. New York: Knopf, 1977.

Current, Richard N. (ed.). *Encyclopedia of the Confederacy*. 4 vols. New York: Simon & Schuster, 1993.

Davis, Burke. *Gray Fox: Robert E. Lee and the Civil War*. New York: Rinehart & Co., 1956.

Davis, William C. (ed.). *The Confederate General*. 6 vols. N.p.: National Historical Society, 1991.

Freeman, Douglas Southall. *Lee*. Ed. by Richard Harwell. New York: Charles Scribner's Sons, 1961.

———. *Lee of Virginia*. New York: Charles Scribner's Sons, 1958.

———. *Lee's Lieutenants: A Study of Command*. 3 vols. New York: Charles Scribner's Sons, 1942–1944.

———. *R. E. Lee*. 4 vols. New York: Charles Scribner's Sons, 1934.

Gallagher, Gary W. (ed.). *R. E. Lee, The Soldier*. Lincoln: University of Nebraska Press, 1995.

Grimsley, Mark. "Robert E. Lee: The Life and Career of the Master General," *Civil War Times Illustrated*, 24 (November 1985), [Special Issue].

Lesser, W. Hunter. *Battle at Carrick's Ford: Confederate Disaster and Loss of a Leader*. Parsons, W.Va.: McCain Printing Co., 1993.

Lowry, Terry. *September Blood: The Battle of Carnifex Ferry*. Charleston, W.Va.: Pictorial Histories Publishing Co., 1985.

McKenzie, John D. *Uncertain Glory: Lee's Generalship Re-Examined*. New York: Hippocrene Books, 1997.

McKinney, Tim. *Robert E. Lee at Sewell Mountain: The West Virginia Campaign*. Charleston, W.Va.: Pictorial Publishing Co., 1990.

Newell, Clayton R. *Lee vs. McClellan: The First Campaign*. Washington, D.C.: Regnery Publishing, 1996.

Nolan, Alan T. *Lee Reconsidered: General Robert E. Lee and Civil War History*. Chapel Hill: University of North Carolina Press, 1991.

Parrish, T. Michael. "The R. E. Lee 200: An Annotated Bibliography of Essential Books on Lee's Military Career," in Gary W. Gallagher, (ed.). *R. E. Lee, the Soldier*. Lincoln: University of Nebraska Press, 1995.

Poulter, Keith (ed.). "Robert E. Lee Special Issue," *North & South*, 3 (June 2000).

Riley, Harris D., Jr. "Robert E. Lee's Battle with Disease," *Civil War Times Illustrated*, 18 (January 1980), 12–22.

Rollins, Richard. "Understanding Lee's Audacity," *North & South*, 5 (December 2001), 30–41.

Sears, Stephen W. "Getting Right with Robert E. Lee," *American Heritage*, 42 (May/June 1991), 58–72, *passim*.

Tucker, Glenn. "An Appraisal of Robert E. Lee," *Civil War Times Illustrated*, 4 (April 1965), 4–11, 35–38.

Warner, Ezra J. *Generals in Gray: Lives of Confederate Commanders*. Baton Rouge: Louisiana State University Press, 1959.

Wert, Jeffry D. "Lee and His Staff," *Civil War Times Illustrated*, 11 (July 1972), 10–19.

Woodworth, Steven E. *Davis and Lee at War*. Lawrence: University Press of Kansas, 1995.

LIBERAL REPUBLICANISM

Dobson, John M. *Politics in the Gilded Age: A New Perspective on Reform*. New York: Praeger, 1972.

Hofstadter, Richard. *The Age of Reform*. New York: Vintage Books, 1955.

Hoogenboom, Ari A. *Outlawing the Spoils: A History of the Civil Reform Movement*. Urbana: University of Illinois Press, 1961.

Hoogenboom, Ari A. *The Presidency of Rutherford B. Hayes*. Lawrence: University Press of Kansas, 1988.

Morgan, H. Wayne. *From Hayes to McKinley: National Party Politics, 1877–1896*. Syracuse, N.Y.: Syracuse University Press, 1968.

Polakoff, Keith Ian. *The Politics of Inertia: The Election of 1876 and the End of Reconstruction*. Baton Rouge: Louisiana State University Press, 1973.

Riddleberger, Patrick W. "The Break in the Radical Ranks: Liberals vs. Stalwarts in the Election of 1872," *Journal of Negro History*, 44 (1959), 136–57.

Smith, Ronald D., and William L. Richter. *Fascinating People and Astounding Events from American History*. Santa Barbara: ABC-Clio, 1993.

LINCOLN, ABRAHAM (1809–1865)

Ambrose, Stephen E. "An Appraisal of Lincoln: 'The Savior of the Union,'" *Civil War Times Illustrated*, 6 (February 1968), 27–33.

Basler, Roy P., *et al.* (eds.). *The Collected Works of Abraham Lincoln*. 9 vols. New Brunswick, N.J.: Rutgers University Press, 1953–1955.

———, and Christian O. Basler (eds.). *The Collected Works of Abraham Lincoln: Second Supplement, 1848–1865*. New Brunswick, N.J.: Rutgers University Press, 1990.

———. (eds.). *The Collected Works of Abraham Lincoln: Supplement, 1832–1865*. New Brunswick, N.J.: Rutgers University Press, 1974.

Bennett, Lerone, Jr., *Forced into Glory: Abraham Lincoln's White Dream*. Chicago: Johnson Publishing, 2000.

———. "Was Abe Lincoln a White Supremacist?" *Ebony*, 23 (1968), 35–38, 40, 42.

Blue, Frederick J. "Friends of Freedom: Lincoln, Chase, and the Wartime Racial Policy," *Ohio History*, 102 (1993), 85–97.

Bradford, M. E. "Against Lincoln: A Speech at Gettysburg," in Bradford (ed.), *The Reactionary Imperative: Essays Literary and Political*. Peru, Ill.: Sherwood Sudgen, 1990, 219–27.

———. "The Lincoln Legacy: A Long View," in M. E. Bradford, *Remembering Who We Are: Observations of a Southern Conservative*. Athens: University of Georgia Press, 1985, 143–56.

Charnwood, Godfrey Rathbone Benson, Lord. *Abraham Lincoln*. New York: Henry Holt & Co., 1916.

Cox, LaWanda. *Lincoln and Black Freedom: A Study in Presidential Leadership*. Columbia: University of South Carolina Press, 1981.

Current, Richard N. *The Lincoln Nobody Knows*. New York: McGraw-Hill Book Co., 1958.

Donald, David H. *Lincoln*. New York: Simon & Schuster, 1996.

———. *Lincoln Reconsidered*. 2nd ed. New York: Vintage Books, 1956.

Fehrenbacher, Don E. *Prelude to Greatness: Lincoln in the 1850s*. Palo Alto, Calif.: Stanford University Press, 1962.

Fleming, Thomas. "Lincoln's Tragic Heroism," *National Review*, 41 (December 8, 1989), 38–40.

Graebner, Norman A. (ed.). *The Enduring Lincoln*. Urbana: University of Illinois Press, 1959.

Herndon, William H., and Jesse Weik. *Herndon's Life of Lincoln: The History and Personal Recollections of Abraham Lincoln*. Ed. by Paul M Angle. New York: Albert and Charles Boni, 1930.

Hesseltine, William B. *Lincoln's Plan of Reconstruction*. Tuscaloosa, Ala.: Confederate Publishing Company, 1960.

Holzer, Harold. "Abraham Lincoln: American Hero," *North & South*, 8 (September 2005), 50–59.

Jaffa, Harry V. "Lincoln's Character Assassins," *National Review*, 42 (January 22, 1990), 34–38.

Kushlan, Jim (ed.). "Abraham Lincoln," *Civil War Times Illustrated*, 34 (November 1995), [Special Issue].

——— (ed.). "Abraham Lincoln at War," *Civil War Times Illustrated*, 39 (February 2001), [Special Issue].

McPherson, James M. *Abraham Lincoln and the Second American Revolution*. New York: Oxford University Press, 1990.

Nevins, Allan. *The War for the Union*. 4 vols. New York: Charles Scribner's Sons, 1959–1971.

Neely, Mark E., Jr. *The Abraham Lincoln Encyclopedia*. New York: McGraw-Hill, 1982.

Nicolay, John G., and John Hay. *Abraham Lincoln: A History*. New York: Century, 1890.

Oates, Stephen B. *Abraham Lincoln: The Man Behind the Myths*. New York: Harper & Row, 1984.

———. *With Malice toward None: The Life of Abraham Lincoln*. New York: Harper & Row, 1977.

Olsen, Otto H. "Abraham Lincoln as Revolutionary," *Civil War History*, 24 (1978), 213–24.

Paludan, Philip S. *The Presidency of Abraham Lincoln*. Lawrence: University Press of Kansas, 1994.

Randall, James G. *Lincoln the President*. 4 vols. New York: Dodd, Mead & Co., 1945–1955.

Randall, Ruth Painter, *Mary Lincoln: Biography of a Marriage*. Boston: Little, Brown, 1953.

Sandburg, Carl. *Abraham Lincoln*. 6 vols. New York: Harcourt, Brace & Co., 1926–1939.

Simpson, Brooks D. *The Reconstruction Presidents*. Lawrence: University Press of Kansas, 1998.

Stanchak, John (ed.). "Lincoln," *Civil War Times Illustrated*, 22 (February 1984), [Special Issue].

Thomas, Benjamin. *Abraham Lincoln: A Biography*. New York: Alfred A. Knopf, 1953.

Williams, T. Harry. "Lincoln and the Radicals," in Grady McWhiney (ed.), *Grant, Lee, Lincoln, and the Radicals*. Evanston, Ill.: Northwestern University Press, 1964, 92–117.

———. *Lincoln and His Generals*. New York: Alfred A. Knopf, 1952.

———. *Lincoln and the Radicals*. Madison: University of Wisconsin Press, 1941.

Wright, John S. *Lincoln and the Politics of Slavery*. Reno: University of Nevada Press, 1970.

Zilversmit, Arthur (ed.). *Lincoln on Black and White: A Documentary History*. Belmont, Calif.: Wadsworth Publishing Company, 1971.

LINCOLN, ABRAHAM AND BISEXUALISM

Alarik, Scott. "Overreaching Limits Lincoln Biography," *The Boston Globe*, January 23, 2005.

Brookhiser, Richard. "Was Lincoln Gay?" *New York Times Book Review*, January 9, 2005.

Epstein, Daniel Mark. "The Real Lincoln Bedroom: Love in a Time of Strife," *New York Times*, July 3, 2008, B1.

Ewers, Justin. "The Real Lincoln," *U.S. News & World Report*, 126 (February 21, 2005), 66.

Greenburg, Paul. "The Essential Lincoln: Reflections on a Great President's Birthday," *Jewish World Review*, February, 11 2005.

Nobile, Philip. "A Dishonest Book Claims Lincoln as the First Log Cabin Republican," *The Weekly Standard*, 10 (January 17, 2005).

Smith, Dinitia. "Finding Homosexual Threads in Lincoln's Legend," *New York Times*, December 16, 2004, B1.

Tripp, C. A. *The Intimate World of Abraham Lincoln*. New York: Free Press, 2005.

LINCOLN, ABRAHAM—A DIFFERENT VIEW

DiLorenzo, Thomas J. *The Real Lincoln: A New Look at Abraham Lincoln, His Agenda, and an Unnecessary War*. Roseville, Calif.: Forum, 2002.

———, and Gerald Prokopowicz. "Abraham Lincoln: Savior or Tyrant?" *North & South*, 7 (February 2004), 44–55.

Greenburg, Paul. "The Essential Lincoln: Reflections on a Great President's Birthday," *Jewish World Review*, February, 11 2005.

Richter, William L. "How Did Anakin Skywalker Become Darth Vader?: The Lincoln John Wilkes Booth Knew," in Richter, *Sic Semper Tyrannis: Why John Wilkes Booth Shot Abraham Lincoln*. Indianapolis: iUniverse, 2009, 1–78.

LINCOLN AND THE EXECUTIVE PROCLAMATION—CREATING A NEW REGULAR ARMY AND CALLING UP THE VOLUNTEERS

Herndon, William H., and Jesse Weik. *Herndon's Life of Lincoln: The History and Personal Recollections of Abraham Lincoln*. Ed. by Paul M Angle. New York: Albert and Charles Boni, 1930.

Nicolay, John G., and John Hay. *Abraham Lincoln: A History*. New York: Century, 1890.

LINCOLN AND THE EXECUTIVE PROCLAMATION—DECLARING THE WAR OF THE REBELLION

Herndon, William H., and Jesse Weik. *Herndon's Life of Lincoln: The History and Personal Recollections of Abraham Lincoln*. Ed. by Paul M Angle. New York: Albert and Charles Boni, 1930.

Nicolay, John G., and John Hay. *Abraham Lincoln: A History*. New York: Century, 1890.

Ostrowski, James. "Was the Union Army's Invasion of the Confederate States a Lawful Act? An Analysis of President Lincoln's Legal Arguments Against Secession," in David Gordon (ed.), *Secession State and Liberty*. New Brunswick, N.J.: Transaction Publishers, 1998, 155–90.

LINCOLN AND THE EXECUTIVE PROCLAMATION—IN GENERAL

Belz, Herman. *Lincoln and the Constitution: The Dictatorship Question Reconsidered*. Ft. Wayne, Ind.: Louis A. Warren Lincoln Library and Museum, 1984.

Bensel, Richard F. *Yankee Leviathan: The Origins of Central State Authority in America*. New York: Cambridge University Press, 1990.

DiLorenzo, Thomas J. "The Great Centralizer: Abraham Lincoln and the War Between the States," *Independent Review*, 3 (No. 2, Fall 1998), 243–71.

Goldin, Claudia D. "The Economics of Emancipation," *Journal of Economic History*, 33 (1973), 66–85.

Herndon, William H., and Jesse Weik. *Herndon's Life of Lincoln: The History and Personal Recollections of Abraham Lincoln*. Ed. by Paul M Angle. New York: Albert and Charles Boni, 1930.

Hyman, Harold M. *"A More Perfect Union": The Impact of the Civil War and Reconstruction on the Constitution*. New York: Knopf, 1973.

———, and William Wiecek. *Equal Justice under Law: Constitutional Development, 1835–1875*. New York: Harper & Row, 1982.

Marszalek, John F., Jr. "Lincoln's Special Session," *Civil War Times Illustrated*, 10 (June 1971), 30–37.

Nicolay, John G., and John Hay. *Abraham Lincoln: A History*. New York: Century, 1890.

Ostrowski, James. "Was the Union Army's Invasion of the Confederate States a Lawful Act? An Analysis of President Lincoln's Legal Arguments Against Secession," in David Gordon (ed.), *Secession State and Liberty*. New Brunswick, N.J.: Transaction Publishers, 1998, 155–90.

Randall, James G. *Constitutional Problems under Lincoln*. Urbana: University of Illinois Press, 1951.

Williams, T. Harry. "Abraham Lincoln: Principle and Pragmatism in Politics," *Mississippi Valley Historical Review*, 40 (June 1953), 89–108.

LINCOLN AND THE EXECUTIVE PROCLAMATION—PRIZE CASES AND NAVAL BLOCKADE

Bernath, Stuart L. *Squall Across the Atlantic: American Civil War Prize Cases and Diplomacy*. Los Angeles: University of California Press, 1970.

Flannery, Michael A. "Hapless or Helpmate? The Effectiveness of the Union's Blockade of the Confederacy from a Medical Perspective," *North & South*, 8 (May 2005), 72–80.

Herndon, William H., and Jesse Weik. *Herndon's Life of Lincoln: The History and Personal Recollections of Abraham Lincoln*. Ed. by Paul M Angle. New York: Albert and Charles Boni, 1930.

Johnson, Ludwell H., III. "Abraham Lincoln and the Development of Presidential War-Making Powers: Prize Cases (1863) Revisited," *Civil War History*, 35 (1989), 208–24.

———. "The Confederacy: What Was It? A View from the Federal Courts," *Civil War History*, 32 (1986), 5–22.

Jones, V. C. "Mr. Lincoln's Blockade," *Civil War Times Illustrated*, 10 (December 1971), 10–24.

Neely, Mark E., Jr. "The Perils of Running the Blockade: The Influence of International Law in an Era of Total War," *Civil War History*, 32 (1986), 101–18.

Nicolay, John G., and John Hay. *Abraham Lincoln: A History*. New York: Century, 1890.

Weddle, Kevin J. "The Blockade Board of 1861 and Union Naval Strategy," *Civil War History*, 48 (2002), 123–142.

LINCOLN AND THE EXECUTIVE PROCLAMATION—RULES OF WAR

Freidel, Frank. "Francis Lieber, Charles Sumner, and Slavery," *Journal of Southern History,* 9 (1943), 75–93.

———. "General Orders No. 100 and Military Government," *Mississippi Valley Historical Review*, 32 (1945–1946), 541–56.

Garner, James W. "General Orders 100 Revisited," *Military Law Review*, 27 (1965), 1–48.

LINCOLN AND THE EXECUTIVE PROCLAMATION—WRIT OF *HABEAS CORPUS* SUSPENSION

Belz, Herman. *Lincoln and the Constitution: The Dictatorship Question Reconsidered*. Ft. Wayne, Ind.: Louis A. Warren Lincoln Library and Museum, 1984.

Duker, William F. *A Constitutional History of Habeas Corpus*. Westport, Conn.: Greenwood, 1980.

Herndon, William H., and Jesse Weik. *Herndon's Life of Lincoln: The History and Personal Recollections of Abraham Lincoln*. Ed. by Paul M Angle. New York: Albert and Charles Boni, 1930.

Neely, Mark E., Jr., *The Fate of Liberty: Abraham Lincoln and Civil Liberties*. New York: Oxford University Press, 1991.

Nicolay, John G., and John Hay. *Abraham Lincoln: A History*. New York: Century, 1890.

Oaks, Dallin H. "Habeas Corpus in the States, 1776–1865," *University of Chicago Law Review*, 33 (1965), 243–88.

Spragus, Dean. *Freedom under Lincoln*. Boston: Houghton Mifflin, 1965.

Tarrant, Catherine W. "A Writ of Liberty or a Covenant with Hell? *Habeas Corpus* in the War Congresses, 1861–1867." Ph.D. dissertation, Rice University, 1972.

LINCOLN ASSASSINATION

Evans, C. Wyatt. "Lafayette C. Baker and Civil War Security in the North," *North & South*, 11 (March 2009), 44–51.

Fowler, Robert F. (ed.). "Album of the Lincoln Murder, Illustrating How It Was Planned, Committed, and Avenged," *Civil War Times Illustrated*, 4 (July 1965), [Special Issue].

———. "New Evidence in the Lincoln Murder Conspiracy," *Civil War Times Illustrated*, 3 (February 1965), 4–11.

George, Joseph, Jr. "Black Flag Warfare: Lincoln and the Raid against Richmond and Jefferson Davis," *Pennsylvania Magazine of History and Biography*, 115 (1991), 291–318.

Hanchett, William. "The Lincoln Assassination Revisited," *North & South*, 3 (September 2000), 33–39.

———. *The Lincoln Murder Conspiracies*. Urbana: University of Illinois Press, 1983.

———. "Lincoln's Murder: The Single Conspiracy Theory," *Civil War Times Illustrated*, 30 (Nov./Dec.), 28–35, 70–71.

Hyman, Harold M. "Hitting the Fan(s) Again: or, Sic Semper Conspiracies," *Reviews in American History*, 12 (1984), 388–92.

———. *With Malice Toward Some: Scholarship (or Something Less) on the Lincoln Murder*. Pamphlet. Springfield, Ill: Abraham Lincoln Association, 1978.

Kauffman, Michael W. "John Wilkes Booth's Escape Route," *Blue and Gray*, 8 (April 1991).

———. "The Lincoln Assassination," *Blue and Gray*, 8 (February 1991).

Lange, James E. T., and Katherine DeWitt, Jr. "Who Ordered Lincoln's Death?" *North & South*, 1 (No. 6, 1998), 16–33.

McAuliffe, Kieran. "Portrait of an Historical Detective [James O. Hall]," *North & South*, 5 (April 2002), 74–80.

Steers, Edward, Jr. *Blood on the Moon: The Assassination of Abraham Lincoln.* Lexington: University of Kentucky Press, 2001.

————. "Maryland, My Maryland!" *North & South*, 6 (February 2003), 42–51.

Swanson, James L., and Daniel R. Weinberg. *Lincoln's Assassins.* Santa Fe, N.Mex.: Arena Editions, 2001.

Tidwell, William A. *April '65: Confederate Covert Action in the American Civil War.* Kent, Ohio: Kent State University Press, 1995.

————, with James O. Hall and David Winfred Gaddy. *Come Retribution: The Confederate Secret Service and the Assassination of Lincoln.* Jackson: University of Mississippi Press, 1988.

Turner, Thomas R. *Beware the People Weeping: Public Opinion and the Assassination of President Lincoln.* Baton Rouge: Louisiana State University Press, 1982.

LINCOLN ASSASSINATION, BALTIMORE PLOT, AND THE CITY'S REBEL SYMPATHIES

Betterly, Richard. "Seize Mr. Lincoln [the Baltimore Plot]," *Civil War Times Illustrated*, 25 (February 1987), 14–21.

Clark, Charles B. "Baltimore and the Attack on the Sixth Massachusetts Regiment, April 1861," *Maryland Historical Magazine*, 56 (1961), 39–71.

Hall, James O. "Butler Takes Baltimore," *Civil War Times Illustrated*, 17 (August 1978), 4–10, 44–46.

Herndon, William H., and Jesse Weik. *Herndon's Life of Lincoln: The History and Personal Recollections of Abraham Lincoln.* Ed. by Paul M Angle. New York: Albert and Charles Boni, 1930.

Klugewicz, Stephen M. "'The First Martyrs': The Sixth Massachusetts and the Baltimore Riot of 1961," *Southern Historian*, 20 (Spring 1999), 5–24.

Lanis, Edward Stanley. "Allen Pinkerton and the Baltimore 'Assassination' Plot against Lincoln," *Maryland Historical Magazine*, 45 (March 1950), 1–13.

Nicolay, John G., and John Hay. *Abraham Lincoln: A History.* New York: Century, 1890.

Potter, John Mason. *Thirteen Desperate Days.* New York: Ivan Obolensky, 1964.

Newman, Harry Wright. *Maryland and the Confederacy.* Annapolis, Md.: Harry Wright Newman, 1976.

Steers, Edward, Jr. "Mac Lincoln's Highland Fling [Baltimore Assassination Plot]," *North & South*, 6 (April 2003), 50–59.

Verge, Laurie. "The Baltimore Plot," in Michael Kauffman (ed.), *In Pursuit of . . . Continuing Research in the Field of the Lincoln Assassination.* Clinton, Md.: Surratt Society, 1990, 137–40.

Williams, Glenn F. "Under the Despot's Heel [Baltimore]," *America's Civil War*, 13 (May 2000), 22–28.

LINCOLN ASSASSINATION, THE CONFEDERACY AND

George, Joseph, Jr. "Black Flag Warfare: Lincoln and the Raid against Richmond and Jefferson Davis," *Pennsylvania Magazine of History and Biography*, 115 (1991), 291–318.

Hanchett, William. *The Lincoln Murder Conspiracies*. 1983.

———. "Lincoln's Murder: The Single Conspiracy Theory," *Civil War Times Illustrated*, 30 (November/December), 28–35, 70–71.

Long, David E. "Lincoln, Davis, and the Dahlgren Raid," *North & South*, 9 (October 2006), 70–83.

Singer, Jane. *The Confederate Dirty War: Arson, Bombings, Assassination, and Plots for Chemical and Germ Attacks on the Union*. Jefferson, N.C.: McFarland & Co., 2005.

Steers, Edward, Jr. "Terror—1860s Style," *North & South*, 5 (May 2002), 12–18.

Tidwell, William A. *April '65: Confederate Covert Action in the American Civil War*. Kent, Ohio: Kent State University Press, 1995.

———, James O. Hall, and David W. Gaddy. *Come Retribution: The Confederate Secret Service and the Assassination of Lincoln*. Jackson: University Press of Mississippi, 1988.

Turner, Thomas R. *Beware the People Weeping: Public Opinion and the Assassination of President Lincoln*. Baton Rouge: Louisiana State University Press, 1982.

LINCOLN ASSASSINATION, THE NEW YORK CONNECTION OF

Evans, C. Wyatt. "Lafayette C. Baker and Civil War Security in the North," *North & South*, 11 (March 2009), 44–51.

Stelnick, Rick. *Dixie Reckoning: A Reassessment of the Lincoln Assassination and the Lost Confederate Treasury*. Lanham, Md.: University Press of America, forthcoming.

Tidwell, William A., James O. Hall, and David W. Gaddy. *Come Retribution: The Confederate Secret Service and the Assassination of Lincoln*. Jackson: University Press of Mississippi, 1988.

LINCOLN–DOUGLAS DEBATES (1858)

Angle, Paul M. (ed.). *Created Equal? The Complete Lincoln-Douglas Debates*. Chicago: University of Chicago, 1958.

Auer, J. Jeffry (ed.). *Antislavery and Disunion, 1857–1861: Studies in Rhetoric of Compromise and Conflict*. New York: Harper & Row, 1963.

Heckman, Richard Allen. *Lincoln vs. Douglas: The Great Debates Campaign*. Washington, D.C.: Public Affairs Press, 1967.

Jaffa, Harry V., and Robert W. Johannsen (eds.). *In the Name of the People: Speeches and Writings of Lincoln and Douglas in the Ohio Campaign of 1859.* Columbus: Ohio State University Press, 1959.

Johanssen, Robert W. *The Lincoln Douglas Debates.* New York: Oxford University Press, 1965.

———. *Stephen A. Douglas.* New York: Oxford University Press, 1973.

———. "Stephen A. Douglas, 'Harper's Magazine,' and Popular Sovereignty," *Mississippi Valley Historical Review*, 45 (1959), 606–31.

Johnson, Allen. *Stephen A. Douglas: A Study in American Politics.* New York: Macmillan, 1908.

Milton, George Fort. *Eve of Conflict: Stephen A. Douglas and the Needless War.* Boston: Houghton Mifflin, 1934.

Pratt, Harry E. *The Great Debates of 1858.* rev. ed. Springfield: Illinois State Historical Library, 1956.

Sparks, Edwin Erle (ed.). *The Lincoln-Douglas Debates of 1858.* Springfield: Illinois State Historical Library, 1908.

LITTLEFIELD, MILTON

Daniels, Jonathan. *Prince of Carpetbaggers.* Philadelphia: J. B. Lippincott Co., 1958.

Fenlon, Paul E. "The Notorious Swepson-Littlefield Fraud: Railroad Financing in Florida, 1868–1871," *Florida Historical Quarterly*, 32 (1954), 231–61.

LONGSTREET, JAMES (1821–1904)

Current, Richard N. (ed.). *Encyclopedia of the Confederacy.* 4 vols. New York: Simon & Schuster, 1993.

Davis, William C. (ed.). *The Confederate General.* 6 vols. N.p.: National Historical Society, 1991.

Eckenrode, Hamilton J., and Bryan Conrad. *James Longstreet: Lee's War Horse.* Chapel Hill: University of North Carolina Press, 1936.

Longstreet, Helen D. *Lee and Longstreet at High Tide.* Gainesville, Ga.: Helen D. Longstreet, 1904.

Longstreet, James. *From Manassas to Appomattox: Memoirs of the Civil War in America.* Philadelphia: J. B. Lippincott, 1896.

Pearce, Haywood J., Jr. "Longstreet's Responsibility on the Second Day at Gettysburg," *Georgia Historical Quarterly*, 10 (1926), 26–45.

Piston, William G., *Lee's Tarnished Lieutenant: James Longstreet and His Place in Southern History.* Athens: University of Georgia Press, 1987.

Richter, William L. "James Longstreet: From Rebel to Scalawag," *Louisiana History*, 11 (1970), 215–29.

Sanger, Donald B., and Thomas R. Hay. *James Longstreet*. 2 vols. Baton Rouge: Louisiana State University Press, 1952.

Tucker, Glenn, *Lee and Longstreet at Gettysburg*. Indianapolis: Bobbs-Merrill, 1968.

———. "Longstreet: Culprit or Scapegoat?" *Civil War Times Illustrated*, 1 (April 1962), 5–7, 39–44.

Wakelyn, Jon L. *Biographical Dictionary of the Confederacy*. Westport, Conn.: Greenwood Press, 1977.

Warner, Ezra J. *Generals in Gray: Lives of Confederate Commanders*. Baton Rouge: Louisiana State University Press, 1959.

Wert, Jeffrey D. *General James Longstreet: The Confederacy's Most Controversial Soldier—A Biography*. New York: Simon & Schuster, 1993.

LOUISIANA UNIFICATION MOVEMENT

Williams, T. Harry. "The Louisiana Unification Movement of 1873," *Journal of Southern History*, 11 (1945), 349–69.

LYNCH, JAMES (1838–1872)

Harris, William C. "James Lynch: Black Leader in Southern Reconstruction," *Historian*, 34 (1971), 40–61.

LYNCH, JOHN R. (1847–1939)

Franklin, John Hope. "John Roy Lynch: Republican Stalwart from Mississippi," in Howard N. Rabinowitz (ed.), *Southern Black Leaders of the Reconstruction Era*. Urbana: University of Illinois Press, 1982, 39–58.

Lynch, John R. *The Facts of Reconstruction*. New York: Neale Publishing Co., 1913.

———. *Reminiscences of an Active Life: The Autobiography of John Roy Lynch*. Ed. by John Hope Franklin. Chicago: University of Chicago Press, 1970.

———. "Some Historical Errors of James Ford Rhodes," *Journal of Negro History*, 2 (1917), 345–67.

———. *Some Historical Errors of James Ford Rhodes*. Boston: Cornhill Publishing Co., 1922.

McFarlin, Annjeannette Sophia. *Black Congressional Reconstruction Orators and Their Orations*. Metuchen, N.J.: Scarecrow Press, 1976.

MANASSAS, BATTLE OF FIRST (1861)

Beatie, R. H. *Road to Manassas: The Growth of Union Command in the Eastern Theater from the Fall of Fort Sumter to the First Battle of Bull Run*. New York: Cooper Square, 1961.

Davis, William C. *Battle at Bull Run: A History of the First Major Campaign of the Civil War*. New York: Doubleday, 1977.

———. *First Blood: Fort Sumter to Bull Run*. Alexandria, Va.: Time-Life Books, 1983.

Freeman, Douglas Southall. *Lee's Lieutenants: A Study of Command*. 3 vols. New York: Charles Scribner's Sons, 1942–1944.

Hennessy, John. *The First Battle of Manassas: And End to Innocence, July 18–21, 1861*. Lynchburg, Va.: H. E. Howard, 1989.

Jones, Virgil Carrington. "First Bull Run," *Civil War Times Illustrated*, 19 (July 1980), [Special Issue].

McPherson, James M. (ed.). *Battle Chronicles of the Civil War*. 6 vols. New York: Macmillan, 1989.

Rafuse, Ethan S. *A Single Grand Victory: The First Camapign and Battle of Manassas*. Wilmington, Del.: SR Books, 2002.

Shier, Maynard J. "The Battle of Falling Waters," *Civil War Times Illustrated*, 15 (February 1977), 16–22.

Wert, Jeffry D. "Johnston vs. Patterson: The Valley Campaign of 1861," *Civil War Times Illustrated*, 17 (December 1978), 4–11, 41–44.

MANASSAS CAMPAIGN, SECOND (1862)

Carse, Robert. *Hilton Head Island in the Civil War: Department of the South*. Columbia, S.C.: The State Printing Co., 1961.

Casdorph, Paul D. *Lee and Jackson: Confederate Chieftains*. New York: Paragon House, 1992.

Connelly, Thomas L. *The Marble Man: Robert E. Lee and His Image in American Society*. New York: Knopf, 1977.

Current, Richard N. (ed.). *Encyclopedia of the Confederacy*. 4 vols. New York: Simon & Schuster, 1993.

Davis, Burke. *Gray Fox: Robert E. Lee and the Civil War*. New York: Rinehart & Co., 1956.

Davis, William C. (ed.). *The Confederate General*. 6 vols. N.p.: National Historical Society, 1991.

Freeman, Douglas Southall. *Lee*. Ed. by Richard Harwell. New York: Charles Scribner's Sons, 1961.

———. *Lee of Virginia*. New York: Charles Scribner's Sons, 1958.

———. *Lee's Lieutenants: A Study of Command*. 3 vols. New York: Charles Scribner's Sons, 1942–1944.

———. *R. E. Lee*. 4 vols. New York: Charles Scribner's Sons, 1934.

Gallagher, Gary W. (ed.). *R. E. Lee, The Soldier*. Lincoln: University of Nebraska Press, 1995.

Grimsley, Mark. "Robert E. Lee: The Life and Career of the Master General," *Civil War Times Illustrated*, 24 (November 1985), [Special Issue].

Lesser, W. Hunter. *Battle at Carrick's Ford: Confederate Disaster and Loss of a Leader*. Parsons, W.Va.: McCain Printing Co., 1993.

Lowry, Terry. *September Blood: The Battle of Carnifex Ferry*. Charleston, W.Va.: Pictorial Histories Publishing Co., 1985.

McKenzie, John D. *Uncertain Glory: Lee's Generalship Re-Examined*. New York: Hippocrene Books, 1997.

McKinney, Tim. *Robert E. Lee at Sewell Mountain: The West Virginia Campaign*. Charleston, W.Va.: Pictorial Publishing Co., 1990.

Newell, Clayton R. *Lee vs. McClellan: The First Campaign*. Washington, D.C.: Regnery Publishing, 1996.

Nolan, Alan T. *Lee Reconsidered: General Robert E. Lee and Civil War History*. Chapel Hill: University of North Carolina Press, 1991.

Parrish, T. Michael. "The R. E. Lee 200: An Annotated Bibliography of Essential Books on Lee's Military Career," in Gary W. Gallagher, (ed.). *R. E. Lee, The Soldier*. Lincoln: University of Nebraska Press, 1995.

Poulter, Keith (ed.). "Robert E. Lee Special Issue," *North & South*, 3 (June 2000).

Pryor, Elizabeth Brown. "Robert E. Lee and Slavery," *Civil War Times Illustrated*, 48 (February 2009), 30ff.

Riley, Harris D., Jr. "Robert E. Lee's Battle with Disease," *Civil War Times Illustrated*, 18 (January 1980), 12–22.

Rollins, Richard. "Understanding Lee's Audacity," *North & South*, 5 (December 2001), 30–41.

Sears, Stephen W. "Getting Right with Robert E. Lee," *American Heritage*, 42 (May/June 1991), 58–72, *passim*.

Tucker, Glenn. "An Appraisal of Robert E. Lee," *Civil War Times Illustrated*, 4 (April 1965), 4–11, 35–38.

Warner, Ezra J. *Generals in Gray: Lives of Confederate Commanders*. Baton Rouge: Louisiana State University Press, 1959.

Wert, Jeffry D. "Lee and His Staff," *Civil War Times Illustrated*, 11 (July 1972), 10–19.

Woodworth, Steven E. *Davis and Lee at War*. Lawrence: University Press of Kansas, 1995.

MARCH TO THE SEA

Churchill, Edward. "Betrayal at Ebenezer Creek," *Civil War Times Illustrated*, 37 (October 1998), 52–56, 58–59.

Davis, Burke. *Sherman's March*. New York; Random House, 1980.

Gibson, John M. *Those 163 Days: A Southern Account of Sherman's March from Atlanta to Raleigh*. New York: Coward-McCann, 1961.

Glatthaar, Joseph T. *The March to the Sea and Beyond: Sherman's Troops in the Savannah and Carolinas Campaigns*. New York: New York University Press, 1985.

Kennett, Lee. *Marching through Georgia: The Story of Soldiers and Civilians during Sherman's Campaign*. New York: HarperCollins, 1995.

McMurry, Richard M. "On the Road to the Sea: Sherman's Savannah Campaign,' *Civil War Times Illustrated*, 21 (January 1983), 8–25.

Miers, Earl Schenck. *The General Who Marched to Hell: William Tecumseh and His March to Fame and Infamy*. New Brunswick, N.J.: Rutgers University Press, 1948.

Savas, Theodore, and David A. Woodbury (eds.). *Campaign for Atlanta and Sherman's March to the Sea*. 2 vols. Campbell, Calif.: Savas Publishers, 1994–1997.

Scaife, William. "Sherman's March to the Sea," *Blue & Gray*, 7 (1989–1990), [Special Issue].

MARYLAND CAMPAIGN

Alexander, Ted. "Antietam: The Bloodiest Day," *North & South*, 5 (October 2002), 76–89.

Bailey, Ronald H. *The Bloodiest Day: The Battle of Antietam*. Alexandria, Va.: Time-Life Books, 1984.

Brooksher, William R., and David K. Snider. "Around McClellan Again," *Civil War Times Illustrated*,13 (August 1974), 4–8, 39–44.

Cannan, John. *The Antietam Campaign, August–September 1862*. Conshohocken, Pa.: Combined Books, 1990.

Catton, Bruce. *Mr. Lincoln's Army*. New York: Doubleday and Co., 1951.

Chiles, Paul. "Artillery at Antietam," *Blue & Gray*, 16 (1998–1999), [Special Issue].

Fowler, Robert H. (ed.). "Antietam," *Civil War Times Illustrated*, 1 (August 1962), [Special Issue].

Freeman, Douglas Southall. *Lee's Lieutenants: A Study of Command*. 3 vols. New York: Charles Scribner's Sons, 1942–1944.

Frye, Dennis E. "Stonewall Attacks! The Siege of Harper's Ferry," *Blue and Gray*, 5 (September 1987).

Gallagher, Gary W. (ed.). *Antietam: Essays on the 1862 Maryland Campaign*. Kent, Ohio: Kent State University Press, 1989.

Grimsley, Mark. "In the Edge of Disaster [at South Mountain]," *Civil War Times Illustrated*, 24 (November 1986), 18–23, 44–46, 49–50.

McPherson, James M. *Crossroads of Freedom: Antietam*. New York: Oxford University Press, 2002.

——— (ed.). *Battle Chronicles of the Civil War*. 6 Vols. New York: Macmillan, 1989.

Murfin, James V. "Along Antietam Creek, September 17, 1862," *Blue and Gray*, 3 (September 1985).

———. "Battle of Antietam—Part 1," *Blue & Gray*, 3 (1985–1986), [Special Issue].

———. "Battle of Antietam, Part 2," *Blue & Gray*, 3 (1985–1986), [Special Issue].

———. *The Gleam of Bayonets: The Battle of Antietam and the Maryland Campaign of 1862*. New York: A. S. Barnes and Co., 1965.

Poulter, Keith (ed.). "Official 140th Antietam Commemorative Issue," *North & South*, 5 (October 2002).

Priest, John M. *Antietam: The Soldiers' Battle*. Shippensburg, Pa.: White Mane Publishing Co., 1989.

———. *Before Antietam: The Battle for South Mountain*. Shippensburg, Pa.: White Mane Publishing Co., 1992

Sears, Stephen W. "America's Bloodiest Day: The Battle of Antietam," *Civil War Times Illustrated*, 26 (April 1987).

———. "Battle of South Mountain, September 14, 1862," *Blue and Gray*, 5 (January 1987).

———. "Battles for South Mountain," *Blue & Gray*, 4 (1986–1997), [Special Issue].

———. *Landscape Turned Red: The Battle of Antietam*. New York: Ticknor & Fields, 1983.

———. "McClellan at Antietam," *Blue and Gray*, 3 (November 1985).

Stackpole, Edward J. *From Cedar Mountain to Antietam, August–September 1862*. Harrisburg, Pa.: The Stackpole Co., 1959.

Stanchak, John (ed.). "Antietam," 26 (April 1987), [Special Issue].

Thiele, Gregory A. "McClellan at Antietam: Another View," *North & South*, 12 (No. 4, 2010), 31–37.

Wert, Jeffry D. "Lee and His Staff," *Civil War Times Illustrated*, 11 (July 1972), 10–19.

Williams, Kenneth P. *Lincoln Finds a General: A Military Study of the Civil War*. 5 vols. New York: Macmillan, 1949–1959.

MCCLELLAN, GEORGE BRINTON (1826–1885)

Castel, Albert. "George B. McClellan: "Little Mac,'" *Civil War Times Illustrated*, 13 (May 1974), 4–11, 44–45.

Curry, Richard Orr. "McClellan's Western Virginia Campaign of 1861," *Ohio History*, 71 (1962), 83–96.

Eckenrode, H. J., and Bryan Conrad. *George B. McClellan: The Man Who Saved the Union*. Chapel Hill: University of North Carolina Press, 1941.

Fleming, Martin K. "The Northwestern Virginia Campaign of 1861," *Blue & Gray*, 11 (August 1993).

Harsh, Joseph L. "On the McClellan-Go-Round," *Civil War History*, 19 (1973), 101–18.

Hassler, Warren W., Jr. *General George B. McClellan: Shield of the Union*. Baton Rouge: Louisiana State University Press, 1957.

McClellan, George B. *McClellan's Own Story: The War for the Union, the Soldiers Who Fought It, the Civilians Who Directed It, and His Relationship to It and Them.* New York: C. L. Webster, 1887.

Mitchie, Peter S. *General McClellan.* New York: Appleton, 1901.

Myers, William S. *General George Brinton McClellan: A Study in Personality.* New York: Appleton-Century, 1934.

Newell, Clayton R. *Lee vs. McClellan: The First Campaign.* Washington, D.C.: Regnery Publishing, 1996.

Rafuse, Ethan S. "Toward a Better Understanding of George McClellan: [His Whig Party Roots]," *Civil War Times Illustrated,* 48 (June 2009), 28–33.

Rowland, Thomas J. *George B. McClellan and Civil War History: In the Shadow of Grant and Sherman.* Kent, Ohio: Kent State University Press, 1998.

Sears, Stephen W. *George B. McClellan: The Young Napoleon.* New York: Ticknoe & Fields, 1988.

Sears, Stephen W. "Little Mac and the Historians," *North & South,* 2 (March 1999), 61–71.

Thiele, Gregory A. "McClellan at Antietam: Another View," *North & South,* 12 (No. 4, 2010), 31–37.

Williams, T. Harry. *Lincoln and His Generals.* New York: Knopf, 1952.

MEADE, GEORGE GORDON (1815–1872)

Agassiz, George R (ed.). *Meade's Headquarters, 1863–1865: Letters of Colonel Theodore Lyman from the Wilderness to Appomattox.* Boston: Atlantic Monthly Press, 1922.

Cleaves, Freeman. *Meade of Gettysburg.* Norman: University of Oklahoma Press, 1960.

Cullen, Joseph P. "George Gordon Meade," *Civil War Times Illustrated,* 14 (May 1975), 4–9, 41–46.

Haggerty, Charles. "George Who? [Meade]," *Civil War Times Illustrated,* 41 (August 2002), 20–28.

Himmer, Robert. "Meade at Gettysburg (I)," *North & South,* 9 (March 2006), 52–64.

———. "Meade at Gettysburg (II)," *North & South,* 9 (May 2006), 52–64.

Meade, George G., Jr. *The Life and Letters of George Gordon Meade, Major-General United States Army.* New York: Charles Scribner's Sons, 1913.

MEDICINE, CIVIL WAR

Adams, George W. *Doctors in Blue: The Medical History of the Union Army in the Civil War.* New York: H. Schuman, 1952.

Bollet, Alfred Jay, M.D.. *Civil War Medicine: Challenges and Triumphs.* Tucson, Ariz.: Galen Press, 2000.

———. "The Truth about Civil War Surgery," *Civil War Times Illustrated*, 43 (October 2004), 26ff.

Courtwright, David T. "Opiate Addiction as a Consequence of the Civil War," *Civil War History*, 24 (1978), 101–11.

Cullen, Joseph P. "Chimborazo Hospital," *Civil War Times Illustrated*, 19 (January 1981), 36–42.

Cunningham, Horace H. *Doctors in Gray: The Confederate Medical Service*. Baton Rouge: Louisiana State University Press, 1958.

Denney, Robert E. *Civil War Medicine: Care and Comfort of the Wounded*. New York: Sterling, 1994.

Eisenschiml, Otto. "Medicine in the Civil War," *Civil War Times Illustrated*, 1 (May 1962), 4–7, 26–32.

Faust, Drew Gilpin. "The Civil War Soldier and the Art of Dying," *Journal of Southern History*, 67 (2001), 3–38.

Freemon, Frank R. *Gangrene and Glory: Medical Care during the American Civil War*. Teaneck, N.J.: Fairleigh Dickinson University Press, 1998.

———. "The Medical Support System for the Confederate Army of Tennessee in the Georgia Campaign, May–September 1864," *Tennessee Historical Quarterly*, 52 (1993), 46–52.

Hawk, Alan. "An Ambulating Hospital: or, How the Hospital Train Transformed Army Medicine," *Civil War History*, 48 (2002), 197–219.

Jones, Gordon W. "Sanitation—100,000 Needless Deaths," *Civil War Times Illustrated*, 5 (November 1966), 12–18.

———. "Surgery in the Civil War," *Civil War Times Illustrated*, 2 (May 1963), 7–9, 28–30.

Maxwell, William Q. *Lincoln's Fifth Wheel: The Political History of the United States Sanitary Commission*. New York: Longmans, Green, 1956.

Oates, Stephen. *A Woman of Valor: Clara Barton and the Civil War*. New York: Free Press, 1994.

O'Brien, Jean Getman. "Mother Bickerdyke—A Profile," *Civil War Times Illustrated*, 1 (January 1963), 21–24.

Reimer, Terry. "'Poisonous Techniques and Dressing'," *North & South*, 5 (December 2001), 66–75.

Riley, Harris D., Jr. "Medicine in the Confederacy," *Military Medicine*, 158 (1956), 53–63, 145–53.

Schroder-Lein, Patricia. "'To Be Better Supplied Than Any Hotel in the Confederacy': The Establishment and Maintenance of the Army of Tennessee Hospitals in Georgia, 1863–1865," *Georgia Historical Quarterly*, 76 (1993), 809–36.

Stein, Alice F. "The North's Unsung Sisters of Mercy," *America's Civil War*, 12 (September 1999), 38–44.

Steiner, Paul E. *Diseases in the Civil War: Natural Biological Warfare in 1861–1865*. Springfield, Ill.: Charles C. Thomas, 1996.

Wilbur, C. Keith. *Civil War Medicine*. Old Saybrook, Conn.: The Globe Pequot Press, 1998.

Wood, Ann D. "The War within a War: Women Nurses in the Union Army," *Civil War History*, 18 (1972), 197–212.

Zeidenfelt, Alex. "Surgeon General William Hammond," *Civil War Times Illustrated*, 17 (October 1978), 24–32.

Zeller, Bob. "Snaketown Hospital," *Civil War Times Illustrated*, 35 (May 1996), 36–43.

MEN IN THE FIELD

Barton, Michael. *Good Men: The Character of Civil War Soldiers*. University Park: Pennsylvania State University Press, 1981.

Brooks, Charles E. "The Social and Cultural Dynamics of Soldiering in Hood's Texas Brigade," *Journal of Southern History*, 67 (2001), 535–72.

Browning, Judkin. "'I Am Not So Patriotic as I Was Once': The Effects of Military Occupation on the Occupying Union Soldiers during the Civil War," *Civil War History*, 55 (2009), 217–243.

Faust, Drew Gilpin. "The Civil War Soldier and the Art of Dying," *Journal of Southern History*, 67 (2001), 3–38.

Huebner, Michael. "The Regulars," *Civil War Times Illustrated*, 39 (June 2000), 24–34.

Linderman, Gerald F. *Embattled Courage: The Experience of Combat in the American Civil War*. New York: Free Press, 1987.

McPherson, James M. *What They Fought For*. Baton Rouge: Louisiana State University Press, 1994.

McWhiney, Grady, and Perry D. Jamieson. *Attack and Die: Civil War Military Tactics and the Southern Heritage*. Tuscaloosa: University of Alabama Press, 1982.

Mitchell, Reid. *Civil War Soldiers: Their Expectations and Their Experiences*. New York: Viking, 1988.

Paskoff, Paul F. "Measures of War: A Quantitative Examination of the Civil War's Destructiveness in the Confederacy," *Civil War History*, 54 (2008), 35–62.

Robertson, James I., Jr. *Soldiers in Blue and Gray*. New York: Warner Books, 1988.

Wiley, Bell I. "The Common Soldier of the Civil War," *Civil War Times Illustrated*, 12 (July 1973), [Special Issue].

———. *The Life of Billy Yank: The Common Soldier of the Union*. Baton Rouge: Louisiana State University Press, 1953.

———. *The Life of Johnny Reb: The Common Soldier of the Confederacy*. Baton Rouge: Louisiana State University Press, 1943.

MILITARY RECONSTRUCTION ACTS

Kincaid, Larry G. "The Legislative Origins of the Military Reconstruction Act, 1865–1867." Ph.D. dissertation, The Johns Hopkins University, 1968.

MISSOURI CAMPAIGN, 1861

Bearss, Edwin C. *The Battle of Wilson's Creek*. N.p.: George Washington Carver Birthplace District Association, 1975.

Brown, D. Alexander. "Pea Ridge: 'Gettysburg of the West,'" *Civil War Times Illustrated*, 6 (October 1967), 4–11, 46–47.

Brown, Dee. "Wilson's Creek," *Civil War Times Illustrated*, 11 (April 1972), 11–18.

Brownlee, Richard S. *Gray Ghosts of the Confederacy: Guerrilla Warfare in the West, 1861–1865*. Baton Rouge: Louisiana State University Press, 1958.

Burkhardt, George S. "No Quarter! Black Flag Warfare, 11863–1865," *North & South*, 10 (May 2007), 12–29.

Castel, Albert. *General Sterling Price and the Civil War in the West*. Baton Rouge: Louisiana State University Press, 1968.

———. "The Guerrilla War," *Civil War Times Illustrated*, 13 (October 1974), [Special Issue].

———. "The Siege of Lexington," *Civil War Times Illustrated*, 8 (August 1969), 4–13.

Christ, Mark (ed.). *Rugged and Sublime: The Civil War in Arkansas*. Fayetteville: University of Arkansas Press, 1994.

Cozzens, Peter. "Hindman's Grand Delusion [Prairie Grove]," *Civil War Times Illustrated*, 39 (October 2000), 28–35, 66–69.

Cutrer, Thomas W. *Ben McCulloch and the Frontier Military Tradition*. Chapel Hill: University of North Carolina Press, 1993.

Davis, William C. "The Battle of Prairie Grove," *Civil War Times Illustrated*, 7 (July 1968), 10–19.

Downey, Fairfax. "The Blue, the Gray, and the Red—Indians in the Civil War," *Civil War Times Illustrated*, 1 (July 1962), 7–9, 26–34.

Ethier, Eric. "Firebrand in a Powder Keg: [Nathaniel Lyon in St. Louis, 1861]," *Civil War Times Illustrated*, 44 (June 2005), 50–56, 81.

Fellman, Michael. *Inside War: The Guerrilla Conflict in Missouri during the American Civil War*. New York: Oxford University Press, 1989.

Frémont, John Charles. *Memoirs of My Life*. Chicago: Bedford, Clark, 1887.

Gaines, W. Craig. *The Confederate Cherokees: John Drew's Regiment of Mounted Rifles*. Baton Rouge: Louisiana State University Press, 1989.

Hatcher, Richard, and William Garrett Piston. "Battle of Wilson's Creek," *Blue & Gray*, 14 (1996–1997), [Special Issue].

Huff, Leo E. "Guerrillas, Jayhawkers, and Bushwackers in Northern Arkansas during the War," *Arkansas Historical Quarterly*, 24 (1965), 127–48.

Hughes, Michael A. "Battle of Pea Ridge," *Blue & Gray*, 5 (1987–1988), [Special Issue].

Josephy, Alvin M. Jr. *The Civil War in the American West*. New York: Knopf, 1991.

Knight, Wilfred. *Red Fox: Stand Watie and the Confederate Indian Nations during the Civil War Years in Indian Territory*. Glendale, Calif.: Arthur C. Clark Co., 1988.

Kushlan, Jim (ed.). "Indians in Blue and Gray," *Civil War Times Illustrated*, 35 (February 1997), [Special Issue].

Monachello, Anthony. "Struggle for St. Louis," *America's Civil War*, 11 (March 1998), 44–49, 74.

Monaghan, Jay. *Civil War on the Western Border, 1854–1865*. Boston: Little, Brown & Co., 1955.

Neal, Diane, and Thomas W. Kremm. *The Lion of the South: General Thomas C. Hindman*. Macon, Ga.: Mercer University Press, 1993.

Nevins, Allan. *Frémont: The World's Greatest Adventurer*. 2 vols. New York: Harper, 1828.

Oates, Stephen B. *Confederate Cavalry West of the River*. Austin: University of Texas Press, 1992, repr.

———. "A Personality Profile of Nathaniel Lyon," *Civil War Times Illustrated*, 6 (February 1968), 15–26.

Owens, Richard H. "Battle of Pea Ridge: Deciding the Future of Missouri," *America's Civil War*, 13 (January 2000), 44–49.

Parrish, William E. "Frémont in Missouri," *Civil War Times Illustrated*, 17 (April 1978), 4–10. 40–45.

Phillips, Christopher. *Damned Yankee: The Life of General Nathaniel Lyon*. Columbia: University of Missouri Press, 1990.

Piston, William Garrett. "Struggle for the Trans-Mississippi," *North & South*, 11 (October 2009), 14–21, 67.

———, and Richard W. Hatcher III. *Wilson's Creek: The Second Battle of the Civil War and the Men Who Fought It*. Chapel Hill: University of North Carolina Press, 2000.

Rolle, Andrew. *John Charles Frémont: Character as Destiny*. Norman: University of Oklahoma Press, 1991.

Sallee, Scott. "The Battle of Prairie Grove: War in the Ozarks," *Blue & Gray*, 21 (2003–2004), [Special Issue].

Shalhope, Robert E. *Sterling Price: Portrait of a Southerner*. Columbia: University of Missouri, 1971.

Shea, William L. "Thunder in the Ozarks: The Battle of Prairie Grove," *North & South*, 9 (March 2006), 12–23.

———. "'Whipped and Routed': Blunt Strikes Marmaduke at Cane Hill," *North & South*, 7 (February 2004), 26–39.

———, and Earl J. Hess. *Pea Ridge: Civil War Campaign in the West*. Chapel Hill: University of North Carolina Press, 1992.

Starr, Stephen Z. *The Union Cavalry in the Civil War: The War in the West, 1861–1865*. Vol. 3. Baton Rouge: Louisiana State University Press, 1985.

Sutherland, Daniel E. "Guerrilla Warfare, Democracy, and the Fate of the Confederacy," *Journal of Southern History*, 68 (2002), 259–92.

———. "Guerillas: The Real War in Arkansas," *Arkansas Historical Quarterly*, 52 (1993), 257–85.

————. "Without Mercy and Without the Blessings of God: [Guerrilla Operations during the Civil War]," *North & South*, 1 (September 1998), 12–21.

MOBILE CAMPAIGN

Bergeron, Arthur W. *Confederate Mobile*. Jackson: University of Mississippi Press, 1991.

Boatner, Mark M., III. *The Civil War Dictionary*. New York: D. McKay and Company, 1959.

Heyman, Max L., Jr. *Prudent Soldier: A Biography of Major General E. R. S. Canby, 1817–1873*. Glendale, Calif.: A. H. Clark, 1959.

Huffstodt, James. "Campaign for Mobile," 21 (March 1982), 8–17.

Jones, Virgil Carrington. *The Civil War at Sea*. 3 vols. New York: Rinehart and Winston, 1960–1962.

————. "Preparation Paid Off for Farragut at Mobile Bay," *Civil War Times Illustrated*, 3 (1964), 7–14.

Rogers, Thomas G. "Last Stand at Fort Blakely," *America's Civil War*, 11 (November 1998), 48–53, 90.

Still, William N., Jr. "Confederate Naval Strategy: The Ironclad," *Journal of Southern History*, 27 (1961), 330–43.

————. *Iron Afloat: The Story of the Confederate Armorclads*. Nashville, Tenn.: Vanderbilt University Press, 1985.

Thomas, Emory. "'Damn the Torpedoes . . .': The Battle of Mobile Bay," *Civil War Times Illustrated*, 16 (April 1977), 4–10, 43–45.

MORGAN, ALBERT T. (1842–1922)

Current, Richard N. *Those Terrible Carpetbaggers: A Reinterpretation*. New York: Oxford University Press, 1988.

Harris, William C. "The Creed of the Carpetbaggers: The Case of Mississippi," *Journal of Southern History*, 40 (1974), 199–224.

Morgan, Albert T. *Yazoo; or, On the Picket Line of Freedom in the South*. New York: Russell & Russell, 1968 repr.

Overy, David H., Jr. "The Wisconsin Carpetbagger: A Group Portrait," *Wisconsin Magazine of History*, 44 (1960), 15–49.

MORMON WAR (1858)

Archer, Jules. *Indian Foe, Indian Friend: The Story of William S. Harney*. New York: Crowell-Collier, 1970.

Brooks, Juanita. *John Doyle Lee: Zealot—Pioneer—Scapegoat.* Glendale, Calif.: A. H. Clark, 1961.

———. *Mountain Meadows Massacre.* Stanford, Calif.: Stanford University Press, 1950.

Denton, Sally. "What Happened at Mountain Meadows?" *American Heritage,* 52 (October 2001), 76–85.

Furniss, Norman F. *The Mormon Conflict, 1850–1859.* Westport, Conn.: Greenwood, 1977.

Moorman, Donald R., and Gene Allred Sessions. *Camp Floyd and the Mormons: The Utah War.* Salt Lake City: University of Utah Press, 1992.

Poll, Richard D. "The Move South," *BYU Studies,* 29 (Fall 1989), 65–88.

———. *Quixotic Mediator: Thomas L. Kane and the Utah War.* Ogden, Utah: Weber University Press, 1985.

Prior, David. "Civilization, Republic, Nation: Contested Keywords, Northern Republicans, and the Forgotten Reconstruction of Mormon Utah," *Civil War History,* 56 (2010), 283–310.

Varley, James F. *Brigham and the General: General Patrick Connor and His California Volunteers in Utah and Along the Overland Trail.* Tucson, Ariz.: Westernlore Press, 1989.

Wise, William. *Massacre at Mountain Meadows: An American Legend and a Monumental Crime.* New York: Crowell, 1976.

MORRILL, JUSTIN M. (1810–1898)

Fuess, Claude M. "Justin Smith Morrill," in Allen Johnson *et al.* (eds.), *Dictionary of American Biography* (10 double vols. + 9 supplements, 1964–1981), XII, 198–99.

Nevins, Allan. *The Origins of the Land-grant Colleges and Universities: A Brief Account of the Morrill Act of 1862 and Its Results.* Washington, D.C.: Civil War Centennial Commission, 1962.

MOSES, FRANKLIN J., JR. (1838–1906)

Carter, Hodding. *The Angry Scar: The Story of Reconstruction.* Garden City, N.Y.: Doubleday & Company, Inc., 1959.

Reynolds, John S. *Reconstruction in South Carolina.* Columbia: University of South Carolina Press, 1905.

Simkins, Francis B., and Robert W. Woody. *South Carolina during Reconstruction.* Chapel Hill: University of North Carolina Press, 1932.

Woody, Robert H. "Franklin Moses, Jr., Scalawag Governor of South Carolina," *North Carolina Historical Review,* 10 (1933), 111–33.

Zuczek, Richard. *State of Rebellion: Reconstruction in South Carolina*. Columbia: University of South Carolina Press, 1996.

NASHVILLE CAMPAIGN

Brennan, Patrick. "The Battle of Franklin," *North & South*, 8 (January 2005), 26–46.
———. "Last Stand in the Heartland [Battle of Nashville]," *North & South*, 8 (January 2005), 20–45.
Connelly, Thomas M. *Autumn of Glory: The Army of Tennessee, 1862–1865*. Baton Rouge: Louisiana State University Press, 1971.
Daniel, Larry J. *Soldiering in the Army of Tennessee: A Portrait of Life in a Confederate Army*. Chapel Hill: University of North Carolina Press, 1991.
Dolzall, Gary W. "Union Stand That Destroyed an Army [Franklin]," *America's Civil War*, 13 (January 2001), 46–52, 88.
Fowler, Robert H. "Hood's Nashville Campaign," *Civil War Times Illustrated*, 3 (December 1964), [Special Issue].
Hay, Thomas Robeson. *Hood's Tennessee Campaign*. New York: W. Neale, 1929.
Horn, Stanley F. *The Decisive Battle of Nashville*. Baton Rouge: Louisiana State University Press, 1956.
———. "The Spring Hill Legend—A Reappraisal," *Civil War Times Illustrated*, 8 (April 1969), 20–32.
McDonough, James Lee. "Battle of Franklin," *Blue & Gray*, 2 (1984–1985), [Special Issue].
———, and Thomas L. Connelly. *Five Tragic Hours: The Battle of Franklin*. Knoxville: University of Tennessee Press, 1983.
Pratt, Fletcher. *Eleven Generals: Studies in American Command*. New York: W. Sloane Associates, 1949.
Roth, Dave. "Mysteries of Spring Hill," *Blue & Gray*, 2 (1984–1985), [Special Issue].
Sword, Wiley. "Battle of Nashville," *Blue & Gray*, 11 (1993–1994), [Special Issue].
———. *Embrace an Angry Wind: The Confederacy's Last Hurrah: Spring Hill, Franklin, and Nashville*. New York: HarperCollins, 1992.

NEGRO MILITIAS AND RECONSTRUCTION

Severance, Ben H. *Tennessee's Radical Army: The State Guard and Its Role in Reconstruction, 1867–1869*. Knoxville: University of Tennessee Press, 2005.
Singletary, Otis A. "Military Disturbances in Arkansas during Reconstruction," *Arkansas Historical Quarterly*, 15 (1956), 140–50.
———. *Negro Militia and Reconstruction*. Austin: University of Texas Press, 1957.

———. "The Negro Militia during Radical Reconstruction," *Military Affairs*, 19 (1955), 177–86.

———. "The Texas Militia during Reconstruction," *Southwestern Historical Quarterly*, 60 (1855–56), 23–35.

NEW DEPARTURE YEARS AFTER RECONSTRUCTION

Beatty, Bess. *A Revolution Gone Backward: The Black Response to National Politics, 1876–1896*. New York: Greenwood Press, 1987.

DeSantis, Vincent P. "Negro Dissatisfaction with Republican Policy in the South," *Journal of Negro History*, 36 (1951), 148–59.

———. "President Arthur and the Independent Movements in the South," *Journal of Southern History,* 19 (1953), 346–63.

———. "President Hayes's Southern Policy," *Journal of Southern History*, 21 (1955), 476–94.

———. "The Republican Party and the Southern Negro, 1877–1897," *Journal of Negro History*, 45 (1960), 71–87.

———. *Republicans Face the Southern Question: The New Departure Years, 1877–1897*. Baltimore, Md.: The Johns Hopkins University Press, 1959.

———. "Rutherford B. Hayes and the Removal of the Troops and the End of Reconstruction," in J. Morgan Kousser and James M. McPherson (eds.), *Region, Race, and Reconstruction: Essays in Honor of C. Vann Woodward.* New York: Oxford University Press, 1982, 417–50.

Fishel, Leslie H., Jr. "The Negro in Northern Politics, 1870–1900," *Mississippi Valley Historical Review,* 42 (1955–1956), 466–89.

Kelly, Patrick J. "The Election of 1896 and the Restructuring of Civil War Memory," *Civil War History*, 49 (2003), 254–280.

Lewis, Elsie M. "The Political Mind of the Negro, 1865–1900," *Journal of Southern History*, 21 (1955), 189–202.

Lewinson, Paul. *Race, Class, and Party: A History of Negro Suffrage and White Politics in the South.* New York: Grosset & Dunlap, 1965.

Logan, Rayford W. *The Betrayal of the Negro: From Rutherford B. Hayes to Woodrow Wilson.* New York: Collier Books, 1965.

Midgette, Nancy Smith. "What Students Need to Know About the 'New South'," *OAH Magazine of History*, 4 (Winter 1989), 51–55.

Wesley, Charles H. "Negro Suffrage in the Period of Constitution-Making, 1787–1865," *Journal of Negro History*, 32 (1947), 143–86.

———. "The Participation of Negroes in Anti-slavery Political Parties," *Journal of Negro History*, 29 (1944), 32–74.

Woodward, C. Vann. "Seeds of Failure in Radical Race Policy," in Harold M. Hyman (ed.), *New Frontiers of the American Reconstruction.* Urbana: University of Illinois Press, 1966, 125–47.

NEW MEXICO AND ARIZONA CAMPAIGN, 1861–1862

Alberts, Don E. *The Battle of Glorieta: Union Victory in the West.* College Station: Texas A&M University Press, 1998.

Bellah, James Warner. "California to the Rescue," *Civil War Times,* 3 (April 1961), 9.

———. "The Desert Campaign," *Civil War Times,* 4–6, 24.

Clendenen, Clarence C. "The Column from California," *Civil War Times Illustrated,* 9 (December 1970), 20–28.

Colton, Ray. *The Civil War in the Western Territories.* Norman: University of Oklahoma Press, 1959.

Craig, Reginald S. *Fighting Parson: The Biography of Colonel John M. Chivington.* Los Angeles: Westernlore Press, 1959.

Donnell, F. S. "The Confederate Territory of Arizona," *New Mexico Historical Review,* 17 (1942), 148–63.

Finch, L. Boyd. *Confederate Pathway to the Pacific: Major Sherrod Hunter and Arizona Territory, C.S.A.* Tucson: Arizona Historical Society , 1996.

Frazier, Donald S. *Blood and Treasure: Confederate Empire in the Southwest.* College Station: Texas A&M University Press, 1995.

Hall, Martin H. *The Confederate Army of New Mexico.* Austin, Tex.: Presidial Press, 1978.

Heyman. Max L. *Prudent Soldier: A Biography of Major General E. R. S. Canby, 1817–1873.* Glendale, Calif.: Arthur H. Clark, 1959.

Josephy, Alvin M., Jr. *The Civil War in the American West.* New York: Knopf, 1991.

Kerby, Robert L. *The Confederate Invasion of New Mexico and Arizona, 1861–1862.* Los Angeles: Westernlore Press, 1958.

Kliger, Paul. "New Mexico Campaign," *Blue & Gray,* 11 (1993–1994), [Special Issue].

Lowry, Thomas P. "The Irish Desert Fox [Paddy Graydon]," *Civil War Times Illustrated,* 42 (April 2003), 26–31.

O'Brien, Tom, and John Taylor. "Battle for the Rio Grand [Valverde]," *Civil War Times Illustrated,* 34 (September 1995), 56–68.

Oder, Broech N. "Sibley's New Mexico Campaign," *Civil War Times Illustrated,* 17 (August 1978), 22–28.

Rosenberg, David H. "Rebel Invasion of New Mexico," *America's Civil War,* 13 (July 2000), 50–57.

Santee, J. F. "The Battle of Glorita Pass," *New Mexico Historical Review,* 6 (1931), 66–75.

Smith, Dean. "Shoot Out at Picacho Pass," *Civil War Times Illustrated,* 18 (October 1979), 5–9, 44–47.

Thompson, Jerry D. (ed.). *Civil War in the Southwest: Recollections of the Sibley Brigade.* College Station: Texas A&M University Press, 2001.

————. *Colonel John Robert Baylor: Texas Indian Fighter and Confederate Soldier.* Hillsboro, Tex.: Hill Junior College Press, 1971.

————. *Desert Tiger: Captain Paddy Graydon and the Civil War in the Far Southwest.* El Paso: Texas Western University Press, 1992.

————. *Henry Hopkins Sibley: Confederate General of the West.* Natchitoches, La.: Northwestern State University Press, 1987.

Waggoner, Jay J. *Early Arizona: Prehistory to Civil War.* Tucson: University of Arizona Press, 1977.

Westphal, David. "The Battle of Glorieta Pass: Its Importance in the Civil War," *New Mexico Historical Review,* 44 (1969), 137–51.

Whitford, William C. *Colorado Volunteers in the Civil War: The New Mexico Campaign in 1862.* Glorieta, N.Mex.: Rio Grande Press, 1971.

Wilson, John P. *When the Texans Came: Missing Records from the Civil War in the Southwest.* Albuquerque: University of New Mexico Press, 2001.

Wright, Arthur A. "Colonel John P. Slough and the New Mexico Campaign, 1862." *Colorado Magazine,* 39 (April 1962), 49–52.

NULLIFICATION

Freehling, William W. *Prelude to Civil War: The Nullification Controversy in South Carolina.* New York: Harper & Row, 1965.

OVERLAND CAMPAIGN ON RICHMOND, 1864

"Battles at Spotsylvania Court House," *Blue & Gray,* 1 (1983–1984), [Special Issue].

Baltz, Louis J. III. *The Last Battle of Cold Harbor: May 27–June 13, 1864.* Lynchburg, Va.: H. E. Howard, 1994.

Cannan, John. *The Wilderness Campaign, May 1864.* Conschohocken, Pa.: Combined Books, 1993.

Catton, Bruce. *A Stillness at Appomattox.* New York: Doubleday & Co., 1953.

Cullen, Joseph P. "The Battle of Cold Harbor," *Civil War Times Illustrated,* 2 (November 1963), 11–17.

————. "Battle of the Wilderness," *Civil War Times Illustrated,* 10 (April 1971), 4–11, 42–47.

————. "Spotsylvania," *Civil War Times Illustrated,* 10 (May 1971), 4–9, 46–48.

————. "When Grant Faced Lee Across the North Anna," *Civil War Times Illustrated,* 3 (February 1965), 16–23.

Davis, William C. *The Battle of New Market.* New York: Doubleday, 1975.

————. "The Day at New Market," *Civil War Times Illustrated,* 10 (July 1971), 4–11. 43–47.

Dowdey, Clifford. *Lee's Last Campaign: The Story of Lee and His Men against Grant.* Boston: Little, Brown, 1960.

Freeman, Douglas Southall. *Lee's Lieutenants: A Study of Command.* 3 vols. New York: Charles Scribner's Sons, 1942–1944.

Gallagher, Gary W. "The Army of Northern Virginia in 1864: A Crisis of High Command," *Civil War History*, 36 (1990), 101–18.

———. "'The Most Memorable Day of Our War' [Muleshoe at Spotsylvania]," *Civil War Times Illustrated*, 27 (May 1988), 22–29.

Hassler, Warren W. "The Battle of Yellow Tavern," *Civil War Times Illustrated*, 5 (November 1966), 5–11, 46–49.

Historian Staff of Richmond National Battlefield Park. "North Anna to the Crossing of the James," *Blue & Gray*, 11 (1993–1994), [Special Issue].

Holsworth, Jerry. "Battle of New Market," *Blue & Gray*, 16 (1998–1999), [Special Issue].

Jaynes, Gregory. *The Killing Ground: Wilderness to Cold Harbor.* Alexandria, Va.: Time-Life Books, 1986.

Krick, Robert E. L., Michael Andrus, and David Ruth. "Grant and Lee, 1864: From the North Anna to the Crossing of the James," *Blue and Gray*, 11 (April 1994).

Long, David E. "Cover-up at Cold Harbor," *Civil War Times Illustrated*, 36 (June 1997), 50–59.

Longacre, Edward G. "The Long Run for Trevilian Station," *Civil War Times Illustrated*, 18 (November 1979), 28–39.

Lowry, Don. *No Turning Back: The Beginning of the End of the Civil War, March–June 1864.* New York: Hippocrene Books, 1991.

Maney, R. Wayne. *Marching to Cold Harbor: Victory or Failure, 1864.* Shippensburg, Pa.: White Mane Publishing Co., 1994.

Matter, William D. *If It Takes All Summer: The Battle of Spotsylvania.* Chapel Hill: University of North Carolina Press, 1988.

Mertz, Gregory A. "Battle of the Wilderness, Part 1," *Blue & Gray*, 12 (1994–1995), [Special Issue].

———. "Battle of the Wilderness, Part 2," *Blue & Gray*, 12 (1994–1995), [Special Issue].

———. "Upton's Attack at Spotsylvania," *Blue & Gray*, 18 (2000–2001), [Special Issue].

Miers, Earl Schenck. *The Last Campaign: Grant Saves the Union.* Philadelphia: J. B. Lippincott, 1972.

Miller, J. Michael. "Battle of North Anna," *Blue & Gray*, 10 (1992–1993), [Special Issue].

———. "Blood at the [North Anna] River: The Ox Ford Story," *Civil War Times Illustrated*, 26 (November 1987), 16–18, 20–25, 45, 49.

———. *The North Anna Campaign: "Even to Hell Itself," May 21–26, 1864.* Lynchburg, Va.: H. E. Howard, 1989.

Naisawald, L. VanLoan. "What VMI Cadets Did at New Market," *Civil War Times*, 3 (February 1962), 6–8, 23–24.

Rhea, Gordon C. *The Battle of the Wilderness, May 5–6, 1864*. Baton Rouge: Louisiana State University Press, 1995.

———. *The Battles for Spotsylvania Court House and the Road to Yellow Tavern, May 7–12. 1864*. Baton Rouge: Louisiana State University Press, 1997.

———. "'Butcher' Grant and the Overland Campaign," *North & South*, 4 (November 2000), 44–55.

———. *Cold Harbor: Grant and Lee, May 26–June 3, 1864*. Baton Rouge: Louisiana State University Press, 2002.

———. *To the North Anna River: Grant and Lee, May 13–25, 1864*. Baton Rouge: Louisiana State University Press, 2000.

Robertson, William Glenn. *Back Door to Richmond: The Bermuda Hundred Campaign*. Newark: University of Delaware Press, 1987.

Ross, Robert. "Tactics in the Wilderness," *North & South*, 11 (August 2009), 22–41.

Ryckman, W. G. "Clash of the Cavalry at Trevilian's," *Virginia Magazine of History and Biography*, 75 (1967), 443–58.

Schiller, Herbert M. *The Bermuda Hundred Campaign: Operations of the South Side of the James River—May 1864*. Dayton, Ohio: Morningside Press, 1988.

Scott, Robert Garth. *Into the Wilderness with the Army of the Potomac*. Bloomington: Indiana University Press, 1985.

Steere, Edward. *The Wilderness Campaign*. Harrisburg, Pa.: Stackpole Co., 1960.

Trudeau, Noah Andre. *Bloody Roads South: The Wilderness to Cold Harbor, May–June 1864*. Boston: Little, Brown, 1989.

———. "Lee's Struggle in the Wilderness," *America's Civil War*, 13 (September 2000), 26–32, 80.

Wert, Jeffry D. "Lee and His Staff," *Civil War Times Illustrated*, 11 (July 1972), 10–19.

———. "One Great Regret: Cold Harbor," *Civil War Times Illustrated*, 17 (February 1979), 22–35.

———. "Spotsylvania: Charge on the Mule Shoe," *Civil War Times Illustrated*, 22 (April 1983), 12–15, 19–21.

Williams, Robert A. "Haw's Shop: A 'Storm of Shot and Shell,'" *Civil War Times Illustrated*, 9 (December 1970), 12–19.

Young, Alfred, III. "Numbers and Losses in the Army of Northern Virginia," *North & South*, 3 (March 2000), 14–29.

PALMETTO RANCH, BATTLE OF

Marvel, William. "Last Hurrah at Palmetto Ranch," *Civil War Times Illustrated*, 44 (January 2006), 66–73.

Young, Kevin R. *To the Tyrants Never Yield: A Texas Civil War Sampler*. Plano, Tex.: Wordware Publishing, 1992.

PARDON, AMNESTY, AND PAROLE

Carter, Dan T. *When the War Was Over: The Failure of Self-Reconstruction in the South, 1865–1867.* Baton Rouge: Louisiana State University Press, 1985.

Dorris, Jonathan Truman. *Pardon and Amnesty under Lincoln and Johnson: The Restoration of Confederates to Their Rights and Privileges, 1861–1898.* Chapel Hill: University of North Carolina Press, 1953.

———. "Pardon Seekers and Brokers: A Sequel to Appomattox," *Journal of Southern History*, 1 (1935), 276–92.

———. "Pardoning the Leaders of the Confederacy," *Mississippi Valley Historical Review*, 15 (1928), 3–21.

Perman, Michael. *Reunion without Compromise: The South and Reconstruction, 1865–1868.* New York: Cambridge University Press, 1973.

Rawley, James A. "The General Amnesty Act of 1872: A Note," *Mississippi Valley Historical Review*, 47 (1960), 480–84.

PEASE, ELISHA MARSHALL (1812–1883)

Baggett, James Alex. "Birth of the Texas Republican Party," *Southwestern Historical Quarterly*, 78 (1974–1975), 1–20.

———. "Origins of Early Texas Republican Party Leadership," *Journal of Southern History*, 40 (1974), 441–50.

Baum, Dale. *The Shattering of Texas Unionism: Politics in the Lone Star State During the Civil War Era.* Baton Rouge: Louisiana State University Press, 1998.

Campbell, Randolph B. "Carpetbagger Rule in Reconstruction Texas: An Enduring Myth," *Southwestern Historical Quarterly*, 97 (1993–1994), 586–96.

Carrier, John P. "A Political History of Texas during the Reconstruction, 1865–1874." Ph.D. dissertation, Vanderbilt University, 1971.

Crouch, Barry A. "'Unmanacling' Texas Reconstruction: A Twenty Year Perspective," *Southwestern Historical Quarterly*, 93 (1989–1990), 275–302.

Richter, William L. *The Army in Texas During Reconstruction, 1865–1870.* College Station: Texas A&M University Press, 1987.

PENINSULA CAMPAIGN

Bailey, Ronald H. *Forward to Richmond: McClellan's Peninsula Campaign.* Alexandria, Va.: Time-Life Books, 1983.

Burton, Brian K. *Extraordinary Circumstances: The Seven Days Battles.* Bloomington: University of Indiana Press, 2001.

Cullen, Joseph P. "The McClellan-Lincoln Controversy," *Civil War Times Illustrated*, 5 (November 1966), 34–43.

———. *The Peninsula Campaign: McClellan and Lee Struggle for Richmond.* Harrisburg, Pa.: Stackpole Company, 1973.

Longacre, Edward G. "All the Way Around [Stuart's Raid]," *Civil War Times Illustrated*, 41 (August 2003), 22–29, 59.

Martin, David G. *The Peninsula Campaign, March–July 1862.* Conshohocken, Pa.: Combined Books, 1992.

McPherson, James M. (ed.). *Battle Chronicles of the Civil War.* 6 vols. New York: Macmillan, 1989.

Mewborn, Horace. "Stuart's Ride Around McClellan," *Blue & Gray*, 15 (1997–1998), [Special Issue].

Miller, William J. (ed.). *The Peninsula Campaign of 1862: Yorktown to the Seven Days.* Campbell, Calif.: Savas Publishers, 1993.

Moore, J. Michael. "That Dam Failure," *North & South*, 5 (July 2002), 62–71.

Newton, Steven H. *The Battle of Seven Pines.* Lynchburg, Va.: H. E. Howard, 1993.

Sears, Stephen W. *To the Gates of Richmond: The Peninsula Campaign.* New York: Ticknoe & Fields, 1992.

Starr, Stephen W. *The Union Cavalry in the Civil War: From Fort Sumter to Gettysburg.* Vol. 1. Baton Rouge: Louisiana State University Press, 1979.

Stinson, Dwight E. "The Battle of Eltham's Landing," *Civil War Times Illustrated*, 1 (February 1963), 38–41.

Thomas, Emory. "The Peninsula Campaign." *Civil War Times Illustrated*, 17 (February 1979), 4–9, 40–45; 18 (April 1979), 28–35; 18 (May 1979), 12–18; 18 (June 1979), 10–17; 18 (July 1979), 14–24.

Wert, Jeffry. "[Seven Pines]," *Civil War Times Illustrated*, 27 (October, November 1988), 20–28; 20–29.

PENNSYLVANIA INVASION

Albright, Harry. *Gettysburg: Crisis of Command.* New York: Hippocrene Books, 1989.

Alexander, Ted. "Gettysburg Cavalry Operations," *Blue & Gray*, 6 (1988–1989), [Special Issue].

———. "'A Regular Slave Hunt': The Army of Northern Virginia and Black Civilians in the Gettysburg Campaign," *North & South*, 4 (September 2001), 82–89.

Bellah, James Warner. *Soldiers' Battle: Gettysburg.* New York: David McKay Co., 1962.

Brann, James R. "Defense of Little Round Top: The Full Story," *America's Civil War*, 12 (November 1999), 34–40.

Brennan, Patrick. "Thunder on the Plains of Brandy," *North & South*, 5 (April 2002), 14–34; *North & South*, 5 (May 2002), 32–51.

Busey, John W. *These Honored Dead: The Union Casualties at Gettysburg.* Highstown, N.J.: Longstreet House, 1988.

————, and David G. Martin. *Regimental Strengths at Gettysburg*. Baltimore, Md.: Gateway Press, 1982.

Campbell, Eric A. "Death of [Sickles'] III Corps [at Gettysburg]," *Civil War Times Illustrated*, 48 (August 2009), 34–37.

Cannan, John. *The War in the East: Chancellorsville to Gettysburg, 1863*. New York: New York: Gallery Books, 1990.

Catton, Bruce. *Gettysburg: The Final Fury*. Garden City, N.Y.: Doubleday, 1974.

————. *Glory Road: The Bloody Route from Fredericksburg to Gettysburg*. New York: Doubleday and Co., 1952.

Christ, Elwood W. *The Struggle for Bliss Farm at Gettysburg, July 2nd and 3rd, 1863*. Baltimore, Md.: Butternut & Blue Press, 1993.

Clark, Champ. *Gettysburg: The Confederate High Tide*. Alexandria, Va.: Time-Life Books, 1985.

Coco, Gregory A. *A Vast Sea of Misery: A History and Guide to the Union and Confederate Field Hospitals at Gettysburg, July 1–November 20, 1863*. Gettysburg, Pa.: Thomas Publications, 1988.

————. *Wasted Valor: The Confederate Dead at Gettysburg*. Gettysburg, Pa.: Thomas Publications, 1990.

Coddington, Edwin B. *The Gettysburg Campaign: A Study in Command*. New York: Charles Scribner's Sons. 1968.

Daniels, Elizabeth. "The Children of Gettysburg," *American Heritage*, 40 (May/June 1989), 97–107, *passim*.

Dowdey, Clifford. *Death of a Nation: Lee and His Men at Gettysburg*. New York: Knopf, 1958.

Downey, Fairfax. *The Guns at Gettysburg*. New York: David McKay, 1958.

Eden, Stephen J. "The War's Hottest Half-hour [Herbst's Woods]," *Civil War Times Illustrated*, 42 (August 2003), 56–65.

Epperson, James F. "Lee's Slave-Makers," *Civil War Times Illustrated*, 41 (August 2002), 44–51.

Foote, Shelby. *The Civil War: A Narrative*. New York: Random House, 1958–1974.

Fowler, Robert H. "Gettysburg," *Civil War Times Illustrated*, 2 (July 1963), [Special Issue].

Freeman, Douglas Southall. *Lee's Lieutenants: A Study of Command*. 3 vols. New York: Charles Scribner's Sons, 1942–1944.

Gallagher, Gary W. (ed.). *The First Day at Gettysburg: Essays on Confederate and Union Leadership*. Kent, Ohio: Kent State University Press, 1992.

———— (ed.). *The Second Day at Gettysburg: Essays on Confederate and Union Leadership*. Kent, Ohio: Kent State University Press, 1993.

———— (ed.). *The Third Day at Gettysburg and Beyond*. Chapel Hill: University of North Carolina Press, 1994.

Georg Harrison, Kathleen. "Battle of Gettysburg, Day 3," *Blue & Gray*, 5 (1987–1988), [Special Issue].

————, and John W. Busey. *Nothing But Glory: Pickett's Division at Gettysburg*. Highstown, N.J.: Longstreet House, 1987.

Gottfried, Bradley M. *Brigades of Gettysburg: The Union and Confederate Brigades at the Battle of Gettysburg.* Cambridge, Mass.: Da Capo, 2002.

Graham, Martin F., and George F. Skoch. *Mine Run: A Campaign of Lost Opportunities, October 21, 1863–May 1, 1864.* Lynchburg, Va.: H. E. Howard, 1987.

Grimsley, Mark. "Review Essay: The Continuing Battle of Gettysburg," *Civil War History,* 49 (2003), 181–87.

Hall, Clark B. "The Winter Encampment of the Army of the Potomac, December 1, 1863–May 1, 1864," *Blue and Gray,* 8 (April 1991).

Harman, Troy D. *Cemetery Hill: "The Plan Was Unchanged."* Baltimore, Md.: Butternut and Blue, 2001.

Harrison, Kathleen Georg. "Ridges of Grim War: Gettysburg, July 1, July 2, July 3," *Blue and Gray,* 5 (1987–1988).

Hassler, Warren W., Jr. *Crisis at the Crossroads: The First Day at Gettysburg.* Tuscaloosa: University of Alabama Press, 1970.

———. "Slaughter Pen at Bristoe Station," *Civil War Times Illustrated,* 1 (May 1862), 8–17.

Henderson, William D. *The Road to Bristoe Station: Campaigning with Lee and Meade, August 1–October 20, 1863.* Lynchburg, Va.: H. E. Howard, 1987.

Herdegen, Lance Jr., and William J. K. Beaudot. *In the Bloody Railroad Cut at Gettysburg.* Dayton, Ohio: Morningside Press, 1990.

Hollingsworth, Alan M., and James M. Cox. *The Third Day at Gettysburg: Pickett's Charge.* New York: Henry Holt and Co., 1959.

Klein, Frederic S. "Westminster: Little Skirmish, Big Affair?" *Civil War Times Illustrated,* 7 (August 1968), 32–38.

Krolick, Marshall D. "Battle of Gettysburg, Day 1," *Blue & Gray,* 5 (1987–1988), [Special Issue].

Kross, Gary. "Battle of Gettysburg, Day 2," *Blue & Gray,* 5 (1987–1988), [Special Issue].

———. "Gettysburg Vignettes 1—Buford-Iverson-Ewell," *Blue & Gray,* 12 (1994–1995), [Special Issue].

———. "Gettysburg Vignettes 2—Chamberlain-Oates-Farnsworth," *Blue & Gray,* 13 (1995–1996), [Special Issue].

———. "Gettysburg Vignettes 3—Eastern Flank," *Blue & Gray,* 14 (1996–1997), [Special Issue].

———. "Gettysburg Vignettes 4—Sickles' Front," *Blue & Gray,* 15 (1997–1998), [Special Issue].

———. "Gettysburg Vignette 5—Pickett's Charge," *Blue & Gray,* 16 (1998–1999), [Special Issue].

Kushlan, Jim (ed.). "Gettysburg," *Civil War Times Illustrated,* 37 (August 1998), [Special Issue].

——— (ed.). "Inside the Mind of Lee the Invader," *Civil War Times Illustrated,* 42 (August 2003), 30–40.

LaFantasie, Glenn W. "Gettysburg," *North & South,* 6 (July 2003), [Special Issue].

Longacre, Edward G. *The Cavalry at Gettysburg: A Tactical Study of Mounted Operations during the Civil War's Pivotal Campaign, 9 June-14 July, 1863.* Rutherford, N.J.: Fairleigh Dickinson University Press, 1986.

Luvaas, Jay. "Lee at Gettysburg: A General without Intelligence," *Intelligence and National Security*, 5 (1990), 116–35.

Martin, Samuel J. "Did 'Baldy' Lose Gettysburg?" *America's Civil War*, 10 (July 1997), 34–40.

Mackowski, Chris, and Kristopher D. White. "Second-Guessing Dick Ewell," *Civil War Times Illustrated*, 49 (August 2010), 34–41.

McLaughlin, Jack. *Gettysburg: The Long Encampment.* New York: Bonanza, 1963.

McLean, James L. *Cutler's Brigade at Gettysburg.* Baltimore, Md.: Butternut & Blue Press, 1987.

———, and Judy McLean (eds.). *Gettysburg Sources.* 3 vols. Baltimore, Md.: Butternut & Blue Press, 1986–1990.

McPherson, James M. (ed.). *Battle Chronicles of the Civil War.* 6 vols. New York: Macmillan, 1989.

Miers, Earl Schenck, and Richard A. Brown. *Gettysburg.* New Brunswick, N.J.: Rutgers University Press, 1948.

Motts, Wayne E. "Pickett's Charge Revisited: A Brave and Resolute Force," *North & South*, 2 (June 1999), 27–34.

Nesbitt, Mark. *Saber and Scapegoat: J. E. B. Stuart and the Gettysburg Controversy.* Mechanicsburg, Pa.: Stackpole Books, 2002.

Nye, Wilbur S. "The Affair at Hunterstown," *Civil War Times Illustrated*, 9 (February 1971), 22–34.

———. *Here Come the Rebels!* Baton Rouge: Louisiana State University Press, 1965.

Persico, Joseph E. *My Enemy, My Brother: Men and Days at Gettysburg.* New York: Macmillan, 1977.

Pfanz, Harry. *Gettysburg: Culp's Hill and Cemetery Hill.* Chapel Hill: University of North Carolina Press, 1993.

———. *Gettysburg: The First Day.* Chapel Hill: University of North Carolina Press, 2001.

———. *Gettysburg: The Second Day.* Chapel Hill: University of North Carolina Press, 1987.

Poulter, Keith (ed.). "140th Gettysburg Commemorative Issue," *North & South*, 6 (July 2003).

——— (ed.). "Special Edition: Retreat from Gettysburg," *North & South*, 2 (August 1999).

Priest, John Michael. "Lee's Gallant 6,000?" *North & South*, 1 (No. 6, 1998), 42–56.

Raus, Edmund J., Jr. *A Generation on the March—The Union Army at Gettysburg.* Lynchburg, Va.: H. E. Howard, 1987.

Rice, Gary R. "Devil Dan Sickles' Deadly Salient," *America's Civil War*, 11 (November 1998), 38–45.

Roland, Charles P. "Lee's Invasion Strategy," *North & South*, 1 (June 1998), 34–39.

Rollins, Richard. "The Failure of the Confederate Artillery in Pickett's Charge," *North & South*, 3 (April 2000), 26–42.

———. "Lee's Artillery Prepares for Pickett's Charge," *North & South*, 2 (September 1999). 41–55.

———. "Ordinance and Logistics: The Failure of Confederate Artillery at Gettysburg," *North & South*, 3 (January 2000), 44–54.

——— (ed.). *Pickett's Charge! Eyewitness Accounts*. Redondo Beach, Calif.: Rank and File Publications, 1994.

———, and Dave Schultz. "A Combined and Concentrated Fire: The Federal Artillery at Gettysburg, July 3, 1863," *North & South*, 3 (March 1999), 39–60.

Samito, Christian G. "Lost Opportunity at Gettysburg," *America's Civil War*, 11 (July 1998), 46–53, 88.

Sapperson, James F. "Lee's Slave-makers," *Civil War Times Illustrated*, 41 (August 2002), 44–51.

Sauers, Richard Allen. *A Caspian Sea of Ink: The Meade-Sickles Controversy*. Baltimore, Md.: Butternut & Blue Press, 1989.

———. *The Gettysburg Campaign, June 3–August 1, 1863: A Comprehensive, Selectively Annotated Bibliography*. Westport, Conn.: Greenwood Press, 1982.

Stackpole, Edward J. *They Met at Gettysburg*. Harrisburg, Pa.: Stackpole Co., 1956.

Stanchak, John (ed.). "Gettysburg," *Civil War Times Illustrated*, 27 (Summer 1988), [Special Issue].

Stewart, George R. *Pickett's Charge: A Microhistory of the Final Attack at Gettysburg, July 3, 1863*. Boston: Houghton Mifflin, 1959.

Taylor, John M. "The Question: What Went Wrong at Gettysburg?" *Civil War Times Illustrated*, 41 (March 2002), 24–31.

Tucker, Glenn. "Brandy Station: Where Stuart Learned that Federals Could Fight," *Civil War Times*, 2 (December 1960), 5–6, 18–19.

———. *High Tide at Gettysburg: The Campaign in Pennsylvania*. Indianapolis: Bobbs-Merrill, 1958.

———. *Lee and Longstreet at Gettysburg*. Indianapolis: Bobbs-Merrill, 1968.

———. "Longstreet: Culprit or Scapegoat?" *Civil War Times Illustrated*, 1 (April 1962), 5–7, 39–44.

Wert, Jeffry D. "Gettysburg," *Civil War Times Illustrated*, 28 (Summer 1988).

———. *Gettysburg: Day Three*. New York: Simon & Schuster, 2001.

———. "Lee and His Staff," *Civil War Times Illustrated*, 11 (July 1972), 10–19.

———. "Rappahannock Station," *Civil War Times Illustrated*, 15 (December 1976), 5–8, 40–46.

Wittenberg, Eric J. *Gettysburg's Forgotten Cavalry Actions*. Gettysburg, Pa.: Thomas Publications, 1998.

PERRYVILLE AND STONE'S RIVER CAMPAIGNS

Bogle, James G. "Great Locomotive Chase," *Blue & Gray*, 4 (1986–1987), [Special Issue].

Cheeks, Robert C. "Rout of the Union Rights at Stone's River," *America's Civil War*, 12 (September 1999), 30–36.

Connelly, Thomas M. *Army of the Heartland: The Army of the Tennessee, 1861–1862*. Baton Rouge: Louisiana State University Press, 1967.

———. *Autumn of Glory: The Army of Tennessee, 1862–1865*. Baton Rouge: Louisiana State University Press, 1971.

Cozzens, Peter. *No Better Place to Die: The Battle of Stone's River*. Urbana: University of Illinois Press, 1990.

Daniel, Larry J. *Soldiering in the Army of Tennessee: A Portrait of Life in a Confederate Army*. Chapel Hill: University of North Carolina Press, 1991.

Hafendorfer, Kenneth. *Perryville: The Battle for Kentucky*. Owensboro, Ky.: McDowell, 1981.

Harrison, Lowell H. "The Battle of Munfordville," *Civil War Times Illustrated*, 13 (June 1974), 12–27.

———. "Perryville: Death on a Dry River," *Civil War Times Illustrated*, 18 (May 1979), 4–9, 44–47.

Hess, Earl J. *Banners to the Breeze: The Kentucky Campaign, Corinth, and Stone's River*. Lincoln: University of Nebraska Press, 2000.

Horn, Stanley F. "The Battle of Perryville," *Civil War Times Illustrated*, 4 (February 1966), 4–11, 42–47.

———. "The Battle of Stone's River," *Civil War Times Illustrated*, 2 (February 1964), 7–11, 34–39.

McDonough, James Lee. "Cold Days in Hell: The Battle of Stone's River, Tennessee," *Civil War Times Illustrated*, 25 (June 1986), [Special Issue].

———. *Stone's River: Bloody Winter in Tennessee*. Knoxville: University of Tennessee Press, 1983.

———. *War in Kentucky From Shiloh to Perryville*. Knoxville: University of Tennessee Press, 1994.

Noe, Kenneth W. "Last Stand Ridge: The Other Highwater Mark [at Perryville]," *North & South*, 4 (September 2001), 64–77.

———. *Perryville: The Grand Havoc of Battle*. Lexington: University of Kentucky Press, 2001.

Prokopowicz, Gerald J. "Tactical Stalemate: The Battle of Stone's River," *North & South*, 2 (September 1999), 10–28.

Roth, Dave. "Battle of Perryville," *Blue & Gray*, 1 (1983–1984), [Special Issue].

Sanders, Stuart. "The 1862 Kentucky Campaign and the Battle of Perryville," *Blue & Gray*, 22 (2004–2005), [Special Issue].

Spearman, Charles M. "Battle of Stone's River," *Blue & Gray*, 6 (1988–1989), [Special Issue].

Walsh, John P., Jr. "'I Tell You, Sir, They Are Yankees! [Perryville]," *North & South*, 5 (September 2002), 56–69.

Williams, Kenneth P. *Lincoln Finds a General: A Military Study of the Civil War.* 5 vols. New York: Macmillan, 1949–1959.

PETERSBURG, SIEGE OF

Brooksher, William, and David K. Snyder. "Wade Hampton Turns Cattle-Rustler: A Piece of Rebel Rascality," *Civil War Times Illustrated*, 23 (June 1984), 10–19.

Calkins, Chris. "Action in the Petersburg Campaign: Weldon Railroad (Globe Tavern) and Reams' Station," *Blue & Gray*, 23 (2005–2006), [Special Issue].

Catton, Bruce. *A Stillness at Appomattox*. New York: Doubleday & Co., 1953.

Cavanaugh, Michael A., and William Marvel. *The Petersburg Campaign: The Battle of the Crater: "The Horrid Pit," June 25–Auust 6, 1864*. Lynchburg, Va.: H. E. Howard, 1989.

Cullen, Joseph P. "Petersburg!" *Civil War Times Illustrated*, 9 (August 1970), [Special Issue].

———. "The Siege of Petersburg," *Civil War Times Illustrated*, 27 (Summer 1988). [Special Issue].

Davis, William C. *Death in the Trenches: Grant at Petersburg*. Alexandria, Va.: Time-Life Books, 1986.

Freeman, Douglas Southall. *Lee's Lieutenants: A Study of Command*. 3 vols. New York: Charles Scribner's Sons, 1942–1944.

Guelzo, Allen C. "As Plain as a Deep Scar: Disaster at Reem's Station, August 25, 1864," *North & South*, 9 (May 2006), 26–36.

Guttman, Jon. "Beauregard Battles the Beast [Drewry's Bluff, 1864]," *America's Civil War*, 11 (March 1998), 26–32.

Helniak, Roman J., and Lawrence L. Hewitt (eds.). *The Confederate High Command and Related Topics: The 1988 Deep Delta Civil War Symposium*. Shippensburg, Pa.: White Mane Publishing Co., 1990.

Horn, John. *The Petersburg Campaign: The Destruction of the Weldon Railroad—Deep Bottom, Globe Tavern, Reams' Station, August 14–25, 1864*. Lynchburg, Va.: H. E. Howard, 1991.

———. *The Petersburg Campaign: June 1864–April 1865*. Conshohocken, Pa.: Combined Books, 1993.

Howe, Thomas J. *The Petersburg Campaign: Wasted Valor, June 15–18, 1864*. Lynchburg, Va.: H. E. Howard, 1988.

Klein, Frederic S. "Butler at Bermuda Hundred," *Civil War Times Illustrated*, 6 (November 1967), 4–11, 45–47.

Levin, Kevin M. "'Until Every Negro Has Been Slaughtered!' Did Southerners See the Battle of the Crater as a Slave Rebellion?" *Civil War Times Illustrated*, 49 (October 2010), 32–37.

Longacre, Edward G. "The Blackest of All Days [Ream's Station]," *Civil War Times Illustrated*, 25 (March 1986), 12–19.

———. "[Butler's] Petersburg Follies," *Civil War Times Illustrated*, 19 (January 1980), 4–9, 34–41.

Pfanz, Donald C. *The Petersburg Campaign: Abraham Lincoln at City Point, March 20–April 9, 1865*. Lynchburg, Va.: H. E. Howard, 1989.

Robertson, William Glenn. *The Petersburg Campaign: The Battle of Old Men and Young Boys, June 9, 1864*. Lynchburg, Va.: H. E. Howard, 1989.

Sommers, Richard J. "Fury at Fort Harrison," *Civil War Times Illustrated*, 19 (October 1980), 12–23.

———. "'Only a Miracle Can Save Us': Second Battle of Deep Bottom, Virginia, August 14–20, 1864," *North & South*, 4 (January 2001), 12–32.

———. *Richmond Redeemed: The Siege at Petersburg*. Garden City, N.Y.: Doubleday, 1981.

Sudarow, Bruce. "Glory Denied: First Deep Bottom,: *North & South*, 3 (September 2000), 17–32.

———. "War Along the James," *North & South*, 6 (April 2003), 12–23.

Trudeau, Noah Andre. *The Last Citadel: Petersburg, Virginia, June 1864–April 1865*. Boston: Little, Brown, 1991.

Wert, Jeffry D. "Lee and His Staff," *Civil War Times Illustrated*, 11 (July 1972), 10–19.

PINCHBACK, PINCKNEY BENTON STEWART (1837–1921)

Grosz, Agnes Smith. "The Political Career of Pinckney Benton Stewart Pinchback," *Louisiana Historical Quarterly*, 27 (1944), 527–612.

Haskins, James. *Pinckney Benton Stewart Pinchback*. New York: Macmillan, 1973.

Low, W. Augustus, and Virgil A. Clift. *Encyclopedia of Black America.* New York: McGraw-Hill Book Company, 1981.

Vincent, Charles. *Black Legislators in Louisiana during Reconstruction*. Baton Rouge: Louisiana State University Press, 1976.

PRICE, STERLING (1809–1867)

Boatner, Mark M. *The Civil War Dictionary.* New York: David McKay Co., Inc., 1959.

Castel, Albert. *General Sterling Price and the Civil War in the West*. Baton Rouge: Louisiana State University Press, 1968.

Monaghan, Jay. *Civil War on the Western Border, 1854–1865.* New York: Bonanza Books, 1955.

Ross, Reid. "Price's Raid," *North & South*, 12 (No. 4, 2010), 11–26.

PRICE'S MISSOURI RAID (1864)

Boatner, Mark M. *The Civil War Dictionary.* New York: David McKay Co., Inc., 1959.

Castel, Albert. *General Sterling Price and the Civil War in the West.* Baton Rouge: Louisiana State University Press, 1968.

Monaghan, Jay. *Civil War on the Western Border, 1854–1865.* New York: Bonanza Books, 1955.

Piston, William Garrett. "Struggle for the Trans-Mississippi," *North & South*, 11 (October 2009), 14–21, 67.

Ross, Reid. "Price's Raid," *North & South*, 12 (No. 4, 2010), 11–26.

Sallee, Scott E. "Price's Missouri Raid, 1864," *Blue & Gray*, 8 (1990–1991), [Special Issue].

PRISONERS OF WAR

Beitzell, Edwin W. *Point Lookout Prison Camp for Confederates.* Leonardtown, Md.: St. Mary's County Historical Society, 1972.

Blakley, Arch Frederic. *General John H. Winder, C.S.A.* Gainesville: University of Florida Press, 1990.

Brown, Louis A. *The Salisbury Prison: A Case Study of Confederate Military Prisons, 1861–1865.* Wendell, N.C.: Broadfoot, 1980.

Bryant, William O. *Cahaba Prison and the Sultana Disaster.* Tuscaloosa: University of Alabama Press, 1990.

Byrne, Frank L. "Libby Prison: A Study in Emotions," *Journal of Southern History*, 24 (1958), 430–444.

Catton, Bruce. "Prison Camps of the Civil War," *American Heritage*, 10 (August 1959), 4–13, 96–97.

Cross, David F., M.D. "What Killed the Yankees at Andersonville?" *North & South*, 6 (September 2003), 26–32.

Denney, Robert E. *Civil War Prisons and Escapes: A Day by Day Chronicle.* New York: Sterling, 1993.

Downer, Edward T. "Johnson's Island," *Civil War History*, 8 (1962), 202–17.

Futch, Ovid L. *History of Andersonville Prison.* Gainesville: University of Florida Press, 1968.

Gillespie, James. "Guests of the Yankees," *North & South*, 5 (July 2002), 40–49.

———. "Postwar Mythmaking: The Case of the POWs," *North & South*, 6 (April 2003), 40–49.

Hesseltine, William B. *Civil War Prisons: A Study in War Psychology.* 2nd ed. Ungar, 1930.

Kaufhold, John. "The Elmira Observatory," *Civil War Times Illustrated*, 16 (July 1977), 30–35.

Keen, Nancy Travis. "Confederate Prisoners of War at Fort Delaware," *Delaware History*, 13 (1968), 1–27.

Lawrence, F. Lee, and Robert W. Glover. *Camp Ford, C.S.A.* Austin, Tex.: Civil War Centennial Advisory Committee, 1964.

Long, Roger. "Johnson's Island Prison," *Blue & Gray*, 4 (1986–1987), [Special Issue].

Marvel, William. *Andersonville: The Last Depot.* Chapel Hill: University of North Carolina Press, 1994.

Miller, Robert Earnest. "War within Walls: Camp Chase and the Search for Administrative Reform," *Ohio History*, 96 (1987), 35–56.

Parker, Sandra V. *Richmond's Civil War Prisons.* Lynchburg, Va.: H. E. Howard, 1990.

Perry-Mosher, Kate E. "The Rock Island P.O.W. Camp," *Civil War Times Illustrated*, 8 (July 1969), 28–36.

Robertson, James I., Jr. "House of Horror: Danville's Civil War Prison," *Virginia Magazine of History and Biography*, 69 (1961), 329–45.

———. "Old Capitol: Eminence to Infamy," *Maryland Historical Magazine*, 65 (1970), 394–412.

———. "The Scourge of Elmira," *Civil War History*, 8 (1962), 184–201.

Robins, Glenn. "Race, Repatriation, and Galvanized Rebels: Union Prisoners and the Exchange Question in Deep South Prison Camps," *Civil War History*, 53 (2007), 117–40.

Sanders, Charles W., Jr. "'A Most Horrible National Sin': The Treatment of Prisoners in the American Civil War," *North & South*, 9 (October 2006), 12–30.

Shriver, Philip R., and Donald J. Breen. *Ohio's Military Prisons in the Civil War.* Columbus: Ohio Historical Society, 1964.

Soodalter, Ron. "Last Raid of a Rebel Pirate [John Yates Bealeand the Raid on Johnson's Island POW Camp in Lake Erie]," *Civil War Times Illustrated*, 48 (April 2009), 42–47.

Speer, Lonnie R. "'Hell on Earth' [Gratiot Street Prison in St. Louis]," *Civil War Times Illustrated*, 34 (July 1995), 58–66.

———. *Portals to Hell: Military Prisons of the Civil War.* Mechanicsburg, Pa.: Stackpole Books, 1997.

———. *War of Vengeance: Acts of Retaliation Against Civil War POWs.* Mechanicsburg, Pa.: Stackpole Books, 2002.

Walker, T. R. "Rock Island Prison Barracks," *Civil War History*, 8 (1962), 152–63.

Wilson, W. Emerson. *Fort Delaware.* Newark: University of Delaware Press, 1957.

———. "Fort Delaware: Northern Andersonville," *Civil War Times*, 2 (November 1960), 14–15.

Winslow, Hattie Lou, and Joseph R. Moore. *Camp Morton, 1861–1865, Indianapolis Prison Camp.* Indianapolis: Indiana Historical Society, 1940.

RACE RIOTS THAT INFLUENCED THE RECONSTRUCTION ACTS

Carter, Dan T. *When the War Was Over: The Failure of Self-Reconstruction in the South, 1865–1867.* Baton Rouge: Louisiana State University Press, 1985.

Edwards, John Carver. "Radical Reconstruction and the New Orleans Riot of 1866," *Journal of History and Politics*, 11 (1973), 48–64.

Franklin, John Hope. *The Militant South*. Cambridge, Mass.: Harvard University Press, 1956.

Hardwick, Kevin R. "'Your Father Abe Lincoln Is Dead and Damned': Black Soldiers and the Memphis Race Riot of 1866," *Journal of Social History*, 27 (1993), 109–28.

Holmes, Jack D. L. "The Underlying Causes of the Memphis Race Riot of 1866," *Tennessee Historical Quarterly*, 17 (1958), 195–225.

Lovett, Bobby L. "Memphis Riots: White Reactions to Blacks in Memphis, May 1865–July 1866," *Tennessee Historical Quarterly*, 38 (1979), 9–33.

Moore, John Hammond. "The Norfolk Riot: April 16, 1866," *Virginia Magazine of History and Biography*, 90 (182), 155–64.

Nieman, Donald G. (ed.). *Black Freedom/White Violence, 1865–1900*. New York: Garland Publishing, Inc., 1994.

Rable, George C. *But There Was No Peace: The Role of Violence in the Politics of Reconstruction*. Athens: University of Georgia Press, 1984.

Reynolds, Donald E. "The New Orleans Riot of 1866, Reconsidered," *Louisiana History*, 5 (1964), 5–27.

Riddleberger, Patrick W. *1866: The Critical Year Revisited*. Carbondale: Southern Illinois University Press, 1979.

Ryan, James Gilbert. "The Memphis Riot of 1866: Terror in a Black Community During Reconstruction," *Journal of Negro History*, 62 (1977), 243–57.

Vandall, Gilles. *The New Orleans Riot of 1866*. Lafayette: University of Southwestern Louisiana Press, 1983.

———. "The Origins of the New Orleans Riot of 1866, Revisited," *Louisiana History*, 22 (1981), 135–65.

Waller, Altina L. "Community, Class, and Race in the Memphis Riot of 1866," *Journal of Social History*, 18 (1984), 233–46.

RAINEY, JOSEPH H. (1832–1887)

Simkins, Francis B. "Joseph Hayne Rainey," in Allen Johnson *et al.* (eds.), *Dictionary of American Biography* (10 double vols. + 9 supplements, 1964–1981), XV, 327–28.

Low, W. Augustus, and Virgil A. Clift. *Encyclopedia of Black America*. New York: McGraw-Hill Book Company, 1981.

McFarlin, Annjeannette Sophia. *Black Congressional Reconstruction Orators and Their Orations*. Metuchen, N.J.: Scarecrow Press, 1976.

REBEL SURRENDER

Ash, Stephen V. *A Year in the South: Four Lives in 1865*. New York: Palgrave Macmillan, 2002.

Bearss, Edwin C., and Chris Caulkins. *The Battle of Five Forks*. Lynchburg, Va.: H. E. Howard, 1985.

Bellware, Daniel A. "The Last Battle. Period. Really," *Civil War Times Illustrated*, 42 (April 2003), 48–56.

Bradley, Mark L. "Surrender at Bennet Place [Durham Station]," *Blue & Gray*, 17 (1999–2000), [Special Issue].

————. *This Astounding Close: The Road to Bennett Place*. Chapel Hill: University of North Carolina Press, 2000.

Cauble, Frank P. *The Surrender Proceedings: April 9, 1865–Appomattox Court House*. Lynchburg, Va.: H. E. Howard, 1987.

Caulkins, Chris M. "Battle of Five Forks," *Blue & Gray*, 9 (1991–1992), [Special Issue].

————. *The Battles of Appomattox Station and Appomattox Court House, April 8–9, 1865*. Lynchburg, Va.: H. E. Howard, 1987.

————. "Hurtling Toward the End [the Battle of Sayler's Creek]," *Civil War Times Illustrated*, 44 (January 2006), 42–49.

Clark, James C. *Last Train South: The Flight of the Confederate Government from Richmond*. Jefferson, N.C.: McFarland & Co., 1984.

Davis, Burke. *The Long Surrender*. New York: Random House, 1985.

————. *To Appomattox: Nine April Days, 1865*. New York: Rinehart & Co., 1959.

Davis, William C. "The Campaign to Appomattox," *Civil War Times Illustrated*, 14 (April 1975), [Special Issue].

Greene, A. Wilson. "Breakthrough at Petersburg: Pamplin Park," *Blue & Gray*, 18 (2000–2001), [Special Issue].

Hoeling, A. A., and Mary Hoeling. *The Last Days of the Confederacy*. New York: Fairfax Press, 1981.

King, Curtis S. "'Reconsider, Hell!' [Sheridan at Five Forks]," *Civil War Times Illustrated*, 44 (January 2006), 24–32.

Kurtz, Henry I "Five Forks—The South's Waterloo," *Civil War Times Illustrated*, 3 (October 1964), 5–11, 36–41.

Kushlan, Jim (ed.). "The Last Days of the Civil War [in Virginia]," *Civil War Times Illustrated*, 39 (May 2000), [Special Issue].

Luvaas, Jay. "Bentonville—Last Chance to Stop Sherman," *Civil War Times Illustrated*, 44 (January 2006), 16–22.

Marszalek, John F., Jr. "The Sherman-Stanton Controversy," *Civil War Times Illustrated*, 9 (October 1970), 4–12.

Marvel, William. *Lee's Last Retreat: The Flight to Appomattox*. Chapel Hill: University of North Carolina Press, 2002.

————. "Lee's Retreat to Appomattox," *Blue & Gray*, 18 (2000–2001), [Special Issue].

Mitchell, Joseph B. "The Battle of Sayler's Creek," *Civil War Times Illustrated*, 4 (October 1964), 9–16.

Patrick, Rembert W. *The Fall of Richmond*. Baton Rouge: Louisiana State University Press, 1960.

Reed, Liz Carson. "Battle in Desperation [Ft. Stedman]," *Civil War Times Illustrated*, 34 (March 1995), 32–38, 80–81.

Ryan, David D. *Four Days in 1865: The Fall of Richmond.* Richmond, Va.: Cadmus Communications Corp., 1993.

Trudeau, Noah Andre. "Last Days of the Civil War," *Civil War Times Illustrated*, 29 (July/August 1990), [Special Issue].

———. *Out of the Storm: The End of the Civil War, April–June 1865.* Boston: Little, Brown, 1994.

Welch, Richard F. "Burning High Bridge: The South's Last Hope [at Sayler's Creek]," *Civil War Times Illustrated*, 46 (March/April 2007), 34–41.

RECONSTRUCTION IN THE NORTHERN STATES

Ahern, Wilbert H. "The Cox Plan of Reconstruction: A Case Study in Ideology and Race Relations," *Civil War History*, 16 (1970), 293–308.

Angle, Paul M. "The Illinois Black Laws," *Chicago History*, 8 (Summer 1967), 65–75.

Berrier, G. Galis. "The Negro Suffrage Issue in Iowa, 1865–1868," *Annals of Iowa*, 39 (1968), 241–60.

Berwanger, Eugene H. *The West and Reconstruction.* Urbana: University of Illinois Press, 1981.

Bonadio, Felice A. *North of Reconstruction: Ohio Politics, 1865–1870.* New York: New York University Press, 1970.

Bradley, Erwin S. "Post-Bellum Politics in Pennsylvania, 1866–1872." Ph.D. dissertation, Pennsylvania State University, 1952.

Current, Richard N. "The Politics of Reconstruction in Wisconsin, 1865–1873," *Wisconsin Magazine of History*, 60 (1976), 83–108.

Dante, Harris L. "Western Attitudes and Reconstruction Politics in Illinois, 1865–1872," Illinois State Historical Society, *Journal* (1956), 149–62.

Field, Phyllis F. *The Politics of Race in New York: The Struggle for Black Suffrage in the Civil War Era.* Ithaca, N.Y.: Cornell University Press, 1982.

Fishel, Leslie H. "Northern Prejudice and Negro Suffrage, 1865–1870," *Journal of Negro History*, 39 (1954), 8–26.

Grossman, Lawrence. "The Democratic Party and the Negro: A Study in Northern and National Politics, 1868–1892." Ph.D. dissertation, City University of New York, 1973.

Knapp, Charles Merriam. *New Jersey Politics During the Period of the Civil War and Reconstruction.* Geneva, N.Y.: W. F. Humphrey, 1924.

McLaughlin, Tom L. "Grass-Roots Attitudes Towards Black Rights in Twelve Nonslaveholding States, 1846–1869," *Mid-America*, 56 (1974), 175–81.

Mohr, James C. *Radical Republicans and Reform in New York during Reconstruction.* Ithaca, N.Y.: Cornell University Press, 1973.

——— (ed.). *Radical Republicans in the North: State Politics during Recon-struction*. Baltimore, Md.: The Johns Hopkins University Press, 1976.

Moody, William P. "The Civil War and Reconstruction in California Politics," Ph.D. dissertation, University of California at Los Angeles, 1950.

Murphy, Lawrence R. "Reconstruction in New Mexico," *New Mexico Historical Review*, 43 (1968), 99–115.

Mushkat, Jerome. *The Reconstruction of the New York Democracy, 1861–1874*. Rutherford, N.J.: Fairleigh Dickinson University Press, 1981.

Potts, James B. "Nebraska Statehood and Reconstruction," *Nebraska History*, 69 (Summer 1978), 73–83.

Sawrey, Robert D. *The Dubious Victory: The Reconstruction Debate in Ohio*. Lexington: University Press of Kentucky, 1992.

———. "Ohioans and the Fourteenth Amendment: Initial Perceptions and Ex-pectations," *Old Northwest*, 10 (1984), 3389–407.

Swenson, Philip David. "The Midwest and the Abandonment of Radical Recon-struction, 1864–1877." Ph.D. dissertation, University of Washington, 1971.

Thornbrough, Emma Lou. *Indiana in the Civil War Era, 1850–1880*. Indianapo-lis: Indiana Historical Bureau and Indiana Historical Society, 1965.

Toppin, Edgar A. "Negro Emancipation in Historic Retrospect: Ohio. The Negro Suffrage Issue in Postbellum Ohio Politics," *Journal of Human Relations*, 11 (1963), 232–46.

Voegli, V. Jacque. *Free But Not Equal: The Midwest and the Negro During the Civil War*. Chicago: University of Chicago Press, 1967.

Williams, Helen J., and [T.] Harry Williams. "Wisconsin Republicans and Re-construction, 1865–1870," *Wisconsin Magazine of History*, 23 (1939), 17–39.

RECONSTRUCTION, COX PLAN OF

Ahern, Wilbert H. "The Cox Plan of Reconstruction: A Case Study in Ideology and Race Relations," *Civil War History*, 16 (1970), 293–308.

Bonadio, Felice A. *North of Reconstruction*. New York: New York University Press, 1970.

Sawrey, Robert D. *The Dubious Victory: The Reconstruction Debate in Ohio*. Lexington: University Press of Kentucky, 1992.

RECONSTRUCTION, FIFTEENTH AMENDMENT AND

Benedict, Michael Les. "The Rout of Radicalism: Republicans and the Elections of 1867," *Civil War History*, 18 (1972), 334–44.

Braxton, Allen Caperton. *The Fifteenth Amendment: An Account of Its Enact-ment*. Lynchburg, Va.: N. Pub., ca. 1903.

Brock, W. R. *An American Crisis: Congress and Reconstruction, 1865–1867.* New York: St. Martin's Press, 1969.

Coleman, Charles H. *The Election of 1868: The Democratic Effort to Regain Control.* New York: Columbia University Press, 1933.

Cox, LaWanda, and John H. Cox. "Negro Suffrage and Republican Politics: The Problem of Motivation in Reconstruction Historiography," *Journal of Southern History*, 33 (1967), 303–30.

Gillette, William. *The Right to Vote: Politics and the Passage of the Fifteenth Amendment.* Baltimore, Md.: The Johns Hopkins University Press, 1966, 1969.

Hesseltine, William B. *U. S. Grant: Politician.* New York: Dodd, Mead & Co., 1935.

Logan, Rayford W. *The Betrayal of the Negro: From Rutherford B. Hayes to Woodrow Wilson.* New York: Collier Books, 1965.

Mathews, John M. *Legislative and Judicial History of the Fifteenth Amendment.* Baltimore, Md.: The Johns Hopkins University Press, 1909.

McFeely, William S. *Grant: A Biography.* New York: W. W. Norton, 1981.

Woodward, C. Vann. "Seeds of Failure in Radical Race Policy," in Harold M. Hyman (ed.), *New Frontiers of the American Reconstruction.* Urbana: University of Illinois Press, 1966, 125–47.

RECONSTRUCTION, FOURTEENTH AMENDMENT AND

Avins, Alfred. "The Ku Klux Klan Act of 1871: Some Reflected Light on State Action and the Fourteenth Amendment," *St. Louis University Law Journal*, 11 (1967), 331–81.

Beale, Howard K. *The Critical Year [1866]: A Study of Andrew Johnson and Reconstruction.* New York: Harcourt, Brace & Co., 1930.

Beauregard, Erving E. "John A. Bingham and the Fourteenth Amendment," *Historian*, 50 (1987), 67–76.

Brandwein, Pamela. "Slavery as an Interpretive Issue in the Reconstruction Congresses," *Law & Society Review*, 34 (2000), 315ff.

Clark, John G. "Historians and the Joint Committee of Reconstruction," *Historian*, 23 (1961), 348–61.

———. "Radicals and Moderates in the Joint Committee on Reconstruction," *Mid America*, 45 (1963), 79–98.

Collins, Charles Wallace. "The Fourteenth Amendment and the Negro Race Question," *American Law Review*, 45 (1911), 830–56.

———. *The Fourteenth Amendment and the States: A Study of the Operation of the Restraint Clauses of Section One of the Fourteenth Amendment to the Constitution of the United States.* Boston: Little, Brown & Co., 1912.

Fairman, Charles. "Does the Fourteenth Amendment Incorporate the Bill of Rights?" *Stanford Law Review*, 2 (1952–1953), 5–139.

Flack, Horace E. *The Adoption of the Fourteenth Amendment.* Baltimore, Md.: The Johns Hopkins University Press, 1908.

Frankfurter, Felix. "Memorandum on 'Incorporation' of the Bill of Rights into the Due Process Clause of the Fourteenth Amendment," *Harvard Law Review*, 78 (1964–1965), 746–67.

Graglia, Lino A. "Does Constitutional Law Exist?" *National Review*, 47 (1995), 31–34.

Graham, Howard J. "The 'Conspiracy Theory' of the Fourteenth Amendment," *Yale Law Journal*, 47 (1938), 371–403.

———. "Procedure to Substance—Extra-Judicial Rise of Due Process," *California Law Review*, 40 (1952–1953), 483–500.

James, Joseph B. *The Framing of the Fourteenth Amendment*. Urbana: University of Illinois Press, 1956.

———. "Southern Reaction to the Proposal of the Fourteenth Amendment," *Journal of Southern History*, 22 (1956), 477–97.

Kaczorowski, Robert J. "To Begin the Nation Anew: Congress, Citizenship and Civil Rights after the Civil War," *American Historical Review*, 90 (1987), 45–68.

———. *The Nationalization of Civil Rights: Constitutional Theory and Practice in a Racist Society, 1866–1883*. New York: Garland Publishing, Inc., 1987.

——. "Searching for the Intent of the Framers of the Fourteenth Amendment," *Connecticut Law Review*, 5 (1972–1973), 369–98.

Kendrick, Benjamin B. *The Journal of the Joint Committee of Fifteen on Reconstruction, 39th Congress, 1865–1867*. New York: Columbia University Press, 1914.

Kousser, J. Morgan. *Dead End: The Development of Nineteenth Century Litigation on Discrimination in Schools*. New York: Oxford University Press, 1985.

Lacy, Alex B., Jr. "The Bill of Rights and the Fourteenth Amendment," *Washington and Lee Law Review*, 23 (1966), 37–64.

Lien, Arnold J. *Concurring Opinion: The Privileges and Immunity Clause of the Fourteenth Amendment*. St. Louis: Washington University Press, 1957.

Maltz, Earl M. "Reconstruction without Revolution: Republican Civil Rights Theory in the Era of the Fourteenth Amendment," *Houston Law Review*, 24 (1967), 221–79.

McKitrick, Eric. *Andrew Johnson and Reconstruction*. Chicago: University of Chicago Press, 1960.

Mendelson, Wallace. "A Note on the Cause and Cure of the Fourteenth Amendment," *Journal of Politics*, 43 (1981), 152–58.

Morrison, Stanley. "The Fourteenth Amendment Challenged," *Georgetown Law Journal*, 36 (1948), 398–411.

Richter, William L. "One Hundred Years of Controversy: The Fourteenth Amendment and the Bill of Rights," *Loyola [New Orleans] Law Review*, 15 (1968–1969), 281–95.

Riddleberger, Patrick W. *1866: The Critical Year Revisited*. Carbondale: Southern Illinois University Press, 1979.

Russell, James F. S. "Railroads in the 'Conspiracy Theory' of the Fourteenth Amendment," *Mississippi Valley Historical Review*, 41 (1955), 601–22.

Suthron, W. J. "Dubious Origins of the Fourteenth Amendment," *Tulane Law Review*, 28 (1953–1954), 22–44.

Ten Broek, Jacobus. *Equal Under Law: The Antisalvery Origins of the Fourteenth Amendment*. New York: Collier Books, 1951, 1965.

RECONSTRUCTION, JOINT COMMITTEE OF FIFTEEN ON

Clark, John G. "Historians and the Joint Committee of Reconstruction," *Historian*, 23 (1961), 348–61.

———. "Radicals and Moderates in the Joint Committee on Reconstruction," *Mid America*, 45 (1963), 79–98.

Kendrick, Benjamin B. *The Journal of the Joint Committee of Fifteen on Reconstruction, 39th Congress, 1865–1867*. New York: Columbia University Press, 1914.

Lowe, Richard G. "The Joint Committee on Reconstruction: Some Clarifications," *Southern Studies*, n.s., 3 (1992), 55–66.

U.S., 39th Cong., 1st Sess., H. Rep. 30. "Report of the Joint Committee on Reconstruction." Reprinted, New York: Negro Universities Press, 1969.

RECONSTRUCTION, MODERATE REPUBLICANS AND

Abbott, Richard. *The Republican Party in the South, 1865–1877: The First Southern Strategy*. Chapel Hill: University of North Carolina Press, 1986.

Beale, Howard K. *The Critical Year [1866]: A Study of Andrew Johnson and Reconstruction*. New York: Harcourt, Brace & Co., 1930.

Burgess, John W. *Reconstruction and the Constitution, 1866–1876*. New York: Charles Scribner's Sons, 1902.

Carter, Dan T. *When the War Was Over: The Failure of Self-Reconstruction in the South, 1865–1867*. Baton Rouge: Louisiana State University Press, 1985.

Castel, Albert. *The Presidency of Andrew Johnson*. Lawrence: University Press of Kansas, 1979.

Cox, John, and LaWanda Cox. "Andrew Johnson and His Ghost Writers: An Analysis of the Freedmen's Bureau and Civil Rights Veto Messages," *Mississippi Valley Historical Review*, 48 (1961–1962), 460–79.

———. *Politics, Principles and Prejudice, 1865–1866: Dilemma of Reconstruction America*. New York: Atheneum, 1963.

Kendrick, Benjamin B. *The Journal of the Joint Committee of Fifteen on Reconstruction, 39th Congress, 1865–1867*. New York: Columbia University Press, 1914.

Kincaid, Larry G. "The Legislative Origins of the Military Reconstruction Act, 1865–1867." Ph.D. dissertation, The Johns Hopkins University, 1968.

Lomask, Milton. *Andrew Johnson: President on Trial*. New York: Farrar, Strauss & Cudahy, 1960.

Milton, George F. *The Age of Hate: Andrew Johnson and the Radicals.* New York: Howard-McCann, 1930.

Nieman, Donald G. "Andrew Johnson, the Freedmen's Bureau, and the Problem of Equal Rights, 1865–1866," *Journal of Southern History*, 44 (1978), 399–420.

Perman, Michael. *Reunion without Compromise: The South and Reconstruction, 1865–1868.* New York: Cambridge University Press, 1973.

Rhodes, James Ford. *History of the United States from the Compromise of 1850 to the Final Restoration of Home Rule at the South in 1877.* 7 vols. New York: Macmillan, 1896–1906.

Riddleberger, Patrick W. *1866: The Critical Year Revisited.* Carbondale: Southern Illinois University Press, 1979.

Sefton, James E. *Andrew Johnson and the Uses of Constitutional Power.* Boston: Little, Brown & Co., 1980.

———. *The United States Army and Reconstruction, 1865–1877.* Baton Rouge: Louisiana State University Press, 1967.

Stryker, Lloyd P. *Andrew Johnson: A Study in Courage.* New York: Macmillan, 1929.

Thomas, Lately. *The First President Johnson: The Three Lives of the Seventeenth President of the United States of America.* New York: William Morrow, 1968.

Trefousse, Hans L. *Andrew Johnson: A Biography.* New York: W. W. Norton & Company, 1989.

Winston, Robert W. *Andrew Johnson: Plebeian and Patriot.* New York: Henry Holt, 1928.

RECONSTRUCTION , NEGRO MILITIAS AND

Singletary, Otis A. "Military Disturbances in Arkansas during Reconstruction," *Arkansas Historical Quarterly*, 15 (1956), 140–50.

———. *Negro Militia and Reconstruction.* Austin: University of Texas Press, 1957.

———. "The Negro Militia during Radical Reconstruction," *Military Affairs*, 19 (1955), 177–86.

———. "The Texas Militia during Reconstruction," *Southwestern Historical Quarterly*, 60 (1855–1856), 23–35.

Severance, Ben H., *Tennessee's Radical Army: The State Guard and Its Role in Reconstruction, 1867–1869.* Knoxville: University of Tennessee Press, 2005.

RECONSTRUCTION, RADICAL REPUBLICANS AND

Abbott, Richard. *The Republican Party in the South, 1865–1877: The First Southern Strategy.* Chapel Hill: University of North Carolina Press, 1986.

Benedict, Michael Les. *A Compromise of Principle: Congressional Republicans and Reconstruction, 1863–1869*. New York: W. W. Norton & Co., 1974.

Kincaid, Larry G. "The Legislative Origins of the Military Reconstruction Act, 1865–1867." Ph.D. dissertation, The Johns Hopkins University, 1968.

Sefton, James E. *The United States Army and Reconstruction, 1865–1877*. Baton Rouge: Louisiana State University Press, 1967.

Shortreed, Margaret. "The Antislavery-Radicals: From Crusade to Revolution, 1840–1868," *Past and Present*, 16 (1959), 65–87.

RECONSTRUCTION, THEORIES OF

Benedict, Michael Les. *Fruits of Victory: Alternatives in Restoring the Union, 1865–1877*. Lanham, Md.: University Press of America, 1986.

McKitrick, Eric. *Andrew Johnson and Reconstruction*. Chicago: University of Chicago Press, 1960.

RED RIVER CAMPAIGN AND THE CAMDEN CAMPAIGN

Bearss, Edwin C. *Steele's Retreat from Camden and the Battle of Jenkins' Ferry*. Little Rock: Arkansas Civil War Centennial Commission, 1867.

Bounds, Steve, and Curtis Milbourne. "The Battle of Mansfield," *North & South*, 6 (February 2003), 26–39.

Bradford, James C. (ed.). *Captains of the Old Steam Navy: Makers of the American Naval Tradition, 1840–1880*. Annapolis, Md.: Naval Institute Press, 1986.

Cotham, Edward T., Jr. "The Battle of Galveston," *North & South*, 9 (December 2006), 20–31.

Forsyth, Michael J. *The Red River Campaign and the Loss by the Confederacy of the Civil War*. Jefferson, N.C.: McFarland, 2002.

Gear, Charles D. "Cabin Creek: The One-and-a -Million Dollar Raid," *North & South*, 11 (December 2009), 24–31.

Harrington, Fred Harvey. *Fighting Politician: Major General N. P. Banks*. Philadelphia: University of Pennsylvania Press, 1948.

Johnson, Ludwell H. *Red River Campaign: Politics and Cotton in the Civil War*. Baltimore, Md.: The Johns Hopkins University Press, 1958.

Longacre, Edward G. "Rescue on Red River," *Civil War Times Illustrated*, 14 (October 1975), 4–9, 39–42.

McCartney, Clarence M. *Mr. Lincoln's Admirals*. New York: Funk and Wagnalls, 1856.

Milbourne, Curtis, and Gary Joiner. "The Battle of Blair's Landing [Red River]," *North & South*, 9 (February 2007), 12–21.

Milbourne, Curtis, and Steve Bounds. "The Battle of Pleasant Hill," *North & South*, 8 (November 2005), 70–89.

Piston, William Garrett. "Struggle for the Trans-Mississippi," *North & South*, 11 (October 2009), 14–21, 67.

Reed, Rowena. *Combined Operations in the Civil War*. Annapolis, Md.: Naval Institute Press, 1978.

Sallee, Scott E. "Price's Missouri Raid, 1864," *Blue & Gray*, 8 (1990–1991), [Special Issue].

Still, William N. "'Porter . . . Is the Best Man': This Was Gideon Wells' View of the Man He Chose to Command the Mississippi Squadron," *Civil War Times Illustrated*, 16 (May 1977), 4–9, 44–47.

Urwin, Gregory J. W. "'Cut to Pieces and Gone to Hell': The Poison Springs Massacre," *North & South*, 3 (August 2000), 45–57.

Welcher, Frank J. *The Union Army, 1861–1865*. 2 vols. Bloomington: Indiana University Press, 1993.

West, Richard S., Jr. *The Second Admiral: A Life of David Dixon Porter, 1813–1891*. New York: Coward-McCann, 1937.

REDEEMERS

Benedict, Michael Les. "The Politics of Prosperity in the Reconstruction South," *Reviews in American History*, 12 (1984), 507–14.

Degler, Carl N. *Place over Time: The Continuity of Southern Distinctiveness*. Baton Rouge: Louisiana State University Press, 1977.

Harris, Carl V. "Right Fork or Left Fork? The Section-Party Alignments of Southern Democrats in Congress, 1873–1897," *Journal of Southern History*, 42 (1976), 471–506.

Linden, Glenn M. "'Radicals' and Economic Policies: The Senate, 1862–1873," *Journal of Southern History*, 32 (1966), 189–99.

McDonald, Forrest. "Woodward's Strange Career," *National Review*, 41 (October 27, 1989), 46–47.

McPherson, James M. "Redemption or Counterrevolution? The South in the 1870s," *Reviews in American History*, 13 (1985), 545–50.

O'Brien, Michael. "C. Vann Woodward and the Burden of Southern Liberalism," *American Historical Review*, 78 (1973–1974), 589–604.

Perman, Michael. *The Road to Redemption: Southern Politics, 1869–1879*. Chapel Hill: University of North Carolina Press, 1984.

Phillips, Ulrich B. "The Central Theme of Southern History," *American Historical Review*, 34 (1928–1929), 30–43.

Rable, George C. "Bourbonism, Reconstruction, and the Persistence of Southern Distinctiveness," *Civil War History*, 29 (1983), 135–53.

Roach, Hannah Grace. "Sectionalism in Congress (1870–1890)," *American Political Science Review*, 19 (1925), 500–26.

Seip, Terry L. *The South Returns to Congress: Men, Economic Measures, and International Relationships*. Baton Rouge: Louisiana State University Press, 1983.

Summers, Mark W. *The Era of Good Stealings*. New York: Oxford University Press, 1993.

———. *Railroads, Reconstruction, and the Gospel of Prosperity: Aid Under the Radical Republicans*. Princeton, N.J.: Princeton University Press, 1984.

Williams, George Patrick. "Redeemer Democrats and the Roots of Modern Texas." Ph.D. dissertation, Columbia University, 1996.

Woodward, C. Vann. *The Future of the Past*. New York: Oxford University Press, 1989.

———. *Origins of the New South, 1877–1913*. Baton Rouge: Louisiana State University Press, 1951.

———. *Reunion and Reaction: The Compromise of 1877 and the End of Reconstruction*. Boston: Little, Brown and Company, 1951.

REDEMPTION

Beck, E. M., and Stewart E. Tolnay. "The Killing Fields of the Deep South: The Market for Cotton and the Lynching of Blacks, 1882–1930," *American Sociological Review*, 55 (1990), 526–39.

Carter, Hodding. *The Angry Scar*. Garden City, N.Y.: Doubleday & Co., 1959.

DeLatte, Carolyn E. "The St. Landry Riot: A Forgotten Incident of Reconstruction Violence," *Louisiana History*, 17 (1976), 41–49.

Formwalt, Lee W. "The Camilla Massacre of 1868: Racial Violence as Political Propaganda," *Georgia Historical Quarterly*, 71 (1987), 399–426.

Gillette, William. *Retreat from Reconstruction, 1869–1879*. Baton Rouge: Louisiana State University Press, 1979.

Granade, Ray. "Violence: An Instrument of Policy in Reconstruction Alabama," *Alabama Historical Quarterly*, 30 (1968), 181–202.

Hennessey, Melinda Meek. "Political Terrorism in the Black Belt: The Eutaw Riot," *Alabama Review*, 33 (1980), 35–48.

———. "Racial Violence During Reconstruction: The 1876 Riots in Charleston and Cainhoy," *South Carolina Historical Magazine*, 86 (1985), 100–12.

———. "Reconstruction Politics and the Military: The Eufala Riot of 1874," *Alabama Historical Quarterly*, 38 (1976), 112–25.

———. "To Live and Die in Dixie: Reconstruction Race Riots in the South." Ph.D. dissertation, Kent State University, 1978.

Holmes, William F. "The Leflore County Massacre and the Demise of the Colored Farmers' Alliance," *Phylon*, 34 (1973), 267–74.

Horn, Stanley. *Invisible Empire: The Story of the Ku Klux Klan*. Boston: Houghton Mifflin, 1939.

Johnson, Manie White. "The Colfax Riot of April 1873," *Louisiana Historical Quarterly*, 13 (1930), 391–427.

Kousser, J. Morgan. *The Shaping of Southern Politics: Suffrage Restrictions and the Establishment of the One-Party South, 1880–1910*. New Haven, Conn.: Yale University Press, 1970.

Lestage, Oscar H., Jr. "The White League in Louisiana and Its Participation in Reconstruction Riots," *Louisiana Historical Quarterly*, 18 (1935), 617–95.

Martinez, J. Michael. "An Officer of Great Intelligence: Lewis Merrill, the Man Who Exposed the Ku Klux Klan," *North & South*, 10 (July 2007), 70–79.

Nieman, Donald G. (ed.). *Black Freedom/White Violence, 1865–1900*. New York: Garland Publishing, 1994.

Olsen, Otto H. (ed.). *Reconstruction and Redemption in the South*. Baton Rouge: Louisiana State University Press, 1980.

Perman, Michael. *The Road to Redemption: Southern Politics, 1869–1879*. Chapel Hill: University of North Carolina Press, 1984.

Rabel, George C. *But There Was No Peace: The Role of Violence in the Politics of Reconstruction*. Athens: University of Georgia Press, (1984).

———. "Republican Albatross: The Louisiana Question, National Politics and the Failure of Reconstruction," *Louisiana History*, 23 (1982), 109–30.

Rogers, William Warren. "The Boyd Incident: Black Belt Violence during Reconstruction," *Civil War History*, 21 (1975), 309–29.

Sefton, James E. *The United States Army and Reconstruction, 1865–1877*. Baton Rouge: Louisiana State University Press, 1967.

Simkins, Francis B. "The Election of 1876 in South Carolina," *South Atlantic Quarterly*, 21 (1922), 225–41, 335–51.

Singletary, Otis A. *Negro Militia and Reconstruction*. Austin: University of Texas Press, 1957.

Swinney, Everette. "United States v. Powell Clayton: Use of the Enforcement Acts in Arkansas," *Arkansas Historical Quarterly*, 26 (1967), 143–54.

Trelease, Allan W. *White Terror: The Ku Klux Klan Conspiracy and Southern Reconstruction*. New York: Harper & Row, 1971.

Wetta, Francis Joseph. "'Bulldozing the Scalawags': Some Examples of the Persecution of Southern White Republicans in Louisiana during Reconstruction," *Louisiana History*, 21 (1980), 43–58.

———. "The Louisiana Scalawags." Ph.D. dissertation, Louisiana State University, 1977.

Wiggins, Sarah Woolfolk. "The 'Pig Iron' Kelley Riot at Mobile, May 14, 1867," *Alabama Review*, 23 (1970), 45–55.

Woodward, C. Vann. *The Strange Career of Jim Crow*. 2nd ed. New York: Oxford University Press, 1966.

REDEMPTION OF THE SOUTH BEFORE 1874, THE FIRST MISSISSIPPI OR SHOTGUN PLAN, THE RIFLE CLUBS, AND THE WHITE LINERS

Baenziger, Ann Patton. "The Texas State Police during Reconstruction: A Reexamination," *Southwestern Historical Quarterly*, 72 (1968–1969), 470–91.

Beck, E. M., and Stewart E. Tolnay. "The Killing Fields of the Deep South: The Market for Cotton and the Lynching of Blacks, 1882–1930," *American Sociological Review*, 55 (1990), 526–39.

Bogue, Jessie Parker. "Violence and Oppression in North Carolina During Reconstruction." Ph.D. dissertation, University of Maryland, 1973.

Budiansky, Stephen. "The South Did Rise Again: [Major Lewis Merrill and the Ku Klux Klan]," *Civil War Times Illustrated*, 48 (June 2009), 50–55.

Carter, Hodding. *The Angry Scar: The Story of Reconstruction*. Garden City, N.Y.: Doubleday & Company, Inc., 1959.

Crouch, Barry D., and Donaly E. Brice. *Cullen Montgomery Baker: Reconstruction Desperado*. Baton Rouge: Louisiana State University Press, 1997.

Dauphine, James G. "The Knights of the White Camellia and the Election of 1868: A Benighting Legacy," *Louisiana History*, 30 (1989), 173–90.

DeLatte, Carolyn E. "The St. Landry Riot: A Forgotten Incident of Reconstruction Violence," *Louisiana History*, 17 (1976), 41–49.

Ellem, Warren A. "The Overthrow of Reconstruction on Mississippi," *Journal of Mississippi History*, 54 (1992), 175–201.

Formwalt, Lee W. "The Camilla Massacre of 1868: Racial Violence as Political Propaganda," *Georgia Historical Quarterly*, 71 (1987), 399–426.

Gillette, William. *Retreat from Reconstruction, 1869–1879*. Baton Rouge: Louisiana State University Press, 1979.

Granade, Ray. "Violence: An Instrument of Policy in Reconstruction Alabama," *Alabama Historical Quarterly*, 30 (1968), 181–202.

Hennessey, Melinda Meek. "Political Terrorism in the Black Belt: The Eutaw Riot," *Alabama Review*, 33 (1980), 35–48.

———. "Race and Violence in New Orleans: The 1868 Riot," *Louisiana History*, 20 (1979), 77–91.

———. "Reconstruction Politics and the Military: The Eufala Riot of 1874," *Alabama Historical Quarterly*, 38 (1976), 112–25.

Hogue, James K. "Bayonet Rule: Five Street Battles In New Orleans and the Rise and Fall of Radical Reconstruction." Ph.D. dissertation, Princeton University, 1998.

Horn, Stanley. *Invisible Empire: The Story of the Ku Klux Klan, 1866–1871*. Boston: Houghton Mifflin Company, 1939.

Moneyhon, Carl H. *Texas after the Civil War: The Struggle of Reconstruction*. College Station: Texas A&M University Press, 2004.

Nieman, Donald G. (ed.). *Black Freedom/White Violence, 1865–1900*. New York: Garland Publishing, Inc., 1994.

Perman, Michael. *The Road to Redemption: Southern Politics, 1869–1879*. Chapel Hill: University of North Carolina Press, 1984.

Rable, George C. *But There Was No Peace: The Role of Violence in the Politics of Reconstruction*. Athens: University of Georgia Press, 1984.

Rogers, William Warren. "The Boyd Incident: Black Belt Violence during Reconstruction," *Civil War History*, 21 (1975), 309–29.

Sefton, James E. *The United States Army and Reconstruction, 1865–1877.* Baton Rouge: Louisiana State University Press, 1967.

Singletary, Otis A. *Negro Militia and Reconstruction.* Austin: University of Texas Press, 1957.

Swinney, Everette. "United States *v.* Powell Clayton: Use of the Enforcement Acts in Arkansas," *Arkansas Historical Quarterly,* 26 (1967), 143–54.

Trelease, Allan W. *White Terror: The Ku Klux Klan Conspiracy and Southern Reconstruction.* New York: Harper & Row, 1971.

Tunnell, Ted. *Crucible of Reconstruction: War, Radicalism, and Race in Louisiana 1862–1877.* Baton Rouge: Louisiana State University Press, 1984.

Vandall, Gilles. "'Bloody Caddo': White Violence against Blacks in a Louisiana Parish, 1865–1876," *Journal of Social History,* 25 (1991), 373–88.

Wiggins, Sarah Woolfolk. "The 'Pig Iron' Kelley Riot at Mobile, May 14, 1867," *Alabama Review,* 23 (1970), 45–55.

Wilson, Walter. "The Meridian Massacre of 1871," *Crisis,* 81 (No. 2, 1972), 49–52.

REDEMPTION OF THE SOUTH FROM 1874, THE RED SHIRTS AND THE WHITE LEAGUES

Beck, E. M., and Stewart E. Tolnay. "The Killing Fields of the Deep South: The Market for Cotton and the Lynching of Blacks, 1882–1930," *American Sociological Review,* 55 (1990), 526–39.

Blair, William Alan. "The Use of Military Force to Protect the Gains of Reconstruction," *Civil War History,* 51 (2005), 388–402.

Carter, Hodding. *The Angry Scar: The Story of Reconstruction.* Garden City, N.Y.: Doubleday & Company, Inc., 1959.

Gillette, William. *Retreat from Reconstruction, 1869–1879.* Baton Rouge: Louisiana State University Press, 1979.

Hennessey, Melinda Meek. "Racial Violence during Reconstruction: The 1876 Riots in Charleston and Cainhoy," *South Carolina Historical Magazine,* 86 (1985), 100–12.

———. "To Live and Die in Dixie: Reconstruction Race Riots in the South." Ph.D. dissertation, Kent State University, 1978.

Hogue, James K. "Bayonet Rule: Five Street Battles In New Orleans and the Rise and Fall of Radical Reconstruction." Ph.D. dissertation, Princeton University, 1998.

Holmes, William F. "The Leflore County Massacre and the Demise of the Colored Farmers' Alliance," *Phylon,* 34 (1973), 267–74.

Johnson, Manie White. "The Colfax Riot of April 1873," *Louisiana Historical Quarterly,* 13 (1930), 391–427.

Kousser, J. Morgan. *The Shaping of Southern Politics: Suffrage Restriction and the Establishment of the One Party South, 1880–1910.* New Haven, Conn.: Yale University Press, 1970.

Lestage, Oscar H., Jr. "The White League in Louisiana and Its Participation in Reconstruction Riots," *Louisiana Historical Quarterly*, 18 (1935), 617–95.

Nieman, Donald G. (ed.). *Black Freedom/White Violence, 1865–1900.* New York: Garland Publishing, Inc., 1994.

Olsen, Otto H. (ed.) *Reconstruction and Redemption in the South.* Baton Rouge: Louisiana State University Press, 1980.

Perman, Michael. *The Road to Redemption: Southern Politics, 1869–1879.* Chapel Hill: University of North Carolina Press, 1984.

Rable, George C. *But There Was No Peace: The Role of Violence in the Politics of Reconstruction.* Athens: University of Georgia Press, 1984.

———. "Republican Albatross: The Louisiana Question, National Politics, and the Failure of Reconstruction," *Louisiana History*, 23 (1982), 109–30.

Ross, Michael A. "Obstructing Reconstruction: John Archibald Campbell and the Legal Campaign Against Louisiana's Republican Government, 1868–1873," *Civil War History*, 49 (2003), 235–53.

Sefton, James E. *The United States Army and Reconstruction, 1865–1877.* Baton Rouge: Louisiana State University Press, 1967.

Simkins, Francis B. "The Election of 1876 in South Carolina," *South Atlantic Quarterly*, 21 (1922), 225–41, 335–51.

Singletary, Otis A. *Negro Militia and Reconstruction.* Austin: University of Texas Press, 1957.

Trelease, Allan W. *White Terror: The Ku Klux Klan Conspiracy and Southern Reconstruction.* New York: Harper & Row, 1971.

Tunnell, Ted. *Crucible of Reconstruction: War, Radicalism, and Race in Louisiana 1862–1877.* Baton Rouge: Louisiana State University Press, 1984.

Woodward, C. Vann. *The Strange Career of Jim Crow.* 2nd rev. ed. New York: Oxford University Press, 1966.

Zuczek, Richard. "The Last Campaign of the Civil War: South Carolina and the Revolution of 1876," *Civil War History*, 42 (1996), 18–31.

REED, HARRISON (1813–1899)

Brown, Canter, Jr. *Ossian Bingley Hart: Florida's Loyalist Reconstruction Governor.* Baton Rouge: Louisiana State University Press, 1997.

Current, Richard N. *Those Terrible Carpetbaggers: A Reinterpretation.* New York: Oxford University Press, 1988.

———. *Three Carpetbag Governors.* Baton Rouge: Louisiana State University Press, 1967.

Daniels, Jonathan. *Prince of Carpetbaggers.* Philadelphia: J. B. Lippincott Co., 1958.

Fenlon, Paul E. "The Notorious Swepson-Littlefield Fraud: Railroad Financing in Florida, 1868–1871," *Florida Historical Quarterly*, 32 (1954), 231–61.

Overy, David H., Jr. "The Wisconsin Carpetbagger: A Group Portrait," *Wisconsin Magazine of History*, 44 (1960), 15–49.

Shofner, Jerrell H. "Florida: A Failure of Moderate Republicanism," in Otto H. Olsen (ed.), *Reconstruction and Redemption in the South.* Baton Rouge: Louisiana State University Press, 1980, 13–47.

Smith, George Winston. "Carpetbag Imperialism in Florida, 1862–1868," *Florida Historical Quarterly*, 27 (1948–1949), 99–130, 268–99.

REVELS, HIRAM R. (1822–1901)

Lawson, Elizabeth. *The Gentleman from Mississippi: Our First Negro Congressman* [sic], *Hiram R. Revels.* New York: N. Pub., 1960.

Libby, Billy W. "Senator Hiram Revels of Mississippi Takes His Seat, January–February 1870," *Journal of Mississippi History*, 37 (1875), 381–94.

Low, W. Augustus, and Virgil A. Clift. *Encyclopedia of Black America.* New York: McGraw-Hill Book Company, 1981.

McFarlin, Annjeannette Sophia. *Black Congressional Reconstruction Orators and Their Orations.* Metuchen, N.J.: Scarecrow Press, 1976.

REYNOLDS, JOSEPH J. (1822–1899)

Baggett, James Alex. "Birth of the Texas Republican Party," *Southwestern Historical Quarterly*, 78 (1974–1975), 1–20.

———. "Origins of Early Texas Republican Party Leadership," *Journal of Southern History*, 40 (1974), 441–50.

Boatner, Mark M., III. *The Civil War Dictionary.* New York: D. McKay and Company, 1959.

Carrier, John P. "A Political History of Texas during the Reconstruction, 1865–1874." Ph.D. dissertation, Vanderbilt University, 1971.

Crouch, Barry A. *The Freedmen's Bureau and Black Texans.* Austin: University of Texas, 1992.

Moneyhon, Carl H. *Texas after the Civil War: The Struggle of Reconstruction.* College Station: Texas A&M Unversity Press, 2004.

Ramsdell, Charles W. *Reconstruction in Texas.* New York: Columbia University Press, 1910.

Richter, William L. *The Army in Texas During Reconstruction, 1865–1870.* College Station: Texas A&M University Press, 1987.

———. *Overreached on All Sides: The Freedmen's Bureau Administrators in Texas, 1865–1868.* College Station: Texas A&M University Press, 1991.

———. "'We Must Rubb Out and Begin Anew': The Army and the Republican Party in Texas Reconstruction, 1867–1870," *Civil War History*, 19 (December 1973), 334–52.

Robinson, Charles M., III. *A Good Year to Die: The Story of the Great Sioux War.* New York: Random House, 1995.

Sefton, James E. *The United States Army and Reconstruction, 1865–1877*. Baton Rouge: Louisiana State University Press, 1967.

Shook, Robert W. "Federal Occupation and Administration of Texas, 1865–1870." Ph.D. dissertation, North Texas State University, 1970.

Sinclair, O. Lonnie. "The Freedmen's Bureau in Texas: The Assistant Commissioners and the Negro." Unpublished paper submitted to the Institute of Southern History, the Johns Hopkins University, July 22, 1969.

Vaughn, J. W. *The Reynolds's Campaign on Powder River*. Norman: University of Oklahoma Press, 1961.

Self, Zenobia. "The Court Martial of J. J. Reynolds," *Military Affairs*, 37 (1973), 52–56.

ROSECRANS, WILLIAM STARKE (1819–1898)

Lamers, William M. *The Edge of Glory: A Biography of William S. Rosecrans*. New York: Harcourt, Brace, 1961.

Longacre, Edward G. "The Life of General William Starke Rosecrans: A General Vanquished in the West," *Civil War Times Illustrated*, 24 (October 1985), 16–19, 44–47.

ROUDANEZ, LOUIS CHARLES (1823–1890)

Rouzan, Laura V. "Dr. Louis Charles Roudanez: Publisher of America's First Black Daily Newspaper," theneworleanstribune.com/roudaneztext.htm.

RUBY, GEORGE (1841–1882)

Barr, Alwyn. *Black Texans: A History of Negroes in Texas, 1528–1971*. Austin, Tex.: Jenkins Book Publishing Co., 1973.

Crouch, Barry A. "Black Education in Civil War and Reconstruction Louisiana: George T. Ruby, the Army, and the Freedmen's Bureau," *Louisiana History*, 38 (1997), 287–308.

———. "Self-Determination and Local Black Leaders in Texas," *Phylon*, 39 (1978), 344–55.

Moneyhon, Carl. "George T. Ruby and the Politics of Expediency in Texas," in Howard N. Rabinowitz (ed.), *Southern Black Leaders of the Reconstruction Era*. Urbana: University of Illinois Press, 1982, 363–92.

Pitre, Merline. "George T. Ruby: The Party Loyalist," *Through Many Dangers, Toils, and Snares* (1985), 166–75.

Smallwood, James. "G. T. Ruby: Galveston's Black Carpetbagger in Reconstruction Texas," *Houston Review*, 6 (1983), 24–33.

Woods, Randall B. "George T. Ruby: A Black Militant in the White Business Community," *Red River Valley Historical Review*, 1 (1974), 269–80.

SANDERS, GEORGE N. (1812–1873)

Curti, Merle E. "George Nicholas Sanders," in Dumas Malone (ed.), *Dictionary of American Biography*. New York: Charles Scribner's Sons, 1935, XIV, 334–35.

Galbraith, John S. "George N. Sanders: 'Influence' Man for the Hudson's Bay Company," *Oregon Historical Quarterly*, 53 (September 1952), 159–76.

Gutteridge, Leonard F., and Ray A. Neff. *Dark Union: The Secret Web of Profiteers, Politicians, and Booth Conspirators That Led to Lincoln's Death*. Hoboken, N.J.: John Wiley & Sons, 2003.

Haines, Randall A. "Evidence of a Canadian Connection with Confederate Agents in the Lincoln Assassination," *Surratt Courier*, 29 (July 2004), 3–7.

———. "The Notorious George N. Sanders: His Career and Role in the Lincoln Assassination." Unpublished ms. in the James O. Hall Library, Surratt Museum, 1994.

Higham, Charles. *Murdering Mr. Lincoln: A New Detection of the 19th Century's Most Famous Crime*. Beverly Hills, Calif.: New Millennium Press, 2004.

Keehn, David. "Strong Arm of Secession: The Knights of the Golden Circle in the Secession Crisis of 1861," *North & South*, 10 (June 2005), 42–57.

Mayer, Adam. "St. Lawrence Hall in Montreal," *Civil War Times Illustrated*, 31 (January–February 1993), 44–46, 74.

Morrison, Michael A. "American Reaction to European Revolutions, 1848–1852: Sectionalism, Memory, and the Revolutionary Heritage," *Civil War History*, 49 (2003), 111–32.

Richter, William L. *The Last Confederate Heroes: The Final Struggle for Southern Independence & the Assassination of Abraham Lincoln*. 2nd rev. ed. 2 vols. Ed. with introduction by J. E. "Rick" Smith III. Laurel, Md.: Burgundy Press, 2008.

Stuart, Meriwether. "Operation Sanders: Wherein Old Friends and Ardent Pro-Southerners Prove to be Union Secret Agents," *Virginia Magazine of History and Biography*, 81 (April 1973), 157–99.

SCALAWAGS

Abbott, Richard. *The Republican Party in the South, 1865–1877: The First Southern Strategy*. Chapel Hill: University of North Carolina Press, 1986.

Alexander, Thomas B. "Persistent Whiggery in Alabama and the Lower South, 1860–1867," *Alabama Review*, 12 (1959), 35–52.

———. "Persistent Whiggery in Mississippi: The Hinds County Gazette," *Journal of Mississippi History*, 23 (1961), 71–93.

————. "Persistent Whiggery in the Confederate South, 1860–1877," *Journal of Southern History*, 27 (1961), 305–29.

————. "Whiggery and Reconstruction in Tennessee," *Journal of Southern History*, 16 (1950), 291–305.

Baggett, James Alex. *The Scalawags: Southern Dissenters in the Civil War and Reconstruction*. Baton Rouge: Louisiana State University Press, 2003.

Bowers, Claude. *The Tragic Era: The Revolution After Lincoln*. Boston: Houghton Mifflin, 1929.

Carter, Hodding. *The Angry Scar: The Story of Reconstruction*. Garden City, N.Y.: Doubleday & Company, Inc., 1959.

Coulter, E. Merton. *The South During Reconstruction, 1865–1877*. Baton Rouge: Louisiana State University Press, 1947.

Donald, David H. "The Scalawag in Mississippi Reconstruction," *Journal of Southern History*, 10 (1944), 447–60.

DuBois, W. E. Burghardt. *Black Reconstruction: An Essay Toward a History of the Part Which Black Folk Played in the Attempt to Reconstruct Democracy, 1860–1888*. New York: Harcourt, Brace and Company, 1935.

Ellem, Warren A. "Who Were the Mississippi Scalawags?" *Journal of Southern History*, 48 (1982), 349–72.

Harris, William C. "A Reconsideration of the Mississippi Scalawag," *Journal of Mississippi History*, 32 (1970), 3–42.

Hume, Richard L. "The Arkansas Constitutional Convention of 1868: A Case Study in the Politics of Reconstruction," *Journal of Southern History*, 39 (1973), 183–206.

Kolchin, Peter. "Scalawags, Carpetbaggers, and Reconstruction: A Quantitative Look at Southern Congressional Politics, 1868–1872," *Journal of Southern History*, 45 (1979), 63–76.

Mering, John Vollmer. "Persistent Whiggery in the Confederate South: A Reconsideration," *South Atlantic Quarterly*, 69 (1970–1971), 124–34.

Olsen, Otto H. "Reconsidering the Scalawags," *Civil War History*, 12 (1966), 304–20.

Robinson, Armistead L. "Beyond the Realm of Consensus: New Meanings of Reconstruction for American History," *Journal of American History*, 68 (1981), 276–97.

Rubin, Hyman, III. *South Carolina Scalawags*. Columbia: University of South Carolina Press, 2006.

Sansing, David G. "The Role of the Scalawag in Mississippi Reconstruction." Ph.D. dissertation, University of Southern Mississippi, 1969.

Seip, Terry L. *The South Returns to Congress: Men, Economic Measures, and International Relationships*. Baton Rouge: Louisiana State University Press, 1983.

Stampp, Kenneth M. *The Era of Reconstruction, 1865–1877*. New York: Alfred A. Knopf, 1965.

Storey, Margaret M. *Loyalty and Loss: Alabama's Unionists in the Civil War and Reconstruction*. Baton Rouge: Louisiana University Press, 2004.

Thornton, J. Mills, III. "Fiscal Policy and the Failure of Radical Reconstruction in the Lower South," in J. Morgan Kousser and James M. McPherson (eds.), *Region, Race, and Reconstruction: Essays in Honor of C. Vann Woodward.* New York: Oxford University Press, 1982, 349–94.

Trelease, Allen W. "Republican Reconstruction in North Carolina: A Roll-Call Analysis of the State House of Representatives," *Journal of Southern History,* 42 (1976), 319–44.

Trelease, Allen W. "Who Were the Scalawags?" *Journal of Southern History,* 29 (1963), 445–68.

Wetta, Francis Joseph. "The Louisiana Scalawags." Ph.D. dissertation, Louisiana State University, 1977.

Wiggins, Sarah Woolfolk. "Alabama: Democratic Bulldozing and Republican Folly," in Otto H. Olsen (ed.), *Reconstruction and Redemption in the South.* Baton Rouge: Louisiana State University Press, 1980, 48–77.

Williams, T. Harry. "An Analysis of Some Reconstruction Attitudes," *Journal of Southern History,* 12 (1946), 469–86.

———. "The Louisiana Unification Movement of 1873," *Journal of Southern History,* 11 (1945), 349–69.

Woodward, C. Vann. *Origins of the New South, 1877–1913.* Baton Rouge: Louisiana State University Press, 1951.

———. *Reunion and Reaction: The Compromise of 1877 and the End of Reconstruction.* Boston: Little, Brown and Company, 1951.

Woolfolk, Sarah Van Voorhis. "Five Men Called Scalawags," *Alabama Review,* 17 (1964), 45–55.

———. *The Scalawag in Alabama Politics, 1865–1881.* Tuscaloosa: University of Alabama Press, 1977.

SCHOFIELD, JOHN M. (1831–1906)

Alderson, William T. "The Influence of Military Rule and the Freedmen's Bureau on Reconstruction in Virginia, 1865–1870." Ph.D. dissertation, Vanderbilt University, 1952.

Boatner, Mark M., III. *The Civil War Dictionary.* New York: D. McKay and Company, 1959.

Eckenrode, Hamilton J. *Political History of Virginia during the Reconstruction.* Baltimore, Md.: The Johns Hopkins University Press, 1904.

Gerteis, Louis S. *From Contraband to Freedman: Federal Policy Toward Southern Blacks, 1861–1865.* Westport, Conn.: Greenwood Press, 1973.

Lowe, Richard. *Republicans and Reconstruction in Virginia, 1865–1870.* Charlottesville: University of Virginia Press, 1991

———. "Virginia's Reconstruction Convention: General Schofield Rates the Delegates," *Virginia Magazine of History and Biography,* 80 (1972), 341–60.

Maddex, Jack P., Jr. *The Virginia Conservatives*. Chapel Hill: University of North Carolina Press, 1970.

———. "Virginia: The Persistence of Centrist Hegemony," in Otto H. Olsen (ed.), *Reconstruction and Redemption in the South*. Baton Rouge: Louisiana State University Press, 1980, 113–55.

Majeske, Penelope K. "Virginia after Appomattox: The Unites States Army and the Formation of Presidential Reconstruction Policy," *West Virginia History*, 43 (1982), 95–117.

McDonough, James L. "John Schofield as Military Director of Reconstruction in Virginia," *Civil War History*, 15 (1969), 237–56.

Schofield, John M. *Forty-Six Years in the Army*. New York: Century Co., 1897.

Sefton, James E. "Aristotle in Blue and Braid: General John Schofield's Essays on Reconstruction, *Civil War History*, 17 (1971), 45–57.

———. *The United States Army and Reconstruction, 1865–1877*. Baton Rouge: Louisiana State University Press, 1967.

Smith, James Douglas. "Virginia during Reconstruction, 1865–1870: A Political, Economic, and Social Study." Ph.D. dissertation, University of Virginia, 1960.

Taylor, Joe Gray. *Louisiana Reconstructed, 1863–1877*. Baton Rouge: Louisiana State University, 1974.

SCOTT, ROBERT K. (1826–1900)

Abbott, Martin. *The Freedmen's Bureau in South Carolina, 1865–1872*. Chapel Hill: University of North Carolina Press, 1967.

Boatner, Mark M., III. *The Civil War Dictionary*. New York: D. McKay and Company, 1959.

Current, Richard N. *Those Terrible Carpetbaggers: A Reinterpretation*. New York: Oxford University Press, 1988.

Fowler, Wilton B. "A Carpetbagger's Conversion to White Supremacy," *North Carolina Historical Review*, 43 (1966), 286–304.

Holt, Thomas. *Black over White: Negro Political Leadership in South Carolina during Reconstruction*. Urbana: University of Illinois Press, 1977.

Zuczek, Richard. *State of Rebellion: Reconstruction in South Carolina*. Columbia: University of South Carolina Press, 1996.

SECESSION

Auer, J. Jeffry (ed.). *Antislavery and Disunion, 1857–1861: Studies in Rhetoric of Compromise and Conflict*. New York: Harper & Row, 1963.

Barney, William L. *The Road to Secession: A New Perspective on the Old South*. New York: Praeger, 1972.

————. *The Secessionists Impulse: Alabama and Mississippi in 1860.* Princeton, N.J.: Princeton University Press, 1974.

Buenger, Walter L. *Secession and Union in Texas.* Austin: University of Texas Press, 1984.

Channing, Steven A. *Crisis of Fear: Secession in South Carolina.* New York: Norton, 1970.

Crofts, Daniel. *Reluctant Confederates: Upper South Unionists in the Secession Crisis.* Chapel Hill: University of North Carolina Press, 1989.

Daniel, Larry J. "In Defense of Governor Isham G. Harris," *North & South,* 7 (May 2004), 74–79.

Dumond, Dwight Lowell. *The Secession Movement, 1860–1861.* New York: Macmillan, 1931.

Egnal, Marc. "Rethinking the Secession of the Lower South: The Clash of Two Groups," *Civil War History,* 50 (2004), 261–90.

Ellis, Richard E. *The Union at Risk: Jacksonian Democracy, States' Rights, and the Nullification Crisis.* New York: Oxford University Press, 1987.

Freehling, William W. *Prelude to Civil War: The Nullification Crisis in South Carolina, 1816–1836.* New York: Harper & Row, 1965.

————. *The Road to Disunion: Secessionists at Bay, 1776–1854.* New York: Oxfoed Univwersity Press, 1990.

————. *The Road to Disunion: Secessionmists Triumphant, 1854–1861.* New York: Oxford University Press, 2007.

————, and Craig M. Simpson (eds.). *Secession Debated: Georgia's Showdown in 1860.* New York: Oxford University Press, 1992.

Ford, Lacy K. *Origins of Southern Radicalism: The South Carolina Up Country, 1800–1860.* New York: Oxford University Press, 1988.

Gillespie, Jay. "Slavery and States' Rights in the Old North State [N.C.]," *North & South,* 11 (August 2009), 68–75.

Gordon, David (ed.). *Secession, State, & Liberty.* New Brunswick, N.J.: Transaction Publishers, 1998.

Johnson, Michael. *Toward a Patriarchal Republic: The Secession of Georgia.* Baton Rouge: Louisiana State University Press, 1977.

Keehn, David. "Strong Arm of Secession: The Knights of the Golden Circle in the Crisis of 1861," *North & South,* 10 (June 2008), 42–57.

Kruman, Marc W. *Parties and Politics in North Carolina, 1836–1865.* Baton Rouge: Louisiana State University Press, 1983.

Nagel, Paul C. *One Nation Indivisible: The Union in American Thought, 1776–1861.* New York: Oxford University Press, 1964.

Perkins, Howard Cecil (ed.). *Northern Editorials on Secession.* 2 vols. Gloucester, Mass.: Peter Smith, 1964, repr.

Phillips, Ulrich B. *The Course of the South to Secession: An Interpretation.* New York: Appleton-Century, 1939.

Pithcaithley, Dwight T. Secession of the Upper South: States Rights and Slavery," *North & South,* 12 (February 2010), 14–19.

Potter, David M. *Lincoln and His Party in the Secession Crisis.* 2nd rev. ed. New Haven, Conn.: Yale University Press, 1962.

Reynolds, Donald E. *Editors Make War: Southern Newspapers in the Secession Crisis.* Nashville, Tenn.: Vanderbilt University Press, 1970.

Shanks, Henry Thomas. *The Secession Movement in Virginia, 1847–1861.* Richmond, Va.: Garrett and Massie, 1934.

Sitterson, J. Carlyle. *The Secession Movement in North Carolina.* Chapel Hill: University of North Carolina Press, 1939.

Stampp, Kenneth M. *And the War Came: The North and the Secession Crisis, 1860–1861.* Baton Rouge: Louisiana State University Press, 1950.

Walther, Eric H. *The Fire-Eaters.* Baton Rouge: Louisiana State University Press, 1992.

White, Laura Amanda. *Robert Barnwell Rhett: Father of Secession.* Glouster, Mass.: P. Smith, 1965.

Wood, James M. *Rebellion and Realignment: Arkansas' Road to Secession.* Fayetteville: University of Arkansas Press, 1987.

Wooster, Ralph A. *The Secession Conventions of the South.* Princeton, N.J.: Princeton University Press, 1962.

SECESSION, APOSTLES OF DISUNION AND

Barney, William L. *The Road to Secession: A New Perspective in the Old South.* New York: Praeger, 1972.

Dew, Charles B. *Apostles of Disunion: Southern Secession Commissioners and the Causes of the Civil War.* Charlottesville: University Press of Virginia, 2001.

Dumond, Dwight Lowell, *The Secession Movement, 1860–1861.* New York: Macmillan, 1931.

Kline, Michael J. *The Baltimore Plot: The First Conspiracy to Assassinate Abraham Lincoln.* Yardley, Pa.: Westholme Publishing, 2008.

SECESSION, THE BORDER STATES AND

Baker, Jean H. *The Politics of Continuity: Maryland and Political Parties from 1858 to 1870.* Baltimore, Md.: The Johns Hopkins University Press, 1973.

Castel, Albert. *General Sterling Price and the Civil War in the West.* Baton Rouge: Louisiana State University Press, 1968.

Creason, Joe. "Kentucky's Efforts to Remain Neutral," *Civil War Times,* 2 (January 1961), 8–9.

Crofts, Daniel. *Reluctant Confederates: Upper South Unionists in the Secession Crisis.* Chapel Hill: University of North Carolina Press, 1989.

Curry, Richard Orr. "The Virginia Background for the History of the Civil War and Reconstruction Era in West Virginia: An Analytical Commentary," *West Virginia History,* 20 (1959), 215–46.

Gordon, David (ed.). *Secession, State, & Liberty*. New Brunswick, N.J.: Transaction Publishers, 1998.

Harrison, Lowell. *The Civil War in Kentucky*. Lexington: University of Kentucky Press, 1975.

Kirwan, Albert D. *John J. Crittenden: The Struggle for the Union*. Lexington: University of Kentucky Press, 1962.

McDonough, James Lee. *War in Kentucky From Shiloh to Perryville*. Knoxville: University of Tennessee Press, 1994.

Monaghan, Jay. *Civil War on the Western Border, 1854–1865*. Boston: Little, Brown & Co., 1955.

Morgan, Michael. "The Beast at His Best: [General Butler Saves Maryland, 1861]," *Civil War Times Illustrated*, 42 (February 2004), 2431.

Newman, Harry Wright. *Maryland and the Confederacy*. Annapolis, Md.: Harry Wright Newman, 1976.

Phillips, Christopher. *Damned Yankee: The Life of General Nathaniel Lyon*. Columbia: University of Missouri Press, 1990.

Shalhope, Robert E. *Sterling Price: Portrait of a Southerner*. Columbia: University of Missouri, 1971.

Wright, William C. *The Secession Movement in the Middle Atlantic States*. Rutherford, N.J.: Fairleigh Dickinson University Press, 1973.

SECESSION, BUCHANAN'S CABINET AND THE CRISIS OF

Ambler, Charles Henry. *The Life and Diary of John Floyd, Governor of Virginia, an Apostle of Secession, and the Father of the Oregon Country*. Richmond, Va.: Richmond Press, 1918.

Davis, William C. "The Conduct of 'Mr. Thompson'," *Civil War Times Illustrated*, 9 (May 1970), 4–7, 43–47.

Flower, Frank A. *Edwin McMasters Stanton: The Autocrat of Rebellion, Emancipation, and Reconstruction*. Akron, Ohio: Saalfield Pub. Co., 1905.

Gorham, George C. *Life and Public Services of Edwin M. Stanton*. 2 vols. Boston: Houghton Mifflin and Company, 1899.

Johnson, Z. T. *The Political Policies of Howell Cobb*. Nashville, Tenn.: George Peabody. 1929.

Nicholls, Roy F. *The Disruption of the American Democracy*. New York: Macmillan, 1948.

Pratt, Fletcher. *Stanton: Lincoln's Secretary of War*. Westport, Conn.: Greenwood Press, 1953, reprint 1970.

Robbins, Peggy. "The Greatest Scoundrel [Jacob Thompson]," *Civil War Times Illustrated*, 31 (November/December 1992), 54–59, 89–90.

Simpson, John Eddins. *Howell Cobb: The Politics of Ambition*. Chicago: Adams Press, 1973.

Stampp, Kenneth M. *And the War Came: The North and the Secession Crisis, 1860–1861*. Baton Rouge: Louisiana State University Press, 1950.

Thomas, Benjamin P., and Harold M. Hyman. *Stanton: The Life and Times of Lincoln's Secretary of War*. New York: Alfred A. Knopf, 1962.

SECESSION, COMPROMISE EFFORTS OVER

Grimsley, Mark "Conciliation and Failure, 1861–1862," *Civil War History*, 39 (1993), 317–35.

Gunderson, Robert Gray. *The Old Gentlemen's Convention: The Washington Peace Conference of 1861*. Madison: University of Wisconsin Press, 1961.

Johannsen, Robert W. *Stephen A. Douglas*. New York: Oxford University Press, 1973.

Johnson, Allen. *Stephen A. Douglas: A Study in American Politics*. New York: Macmillan, 1908.

Milton, George Fort. *Eve of Conflict: Stephen A. Douglas and the Needless War.* Boston: Houghton Mifflin, 1934.

Kirwan, Albert D. *John J. Crittenden: The Struggle for the Union*. Lexington: University of Kentucky Press, 1962.

Knupfer, Peter B. *The Union as It Was: Constitutional Unionism and Sectional Compromise, 1787–1861*. Chapel Hill: University of North Carolina Press, 1991.

SELMA RAID (1865)

Davis, William C. (ed.). *The Confederate General*. 6 vols. N.p.: National Historical Society, 1991.

Henry, Robert S. *"First with the Most" Forrest*. Indianapolis: Bobbs-Merrill, 1944.

Jones, James Pickett. *Yankee Blitzkreig: Wilson's Raid through Alabama and Georgia*. Athens: University of Georgia Press, 1976.

Keenan, Jerry. "The Battle of Selma," *North & South*, 8 (May 2005), 60–69.

———. "Wilson's Selma Raid," *Civil War Times Illustrated*, 1 (January 1963), 37–44.

Longacre, Edward G. *Grant's Cavalryman: The Life and Wars of General James Harrison Wilson*. Mechanicsburg, Pa.: Stackpole Books, 1996.

Pratt, Fletcher. *Eleven Generals: Studies in American Command*. New York: W. Sloane Associates, 1949.

Warner, Ezra J. *Generals in Gray: Lives of Confederate Commanders*. Baton Rouge: Louisiana State University Press, 1959.

Wills, Brian Steel. *A Battle from the Start: The Life of Nathan Bedford Forrest*. New York: HarperCollins, 1992.

SEVEN DAYS CAMPAIGN (1862)

Cullen, Joseph P. "The Battle of Gaines' Mill," *Civil War Times Illustrated*, 3 (April 1964), 11–17.

———. "The Battle of Malvern Hill," *Civil War Times Illustrated*, 5 (May 1966), 4–14.

———. "The Battle of Mechanicsville," *Civil War Times Illustrated*, 5 (October 1866), 5–11, 46–49.

———. *The Peninsula Campaign: McClellan and Lee Struggle for Richmond.* Harrisburg, Pa.: Stackpole Company, 1973.

Dowdey, Clifford. *The Seven Days: The Emergence of Lee.* Boston: Little, Brown, & Co., 1964.

Freeman, Douglas Southall. *Lee's Lieutenants: A Study of Command.* 3 vols. New York: Charles Scribner's Sons, 1942–1944.

Guttman, Jon. "Rebel Stand at Drewry's Bluff [1862]," *America's Civil War*, 10 (November 1997), 30–36.

Longacre, Edward G. "First of Seven [Days, the Battle of Oak Grove]," *Civil War Times Illustrated*, 25 (January 1987), 10–19.

McPherson, James M. (ed.). *Battle Chronicles of the Civil War.* 6 vols. New York: Macmillan, 1989.

Mewborn, Horace. "Stuart's Ride Around McClellan," *Blue & Gray*, 15 (1997–1998), [Special Issue].

Schreckengost, Gary. "Gaines' Mill: Costly Confederate Victory," *America's Civil War*, 13 (January 2001), 54–61.

Sears, Stephen W. "Lee's Lost Opportunity: The Battle of Glendale," *North & South*, 5 (December 2001), 12–24.

———. *To the Gates of Richmond: The Peninsula Campaign.* New York: Ticknoe & Fields, 1992.

Thomas, Emory. "The Peninsula Campaign." *Civil War Times Illustrated*, 21 (February–July 1979).

Wert, Jeffry D. "Lee and His Staff," *Civil War Times Illustrated*, 11 (July 1972), 10–19.

Williams, Kenneth P. *Lincoln Finds a General: A Military Study of the Civil War.* 5 vols. New York: Macmillan, 1949–1959.

SEWARD, WILLIAM H. (1801–1872)

Blue, Frederick J. "Friends of Freedom: Lincoln, Chase, and the Wartime Racial Policy," *Ohio History*, 102 (1993), 85–97.

———. *Salmon Chase: A Life in Politics.* Kent, Ohio: Kent State University Press, 1986.

Donald, David H. (ed.). *Inside Lincoln's Cabinet: The Civil War Diaries of Salmon P. Chase.* New York: Longmans, Greene & Co., 1954.

Fairman, Charles. *Reconstruction and Reunion, 1864–1888.* 2 pts. New York: The Macmillan Company, 1971–1987.

Gerteis, Louis S. "Salmon P. Chase, Radicalism, and the Politics of Emancipation, 1861–1864," *Journal of American History,* 60 (1973–1974), 42–62.

Kutler, Stanley I. *Judicial Power and Reconstruction Politics.* Chicago: University of Chicago Press, 1968.

Nevin, John. *Salmon P. Chase: A Biography.* New York: Oxford University Press, 1995.

Sefton, James E. "Chief Justice Chase as an Advisor on Presidential Reconstruction," *Civil War History,* 13 (1967), 242–64.

Silver, David M. *Lincoln's Supreme Court.* Urbana: University of Illinois Press, 1956.

SHENANDOAH VALLEY CAMPAIGN, THE FIRST OR JACKSON'S

Anderson, Paul Christopher. *Blood Image: Turner Ashby and the Civil War in the Southern Mind.* Baton Rouge: Louisiana State University Press, 2002.

Armstrong, Richard L. *The Battle of McDowell, March 11–May 18, 1862.* Lynchburg, Va.: H. E. Howard, 1990.

Beck, Brandon, and Charles Grunder. *The First Battle of Winchester.* Lynchburg, Va.: H. E. Howard, 1992.

Canney, Donald L. "Battle of Port Republic," *Blue & Gray,* 2 (1984–1985), [Special Issue].

Clark, Champ. *Decoying the Yanks: Jackson's Valley Campaign.* Alexandria, Va.: Time-Life Books, 1984.

Collins, Darrell L. *Jackson's Valley Campaign: The Battle of Cross Keys and Port Republic, June 8–9. 1962.* Lynchburg, Va.: H. E. Howard, 1994.

Ecelbarger, Gary L. "Stonewall Jackson's Fog of War," *North & South,* 5 (April 2002), 46–56.

Freeman, Douglas Southall. *Lee's Lieutenants: A Study of Command.* 3 vols. New York: Charles Scribner's Sons, 1942–1944.

Martin, David G. *Jackson's Valley Campaign.* Conshohocken, Pa.: Combined Books, 1988.

Robertson, James I., Jr., "Stonewall in the Shenandoah: The Valley Campaign of 1862," *Civil War Times Illustrated,* 11 (May 1972), [Special Issue].

———. *Stonewall Jackson: The Man, the Soldier, the Legend.* New York: Macmillan, 1997.

Roth, Dave. "Battle of Kernstown," *Blue & Gray,* 3 (1985–1986), [Special Issue].

Stackpole, Edward J. "Stonewall Jackson in the Valley," *Civil War Times Illustrated,* 3 (November 1964), 5–11, 36–41.

Tanner, Robert G. *Stonewall in the Valley: Thomas J. "Stonewall" Jackson's Shenandoah Valley Campaign, Spring 1862.* Garden City, N.Y.: Doubleday, 1976.

———. "'We Are in for It': Jackson at Kernstown," *Civil War Times Illustrated*, *Civil War Times Illustrated*, 15 (November 1976), 16–28.

Williams, Kenneth P. *Lincoln Finds a General: A Military Study of the Civil War.* New York: Macmillan, 1949–1959.

SHENANDOAH VALLEY CAMPAIGN, THE SECOND OR SHERIDAN'S

Albro, Walt. "Forgotten Battle for the Capital [the Monocacy]," *Civil War Times Illustrated*, 31 (November/December 1993), 40–43, 56–61.

Case, David. "The Battle That Saved Washington [the Monocacy]," *Civil War Times Illustrated*, 37 (February 1999), 46–56.

Cooling, Benjamin Franklin. "Battle of [the] Monocacy," *Blue & Gray*, 10 (1992–1993), [Special Issue].

———. *Jubal Early's Raid on Washington, 1864.* Baltimore, Md.: Nautical & Aviation Publishing Company of America, 1989.

Cramer, John Henry. *Lincoln under Enemy Fire: The Complete Account of His Experiences during Early's Attack on Washington.* Baton Rouge: Louisiana State University Press, 1948.

Cullen, Joseph P. "Cedar Creek," *Civil War Times Illustrated*, 8 (October 1969), 4–9, 42–48.

———. "Sheridan Wins at Winchester," *Civil War Times Illustrated*, 6 (May 1967), 5–12, 40–44.

Feis, William B. "Neutralizing the Valley: The Role of Military Intelligence in the Defeat of Jubal Early's Army in the Valley, 1864–1865," *Civil War History*, 39 (September 1993), 199–215.

———. "A Union Military Intelligence Failure: Jubal Early's Raid, June 12–July 14, 1864," *Civil War History*, 36 (1990), 209–25.

Freeman, Douglas Southall. *Lee's Lieutenants: A Study of Command.* 3 vols. New York: Charles Scribner's Sons, 1942–1944.

Gallagher, Gary W. (ed.). *Struggle for the Shenandoah; Essays on the 1864 Valley Campaign.* Kent, Ohio: Kent State University Press, 1991.

Kimball, William J. "The Battle of Piedmont," *Civil War Times Illustrated*, 5 (January 1967), 40–46.

Lewis, Thomas A. *The Guns of Cedar Creek.* New York: Harper & Row, 1988.

———. *The Shenandoah in Flames: The Valley Campaign of 1864.* Alexandria, Va.: Time-Life Books, 1987.

Lowry Don. *Dark and Cruel War: The Decisive Months of the Civil War, September–December 1864.* New York: Hippocrene Books, 1993.

———. *Fate of the Country: The Civil War from June to September 1864.* New York: Hippocrene Books, 1992.

Mahr, Theodore C. *Early's Valley Campaign: The Battle of Cedar Creek—Showdown in the Shenandoah, October 1–30, 1864.* Lynchburg, Va.: H. E. Howard, 1992.

Morsberger, Robert E. "The Battle That Saved Washington," *Civil War Times Illustrated*, 13 (May 1974), 12–27.

Patchan, Scott C. "The Battle of Cedar Creek," *Blue & Gray*, 24 (2006–2007), [Special Issue].

———. "The Battle of Fisher's Hill," *Blue & Gray*, 24 (2006–2007), [Special Issue].

———. "Piedmont: The Forgotten Battle," *North & South*, 6 (April 2003), 62–75.

Pratt, Fletcher. *Eleven Generals: Studies in American Command.* New York: W. Sloane Associates, 1949.

Ray, Fred L. "Mimic War No More: Battle of Charles Town, [W. Va., August 1864]," *Civil War Times Illustrated*, 49 (February 2010), 52–58.

Stuart, Meriwether. *Sheridan in the Shenandoah: Jubal Early's Nemesis.* Harrisburg, Pa.: Stackpole Co., 1961.

Swift, Gloria Baker, and Gail Stephens. "Honor Redeemed: Lew Wallace's Military Career and the Battle of [the] Monocacy," *North & South*, 4 (January 2001), 34–46.

Vandiver, Frank. *Jubal's Raid: General Early's Famous Attack on Washington in 1864.* New York: McGraw-Hill, 1960.

Wert, Jeffry. "'First Fair Chance' [Fisher's Hill]," *Civil War Times Illustrated*, 18 (August 1979), 4–9, 40–45.

———. *From Winchester to Cedar Creek: The Shenandoah Campaign of 1864.* Carlisle, Pa.: South Mountain Press, 1987.

———. "Woodstock Races," *Civil War Times Illustrated*, 19 (May 1980), 8–12. 38–40.

SHERIDAN, PHILIP H. (1831–1888)

Boatner, Mark M., III. *The Civil War Dictionary.* New York: D. McKay and Company, 1959.

Carrier, John P. "A Political History of Texas during the Reconstruction, 1865–1874." Ph.D. dissertation, Vanderbilt University, 1971.

Dawson, Joseph Green, III. *Army Generals and Reconstruction: Louisiana, 1862–1977.* Baton Rouge: Louisiana State University Press, 1982.

———. "General Phil Sheridan and Military Reconstruction in Louisiana," *Civil War History*, 24 (1978), 133–51.

Gard, Wayne. *The Great Buffalo Hunt.* New York: Alfred A. Knopf, 1960.

Hutton, Paul Andrew. *Phil Sheridan and His Army.* Lincoln: University of Nebraska Press, 1985.

King, Curtis S. "'Reconsider, Hell!' [Sheridan at Five Forks]," *Civil War Times Illustrated*, 44 (January 2006), 24–32.

Ramsdell, Charles W. *Reconstruction in Texas.* New York: Columbia University Press, 1910.

Richter, William L. *The Army in Texas During Reconstruction, 1865–1870.* College Station: Texas A&M University Press, 1987.

―――. "General Phil Sheridan, the Historians, and Reconstruction," *Civil War History,* 33 (1987), 131–54.

Robinson, Charles M., III. *A Good Year to Die: The Story of the Great Sioux War.* New York: Random House, 1995.

Sefton, James E. *The United States Army and Reconstruction, 1865–1877.* Baton Rouge: Louisiana State University Press, 1967.

Shook, Robert W. "Federal Occupation and Administration of Texas, 1865–1870." Ph.D. dissertation, North Texas State University, 1970.

Taylor, Joe Gray. *Louisiana Reconstructed, 1863–1877.* Baton Rouge: Louisiana State University, 1974.

Weigley, Russell F. "Philip H. Sheridan: A Personality Profile," *Civil War Times Illustrated,* 7 (July 1968), 5–9, 46–48.

SHERMAN, JOHN (1823–1900)

Bridges, Roger D. "John Sherman and the Impeachment of Andrew Johnson," *Ohio Historical Quarterly,* 82 (1973), 176–91.

Burton, Theodore E. *John Sherman.* Boston: Houghton Mifflin & Co., 1906.

Kerr, Winfield Scott. *John Sherman: His Life and Public Services.* 2 vols. Boston: Sherman, French & Co., 1906.

Nichols, Jeannette P. "John Sherman," in Allen Johnson *et al.* (eds.), *Dictionary of American Biography* (10 double vols. + 9 supplements, 1964–1981), XVII, 84–88.

Randall, James G. "John Sherman and Reconstruction," *Mississippi Valley Historical Review,* 19 (1932–1933), 382–93.

Sherman, John. *Recollections of Forty Years in the House, Senate, and Cabinet: An Autobiography.* Chicago: Herner Co., 1895.

SHERMAN, WILLIAM TECUMSEH (1920–1891)

Castel, Albert. "The Life of a Rising Son [William T. Sherman]," *Civil War Times Illustrated,* 18 (July 1979), 4–7, 42–46; 18 (August 1979), 12–22; 18 (October 1979), 10–21.

Kitrell, Irvin, III. "40 Acres and a Mule: [Sherman's Special Field Orders, No. 15, 16 January 1865]," *Civil War Times Illustrated,* 41 (May 2002), 54–61.

Lewis, Lloyd. *Sherman, Fighting Prophet.* New York: Harcourt, Brace, 1932.

Liddell-Hart, B. H. "Sherman—Modern Warrior," *American Heritage,* 13 (August 1962), 21–22. 102–106.

―――. *Sherman: Soldier, Realist, American.* New York: Dodd, Mead, 1929.

Lucas, Marion B. *Sherman and the Burning of Columbia.* College Station: Texas A&M University Press, 1976.

Marszalek, John F., Jr. *Sherman: A Soldier's Passion for Order.* New York: Free Press, 1993.

———. *Sherman's Other War: The General and the Civil War Press*, Memphis, Tenn.: Memphis State University Press, 1981.

Royster, Charles. *The Destructive War: William Tecumseh Sherman, Stonewall Jackson, and the Americans.* New York: Knopf, 1991.

Sherman, William T. *Memoirs of General W. T. Sherman.* New York: Library of America, 1990, repr.

SHILOH CAMPAIGN

Allen, Stacy. "Battle of Shiloh, Part 1," *Blue & Gray*, 14 (1996–1997), [Special Issue].

———. "Battle of Shiloh, Part 2," *Blue & Gray*, 14 (1996–1997), [Special Issue].

Ambrose, Stephen E. "Fort Donelson: 'Disastrous Blow to the South,'" *Civil War Times Illustrated*, 5 (June 1966), 4–13, 42–45.

Catton, Bruce. *Grant Moves South.* Boston: Little, Brown & Co., 1960.

Cimprich, John. "Fort Pillow during the Civil War," *North & South*, 9 (December 2006), 60–70.

Connelly, Thomas M. "The [Albert Sidney] Johnston Mystique—A Profile," *Civil War Times Illustrated*, 5 (February 1967), 15–23.

———. *Army of the Heartland: The Army of the Tennessee, 1861–1862.* Baton Rouge: Louisiana State University Press, 1967.

———. *Autumn of Glory: The Army of Tennessee, 1862–1865.* Baton Rouge: Louisiana State University Press, 1971.

Cooling, Benjamin Franklin. "Forts Henry and Donelson," *Blue & Gray*, 9 (1991–1992), [Special Issue].

———. *Forts Henry and Donelson: The Key to the Confederate Heartland.* Knoxville: University of Tennessee Press, 1987.

Cozzens, Peter. "Roadblock on the Mississippi, [Island No. 10]," *Civil War Times Illustrated*, 41 (March 2002), 40–49.

Daniel, Larry J. *Soldiering in the Army of Tennessee: A Portrait of Life in a Confederate Army.* Chapel Hill: University of North Carolina Press, 1991.

Eisenchiml, Otto. "Shiloh—The Blunders and the Blame," *Civil War Times Illustrated*, 2 (April 1983), 4–13, 30–34.

Frank, Joseph Allan, and George A. Reeves. *"Seeing the Elephant": Raw Recruits at the Battle of Shiloh.* Westport, Conn.: Greenwood Press, 1989.

Gauthreaux, Alan G. "Lost in the Fog of War [Battle of baton Rouge]," *Civil War Times Illustrated*, 49 (April 2010), 54–58.

Gott, Kendall D. "Gateway to the Heartland [Fts. Henry and Donelson]," *North & South*, 7 (March 2004), 46–59.

Hamilton, James T. *The Battle of Fort Donelson*. New York: Thomas Yoseloff, 1968.

Harrison, Lowell H. "Mill Springs: 'The Brilliant Victory,'" *Civil War Times Illustrated*, 10 (January 1972), 4–9, 44–47.

Horn, Stanley F. *The Army of Tennessee*. Norman: University of Oklahoma Press, 1941.

Huffstot, Robert S. "The Story of the CSS *Arkansas*," *Civil War Times Illustrated*, 7 (July 1968), 20–27.

Hughes, Nathaniel Cheairs. *The Battle of Belmont: Grant Strikes South*. Chapel Hill: University of North Carolina Press, 1991.

Keller, Allan. "Admiral Andrew Hull Foote," *Civil War Times Illustrated*, 18 (December 1979), 6–11, 43–47.

Kushlan, Jim (ed.). "[General Albert Sidney Johnston and the Battle of Shiloh]," *Civil War Times Illustrated*, 36 (March 1997), [Special Issue].

Long, E. B. "Plum Run Bend," *Civil War Times Illustrated*, 11 (June 1972), 4–11, 40–45.

McDonough, James Lee. *Shiloh: In Hell before Night*. Knoxville: University of Tennessee Press, 1877.

McMurry, Richard M. *Two Great Rebel Armies: An Essay in Confederate Military History*. Chapel Hill: University of North Carolina Press, 1989.

McWhiney, Grady. "General Beauregard's 'Complete Victory' at Shiloh: An Interpretation," *Journal of Southern History*, 49 (1983), 421–34.

Melton, Maurice. "The Struggle for Island No. 10," *Civil War Times Illustrated*, 18 (April 1979), 4–11, 43–46.

Melville, Phillips. "The *Carondelet* Runs the Gauntlet [at Island No. 10]," *American Heritage*, 10 (October 1959), 66–72. 77.

Nash, Howard P., Jr. "The Story of Island No. 10," *Civil War Times Illustrated*, 5 (December 1966), 42–47.

Starr, Stephen Z. *The Union Cavalry in the Civil War: The War in the West*. Vol. 3. Baton Rouge: Louisiana State University Press, 1985.

Sword, Wiley. "The Battle of Shiloh," *Civil War Times Illustrated*, 17 (May 1978), [Special Issue].

———. *Shiloh: Bloody April*. New York: Morrow, 1974.

Tate, Roger. "Battle of Mill Springs," *Blue & Gray*, 10 (1992–1993), [Special Issue].

Williams, Kenneth P. *Lincoln Finds a General: A Military Study of the Civil War*. 5 vols. New York: Macmillan, 1949–1959.

SICKLES, DANIEL E. (1819–1914)

Beckman, W. Robert. "Daniel Edgar Sickles," in David S. Heidler and Jeanne T. Heidler (eds.), *Encyclopedia of the American Civil War: A Political, Social, and Military History*. New York: W. W. Norton & Company, 2000.

Brandt, Nat. *The Congressman Who Got Away With Murder*. Syracuse, N.Y.: Syracuse University Press, 1991.

Campbell, Eric A. "Death of [Sickles'] III Corps [at Gettysburg]," *Civil War Times Illustrated*, 48 (August 2009), 34–37.

Coddington, Edwin B. *The Gettysburg Campaign; a Study in Command*. New York: Scribner's, 1968.

Keneally, Thomas. *American Scoundrel: The Life of the Notorious Civil War General Dan Sickles*. New York: Nan A. Talese/Doubleday, 2002.

Sauers, Gettysburg: *The Meade-Sickles Controversy*. Dulles, Va.: Brassey's, 2003.

Swanberg, W. A. *Sickles: The Incredible*. New York: Charles Scribner's Sons, 1956.

Tagg, Larry. *The Generals of Gettysburg*. Campbell, Calif.: Savas Publishing, 1998.

Warner, Ezra J. *Generals in Blue: Lives of the Union Commanders*. Baton Rouge: Louisiana State University Press, 1964.

SIOUX WAR IN MINNESOTA AND ITS AFTERMATH ON THE PLAINS

Brown, Dee. *The Galvanized Yankees*. Lincoln: University of Nebraska Press, 1963.

———. "The Galvanized Yankees," *Civil War Times Illustrated*, 4 (February 1966), 12–20.

Jones, Robert H. *The Civil War in the Northwest: Nebraska, Wisconsin, Iowa, Minnesota, and the Dakotas*. Norman: University of Oklahoma Press, 1960.

Josephy, Alvin M., Jr. *The Civil War in the American West*. New York: Knopf, 1991.

Kachuba, John B. "Sioux Terror on the Prairie," *America's Civil War*, 10 (March 1997), 30–38.

Robrock, David P. "The Eleventh Ohio Cavalry on the Central Plains," *Arizona and the West*, 25 (1983), 23–48.

SLAVERY IN THE TERRITORIES—THE WILMOT PROVISO

Brauer, Kinley. *Cotton versus Conscience: Massachusetts Whig Politics and Southwestern Expansion, 1843–1848*. Lexington: University of Kentucky Press, 1967.

Franklin, John Hope, "The Southern Expansionists of 1846," *Journal of Southern History*, 25 (1959), 323–38.

Going, Charles B. *David Wilmot, Free Soiler: A Biography of the Great Advocate of the Wilmot Proviso*. New York: D. Appleton & Co., 1924.

Morrison, Chaplain. *Democratic Politics and Sectionalism: The Wilmot Proviso Controversy*. Chapel Hill: University of North Carolina Press, 1967.

Potter, David. *The Impending Crisis, 1848–1861*. New York: Harper & Row, 1976.

Sewell, Richard. *Ballots for Freedom: Antislavery Politics in the United States.* New York: Oxford University Press, 1976.

Sibley, Joel. *The Shrine of Party: Congressional Voting Behavior, 1841–1852.* Pittsburgh: University of Pittsburgh Press, 1967.

SMALLS, ROBERT (1839–1915)

Bryant, Lawrence C. *South Carolina Negro Legislators: State and Local Office-holders, Biographies of Negro Representatives, 1868–1902.* Orangeburg, S.C.: L. C. Bryant, 1974.

Gibbons, Tony. *Warships and Naval Battles of the US Civil War.* Limpsfield, Surry, G.B.: Dragon's World Ltd., 1989.

Holt, Thomas. *Black over White: Negro Political Leadership in South Carolina during Reconstruction.* Urbana: University of Illinois Press, 1977.

Low, W. Augustus, and Virgil A. Clift. *Encyclopedia of Black America.* New York: McGraw-Hill Book Company, 1981.

McFarlin, Annjeannette Sophia. *Black Congressional Reconstruction Orators and Their Orations.* Metuchen, N.J.: Scarecrow Press, 1976.

Quarles, Benjamin. "The Abduction of the *Planter*," *Civil War History*, 4 (1958), 5–10.

Simkins, Francis B. "Robert Smalls," in Allen Johnson *et al.* (eds.), *Dictionary of American Biography* (10 double vols. + 9 supplements, 1964–1981), XVII, 224–25.

Uya, Okun Edet. *From Slavery to Public Service, Robert Smalls, 1839–1915.* New York: Oxford University Press, 1971.

Westwood, Howard. "Mr. Smalls: A Slave No More," *Civil War Times Illustrated*, 25 (1986), 20–23, 28–31.

SMITH, EDMUND KIRBY (1824–1893)

Current, Richard N. (ed.). *Encyclopedia of the Confederacy.* 4 vols. New York: Simon & Schuster, 1993.

Davis, William C. (ed.). *The Confederate General.* 6 vols. N.p.: National Historical Society, 1991.

Freeman, Douglas Southall. *Lee's Lieutenants: A Study of Command.* 3 vols. New York: Charles Scribner's Sons, 1942–1944.

Holladay, Florence Elizabeth. "The Extraordinary Powers and Functions of the General Commanding the Trans-Mississippi Department of the Southern Confederacy." M.A. thesis, University of Texas, 1914. Partially published as "The Powers of the Commander of the Confederate Trans-Mississippi Department, 1863–1865," *Southwestern Historical Quarterly*, 21 (1918), 279–98, 333–59.

Kerby, Robert L. *Kirby Smith's Confederacy: The Trans-Mississippi South, 1863–1865.* New York: Columbia University Press, 1972.

Parks, Joseph H. *General Edmund Kirby Smith, C.S.A.* Baton Rouge: Louisiana State University Press, 1954.

Prushankin, Jeffery S. "'To This Fatal Blunder, [Kirby Smith]," *North & South*, 5 (September 2002), 76–91.

Warner, Ezra J. *Generals in Gray: Lives of Confederate Commanders.* Baton Rouge: Louisiana State University Press, 1959.

Woodworth, Steven E. "'Dismembering the Confederacy': Jefferson Davis and the Trans-Mississippi West," *Military History of the Southwest*, 20 (1990), 1–22.

SOCIAL THOUGHT DURING AND AFTER RECONSTRUCTION

Abell, Aaron Ignatius. *Urban Impact on American Protestantism.* Cambridge, Mass.: Harvard University Press, 1943.

Clark, Clifford E. *Henry Ward Beecher: Spokesman for a Middle-Class America.* Urbana: University of Illinois Press, 1978.

Curti, Merle E. *The Growth of American Thought.* New York: Harper & Brothers, 1943.

Dombrowski, James A. *Early Days of Christian Socialism in America.* New York: Octagon, 1936, repr. 1966.

Gabriel, Ralph H. *The Course of American Democratic Thought.* 2nd ed. New York: Rondell Press, 1956.

Harlow, Alvin F. "Victoria Claflin Woodhull," in Allen Johnson *et al.* (eds.), *Dictionary of American Biography* (10 double vols. + 9 supplements, 1964–1981), XX, 494–95.

Hibben, Paxton. *Henry Ward Beecher: An American Portrait.* New York: Press of the Readers Club, 1942.

Higham, John. *From Boundlessness to Consolidation: The Transformation of American Culture, 1848–1860.* Ann Arbor: University of Michigan Press, 1969.

Hopkins, C. H. *The Rise of Social Gospel in American Protestantism.* New Haven, Conn.: Yale University Press, 1940.

Howe, Daniel W. "American Victorianism as a Culture," *American Quarterly*, 27 (1975), 507–32.

Knox, Thomas W. *Life and Work of Henry Ward Beecher.* Hartford, Conn.: Hartford Publishing Co., 1887.

May, Henry Farnham. *Protestant Churches and Industrial America.* New York: Harper & Brothers, 1949.

McLoughlin, William G. *The Meaning of Henry Ward Beecher.* New York: Knopf, 1970.

Muraskin, William A. "The Social-Control Theory in American History: A Critique," *Journal of Social History*, 9 (1976), 559–69.

Parrington, V. L. *The Main Currents in American Thought.* 3 vols. New York: Harcourt-Brace, 1927–1930.

Ryan, Halford R. *Henry Ward Beecher: Peripatetic Preacher.* New York: Greenwood Press, 1990.

Starr, Harris Elwood. "Henry Ward Beecher," in Allen Johnson *et al.* (eds.), *Dictionary of American Biography* (10 double vols. + 9 supplements, 1964–1981), II, 129–35.

Wallace, Irving. *The Nympho and Other Maniacs: The Lives, the Loves, and the Sexual Adventures of Some Scandalous and Liberated Ladies.* New York: Simon & Schuster, 1971.

Waller, Altina L. *Reverend Beecher and Mrs. Tilton: Sex and Class in Victorian America.* Amherst: University of Massachusetts Press, 1982.

Wish, Harvey A. *Society and Thought in America.* 2 vols. New York: Longmans, Green, 1950–1952.

SOUTHERN CARPETBAGGERS IN THE NORTH

Buck, Paul H. *The Road to Reunion, 1865–1890.* Boston: J. B. Lippincott, 1937.

Gaston, Paul M. *The New South Creed: A Study in Southern Mythmaking.* New York: Alfred A. Knopf, 1970.

Sutherland, Daniel E. *The Confederate Carpetbaggers.* Baton Rouge: Louisiana State University Press, 1988.

———. "Former Confederates in the Post-Civil War North: An Unexplored Aspect of Reconstruction History," *Journal of Southern History*, 47 (1981), 393–410.

SOUTHERN CLAIMS COMMISSION

Klingberg, Frank Wysor. *The Southern Claims Commission.* Berkeley: University of California Press, 1955.

Moore, John Hammond. "Getting Uncle Sam's Dollars: South Carolinians and the Southern Claims Commission," *South Carolina Historical Magazine*, 82 (1981), 248–62.

Randall, James G. *The Confiscation of Property during the Civil War.* Indianapolis: Bobbs-Merrill, 1913.

SOUTHERN CULTURE, POLITICAL THOUGHT, AND PROSLAVE DOCTRINE

Carpenter, Jesse T. *The South as a Conscious Minority, 1789–1861: A Study in Political Thought.* New York: New York University Press, 1930.

Carwardine, Richard J. *Evangelicals and Politics in Antebellum America.* New Haven, Conn.: Yale University Press, 1993.

Cecil-Fransman, Bill. *Common Whites: Class and Culture in Antebellum North Carolina.* Lexington: University of Kentucky Press, 1992.

Collins, Bruce. *White Society in the Antebellum South.* London: Longmans, 1985.

Cooper, William J. *Liberty and Slavery: Southern Politics to 1860.* New York: Knopf, 1983.

————. *The South and the Politics of Slavery, 1852–1856.* Baton Rouge: Louisiana State University Press, 1978.

Craven, Avery O. *The Growth of Southern Nationalism, 1848–1861.* Baton Rouge: Louisiana State University Press, 1953.

Davis, Davis Brion. *The Slave Power Conspiracy and the Paranoid Style.* Baton Rouge: Louisiana State University Press, 1969.

Eaton, Clement. *The Freedom-of-Thought Struggle in the Old South.* rev. ed. New York: Harper & Row, 1964.

————. *The Growth of Southern Civilization, 1790–1860.* New York: Harper & Row, 1961.

————. *The Mind of the Old South.* rev. ed. Baton Rouge: Louisiana State University Press, 1967.

Faust, Drew Gilpin. *The Ideology of Slavery: Proslavery Thought in the Antebellum South, 1830–1869.* Baton Rouge: Louisiana State University Press, 1981.

Freehling, William W. *The Reintegration of American History: Slavery and the Civil War.* New York: Oxford University Press, 1994.

————. *The Road to Disunion: Secessionists at Bay.* New York: Oxford University Press, 1990.

Genovese, Eugene D. *The Slaveholder's Dilemma: Freedom and Progress in Southern Conservative Thought, 1820–1860.* Columbia: University of South Carolina, 1992.

————. *The World the Slaveholders Made: Two Essays in Interpretation.* New York: Pantheon Books, 1969.

Greenberg, Kenneth. *Masters and Statesmen: The Political Culture of American Slavery.* Baltimore, Md.: The Johns Hopkins University Press, 1985.

Hahn, Steve. *The Roots of Southern Populism: Yeoman Farmers and the Transformation of the Georgia Upcountry, 1850–1890.* New York: Oxford University Press, 1983.

Harris, J. William. *Plain Folk and Gentry in a Slave Society: White Liberty and Black Slavery in Augusta's Hinterlands.* Middletown, Conn.: Wesleyan University Press, 1985.

Hill, Samuel S. *The South and North in American Religion.* Athens: University of Georgia Press, 1980.

Inscoe, John C. *Mountain Masters, Slavery, and the Sectional Crisis in Western North Carolina.* Knoxville: University of Tennessee Press, 1989.

Jenkins, William Sumner. *Pro-Slavery Thought in the Old South.* Chapel Hill: University of North Carolina Press, 1935.

Levine, Bruce. *Half Slave and Half Free: The Roots of the Civil War.* New York: Hill and Wang, 1992.

Loveland, Anne C. *Southern Evangelicals and the Social Order, 1800–1860*. Baton Rouge: Louisiana State University Press, 1980.

McCardle, John. *The Idea of a Southern Nation: Southern Nationalists and Nationalism, 1830–1860*. New York: Norton, 1979.

Osterweis, Rollin G. *Romanticism and Nationalism in the Old South*. New Haven, Conn.: Yale University Press, 1949.

Owsley, Frank. *Plain Folk of the Old South*. Baton Rouge: Louisiana State University Press, 1949.

Phillips, Kevin. *The Cousins' Wars: Religion, Politics, and the Triumph of Anglo-America*. New York: Basic Books, 1999.

Ransom, Roger L. *Conflict and Compromise: The Political Economy of Slavery, Emancipation and the Civil War*. Cambridge, GB: Cambridge University Press, 1989.

Snay, Mitchell. *Gospel of Disunion: Religion and Separatism in the Antebellum South*. Cambridge, GB: Cambridge University Press, 1993.

Taylor, William R. *Cavalier and Yankee: The Old South and the American National Character*. Garden City, N.Y.: Doubleday, 1963, repr.

Wyatt-Brown, Bertram. *Yankee Saints and Southern Sinners*. Baton Rouge: Louisiana State University Press, 1985.

SOUTHERN HOMESTEAD ACT OF 1866

Abbott, Martin. "Free Land Free Labor, and the Freedmen's Bureau," *Agricultural History*, 30 (1956), 150–56.

Bleser, Carol Rothrock. *The Promised Land: The History of the South Carolina Land Commission, 1869–1890*. Columbia: University of South Carolina Press, 1969.

Cox, LaWanda. "The Promise of Land for the Freedmen," *Mississippi Valley Historical Review*, 49 (1958), 413–40.

Gates, Paul W. "Federal Land Policy in the South, 1866–1880," *Journal of Southern History*, 6 (1940), 303–60.

Hoffman, Edwin D. "From Slavery to Self Reliance," *Journal of Negro History*, 41 (1956), 8–42.

Oubre, Claude F. *Forty Acres and a Mule: The Freedmen's Bureau and Black Land Ownership*. Baton Rouge: Louisiana State University Press, 1978.

Randall, James G. *Constitutional Problems Under Lincoln*. rev. ed. Urbana: University of Illinois Press, 1964.

Roark, James L. "George W. Julian: Radical Land Reformer," *Indiana Magazine of History*, 64 (1968), 25–38.

Summers, Mark W. *The Era of Good Stealings*. New York: Oxford University Press, 1993.

"SPREAD EAGLE" FOREIGN POLICY, YOUNG AMERICA, AND FILIBUSTERING

Bridges, C. A. "The Knights of the Golden Circle: A Filibustering Fantasy," *Southwestern Historical Quarterly*, 287–302.

Crenshaw, Ollinger. "The Knights of the Golden Circle," *American Historical Review*, 47 (1941), 23–50.

Curti, Merle E. "'Young America,'" *American Historical Review*, 32 (October 1926), 34–55.

Curtis [sic], Merle E. "George Sanders—American Patriot of the Fifties," *South Atlantic Quarterly*, 27 (January 1928), 79–87.

DeForest, Tim. "Southern Attempts to Annex Cuba," *America's Civil War*, 10 (May 1997), 38–44.

Hall, James O. "A Magnificent Charlatan: George Washington Lafayette Bickley Made a Career of Deceit," *Civil War Times Illustrated*, 18 (February 1980), 40–42.

Johannsen, Robert W. *Stephen A. Douglas*. New York: Oxford University Press, 1973.

Johnson, Allen. *Stephen A. Douglas: A Study in American Politics*. New York: Macmillan, 1908.

May, Arthur J. *Contemporary American Opinion of the Mid-Century Revolutions in Central Europe*. Philadelphia: University of Pennsylvania, 1927.

May, Robert E. *The Southern Dream of a Caribbean Empire, 1854–1861*. Baton Rouge: Louisiana State University Press, 1973.

Nichols, Roy F. *The Democratic Machine, 1850–1854*. New York: Columbia University Press, 1923.

———. *Franklin Pierce: Young Hickory of the Granite Hills*. Philadelphia: University of Pennsylvania, 1931.

Oliver, John W. "Louis Kossuth's Appeal to the Middle West," *Mississippi Valley Historical Review*, 14 (1828), 481–95.

Riepma, Siert F. "Young America: A Study in American Nationalism before the Civil War." Ph.D. dissertation, Western Reserve University, 1939.

Shippee, Lester Burrell. *Canadian-American Relations, 1848–1974*. New Haven, Conn.: Yale University Press, 1939.

Stout, Joe A., Jr. *The Liberators: Filibustering Expeditions into Mexico, 1848–1862, and the Last Gasp of Manifest Destiny*. Los Angeles: Westernlore Press, 1973.

STANTON, EDWIN MCM. (1814–1869)

Flower, Frank A. *Edwin McMasters Stanton, The Autocrat of Rebellion, Emancipation, and Reconstruction*. Akron, Ohio: Saalfield Pub. Co., 1905.

Gorham, George C. *Life and Public Services of Edwin M. Stanton*. 2 vols. Boston: Houghton Mifflin and Company, 1899.

Meneely, A. Howard. "Edwin McMasters Stanton," in Allen Johnson *et al.* (eds.), *Dictionary of American Biography* (10 double vols. + 9 supplements, 1964–1981), XVII, 517–21.

Pratt, Fletcher. *Stanton: Lincoln's Secretary of War.* Westport, Conn.: Greenwood Press, 1953, reprint 1970.

Thomas, Benjamin P., and Harold M. Hyman. *Stanton: The Life and Times of Lincoln's Secretary of War.* New York: Alfred A. Knopf, 1962.

STATE SOVEREIGNTY AND SLAVERY—THE U.S. SUPREME COURT VINDICATES THE SOUTH AND THE NON-EXCLUSION DOCTRINE

Allen, Austin. "The Political Economy of Blackness: Citizenship, Corporations, and Race in Dred Scott," *Civil War History*, 50 (2004), 229–260.

Bestor, Arthur. "The American Civil War as a Constitutional Crisis," *American Historical Review*, 69 (1964), 327–54.

————. "State Sovereignty and Slavery: A Reinterpretation of Proslavery Constitutional Doctrine, 1846–1860," Illinois State Historical Society, *Journal*, 53 (1960), 117–80.

Campbell, Stanley. *The Slave Catchers: Enforcement of the Fugitive Slave Law, 1850–1860.* Chapel Hill: University of North Carolina Press, 1970.

Cover, Robert M. *Justice Accused: Antislavery and Judicial Process.* New Haven, Conn.: Yale University Press, 1975.

Fehrenbacher, Don. *The Dred Scott Case: Its Significance in American Law and Politics.* New York: Oxford University Press, 1978.

Finkelman, Paul. *An Imperfect Union: Slavery, Federalism, and Comity.* Chapel Hill: University of North Carolina Press, 1981.

————. "The Nationalization of Slavery: A Counter-Factual Approach to the 1860s," *Louisiana Studies*, 14 (1975), 213–40.

Gara, Larry. "Results of the Fugitive Slave Law," *Civil War Times Illustrated*, 2 (October 1963), 30–37.

Hopkins, Vincent C. *Dred Scott's Case.* New York: Fordham University Press, 1951.

Hyman, Harold M., and William Wiecek. *Equal Justice under Law: Constitutional Development, 1835–1875.* New York: Harper & Row, 1982.

Kutler, Stanley I. (ed.). *The Dred Scott Decision: Law or Politics?* Boston: Houghton Mifflin Co., 1967.

McCormick, E. I. "Justice Campbell and the Dred Scott Decision," *Mississippi Valley Historical Review*, 19 (1933), 565–71.

Meerse, David E. "James Buchanan, the Patronage, and the Northern Democratic Party, 1857–1858." Ph.D. dissertation, University of Illinois, 1969.

Morris, Thomas D. *Free Men All: The Personal Liberty Laws of the North, 1780–1861.* Baltimore, Md.: The Johns Hopkins University Press, 1974.

Nevins, Allan. *The Constitution, Slavery, and the Territories.* Boston: Boston University Press, 1953.

Paludan, Phillip S. *A Covenant with Death: The Constitution, Law, and Equality in the Civil War Era*. Urbana: University of Illinois University Press, 1975.

Quaife, Milo M. *The Doctrine of Non-Intervention with Slavery in the Territories*. Chicago: M. C. Chamberlain, 1910.

Russel, Robert. "Constitutional Doctrines with Regard to Slavery in the Territories," *Journal of Southern History*, 32 (1966), 466–85.

Stampp, Kenneth M. *America in 1857: A Nation on the Brink*. New York: Oxford University Press, 1990.

Wallance, Gregory J. "The Lawsuit That Started the Civil War [Dred Scott *v.* Sanford, 1857]," *Civil War Times Illustrated*, 45 (March/April 2006), 46–52.

Wiecek, William. "Slavery and Abolition before the United States Supreme Court," *Journal of American History*, 65 (1978), 34–59.

———. *The Sources of Antislavery Constitutionalism in America, 1760–1848*. Ithaca, N.Y.: Cornell University Press, 1877.

STEVENS, THADDEUS (1792–1868)

Bowers, Claude. *The Tragic Era: The Revolution After Lincoln*. Boston: Houghton Mifflin, 1929.

Brodie, Fawn. *Thaddeus Stevens: Scourge of the South*. New York: W. W. Norton, 1966.

Bryant-Jones, Mildred. "The Political Program of Thaddeus Stevens," *Phylon*, 2 (1941), 147–54.

Callender, Edward B. *Thaddeus Stevens: Commoner*. New York: AMS Press, 1972, repr.

Current, Richard N. *Old Thad Stevens: A Story of Ambition*. Madison: University of Wisconsin Press, 1942.

DuBois, W. E. Burghardt. *Black Reconstruction: An Essay toward a History of the Part which Black Folk Played in the Attempt to Reconstruct Democracy, 1860–1888*. New York: Harcourt, Brace and Company, 1935.

Klein, Frederic S. "Thaddeus Stevens—A Personality Profile," *Civil War Times Illustrated*, 2 (February 1964), 19–23.

Korngold, Ralph. *Thaddeus Stevens: A Being Darkly Wise and Rudely Great*. New York: Harcourt, Brace & Co., 1955.

McCall, Samuel W. *Thaddeus Stevens*. Boston: Houghton-Mifflin & Co., 1899.

Morrill, George P. "The Best White Friend Black Americans Ever Had," *Reader's Digest*, 99 (July 1971), 169–74.

Nevins, Allan. "Thaddeus Stevens," in Allen Johnson *et al.* (eds.), *Dictionary of American Biography* (10 double vols. + 9 supplements, 1964–1981), XVII, 620–25.

Pickens, Donald K. "The Republican Synthesis and Thaddeus Stevens," *Civil War History*, 31 (1985), 57–73.

Woodburn, James A. *The Life of Thaddeus Stevens*. Indianapolis: Bobbs-Merrill, 1913.

Woodley, Thomas Frederick. *Thaddeus Stevens, 1792–1868*. Harrisburg: Telegraph Press, 1934.

STRATEGY, COMMAND, AND LOGISTICS—CONFEDERATE

Ball, Douglas B. *Financial Failure and Confederate Defeat*. Urbana: University of Illinois Press, 1991.

Beringer, Richard E., Herman Hattaway, Archer Jones, and William N. Still, Jr. *Why the South Lost the Civil War*. Athens: University of Georgia Press, 1986.

Black, Robert C., III. *The Railroads of the Confederacy*. Chapel Hill: University of North Carolina Press, 1952.

Castel, Albert. "The Historian and the General: Thomas L. Connelly versus Robert E. Lee," *Civil War History*, 16 (1970), 50–63.

Connelly, Thomas M. "Robert E. Lee and the Western Confederacy: A Criticism of Lee's Strategic Ability," *Civil War History*, 15 (1969), 116–32.

———, and Archer Jones. *The Politics of Command: Factions and Ideas in Confederate Strategy*. Baton Rouge: Louisiana State University Press, 1973.

Doster, James F. "Were Southern Railroads Destroyed by the Civil War?" *Civil War History*, 7 (1961), 310–20.

Epstein, Robert M. "The Creation and Evolution of Army Corps in the Civil War," *Civil War History*, 7 (1961), 310–20.

Goff, Richard D. *Confederate Supply*. Durham, N.C.: Duke University Press, 1969.

Gow, June I. "Theory and Practice in Confederate Military Administration," *Military Affairs*, 21 (1975), 118–23.

Hagerman, Edward. *The American Civil War and the Origins of Modern Warfare*. Bloomington: Indiana University Press, 1988.

Hay, Thomas Robeson. "Lucius B. Northrop: Commissary General of the Confederacy," *Civil War History*, 9 (1963), 5–23.

Helniak, Roman J., and Lawrence L. Hewitt (eds.). *The Confederate High Command and Related Topics: The 1988 Deep Delta Civil War Symposium*. Shippensburg, Pa.: White Mane Publishing Co., 1990.

———, and Lawrence L. Hewitt (eds.). *The Confederate High Command and Related Topics: Themes in Honor of T. Harry Williams*. Shippensburg, Pa.: White Mane Publishing Co., 1988.

Jones, Archer. "Some Aspects of George W. Randolph's Service as Confederate Secretary of War," *Journal of Southern History*, 26 (1960), 299–314.

Johnston, Angus J. *Virginia Railroads in the Civil War*. Chapel Hill: University of North Carolina Press, 1961.

Lerner, Eugene M. "The Monetary and Fiscal Programs of the Confederate Government, 1861–1865," *Journal of Political Economy*, 62 (1954), 506–22.

McWiney, Grady. "Jefferson Davis and the Art of War," *Civil War History*, 21 (1975), 101–12.

Minter, Winifred P. "Confederate Military Supply," *Social Science*, 34 (1959), 163–71.

Moore, John G. "Mobility and Strategy in the Civil War," *Military Affairs*, 24 (1960), 68–77.

Poulter, Keith (ed.). "Confederate Strategy Considered," *North & South*, 4 (September 2001), 14–22.

Ramsdell, Charles W. "The Control of Manufacturing by the Confederate Government," *Mississippi Valley Historical Review*, 8 (1921), 2349.

———. "General Robert E. Lee's Horse Supply, 1862–1865," *American Historical Review*, 35 (1930), 758–77.

Rollins, Richard. "Understanding Lee's Audacity," *North & South*, 5 (December 2001), 30–41.

Royster, Charles. *The Destructive War: William Tecumseh Sherman, Stonewall Jackson, and the Americans*. New York: Knopf, 1991.

Vandiver, Frank E. *Rebel Brass: The Confederate Command System*. Baton Rouge: Louisiana State University Press, 1956.

Woodward, Steven E. *Jefferson Davis and His Generals: The Failure of Confederate Command in the West*. Lawrence: University Press of Kansas, 1990.

STRATEGY, COMMAND, AND LOGISTICS—UNION

Ballard, Colin R. *The Military Genius of Abraham Lincoln: An Essay*. London: Oxford University Press, 1926.

Clark, John E., Jr. *Railroads in the Civil War: The Impact of Management on Victory and Defeat*. Baton Rouge: Louisiana State University Press, 2001.

Dean, Eric T., Jr. "Rethinking the Civil War: Beyond 'Revolutions,' 'Reconstruction,' and the 'New Social History,'" *Southern Historian*, 15 (1994), 28–50.

Donald, David H. (ed.). *Why the North Won the Civil War*. Baton Rouge: Louisiana State University Press, 1960.

East, Sherrad E. "Montgomery C. Meigs and the Quartermaster Department," *Military Affairs*, 26 (1962), 183–97.

Epstein, Robert M. "The Creation and Evolution of Army Corps in the Civil War," *Civil War History*, 7 (1961), 310–20.

Espanet, O. "The Art of Supplying Armies in the Field as Exemplified during the Civil War," *Journal of the Military Service Institution of the United States*, 45–90.

Freidel, Frank. "General Orders No. 100 and Military Government," *Mississippi Valley Historical Review*, 32 (1946), 541–56.

Garner, James W. "General Orders 100 Revisited," *Military Law Review*, 27 (1965), 1–48.

Grimsley, Mark. "Conciliation and Failure, 1861–1862," *Civil War History*, 39 (1993), 317–35.

————. *The Hard Hand of War: Union Military Policy toward Southern Civilians, 1861–1865.* New York: Cambridge University Press, 1995.

Hagerman, Edward. *The American Civil War and the Origins of Modern Warfare.* Bloomington: Indiana University Press, 1988.

Hattaway, Herman, and Archer Jones. *How the North Won.* Urbana: University of Illinois Press, 1983.

Huston, James A. "Logistical Support of Federal Armies in the Field," *Civil War History*, 7 (1961), 36–47.

Janda, Lance. "Shutting the Gates of Mercy: The American Origins of Total War, 1860–1880," *Journal of Military History*, 59 (1995), 7–26.

Lord, Francis A. *Lincoln's Railroad Man: Herman Haupt.* Rutherford, N.J.: Fairleigh Dickinson University Press, 1969.

McKitrick, Eric I. "Party Politics and the Union and Confederate War Efforts," in William Nesbit Chambers and Walter Dean Burnham (eds.), *The American Party Systems: Stages of Development.* New York: Oxford University Press, 1967, 117–51.

Meredith, Roy, and Arthur Meredith. *Mr. Lincoln's Military Railroads.* New York: Norton, 1979.

Moore, John G. "Mobility and Strategy in the Civil War," *Military Affairs*, 24 (1960), 68–77.

Mruck, Armin E. "The Role of Railroads in the Atlanta Campaign," *Civil War History*, 7 (1961), 264–71.

Neely, Mark E., Jr. "Was the Civil War a Total War?" *Civil War History*, 37 (1991), 5–28.

Royster, Charles. *The Destructive War: William Tecumseh Sherman, Stonewall Jackson and the Americans.* New York: Knopf, 1991.

Shannon Fred A. *The Organization and Administration of the Union Army, 1861–1865.* 2 vols. Cleveland: Arthur H. Clark Co., 1928.

Sutherland, Daniel E. "Abraham Lincoln, John Pope, and the Origins of Total War," *Journal of Military History*, 56 (1992), 567–86.

Turner, George E. *Victory Rode the Rails.* Indianapolis: Bobbs-Merrill, 1953.

Walters, John Bennett. *Merchant of Terror: General Sherman and Total War.* Indianapolis: Bobbs-Merrill, 1973.

Ward, James A. *That Man Haupt! A Biography of Herman Haupt.* Baton Rouge: Louisiana State University Press, 1973.

Weber, Thomas. *The Northern Railroads in the Civil War.* New York: King's Crown, 1952.

Weigley, Russell F. *Quartermaster General of the Union Army: A Biography of M. C. Meigs.* New York: Columbia University Press, 1959.

Williams, T. Harry. *Lincoln and His Generals.* New York: Knopf, 1952.

Woodworth Steven E. "The Army of Tennessee and the Elements of Military Success," *North & South*, 6 (May 2003), 44–55.

SUMNER, CHARLES (1811–1874)

Donald David H. *Charles Sumner and the Coming of the Civil War.* New York: Alfred A. Knopf, 1968.

———. *Charles Sumner and the Rights of Man.* New York: Alfred A. Knopf, 1970.

Freidel, Frank. "Francis Lieber, Charles Sumner, and Slavery," *Journal of Southern History*, 9 (1943), 75–93.

Haynes, George H. "Charles Sumner," in Allen Johnson *et al.* (eds.), *Dictionary of American Biography* (10 double vols. + 9 supplements, 1964–1981), XVIII, 208–14.

Hoar, G. F. (ed.). *Charles Sumner: His Complete Works.* 20 vols. New York: Lee & Shepard, 1900.

Hoffert, Sylvia. "The Brooks-Sumner Affair, *Civil War Times Illustrated*, 11 (October 1972), 35–40.

Osofsky, Gilbert. "Cardboard Yankee: How Not to Study the Mind of Charles Sumner," *Reviews in American History*, 1 (1973), 595–605.

Ruchames, Louis. "Charles Sumner and American Historiography," *Journal of Negro History*, 38 (1953), 139–60.

Sefton, James E. "Charles Sumner for Our Time: An Essay Review," *Maryland Historical Magazine*, 66 (1971), 456–61.

SUPREME COURT, U.S., IN CIVIL WAR AND RECONSTRUCTION

Currie, David P. "The Constitution and the Supreme Court: Civil War and Reconstruction, 1865–1873," *University of Chicago Law Review*, 51 (1984), 131–86.

Fairman, Charles. *Reconstruction and Reunion, 1864–1888.* 2 pts. New York: The Macmillan Company, 1971–1987.

Fried, Joseph P. "The U.S. Supreme Court during the Civil War," *Civil War Times Illustrated*, 1 (February 1963), 28–35.

Goldman, Robert Michael. *Reconstruction and Black Suffrage: Losing the Vote in Reese and Cruikshank.* Lawrence: University Press of Kansas, 2001.

Hyman, Harold M. *A More Perfect Union: The Impact of the Civil War and Reconstruction on the Constitution.* New York: Alfred A. Knopf, 1973.

———. *The Reconstruction Justice of Salmon P. Chase: In Re Turner and Texas v. White.* Lawrence: University Press of Kansas, 1997.

Johnson, Ludwell H., III. "Abraham Lincoln and the Development of Presidential War-Making Powers: Prize Cases (1863) Revisited," *Civil War History*, 35 (1989), 208–24.

———. "The Confederacy: What Was It? The View from the Federal Courts," *Civil War History*, 32 (1986), 5–22.

Kutler, Stanley I. "*Ex Parte McCardle*: Judicial Impotency? The Supreme Court and Reconstruction Reconsidered," *American Historical Review*, 72 (1967), 835–51.

———. *Judicial Power and Reconstruction Politics*. Chicago: University of Chicago Press, 1968.

———. "Reconstruction and the Supreme Court: The Numbers Game Reconsidered," *Journal of Southern History*, 32 (1966), 42–58.

Lucie, Patricia M. L. "Confiscation: Constitutional Crossroads," *Civil War History*, 23 (1977), 307–21.

Myers, Lewis. "The Habeas Corpus Act of 1867: The Supreme Court as Legal Historian," *University of Chicago Law Review*, 33 (1965), 31–59.

Pierson, William Wately. "Texas *Versus* White," *Southwestern Historical Quarterly*, 18 (1914–1915), 341–67; 19 (1915–1916), 1–36, 142–58.

Randall, James G. *Constitutional Problems Under Lincoln*. rev. ed. Urbana: University of Illinois Press, 1964.

Silver, David M. *Lincoln's Supreme Court*. Urbana: University of Illinois Press, 1956.

Warren, Charles. *The Supreme Court in United States History*. 2 vols. Boston: Little Brown & Co., 1922.

Wiecek, William M. "The Great Writ and Reconstruction: The Habeas Corpus Act of 1867," *Journal of Southern History*, 36 (1970), 530–48.

———. "The Reconstruction of the Constitution," *Reviews in American History*, 1 (1973), 548–53.

———. "The Reconstruction of the Federal Judicial Power, 1863–1875," *American Journal of Legal History*, 13 (1969), 333–59.

SUPREME COURT, U.S., IN REDEMPTION

Avins, Alfred. "Racial Segregation in Public Accommodations: Some Reflected Light on the Fourteenth Amendment from the Civil Rights Act of 1875," *Case Western Law Review*, 18 (1967), 1251–83.

Donald David H. *Charles Sumner and the Rights of Man*. New York: Alfred A. Knopf, 1970.

Emerson, Thomas I., *et al*. *Political and Civil Rights in the United States*. 3rd ed. Boston: Little, Brown & Co., 1967.

Fairman, Charles. *Reconstruction and Reunion, 1864–1888*. 2 pts. New York: The Macmillan Company, 1971–1987.

Fischer, Roger A. *The Segregation Struggle in Louisiana, 1862–1877*. Urbana: University of Illinois Press, 1974.

Franklin, John Hope. *Race and History: Selected Essays, 1938–1988*. Baton Rouge: Louisiana State University, 1989.

Frantz, Laurent B. "Fourteenth Amendment against Private Acts," *Yale Law Journal*, 73 (1964), 1353–84.

Gaffney, Edward M., Jr. "History and Legal Interpretation: The Early Distortion of the Fourteenth Amendment by the Gilded Age Courts," *Catholic University Law Review*, 25 (1976), 207–49.

Gillette, William. *Retreat from Reconstruction, 1869–1879.* Baton Rouge: Louisiana State University Press, 1979.

Hyman, Harold M. *A More Perfect Union: The Impact of the Civil War and Reconstruction on the Constitution.* New York: Alfred A. Knopf, 1973.

Kaczorowski, Robert J. *The Nationalization of Civil Rights: Constitutional Theory and Practice in a Racist Society, 1866–1883.* New York: Garland Publishing, Inc., 1987.

Kelly, Alfred H. "The Congressional Controversy over School Segregation, 1867–1875," *American Historical Review,* 64 (1959), 537–63.

———, and Wilfred A. Harbison. *The American Constitution: Its Origins and Development.* 4th ed. New York: W. W. Norton, 1970.

Kutler, Stanley I. *Judicial Power and Reconstruction Politics.* Chicago: University of Chicago Press, 1968.

Logan, Rayford W. *The Betrayal of the Negro: From Rutherford B. Hayes to Woodrow Wilson.* New York: Collier Books, 1965.

McPherson, James M. "Abolitionists and the Civil Rights Act of 1875," *Journal of American History,* 52 (1965), 493–510.

Murphy, L. E. "The Civil Rights Law of 1875," *Journal of Negro History,* 12 (1927), 110–27.

Nathan, Hans. *Dan Emmett and the Rise of Early Negro Minstrelsy.* Norman: University of Oklahoma Press, 1962.

Olsen, Otto H. (ed.). *The Thin Disguise: Turning Point in Negro History—Plessy v. Ferguson, a Documentary Presentation, 1864–1896.* New York: Humanities Press, 1967.

Palmer, Robert C. "The Parameters of Constitutional Reconstruction: Slaughter-House, Cruikshank, and the Fourteenth Amendment," *University of Illinois Law Review,* no vol. (1984), 739–70.

Perman, Michael. *Reunion without Compromise: The South and Reconstruction, 1865–1868.* New York: Cambridge University Press, 1973.

———. *The Road to Redemption: Southern Politics, 1869–1879.* Chapel Hill: University of North Carolina Press, 1984.

Warren, Charles. *The Supreme Court in United States History.* 2 vols. Boston: Little Brown & Co., 1922.

Weaver, Valerie W., "The Failure of Civil Rights 1875–1883 and Its Repercussions," *Journal of Negro History,* 54 (1969), 368–82.

Woodward, C. Vann. *The Strange Career of Jim Crow.* 2nd rev. ed. New York: Oxford University Press, 1966.

SWING AROUND THE CIRCLE

McKitrick, Eric. *Andrew Johnson and Reconstruction.* Chicago: University of Chicago Press, 1960.

TAYLOR, RICHARD (1826–1879)

Current, Richard N. (ed.). *Encyclopedia of the Confederacy*. 4 vols. New York: Simon & Schuster, 1993.

Davis, William C. (ed.). *The Confederate General*. 6 vols. N.p.: National Historical Society, 1991.

Freeman, Douglas Southall. *Lee's Lieutenants: A Study of Command*. 3 vols. New York: Charles Scribner's Sons, 1942–1944.

Parrish, T. Michael. *Richard Taylor: Soldier Prince of Dixie*. Chapel Hill: University of North Carolina Press, 1992.

Prushankin, Jeffery S. "'To This Fatal Blunder'," *North & South*, 5 (September 2002), 76–91.

Warner, Ezra J. *Generals in Gray: Lives of Confederate Commanders*. Baton Rouge: Louisiana State University Press, 1959.

TENURE OF OFFICE ACT

Sefton, James E. *The United States Army and Reconstruction, 1865–1877*. Baton Rouge: Louisiana State University Press, 1967.

Thomas, Benjamin P., and Harold M. Hyman. *Stanton: The Life and Times of Lincoln's Secretary of War*. New York: Alfred A. Knopf, 1962.

TILDEN, SAMUEL J. (1814–1886)

Barnard, Harry. *Rutherford B. Hayes and His America*. Indianapolis: Bobbs-Merrill, 1954.

Eckenrode, Hamilton J. *Rutherford B. Hayes: Statesman of Reunion*. New York: Dodd, Mead & Co., 1930.

Haworth, Paul L. *The Hayes-Tilden Disputed Presidential Election of 1876*. Cleveland, Ohio: Arthur H. Clark Co., 1906.

Hoogenboom, Ari A. *The Presidency of Rutherford B. Hayes*. Lawrence: University Press of Kansas, 1988.

———. *Rutherford B. Hayes: Warrior and President*. Lawrence: University Press of Kansas, 1995.

Nevins, Allan. "Rutherford Birchard Hayes," in Allen Johnson *et al.* (eds.), *Dictionary of American Biography* (10 double vols. + 9 supplements, 1964–1981), VIII, 446–51.

Simpson, Brooks D. *The Reconstruction Presidents*. Lawrence: University Press of Kansas, 1998.

Williams, T. Harry. *Hayes of the Twenty-Third: The Life of a Volunteer Officer*. New York: Alfred A. Knopf, 1965.

———— (ed.). *Hayes: The Diary of a President, 1875–1881, Covering the Disputed Election, the End of Reconstruction, and the Beginning of Civil Service.* New York: D. McKay Co., 1964.

TORPEDOES (CIVIL WAR LAND AND NAVAL MINES)

Crowley, R. O. "Making the Infernal Machines," *Civil War Times Illustrated*, 12 (June 1973), 24–35.
Snyder, Dean. "Torpedoes for the Confederacy," *Civil War Times Illustrated*, 24 (March 1985), 40–45.

TOURGÉE, ALBION W. (1838–1905)

Current, Richard N. *Those Terrible Carpetbaggers: A Reinterpretation.* New York: Oxford University Press, 1988.
Currie-McDaniel, Ruth. "The Wives of the Carpetbaggers," in Jeffrey J. Crow *et al.* (eds.), *Race, Class, and Politics in Southern History.* Baton Rouge: Louisiana State University Press, 1989, 35–78.
Daniels, Jonathan. *Prince of Carpetbaggers.* Philadelphia: J. B. Lippincott Co., 1958.
Dibble, Roy F. *Albion W. Tourgée.* Port Washington, N.Y.: Kennikat Press, 1968, repr.
Gross, Theodore L. "The Fool's Errand of Albion W. Tourgée," *Phylon*, 24 (1963), 240–54.
————. "The Negro in the Literature of Reconstruction," *Phylon*, 22 (1961), 5–14.
Harris, William C. *William Woods Holden: Firebrand of North Carolina Politics.* Baton Rouge: Louisiana State University Press, 1987.
Olenick, Monte M. "Albion W. Tourgée: Radical Republican Spokesman of the Civil War Crusade," *Phylon*, 23 (1962), 332–45.
Olsen, Otto H. *Carpetbagger's Crusade: The Life of Albion W. Tourgée.* Baltimore, Md.: The Johns Hopkins University Press, 1965.
————. "North Carolina: An Incongruous Presence," in Otto H. Olsen (ed.), *Reconstruction and Redemption in the South.* Baton Rouge: Louisiana State University Press, 1980, 156–201.
Weissbuch, Ted N. "Albion W. Tourgée: Propagandist and Critic of Reconstruction," *Ohio Historical Quarterly*, 71 (1961), 27–44.

TRUMBULL, LYMAN (1813–1896)

Ellis, L. Ethan. "Lyman Trumbull," in Allen Johnson *et al.* (eds.), *Dictionary of American Biography* (10 double vols. + 9 supplements, 1964–1981), XIX, 19–20.

Krug, Mark M. *Lyman Trumbull: Conservative Radical.* New York: A.S. Barnes, 1965.
White, Horace. *The Life of Lyman Trumbull.* Boston: Houghton-Mifflin, 1913.

TWEED RING

Bowen, Croswell. *The Elegant Oakey.* New York: Oxford University Press, 1956.
Callow, Alexander B. *The Tweed Ring.* New York: Oxford University Press, 1966.
Harlow, Alvin F. "William Marcy Tweed," in Allen Johnson *et al.* (eds.), *Diction-ary of American Biography* (10 double vols. + 9 supplements, 1964–1981), XIX, 79–82.
Hershkowitz, Leo. *Tweed's New York: Another Look.* Garden City, N.Y.: Double-day & Co., 1977.
Hoogenboom, Ari, and Olive Hoogenboom. "Was Boss Tweed Really Snow White?" *Reviews in American History,* 5 (1977), 360–66.
Lewis, Alfred Henry. *Richard Croker.* New York: Life Publishing Company, 1901.
Mandelbaum, Seymour J. *Boss Tweed's New York.* New York: John Wiley & Sons, Inc., 1965.
Summers, Mark W. *The Era of Good Stealings.* New York: Oxford University Press, 1993.

TWEED, WILLIAM MARCY (MAGEAR) "BOSS" (1823–1878)

Callow, Alexander B. *The Tweed Ring.* New York: Oxford University Press, 1966.
Harlow, Alvin F. "William Marcy Tweed," in Allen Johnson *et al.* (eds.), *Diction-ary of American Biography* (10 double vols. + 9 supplements, 1964–1981), XIX, 79–82.
Hershkowitz, Leo. *Tweed's New York: Another Look.* Garden City, N.Y.: Double-day & Co., 1977.
Hoogenboom, Ari, and Olive Hoogenboom. "Was Boss Tweed Really Snow White?" *Reviews in American History,* 5 (1977), 360–66.

TWITCHELL, MARSHALL H. (1840–1905)

Shoalmire, Jimmie G. "Carpetbagger Extraordinary: Marshall Harvey Twitchell, 1840–1905." Ph.D. dissertation, Mississippi State University, 1969.
Tunnell, Ted (ed.). *Carpetbagger from Vermont: The Autobiography of Marshall Harvey Twitchell.* Baton Rouge: Louisiana State University Press, 1989.
———. *Edge of the Sword: The Ordeal of Carpetbagger Marshall Harvey Twitchell in the Civil War and Reconstruction.* Baton Rouge: Louisiana State University Press, 2001.

UNION LOYAL LEAGUES

Drumm, Austin M. "The Union League in the Carolinas." Ph.D. dissertation, 1955.

Fitzgerald, Michael W. *The Union League Movement in the Deep South: Politics and Agricultural Change during Reconstruction.* Baton Rouge: Louisiana State University Press, 1989.

Fleming, Walter Lynwood. "The Formation of the Union Leagues in Alabama," *Gulf States Historical Magazine*, 2 (1903), 73–89.

Lawson, Melinda. "'A Profound National Devotion': The Civil War Union Leagues and the Construction of a New National Patriotism," *Civil War History*, 48 (2002), 338–62.

Owens, Susie Lee. *The Union League of America: Political Activities in Tennessee, the Carolinas, and Virginia.* Ann Arbor: University of Michigan Press, 1947.

VICKSBURG CAMPAIGN

Baradell, Lang. "Mushroom Cloud at Vicksburg: Union Miners Tunnel under Confederate Fortifications," *Civil War Times Illustrated*, 44 (October 2005), 50–56, 62.

Barton, Dick. "Charge at Big Black River," *America's Civil War*, 12 (September 1999), 54–61.

Bearss, Edwin C. *Decision in Mississippi: Mississippi's Important Role in the War Between the States.* Jackson: Mississippi Commission on the War Between the States, 1962.

———. *Rebel Victory at Vicksburg.* Vicksburg, Miss.: Vicksburg Centennial Commemoration Commission, 1963.

———. *The Vicksburg Campaign.* 3 vols. Dayton, Ohio: Morningside, 1985–1986.

———. "Vicksburg Campaign, Part 1—Grant Moves Inland: The Battles of Raymond and Jackson," *Blue & Gray*, 17 (1999–2000), [Special Issue].

———. " Vicksburg Campaign, Part 2—Grant Moves Inland: The Battles of Champion's Hill and the Big Black River Bridge," *Blue & Gray*, 18 (2000–2001), [Special Issue].

Brooksher, William R., and David K. Snider. "A Visit to Holly Springs," *Civil War Times Illustrated*, 14 (June 1975), 4–9, 40–44.

Brown, D. Alexander. "Battle at Chickasaw Bluffs," *Civil War Times Illustrated*, 9 (July 1970), 4–9. 44–48.

———. *Grierson's Raid.* Urbana: University of Illinois Press, 1954.

———. "Grierson's Raid: 'Most Brilliant' of the War," *Civil War Times Illustrated*, 3 (January 1965), 4–11, 30–32.

Carter, Samuel, III. *The Final Fortress: The Campaign for Vicksburg, 1862–1863.* New York: St. Martin's Press, 1980.

Connelly, Thomas. "Vicksburg: Strategic Point or Propaganda Device?" *Military Affairs*, 34 (1970), 49–53.

Dinges, Bruce J. "The Making of a Cavalryman: Benjamin Grierson and the Civil War Along the Mississippi, 1861–1865." Ph.D. dissertation, Rice University, 1978.

———. "Running Down Rebels [Van Dorn's Raid on Holly Springs]," *Civil War Times Illustrated*, 19 (April 1980), 10–18.

Fowler, Robert F. (ed.). "Struggle for Vicksburg," *Civil War Times Illustrated*, 6 (July 1967), [Special Issue].

Hattaway, Herman, and Archer Jones. *How the North Won: A Military History of the Civil War*. Urbana: University of Illinois Press, 1983.

Hoehling, A. A. *Vicksburg: 47 Days of Siege*. Englewood Cliffs, N.J.: Prentice-Hall, 1969.

Jones, Archer. *Confederate Strategy from Shiloh to Vicksburg*. Baton Rouge: Louisiana State University Press, 1961.

Kushlan, Jim (ed.). "July 1863: America Explodes," *Civil War Times Illustrated*, 42 (August 2003), 30–40.

Leonard, Phillip A. B. "Forty-seven Days [Siege of Vicksburg]," *Civil War Times Illustrated*, 39 (August 2000), 40–49, 68–69.

Lowery, Don. "Grierson's Other Cavalry Raid [1864]," *America's Civil War*, 13 (September 200), 34–40.

Miers, Earl Schenck. *The Web of Victory: Grant at Vicksburg*. New York: Knopf, 1955.

Milligan, John. "Expedition into the Bayou," *Civil War Times Illustrated*, 15 (January 1977), 12–21.

Northrop, L. B. "Hill of Death [Champion's Hill]," *Civil War Times Illustrated*, 24–33, 62–67.

Pemberton, John C. *John C. Pemberton: Defender of Vicksburg*. Chapel Hill: University of North Carolina Press, 1942.

Roth, Dave. "Grierson's Raid," *Blue & Gray*, 10 (1992–1993), [Special Issue].

Starr, Stephen Z. *The Union Cavalry in the Civil War: The War in the West*. Vol. 3. Baton Rouge: Louisiana State University Press, 1985.

Williams, Kenneth P. *Lincoln Finds a General: A Military Study of the Civil War*. 5 vols. New York: Macmillan, 1949–1959.

Winschel, Terrence J. "Port Gibson," *Blue & Gray*, 11 (1993–1994), [Special Issue].

———. "The Siege of Vicksburg," *Blue & Gray*, 20 (2002–2003), [Special Issue].

———. "A Tragedy of Errors: The Failure of the Confederate High Command in the Defense of Vicksburg," *North & South*, 8 (January 2006), 40–58.

———. "Vicksburg the Key," *North & South*, 7 (November 2004), 58–67.

WADE, BENJAMIN F. (1800–1878)

Meneely, A. Howard. "Benjamin Franklin Wade," in Allen Johnson *et al.* (eds.), *Dictionary of American Biography* (10 double vols. + 9 supplements, 1964–1981), XIX, 303–5.

Shover, Kenneth B. "Maverick at Bay: Ben Wade's Senate Re-election Campaign, 1862–1863," *Civil War History*, 12 (1966), 23–42.

Trefousse, Hans L. "Ben Wade and the Failure of the Impeachment of Andrew Johnson," Historical and Philosophical Society of Ohio, *Bulletin*, 18 (1960), 241–52.

———. *Benjamin Franklin Wade: Radical Republican from Ohio.* New York: Twayne Publishers, 1963.

WAITE, MORRISON R. (1816–1888)

Fairman, Charles. *Reconstruction and Reunion, 1864–1888.* 2 pts. New York: The Macmillan Company, 1971–1987.

McGrath, C. Peter. *Morrison R. Waite: The Triumph of Character.* New York: Macmillan, 1963.

WAR ON THE HIGH SEAS—CONFEDERATE CRUISERS, THE BLOCKADE, AND SUBMARINES, THE

Anderson, Bern. *By Sea and River: The Naval History of the Civil War.* New York: Knopf, 1962.

Balch, Thomas Willing, *The Alabama Arbitration.* Philadelphia: Allen, Lane and Scott, 1900.

Bowker, R. R. *Danger Beneath the Waves: History of the Confederate Submarine H. L. Hunley.* Orangeburg, S.C.: Sandlapper Publishing Co., 1992.

Bradlee, Francis B. Blockade *Running during the Civil War and the Effect of Land and Water Transportation on the Confederacy.* Salem, Mass.: Essex Institute, 1925.

Browning, Robert M. *From Cape Charles to Cape Fear: The North Atlantic Blockading Squadron during the Civil War.* Tuscaloosa: University of Alabama Press, 1993.

Buker, George E. *Blockaders, Refugees, and Contrabands: Civil War on Florida's Gulf Coast, 1961–1865.* Tuscaloosa: University of Alabama Press, 1993.

Bulloch, James D. *The Secret Service of the Confederate States in Europe; or, How the Confederate Cruisers Were Equipped.* New York: Thomas Yoseloff, 1959, repr.

Delaney, Norman. "The Strange Occupation of James Bulloch: 'When Can You Start?'," *Civil War Times Illustrated*, 21 (March 1982), 18–27.

Donnelly Ralph W. *Confederate States Marine Corps.* Shippensburg, Pa.: White Mane Press, 1989.

Durkin, Joseph T. *Stephen R. Mallory: The Confederate Navy Chief.* Chapel Hill: University of North Carolina Press, 1954.

Ekelund, Robert B., Jr., and Mark Thornton. "The Union Blockade and the Demoralization of the South: Relative Prices in the Confederacy," *Social Science Quarterly*, 73 (1992), 890–902.

Fowler, William M. *Under Two Flags*. New York: Norton, 1990.

Gibbons, Tony. *Warships and Naval Battles of the U.S. Civil War*. Limpsfield, Surry, GB: Dragon's World, 1989.

Harlowe, Jerry. *Monitors: The Men, Machines, and Mystic*. Gettysburg: Thomas Publications, 2001.

Hay, John D., and Joan Hay. *The Last of the Confederate Privateers*. New York: Crescent Books, 1977.

Heath, Chester G. *Gray Raiders of the Sea: How Eight Confederate Warships Destroyed the Union's High Sea Commerce*. Camden, Maine: Provincial Press, 1992.

Jones, Virgil Carrington. *The Civil War at Sea*. 3 vols. New York: Rinehart and Winston, 1960–1962.

———. "How the South Created a Navy," *Civil War Times Illustrated*, 8 (July 1969), 4–9, 42–48.

———. "Mr. Lincoln's Blockade," *Civil War Times Illustrated*, 10 (December 1971), 10–24

Jones, Wilbur Devereaux. *The Confederate Rams at Birkenhead: A Chapter in Anglo-American Relations*. Tuscaloosa: Confederate Publishing Co., 1961.

Lamgenberg, William H. "Perapetic Coffin: Last Voyage of *CSS Hunley*," *America's Civil War*, 11 (July 1998), 54–60.

Lester, Richard I. *Confederate Finance and Purchasing in Great Britain*. Charlottesville: University of Virginia Press, 1975.

Luraghi, Raimondo. *The Southern Navy: The Confederate Navy and the American Civil War*. Annapolis, Md.: Naval Institute Press, 1995.

McCartney, Clarence E. *Mr. Lincoln's Admirals*. New York: Funk and Wagnalls, 1956.

Merli, Frank J. *Great Britain and the Confederate Navy, 1861–1865*. Bloomington: Indiana University Press, 1970.

———. "The South on the Seas," *Civil War Times Illustrated*, 11 (November 1972), 4–8, 39–45.

———, and Thomas W. Green. "Could the Laird Rams Have Lifted the Blockade?" *Civil War Times Illustrated*, 2 (April 1963), 14–17.

Miller, Edward D. *USS Monitor: The Ship That Launched a Modern Navy*. Annapolis, Md.: Leeward Publications, 1987.

Nash, Howard P., Jr. "The CSS *Alabama*: Roving Terror of the Seas," *Civil War Times Illustrated*, 2 (August 1963), 5–9, 34–39.

Niven, John. *Gideon Welles: Lincoln's Secretary of the Navy*. New York: Oxford University Press, 1973.

Perry, Milton F. *Infernal Machines: The Story of Confederate Submarine and Mine Warfare*. Baton Rouge: Louisiana State University Press, 1965.

Ragan, Mark K. "Union and Confederate Submarine Warfare," *North & South*, 2 (March 1999), 72–83.

Robbins, Peggy. "Caleb Huse," *Civil War Times Illustrated*, 17 (August 1978), 31–40.

Robinson, William M. *The Confederate Privateers.* New Haven, Conn.: Yale University Press, 1928.

Schneller, Robert J., Jr. *A Quest for Glory: John A. Dahlgren, American Naval Ordnance and the Civil War.* Annapolis, Md.: Naval Institute Press, 1995.

Silverstone, Paul H. *Warships of the Civil War Navies.* Annapolis, Md.: Naval Institute Press, 1989.

Smith, Myron J. *American Civil War Navies.* Metuchen, N.J.: Scarecrow Press, 1972.

Spencer, Warren F. *The Confederate Navy in Europe.* Tuscaloosa: University of Alabama Press, 1983.

Still, William N., Jr. "The Common Sailor: The Civil War's Uncommon Man— Yankee Blue Jackets and Confederate Tars," *Civil War Times Illustrated,* 23 (February 1985), 24–39; 24 (March 1985), 12–19, 36–39.

———. "Confederate Naval Strategy: The Ironclad," *Journal of Southern History,* 27 (1961), 330–43.

———. *Iron Afloat: The Story of the Confederate Armorclads.* Nashville, Tenn.: Vanderbilt University Press, 1985.

———. "The Iron Rebel Navy," *Civil War Times Illustrated,* 19 (June 1980), 22–31.

———. "A Naval Sieve: The Union Blockade in the Civil War," *Naval War College Review,* 36 (1983), 38–45.

Surdam, David G. *Northern Naval Superiority and the Economics of the American Civil War.* Columbia: University of South Carolina Press, 2001.

Tucker, Spencer C. *A Short History of the Civil War at Sea.* Wilmington, Del.: SR Books, 2001.

West, Richard S. *Gideon Welles: Lincoln's Navy Department.* Indianapolis: Bobbs-Merrill, 1943.

———. *Mr. Lincoln's Navy.* New York: Longmans, Green, 1957.

WAR ON THE INLAND AND COASTAL WATERS—GUNBOATS AND IRONCLADS, THE

Anderson, Bern. *By Sea and River: The Naval History of the Civil War.* New York: Knopf, 1962.

Baxter, James Phinney. *The Introduction of the Ironclad Warship.* Cambridge, Mass.: Harvard University Press, 1933.

Coryell, Janet L. *Neither Heroine nor Fool: Anna Carroll of Maryland.* Kent, Ohio: Kent State University Press, 1990.

Crandall, Warren Daniel. *History of the Ram Fleet and the Mississippi Marine Brigade in the War for the Union on the Mississippi and Its Tributaries.* St. Louis: Burchart Bros., 1907.

Dufour, Charles L. *The Night the War Was Lost.* Garden City, N.Y.: Doubleday, 1960.

Durkin, Joseph T. *Stephen R. Mallory: The Confederate Navy Chief.* Chapel Hill: University of North Carolina Press, 1954.

Gibbons, Tony. *Warships and Naval Battles of the U.S. Civil War.* Limpsfield, Surry, GB: Dragon's World, 1989.

Gibson, Charles Dana, and E. Kay Gibson. *Assault and Logistics: Union Coastal and River Operations.* Camden, Maine: Ensign Press, 1995.

Gosnell, H. Allen. *Guns on the Western Waters: The Story of River Gunboats in the Civil War.* Baton Rouge: Louisiana State University Press, 1949.

Hoppin, James M. *Life of Andrew Hull Foote, Rear Admiral, United States Navy.* New York: Harper, 1874.

Johnson, Ludwell H. *Red River Campaign: Politics and Cotton in the Civil War.* Baltimore, Md.: The Johns Hopkins University Press, 1958.

Jones, Virgil Carrington. *The Civil War at Sea.* 3 vols. New York: Rinehart and Winston, 1960–1962.

Keller, Allan. "Admiral Andrew Hull Foote," *Civil War Times Illustrated*, 18 (December 1979), 6–11, 43–47.

MacBride, Robert. *Civil War Ironclads: The Dawn of Naval Armor.* Philadelphia: Chilton, 1962.

Melton, Maurice. *The Confederate Ironclads.* South Brunswick, N.J.: Thomas Yoseloff, 1968.

Merrill, James M. *Battle Flags South: The Story of the Civil War Navies on Western Waters.* Rutherford, N.J.: Fairleigh Dickinson University Press, 1970.

Niven, John. *Gideon Welles.* New York: Oxford University Press, 1973.

Pratt, Fletcher. *Civil War on Western Waters.* New York: Holt, 1956.

Reed, Rowena. *Combined Operations in the Civil War.* Annapolis, Md.: Naval Institute Press, 1978.

Silverstone, Paul H. *Warships of the Civil War Navies.* Annapolis, Md.: Naval Institute Press, 1989.

Soley, James Russell. *Admiral Porter.* New York: D. Appleton, 1903.

Still, William N., Jr. *Iron Afloat: The Story of the Confederate Ironclads.* Nashville, Tenn.: Vanderbilt University Press, 1971.

_____. "'Porter . . . Is the Best Man': This Was Gideon Wells' View of the Man He Chose to Command the Mississippi Squadron," *Civil War Times Illustrated*, 16 (May 1977), 4–9, 44–47.

Welcher, Frank J. *The Union Army, 1861–1865: Organization and Operations.* 2 vols. Bloomington: Indiana University Press, 1993.

Wells, Tom Henderson. *The Confederate Navy: A Study in Organization.* Tuscaloosa: University of Alabama Press, 1971.

West, Richard S. *Gideon Welles: Lincoln's Navy Department.* Indianapolis: Bobbs-Merrill, 1943.

_____. *Mr. Lincoln's Navy.* New York: Longmans, Green, 1957.

_____. *The Second Admiral: A Life of David Dixon Porter, 1813–1891.* New York: Coward-McCann, 1937.

WARMOTH, HENRY CLAY (1842–1931)

Binning, Francis W. "Henry Clay Warmoth and Louisiana Reconstruction." Ph.D. dissertation, University of North Carolina, 1969.

Current, Richard N. *Three Carpetbag Governors.* Baton Rouge: Louisiana State University Press, 1967.

Current, Richard N. *Those Terrible Carpetbaggers: A Reinterpretation.* New York: Oxford University Press, 1988.

Dufour, Charles L. "The Age of Warmoth," *Louisiana History,* 6 (1965), 335–64.

Harris, Francis B. "Henry Clay Warmoth, Reconstruction Governor of Louisiana," *Louisiana Historical Quarterly,* 30 (1947), 523–652.

Taylor, Joe Gray. "Louisiana: An Impossible Task," in Otto H. Olsen (ed.), *Reconstruction and Redemption in the South.* Baton Rouge: Louisiana State University Press, 1980, 202–36.

Warmoth, Henry Clay. *War Politics and Reconstruction: Stormy Days in Louisiana.* New York: Macmillan, 1930.

Wilson, James D. "The Donaldsonville Incident of 1870: A Study of Local Party Dissention and Republican Infighting in Reconstruction Louisiana," *Louisiana History,* 38 (1997), 329–45.

WARTIME POLITICS IN THE NORTH–CAPTURED AND ABANDONED PROPERTY ACT OF 1863

Abbott, Martin. "Free Land Free Labor, and the Freedmen's Bureau," *Agricultural History,* 30 (1956), 150–56.

Cox, LaWanda. "The Promise of Land for the Freedmen," *Mississippi Valley Historical Review,* 49 (1958), 413–40.

Gates, Paul W. "Federal Land Policy in the South, 1866–1880," *Journal of Southern History,* 6 (1940), 303–60.

Hoffman, Edwin D. "From Slavery to Self Reliance," *Journal of Negro History,* 41 (1956), 8–42.

Johnson, Ludwell H., III. "Contraband Trade during the Last Year of the Civil War," *Mississippi Valley Historical Review,* 49 (1963), 635–41.

———. "Northern Profit and Profiteers: The Cotton Rings of 1864–1865," *Civil War History,* 12 (1966), 101–15.

Oubre, Claude F. *Forty Acres and a Mule: The Freedmen's Bureau and Black Land Ownership.* Baton Rouge: Louisiana State University Press, 1978.

Randall, James G. *The Confiscation of Property during the Civil War.* Indianapolis: Bobbs-Merrill, 1913.

———. *Constitutional Problems Under Lincoln.* rev. ed. Urbana: University of Illinois Press, 1964.

WARTIME POLITICS IN THE NORTH–CONFISCATION ACTS

Bradley, Michael R. "In the Crosshairs: Southern Civilians Targeted by the U.S. Army," *North & South*, 10 (March 2008), 46–61.

Lucie, Patricia M. L. "Confiscation: Constitutional Crossroads," *Civil War History*, 23 (1977), 307–21.

Newton, Steven H. "What Kind of War? [Destruction of Civilian Property]," *North & South*, 10 (October 2007), 16–24.

Randall, James G. *The Confiscation of Property during the Civil War*. Indianapolis: Bobbs-Merrill, 1913.

———. *Constitutional Problems Under Lincoln*. rev. ed. Urbana: University of Illinois Press, 1964.

Siddali, Silvana R. *From Property to Person: Slavery and the Confiscation Acts, 1861–1862*. Baton Rouge: Louisiana State University Press, 2005.

———. "'Must We Not Punish to Conquer?': The Militant Northern Home Front and the Early Development of Hard War Ideas," *North & South*, 8 (May 2005), 46–56.

WARTIME POLITICS IN THE NORTH—DEMOCRATIC PARTY

Baker, Jean H. *Affairs of Party: The Political Culture of Northern Democrats in the Mid-Nineteenth Century*. Ithaca, N.Y.: Cornell University Press, 1983.

———. "A Loyal Opposition: Northern Democrats in the Thirty-seventh Congress," *Civil War History*, 25 (1979), 139–55.

Cowden, Joanna D. "The Politics of Dissent: Civil War Democrats in Connecticut," *New England Quarterly*, 56 (1983), 538–54.

Curry, Leonard P. "Congressional Democrats, 1861–1863," *Civil War History*, 12 (1966), 213–29.

Mitchell, Stewart. *Horatio Seymour of New York*: Cambridge, Mass.: Harvard University Press, 1938.

Mushkat, Jerome. *The Reconstruction of the New York Democracy, 1861–1874*. Rutherford, N.J.: Fairleigh Dickinson University Press, 1981.

Tredeway, G. R. *Democratic Opposition to the Lincoln Administration in Indiana*. Indianapolis: Indiana Historical Bureau, 1973.

Wainwright, Nicholas B. "The Loyal Opposition in Civil War Philadelphia," *Pennsylvania Magazine of History and Biography*, 88 (1964), 294–315.

Sibley Joel. *A Respectable Minority: The Democratic Party in the Civil War Era*. New York: Norton, 1977.

WARTIME POLITICS IN THE NORTH–ELECTION OF 1862

Downs, Lynwood G. "The Soldier Vote and Minnesota Politics, 1862–1865," Minnesota Historical Society, *Publications*, 26 (1945), 187–210.

Harbison, Winfred A. "The Election of 1862 as a Vote of Want of Confidence in President Lincoln," Michigan Academy of Sciences, Arts, and Letters, *Papers* (1930), 499–513.

McKitrick, Eric L. "Party Politics and the Union and Confederate War Efforts," in William N. Chambers and Walter D. Burnham (eds.), *The American Party Systems: Stages of Development.* New York: Oxford University Press, 1967, 117–51.

McSeveney, Samuel T. "Winning the Vote for Connecticut Soldiers in the Field, 1862–1864: A Research Note and Historiographical Comment," *Connecticut, History*, 26 (1985), 115–24.

Naisawald, L. VanLoan. "The FitzJohn Porter Case." *Civil War Times Illustrated,* 7 (June 1968), 4–9, 42–48.

Pratt, Harry E. "The Repudiation of Lincoln's War Policy in 1862—Stuart-Swett Congressional Campaign," Illinois State Historical Society, *Journal*, 24 (1931), 129–40.

WARTIME POLITICS IN THE NORTH—ETHRIDGE CONSPIRACY OF 1863

Belz, Herman. "The Ethridge Conspiracy of 1863: A Projected Conservative Coup," *Journal of Southern History*, 36 (1970), 549–67.

WARTIME POLITICS IN THE NORTH—INCOME TAX

McPherson, James M. *Battle Cry of Freedom: The Civil War Era.* New York: Ballantine Books, 1988.

Meese , Edwin, *et al. The Heritage Guide to the Constitution.* Washington, D.C.: The Heritage Foundation, 2005.

Randall, James G. *Constitutional Problems Under Lincoln.* rev. ed. Urbana: University of Illinois Press, 1964.

WARTIME POLITICS IN THE NORTH—LINCOLN AND PRESIDENTIAL RECONSTRUCTION OR TEN PERCENT PLAN

Belz, Herman. *Emancipation and Equal Rights: Politics and Constitutionalism in the Civil War Era.* New York: W. W. Norton, 1978.

Brown, Norman D. "A Union Election in Civil War North Carolina," *North Carolina Historical Review*, 43 (1966), 381–400.

Donald, David H. *Lincoln Reconsidered.* 2nd ed. New York: Vintage Books, 1956.

Graebner, Norman A. (ed.). *The Enduring Lincoln.* Urbana: University of Illinois Press, 1959.

Gunderson, Robert Gray. *Old Men's Convention: The Washington Peace Conference of 1861.* Madison: University of Wisconsin Press, 1961.

Harris, William C. *With Charity for All: Lincoln and the Restoration of the Union.* Lexington: University of Kentucky Press, 1997.

Hesseltine, William B. *Lincoln's Plan of Reconstruction.* Tuscaloosa: Confederate Publishing Company, 1960.

Hofstadter, Richard. *The American Political Tradition and the Men Who Made It.* New York: Alfred A. Knopf, 1948.

Hyman, Harold M. *The Era of the Oath: Northern Loyalty Tests during the Civil War and Reconstruction.* Philadelphia: University of Pennsylvania Press, 1954.

———. *Lincoln's Reconstruction: Neither Failure of Vision Nor Vision of Failure.* Ft. Wayne, Ind.: Louis A. Warren Lincoln Library and Museum, 1980.

Mallin, William D. "Lincoln and the Conservatives," *Journal of Southern History*, 28 (1962), 31–45.

McCrary, Peyton. *Abraham Lincoln and Reconstruction: The Louisiana Experiment.* Princeton, N.J.: Princeton University Press, 1978.

Morris, Robert L. "The Lincoln-Johnson Plan for Reconstruction and the Republican Convention of 1864," *Lincoln Herald*, 71 (Spring 1969), 33–39.

Oates, Stephen B. *With Malice Toward None: The Life of Abraham Lincoln.* New York: Harper & Row, 1977.

Paludan, Philip S. "The American Civil War: Triumph through Tragedy," *Civil War History*, 20 (1974), 239–50.

Randall, James G. *Lincoln the President.* 4 vols. New York: Dodd, Mead & Co., 1945–1955.

Rosenberg, John S. "Toward a New Civil War Revisionism," *The American Scholar*, 38 (1969), 250–72.

Stampp, Kenneth M. *The Era of Reconstruction, 1865–1877.* New York: Alfred A. Knopf, 1965.

Thomas, Benjamin P., and Harold M. Hyman. *Stanton: The Life and Times of Lincoln's Secretary of War.* New York: Alfred A. Knopf, 1962.

Wade, Michael G. "'I Would Rather Be Among the Comanches': The Military Occupation of Southwest Louisiana, 1865," *Louisiana History*, 39 (1998), 45–64.

Williams, T. Harry. "Abraham Lincoln: Principle and Pragmatism in Politics," *Mississippi Valley Historical Review*, 40 (June 1953), 89–108.

WARTIME POLITICS IN THE NORTH—OATHS OF ALLEGIANCE

Hyman, Harold M. *The Era of the Oath: Northern Loyalty Tests during the Civil War and Reconstruction.* Philadelphia: University of Pennsylvania Press, 1954.

WARTIME POLITICS IN THE NORTH—RADICAL REPUBLICANS

Howard, Victor. *Religion and the Radical Republican Movement.* Lexington: University of Kentucky Press, 1990.

Hunt, H. Draper. *Hannibal Hamlin of Maine: Lincoln's First Vice President.* Syracuse, N.Y.: Syracuse University Press, 1969.

Montgomery, David. *Beyond Equality: Labor and the Radical Republican*s. New York: Vintage. 1967.

Trefousse, Hans L. *Benjamin Franklin Wade: Radical Republican from Ohio.* New York: Twayne, 1963.

———. *The Radical Republicans: Lincoln's Vanguard for Justice.* New York: Knopf, 1968.

Williams, T. Harry. *Lincoln and the Radicals.* Madison: University of Wisconsin Press, 1941.

———. "Lincoln and the Radicals," in Grady McWhiney (ed.), *Grant, Lee, Lincoln, and the Radicals.* Evanston, Ill.: Northwestern University Press, 1964, 92–117.

WARTIME POLITICS IN THE NORTH—REPUBLICAN PARTY

Albright, Rebecca G. "The Civil War Career of Andrew Gregg Curtin, Governor of Pennsylvania," *Western Pennsylvania Magazine of History,* 47 (1964), 321–41; 48 (1965), 19–42, 151–73.

Blue, Frederick J. "Friends of Freedom: Lincoln, Chase, and the Wartime Racial Policy," *Ohio History,* 102 (1993), 85–97.

Bogue, Allan G. *The Congressman's Civil War.* New York: Cambridge University Press, 1989.

———. *The Earnest Men: Republicans of the Civil War Senate.* Ithaca, N.Y.: Cornell University Press, 1981.

Bradley, Erwin S. *The Triumph of Militant Republicanism: A Study of Pennsylvania and Presidential Politics, 1860–1872.* Philadelphia: University of Pennsylvania Press, 1964.

Wells, Jonathan. "The Transformation of John Pendleton Kennedy: Maryland, the Republican Party, and the Civil War," *Maryland Historical Magazine,* 95 (2000), 291–307.

WARTIME POLITICS IN THE NORTH—REPUBLICAN PLATFORM ENACTED

Ambrose, Stephen E. *Nothing Like It in the World: The Men Who Built the Transcontinental Railroad, 1863–1869.* New York: Simon & Schuster, 2000.

Barrett, Don C. *The Greenbacks and the Resumption of Specie Payments, 1862–1879.* Cambridge, Mass.: Harvard University Press, 1931.

Bensel, Richard F. *Yankee Leviathan: The Origins of Central State Authority in America.* New York: Cambridge University Press, 1990.

Borritt, Gabor S. *Lincoln and the Economics of the American Dream.* Memphis, Tenn,: Memphis State University Press, 1978.

Dean, Eric T., Jr. "Rethinking the Civil War: Beyond 'Revolutions,' 'Reconstruction,' and the 'New Social History,'" *Southern Historian,* 15 (1994), 28–50.

DiLorenzo, Thomas J. "The Great Centralizer: Abraham Lincoln and the War Between the States," *Independent Review,* 3 (No. 2, Fall 1998), 243–71.

———. *The Real Lincoln: A New Look at Abraham Lincoln, His Agenda, and an Unnecessary War.* Roseville, Calif.: Forum, 2002.

DuBois, James T., and Gertrude S. Mathews. *Glausha Grow: Father of the Homestead Law.* Boston: Houghton Mifflin, 1917.

Engermann, Stanley. "The Economic Impact of the Civil War," *Explorations in Economic History,* 3 (1966), 176–99.

Gallman, J. Matthew. *The North Fights the Civil War: The Home Front.* Chicago: Ivan R. Dee, 1994.

Gates, Paul W. *Agriculture and the Civil War.* New York: Knopf, 1965.

Graham, Frank D. "International Trade Under Depreciated Paper: The United States, 1862–1879," *Quarterly Journal of Economics,* 36 (1922), 220–73.

Gunderson, Gerald. "The Origin of the American Civil War," *Journal of Economic History,* 34 (1974), 915–50.

Hammond, Bray. *Banks and Politics in America: From the Revolution to the Civil War.* Princeton, N.J.: Princeton University Press, 1957.

———. *Sovereignty and an Empty Purse: Banks and Politics in the Civil War.* Princeton, N.J.: Princeton University Press, 1970.

James, John A. "The Optimal Tariff in the Antebellum United States," *American Economic Review,* 71 (1981), 726–34.

Larson. Henrietta M. *Jay Cooke, Private Banker.* Cambridge, Mass.: Harvard University Press, 1936.

DuBois, James T., and Gertrude S. Mathews. *Glausha Grow: Father of the Homestead Law.* Boston: Houghton Mifflin, 1917.

McCrary, Peyton. "The Party of Revolution: Republican Ideas about Politics and Social Change, 1862–1867," *Civil War History,* 30 (1984), 330–50.

McKitrick, Eric L. "Party Politics and the Union and Confederate War Efforts," in William Nesbit Chambers and Walter Dean Burnham (eds.), *The American Party Systems: Stages of Development.* New York: Oxford University Press, 1967, 117–51.

Mercer, Lloyd J. *Railroads and Land Grant Policy: A Study in Government Intervention.* New York: Academic Press, 1982.

Montgomery, David. *Beyond Equality: Labor and the Radical Republicans.* New York: Vintage. 1967.

Oberholtzer, Ellis P. *Jay Cooke: Financier of the Civil War.* New York: Burt Franklin, 1970, repr.

Olmstead, Alan. "The Civil War as a Catalyst of Technological Change in Agriculture," *Business and Economic History*, 5 (1976), 36–50.

Rasmussen, Wayne. "The Civil War: A Catalyst of Agricultural Revolution," *Agricultural History*, 39 (1965), 187–95.

Rawley, James A. *The Politics of Union: Northern Politics during the Civil War*. Hillsdale, Ill.: Dryden Press, 1974.

Roark, James L. "George W. Julian: Radical Land Reformer," *Indiana Magazine of History*, 64 (1968), 25–38.

Russel, Robert R. *Improvement in Communication with the Pacific Coast as an Issue in American Politics, 1783–1864*. Cedar Rapids, Iowa: Torch Press, 1948.

Sharkey, Robert P. *Money, Class, and Party: An Economic Study of the Civil War and Reconstruction*. Baltimore, Md.: The Johns Hopkins University Press, 1959.

Summers, Mark W. *Railroads, Reconstruction, and the Gospel of Prosperity: Aid under the Radical Republicans*. Princeton, N.J.: Princeton University Press, 1984.

———. "The Spoils of War," *North & South*, 6 (February 2003), 82–89.

Unger, Irwin. "Businessmen and Specie Resumption," *Political Science Quarterly*, 74 (1959), 46–70.

———. *The Greenback Era: A Social and Political History of American Finance*. Princeton, N.J.: Princeton University Press, 1964.

WARTIME POLITICS IN THE NORTH—STATE POLITICS

Baker, Jean H. *The Politics of Continuity: Maryland Political Parties from 1858 to 1870*. Baltimore, Md.: The Johns Hopkins University Press, 1973.

Barnhart, John D. "The Impact of the Civil War in Indiana," *Indiana Magazine of History*, 57 (1961), 185–224.

Baum, Dale. *The Civil War Party System: The Case of Massachusetts, 1848–1876*. Chapel Hill: University of North Carolina Press, 1984.

Benton, Josiah H. *Voting in the Field: A Forgotten Chapter of the Civil War*. Boston: Plimpton Press, 1915.

Bradley, Erwin S. *The Triumph of Militant Republicanism: A Study of Pennsylvania and Presidential Politics, 1960–1872*. Philadelphia: University of Pennsylvania Press, 1964.

Brummer, Sidney D. *Political History of New York State during the Period of the Civil War*. New York: Columbia University Press, 1911.

Castel, Albert E. *A Frontier State at War: Kansas, 1861–1865*. New York: Cornell University Press, 1958.

Clark, Charles B. *Politics in Maryland during the Civil War*. Chestertown, Md.: N. pub., 1952.

Cowden, Joanna D. "Civil War and Reconstruction Politics in Connecticut, 1863–1868." Ph.D. dissertation, University of Connecticut, 1975.

Current, Richard N. *The History of Wisconsin: The Civil War Era, 1848–1873*. Madison: The State Historical Society of Wisconsin, 1976.

Curry, Richard O. *A House Divided: A Study of Statehood Politics and the Copperhead Movement in West Virginia*. Pittsburgh: University of Pittsburgh Press, 1964.

Davis, Stanton L. *Pennsylvania Politics, 1960–1863*. Cleveland, Ohio: Case Western Reserve University, 1935.

Downs, Lynwood G. "The Soldier Vote and Minnesota Politics, 1862–1865," Minnesota Historical Society, *Publications*, 26 (1945), 187–210.

Dusinberre, William. *Civil War Issued in Philadelphia, 1856–1865*. Philadelphia: University of Pennsylvania Press, 1965.

Field, Phyllis F. *The Politics of Race in New York: The Struggle for Black Suffrage in the Civil War Era*. Ithaca, N.Y.: Cornell University Press, 1982.

Gallman, J. Matthew. *Mastering Wartime: A Social History of Philadelphia during the Civil War*. Cambridge, GB: Cambridge University Press, 1990.

Gray, Leslie B. *The Source and the Vision: Nevada's Role in the Civil War*. Sparks, Nev.: The Gray Trust, 1990.

Hancock, Harold. *Delaware during the Civil War*. Wilmington: Historical Society of Delaware, 1961.

Hershock, Martin J. "Copperheads and Radicals: Michigan Politics during the Civil War," *Michigan Historical Review*, 18 (1992), 28–69.

Hesseltine, William B. *Lincoln and the War Governors*. New York: Knopf, 1948.

Hodnett, Mary P. "Civil War Issues in New York State Politics." Ph.D. dissertation, New York University, 1970.

Holliday, John W. *Indianapolis during the Civil War*. Indianapolis: E. J. Hecker, 1911.

Jackson, W. Sherman. "Emancipation, Negrophobia, and Civil War Politics in Ohio," *Journal of Negro History*, 65 (1980), 250–60.

Kamphoefner, Walter D. "German-Americans and Civil War Politics: A Reconsideration of the Ethnocultural Thesis," *Civil War History*, 37 (1991), 232–46.

Klement, Frank L. "The Soldier Vote in Wisconsin during the Civil War," *Wisconsin Magazine of History*, 28 (1944), 37–47.

———. *Wisconsin and the Civil War*. Madison: State Historical Society of Wisconsin, 1963.

Kleppner, Paul. *The Third Electoral System, 1853–1892: Parties, Voters, and Political Culture*. Chapel Hill: University of North Carolina Press, 1979.

Knapp, Charles M. *New Jersey Politics during the Period of the Civil War and Reconstruction*. Geneva, N.Y.: W. F. Humphrey, 1924.

Kane, Jarlath R. *A Political History of Connecticut during the Civil War*. Washington, D.C.: Catholic University Press, 1941.

Karamanski, Theodore J. *Rally 'Round the Flag: Chicago and the Civil War*. Chicago; Nelson Hall, 1993.

Laughlin, Sceva. *Missouri Politics during the Civil War*. Salem, Oreg.: N. pub., 1930.

Long, E. B. *The Saints and the Union: Utah Territory during the Civil War*. Urbana: University of Illinois Press, 1981.

McKay, Ernest A. *The Civil War in New York City*. Syracuse, N.Y.: Syracuse University Press, 1990.

McKitrick, Eric L. "Party Politics and the Union and Confederate War Efforts," in William N. Chambers and Walter D. Burnham (eds.), *The American Party Systems: Stages of Development*. New York: Oxford University Press, 1967, 117–51.

Mitchell, Stewart. *Horatio Seymour of New York*. Cambridge, Mass.: Harvard University Press, 1938.

Niven John. *Connecticut for the Union: The Role of the State in the Civil War*. New Haven, Conn.: Yale University Press, 1965.

Parrish, William E. *Turbulent Partnership: Missouri and the Union, 1861–1865*. Columbia: University of Missouri Press, 1963.

Phillips, Christopher. "'The Crime against Missouri': Slavery, Kansas, and the Cant of Southernness in the Border West," *Civil War History*, 48 (2002), 60–81.

Pleasants, Samuel A. *Fernando Wood of New York*. New York: Columbia University Press, 1948.

Porter, George H. *Ohio Politics during the Civil War Period*. New York: Longmans, Green, and Co., 1911.

Rawley, James A. *The Politics of Union: Northern Politics during the Civil War*. Hillsdale Ill.: Dryden Press, 1974.

Renda, Lex. "Credit and Culpability: New Hampshire State Politics during the Civil War," *Historical New Hampshire*, 48 (1993), 2–84.

Roseboom, Eugene H. *The Civil War Era, 1850–1873*. Columbus: Ohio State Archeological and Historical Society, 1944.

Stampp, Kenneth M. *Indiana Politics during the Civil War*. Indianapolis: Indiana Historical Bureau, 1949.

Stanley, Gerald. "Civil War Politics in California," *Southern California Quarterly*, 64 (1982), 115–32.

Stewart, Mitchell. *Horatio Seymour of New York*. Cambridge, Mass.: Harvard University Press, 1938.

Sylvester, Lorna L. "Oliver P. Morton and Hoosier Politics during the [Civil] War." Ph.D. dissertation, Indiana University, 1968.

Thornbrough, Emma Lou. *Indiana in the Civil War Era, 1850–1880*. Indianapolis: Indiana Historical Bureau and Indiana Historical Society, 1965.

Wells, Jonathan. "The Transformation of John Pendleton Kennedy: Maryland, the Republican Party, and the Civil War," *Maryland Historical Magazine*, 95 (2000), 291–307.

WARTIME POLITICS IN THE NORTH—WADE–DAVIS MANIFESTO AND ELECTION OF 1864

Belz, Herman. *Reconstructing the Union: Theory and Practice during the Civil War*. Ithaca, N.Y.: Cornell University Press, 1969.

Benedict, Michael Les. *A Compromise of Principle: Congressional Republicans and Reconstruction, 1863–1869*. New York: W. W. Norton & Co., 1974.

Cox, LaWanda. *Lincoln and Black Freedom: A Study in Presidential Leadership.* Columbia: University of South Carolina Press, 1981.

Downs, Lynwood G. "The Soldier Vote and Minnesota Politics, 1862–1865," Minnesota Historical Society, *Publications*, 26 (1945), 187–210.

Foner, Eric. *Reconstruction: America's Unfinished Revolution, 1863–1877*. New York: Harper & Row, 1988.

Grimsley, Mark. "The 'Dump Lincoln' Movements of 1864," *North & South*, 8 (January 2006), 28–37.

Harbison, Winfred A. "Indiana Republicans and the Reelection of President Lincoln," *Indiana Magazine of History*, 33 (1937), 277–303.

Hesseltine, William B. "Lincoln and the Politicians, *Civil War History*, 6 (1960), 43–55.

———. *Lincoln's Plan of Reconstruction*. Tuscaloosa, Ala.: Confederate Publishing Company, 1960.

Long, David E. *The Jewel of Liberty: Abraham Lincoln's Re-election and the End of Slavery*. Mechanicsburg, Pa.: Stackpole, 1994.

McCrary, Peyton. *Abraham Lincoln and Reconstruction: The Louisiana Experiment*. Princeton, N.J.: Princeton University Press, 1978.

McSeveney, Samuel T. "Re-electing Lincoln: The Union Party Campaign and the Military Vote in Connecticut," *Civil War History*, 32 (1986), 139–58.

Morris, Robert L. "The Lincoln-Johnson Plan for Reconstruction and the Republican Convention of 1864," *Lincoln Herald*, 71 (Spring 1969), 33–39.

Sears, Stephen W. "McClellan and the Peace Plank of 1864: A Reappraisal," *Civil War History*, 40 (1994), 57–64.

Spencer, Ivor D. "Chicago Helps to Reelect Lincoln," Illinois State Historical Society, *Journal*, 63 (1970), 167–79.

Waugh, John C. *Reelecting Lincoln: The Battle for the 1864 Presidency*. New York: Crown, 1997.

Winther, Oscar O. "The Soldier Vote in the Election of 1864," *New York History*, 15 (1944), 440–58.

Wright, John S. *Lincoln and the Politics of Slavery*. Reno: University of Nevada Press, 1970.

WARTIME POLITICS IN THE NORTH—WADE–DAVIS PLAN OF RECONSTRUCTION

Belz, Herman. "Henry Winter Davis and the Origins of Congressional Reconstruction," *Maryland Historical Magazine*, 67 (1972), 129–43.

Belz, Herman. *Reconstructing the Union: Theory and Practice during the Civil War*. Ithaca, N.Y.: Cornell University Press, 1969.

Benedict, Michael Les. *A Compromise of Principle: Congressional Republicans and Reconstruction, 1863–1869.* New York: W. W. Norton & Co., 1974.

Cox, LaWanda. *Lincoln and Black Freedom: A Study in Presidential Leadership.* Columbia: University of South Carolina Press, 1981.

Foner, Eric. *Reconstruction: America's Unfinished Revolution, 1863–1877.* New York: Harper & Row, 1988.

Hentig, Gerald S. *Henry Winter Davis: Antebellum and Civil War Congressman from Maryland.* New York: Twayne, 1973.

Hesseltine, William B. "Lincoln and the Politicians, *Civil War History*, 6 (1960), 43–55.

———. *Lincoln's Plan of Reconstruction.* Tuscaloosa, Ala.: Confederate Publishing Company, 1960.

McCrary, Peyton. *Abraham Lincoln and Reconstruction: The Louisiana Experiment.* Princeton, N.J.: Princeton University Press, 1978.

Wright, John S. *Lincoln and the Politics of Slavery.* Reno: University of Nevada Press, 1970.

WARTIME RECONSTRUCTION—DAVIS BEND EXPERIMENT

Benedict, Michael Les, "The Rout of Radicalism: Republicans and the Elections of 1867," *Civil War History*, 18 (1972), 176–77.

Hermann, Janet S. *The Pursuit of a Dream.* New York: Oxford University Press, 1981.

———. "Reconstruction in Microcosm: Three Men and a Gin," *Journal of Negro History*, 65 (1980), 312–35.

Hesseltine, William B. "Economic Factors in the Abandonment of Reconstruction," *Mississippi Valley Historical Review*, 22 (1935–1936), 191–210.

Ross, Stephen Joseph. "Freed Soil, Freed Labor, Freed Men: John Eaton and the Davis Bend Experiment," *Journal of Southern History*, 44 (1978), 213–32.

WARTIME RECONSTRUCTION—LOUISIANA EXPERIMENT

Berlin, Ira, *et al. Slaves No: Three Essays on Emancipation and the Civil War.* New York: Cambridge University Press, 1992.

Capers, Gerald. *Occupied City: New Orleans under the Federals, 1862–1865.* Lexington: University of Kentucky Press, 1965.

Cornish, Dudley T. *The Sable Arm: Negro Troops in the Union Army.* New York: W. W. Norton, 1966.

Cox, LaWanda. *Lincoln and Black Freedom: A Study in Presidential Leadership.* Columbia: University of South Carolina Press, 1981.

Dawson, Joseph Green, III. *Army Generals and Reconstruction: Louisiana, 1862–1977.* Baton Rouge: Louisiana State University Press, 1982.

Garcia, Pedro. "Losing the Big Easy: [Second Battle of New Orleans, 1862]," *Civil War Times Illustrated*, 41 (May 2002), 46–53, 64–65.

Gerteis, Louis S. *From Contraband to Freedman: Federal Policy Toward Southern Blacks, 1861–1865*. Westport, Conn.: Greenwood Press, 1973.

Johnson, Ludwell H., III. "Contraband Trade during the Last Year of the Civil War," *Mississippi Valley Historical Review*, 49 (1963), 635–41.

Johnson, Ludwell H., III. "Northern Profit and Profiteers: The Cotton Rings of 1864–1865," *Civil War History*, 12 (1966), 101–15.

May, J. Thomas. "Continuity and Change in the Labor Program of the Union Army and the Freedmen's Bureau," *Civil War History*, 17 (1971), 245–54.

McCrary, Peyton. *Abraham Lincoln and Reconstruction: The Louisiana Experiment*. Princeton, N.J.: Princeton University Press, 1978.

Messner, William F. "Black Violence and White Response: Louisiana, 1862," *Journal of Southern History*, 41 (1975), 19–38.

Ripley, C. Peter. *Slaves and Freedmen in Civil War Louisiana*. Baton Rouge: Louisiana State University Press, 1978.

Robbins, Peggy. "When the Rebels Lost Ship Island," *Civil War Times Illustrated*, 17 (January 1979), 4–9, 42–45.

Robinson, Armistead, "Reassessing the First Reconstruction: Lost Opportunity or Tragic Era?" *Reviews in American History*, 6 (1978), 80–86.

Smith, David R. "The Beast of New Orleans," *Civil War Times Illustrated*, 8 (October 1969), 10–21.

Treagle, Joseph G., Jr. "Thomas J. Durant, Utopian Socialism and the Failure of Presidential Reconstruction in Louisiana," *Journal of Southern History*, 45 (1979), 485–512.

Wetta, Francis Joseph. "The Louisiana Scalawags." Ph.D. dissertation, Louisiana State University, 1977.

Wiley, Bell I. "Vicissitudes of Early Reconstruction Farming in the Lower Mississippi Valley," *Journal of Southern History*, 3 (1937), 441–52.

Williams, T. Harry, "General Banks and Radical Republicans in the Civil War," *New England Quarterly*, 12 (1939), 268–80.

Wright, John S. *Lincoln and the Politics of Slavery*. Reno: University of Nevada Press, 1970.

WARTIME RECONSTRUCTION—MISSISSIPPI VALLEY EXPERIMENT

Berlin, Ira, *et al. Slaves No: Three Essays on Emancipation and the Civil War*. New York: Cambridge University Press, 1992.

Bigelow, Martha M. "Freedmen of the Mississippi Valley, 1862–1865," *Civil War History*, 8 (1962), 38–47.

———. "Vicksburg: Experiment in Freedom," *Journal of Mississippi History*, 26 (1964), 28–44.

Currie, James T. *Enclave: Vicksburg and Her Plantations, 1863–1870.* Jackson: University Press of Mississippi, 1980.

Davis, Ronald L. F. *Good and Faithful Labor: From Slavery to Sharecropping in the Natchez District, 1860–1890.* Westport, Conn.: Greenwood Press, 1982.

———. "The U. S. Army and the Origins of Sharecropping in the Natchez District: A Case Study," *Journal of Negro History,* 62 (1977), 60–80.

Gerteis, Louis S. *From Contraband to Freedman: Federal Policy Toward Southern Blacks, 1861–1865.* Westport, Conn.: Greenwood Press, 1973.

Hermann, Janet S. *The Pursuit of a Dream.* New York: Oxford University Press, 1981.

———. "Reconstruction in Microcosm: Three Men and a Gin," *Journal of Negro History,* 65 (1980), 312–35.

May, J. Thomas. "Continuity and Change in the Labor Program of the Union Army and the Freedmen's Bureau," *Civil War History,* 17 (1971), 245–54.

Wiley, Bell I. "Vicissitudes of Early Reconstruction Farming in the Lower Mississippi Valley," *Journal of Southern History,* 3 (1937), 441–52.

WARTIME RECONSTRUCTION—PORT ROYAL EXPERIMENT

Berlin, Ira, *et al. Slaves No: Three Essays on Emancipation and the Civil War.* New York: Cambridge University Press, 1992.

Cimbala, Paul A. "The Freedmen's Bureau, the Freedmen, and Sherman's Grant in Reconstruction Georgia, 1865–1867," *Journal of Southern History,* 55 (1989), 597–632.

Gerteis, Louis S. *From Contraband to Freedman: Federal Policy Toward Southern Blacks, 1861–1865.* Westport, Conn.: Greenwood Press, 1973.

Johnson, Ludwell H., III. "Contraband Trade during the Last Year of the Civil War," *Mississippi Valley Historical Review,* 49 (1963), 635–41.

———. "Northern Profit and Profiteers: The Cotton Rings of 1864–1865," *Civil War History,* 12 (1966), 101–15.

Kitrell, Irvin, III. "40 Acres and a Mule," *Civil War Times Illustrated,* 41 (June 2002), 54–61.

Pease, William H. "Three Years Among the Freedmen: William C. Gannett and the Port Royal Experiment," *Journal of Negro History,* 42 (1957), 98–117.

Robinson, Armistead. "Reassessing the First Reconstruction: Lost Opportunity or Tragic Era?" *Reviews in American History,* 6 (1978), 80–86;

Rose, Willie Lee. *Rehearsal for Reconstruction: The Port Royal Experiment.* Indianapolis: Bobbs-Merrill Company, Inc., 1964.

Saville, Julie. *The Work of Reconstruction: From Slave to Wage Laborer in South Carolina, 1860–1870.* New York: Cambridge University Press, 1994.

WARTIME RECONSTRUCTION—SPECIAL FIELD ORDERS NO. 15

Berlin, Ira, *et al. Slaves No: Three Essays on Emancipation and the Civil War.* New York: Cambridge University Press, 1992.

Cimbala, Paul A. "The Freedmen's Bureau, the Freedmen, and Sherman's Grant in Reconstruction Georgia, 1865–1867," *Journal of Southern History,* 55 (1989), 597–632.

Kitrell, Irvin, III. "40 Acres and a Mule: [Sherman's Special Field Orders, No. 15, 16 January 1865]," *Civil War Times Illustrated,* 41 (May 2002), 54–61.

Oubre, Claude F. *Forty Acres and a Mule: The Freedmen's Bureau and Black Land Ownership.* Baton Rouge: Louisiana State University Press, 1978.

WARTIME RECONSTRUCTION—VIRGINIA EXPERIMENT AND CONTRABANDS

Ash, Steven V. "White Virginians under Federal Occupation, 1861–1865," *Virginia Magazine of History and Biography,* 98 (1990), 162–92.

Berlin, Ira, *et al. Slaves No: Three Essays on Emancipation and the Civil War.* New York: Cambridge University Press, 1992.

Gerteis, Louis S. *From Contraband to Freedman: Federal Policy Toward Southern Blacks, 1861–1865.* Westport, Conn.: Greenwood Press, 1973.

Randall, James G. *Constitutional Problems Under Lincoln.* rev. ed. Urbana: University of Illinois Press, 1964.

WASHINGTON'S BIRTHDAY SPEECH

McKitrick, Eric. *Andrew Johnson and Reconstruction.* Chicago: University of Chicago Press, 1960.

"WAVING THE BLOODY SHIRT"

Carter, Hodding. *The Angry Scar: The Story of Reconstruction.* Garden City, N.Y.: Doubleday & Co., 1959.

WEAPONS AND ORDNANCE

Austerman, Wayne R. "Abhorrent to Civilization: The Explosive Bullet in the Civil War," *Civil War Times Illustrated,* 24 (September 1985), 36–40.

———. "Case Shot and Cannister," *Civil War Times Illustrated,* 26 (September 1987), 16–29, 43–48.

Bruce, Robert V. *Lincoln and the Tools of War*. Indianapolis: Bobbs-Merrill, 1956.

Coggins, Jack. *Arms and Equipment of the Civil War*. New York: Fairfax Press, 1983, repr.

Daniel, Larry J. *Cannoneers in Gray: The Field Artillery of the Army of Tennessee, 1861–1865*. Tuscaloosa: University of Alabama Press, 1984.

Edwards, William Bennett. *Civil War Guns: The Complete Story of Federal and Confederate Small Arms.* . . . Harrisburg, Pa.: Stackpole, 1962.

Fuller Claud E. *The Rifled Musket*. Harrisburg, Pa.: Stackpole, 1958.

Garavaglia, A., and Charles G. Worman. "Fast Firing by the Rank and File," *North & South*, 2 (November 1998), 76–79.

Hazlett, James C. "The Federal Napoleon Gun," *Military Collector and Historian*, 15 (1963), 103–108.

———. "The 3-Inch Ordnance Rifle," *Civil War Times Illustrated*, 7 (December 1968), 30–36.

Howey, Allan W. "The Widow-Makers [Springfield Rifled Musket]," *Civil War Times Illustrated*, 38 (October 1999), 46–51, 60.

Longacre, Edward G. "'The Soul of Our Artillery': General Henry Hunt," *Civil War Times Illustrated*, 12 (June 1973), 4–7, 10–11, 42–47.

Lord, Francis A. *Civil War Collector's Encyclopedia: Arms, Uniforms, and Equipment of the Union and the Confederacy*. Secaucus, N.J.: Castel Books, 1982, repr.

McClelland, Russ. "Load by the Numbers," *American Rifleman*, 136 (February 1988), 38–40, 90–93.

Naisawald, Louis Van Loan. *Grape and Cannister: The Story of the Field Artillery of the Army of the Potomac, 1861–1865*. New York: Oxford University Press, 1960.

Nye, Wilbur S. "How Artillery Was Aimed," *Civil War Times Illustrated*, 3 (August 1964), 22–25.

Phillips, Stanley S. *Bullets Used in the Civil War, 1861–1865*. Laurel, Md.: Wilson's Specialty Co., 1971.

Rollins, Richard. "The Failure of the Confederate Artillery in Pickett's Charge," *North & South*, 3 (April 2000), 26–42.

———. "Lee's Artillery Prepares for Pickett's Charge," *North & South*, 2 (September 1999). 41–55.

———. "Ordinance and Logistics: The Failure of Confederate Artillery at Gettysburg," *North & South*, 3 (January 2000), 44–54.

———, and Dave Schultz. "A Combined and Concentrated Fire: The Federal Artillery at Gettysburg, July 3. 1863," *North & South*, 3 (March 1999), 39–60.

Thomas, Dean S. *Cannons: An Introduction to Civil War Artillery*. Arendtsville, Pa.: Thomas Publications, 1986.

Trout, Robert J. "Galloping Thunder: Horse Artillery of the Army of Northern Virginia," *North & South*, 3 (September 2000), 74–84.

Vandiver, Frank E. *Ploughshares into Swords: Josiah Gorgas and the Confederate Ordnance*. Austin: University of Texas Press, 1952.

Wise, Jennings Cropper. *The Long Arm of Lee: or, the History of the Artillery of the Army of Northern Virginia.* . . . 2 vols. Lynchburg, Va.: J. P. Bell Co., 1915.

Woodhead, Henry (ed.). *Arms and Equipment of the Confederacy.* Alexandria, Va.: Time-Life Books, 1991.

———— (ed.). *Arms and Equipment of the Union.* Alexandria, Va.: Time-Life Books, 1991.

WIGFALL, LOUIS T. (1816–1873)

Connelly, Thomas Lawrence, and Archer Jones. *The Politics of Command: Factions and Ideas in Confederate Strategy.* Baton Rouge: Louisiana State University Press, 1973.

Cooper, Edward S. *Traitors: The Secession Period, November 1860–July 1861.* Madison-Teaneck, N.J.: Fairleigh Dickinson University Press, 2008.

King, Alvy L. *Louis T. Wigfall.* Baton Rouge: Louisiana State University Press, 1970.

Kline, Michael J. *The Baltimore Plot: The First Conspiracy to Assassinate Abraham Lincoln.* Yardley, Pa.: Westholme Publishing, 2008.

Ledbetter, Billy D. "The Election of Louis T. Wigfall, 1859: A Reevaluation," *Southwestern Historical Quarterly,* 77 (1972–73), 241–54.

WOMEN BEFORE, DURING, AND AFTER THE CIVIL WAR

Beard, Mary R. *Woman as a Force in History: A Study in Traditions and Realities.* New York: Macmillan, 1946.

Bercaw, Nancy. *Gendered Freedoms: Race, Rights, and the Politics of Household in the Delta, 1861–1875.* Gainesville: University of Flodida Press, 2003.

Bleser, Carol K., and Lesley J. Gordon (eds.). *Intimate Strategies of the Civil War: Military Commanders and Their Wives.* New York: Oxford University Press, 2001.

Boatwright, Eleanor M. "The Political and Civil Status of Women in Georgia, 1783–1860," *Georgia Historical Quarterly,* 25 (1941), 301–24.

Brown, Elizabeth G. "Husband and Wife—A Memorandum on the Mississippi Woman's Law of 1839," *Michigan Law Review,* 42 (1944), 1110–21.

Censer, Jane Turner. *The Reconstruction of White Southern Womanhood, 1865–1895.* Baton Rouge: Louisiana State University Press, 2003.

Clinton, Catherine, and Nina Silber (eds.). *Divided Houses: Gender and the Civil War.* New York: Oxford University Press, 1992.

Culpepper, Marilyn Mayer, (ed.). *Trials and Triumphs: The Women of the American Civil War.* East Lansing: Michigan State University Press, 1991.

Edwards, Laura F. *Gendered Strife and Confusion: The Political Culture of Reconstruction.* Urbana: University of Illinois Press, 1997.

Frankel, Noralee. *Freedom's Women: Black Women and Families in Civil War Era Mississippi.* Bloomington: University of Indiana Press, 1999.

———. "From Slave Women to Free Women: The National Archives and Black Women's History in the Civil War Era," *Prologue*, 29 (1997), 100–104.

Hewitt, Nancy. "Did Women Have a Reconstruction? Gender in the Rewriting of Southern History," Georgia Association of Historians, *Proceedings and Papers*, 14 (1993), 1–11.

Hodes, Martha. "The Sexualization of Reconstruction Politics: White Women and Black Men in the South After the Civil War," *Journal of the History of Sexuality*, 3 (1993), 402–17.

Johnston, John D., Jr. "Sex and Property: The Common Law Tradition, the Law School Curriculum, and Developments Toward Equality," *New York University Law Review*, 47 (1972), 1033–92.

Jones, Jacqueline. "Encounters, Likely and Unlikely, Between Black and Poor White Women in the Rural South, 1865–1940," *Georgia Historical Quarterly*, 76 (1992), 332–53.

Kushlan, Jim (ed.). "Women in the Civil War," *Civil War Times Illustrated*, 38 (August 1999), [Special Issue].

Lebsock, Suzanne D. "Radical Reconstruction and the Property Rights of Southern Women," *Journal of Southern History*, 43 (1977), 195–215.

Leonard, Elizabeth D. *Yankee Women: Gender Battles in the Civil War.* New York: Norton 1994.

Massey, Mary Elizabeth. *Bonnet Brigades: American Women and the Civil War.* Lincoln: University of Nebraska Press, 1994, repr.

Rabkin, Peggy. "The Origins of Law Reform: The Social Significance of the Nineteenth-Century Codification Movement and Its Contribution to the Passage of the Early Woman's Property Acts," *Buffalo Law Review*, 24 (1975), 683–760.

Rable George C. *Civil Wars: Women and the Crisis of Southern Nationalism.* Urbana: University of Illinois Press, 1989.

Schuler, Kathryn Reinhart. "Women in Public Affairs in Louisiana During Reconstruction," *Louisiana Historical Quarterly*, 19 (1936), 668–750.

Schultz, Jane E. "Race, Gender, and Bureaucracy: Civil War Army Nurses and the Pension Bureau," *Journal of Women's History*, 6 (1994), 45–69.

Schwalm, Leslie A. *A Hard Fight for We: Women's Transition from Slavery to Freedom in South Carolina.* Urbana: University of Illinois Press, 1997.

Silber, Nina. "Loosening the Ties that Bind: The Conflicting Moral Visions of the Men and Women in the Civil War North," *North & South*, 9 (March 2006), 24–33.

Smallwood, James M. "Black Freedwomen after Emancipation: The Texas Experience," *Prologue*, 27 (1995), 303–17.

Sommerville, Diane Miller. "The Rape Myth in the Old South Reconsidered," *Journal of Southern History*, 61 (1995), 481–518.

Sterming, Dorothy (ed.). *We Are Your Sisters: Black Women in the Nineteenth Century.* New York: Norton, 1984.

Venet, Wendy Hamand. *Neither Ballots nor Bullets: Women Abolitionists and the Civil War*. Charlottesville: University of Virginia Press, 1991.

Wallenstein, Peter. "Race, Marriage, and the Law of Freedom: Alabama and Virginia, 1860–1960s," *Chicago-Kent Law Review*, 70–2 (1994), 371–437.

Young, Agatha. *Women and the Crisis: Women of the North in the Civil War*. New York: McDowell, Obolensky, 1959.

About the Author

WILLIAM L. RICHTER (B.A., M.A., Arizona State University; M.L.S., University of Arizona; Ph.D., Louisiana State University) is an academically trained historian-turned-cowboy, operating his own horseshoeing business out of Tucson, Arizona. He has researched and written extensively in the areas of the antebellum South, the Civil War, and Reconstruction. He has two dozen articles and book reviews to his credit and is the author of 10 books, including the *Historical Dictionary of the Old South* (Scarecrow, 2006). His most recent work is a historical novel, *The Last Confederate Heroes: The Final Struggle for Southern Independence & The Assassination of Abraham Lincoln* (2002), about the people who assassinated Abraham Lincoln and why they did it, and a nonfiction study, *Sic Semper Tyrannis: Why John Wilkes Booth Shot Abraham Lincoln* (2009). He can be reached at www.williamrichter.com.